T0326327

THE ROUTLEDGE HANDBOOK OF TAXATION AND PHILANTHROPY

The Routledge Handbook of Taxation and Philanthropy ventures into a territory that is still widely unexplored. It contains 30 academic contributions that aim to provide a better understanding of whether, why, and how philanthropic initiatives, understood as voluntary contributions for the common good, can and should be fostered by states through tax incentives. The topic has been addressed from a multidisciplinary and multicultural perspective – covering neuroeconomics, sociology, political science, psychology, affective sciences, philosophy, behavioral economy, and law – because of its global and multifaceted nature. It also contains the OECD report on Taxation and Philanthropy released in November 2020, which was prepared in this context as a result of a collaboration with the Geneva Centre for Philanthropy of the University of Geneva.

The book is divided into four sections, exploring, respectively, the justification of tax incentives for philanthropy, theoretical and empirical insights about taxes, efficiency and donor behavior in that context, and tax incentives for cross-border philanthropy and for hybrid entities and social entrepreneurship. It is believed that this volume will be a landmark yet only the beginning of a journey in which a lot remains to be studied, learned, and said.

Henry Peter is a full professor at the University of Geneva, Faculty of Law, and, since 2017, the head of the university's Geneva Centre for Philanthropy. For more than 20 years, his teaching and numerous publications have focused on companies' structure and governance, as well as their social responsibility and purpose. In 2014, he launched the "Philanthropy Series" public conferences at the university. He is a member of several organizations dealing with governance and ethical issues and sits on several boards of foundations, associations, and private companies.

Giedre Lideikyte Huber is a senior lecturer of tax law at the University of Geneva, Faculty of Law, and considering her activities in that context, works in collaboration with the Geneva Centre for Philanthropy. Her research focuses on tax law, tax policies, and sustainable taxation, such as climate and gender issues in fiscal systems. She participated as an expert in the elaboration of the 2020 OECD Report "Taxation and Philanthropy" and on the advisory committee of the Philanthropy Advocacy's project "Legal Environment for Philanthropy in Europe." She is also a board member of the Geneva supervisory authority of foundations and pension funds.

THE ROUTLEDGE HANDBOOK OF TAXATION AND PHILANTHROPY

Edited by Henry Peter and Giedre Lideikyte Huber

LONDON AND NEW YORK

Cover image: © pict rider / iStock

First published 2021
by Routledge
4 Park Square, Milton Park, Abingdon, Oxon OX14 4RN

and by Routledge
605 Third Avenue, New York, NY 10158

Routledge is an imprint of the Taylor & Francis Group, an informa business

British Library Cataloguing-in-Publication Data
A catalogue record for this book is available from the British Library

Library of Congress Cataloging-in-Publication Data
Names: Peter, Henry, editor. | Lideikyte Huber, Giedre, editor.
Title: The Routledge handbook of taxation and philanthropy / edited by Henry Peter and Giedre Lideikyte Huber.
Description: 1 Edition. | New York, NY : Routledge, 2022. | Series: Routledge international handbooks | Includes bibliographical references and index.
Identifiers: LCCN 2021032961 (print) | LCCN 2021032962 (ebook) | ISBN 9780367688271 (hardback) | ISBN 9780367688288 (paperback) | ISBN 9781003139201 (ebook)
Subjects: LCSH: Taxation. | Tax incentives—Law and legislation. | Charities.
Classification: LCC HJ2305 .R68 2022 (print) | LCC HJ2305 (ebook) | DDC 336.2—dc23
LC record available at https://lccn.loc.gov/2021032961
LC ebook record available at https://lccn.loc.gov/2021032962

ISBN: 978-0-367-68827-1 (hbk)
ISBN: 978-0-367-68828-8 (pbk)
ISBN: 978-1-003-13920-1 (ebk)

DOI: 10.4324/9781003139201

Typeset in Bembo
by Apex CoVantage, LLC

CONTENTS

FIGURES

TABLES

DIAGRAMS AND ANNEXES, APPENDIXES, AND BOXES

CONTRIBUTORS

Maja Adena is a senior researcher and vice director of the research unit "Economics of Change" at the Wirtschaftszentrum (WZB) in Berlin, Germany.

Brigitte Alepin is Professor of Taxation at the University of Quebec in Outaouais and the Cofounder of TaxCOOP.

James Andreoni is a distinguished professor of economics at the University of California in San Diego and a research associate at NBER, Cambridge, Massachusetts, USA.

Rob Atkinson is Greenspoon Marder Professor at the Florida State University College of Law, USA.

Philip Balsiger is Professor of Sociology at the University of Neuchâtel, Switzerland.

René Bekkers is a professor in the Department of Sociology, Faculty of Social Sciences, and director of the Center for Philanthropic Studies at Vrije Universiteit Amsterdam in the Netherlands.

Ursa Bernardic is a PhD candidate at Geneva School of Economics and Management at the University of Geneva, Switzerland.

Dana Brakman Reiser is Centennial Professor of Law at Brooklyn Law School in Brooklyn, New York, USA.

Renate Buijze PhD is Researcher at the Erasmus School of Law at Erasmus University in Rotterdam, The Netherlands.

Calum M. Carmichael is Associate Professor of Public Policy and Administration at Carleton University in Ottawa, Canada.

Romain Carnac is Research Associate at the University of Applied Sciences and Arts Western Switzerland, Faculty of Social Work (HETSL | HES-SO), Switzerland.

Emanuela Ceva is Professor of Political Theory, Department of Political Science & International Relations at the University of Geneva, Switzerland.

Malini Chakravarty is the Thematic Lead for Research on Tax Equity at the Centre for Budget and Governance Accountability (CBGA) in New Delhi, India.

Jo Cutler is a postdoctoral research fellow in psychology, Centre for Human Brain Health at the University of Birmingham, UK.

Steven Dean is Professor of Law at Brooklyn Law School in Brooklyn, New York, USA.

Laurence de Nervaux was Head of Research and International Affairs at Fondation de France, France until July 2021.

Nicolas J. Duquette is Associate Professor of Public Policy at the University of Southern California in Los Angeles, California, USA.

Philippe Durand is a partner at PWC law firm; he was formerly Head of the legal department of the French Tax Administration and a member of the board of the Fondation de France, France.

Nicolas Duvoux is Professor of Sociology at the University of Paris 8 Vincennes Saint-Denis and Senior Researcher at the CRESPPA-LabTop, Paris, France.

Raphaël Gani is Judge at the Swiss Federal Administrative Court (Tax Court) and holds a PhD from the University of Lausanne, Switzerland.

Sigrid Hemels is Professor of Tax Law at Erasmus University Rotterdam School of Law, The Netherlands; Visiting Professor in Tax Law at Lund University School of Economics and Management, Sweden; and PSL Counsel at Allen & Overy LLP, Amsterdam.

Caroline Honegger is Research Associate at the University of Applied Sciences and Arts Western Switzerland, Faculty of Social Work (HETSL | HES-SO), Switzerland.

Stephanie Koolen-Maas is a postdoctoral researcher at the Centre for Philanthropic Studies at Vrije Universiteit Amsterdam and at the Rotterdam School of Management, Erasmus University in the Netherlands.

Alexandre Lambelet is Associate Professor at the University of Applied Sciences and Arts Western Switzerland, Faculty of Social Work (HETSL | HES-SO), Switzerland.

Maël Lebreton is the Senior Research Associate at the Swiss Center for Affective Sciences and the Department of Basic Neuroscience, University of Geneva, Switzerland.

Dominique Lemaistre is former Head of Programs and Donor Advised Fonds at the Fondation de France, France.

Giedre Lideikyte Huber is a senior lecturer of tax law at the Faculty of Law at the University of Geneva, Switzerland.

Johannes Lohse is Associate Professor of Economics, Economics Department at the University of Birmingham, UK.

Fiona Martin is Emeritus Professor of the University of New South Wales in Sydney, Australia.

Jennifer Mayo is a PhD student, Department of Economics at the University of Michigan, USA.

Ian Murray is Associate Professor of Law at the University of Western Australia in Perth, Australia.

Xavier Oberson is Professor of Law at the University of Geneva, Switzerland, and a partner at Oberson Abels SA.

Ann O'Connell is Professor of Taxation at the Law School, University of Melbourne, Australia.

Henry Peter is Professor at the Law School and Head of the Geneva Centre for Philanthropy, both at the University of Geneva, Switzerland.

Marta Pittavino is a senior lecturer of statistics at the Research Center for Statistics of the Geneva School of Economics and Management at the University of Geneva, Switzerland.

Kimberley Scharf is Professor of Economics and Public Policy at the University of Birmingham, UK.

Charles Sellen is the inaugural Global Philanthropy Fellow at the Indiana University Lilly Family School of Philanthropy in Indianapolis, USA.

Natalie Silver is a lecturer at the University of Sydney Law School, Australia.

Priyadarshini Singh is a senior visiting fellow at the Center for Social Impact and Philanthropy (CSIP) at Ashoka University and a research fellow at the Center for Policy Research (CPR), where she leads a research program on democracy and state capacity.

Sarah Smith is Professor of Economics, University of Bristol, and a research associate at the Institute for Fiscal Studies in London, UK, and at the Centre for Economic Policy and Research in London, UK.

Richard Steinberg is Professor of Economics and Philanthropic Studies at the IUPUI in Indianapolis, USA.

Emma Tieffenbach is Adjunct Lecturer and Researcher in Philosophy at the University of Geneva, Switzerland.

Giuseppe Ugazio is the Edmond de Rothschild Foundations Assistant Professor in Behavioral Philanthropy at the Geneva Finance Research Institute, University of Geneva, Switzerland.

Claire van Teunenbroek is a postdoctoral researcher and data manager for Giving in the Netherlands at the Center for Philanthropic Studies at Vrije Universiteit Amsterdam in the Netherlands.

Eric M. Zolt is Michael H. Schill Distinguished Professor Emeritus at the UCLA School of Law in Los Angeles, USA.

PREFACE

We are delighted to publish this *Routledge Handbook of Taxation and Philanthropy*, a project we conceived in 2019. It started with the choices the University of Geneva's Geneva Centre for Philanthropy (GCP) had to make shortly after it was established in September 2017. We wanted to focus on topics that were still largely unexplored from an academic standpoint; that had the potential to bring added theoretical and practical value in the philanthropy field; and that required, or at least deserved, a multidisciplinary perspective. The relationship between taxation and philanthropic initiatives was at the top of the list. Thus, our sense of pride when the Swiss National Science Foundation granted four-year funding for this project.

Initially, we had planned to focus on the data coming from Swiss federal and cantonal sources, but it quickly became clear that limiting the analysis to Switzerland would be of insufficient interest. So, we decided to get in touch with Pascal Saint-Amans, director of the OECD's Centre for Tax Policy and Administration (CTPA). Thanks to the support of Ulrich Lehner (then Swiss ambassador to the OECD in Paris), Pascal Saint-Amans confirmed his interest in what he immediately perceived as a study with global and societal significance. In November 2019, the OECD, in collaboration with the GCP, launched an ambitious project to collect and analyze data from OECD members and other countries. The objective was to prepare a report on taxation and philanthropy to be published in OECD *Tax Policies Studies*. The project quickly gained momentum and attracted the interest of many more countries than initially expected. Forty countries responded to the detailed OECD questionnaire.

In parallel, the GCP organized an international academic conference in Geneva in November 2020. We decided to present the OECD report at that conference. The delegates would be experts from various academic disciplines with the expertise and ability to contribute to whether, why, and how states should grant tax incentives to support philanthropic initiatives. About 60 academics volunteered to contribute. This led to 25 papers being selected for the event. Because of what we will all remember as the gloomy COVID-19 period, the conference was held virtually instead of physically. However, this cloud had a silver lining, as it enabled a vast international community to attend.

Routledge enthusiastically agreed to publish a handbook mainly containing the leading papers prepared for the conference. Thanks to the contributors' discipline and interest in the project, this was done remarkably quickly. The Handbook contains an introduction and 30 contributions, written by 45 authors. They are leading experts in the field, representing a wide range of disciplines: economics, sociology, political science, psychology, affective sciences, philosophy, behavioral economics, cognitive neuroscience, and law. They also come from many different countries and cultures, including North America, Europe, India, Australia, and New Zealand. The Handbook also contains the landmark OECD report as an integral part of the project.

Its editors cannot conclude this introduction without thanking the many people who made it possible. All the authors, of course, who prepared an impressive series of outstanding papers on a topic still widely unexplored, but also the CTPA team, from Pascal Saint-Amans to David Bradbury, head of the Tax Policy and Statistics Division; Bert Brys, head of the Country Tax Policy team and of the Personal and Property Taxes unit in the Tax Policy and Tax Statistics Division; Alastair Thomas, senior economist; and Daniel Fichmann, junior economist. It was a privilege to collaborate with them for over a year. Our gratitude also goes to the Swiss National Science Foundation for the grant that made this project possible. And, last but not least, to the GCP team that supported us efficiently since this project began. Our special thanks go to Sémia Bey, project manager, for her meticulous work in managing this project from its outset; Anne-Françoise Ritter, who is in charge of Publications, for her professional assistance during the editing phase; Laetitia Gill, executive director; and Pauline Guédon, administrative assistant, for their constant support in so many ways. We are also grateful to the Routledge team, particularly Kristina Abbotts and Christiana Mandizha, for their extremely professional support and availability. And, of course, for believing in this project.

Henry Peter and Giedre Lideikyte Huber
June 14, 2021

EDITORS' INTRODUCTION TO THE VOLUME

Taxation of philanthropy is a heterogeneous topic that extends to multiple scientific disciplines. For academics and practitioners working in philanthropy, it is not uncommon to turn to branches such as philosophy, law, sociology, and economics to obtain thorough answers to the questions they encounter in their research and work. To date, however, there has been no comprehensive multidisciplinary analysis of the interaction between taxation and philanthropy. The present volume seeks to fill this gap. Through this handbook, the editors also endeavored to contribute to the emerging multidisciplinary domain that can be referred to as "the science of philanthropy." It is hoped that the readers will find the contributions in this volume not only useful but also thought provoking and that they will be encouraged to pursue such studies further.

Due to the diversity of the questions and scientific fields involved, we, the editors, have decided to structure the present handbook around four topics. The first part consolidates contributions to the justification of tax incentives for philanthropic initiatives. The second part ventures into the economic and technical aspects of tax incentives for philanthropy, exploring and comparing various models and their respective efficiencies. The third part addresses tax issues arising from cross-border philanthropy. Finally, the last part of the handbook explores the phenomena of corporate philanthropy and social entrepreneurship, inquiring into, among other things, the rationale of the traditional distinction between charity and business, which is now often blurred.

Annexed to this handbook is the OECD report "Taxation and Philanthropy," which was published in November 2020 in the context of the research project that led to this book (hereafter the "OECD report"). It is the first in-depth comparative analysis of the legal norms and practices in the field. Based on the data gathered through country questionnaires by the OECD, it provides a detailed review of the tax treatment of philanthropic entities and philanthropy as applied by 40 OECD members and participating countries. It was carried out as part of a collaboration between the OECD and the Geneva Centre for Philanthropy at the University of Geneva.

In this introduction, the contributions of all four sections of this handbook are briefly presented.

 DOI: 10.4324/9781003139201-1

1 Justification of tax incentives for philanthropy

One cannot analyze the taxation of philanthropic initiatives without addressing the fundamental question of the rationale behind the tax incentives for philanthropy. This justification raises controversies; in essence, tax incentives for private philanthropy amount to channeling public funds into support for private activities that have been decided and structured by bypassing democratic governance mechanisms. Why would legislators delegate some of their budgetary prerogatives to private actors? How can one reconcile different views on what constitutes philanthropic activity? Can a clear distinction be drawn between philanthropic and political goals? In the first part of the handbook, authors from diverse scientific fields offer perspectives on these and many other questions.

This first part of the volume opens with the contribution of **Rob Atkinson**, who looks at the OECD and its concept of philanthropy from a historical perspective. What was the global vision of philanthropy almost 100 years ago during the era of the Marshall Planners? Has this vision changed? Atkinson argues that philanthropy was seen as an international alliance between states, and this vision must subsist today, with activist states being the only agents of philanthropy truly capable of doing work of a global scope and scale.

Caroline Honegger, **Romain Carnac**, **Philip Balsiger**, and **Alexandre Lambelet** study the concept of philanthropy in Switzerland from the perspective of policymakers. After conducting and analyzing multiple interviews with politicians, they dig deep into the specific rationales and frames used by Swiss policymakers to support tax incentives for philanthropy and their understanding of the notion of public interest. These authors observe that the reasons for supporting philanthropy are diverse and sometimes contradictory due to the very different realities of philanthropy, such as the variety of types and sizes of philanthropic entities and the diversity of their goals. They suggest that when taken together and linked to discourse focused on efficiency, these arguments lead political actors to increase the incentives for philanthropy.

Emanuella Ceva's chapter offers readers a perspective on the justification of philanthropy from a political theory viewpoint. Ceva submits that members of society have reasons to be vigilant regarding and responsive to institutional failures that may threaten the general social order. When the institutional system is dysfunctional, it is justified to sustain public institutional action through donations. When such donations become crucial for proper institutional functioning, not only are they justified, but there are good reasons to incentivize them – for instance, through tax benefits. Exploring the same question from another perspective, philosopher **Emma Tieffenbach** analyzes the justification of tax incentives for philanthropy through the "gifting puzzle," which refers to the attempt to explain in terms of maximizing utility theory the donors' inherently costly choice to unilaterally transfer their financial resources. As Tieffenbach shows, many of the solutions offered to that puzzle amount to displacing, sometimes even erasing, the conceptual boundaries between acts of gifting and acts of consumption. Examining these solutions thus proves relevant to the actual practice of tax deductions being granted in much legislation on conditions that donations be non-profit activities of general interest.

Nicolas Duvoux offers a sociological perspective on certain aspects of taxes and giving. He delivers a qualitative study on the way philanthropic donors perceive the taxation of wealth in France. He analyzes the "elite" households that are at the top of wealth distribution and are usually considered major philanthropic donors (see also the analysis based on top income conducted by Lideikyte Huber, Pittavino, and Peter in this book). Duvoux analyzes the elite class, taking into account its diversity, and observes that the aspects of economic capital as well as occupational status, both former and current (e.g., businessmen, managers), appear to be salient in framing philanthropists' relationship with the wealth tax – for instance, in relation to dismissing its legitimacy. Duvoux also observes that families with larger and more dynastic wealth value tax deductions for their contribution to pluralism.

Distinguishing between charitable and political activities is often difficult, and **Calum M. Carmichael** addresses this topic in his chapter. The unregulated use of private monies to finance political activities is commonly identified as constituting a risk to democracy. Carmichael seeks to clarify whether governments, in regulating the political activities that charitable organizations perform without losing their fiscal privileges, take a similarly restrictive or permissive stance as they take in regulating the private financing of politics. He finds that in all but 3 of the 16 countries that he compares, the stance toward regulating the *political activities* performed by charitable organizations differs from the stance toward regulating the *private donations* received by political entities. According to Carmichael, such inconsistencies suggest that in their regulation of charities, governments are guided by considerations apart from the use of private monies to finance political activities, and he offers examples of these.

Closing the first part of the handbook, two chapters discuss specific aspects of charitable entity exemption regimes that are potentially difficult to justify: benefits given to members and the control of the entity retained by the donor. In general, membership-based charities are almost never tax exempt, as one can also observe from the OECD report (p. 46). However, **Ann O'Connell** shows that the Australian legal framework diverges from this general trend because some entities that provide significant benefits to their members are recognized as charities. She explains the legal foundations of this trend and provides a critical overview. She also highlights that the Australian experience serves as a reminder to other countries of the importance of transparency and the need for ongoing vigilance in relation to eligibility for tax relief. **Ian Murray** examines a different aspect of the justifications of tax concessions for charitable entities. He presents a new take on different tax regulations (United States, Australia, Canada, England, and Wales), exploring the extent to which they encourage donor autonomy and control of charitable foundations' assets. Murray notes that, to the detriment of public benefit, tax laws are often overly focused on restricting marketable private benefits but not on intangible control rights, and that tax regulators generally lack the tools to reform the use of charity assets to reduce donor control. He proposes several possible reforms, such as strengthening the distinction between public and private charities, providing the tax authority with access to tools to modify a charity – such as administrative or *cy-près* schemes – and better support for or encouragement of charity trustees and directors to themselves access such schemes to remove donor controls.

2 Taxes, efficiency, and donor behavior: theoretical and empirical insights

Tax incentives in the field of philanthropy can take many forms, such as tax deductions, tax credits, tax assignments, or tax refunds to charitable organizations (Hemels, 2017: 39 et seq.;). Deduction is arguably the most-used instrument (OECD report, p. 79). The choice of approach depends on multiple factors, such as legal tradition or political motives, which do not necessarily result from an in-depth efficiency analysis. Nonetheless, the question of the efficiency of a tax incentive is a key factor in systems based on the ability to pay (Lideikyte Huber, pp. 635–638). As tax incentives for philanthropy diverge from this fundamental principle of taxation, they should, at a minimum, provide society with benefits that are larger than the concessions granted by the state to private philanthropic donors. However, it is not uncommon for states to be unclear about their objectives in this context. In addition, states do not systematically evaluate the efficiency of the incentives that they put in place (Chapter 13, Chakravarty/

Singh; Chapter 14, Lideikyte Huber/Pittavino/Peter). One reason for this is that the discussion regarding the efficiency of tax incentives for charitable giving (and, more generally, the efficiency of *any* tax incentive) is complex due, inter alia, to diverging views about the definition of efficiency. The authors in this section study various aspects of these issues, which are briefly presented in the following.

James Andreoni and **Sarah Smith** open this technical topic with their chapter on two issues relevant to policymakers in designing incentives for giving: tax efficiency and the social efficiency of tax incentives. They suggest that policymakers should not only focus on tax-price elasticities but also, as recent behavioral insight has shown, on the design and framing of tax incentives, including salience, fixed costs, minimum threshold, social norms, and social information. They further submit that the definition of social benefit goes beyond channeling giving to the most cost-effective charities and should also encompass discussing what it means to have a healthy charitable sector and a strong civil society. Andreoni and Smith suggest that by allowing citizens to have a say in the allocation of government funding via tax-subsidized donations, governments may help build support for tax and spending more generally.

Richard Steinberg's chapter provides a theoretical analysis that challenges several mainstream ideas frequently discussed in studies of tax incentives for philanthropy. He questions three widely reported academic findings on tax design in that context, arguing that they are wrong or misleading. He specifically argues (i) that although charitable tax deductions are, in some sense, favorable to those with higher income, they are not regressive; (ii) that the traditional treasury efficiency test is incorrect; and (iii) that the correct treasury efficiency test does not lead to social efficiency. Steinberg then discusses various policy options and trade-offs. Although the economic case for the favorable tax treatment of charitable donations is uneasy, he supports favorable tax treatment of giving, following some reforms, on noneconomic grounds.

Certain chapters in this section focus specifically on the structure and efficiency of national tax incentives that make them of particular interest to the respective countries. The contribution by **Brigitte Alepin** studies the Canadian tax system and concludes that it is currently inefficient. The reason for this is that the disbursement quota of foundations is too low – in other words, foundations do not spend enough annually on public utility purposes; their disbursement to society is not close to what the state currently spends on them. Therefore, this quota must be increased to make the system more efficient and justified from a policy perspective.

Maja Adena examines the treasury efficiency of German tax incentives. She analyzes German taxpayer data, alleviating the scarcity of studies on the tax-price elasticity of charitable giving behavior in European countries in comparison to numerous studies on the United States. Adena estimates the tax-price and income elasticity of charitable giving in Germany and provides evidence that donors adjust their donations gradually after changes in the tax schedule and respond to future predictable changes in price. In addition, they respond mainly to changes in current and, to a smaller extent, future income. She concludes that German tax incentives are effective overall.

Malini Chakravarty and **Priyadarshini Singh** provide a rare study of the Indian tax incentive regime. They argue that tax incentives in India primarily incentivize donations to government entities, and their design is conservative when compared to 11 other selected countries across the developed and developing world. Still, these authors highlight that such incentives are an important source of financial stability for smaller NGOs, which form the bulk of the sector, and a factor of recognition. On the other hand, based on analysis of available data, they also argue that such tax incentives do not cost the government much. Overall, they stress that the Indian context lacks a systematic evaluation of whether tax incentives can effectively increase donations to the non-profit sector as well as their legal and regulatory implications.

Two chapters study national tax incentives for giving using longitudinal data. **Giedre Lideikyte Huber**, **Marta Pittavino**, and **Henry Peter** observe taxpayers' giving behavior in the canton of Geneva from 2001 to 2011 using tax data of the entire Geneva population. As Geneva is one of the most important cantons for philanthropic activities in Switzerland, studying taxpayers' giving patterns provides important indications about the philanthropic sector in general. The authors observe that the number of taxpayers deducting charitable donations significantly increased during the study period, and the median deduction decreased among all income classes. In other words, more taxpayers deduct charitable donations, but they deduct smaller amounts. In addition, studying the years 2001 and 2011, the authors observe that both the size and frequency of deductions for charitable donations increase sharply with taxpayers' income class.

Nicolas J. Duquette and **Jennifer Mayo** study the long-run distribution of philanthropy in the United States from both donor and beneficiary perspectives. They find that over several decades giving by the biggest donors increased, and those households were more likely to be married, older, and have children than households that were not top donors. The concentration of giving across charitable organizations has been more modest, suggesting that much of the concentration of donations has happened within, rather than across, charities (i.e., the charities are chaining slowly in the aggregate, but the donor base of each organization individually is becoming more top-heavy on average). Duquette and Mayo conclude with a review of tax policies that affect the composition of donors and donees as well as with proposals for tax policy reforms that would broaden the donor base.

Donor motivations play an important role in charitable giving, but do tax incentives boost them? **Jo Cutler** explores the psychological factors that determine donors' motivations and reviews the key findings in the fields of psychology and neuroscience. She describes the main concepts and major experimental techniques and discusses potential future research directions. **Charles Sellen** questions the importance of financial motivations for increasing giving. He highlights a certain fatigue in the public discourse around philanthropy, including its definition and related concepts, and suggests revitalizing it. Would placing less emphasis on the financial costs associated with giving (such as tax incentives) and instead highlighting the noneconomic benefits derived from altruism spur generosity? Sellen says yes and proposes a new paradigm centered on happiness and wellbeing, putting forth a conceptualization of philanthropy as a form of voluntary self-taxation that generates lasting inner satisfaction for the donor.

The chapter by **Kimberly Scharf** and **Johannes Lohse** pushes the boundaries of field efficiency studies, exploring questions beyond fundraising and tax incentives for giving. In particular, what *motivates charities* (as opposed to donors) and makes them efficient? To answer this question, Scharf and Lohse consider the implications of inter-charity competition in relation to different factors, such as the distribution of donations, charities' outputs, and the structure of charitable markets. They show that, in contrast to competition in private markets, inter-charity competition does not eliminate all inefficiencies and may even exacerbate them. They then discuss the scope of government policies and tax incentives using these insights.

What are the technical means for lawmakers to test the effects of tax incentives that have not yet been introduced in a given jurisdiction? **Maja Adena** highlights that the treatment of donations in tax codes and fundraising strategies, respectively, share a number of design elements. Thus, lawmakers could turn to experimental research on fundraising when looking for ways to improve tax incentives. Adena provides an overview of the experimental field literature in the economics of philanthropy, explaining what such results could suggest for tax laws and indicating research gaps.

The section closes with an interdisciplinary study by **Ursa Bernardic**, **Maël Lebreton**, **Giedre Lideikyte Huber**, **Henry Peter**, and **Giuseppe Ugazio** introducing behavioral philanthropy and its relationship with tax incentives. The authors note that the behavioral philanthropy perspective and methods are particularly relevant to policymakers and law researchers who design tax-based incentives to stimulate private engagement in philanthropy. They highlight the benefits of producing data in controlled environments, such as laboratory settings. In particular, this approach promotes the understanding of the psychological and affective mechanisms supporting philanthropic decision-making, helps build new sound theories that rely on precise computational models, and provides implications for informed policy that could help design efficient tax schemes to generate the most impactful giving and welfare systems across the globe.

3 Tax incentives for cross-border philanthropy

Historically, tax subsidies for philanthropic activities limit tax relief for charitable donations outside national borders. There are two main reasons for this restriction. First, the driving principle is that to be justified, such relief has to produce a positive impact on the national budget, which can only happen if the receiving entity is in the same jurisdiction. In addition, cross-border philanthropic activities are more difficult to control and, therefore, potentially subject to the misallocation of funds (money laundering, terrorism funding, etc.; Silver and Buijze, 2020, p. 112). The situation is slightly different in the EU, where the European Court of Justice has issued several landmark decisions that greatly facilitate cross-border philanthropic transfers within the common market (Buijze, 2016). However, in practice, cross-border payments still encounter multiple obstacles, even in the EU, where cross-border restrictions on tax relief are still present in all jurisdictions (OECD report, p. 110). In this section, the authors outline the tax treatment of cross-border philanthropy in their respective jurisdictions as well as national and global solutions.

The opening chapter confronts the readers with the following question: Can double taxation conventions solve or alleviate the potential tax burdens of cross-border charitable giving? **Xavier Oberson** considers that they could indeed play a more important role in this context. Oberson bases his reasoning on various double taxation treaties, and by giving examples, he suggests new clauses that can be inserted into the treaties. For instance, the states could recognize non-profit entities as residents for convention purposes, introduce specific clauses on the deductibility of cross-border philanthropic gifts, or even in the longer term, create a multilateral approach to the problem.

Providing insight into the specific aspects of cross-border giving in the domain of art, **Renate Buijze** compares theory and practice, looking into the experiences of philanthropic art organizations. She concludes that, despite the relaxing of EU rules, donors face practical difficulties in cross-border giving. According to Buijze, giving intermediaries emerge as the current best solution until legislation (ideally) introduces a provision at either the national, bilateral, or supranational level that allows for tax-efficient cross-border giving to equivalent foreign philanthropic organizations based on an *ex-ante* approach and home country control.

Exploring cross-border philanthropy from the U.S. perspective, **Eric M. Zolt** poses two questions: (i) whether tax benefits should support charitable activities outside the United States and (ii) whether contributions to foreign charities should be treated differently by the U.S. tax system from contributions to domestic charities. In answering these questions, the author provides an in-depth presentation of the U.S. legal framework, showing that tax law provides relatively low barriers for U.S. donors who engage in cross-border philanthropy. The theoretical analysis of such a tax framework is difficult, as the United States lacks a comprehensive theory on the rationale behind tax subsidies for domestic charities engaged in domestic charitable activities. Therefore, the author discusses different factors that policymakers may find useful when considering options to either reduce or increase barriers to cross-border philanthropy.

As few countries have removed tax barriers to cross-border philanthropy, **Natalie Silver**'s analysis of the Australian example is interesting. Silver examines the implications of Australia's shift in its policy approach from a very restrictive to a more permissive one. The chapter also assesses the lessons for other countries seeking to achieve an appropriate balance between facilitating tax-effective cross-border philanthropy and ensuring appropriate oversight of domestic entities engaged in international charitable activities.

4 Tax incentives for hybrid entities and social entrepreneurship

Traditionally, the legal status of a philanthropic organization, which allows it to operate under special favorable tax conditions (e.g., exempt from profit or other taxes), has stood under the assumption that such an organization does not engage in commercial activities. Over the last two decades, however, an entirely new sector that does not fit into the distinction between traditional business and charity has emerged. This new sector is usually called "social entrepreneurship" or "for-profit charity." The so-called "social enterprises" operating in this context (for instance, "hybrid entities" or "B-corporations") blur the line between the profit and non-profit sectors, as they derive revenues from commercial activities, but their main – or, in any event, substantial – objective is to have a positive social impact rather than merely to maximize their owners' profit. Certain countries (e.g., the United States and Italy) have adopted new legal forms of entities to accommodate these "hybrid" goals without granting them any tax benefits.[1] Thus, social entrepreneurs may be confronted with the following dilemma: Either operate via a tax-exempt organization, without the possibility to self-finance their activities, or choose a taxable business entity and face potential difficulty finding investors to fund their socially responsible activities.

Authors from four jurisdictions – the Netherlands, the United States, Australia, and Switzerland – discuss various aspects of this emerging phenomenon.

Showing that companies and corporate foundations have become important players in philanthropy, Dutch scholar **Sigrid Hemels** analyzes the general business rationale driving corporate philanthropy, questioning, for instance, the distinction between sponsorship and donations. Furthermore, Hemels illustrates the challenges the Netherlands faces in trying to fit the entrepreneurial forms of philanthropy into its system for gift deductions and charities. In particular, she highlights problems in relation to the deductibility of corporate gifts, donations of shares, donations to for-profit entities, as well as program-related investments, and describes existing and potential solutions to such problems. She also highlights the threats represented by the EU Common Consolidated Corporate Tax Base (CCCTB) directive. It could harm corporate philanthropy in the Netherlands because of its interplay with the Dutch national legislation, which would, in effect, result in limiting corporate deductions.

Stephanie Koolen-Maas, **Claire van Teunenbroek**, and **René Bekkers** explore the 2012 tax reform on charitable donations in the Netherlands, which enhanced the deductibility of gifts to cultural organizations and allowed cultural organizations to earn more commercial income. The goal of the reform was to encourage the cultural sector to reduce its historical dependency on government grants, become more entrepreneurial, and increase philanthropic giving by private donors and corporations. Using survey data, the authors find that giving to culture has increased but probably not as a result of the tax reform. Among cultural nonprofit organizations, they observe an increase in entrepreneurial orientations but not more diversification of income. They also observe a Matthew effect, as larger cultural nonprofit organizations prove more successful in attracting other forms of income.

Addressing the same question from the U.S. perspective, **Steven Dean** and **Dana Brakman Reiser** consider why socially responsible business struggles to attract investors and what the importance of trust between philanthropists and society is. They outline the last half-century history of American philanthropy from the perspective of Stanley Surrey, highlighting that often philanthropists hope to retain access to their wealth. To re-establish trust, the authors suggest using a wealth tax that falls more lightly on assets placed in private foundations than on assets lodged in alternative vehicles that are currently popular among U.S. philanthropists, such as philanthropy LLCs. In fact, such a tax scheme may nudge elites to donate rather than burden them.

Fiona Martin analyzes the framework for social enterprises in Australia. She shows that currently, there is no separate legal structure for social enterprises in the Australian legal system, and that such enterprises are commonly operated by charities. The social enterprises may be either an income-tax exempt or for-profit company limited by shares. Martin discusses the overlap, limitations, and advantages of carrying out a social enterprise through charity and uses case studies to demonstrate the advantages and disadvantages of this approach in Australia.

Raphaël Gani then discusses the Swiss legal framework as well as the general rationale for social enterprises, focusing on the conditions under which entrepreneurial activities can claim tax exemptions. Analyzing the current tax and competition laws in Switzerland, Gani advocates for a larger exemption framework in favor of social enterprises.

In the final chapter of the handbook, **Philippe Durand**, **Dominique Lemaistre**, and **Laurence de Nervaux** address the French approach as to which entity and, more generally, which activity should be considered of public interest and should thus enjoy privileged tax treatment. As in other countries, the test includes whether and to what extent such entities carry out economic activities, on the one hand, and, on the other, whether competition law is complied with, both issues being intertwined. They review the development of the French requirements and argue that the current French system needs to be amended in order to take better account of the growing social impact of economic activities.

The OECD 2020 Taxation and Philanthropy policy study[2]

This book also contains the OECD 2020 report entitled "Taxation and Philanthropy" (hereafter "the report"), the first-ever OECD study on the tax treatment of philanthropy, issued in collaboration with the GCP. The report acknowledges that in most countries philanthropy plays an important role in mobilizing private support for the public good. Some cross-country studies estimate the economic contribution of the non-profit sector at as much as 5% of the global GDP, and this support is especially vital in times of hardship and crisis, such as during the COVID-19 pandemic. The report undertakes a detailed study of the legal frameworks related to tax incentives for the charitable sector. 40 countries took part in this survey.

The fundamental question in the report is as follows: How can governments design tax rules that support philanthropy in a manner that aligns with the public interest? An overview of related doctrines shows that striking the right balance can be difficult, as certain theoretical and practical difficulties exist with regard to the justification of such incentives. In particular, tax support for philanthropy can raise inequality and democracy concerns, as such policy measures could give a small number of wealthy donors disproportionate influence over how public resources are allocated. This apprehension is highlighted by the rise in the number of very large private philanthropic foundations established by ultra-high-net-worth individuals, who are able to channel substantial resources into their own priorities while significantly minimizing their tax liabilities. While risks of abuse should be addressed, this concern should not overshadow the overwhelmingly positive contributions of philanthropy in general.

Nonetheless, the report suggests that there are ways to safeguard tax systems and allow governments to continue providing support to the philanthropic sector. It highlights a number of important considerations for policymakers to help them strike a balance. First, the report suggests that policymakers should *reassess the activities eligible for tax support.* In particular, across the countries surveyed, the activities eligible for tax support were very broad. Countries should ensure that the range of activities eligible for tax support is limited to those areas that are consistent with their underlying policy goals. In addition, the OECD suggests the *use of tax credits and fiscal caps* for this purpose. The report highlights that, among the countries surveyed, the most popular tax incentive for philanthropic giving is tax deductions. However, this can disproportionately benefit higher-income taxpayers. A tax credit coupled with a percentage-based cap may be fairer and more closely aligned with democratic principles. Furthermore, *reassessing the extent of tax exemptions for the commercial income* of philanthropic entities could also be considered. Exempting income from commercial activities could be limited to the extent that they are related to the purpose of the entity. Taxing unrelated commercial income would minimize any competitive disadvantage faced by for-profit businesses. The report also suggests *reducing the complexity of tax rules and related compliance costs* that disproportionately affect low-income donors and smaller philanthropic entities. For this purpose, the countries could, for example, align the eligibility requirements for tax incentives, simplify the tax rules for non-monetary donations, and facilitate payroll schemes for philanthropic giving. Another important policy measure could be *to improve the oversight of tax concessions.* Increased transparency, such as public registers of approved philanthropic entities, annual reporting, differentiating between donating and sponsoring, and publishing tax expenditure data, would help safeguard public trust in the sector and ensure that tax concessions used to subsidize philanthropy are better understood by the public at large and not abused through tax avoidance and evasion schemes. Finally, the OECD report suggests *reassessing restrictions imposed on cross-border philanthropic activities.* Responding to global issues such as poverty, environmental concerns, and pandemics may require countries and institutions to cooperate across borders. With appropriate requirements, equivalent tax treatment can be provided to domestic and cross-border philanthropy.

***

As can be seen, the authors participating in this volume cover extremely diverse questions and perspectives related to taxation and philanthropy. The OECD report presents an additional in-depth comparative study on this topic. A number of the issues and problems raised remain open for further analysis and potential solutions, as not all contributions provide final answers. However, we believe that these works offer a number of promising ways to contribute to the further development of the complex field of taxation related to philanthropic activities, and we hope that they build solid foundations for further studies on this topic.

Giedre Lideikyte Huber and Henry Peter

Notes

1 L. Ventura, *Le "società benefit" nel mondo: Un'analisi comparata, in Societa' Benefit: Profili giuridici ed economico-aziendali*, ed. by C. Bellavite Pellegrini, R. Caruso, EGEA, Milano, 2020, 115–126.

2 This section mirrors the article authored by Pascal Saint-Amans and Henry Peter and published as a blog on the OECD forum network platform.

References

Buijze, Renate. 'Approaches towards the application of tax incentives for cross-border philanthropy', *Intertax*, 44(1), 2016.

Hemels, Sigrid. Tax Incentives as a Creative Industries Policy Instrument, in *Tax Incentives for the Creative Industries*. Singapore: Springer, 2017, pp. 33–64.

Silver, Natalie, and Renate Buijze. 'Tax incentives for cross-border giving in an era of philanthropic globalization: A comparative perspective', *Canadian Journal of Comparative and Contemporary Law*, 6, 2020, 109–150.

PART I

Justification of tax incentives for philanthropy insights

1

THE PROPER RELATIONSHIP OF PRIVATE PHILANTHROPY AND THE LIBERAL DEMOCRATIC STATE

The inquiry and the inquirers as the answer

Rob Atkinson

Introduction: back to which future, forward in which tradition?

> In public affairs, as in the humbler departments of human life, questions of ends and questions of means inevitably intersect. Disputes as to the former commonly produce more sparks than light, and more heat than either. If a man affirms that his heart leaps up at the spectacle either of a society in which the common good is defined by the decisions of a totalitarian bureaucracy, or of one – like, to mention only one example – the England of a century ago, where, in the unceasing struggle of individuals for personal gain, a conception of the common good cannot easily find a foothold, it may readily be admitted that no logic exists which can prove these exhilarating palpitations either right or wrong. One cannot argue with the choice of a soul.
>
> *(Tawney, 1964)*

> Beware of false prophets, who come to you in sheep's clothing but are ravenous wolves. You will know them by their fruits. Are grapes gathered from thorns, or figs from thistles? In the same way, every good tree bears good fruit, but the bad tree bears bad fruit.
>
> *(Matthew 7:15–17)*

Taxation and Philanthropy (OECD, 2020), jointly produced by the OECD Centre for Tax Policy and Administration and the University of Geneva Centre for Philanthropy, surveys and assesses the tax policies that member states, donee states, and others might want to use to encourage both private philanthropic organizations and donations to those organizations from private individuals and for-profit entities. The point of this chapter is to identify and unpack several apparent paradoxes in the Report's position, admittedly in an apparently paradoxical way. I argue that the Report is, in several important respects, at odds with the basic mission of the OECD itself; I mean that deep criticism in the most friendly possible way, and I mean

 DOI: 10.4324/9781003139201-3

to explain why. This chapter offers not just friendly amendments but a comradely salute (or at least a word, with a wink, to the wise who would set global policy for the good of all humankind).

The Report's most basic proposal poses the deepest paradox: A collaborative report by two public institutions, one a consortium of liberal democratic states and the other an old and renowned state university, suggests to states that they may want to use their fiscal systems to encourage non-state institutions to do the philanthropic work that states themselves have done and to do that work financed by voluntary contributions rather than by the state's own method of finance, taxing and spending. In both respects, the financing and the delivering of public services, the Report's cosponsors seem to suggest ways of doing philanthropy better than their own. They seem to propose, if not quite to preach, something very different from what they practice, what both the OECD and public universities have always practiced: tax-financed, state-delivered works for the common good.

The collection of essays published along with the Report poses a second, and almost equally deep, paradox: The wisdom of a policy to be recommended to democratic nations is to be assessed not by submission to the voters of those nations, or even to their elected leaders, but by academics and civil servants, agents of meritocraticly elitist, and thus implicitly undemocratic, institutions. This anthology thus has a distinct ring to it: "inside the Beltway," in the idiom of the United States; "over there in Brussels," in that of the United Kingdom.

Unpacking those two paradoxes – the paradox of the Report's recommendations and the paradox of this volume's commentary on those recommendations – produces a double paradox of its own. On the one hand, this chapter offers the strongest possible praise for the Report; on the other hand, it raises a very deep qualification. Compounding, perhaps more than doubling, that paradox, it spends far more time on the qualification than on the praise. Its praise is not faint, and the very opposite of damning, but that praise may seem overshadowed by its heavy qualification.

This is the praise: The joint Report is a really fine example of the ethos of the Marshall Planners, the OECD's long-standing tradition of collaboration between career civil servants and mainstream academics in addressing major issues of public concern. This is the qualification: The Report might have gone further in advancing that very tradition. At the end, the praise and the qualification are not at odds; if they are not essentially the same, they demonstrably derive from the same source, the ethos of the original Marshall Planners. The proper answer to the relationship of the modern state and private philanthropy is for both to serve the two related goals of the Marshall Plan: at the very least, the maintenance of peace as the minimal condition of human flourishing; at the very best, the active promotion of those conditions that encourage human flourishing itself, an essential collaboration of modern states and traditional universities to advance the fullest possible realization of the core of philanthropy: the love of humankind.

Those truly Good Shepherds, the original Marshall Planners, knew very well the wolves that were at the door of the nations of Europe and Asia, the victorious allies as well as the defeated Axis, in the ruins of World War II. On the one hand loomed a new and emboldened species of totalitarian bureaucracy, Soviet and Chinese Communism, in place of the old and defeated species, Nazism and Fascism. This was the first alternative to the ethos of the Marshall Plan that R. H. Tawney mentioned in our first epigraph. Thanks in no small part to the Marshall Plan, Stalinism and Maoism, like Nazism and Fascism, have slunk back to their lairs.

On the other hand, the second alternative that Tawney identified is still very much with us, even among us: equating the common good with either aggregate consumer satisfaction or unexamined popular political preference. As the Marshall Planners knew from the most painful possible experience, the market's "invisible hand" can, in the wrong hands, dangerously misdirect economic gains to the few, even as demagogues can distort the political preferences of the many. These are the false prophets, the wolves in sheep's clothing, that the very Gospels warn us about. And here we have yet another paradox, itself both deep and double, that we must unpack: These false prophets approach us in the very garb of both philanthropy and philosophy themselves; they preach a gospel all their own, often grounded in the best universities. We, like the Marshall Planners, must know them by their fruits: Who best advances the vision of universal human flourishing embraced by the victorious allies, East and West?

Only when we have unpacked all these paradoxes – the paradoxes of the Report's proposals and the paradoxes of my friendly criticism – can we properly appreciate a final paradox. This last one lies at the intersection of the other two. On the one hand, I imagine that, for their part, the co-producers of the Report and the sponsors of this symposium, the OECD and the University of Geneva, not only anticipated my criticisms but also embraced them – all before I had even written them down. On the other hand, I cannot fault them for not raising these objections themselves; I must salute them for the very great wisdom of their forbearance. Unpacking this final paradox is perhaps this chapter's ultimate homage to the Reports' authors and this symposium's sponsors. It is a salute that is more a whisper (with a wink): Well done, good and faithful fellow laborers in the vineyards of the Marshall Planners (and perhaps – a matter I must leave to still other fellow laborers – the Master Planner).

To unpack all these paradoxes, we must situate the Report in three related contexts. Part I examines the debate on the effectiveness of taxation as a means of promoting private philanthropy, Part II takes up the theory of private philanthropy's function, and Part III traces the historical links between private philanthropy and the ethos of the Marshall Planners.

This chapter's conclusion is the paradox of its subtitle: The inquiry and the inquirers are the answer. The question that the OECD and the University of Geneva pose can only be answered, in the ethos of the original Marshall Planners and traditional academics, by exactly the kind of inquiry they have invited us to join them in undertaking. As the work of the OECD and its academic partners has long demonstrated, the role of private philanthropy in advancing the ethos of the Marshall Planners has always been decidedly secondary and, ironically, sometimes not only unhelpful but actively opposed. If the work of global humanitarianism must depend, in a dark time, on handouts from the wealthy, virtuous or vicious, we can nonetheless hope for a brighter day, a day that seems already to be dawning.

I Situating the report in tax theory: are tax favors effective in encouraging private philanthropy?

The basic position of the Report is that states may want to support private philanthropy by means of favorable tax treatment. Much of the Report is taken up with evaluating whether various forms of favorable tax treatment are effective means of advancing that end, private philanthropy. Plausibly enough, the Report begins with an effort to identify what the end to be advanced, private philanthropy, actually is. It next proceeds to a detailed analysis of the scholarly literature on effectiveness of tax favors in promoting private philanthropy. As we examine this analysis, we can only conclude that it inevitably raises questions that it studiously declines to answer: whether particular private philanthropic purposes, or even private philanthropy in general, actually advance the public good – including the public good as identified and advanced by the Marshall Planners.

a The meaning of philanthropy: a working definition (with real and recognized limits)

At the outset, after noting the term's derivation from the Greek term meaning "love of humanity," the Report identifies what will prove to be a very serious problem: "The term 'philanthropy' does not have a universally accepted meaning" (OECD, 2020, Section 1.1, p. 11). In a telling understatement, the Report notes that "Various attempts have been made to define the term" (OECD). After a dutiful review of those efforts, the Report ventures its own:

> Despite the divergent uses of the term, there are some common threads: philanthropy is concerned with "giving", and with "worthy" and "public", rather than private, causes. . . . The focus then, is on "gifting" – the making of voluntary contributions without expectation of return; and on identification of appropriate worthy causes or purposes. This identification of "worthy purposes" is likely to differ between jurisdictions and is an important part of the tax framework in this area.
>
> *(OECD, 2020)*

In this last detail, identifying worthy purposes, lies either God or the devil, depending on one's point of view – particularly one's view of philanthropy.

As we shall see, and as the authors of the report seem to recognize, their definition, particularly its last detail, raises at least as many questions as it answers. It works quite well enough, however, as a kind of algebraic "x" at the next level of their analysis: If you want to promote philanthropy's "worth purposes" (whatever you think those are), here is our assessment of how various tax favors will work.

b Favorable tax treatment as a means of encouraging private philanthropy

It would be hard to over-praise the Report's diligence in reviewing the vast literature on the efficacy of various tax treatments of philanthropy. Its analysis is long and detailed and clear and compelling. But that analysis also has to be awarded a more ambiguous accolade: It is clear, and clearly inconclusive. On balance, it is clearly unclear whether tax favors are really all that effective in promoting private philanthropy. As our epigraph from Tawney implies, proper inquiry into questions like this, questions of means, often sheds a great deal of light, without generating much friction, much igniting of heated disagreement. Here, however, what the cool light of careful analysis reveals about the efficacy of tax favors as a means of promoting philanthropic ends is very nearly a Scots verdict: not proved.

Nor, alas, is that the end of the matter. If a state decides to use tax favors to that end anyway, it will have to return to a hugely difficult problem that the Report has already flagged: It will have to decide whether the purposes that nonprofit, nongovernmental organizations claim to be philanthropic, and thus entitled to tax favors, are really the kind of benefits that the government itself wants to encourage. To answer that question, as the Report implicitly notes, one must turn from an analysis of the effectiveness of tax favors to the function of nonprofit, nongovernmental organizations, to the kinds of public benefits they promise, the kinds of worthy purposes they purport to serve – and to the still more difficult question of whether they deliver on those promises, actually serve those purposes. Before a state decides whether to encourage private philanthropy, it will need to know what private philanthropy does and what it does well (OECD, 2020, p. 22, note 1).

Here we move from questions of means to questions of ends; here, as Tawney also reminds us, we may expect our inquiry to produce friction as well as light, to spark debate that is political, even existential, not merely technical or descriptive.

II Situating the report in positive economic, political, and sociological theory: what is the function of nonprofit, nongovernmental entities?

Here again, the Report does an admirable job of surveying, summarizing, and evaluating a vast scholarly literature. We need to review the Report's review the better to appreciate a problem that the Report identified at the outset: In important respects, philanthropy is in the eye of the beholder. As we shall see, and as the Report clearly appreciates, the relevant beholders are not only the private individuals who operate and support private philanthropy but also the states that must decide their proper relationship with those entities, including whether to try to encourage them with favorable tax treatment.

a The Standard Model of positive economics and political science

Here we must, alas, summarize aggressively. Here is the basic point, something of a good news, bad news situation. First, the good news: Positive economic analysis and positive political theory have offered complementary theories of how private philanthropy functions, two sides of essentially the same coin. Each theory assumes a particular kind of four-sector modern society. One sector is the liberal democratic state; a second sector is the capitalist market economy. The third sector includes private philanthropy; the fourth sector comprises households, or nuclear families. The identification of these sectors involves the intersection of two variables: whether the sector's constituent institutions are voluntary and whether they are for profit.

Four Societal Sectors

		For Profit?	
		Yes	No
Voluntary?	Yes	For-Profit Sector	Nonprofit Sector
	No	Household Sector	Governmental Sector

(Harding and Pascoe, 2018, p. 50).
Diagram.

According to this Standard Model (Diagram), each sector in this four-part social system has certain distinct advantages over the others in providing goods and services, advantages traceable to their two defining characteristics: for profit (or not); voluntary (or not). What is more, two of these four social sectors, the liberal democratic state and the capitalist market economy, have their own intrinsic standards of performance. The standard of positive economics is economic efficiency: giving consumers, in the aggregate, the most of what they want at the lowest possible cost. The standard of positive political science is democratic legitimacy: giving a majority of voters what they want, subject to constraints imposed by the majority voters on what the state is allowed to do, and how.

Each of these disciplines, economics and politics, accounts for the function of the others as providing goods or services that the institutions of its own sector fail to provide by that sector's own standard. Thus economic theory holds that when private firms cannot produce a good or service at optimal efficiency, individuals will seek that good in one of the other sectors. Similarly, political theory holds that if the majority of voters do not provide a good or service at the level preferred by an individual voter, that dissatisfied voter can turn to one of the other sectors. Since the Standard Model thus defines the function of the nonprofit, nongovernmental sector by default of the market and governmental sectors, it is sometimes called the Twin Failure theory.

Even this briefest outline should convey some of the elegance of the Standard Model. It explains the function of not just the nonprofit, nongovernmental sector, but also the other three sectors as well. It is, essentially, social science's equivalent of a Grand Unified Theory; it is as if physicists had managed to unify the microcosmic theory of quantum mechanics with the macrocosmic theory of general relativity. If there were a Nobel Prize for positive social science, the economists and political scientists of the Standard Model should have shared it long ago. That, obviously enough, is the good news

Now the other shoe must drop; here's the bad news: The Standard Model, for all its elegance as a sectoral map, is no guide through the relevant policy maze. The Standard Model, for all its descriptive elegance, offers the policy makers whom the Report is addressing very little guidance in the task at hand: whether to try to encourage private philanthropy with favorable tax treatment. The full elaboration of this bad news, alas, is a very long story. But it only takes a slightly closer look to reveal several limitations of the Standard Model's usefulness as a guide to policy-making in general and thus to the policy planning of the states to which the Report has directed its own policy recommendations.

Most obviously, the Standard Model is, by its own terms, limited to a particular kind of society: liberal democratic polities with capitalist market economies. Its insights, accordingly, apply with much less force in other kinds of societies. This is a very big limitation: Some of the OECD's donees do not have liberal democratic polities; some do not have capitalist market economies; some have neither of the two. (And, complicating matters even more, the current democratically elected leaders of Poland and Hungary – members of not only of the OECD but also of both NATO and the EU – openly aspire to make their countries "illiberal democracies.")

A second important limitation to the Standard Model as a policy guide applies even with respect to countries that have, and hope to retain, both liberal democratic polities and capitalist market economies. To appreciate this limit, we must notice something odd about how positive economics and positive political theory both define and measure the public good. Both disciplines measure the public good as an aggregation of unexamined individual preferences: In economics, these are the goods and services that consumers are both willing and able to pay for, quantified in monetary units; in politics, these are the politicians and policies that a majority of citizens prefer, quantified in terms of the ballots they cast. It is this common metric, aggregated individual preference, that allows economists and political scientists to produce their Grand Unified Theory (of, as we have seen, a certain kind of society).

A moment's thought will reveal that, as a guide to choosing policy ends, as a means of identifying the public good, the Standard Model is wholly unhelpful to policy makers in two diametrically opposite ways. On the one hand, if policy makers identify the public good with what the people want, then the policy makers do not need the Standard Model to tell them what they need to know: That is what free markets and free elections already do. On the other hand, if policy makers want to know what is really good for the people, not just what the people want, then the Standard Model offers them no guidance at all, and they will have to look elsewhere, beyond not only the market and the ballot box but also the Standard Model.

This radical limitation of the Standard Model is not just demonstrably true; it is also readily conceded by the Model's architects. But, though entirely true, this criticism is a bit overly harsh. Even if the Standard Model is no help to policy makers in identifying ends, what the public good is, it might be quite helpful in identifying means to ends not otherwise accounted for, how to go about achieving the public good without evaluating that good by standards other than their own (aggregate consumer satisfaction and majority voter preference). The Standard Model could, in that strictly instrumentalist way, help both kinds of policy makers, those who want to give people what they want and also those who want to give people what they need, what they should want (as identified by standards supplementing those of positive economics and political science).

In fairness, this is what the Standard Model primarily purports to do; its main purpose is to explain how society works, not how to make society work better. As we have seen, the Standard Model purports to explain why each sector is better at providing some kinds of good and services than others. It is particularly insightful about two broad categories of goods and services that capitalist firms, left to their own devices, are likely not to produce efficiently – so as to give consumers more bang for their buck – on their own.

Let's look at the two kinds of goods and services that the Standard Model identifies as particularly relevant here. The first, and most obvious, are what economists call public goods. Classic example are lighthouses and radio broadcasts. Private firms have a hard time making a profit providing these goods and services, because they have no effective way of charging consumers for them. With respect to the second kind of products, the shoe is basically on the other foot. Private firms can quite easily deny the benefits of these products to those who don't buy them, but those who do buy them are not in a position to evaluate whether they are, in fact, getting what they pay for. This is especially true of services involving highly technical knowledge, like medicine or law or advanced education; unless you're a doctor or a lawyer or a professor, it is hard to know if your doctor or lawyer or professor really knows what he or she is doing (for you – or to you).

In both these classic cases of "market failure," externalities and information asymmetries, private firms are not likely to give consumers in the aggregate the most of what they are willing and able to pay for at the lowest possible price. In these cases, then, for-profit private firms fail to function optimally by the standard of positive economic analysis itself. Provision by another sector might, in those very terms, be a better means of meeting consumer demand.

But notice that, in such a situation, consumers may have an embarrassment of riches: They could avoid their problems with private firms by turning to providers in either of the other two public sectors, state agencies on the one hand or private philanthropies on the other – assuming, of course, that suppliers were available in both alternative sectors and that those alternative suppliers offered consumers a comparable product at a competitive price.

Here, alas, the consumer may find further problems. Maybe the product is available from only a private philanthropy or the state. Or maybe the product is available from both, but the consumer is no better able to tell which of the two is producing it at the ideal price/quality point than he or she was in the case of private, for-profit providers. Why might this problem arise again outside the for-profit sector? Because governments and private philanthropies, though less tempted than non-profits to skimp on quality to increase their profit margins, may be tempted to skimp on quality for other reasons; without net profit as an incentive to lower costs, maybe they will "slack off" rather than "skim off."

Here policy makers might be a real help making sure consumers get what they are paying for. If they knew which nonprofit suppliers, state agencies or private philanthropies, were likely to be the lowest-cost, highest-quality provider, they could direct consumers to that alternative. If none, or too few, were available, they could have the state subsidize those providers or provide the relevant product themselves.

But here policy makers would have, alas, yet another problem. Although that course would seem to be the economically appropriate course of action, it might not be the politically appropriate course. Individual consumers might prefer the less economically reliable alternative to for-profit suppliers because they have a preference for that provider independent of its economic efficiency. Some consumers, in fact, may prefer private for-profit providers over either governmental or private non-profit suppliers, even though both of the latter are the most cost-effective providers.

And that (alas yet again) is not just an academic hypothetical; it seems to be the case in a great deal of the "real world." Individual consumers do seem to have preferences not just for products but also for the sector that provides the product. And, what is more, these preferences as to both providers and product seem to vary with consumers from country to country. As a result, the Standard Model, though quite elegant in showing which sectoral providers – state, private nonprofits, or private for-profits – consumers would choose *if* getting the most for their money were their only concern, is a pretty poor predictor of which sectoral providers they actually do choose.

Here is the trouble. The Standard Model takes preferences for particular goods and services as exogenous but assumes that consumers will want their preferences met by the lowest-cost provider not only within each sector but among all four sectors. Inconveniently for the Standard Model, consumers have preferences not only for particular goods and services but also for particular sectoral providers. The Standard Theory has, in its own terms, no way to account for individual preferences; this is fine at the level of particular products, but, at the level of sectoral choice, it seriously affects the predictive power of the model.

b Social Origins Theory

As the Report nicely notes, insights from a third descriptive social science, sociology, give a very powerful improvement here. These insights, aptly called Social Origins Theory, trace individual countries' preference for particular combinations of state or nonprofit provision of social services to a critical moment in the state's development (OECD, p. 12, citing Anheier and Salamon, 1996, pp. 213–248). That critical moment is when the state actually becomes modern; the critical variable at that moment is the social group most politically empowered. Social Origins Theory identifies four distinctive kinds of states that emerge in that moment, each of which has a distinctive kind of relationship with private philanthropy in the provision of social services.

With one terminological qualification,[1] the Report's own summary cannot be improved upon:

- "[Negative] liberal states" – where democratic government developed before the welfare state. The welfare state may be limited but available to the "deserving poor". These countries are likely to have a larger philanthropic sector;
- "social-democratic [or Positive Liberal] states" – where the working class gained power and pushed for a universal welfare state. As a result of the high level of welfare, these countries tend to have smaller philanthropic sectors;

- "corporatist states" – where the welfare state developed under the control of non-democratic states that later became democratic. These countries tend to have low welfare and large philanthropic sectors;
- "statist states" – where a country's elites are in control of the public good provision, and this leads to both low government spending on social welfare and a small philanthropic sector.

(OECD, p. 12) (Salamon, Sokolowski and Anheier, 2000, at 16–17)

Social Origins Theory claims, plausibly enough, to account far better for the actual mix of state and private delivery of social services than does the Standard Model alone. By its account, the predictable pattern is Negative Liberal in the United Kingdom and the United States; Positive Liberal in Scandinavia; Corporatist in Germany, France, Belgium, and the Netherlands; and Statist in Japan and Latin America.

Social Origins Theory also analyzes another variable that is critical both to its own predictive power and to our present purposes: the predominant kind of private philanthropy at the time that the modern state decides to assume modern welfare functions. Thus, for example, in the nineteenth century, the critical period in both Germany and France, a very powerful and oppositional Roman Catholic Church managed to retain an extensive role in the provision of social services not found in Scandinavia, where legally established Protestant churches were not only state supported, but also state supporting.

Here, then, the policy makers who are interested in giving consumers and voters what they want would seem to have the guidance that they need. If citizens in their country show a preference for provision of a good or service from private philanthropies, and if the policy makers conclude that tax incentives actually encourage private philanthropy, then they should supply those incentives; if they prove wrong on either point – the efficacy of the incentives or the preferences of their citizens – then their citizens can correct them.

That would, alas, be no help to the other kind of policy maker, those who want to give the people not just what they want but also what they need. Nor, upon still closer inspection, would it give the preference-serving policy makers quite what they need, either. Three insights of Social Origins Theory are especially relevant here.

First, and most basically, society is not static. The starting point of Social Origins Theory, the emergence of the modern state itself, represented a radically new prospect in the relationship of the public sector and the private non-profit sector: Modern societies, with modern states, generate a great deal more wealth than traditional societies. As the Social Origins model reminds us, the state can deal with that new wealth in several distinct ways. Thus, for example, statist states tend to hoard it in the hands of political elites; liberal states tend to leave it in the hands of economic elites; social democratic societies tend to redistribute it across their entire population on the basis of democratic politics; corporatist states tend to allocate it across social classes by the lights of *soi-disant* publicly spirited elites.

Second, as the Social Origins theory clearly implies, these ideal-type states themselves, each with its own pattern of wealth allocation and relationship with private philanthropy, are dynamic, not static. This is clear in the Report's own description of Positive Liberal states and Negative Liberal states: In the former, "democratic government developed before the welfare state"; in the latter, "the working class gained power and pushed for a universal welfare state." It is bracing to be reminded that fundamental institutional choices, both individual and collective, are not what they once were and thus may not remain what they now are.

This brings us to the third insight implicit in Social Origins Theory, in considerable tension with the first two. True, social institutions change; also true, human beings, individually and collectively, are profoundly significant agents of social change. And yet, as Social Origins

Theory also reminds us, individuals' preferences are not entirely chosen; they are also shaped, and they are shaped to a very large extent not by pure or unencumbered individual choice but by exogenous factors that both constrain and condition, even implant, individual inclinations toward particular choices. More specifically – and far more significant for our purposes – is this: Among the primary shapers and limiters of individual choice are precisely the two kinds of entities with whose proper function in relationship to each other that the Report and the policy makers it addresses must be most concerned: contemporary states and private philanthropies.

c Summary of positive social scientific functional theories

The Report's examination of positive social theory – economic, political, and sociological – sheds admirable light on our understanding of the basic topic the Report addresses: tax support for private philanthropy. For this it is, once again, very much to be commended. The light that positive social theory sheds on that topic sharpens our focus even as it reveals an essential second phase of our analysis. We now have a much better sense of how, and how well, tax favors might be used, and best used, to support private philanthropy.

Beyond that, we have a much better sense of what private philanthropy actually is and does, of how it functions alongside the other three sectors of a modern state: the private for-profit sector, the governmental sector, and the household sector. But here, if you'll forgive me, we find another paradox: That we know more about both the modern state and private philanthropy is good news; what we now know about each of them is by no means entirely good – at least from the perspective of those of us committed to the traditional work of both the Report's sponsors, the liberal democratic states of the OECD and modern research universities like the home of the Geneva Center on Philanthropy.

Let's pause to look at that news, the good and bad, with respect to both institutions in question, private philanthropy and the modern state. Let us begin with the lessons learned, first about philanthropy, then about the modern state. With those lessons in mind, we can better appreciate where we need to go next – where we might be forgiven for wishing, if only provisionally, that the Report had taken us.

The Report, much to its credit, begins with an effort to understand exactly what we mean by philanthropy. No beginning could be better rooted in the best of academic traditions. For both Socrates and Confucius, much turns on proper terminology, and no concept is more important than the loving care of humankind, in both oneself and others. The Report's provisional definition of philanthropy focused on two factors: private voluntary efforts for publicly beneficial purposes. Both halves of this definition, we can now see, need considerable amendment.

On the one hand, the focus on private agency is seriously distorting. Some modern states do much of the work once done by private philanthropy; to award the very positive associations of the term "philanthropy" to one set of sectoral providers to the exclusion of another is doubtlessly an innocent oversight in the OECD report; elsewhere, unfortunately, it is a most artful rhetorical move. Whatever the motive, the effect tends to be the same: to suggest that one of the two sometimes competing sectors serves the public good essentially; the others, at best, only incidentally.

This suggestion is doubly dubious.

This becomes even clearer when we look more closely at the second element of the Report's definition, serving the public good. As we have seen, and as the Report quite rightly acknowledges, what counts as "public benefit" is often very much in the eye of the beholder. One person's meat is another's poison; the Trojan horse was nothing if not a gift, but its goodness depended entirely on the side of the relevant wall from which one saw it.

In our case, the relevant walls are those that divide the most distinctive kinds of modern states. As Social Origins Theory points out, some modern states are more likely to rely on the organizations in the non-profit, non-governmental sector than others. But that insight, useful though it is, is only the beginning. Basically, the OECD Report's tendency to take "philanthropy" as synonym for nonprofit, non-governmental organizations implicitly begs two important questions.

On the one hand, using the term "philanthropic" to describe all third-sector organizations implies that all third-sector organizations are "philanthropic" in a meaningful sense, a sense that has to do with genuine "love of humanity." To the contrary, as we shall see, some third-sector organizations are "philanthropic" only in a technical, or perhaps deceptive, sense. Some *soi-disant* "philanthropies" are false prophets, wolves in sheep's clothing. On the other hand, using "philanthropy" to cover all third-sector organizations tends to obscure a very old human aspiration and a very real possibility: The state itself may be philanthropic, in the fullest possible way. Such, so we might remember, was the ideal polis of classical philosophy; so, too, were the states that formed the precursor of the OECD and eventually the OECD itself.

We are back – much better informed, to be sure! – to the questions with which we began: whether the state should encourage private philanthropy, and, if so, which ones? Here, I have to suggest, the Report needs to look past the social science of both the efficacy of tax favors to private "philanthropy" and the function of private philanthropy in relationship to our society's other three sectors. In addition to the social sciences, the physical sciences offer hugely helpful insights. This is especially true of evolutionary psychology, where there is increasingly compelling evidence of our capacity for both selfish and pro-social orientation. For our purposes, though, the most important place to look must be the humanities.

Here the obvious choice might seem normative philosophy, particularly the classical subjects of ethics and politics, those ancient and perennial inquiries into the basic question of philanthropy: how to be the best possible human beings, individually and collectively. I myself have spent a good bit of time trying to show how a neo-classical understanding of philanthropy has much to commend it.

But here, in commenting on the OECD's joint proposal, the discipline to turn to, I hope to convince you, is history, in particular the history of the OECD itself and the relationship of the OECD and its members and donees with private philanthropy. Before turning from social science to history, though, I want to note what I think is a most important point: These are all disciplines centered in the university; this turn to yet another academic discipline, like the course of our study so far, is very much in the tradition of the OECD, approaching the solution to complex social problems in conversations between policy makers and academics. So: In turning to the history of the OECD and private philanthropy, we remain well within the tradition of the OECD (and, at the deepest possible level, the Academy).

III Situating the OECD Report in history: the affairs of Marshall Plan members and private philanthropy as a drama in three acts

> The life of the law has not been logic: it has been experience. The felt necessities of the time, the prevalent moral and political theories, institutions of public policy, avowed or unconscious, even the prejudices which judges share with their fellow-men, have had a good deal more to do than the syllogism in determining the rules by which men should be governed. The law embodies the story of a nation's development through many centuries, and it cannot be dealt with as if it contained only the axioms and corollaries of a book of mathematics. In order to know what it is, we must

> know what it has been, and what it tends to become. We must alternately consult history and existing theories of legislation. But the most difficult labor will be to understand the combination of the two into new products at every stage.
>
> *(Holmes, 1881, p. 1)*

> And if you want biographies, do not look for those with the legend "Mr. So-and-so and his times" but for one whose title-page might be inscribed "A fighter against his time." Feast your souls on Plutarch, and dare to believe in yourselves when you believe in his heroes. A hundred such men – educated against the fashion of today, made familiar with the heroic, and come to maturity – are enough to give an eternal quietus to the noisy sham education of this time.
>
> *(Nietzsche, 1957, pp. 41–42)*

As Social Origins Theory reminds us, in any particular country at any particular time, the relationship between the modern state and private philanthropy will be, to a more or less substantial degree, path dependent. In approaching the work of philanthropy in their own time, both private individuals and public policy makers find their choice of means to the great end of global human flourishing influenced, even constrained, by inherited institutions and customary modes of institutional relationships. Properly to understand the context in which the OECD Report has appeared, and thus the constraints under which policy makers who read it have to operate, we need to focus our analysis on a particular era and two particular nations. The relevant era is the twentieth century; the relevant nations are the United Kingdom and the United States.

This latter focus requires a word of explanation, though I think not apology. By historical accident – happy or not – the United States and the United Kingdom have loomed especially large in two critical developments: first, the "Social Democratic," or "Positive Liberal," mode of domestic interaction between states and private philanthropy and, second, the Marshall Plan as the expansion of that mode into the international arena. The basic story line is this: At the turn of the twentieth century, even as Social Origins Theory has pointed out, both the United States and the United Kingdom were paradigms of the Negative Liberal mode of state and private philanthropic interaction (SSA, p. 19). As a result, traditions and institutions of private philanthropy were particularly strong and well-developed in the United Kingdom and United States, and, as the Report acknowledges, scholarly focus long centered on the latter (OECD, 2020, p. 12).

In both nations, that pattern changed dramatically (but not permanently) in the wake of World War I and especially in response to the global economic depression of the 1930s. Reliance on vastly expanded central government provision of essential goods and services, very much in the Positive Liberal pattern, became the practice and the expectation in both the United States and the United Kingdom.

That pattern continued, perforce, through World War II. The states allied against the fascism of the Axis Powers were neither "night watchmen" nor "nannies." And, through the Marshall Plan, the victorious allies made the Positive Liberal domestic model of the United States and the United Kingdom not only the template of post-war recovery but also the pattern of collective defense and international development for next three decades.

By the 1970s, a distinct reaction had set in not only in the United States and United Kingdom but across much of the rest of the Western Alliance and the world, a reaction that accelerated with the collapse of the Soviet threat. If you'll pardon the eponyms, it went like this: The Marshall Plan ethos, the ethos of Roosevelt and Attlee, gave way to a very different ethos, first of Reagan and Thatcher, then of Clinton and Blair, and finally of Trump and Johnson. Understandably enough, these developments cannot but have affected the position of the OECD and its supporters toward private philanthropy in both domestic politics and international relations.

To put the change most bluntly: A new generation of vastly wealthy private, purportedly philanthropic, foundations, some of which had grown extremely large in the unraveling of the domestic and international order of the Marshall Planners, became one of the few available sources of financial and technical support for international development once done by the OECD and its member states themselves, with limited but significant aid from older and closely allied private foundations.

As we have said, the main theme of this historical review is the shift in relations in the relationship between the state and private philanthropy as the governments of the United Kingdom and United States went from Negative Liberal to Positive Liberal (Social Democratic) and then back. As we examine this cycle, we also need to watch the other side of the relationship, private philanthropy. On this side, we need to be particularly mindful of the role of three significant institutions: religious organizations, especially Protestant Christian churches; universities, both private and public; and private philanthropic foundations, both those favoring Positive Liberalism and those favoring Negative Liberalism.

a In the beginning (as identified by Social Origins Theory): the amazing rise and spectacular fall of the (Negative) Liberal state

> Radicals and conservatives, after all, necessarily share some ground in common. . . . Radicals, for example, are traditionalists, just as conservatives are; it is simply that they adhere to entirely different traditions.
>
> *(Eagleton, 1996, p. 6)*

> [I]f this faith is truly liberal, then somewhere in it lies a deep strain of political conservatism.
>
> *(Rossiter, 1955, p. 71)*

The era that set what Social Origins Theory identifies as the distinctive mode of state interaction with private philanthropy in the United States and United Kingdom, our Negative Liberalism, is often and tellingly known, especially in the United States, as the Gilded Age. It was an age of astonishing industrial, commercial, and financial expansion; particularly savvy entrepreneurs, often neither morally scrupulous nor socially conscious, amassed hitherto unimaginable private fortunes. Collectively, and hardly affectionately, called robber barons, their ranks included names that are still household words, if no longer watch-words, today: Ford and Carnegie, Rockefeller and Mellon. At the time these magnates amassed their vast fortunes in steel and oil, assembly-line production, and international banking, the state, decidedly Negative Liberal, imposed minimum regulation on their profit-making conduct and virtually no control over the disposition of their accumulated wealth (SSA, p. 19). To say that these private fortunes conferred a considerable say in state policy in these and other matters is to strain understatement to the point of self-parody.

The insulation from state interference of these "Captains of Industry" did not depend entirely on their direct political influence. They received considerable support from two significant sources: mainstream Protestant churches and universities, particularly the newly emerging economics departments of those universities R.L. Heilbroner (1972). But, quite significantly, neither church nor academic support was ever unanimous, and, as the effect of essentially unregulated capitalism became increasingly apparent, opposition in both churches and universities increased.

Partly in response to that criticism and its feared effect on public policy, though surely in part out of genuine good will, several of the great magnates developed a significant new form of private philanthropy, the private foundation. The foundation was to do for private charity what the magnates' *soi-disant* genius had done for capitalism itself: introduce new levels of scale and new methods of scientific management. In the view of these Captains of Industry, just as capitalism, before their age of industrial consolidation, had been a wasteful battleground of petty competition, so private charity had remained an amateurish, ill-guided social enterprise. Private foundations were to change all that. And, to a considerable extent, they did, in two particularly important ways: They became, functionally speaking, old-style charities' consulting firms and investment bankers; private foundations' permanent and increasingly professional staffs gave expert advice not only on how best to undertake traditional philanthropic operations like poor relief, primary education, and hospital care but also on getting at the roots of traditional problems like poverty, ignorance, and disease.

And, it has to be noted, many of the giant first-generation private foundations had the explicit goal, and all of them the cumulative effect, of performing functions that, as early skeptics duly noted, might have been undertaken by a more active state itself. Private foundations were, in theory as well as in effect, the archangels of Andrew Carnegie's *Gospel of Wealth:* Best to let the titans of industry control not only the making of money but also its ultimate direction and distribution (Carnegie, 2017). Some unfortunate souls, to be sure, would fall by the wayside, in the happier future as in the less fortunate past. But now, to quote a reluctant private philanthropist, fictitious but famous, this decrease of the excess population could be seen not as the tragic outworkings of Professor Malthus's inscrutable mathematics and mankind's manifestly fallen nature but as the social implications of the Reverend Darwin's accessible insights into the progressive improvement of all surviving species, not excluding *Homo sapiens*.

These assuredly wholesome, if sometimes stern, domestic arrangements had important implications for foreign affairs. The Titans of Industry, with their supportive lawyers and policy makers, were committed to free international trade and open global markets among nearly absolutely sovereign nation-states (once their own nascent industries were safe against older industries established elsewhere earlier). Nation-states, as sovereign legal agents, were free to regulate their internal affairs as they chose; in their relations with each other, they were to keep their borders open to the free movement of goods and capital (though not, significantly, labor). Their disputes were to be resolved peaceably, if not by the disputants themselves, then by neutral international tribunals they themselves created to apply universal principles of law dutifully fashioned by university-based law faculties in a remarkably formalized conceptual system (Giovanopoulou, forthcoming, 2021, pp. 11–12).

This story is hard to tell with a completely straight face, and, no matter how one tells it, it does not have a surprise ending. It all came crashing down in two watershed events: the Great War and the Great Depression. As we look back upon these ruins, we must be careful not to commit the post hoc fallacy; indeed, some still assert, in what we must in all charity take to be good faith, that unregulated capitalism itself was not a major cause of either the War or the Depression. For our purposes, it is enough to note that many observers, then and now, have taken quite a different view and acted on those convictions. Their legacy includes, as most relevant here, the Marshall Plan and its direct descendant, the OECD.

b *The post-war realignments: Positive Liberalism's ascendancy, domestically and internationally*

> It is logical that the United States should do whatever it is able to do to assist in the return of normal economic health in the world, without which there can be no political stability and no assured peace. Our policy is directed not against any country or doctrine but against hunger, poverty, desperation and chaos.
>
> *(Marshall, 1947)*

> Injustice anywhere is a threat to justice everywhere.
>
> *(King, 1963)*

In the wake of the global catastrophe of WWII, as the great English Social Democrat R.H. Tawney was writing his fellow socially conscious Christians across the Atlantic, other leaders of the Western Alliance were laying the foundations of the post-war world order. A cornerstone of that order was the Marshall Plan; out of the Marshall Plan, of course, grew the OECD. For our purposes, several aspects of that new order are especially salient. We will look first at the role of the relevant states, focusing still on the United States and the United Kingdom, then at those states' relationships with three particular institutions: universities, private foundations, and Protestant churches.

As in the preceding era of Negative Liberalism in the United States and the United Kingdom, the domestic and foreign policies of the relevant nations were critically linked. The Marshall Planners saw the need to respond militarily to the threat of the Soviet Union. This, quite by itself, would require a rebuilding of both the Western Allies and former enemies Germany, Italy, and Japan. The Marshall Planners knew this would involve massive infusions of North American money, material, and technical assistance; they also knew that this aspect of the Plan was a necessary but not sufficient condition.

In addition to ensuring a military response to the Stalinist threat, the Marshall Planners believed they had to appeal to the "hearts and minds" of the citizens of then-donee countries, the previously industrialized countries, friend and foe, devastated by the war. Again, Tawney's insight is instructive:

> [T]he task of reconstruction, both for England and for several of her continental neighbors, is more subtle and exacting than the mere reparation of a shattered edifice.
>
> *(Tawney, 1964, p. 139)*

Tawney and his Marshall Plan allies looked ahead, then, not merely to restoring the pre-War domestic arrangements. That regime, they believed, had broken down in two world wars and an intervening global economic collapse. Against the backdrop of that failure, the architects of the new order worked address the reasons why the old had failed. In persuading the United States to join the Allied war effort, Roosevelt had promised freedom from fear (Roosevelt, 1941). After the war, any tenant farmer or factory worker might well have known, many from quite bitter experience, that what they had to fear along with the Communists in Moscow was not an activist government in Washington or Westminster, Paris, or Bonn but the Boss and the Man, the Sir and the Seigneur, very much closer to home.

And so, in a fundamental sense, the Marshall Plan was, from the perspective of both sponsors in the United States and its participants abroad, an extension of the Roosevelt's New Deal onto the international stage (Priestland, 2012, p. 156; Giovanopoulou, forthcoming, 2021, pp. 13–16). And, as the Cold War with the Soviet Union expanded beyond Eastern Europe and into less economically advanced countries outside Europe, particularly in Latin America, Africa, and South Asia, the Marshall Planners expanded their basic development program, both economic and political, into those areas as well (Machado and Marshall, 2007, Giovanopoulou, forthcoming, 2021, p. 25).

Seen through the very useful lens of Social Origins Theory, the Marshall Planners' new world order was far closer to the Positive Liberal, or social democratic, model first established in the Nordic countries than to the Negative Liberal model dominant in the United Kingdom and the United States at the turn of the twentieth century. Two aspects of this change from the prior period are critical for our analysis. First, for the Positive Liberal direction of the Marshall Planners to enjoy the necessary international cooperation of its member countries, it had also to have very broad political support within those countries. It did. Second, it did not need to rely on private philanthropy in either the design or the implementation of its program, domestically or internationally. It did not.

The Positive Liberal ethos of the Marshall Planners was not merely the position of the parties of the West's democratic Left, parties like Labor in the United Kingdom and the Democrats in the United States. That ethos also became, in basic outline, the position of center-right parties like the Conservatives in the United Kingdom and the Republican Party in the United States. (And so, too, it was across Europe the consensus position of not only the moderately leftist social democratic parties, but also center-right parties like the Christian Democrats.) Thus, in the United States, as one prominent scholar of the period has observed,

> Under President Dwight Eisenhower, the [Republican] party had made peace with New Deal social provisioning and backed large-scale federal spending on infrastructure and education. Even as late as the 1970s, President Richard Nixon passed legislation expanding federal regulatory agencies.
>
> *(McGirr, 2021)*

This convergence of mainstream political parties toward the social democratic center-left was even older and more secure in Britain. Thus, as Tawney noted, in the interwar years, the United Kingdom had more than doubled real spending on social programs, mainly under Conservative governments (145).

Of equal importance was a parallel development: In both countries, the political position of the nineteenth century's Negative Liberalism had all but collapsed. In the United Kingdom, the nominally Liberal Party came apart at the seams (Dangerfield, 2012). In the United States, the Republican Party lost the presidency in 1932 and regained it only in 1952. For more than a generation after the war, both the Conservative Party and the Republican Party accepted the social democratic status quo of the Roosevelt and Attlee years.

A second feature of the new era was, for our purposes, every bit as important. As it was for the paradigmatic Social Democratic states in the Social Origins Theory of philanthropy, so it was with the corresponding but later phase of Positive Liberalism in American and British politics: It had no particularly large place for private philanthropy as such. The reason is radically significant: The Positive Liberal state is *itself* actively philanthropic. A chapter title from David Owens's contemporary survey of English philanthropy in this period nicely captures the situation: *Junior Partner in the Welfare Firm* (1964, p. 527). And, at least in the early post-war period, it seemed that the trend toward less reliance on private philanthropy would continue: "Not only did the State emerge as the predominant partner, but for a time there was grave doubt as to what might be left for its older but now junior associate" (p. 526).

A closer look, however, reveals that there was quite a lot. The Marshall Planners' broad political consensus, it is important to note, rested on a social consensus that was equally broad and quite likely even deeper. And this social consensus included, quite critically, two particular kinds of traditionally philanthropic organizations, universities and churches, as well as that newer innovation, the private foundation.

Take the oldest, the churches, first. The academic leadership of mainstream Protestant denominations in the United States was solidly behind the New Deal and the Marshall Plan – when not ahead of them. And these mainstream denominations – Presbyterians, Episcopalians, Congregationalists, Lutherans, and, increasingly, Methodists – insisted that their clergy hold graduate-level university degrees, which their academic leadership, through its professional organization, hoped to make the norm in other prominent denominations as well (as it had long been, of course, in the Catholic communion) (Niebuhr et al., 1957, p. 203). The leadership of the Catholic Church was considerably slower in accepting secular liberalism in politics, but it was at least equally reluctant to embrace laissez-faire liberalism in economics (Leo XIII, 1891). And the Catholic laity in the United States, particularly those of the urban working class, became essential constituents of the New Deal coalition (until, in the next period, that coalition turned further left on social as well as economic issues, particularly abortion and same-sex marriage).

Even as the academic elite of Protestants in the United States supported social democratic programs, so those programs drew heavily from universities for both their inspiration and their implementation. Felix Frankfurter at Harvard Law School was a particular significant "talent scout" before Roosevelt elevated him to the Supreme Court (and almost certainly afterward) (Urofsky, 1991, p. 62). Nor were elite private Eastern universities like Harvard the sole, perhaps even the principal, source of intellectual talent. The great public universities of the West and South also provided both ideas and leadership. When George Marshall himself announced what was to be his namesake plan at Harvard, one of the premier private universities in the United States, he spoke as a graduate of the Virginia Military Institute, a university founded and funded by the Commonwealth of Virginia. Far more of the United States military officer corps were graduates of the nation's own military academies. And the same, of course, was true in the United Kingdom as well.

This relationships among the Positive Liberal state, the mainstream Protestant churches, and the universities had an equally important additional dimension: It was deep as well as broad. The academic elites of the movement were, for both practical and theoretical reasons, reticent about the ultimate foundations of their political faith. But they were quite clear that, secular though many among them certainly were, their basic values were quite compatible with those of their more traditionally religious allies, if not the very same. Tawney was, famously, prominent in the leadership of both social democrats and socially progressive Christians (Sifton, 2003, pp. 198–199). Among the latter, it was the daughter of the theologian Reinhold Niebuhr who paid him perhaps the highest compliment: "Tawney is my idea of a really effective Christian, not least because he never talked about being one" (Ibid.).

Another example captures the Marshall Planners' ecumenical spirit even more nicely. Jerome Frank was one of the more prominent, as well as one of the more theoretically radical, of the New Dealers, first as a Harvard law professor, then as a federal judge. And yet, when pressed on what his basic values were, he replied, "I do not understand how any decent man today can refuse to adopt, as the basis of any modern civilization, the fundamental principles of Natural

Law, relative to human conduct, as stated by Thomas Aquinas" (Frank, 1963, p. xx). Thus the most secular of Positive Liberals had no trouble reconciling their political principles with those of the most orthodox doctor of the Catholic Church.

The relationship between private foundations and the post-war Marshall Plan consensus was less significant than that of either churches or universities. It was, however, profoundly significant in comparison with what had gone before, in the era of the Negative Liberal state's original ascendancy and even more significant in comparison with what was to come after, the era of the Negative Liberal state's revival. All the major foundations, even those founded and funded by laissez-faire proponents like Ford, Rockefeller, and Carnegie, eventually espoused, even advanced, an essentially state-supportive role. Ironically, the namesake foundations of the Captains of Industry, established as bulwarks against the Positive Liberal state, came to be an important part of its vanguard: seeking out new areas of human need for it to enter, providing "seed money" until it got there. (And, as we shall see, later acting as "stop-gaps" when it left.) This was equally true of their counterparts in the United Kingdom (Owen, 1964, p. 553).

This new role of the great private foundations as vanguards of the newly activist, Positive Liberal state points us, finally, to a most significant aspect of that state's political leaders: They were both democrats and leaders but only in very distinctive meanings of those two words. They rallied their electorates behind policies that they themselves believed were for the common good; they were, if you will, modern democrats in practical politics but neo-classical republicans in political ideology. To paraphrase Lincoln, a real as well as nominal republican, they practiced government "for the people," and they mastered enough of the common touch to make it seem as "of the people" as necessary. But they took "by the people" as better politics than policy. They had seen the direst dangers of demagoguery; they were interested neither in following the angry mob down dark paths that end in "blood and soil" populism nor in leading the tractably gullible into schemes that could only benefit their promoters' own narrow class or partisan interest. They were too wise to preach the rule of the wise for the good of all; they were too good not to practice it.

The achievements, domestic and foreign, of the post-war center-left coalitions within and among the Marshall Plan's donor and donee nations call to mind Thucydides' observation about democratic Athens under Pericles:

> In short, what was nominally a democracy became in his hands government by the first citizen. With his successors it was different.
>
> *(Thucydides, Crawley and Gavorse, 1951, pp. 120–121)*

As classical Athens passed from Pericles to Cleon the tanner and Alcibiades the turn-coat, so, alas, the Positive Liberalism of the Marshall Planners would have its own populist epigones.

c The recrudescence of Negative Liberalism: the tragi-comic third act in three scenes

> History repeats itself, first as tragedy, then as farce.
>
> *(Marx and De Leon, 1898)*

Even as Tawney and his counterparts early in the post-war period championed the path of Positive Liberalism and the Marshall Plan, they knew there were other paths ahead, ways that looked back to very different traditions. Two of these troubled them the most: on the one hand,

Soviet-style totalitarian communism; on the other, Anglo-American-style laissez-faire capitalism, our Negative Liberalism. The Marshall Planners and their fellow Positive Liberals held the middle ground – I daresay the high ground – for the better part of four decades.

By the last decade of the twentieth century, the threat from the radical "Left," Soviet Communism, was collapsing. In 1989, the Berlin Wall, symbol of the Soviet threat that the Marshall Plan had initially anticipated, had fallen. But by then, the threat from the radical right was already looming large. At the beginning of the prior decade, the Anglo-American form of laissez-faire capitalism and negative Political Liberalism returned with what can only be called a vengeance. Ronald Reagan was elected US president in 1980; his political soul-mate, Margaret Thatcher, had been elected UK prime minister the year before. The epigraphs to their era, which we must take up next, can only offer an aftertaste of that bitter revanchism.

i. The Reagan-Thatcher Negative Liberal counter-revolution

> The nine most terrifying words in the English language are: *I'm from the Government, and I'm here to help.*
>
> *(Reagan, 1986)*

> They are casting their problems at society. And, you know, there's no such thing as society. There are individual men and women and there are families. And no government can do anything except through people, and people must look after themselves first.
>
> *(Thatcher, 1987)*

Both Reagan and Thatcher were too nearly two-dimensional characters to be classically tragic figures themselves; Reagan quite literally became a public figure through the medium of the movie screen, in roles that were, themselves, decidedly flat.[2] The tragedy repeated first in the scene they shared was not personal but institutional, a repeat of the old Negative Liberalism of the Gilded Age with which our historical survey, following Social Origins Theory's account of the role of private philanthropy in the United States and the United Kingdom, began.

We need only review the main script in mercifully brief outline. Under Reagan and Thatcher's remarkably charismatic leadership, majorities in both the United States and the United Kingdom voted to dismantle the three basic domestic pillars of the Marshall Planners' Positive Liberal ethos: aggressive state regulation to keep capitalism both efficient and competitive, generous social programs to alleviate misery and promote opportunity, and aggressively progressive taxation to fund both of the other two.

A key component of Reaganism and Thatcherism's success was raising social over economic issues as a means of splitting the core coalitions of both the New Deal and the Labor Party: setting working-class people against Positively Liberal, often university-based, intellectuals. Both Reagan and Thatcher preached a decidedly old-fashioned brand of self-reliance, even as they caricatured the beneficiaries of the welfare state as idlers (Reaganism's "welfare queens") and the agents of the welfare state as elitist meddlers (Thatcherism's "nanny state"). In international affairs, both Reagan and Thatcher defended, even redoubled, the NATO opposition to the Soviet Union and generally pressed for the traditional Negative Liberal line on unregulated trade, even as they more quietly reduced support for the OECD's global development goals.

With respect to private philanthropy, both Reaganism and Thatcherism preached a return to the model of the Negative Liberal state that, as we have seen, Social Origins Theory identifies as characteristic of the modern state's first phase in the United States and the United Kingdom.

This involved important shifts in the relationship between the state and the three institutions on which we have been focusing: churches, universities, and especially private foundations.

Churches were critical in shifting the attention of working-class voters, the basis of both the Labor Party and the New Deal Democratic coalition, away from economic issues and onto social issues. This generally involved divisions *within* Protestant denominations and the Catholic Church as much as *between* them. Mainstream Protestant denominations with traditions of university-educated clergy tended to divide along urban/rural and higher-income/lower-income lines; other Protestant denominations remained divided along lines of both class and race. And, especially after Vatican II, Catholics tended to divide into traditionalists and progressives.

The most interesting development for our purposes was the role of private foundations. The older flagship foundations – Ford, Rockefeller, and Carnegie, for example – continued their post-war supporting role in the Positive Liberal political consensus. A new generation joined them in that general political orientation, but with a critical difference: They saw themselves less as leading the welfare state into new areas and filling gaps in areas of critical need until the state arrived. Instead, the newer positively liberal foundations tended to take that role as permanent. This is nicely reflected in Bill Gates's response to a question about the role of private foundations, a question prefaced by the implication that more of his wealth might better have gone into the hands of the Positive Liberal state:

> [w]e think there's always going to be a unique role for foundations. They're able to take a global view to find the greatest needs, take a long-term approach to solving tough problems and manage high-risk projects that governments can't take on and corporations won't.
>
> *(Gates, AP News, 2018)*

Among private foundations engaged in international development, the Gates Foundation has accounted for very nearly half the private funding (OECD, 2018, p. 16). Here is a voice very likely to be listened to. And perhaps listened to too intently, as the OECD has itself commendably noted (PPD at 96) and pointed out to donor states (PPD at 96). Surely the Marshall Planners would have balked at the "conventional wisdom" of the Gates generation of private foundations: The Positive Liberal State is too parochial, too short sighted, and too risk averse for major projects.

At risk of belaboring the obvious, two further points bear emphasis here. First, and most obviously, it is hard to imagine a project bigger than that of re-building Europe after World War II, even as it is inconceivable that such a project might have been funded by private philanthropy. Nor, as we have seen, did the Marshall Planners find themselves reliant upon private philanthropy either to show them the strategic, global perspective or to provide them with the necessary tactical, boots-on-the-ground expertise. Second, it only takes a glance at the OECD's impressive statistical survey to see how large big private foundations in general, and the Gates Foundation in particular, now figure in the funding and implementation of projects that the Marshall Planners would surely have thought to be within the proper purview of states and their agencies, particularly interstate institutions like the OECD itself, and allied universities, public as well as private.

Nor, with respect to private foundations, is that the most notable departure from the pattern of the Marshall Planners. As Positively Liberal foundations like Gates seemed ready to displace the work of the state with their own, a new brand of Negative Liberal foundations arose to challenge the very ethos of the Marshall Planners themselves. It is difficult to summarize this vital phase of the relevant history without sounding at least a little like something of a conspiracy theorist. To redress that problem fully would require providing far more detail than appropriate here. A very brief outline must suffice, backed with references to long and deeply documented accounts (Andersen, 2020; Mayer, 2017). Newly minted billionaires essentially retro-engineered the work of the post-war private foundations: They funded populist movements like the Tea Party, they promoted the social agenda of more Negatively Liberal Christians, and, perhaps most significantly, they fostered an alternative intellectual establishment of Negative Liberalism, particularly in law and economics.

For our purposes, the point is this: These new Negative Liberal foundations did not mean to be partners in advancing the Positive Liberal ethos of the Marshall Planners; they meant to destroy that ethos, root and branch. Here we have, then, a particularly important example in very recent history of a more general point long ago announced in theory: When it comes to philanthropy's core mission of advancing the public good, opinions can be not only divergent as to the best means but even diametrically opposed on the end itself.

ii The interlude of Neo-Liberalism lite: the Negative Liberal consolidation of the Clinton-Blair "New Left"

> The era of big government is over, but we cannot go back to the time when our citizens were left to fend for themselves.
>
> *(Clinton, 1996)*

One has to say that, for better or worse, President Reagan and Prime Minister Thatcher were charismatic leaders with the courage of their convictions. One also has to say that, surely for the worst, President Clinton and Prime Minister Blair, if almost their predecessors' equals in charisma, seem considerably less graced with either courage or conviction. Their political home bases, more inherited than chosen, were on the port side of Positive Liberalism; the timing of their political ascendancy made them tack, reluctantly or not, rather far toward the starboard side of Negative Liberalism. This is not the place to say whether their tacks were motivated more by the felt need to keep their parties from totally floundering or by their own overweening personal ambition to sail first past the farthest political post, leadership positions in their respective parties and countries. The fuller record, suffice it to say, speaks quite loudly enough for itself.

What matters here is that, in matters of both economic regulation and wealth redistribution, the rightward trim of Clinton and Blair's rigging helped both to consolidate and to legitimate the Reagan-Thatcher Negative Liberal counter-revolution against the United States and the United Kingdom's generation-long commitment to the Positive Liberalism of the Marshall Planners.

iii The denouement of Donald Trump and Boris Johnson: illiberal democracy in the lands of the Marshall Plan

> For they sow the wind, and they shall reap the whirlwind.
>
> *(Hosea 8:7)*

The minimalist, negative liberal state dominant in both the United States and the United Kingdom at the turn of the twentieth century first repeated itself, as we have seen, in the tragedy, at least in philanthropic terms, of the Reagan and Thatcher years. The rich got richer, and the poor poorer. We now have its farcical second repetition, the triumph of Trumpism in the United States and Brexitism in the United Kingdom, the rejection of the ethos of the Marshall Planners. As we have seen, Reaganism and Thatcherism quietly abandoned President Roosevelt's pre-War promise to end fear and want everywhere on the globe, abroad as well as at home. But Reagan and Thatcher carefully kept intact two other elements of that ethos, those most important to their wealthy patrons: opposition to the Soviet Union and expansion of free trade (again, in goods and capital, not in labor).

President Trump infamously campaigned on the slogan of the very isolationists who opposed the United States' opposition to the Axis Powers: *America First!* He openly admires former KGB agent Putin, even as he openly questions the continued utility of the NATO alliance, bringing the embrace of Marshall Plan foes and the abandonment of its friends together in a musing once unimaginable for a president of the United States: Why would we defend tiny Estonia against a Russian invasion? (Kramer, 2016). Reagan famously demanded that Gorbachev tear down the Berlin War, symbol of Soviet occupation; Trump virtually invites Putin to move it further West. And President Trump both actively promoted protective tariffs and openly favored bilateral trade agreements over regional economic integration and multilateral free trade arrangements; this latter position, with the prospect of a special U.S./UK trade relationship, was a major selling point of Boris Johnson and the Brexiteers.

In Trump and Johnson, those who worked to reverse the ethos of the Marshall Planners have become the victims of their own success. With barely disguised "blood and soil" populism, they lured rank-and-file voters out of the Labor Party's worker-intellectual alliance and New Deal's economically progressive coalition and into parties that preached social conservatism while practicing plutocracy. Then the establishment of those very parties lost control of the beast they had waken and ridden to power; the angry body of populist voters turned on the neo-liberals themselves – the Republicans in the United States and the Conservatives in the United Kingdom – and the unholy alliance of plutocrats and populists ripped along its unseemly seam.

Hardly the least obvious element of this farce: In the United States, the populist leader was a self-proclaimed billionaire; in the United Kingdom, the product of the public school and Oxbridge establishment.

d Unpacking the final paradox: Marshall Planners' ends, Fabius's means

> For the right moment you must wait, as Fabius did most patiently, when warring against Hannibal, though many censured his delays; but when the time comes you must strike hard, as Fabius did, or your waiting will be in vain, and fruitless.
>
> *(Fabians.org.uk, 2010)*

> I know the comments that some people will make on our Fabian conduct. . . . But the more discerning, I trust, will not find it difficult to conceive that it proceeds from the truest policy.
>
> *(Alexander Hamilton, quoted in Ricks, 2020, p. 154)*

Against this background, we can now unpack the final paradox we noted at the beginning. This, remember, was the paradox: In its suggestion that policy makers may want to support private philanthropy with public finances, particularly favorable tax treatment, the EOCD Report does not go far enough in its own direction. This is the unpacking: The Report goes no further, because the way is blocked. In the ethos of the Marshall Planners, private philanthropy played no essential part. Their vision of global peace and prosperity, of universal economic and social justice, was to be the work of Positive Liberal, social democratic states, at home and abroad – independently if necessary, cooperatively if possible.

When Positive Liberalism lost the United States and the United Kingdom to a Negative Liberalism that was both isolationist and anti-statist, then private philanthropy, especially the great private foundations, seemed an essential, if stop-gap, source for even the most basic work of organizations like the OECD itself (OECD, 2018, p. 29). In the candid words of the OECD,

> As the ambitious priorities of the Sustainable Development Goals [for 2030] come face-to-face with limited economic resources exacerbated by the 2007 financial crisis, the time is ripe to harness the promise of philanthropy.
>
> *(Ibid., p. 3)*

This reliance on private philanthropy is a decidedly second-best solution, a distant and dim reflection of the Positive Liberal ethos of the Marshall Planners. The OECD's own report, Private Philanthropy for Development, bears sad testimony to the novelty of this departure:

> Several major declarations on global development policy and financing were endorsed between 2000 and 2010, including the 2000 Millennium Development Goals (MDGs), the 2002 *Monterrey Consensus on Financing for Development*, the 2005 *Paris Declaration on Aid Effectiveness* and the 2008 *Accra Agenda for Action. None mentioned philanthropy as a development actor or as a source of finance.*
>
> *OECD/ PPD at 93–94 (emphasis added)*

Still and all, half a loaf is better than no bread – and today it is real loaves and literal starvation that all too often measure the success and failure of global development. In these dark times, it is good policy not to bite any hand that feeds the hungry[3] – even hands that would keep the hungry on very short rations indeed, as they help themselves to the lion's share of social resources. But, even in dark times, it is wisest to work for better days, when – claiming no originality here! – the wise rule, as they did in the West in the wake of World War II, for the good of all.

And this day may be dawning even now. In the words of Paul Krugman, Nobel Laureate in economics,

> For the lesson of 2020 is that in a crisis, and to some extent even in calmer times, the government can do a lot to improve people's lives. And what we should fear most is a government that refuses to do its job.
>
> *(Krugman, 2020)*[4]

Conclusion: what is to be done now?

> I have the audacity to believe that peoples everywhere can have three meals a day for their bodies, education and culture for their minds, and dignity, equality and freedom for their spirits.
>
> *(King, 1964)*

One cannot help but be at least a little hopeful, as we enter the first hundred days of President Biden's administration, to learn that his role model is Franklin Roosevelt. Then again, one cannot but be a bit leery of the aspiration's likely fulfillment. It calls to mind the response of the Archbishop of York to the remark that "what we need are a few more people like Tawney": "There are no more men like Tawney" (Gaitskell, 1964, pp. 211, 214).

It would be immodest, if not worse, to think of ourselves as agents of philanthropy, lovers of humankind, on the order of the Marshall Planners, much less that of their leaders, humanitarian heroes like Roosevelt, Tawney, and Marshall himself. Then again, we would do well to remember that we may stand on their very shoulders and, so standing, see even further and clearer than they could. So, too, we may build upon the foundations they and their fellow laborers have laid. And we would do well to remember words in which they themselves must have taken comfort, in their time, a time far more fraught than even our own:

> Therefore, since we are surrounded by so great a cloud of witnesses, let us also lay aside every weight and sin that easily distracts, and let us run with perseverance the race that is set before us.
>
> *(Hebrews 12:1)*

Amen.

Notes

My thanks to Kat Klepfer of the F.S.U. College of Law Research Center and Peter Meisenbacher (F.S.U., J.D. 2022) for their invaluable research assistance. My thanks, too, to my editors for allowing me to post on SSRN, under the same title and with the same text, a version of this chapter that lets me indulge United States law academics' over-fondness for fulsome footnotes.

1 The Report follows Social Origins Theory itself in using the terms "social democratic" and "liberal." In view of the different meanings of "liberal" in the United States and the rest of the world and the sadly negative connotations of "social democracy" in the United States, I will use instead the terms "Negative Liberal" and "Positive Liberal," respectively. Positive liberty as used here actually comes closer to a third alternative, republican liberty. See Pettit, P. (1997). *Republicanism: a theory of freedom and government.* Oxford: Oxford University Press, pp. 16–21.

2 Perhaps most fittingly, in *Bedtime for Bonzo,* he played second fiddle to a show-stealing chimpanzee.

3 It has to be noted – yet again, very much to its credit – that, although the OECD seems never to bite, it has shown an admirable willingness to bark, sometimes rather insistently. Thus, in its OECD PPD, it offers a number of recommendations to donor foundations that are a long way from obsequious. PPD at 116–119 ("Recommendations for Foundations"). And, as we have already seen, the OECD has also pointed out to donor nations the need to address the risk of giving too much influence to a relatively small number of mostly North American donor foundations. PPD at 120.

4 And yet, even as I thus reconcile myself with my hosts, do I not pose a final, perhaps fatal, paradox? In highlighting our common commitment to the Positive Liberal vision of the Marshall Planners, do I not risk undermining that very position? In articulating our shared commitment to Positive Liberal State action as the first-best solution to humanity's largest problems, and private philanthropy a distant second, am I not playing into the very hands that would denounce us all as "socialists" and "internationalists"? For my response, which requires a bit of an excursion in Aristotle's Rhetoric, see the Appendix to the version of this chapter posted on SSNR, note 1, supra.

References

Andersen, K. (2020). *Evil geniuses the unmaking of America: a recent history.* London: Ebury Press.

Anheier, H. and Salamon, L. (1996). The social origin of civil society: explaining the nonprofit sector cross-nationally. *International Journal of Voluntary and Nonprofit Organizations,* vol. 9, pp. 213–248.

AP News. (2018). *The Gates explain reason for giving their money away* [online]. Available at: https://apnews.com/article/ccce75e95c27497ab9c9b67f73b0c4c9 [Accessed 9 Feb. 2021].

Carnegie, A. (2017). *The gospel of wealth.* New York: Carnegie Corporation of New York.

Clinton, W. (1996). *State of the union address,* 23 Jan. [online]. Available at: https://en.wikipedia.org/wiki/1996_State_of_the_Union_Address#:~:text=The%201996%20State%20of%20the,the%20104th%20United%20States%20Congress.

Dangerfield, G. (2012). *The strange death of liberal England.* London: Serif.

Eagleton, T. (1996). *The illusions of postmodernism.* Oxford: Wiley-Blackwell, 1st ed.

Fabians.org.uk. (2010). *Our history | Fabian society* [online]. Available at: https://fabians.org.uk/about-us/our-history/.

Frank, J. (1963). *Law and the modern mind.* Gloucester, MA: Peter Smith.

Gaitskell, H. (1964). Postscript: an appreciation. In: *The radical tradition,* ed. by Tawney, R.H. London: George Allen & Unwin Ltd.

Giovanopoulou, A. (forthcoming 2021). Pragmatic legalism: revisiting America's order after World War II. *Harvard International Law Journal*, vol. 62.
Harding, M. and Pascoe, S. (2018). *Research handbook on not-for-profit law*. Cheltenham: Edward Elgar Publishing.
Hebrews 12:1, Holy Bible: Revised Standard Version.
Heilbroner, R. L. (1972). *The worldly philosophers: the lives, times, and ideas of the great economic thinkers* (4th ed.), p. 166. New York: Simon and Schuster.
Holmes, O. (1881). *The common law*. S.L.: Wilder Publications.
Hosea 8:7, Holy Bible: Revised Standard Version.
King, Jr., M.L. (1963). *Letter from a Birmingham Jail*, 16 Apr.
King, Jr., M.L. (1964). *Nobel Peace Prize acceptance speech*, 11 Dec.
Kramer, A.E. (2016). Spooked by Russia, Tiny Estonia trains a nation of insurgents. *The New York Times*, 31 Oct. [online]. Available at: https://www.nytimes.com/2016/11/01/world/europe/spooked-by-russia-tiny-estonia-trains-a-nation-of-insurgents.html [Accessed 9 Feb. 2021].
Krugman, P. (2020). Opinion | 2020 was the year Reaganism died. *The New York Times*, 29 Dec. [online]. Available at: https://www.nytimes.com/2020/12/28/opinion/reagan-economy-covid.html?smid=em-share [Accessed 9 Feb. 2021].
Leo XIII. (1891). *Rerum novarum: on capital and labor*.
Machado, B. and Marshall, G.C. (2007). *In search of a usable past: the Marshall Plan and postwar reconstruction today*. Lexington, VA: George C. Marshall Foundation.
Marshall, G.C. (1947). *Marshall Plan Speech*. Harvard University, 5 June.
Marx, K. and De Leon, D. (1898). *The eighteenth Brumaire of Louis Bonaparte*. New York: International Publishing Co.
Matthew, Bible: Revised Standard Version.
Mayer, J. (2017). *Dark money: the hidden history of the billionaires behind the rise of the radical right*. New York: Anchor Books, a Division of Penguin Random House LLC.
McGirr, L. (2021). Opinion | Trump is the Republican party's past and its future. *The New York Times*, 13 Jan. [online]. Available at: https://www.nytimes.com/2021/01/13/opinion/gop-trump.html [Accessed 19 Feb. 2021].
Niebuhr, H.R. et al. (1957). *The advancement of theological education*. New York: Harper.
Nietzsche, F.W. (1957). *On the use and abuse of history for life*, trans. by Collins, A. New York: The Liberal Arts Press, 2nd revised ed.
OECD. (2008). *The Marshall Plan: lessons learned for the twenty-first century*. Paris: OECD Publishing.
OECD. (2018). *Private philanthropy for development, the development dimension*. Paris: OECD Publishing. http://doi.org/10.1787/9789264085190-en.
OECD. (2020). *Taxation and philanthropy*. OECD Tax Policy Studies No. 27. Paris: OECD Publishing. https://doi.org/10.1787/df434a77-en.
Owen, D. (1964). *English philanthropy 1660–1960*. Cambridge: Belknap Press of Harvard University Press.
Pettit, P. (1997). *Republicanism: a theory of freedom and government*. Oxford: Oxford University Press.
Priestland, D. (2012). *Merchant, soldier, sage: a new history of power*. London: Allen Lane.
Reagan, R. (1986). *The president's news conference*, 12 Aug. [online]. Available at: https://www.reaganlibrary.gov/archives/speech/presidents-news-conference-23.
Ricks, T.E. (2020). *First principles: what America's founders learned from the Greeks and Romans and how that shaped our country*. New York: Harper, an Imprint of Harpercollins Publishers.
Roosevelt, F.D. (1941). *Eighth state of the union address* [online]. Available at: https://millercenter.org/the-presidency/presidential-speeches/january-6-1941-state-union-four-freedoms.
Rossiter, C. (1955). Conservatism in America. *Journal of American History*, vol. 42, p. 3.
Salamon, L.M., Sokolowski, S.W. and Anheier, H.K. (2000). *Social origins of civil society: an overview*. Working papers of the Johns Hopkins comparative nonprofit sector project no. 38. Baltimore: The Johns Hopkins Center for Civil Society Studies.
Sifton, E. (2003). *The serenity prayer: faith and politics in times of peace and war*. London: W. W. Norton & Company.
Tawney, R.H. (1964). Social democracy in Britain. In: *The radical tradition*. London: George Allen & Unwin Ltd., pp. 138–166.
Thatcher, M. (1987). *Interview by women's own*, 27 Sep.
Thucydides, Crawley, R. (1951). *The complete writings of Thucydides: the Peloponnesian war, the unabridged Crawley translation with an introduction by John H. Finley, Jr.* New York: The Modern Library, Random House.
Urofsky, M.I. (1991). *Felix Frankfurter: judicial restraint and individual liberties*. Boston: Twayne.

2

WHY FISCALLY ENCOURAGE PHILANTHROPY?

Analyzing discourses and issues of political actors who legislate on philanthropy in Switzerland

Caroline Honegger, Romain Carnac, Philip Balsiger and Alexandre Lambelet

Introduction[1]

Philanthropy, that is, the giving of money (or time) for public purposes, is often co-financed by public authorities through tax exemptions to the benefit of public utility organizations and donors. Philanthropy is thus not only a social practice but also as a public policy tool (Steinmo, 1986; McDaniel, 1989; Salamon, 1989; Howard, 1993) whose development and support by public authorities has been the subject of much controversy (Brilliant, 2000; McGravie, 2003; Reich, 2018; Zunz, 2011). Studies have shown that the institutional underpinnings of philanthropy vary depending on different non-profit regimes (Salamon and Anheiner, 1998; Salamon and Toepler, 2000; Layton, 2015); at the same time, a trend towards increased public and fiscal encouragement of philanthropy has been observed in many countries (Lambelet, 2014).

Charities and their advocates agree on the importance of fiscal incentives to promote donations (Bekkers and Wiepking, 2011; Layton, 2015), but there are vivid debates about the economic effectiveness of incentives and their legitimacy from a democratic point of view (OECD, 2020). Many studies, in particular by economists, have analyzed whether tax exemptions are more or less efficient than direct subsidies and whether fiscal incentives crowd out other forms of giving (Ariely, Bracha and Meier, 2009; Bakija and Heim, 2011; Lideikyte Huber, 2020; Monnet and Panizza, 2017). Other authors have discussed tax exemptions' legitimacy in terms of justice, revealing the problem of the potential *non-alignment* between the beneficiaries of donations and the goals of public policies (McDaniel, 1989), as well as the effects that tax exemptions may have on the democratic functioning of countries, in particular because of the *plutocratic bias* linked to exemption systems (Thaler, 2010; Reich, Cordelli and Bernholz, 2016; Leat, 2016; Reich, 2018; Saez and Zucman, 2019; Cagé, 2020).

Yet while political philosophers have discussed the possible justifications or rationales of fiscal incentives for philanthropy and philanthropic giving (Benshalom, 2008; Reich, 2018), there are

DOI: 10.4324/9781003139201-4

few empirical studies looking at how political actors justify the use of fiscal tools to encourage philanthropy. How do they conceive of the role of philanthropy, and what arguments do they use to justify the legal and tax treatment that governs it? Taking Switzerland as a case study, this chapter opens this 'black box' in order to know more about the motivational dynamics of increasing (or not) tax expenditures for charitable giving and volunteering and widening the boundaries of what is recognized as being of public interest and should benefit from tax incentives. Since political actors are the ones who make the legislation that governs philanthropic practices and decide on the tax exemptions from which these organizations and donations may or may not benefit, it is crucial to question these actors in order to understand the place of philanthropy today.

Through a qualitative study of 48 interviews with Swiss political actors (parliamentarians and members of cantonal executive bodies), the chapter analyzes how these actors problematize philanthropy[2] and decide on the legislative developments that should frame it. Switzerland's non-profit regime can be characterized as 'liberal' (Helmig *et al.*, 2017) or as between a liberal and social-democratic model (Schnurbein and Perez, 2018), with a large third sector, large subsidies from public authorities (Helmig, Lichtsteiner and Gmür, 2010), deductible donations for donors and a broad eligibility for organizations (Lideikyte Huber, 2018).[3] In comparison with other countries (European Foundation Center, 2015), not all non-profit organizations are tax exempt and can benefit from tax-deductible donations: Sports clubs or self-help organizations are excluded. And although philanthropic organizations have to be registered officially, no further public reporting obligations exist. Since the early 2000s, there have been a few important reform proposals, most aiming at further liberalization (to broaden the type of organizations that can benefit from the recognition of public utility, to fiscally support volunteering or to increase tax incentives for donations) but some also seeking to increase the transparency of philanthropic organizations. In this context of a liberal regime, we found that to speak about the fiscal encouragement of philanthropy, political actors' reasons for supporting philanthropy are diverse and refer to very different realities of philanthropic organizations. The analysis identifies five ways of framing philanthropy: civic, liberal, pragmatic, wary and critical. We also see, however, that while political actors draw on different rationales and frame the issue differently, arguments related to the efficiency of philanthropic giving are most commonly used to justify fiscal incentives.

The next two sections detail the theoretical framework and the methodological approach used in this chapter. The following empirical part proceeds in two steps: A first part presents the arguments used by political actors and groups them into four rationales they refer to. A second part analyzes the interviews to develop a typology of five frames Swiss political actors use when speaking about philanthropy and tax exemptions. Because we have observed that these frames are linked with the experiences of the third sector the political actors have, we will discuss the link between their way of framing the issue and the positions they have in the third sector and as political actors.

Conceptual framework: rationales, frames and arguments

Approaches on philanthropy by political philosophers have shown different rationales, that is to say 'higher common principles,' that can be viewed as ensembles of higher-order meanings people (including political actors) have to deal with (for example, in a democracy: liberty or equality). In his theoretical and philosophical work on philanthropy, Benshalom (2008) identifies two rationales for the deductibility of donations: 1) they encourage more and/or better spending of public goods; 2) they are desirable because they allow taxpayers to 'vote with their dollars' and to express their preferences regarding the allocation of public goods in society. More recently, Reich (2013, 2018) distinguished three rationales: 1) a 'tax base rationale' that stems from the principle that donations for public-interest organizations are voluntary means of giving up part of one's income for the public good. Consequently, this donation should not be taxed. 2) An 'efficiency rationale' based on the idea that the state can encourage philanthropic activity in order to stimulate the production of collective goods of greater social value than those that the state alone can produce. 3) A 'pluralism rationale'; In this argument, the tax exemption is justified by its role in the promotion of a diversified, pluralist and decentralized third sector, the basis of a liberal democracy. This argument also contends that pluralism, while decentralizing political decision-making, also favors the emergence of new and innovative solutions.

These rationales are interesting for understanding the kind of conceptual debates in which philanthropy is caught. But they tell us little about how political actors respond concretely to proposals for legislative or tax changes that surround the issue of philanthropy. Coming out of theoretical debates, this chapter goes one step further to study the concrete frames the political actors who make the laws governing philanthropy use. Following a constructivist approach in the field of social problems research, we want to study, in this chapter, the more specific frames (Goffman, 1974; Gamson and Modigliani, 1989; Reese, Gandy and Grant, 2001) political actors use concretely when they have to speak on philanthropy. Frames are articulations of arguments that can be drawn from the different rationales and that shape the meaning individuals give to the problems they face. Frames can be linked with rationales, but it is the arrangement or hierarchy of the elements drawn from the latter that makes different frames specific and that promote particular definitions of legitimacy or conceptions of the common good. If the frames are different from the rationales identified by political philosophy works, it is because, for political actors, philanthropy does not exist outside – or is not thought of independently of – particular conceptions of the state, taxation or the functioning of democracy. They do not think of philanthropy as an isolated phenomenon but read philanthropy together with other questions that also involve the place of the state or the equality between citizens.

We thus have to look at the arguments used by the political actors during the interviews, at the pros and cons of tax incentives in favor of philanthropy or the pros and cons of the enlargement of the type of organizations that can benefit from them. Doing so, we use an inductive approach to identify the rationales political actors rely on in their arguments. We then study how political actors combine different arguments and standards of evaluation in order to produce frames. Constructivist approaches in the field of social problems research have shown how different actors frame problems and public policies in different ways (Best, 2008). We see frames as a 'central organizing idea (. . .) for making sense of relevant events, suggesting what is at issue' (Gamson and Modigliani, 1989, p. 3). They are at the center of 'interpretative packages' that 'give meaning to an issue' (ibid.). In other words, frames as interpretative packages combine different elements – arguments referring to different rationales, representations of the respective role of the state and civil society, views of the policy-making process, conceptions of the public interest, and so on – in a specific way. Using this type of analysis, our goal is to uncover the different interpretative packages underlying discourses on philanthropy in a liberal welfare state like Switzerland.

Methods and data

Using the term 'public utility' in the search engines of the parliaments at the federal level and in three cantons,[4] we have listed the proposals for reform of tax exemptions for philanthropy over the period from 2000 until 2018, that is, 39 interventions at the federal level and the same number at the cantonal level for the three cantons. They concern themes as varied as the thresholds of deductibility of donations to philanthropic organizations, the calling into question of fiscal advantages for major sports federations, the opportunity to permit volunteers to enjoy tax reductions, the improvement of Switzerland's attractiveness in the sector of philanthropy, the recognition of the public interest of cultural organizations or of political parties, the possibility of spreading an exceptional donation over a number of fiscal years and the fight against tax fraud and money laundering in non-governmental organizations. Since these themes have a common denominator of questioning the definition of philanthropy and the fiscal and legal framework from which it must benefit, debates on these different parliamentary objects were incorporated into the body of the research.

On the basis of this data, we identified the political actors who played a leading role, either because they made an intervention or participated significantly in political debates or because, at this point in time, they occupied a key position (president or vice-president of the tax commission, state councilor in charge of the Department of Finance, etc.). Of the 88 individuals thus identified, 48 responded favorably to our interview request. They belong to different bodies, political formations and cantons. With these political actors, we conducted semi-directive interviews, following a single grid, for a period of time ranging from 40 minutes to 3 hours. In the grid, we focused on discussing the intervention they were involved in and asked more general questions about philanthropy and tax exemption policies. In a first step, we used content analysis (Krippendorf, 2004) to list all the arguments given in favor of or against tax exemptions. We then analyzed this list to identify what underlying rationales they build upon. This led us to class them into four groups. In a second step, we analyzed the interviews internally and in comparison with each other to characterize the way each interviewee frames philanthropy. In this step, we intersected discursive data on arguments and opinions given by interviewees with elements objectifying their personal trajectories and political, professional and community engagements. This led us to the development of a typology around five interpretative frames, related to different views of philanthropy.

Arguments for and against tax incentives for philanthropy: underlying rationales

Interviewing political actors on the theme of tax incentives for philanthropy first led to astonishment at the great diversity of their remarks: Not only do their positions and arguments differ, but they rarely speak about the same object. Nonetheless, there are some recurring themes in the discourse. The systematic coding of the interview transcripts allowed us to extract argument types which point at four distinct categories. Each of these categories evaluates the tax measures supporting philanthropy in light of a different rationale: The first category assesses the measures discussed from the point of view of (fiscal) justice, the second evaluates their efficiency, the third takes democracy as a frame of reference and the last judges them through the prism of virtue. The left side of Figure 2.1 lists the arguments identified and the rationale they refer to. For each of these categories, we illustrate the layout of themes and arguments, with an emphasis on some salient tendencies amongst the interviews.

Justice

The donation is another way to pay one's taxes: through directly supporting social goods that the state will not be financing.

The normal taxation system is 'confiscatory'; unfair; anything that allows one to ease the burden is good.

Deductions are not fair because they advantage certain taxpayers (the more fortunate ones).

Deductions may be diverted from their original purpose and used as an instrument of fiscal optimizations.

Efficiency

It is in the state's interest to maximize the volume of donations to philanthropic organizations/one has to look for the money where it can be found.

Incentives are effective in increasing the number and the size of donations.

Philanthropic organizations are less expensive than state services in certain domains, especially thanks to volunteer work.

Philanthropic organizations are more effective, more reactive, closer to the grassroots than state services in certain domains.

The state, on its own, lacks the means to provide all the public and social services desired.

It is necessary to put forward a system of advantageous tax deductions to be more attractive than rival cantons/countries.

Certain social problems cannot be resolved by philanthropy since they are not very visible or evoke little sympathy.

Tax deductions tend to aggravate inequalities in preventing redistribution.

Deductions generate major fiscal losses; they empty state coffers.

Virtue

It is fair that those who give to good causes be recompensed/thanked by the collectivity.

The role of the state is to recognize, highlight and recompense virtuous behavior.

A donation is never disinterested; one always receives in return psychological, symbolic or social gratification.

It is immoral or antisocial to not pay taxes; the principle of universality of taxation is symbolically important and must be respected.

Democracy

The tax incentive is a means to support the dynamism of the third sector/civil society/private initiatives, which are good in themselves.

The deductibility of donations gives decision-making power to citizens, who 'vote for projects'; this is a mechanism of direct democracy.

It is not desirable that the state concentrate all the decision-making power and means of implementing social policies in its own hands.

Philanthropic organizations escape democratic control; their actions are not controlled or are insufficiently controlled by political authorities.

Figure 2.1 Collection of arguments according to rationales and types of framing

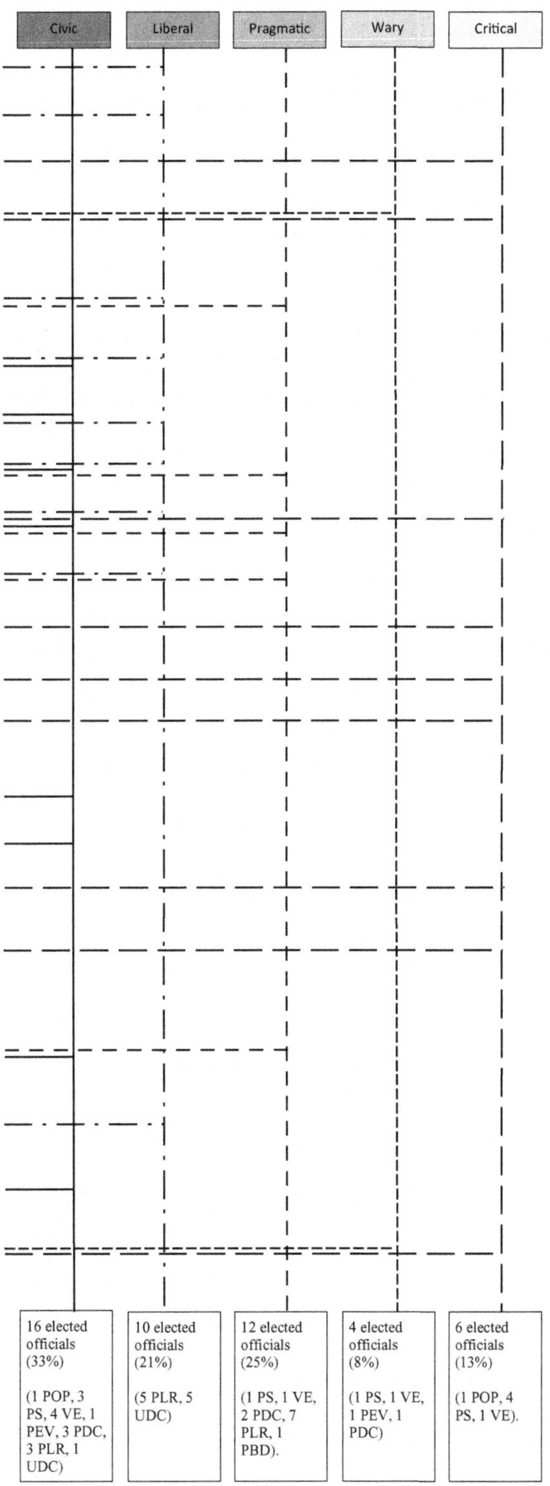

Figure 2.1 Continued

Justice

The tax exemption for philanthropy is generally presented as obvious by Swiss politicians: 'it would be 'completely absurd and . . . scandalous to work not for profit and then have to pay taxes' (Interviewee 28, VE).[5] Similarly, it would be unfair to pay taxes on money which one had given away: 'the people who give this away no longer have this money in their own bag' (Interviewee 42, PEV). This perspective, which comes back to what Reich (2013) calls 'tax-base rationale', considers that, for the donation affecting the tax base, the latter must be calculated after the donation and not before. Finally, the donation often seems like another means of paying one's taxes, since one is financing social goods that the state will not then have to finance. Therefore, the focus is the equitable treatment of the donor; it would not be fair to make someone pay tax on a sum of money given to a public-interest organization.

The rationale of fiscal justice as it appears in the Swiss political discourse contains further arguments: For instance, some politicians see tax incentives for philanthropy simply as a means of providing tax relief: 'the more we can lower it, the better' (Interviewee 18, PLR) and 'the state's appetite for taxes is exaggerated' (Interviewee 31, UDC). Other politicians use arguments referring to fiscal justice to criticize fiscal advantages. To them, deductions are an instrument of fiscal optimization, and the donation becomes 'a means to avoid taxes,' especially for the 'ultra-rich' (Interviewee 29, PDC). Some politicians also emphasize that the risk of creating unfair situations is increased by the fact that deductions, due to the role of progressive tax rates, benefit the wealthiest taxpayers more.

Efficiency

The second rationale identified roughly overlaps with what Reich calls 'subsidy rationale'. Here, the idea is that the state encourages philanthropic activity in order to stimulate the production of a collective good of greater social value than if the state alone had done this. The encouragement is thus effective in promoting the public good; what matters is the impact of the donation. This argument is part of the classic critique of government, especially advanced by proponents of new public management, who see the public sector as being slow, bureaucratic and unresponsive to the needs of its beneficiaries, as opposed to the private sector, which is closer to the people, more reactive and more results oriented.

The efficiency rationale as it appears in the Swiss political discourse on philanthropic organizations covers a wide range of arguments, which all converge on the objective of maximizing the quantity and quality of services delivered for the least possible cost to the state. Efficiency refers to two different notions (Monnet and Panizza, 2017): *treasury efficiency* (purely from a budgetary perspective, measured by comparing the amounts foregone by the public treasury due to deductions and the amounts of donations to public-interest organizations due to this fiscal encouragement) and *social efficiency* (which cross-references the loss of fiscal tax revenues for the state, the quality of social goods produced and the cost to the state if it had had to produce them). These two dimensions of efficiency can be found in the discourse of political actors: Thus, one can distinguish, on the one hand, the arguments which proceed from a budgetary rationale and those which relate to the effectiveness of tax incentives in financing public-interest organizations and, on the other hand, those bearing on the efficiency of these organizations themselves, that is, their capacity to deliver more and better services than the state could provide, at a fixed cost.

Arguments referring to efficiency are also used by Swiss politicians to criticize tax incentives for philanthropy. Some of them highlight the fact that certain social problems cannot be resolved by philanthropy since they are not very visible or evoke little sympathy, while others emphasize the fiscal losses generated by tax deductions and the negative consequences for the state budget. Another critique expressed by Swiss politicians refers to the fact that tax deductions tend to aggravate inequalities by preventing redistribution.

Democracy

The third rationale identified, that of democracy, also covers arguments in favor of tax incentives for philanthropy and criticisms of this measure. It corresponds approximately with what Reich calls 'pluralism rationale'. In this argument, the tax exemption is justified by its role in the promotion of a diversified, pluralist and decentralized third sector, the basis of a liberal democracy. This argument also contends that by decentralizing political decision-making, one favors the emergence of new and innovative solutions. However, democracy is also used as an argument by some politicians to contest the fiscal encouragement of philanthropy. The third sector is denounced as escaping the control of political authorities and therefore of democracy. Through the mechanism of tax relief, the sector's financing escapes the 'political, public and democratic realm' (Interviewee 40, PS) and 'the state loses control of its public policy' (Interviewee 47, PS).

This phenomenon is reinforced by the lack of transparency, the activity of foundations being described at times as 'completely opaque' (Interviewee 9, POP), and by the 'lobbying' (Interviewee 45, PS) of the sector of foundations which contributes to removing even more democratic control.[6] Finally, in 'permitting people or entities with the means to not contribute to the common pot' (Interviewee 40, PS) to 'circumvent the state . . . in deciding themselves where to put their dough' (Interviewee 47, PS), it is the very democratic culture itself which is threatened: The risk is then that of seeing a form of 'individual democracy' emerge (Interviewee 40, PS) which would reject the redistributive dimension of taxes.

Virtue

In addition to the three rationales identified by Reich, a fourth category of argumentation referring to the principle of virtue appeared in the discourse of Swiss political actors on philanthropic activities. A priori, philanthropic activity usually plays a very positive role in moral terms, and the political actors interviewed do not really disagree with this widely held view. Public-interest efforts are often defined as 'helping people' (Interviewee 5, VE) and are linked to the idea of 'gift of self' (Interviewee 3, PDC). Some people base this on 'Christian values' (Interviewees 30, PLR, and 36, VE) and others more generally on the 'concern for other people' (Interviewee 33, PS). From this perspective, which takes moral evaluation of the 'altruistic' commitment as its point of departure, plans for tax relief for philanthropy are defended as a means to highlight those who do good, whether public interest organizations, generous donors or volunteers.

Thus, the fact that philanthropic activity is considered virtuous justifies it being 'treated in a special way' (Interviewee 39, PDC) by the state. The donation of money to public-interest organizations is perceived as an integral part of this philanthropic activity. Unlike taxes, which constitute an obligatory contribution to the common good, the donation is part of an 'interpersonal' relation (Interviewee 25, PDC). 'There is a stronger human gesture which is not at all anonymous' (Interviewee 36, VE).

Another virtue of the donation is also related to what it gives the donor: 'The donation benefits the recipient, in addition to the one who gives' (Interviewee 36, VE). This holds true, too, for the donation of time. One political actor, smiling, refers to 'a study which shows that the more volunteer work you do, the happier you are in life' (Interviewee 30, PLR). Yet many political actors deplore the fact that awareness of the mutual advantage of altruistic commitment has tended to fade away. The prevailing perception of those interviewed is that we are living 'in a society where people are increasingly individualistic' (Interviewee 3, PDC). Consequently, it is necessary for the state to guide them towards the path of charitable works, and tax benefits serve this purpose. However, certain remarks made during the interviews serve to tarnish the popular image of the noble philanthropist. Thus, philanthropic organizations are accused of 'making money from the suffering of others' (Interviewee 1, PEV). As for the donation itself, it is sometimes depicted as a means of enhancing an individual's 'personal prestige' (Interviewee 37, VE) or of 'giving oneself a reputation as a benefactor' (Interviewee 47, PS), with the donation seen as a 'marketing' tool (Interviewee 40, PS).

Another critique, on the question of virtue, arises with regard to tax incentives for philanthropy: that it is immoral that some not pay taxes, whatever the reason. Here, indeed, the very principle of tax incentives as a tool of public policy is being criticized: 'taxation should not be jeopardized' (Interviewee 36, VE). The problem with deductions and exemptions is that they create a multitude of specific fiscal situations liable to threaten this principle of universal taxation.

Five frames on philanthropy

As the analysis so far has established, political actors refer to a wide range of arguments to express their positions for or against tax advantages for philanthropy. However, all these arguments are not drawn upon in an identical fashion in each interview; the political actors select, combine and rank-order them according to different modalities. The coding of the interviews allows us to see a structure behind this diversity: it brings out various recurring argumentative patterns, which define five types of frames on philanthropy. Their graphic representation permits us to visualize their differences (see right half of Figure 2.1) but also the basis of ideas, values and representations that they share.

The left side of Figure 2.1 classifies the arguments of political actors as presented in the first part of this chapter by rationales, in favor of fiscal advantages (bright) and opposed (dark). Each trait linking an argument to a frame signifies that this argument is employed by the majority of political actors using this frame: for example, the majority of the political actors whose discourse is 'liberal' use the first positive argument of the justice category, 'The donation is another means of paying one's taxes'. In this same category, the negative argument 'deductions may be diverted from their original purpose' is used by the majority of those whose discourse is 'wary', as well as most of those whose discourse is predominantly 'critical'.

Figure 2.1 reveals that political actors largely share a positive view of fiscal advantages for public-interest organizations: Three of the five frames are based exclusively on arguments in favor of these measures; and these three frames were employed by 38 political actors, that is, 79% of all political actors interviewed. It follows that arguments in favor of fiscal advantages are much more often employed (there are 23 uses of positive arguments, marked by horizontal lines towards the bright cases) than counterarguments (10 uses of negative arguments). Analysis of Figure 2.1 then shows an overwhelming predominance of the rationale of efficiency in political actors' discourse: out of a total of 33 uses of arguments in the five categories, more than half fall into this category. It is principally in reference to this rationale that the role and place of Swiss philanthropic organizations and the legitimacy of fiscal measures designed to support them are evaluated. Even in the discourse of political actors more critical of or even hostile to tax incentives for philanthropy, efficiency structures the frame of reference of their argumentation and tends to be seen as obvious.

While political actors largely approve of fiscal advantages for public-interest organizations, based particularly on efficiency arguments, they do not all do so for the same reasons. In the first type of discourse, the 'civic' frame, fiscal advantages are perceived as a means of supporting the third sector. In the 'liberal' frame, these advantages serve to reduce taxes and the ascendancy of the state, and in the 'pragmatic' frame, they represent a measure of good management of public finances rather than an option reflecting a political orientation. To these first three categories can be added two frames composed essentially of negative arguments: In the 'wary' frame, the fiscal advantages constitute a risk factor for abuse and fraud; the 'critical' frame, for its part, interprets these advantages as undermining equality (between taxpayers and between organizations). Finally, each of these frame types is distinguished by a particular view of philanthropic organizations, linking them to a specific issue. We now propose to examine them in greater detail.

Fiscal policies in favor of public-interest organizations, a solution to support the dynamism of civil society: the 'civic' frame

'Civic' discourse frames fiscal advantages for philanthropic organizations as a good way to support the third sector. Many political actors adopting this frame are thus favorable to broadening the criteria of philanthropic organizations and to raising the threshold of deductibility of donations to them. Some of those employing this discourse, however, are less enthusiastic about the idea of such increases, fearing significant losses of revenues for the state and worrying about the social injustice caused by such a measure. Therefore, a number of those interviewed, notably on the left, explain that the choice between these two options constitutes a dilemma for them.

In addition to drawing upon the category of efficiency, the 'civic' frame is primarily composed of positive arguments from the value categories of democracy and virtue. Regarding the value of democracy, 'civic' discourse highlights pluralism in society and sees the associative life as a guarantee of that. Tax incentives are then perceived as a condition for this associative dynamism and should be extended, for example, to all types of associations, to increase the means at their disposal:

> Numerous sports clubs would have fewer problems if you could say, at the end of the year: 'Let's make a donation of 10,000 francs and we will then be able to deduct that from our taxes'. . . . Maybe there is a person here and there who would really like to make a donation, because, in fact, it is very attractive if one can deduct it all.
>
> *(Interviewee 43, PLR)*

Political actors with this frame also stress the fact that it is not desirable that all decision-making power and all means available for establishing social policies be concentrated in the state. They prefer 'bottom-up' initiatives, stemming from civil society, to the verticality of state power:

> The state cannot be everywhere. This is not its role! . . . Otherwise, we cannot escape; we find ourselves caught in the tentacles of an expanding state. . . . A bit like in France, where, in fact, the system has become completely blocked because the state is ubiquitous.
>
> *(Interviewee 5, VE)*

As for virtue, political actors with this frame agree on the fact that it is fair that those who give to good causes be recompensed and that the role of the state is to recognize and promote virtuous behavior. 'Civic' discourse is that which most emphasizes the virtuous nature of tax benefits.

This frame is that of a very heterogeneous group of political actors in terms of their party affiliation: we find amongst them as many political actors of the left as those of the right. Among the 16 political actors with this type of discourse, we find 8 from left-wing parties – one Parti ouvrier populaire (POP), three Parti socialiste (PS), four Greens, 4 from the center – one Parti évangélique suisse (PEV), three Parti démocrate-chrétien (PDC) – and 4 on the right – three Parti liberal-radical (PLR) and one Union démocratique du centre (UDC). These political actors are characterized by the fact that they are very committed to the world of associations and foundations. This commitment is an integral part of their identity: during interviews, they often refer to this, even before mentioning their political mandates. Particularly preoccupied by the difficulties encountered by small organizations (which they have generally observed in the context of their own involvement), they especially regret the administrative burden for the organizations incurred in the increased requirements of control, as well as the difficulties of recruiting volunteers. A number of them have, moreover, intervened in the political debate to ask for fiscal advantages for volunteers.

Fiscal policies in favor of public-interest organizations, a means of reducing taxes and limiting the role of the state: the 'liberal' frame

In the 'liberal' frame, the tax exemption of donations to philanthropic organizations is perceived, above all, as a means to limit public expenditures, taxes and state power. The common objective of these parliamentarians being 'a maximum reduction in taxes' (Interviewee 14, UDC), they consider, on the one hand, that the threshold of deductibility of donations is too low and, on the other hand, that it would be desirable to broaden the criteria of public-interest organizations: 'Yes, I would like to develop as many tax deduction schemes as possible. . . . Every Swiss franc that is not controlled by the State is actually a gain' (Interviewee 31, UDC).

The 'liberal' frame combines different positive arguments from the categories of efficiency and democracy, as well as that of justice. Moreover, this is the only frame in which this category is drawn upon to favor tax incentives: the arguments which claim that 'a donation is another means of paying one's taxes, because it allows for the direct financing of social goods which the state will not be able to finance' and that 'the usual tax system is "confiscatory" and unjust, and anything which serves to alleviate this is good' are central. As one politician said: 'People give money, and then some of this money comes back into state coffers. For me this [is] absurd' (Interviewee 7, UDC).

This discourse focuses on the onerousness of the 'state bureaucracy': Philanthropic organizations are described as less expensive and more efficient than state services. The argument of tax competition is also more often drawn upon than in the other types of discourse, principally in raising the threat of major taxpayers going elsewhere.

These tax measures are also presented as a mechanism of direct democracy. They must permit 'the giving of greater liberty to individuals' (Interviewee 19, PLR) and are opposed to 'the optic of the left which considers that only policy or politics is capable of having the wisdom to know where to put the money' (ibid.). Tax even constitutes a danger: 'There is no longer individual responsibility. If worst comes to worst, it's communism! . . . We trust the state, and then after there's shouting because they have to raise taxes' (Interviewee 7, UDC).

This 'liberal' frame is particularly widespread on the right of the political chessboard. It is utilized by ten political actors, five of whom belong to the PLR and five to the UDC. They are generally not very involved in the third sector.

Tax policies in favor of public-interest organizations, a measure of good management of public funds: the 'pragmatic' frame

The 'pragmatic' frame presents tax exemptions for donations as a measure of good management and defends a 'moderate' approach in order to depoliticize the debate and avoid 'ideological postures'. The desire to find a 'happy medium' and avoid the 'extremes' generally translates into an attachment to the existence of a threshold of deductibility, even if the existing threshold is sometimes considered a little low.

Very clearly dominated by positive arguments from the value of efficiency, this frame is based, in particular, on two key arguments: 'you have to take the money where you find it' and 'the state alone cannot assume responsibility for every desirable policy'. Then, the idea of public-private complementarity often comes up as a 'common sense' position, 'to everyone's advantage'. The financing of public or para-public institutions (such as universities or hospitals) is often cited as an example:

> Let's imagine that I win 20 million in the lottery. . . . If I were living in the canton of Baselland [a canton in which one may deduct up to 100% of one's income], I could probably use this 20 million to serve a public interest organization without paying any tax. That could be the University of Basel, maybe with certain demands, like, for example: I would like this to be used in X or Y medical research. . . . In all the other cantons [where one can only deduct between 5 and 20% of one's income] I could not do the same thing, because I would first have to pay taxes.
>
> *(Interviewee 38, PLR)*

The predominance of the category of efficiency over other argumentative categories is expressed in the discourse through the demand for a 'utilitarian' stance: 'the goal is not to have greater fiscal justice . . . ; it is only to have more donations', this justifying '[making] an exception to the principle of taxation based on the amount of income or fortune [and admitting] that this taxation could be somewhat reduced with the goal of encouraging grants and donations' (Interviewee 21, PLR).

While this frame is often critical of fiscal competition, it takes seriously the issue of 'attractiveness', in particular among members of cantonal executive bodies. Thus, a state councilor in charge of finances presents his mission as being a manager before being a politician: He explains that the dominant policy objective of tax exemptions is to 'maintain the tax substance' (Interviewee 8, PDC), that is, tax revenues, which he reminds us are dependent in large part on the wealthiest taxpayers. Proposing to these taxpayers advantages such as the possibility of deducting their philanthropic donations is a means of avoiding their departure for cantons with lower tax rates and at the same time allows the state to make substantial savings, since the third sector benefits from resources which allow it to carry out missions which would not be taken on by the public service. And, like those adhering to the 'civic' discourse, the 'pragmatic' ones think that tax incentives are a means of supporting dynamism in civil society and thus perceive them as inherently positive.

Parties from the center and the right, in particular the PLR, are overrepresented among those who adopt this discourse: among the 12 political actors with a 'pragmatic' frame, 7 are part of the PLR (the majority among them come from the former Radical Party), 2 from the PDC, 1 from the PBD, 1 from the PS and 1 from the Greens. This type of discourse is also most frequently heard, independently of party attachment, among political actors with executive responsibilities (cantonal ministers of finance), presidents/vice-presidents of tax commissions and members of the Council of States; these positions predispose them to adopt a discourse which puts 'the interest of the canton' in the forefront rather than the defense of a given political vision.

Fiscal policies in favor of public-interest organizations, a risk factor for abuse and fraud: the 'wary' frame

The 'wary' frame tends to present fiscal advantages for public-interest organizations as a risk: characterized by suspicion, it is focused on fraud, abuse and dysfunction. The criticism does not center on the principle of philanthropy or that of tax incentives in general but only on certain problematic aspects of the functioning of the third sector and of taxation. In this sense, the legislators whose discourse is of this type are not very interested in the question of the deductibility of donations and of the maximum thresholds for this.

Instead, they often turn their attention to 'scandals' of which they have become aware, and their remarks frequently take the form of commentary on the events of the day. For example, with respect to the risk of tax evasion:

> What is very difficult in these questions is that they are not going to tell you the truth. It's true that tax evasion by means of foundations. . . . I question this. Still, there are some indications that prove that it's true. You tell me that they're obliged to say to whom they have donated but there can be some false statements; they can fiddle with the accounts. . . . Then, it's almost impossible to verify.
>
> *(Interviewee 45, PS)*

This frame is essentially based on two negative arguments which belong to the categories of justice and of democracy: 'Deductions may be diverted from their purpose and used as an instrument of fiscal optimization' and 'Philanthropic organizations escape democratic control; their actions are not controlled or not controlled sufficiently by the political authorities'. This is maintained by a small number of political actors, gravitating around the center-left (one PS, one Greens, one PEV and one PDC). Two of them filed interventions against the exemption for major sports federations, developed in the particular context of the European Championship of football organized in Switzerland in 2008.

Finally, we will note that, while these politicians are very critical of abuses and question the criteria for recognizing public-interest organizations, they are rather reticent in terms of requiring more significant controls; in particular, they are afraid of the excess of the administrative work for the small associations. One explanation of this paradox can probably be found in the fact that these political actors divide the third sector into categories: for them, there are the 'good organizations' and, on the other side, the 'bad' ones. This division into good and bad is expressed in various ways by political actors, with other dualities, for example, large organizations vs. small ones or foundations vs. associations.

> There are private law organizations where there is not even control of the surveillance of foundations. . . . So, while other organizations which are also tax exempt, like, for example, the railway museum in Zurich, of which I was the president until just

> last year. . . . There, I also saw what the canton demands in order to receive this tax exemption. We have to report on everything that we earn with this steam locomotive, guarantee perfect accounting, everything must be invested, there is no compensation for the people who get up at 4 in the morning to warm up these steam locomotives and who return in the evening with a dirty face at any hour. . . . That's different, . . . there, that's perfectly alright. But in the case of organizations who operate as a kind of business, at the international level . . ., that's problematic.
>
> *(Interviewee 1, PEV)*

Fiscal policies in favor of public-interest organizations, a vector of political, economic and social inequality: the 'critical' frame

Finally, those who hold to the 'critical' frame are the only ones to condemn the fiscal measures encouraging philanthropy. For them, they constitute a violation of equality between individuals (rich and poor) and between organizations (those who can easily collect donations and those which defend less popular causes). Therefore, they are strongly opposed to political plans to increase the threshold of deductibility of donations or to extend the domain of public-interest organizations.

The 'critical' frame combines a multitude of negative arguments from each of the four categories. The concern with equality and universalism leads to criticism of the fact that the decisions of public-interest organizations escape democratic control:

> Instead of paying taxes, you decide where the money goes; so, this contradicts the democratic principle. The democratic principle means that the public authority collects the money for the basics and decides on how much goes to schools, how much to roads, how much to hospitals.
>
> *(Interviewee 36, VE)*

'Critical' discourse especially stresses tax losses due to tax exemptions and deductions – an issue relegated to the background in the other types of discourse:

> Should we limit this? Yes, probably, because the canton's budget simply must be put in order. When there's nobody left to pay taxes because everyone. . . . This is certainly not desirable.
>
> *(Interviewee 12, PS)*

To criticize tax advantages, this discourse draws from the category of virtue, claiming that the failure to pay taxes is an immoral or unsociable act and that the principle of universality must be respected. However, it is interesting to observe that the 'critical' discourse does not go as far as to question the idea that 'the state on its own lacks the means to provide all desirable public and social services', which seems to be a view on which all agree.

This frame is that of a small number of politicians who all belong to parties of the left (four PS, one Greens and a POP) and are very active in the associative environment. Their position in the field of public-interest organizations (often close to umbrella organizations and association networks) and/or their experience with social work makes them more sensitive to questions related to financing and to the independence of associative structures. Quite isolated on these matters – including in their own parties – they deplore the fact that they are not understood by their colleagues, who, for lack of having invested sufficient time to grasp the profound political issues related to these technical fiscal questions, 'just don't get it' (Interviewee 36, VE).

Discussion: philanthropy, the product of an accumulation rather than a confrontation of arguments

Examining the discourse of politicians allows us to show the way in which 'philanthropy' as a political object is constructed by the actors who legislate on the subject. These empirical results also lead us to enrich the theoretical literature on philanthropy and tax exemptions and to question a number of its assumptions, in particular with regard to two aspects: the rationales the discourses refer to and the role played by different representations of philanthropic organizations to explain variations in the way political actors frame tax exemptions for philanthropy.

In terms of rationales, the Swiss case shows the use of varied argumentation based on four rationales: fiscal justice, efficiency, democracy and virtue. While the first three rationales have been identified in other studies – Benshalom (2008) discusses efficiency (to encourage more and/or better spending of public goods) as well as civism or commitment (to allow taxpayers to express their preferences regarding the allocation of public goods in society), and Reich (2018) adds the question of tax justice – a fourth rationale appears in the comments of our interviewees. In this type of argumentation, the act of philanthropic giving as such is seen as inherently virtuous, and it is for this reason that it is seen as worthy of recognition and encouragement by the state. Contrary to the other rationales, which build on a broader general principle to which philanthropy contributes, the rationale of virtue recognizes the value of the act for itself.

The study also gives empirical insight into which rationales are used most often. It suggests that among the various rationales, efficiency is by far the most important, mobilized in all the identified discourses – well before those of democracy and justice. Philanthropy then seems to benefit from a more general trend – which goes beyond this single object – which sees politicians increasingly relying on purely economic concepts (Lebaron, 2013, p. 11; Weil, 2017) and which profoundly modifies the decision makers' perception and appreciation of social realities: efficiency rather than justice. But beyond this general trend, this finding also indicates that political actors apply the efficiency lens to a broader range of objects than what is commonly discussed in the literature. Most studies focus on the financial efficiency of tax incentives, but for many political actors, efficiency also relates to the greater capacity of philanthropic organizations to achieve their goals. If the discourse of efficiency occupies such a place, it is also because it mixes these two different dimensions which, as this study shows, are less seen as diverse and potentially contradictory than working together in favor of legal and fiscal reforms.

The second contribution of this study concerns the role of representations of philanthropic organizations for the frames political actors use to argue about it. The existing literature discusses the question of 'why fiscally encourage philanthropy'; the focus is on the distribution effects of tax exemption. Yet if we look at political actors' discourses, we see that beyond partisan cleavages on purported benefits of fiscal tools, their positions and arguments are very much related to the very heterogeneous depictions of philanthropy. As our interviews show, the ways of depicting philanthropy usually seem to be piecemeal and limited. This is as if, in the absence of established discourse on what this sector of public-interest organizations really is, each individual approached this through their own personal experience and with respect to their own preoccupations. This phenomenon is maybe particularly pronounced in the debates on public interest, because the third sector is an extremely plural one. It is composed of structures that are sometimes so different from one another that, strictly speaking, they do not have much in common. A great variety of organizations active in many different domains populate this sector in Switzerland: from small environmental NGOs to the Red Cross; from theater associations and local football clubs to huge international sports organizations like FIFA or UEFA, which are considered of public interest in Switzerland.

The perception of the third sector and even the definition of public interest by Swiss politicians depend therefore widely on the type of organizations that they have in mind. The parliamentarians may or may not be involved in associations or foundations; some raise this question in thinking about donors, while others are thinking about the beneficiaries. When they think about these donors, some think about those who make monetary donations, while others, on the contrary, speak about those who give their time in volunteer activities. When they think about beneficiaries, some think of public and para-public establishments (such as universities or hospitals), others of small local associations, while still others make reference to the major international sports organizations. Some broached the subject because they were personally confronted with a practical incomprehension in the context of an involvement in public-interest organizations, while others interject following a media scandal or to make themselves the spokesperson for an association of public-interest organizations.

It is the way actors delimit the subject, in this case philanthropy, which matters when one wants to understand the positions taken and the frames used. The politicians adopting a 'wary' frame, for example, are not fundamentally opposed to tax incentives for philanthropy. They are simply interested, for one reason or another, in big international organizations and the supposedly negative effects of their fiscal advantages. Or, to take another example, the 'pragmatic' frame is mainly adopted by executive politicians at the cantonal level. When they speak of public interest, they think of organizations they encounter in their day-to-day work: During interviews, they speak of donations made for research but also of para-public organizations like regional home care services. Politicians embracing a 'civic' frame, on the other hand, are especially committed to the world of associations and foundations and are personally involved in the non-profit sector, mainly in small organizations. The lens through which they approach public interest as a political object is the concrete challenges encountered by these organizations and the strategies to facilitate their work.

In sum, while the literature often seems to confine the issue of philanthropy to the question of tax incentives for donations, our study shows, on the contrary, that when political actors think about philanthropy, they do not only think about donations (or donors) but just as much about philanthropic organizations, which are also tax exempt. Is it the fact that FIFA and UEFA have their headquarters in Switzerland? The question of their tax exemption is omnipresent, as is the comparison of their status vis-à-vis small sports clubs whose social utility seems no less important. As a counterpoint to a literature that most often focuses only on tax exemptions for donations, this study shows the extent to which, for political actors, the discussion on the legal and fiscal frameworks governing philanthropy concerns just as much – and even more importantly – the equity between organizations that benefit or not from these exemptions and the justification of these exemptions for such organizations.

Notes

1 The authors would like to thank the attentive reviewers of a previous version of this chapter for their insightful comments.

2 The term 'philanthropy' does not have a legal definition in Swiss law. Regarding direct taxes, Swiss federal law exempts legal entities that are pursuing public-service or public-interest purposes from the federal income tax on profits that are exclusively and irrevocably affected to such purposes (Art. 56 lit. 6 LIFD) and allows donations in favor of these entities to be deducted of income (or net profit) up to a maximum of 20% (Art. 33a and 59 let. c LIFD). In the present analysis, the term 'philanthropy' is used in its two possible linguistic meanings, that is, regarding the taxation of 1) philanthropic organizations and of 2) philanthropic transfers of funds or other property (donor taxation).

3 Regarding direct taxes, Switzerland exempts legal entities that have: 1) purpose of general interest, 2) unlimited circle of beneficiaries, 3) exclusive and irrevocable contribution of the funds, 4) disinterest and 5) actual non-profit activity.

4 We focused on the parliamentary activity of three cantons in particular: Geneva, Neuchâtel and Baselland. These three cantons were chosen due to different limits on the deductibility of donations which they adopted or modified in the 2000s (5% of taxable income or profits in Neuchâtel, 20% in Geneva and no limit in Baselland).

5 For a detailed list of the interviewees and their interventions, we refer the reader to Lambelet et al. (2021). We indicate here the political party of the interviewees using party acronyms. Switzerland has a multiparty system whose political parties can be categorized in three groups. Parties of the left: POP (Parti ouvrier et Populaire [Swiss Labour Party]), PS (Parti socialiste [Social Democratic Party]), VE (Les Verts [Green Party]). Parties of the centre: PDC (Parti démocrate-chrétien [Christian Democrats]), PEV (Parti évangélique [Evangelical People's Party]), PBD (Parti bourgeois-démocratique [Conservative Democratic Party]). Parties on the right: PLR (Parti libéral-radical [The Liberals]), UDC (Union démocratique du centre [Swiss People's Party]).

6 In contrast with the long US tradition of making public financial forms and annual reports, Swiss foundations have to report only to the state supervisory authority, which does not make the information public (Schnurbein and Perez, 2018).

References

Ariely, D., Bracha, A. and Meier, S. (2009). 'Doing good or doing well? Image motivation and monetary incentives in behaving prosocially'. *American Economic Review*, 99(1), pp. 544–555.

Bakija, J. and Heim, B. T. (2011). 'How does charitable giving respond to incentives and income? New estimates from panel data'. *National Tax Journal*, 64(2, Part 2), pp. 615–650.

Bekkers, R. and Wiepking, P. (2011). 'A Literature Review of Empirical Studies of Philanthropy: Eight Mechanisms That Drive Charitable Giving'. *Nonprofit and Voluntary Sector Quarterly*, 40(5), pp. 924–973.

Benshalom, I. (2008). 'The Dual Subsidy Theory of Charitable Deductions'. *Indiana Law Journal*, 84, pp. 1047–1097.

Best, J. (2008). *Social Problems* (1st ed.). New York, NY: W.W. Norton & Company.

Brilliant, E. (2000). *Private Charity and Public Inquiry: A History of the Filer and Peterson Commissions*. Bloomington, IN: Indiana University Press.

Cagé, J. (2020). *The Price of Democracy: How Money Shapes Politics and What to Do About It*. Cambridge, MA: Harvard University Press.

European Foundation Center. (2015). *Comparative Highlights of Foundation Laws*. Bruxelles: EFC.

Gamson, W.A. and Modigliani, A. (1989). 'Media Discourse and Public Opinion on Nuclear Power: A Constructionist Approach'. *American Journal of Sociology*, 95(1), pp. 1–37.

Goffman, E. (1974). *Frame Analysis: An Essay on the Organisation of Experience*. New York, NY: Harper.

Helmig, B., Gmür, M., Bärlocher, Ch., von Schnurbein, G., Degen, B., Nollert, M., Wojciech Sokolowski, S. and Salamon, L. (2017). 'Switzerland: A Liberal Outlier for Europe'. In *Explaining Civil Society Development: A Social Origins Approach*. Baltimore, MD: Johns Hopkins University Press, pp. 131–142.

Helmig, B., Lichtsteiner, H. and Gmür, M. (2010). *Der Dritte Sektor der Schweiz: die Schweizer Länderstudie im Rahmen des Johns Hopkins Comparative Nonprofit Sector Project (CNP)* (1. Auf.). Bern: Haupt Verlag.

Howard, Ch. (1993). 'The Hidden Side of the American Welfare State'. *Political Science Quarterly*, 108(3), pp. 403–436.

Krippendorff, K. (2004). *Content Analysis: An Introduction to Its Methodology* (2nd ed.). Thousand Oaks, CA: Sage.

Lambelet, A. (2014). *La Philanthropie*. Paris: Presses de Sciences Po.

Lambelet, A., Balsiger, P., Carnac, R. and Honegger C. (2021). *Reconnaître l'utilité publique. Parlementaires et personnel des administrations fiscales face à la philanthropie en Suisse*. Lausanne: HETSL Editions.

Layton, M. (2015). 'The Influence of Fiscal Incentives on Philanthropy Across Nations'. In Wiepking, P. and Handy, F. (eds). *The Palgrave Handbook of Global Philanthropy*. London: Palgrave Macmillan, pp. 540–557.

Leat, D. (2016). *Philanthropy Foundations, Public Good and Public Policy*. London: Palgrave Macmillan.

Lebaron, F. (2013). 'Pour une sociologie de la production et de la diffusion des discours économiques: Réflexion à partir de l'exemple de la notion de modèle social'. In Temmar, M., Angermüller, J. and Lebaron, F. (eds). *Les discours de l'économie*. Paris: Presses Universitaires de France, pp. 13–32.

Lideikyte Huber, G. (2018). 'Philanthropy and Taxation: Swiss Legal Framework and Reform Perspectives'. *Expert Focus*, 3, pp. 209–213.

Lideikyte Huber, G. (2020). 'Tax Incentives for Charitable Giving as a Policy Instrument: Theoretical Discussion and Latest Economic Research'. *World Tax Journal*, 12, p. 3.

McDaniel, P.R. (1989). 'Tax Expenditures as Tools of Government Action'. In L.M. Salamon (ed). *Beyond Privatization: The Tools of Government Action*. Washington, DC: The Urban Institute Press, pp. 167–195.

McGravie, M. (2003). 'The Dartmouth College Case and the Legal Design of Civil Society'. In Friedman, L. and McGravie, M. (ed). *Charity, Philanthropy and Civility in American History*. New York, NY: Cambridge University Press, pp. 91–105.

Monnet, N. and Panizza, U. (2017). *A Note on the Economics of Philanthropy*. IHEID Working Papers No. 19. Genève: Economics Section, The Graduate Institute of International Studies.

OECD. (2020). *Taxation and Philanthropy*. OECD Tax Policy Studies No. 27. Paris: OECD Publishing. https://doi.org/10.1787/df434a77-en

Reese, S.D., Gandy, O. and Grant, A.E. (eds). (2001). *Framing Public Life: Perspectives on Media and Our Understanding of the Social World*. New York, NY: Routledge.

Reich, R. (2013). 'Philanthropy and Caring for the Needs of Strangers'. *Social Research: An Internal Quarterly*, 80(2), pp. 517–538.

Reich, R. (2018). *Just Giving: Why Philanthropy Is Failing Democracy and How It Can Do Better*. Princeton, NJ: Princeton University Press.

Reich, R., Cordelli, C. and Bernholz, L. (eds). (2016). *Philanthropy in Democratic Societies: History, Institutions, Values*. Chicago and London: University of Chicago Press.

Saez, E. and Zucman, G. (2019). *The Triumph of Injustice: How the Rich Dodge Taxes and How to Make Them Pay*. New York, NY: W.W. Norton & Company.

Salamon, L.M. (1989). 'The Changing Tools of Government Action: An Overview'. In Salamon L. (ed). *Beyond Privatization: The Tools of Government Action*. Washington, DC: The Urban Institute Press.

Salamon, L.M. and Anheiner, H.K. (1998). 'Social Origins of Civil Society: Explaining the Nonprofit Sector Cross-Nationally'. *Voluntas: International Journal of Voluntary and Nonprofit Organizations*, 9(3), pp. 213–248.

Salamon, L.M. and Toepler, S. (2000). *The Influence of the Legal Environment on the Development of the Nonprofit Sector*. Working Paper Series No. 17. Baltimore, MD: The Johns Hopkins University Institute for Policy Studies/Center for Civil Society Studies.

Schnurbein von, G. and Perez, M. (2018). 'Foundations in Switzerland: Between the American and the German Cases'. *American Behavioral Scientist*, 62(13), pp. 1919–1932.

Steinmo, S. (1986). 'So What's Wrong with Tax Expenditures? A Reevaluation Based on Swedish Experience'. *Public Budgeting & Finance*, 6(2), pp. 27–44.

Thaler, R. H. (2010). 'It's Time to Rethink the Charity Deduction'. *The New York Times*, 18 December.

Weil, S. (2017). *25 Jahre New Public Management in der Schweiz. Zehn Gestalter erzählen*. Cahier de l'IDHEAP. Cahier de l'IDHEAP 300. Lausanne: IDHEAP.

Zunz, O. (2011). *Philanthropy in America: A History*. Princeton, NJ: Princeton University Press.

3

INSTITUTIONAL SHORTCIRCUITS

When should philanthropy be incentivised?[1]

Emanuela Ceva

1 Introduction

The practice of philanthropy has been sitting uncomfortably with the credentials of the liberal democratic state. One of the main concerns has been with the uneven distribution of political power that philanthropy may entail when the state's political agenda and priorities respond to the particular interests of some wealthy donors rather than to the general interests of the citizenry (Cordelli 2016; Greaves and Pummer 2019; Lambelet et al. 2019; Reich 2018). To the extent that philanthropy exposes the state's political agenda to the uneven influence of certain (individual or corporate) personal agendas, it may even be censored as a form of political corruption (Ceva and Ferretti 2021, 2018, 2017).

Philanthropy can perform many functions in society. It can, for example, address resources to socially innovative practices (e.g., sponsoring new research and start-ups), alert to neglected causes or issues that have fallen out of the state's political agenda (e.g., supporting environmental initiatives), or act quickly to address unexpected social needs (e.g., financing infrastructures to deal with a health emergency). Against this composite background (for an overview, see Anheier 2018), this chapter adopts a normative point of view to discuss the justification of tax incentives for philanthropy when philanthropy performs one particular function. This is a remedial function that philanthropy may be called to perform in the face of institutional failures in the nonideal circumstances of concrete public institutional action. Ideally, public institutional action should be capable of developing and pursuing a political agenda that caters to shared needs (and adjudicates between competing ones). However, in the nonideal circumstances of concrete public institutional action, public institutions may fail, and philanthropic initiatives might inject valuable skills and resources, thus compensating (at least in part) for some institutional failures. The announcement of the commitment of such eminent philanthropists as Bill Gates in the immediate afermath of the COVID-19 pandemic outbreak to finance the production and distribution of vaccines is but one recent illustration of philanthropy's possible remedial function. Insofar as philanthropy can play this remedial function, the state seems to be justified to incentivise it in nonideal conditions. But when these incentives occur through taxation, they may have the adverse effect of draining resources from the state, thus further undercutting its action (see, e.g., Reich 2016, pp. 70–71). An institutional short-circuit may thus occur.

DOI: 10.4324/9781003139201-5

In this chapter, I set out to assess the fear that offering tax incentives for philanthropy may trigger vicious institutional short-circuits by discussing the justification of philanthropy from the point of view of a liberal democratic institutional ethics. I start from a conception of this institutional ethics as grounded in the normative idea of 'office accountability', the idea that officeholders in public institutions should always be in the position of justifying the rationale of the agenda they pursue by their conduct in their institutional capacity as coherent with the terms of their power of office mandate (§2). A public institution that realises office accountability can draw on the interrelated action of officeholders as an *internal* resource to sustain its functioning. When there is a deficit of office accountability, this internal mechanism fails, and remedial action should be taken. I proceed (§3) by distinguishing between two types of remedial action of this sort, internal and external, and present philanthropy as an instance of this latter (§4). I then argue that remedial philanthropic initiatives may be justified within this ethical framework insofar as they occur in such a way that enhances their compatibility with a commitment to office accountability. Failing this condition, such philanthropic initiatives risk being disqualified as a form of political corruption (§5).

This discussion serves as a basis for exploring the boundaries of the justification of tax incentives for a particular set of philanthropic initiatives. While this argument has thus a limited scope, it points at a circumscribed but significant domain of institutional action where the allegiance between the state and philanthropy is fully (albeit nonideally) justified. Within this particular domain, I will argue, remedial philanthropic initiatives play the important instrumental function of upholding public institutional action from the *outside* public institutions when the interrelated action of officeholders fails to sustaining it from their *inside*.

2 Institutional functioning and the ethics of office accountability

To describe an institution means to describe the action of a group of agents, the officeholders, who act in a special capacity in virtue of the powers entrusted to the institutional roles they occupy.[2] The discussion in this chapter mainly concerns the functioning of public institutions; but this basic description applies to any kind of institution understood as a system of roles. More specifically, institutions are not just a set of *procedural mechanisms* and formal rules, nor may institutional action be identified straightforwardly with the joint action of *individual* institutional members. An institution is a system of *interrelated embodied rule-governed roles* (the offices) to which powers are entrusted with a mandate (Ceva and Ferretti 2021, 2018). Let us pause to consider the elements of this definition.

First, notice that each *role* within an institution is established and governed by a set of *rules* (the constitutive rules of an institution), which spells out the normative powers (the rights and duties) and the tasks associated with each role. Second, take note that each role is *embodied* in the sense that it is occupied by a human person (the officeholder), whose conduct in her institutional capacity is governed by the constitutive rules of an institution. Consider, third, that the embodied rule-governed roles of an institution are *interrelated* in the sense that the capacity of each officeholder to exercise her powers of office and perform her tasks *structurally* depends on the other officeholders' conduct in their institutional capacity. Finally, note that an institution is grounded in a raison d'être which comprises the normative ideals that motivate its establishment and, consequently, its internal structure of roles and related tasks. An institution's raison d'être informs what powers are entrusted to the various institutional roles with what mandate. From all this, it follows that to see whether an institution functions, we should be looking at the officeholders' interrelated conduct in their institutional capacity, whether the occupants of institutional roles exercise their powers of office in keeping with an agenda whose rationale is coherent with the terms of their power mandate.

It is important to point out that the very fact of occupying an institutional role entrusts people with normative powers, in the form of rights and duties, that they do not normally have (Rawls 1955; Searle 1995). As a university professor, I have the right to demand that certain people, the students, read and write certain things and to assess their performance on that ground; correspondingly, the students have a duty to read and write what I demand of them and a right to expect a fair evaluation of their work. This set of normative relations does not normally hold between people as 'bare agents' – I can recommend a book to friend, but I cannot *demand* that she read it and write a commentary about it. Institutional membership therefore creates an order of rights and duties that binds together the occupants of institutional roles and regulates their interactions *inside* an institutional context. This internal perspective is of paramount importance for the discussion in the chapter; we will revisit it in §3.

There is a further important point about the nature of institutions to revisit: all roles in an institution are interrelated. As anticipated, the interrelatedness of institutional roles means that the performance of any officeholder in her institutional capacity structurally depends on the performances of the other officeholders and the uses they make of the powers entrusted to their roles. To understand officeholders' actions, and assess the uses of powers they make, it is essential to see them in the context of and as interrelated with the other officeholders' actions and the performance of their tasks. This perspective of interrelatedness gives meaning to the officeholders' actions in their institutional capacity, whose interrelated work is definitive of institutional action. So, for example, to assess the functioning of an authority responsible for the marketing of new drugs, it is not enough to look at its statutory regulations and the formal rules that govern its procedural mechanisms on paper. We need, rather, to look at the interrelated conduct of the holders of the various offices implicated in the authorisation procedure, from those entrusted with the power to seek experts' opinions on the health risks of the drug or on its marketability, including those who are called to collect and analyse those opinions, down to those responsible for signing off the final authorisation. None of these tasks can be appropriately understood, exercised, or assessed in isolation, as the failure of one of them may cause the failure of all the others and therefore of the entire institution (for example, when a decision on a drug's marketability is based on a more or less intentionally biased analysis of the experts' opinion). To understand and assess an institution means, therefore, to look at how it works in practice through the interrelated action of the officeholders. To wit, this understanding and assessment require taking an internal perspective capable of offering an insight about the actual interrelated conduct of the officeholders in the exercise of their institutional tasks.

From the general consideration regarding the interrelatedness of institutional roles, two more specific claims follow. Fist, the functioning of an institution depends on the capacity of the officeholders' interrelated action to honour the raison d'être of their institution by acting in keeping with the terms of their power mandate. Second, the exercise of one officeholder's rights and duties in her institutional capacity (as established by the power mandate entrusted to her role) structurally and fundamentally requires that the other officeholders perform their rights and duties in keeping with the terms of their power mandate. The main entailment of this claim is that, when officeholders act in their institutional capacity, they are *mutually accountable* for the uses they make of their powers of office. This is the idea of 'office accountability' (Ceva 2019). Office accountability is thus the pivot of an institutional ethics of office because it is the normative practical principle that ought to guide the action of officeholders in their institutional capacity. Taken together, these claims result in the statement that the functioning of an institution is premised on an institutional ethics of office accountability.

What we have seen so far is sufficient to qualify a necessary condition for an institution to be well functioning. A well-functioning institution is necessarily one in which the officeholders are in the position of giving each other an account of the rationale of the agenda that underpins the uses they make of their power of office *when they act in their institutional capacity* and show its coherence with the terms of that power mandate (see also Applbaum 1999; Ceva and Ferretti 2021; Emmet 1966; Winston 1999). We can now get a better grasp of the meaning of the condition that officeholders are mutually accountable when they act in their institutional capacity as a requirement of an institutional ethics of office. Notably, office accountability is the centrepiece of a set of normative prescriptions that guide the officeholders' interactions *inside* an institutional context. As participants in such a context, officeholders share the normative standing to require one another to 'give an account' of their action (see also Bovens, Goodin and Schillemans, 2014, p. 6). I call this ethics of office 'institutional', as it refers to the terms of mandate within an institution and is, thus, different from the 'personal' ethics that may guide people's interaction in other capacities, for instance, as friends or lovers.

3 Institutional failures and their internal correction

To summarise the argument so far, a well-functioning institution is one sustained by an institutional ethics of office accountability; it is an institution where the officeholders are in the position of giving to each other an account of the rationale of their action in their institutional capacity which is coherent with the terms of their power mandate. In so doing, their interrelated conduct can uphold the raison d'être of their institution. An institution that realises office accountability can draw on the interrelated action of officeholders as an *internal* resource to sustain its functioning. In this sense, think of institutional functioning as that of a sports team, structured according to various rule-governed interrelated specific roles, which are definitive of the team's action. In this context, what a player does (how she makes use of the powers given to her by occupying a certain role) necessarily affects the action of the whole team and its capacity to perform its function.

Unfortunately, in the nonideal circumstances of concrete institutional action, institutional functioning hardly ever proceeds so smoothly. In many circumstances, institutions may fail, including because of a lack of material resources, incompetence, systemic inefficiencies, as a result of the malicious intent of some bad apple, or because of the deterioration of the institutional patterns of officeholders' interaction (Ferretti 2019; Ceva and Ferretti 2021). For instance, institutions may fail as the summative result of the officeholders' individual actions. When several officeholders individually fail to perform their tasks (on various grounds), the institution as a whole may fail. Consider the example of a border control agency where a good number of inspectors regularly allow bulk cash smuggling, so that the borders supposedly controlled by the agency become a safe channel for money smugglers, and an informal bribe-and-smuggle practice becomes characteristic of the work of the entire agency. This practice, initiated by the discrete actions of a number of individuals, impairs the agency's functioning as a whole by working from its inside.

On a different count, an institutional failure may depend on the particular morphology of the interrelatedness of roles within an institution. Consider, for example, the case of an authority for the marketing of new drugs (Ceva and Ferretti 2021, pp. 65–67). The officeholder who has the task of selecting the experts to seek advice on the drug's weighted dangers is the husband of the head of a pharmaceutical company that is leading the research on the drug. He selects the experts in such a way to obtain a favourable advice on its safety. Now, some of this officeholders' colleagues who have not been involved in the selection procedure are called to decide on the drug's marketability. Per their power mandate, they base their judgment on the experts' report and find evidence in support of the marketing authorisation. In doing so, the marketing officeholders act according to the rules of their office. However, the rationale of the entire institutional action has been compromised by the behaviour of the first officeholder, who acted in the pursuit of a familistic agenda that is totally extraneous to the rationale of his power of office mandate (which is certainly not that to favour his dear and near ones by his institutional action). Because of the interrelatedness of institutional roles, the officeholders responsible for the marketing authorisation procedure can function or fail only together. Because, as seen in the previous section, an institution *is* a system of interrelated rule-governed embodied roles, and the assessment of institutional action *is* the assessment of the officeholders' interrelated conduct, when this latter fails, the institution itself fails.

The illustration of institutional failures suggests the importance for institutional functioning that officeholders be constantly vigilant not only as concerns their own conduct but also, and perhaps most importantly, with respect to the conduct of the other occupants of institutional roles in their institutions. The primary resource for counteracting institutional failures should therefore come from the inside of an institution. This thought reinforces the idea that institutional functioning (and the correction of institutional failures) is first and foremost a matter of an institutional ethics of office accountability. As seen, at the core of this institutional ethics is a general commitment to making officeholders mutually accountable for their conduct in their institutional capacity. I want to add now that, whenever a deficit of office accountability is suspected, this general commitment translates into the specific requirement that officeholders engage in good faith in practices of *answerability*.

To ensure its functioning and address possible partial or systemic failures, institutions should set up internal answerability practices through which officeholders may call on each other to honour their professional duties and sustain institutional action as an interrelated body of agents. Such practices may include organisational codes of conduct, transparency mechanisms, and whistleblowing (Ceva and Bocchiola 2018). These practices are aimed at establishing and assigning retrospective and prospective responsibilities for institutional failures to officeholders, severally and as interrelated agents (for instance, per the summative and morphological patterns of interaction illustrated previously). This exercise is crucial to engage officeholders in a communicative practice, thus calling them to respond to the threats that their conduct may pose to the capacity of their institution to be faithful to its raison d'être. By engaging in this practice, officeholders can either rebut, in part or in full, or accept their implication in institutional failures and also take up the prospective responsibility of sustaining the functioning of their institution in the future.

4 Institutional failures and their external correction: the contribution of philanthropy

While the presence of internal answerability practices is essential to mobilise an institution's internal resources of self-correction, sometimes the relationships between officeholders and their dynamics of interaction are compromised to an extent that makes the resort to external resources necessary, too. To be sure, for starters, in any institutional setup, officeholders are generally expected to respond for their institutional action to third-party authorities such as the judiciary or, in a democracy, the citizenry. In some such major instances of institutional failure as in cases of systemic corruption, for example, it seems hard to imagine that an entrenched system of dysfunctional interactions that is prey – say – to clientelism or other forms of regulatory capture may be transformed without an external 'shock'. This predicament may be due to very high peer pressure to maintain the corrupt network in place to salvage the privileges of sharing the profits that derive from a well-established network of personal connections, which sometimes also sees collusion with organised crime. A change of pace requires a substantial transformation, possibly including the appointment of new officials with a clean personal record.

On other occasions, external hurdles may join such internal obstacles as the deterioration of the officeholders' relationships dynamics to exacerbate the difficulty of initiating the officeholders' reaction to institutional failures. Relying on an institution's internal resources of self-correction might prove particularly difficult in circumstances plagued by a scarcity of material resources or the lack of the infrastructural and planning capacity to implement certain actions in a given territory; external and extraordinary circumstances, including natural calamities or a pandemic, may strain the context in which officeholders operate and undercut their capacity to undertake corrective actions by their own efforts. When such factors impinge upon the functioning of public institutions and their internal reactive resources, as it were, philanthropic individual and corporate initiatives may enter the picture to sustain public institutional action. Such nonideal circumstances thus provide a fruitful context to explore the justification of a particular form of philanthropy consisting of remedial initiatives.

In broad brushes, I take philanthropy as essentially characterised by the voluntary commitment of someone's private resources for the pursuit of some public goal (or to sustain an agency engaged in such a pursuit).[3] Philanthropic initiatives are manifold. They may be individual, in the form of gifts by single wealthy donors, or corporate, when they see the engagement of charitable organisations or private foundations. Philanthropy may not only take many different forms, but it can perform various functions in society that are more or less complementary to the action of public institutions (see, e.g., Anheier 2018). I shall expound on and revisit the many possible functions of philanthropy in the next section. I would like to draw the reader's attention now to one particular function that philanthropy may perform in the context of the nonideal circumstances of institutional action we have just seen. An immediate illustration of this particular function comes by observing the COVID-19 pandemic context, which has clearly opened a window on one particular form of philanthropy's contribution to public institutional action. In that exceptional context, nonprofit agencies, foundations, or single donors have sustained the development (and committed to the distribution) of vaccines, as well as offering contributions for the assistance of the most vulnerable sectors of the population (e.g., homeless people or the elderly). This contribution has proved particularly important given the difficulties of coordinating and activating prompt institutional responses to an unprecedented and (partially) unforeseeable emergency. For example, philanthropy's contribution has been crucial in this sense to complement and sustain the action of public institutions, which has sometimes left vulnerable minorities behind in an effort to manage the sanitary situation for the majority of the population. This particular complementary function qualifies what I call 'remedial philanthropic initiatives'.

To be true, philanthropy's complementary contribution to public institutional action is far from being a novel phenomenon that emerged in the pandemic times. From being primarily a church- or religion-based initiative, philanthropy has gradually come to permeate many domains traditionally the preserve of public institutional action, including education, health, arts, science, and innovation, as well as the protection of people's social and civil rights (Bremner 1988; Hall 2006). Because of its enhancing contribution to many domains of people's personal, social, cultural, and political life, the role of individual philanthropists and of philanthropic foundations may be seen as an important complement to the action of public institutions. In a democracy, philanthropy may have the additional value of sustaining and moving forward specific projects or endeavours that might be too marginal or controversial to be pursued by public institutional action or whose priority is not recognised by the political and social majority of citizens. The action of advocacy and social campaigning that may be sustained by philanthropic initiatives may thus contribute also to enrich the democratic public sphere and contribute to a pluralistic political discourse in keeping with one of the pivotal commitments of a democratic institutional setting (Reich 2016, pp. 73–76, 2018).

In view of these positive grounds for the assessment of philanthropy's contribution to public institutional action, good reasons seem to hold to justify the public incentivisation of philanthropic initiatives, especially in nonideal circumstances that threaten the functioning of public institutions (both from the inside and the outside, as seen previously). Incentives for philanthropic initiatives may be manifold, but they almost ubiquitously include provisions of tax incentives for private and corporate donors. Tax incentives may take the form of either tax reductions or tax credits, and they may concern either income or estate taxes. Moreover, tax incentives may come in degrees depending on the fiscal level where they occur – federal, state, or local (see Greene and McClelland 2001). Among the countries where tax incentives for philanthropy are sizable and widespread are certainly the United States of America and the United Kingdom. But Switzerland, where philanthropy is a major instance of the general commitment to subsidiarity, also provides an illustration of the multiple layers of this mode of incentivisation for philanthropic initiatives. In the confederation, tax deductions for philanthropic donations apply to foundations and individual citizens. Philanthropic foundations enjoy a total tax exemption from the federal income tax and may also benefit from variable tax exemptions on a cantonal and communal level. These exemptions may concern the income and/or capital tax and the real estate income tax as well as the inheritance tax. The exemptions for individual citizens who donate to philanthropic foundations apply at the same twofold federal (up to 20% of the total taxable income) and cantonal/ municipal level.

However, the story of the supposed allegiance between philanthropic and public institutional actions is far from being rosy. In periods of fiscal austerity and political polarisation, the choice of what social causes and interests to promote and prioritise is particularly arduous, and philanthropic initiatives may seem a way to force the hands of public institutions in particular directions, as they sidestep the ordinary democratic process for giving political orientation. The criticism may be pressed to the point of pinpointing the essential incompatibility between democracy and philanthropy as an instance of plutocracy (Reich 2013). The question concerns whether and to what extent democracies may afford the condition that private property and wealth become the guidance for the promotion and prioritisation of public purposes, thus sanctioning the influence of background inequalities on public decisions. The very freedom of philanthropic initiatives to choose what issues to press and sustain by the employment of private funds is frequently indicated as a source of democratic risk. Sometimes pet causes or marginal cultural initiatives may erratically get pride of place, overshadowing more urgent economic or social needs. Moreover, there is a risk of cacophony, as the most disparate initiatives may attract donors' idiosyncratic support, thus causing inefficient expenditures that a careful political strategy of coherent public investments could easily avoid. The underlying fear concerns a general lack of public control and transparency on philanthropic initiatives that risks exposing public institutional action to private and partisan interests, outside the usual mechanisms of checks and balances proper of a democracy.

These shadows over the justifiability of the allegiance between philanthropic and public institutional action have also cast more than a doubt concerning the justification of such forms of support as tax incentives for private (individual or corporate) donors. At a basic individual-centred level, one may ask why and to what extent the state is ever justified to subsidise (with a loss of tax revenue) people's exercise of their freedom to give their private money away (see Reich 2011). To use Rob Reich's eloquent words, in reference to the American context, philanthropy

> is not just the voluntary activity of a donor, the result of people exercising a freedom to do what they wish with their private property. Philanthropy . . . is generously tax subsidized. . . . So foundations do not simply express the individual liberty of wealthy people. Citizens pay, in lost tax revenue, for foundations, and, by extension, for giving public expression to the preferences of rich people.
>
> *(Reich 2016, pp. 70–71)*

But this individualistic, broadly liberal questioning does not exhaust the qualms with justifying tax incentives for philanthropy. From the institution-centred internalist perspective I have adopted in this chapter, more can be said to explore the possible tensions between philanthropic and public institutional action. For starters, there is a risk that by 'throwing money at' certain causes, philanthropy more or less subtly interferes with an institution's self-control on how its action furthers its grounding ideals (and perhaps even questions such ideals on grounds of pleasing the philanthropist). Also, philanthropy may endanger the mutuality of the accountability relations we have seen as pivotal to an institutional ethics of office. To be sure, any philanthropist would want to know what has been done with their money and so hold the officeholders accountable to them in ways in which the philanthropists are not really accountable to the officeholders (in view of their freedom to donate for causes of their choosing). Finally, especially when philanthropy steps in to respond to institutional failures, tax incentives for philanthropy may come under attack as the source of a potential viciously self-defeating institutional short-circuit. Fiscal benefits of this kind, especially if widespread, may have the adverse effect of draining resources from the state, thus further undercutting public institutional action. An institutional short-circuit may thus occur by which public institutional action risks being entangled in a viciously self-defeating circularity, thus surrendering its raison d'être.

In the remainder of the chapter, I address these criticalities concerning the justification of the allegiance between philanthropic and public institutional action and the sanctioning of such an allegiance by means of tax incentives. I will do that with reference to a specific remedial function that philanthropy may perform in the face of institutional failures within the framework of an institutional ethics of office accountability (as presented in the first part of the chapter).

5 Remedial philanthropic initiatives as external props for public institutional action

The question of whether tax incentives for philanthropy are justified necessarily depends on the answer we give to the more general question of the justification of the very place of philanthropy in the context of public institutional action. I want to suggest a particular answer to this general question with reference to a specific remedial function that philanthropy can perform within the institutional ethics of office accountability I have presented in the first part of the chapter. I have argued there that the key structural feature for having a functioning public institution is that the officeholders within it always act in their institutional capacity for the pursuit of an agenda whose rationale may be vindicated as coherent with the terms of their power mandate. This thought is summarised in the normative idea of office accountability. The commitment to office accountability is key to institutional functioning because it emphasises the importance of officeholders' mutual reliance to uphold by their interrelated action the raison d'être of their institution. As we have seen in §3, when public institutional action fails, office accountability grounds the expectation that officeholders be ready to engage in practices of institutional answerability as a self-reflective communicative exercise aimed to gain a shared understanding of what went wrong and how it could be remedied.

However, sometimes internal or external hurdles may impair the mobilisation of an institution's internal resources of self-correction. When these predicaments occur, the prompt for remedial action may well come from outside a failing public institution. My suggestion is that one important ground for the justification of philanthropy emerges whenever philanthropy takes on such a remedial function in the face of failures of public institutional action. This is a *normative*, not a descriptive, claim, and, most importantly, it concerns a *particular* set of philanthropic initiatives. Of course, we may have philanthropic initiatives of other kinds that claim for themselves either a more or a less ambitious role. More ambitious philanthropic initiatives would claim a more pronounced action-guiding function as they offer their support for activities aimed at (re-)orienting political action or (re)setting political priorities (e.g., through advocacy or lobbying).[4] Other forms of philanthropy may have greater modesty as they operate to sustain 'additional' activities that are normally not considered definitional of public institutional action (e.g., artistic activities or sports events).[5] Of course, we may have reasons to cherish (or, in fact, dread) philanthropy even under such richer or more modest descriptions. We should also be mindful of the general liberal presumption in favour of people's freedom to dispose of their own personal resources as they see fit (within basic limits such as those set by the harm principle). My argument is more specific. Whatever we may think about the general complementarity between philanthropy and public institutional action (in a democracy or more in general), there are reasons for justifying certain philanthropic initiatives in the nonideal circumstances of institutional failures, which require an external prop to be addressed and redressed in ways capable of sustaining institutional functioning.

To the extent that philanthropy serves this circumscribed but important remedial role for the functioning of the public institutional system, it is justified, and so are provisions that incentivise it, including by means of tax incentives. The simple thought behind this seemingly bold claim is that taxation should serve to sustain the basic functioning of public institutions; there is nothing surprising about this thought, as we normally accept that taxpayer money is used, inter alia, to pay officeholders' salaries and cover the indirect costs of their action (by catering to their working tools and facilities). To the extent that some philanthropic initiatives target failures of public institutional action, they attend to a sufficiently analogous role of propping up institutional functioning from the outside. From this point of view, there does not seem to be anything outrageous in the thought that those who use their own private resources to this end should be sustained, encouraged, and relieved from paying twice, as it were, for their contribution to the functioning of the public institutional system in which they partake.

The claim can be made in yet stronger terms. To the extent that a well-ordered society rests on a network of functioning public institutions, we can safely say that all those who value living in such a society have reasons to be vigilant about and responsive to institutional failures that may threaten the general social order. When the officeholders, who are directly implicated in the action of public institutions, fail to sustain institutional functioning by their interrelated conduct, the members of that society acquire a reason to act to ensure that the institutional system as a whole is functioning, which entails their having reasons to sustain public institutional action by their conduct, including through donations. Because such donations become a crucial prop for institutional functioning, they are not only justified, but there are general reasons to incentivise them (e.g., through tax benefits). Seen in this light, remedial philanthropic initiatives do not necessarily indicate the surrender of public institutional action or the 'outsourcing' of citizens' responsibilities to some private provider (Beerbohm 2016). Insofar as philanthropists are members of a well-ordered society, they have stakes and certain obligations in upholding the functioning of the public institutional system. Many (but not all) of their initiatives may therefore be rightfully justified and incentivised in this contributive spirit.[6]

Two corollaries immediately follow from my claim about the justification of remedial philanthropic initiatives and their incentivisation. The first corollary concerns the *site* of my proposed normative view. The argument I have offered for the justification and incentivisation of philanthropy is situated within a nonideal theory of institutional action. In ideal circumstances, characterised by a perfect officeholders' compliance with office accountability, the functioning of public institutions rests on internal resources, as it relies upon the officeholders' interrelated action. Deficits of office accountability in the officeholders' conduct trigger institutional dysfunctions that undermine the capacity of an institution to engage in a reflexive process of self-correction. These threats to institutional functioning mark the transition to a nonideal situation, which sets the condition for initiating a corrective action of institutional dysfunctions to (re-) establish office accountability. I have suggested that we can understand and justify the remedial role of philanthropy and of provisions intended to encourage it in these conditions as an external prop for institutional functioning.

This first corollary signposts one specificity of the argument I have put forward in this chapter: Specific measures to sustain certain philanthropic initiatives through (fiscal) incentives are justified as a remedial (possibly transitory?) measure in support of the action of public institutions when office accountability fails to sustain institutional functioning from the inside of those institutions. The incentivisation of remedial philanthropic initiatives through the investment of public funds (e.g., in the form of subsidies granted through tax benefits) is thus a measure justified in special nonideal circumstances. This said, to the extent that such nonideal circumstances are frequent (and easily predictable) in normal politics (whereas ideal conditions are hardly ever satisfied), the incentivisation of remedial philanthropic initiatives may be rightfully considered part of the ordinary business of a well-ordered society.

The second corollary of my proposed normative view of philanthropy concerns the *type* of philanthropic initiatives that are justifiably the object of incentives. The type of philanthropy justifiable on the institution-centred grounds I have presented (and for which tax incentives are equally justified) is that specifically targeted at enhancing institutional functioning by remedying the failures of the officeholders' interrelated action and that is itself informed by an agenda whose rationale may withstand public scrutiny as coherent with the raison d'être of the institution in question.[7] This corollary has two specific implications. First, as anticipated, whatever specific form they take, remedial philanthropic initiatives are justified within this framework insofar as they contribute to remedying deficits that may make a public institution fail its raison d'être. Justifiable remedial philanthropic initiatives should aim at upholding office accountability by sustaining officeholders in their effort to discharge their tasks, exercise their powers of office in keeping with the terms of their power mandates, and therefore uphold the raison d'être of their institution. This implication is not to suggest that other forms of philanthropy are necessarily unjustifiable on any normative ground. What it certainly means is that the normative resources for justifying them must be found elsewhere.

Moreover, remedial philanthropic initiatives may be justified within this institutional framework insofar as they are organised in such a way that enhances the compatibility with a commitment to office accountability. To wit, philanthropic initiatives should themselves be moved by the pursuit of agendas whose rationale may be vindicated as coherent with the raison d'être of the targeted institution. This requirement is of the utmost importance to resist two allegations that may be levelled against philanthropy. The first concerns the frequently heard challenge that philanthropy is unjustifiable, as it defies normal standards of accountability (Reich 2016, pp. 68–69). Because, by definition, philanthropy consists in a voluntary donation of private resources, donors are (and claim to be) characteristically free to choose the causes they want to support and, in so choosing, they are not expected to respond to any particular public commitment, democratically deliberated agenda, or – in fact – constituency. This characteristic unboundedness of philanthropic action has often been presented as a source of tension with the democratic ethos. The argument I have offered in this chapter shows that there are in fact solid normative bases to justify and incentivise certain forms of philanthropy that honour a specific form of office accountability. For instance, one may think of ways to engage officeholders to draw up a list of institutional problems that need outside help from which philanthropists can choose. In this way, philanthropists' commitment to office accountability could be enhanced in keeping with the commitment to maintaining the officeholders' responsibility engaged.[8] Philanthropists might still not be accountable in the same sense in which elected officials are accountable to their constituency in a democracy. But this does not mean or entail that they can do away with being called to account for the causes they choose or claim for being recognised and supported only to the extent that they pursue certain causes in certain ways.

Second, the specifications I have hitherto introduced are geared to ensuring that remedial philanthropic initiatives uphold without hijacking public institutional action, thus steering clear of the allegation of being tantamount to a form of corruption. Quite apparently, philanthropy runs the risk of being categorised as a form of corruption on either of the primary understandings of this pathology of the public function in the current philosophical debate. On one count, philanthropy may be viewed as a form of 'institutional corruption' to the extent that public institutions become dependent on the undue influence of the donors' private interests, thus compromising their integrity as they are distracted from the pursuit of the public good (Lessig 2013, 2018; Miller 2017; Sandel 2012; Thompson 2018). But philanthropy may also be seen as instantiating a form of 'political corruption' insofar as it advocates for certain partisan causes that pressure officeholders to make use of their powers of office in ways incoherent with the terms of their mandate (Ceva and Ferretti 2021, 2018). The restricted view and justification of philanthropy I have laid out in these pages has the resources to resist both allegations because it does not lend support to the justification (let alone the incentivisation) of philanthropic initiatives that have the ambition of either giving new direction to public institutional action by playing with its agenda or in fact accomplishing certain tasks instead of public institutions. To steer away from the risk of initiating viciously self-defeating institutional short-circuits, remedial philanthropic initiatives are themselves justified and may be justifiably incentivised when they work as an external prop to enable officeholders to perform their tasks and uphold the functioning of their institution, not when they replace their actions.

While my defence of philanthropy and its incentivisation is conditional and targeted to specific types of initiatives, it is by no means marginal or residual. There are many instances of philanthropy that could qualify (whereas some, as seen previously, are excluded). For example, a growing number of foundations has long recognised the importance of investing in leadership development, capacity-building, and innovation. While this recognition has primarily originated and been consolidated in the domain of private corporations, it also matters for governmental action. The Broad Foundation,[9] for example, is characterised by a commitment to developing leadership- and capacity-building programmes for government employees. In particular, the Broad Residency in Urban Education and the Broad Superintendents Academy have gradually come to uphold the American public educational system as concerns the provision of training for central-office executives. By upholding the development of officeholders' skills, this action seems to qualify as a form of external prop for public institutional action along the lines I have suggested previously. Because public education is one of the main government's expenditures, the support of this type of philanthropic action through such incentives as fiscal benefits seems by no means misplaced.

Remedial philanthropic initiatives may also work to support the working of political processes. Another example from the American context is helpful here. In 2007, five major foundations joined forces to examine the hurdles in the decision-making process that were causing the California state government to make fewer and fewer major policy and budgetary decisions. The joint efforts of these foundations managed to attract more than $30 million from private donors willing to launch California Forward,[10] a bipartisan organisation aimed to promote actions of revision and enhancement of the state government's capacity to make pragmatic, fiscally sound public policy decisions capable to respond to Californians' claims and needs. Also in this case, we can see a remedial philanthropic initiative that, far from forcing the hand of public institutions into specific directions, contributes to making officeholders more responsive to popular demands, coherently with the raison d'être of a governmental institution in a democracy. In this case, too, philanthropy seems to perform an important remedial task, which is reasonable to incentivise, as it upholds an institutional ethics of office accountability, thus propping public institutional action.

These two examples serve the illustrative purpose of showing how the institution-centred argument I have presented in this chapter, while targeted at specific types of philanthropic initiatives in the nonideal circumstances of public institutional failures, may make some normative space for the justification of philanthropy and its incentivisation within an ethics of institutional action for democracies. The main claim I have defended in the chapter is that when remedial philanthropic initiatives are within the boundaries of office accountability, they fall short of generating any viciously self-defeating institutional short-circuit. What is more, there are general normative reasons to uphold remedial philanthropic initiatives that meet this condition as a means to uphold public institutional action from the *outside* a public institution when the interrelated action of officeholders fails to sustain it from the *inside*.

Notes

1 An earlier version of this chapter was discussed at the Taxation and Philanthropy conference organised by the Geneva Centre for Philanthropy. I am particularly grateful to Pamala Wiepking for the comments offered on that occasion. I am indebted also to Andrei Poama for his detailed written comments on an earlier draft.

2 For a classic presentation of an institution as a 'pattern of roles', whereby roles are capacities 'in which someone acts in relation to others', see Emmet 1966. For an overview, see Miller 2014.

3 For an analytical philosophical discussion of what philanthropy is see Reich, Cordelli and Bernholz (2016), where philanthropy is presented as an act or a structure consisting of a 'voluntary donation aimed at providing some other-regarding or prosocial benefit' (p. 7).

4 For example, Reich (2016, pp. 73–81) defends the role of foundations in democracies on the ground that the freedom of philanthropic initiatives may enrich the pluralism of the political agenda and enhance the discovery capacity of the payoffs of new approaches to social policy precisely by virtue of the foundations' more ambitious function of giving visibility to marginal or neglected causes and resources for social innovation.

5 In this spirit, for instance, Pevnick (2016, pp. 232–238) sees philanthropy as a particularly apt provider of cultural goods. Because of the egalitarian commitment that should inform the direct action of democratic governments, the support of particular cultural initiatives may be discriminatory or disrespectful. However, for Pevnick, insofar as we recognise the importance of furthering cultural interests, philanthropists may perform this role free from the constraint of government action.

6 In this sense, my argument can be seen as addressed to the justification of what Horvath and Powell (2016) have called 'contributive philanthropy', as distinguished from 'disruptive philanthropy', which is

instead 'an activity that through the magnitude of donations either explicitly or by consequence alters the public conversation about which social issues matter, and specifies who is the preferred providers of services to address these issues without any engagement with the deliberative processes of civil society' (p. 90).

7 This restriction concerning the type of justifiable philanthropic initiative goes in the direction of taking issue with what Cordelli (2016) has called the 'discretionary view' for which philanthropy should be the expression of individual free decisions to support whatever cause is closer to their hearts, as it were (p. 245).

8 I owe this suggestion to Andrei Poama.

9 See https://broadfoundation.org. Discussions in this direction are happening in Europe, too, where the role of philanthropy as a complement to state's action has so far been less explored – see, for example, the European Economic and Social Committee (EESC)'s 2019 opinion on 'European philanthropy: An untapped potential', https://www.eesc.europa.eu/en/our-work/opinions-information-reports/opinions/european-philanthropy-untapped-potential-exploratory-opinion-request-romanian-presidency

10 See https://www.cafwd.org

References

Anheier, H. K., 2018. 'Philanthropic Foundations in Cross-National Perspective: A Comparative Approach'. *American Behavioral Scientist* 62 (12): 1591–1602.

Applbaum, A., 1999. *Ethics for Adversaries: The Morality of Roles in Public and Professional Life* (Princeton, NJ: Princeton University Press).

Beerbohm, E., 2016. 'The Free-Provider Problem: Private Provision of Public Responsibilities'. In R. Reich, C. Cordelli, L. Bernholz (eds.). *Philanthropy in Democratic Societies* (Chicago: University of Chicago Press).

Bovens, M., Goodin, R. E., Schillemans, T. (eds.), 2014. *The Oxford Handbook of Public Accountability* (Oxford: Oxford University Press).

Bremner, R. H., 1988. *American Philanthropy* (Chicago: University of Chicago Press).

Ceva, E., 2019. 'Political Corruption as a Relational Injustice'. *Social Philosophy & Policy* 35 (2): 118–137.

Ceva, E., Bocchiola, M., 2018. *Is Whistleblowing a Duty?* (Cambridge: Polity).

Ceva, E., Ferretti, M. P., 2017. 'Political Corruption'. *Philosophy Compass* e12461.

Ceva, E., Ferretti, M. P., 2018. 'Political Corruption, Individual Behaviour, and the Quality of Institutions'. *Politics, Philosophy & Economics* 17 (2): 216–231.

Ceva, E., Ferretti, M. P., 2021. *Political Corruption: The Internal Enemy of Public Institutions* (New York: Oxford University Press).

Cordelli, C., 2016. 'Reparative Justice and the Moral Limits of Discretionary Philanthropy.' In R. Reich, C. Cordelli, L. Bernholz (eds.). *Philanthropy in Democratic Societies* (Chicago: University of Chicago Press).

Emmet, D., 1966. *Rules, Roles and Relations* (London: Palgrave Macmillan).

Ferretti, M. P., 2019. 'Towards a Taxonomy of Institutional Corruption'. *Social Philosophy & Policy* 35 (2): 242–263.

Greaves, E.H., Pummer, T. (eds.), 2019. *Effective Altruism: Philosophical Issues* (Oxford: Oxford University Press).

Greene, P., McClelland, R., 2001. 'Taxes and Charitable Giving'. *National Tax Journal* LIV (3): 433–449.

Hall, P. D. 2006. 'A Historical Overview of Philanthropy, Voluntary Associations, and Nonprofit Organizations in the United States, 1600–2000'. In W. W. Powell, R. Steinberg (eds.). *The Nonprofit Sector: A Research Handbook* (New Haven: Yale University Press).

Horvath, A., Powell, W. W., 2016. 'Contributory or Disruptive: Do New Forms of Philanthropy Erode Democracy?'. In R. Reich, C. Cordelli, L. Bernholz (eds.). *Philanthropy in Democratic Societies* (Chicago: University of Chicago Press).

Lambelet, A., Balsiger, P., Carnac, R., Honegger, C., 2019. 'Tax Incentives in Favour of Public Utility in Switzerland: An Incomplete Debate?' *L'Année PhiLanthropic – The PhiLanthropic Year* 1 (15): 31–45.

Lessig, L., 2013. 'Institutional Corruptions'. *Edmond J. Safra Research Lab Working Papers* 1: 1–20.

Lessig, L., 2018. *America, Compromised* (Chicago: University of Chicago Press).

Miller, S., 2017. *Institutional Corruption* (Cambridge: Cambridge University Press.

Miller, S., 2014. 'Social Institutions'. In E. Zalta (ed.). *The Stanford Encyclopedia of Philosophy*. https://plato.stanford.edu/archives/win2014/entries/social-institutions.
Pevnick, R., 2016. 'Philanthropy and Democratic Ideals'. In R. Reich, C. Cordelli, L. Bernholz (eds.). *Philanthropy in Democratic Societies* (Chicago: University of Chicago Press).
Rawls, J., 1955. 'Two Concepts of Rules'. *Philosophical Review* 64: 3–32.
Reich, R., 2011. 'Towards a Political Theory of Philanthropy'. In P. Illingworth, T. Pogge, L. Wenar (eds.). *Living Well: The Ethics of Philanthropy* (Oxford: Oxford University Press).
Reich, R., 2013. 'What Are Foundations for?'. *Boston Review* 38, March–April.
Reich, R., 2016. 'On the Role of Foundations in Democracies'. In R. Reich, C. Cordelli, L. Bernholz (eds.). *Philanthropy in Democratic Societies* (Chicago: University of Chicago Press).
Reich, R., 2018. *Just Giving: Why Philanthropy Is Failing Democracy and How It Can Do Better* (Princeton, NJ: Princeton University Press).
Reich, R., Cordelli, C., L. Bernholz (eds.), 2016. *Philanthropy in Democratic Societies* (Chicago: University of Chicago Press).
Sandel, M., 2012. *What Money Can't Buy: The Moral Limits of the Market* (London: Penguin).
Searle, J., 1995. *The Construction of Social Reality* (London: Penguin).
Thompson, D., 2018. 'Theories of Institutional Corruption'. *Annual Review of Political Science* 21 (26): 1–19.
Winston, K., 1999. 'Constructing Law's Mandate'. In D. Dyzenhaus (ed.). *Recrafting the Rule of Law: The Limits of Legal Order* (Portland: Hart Publishing).

4
THE GIFTING PUZZLE

Emma Tieffenbach

1 Introduction

In both ordinary language and in economics, "gifting" refers to diverse acts, such as the exchange of in-kind gifts (such as "Christmas gifts"), monetary transfers to philanthropic organizations, organ donations, bequests, giving alms to beggars, and so on, apart from volunteering activities, care-giving acts such as child-rearing, and exchanging favors between friends or spouses. While these activities are often grouped within the same term, it is worth questioning whether they have anything in common (Zimmerman 1990, pp. 477–507; Martin 1994; Daly 2012; Elder-Vass 2020). In this chapter, I use gifting to imply a unilateral transfer of a certain amount of money to a non-profit cause. Signing a check to the Red Cross, alumni making donations to their alma maters, contributing to public radio, religious tithes, patronage of the arts, taking the "Giving (what you can) pledge," and so on are all instances of gifting. For simplicity, I consider "gifting" a three-pronged act, involving a "gift-giver," a "gift-receiver" or a giftee, and the amount of money transferred between these two parties.

From a behavioral perspective, gifting is often considered incompatible with the conventional model of economic agents acting to maximize their "utility," which refers to qualities that make a particular action subjectively profitable or preferable to these agents. Thus, the gifting puzzle stems from the fact that gifting is inherently unprofitable, which is exemplified through its three widely recognized features. The first is the transfer of a certain amount of money from a gift-giver to a receiver,[1] which precludes the former from any form of self-expenditure. A gift necessarily involves a loss in consumption. The second feature of gifting is that it constitutes of a unilateral transfer of money, unlike bilateral transfers that are central to economic exchanges. Therefore, a gift-giver's loss in consumption is not compensated by any goods or services received in return. The third feature is that gifting involves a voluntary transfer, unlike taxation, which involves a compulsory transfer of money. The gifting puzzle asks why rational consumers, who are competent in conducting a cost-benefit analysis, would consider undertaking such an unproductive activity instead of avoiding their losses. Neglected for a long time,[2] the gifting puzzle has recently inspired a variety of solutions, which are discussed in this chapter.

The existing literature proposes three solutions to the gifting puzzle. One is to concede that the act of gifting is unproductive and yet that it does not refute the model of utility maximization. Carl Menger uses this strategy while defending the relevance of the "dogma of

DOI: 10.4324/9781003139201-6

ever constant self-interest" as "the expression of the most original and most general forces and impulses of human nature" (1985, p. 86). Menger admits that "[g]oodwill toward others" leads people to "not protect their economic interest at all in some cases, and in some cases incompletely" (1985, p. 71), and that real agents do not always guide "their economic activity exclusively by consideration of their individual interests" (1985, p. 83). If acts of gifting are such cases, they should be treated as not falling within the scope of the dogma of constant self-interest, rather than as exceptions to the latter behavioral rule.

However, it is not obvious that the acts of gifting are not a relevant subject matter for the economic realm. No less than exchanges, gifting is arguably a significant concept of economics, traditionally defined as the science of allocation of scarce resources (Robbins 1935). If so, acts of gifting do not exemplify the limitations of the attempt to apply maximizing utility theory to the most varied aspects of human behavior. Rather, what acts of gifting reveal is that the latter theory may fail at heart.

A second way to attempt to solve the gifting puzzle will examine the hidden motivation of gift-givers, which has been the focus of several studies. Consider, for example, Julie's donation of 100 CHF to the Red Cross. While it is possible that her donation is motivated by an expectation of making a difference to the health condition of the medically poor, she could also be motivated by her desire to be seen by others as a concerned benefactor (West 2004), to conform to peer pressure (Shang and Croson 2009), to attract the members of the opposite sex (Landry *et al.* 2005), "to gratify an inner audience" (Elster 2006), or to "buy" salvation. If self-interested motivations can "mimic" altruistic ones (Elster 2006) so that altruistic actions bear no trace of their motivations, it is vain, one may conclude, to investigate whether acts of gifting conform with the theory of utility maximization.

Against this strategy, one may reply that the gifting puzzle is not the epistemological problem of discerning what truly, despite confounding appearance, motivates real donors. The puzzle is rather to figure whether someone can consistently maximize his utility by gifting – not to reckon whether one can ever be certain about whether that is the case. The gifting puzzle is the theoretical puzzle of trying to reconcile an apparently unprofitable course of action within the constraints of a theory that assumes that economic agents tend to prioritize the most profitable course of action.

A third way to attempt to provide a solution to the gifting puzzle is to argue that the puzzle itself rests on a misconstruction of the concept of gifting. Those who employ this strategy argue that once gifting acts are recognized for what they truly are, they turn out to be the productive activity that a rational economic agent may prefer to perform after a cost-benefit analysis (Sections 2–4). Still another way of dealing with the gifting puzzle is to argue that the puzzle itself rests on a narrow definition of "utility" and that expanding its definition would clarify that the act of gifting does enable utility maximization (Sections 5–8). The following sections present an in-depth analysis of these last two strategies.

2 Gifting need not be costly

The gifting puzzle rests on the assumption that gifting is unattractive because it is inherently costly. Conventional economic theories also perpetuate the idea that gifting cannot occur without incurring some cost. For example, the charity law assumes that individuals respond to the "price"[3] of gifting; therefore, a favorable tax treatment incentivizes gifting by making it less costly. The claim that gifting is costly also appears in ethical debates on the moral obligation of charity. For example, Peter Singer assumes that gifting must involve a certain amount of "sacrifice", which, according to him, one is individually morally obligated to bear if doing so enables an increase of the total wellbeing (1972). Effective altruists, who insist on making donations to cost-effective charities that provide the highest benefits or goods per unit of currency received, also assume that gifting is costly (MacAskill 2015). Furthermore, the so-called "demandingness objection" to the utilitarian approach also relies on the same assumption while also presupposing that the cost of gifting borne by the well-off is more important than that borne by the poor (in terms of death rates, disease, poverty, etc.; McElwee 2017). Another common claim is that one's duty to donate is limited by the cost one has already incurred (Kamm 1992, p. 356). The costliness of gifting is assumed even by those who argue that gifting is not as demanding (or costly) as one may intuitively presume (MacAskill, Mogensen, and Ord 2018). In sum, the diverse viewpoints on the nature and extent of our duty to donate hinge on an uncontested assumption that such a duty cannot be fulfilled without incurring some cost.[4]

Nevertheless, one may object that gifting need not be inherently costly and, therefore, the unproductive choice that a rational consumer should disprefer. The claim that gifting entails a consumption loss relies on the assumption that the utility derived from spending $n+1$ unit of one's money is always greater than that derived from gifting the same.[5] However, the decreasing marginal value of money implies that not all donors are equally burdened by the cost of gifting. In particular, ultra-rich donors are most likely to be spared of the costs of gifting. Excessive wealth helps these donors satisfy most of their desires; therefore, between two competing uses of an additional unit of their wealth, spending money on themselves may not necessarily lead to greater utility than gifting it to others. This implies that gifting by the wealthy does not destroy utility, as supposed by the gifting puzzle. Therefore, one solution to the gifting puzzle is to determine cases where gifting is nearly costless, thus making it a rational choice.

In practice, whether the unequally distributed cost of gifting determine the rates of tax breaks warrants greater examination. In many countries, the variable costs of each donor's per-unit donation amount is not a relevant consideration in determining the country's tax incentive rates. Lambelet *et al.* (2019) explain that in Switzerland, since the tax deduction offered to donors lowers their taxable income by the donation amount, "the financial benefit (of a tax deduction) proportionally increases according to the income and the tax-bracket of the person" (p. 35). For instance, a donation of 5,000 CHF will incur a cost of 4,867.01 CHF to someone with a federal taxable income of 50,000 CHF, and 4,450 CHF to someone with a federal taxable income of 150,000 CHF (Lambelet *et al.* 2019, p. 35). Therefore, given the decreasing marginal utility of money, this country follows the system of lowering the burden of the cost of gifting, the greater the benefit of tax deductions. Scholars have debated the rationale behind such a tax policy and object to its "plutocratic bias" (Reich 2018, p. 120; Lambelet *et al.* 2019). If tax breaks are meant to make gifting cheaper, they are also designed to favor those who are already less affected by its financial costs. There is here a trade-off between the *efficiency* of a system that intends to increase the distribution of public goods by encouraging wealthy individuals to increase their donation amounts in absolute terms and the *fairness* of a system that ascribes them greater power.

The previous solution to the gifting puzzle involves rejecting the assumption that gifting is costly due to the negligible cost incurred by ultra-rich donors. This solution is unsuitable because it unduly restricts rational gifting to billionaires. It entails that other profiles of donors, those whose desires are chronically left unsatisfied by their more modest income but who nonetheless choose to gift, fail to act rationally. However, the claim that only the ultra-rich can rationally choose to gift is to posit a very demanding condition. Therefore, before conceding it, we must examine the possibility that gifting could also be the rational choice for those less fortunate donors who have to bear its costs.

3 Gifting is an act of consumption

The gifting puzzle relies on the assumption that utility accrues to an agent through the consumption of physical goods such as foodstuff, medicine, cars, and houses. However, as Ariely and Norton (2009) argue, consumption may also include consumption of "concepts," through activities such as reading information or blogs, listening to gossip, and hearing stories. Additionally, "conceptual consumption is implicated in even the most basic consumption acts, such as eating or drinking, and is therefore paramount" (Ariely and Norton 2009, p. 477). They state that the experience of eating a chocolate chip cookie, for example, is not just a case of physical consumption but also a case of conceptual consumption in view of the number of thoughts elicited by the act of consumption. They further explain:

> In this example, notice that regardless of the questions the consumer asks – the concepts brought to mind – the physical consumption object (the cookie) remains exactly the same; conceptual consumption, on the other hand, will be markedly different depending on whether consumers are thinking about a goal to lose weight as compared to a desire to promote fair labor practices.
>
> *(Ariely and Norton 2009, p. 477)*

Thus, however loosely defined, the notion of conceptual consumption encapsulates certain "psychological aspects of consumption."

According to Ariely and Norton, gifting is a case "where physical consumption is sacrificed for the sake of conceptual consumption." They argue:

> From our perspective, charitable donations offer an interesting case of foregoing positive physical consumption, since any donation to another person necessarily precludes givers from using that money to pursue their own happiness . . . they do so to engage in conceptual consumption, to consume a view of themselves as altruistic individuals, leading to the benefit of increased well-being.
>
> *(Ariely and Norton 2009, p. 487)*

If a conceptual consumption of a moral satisfaction can compensate for the loss from a physical consumption, the option of gifting would then become profitable to a rational consumer.

Nevertheless, the aforementioned solution to the gifting puzzle does not withstand scrutiny. This is because the boundaries of what is "consumable" have some restraints, which can rule out a good self-image or moral satisfaction as a genuine act of consumption. In his discussion of conceptual disappointment, Albert Hirschman notes that

> [o]riginally we consumed turnips and candles whereas we owned and used gowns and carriages; but with time (and the progress of macroeconomics), consumption came to refer to all the goods and services people produced or purchase for their own goods.
>
> *(2002, p. 30)*

A "consumable" item was first a "non-durable good," that is, a good that "deteriorates in the performance of its function" (Hirschman 2002, p. 29). Later, the category of "consumables" was extended to also include durable goods (e.g., cars and houses). However, even with a less restricted definition, not anything can be counted as a consumable item. Consumables are things that are "transferable," that have the capacity to a life of their own, and that can be owned and piled up. But if a consumable is that sort of physical "thing," it cannot be the intangible, psychological experiences that sometimes accompany an act of physical consumption, including the gift-giver's enjoyment of a good opinion of oneself. In sum, I argue that the term "conceptual consumption" misconstrues the concept of consumption and its introduction represents a failed attempt to subsume acts of gifting under the latter category.

4 Gifting as another form of economic exchange

According to Kenneth Boulding, what makes gifting a puzzle for economists is that it fails to display the quid pro quo involved in most economic exchanges (Boulding 1962). Boulding argues:

> Exchange is a reciprocal transfer. Philanthropy, apparently, represents a unilateral transfer. In an exchange, something is transferred from party A to party B and something else from B to A. The ratio of these two quantities is, of course, the ratio of exchange and if one of the exchangeables is money, then this ratio is a price. The price system is a basic one for the economist and he tends to regard society as being organized by it. This is true even in national income economics for money income always represents quantity of commodity multiplied by its price. In a single transfer or gift, however, there is no price, for nothing is given in exchange. The economist, hence, feels rather at sea. When he finds himself in an area of social life which is apparently priceless, he hardly knows what to do.
>
> *(1962, p. 57)*

Some scholars have objected to Boulding's definition of gifting as a unilateral transfer of money in light of the various "private benefits" that gift-givers often receive from their beneficiaries in return. Lisa Vesterlund lists several types of counter-gifts (or "benefits," "quid pro quo contributions") such as of

> recognition, welcoming or thank-you gifts, membership benefits like free tickets to events, updates on shows and exhibits . . . large contributors may have buildings named after them, receive exclusive dinner invites, be invited to have lunch with powerful politicians, and so on.
>
> *(2004, p. 573)*

In light of these reciprocal gestures, Vesterlund concludes that "the choice to give is not conceptually different from any act of purchasing a good" (2004, p. 573). From this point of view, gifting is a sub-case of economic exchanges and can be potentially profitable as the latter.

Nevertheless, one may insist on not conflating gifting with exchanging. Consider the case of donors who choose to contribute to gain membership into a club or a certain social circle. Vesterlund argues that in this case, the donation is equivalent to the payment of a "membership fee" to be part of the community surrounding the charity (2004 p. 173), because it involves the bilateral, mutually related kind of transfers that pertain to economic exchanges. However, a donation that is followed by a good in return (in the form of a club membership) need not constitute as a "payment" for that good. Additionally, these counter-gifts are not mandatory or certain (Elder-Vass 2020). Even when they occur, they do not by themselves indicate that they have been bought.

The difficulty in sorting out gifting from an exchange arises from the fact that both acts can be performed simultaneously. Consider, for example, tipping. Diego Gambetta implicitly endorses that tipping is an instance of an economic exchange by defining it as "the discretionary payments we make to certain occupations over and above the price of service" (2014). Thus, according to Gambetta's definition, tipping is an overpayment for the price asked and is still a part of the consumer's purchase of the server's services.[6] Alternatively, tipping may be approached as an instance of gifting. The amount of money tipped is not price-tagged and therefore is not part of the amount of money that the consumer is committed to transfer.

Why one should consider the transfer of a good from A to B followed by a transfer of another good (or service) from B to A as two separate gifts rather than a single instance of a trade remains a relevant question. A successive transfer from a gift-giver to a receiver and vice versa is not a sufficient justification for subscribing to such a reductionist view. Moreover, unlike a trade, an expectation of receiving something in return is not a precondition for gifting. Here, while the non-satisfaction of these expectations can cause a disappointment, all a gift-giver can do is express it and maybe remind the recipient of the prevalent norms of social reciprocity. In contrast, traders have the right to coerce their recipients to fulfill their obligations by rightfully demanding them to transfer the good (or payment) in exchange for their payment (or good) while reserving the right to claim their share of the transfer.

Proponents of the reductive view typically respond that counter-gifting is no less obligatory than paying for a good that one intends to purchase. Following Marcel Mauss, they argue that norms of reciprocity make counter-gifting compulsory. Elder-Vass (2020) objects to this view and argues that, unlike in trade, the norms of reciprocity that govern counter-gifting are not truly "compulsory."

> If I give you a birthday present, it is entirely possible that you will later give one to me, and the fact that I gave you one may influence you to reciprocate, but the original gift does not create a binding requirement to do so. By the time my birthday comes around, we may have drifted apart, or you may be too poor to buy me a gift, or too ill to buy me a gift, or just too mean to buy me a gift, and there is no sanction that compels you to do so.
>
> *(2020, p. 681)*

Elder-Weiss claims that gifting, unlike economic exchange, does not require "a compulsory transfer in return" (2020, p. 681). However, a failure to reciprocate a gift may at times trigger indirect sanctions that are so harsh that counter-gifting may become a requirement. What distinguishes gifting from exchanging, I submit, is that only the latter involves an offer, that is, a conditional promise (Massin and Tieffenbach 2017). In the conceptual analysis we proposed of an economic exchange, we argue that when a seller price-tags an item, what she actually does is make a promise to whomever is willing to consider her offer that, if he transfers to her the price-tagged amount of money, she will transfer the good to him. To accept this offer, we further suggested, is something that is done by simply satisfying the condition of the promise through a voluntary transfer of the requested amount. Transferring the money simultaneously activates the seller's obligation to deliver the good while giving the buyer a rightful claim on that good. In sum, the seller's obligation to transfer the good is grounded on a conditional promise to deliver it to anyone who satisfies the condition of transferring the requested amount of money. Doing so entitles the buyer to receive the good purchased. In contrast, a gift-giver and a giftee do not share a similar obligatory and reciprocal relationship; a gift-giver is not obligated to provide a gift nor entitled to receive a reciprocal counter-gift from a giftee.

The question of whether a thank-you gesture for a donation disqualifies it from being tax-deductible is worth asking because the eligibility of receiving a tax incentive on a charitable transfer is conditional upon satisfying the legal definition of charity (Harding 2013). There is a "not for profit" requirement (Lideikyte Huber 2018), which could potentially exclude donors from receiving certain types of goods and services as quid pro quo. Some legislation stipulates that the "fair market value" of the counter-gifts ought to be "insubstantial" and should not exceed 2% of the donation. However, this condition may not strictly guarantee the "non-profit" dimension of the donation. As marginalist economists have discovered, an inverse preference for each other's good is sufficient to characterize the related exchange as subjectively profitable to both parties. For someone dying of thirst in the desert, paying 1,000 USD to a Bad Samaritan for a glass of water is beneficial, despite being overpriced. The glass of water is not a counter-gift for a payment of 1,000 USD, even if its real market value is "insubstantial." Moreover, the fair market value of counter-gifts is not always readily available. Suppose a donor donates their private collection of avant-garde art to a prestigious art institution, which in turn rewards them with favorable publicity by inscribing their name on the entrance of the institutional building. In this case, what is the "fair market price" of the favorable publicity in response to the price of the art collection donated to the institution?

Determining whether counter-gifting always turns gifting into an economic exchange (thus casting doubt on its tax deductibility) requires an examination of the constitutive elements of such an exchange. Consider two scenarios of a donor enjoying a private concert for a donation made to an opera foundation. The first case involves an ex ante promise of the private concert, conditional upon the transfer of the donation amount. Here, the concert is a service that the foundation sells to its benefactors in the misleading form of a counter-gift. In contrast, in the second case, the concert is provided ex post. As described by Reinhard Zimmerman:

> A benefit may have been transferred as a remuneration for a certain service rendered by the other party or as a reward for an act of rescue, or the donor may have wished to induce the donee to act in a certain way or to produce a certain result. In this latter instance, the donor will often impose a charge on the gift (donatio sub modo), with the result that the transaction includes a strong element of exchange.
>
> *(1990, pp. 477–478)*

According to Zimmerman, these ambiguous cases require an examination of the transfer of gratuitous benefits. He also argues that the charity law requires an acute understanding of the definition of a donation and its differences with other forms of transactions, such as economic transactions. Hopefully, some of the observations made in this section have contributed to highlighting the conceptual boundaries between these two notions.

5 Utility as mere representation of preferences

Thus far, I have assumed that a utility maximizer evaluates the personal costs and benefits of various courses of actions and chooses the least costly (or the more beneficial) of these. The implicit assumption has been that the more "utility" an individual derives from a certain course of action, the better off she is. John Broom disagrees with those economists who tacitly endorse such a definition of the notion of "utility" (1991). As he argues, such an erroneous definition may have stemmed from an ambiguity in the word "utility" itself. According to Broom, the "official meaning" of utility is "the value of a function that represents preferences," which refers to any aspects of an option that make it preferable (for whatever subjective reasons) to another option. However, due to a shift in meaning, utility has instead come to refer to the "good," "pleasure," "benefit," "happiness," "satisfaction," "well-being," and "welfare" produced by certain actions for those who perform them.[7] One argument Broom offers for the official (or value-neutral) definition of utility is that it accommodates the "preferences that are partly altruistic: directed toward the good of others" (1991, p. 5). An altruistic preference for gifting does not necessarily bring any benefits, even if acting on such preference does bring oneself a certain amount of utility. Therefore, the official meaning provides a solution to the gifting puzzle by freeing the gift-givers from the need to identify the aspects of gifting that could make it beneficial or costly for them. This conception of utility is advantageous because it is accommodative of widely different donor profiles, from the self-interested donor (who finds it onerous to donate more than 100 CHF to the Red Cross annually) to the generous one (who enjoys spending 50% of their annual income in humanitarian aid). Supposing both have the same annual income and can both derive utility from gifting, their donation amounts will be widely different based on the threshold at which they stop deriving more utility from donating their next 10 CHF.

However, endorsing the official meaning of utility has three unappealing implications. As previously discussed (Guth and Kliemt 2007; Engelen 2017), one implication is that it deprives the notion of utility of any substantial explanatory power. On the official meaning, the option of gifting is not preferred because it has a high utility. Rather it is because the option of gifting is preferred (for whatever subjective reasons) that it has a high utility. There is a reverse of the natural order of the explanation, which appears to be the most significant objection against endorsing the official meaning.

Second, the official meaning precludes gift-givers (or any agent) from making a wrong decision, because an individual's preference for A over B does not mean that A is the better option than B. Once the preferences are understood as not tracking the betterness of an option, they cannot be disputed, and the grounds for assessing whether they rationally motivate gifting (or any action) is lost. However, if the donors (or for that matter, any economic agents) are immune from error, maximizing utility theory can no longer be used to assess the rationality of human actions. Interestingly, the immunity is a point in favor of utility theory when it is applied to the preferences that motivate the buying and selling of goods and services. In the latter case, merely having a preference for the other trader's good suffices to make it rational to choose to buy it. As Austrian economists have shown, the productivity of exchanges merely depends on the exchangers' inverse valuations of each other's goods (Massin and Tieffenbach 2017). Apart from the risk of a long-term bankruptcy from having inconsistent preferences, the exchangers' preferences cannot be wrong. In contrast, absent a good (or a service) from either the giftee or from any third party that could make their act of gifting expectedly profitable, gift-givers do not enjoy the same immunity.

The third implication is that the official meaning of utility is at odds with the practice of determining particular taxation rates (Barry and Lawford-Smith 2019). Consider the example of a price-sensitive individual who is deeply affected by the cost of gifting 100 CHS annually versus someone who derives a moral satisfaction from gifting 50% of their income during the same period. Barry and Lawford-Smith note that using the proportional (and subjective) impact of the cost of gifting on the donors to grant the miser a greater tax deduction seems unfair. Although the official meaning of utility, as endorsed by Broom and others, would solve the gifting puzzle, making it a rational choice, it has no practical value in determining the rates of tax incentives.

6 Utility derived from being seen as gifting

An alternative way of addressing the gifting puzzle is to analyze yet another over-restricting assumption about how utility accrues to gift-givers. The assumption is that utility can only be derived from performing an action, such as eating cake or playing tennis, or more leisurely activities, such as sleeping or watching movies. Note that an agent receiving utility need not be the one to perform the utility-creating action. Instead, utility may be derived from someone else's actions – for example, from being massaged, consoled, entertained, or told the truth. Philipp Pettit refers to such categories of goods as "action-dependent goods," that is, "goods I get by grace of what I or others do" (1993, p. 331). However, besides action-dependent goods, as Pettit stresses there are "goods I get by grace of what I or others think," which he names "attitude-dependent goods" (1993, p. 331). These are the goods that one enjoys by virtue of others' favorable attitude toward oneself and result from others' positive opinions. Pettit also stresses that attitude-dependent goods are not as easily tractable as action-dependent goods; this is because giving or receiving positive attitudes from others cannot be determined at will.

However, attitude-dependent goods are quite useful in determining donors' hidden motivation. Several scholars have empirically tested and established the impact of prospective attitude-dependent goods (such as a favorable reputation) over donor's actions. The effects of being watched (Brook *et al.* 2006), eye contact with a solicitor (Bull and Gibson-Robinson 1981), being questioned (Andreoni, Rao, and Trachtman 2017), and, correlatively, the statistical paucity (1%) of anonymous donations all point to the motivating power of attitude-dependent goods. However, since the desire to be admired is often condemned, a donation driven by such a desire could be self-defeating. Nevertheless, once it is recognized that gifting could lead to positive recognition from others, it can become a profitable activity, making it the valid content of an economic preference. A utility maximizer will choose to gift if the value ascribed to gaining others' favorable opinions offsets the costs of gifting.

However, focusing on the motivating role of attitude-dependent goods cannot solve the gifting puzzle, because such goods are only contingently related to acts of gifting. Surely, it is often the case that when someone deliberates as to whether she should or should not gift her money,

1. she believes that others will find the gesture admirable,
2. she is seen as someone admirable if she gifts her money,
3. others who see her as admirable will express a positive opinion about her if she gifts her money,
4. she enjoys being seen and publicly described as someone who is admirable,
5. those who see her are sufficiently influential share their good opinion of the donor to elicit further commitments to gifting,
6. and, in view of 1–5, she assesses gifting to be the best possible option.

However, aspects 1–5 are contingent claims that may apply only to some cases of gifting and not all. Several factors could disrupt the donors' expectations of eliciting public admiration. For example, the act of gifting may not be sufficiently visible in the public eye; those who see gift-givers as admirable may not openly express their view; or those who were expected to see gift-givers as admirable may instead express contempt toward them. The contingency of a favorable public image challenges the assumption that the expected productivity of gifting in terms of a good image is inherently profitable.

7 Utility derives from other's wellbeing ("pure altruism")

The gifting puzzle itself can be criticized as hinging on a restricted view of the conditions that determine a gift-giver's utility. In particular, it assumes "self-centred welfare," as defined by Amartya Sen as "a person's utility depends on his or her own consumption, which rules out sympathy or antipathy toward others" (2007, p. 18). Additionally, he notes that a utility maximizer can simultaneously be sensitive to others' welfare (also see Arrow 1972, p. 348), which happens when sympathy for others' welfare attunes one's welfare toward others. Thus, Sen's concept of an "other-centered welfare" could help to solve the gifting puzzle. If a gift-giver's welfare is tuned to others' welfare, the opportunity of relieving others' suffering also helps to relieve one's own suffering, which provides the donor with indirect benefits. The following testimony by Thomas Hobbes on how pity and compassion motivate a gift-giver to give alms to a beggar can be considered an example of an other-centered welfare:

> One time, I remember, going into the Strand. A poor and infirm old man craved his alms. He beholding him with eyes of pity and compassion, put his hands in his pocket, and gave him 6d. Would you have done this if it had not been Christ's command? Yes, because I was in pain to consider the miserable condition of the old man, and now my alms, giving him some relief, does also ease me.
>
> *(John Aubrey, Brief Lives 2015, pp. 158–159)*

The capacity to find relief in others' relief makes gifting a rational choice if, by one's own calculation, the relief thus compensates one's consumption loss. Once other-centered welfare is granted, gifting can become the kind of productive activity that a competent cost and benefit agent will rightly engage in.

However, some economists argue that donors cannot be rationally motivated to find relief in others' relief. This is because if everyone had a "purely" altruistic disposition, the outcome of everyone's gifting becomes a "public good," or a good that is both non-excludable (each can find relief in through another donor's gift-giving) and non-rival (one individual's relief is not derived at the cost of another person's relief). This situation displays the characteristics of the prisoner's dilemma situation, where free-riding on others' contributions becomes the rational course of action.

It is worth emphasizing that this objection to the hypothesis of other-centered welfare (a.k.a. "pure altruism") introduces two additional assumptions. One assumption is that gifting is a strategic choice that donors make by considering other's actions. The second assumption is that an individual act of gifting is insufficient to make a significant difference with regard to the desired outcomes. Under these assumptions, gifting could either entail an enjoyment of benefits without incurring any costs or may render the cost of giving futile if the total amount of donations is insufficient to bring about the desired benefits. However, none of these assumptions inform the gifting puzzle, as this puzzle does not consider the act of gifting an interactive choice. Gifting is presumed to be both an individual act and an act that is instrumentally powerful by itself. Following effective altruists, I assume that, unlike a single vote in a country's presidential election, a single act of gifting can make a significant difference to meet a desired outcome (MacAskill 2015). Therefore, an other-centered welfare cannot be challenged as a solution to the gifting puzzle for giving rise to a collective action problem.

A more relevant objection to other-centered welfare ("pure altruism") as a solution to the gifting puzzle is that it construes an individual's act of gifting as a means of relieving his or her own pity or compassion. Means are fungible, such that an individual would prefer to address his or her pity or compassion through the cheapest means possible. Consider again Hobbes' act of charity and suppose, as a variant of Jon Elster's guilt-erasing pill argument (1998, p. 303), that an individual can relieve the painful pity he has for the beggar by swallowing a "pity-erasing pill" at no cost. The pill is free and functions to make an individual insensitive to the misery of the beggar, and therefore it is a rational means to avoid the personal cost of gifting. However, someone who is sensitive to others' suffering will only swallow the pill if he or she considers their pity a pointless cost. While taking the pill or ignoring the beggar's condition remains a worthwhile option, a rational individual would consider pity an affective disposition of one's moral worth and will find the inability to act on such a disposition morally unattractive. The trade-off between the benefit of finding relief in others' relief on the one hand and losing consumption power on the other is complicated by the prospect of canceling such moral disposition upon taking the pill.

In short, other-centered welfare cannot solve the gifting puzzle, because it wrongly presupposes that an individual moved by a sympathy toward the needy will weigh the impact of pity on his or her choice similar to weighing the loss of consumption.

8 Utility derives from gifting itself ("impure altruism")

In economic theory, preferences are often outcome-oriented. Option A will be preferred over option B if it brings about better outcomes than option B. Per standard definitions, an individual's preferences depend on the output of her or his action. Purchasing, say, a bottle of wine, is an inherently costly means to reach the ultimate utility-supply state of drinking the wine. So far, the same means-end relationship has been taken to apply to acts of gifting: transferring one's money, it was assumed, entered the negative side of the calculation. Gifting, thus construed, is doomed to remain a non-profitable activity, because any external private benefits gleaned from the act are contingently related to its performance.

Could economic preferences be construed to bear on the action itself, regardless of outcomes? In a series of influential articles, Andreoni (1989, 1990, 2006) departed from the utility maximization model to propose that the act of gifting, apart from its consequences, directly enters an individual's utility function[8] and can elicit utility by itself through a feeling of a "warm glow" or inner satisfaction. However, this only happens when the warm glow derived from gifting offsets its costs. Unlike prestige or any other extrinsic incentives, the desire to experience this feeling makes gifting intrinsically rewarding, as it only depends on the gift-giver's disposition to derive a certain hedonic experience from the performance of the act of gifting itself.

The warm glow that donors derive from gifting often appears in the debate surrounding tax deductions for philanthropic donations and is used to challenge the view that donations are conceptually different from personal consumption. Proponents of the opposite viewpoint claim that donating one's money is not equivalent to personal consumption, which justifies discounting donations from taxable income. Andrews (1972) argues that donations are not acts of consumption because they are not a "preclusive" use of one's money (pp. 362–363). Robert Reich objects that "whatever a person decides to do with [his or her] resources – spend it on luxury goods or give it to charity – is, by definition, tautologically, consumption" (2011, p. 180). However, Reich's argument that a transfer of money from A to B can be categorized as A's consumption only if the transfer results in a purchase of a good or a service sold by B can be objected to on the grounds that a gift-giver and giftee's relationship is different from a buyer-seller relationship, as discussed in Section 4.

Nevertheless, Reich argues that the satisfaction received from gifting leads toward refuting the distinction between gifting and consumption. Even if, as Reich first concedes, the warm glow is "non-preclusive" since "purchasing joy through a charitable contribution does not diminish the ability of others to do the same," Reich also claims that experiencing the warm glow amounts to "consuming the benefit of altruism" (2011, p. 180). As far as "a warm glow is undeniably private rather than public," experiencing it makes donations genuine acts of consumption.

However, the distinction between the pleasure of consumption and the warm glow from gifting is significant enough to challenge this claim. As has been stressed before, warm-glow givers are not moved by how the donations help others but by what their donations reveal about themselves. In contrast, pleasure consumption accrues on consumers upon eating the meal, driving the new car, or wearing the newly bought clothes and not just by transferring the money required for purchasing these goods. Therefore, the pleasure of consumption is the pleasure of actually making use of goods. These are two conceptually distinct pleasures.

What the pleasure of gifting precisely amounts to requires further analysis, especially on whether it can be described as a feeling, an emotional state, or a mood. As James Andreoni admits, "the warm-glow hypothesis provides a direction for research rather than an answer to the puzzle of why people give – the concept of warm-glow is a placeholder for more specific models of individual and social motivations" (Andreoni, Rao, and Trachtman 2017).

Bodner and Prelec (2002) propose viewing the warm glow as "acts of self-signaling" defined as "acts done partly for gathering information about oneself." A case in point is a proud donor who sees gifting as proof of his or her capacity to suppress a selfish desire to spend money on oneself. The warm glow would then constitute the egocentric satisfaction from the proof of one's moral worth demonstrated through one's act of gifting.

While the warm glow provides a promising solution for the gifting puzzle, it is worth stressing that this hypothesis comes with a substantive revision of the traditional model of utility maximization. Because it hinges on consumption loss, utility (the warm glow) and disutility (consumption loss) are no longer independent features of the same course of action. This is because the private benefit of gifting does not come despite the costs but because of these costs, which is an important departure from the theory of utility maximization. Instead of treating them as unrelated features of the same act, a donation's utility is considered to rely on its disutility. One may even ask whether gifting becomes more profitable by being costlier.

Some scholars question whether the warm glow can be the treated as a rational aim of gifting. One skeptical answer is that, as in any case of pleasure-seeking, gifting for the sake of experiencing the warm glow is doomed to fail. The reason gifting for the sake of the warm glow is self-defeating, skeptics argue, is that the enterprise turns into the aim of giving what can only come as its by-product (Feinberg 2007; Elster 2011). However, whether it is vain to aim at getting a warm glow from one's philanthropic contribution requires a better understanding of this phenomenon (Tieffenbach 2019).

9 Conclusion

Economic models explain self-serving human behavior through utility maximization, where individuals maximize their utility by choosing the most productive course of actions after a cost-benefit analysis. While this model is valuable for explaining individuals' purchase decisions for specific goods or services, it has been found to be ill suited to explain why they would voluntarily gift some of their financial resources. This chapter critically reviewed various solutions to the gifting puzzle by examining whether conventional economics models can accommodate gifting acts. Some of these solutions that seek to either exclude or integrate gifting within the scope of economics or seek to blur the conceptual boundaries between gifting and trading have been proved mostly conservative. In contrast, more fruitful ways of addressing this conundrum consist of broadening the notion of economic preferences to make it theoretically possible to maximize one's utility by gifting. I have also discussed the relevance of some of these strategies to the practice and justification of the tax deductibility of philanthropic donations. These fiscal advantages are granted on certain conditions such as the transfer of financial resources and should be made for a non-profit activity of general interest with non-preclusive uses (Lideikyte Huber 2018, p. 20). This, in turn, relies on the theoretical and practical differences between donations and other economic activities such as paying for, consuming, exchanging, or bartering goods or services. Therefore, while there are many reasons for inciting gifting, there are also plenty of reasons for policing the related voluntary and unilateral transfer of resources, both of which require an accurate and consensual understanding of what gifting fundamentally is. Despite the difficulties of drawing accurate conceptual boundaries between these notions, I have also highlighted the drawbacks of lumping these notions together.

Among the various solutions for the gifting puzzle, the hypothesis of the warm glow could be the most promising, provided that its concept is thoroughly clarified. However, this hypothesis has a negative strategic implication for the gifting puzzle. That is, if the warm glow is treated as the pleasure derived from the conscious choice of foregoing one's consumption power, then it implies that utility and disutility of gifting are the two sides of the same coin.

Notes

1 The assumption that a "giftable" item is "transferable" is both widespread and uncontested. It imposes two constraints on a gift, namely that it can be owned exclusively and retained over a long period. I have recently argued that these two conditions fail to accommodate gratuitous work as bona fide instance of gifts (Tieffenbach, 2020, "The Metaphysics of Gifting," unpublished manuscript).

2 Mirowski (2001). According to Robert Garnett, the neglect of philanthropy is due to an increasing faith in market exchanges as the most important mechanism of wealth redistribution in contrast to charity and other forms of philanthropic giving, which are seen as "outmoded, inefficient, and ad hoc" (Garnett 2010, p. 112).

3 Lisa Vesterlund rightly stresses that the term "price," when applied to donations, does not have the same meaning as the price of a commodity on sale. As she explains, "[t]ypically the price of an object refers to what we must pay to obtain a particular good. For charitable giving, the price of giving refers to what it costs us to give the organization an additional dollar" (2004, p. 569). However, if the "price of gifting" is just the consumption loss incurred by the donors, the term misguidedly assimilates donations to other forms of payment. See Section 4 of the present chapter for an extended discussion of this topic.

4 Apart from the loss in consumption, the cost of gifting also comprises an opportunity cost of spending scarce time or effort. This chapter does not examine the opportunity cost of gifting while discussing the gifting puzzle.

5 The full sentence is "an individual will always derive more utility from spending n+1 unit of her money on a good, which possesses the quality that is needed for satisfying an unsatisfied desire of him than from gifting it."

6 Tipping can be correctly described as a form of payment only when it is institutionalized into a service charge, making it a part of the price paid for a service.

7 Likewise, Daniel Hausman and Michael S. McPherson stress the same misconception of the notion of utility and write that "utility does not refer to usefulness or pleasure. A utility function is only a way of representing a preference ranking – that is, a ranking of alternatives with respect to everything relevant to choose. . . . Maximizing utility is just doing what one most prefers to do" (Hausman and McPherson 2006, p. 48).

8 Kenneth Arrows comes close to that hypothesis when, discussing altruistic motivations of blood donations, he conceives of cases where "the welfare of each individual depends not only on the utilities of himself and others but also on his contributions to the utilities of others" (1972, p. 348).

References

Andreoni, James (1989). "Giving with Impure Altruism: Applications to Charity and Ricardian Equivalence", in *Journal of Political Economy*, 97(6), 1447–1458.

Andreoni, James (1990). "Impure Altruism and Donations to Public Goods: A Theory of Warm-Glow Giving", *The Economic Journal*, 100(401), 464–477.

Andreoni, James (2006). "Chapter 18, 'Philanthropy'", in L.-A. Gerard-Varet, Serge-Christophe Kolm, Jean Mercier Ythier (eds.), *Handbook of Giving, Reciprocity and Altruism*, North-Holland: Elsevier, 1st edition, volume 1, 1201–1269.

Andreoni, James, Justin M. Rao, Hannah Trachtman (2017). "Avoiding the Ask: A Field Experiment on Altruism, Empathy, and Charitable Giving", *Journal of Political Economy*, 125(3), 625–653.

Andrews, Williams (1972). "Personal Deductions in an Ideal Income Tax", *Harvard Law Review*, 86(2), 309–385.

Ariely, Dan, Michael I. Norton (2009). "Conceptual Consumption", *Annual Review of Psychology*, 60, 475–499.

Arrow, Kenneth (1972). "Gifts and Exchanges", *Philosophy and Public Affairs*, 1(4), 343–362.

Aubrey, John (2015). *John Aubrey: Brief Lives with an Apparatus for the Lives of Our English Mathematical Writers*, Kate Bennett (ed.), Oxford: Oxford University Press.

Barry, Christian, Lawford-Smith Holly (2019). "On Satisfying Duties to Assist", in Hilary Greaves, Theron Pummer (eds.), *Effective Altruism: Philosophical Issues*, Oxford: Oxford University Press, 150–165.

Bodner, Robert, Prelec Dan (2002). "Self-Signaling and Diagnostic Utility in Everyday Decision Making", in I. Brocas, J.D. Carrillo (eds.), *Collected Essays in Psychology and Economics*, Oxford: Oxford University Press, 105–126.

Boulding, Kenneth E. (1962). "Notes on a Theory of Philanthropy", *Philanthropy and Public Policy*, 57–62.

Brook, Robert H., Emmett B. Keeler, Kathleen N. Lohr, Joseph P. Newhouse, John E. Ware, William H. Rogers, Allyson Ross Davies, Cathy D. Sherbourne, George A. Goldberg, Patricia Camp, Caren Kamberg, Arleen Leibowitz, Joan Keesey, David Reboussin (2006). *The Health Insurance Experiment: A Classic RAND Study Speaks to the Current Health Care Reform Debate*, Rand Research Brief RB-9174-HHS, Santa Monica, CA: Rand Corporation, at: http://www.rand.org/pubs/research_briefs/RB9174.html.

Broom, John (1991). "Utility", *Economics and Philosophy*, 7(1), 1–12.

Bull, Ray, Elizabeth Gibson-Robinson (1981). "The Influences of Eye-Gaze, Style of Dress, and Locality on the Amounts of Money Donated to a Charity", *Human Relations*, 34(10), 895–905.

Daly, Siobhan (2012). "Philanthropy as an Essentially Contested Concept", *Voluntas: International Journal of Voluntary and Nonprofit Organizations*, 23(3), 535–557.

Elder-Vass, Dave (2020). "Defining the Gift", *Journal of Institutional Economics*, 16(5), 675–685.

Elster, Jon (1998). *Alchemies of the Mind: Rationality and the Emotions*, Cambridge: Cambridge University Press.

Elster, Jon (2006). "Altruistic Behavior and Altruistic Motivations", in L.-A. Gerard-Varet, Serge-Christophe Kolm, Jean Mercier Ythier (eds.), *Handbook of Giving, Reciprocity and Altruism*, North-Holland: Elsevier, 1st edition, volume 1, 183–206.

Elster, Jon (2011). "The Valmont Effect: The Warm-Glow Theory of Philanthropy", in Patricia Illingworth, Leif Wenar (eds.), *Giving Well: The Ethics of Philanthropy*, Oxford: Oxford University Press, 67–83.

Engelen, Bart (2017). "A New Definition of and Role for Preferences in Positive Economics", *Journal of Economic Methodology*, 24(3), 254–273.

Feinberg, Joël (2007). "Psychological Egoism", *Reason and Responsibility*, 183–197.

Gambetta, Diego (2014). "What Makes People Tip", in *Rationality, Democracy, and Justice: The Legacy of Jon Elster, Claudio Lopez-Guerra and Julia Maskiver*, New York: Cambridge University Press, European University Institute Research Repository, Cadmus, 97–114, at: http://hdl.handle.net/1814/35119.

Garnett, Robert (2010). "Philanthropy and the Invisible Hand: Hayek, Boulding, and Beyond", in M.D. White (ed.), *Accepting the Invisible Hand: Market-Based Approaches to Social-Economic Problems*, New York: Palgrave Macmillan, 111–137.

Guth, Werner, Kliemt Hartmut (2007). "The Rationality of Rational Fools: The Role of Commitments, Persons, and Agents in Rational Choice Modelling", in F. Peter, H.-B. Schmid (eds.), *Rationality and Commitment*, Oxford: Oxford University Press, 124–149.

Harding, Matthew (2013). "What is the Point of Charity Law?", in K. Barker, D. Jensen (eds.), *Private Law: Key Encounters with Public Law*, Cambridge: Cambridge University Press, 147–170.

Hausman, Daniel, Michael S. McPherson (2006). *Economic Analysis, Moral Philosophy, and Public Policy*, Cambridge: Cambridge University Press, 2nd edition.

Hirschman, Albert O. (2002). *Shifting Involvements: Private Interest and Public Action*, Princeton, NJ: Princeton University Press.

Kamm, Frances (1992). "Non-Consequentialism, the Person as an End-in-Itself, and the Significance of Status", *Philosophy and Public Affairs*, 21(4), 354–389.

Lambelet, Alexandre, Philip Balsiger, Romain Carnac, Caroline Honegger (2019). "Tax Incentives in Favour of Public Utility in Switzerland: An Incomplete Debate?", *The Philanthropic Year*, 1, 31–45.

Landry, Craig, Andreas Lange, John A. List, Michael K. Price, Nicholas G. Rupp (2005). *Toward an Understanding of the Economics of Charity: Evidence from a Field Experiment*, Working Paper, Cambridge, MA: National Bureau for Economic Research (NBER) and Washington, DC: Resources for the Future (RFF).

Lideikyte Huber, Giedre (2018). "Philanthropy and Taxation: Swiss Legal Framework and Reform Perspectives", *Expert Focus*, 3, 20–24, at: https://archive-ouverte.unige.ch/unige:134900.

MacAskill, William (2015). *Doing Good Better: How Effective Altruism Can Help You Make a Difference*, New York: Avery.

MacAskill, William, Andreas Mogensen, Ord Toby (2018). "Giving Isn't Demanding", in Paul Woodruff (ed.), *The Ethics of Philanthropy: Philosophers' Perspectives on Philanthropy*, New York: Oxford University Press, 178–203.

Martin Mike, W. (1994). *Virtuous Giving: Philanthropy, Voluntary Service, and Caring*, Bloomington, IN: Indiana University Press.

Massin, Olivier, Emma Tieffenbach (2017). "The Metaphysics of Economic Exchanges", *Journal of Social Ontology*, 3(2), 167–205.

McElwee, Brian (2017). "Demandingness Objections in Ethics", *The Philosophical Quarterly*, 67(266), 84–105.

Menger, Carl (1883) [1985]. *Investigations into the Method of the Social Sciences*, Louis Schneider ed., Francis J. Nock, trans., New York and London: New York University Press.

Mirowski, Philip (2001). "Refusing the Gift", in S. Cullenberg, J. Amariglio, D.F. Ruccio (eds.), *Postmodernism, Economics and Knowledge*, Abingdon: Routledge, 431–458.

Pettit, Philip (1993). *The Common Mind, an Essay on Psychology, Society and Politics*, Oxford: Oxford University Press.

Reich, Robert (2011). "Toward a Political Theory of Philanthropy", in Patricia Illingworth, Thomas Pogge, Leif Wenar (eds.), Giving Well: The Ethics of Philanthropy, New York: Oxford University Press, 177–195.

Reich, Robert (2018). *Just Giving, Why Philanthropy Is Failing Democracy and How It Can Do Better*, Princeton, NJ: Princeton University Press.

Robbins, Lionel (1935). *An Essay on the Scope and Nature of Economic Science*, London: Palgrave Macmillan, 2nd edition.

Sen, Amartya (2007). "Why Exactly Is Commitment Important for Rationality", in F. Peter, H.B. Schmid (eds.), *Rationality and Commitment*, Oxford: Oxford University Press, 17–27.

Shang, Jen, Rachel Croson (2009). "A Field Experiment in Charitable Contribution: The Impact of Social Information on the Voluntary Provision of Public Goods", *The Economic Journal*, 119(540), 1422–1439.

Singer, Peter (1972). "Famine, Affluence and Morality", *Philosophy and Public Affairs*, 1, 229–243.

Tieffenbach, Emma (2019). "La Science du Don, Le Warm-Glow Feeling, Une Théorie de l'Altruisme Impur", *Expert Focus*, 116–120.

Tieffenbach, Emma (2020). *The Metaphysics of Gifting*, Unpublished Manuscript.

Vesterlund, Lisa (2004). "Why Do People Give?", *The Nonprofit Sector: A Research Handbook*, 2, 168–190.

West, Patrick (2004). *Conspicuous Compassion: Why Sometimes it Really is Cruel to be Kind*, Civitas: Institute for the Study of Civil Society.

Zimmermann, Reinhard (1990). *The Law of Obligations Roman Foundations of the Civilian Tradition*, Cape Town: Juta and Co.

5

PHILANTHROPY, CLASS, AND TAX IN FRANCE

Nicolas Duvoux

Introduction

Research on tax deduction for philanthropic purposes has developed in two main directions. First, following the concept of different countries belonging to non-profit regimes (Salamon and Anheier, 1998), the literature tends to highlight the 'crowding out' effect of high government expenditure on private philanthropic donations (Abrams and Shitz, 1978). Conversely, Arts and van Oorschot (2005) argue that high government expenditure coincides with a strong civil society. Second, the low price elasticity of donations (Fack and Landais, 2009) highlights that the majority of donations and higher gifts are concentrated at the top of the income distribution, eliciting sharp criticism about the plutocratic bias (Cagé, 2020). These developments resonate with critiques from the American context, on which the bulk of research on this subject is focused – most notably by Rob Reich (2018).

Economists focus on income and wealth as criteria for socio-economic inequality. However, occupational background matters for analysing income, wealth accumulation, and social status. Occupational backgrounds are important, as they define the hierarchy of autonomy at work and prestige, as argued by Goldthorpe (1996); these backgrounds also frame structured and stabilised perceptions of oneself and the world at large. Sociologist Michèle Lamont (2002) examines the different sets of values embraced by working-class members and managers in France and in the United States. The present chapter asserts that class is important with respect to perceptions of tax deduction for philanthropy. Thus, the diversity of relationships that donors at the top of the socio-economic ladder of France have with tax deductions is highlighted.

To do so, I draw on a qualitative set of ethnographic observations and semi-structured interviews with donors who created family foundations and enrolled them as big philanthropic players in France. These organisations have peculiarities which are detailed later in the chapter. These peculiarities allow an in-depth preliminary analysis of the diverse perceptions of tax deductions.

The cultural sociology of the relationship between tax deductions and donations

This section distinguishes this study from others on the impact of tax incentives for philanthropy in France. The latter are based more in economics and stem from the question regarding the

 DOI: 10.4324/9781003139201-7

relationship between public provision and private funding of the common good. Two concepts, namely the 'crowding in' and 'crowding out' effects, are defined in this field. France's position in cross-country comparison in terms of the share of GDP devoted to publicly financed social provision is high. It is among the countries with a low rate of donors, low percentage of philanthropic donations relative to the GDP, and, most significantly, low number of foundations related to the population (Salamon and Anheier, 1998). It is therefore quite logical that few researchers have studied the impact of tax deductions on philanthropy in this context. Fack and Landais's (2009) analysis shows that the efficacy of tax deductions is dubious. However, they also show that the higher the donor is in the income distribution, the greater is the impact of tax incentives on them. These two studies are dated and neither provide insights on the rapidly growing field of philanthropy nor illuminate the meaning-making processes through which donors perceive the role and the legitimacy of private funding for the common good as well as tax deductions for philanthropic giving (Box 5.1).

Box 5.1 Tax deduction for philanthropic giving in France

All organisations defined as "d'intérêt general" (general interest) are eligible for donations that can be deducted from the donor's taxes. There are three main incentives:

- For private individual donors: a tax deduction of 66% of the amount of the donation, up to a maximum of 20% of the taxable income;
- For companies: a corporate tax deduction of 60% of their donations, up to a maximum of 0.5% of their annual turnover (Source: French General Tax Code (CGI), articles 200 & 238b;
- For individuals who own a real estate whose net worth is 1.3 million€+: a tax deduction of 75% the amount of the donation, up to 50,000€. The wealth tax is the result of reform that took place in 2018. Before 2018, the wealth tax concerned individuals who own a patrimony worth 1.3 million€+ be it composed of financial or real estate assets.

In this chapter, I will focus on this last tax deduction on a wealth tax that concerns the top 3% of wealth concentration in France.

Broadening the scope and considering a wider set of tax deductions makes more data available. Sociologist and political scientist Alexis Spire (2018) presents one of the key insights provided by quantitative research. Using data representative of the adult population, he shows that those who pay more taxes also are, counterintuitively, those who accept higher taxation by the state. This paradox is resolved when tax deductions are considered because the wealthiest can take advantage of a wide range of tax deductions and exemptions for housing interest rests or repairs, for instance, home help services. This category consists of philanthropic donors. The most important thing is to consider, following Bourdieu's view (1979), that class does not only secure access to economic resources but also frames one's perceptions of themselves and of others; of one's identity and correlatively of their position in the outside world. The two are closely related in Bourdieu's relational sociology of positions in a field analysis. Empirically, Bourdieu's analysis of cultural capital can help create a better understanding of why philanthropy matters as a tool of distinction for the elite (Ostrower, 1995).

Spire (2018) provides important insights on the social stratification of the relationship between philanthropy and tax deduction as a general category. However, the study does not analyse the variety of meaning-making processes associated with tax deduction for philanthropy. Therefore, I turn to a different analytical lens, using the tools of cultural sociology. Cultural sociology is a very dynamic field of research, notably in the American context, where the 'Culture' section of the American Sociological Association has evolved into one of the most important sections in quantitative terms. To provide a general overview of this field, it can be said, like Mohr et al. (2020:3) did, that:

> Over the past few decades, cultural sociologists have amassed an impressive array of theoretical insights and modes of empirical investigation about how people create and interpret the meaning of the world around them. A central theme of this work is unpacking what meaning-making actually entails. Culture has turned from something that everybody in a given society has – whether that society is defined by national boundaries, language, or history – into a more stratified and segmented category. In this view, culture is not only the environment that enables the meaningfulness of social life but also a more specific set of scripts, narratives, embodied practices and schemas.

Among the various concepts put forward by this subject, I focus on 'frameworks'. This concept, inspired by sociologist E. Goffman's work (1974), can be defined as proposed by Lamont, Harding, and Small (2010):

> How people act depends on how they cognitively perceive themselves, the world or their surroundings.

Cultural sociology aims at giving room to a variety of perceptions of one set of practices or institutions. More recently, cultural sociology has been blended with a neo-institutionalist agenda to broaden the understanding of inequality in the post-Piketty era (Lamont and Pierson, 2019). In our field of research, several studies show the relevance of this conceptual toolbox to create a better understanding of philanthropy. In her research on the anxieties of affluence, Sherman (2017) highlights the different meanings that wealthy families accord to philanthropy. Luna Glucksberg has studied the role of philanthropy in framing unequal gender relationships among the wealthiest families and how family offices have been used to secure a dynastic transmission of wealth (Glucksberg and Burrows, 2016). However, few studies have focused on the perception of tax deductions by families who benefit from them. From 2015 to 2017, I led in-depth ethnographic research, which provides elements to enrich our understanding of these processes. The bulk of this research draws on the seminal works of Lamont, which underline that class shapes perceptions and frameworks and self-understanding, as well as the perceptions of the world (2002). Precisely, the study of socioeconomics has become a more integrated field and has underlined the causal power of class on positions in the income distribution. This power remains strong and continues to grow over time (Albertini, Ballarino, and de Luca, 2020). We hypothesise that class is also important in shaping subjective views and is therefore important in shaping views on tax deductions. The distinction between small entrepreneurs and managers and professionals helps explain the diversity of meanings related to tax deduction for philanthropy among elite groups within the occupational structure.

Data

My starting point is the idea that 'to study how individual giving responds to governments, information about the individual level of donations is required' (De Wit, Neumayr, Handy, and Wiepking, 2018:2) Few studies examine the formation of the cognitive mechanisms through which tax deductions for donations are perceived by individuals. To examine these mechanisms, I draw on a long-term ethnographic study led by one of the key French players in philanthropy. Through its grants, this foundation has funded a wide variety of non-profits and non-governmental organisations dedicated to fighting poverty and social exclusion in France and the world. Furthermore, it shelters small foundations created by wealthy families. It delegates its own entitlement to the maximum tax deduction available to them for individuals and households in France, 75% (up to 50,000€ on wealth tax). Only foundations recognised by the French Council of State, which is in charge of authorising the incorporation of non-profit organisations, can benefit from this deduction. Families who neither have the expertise nor the time to go through this very complex and time-consuming procedure are provided enrolment by big foundations which are already incorporated as 'RUPs' (reconnues d'utilité publique/recognised public-interest organisations). As a historian specialising in examining this procedure, Chloé Gaboriaux explains that the 'RUP' status has a centuries-long legacy in the French law system:

> In France, 'Reconnaissance d'utilité publique' (RUP) has for a long time been the only way for foundations – endowment funds managed by a board of trustees – to exist and for associations – a group of people working together to achieve a common set of goals – to acquire a legal entity. It stems from a very ancient principle of medieval Roman law, which says that an organization cannot exist and act as a moral entity without being authorized by the State. In the 19th century, associations with more than 20 members could not be established without a prefectoral authorization (Article 291 of the Penal Code of 1810) and needed RUP to acquire legal capacity (or incorporation) – in order, that is, to hold property in their own name and to exist as a collective entity before the law.
>
> *(2019)*

I draw on a long-term ethnographic study of a group of wealthy Parisian families who enrolled their foundations under the main foundation of interest. The relationship established with the foundation should be considered in order to understand how the material was collected. This foundation first asked me to lead the study with the explicit aim of interviewing some of the most important families among its clientele to anticipate the effects of a reform regarding the wealth tax on philanthropic donations. The foundation's manager wanted to know who, among its donors, would continue donating after a sharp decrease of charitable contribution deduction.

For two years, I was allowed to attend confidential meetings between donors and the staff regarding grant strategy, investments regarding the foundation's financial assets, expertise, and mentoring. I also attended most events organised for the donors' welfare, which included dinners, private concerts, work gatherings, and special events. These observations allowed me to obtain inside knowledge of the daily activities of the foundation and afforded me a certain level of familiarity with the families, which would be interviewed at the second step. In the late 2010s, the wealth tax was heavily criticised for imposing a burden on wealth, and it resulted in wealthy families leaving the country and creating businesses abroad. These arguments have been very important in conceptualising the wealth tax that was supported by Macron during the first year of his term, despite the fact that there is little evidence supporting them. Big foundations were nervous about the effects of such a possible outcome and were consequently willing to better know the families enrolled to be able to navigate these legal transformations. This prompted the foundation to open their doors to me. Therefore, in the semi-structured interviews, I focused on the donors' perceptions of the tax deduction. The questions were about the size and composition of wealth, structure of investments (housing, risky and non-risky financial assets), philanthropic strategy developed, and relationship with the sheltering foundation. A sample of twenty families was constituted progressively, and I recorded interviews of more than two hours with each of them. I was able to follow five families more closely and had regular follow-up interviews and meetings with them at their homes. These families were selected because they presented very diverse objective as well as subjective features. The size of their wealth varied considerably, ranging from retired professionals who had accumulated wealth during their working years to industrial heirs or players in the financial sector. However, such a small dataset had obvious limitations and thus cannot be considered representative of wealthy French donors. The sample comprises organisations affiliated with a foundation having a peculiar position in the philanthropic sector. Being relatively open socially and liberal religiosity are the key features that distinguish the interviewed families from other philanthropists in France.

Results

This study draws on a qualitative subset of semi-structured interviews. Therefore, it does not aim at providing a representative picture of the way donors perceive the tax deduction they are benefited by. However, these data help create a better understanding of the arguments that structure the perceptions of philanthropy among the subgroups of donors that adopt different frameworks and of how their support of the common good is related to a wider perception of the role of the state.

a A critic of the wealth tax

The first subgroup was strongly and explicitly opposed to the principle of a wealth tax. The legitimacy of this fiscal tool was heavily contested. At the time when the fieldwork was undertook, the wealth tax (*Impôt de Solidarité sur la Fortune*) was being criticised. This political context may have, therefore, favoured the expression of such a critique. The wealth tax was regarded as a predation by the state vis-à-vis entrepreneurs' legitimate gains:

> People simply hate paying taxes. There is an extreme polarization on the wealth tax as you have to pay a share of your wealth yearly. For entrepreneurs like me who have worked to accumulate wealth, it is senseless to give it to a spendthrift state.

This kind of opinion is rarely expressed so bluntly. However, one should not underestimate the fact that it represents the collective view of a social group about the wealth tax. In her ethnographic research on the family offices that take care of the wealth of families, sociologist Camille Herlin-Giret notes the insistence on tax optimisation through various legal schemes (2019). Among these, some private bankers or family office employees recognise that the motivation for some philanthropic givers does not go far beyond the avoidance of the wealth tax. Taxpayers prefer to pay 25% more rather than pay the remaining percentage (75%) to the state. Donating is, in this case, an ideological statement. It structures networks of friends and family members.

As mentioned by a family foundation leader, the wealth tax avoidance helps structuring a network of donors. The leader details the annual contribution of one of his sons:

> Among the six children of the family, one started his own business, which grew rapidly. It boomed over the years; he then sold the company. His cheque to the foundation represents his wealth tax. It is the most important resource of our foundation.

Another one clearly relates the occupational status of an entrepreneur with the avoidance of taxes:

> Pay less tax. It is really the first motivation of entrepreneurs, therefore, it goes together.

A key feature of this framework is denying a sense of generality to the state. The state is personified to lower its legitimacy regarding tax raises on behalf of the people:

> It is a bit senseless to give money to Mr Hollande or Mr Sarkozy. I prefer to make my choices.

Political leaders seem to view taxes as personal gains rather than contributions to the state's budget. State-sponsored taxation is considered an illegitimate predation by entrepreneurs who have spent their lifetime running businesses.

b A search for efficacy

Although various frameworks can be mixed in the discourse of a single interviewee, a second group of donors refers not so much to a refusal of the legitimacy given to tax but rather to a will to secure a greater efficiency of the money donated. As a matter of fact, donors often mention a consideration for impact. They want their money to be useful to the community and consider that private provision is a better means to achieve this goal. This is consistent with Bekkers and Wiepking's (2011) explanation of philanthropy driven by the quest for efficiency. Even though I do not focus on the motivations of donors per se and the way they perceive the tax deductions they are entitled to, my findings converge with those from a wide body of literature. Vis-à-vis tax deductions, the most important point is that donors do not value the absolute efficacy of their donation but rather the relative efficacy of their donation vis-à-vis the same amount of money dedicated to tax.

> They think that the state has failed, and that poverty and inequality are growing. Paying taxes equals subsidizing a machine that is also broken. Donors are willing to pay a little bit more in order to have an impact on the ground thanks to the non-profits they have chosen and projects they know about.

Efficacy is therefore a strong element of the donor's perception of tax deductions for philanthropic purposes. They allow philanthropists to choose projects and to fund non-profits that emulate corporate values because they think that, however controversial this view might be, the latter are more prone to helping people to move out of poverty, for instance. While explaining to me the core principles driving his own foundation, a donor underlined the distinction between an environment that provides money and creates dependency and an environment which creates social mobility through training:

> Our principle states that if a person is unwilling, even if the environment provides them with resources, they will not change their fate. Conversely, if a person is willing but the environment is not conducive, they will be impotent. . . . My foundation is not dedicated to give a hand-out or to send cash to southern countries. We want people to thrive and lift the barriers that keep them from doing so.

Similarly, managers and professionals tend to think that tax deductions allow a greater efficacy for the money donated. They highlight the fact that the non-profits they fund replicate the impact measurement strategies (through the use of metrics) which they consider essential for running a corporation successfully. They are interested in the technicalities of implementation and often closely know the leaders of the non-profits. Tax deductions allow them to be involved in various projects and initiatives dedicated to eradicating poverty in France and abroad.

This last example shows how efficacy and values are intertwined. A last set of donors, often, if not always, the wealthiest of the families, tend to value the fact that through tax deductions, the state is providing a recognition of their own values, hence contributing to genuine pluralism.

c Values and authenticity

Tax deductions are a form of recognition of different sets of values by the state. This perception is common among families which are wealthy enough to continue giving without tax deductions. Moreover, one could argue that because they are high enough in income distribution, they are concerned not only for their positions but have also developed a concern for the welfare of the philanthropic sector itself. Therefore, their position vis-à-vis tax is both detached, because the social status and intrinsic gratifications attached to philanthropy do not depend on these tax deductions, and concerned, because they have a strong interest in influencing public choices. They can afford to give without being supported. However, they attach extreme importance to the fact that through tax deductions, the state is promoting a kind of pluralism, which is difficult to find in other fields of public intervention. This is consistent with the fact that for civil society organisations, non-profits, and foundations alike, government subsidies are seen as a 'seal of approval' (Schiff, 1990). During an interview, a foundation leader told me that:

> The label is very important. Getting recognition for our contribution to the common good matters a lot. It makes the project credible for partners and sponsors. It is also a way to acknowledge that we are doing good work and that there is room for the kind of initiatives we have launched.
>
> We are entitled and have supported promoting a certain vision of the world and of how its problems should be settled. We are not particulars, we are acting by our own convictions, on behalf of the state. In poverty relief, religious convictions are crucial.

The attachment to pluralism is very close to an argument put forward by Rob Reich. In his book, as in previous works, he asks if fiscal support for philanthropy and, ultimately, the contributions philanthropic foundations make to democracy can be justified and, if so, how. He believes they are. He considers two arguments often put across in this debate: that of pluralism and that of discovery. The argument on pluralism expresses that foundations contribute to a pluralistic conception of the common good and diversify the agents involved in defining it, making it possible to overcome a univocal and centralised conception of the public interest. However, while this argument is acceptable to a degree, it suffers a rather obvious plutocratic bias. The discovery argument argues that, contrary to the state and market, philanthropy can invest for the longer term and help discovering new paths, as in science, where interests are detached from immediate outcomes.

Even if it was possible to identify this plutocratic bias in the data I collected, I do not wish to make an argument for or against philanthropy. I simply wish to show that the attachment to pluralism is related to Catholic faith and a will to see Catholic welfare services as contributing to the common good. In a republic with a strong commitment to a neat distinction between religion and public affairs labelled and put forward under the banner of the defence of 'Laïcité', (secularism), tax deductions convey a discreet yet subjectively and objectively important contribution to a pluralistic implementation of various organisations. With the exception of the Foundation of France, the main players of the philanthropic sector are influenced by religion, be it a liberal or conservative Catholicism, Judaism, or Protestantism. This point is, therefore, a more general one: religious domination structures the philanthropic sector. This is also a point that is valid in the 'longue durée' (long duration) of history, as research has shown that the philanthropic networks of the 1900s Paris displayed, in a country heavily fragmented by an open crisis between the Republican State and the Catholic church, a peaceful coexistence of Republican and Catholic elites (Topalov, 2020).

Discussion

These results bring a descriptive and value-added view on the diversity of perceptions of tax deduction for philanthropic purposes displayed by a small set of donors enrolled in a liberal Catholic foundation. These results must be considered carefully, given the limitations of the qualitative sample, and must be contextualised against an era when the bulk of the wealth tax was still in place – which is no longer the case today. Nonetheless, they do provide insights on philanthropic initiatives and on the way donors perceive the tax deductions they benefit from. Understanding state support through fiscal deductions is not the same as understanding the motivations of donors, which are significantly more diverse. Obviously, studying the perceptions of tax deduction enhances the importance of the latter and may suggest that they are key for motivating donors as well as for unfairly obscuring the concern for the needs of those helped or the peer pressure to donate. However, as has been seen after the introduction of the wealth tax, tax deductions are crucial for forming positive perceptions of philanthropic donation.

A second value-added factor is to bring class back in the way we relate these perceptions with specific subgroups. Once again, I do not have the means to show a causal relationship between a given class and a given framework. Nonetheless, it is interesting to note that among the groups overrepresented at the top of the income and wealth distribution, two different frames of perception of tax deductions appear, and they are closely related to two different occupational backgrounds. On the one hand, the blunt dismissal of the legitimacy of the wealth tax comes from entrepreneurs, be they small or big. This is consistent with the longstanding political positioning of this group to defend oneself against taxation as well as mandatory social protection. On the other hand, professionals and managers who implement – or have implemented when retired – bureaucratic or economic rationality in their corporations display a strong attachment to efficacy and consider that the efficacy of donations privately is higher than when the state implements social services. As has been seen in the critique of cash transfers, consideration for values is not separated from consideration of efficacy. However, a specific subgroup, consisting of families with higher and more dynastic wealth, values tax deductions for their contribution to pluralism.

The latter finding has several important theoretical implications. For more than a decade, European sociology in general, and British sociology in particular, has debated the definition of class. Does the 'employment aggregate approach' (Crompton, 1993) capture a social stratification where wealth inequality plays a bigger role, as has compellingly been shown by Piketty (2014)? He argues that a social class map needs to take wealth into account for determining class (2020). This can lead to what Savage et al. (2013) called a new class map, inductively built and considering various dimensions of capital. This study aims to contribute to this agenda by taking another route, which is continuing to use occupations to examine class but doing it via cultural sociology, because it helps distinguish various meaning-making processes related to wealth through the study of the relationship the wealthy have to wealth tax. The aspects of economic capital as well as occupational status (former or current) appear to be salient in framing philanthropists' relationship to the wealth tax. These preliminary results call for a more integrated research agenda on the intertwining of class and wealth. It could provide additional knowledge in two main directions: on the one hand considering the impact of wealth all along the socio-economic ladder and, on the other, as this study shows, distinguishing the diverse social worlds that are composed by the top 1% of the income and wealth distribution. In this context, a predominantly qualitative, culturally sociological approach could contribute to highlight the varieties of meaning-making processes related to class at the top of the socio-economic ladder and conversely to make room for the multidimensional effects of wealth on class-based perceptions of oneself, other people, and the world at large.

References

Abrams, B.A.; M.D. Shitz, 'The "crowding-out" effect of governmental transfers on private charitable contributions', *Public Choice*, 33(1), 1978, 29–39.

Albertini, M.; G. Ballarino; D. De Luca, 'Social class, work-related incomes and socio-economic polarization in Europe, 2005–2014', *European Sociological Review*, 36(4), 2020, 1–20.

Arts, W.A.; W.J.H. van Oorschot, 'The social capital of European welfare states: The crowding out hypothesis revisited', *Journal of European Social Policy*, 15(1), 2005, 5–26.

Bekkers, R.; P. Wiepking, 'A literature review of empirical studies of philanthropy: Eight mechanisms that drive charitable giving', *Nonprofit and Voluntary Sector Quarterly*, 40(5), 2011, 925–973.

Bourdieu, P., *La distinction: Critique sociale du jugement*, Paris: Editions de Minuit, 1979.

Cagé, J., *The Price of Democracy: How Money Shapes Politics and What to Do About It*, Cambridge, MA: Harvard University Press, 2020.

Crompton, R., *Class and Stratification*, Cambridge: Polity Press, 1993.

De Wit, A.; M. Neumayr; F. Handy; P. Wiepking, 'Do government expenditures shift private philanthropic donations to particular fields of welfare? Evidence from cross-country data', *European Sociological Review*, 34(1), 2018, 6–21.

Fack, G.; C. Landais, 'Les incitations fiscales au dons sont-elles efficaces?', *Economie et Statistique*, 427–428, 2009, 101–121.

Gaboriaux, C., 'A social construction of public interest: The "Reconnaissance d'Utilité Publique" of associations and foundations by the Council of State (1870–1914)', *Histphil Blog*, May 10, 2019.

Glucksberg, L.; R. Burrows, 'Family offices and the contemporary infrastructures of dynastic wealth', *LSE Research Online Documents on Economics*, 75899, 2016.

Goffman, E., *Frame Analysis: An Essay of the Organization of Experience*, New York: Harper, 1974.

Goldthorpe, J., 'Class analysis and the reorientation of class theory: The case of persisting differentials in educational attainment', *The British Journal of Sociology*, 47(3), 1996, 481–505.

Harding, D.J.; M. Lamont; M.L. Small, 'Reconsidering culture and poverty', *The Annals of the American Academy of Political and Social Science*, 629(1), 2010, 629.

Herlin-Giret, C., *Rester Riche: Enquête sur les Gestionnaires de Fortune et Leurs Clients*, Paris: Le bord de l'eau, 2019.

Lamont, M., *The Dignity of Working Men: Morality and the Boundaries of Race, Class and Immigration*, Cambridge, MA: Harvard University Press, 2002.

Lamont, M.; P. Pierson, 'Inequality as a multidimensional process', Special Issue of *Daedalus: Journal of the American Academy of Arts and Science*, 148(3), 2019, 5–19.

Mohr, J.W.; C.A. Bail; M. Frye; J.C. Lena; O. Lizardo; T.E. McDonnell; A. Mische; I. Tavory; F.F. Wherry, *Measuring Culture*, New York: Columbia University Press, 2020.

Ostrower, F., *Why the Wealthy Give: The Culture of Elite Philanthropy*, Princeton, NJ: Princeton University Press, 1995.

Piketty, T., *Capital and Ideology*, Cambridge, MA: Harvard University Press, 2020.

Piketty, T., *Capital in the Twentieth Century*, Cambridge, MA: Harvard University Press, 2014.

Reich, R., *Just Giving: How Philanthropy Is Failing Democracy and How It Can Do Better*, Princeton, NJ: Princeton University Press, 2018.

Salamon, L.; H.K. Anheier, 'Social origins of civil society: Explaining the nonprofit sector cross-nationally', *Volontas: International Journal of Voluntary and Nonprofit Organizations*, 9(2), 1998, 213–248.

Savage, M.; F. Devine; N. Cunningham; M. Taylor; L. Yaojun; J. Hjellbreke; B. Le Roux; S. Friedman; A. Miles, 'A new model of social class? Findings from the BBC's Great British class survey experiment', *Sociology*, 47(2), 2013, 219–250.

Schiff, J., *Charitable Giving and Government Policy: An Economic Analysis*, New York: Greenwood Press, 1990.

Sherman, R., *Uneasy Streets: The Anxieties of Affluence*, Princeton, NJ: Princeton University Press, 2017.

Spire, A., *Résistances à l'impôt, attachement à l'Etat. Enquête sur les contribuables français*, Paris: Le Seuil, 2018.

Topalov, C., ed., *Philanthropes en 1900. Londres, New York, Paris, Genève*, Paris: Créaphis, 2020.

6

CHARITABLE ENDS (PERHAPS) BY POLITICAL MEANS

What are governments regulating?

Calum M. Carmichael

1 Introduction

As documented by the OECD (2020), many governments award fiscal privileges to the organisations they have granted "charitable" or "public-benefit" status.[1] To be eligible for this status and these privileges, the organisations must pursue certain purposes and undertake or forgo certain activities.[2] In defining those activities, governments typically distinguish charitable from political ones and require the organisations to forgo forms or levels of the latter. Such requirements raise questions not only about why governments consider some political activities incompatible with charitable status and its fiscal privileges but also about what they intend to accomplish by restricting them. Do they intend to regulate the definition of charitable purposes and the types of activities that may advance them and hence take an approach specific to charitable organisations? Or do they intend to regulate the donations of individuals, groups and corporations that privately finance political activities and hence take a more general approach that is consistent across both the political entities and charitable organisations performing them?

This chapters addresses these questions of why and what. The answers are particularly relevant to governments intending to pursue the second task – that of comprehensively regulating the use of private monies to finance politics. The importance of that task has received international attention given the challenges to democracy that could arise, particularly in an era of increasing income inequality (OECD 2016). To date, however, that attention has focused on the private financing of political entities – parties, candidates or independent political outfits – rather than the private financing of political activities as performed across a broader range of organisations, including charitable ones. The problems of such a narrow focus can be inferred from the "hydraulics" of political monies as described by Issacharoff and Karlan (1999) – a phenomenon that can turn regulatory reform into "a graveyard of well-intentioned plans gone awry . . . [where] reforms could exacerbate the very political pathologies they are designed to combat. Far from making politics more accountable to democratic control, they may make it less so" (1705–07) – for reasons akin to the laws of physics. In their judgement:

> It doesn't take an Einstein to discern a First Law of Political Thermodynamics – the desire for political power cannot be destroyed, but at most, channeled into different forms – nor a Newton to identify a Third Law of Political Motion – every reform

 DOI: 10.4324/9781003139201-8

> effort to constrain political actors produces a corresponding series of reactions by those with power to hold onto it. . . . Our account, then, is "hydraulic" in two senses. First, we think political money, like water, has to go somewhere. It never really disappears into thin air. Second, we think political money, like water, is part of a broader ecosystem. Understanding why it flows where it does and what functions it serves when it gets there *requires thinking about the system as a whole.*
>
> (1705, italics added)

As described here, that broader system comprises not only political entities but charitable organisations as well.

This chapter proceeds as follows. Part 2 structures and summarises the debates in the charity finance literature on whether charitable organisations receiving fiscal privileges and relying on private donations should forgo at least some political activities. Part 3 structures and summarises the debates in the campaign finance/political finance literature on whether political entities should forgo at least some private donations. Part 4 identifies in each literature the same opposing pairs of political ideologies and models of democracy – egalitarianism and deliberative democracy versus libertarianism and pluralism – of which the first pair supports more restrictions on both the political activities of charitable organisations and the private donations to political entities, and the second pair supports fewer restrictions. To see whether governments take similarly restrictive or permissive stances toward regulating the private financing of political activities by charitable organisations and political entities, Part 5 categorises and compares the approaches of 16 countries. In some countries (e.g., Canada, Italy, Singapore), the stances appear similar, as would be the case with governments regulating not charitable organisations and political entities specifically and separately but rather the private financing of politics generally and comprehensively. However, in other countries (e.g., India, United States) the stances appear very different. For the rest, various degrees of difference hold, suggesting that most of the sampled governments interpret and respond differently to the use of private monies to finance political activities depending on the organisation or entity performing them – and thus either fail or do not intend to regulate that use comprehensively and consistently. Part 6 offers several explanations for why such differences might exist and draws inferences for governments intending to be comprehensive.

2 Framing the debate in the charity finance literature: are political activities incompatible with charitable status?[3]

The legal literature on charity finance literature focuses on the regulation and resourcing of organisations officially recognised as charitable. The central debate within that literature considers whether such organisations, which receive fiscal privileges and rely on private donations, should forgo political activities. It can be framed according to whether charitable and political purposes are incompatible, either because charitable purposes and activities are inherently different from political ones, or because political activities performed by charitable organisations would harm charitable or political purposes. Here, charitable *purposes* are interpreted as being to improve societal wellbeing by providing persons in need or society in general with certain publicly beneficial goods and services otherwise not available from government or the for-profit sector. Charitable *activities* are limited to the direct provision of those goods and services. Political *purposes* are interpreted systemically as being to establish, uphold and operate the principles and institutions that compose the official processes whereby legitimate collective decisions are made. Political *activities* are limited to the ones potentially available to charitable organisations.

They include attempts to affect the formation of governments by influencing the outlook and actions of potential voters and volunteers in elections (electioneering). And they include attempts to affect the decisions of governments by influencing either the outlook and actions of the community at large (advocacy) or the outlook and actions of elected and government officials (lobbying).

The debate over inherent incompatibilities

Some scholars and practitioners argue that political activities are inherently different from charitable ones. Under common law, political purposes and activities have traditionally been deemed non-charitable for reason that courts could not or should not determine whether any prescribed change in law or government would be for the public benefit (Chisolm 1990, 344–346; Brunson 2011, 140; Colinvaux 2012, 702–703). In those terms, prohibiting charitable organisations from performing political activities constitutes a form of "border control" to distinguish the organisations that deserve fiscal privileges from those that do not (Carroll 1992, 253–254; Simon, Dale and Chisolm 2006, 284–288; Tobin 2007, 1330; Colinvaux 2012, 704, 709–712). Charitable activities are publicly beneficial and capable of generating "positive externalities" which benefit individuals and groups broadly. In comparison, political activities are only of private benefit and capable of generating "negative externalities" which harm the individuals or groups aligned with opposing causes (Buckles 2007, 1086, 1091–1092; Tobin 2007, 1336). Charitable activities are noble and ennobling, whereas political activities are sullied and sullying (Houck 2003, 85–86; Colinvaux 2012, 706–707, 756; Crimm and Winer 2013, 106). If undertaken, they would debase charitable organisations – whether actually or in the public eye – as well as compromising and corrupting their executives and board (Dessingue 2001, 925–926; Tobin 2007, 1319–1323, 1329–1330, 1337, 1341–1342). Just as politicians and governments should not "do politics and government" through charities, charities should not "do charity" through politics and government (Parachin 2016, 1075–1077).

There are arguments that counter these. The observation that political *purposes* are not legally charitable does not prevent political *activities* from being instrumental to charitable purposes (Chisolm 1990, 346–347; Carroll 1992, 252–253; Houck 2003, 4–8; Buckles 2007, 1090; Brunson 2011, 141–142). Moreover, political activities might generate public benefits through legitimising collective decisions, fostering citizenship and social capital or facilitating peaceful transitions of power. On the other hand, charitable activities – say, in areas of religion, reproductive health, human rights or the environment – might be as rivalrous as political activities, such that one cause's gain imposes another's loss (Chisolm 1990, 350–355; Buckles 2008, 1111–1112). Both the charitable and political sectors focus on the definition and promotion of the common good – concepts of which might differ as much within each sector as between them (Dunn 1999, 306–307). Besides, separating the two sectors would undercut the strength that each could draw from their interdependence and sharing of means (Salamon and Toepler 2015).

The debate over the harm to charitable purposes caused by charitable organisations performing political activities

Some argue that political activities performed by charitable organisations would harm societal wellbeing. The benefits of such activities are uncertain, whereas the administrative and resource costs are immediate and concrete (Buckles 2008, 1087; Galle 2013, 1561, 1576–1580). Politically motivated and monied donors increase the risk of political capture that would narrow the organisation's priorities, making it partisan and thus less able to collaborate with others in pursuing a common purpose – say, the relief of poverty (Tobin 2007, 1329–1330; Buckles 2008, 1110; Colinvaux 2012, 754; Galle 2013, 1610; Wolpe 2017). By steering a transformation toward greater political involvement, the organisation's executive could benefit professionally, gaining notoriety and opportunities for advancement (Buckles 2008, 1098–1106; Galle 2013, 1604–1607). Hence, the decision of whether to undertake political activities should not be left to their discretion and abilities to persuade the board but rather constrained by regulation.

There are arguments that counter these. The executive and board, not the government, are best able to judge the mix of activities that would best allow the organisation to advance its charitable purpose (Clark 1960, 465–466; Buckles 2008, 1087, 1099–1101; Brunson 2011, 142). By their nature, charitable purposes involve ideas that are controversial and disputable (Sacks 1960, 528–533). Pursuing them requires entering those controversies, publicly endorsing what is good and admonishing what is bad (Klapach 1999, 506, 538; Colinvaux 2012, 699–700). As to the encroachment of monied interests or the risk of capture: such challenges confront all charitable organisations, regardless of their political involvement. Instead, that involvement might help deflect one form of co-optation: the silence preferred by government (Garnett 2001, 797–798; Buckles 2008, 1091–1094; Brunson 2011, 149).

The debate over the harm to political purposes caused by charitable organisations performing political activities

Some argue that political activities performed by charitable organisations would harm the democratic processes whereby collective decisions are made. Those processes rely on a conceptual framework that all citizens can endorse: the common ground offered by secular (as opposed to irreligious) public reason (Audi 1993, 687–697; Rawls 2005). And they benefit from terms of deliberation that are dispassionate, allowing differences to be aired and understood without foreclosing compromise or agreement (Galle 2013, 1584–1585). The political involvement of charitable organisations – particularly those that are dedicatedly religious or single issue – threatens that common ground and those terms. It could make public dialogue more fragmented and inflammatory, the decision-making processes more deadlocked, politics more sectarian and policies less coherent – fostering political disengagement among citizens (Galston 1993, 1315–1317; Tobin 2007, 1326–1329; Trotter 2012, 21; Cafardi, 2005, 538–542; Galle 2013, 1583–1585). By avoiding political involvement, charitable organisations are better able to cultivate an educated and discerning electorate. Within their areas of expertise, they would serve as independent and trusted clearing houses of political information and interpretation, relied upon to highlight important issues and outline alternative positions and their implications – without taking sides (Tobin 2007, 1337; Galle 2013, 1628–1629). Again, however, the organisation's executive could benefit professionally from undertaking political activities. Thus, to protect and promote systemic political purposes, the decision of whether to undertake them should be constrained by regulation.

There are arguments that counter these. Liberal democracies rely upon public debate that does not suppress from the outset certain convictions or world views – including ones rooted in religious or single-issue perspectives (Habermas 2006, 6–12; Dworkin 2016, 63–66). Those perspectives might morally inform and enrich the debate, as well as be informed and broadened by it (Dessingue 2001, 923–925; Garnett 2001, 798–801; Habermas 2006, 18–20; Totten 2007, 310–313). Religious convictions are no more prone to making debate more fractious and intolerant than are certain secular ones (McConnell 1999, 648–656). Rather than contributing to political disengagement, the political involvement of charitable organisations might forestall it by recruiting an otherwise disaffected citizenry (Dunn 2008). It could balance the presence of business organisations or bring to the fore otherwise overlooked problems that are longer term or affect the disadvantaged (Chisolm 1990, 348–349; Houck 2003, 84; Buckles 2008, 1108–1109; Colinvaux 2012, 705; Galston 1993, 1318–1322, 1335–1353; Parachin 2016, 1070–1071). Moreover, regulations limiting the types and levels of political activity available to charitable organisations could contravene constitutional rights by encumbering freedom of speech or religion (Chisolm 1990, 320–337; Carroll 1992, 254–259; Klapach 1999, 513–519; Guinane, 2007; Leff 2009, 685–696; Brunson 2011, 145–147; Galston 2011, 903–911, 918–928; Weitzel 2011, 157–158; Fresco 2012, 3026–3045; for a retort, see Tobin 2007, 1342–1349).

3 Framing the debate in the political finance literature: are private donations compatible with democratic principles?

The legal literature on political finance focuses on the regulation and resourcing of electioneering by political parties and candidates. The central debate within that literature considers whether the protection of liberty or equality should determine how the private donations to such entities are regulated. The scholars and practitioners who uphold political liberty argue that the donations of natural and legal persons constitute speech, enabling them to express their support for a political entity and signal its intensity (BeVier 1994, 1277; Sullivan 1997, 671–675; Redish 2001, 125–128; Smith 2001, 109–121; Samples 2006, 31–40). Moreover, unlimited campaign spending allows political parties and candidates to deal with more issues, handle them at greater depth and reach wider audiences. Constraining who spends and the amounts spent would leave the electorate less informed and introduce arbitrary judgements over what types and amounts of information are excessive (*ibid*, 1266–1267, 675–678, 135–136, 41–45, 175–179). Thus, to protect the freedom of speech and the benefits of unrestrained information, those who uphold liberty recommend a "liberalising agenda" for the regulation of political finance (Samples 2006, 266–297): one that would allow natural and legal persons to give and political entities to spend whatever they wish and one that would reduce or remove public funding, thereby neither imposing this burden on taxpayers nor compelling them to support candidates apart from those of their choosing.

There are arguments that counter these. Money is a form of property that purchases things other than speech; hence, giving and spending are acts tied to property rights that can be regulated without regulating speech *per se* (Wright 1976; Hellman 2011). In the context of electioneering, the purpose of free speech is not to create an unregulated "marketplace of ideas" easily dominated by those with greater resources but to support a public discourse among political equals, each having the same opportunity to speak and be heard (Sunstein 1993, 244–250; Fiss 1996, 15–16). More information does not make the electorate more informed. The communications and causes backed by greater resources will "drown out" the others, thereby narrowing the range of issues that occupies the electorate's attention (Rawls 1971, 225; Wright 1982, 624–625).

The scholars and practitioners who uphold political equality argue that it is threatened by income inequality – echoing the concerns of the OECD (2016). Income conveys influence, encouraging or enabling individuals to be more politically active, whether by donating, volunteering, communicating with peers or candidates, voting or running for office (Raskin and Bonifaz 1994, 1174–1183; Overton 2004, 85–104; de Figueiredo and Garrett 2005, 627–634). Natural or legal persons make campaign donations either for the "consumption" purpose of endorsing the image projected and the policy platform put forward or for the "investment" purpose of altering that platform to serve their interests (Ansolabehere, de Figueiredo and Snyder 2003). Candidates and parties that rely on donations could adjust their platforms to attract the support of those most able and willing to give (Hasen 1996, 8–35; Garrett and Smith 2005, 296–299; Issacharoff 2010, 126–130). Greater donations enable them to mount campaigns that could broaden their appeal by shifting political messaging away from platforms that ignore the poor and toward the symbols and personal qualities that promote their own image or demean that of their opponents (Mazo 2014, 284; Fowler, Franz and Ridout, 2016, 141–147). Such strategies would be reinforced by sections of the electorate being politically alienated and apathetic or malleable and credulous (Dworkin 1996; Ortiz 1998; Hardin 2004; Achen and Bartels 2016). Thus, to prevent income inequality from skewing political participation, platforms and powers of persuasion, those who uphold equality recommend regulations that would provide greater public funding for party and candidate campaigns, as well as measures to increase the number of individuals donating, level up or level down the amounts they donate, cap or prohibit the donations or expenditures of corporations and independent political outfits and encourage or require limits on campaign spending (Foley 1994; Hasen 1996; Briffault 1999; Ackerman and Ayers 2002; Cmar 2005; Sarbanes and O'Mara 2016).

Again, there are arguments that counter these. As a source of influence, income is not unique, somehow illegitimate or necessarily skewed across the political spectrum; besides, efforts to neutralise its effects would simply enhance the relative effects of other unevenly distributed sources (BeVier 1994, 1266–1269; Sullivan 1997, 680; Redish 2001, 9; Smith 2001, 45–48, 79–83, 201–213; Samples 2006, 131–134, 140–145). There are no clear standards to measure the extent to which platforms and persuasive powers favour the wealthy. And even if they were, there is no clear evidence of this being attributable to private donations (*ibid*, 1268–1269, 675–685, 48–63, 121–136, 213–215, 88–106).

4 Linking the political and charity finance debates

The central debates of the charity finance and political finance literatures have been conducted in relative isolation. And yet in each one, can recognise the same opposing pairs of political philosophies and models of democracy: libertarianism and classical pluralism versus egalitarianism and deliberative democracy.[4] Libertarianism and classic pluralism underlie not only the political finance arguments that uphold liberty but also the charity finance arguments countering the claims that the political activities of charitable organisations would harm political purposes. Both sets of arguments place importance on freedom of speech and conscience for natural and legal persons and thus oppose limits to that freedom apart from ones needed to prevent violating the rights of others (Mill 2003, 139; Vallier 2018, 402).[5] Such freedom extends to persons being able to give to charitable organisations and political entities and to those organisations and entities being able to perform political activities and spend on them. Both sets of arguments envisage those organisations and entities joining other groups and associations, each working with distinct priorities and specialised information, striving to promote its cause and frustrate the causes of others and adding to the array of competing interests and demands that ultimately needs to be adjudicated either by the electorate to form a government or by the government to formulate policy (Dahl 1956, 131–135; Held 2006, 158–169).[6] Such competition and bargaining across groups can operate alongside the "passive acquiescence or indifference of a majority of adults or voters" (*ibid*, 133; 166).

In comparison, egalitarianism and deliberative democracy underlie not only the political finance arguments that uphold equality but also the charity finance arguments that support the claims that by performing political activities charitable organisations would harm political purposes. Both sets of arguments envisage all citizens having equal opportunities to follow and participate in processes of reasoned and reflective public discourse and decision-making. Although such processes would not necessarily eliminate differences in priority or outlook, they could accommodate them and lead to decisions and actions that could be understood by and justified to all (Rawls 1971, 221–234, 239 n 23; Held 2006, 231–255).[7] In spite of these common elements, each set of arguments has a different focus. That from political finance recommends regulations to restrict the giving to and spending of political entities in order to counter the threats that income poses to political equality.[8] In contrast, the set from charity finance recommends regulations to restrict the political activities available to charitable organisations in order to counter threats to public reason, dispassionate discourse and citizen discernment.[9]

5 Categorising and comparing international approaches to regulating privately financed political activities

How can one characterise international approaches to regulating the private financing of political activities? To address that question, this part categorises and compares the approaches taken by a sample of countries to regulate the political activities that charitable organisations may perform and the private donations that political entities may receive. The sample comprises 16 democracies from Europe, Africa, the Americas and Asia-Pacific; half are common-law jurisdictions (Australia, Canada, England-Wales, India, Kenya, Nigeria, Singapore and the United States) and half civil-law (Brazil, France, Germany, Italy, Japan, Mexico, Portugal and Sweden); four are middle income (Brazil, India, Kenya and Nigeria) and the rest high income. All 16 countries provide charitable organisations and political entities with fiscal privileges that include exempting their income from taxation. And, as presented in Table 6.1, all 16 permit private donations from individuals and corporations to charitable organisations, and indeed encourage them by offering at least some donors tax credits, deductions or matching grants. For these organisations, regulating their use of private monies to finance political activities involves restricting the types and levels of activities they may perform. All of the countries also permit private donations from individuals to political entities. Some permit donations from corporations. And some encourage certain donations again by offering donors tax credits or deductions. For these entities, regulating their use of private monies to finance political activities involves restricting the levels and sources of donations they may receive. As outlined in the following, the regulatory approaches taken by each country in limiting both the activities of charitable organisations and the donations to political entities can be characterised by stances that are either more permissive, in keeping with libertarianism and pluralism, or more restrictive, in keeping with egalitarianism and deliberative democracy. To be sure, these stances are based on actions or indicators that are stated in legislation or regulatory guidelines rather than on what is necessarily enforced or followed. And inevitably the job of assigning them requires discretionary judgement. Nevertheless, patterns emerge across what are at least practices *de jure*.

Regulating the political activities of charitable organisations

Table 6.2 describes the regulatory treatment of electioneering, advocacy and lobbying by charitable organisations as being either prohibited, restricted, permitted conditionally or permitted with no formal limitations. In general, the limitations placed on electioneering are at least as great as those on advocacy and lobbying. They are greatest – amounting to prohibition – in Canada, Germany, India, Mexico and the United States. They are lowest in Italy, Portugal, Singapore and Sweden: registered nonprofit third sector entities in Italy may donate to political parties but are subject to transparency requirements if the amounts exceed €5,000; associations and foundations in Portugal may engage with political parties but must stop short of

Table 6.1 Fiscal treatment of donations from individuals and corporations to charitable organisations and political entities

Country	*Donations from individuals to:*						*Donations from corporations to:*					
	Charitable organisations		*Political entities*				*Charitable organisations*		*Political entities*			
	Subsidy	*Cap*	*Permitted*	*Limit*	*Subsidy*	*Cap*	*Subsidy*	*Cap*	*Permitted*	*Limit*	*Subsidy*	*Cap*
Australia	Deduction	None	Yes	None	Deduction	$1,500	Deduction	None	Yes	None	None	NA
Brazil	Credit	8%[1]	Yes	10%[2]	None	NA	Credit	1–4%[3]	No	NA	NA	NA
Canada	Credit	75%[4]	Yes	$1,625[5]	Credit	$1,275	Deduction	75%[4]	No	NA	NA	NA
England	Grant[6]	None	Yes	None	None	NA	Deduction	None	Yes	None	None	NA
France	Credit	20%[7]	Yes	€7,500	Credit	€7,500	Credit	.5%[8]	No	NA	NA	NA
Germany	Deduction	20%[7]	Yes	None	Deduction	€1,650	Deduction	20%[7]	Yes	None	None	NA
India	Deduction	10%[9]	Yes	None	Deduction	None	Deduction	10%[9]	Yes	None	Deduction	None
Italy	Credit	€30,000	Yes	€100,000	Credit	€30,000	Deduction	10%[7]	Yes	€100,000	Credit	€30,000
Japan	Deduction	40%[7]	Yes	¥20M	Deduction	40%[7]	Deduction	3.125%[10]	Yes	¥30M[11]	None	NA
Kenya	Deduction	None	Yes	5%[12]	None	NA	Deduction	None	Yes	5%[12]	None	NA
Mexico	Deduction	7%[7]	Yes	.5%[13]	Deduction	None	Deduction	7%[7]	No	NA	NA	NA
Nigeria	None	NA	Yes	₦1M	None	NA	Deduction	10%[14]	Yes	₦1M	None	NA
Portugal	Credit	15%[15]	Yes	€11,000[16]	None	NA	Deduction	6–8%[17]	No	NA	NA	NA
Singapore	Deduction	None	Yes	None	None	NA	Deduction	None	Yes	None	None	NA
Sweden	Deduction	1,500kr	Yes	None	None	NA	None	NA	Yes	None	None	NA
U.S.	Deduction	50%[18]	Yes	None[19]	None	NA	Deduction	10%[7]	Yes[20]	None	None	NA

1 Cumulative, calculated on total tax liability.
2 Calculated on gross income earned over year before election.
3 Varies by project or program, calculated on operating profit.
4 Calculated on net income.
5 Circa 2020.
6 Combined with credit for individuals paying more than the basic tax rate.
7 Calculated on taxable income.
8 Calculated on annual turnover.
9 Calculated on gross income.
10 Calculated on taxable income, plus 1875% of stated capital and capital surplus.
11 Lower limits for corporations with capital below ¥5B.
12 Calculated on party's expenditure.
13 Calculated on ceiling for total party spending in preceding election. Applies to total donations.
14 Calculated on total profits.
15 Calculated on taxes paid.
16 Approximate limit for 2020, calculated as 25 times the annually adjusted "social support index" used to set social security benefits.
17 Calculated on revenues.
18 For donations to public charities, calculated adjusted gross income.
19 Applies to aggregate donations.
20 Applies to donations to independent-expenditure political action committees.

Table 6.2 Regulatory treatment of political activities performed by charitable organisations

Country	*← More egalitarian/deliberative restrictive*		*More libertarian/pluralist permissive →*	
	Prohibited	*Restricted*	*Conditionally permitted*	*Permitted or no formal limitations*
Australia			Electioneering, advocacy, lobbying[1]	
Brazil		Electioneering[2]		Advocacy, lobbying[3]
Canada	Electioneering[4]		Advocacy, lobbying[5]	
England			Electioneering, advocacy, lobbying[6]	
France			Electioneering, advocacy, lobbying[7]	
Germany	Electioneering[8]		Advocacy, lobbying[9]	
India	Electioneering, advocacy[10]		Lobbying[11]	
Italy				Electioneering, advocacy, lobbying[12]
Japan		Electioneering[13]	Advocacy, lobbying	
Kenya	Electioneering[14]		Advocacy, lobbying[15]	Electioneering[16]
Mexico	Electioneering[17]		Advocacy, lobbying[18]	
Nigeria		Electioneering[19]	Advocacy, lobbying[20]	
Portugal				Electioneering, advocacy, lobbying[21]
Singapore				Electioneering, advocacy, lobbying[22]
Sweden				Electioneering, advocacy, lobbying[23]
U.S.	Electioneering[24]	Advocacy, lobbying[25]		

1 Advocacy and lobbying are charitable if undertaken by a charity to further its charitable purpose (Aid/Watch Incorporated v Commissioner of Taxation [2010] HCA 42). The Australian Charities and Not-for-Profits Commission recognises "campaigning" as a legitimate way of furthering a charity's charitable purpose. This includes supporting the stance of a political party or candidate on an issue without promoting or opposing a particular party or candidate *per se* (ACNC, *Charities, elections and advocacy* April 2016). Charities making "electoral expenditures" above tiered thresholds must disclose them at different levels of detail to the Australian Electoral Commission (Commonwealth Electoral Act 1918).

2 Public Interest Civil Society Organisations (PISCOs) may not participate in political campaigns or support political parties or politicians (Law 9.790/99 Article 16). Corporate donations to any PICSO cannot be deducted from taxable income (Law 13.019/2014 Art. 16-C).

3 Brazilian law generally imposes no restrictions on – or protections of – the ability of civil society organisations to lobby or advocate (International Centre for Non-for-Profit Law. Civic Freedom Monitor – Brazil, July 2020: https://www.icnl.org/resources/civic-freedom-monitor/brazil#glance accessed 20 September 2020).

4 Charities may not devote any of their resources to the direct or indirect support of, or opposition to, any political party or candidate for public office [Income Tax Act Section 149.1 (6.1), (6.2)].

5 Advocacy and lobbying constitute "public policy dialogue and development activities" that are charitable if undertaken by a charity to further its charitable purpose (Canada Revenue Agency, Guidance Reference number CG-027, 21 January 2019).

6 The Charity Commission for England and Wales recognises advocacy and lobbying as ways a charity may further its charitable purpose and permits charities to focus most of their resources on those activities for a finite period (Campaigning and Political Activity Guidance for Charities, publication CC9). To further its charitable purpose, a charity may engage with political parties and candidates and endorse or oppose their policies but cannot endorse or oppose them categorically.

(*Continued*)

Table 6.2 (Continued)

7 General interest associations may engage in political activities, whereas public utility associations and foundations may not primarily engage in them (State Council Opinion No. 322894, 13 June 1978). These organisations cannot directly fund the campaign activities of parties or candidates (Article 11.4, Law No. 88–227 of 11 March 1988; Electoral Code L.52–8).
8 Tax-privileged organisations may not use their assets for the direct or indirect benefit of political parties (General Fiscal Law Article 55–1).
9 Tax-privileged organisations may comment publicly on and communicate with legislators about policies related to their tax-privileged purposes (General Fiscal Law Articles 52, 55–1).
10 The governing documents of institutions established for charitable purposes must prohibit the use of assets for purposes other than charitable ones [Income Tax Act Section 80G 5(ii)]. Indian courts hold political purposes or activities not to be charitable [e.g., CIT v. All India Hindu Mahasabha [1983] 140 ITR 748 (Delhi)].
11 Institutions established for charitable purposes are not prohibited from communicating with legislators on issues tied to their purpose or to "general public utility", provided such activities remain incidental to achieving their charitable objects.
12 There are no formal limits to registered nonprofit third sector entities performing political activities to further the general interest they serve (Legislative Decree No. 117 of 3 July 2017). However, such entities are subject to the same transparency requirements as political parties (i.e., submitting their budget to the relevant parliamentary committee) if they donate in cash or kind more than €5,000 to political parties, political movements or to persons holding a position in government or elected office (Legislative Decree No. 34 of 28 June 2019).
13 Special Nonprofit Corporations are prohibited from "promoting, supporting, or opposing a political principle" and from "recommending, supporting, or opposing a candidate for public office, a person holding a public office, or a political party" [Law to Promote Specified Nonprofit Activities 25 March 1998 Article 2–2(ii b,c)]. Otherwise, nonprofit organisations may engage in political activities as means to pursue their authorised purposes.
14 The yet-to-be enacted Public Benefits Organisations Act 2013 defines a registered organisation as "autonomous, nonpartisan, non-profit making" [Sect. 5(1)] that "may not engage in fundraising or campaigning to support or oppose any political party or candidate for appointive or elective public office, nor may it propose or register candidates for elective public office" [Sect. 66(3)].
15 The yet-to-be-repealed Non-Governmental Organisations Co-Ordination Act 1990 does not prohibit advocacy or lobbying, whereas the pending Public Benefits Organisations Act 2013 explicitly endorses them, defining "public benefit activity" as "an activity that supports or promotes public benefit by enhancing or promoting the economic, environmental, social or cultural development or protecting the environment or lobbying or advocating on issues of general public interest or the interest or well-being of the general public or a category of individuals or organisations" [Section 2(1)].
16 In contrast with the PBO Act 2013, the NGO Act 1990 prohibits a registered organisation from affiliating with political entities established outside Kenya (Section 21–1b) but does not prohibit affiliations with domestic entities or political activities "for the benefit of the public at large and for the promotion of social welfare, development charity or research in the areas inclusive of, but not restricted to, health, relief, agriculture, education, industry and the supply of amenities and services" (Section 2).
17 Nonprofit organisations authorised to receive deductible donations must fulfil "their social object, without being able to intervene in political campaigns or get involved in activities of propaganda" [Income Tax Act 2013 Article 82(II)].
18 Such organisations "may carry out activities designed to influence legislation, provided that such activities are not remunerated and are not carried out for of persons or sectors who have made donations to them" [Ibid., Article 82(III)].
19 The Companies and Allied Matters Act 2020 Section 38(2) prohibits companies limited by guarantee from making "a donation or gift of any of its property or funds to a political party or political association, or for any political purpose" but does not prohibit other forms of nonprofit organisations from endorsing political parties or candidates.
20 Institutions or bodies authorised to receive deductible donations are not formally prohibited from advocacy or lobbying; however, certain subjects are or could be excluded. The Constitution of Nigeria Sections 39, 40 guarantee rights to receive and impart information and to assemble freely and associate, but Section 45(1) permits restricting these rights "in the interest of defence, public safety, public order, public morality or public health". The Criminal Code Act 1916 Section 62 declares unlawful any society for "interfering with, or resisting, or encouraging interference with or resistance to the administration of the law". More specifically, the Same Sex Marriage Act 2014 Section 5(3) makes it an offence for a person or group to support "the registration, operation and sustenance of gay clubs, societies, organisations, processions or meetings".
21 There are no formal limits to private institutions of social solidarity or public utility associations and foundations engaging in political activities to further their purposes of social interest. Associations and foundations may engage with political parties but not elaborate a political program or run candidates for election (Decree Law no. 594/74 Article 12).

22 There are no formal limits to Institutions of a Public Character engaging in political activities to further their charitable purposes.
23 There are no formal limits to nonprofit organisations engaging in political activities.
24 Public charities and private foundations cannot participate in any campaign for elective or appointive public office [Internal Revenue Code [1986] §501(c)(3)].
25 Churches and foundations cannot make lobbying or advocacy expenditures to influence legislation; other organisations can make "insubstantial" expenditures calculated as percentages of "exempt purpose expenditures" up to a maximum of USD 1M [Internal Revenue Code [1986] §501(h)].

presenting a political platform or running candidates; both Institutions of a Public Character in Singapore and registered nonprofit organisations in Sweden face no formal limitations on political activities related to their charitable purposes. The treatment of electioneering in the other seven countries appears intermediate. In Brazil, Japan and Nigeria, it is restricted in that any prohibitions apply only to specified organisations: Public Interest Civil Society Organisations in Brazil, Special Nonprofit Corporations in Japan and companies limited by guarantee in Nigeria. In Australia, England and France, organisations may campaign to support or oppose the policies or positions of parties and candidates on condition that this furthers their charitable purposes or general interests and that their support or opposition does not apply to the parties or candidates *per se*. For Kenya, the status of electioneering is uncertain: under the non-repealed 1990 Non-Governmental Organisations Co-ordination Act (Section 21(1b)), they must only avoid affiliations with "political entities established outside Kenya", whereas under the not-yet-ratified 2013 Public Benefits Organisations Act (Section 66(3)), registered organisations "may not engage in fundraising or campaigning to support or oppose any political party or candidate"– raising concerns that the proposed legislation seeks to silence the charitable sector on issues related to the International Criminal Court or politicians' salaries (Churchill 2013).

With respect to advocacy, the limitations are as least as great as those on lobbying. They are greatest in India and to a lesser degree in the United States: Indian courts prohibit advocacy, considering it non-charitable for reason that they could not or should not decide if a change in law would be for the public benefit; American religious institutions and foundations can make no expenditures to influence legislation, and other charitable organisations can only make "insubstantial" expenditures. In Australia, Canada, England, France, Germany, Japan, Kenya, Mexico and Nigeria, advocacy is permitted on condition that it further the charitable, tax-privileged, authorised or general-interest purposes of registered organisations. That said: in England and France, there are limits to the share of resources that can be so devoted; in Mexico, advocacy cannot be at the behest of donors; and in Nigeria, certain areas of policy (e.g., those related to sexual orientation) are ruled out by law. There are no formal prohibitions or conditions on advocacy in Brazil, Italy, Portugal, Singapore and Sweden. In general, the treatment of lobbying follows that of advocacy, India being the exception. There, although advocacy is prohibited, lobbying is permitted on condition that the issues be tied to the organisations' charitable purpose and that the activity remain incidental.

Regulating private donations to political entities

Table 6.3 describes the regulatory treatment of private donations to political entities, using indicators that represent either a permissive stance tied to libertarianism and classical pluralism or a restrictive stance tied to egalitarianism and deliberative democracy. The indicators representing a permissive stance are: high or no limits on private donations to political candidates and parties from individuals, corporations and other entities; high or no limits on anonymous donations; high or no limits on third-party election spending; and limited or no public funding for election

Table 6.3 Regulatory treatment of political finance

Country	*Egalitarian/deliberative restrictive indicators*								*Libertarian/pluralist permissive indicators*						
	No or limited private donations to parties, candidates or political committees from:				*Significant public funding for parties or candidates, based on:*		*Limited or no spending by third parties*	*Limited or no anonymous donations*	*Private contributions with high or no limits from:*				*Limited or no public funding of parties or candidates*	*High or no limits on third party spending*	*High or no limits on anonymous donations*
	Candi-dates	*Individ-uals*	*Corpora-tions*	*other entities*	*votes, seats, flat amount*	*Donations, other*			*Candi-dates*	*Individ-uals*	*Corpora-tions*	*other entities*			
Australia					X[1]				X	X	X	X		X	X[2]
Brazil			X	X	X[3]			X[4]	X	X[5]				X	
Canada	X	X[6]	X[6]	X[6]		X[7]		X[8]						X[9]	
England								X[10]	X[11]	X[11]	X[11]	X[11]	X[12]	X[13]	
France	X	X[14]	X[15]	X[15]	X[16]			X[17]						X	
Germany				X[18]	X[19]	X[19]		X[20]	X	X[21]	X[22]	X[23]		X	
India									X[24]	X[25]	X[26]	X[27]	X	X	X[28]
Italy								X[29]	X[30]	X[31]	X[32]	X[33]	X[34]	X	
Japan					X[35]			X[36]	X[37]	X[38]	X[39]	X[40]		X	
Kenya					X[41]			X[42]	X[43]	X[44]	X[44]	X[45]	X[46]	X	
Mexico			X[47]	X[48]	X[49]		X[50]	X[51]	X	X[52]					
Nigeria									X	X[53]	X[53]	X[54]	X	X	X[55]
Portugal			X[56]	X[56]	X[57]		X[58]	X[58]		X[59]					
Singapore	X[60]			X[61]					X	X	X		X	X[62]	X[63]
Sweden					X[64]			X[65]	X[66]	X	X	X		X	
U.S.			X[67]	X[67]				X[68]	X[69]	X[69]	X[70]	X[70]	X[71]	X[71]	

1 Calculated as the total number of formal first preference votes received times the current electoral rate (set at AUD 2.829 for 2020). Electoral Legislation Amendment (Electoral Funding and Disclosure Reform) Act 2018.
2 Donations must be disclosed if above annually adjusted threshold (AUD 14,300 for 2020). Donors can avoid disclosure requirement by making multiple donations below the threshold.
3 Campaign Fund established by Law No. 13.487/2017 and Law No. 9.096/2018.
4 Law No. 9.504/1997 Article 28.
5 Limited to 10% of annual income (Law No. 13.165 29 September 2015).
6 Only natural persons who are Canadian citizens or permanent residents may donate to a registered party, a registered association, a nomination contestant, a candidate or a leadership contestant [Canada Elections Act 2000 Section 363(1)]. Annual contributions are limited to an amount that increases by CAD 25 yearly (the limit for 2020 is CAD 1,625). Contributions capped at CAD 1,275 receive a tax credit [Income Tax Act Section 42(2)].
7 Public funding covers 50% of the election expenses incurred by parties and 60% of those by candidates; these expenses otherwise financed by donations from natural persons [Canada Elections Act 2000 Sections 444(1), 477.74(2)].
8 Canada Elections Act 2000 Section 366(2).

9 CAD 350,000 overall, of which no more that CAD 3,000 can be spent for or against any candidate (Canada Elections Act 2000 Section 350(1)).
10 Parties and candidates must report the identities of donors to confirm they are among those "permissible" [Parties and Referendums Act 2000 Section 54(2)].
11 Political Parties and Referendums Act 2000 Article 54.
12 Parliament annually distributes £2M across parties for the purpose of policy development (https://www.electoralcommission.org.uk/who-we-are-and-what-we-do/financial-reporting/donations-and-loans/public-funding-political-parties accessed 20 September 2020).
13 Political Parties and Referendums Act 2000 Article 85.
14 Limit is €7,500 for a party, €4,600 for a candidate (Law No, 88.227 11 March 1988 Article 11.4). Contributions receive a tax credit.
15 Donations from legal persons, except other political parties, prohibited (Law No. 88.227 11 March 1988 Article 11.4).
16 Law No. 88.227 11 March 1988 Article 119.
17 Donors must be identified if donation exceeds €150 (Law No. 88.227 11 March 1988 Article 11.4).
18 Public benefit, benevolent or church-related nonprofit organisations prohibited (Political Parties Act Section 2).
19 Formula depends on number of votes received in last election and the donations up to €3,300 from individuals (Political Parties Act Section 18).
20 Donors must be identified if donation exceeds €500 and disclosed if annual total exceeds €10,000 [Political Parties Act Section 25(2,3)].
21 There are no limits to the donations from individuals, but the amount eligible for a deduction is capped at €1,650 (Income Tax Act Articles 10b).
22 Corporations must be headquartered in the European Union or be more than 50% owned by citizens of the European Union (Political Parties Act Article 2).
23 Trade unions not prohibited.
24 Contingent upon the candidate's campaign spending not exceeding prescribed limit [Representation of the People Act Sections 77, 123(6) and Conduct of Election Rules Section 90].
25 There is neither a limit to the donations from individuals nor a cap on the amount that can be deducted (Income Tax Act Section 80GGB).
26 There is neither a limit to the donations from corporations in existence for more than three years nor a cap on the amount that can be deducted (Companies Act Section 182, Income Tax Act Section 80GGC).
27 Trade unions not prohibited.
28 Parties and candidates not required to disclose total contributions.
29 Donors must be identified if donation exceeds €500 (Law No. 3/2019).
30 Candidates' contributions limited to €100,000, as for individuals' donations.
31 Donations from individuals are limited to €100,000, of which a cap of €30,000 can receive a credit of 26% (Legislative Decree No. 13 of 21 February 2014 Article 10).
32 Donations from corporations are limited to €100,000, of which a cap of €30,000 can receive a credit of 26% (Legislative Decree No. 13 of 21 February 2014 Article 11).
33 Trade unions or nonprofit organisations not prohibited.
34 Legislative Decree No. 149 of 28 December 2013.
35 Total funds calculated as ¥250 yen per capita are distributed among parties according to their number of Diet seats and their proportion of the total vote (Political Party Subsidies Act Articles 3, 7, 8).
36 Identity of donors must be disclosed for donations exceeding ¥50,000 [Political Funds Control Act 1948 Articles 12, 22(6)].
37 Contingent upon candidate's campaign spending not exceeding prescribed limit (Public Offices Election Act Article 194).
38 Donations from individuals are limited to ¥20M, of which a cap of 40% of taxable income exceeding ¥2,000 can be deducted [Political Funds Control Act Article 21–3(2)].
39 The limits for corporate donations range from ¥7.5M to ¥30M depending on its capitalisation (Political Funds Control Act Article 21–3).
40 The limits for trade union donations range from ¥7.5M to ¥30M depending on its membership (Political Funds Control Act Article 21–3).
41 Outside of an election, parties receiving at least 3% of the votes cast in the previous election and having no more than two-thirds of its registered office bearers of the same gender receive annual payments from a Political Parties' Fund, 80% of which are proportional to the distribution of votes across those parties (Political Parties Act 2011 Section 25).
42 Elections Campaign Financing Act 2013 Section 13.
43 Contingent upon candidate's campaign spending not exceeding prescribed limit (Election Campaign Financing Act 2013 Section 18).
44 No individual or corporate donor may donate more than 5% of a party's expenditures as recorded in the audited accounts of the previous year (Political Parties Act 2011, Section 28–2, 3). For an election

(*Continued*)

Table 6.3 (Continued)

campaign, no single course shall donate more than 20% of total contributions received by a party or candidate (Election Campaign Finance Act 2013 Section 12).

45 Trade unions or other organisations can contribute to a candidate or party with their written consent (Election Campaign Financing Act 2013 Section 15).

46 Parties or candidates receive no public funding (Election Campaign Financing Act 2013 Section 14).

47 General Law on Political Parties 2014 Articles 54.

48 Trade unions and religious or social organisations are among those that cannot contribute [Electoral Auditing Rules 2018 Article 401(1)].

49 Total funds to support political parties are calculated annually by multiplying the total number of citizens in a federal or local registry times 65% of the minimum wage there. Thirty percent of the total is allocated equally across the parties and 70% in proportion to the distribution of votes in the last election. In an election year, the amount is increased by 50% (Political Constitution of the United Mexican States 2016 Article 41; General Law on Political Parties 2014 Articles 51).

50 General Law on Electoral Institutions and Procedures 2020 Article 159.

51 General Law on Political Parties 2014 Articles 55, 56; Electoral Auditing Rules 2018 Article 121.

52 No individual may annually donate more than .5% of the expenditure ceiling from the previous election, with total contributions from individuals and candidates not exceeding 10% of that ceiling in an election year [General Law on Political Parties 2014 Articles 56(2)].

53 Corporations cannot donate to political parties [Companies and Allied Matters Act 2004 Section 38(2)]. Annual donations from individuals and corporations to candidates are limited to ₦1M. Individuals can donate to political parties, which must record their names and addresses if the donation exceeds ₦1M [Electoral Act 2010, Section 91(9), 93(2b)].

54 Nonprofit organisations – specifically, companies limited by guarantee – are an exception: they are prohibited from donating to political parties [Companies and Allied Matters Act 1990 Section 38(2)].

55 Parties are prohibited from anonymous donations, but not candidates (Electoral Act 2010 Sections 92, 93).

56 Donations from legal persons prohibited (Law No. 19/2003 20 June 2003 Article 8).

57 Law No. 19/2003 20 June 2003 Articles 5, 16, 17, 18.

58 Law No. 19/2003 20 June 2003 Article 8.

59 Law No. 19/2003 20 June 2003 Articles 7, 16(4). Donations from individuals are limited to 25 times the annually adjusted "social support index" for a party, or 60 times for an election campaign or a presidential candidate. For 2020, the index was €438.81.

60 Candidates can receive donations only from the party for which they are standing (Political Donations Act 2011 Section 2).

61 "Permissible donors" comprise individuals who are citizens of Singapore and at least 21 years old, and Singapore-controlled corporations (Political Donations Act 2011 Section 2).

62 Trade unions are an exception: political objects are not among those on which they can spend (Trade Unions Act 1992 Section 2).

63 Parties and candidates can accept anonymous donations under SD 5,000, allowing multiple donations below threshold (Political Donations Act 2011 Section 2).

64 Parties receive a fixed grant for each seat in the Rikstag won in the last two elections to support their secretariats, as well as basic and supplementary support for their Parliamentary activities: the former being a fixed amount for each party receiving at least 4% of the votes cast, the latter a per-seat amount that is higher if the party is not represented in the government (Act on State Support for Political Parties 8 December 1972 Sections 3, 6, 8).

65 Anonymous donations are prohibited above 0.05 price base amount (Act on Transparency of Party Financing 15 February 2018 Section 9). For 2020, the annually price-adjusted price base amount was 47,300kr.

66 The Act on Transparency of Party Financing 15 March 2018 outlines the reporting of donations but places no limitations on their source or amount.

67 Contributions to parties or candidates by corporations or trade unions are prohibited (Title 2 U.S. Code Section 441b).

68 Candidates, political parties and political action committees must identify donors for contributions above USD 200 (United States Code Title 2 Paragraph 434b).

69 There is no ceiling on the aggregate contributions of a single donor to different candidates, national party committees and independent third parties (*McCutcheon v FEC* [2014] 572 US 185).

70 There is no ceiling on the contributions of corporations and trade unions to independent and uncoordinated political action committees (*Citizens United v FEC* [2009] 588 US 310; *SpeechNow.org v FEC* [2010] 599 F3d 686).

71 For presidential campaigns: the federal government will match up to USD 250 of an individual's total contributions to an eligible primary candidate; each major political party receives USD 4M (circa 1974 adjusted for inflation) to finance its national nominating convention, and the candidate for each major party is eligible for USD 20M for campaigning on condition of refusing private contributions – and offer declined in recent history (Title 26 US Code Sections 9001 to 9042).

campaigns. Conversely, the indicators representing a restrictive stance are: no or limited private donations to political candidates and parties from individuals, corporations and other entities; limited or no anonymous donations; limited or no third-party election spending; and significant public funding for election campaigns.

The stances of Canada and France appear egalitarian and restrictive. Corporate and trade union donations are prohibited; donations from individuals receive a tax credit and are limited, albeit at higher level in France; and public funding for campaigns is significant. The only exception is the amount of spending by unaffiliated non-party (i.e., third-party) political outfits: Canada sets a relatively high limit (CAD 350,000), whereas France imposes no limits. In contrast, the stances of England, India, Italy, Nigeria, Singapore and the United States appear libertarian and permissive. Public funding for campaigns is limited or nonexistent, and spending by third parties is unlimited. Individual and corporate donations are permitted, with no limits in England, India, Singapore and the United States (for individuals' aggregate donations and for corporate donations to political action committees) and high limits in Italy and Nigeria (for donations to candidates, not parties). The stances of the other countries appear intermediate. Those of Brazil, Mexico and Portugal tilt toward the egalitarian: although the limits on donations from individuals are high, and there are no limits on third-party spending in Brazil, all three countries prohibit corporate donations and provide significant public funding. In comparison, the stances of Australia, Germany, Japan, Kenya and Sweden tilt toward the libertarian. All five countries provide significant public funding; however, they set high or no limits on the spending of third parties and donations from individuals and corporations.

Comparing regulatory approaches toward charitable organisations and political entities

In regulating the use of private monies to finance political activities, do governments take a similar approach regardless of whether those activities are performed by charitable organisations or political entities? To address that question, Table 6.4 categorises and compares the regulatory stances of each country, inferring these from the assignment of indicators in Table 6.2 and the assignment of gradations in Table 6.3 for which the treatment of electioneering receives greatest weight. The range of stances follows a rough continuum running from a strong to weak restrictive stance and from a weak to strong permissive stance.

Similar approaches appear for Canada, Italy and Singapore. In regulating both political entities and charitable organisations, Canada adopts a relatively strong restrictive stance: it encourages but limits the donations of individuals to political entities, prohibits corporate donations and offers substantial public funding for campaigns; in addition, it prohibits charities from electioneering but permits advocacy and lobbying on condition that they further the organisations' charitable purpose. Italy and Singapore adopt a relatively strong permissive stance in both contexts: they permit and place no limits on the donations of individuals and corporations to political entities and provide no or little public funding for campaigns; in addition, they place slight or no formal limits on the political activities available to registered nonprofit third-sector entities or Institutions of a Public Character. In contrast, very different approaches appear for India and the United States. In regulating political entities, both adopt a relatively strong permissive stance. But in regulating charitable organisations, they adopt a relatively strong restrictive stance: both prohibit electioneering but permit lobbying on condition that it further the organisations' political purpose and remain insubstantial; India prohibits advocacy, whereas the United States permits it conditionally. For the other 11 countries, varying degrees of difference appear between the stances they take toward regulating the use of private monies to finance the political activities of charitable organisations and political entities. Some countries – such as

Table 6.4 Regulatory stance toward privately-financed political activities of political entities (P) and charitable organisations (C)

Country	*Regulatory stance*			
	Egalitarian/deliberative restrictive		*Libertarian/pluralist permissive*	
	Strong	*Weak*	*Weak*	*Strong*
Australia		C	P	
Brazil		P	C	
Canada	P C			
England			C	P
France	P		C	
Germany	C		P	
India	C			P
Italy				P C
Japan		C	P	
Kenya	C		P	C
Mexico	C	P		
Nigeria		C		P
Portugal		P		C
Singapore				P C
Sweden			P	C
U.S.	C			P

France and Portugal – take a more permissive stance toward charitable organisations, whereas others – such as Germany and Nigeria – take a more restrictive stance.

6 Implications for the regulation of privately financed political activities

For all but three of the sample countries, the stance toward regulating the political activities performed by charitable organisations differs from the stance toward regulating the private donations received by political entities. Such differences suggest that what matters most to those governments is not the general task of regulating the use of private monies to finance political activities. Accounting for this on a country-by-country basis exceeds the scope of this chapter. However, a range of considerations could conceivably contribute to differences between the regulatory stances – considerations apart from the opposing pairs of political philosophies and models of democracy that, if applied consistently, would result in the stances being similar.

By way of illustration, governments might take a relatively more restrictive stance toward charitable organisations if they interpret charitable purposes and activities as being inherently different from political ones or if they envisage political activities performed by charitable organisations as harming charitable purposes – positions found in the charity finance literature, as outlined in part 2. Alternatively, governments might perceive civil society and the charitable organisations within it as rivalling its own abilities to mobilise and represent the interests and values of citizens. In recent decades, for example, multiple countries have introduced laws and regulations that restrict the operations of civil society and curtail international funding – allegedly to protect and enforce state sovereignty against foreign influence, promote accountability, co-ordinate sources of aid and prevent money laundering (Rutzen 2015). Or it could be that governments perceive the prominence of very rich philanthropists as generating forms of philanthropy that are "disruptive" or plutocratic – ones that threaten democracy by enabling the rich to have a disproportionate say in which public purposes receive attention and which public programs receive resources (Horvath and Powell 2016; Saunders-Hastings 2018). Such governments might see a need "to craft, through various policies and social norms, a framework that domesticates plutocrats to serve democratic ends" (Reich 2019, 28) – a framework that could include restricting the political activities that charitable organisations perform.

On the other hand, governments might take a relatively more permissive stance toward charitable organisations if they perceive them as advancing democracy. Theorists of civil society typically present it as playing two broad roles: that of producing and delivering goods and services which complement those of the market and state and that of assembling and expressing the collective priorities and interests of individuals, groups and communities which compose society (Rathgeb Smith and Grønbjerg 2006, 223–238). Those who focus on the latter role typically refer to Tocqueville's 19th-century portrayal of American voluntary associations encouraging and enabling individual citizens to find common cause, as well as joint opportunities for them to promote the social good (Clemens 2006, 207–217). Thus, governments might take a more permissive stance toward charitable organisations if they perceive them as facilitating democracy – a role that could be strengthened by giving them a greater voice in the processes by which collective decisions are structured, debated and made.

Finally, it might be that governments are simply unwilling or unable to define clear policy goals and act on them comprehensively – whether such goals are to promote particular pairs of political philosophies and models of democracy, respond to certain incompatibilities between charitable organisations and political activities, suppress the abilities of charitable organisations to undercut state authority or strengthen their abilities to engage citizens in democratic processes. The individuals who set the policy agenda, or design and implement regulations, might variously seek to please certain stakeholders, pursue personal advantage or resist change. Their information and knowledge might be incomplete or inaccurate. And their administrative capabilities might be limited, such that any reforms are piecemeal, patching new elements onto previous regimens or stretching existing instruments and procedures to handle goals or conditions for which they were not meant. In other words, governments might exercise a low level of policy design (Howlett and Mukerjee 2014). If so, then they might be inconsistent in how they approach regulating the use of private monies to finance the political activities of charitable organisations and political entities simply because they have neither the incentives, knowledge nor capabilities to do otherwise.

As noted in the introduction, the use of private monies to finance political activities has received international attention given the possible risks to democracy (OECD 2016). Regulating that use effectively and comprehensively is made more complex by the wide range of entities and organisations that compose the broader system able to perform political activities and finance them privately (Issacharoff and Karlan 1999). Several of the 16 countries included in this chapter evidently seek to restrict the use of private monies to finance political entities by prohibiting donations from legal persons, limiting those from natural persons and providing public funding. For Canada and to some extent Mexico, their restrictive stances toward political entities are matched by those toward charitable organisations, suggesting that their regulatory approach applies consistently across the broader political system. But this is not the case for France, Portugal and to some extent Brazil: although their stances toward political entities are restrictive, those toward charitable organisations are relatively permissive, leaving open a channel for private monies to flow into the broader political system. Several of the countries evidently do not seek to restrict the use of private monies to finance political entities. For Italy, Singapore and to some extent England, their permissive stances toward political entities are matched by those toward charitable organisations, again suggesting consistency in their regulatory approach. However, should any of those countries pursue regulatory reform to restrict the use of private monies to finance politics, then – following the hydraulics arguments of Issacharoff and Karlan – their attentions should extend beyond political entities to include charitable organisations as well.

Notes

1 The title of this status varies across countries. For the sake of brevity, I refer to the organisations and their purposes and activities as "charitable" – despite this term having legal meaning only in common law jurisdictions.
2 For a comparison of practices across eight countries circa 2012, see Carmichael (2016).
3 Parts 2 and 3 draw from the more detailed account in Carmichael (2020).
4 The contending philosophies – egalitarianism and libertarianism – distinguish the Supreme Courts of Canada and of the United States in their decisions over the constitutionality of political finance regulations (Carmichael 2020, n 110).
5 Within the political finance literature, see BeVier 1994, 1277; Sullivan 1997, 671–675; Redish 2001, 125–128; Smith 2001, 109–121; Samples 2006, 31–40. Within the charity finance literature, see Chisolm 1990, 320–337; Carroll 1992, 254–259; Klapach 1999, 513–519; Guinane, 2007; Leff 2009, 685–696; Brunson 2011, 145–147; Galston 2011, 903–911, 918–928; Weitzel 2011, 157–158; Fresco 2012, 3026–3045.
6 Within the political finance literature, see BeVier 1994, 1274–1275; Sullivan 1997, 681–682; Wright 1976, 1015–1017. Within the charity finance literature, see those cited previously who counter the argument that charitable organisations harm political purposes by performing political activities.
7 Within the political finance literature, see Wright 1976, 1017–1021; Sunstein 1993, 241–252.
8 Within the political finance literature, see those cited previously who hold political equality paramount.
9 Within the charity finance literature, see those cited previously who support the argument that charitable organisations harm political purposes by performing political activities.

References

Achen, C.H. and Bartels, L.M. (2016). *Democracy for Realists: Why Elections Do Not Produce Responsive Government.* Princeton: Princeton University Press.

Ackerman, B. and Ayers, I. (2002). *Voting with Dollars: A New Paradigm for Campaign Finance.* New Haven: Yale University Press.

Ansolabehere, S., de Figueiredo, S.M. and Snyder, Jr., J.M. (2003). Why is there so little money in U.S. politics? *The Journal of Economic Perspectives* 17, 105–130.

Audi, R. (1993). The place of religious argument in a free and democratic society. *San Diego Law Review* 30, 677–702.

BeVier, L.R. (1994). Campaign finance reform: specious arguments, intractable dilemmas. *Columbia Law Review* 94, 1258–1280.

Briffault, R. (1999). Public funding and democratic elections. *University of Pennsylvania Law Review* 148, 563–590.

Brunson, S.D. (2011). Reigning in charities: using an intermediate penalty to enforce the campaigning prohibition. *Pittsburgh Tax Review* 8, 125–170.

Buckles, J.R. (2007). Not even a peep? The regulation of political campaign activity by charities through federal tax law. *University of Cincinnati Law Review* 75, 1071–1111.

Buckles, J.R. (2008). Is the ban on participation in political campaigns by charities essential to their vitality and democracy? A reply to Professor Tobin. *University of Richmond Law Review* 42, 1057–1127.

Cafardi, N.P. (2005). Saving the preachers: the tax code's prohibition on church electioneering. *Duquesne Law Review* 50, 503–544.

Carmichael, C.M. (2016). The fiscal treatment of philanthropy from a comparative perspective. In: T. Jung, S.D. Phillips and J. Harrow, eds. *The Routledge Companion to Philanthropy.* London: Routledge, 244–259.

Carmichael, C.M. (2020). We should talk: framing and connecting the legal literatures on charity finance and campaign finance. *King's Law Journal* 31, 402–425.

Carroll, A.B. (1992). Religion, politics and the IRS: defining the limits of tax law controls on political expression by churches. *Marquette Law Review* 76, 217–263.

Chisolm, L.B. (1990). Politics and charity: a proposal for peaceful coexistence. *The George Washington Law Review* 58, 308–367.

Churchill, S. (12 June 2013). Why NGOs are jittery over public benefits organizations act. *Pambazuka News* <https://www.pambazuka.org/governance/why-ngos-are-jittery-over-public-benefits-organizations-act> retrieved 20 September 2020.

Clark, E. (1960). The limitation on political activities: a discordant note in the law of charities. *Virginia Law Review* 46, 439–466.

Clemens, E.S. (2006). The constitution of citizens: political theories of nonprofit organisations. In: W.W. Powell and R. Steinberg, eds. *The Nonprofit Sector: A Research Handbook*, 2nd edition. New Haven: Yale University Press, 207–220.

Cmar, T. (2005). Toward a small donor democracy: the past and future of incentive programs for small political contributions. *Fordham Urban Law Journal* 32, 443–505.

Colinvaux, R. (2012). The political speech of charities in the face of *Citizens United*: a defense of prohibition. *Case Western Reserve Law Review* 62, 685–756.

Crimm, N.J. and Winer, L.H. (2013). The law bans on political campaign speech by houses of worship: inappropriate government censorship and intrusion on religion. *Journal of Law, Religion and State* 2, 101–136.

Dahl, R.A. (1956). *A Preface to Democratic Theory*. Chicago: University of Chicago Press.

de Figueiredo, J.M. and Garrett, E. (2005). Paying for politics. *Southern California Law Review* 78, 591–667.

Dessingue, D. (2001). Prohibition in search of a rationale: what the tax code prohibits; why: to what end? *Boston College Law Review* 42, 903–929.

Dunn, A. (1999). Charity as a political option for the poor. *Northern Ireland Legal Quarterly* 50, 298–317.

Dunn, A. (2008). Charities and restrictions on political activities: developments by the Charity Commission for England and Wales in determining the regulatory barriers. *International Journal of Not-for-Profit Law* 11, 51–66.

Dworkin, R. (1996). The curse of American politics. *The New York Review of Books* 43, 19–24.

Dworkin, R. (2016). *Is Democracy Possible Here? Principles for a New Political Debate*. Princeton: Princeton University Press.

Fiss, O.M. (1996). *Liberalism Divided*. Boulder: Westview Press.

Foley, E.B. (1994). Equal-dollars-per-voter: a constitutional principle of campaign finance. *Columbia Law Review* 94, 1204–1257.

Fowler, E.F., Franz, M.M. and Ridout, T.N. (2016). *Political Advertising in the United States*. Boulder: Westview Press.

Fresco, M. (2012). Getting to "exempt!": putting the rubber stamp on section 501(c)(3) political activity prohibition. *Fordham Law Review* 80, 3015–3055.

Galle, B. (2013). Charities in politics: a reappraisal. *William and Mary Law Review* 541, 1561–1632.

Galston, M. (1993). Lobbying and the public interest: rethinking the internal revenue code's treatment of 501(c)(3) legislative activities. *Texas Law Review* 71, 1269–1354.

Galston, M. (2011). When statutory regimes collide: will *Citizens United* and *Wisconsin Right to Life* make federal tax regulation of 501(c)(3) campaign activity unconstitutional? *Journal of Constitutional Law* 13, 867–930.

Garnett, R.W. (2001). A quiet faith? Taxes, politics and the privatisation of religion. *Boston College Law Review* 42, 771–803.

Garrett, E. and Smith, D.A. (2005). Veiled political actors and campaign disclosure laws in direct democracy. *Election Law Journal* 4, 295–328.

Guinane, K. (2007). Wanted: a bright-line test defining prohibited intervention in elections by 501(c)(3) organisations. *First Amendment Law Review* 6, 142–170.

Habermas, J. (2006). Religion in the public sphere. *European Journal of Philosophy* 14, 1–25.

Hardin, R. (2004). Representing ignorance. *Journal of Social Philosophy and Policy* 21, 76–99.

Hasen, R.L. (1996). Clipping coupons for democracy: an egalitarian/public choice defense of campaign finance vouchers. *California Law Review* 84, 1–59.

Held, D. (2006). *Models of Democracy*, 3rd edition. Stanford: Stanford University Press.

Hellman, D. (2011). Money talks but it isn't speech. *Minnesota Law Review* 95, 935–1002.

Horvath, A. and Powell, W.W. (2016). Contributory or disruptive: do new forms of philanthropy erode democracy? In: R. Reich, C. Cordelli and L. Bernholz, eds. *Philanthropy in Democratic Societies: History, Institutions, Values*. Chicago: University of Chicago Press, 87–122.

Houck, O.A. (2003). On the limits of charity: lobbying, litigation, and electoral politics by charitable organisations under the internal revenue code and related laws. *Brooklyn Law Review* 69, 1–89.

Howlett, M. and Mukerjee, I. (2014). Policy design and non-design: towards a spectrum of policy formulation types. *Politics and Governance* 2, 57–71.

Issacharoff, S. (2010). On political corruption. *Harvard Law Review* 124, 118–142.

Issacharoff, S. and Karlan, P.S. (1999). The hydraulics of campaign finance reform. *Texas Law Review* 77, 1705–1738.

Klapach, J.S. (1999). Thou shalt not politic: a principled approach to section 501(c)(3)'s prohibition of political campaign activity. *Cornell Law Review* 84, 504–542.

Leff, B.M. (2009). "Sit down and count the cost": a framework for constitutionally enforcing the 501(c)(3) campaign intervention ban. *Virginia Tax Review* 28, 673–731.

Mazo, E.D. (2014). The disappearance of corruption and the new path forward for campaign finance. *Duke Journal of Constitutional Law and Public Policy* 9, 259–313.

McConnell, M.W. (1999). Five reasons to reject the claim that religious arguments should be excluded from democratic deliberation. *Utah Law Review* 639–657.

Mill, J.S. (2003). *On Liberty*. New Haven: Yale University Press.

OECD. (2016). *Financing Democracy: Funding of Political Parties and Election Campaigns and the Risk of Policy Capture*. Paris: OECD Publishing.

OECD. (2020). *Taxation and Philanthropy*. OECD Tax Policy Studies No. 27. Paris: OECD Publishing.

Ortiz, D.R. (1998). The democratic paradox of campaign finance reform. *Stanford Law Review* 50, 893–914.

Overton, S. (2004). The donor class: campaign finance, democracy, and participation. *University of Pennsylvania Law Review* 153, 73–118.

Parachin, A. (2016). Reforming the regulation of political advocacy by charities: from charity under siege to charity under rescue? *Chicago-Kent Law Review* 91, 1047–1078.

Raskin, J. and Bonifaz, J. (1994). The constitutional imperative and practical superiority of democratically financed elections. *Columbia Law Review* 94, 1160–1203.

Rathgeb Smith, S. and Grønbjerg, K.A. (2006). Scope and theory of government-nonprofit relations. In: W.W. Powell and R. Steinberg, eds. *The Nonprofit Sector: A Research Handbook*, 2nd edition. New Haven: Yale University Press, 221–242.

Rawls, J. (1971). *A Theory of Justice*. Cambridge, MA: Belknap Press.

Rawls, J. (2005). The idea of public reason revisited. *The University of Chicago Law Review* 64, 765–807.

Redish, M.H. (2001). *Money Talks: Speech, Economic Power, and the Values of Democracy*. New York: New York University Press.

Reich, R. (2019). Philanthropy in the service of democracy. *Stanford Social Innovation Review* Winter, 26–33.

Rutzen, D. (2015). Civil society under assault. *Journal of Democracy* 26, 28–39.

Sacks, A. (1960). The role of philanthropy: an institutional review. *Virginia Law Review* 46, 516–538.

Salamon, L.M. and Toepler, S. (2015). Government-nonprofit cooperation: anomaly or necessity? *Voluntas* 26, 2155–2177.

Samples, J. (2006). *The Fallacy of Campaign Finance Reform*. Chicago: The University of Chicago Press.

Sarbanes, J.P. and O'Mara III, R. (2016). Power and opportunity: campaign finance reform for the 21st century. *Harvard Journal on Legislation* 53, 1–38.

Saunders-Hastings, E. (2018). Plutocratic philanthropy. *Journal of Politics* 80, 149–161.

Simon, J., Dale, H. and Chisolm, L. (2006). The federal tax treatment of charitable organisations. In: W.W. Powell and R. Steinberg, eds. *The Nonprofit Sector: A Research Handbook*, 2nd edition. New Haven: Yale University Press, 267–306.

Smith, B.A. (2001). *Unfree Speech: the Folly of Campaign Finance Reform*. Princeton: Princeton University Press.

Sullivan, K.M. (1997). Political money and freedom of speech. *UC Davis Law Review* 30, 663–690.

Sunstein, C.R. (1993). *Democracy and the Problem of Free Speech*. New York: The Free Press.

Tobin, D.B. (2007). Political campaigning by churches and charities: hazardous for 501(c)(3)s, dangerous for democracy. *The Georgetown Law Journal* 95, 1313–1363.

Totten, M. (2007). The politics of faith: rethinking the prohibition on political campaign intervention. *The Stanford Law and Policy Review* 18, 298–323.

Trotter, R.W. (2012). Lobbying by religious non-profit entities: its impact, theoretical inconsistency, and how to prevent it. *The Dartmouth Law Journal* 10, 12–55.

Vallier, K. (2018). Religion and politics. In: J. Brennan, B. van der Vossen and D. Schmidtz, eds. *The Routledge Handbook of Libertarianism*. London: Routledge, 390–404.

Weitzel, P. (2011). Protecting speech from the heart: how *Citizens United* strikes down political speech restrictions on churches and charities. *The Texas Review of Law and Politics* 16, 155–174.

Wolpe, D. (19 February 2017). A rabbi defends the Johnson amendment. *The Atlantic* <https://www.theatlantic.com/politics/archive/2017/02/a-rabbi-defends-the-johnson-amendment/516981/> retrieved 20 September 2020.

Wright, J.S. (1976). Politics and the constitution: is money speech? *Yale Law Journal* 85, 1001–1021.

Wright, J.S. (1982). Money and the pollution of politics: is the first amendment an obstacle to political equality? *Columbia Law Review* 82, 609–645.

7

IS IT REALLY A CHARITY? MEMBERSHIP-BASED ENTITIES AS CHARITIES

The Australian experience

Ann O'Connell

> The application of the word 'charity' in this connection is not confined to the objects that come within the quaint catalogue of the Statute of Elizabeth, but applies also to cases analogous, and what seems to be more alarming, to cases analogous to cases which have been adjudged to be analogous, thereby making the development of the law perpetual . . . the pursuit of these analogies obviously requires caution and circumspection.
>
> (Commissioners of Inland Revenue v Yorkshire Agricultural Society *(1927) 13 TC 58: 65* per Rowlatt J)

1 Introduction

The not-for-profit (NFP) sector in Australia, as elsewhere, is incredibly diverse. In addition to diversity related to purpose, there are significant differences related to size, legal form, reliance on volunteers and/or employees and geographic coverage. Those differences are also reflected in charities, an important subgroup of NFPs. Another possible difference relates to whether the entity has members. Some NFPs have 'members' and some do not. Indeed, some NFPs are deliberately established and operated for the benefit of members, for example, social clubs and societies, and might appropriately be referred to as 'member benefit organisations'. Some charities also have members, but a distinguishing feature of charity is that the charity must provide 'public benefit'. If there are any benefits to members of the charity, they must be incidental to the public benefit. This means that although having members does not preclude the entity from being a charity, it does raise the question about whether those members are receiving benefits and, if so, whether those benefits are incidental.

The federal taxing statute, the Income Tax Assessment Act 1997 (ITAA 1997), provides a number of tax concessions to charities, but it also provides concessions to many NFPs that are not charities (non-charitable NFPs). Given that legislative scheme, it is interesting to consider why entities that appear to be primarily for the benefit of members, and perhaps eligible for income tax exemption, would seek to be classified as charities and why courts or regulators would extend charitable status to entities that appear to be covered by specific legislative provisions. This chapter considers some different types of membership-based NFPs and asks whether

 DOI: 10.4324/9781003139201-9

they are appropriately 'charities' for federal, and perhaps state and territory, tax purposes. The Australian experience demonstrates that having information about tax-preferred entities, as now occurs as a result of a searchable register, allows questions to be raised about eligibility and, indeed, suitability for those concessions.

This chapter will proceed as follows: Section 2 will consider the different types of NFP membership-based entities. Section 3 will consider the legislative context for the granting of tax concessions to charities and to non-charitable NFPs. Section 4 will consider what is required to be a charity under the Charities Act 2013 (Cth) (Charities Act). Section 5 will consider three case studies of membership-based entities that have sought relief as charities – agricultural associations, business associations and professional associations. Section 6 will draw some conclusions and offer some suggestions for reform going forward.

2 Different types of membership-based entities

One of the problems of examining membership-based entities that receive tax concessions is that there is little data collected on this characteristic, and, indeed, little has been written about the significance of a NFP entity having members. Neither the Australian charities regulator, the Australian Charities and Not-for-profits Commission (ACNC), or the Australian Taxation Office (ATO) collect data on how many entities have members. Analysis from the United States suggests that approximately 33% of all NFPs have members and that this increases to 60% if religious congregations are included (Tschirhart 2006). A report of the Charity Commission for England and Wales in 2004, based on a survey of registered charities, found that 44% of charities surveyed had members (Charity Commission for England and Wales, 2004, p. 44). The report also noted that 80% of charities surveyed had voting members (ibid: 5), meaning that the membership had some say in the governance of the charity.[1] The charities that had both voting and non-voting members used a variety of terms to refer to non-voting members, such as 'sponsors', 'friends' and 'associate members' (ibid: 44). There are currently approximately 140,000 non-charitable NFPs in Australia in receipt of some tax concessions[2] and 58,800 charities,[3] but it is not possible to say what percentage of those entities are membership-based.[4] It is however clear that some entities, in receipt of tax concessions will be membership based. Indeed, this is contemplated by the governance standards set out in the Australian Charities and Not-for-profits Regulations 2013, which mandate disclosure by the entity to members.[5]

A NFP entity may have members or may be formed without members. It seems likely, however, that the majority of non-charitable NFPs will have members, such as sporting clubs and community service organisations. On the other hand, it seems likely that many registered charities will not have members, such as hospitals and educational institutions. Although there is no data available on either non-charitable or charitable NFP membership, two factors may give an indication, that is, the type of charity and the legal form of the entity. According to the latest Australian Charities and Not-for-Profits Commission Charities Report (2018), the most significant types (or sub-types) of charities are religious entities, educational entities and welfare and public benevolent institutions (PBIs). While many religious entities will have congregations, educational entities and welfare entities are unlikely to. On the other hand, other types of entities such as cultural, environmental, human rights, animal protection and reconciliation-focused entities are more likely to have members. In relation to legal form, unincorporated associations[6] are likely to have members; incorporated entities (either companies limited by guarantee or incorporated associations) may generally choose whether to have members beyond some statutory minimums, and trusts will not have members.

Membership structures do ensure some accountability of the entity and its officers. This can be an issue for NFP entities where the membership does not have the same sort of interest as shareholders in a company and may not, therefore, provide the same level of accountability. Where charities have a choice about ownership structure, it may be that adopting a closely held membership structure will avoid the need to comply with ACNC Governance Standard 2 relating to accountability to members. This suggests that there are tensions between accountability and the additional costs that this imposes.

Of more significance is whether the membership confers benefits on members, with or without also conferring governance authority. It is possible to identify at least three scenarios: where membership does not confer any benefits (e.g., where the member is effectively a donor or supporter of the entity), where membership confers minor benefits (e.g., access to a newsletter or reduced entry to events) and where membership confers significant benefits (e.g., a social club where members receive reduced prices on goods and services).

Some common types of NFP membership-based entities include the following:

- Community service organisations (CSOs),
- Professional and business associations,
- Non-distributing co-operatives,
- Self-help groups and
- Sporting and recreational clubs.

It is useful to consider how these different types of entities might be taxed, either as charities or as non-charitable entities.

Community service organisations

A CSO is the term used to describe an organisation that is income tax exempt under s 50–10 of the ITAA (1997). The exemption applies to a 'society, association or club established for community service purposes (except political or lobbying purposes)'. The exemption was included in the legislation in 1990, with the Explanatory Memorandum noting that 'many entities are not charitable, and so such bodies as the traditional community service clubs – Apex, Rotary, Lions, Zonta, Quota and the like have not qualified for exemption' (Explanatory Memorandum, Taxation Laws Amendment Bill (No 2) 1990 (Cth): 20). The Explanatory Memorandum addressed what was intended to be covered by the exemption:

> The words 'for community service purposes' are not defined but are to be given a wide interpretation. The words are not limited to those purposes beneficial to the community which are also charitable. They extend to a range of altruistic purposes. The words would extend to promoting, providing or carrying out activities, facilities or projects for the benefit or welfare of the community, or of any members of the community who have particular need of those activities, facilities or projects by reason of their youth, age, infirmity or disablement, poverty or social or economic circumstances.
>
> *(ibid: 21)*

The Explanatory Memorandum also noted that organisations such as the Country Women's Association of Australia and its constituent Associations would be exempt under the provision. It might be thought that the reason these types of entities would not be charities is because they also provide benefits to their members. Despite that – and based on the examples in the Explanatory Memorandum – the government wanted to extend tax exemption to them but did not deem them charities.

Professional and business associations

An association, whether incorporated or unincorporated, will be a company for tax purposes (ITAA 1997: s. 995-1)[7] and, in the absence of an exemption, will generally be liable to pay tax on taxable income even though it is NFP. There is no specific exemption from income tax for professional associations, although employer and employee associations are exempt (ibid: s. 50–15) (the exemption also covers trade unions). These types of entities may be able to rely on the principle of mutuality to exclude payments received from members from taxable income.[8] Some professional associations have been able to become registered charities (for example, the Law Institute of Victoria is an ACNC-registered charity), but the state and territory tax concessions have generally not been extended (see business association cases subsequently, Section 5).

Non-distributing co-operatives

Co-operatives are companies for tax purposes (ibid: s. 995–1). Distributing co-operatives can either pay members franked dividends or claim a deduction for payments to members (Income Tax Assessment Act 1936 (Cth) (ITAA 1936): ss. 117–120). A non-distributing co-operative (e.g., a child care co-operative) may be a charity if it meets the definition in the Charities Act (2013, see Section 4). The case of Co-operative Bulk Handling Limited (CBH), discussed in the following, considers the notion of a non-distributing co-operative.

Self-help groups

Self-help groups are likely to be unincorporated associations formed primarily for the benefit of members. Whatever the legal form, such an entity will be a company for tax purposes (ITAA 1997: s. 995–1). Self-help groups were described in the *Report of the Inquiry into the Definition of Charities and Related Organisations* (*Charities Definition Inquiry Report*) as:

> [M]ade up of and controlled by people who are directly affected by the particular disadvantage, discrimination or unmet need that draws the members together.
>
> *(Sheppard, Fitzgerald and Gonski 2001: 126)*

Examples given were groups formed by people directly or indirectly affected by a disease or disability but could also include a community centre or neighbourhood house which through mutual support assists people seeking to overcome some form of economic or social disadvantage (ibid). The Charities Definition Inquiry Report recognised that many such groups would have difficulty meeting the 'public benefit' requirement of being a charity and recommended that if certain conditions were met, such entities should be regarded as having met the public benefit test (ibid: 127). This recommendation finds form in the Charities Act s 10, which provides that if the entity has an open and non-discriminatory membership and the entity is made up of, and controlled by, individuals who are affected by the disadvantage, discrimination or need, the requirement in s 5 that a purpose of an entity be for the public benefit can be disregarded.

A self-help group will therefore need to be NFP and demonstrate a charitable purpose but will not be required to demonstrate that there is public benefit. Other self-help groups, for example, a public speaking club that seeks to help to improve the self-esteem of members, will not qualify, as it will not be able to demonstrate the requisite charitable purpose (ibid: 126).

Sporting and recreational clubs

Sporting and recreational clubs, societies or associations will, regardless of legal form, be companies for tax purposes (ITAA 1997: s. 995-1). Some clubs may be income tax exempt under s 50–45 of the ITAA 1997, that is, a society, association or club established for the encouragement of animal racing, art, a game or sport or literature or for musical purposes. Such clubs are unlikely to be charities, as their purposes are not recognised as charitable. It has been argued that amateur sport should be recognised as charitable in line with the position in England, Wales and Scotland (Batrouney and Lee 2018: 41–44). Many clubs that do not come within s 50–45, for example, social clubs, will be able to rely on the principle of mutuality[9] to exclude payments from members in their taxable income.

3 Tax treatment of charities and non-charitable NFPs

The notion of what constitutes a charity will be considered in more detail in Section 4. This part considers the tax concessions that are available to charities and to NFPs that are not charities.

Charities

A registered charity, that is, a charity as defined in Charities Act s 5, that is registered under the Australian Charities and Not-for-Profits Commission Act 2012 (Cth) s 25–5 (ACNC Act), will be entitled to a range of Commonwealth tax concessions. The most significant, for the purposes of membership entities,[10] are:

- income tax exemption,
- refunds of franking credits, and
- fringe benefits tax (FBT) concessions.

Income tax exemption arises under s 50-5 of the ITAA 1997. A registered charity will be exempt from income tax on all income – ordinary income and statutory income (ITAA 1997: s. 50-51). Ordinary income includes income from business and investment income, for example, interest, rent and royalties.[11] Statutory income includes amounts that are income under a statutory provision (ibid: s. 6-10), for example, capital gains (ibid: pts. 3-1 and 3-3) and dividends (ITAA 1936 (Cth): s. 44). Unlike many other countries, trading or business income is also exempt. There are a number of conditions that must be satisfied: for example, the 'in Australia' condition (ITAA 1997: s. 50-50(1)(a)).

A registered charity may also be entitled to refunds of franking credits (ibid: divs. 67, 207), where the entity receives dividends from a corporation that has paid sufficient tax to enable a shareholder to claim a credit for the tax paid. The receipt of a franked distribution[12] by a tax-paying shareholder would allow the franking credit to be offset against any tax liability (ibid: s. 207-220). In the case of tax-exempt entities that have no liability to pay tax, the franking credits could potentially be wasted. However, 'charities', but not other NFPs unless they are deductible gift recipients under div 30 of the ITAA 1997 (ibid: ss. 67-25, 207-115), are entitled to claim a refund of the amount of tax paid by the distributing company. Many philanthropic trusts that invest corpus to produce a return in order to make grants rely on the refunds of franking credits as a major source of revenue, but other, probably larger, charities also derive significant benefit from this concession. The ability of charities to claim these refunds is likely a major reason a NFP entity might seek to become a charity.

A further concession available to income tax-exempt entities that have employees arises under the Fringe Benefits Tax Assessment Act 1986 (Cth) (FBTAA). A subgroup of entities are entitled to an exemption from FBT: PBIs, health promotion charities, public and NFP hospitals and public ambulance services are exempt from the tax, subject to caps (FBTAA: ss. 5E, 57A). There are also a number of concessions for religious practitioners and religious entities (ibid: s. 57). Most registered charities that do not come within the exemption are, however, entitled to a rebate of 47% of the FBT otherwise payable, subject to caps (ibid: s. 65J). Some charities are excluded from the exemption and the rebate, including charities that are considered government-controlled entities, such as universities (ibid: s. 65J(1)).

A charity, as that term applies at common law (see Part 3), may also be entitled to tax concessions at the state and territory level. Perhaps the most significant of the concessions is the exemption from payroll tax – a tax imposed on the employer's total payroll.[13] Some charities, notably universities, are generally excluded from the exemption (perhaps reflecting the fact the federal government rather than state government, has fiscal responsibility for universities), and there are also requirements relating to the nature of the work being performed.[14] There are also other state and territory tax concessions for charities (subject to some exceptions) such as from land tax,[15] municipal rates,[16] and stamp duties.[17]

The legislative scheme in Australia since the first income tax legislation has been to have a list of eligible types of entities that are income tax exempt, including but not limited to charities.[18] It has been suggested that this may have been because the drafters assumed that charity would have its ordinary meaning (*Chesterman v Federal Commissioner of Taxation* (1923) 32 CLR 362). That approach was disabused by the Privy Council in 1925 (*Chesterman v Federal Commissioner of Taxation* (1925) 37 CLR 317), but the legislature continued to spell out the types of entities that were eligible, including some types that would clearly come within the technical meaning of charity – such as religious entities and public educational institutions.

Non-charitable NFPs

As noted previously, a range of other types of NFP entities that would generally not qualify as charities are also entitled to exemption from income tax, including:

- CSOs (ITAA 1997: s. 50-10);
- employer and employee associations (ibid: s. 50-15);
- associations for the promotion of primary and secondary resources and tourism (ibid: s. 50-40); and
- sporting, cultural and recreational associations (ibid: s. 50-45).

According to the ATO, there are approximately 200,000 NFPs that are eligible for income tax exemption under div 50 (ATO-supplied data – see n 2).

Non-charitable NFPs that are not income tax exempt under div 50 of the ITAA 1997 may be able to rely on the common law principle of mutuality. For example, a social club that receives monies from members either as membership dues, or for goods and services, will not be required to include those receipts as assessable income. A non-profit company that earns less than $A417 will not pay tax (Income Tax Rates Act 1986 (Cth): s. 23(6)). There may also be a specialist regime available, for example, for co-operatives (ITAA 1936: ss. 117–120) or small credit unions (ibid: s. 23G). Being income tax exempt also allows an entity to access FBT concessions, notably the FBT rebate of 47% of FBT payable (FBTAA: s. 65J).

However, the other concession available to charities, refunds of franking credits (ITAA 1997: divs. 67, 207), is not available to most non-charitable NFPs. As noted previously, this may provide an incentive to seek charitable status.

Some state and territory concessions, such as the payroll tax exemption, are only available to charities. This may be another reason a NFP entity could wish to be treated as a charity. For example, in Victoria, the payroll tax exemption is available to 'a religious institution; a public benevolent institution or a non-profit organisation having as its whole or dominant purpose a charitable, benevolent, philanthropic or patriotic purpose (but not including a school or an educational institution' (Payroll Tax Act 2007 (Vic): s. 48(1)). Interestingly, some states and territories have responded to the expansion of fourth-head charities by restricting the concessions. This is discussed further in the following.

4 Meaning of charity for federal tax purposes

The meaning of the term 'charity' differs for federal tax purposes and for state and territory tax purposes. This is because in 2013, the federal government enacted a statutory definition in the Charities Act. The states and territories still rely on the common law meaning of the term. Despite this, there is a fair amount of commonality, since the aim of the Charities Act was said to be to restate the common law,[19] but the legislature also took the opportunity to 'modernise' the definition (Explanatory Memorandum, Charities Bill 2013 (Cth) 2013: 3). To be a charity either under the statute or at common law, the entity must:

- be not for profit,
- have a charitable purpose and
- be for the public benefit.

i Not-for-profit requirement

This requirement is common to the Charities Act and the common law. The requirement is also common to non-charitable and charitable entities. The term 'NFP' is not defined, although in 2012, there was a proposal to include a definition in the tax legislation (Tax Laws Amendment (Special Conditions for Not-for-Profit Concessions) Bill 2012 (Cth)). A decision not to proceed was made following a change of government (Sinodinos 2013). In any event, the NFP requirement is fairly easily satisfied. The entity simply needs to demonstrate that it does not distribute any profit or surplus to persons or entities associated with the entity. It is usual to include standard non-distribution clauses in the governing documents (Commissioner of Taxation 1997).

Although charities and non-charitable NFPs are required to have non-distribution requirements, as Dal Pont notes, distributions of profits may occur other than as a result of a formal distribution of profit, for example, as payments to management or staff or to suppliers or associates (2017). This is significant where an entity has members, as it is necessary to consider whether there are informal distributions to those members.

ii Charitable purpose

Charities at common law, and under the Charities Act, must have a charitable purpose. In both cases, the purpose or purposes must be exclusively charitable. At common law, this is said to require the charitable purpose be the *sole* purpose. This means that if the entity has another purpose which is not charitable, it will not be a charity. This apparently strict requirement has been ameliorated to some extent by an acceptance that the entity may have purposes that are merely incidental or ancillary to its main charitable purpose. Where a charity has more than one purpose, it is therefore necessary to consider whether any of its purposes are non-charitable and, if so, whether any non-charitable purpose can appropriately be described as 'incidental or ancillary'.

The recognised categories of purpose at common law are: relief of poverty, advancement of education, advancement of religion and other purpose beneficial to the community that are 'within the spirit and intendment of the Preamble to the Statute of Elizabeth 1601' (*Commissioners for Special Purposes of the Income Tax v Pemsel* [1891] AC 531) (*Pemsel*). The latter category, sometimes referred to as the 'fourth head of charity' (*Aid/Watch Inc v Federal Commissioner of Taxation* (2010) 241 CLR 539: 556–557, para. 46), is the one most often relied on by membership entities seeking to establish charitable status.

The Charities Act expanded the categories of 'charitable purposes' beyond health, education, welfare and religion to include culture, reconciliation, human rights, security and safety, animal welfare and the environment. It also includes:

> (k) any other purpose beneficial to the general public that may reasonably be regarded as analogous to, or within the spirit of, any of the [stated] purposes.
>
> *(Charities Act: s. 12(1))*

The list of charitable purposes in the Charities Act was compiled over a considerable period of time, starting with the *Charities Definition Inquiry Report* in 2001 (Sheppard, Fitzgerald and Gonski 2001). Interestingly, although the Inquiry considered one option of including a purpose of 'the promotion of community development to enhance social and economic participation', there was no express reference to promotion of agricultural, business or professional associations. Paragraph (k) serves the same purpose as the fourth head at common law and allows courts, and presumably the regulator, to determine that even though a purpose is not expressly referred to, it may be charitable, if it is reasonably analogous to the listed purposes. The 'fourth head' has been relied on in a number of cases involving membership-based NFP entities that do not fall within the recognised categories.

iii Public benefit

The third requirement for an entity to be a charity is that it needs to satisfy the requirement of public benefit. This requires identification of benefit or benefits and consideration of whether the benefits satisfy the public element. Where the relevant charitable purpose is para. (k), there seems to be some overlap between the requirements. Dal Pont's view is that the extent to which the phrase 'beneficial to the community' can be equated with the phrase 'public benefit' is unclear (2017: para. 11.4). What is clear is that under both phrases, there must be 'benefit', and the benefit must be available to the 'public'.

Certain purposes are presumed to be for the public benefit. This is stated in s 10 of the Charities Act and appears to go further than the common law presumption that applied to the 'public' element rather than the 'benefit' element. Where the public benefit cannot be presumed, it must be demonstrated. In *Grain Growers Ltd v Chief Commissioner of State Revenue* [2015] NSWSC 925, Black J did not believe it was necessary to require proof of benefit despite counsel for the Commissioner for State Revenue arguing that it was required. Black J concluded that:

> I can, without specific proof, infer that agricultural activity benefits society generally, and Australian agricultural activity benefits Australian society generally, and no evidence was led to suggest that the benefit that has previously existed in such activity has ceased to exist.
>
> *(ibid: para. 27)*

Black J did, however, refer to evidence of the value of the grain industry to the Australian economy, including that the Australian grain industry contributes approximately $15 billion to Australia's exports and approximately $26 billion to Australia's gross domestic product, presumably on an annual basis (ibid).

The benefit element

According to s 10 of the Charities Act, the 'benefit' can be tangible or intangible but must be identifiable and must take into account any possible detriment. One commentator, Professor Rossman, has considered the benefit of a type of entity in the United States called a 'regional economic development organisation', which he describes as 'running venture capital funds, recruiting companies to major metropolitan areas, providing technical assistance to business owners, and in a multitude of other ways facilitating targeted economic growth in urban, suburban, and rural areas throughout the country' (2014: 1457). Although Rossman accepts that these entities might have social value, he is critical of the acceptance of indirect or remote benefits, which he describes as 'trickle down' benefits, as such entities are recognised as charities even though they are providing direct assistance to for-profit businesses (ibid: 1459). A number of recent cases appear to adopt this 'trickle down' notion of benefit.

The public element: public or a section of the public

At common law, the public element has been interpreted to include 'a sufficient section of the community to amount to the public' (*Lloyd v Federal Commissioner of Taxation* (1955) 93 CLR 645: 662, 667, 670). Under the Charities Act, the benefit must be available to the public or a section of the public (Charities Act: s. 6). The sub-heading in s 6 refers to the benefit being 'widely available'. The reference to a section of the public means that it is necessary to identify whether a group of individuals constitutes a section of the public or whether they are a group of private individuals. This has been said to require that the section of the public must be sufficiently defined and identifiable by some quality of a public nature. In any event, the cases in the next part do not rely on the membership constituting a section of the public but rather argue that the benefit that arises from the promotion of agriculture, or from a business or professional association, is available to the whole community – a version of the trickle-down argument noted previously.

Any private benefit must be incidental

The public benefit requirement for charity is sometimes expressed as prohibiting private profit or private benefit. This will exclude entities that may be formed for otherwise charitable purposes where the profits accrue to private individuals, for example, for-profit schools or for-profit hospitals. It will also exclude clubs or societies where the benefit is only available to the members, for example, a social club. In this way, the requirement of public benefit is linked to the notion that private profit or gain is inconsistent with the notion of charity.

In Taxation Ruling 2011/4 (2011: para. 258), the Commissioner notes that:

> Private benefits that are no more than incidental or ancillary to a purpose of benefiting the community do not detract from the charitable status of an institution. *Benefits are incidental if they are a minor by-product of activities undertaken to carry out the institution's purpose. They are ancillary if they are conferred only as a means of achieving an institution's charitable purpose.* The greater the scope to provide private benefits, the greater the concern that the purpose is not to benefit the public, but to provide those private benefits.
>
> *(emphasis added)*

In this regard, it is important to emphasise that the test is not whether the private benefits are minor in nature but whether they are *incidental* to achieving the main (charitable) purpose. However, the size of the benefits may indicate something about the purpose of the entity.

5 Stretching the concept of charity – case studies

There have been a number of cases recently dealing with whether different types of membership-based entities are charities in Australia. These cases relate to: agricultural associations, business associations and professional associations.

a Agricultural associations

The importance of agriculture in Australia is of long standing.[20] Tax relief for agricultural associations in Australia can be traced to a specific exemption being included in the Income Tax Assessment Act 1922 (Cth) (ITAA 1922). It provided an exemption for:

> [A]ny society or association not carried on for the purposes of profit or gain to the individual members thereof, established for the purpose of promoting the development of the agricultural, pastoral, horticultural, viticultural, stock-raising, manufacturing or industrial resources of Australia.
>
> (ITAA 1922*: s. 14(1)(j)*)

This was in addition to the existing exemption for the income of a religious, scientific, charitable or public educational institution (ibid: s. 14(1)(d)), which suggests that the legislature did not believe that agricultural associations would be charities. The income tax exemption for agricultural and similar associations is now in s 50-40, item 8.2 of the ITAA 1997, which provides an exemption for:

> a society or association established for the purpose of promoting the development of any of the following Australian resources:
>
> (a) agricultural resources;
> (b) horticultural resources;

(c) industrial resources;
(d) manufacturing resources;
(e) pastoral resources;
(f) viticultural resources;
(g) aquacultural resources;
(h) fishing resources.

The exemption is subject to a 'special condition' that the society or association be 'not carried on for the profit or gain of its individual members' (ITAA 1997: s. 50-40(1) item 8.2). The fact that this is now a condition rather than the initial requirement may dilute its significance.

It is not clear when agricultural associations started to be recognised as *charities* in Australia. Until 2000, entities self-assessed their entitlement to income tax exemption and, generally, it would not have made much difference whether the entity was a charity or exempt under the specific exemption. In 2012, the ACNC grandfathered all of the charities that had been endorsed by the ATO. The ACNC Register lists a number of entities that have the stated purpose of 'promoting the development of agricultural resources'. For example, there are more than 140 entities with the words 'agriculture' or 'agricultural' in their name, many of which run annual shows. But there are also entities that provide significant benefits to their members and are nevertheless recognised as charities. It is interesting to consider how this has come about.

The main case that has been relied on for recognising societies and associations for the promotion of agriculture in Australia as charities is the United Kingdom Court of Appeal case of *Commissioners of Inland Revenue v Yorkshire Agricultural Society* [1928] 1 KB 611. The case involved a society formed in 1837 to hold an annual show for the exhibition of farming stock, implements and so on and for 'the general promotion of agriculture'. The Society sought an exemption from income tax with respect to income from its investments – this was because the exemption in the United Kingdom does not apply to trading or business income. At the first instance, Rowlatt J decided against the Society, essentially on the basis that the society was formed for the private enjoyment of the founders and members rather than for charitable purposes (*Commissioners of Inland Revenue v Yorkshire Agricultural Society* (1927) 13 TC 58)). In reaching his conclusion, his Honour accepted that agriculture was of 'great importance' and 'should be promoted', but he cautioned that to be a charity, there must be 'a real public charitable object' (ibid: 67). The Court of Appeal took a different view and concluded that the 'right interpretation to be given to this society is that it has been formed for improvement of agriculture as a whole' (*Commissioners of Inland Revenue v Yorkshire Agricultural Society* [1928] 1 KB 611, 612).

Several comments can be made about this case. First, it should be noted that the cases relied on by the Court of Appeal were wills and trust cases, not taxation cases. It should also be noted that the cost to revenue in the United Kingdom of granting the exemption is much less, as it only applies to investment income and trading income of charities is subject to tax. Finally, it can be noted that the same facts are capable of quite different interpretation. Rowlatt J, contrary to the view of the Court of Appeal, decided that the members of the society were promoting their own businesses ((1927) 13 TC 58, 68)).

There are few Australian cases dealing with these types of entities under the income tax legislation, possibly because of the specific exemption in the income tax legislation since 1922 for societies and associations engaged in 'promotion of agriculture'. There was an obiter reference to the promotion of agriculture in the case of (*Incorporated Council of Law Reporting (Qld) v Federal*

Commissioner of Taxation (1971) 125 CLR 659, a case concerned with whether the production of law reports came within the fourth head of charity under the *Pemsel* case. Barwick CJ noted:

> Agriculture partakes of that fundamental social quality which can give a charitable nature to a trust or purpose relating thereto which is beneficial to the community.
>
> *((1971) 125 CLR 659:* 669*)*

The High Court also referred to this purpose in a case dealing with a bequest in (*Royal National Agricultural and Industrial Association v Chester* (1974) 3 ALR 486). The bequest was to establish an event for pigeon racing. The High Court acknowledged that the society was itself charitable ((1974) 3 ALR 486: 487). But the Court concluded that:

> [T]he breeding of pigeons for racing cannot, either by analogy or by reason of the character of the activity itself, be said to be of benefit to the community in a sense within the preamble.
>
> (ibid: 489)

The Federal Court returned to the issue of agricultural associations in (*Federal Commissioner of Taxation v Co-operative Bulk Handling Ltd* (2010) 189 FCR 322) (*FCT v CBH*). The issue in this case was not whether CBH was a charity but whether it was entitled to income tax exemption under ITAA 1997 s 50-40, item 8-2, that is, whether it was 'a society or association established for the purpose of promoting the development of Australian agricultural resources; and not carried on for the profit or gain of its individual members'. This is significant because it means that there were only two matters being considered: whether CBH had the purpose of 'promoting the development of Australian agricultural resources' and whether CBH was established 'for the profit or gain of its individual members' (*FCT v CBH*: 335, para. 59). It did not need to consider whether 'the promotion of the development of agricultural resources' was a charitable purpose, that is, whether it was 'beneficial to the community' or for the 'public benefit'. The Commissioner had previously issued private rulings in 1971 (and 1996) that accepted that clauses in CBH's constituent documents preventing distributions to members, including on winding up, meant that CBH was entitled to the exemption under s 50-40 (ibid: 330–331, paras. 41–43). In 2008, the Commissioner reviewed the entitlement of CBH to the exemption, arguing that much had changed since 1971 and that the size and scope of the activities of CBH now meant, inter alia, that CBH was not 'established for the purpose of promoting the development of Australian agricultural resources' and that CBH did not satisfy the requirement that it was 'not carried on for the profit or gain of its individual members' in their capacity as members (ibid: 328–329, para. 34).

In relation to the first issue, the majority, Mansfield and McKerracher JJ, noted that CBH had significant revenue and a number of commercial subsidiaries (ibid: 332, para. 48) but concluded that the primary objective of CBH was promoting the development of the Western Australian grain industry, thereby advancing Australia's competitiveness in grain export markets (ibid: 340, para. 76). In relation to the second issue, the majority noted that members would 'gain' from the activities of CBH but said that this was also the case for non-member growers (ibid: 344, para. 95). Further, they noted that where an entity satisfied the first limb (the 'broader community objective'), the fact that there were 'incidental gains or benefits' to members did not disentitle the entity to the exemption (ibid: 343–343, para. 94).

Siopis J dissented (ibid: 350–355, paras. 117–153). He noted that the purpose of promoting agriculture was not included in the objects listed in the constituent documents of

CBH (although it is now: Co-operative Bulk Handling Ltd Rules 2021: cl. 3.2(a)) and that the emphasis in the documents (and in operations) was on conducting the business of bulk handling as its core activity (*FCT v CBH*: 350, para. 123). Further, he noted that CBH is the parent company of a sophisticated international conglomerate which, through subsidiaries, holds investments in flour milling operations in South East Asia as well as shipping and container transportation (ibid: 351, para. 130). That is, CBH is concerned with conducting a business rather than having a broader purpose of promoting Australian agriculture (ibid: 352, para. 132). In his view, the business was carried on for the financial gain of its members despite the fact that some non-members also used the services (ibid: 355, para. 152). Siopis J noted that 90% of customers were members and accounted for 95% of business (ibid: 355, para. 151).

Perhaps what is most surprising about the majority judgment is the conclusion that any benefits to members were 'incidental'. It seems that the fact that there were some non-members that used the services, as well as members, was important in this regard (ibid: 349, para. 112), but, as Siopis J said, the vast majority of business was conducted with and for members. In any event, CBH was retrospectively endorsed by the ATO in 2014 as a *charitable institution*, with effect from 1 July 2000 (CBH 2019: 71).

The recognition of CBH as a charity, now a charity registered by the ACNC, seems to stretch the notion of charity in a number of ways. First, CBH runs a business that is an end in itself. The size of the business is remarkable – in 2019, CBH had gross revenue of $748 million and a 'surplus' of $101 million (CBH 2020). This puts it in the very highest category of registered charities by size – 'extra-large' – with only 0.4% of charities having revenue in excess of $100 million (ACNC 2018: 4). CBH also has assets of $1.9 billion (CBH 2020). It has 15 wholly owned subsidiaries and 2 associated companies (ibid). Of course, many charities run businesses and then apply the profits or surplus towards charitable objects; for example, Word Investments Ltd applied the profits to advance a religious purpose (*Federal Commissioner of Taxation v Word Investments Ltd* (2008) 236 CLR 204), and universities apply their profits to advance education, but CBH does not apply its revenue for a charitable purpose. Second, the labelling of this significant business enterprise as a charity blurs the lines between the charitable and the for-profit sector. The ATO has released data about the non-payment of tax of many of Australia's largest companies, and in 2013–14, CBH was the second largest company to pay no tax (Janda and Anderson 2016).[21] Third, CBH wholly owns a large number of commercial subsidiaries that do pay tax (CBH 2019: 79). However, when they distribute those taxed profits as franked dividends to CBH, CBH is entitled to claim refunds of franking credits as a charity (ITAA 1997: divs. 67, 207), meaning that the profits of the commercial subsidiaries may be effectively tax free. Fourth, CBH has contemplated changing its structure and potentially becoming a listed company. In 2016, a company offered to acquire the interests of members of CBH for $1 billion in cash and scrip (Shepherd 2016). The fact that such a bid was entertained by the board suggests that it is clearly looking at ways to maximise the value of the company rather than to promote agriculture. Fifth, although, as a company limited by guarantee, CBH does not pay dividends, it has operated a program, now called the Grower Patronage Rebate Program, since June 2013 (and a variation on this program in the 2009–2011 income years) where amounts are distributed to growers (including the small percentage of non-member growers) to effectively reduce the amount they pay for the service CBH provides (Grain Central 2019). Although this would not be unusual in a distributing co-operative, it seems anomalous that these distributions would not indicate that there is a gain or benefit to members that is more than incidental.

In 2017, the Productivity Commission was critical of the granting of charitable tax concessions to agricultural trading companies. The Productivity Commission recommended that:

> The Australian Government should legislate to exclude agricultural commodity trading companies from being granted charity status and receiving the associated tax concessions.
>
> *(Productivity Commission 2016: 44)*

b Business association cases

Starting in 2012, there were a number of cases involving state-based Chambers of Commerce claiming eligibility for various state tax concessions. In *Chamber of Commerce and Industry Inc (WA) v Commissioner of State Revenue* (2012) 82 SR (WA) 204 (*CCI v CSR*), the Administrative Tribunal of Western Australia was asked to consider whether the Chamber of Commerce and Industry was a 'charitable body or organisation' for the purposes of the exemption from payroll tax.[22] The legislation defined a charitable body or organisation as one that was 'established or carried on for charitable purposes' (Pay-Roll Tax Assessment Act 2002 (WA): glossary). The Chamber argued that its activities were carried on mainly for the promotion of trade and commerce in Western Australia – a purpose that it argued was beneficial to the wider community, not simply its members.

The Tribunal considered cases such as (*Commissioners of Inland Revenue v Yorkshire Agricultural Society* [1928] 1 KB 611) as well as more recent cases, such as *FCT v CBH* (which, as noted, was not a case about charity). Chaney J accepted that the Chamber devoted extensive resources to the provision of services to its members and to business generally (*CCI v CSR*: 229, para. 90). However, his Honour concluded that the Chamber's main purpose was the promotion of trade and commerce in Western Australia, not serving the private interests of its members (ibid: 229–31, paras. 90–99). The decision in *CCI v CSR* is a first instance decision and therefore not binding on courts in other jurisdictions, although such decisions may be persuasive.[23]

The decision in *CCI v CSR* encouraged similar organisations in other jurisdictions to claim exemptions with mixed results. In (*Queensland Chamber of Commerce and Industry Ltd v Commissioner of State Revenue* (2015) 108 ACSR 334), the issue was whether the Queensland Chamber of Commerce and Industry (QCCI) was entitled to an exemption from payroll tax. The case did not consider whether QCCI was a charitable institution; rather, it appears to have been accepted that QCCI was a charitable institution (ibid: 340, para. 18).[24] The case was concerned with whether 'under its constitution . . . no amount [was] to be distributed, paid or transferred by way of bonus, dividend or other similar payment to its members' (Taxation Administration Act 2001 (Qld): s. 149C(5)). The Commissioner argued that these requirements were not satisfied because there were no express provisions in QCCI's constitution to that effect ((2015) 108 ACSR 334: 340, para. 21). Despite that, Jackson J held that QCCI was entitled to registration as a charitable institution (ibid: 351, para. 94).

In (*South Australian Employers' Chamber of Commerce & Industry Inc v Commissioner of State Taxation* [2017] SASC 127), the Chamber was claiming an exemption from payroll tax as a charitable entity. Blue J concluded that it was not a charity. He accepted that advancement of trade or commerce (or agriculture) can be a charitable purpose, referring to *Commissioners of Inland Revenue v Yorkshire Agricultural Society* [1928] 1 KB 611 ([2017] SASC 127: 37–38, paras. 123–124). He also noted that an entity would not be disqualified if it provided incidental benefits to its members (ibid: 49, para. 163). However, if its main purpose was to benefit members, the entity would not be charitable (ibid). After reviewing the constitution of the Chamber [which he noted was amended in 2012 'to enhance the prospects of the Chamber obtaining tax advantages' (ibid: 7, para. 32)] and its activities, he concluded that the dominant purpose was to advance the interests of its members – South Australian business entities (ibid: 61, para. 217). Blue J recognised that this result was at odds with *CCI v CSR* but distinguished that case on the facts, noting that the South Australian Chambers' policy advocacy activities were of less significance than its counterpart in Western Australia and that the member services provided by the South Australia Chamber were too substantial to be considered ancillary to any charitable purpose of the Chamber (ibid: 64, paras. 231–233, 78, para. 298). The Full Court of the Supreme Court of South Australia affirmed the decision (*South Australian Employers' Chamber of Commerce and Industry Inc v Commissioner of State Taxation* [2019] SASCFC 125). It should be noted that following these decisions, several jurisdictions amended their legislation to exclude 'trade, industry or commerce' bodies (as well as some other types of entities) from the charitable tax concessions. These changes are discussed in Section 6.

c Professional associations

A professional association is a body of persons engaged in the same profession that is formed to promote the interests of its members in the profession. Professional associations often act as a peak body for professionals working in the same or similar fields, representing the interests of members to government and the community. These associations may control the ability to act in a profession to members who have satisfied certain requirements. They will typically assist members through ongoing professional development and seek to maintain standards within a profession, exercising quality control and carrying out research. Although the nature of the entity and the activities it engages in will vary, a professional association, invariably, has as one of its purposes the promotion of the interests of its members.

The case that is often referred to as authority for income tax exemption for professional associations is a United Kingdom decision, (*Commissioners of Inland Revenue v Forrest* (1890) 15 App Cas 334), concerning a civil engineers association. The case was concerned with an exemption from tax which applied to 'property which, or the profits or income whereof' that were 'applied for any purpose connected with any religious persuasion, or for any charitable purpose, or for the promotion of education, literature, science, or the fine arts' ((1890) 15 App Cas 334: 337). The Institution of Civil Engineers (ICE) was incorporated by Royal Charter in June 1828, and its 'objects' were stated to be 'for the general advancement of mechanical science, and more particularly, for promoting the acquisition of that species of knowledge which constitutes the profession of a civil engineer' (ibid: 345). The issue was whether the Institution was established for the promotion of science. There was no discussion about whether the Institution might also be charitable. A majority in the House of Lords concluded that the entity was a scientific institution. In 1931, the status of ICE was again considered, this time under the Income Tax Act 1918 (UK) which provided an exemption to an entity that was formed 'for charitable purposes only' in ([1932] 1 KB 149). Although there was not much discussion of the term 'charitable', it was noted that the fact 'that the promotion of science is a charitable object is not disputed' ([1932] 1 KB 149: 177).

In 1952, the House of Lords considered whether a professional medical association was a charity in (*Royal College of Surgeons of England v National Provincial Bank Ltd* [1952] AC 631);

however, this was not a tax case but a case concerned with whether a bequest was charitable and therefore valid. The House of Lords held that:

> All indications point to the object of the College being the advancement of knowledge and skill necessary for surgery and not the advancement of the professional position of its individual members.
>
> *([1952] AC 631: 661)*

In 1943, the Australian High Court considered whether the Royal Australasian College of Surgeons was entitled to income tax exemption not as a charity but as a scientific institution under ITAA 1936 s 23(e) (now s 50-5 item 1.3 of the *ITAA 1997*) (*Royal Australasian College of Surgeons v Federal Commissioner of Taxation* (1943) 68 CLR 436). The High Court unanimously decided that the College was a scientific institution and did not need to consider whether it was a charity. The Royal Australasian College of Surgeons is now a registered charity.

In 2008, in (*Victorian Women Lawyers' Association Inc v Federal Commissioner of Taxation* (2008) 170 FCR 318), the Federal Court was asked to consider whether the Victorian Women Lawyers' Association Inc (VWL) was entitled to income tax exemption either as a charity or as a community services organisation. The case was heard by French J just prior to taking up his appointment as Chief Justice of the High Court. French J noted that under the fourth head, he was required to find a purpose that was beneficial to the public and analogous to the spirit and intendment of the Preamble, noting that this required some direct and general benefit to the community. He also noted the need to find a public benefit and not just the creation of private benefits. After considering the constituent documents of the association and its activities, he found them to be charitable, commenting that VWL:

> [W]as established to overcome a well-known social deficit, namely the substantial under-representation of women in the legal profession, in its upper reaches and in the judiciary.
>
> *(ibid: 352, para. 148)*

He noted the activities of the Association, including the social and networking functions – which would normally mark an association as being for the benefit of members, but said that 'they were . . . directed to the larger object and in many cases to a larger audience, the legal profession in Victoria' (ibid: 352, para. 149). One reading of the case is that French J was so impressed by the 'worthy' purpose that he was prepared to overlook the fact that the members did receive benefits in the form of career advancement. VWL is now a federally registered charity.

Finally, in 2015, in (*Law Institute of Victoria v Commissioner of State Revenue* [2015] VSC 604), a professional association representing the state's lawyers, which at the time of the case had 18,120 members and more than 100 staff, argued that it was entitled to an exemption from payroll tax as a NFP entity with a sole or dominant charitable purpose. Digby J concluded that the nature of the regulatory and membership activities meant that the Law Institute of Victoria (LIV) could not be charitable. He also noted that the considerable amounts of money generated by the regulatory and membership activities suggested they could not be 'minor, ancillary, incidental, supplemental or subsidiary' to charitable objects. It is of interest to note that LIV was and is a registered charity for federal tax purposes. Digby J noted this but said it provided 'no assistance' because:

> [T]hat recognition and registration was achieved pursuant to a separate and distinct framework and criteria.
>
> *([2015] VSC 604: 40, para. 130)*

6 Conclusions and possible solutions

Consideration of these three case studies raises a number of issues. First, they demonstrate that membership-based entities have at least the possibility of 'private' benefits. This is not necessarily true in all cases – members may receive no benefit and may perform important oversight functions in relation to the entity and its officers. But membership should at least raise a red flag that should be investigated to see if there is private benefit. A second issue concerns the judicial function and perhaps the role of a regulator tasked with determining whether the entity is a charity or is otherwise eligible for tax relief. There are really two sub-issues here: first, although the requirements for eligibility are clear, there is a level of discretion for the decision-maker as to whether those requirements are met. This is particularly the case with the fourth head of charity, where the test of 'beneficial to the community' is so broad that almost any worthwhile purpose could fall within it. A second sub-issue in relation to determining eligibility is that the use of wills cases to determine eligibility for tax relief results in an expansion of the categories of charity, even though the relevant policy considerations are quite different. A third issue is that the doctrine of precedent, and what might be described as 'creeping assumptions', has blurred the lines between for-profit and NFP entities. The initial case discussed, involving the Yorkshire Agricultural Society (*Commissioners of Inland Revenue v Yorkshire Agricultural Society* [1928] 1 KB 611), involved a small society in the United Kingdom holding agricultural shows, with very little taxable income, performing what might be viewed as educational activities, but has led to a very large and profitable entity, CBH, being found eligible for tax relief as a non-charitable entity (*Federal Commissioner of Taxation v Co-operative Bulk Handling Ltd* (2010) 189 FCR 322) that then somehow became a registered charity eligible for additional tax relief. That case also demonstrated how difficult it is to remove a tax concession once it has been granted. A fourth issue relates to the absence of tax policy analysis in relation to the concessions. Tax concessions are equivalent to a government spending program, and it is legitimate to have regard to the 'cost' of those concessions. For example, the significant revenue of CBH (and its subsidiaries) should be a matter of legitimate concern to decision-makers in determining whether such an entity is providing public benefits that would justify those concessions. Similarly, when LIV applied for an exemption from Victorian payroll tax (*Law Institute of Victoria v Commissioner of State Revenue* [2015] VSC 604), it should have been a legitimate concern that LIV had more than 100 employees and that the cost of exempting such an entity was relatively high. By contrast, the amount of revenue forgone in the Yorkshire Agricultural Society case (*Commissioners of Inland Revenue v Yorkshire Agricultural Society* [1928] 1 KB 611) and in the VWL case (*Victorian Women Lawyers' Association Inc v Commissioner of Taxation* (2008) 170 FCR 318) was relatively small. In none of these cases was there any consideration of the underlying tax policy issue. Finally, the cases demonstrate a growing disparity concerning the federal government and the states and territories on the meaning of charity. This is likely to result in uncertainty and potentially increased compliance costs for entities that operate across jurisdictions.

These three case studies demonstrate that although the requirements for charity can be clearly enunciated, the application of the tests by judges and regulators is subjective and that if the decision-maker accepts that the purpose is 'worthy' or even worthwhile, they may overlook the possibility of private benefits arising to members. This may require the tests for charity to be made more rigorous. Three possible ways of seeking to ensure that charities do not provide benefits to their members could be:

i Changing the definition of charity for tax purposes to include benevolence or altruism,
ii Requiring membership-based entities to demonstrate altruism/public benefit, or
iii Excluding certain membership-based entities from concessions (as has occurred in some states and territories).

i Benevolent or altruistic charity

The idea of restricting the notion of charity to those entities that are directed at helping others is not new. It is likely what the legislatures had in mind in colonial times and early in the Federation, when the concessions were granted to 'public benevolent institutions' and 'public charities' as well as religious and public educational institutions. The current position is that PBIs receive some tax concessions that are not available to other charities, that is, deductible gift recipient status and the FBT exemption.

A similar sentiment was expressed by the *Charities Definition Inquiry Report*. The Report recommended that the public benefit test be strengthened by requiring that the dominant purpose of a charitable entity must be altruistic (Sheppard, Fitzgerald and Gonski 2001: rec. 7). The Report noted that the dictionary meaning of that term is 'unselfish concern for the welfare of others' or 'regard for others as a principle for action'. By including altruism or benevolence in the definition of charity, many of the entities that are in reality member serving would be removed from the notion of charity. Of course, this would not preclude the grant of tax exemption if a case could be made.

ii A requirement to demonstrate public benefit

A precedent for requiring certain entities to demonstrate public benefit can be found in the United States. The Internal Revenue Service (IRS) imposes a requirement on 'charitable hospitals' that, to qualify as income tax exempt, a hospital must:

- demonstrate that it provides benefits to a class of persons that is broad enough to benefit the community, and
- operate to serve a public rather than a private interest (IRS 2020).

The inclusion of this requirement (termed the 'Community Benefit' requirement) did not stem from concern about membership interests but rather because of concern that doctors might establish hospitals that treated only their own patients.[25] IRS Revenue Ruling 69–545 (1969) provides the following factors that demonstrate community benefit, including:

- operating an emergency room open to all, regardless of ability to pay;
- providing hospital care for all patients able to pay, including those who pay their bills through public programs such as Medicaid and Medicare;
- using surplus funds to improve facilities, equipment and patient care; and
- using surplus funds to advance medical training, education and research.

The interesting feature of such a test is not so much what is required but that the hospital (or other charity) has the onus of establishing that it meets the public benefit requirement.

iii Excluding some membership-based entities from concessions

Following the decision in 2012 granting charitable status to the Chamber of Commerce and Industry in Western Australia (*CCI v CSR*, 2012), several jurisdictions enacted legislation excluding certain entities from state and territory tax concessions. For example, in Western Australia, the definition of 'charity' excludes a 'relevant body' which is defined as:

- an industrial association;
- a professional association; or
- a body that promotes trade, industry or commerce (Pay-Roll Tax Assessment Act 2002 (WA): s. 42A).

The term 'promotes trade, industry or commerce' is defined to include 'carrying out an undertaking a purpose of which includes the promotion of, or the advocacy for, trade, industry or commerce, whether generally or with respect to any particular kind of trade, industry or commerce' (ibid: glossary).

Similar provisions have been enacted in the Australian Capital Territory (Taxation Administration Act 1999 (ACT): s. 18B) and in the Northern Territory (Revenue and Other Legislation Amendment Act 2015 (NT): s. 48B). In each of these jurisdictions, it is possible to apply to the commissioner for a determination that the organisation is a charity 'within the first three heads' set out in the *Pemsel* case. This effectively requires the entity to demonstrate that it provides public benefits.

It is of course open to any jurisdiction to grant tax concessions to such entities in the same way that the federal tax acts provide concessions to non-charitable NFPs. But by imposing some limits on fourth-head charities, we may avoid the ever-growing number of entities that are regarded as 'charities' and in that way restore integrity to the term.

Notes

1 In a recent case in the United Kingdom, *Children's Investment Fund Foundation (UK) v Attorney-General* [2020] UKSC 33, the Supreme Court held that in some circumstances, members of charities may owe fiduciary duties to act in the best interests of the charitable company. The case was concerned with highly unusual circumstances involving the Children's Investment Fund Foundation and the breakdown of the marriage of the two trustees/directors. A resolution approving a grant to a new charity to be controlled by one spouse needed statutory approval by the members. The one independent member was ultimately held to owe a fiduciary duty (and was required to vote on the resolution in accordance with a direction by the lower court).

2 Data provided by the Australian Taxation Office (ATO) as at April 2020. The figure refers to entities that have an active Australian Business Number registration that self-assess as income tax exempt. The ATO also states that there are an additional 56,000 registered charities and approximately 8,000 NFP entities that are taxable, making a total of approximately 205,000 NFP entities that interact with the federal tax system.

3 Data provided by the ATO as at April 2020. The Australian Charities and Not-for-Profits Commission (ACNC) website states that as at January 2021, there are 58,783 registered charities (ACNC 2021).

4 One category of charities, those that are on the Register of Environmental Organisations, must have at least 50 individual members (ITAA 1997: s. 30–275(1)(b)).

5 Australian Charities and Not-for-profits Regulations 2013, reg 45.10 Accountability to Members.
6 An unincorporated association is an informal group of individuals. An unincorporated association may be a charity (Australian Charities and Not-for-Profits Commission Act 2012 (Cth): s. 205.5) and in the absence of an exemption will be taxable as a company (ITAA 1997 (Cth): s. 995-1).
7 'Company' means a body corporate or any other unincorporated association or body of persons but does not include a partnership.
8 The common law principle of mutuality provides that where a number of persons contribute to a common fund created and controlled by them for a common purpose, such as a social club, any surplus arising from the use of that fund for the common purpose is not income. The principle does not extend to include income that is derived from sources outside that group, so that receipts from non-members will be taxed as income.
9 The mutuality principle has the effect that amounts paid by members of a club or association to the club or association are not income of the entity. Amounts received from non-members will, however, be assessable as income. It has been accepted that the principle applies in Australia (*The Social Credit Savings and Loans Society Ltd v Federal Commissioner of Taxation* (1971) 125 CLR 560 per Gibbs J, referring to *The New York Life Insurance Co v Styles (Surveyor of Taxes)* (1889) 14 App Cas 381 and *The Bohemians Club v Acting Federal Commissioner of Taxation* (1918) 24 CLR 334).
10 A further concession for some charities is the ability to receive gifts that are deductible under div 30 of the ITAA 1997. This is unlikely to be available to NFP entities that provide benefits to members.
11 Ibid s. 6–5 describes ordinary income as income according to ordinary concepts.
12 Ibid s. 995-1 defines a franked distribution as a distribution franked in accordance with s. 202-205.
13 Payroll Tax Act 2011 (ACT); Payroll Tax Act 2007 (NSW); Payroll Tax Act 2009 (NT); Payroll Tax Act 1971 (Qld); Payroll Tax Act 2009 (SA); Payroll Tax Act 2008 (Tas); Payroll Tax Act 2007 (Vic); Pay-Roll Tax Assessment Act 2002 (WA).
14 For example, in Victoria, the wages must be paid or payable to a person engaged exclusively in work of a religious, charitable, benevolent, philanthropic or patriotic nature for the institution or non-profit organisation (Payroll Tax Act 2007 (Vic): s. 48(1)(b)).
15 Land Tax Act 2004 (ACT); Land Tax Management Act 1956 (NSW); Land Tax Act 2010 (Qld); Land Tax Act 1936 (SA); Land Tax Rating Act 2000 (Tas); Land Tax Act 2005 (Vic); Land Tax Act 2002 (WA) (the Northern Territory does not have a land tax).
16 Rates Act 2004 (ACT); Local Government Act 1993 (NSW); Rates Act 1971 (NT); Local Government Act 2009 (Qld); Local Government Act 1999 (SA); Local Government Act 1993 (Tas); Local Government Act 1989 (Vic); Local Government Act 1995 (WA).
17 Duties Act 1999 (ACT); Duties Act 1997 No 123 (NSW); Stamp Duty Act 1978 (NT); Duties Act 2001 (Qld); Stamp Duties Act 1923 (SA); Duties Act 2001 (Tas); Duties Act 2000 (Vic); Duties Act 2008 (WA).
18 The Income Tax Assessment Act 1915 (Cth) s. 11(1)(d) provided an exemption for the income of a religious, scientific, charitable or public educational institution.
19 The Explanatory Memorandum to the Charities Bill 2013 (Cth) noted that 'the statutory definition generally preserves the common law principles by introducing a statutory framework based on those principles but incorporating minor modifications to modernise and provide greater clarity and certainty about the meaning of charity and charitable purpose' (2013: 3).
20 Historian F. K. Crowley in 1973 noted that 'Australian farmers and their spokesman have always considered that life on the land is inherently more virtuous, more healthy, more important and more productive, than living in the towns and cities' (Crowley 1973: 77–78).
21 In 2017–18, 710 companies did not pay any tax, including CBH (Khadem 2020).
22 The Tribunal was also asked to consider whether, if an exemption applied, this would apply to all of the wages paid by the Chamber of Commerce and Industry. This issue is discussed in the following.
23 Although the position may be otherwise with respect to courts of appeal *Farah Constructions Pty Ltd v Say-Dee Pty Ltd* (2007) 230 CLR 89.
24 There was no discussion about why it was common ground that QCCI fell within s 149C(3); however, it is assumed that this was due to the Administrative Tribunal of Western Australia decision in *CCI v CSR* discussed previously.
25 The IRS (2020) notes that 'a hospital that restricts its medical staff privileges to a limited group of physicians is likely to be operating for the private benefit of the staff physicians rather than for the public interest'.

References

Books

Crowley, F. K., *Modern Australia in Documents*, Melbourne: Wren, 1973.
Dal Pont, G. E., *Law of Charity*, Chatswood: LexisNexis Butterworths, 2nd ed., 2017.

Cases

Aid/Watch Inc v Federal Commissioner of Taxation (2010) 241 CLR 539
The Bohemians Club v Acting Federal Commissioner of Taxation (1918) 24 CLR 334
Chamber of Commerce and Industry Inc (WA) v Commissioner of State Revenue (2012) 82 SR (WA) 204
Chesterman v Federal Commissioner of Taxation (1923) 32 CLR 362
Chesterman v Federal Commissioner of Taxation (1925) 37 CLR 317
Children's Investment Fund Foundation (UK) v Attorney-General [2020] UKSC 33
Commissioners for Special Purposes of the Income Tax v Pemsel [1891] AC 531
Commissioners of Inland Revenue v Forrest (1890) 15 App Cas 334
Commissioners of Inland Revenue v Yorkshire Agricultural Society (1927) 13 TC 58
Commissioners of Inland Revenue v Yorkshire Agricultural Society (1928) 1 KB 611
Farah Constructions Pty Ltd v Say-Dee Pty Ltd (2007) 230 CLR 89
Federal Commissioner of Taxation v Co-operative Bulk Handling Ltd (2010) 189 FCR 322
Federal Commissioner of Taxation v Word Investments Ltd (2008) 236 CLR 204
Grain Growers Ltd v Chief Commissioner of State Revenue [2015] NSWSC 925
Incorporated Council of Law Reporting (Qld) v Federal Commissioner of Taxation (1971) 125 CLR 659
Institution of Civil Engineers v Commissioners of Inland Revenue [1932] 1 KB 149
Law Institute of Victoria v Commissioner of State Revenue [2015] VSC 604
Lloyd v Federal Commissioner of Taxation (1955) 93 CLR 645
The New York Life Insurance Co v Styles (Surveyor of Taxes) (1889) 14 App Cas 381
Queensland Chamber of Commerce and Industry Ltd v Commissioner of State Revenue (2015) 108 ACSR 334
Royal Australasian College of Surgeons v Federal Commissioner of Taxation (1943) 68 CLR 436
Royal College of Surgeons of England v National Provincial Bank Ltd [1952] AC 631
Royal National Agricultural and Industrial Association v Chester (1974) 3 ALR 486
The Social Credit Savings and Loans Society Ltd v Federal Commissioner of Taxation (1971) 125 CLR 560
South Australian Employers' Chamber of Commerce & Industry Inc v Commissioner of State Taxation [2017] SASC 127
South Australian Employers' Chamber of Commerce and Industry Inc v Commissioner of State Taxation [2019] SASCFC 125
Victorian Women Lawyers' Association Inc v Federal Commissioner of Taxation (2008) 170 FCR 318

Journal articles

Batrouney, J. and Lee, A., 'Sports: why are they not charitable?', *Law Institute Journal*, 92, April 2018.
Rossman, M. J., 'Evaluating trickle down charity: a solution for determining when economic development aimed at revitalizing America's cities and regions is really charitable', *Brooklyn Law Review* 79, 2014.
Tschirhart, M., 'Nonprofit membership associations', in Powell, W. W. and Steinberg, R. (eds) *The Non-Profit Sector: A Research Handbook*, New Haven: Yale University Press, 2nd ed., 2006.

Legislative materials

Australian Charities and Not-for-Profits Commission Act 2012 (Cth)
Australian Charities and Not-for-Profits Regulations 2013 (Cth)
Charities Act 2013 (Cth)
Duties Act 1997 (NSW)

Duties Act 1999 (ACT)
Duties Act 2000 (Vic)
Duties Act 2001 (Qld)
Duties Act 2001 (Tas)
Duties Act 2008 (WA)
Fringe Benefits Tax Assessment Act 1986 (Cth)
Income Tax Act 1918 (UK)
Income Tax Assessment Act 1915 (Cth)
Income Tax Assessment Act 1922 (Cth)
Income Tax Assessment Act 1936 (Cth)
Income Tax Assessment Act 1997 (Cth)
Income Tax Rates Act 1986 (Cth)
Land Tax Act 1936 (SA)
Land Tax Act 2002 (WA)
Land Tax Act 2004 (ACT)
Land Tax Act 2005 (Vic)
Land Tax Act 2010 (Qld)
Land Tax Management Act 1956 (NSW)
Land Tax Rating Act 2000 (Tas)
Local Government Act 1993 (NSW)
Local Government Act 2009 (Qld)
Local Government Act 1999 (SA)
Local Government Act 1993 (Tas)
Local Government Act 1989 (Vic)
Local Government Act 1995 (WA)
Payroll Tax Act 1971 (Qld)
Payroll Tax Act 2007 (NSW)
Payroll Tax Act 2007 (Vic)
Payroll Tax Act 2008 (Tas)
Payroll Tax Act 2009 (NT)
Payroll Tax Act 2009 (SA)
Payroll Tax Act 2011 (ACT)
Pay-Roll Tax Assessment Act 2002 (WA) http://classic.austlii.edu.au/au/legis/wa/consol_act/ptaa2002279/glossary.html
Rates Act 2004 (ACT)
Rates Act 1971 (NT)
Revenue and Other Legislation Amendment Act 2015 (NT)
Revenue and Other Legislation Amendment Act 2018 (Qld)
Stamp Duties Act 1923 (SA)
Stamp Duty Act 1978 (NT)
Tax Laws Amendment (Special Conditions for Not-for-Profit Concessions) Bill 2012 (Cth)
Taxation Administration Act 1999 (ACT)
Taxation Administration Act 2001 (Qld)

Reports

Australian Charities and Not-for-Profits Commission, 2018, *Australian Charities Report*, ACNC.
CBH Group, 2019, *Annual Report*, CBH Group.
Charity Commission for England and Wales, 2004, *RS7: Membership Charities*, CCEW.
OECD, Taxation and Philanthropy, *OECD Tax Policy Studies*, No. 27, 2020, Paris: OECD Publishing, <https://doi.org/10.1787/df434a77-en>
Productivity Commission, 2016, *Regulation of Australian Agriculture: Productivity Commission Inquiry Report no. 79*, Canberra: Productivity Commission.
Sheppard, I., Fitzgerald, R. and Gonski, D. 2001, *Report of the Inquiry into the Definition of Charities and Related Organisations*, Canberra: Commonwealth Treasury.

Websites

Australian Charities and Not-for-Profits Commission, *Co-Operative Bulk Handling Limited*, viewed 15th January 2021, <https://www.acnc.gov.au/charity/e176f895777280d28621c1671fdf797f>

Australian Charities and Not-for-Profits Commission, *How Can We Help?*, viewed 15th January 2021, <https://www.acnc.gov.au/>

Australian Charities and Not-for-Profits Commission, *Search the ACNC Charity Register*, viewed 15th January 2021, <https://www.acnc.gov.au/charity>

Commissioner of Taxation, 1997, *Taxation Ruling: TR 97/22: Income Tax: Exempt Sporting Clubs*, Australian Taxation Office, viewed 15th January 2021, <https://www.ato.gov.au/law/view/document?DocID=TXR/TR9722/NAT/ATO/00001>

Commissioner of Taxation, 2011, *Taxation Ruling: TR 2011/4: Income Tax and Fringe Benefits Tax: Charities*, Australian Taxation Office, viewed 15th January 2021, <https://www.ato.gov.au/law/view/document?src=hs&pit=99991231235958&arc=false&start=1&pageSize=10&total=35&num=3&docid=TXR%2FTR20114%2FNAT%2FATO%2F00001&dc=false&stype=find&tm=phrase-basic-TR%202011%2F4>

Co-operative Bulk Handling Limited, 2019, *Annual Information Statement 2019*, Australian Charities and Not-for-Profits Commission, viewed 15th January 2021, <https://www.acnc.gov.au/charity/e176f895777280d28621c1671fdf797f#ais-1642a6eb12a2564dc3e2b8ec62263a9f>

Co-operative Bulk Handling Limited, 2020, *Annual Information Statement 2020*, Australian Charities and Not-for-Profits Commission, <https://www.acnc.gov.au/charity/e176f895777280d28621c1671fdf797f#ais-1642a6eb12a2564dc3e2b8ec62263a9f>

Co-operative Bulk Handling Limited, 2021, *Rules of Co-Operative Bulk Handling Limited*, CBH Group, viewed 10th September 2021, <https://www.cbh.com.au/about-cbh/membership/membership-rules>

Grain Central, 2019, *CBH Group Delivers $16 Million Operations Rebate*, viewed 15th January 2021, <https://www.graincentral.com/news/agribusiness/cbh-group-delivers-16-million-operations-rebate/>

Internal Revenue Service, 1969, *Revenue Ruling 69–545*, Internal Revenue Service, viewed 15th January 2021, <https://www.irs.gov/pub/irs-tege/rr69-545.pdf>

Internal Revenue Service, 2020, *Charitable Hospitals – General Requirements for Tax-Exemption Under Section 501(c)(3)*, viewed 15th January 2021, <https://www.irs.gov/charities-non-profits/charitable-hospitals-general-requirements-for-tax-exemption-under-section-501c3>

Janda, M. and Anderson, S., 'ATO says 30 per cent of large private companies pay no corporate tax', *ABC News*, 2016, viewed 15th January 2021, <https://www.abc.net.au/news/2016-03-22/ato-30pc-of-large-private-companies-pay-no-tax/7266454>

Khadem, N., 'ATO data reveals one third of large companies pay no tax', *ABC News*, 2020, viewed 15th January 2021, <https://www.abc.net.au/news/2019-12-12/ato-corporate-tax-transparency-data-companies-no-tax-paid/11789048?nw=0>

Shepherd, B., 'WA grain cooperative CBH offered bid to list on the ASX by ACG consortium', *ABC News*, 2016, viewed 15th January 2021, <https://www.abc.net.au/news/2016-02-17/cbh-presented-with-commercialisation-proposal/7178066>

Sinodinos, A., *Integrity Restored to Australia's Taxation System*, Australian Government Treasury, 2013, viewed 15th January 2021, <https://ministers.treasury.gov.au/ministers/arthur-sinodinos-2013/media-releases/integrity-restored-australias-taxation-system>

Miscellaneous

Explanatory Memorandum, Charities Bill 2013 (Cth)

Explanatory Memorandum, Taxation Laws Amendment Bill (No 2) 1990 (Cth)

8

THE DONOR CONTROL/ PUBLIC BENEFIT BALANCE UNDERLYING PHILANTHROPIC TAX CONCESSIONS

Ian Murray

1 Introduction

While various specific rationales remain contested, in broad terms, many people would accept that charitable donation concessions are provided to support the charity sector. Support is provided to increase the sector's production of particular goods and services and to generate process benefits from the way that charities operate, such as pluralism and altruism. In other words, support is provided to achieve public benefit. However, I argue that in many common law jurisdictions, especially the United States and Canada where revenue authorities are the primary charity regulators, regulation of charities and donors by revenue authorities promotes donor autonomy and control to the detriment of public benefit.

At first glance, this seems strange, especially given tax authorities' goal of protecting the tax base. However, tax regimes and tax authorities often weigh donor autonomy against the public interest, viewed as tax base protection. They thus focus on the leakage of private benefits to donors that have some monetary value. Yet donor control extends well beyond donor extraction of charity resources to include the selection of charitable projects or charity grant recipients, the concomitant allocation of foregone public tax dollars to those projects and the manner in which such projects or charities are to be conducted. In contrast, sector-specific regulators, such as charity commissions in Australia or England and Wales, tend to balance donor autonomy against the public interest viewed through the lens of the proper administration and effective use of charity property. This perspective potentially permits greater attention to the more intangible values and interests that donors may wish to project into the future through charities (Chan 2016: Ch 5; Picton 2018: 192, 196–201).

To investigate the issue, this chapter will look at five areas. First, regulation of the benefits that a donor receives in return for making a gift – an area that tax regulation should be well placed to police. Second, general operational tax rules. Third, the tax law distinction drawn in some jurisdictions between public and private charities, which starts to address questions of donor control but remains focused on private benefits. Fourth, tax restrictions on political activity, which form an exception to the suggestion that tax law is primarily focused on restricting

DOI: 10.4324/9781003139201-10

private benefits. Fifth, the tools available to tax regulators to deal with ineffective use of charity assets as compared with those available to sector-specific regulators.

Before doing so, the chapter discusses the rationale for charitable donation concessions and the tension between protecting donor autonomy and promoting public benefit. It also outlines concerns about material donor control over donated funds, most particularly the risk that this poses for democratic institutions. The chapter concludes with some exploratory thoughts on reforms.

2 The tension between protecting donor autonomy (hence control) and promoting public benefit

Our legal institutions, such as property law and tax law, both shape and are shaped by societal norms and behaviour. Principles such as donor autonomy to freely dispose of property apply and are expressed within these institutions and are thus moulded by those institutions (Reich 2018: ch 1; Saunders-Hastings 2018: 157–158). Donor autonomy is therefore not absolute but regulated in certain ways by tax and related laws. For example, donors have freedom to choose their preferred project amongst the universe of charitable purposes – whether by selection of an existing charity or by creation of a new charity. The legal form of the selected charity can make it easier or harder for future generations to alter that purpose. Rather than a charity that directly carries out its purposes, the recipient charity might be an intermediary foundation, providing further flexibility as to the time at which the donation is ultimately used and as to the selection of recipients. Further, donors have some ability to control the manner in which the charitable project is conducted by imposing gift restrictions under contract, trust or property law; by writing those restrictions in a charity's constitution or trust deed; or by holding a seat on the charity's board or governing body.

To understand how tax law expresses donor autonomy and addresses donor control, we might think it relevant to understand the rationale underlying charitable donation concessions. As noted by Brody (and recently by the OECD), there is 'no single, unified and coherent tax policy with respect to non-profit organizations – and no single rationale' (Brody 2018: 484; OECD 2020: 22). Nevertheless, when introducing income taxes, legislators have typically suggested that donors would reduce their gifts unless a concession was provided (Colinvaux 2018: 445; Brody 2010: 603). Commentators have linked this reason to 'subsidy theories' that focus on the role of tax concessions in supporting the achievement of 'public benefit' by charities (Colinvaux 2018: 445; Duff 2014: 208–214; OECD 2020: 22). I intend to refer broadly to such subsidy theories – being support for the positive externalities of charities, not merely subsidies to finance goods that government would otherwise be expected to provide. For the purposes of this chapter, the positive externalities encompass the public benefits not just from inducing charities to produce goods and services such as health care, education and welfare but also process benefits from the manner in which charities operate, such as charities' role as sites of collective and political action, as well as in the promotion of pluralism or altruism (O'Connell 2018: 395; Atkinson 1997: 403; James & Rose-Ackerman, 1986: 86–87; Hemel 2020: 147–148; Chia et al 2011: 17–20). This link seems especially apt in the many jurisdictions that make donation concessions broadly available to most charities (e.g., United States, United Kingdom, Canada), such that there is substantial overlap between the tax-exempt charities and the donation concession charities (Colinvaux 2018: 447).

Some writers supporting the subsidy theory link with donation concessions also suggest that encouraging donations where taxpayers are able to direct support to the charities of their choice can itself promote pluralism and civic participation (Krever 1991: 11–13; Duff 2014: 213–214). However, donation concessions structured to provide the most benefit to the wealthy (especially so in the United States) undermine equality of opportunity (Fleischer 2018), reducing the degree of added pluralism (Reich 2018: 132–133; Duff 2014: 216–217). Conceiving of public benefit as including process benefits highlights the independence of the charity sector from government, in that the process benefits arise from voluntary selection and/or association rather than government administration. Further, the very form of donation concessions typically involves indirect, not direct, government support and oversight, again emphasising sector independence and autonomy (Gergen 1998: 1399–1403).

Finally, it has also been suggested that the income tax deduction can be justified on the basis that the donated income never formed part of the tax base, but many commentators dispute this by regarding donations as voluntary personal consumption of the donor's income (Duff 2014: 204; Krever 1991: 5–8).

In summary, donation concessions are intended to achieve public benefit but to operate in a manner that leaves substantial autonomy with donors and charities, not least to avoid disincentivising donations. This reflects the general charity law interplay between respecting donor intent and overriding donor intent to achieve a greater or fairer public benefit (Dal Pont 2017: [6.6]; Chan 2016: 53–54; Mulheron 2006: 87–89). Accordingly, I do not propose that tax regulators should have unfettered ability to impose their views on charities about how those charities could more effectively use their resources to achieve public benefit.

Nevertheless, there is some basis for worrying that the balance under income tax rules has shifted too far in favour of donor control and away from public benefit. Reich, Lechterman and Vallely, amongst others, have identified growing inequality, in combination with generous charitable donation tax concessions, as resulting in increased control of the charity sector and its activities by a wealthy elite (Reich 2018; Vallely 2020; Lechterman & Reich 2020: 184). In particular, they warn about the potentially anti-democratic nature of intermediary foundations.[1] See also OECD 2020: 23. Saunders-Hastings adds to this criticism by suggesting that tax legislation, amongst other laws, privileges elite donor views about public benefit over the views of others (2018: 150, 157; see also Pevnick 2013).

Horvath and Powell provide material examples of extensive control exercised over philanthropic undertakings by some of the wealthiest philanthropists such as Gates, Zuckerberg and Bloomberg (Horvath & Powell 2020: 117). They suggest that there has been a return to extensive donor involvement in philanthropic endeavours and infusion of the business practices that proved so successful for the donors in the corporate world – reflecting a return to practices from the time of Carnegie and Rockefeller (Horvath & Powell 2020: 117). This was a time when the U.S. Congress became concerned about and legislated to regulate the activities of private foundations. From an empirical perspective, Teresa Odendahl highlighted several decades ago that elite philanthropy 'support[s] institutions that sustain their culture, their education, their policy formulation, their status – in short, their interests' and that this involves ongoing control over donated funds (1990: 232). More recently, and in keeping with these findings, Susan Ostrander has identified material donor control over donated funds from analysis of the United States professional adviser literature (2007).

If a small group of donors is permitted material control over their donated assets, in addition to the potential harm to democratic institutions, there are further potential detriments to public benefit. Lester Salamon's 'philanthropic paternalism' describes one drawback, in that donors impose their preferences on the public, in contrast to the community discussion about public benefits that should be pursued (1987: 41). This has also been characterised as a failure to build mutual relationships between givers and receivers and the community bonds that some justifications for the charity sector emphasise (Vallely 2020: 466–467, 672–673; Ostrander 2007). There is also an intergenerational dimension, with Fleischer worrying that control over donated assets can enable the intergenerational transfer of political and economic power (2018: 440. See also Odendahl 1990: 4–5, 232). Further, permitting donors in the current generation too much autonomy may breach principles of intergenerational justice about the balance of autonomy between generations (Murray 2021).

Charitable donation concessions are also very large (e.g., US$48.3billion in the United States in 2019 [Treasury (US) 2020], $AU1.8bn in Australia in 2019 [Treasury (Au) 2020]), such that material public benefit should be expected for the material amounts of tax foregone. As well, charitable donation concessions typically benefit wealthier donors to a greater extent.[2] This may be because they constitute a deduction in the context of a progressive income tax system, thus providing a larger tax benefit to higher-rate taxpayers (e.g., Australia, United States), although larger tax benefits are still effectively provided to higher income earners under the UK's hybrid Gift Aid concessions and (assuming that they donate more) under Canada's two-tiered credit system. In the United States, in particular, the high standard deduction under the Tax Cuts and Jobs Act of 2017 has been estimated to mean that only 9% of taxpayers will now itemise – and thus gain a benefit from – their charitable donations (Colinvaux 2019: 1007–1008). Furthermore, the United States provides stunningly concessional treatment for donations of appreciated assets – assets such as company shares whose value reflects unrealised capital gains. A gift of such assets potentially enables a deduction based on the fair market value of the asset but with the donor not required to bring into assessable income the difference between the asset's tax cost and its fair market value (Brody 2018: 500). Canada and the United Kingdom adopt a similar approach for a more limited class of assets (such as listed company shares – and, in the United Kingdom, land) (Duff 2014: 199; Henderson & Fowles 2015: [20–038], [20–046]; Special Senate Committee on the Charitable Sector 2019: 108), and the Canadian Special Senate Committee recently recommended a trial extension to all company shares and to land. Australia generally imposes capital gains tax on inter vivos gifts of property[3] but would potentially provide a corresponding deduction for the market value of the donated property (Income Tax Assessment Act 1997 (Cth) div 30).

3 Tax regulation of donor control

Chan has argued, in relation to the Canada Revenue Agency, that tax regulation and tax regulators seek to balance donor autonomy against the public interest in guarding the breadth and integrity of the tax base (2016: Ch 5). Similar assertions have been made of charity tax regulators in the United States and, before the introduction of Australia's charity commission, of the Australian Taxation Office (ATO) [Colinvaux 2018: 454; Treasury (Au) 2011: 29]. On the other hand, regimes for sector-specific regulators, such as charity commissions in Australia or England and Wales, tend to balance donor autonomy against the public interest viewed through the lens of the proper administration and effective use of charity property, which potentially permits some greater attention to the more intangible values and interests that donors may wish to project into the future through charities (Chan 2016: Ch 5; Picton 2018: 192, 196–201). Given the controversial nature of some of the wider questions of public interest in the effective use of charity property, as opposed to tax base protection (Colinvaux 2018: 454), it is also understandable that tax authorities may shy away from these broader notions of public benefit. Some of these structural barriers are investigated further in the following. First, though, it is important to consider the notion of a 'gift', the private/public distinction and political activities.

3.1 Gifts

Tax laws frequently provide significant attention to charitable donations to ensure that the donor does not receive a material benefit in return, or at least no benefit with respect to amounts that are being claimed as deductions or credits (O'Connell 2018: 413–414; Chan 2016: 113–117). Potentially this means that tax regulators are well placed to monitor control rights obtained by donors. By way of example, in Australia, the income tax law requires either a 'gift' (interpreted by the case law to mean that the donor receives no material benefit or advantage by way of return) (ATO 2005: [37]–[44], [142])[4] or certain contributions for a right to participate in a fundraising event or by way of bid at a charity auction, in which case the deduction is only the difference between the contribution and the market value of the right to participate or the charity auction goods [Income Tax Assessment Act 1997 (Cth) s 30–15(1)]. On their face, these provisions are very broad. However, much of the ATO guidance indicates that breach would occur where something of economic value is received in return and that benefits such as networking opportunities, public recognition and reporting on the use of donated funds, are not captured (ATO 2005: [170], [186], [196], [202]).[5] Nevertheless, the ATO does move beyond marketable benefits to also consider that membership rights and other things that have value to the donor would be caught.[6] Additionally, an anti-avoidance provision denies a deduction where the donor or an associate obtains a right, privilege or benefit other than the benefit of a tax saving [Income Tax Assessment Act 1936 (Cth) ss 78A(2)(c), 78A(3)]. The provision is also deemed to apply where the charity recipient does not immediately receive or have the unconditional right to retain custody and control of the property or does not obtain an immediate, indefeasible and unencumbered legal and equitable title to the property. While the ATO expressly notes that these provisions extend beyond 'pecuniary' and 'proprietary' benefits, the ATO considers that the goal of the provisions is to ensure that 'the benefit to the fund will equal the deduction allowed to the taxpayer' and that they are not intended to apply to 'genuine gifts made in ordinary circumstances' (ATO 2005: [206]–[207]). While reflecting donor control, it is difficult to characterise donor conditions on use of funds for certain purposes within the recipient's overarching purposes or that require expenditure at a particular time as involving the return of a material benefit to the donor (see, e.g., Silver 2021), though unless care is taken, the form of the conditions may raise risks as to receipt of an unencumbered title (see, e.g., O'Connell 2020: 382–383).[7]

In the United States, deductions under Internal Revenue Code §170 are available for gifts (a transfer of property without consideration) or contributions to most §501(c)(3) charities[8] but with the amount of the deduction limited by the market value of benefits received in return (26 CFR §1.170A-1; Fishman, Schwarz, & Mayer 2015: 775–782). Treasury Regulation CFR §1.170A-1(h)(2) focuses especially on the fair market value of benefits received in return, and CFR §1.170A-13 excludes benefits with an 'insubstantial value', such as minor annual membership rights or tokens bearing the charity's logo [26 CFR §1.170A-13(f)(8); IRS 1990]. This indicates that hard-to-value rights to require a charity to use funds for purposes within its overarching charitable purposes or to be expended at a particular time do not sit easily as benefits received in return (Eason 2007: 701–702; Colinvaux 2016: 26–30; Hopkins 2014: 503). However, retained rights to provide ongoing directions to a charity as to the specific application of donated property (e.g., choice of recipients of charity services) are likely to breach the tax requirements on the basis that they reduce or eliminate any contribution in the first place or that they are benefits that materially reduce its value (Eason 2007: 702–703; Hopkins 2014: 505–508).

It is perhaps not surprising, then, that gift agreements do generally permit material conditions or restrictions on the use of funds, many running to tens of pages (Eason 2007: 698–707; Innes & Boyle 2006: 72–74). Further, donors could avoid many of these requirements by first setting up a charity before making a donation. If the constitution or trust deed of the charity sets out the preferred purposes, including rules as to when those purposes should be pursued, it is then simply a matter of making a gift (albeit, as discussed further subsequently, gifts to privately controlled charities are often afforded less generous tax concessions and are subjected to more restrictions) to an existing charity that happens to accord with the donor's views and permits control by way of intergenerational protection of the charitable purposes set out in the constituent documents. Further (and again subject to the public/private charity distinction), donors may retain actual control of the charity to which they donate.

3.2 General organisational and operational rules and control

Other than gift transactions, tax regulators typically pay close attention to charities at the point of registration. As the technical meaning of 'charity' requires that a charity have certain charitable purposes and be for the public benefit, this requires some attention at the initial stages to matters of public benefit and hence means that donors do not have completely unfettered autonomy to determine their projects – they must be charitable. We might now question how rigorous this screening process is in the United States for organisations filing a form 1023-EZ.

Further, most jurisdictions do include some sort of general operational test in their tax rules. In Australia, to be eligible for income tax exemption, a charity must be registered as such by the federal charities commission, the Australian Charities and Not-for-profits Commission [Income Tax Assessment Act 1997 (Cth) s50–55], and meet several special tax conditions, including that the charity must 'comply with all the substantive requirements in its governing rules' and 'apply its income and assets solely for the purpose for which [it] is established' [Income Tax Assessment Act 1997 (Cth) ss50–51, 50–50(2)].

Similarly, United States charities are subject to an 'operational' test due to the wording of Internal Revenue Code §501(c)(3).[9] The Internal Revenue Service (IRS) has interpreted this requirement for organisations that raise and pass on funds to other charities (and potentially organisations that both raise funds and directly pursue their charitable purposes, such as universities) as requiring the organisation to distribute or expend assets 'commensurate in scope with its financial resources' (IRS 1964, 1989: 13–16). In Canada, to be a tax-exempt 'charitable foundation' requires 'a corporation or trust that is constituted and operated exclusively for charitable purposes', while a tax-exempt 'charitable organization' is 'an organization, whether or not incorporated . . . all of the resources of which are devoted to charitable activities carried on by the organization itself' [Income Tax Act, RSC 1985, c 1, s149.1(1)]. This is a very general and vague test (Man 2011: 25–26) and seems chiefly concerned with whether ongoing activities are consistent with the organisation's charitable purpose (Ontario Law Reform Commission 1996: 288; Innes & Boyle 2006: 16–17).

The UK tax legislation contains no blanket income tax exemption for charities. Instead, specific categories of income and gains are rendered exempt, with the exemptions applying to most types of income and gains (HMRC 2020: Annex i, Kessler, Wong & Birkbeck 2019: 285–286). Other than minor exceptions (see Kessler, Wong & Birkbeck 2019: 136–137, 142, 162), and some minor changes in wording, each of the exemptions only applies to income or gains so far as the income or gain is 'applied to charitable purposes only' or 'applied for charitable purposes' [Corporation Tax Act 2010 (UK) c 4, pt 11 chs 2–3; Income Tax Act

2007 (UK) c 3, pt 10; Taxation of Chargeable Gains Act 1992 (UK) c 12, s 256(1)]. This is virtually identical to the Australian 'application-for-purposes' requirement. In addition, the UK rules contain a set of 'charitable expenditure rules', which, in broad terms, reduce the income tax exemptions to the extent that a charity has a 'non-exempt amount' for a tax year [Corporation Tax Act 2010 (UK) c 4, s 492; Income Tax Act 2007 (UK) c 3, s 539; Taxation of Chargeable Gains Act 1992 (UK) c 12, ss 256(3), (3A)]. The aim is to address the fact that, unlike the Australian provisions, the UK primary exemption provisions focus only on a charity's income or gains, not misapplication of its other assets (HMRC 2020: Annex ii). To have a 'non-exempt amount', a charity must have, among other things, 'non-charitable expenditure' for the relevant tax year [Corporation Tax Act 2010 (UK) c 4, s 493; Income Tax Act 2007 (UK) c 3, s 540; Taxation of Chargeable Gains Act 1992 (UK) c 12, ss 256(3), (3A)]. The definition of this phrase includes a range of listed items, including 'expenditure' that is 'not incurred for charitable purposes only' [Corporation Tax Act 2010 (UK) c 4, s 496; Income Tax Act 2007 (UK) c 3, s 543].

These tests focus on whether charity assets are being properly administered. While there is some overlap, they are not concerned with the broader question of whether a charity is effectively using its assets to achieve public benefit. For example, in the context of accumulation of charity assets, the tests seem ill equipped to stop donors from directing charities to save for the future and so project their views well into the future. As set out by Murray (2015), for reasons of policy and doctrinal analysis, the Australian 'application-for-purposes' test is better characterised as being focused on maladministration that affects whether funds are used to promote a charity's purpose. Excessive accumulation or other ineffective uses of charity assets might amount to maladministration where they involve an exercise of power by charity controllers in a way that breaches their duties. However, the starting point is to identify a breach of duty, and a decision to use assets in a less effective way than is possible will not necessarily amount to a breach. Likewise, in the United Kingdom, the application for purposes test has been accepted by commentators and the HMRC as being focused on a class of failures to comply with the charity's rules (Kessler, Wong & Birkbeck 2019: 142–146).

Similarly, in Canada, 'operating' an entity for charitable purposes and 'devoting' funds to 'charitable activities'[10] are sufficiently broad as to encompass an application of funds by way of accumulation (such that they do not impose a temporal requirement to directly spend or distribute funds: Innes & Boyle 2006: 16–17), or to encompass a range of uses that promote the charitable purpose but that are not the optimal use of funds. The United States operational test is differently worded to, and has less clearly defined boundaries than, the Australian focus on maladministration. However, it is arguable that a test focused on whether an entity 'engages primarily in activities which accomplish one or more of [its] exempt purposes' ought to be construed in the same way as the Australian 'application-for-purposes' test, since both examine whether acts are in furtherance of the charitable purposes. This would appear to leave scope for a range of acts that further a charitable purpose but do so in ways that less effectively generate public benefit. In any event, even if the IRS's 'commensurate in scope' interpretation is accepted, commentators suggest that the test would only apply to accumulation in very narrow circumstances, for instance, where distribution/expenditure rates are extraordinarily low or controllers have breached their duties by diverting material funds to their own private benefit (Siegel 2009: 11–12, 16; Simon, Dale & Chisolm 2006: 283).[11]

The United States also applies penalty taxes, and potentially revocation, where 'disqualified persons' receive 'excess benefits' from public charities (Internal Revenue Code §4958). An excess benefit arises where the value of the economic benefit provided by the charity exceeds the value of any consideration provided by the disqualified person (e.g., a low/no-interest loan) [Internal Revenue Code §4958(c)(1)(A)]. Disqualified persons include people in a position to exercise substantial influence over the charity's affairs (and their associates), such as a board member or trustee, a CEO and most likely a founder or substantial contributor [26 CFR §§53.4958–3(c), 53.4958–3(e)(2)(i) and (ii)]. Disqualified persons should thus include donors who exercise control in relation to the charities that they found or to which they donate. However, the rules are focused on economic benefits received by donors (Mayer 2012: 88), not on difficult-to-value rights to project the donor's views (see 26 CFR §§53.4958–4). A similar comment could be made about the Canadian undue benefit penalty taxes [Income Tax Act, RSC 1985, c 1, s 188.1(4)]. 'Undue benefit' is defined broadly to include the 'amount' of property or rights conferred by the charity and would apply to a proprietor, trustee, member, settlor or major contributor to a charity [Income Tax Act, RSC 1985, c 1, s 188.1(5)]. While the Canadian provisions are broader, the need to identify an 'amount' and to calculate a penalty based on this amount also suggests that the Canada Revenue Agency is unlikely to apply the provisions to hard-to-value rights. Again, to similar effect, the Australian public and private ancillary fund rules impose penalties where benefits are provided to those with some ability to control the fund, such as directors of the trustee company, founders and donors [Taxation Administration (Private Ancillary Fund) Guidelines 2019 (Cth) r22; Public Ancillary Fund Guidelines 2011 (Cth) r42]. The penalty must be calculated based on the 'amount' or 'value' of the benefit provided. Moreover, the provisions would not seem to apply where control rights are not received from the charity but are instead built into the charity's formational documents – such as the voting rights of a member or the articulation of a particular charitable purpose and means of pursuing that purpose.

3.3 Public/private charity distinction

An important distinction that is made in several jurisdictions in policing issues of control is to have separate regimes for public charities and more restrictive rules for more tightly controlled private charities/foundations. The United States, for instance, distinguishes 'private foundations' from public charities. Private foundations are, in a broad sense, charities that raise their funds from a limited pool of persons rather than the general public and are controlled by a restricted range of persons (Simon, Dale & Chisolm 2006: 269).[12] In keeping with the 1965 Treasury Report on private foundations, extra requirements apply to private foundations that seek to eliminate private benefits for donors (Fremont-Smith 2004: 76–80; Mayer 2012: 87). A range of penalty taxes may be imposed on the private foundation and/or its controllers motivated largely by concerns around private benefits: provisions concerning self-dealing, excess (i.e., non-portfolio) business holdings and investing in a manner that jeopardises carrying out the charitable purpose (Internal Revenue Code §§4941, 4943, 4944). These rules go some way to replicating controller duties of loyalty and care (Fremont-Smith 2004: 264–300). However, the rules are also intended to extend beyond private benefits to constrain control in various ways (Fremont-Smith 2004: 76–80). Several measures discourage attempts to direct excessive accumulation, as foundations must typically make annual distributions of 5% of 'the fair market value' of their net investment assets (Internal Revenue Code §4942). Private foundations are also subject to a 2% excise tax on net investment income [Internal Revenue Code §4940(a)], although the rate drops to 1% for foundations that sufficiently increase their distributions [Internal Revenue Code §4940(e); and see also Fremont-Smith 2004: 264–265]. Engaging in certain 'taxable expenditures', such as payments for political campaigns and lobbying, can potentially also result in excise taxes (Internal Revenue Code §4945). Further, donation concessions for donations to private foundations are less generous (Madoff 2016: 166–167; Hemel 2020: 159), and disclosure and international grant-making requirements for private foundations are more onerous than for public charities (Hemel 2020: 159; OECD 2020: 124–125).

Australia also distinguishes between public and private 'ancillary funds' and between ancillary funds (which are subject to a disbursement quota) and other (public) deductible gift recipient charities (which are not subject to a disbursement quota). Australian charities do not automatically qualify for donation concessions. However, charitable trusts in the form of public or private ancillary funds can qualify as deductible gift recipients [Income Tax Assessment Act 1997 (Cth) s 30–15(1) item 2]. The public/private distinction relates to the range of persons who may donate to and administer the trust [Taxation Administration (Private Ancillary Fund) Guidelines 2019 (Cth) rr8(c), 12, 24; Public Ancillary Fund Guidelines 2011 (Cth) rr14, 44–45]. Ancillary funds are thus philanthropic intermediaries that receive donations and then (eventually) distribute them to other deductible gift recipients.[13] Public ancillary funds are subject to a less demanding disbursement requirement: 4% (5% for private ancillary funds) of the market value of the fund's net assets as at the end of the preceding financial year [Taxation Administration (Private Ancillary Fund) Guidelines 2019 (Cth) r15; Public Ancillary Fund Guidelines 2011 (Cth) r19]. The public and private ancillary fund guidelines are otherwise very similar, containing rules as to the trustees' degree of care; the need for a member of (private), or a majority of (public), the decision-making committee of the fund to be persons with a degree of responsibility to the community; exclusion from control of a fund for persons convicted of indictable taxation offences; limits on trustee indemnification; disclosure of related party transactions, along with restrictions on such transactions; and various investment limits [Taxation Administration (Private Ancillary Fund) Guidelines 2019 (Cth) rr12, 14, 18(3), 21, 22; Public Ancillary Fund Guidelines 2011 (Cth) rr 13–14, 16, 18, 26.2, 33–40, 41–42].

Canada also differentiates private from public foundations and public charities, with private foundations restricted in their ability to carry on business activities or to incur debts not linked to their charitable operations, restricted in their ability to make non-arms-length investments and subject to excess corporate holdings restrictions and donation concessions being slightly less generous for donations to private foundations (Gillen, Smith & Waters 2012: [14.III]; Income Tax Act, RSC 1985, c 1, ss 38, 149.1(4), 188.1, 189.1). It appears that the main concern with private foundations has been the potential for donors to claim donation concessions but to then maintain some personal benefit from donated property rather than genuinely applying assets to foundation grant expenditure (Gillen, Smith & Waters 2012: [14.III]). All Canadian charities registered for income tax and donation concession purposes are subject to a disbursement quota of 3.5% [Income Tax Act, RSC 1985, c 1, ss 149.1(2)(b), (3)(b), (4)(b)], with that rate applying to the average value of property not used directly in charitable activities or administration over the preceding 24 months (i.e., investment assets).[14] The United Kingdom does not employ a public/private charity tax distinction but does have tainted donation rules that apply where the donor enters into an arrangement with a recipient charity that results in a *financial advantage* to the donor or an associate [Corporation Tax Act 2010 (UK) c 4, pt 21C; Income Tax Act 2007 (UK) c 3, pt 13, ch 8; Kessler, Wong & Birkbeck 2019: Ch 7].

One issue with private foundation restrictions is that they are only partially effective in limiting donor control. In particular, the payout rules are set so low as to enable perpetual existence of private foundations – enabling donors to project their views far into the future. And, as discussed by Murray (2021: Ch 7), if the timing of benefit provision is the issue, payout rules do not necessarily fit with intergenerational justice as a principled basis for approaching the timing issue. Further, lobbying expenditure could simply be provided by way of a (non-earmarked) grant to a third-party organisation to circumvent the United States taxable expenditure rules (Fremont-Smith 2004: 280–281).

More fundamentally, 'donor advised funds' (DAFs), which are seeing increasing use in the United States, United Kingdom, Canada and Australia (Charities Aid Foundation 2020; Murray 2020), represent a breaking down of this distinction. A DAF is a named management account within a charitable foundation (usually a public charitable trust or corporation).[15] A donor makes a gift of property to the charitable foundation and typically obtains a tax deduction or credit. While the donor retains no ownership interest in the property transferred and has no legal power to direct the charitable foundation's dealings with the property, the charitable foundation provides administrative and investment assistance to the donor and gives the donor advisory privileges about how it should deal with the donated property. The charitable foundation thus often acts in accordance with the donor's wishes about when and to whom to distribute. The commercial imperative for charitable foundations to act in accordance with donors' wishes is emphasised where financial services firms provide DAF services as part of their wealth management operations, which is the case for some of the largest DAF sponsors such as Fidelity Charitable and Goldman Sachs Philanthropy Fund. In essence, a DAF is a public charity but with some of the features of donor control that might otherwise be accessed via use of a private foundation. The existence of DAFs also permits United States and Canadian private foundations to effectively avoid their payout rules, as they are permitted to distribute to DAFs (Murray 2020: 271–272, 293–296).

It should be emphasised, as demonstrated by the *Fairbairn v Fidelity Investments Charitable Gift Fund* lawsuit,[16] that donors have less control over a DAF than over a private foundation of which they are the trustee or a director of the trustee company. Thus, despite their recent stratospheric growth, reliance on DAFs may diminish, so leaving a material public/private foundation distinction in place. Further, Australia and Canada apply disbursement requirements to both public and private foundations (indeed, all tax registered charities in Canada). The United States has also taken some steps to maintain the public/private charity distinction as a result of Pension Protection Act 2006 reforms that apply additional self-dealing rules to DAF providers, moving them closer to the treatment of private foundations (Lehmann 2007: 35–37). However, the additional excise taxes on excess benefits transactions, taxable distributions, prohibited benefits and excess business holdings appear largely aimed at benefits derived by donors, their advisors and their affiliates (Mayer 2012: 87). They are not aimed at broader issues of control and timing of benefit provision to ultimate charity beneficiaries (Madoff 2016: Ch 6).

3.4 Political activities

Whether charities ought to be able to engage in campaigning or political lobbying activities is a controversial topic in many jurisdictions (O'Connell 2018: 408–409). It extends well beyond questions of donor control. However, political activities are considered in this chapter, as they provide a relatively unusual instance of tax rules that seek to restrict the projection of donor views. Examining the political activity rules provides insight into whether this type of tax rules is likely to be a successful way of policing intangible control rights held by donors.

Where donations are made to charities in order to carry out political activities, they can be seen – amongst other things – as a projection of donor views and as an attempt to control the use of donated funds to influence public debate and the choice of public benefits pursued. As asserted by Emma Saunders-Hastings, commentators frequently underestimate the similarities between electoral campaign spending by elites and 'elite philanthropy' in the sense that philanthropic donations can act as alternative means of achieving political influence (2018: 150–151). One response, in the United States and, until recently, Canada, has been to limit charity lobbying and to prohibit charity campaigning (that is, electioneering) through tax rules. For instance, in the United States, §501(c)(3) Internal Revenue Code provides that for charity registration, 'no substantial part of the activities of [the charity] is carrying on propaganda, or otherwise attempting to influence legislation', with some ability to elect out of this vague test into a more certain cap or percentage of expenditure test under §501(h), though the caps are relatively low, going up to only the lesser of 20% or $1m of expenditure. In relation to campaigning, §501(c)(3) states that the charity must 'not participate in or intervene in . . . any political campaign on behalf of (or in opposition to) any candidate for public office'. In Canada, the case of *Canada Without Poverty v A-G (Canada)* (2018) ONSC 4147 has led to legislative amendments that retain a prohibition on campaigning [Income Tax Act, RSC 1985, c 1, ss149.1(6.1) and (6.2) provide that a registered charity must not 'devot[e] any part of its resources to the direct or indirect support of, or opposition to, any political party or candidate for public office'] but that expressly permit non-partisan 'public policy dialogue and development activities' – that is, political advocacy [Income Tax Act, RSC 1985, c 1, ss149.1(1), (10.1)].

Constraining tax support in this way is not an attempt to protect tax base integrity but rather a weighing of the benefits and detriments to the public from supporting political activities that advance a charitable purpose and protecting the independence of the charity sector and government (Colinvaux 2018: 448–449). Given the odd role that this imposes on tax regulators, note that the United States and Canadian experience provides some evidence of the difficulties in employing tax regulation of campaigning activities (see also O'Connell 2018: 413–414). For instance, although interpreted broadly in the Treasury regulations, the United States campaign restriction is not always robustly enforced, with the United States IRS still reeling from the fallout over its targeting of politically aligned charities (Fishman, Schwarz & Mayer 2015: 463–497; Treasury Inspector General for Tax Administration 2017). President Trump also issued a vaguely worded executive order to the IRS requesting that it *not* take compliance action against campaigning by religious organisations (Exec Order No 13798, 3 CFR 346 2018). Furthermore, the United States institutional response has included the creation and expansion of tax concession categories for political lobbying and campaigning entities (Internal Revenue Code §527 political organisations) that can remain connected in various ways with registered charities – for example, via Internal Revenue Code §501(c)(4) social welfare organisations and §527 political action committees (Fishman, Schwarz & Mayer 2015: 494–502; Hopkins 2019: 399–400). Moreover, this is in the broader United States context of the existence of some general electoral law regulation of campaign financing but with that regulation materially limited by the *Citizens United* decision (*Citizens United* 558 US 310 (2010)), which effectively removed caps on not-for-profit and for-profit corporation electoral expenditure (Fishman, Schwarz & Mayer 2015: 502–506). In Canada, the *Canada Without Poverty* case resulted from the imposition of increased political activity reporting and audits by the Canada Revenue Agency, which has led to a partial governmental about-face and much public criticism of (and support for) the Agency (Parachin 2016: 1048, 1050–1054).

In keeping with Saunders-Hastings's reflection on the similarities between 'elite philanthropy' and campaign finance, rather than relying on tax rules and tax regulators, it may make more sense to police charity political activities and associated issues of donor control through campaign financing/electoral legislation and regulators like the Federal Election Commission in the United States. In Australia, for example, while the approach is not perfect (see, e.g., Beard 2019: 40–42), Australian electoral legislation requirements apply across the board to charities and other non-party political actors [Commonwealth Electoral Act 1918 (Cth) pt XX]. If electoral expenditure (being certain expenditures on matter communicated or intended to be communicated for the dominant purpose of influencing the way electors vote in a federal election) thresholds are exceeded, then the relevant entity must register and report donations used for that expenditure to the Australian Electoral Commission. Entities that meet 'third party campaigner' or 'political campaigner' thresholds are also required to disclose their 'electoral expenditure', which is to be placed on a public 'transparency register' [Commonwealth Electoral Act 1918 (Cth) pt XX div 1A and div 5A].[17]

The difficulties that regulation of political activities poses for tax regulators are reflected in the next section, which examines more generally the structural barriers that inhibit tax regulators from policing donor control for the public benefit.

3.5 The tools of tax regulators versus charity commissions and other structural barriers to encouraging public benefit

Commentators such as Chan and O'Connell have suggested that some tax regulators are not well established to monitor the 'public-welfare compliance' of charity projects (Chan 2016: 113–117; O'Connell 2018: 416).[18] However, this is only partly due to lack of provisions focusing on the operation of charities. As we have explored previously, there are a number of operational tests that apply under tax legislation, but the general operational tests largely focus on whether a charity is properly administering its assets, not the further question of whether it is effective in its use of assets – and the issue of whether donor control is impeding effectiveness. Rules precluding benefits in return for gifts hold some promise for regulating control rights on gifts to existing charities. However, they typically require tax regulators to form a view of the value of such difficult-to-value rights and, in practice, do not appear to be impeding substantial gift agreements under which donors specify the use of their donated funds. Minimum distribution requirements for private foundations (and public foundations in Australia and all charities in Canada) impose some limits on donor ability to project their views into the future, though the distribution rates are set sufficiently low that no charity is likely to be forced to terminate. The political activity rules also constrain activities, but in a very porous way.

Given that they typically have tools available to deal with some aspects of the 'public welfare compliance' of charity projects, a portion of the criticisms levelled at tax regulators must relate to their practical administration of the tax rules. Part of the problem is that tax regulators, unlike charity commissions, do not have an institutional focus on charities (Owens 2017: 82; Boris & Lott 2017: 97; Gillen 2016: 136, 156–157). The IRS is also underfunded to regulate charities and is still suffering from its regulation of political activities, as discussed previously (Ascher 2014: 1597; Owens 2017: 91). The Canada Revenue Agency has also been affected by its own political activity audits and by perceptions of bias in its role as charity regulator arising from its role as a tax collector (Wyatt 2017: 148–153; Special Senate Committee on the Charitable Sector 2019: 109). Inaction for these reasons will be difficult to resolve, though making it easier to act through more express and better calibrated tools would potentially help.

Second, what is also missing are tools to reform the use of charitable assets to reduce donor control so that they can be applied more effectively. This is not a call for an unbounded tax regulator power to direct the use of charity assets but for a more structured ability to intervene. Administrative/deviation schemes (which alter the administrative machinery of a charity) or cy-près schemes (which vary the charitable purpose) are key 'mechanism[s] by which to prescribe the means to pursue charitable objects and, crucially, to ensure that those objects remain capable of fulfilment over time' (Dal Pont 2017: [14.6]). They help ensure the effective use of charity assets and can be accessed by state and provincial attorneys-general and, in some cases – as for the Charity Commission for England and Wales generally and for the Australian Charities and Not-for-profits Commission in more limited circumstances – by charity commissions. However, many commentators have noted the patchiness of regulation at the level of the United

States and Canadian states and provinces (de March 2017: 127–128; Fremont-Smith 2004: 53; Brody 2004: 946–950). Additionally, the availability of cy-près schemes is more limited in many United States jurisdictions[19] than in Australia or England and Wales and is far more limited in Canada, where cy-près variation is largely limited to the common law circumstances of 'impossibility' or 'impracticability' of purpose (Gillen, Smith & Waters 2012: [14.VI.B]). In Australia and in England and Wales, cy-près can be obtained where the charitable purposes have 'ceased to provide a suitable and effective method of using the trust property' having regard to the 'spirit of the trust' or 'appropriate considerations',[20] or where it is 'impossible, impracticable or inexpedient' to carry out the purpose.[21]

Commentators have noted that even the current expanded administrative scheme and cy-près provisions could go further in limiting donor control and that this could be achieved in ways that retain a degree of respect for donor autonomy (Murray 2021; Picton 2018). For example, this could be achieved by allowing a set time period for greater donor control during which the existing administrative scheme and cy-près scheme rules apply, followed by a broadening of the circumstances in which the effective use of assets to achieve public benefit trumps donor intent.

4 Reform and conclusion

In considering reforms, it is important to remember that the donor autonomy/public benefit balance includes a potential reduction in public benefit if donors give less property because their autonomy is diminished.[22] Further, if the public benefit achieved by charities is viewed as potentially including a range of process benefits linked to the private pursuit of public purposes, then we should favour reforms that are more consistent with the independence of charities from government.

One relatively minor reform would be to strengthen the public/private charity distinction that is made for various tax purposes in the United States, Canada and Australia so that it better accounts for donor advised funds. The public/private charity distinction is not currently made in the United Kingdom and could be considered as an additional tool to regulate private control of charities.

More fundamentally, in jurisdictions such as the United States and Canada, where the tax authority is the primary charity regulator, a further step could be to provide the tax authority with access to tools to modify a charity that mirror the administrative scheme and cy-près provisions. This may not always require new provisions. For instance, it may be that legislative extensions of cy-près or administrative schemes already provide open standing or broad standing for interested persons in some jurisdictions (American Law Institute 2020: §94 cmt g; Murray & Wesson 2020: 1338–1342). It may also be arguable at common law that interested persons extend beyond charity trustees/directors and attorneys-general to tax regulators (American Law Institute 2020: §94 cmt g; Murray & Wesson 2020: 1338–1342). Thus, it may be possible to provide tax regulators with standing – or confirm the existence of standing – to apply to court to use existing cy-près and administrative scheme mechanisms. This could even assist in jurisdictions such as Australia that have a charity commission but where cy-près and administrative scheme reform has chiefly been the domain of state attorneys-general (McClure et al 2018: 34).

This approach would be more consistent with the independence of the charity sector and the autonomy of donors than a confiscatory tax or the imposition of caps on the quantum of donations to individual charities.[23] That is because it would still leave decision-making with the charity board once the administrative or cy-près variation has been applied. As administrative scheme and cy-près provisions already contain elements that seek to protect donor intent to some degree (whilst balancing it against the public benefit achieved by the variation), concerns about loss of donor autonomy and reduced donations should be ameliorated.

However, unlocking new powers for tax regulators does not necessarily mean that they will want them or will use them. In particular, the proposed reform would do little by itself to address tax regulators' lack of institutional focus on charities, lack of funding to regulate charities or perceived revenue bias. Nevertheless, clearly identifying new powers may overcome some lack of institutional focus. Further, if the IRS or Canada Revenue Agency better supported state and provincial regulators through coordinated action and education, this would be appealing on the basis of federalism and would fit with more recent academic work on charity regulation within a federation (Mayer 2016: 944–945; Simon, Dale & Chisolm 2006: 270). This is not likely to prove easy; indeed, even after the Pension Protection Act 2006 expanded the IRS's ability to disclose information to state regulators, information-sharing arrangements between the IRS and state regulators appear virtually non-existent (Owens 2017: 83; Boris & Lott 2017: 106). However, a coordinated approach has the potential to reduce the cost of action for a tax regulator, since it can also rely on the contribution of some resources by state regulators. The involvement of non-revenue authorities could diminish a perceived revenue bias of regulatory action. Further, establishing regular interactions and information sharing with state and provincial regulators – for example, under inter-agency memoranda of understanding – also has the potential to generate a base level of institutional focus on charities.

Finally, tax regulators could also better support or encourage charity trustees and directors to themselves access administrative or cy-près schemes so as to remove donor controls. This would be even more consistent with the autonomy of the charity sector from government. However, it is not proposed as the primary approach, as it is subject to the risk of jurisdiction-shopping by donors keen to find a jurisdiction in which there is little scope for action by trustees or directors.

Notes

1 Reich also outlines functions that charitable foundations could potentially form that would be consistent with democratic institutions: the social innovation and problem solving that foundations and some other charities can engage in due to the long-term and risky approaches that are open to them as a result of limited accountability mechanisms and lack of a profit motive or political cycle: Reich 2018: 152–153, 159–166.

2 For recent overviews of charity donation concessions across these jurisdictions, see Martin 2018; O'Connell 2018; Colinvaux 2019.

3 Capital gains arising from testamentary gifts are disregarded, but generally no corresponding deduction is provided either: Income Tax Assessment Act 1997 (Cth) ss 30–15(2), 118–160.

4 Similarly, in the United Kingdom for Gift Aid, there must be a 'gift', and the Gift Aid provisions also require that there be no 'benefit' for the donor associated with the gift: Kessler et al 2019: ch 15. Sections 110.1(1) and 118.1 of the Income Tax Act, RSC 1985, c 1 (Canada) also require a 'gift' in order for a charitable deduction or credit to be available, though the provisions are premised on a gift existing to the extent of an 'eligible amount' which exceeds an advantage received by the donor: s248(31); Canada Revenue Agency 2020.

5 In the United Kingdom, see also Kessler et al 2019: ch 15; HMRC 2020: ch 3, [3.19].

6 See the HMRC's more forgiving approach to membership rights (HMRC 2020: ch 3, [3.37]).

7 While the imposition of a trust or a charge on the property would breach the provision, the creation of a contractual personal obligation on the charity in the form of a condition subsequent would appear to be permissible.

8 §501(c)(3) public safety organisations are excluded.

9 The provisions and the regulations [26 CFR §§1.501(c)(3)-1(c)(1)] refer to organisations 'organized and operated exclusively for . . . charitable . . . purposes' and provide that 'An organization will be regarded as operated exclusively for one or more exempt purposes only if it engages primarily in activities which accomplish one or more of such exempt purposes specified in section 501(c)(3). An

organization will not be so regarded if more than an insubstantial part of its activities is not in furtherance of an exempt purpose'.

10 The Canadian Supreme Court has interpreted 'charitable activities' by reading in a charitable purpose requirement, noting that it is 'the purpose in furtherance of which an activity is carried out, and not the character of the activity itself, that determines whether or not it is of a charitable nature': *Vancouver Society of Immigrant and Visible Minority Women v MNR* [1999] 1 SCR 10, [152] (Iacobucci J).

11 The IRS's main concern appears to be that charitable assets will be diverted to private purpose (e.g., as remuneration payments to controllers): IRS 1989: 14–15.

12 'Private Foundations' are actually defined in *Internal Revenue Code* §509(a) as a remainder category. That is, all §501(c)(3) organisations that do not fall within four categories of public charities: 'traditional public charities' under §509(a)(1), charities that largely support themselves from sources other than investment income under §509(a)(2), 'supporting organisations' under §509(a)(3) that are closely linked to another public charity and 'testing for public safety' organisations under §509(a)(4).

13 Although they are not permitted to distribute to other ancillary funds.

14 Minimum property value thresholds apply, such that the rate is 0% below the threshold.

15 As to the characteristics of DAFs, see Special Senate Committee on the Charitable Sector 2019: 109–113; Internal Revenue Service 2019; Hussey 2010: 60–61, 64–65; Internal Revenue Code §4966(d)(2).

16 2018 WL 6199684 (ND Cal 2018). The dispute relates to the speed with which Fidelity Charitable disposed of donated shares.

17 Additional restrictions apply to foreign donations.

18 O'Connell notes tax regulators' ability to determine initial eligibility but greater difficulty in monitoring ongoing fulfilment of mission, especially where the entity is not paying any tax.

19 Statutory extensions are less widespread and more varied in the United States, but many states have adopted grounds such as a purpose becoming 'wasteful', 'inexpedient' or 'prejudicial to the public interest': Ascher et al 2006: §39.5.

20 Charitable Trusts Act 1993 (NSW) s9(1); Charities Act (UK) s 62(1)(e)(iii); Trusts Act 1973 (Qld) s105(1)(e)(iii); Trustee Act 1936 (SA) s69B(1)(e)(iii); Variation of Trusts Act 1994 (Tas) s5(3)(e)(iii); Charities Act 1978 (Vic) s2(1)(e)(iii).

21 Charitable Trusts Act 1962 (WA) s7(1)(a); Variation of Trusts Act 1994 (Tas) s5(2); Charitable Trusts Act 1957 (NZ) s32(1).

22 The existence and extent of this reduction is contested. Studies on donation concessions suggest that they generally have a small impact on amounts donated: Heist 2019; Reich 2018: 121–122. On the other hand, reduced giving by plutocrats might actually be of public benefit by permitting a greater plurality of voices: Saunders-Hastings 2018: 159.

23 Such a cap could be an effective restraint on donor control (Odendahl 1990: 239).

References

American Law Institute. *Restatement of the Law of Trusts*, Philadelphia, PA: American Law Institute, 3rd ed., 2020.

Ascher, M. 'Federalization of the Law of Charity', *Vanderbilt Law Review*, 67(6), 2014, 1581.

Ascher, M., A. Scott and W. Fratcher, *Scott and Ascher on Trusts*, New York: Aspen Publishers, 5th ed., 2006.

Atkinson, R. 'Theories of the Federal Tax Exemption for Charities: Thesis, Antithesis, and Syntheses', *Stetson Law Review*, 27(2), 1997, 395.

Australian Taxation Office. *Taxation Ruling TR 2005/13*, 2005. https://www.ato.gov.au/law/view/document?locid=%27TXR/TR200513/NAT/ATO/ft4%27&PiT=20050720000001.

Beard, J. 'Charities, Election Campaigning and the Australian Constitution', *Melbourne University Law Review*, 43(2), 2019, 462.

Boris, E. and C. Lott, 'Reflections on Challenged Regulators', in M. McGregor-Lowndes and B. Wyatt (eds), *Regulating Charities: The Inside Story*, New York: Routledge, 2017, p97.

Brody, E. 'Reforming Tax Policy with Respect to Nonprofit Organizations', in M. Harding (ed), *Research Handbook on Not-For-Profit Law*, Cheltenham: Edward Elgar, 2018, p484.

Brody, E. 'Respecting Foundation and Charity Autonomy: How Public Is Private Philanthropy?', *Chicago-Kent Law Review*, 85(2), 2010, 571.

Brody, E. 'Whose Public? Parochialism and Paternalism in State Charity Law Enforcement', *Indiana Law Journal*, 79(4), 2004, 937.

Canada Revenue Agency. *Income Tax Folio S7-F1-C1: Split-Receipting and Deemed Fair Market Value*, Government of Canada, 2020. https://www.canada.ca/en/revenue-agency/services/tax/technical-information/income-tax/income-tax-folios-index/series-7-charities-non-profit-organizations/series/income-tax-folio-s7-f1-c1-split-receipting-deemed-fair-market-value.html.

Canada Without Poverty v A-G (Canada) (2018) ONSC 4147.

Chan, K. *The Public-Private Nature of Charity Law*, Oxford: Hart Publishing, 2016.

Charities Aid Foundation. *Philanthropy Comes of Age: The Continued Growth of Donor-Advised Giving in the UK*, Kent: Charities Aid Foundation, 2020.

Chia, J., M. Harding, A. O'Connell and M. Stewart. *Taxing Not-for-Profits: A Literature Review: Not-for-Profit Project*, Melbourne: Melbourne Law School, 2011.

Citizens United v Federal Election Commission 558 US 310 (2010).

Colinvaux, R. 'Using Tax Law to Encourage Donor-Imposed Restrictions on Charitable Gifts', Paper presented at the NCPL Annual Conference, New York University, New York, 2016.

Colinvaux, R. 'Ways the Charitable Deduction Has Shaped the US Charitable Sector', in M. Harding (ed), *Research Handbook on Not-For-Profit Law*, Cheltenham: Edward Elgar, 2018, p444.

Colinvaux, R. 'Fixing Philanthropy: A Vision for Charitable Giving and Reform', *Tax Notes*, 162(9), 2019, 1007.

Corporation Tax Act 2010 (UK) c 4.

Dal Pont, G. *Law of Charity*, Chatswood: LexisNexis Butterworths, 2nd ed., 2017.

de March, T. 'The Prevention of Harm Regulator', in M. McGregor-Lowndes and B. Wyatt (eds), *Regulating Charities: The Inside Story*, New York: Routledge, 2017, p119.

Duff, D. 'The Tax Treatment of Charitable Contributions in a Personal Income Tax: Lessons from Theory and the Canadian Experience', in M. Harding, A. O'Connell and M. Stewart (eds), *Not-for-Profit Law: Theoretical and Comparative Perspectives*, Cambridge: Cambridge University Press, 2014, p199.

Eason, J. 'Making and Spending Money in Nonprofits: The Restricted Gift Life Cycle, or What Comes Around Goes Around', *Fordham Law Review*, 76, 2007, 693.

Fishman, J., S. Schwarz and L. Mayer. *Nonprofit Organizations: Cases and Materials*, St Paul: Foundation Press, 5th ed., 2015.

Fleischer, M. 'Subsidizing Charity Liberally', in M. Harding (ed), *Research Handbook on Not-For-Profit Law*, Cheltenham: Edward Elgar, 2018, p418.

Fremont-Smith, M. *Governing Nonprofit Organizations: Federal and State Law and Regulation*, Cambridge, MA: Harvard University Press, 2004.

Gergen, M. 'The Case for a Charitable Contributions Deduction', *Virginia Law Review*, 74(8), 1998, 1393.

Gillen, M. 'A Proposal for Flexibility in Private and Public Express Trust Enforcement', *Canadian Journal of Comparative and Contemporary Law*, 2(1), 2016, 115.

Gillen, M., L. Smith and D. Waters. *Waters' Law of Trusts in Canada*, Toronto: Thomson Reuters, 4th ed., 2012.

Heist, D. *Understanding Donor-Advised Funds: The Behavioural Economics, Macroeconomics and Public Policies Relating to an Emerging Trend in Philanthropy*, PhD Thesis, University of Pennsylvania, Philadelphia, 2019.

Hemel, D. 'Tangled Up in Tax', in W. Powell and P. Bromley (eds), *The Nonprofit Sector: A Research Handbook*, Stanford: Stanford University Press, 3rd ed., 2020, p144.

Henderson, W. and J. Fowles. *Tudor on Charities*, London: Thomson Reuters, 10th ed., 2015.

HMRC. *Charities: Detailed Guidance Notes on How the Tax System Operates*, London: UK Government, 2020.

Hopkins, B. *The Tax Law of Charitable Giving*, Hoboken, NJ: Wiley, 5th ed., 2014.

Hopkins, B. *The Law of Tax Exempt Organizations*, Hoboken, NJ: Wiley, 12th ed., 2019.

Horvath, A. and W. Powell, 'Seeing Like a Philanthropist', in W. Powell and P. Bromley (eds), *The Nonprofit Sector: A Research Handbook*, Stanford: Stanford University Press, 3rd ed., 2020, p81.

Hussey, M. 'Avoiding Misuse of Donor Advised Funds', *Cleveland State Law Review*, 58(1), 2010, 59.

Income Tax Act, RSC 1985 c1 (Canada).

Income Tax Act 2007 (UK) c 3.

Income Tax Assessment Act 1936 (Commonwealth of Australia).

Income Tax Assessment Act 1997 (Commonwealth of Australia).

Innes, W. and P. Boyle. *Charities, Non-Profits and Philanthropy Under the Income Tax Act*, Toronto: CCH Canadian, 2006.

Internal Revenue Service. *Revenue Ruling 64–182 CB 186*, New York: US Government, 1964.

Internal Revenue Service. *Exempt Organizations Continuing Professional Education Technical Instruction Program for Fiscal Year 1989, Special Emphasis Program: Charitable Fund-Raising*, New York: US Government, 1989.

Internal Revenue Service. *Revenue Procedure 90–12, 1990–1 C.B. 471*, New York: US Government, 1990.

Internal Revenue Service. *Donor Advised Funds*, webpage, US Government, March 2019. www.irs.gov/charities-non-profits/charitable-organizations/donor-advised-funds.

James, E. and S. Rose-Ackerman. *The Nonprofit Enterprise in Market Economics*, London: Harwood Academic Publishers, 1986.

Kessler, J., E. Wong and R. Birkbeck. *Taxation of Charities & Non-Profit Organisations*, London: Key Haven Publications, 12th ed., 2019.

Krever, R. 'Tax Deductions for Charitable Donations', in R. Krever and G. Kewley (eds), *Charities and Philanthropic Organisations: Reforming the Tax Subsidy and Regulatory Regimes*, Melbourne: Australian Tax Research Foundation, 1991, p1.

Lechterman, T. and R. Reich. 'Political Theory and the Nonprofit Sector', in W. Powell and P. Bromley (eds), *The Nonprofit Sector: A Research Handbook*, Stanford: Stanford University Press, 3rd ed., 2020, p171.

Lehmann, M. 'Major Changes for Exempt Organizations in the Pension Protection Act of 2006', *Journal of Taxation*, 106(1), 2007, 30.

Madoff, R. 'When Is Philanthropy?: How the Tax Code's Answer to This Question Has Given Rise to the Growth of Donor-Advised Funds and Why It's a Problem', in R. Reich, C. Cordelli and L. Bernholz (eds), *Philanthropy in Democratic Societies*, Chicago: University of Chicago Press, 2016, p158.

Man, T. 'Disbursement Quota Reform: The Ins and Outs of What You Need to Know', Paper delivered at the National Charity Law Symposium, Toronto, 2011.

Martin, F. 'The Major Tax Concessions Granted to Charities', in M. Harding (ed), *Research Handbook on Not-For-Profit Law*, Cheltenham: Edward Elgar, 2018, p463.

Mayer, L. 'Fragmented Oversight of Nonprofits in the United States: Does It Work – Can It Work?', *Chicago-Kent Law Review*, 91(3), 2016, 937.

Mayer, L. 'The Independent Sector: Fee-for-Service Charity and the Limits of Autonomy', *Vanderbilt Law Review*, 65(1), 2012, 49.

McClure, P. et al., *Strengthening for Purpose: Australian Charities and Not-for-Profits Commission Legislation Review 2018*, Canberra: Treasury, 2018.

Mulheron, R. *The Modern Cy-Près Doctrine*, London: UCL Press, 2006.

Murray, I. 'Charity Accumulation: Interrogating the Conventional View on Tax Restraints', *Sydney Law Review*, 37(4), 2015, 541.

Murray, I. 'Donor Advised Funds: What Can North America Learn from the Australian Approach', *Canadian Journal of Comparative and Contemporary Law*, 6, 2020, 260.

Murray, I. *Charity Law and Accumulation: Maintaining an Intergenerational Balance*, Cambridge: Cambridge University Press, 2021.

Murray, I. and M. Wesson, 'Outsourcing to Not-for-Profits: Can Judicial Enforcement of Charity Law Provide Accountability for the Performance of "Public" Functions?', *UNSW Law Journal*, 43(4), 2020, 1309–1348.

O'Connell, A. 'Taxation and the Not-for-Profit Sector Globally: Common Issues, Different Solutions', in M. Harding (ed), *Research Handbook on Not-For-Profit Law*, Cheltenham: Edward Elgar, 2018, p388.

O'Connell, A. *Taxation of Charities and Not-for-Profits*, Chatswood: LexisNexis, 2020.

Odendahl, T. *Charity Begins at Home: Generosity and Self-Interest Among the Philanthropic Elite*, New York: Basic Books, 1990.

OECD. *Taxation and Philanthropy: OECD Tax Policy Studies No 27*, Paris: OECD Publishing, 2020.

Ontario Law Reform Commission. *Report on the Law of Charities*, Toronto: Ontario Law Reform Commission, vol. 1, 1996.

Ostrander, S. 'The Growth of Donor Control: Revising the Social Relations of Philanthropy', *Nonprofit and Voluntary Sector Quarterly*, 36(2), 2007, 356.

Owens, M. 'Challenged Regulators', in M. McGregor-Lowndes and B. Wyatt (eds), *Regulating Charities: The Inside Story*, New York: Routledge, 2017, p81.

Parachin, A. 'Reforming the Regulation of Political Advocacy by Charities: From Charity Under Siege to Charity Under Rescue?', *Chicago-Kent Law Review*, 91, 2016, 1047.

Pevnick, R. 'Democratizing the Nonprofit Sector', *Journal of Political Philosophy*, 21(3), 2013, 260.

Picton, J. 'Donor Intention and Dialectic Legal Policy Frames', in M. Harding (ed), *Research Handbook on Not-For-Profit Law*, Cheltenham: Edward Elgar, 2018, p189.

Reich, R. *Just Giving: Why Philanthropy Is Failing Democracy and How It Can do Better*, Princeton, NJ: Princeton University Press, 2018.

Salamon, L. 'Of Market Failure, Voluntary Failure and Third-Party Government: Toward a Theory of Government-Nonprofit Relations in the Modern Welfare State', *Journal of Voluntary Action Research*, 16, 1987, 29.

Saunders-Hastings, E. 'Plutocratic Philanthropy', *The Journal of Politics*, 80(1), 2018, 149.

Siegel, J. 'Commensurate in Scope: Myth, Mystery, or Ghost? – Part Two', *Taxation of Exempts*, 20(4), 2009, 8.

Silver, N. 'The Tax Treatment of Donor-Restricted Charitable Gifts', *Australian Tax Forum*, 36(1), 2021, 103.

Simon, J., H. Dale and L. Chisolm. 'The Federal Tax Treatment of Charitable Organizations', in W. Powell and R. Steinberg (eds), *The Nonprofit Sector: A Research Handbook*, New Haven: Yale University Press, 2nd ed., 2006, p267.

Special Senate Committee on the Charitable Sector. *Catalyst for Change: A Roadmap to a Stronger Charitable Sector*, Canada: Senate, 2019.

Taxation of Chargeable Gains Act 1992 (UK) c 12.

Treasury (Au). *Scoping Study for a National Not-for-Profit Regulator: Final Report*, Canberra: Commonwealth of Australia, 2011.

Treasury (Au). *Tax Benchmarks and Variations Statement 2019*, 2020. https://treasury.gov.au/sites/default/files/2020-01/complete_tbvs_web.pdf

Treasury (US). *Tax Expenditures Statement*, 2020. https://home.treasury.gov/system/files/131/Tax-Expenditures-2021.pdf

Treasury Inspector General for Tax Administration. *Review of Selected Criteria Used to Identify Tax-Exempt Applications for Review: Final Report No 2017-10-054*, Washington, DC: Department of the Treasury, 2017.

Vallely, P. *Philanthropy: From Aristotle to Zuckerberg*, London: Bloomsbury, 2020.

Vancouver Society of Immigrant and Visible Minority Women v MNR [1999] 1 SCR 10.

Wyatt, B. 'Reflections on the Long and Winding Road of Regulation', in M. McGregor-Lowndes and B. Wyatt (eds), *Regulating Charities: The Inside Story*, New York: Routledge, 2017, p139.

PART II

Taxes, efficiency, and donor behavior

Theoretical and empirical

9

ECONOMICS OF PHILANTHROPIC TAX INCENTIVES

James Andreoni and Sarah Smith

1 Introduction

Most OECD governments offer tax-favorable treatment to charitable donations. In the United States, charitable donations are deducted from taxable income; France offers a non-refundable tax credit with a 66% subsidy rate, while the UK Gift Aid scheme offers a mix of a 'match-style' incentives and deductions. We document the different schemes systematically in Section 2 subsequently. One aim in tax-favoring giving is to encourage donations and support charities. Two important questions for policy-makers are: 1. Are tax incentives, which come at a cost of tax revenue foregone, the best tool for increasing charity incomes, compared to an alternative of funding grants directly to charities? 2. Is subsidizing charitable donations better than the government providing services directly? Addressing these questions requires an understanding of the effect of tax incentives on charity incomes (tax efficiency) and the wider impact of tax incentives for the level and composition of public goods and services (social efficiency). These issues are the focus of this chapter, and our discussion brings together several themes from other chapters in this volume (see also Andreoni, 2006a; Fack and Landais, 2016; Andreoni and Payne, 2013).

We first discuss the tax efficiency of tax incentives for charitable donations (Section 3). By tax efficiency we mean whether the government can increase charities' incomes by 'spending' tax revenue on tax incentives rather than on grants (see Steinberg, this volume). We include a discussion of insights from behavioral science (see Cutler, Adena, and Ugazio et al., this volume) for improving tax efficiency.

We next discuss the social efficiency of tax incentives (Section 4). This moves the discussion away from the 'income pie' to the 'output pie' (see Lohse and Scharf, this volume; Saez, 2004; Diamond, 2006). We touch briefly on a couple of aspects that have not featured prominently in economic discussions of tax incentives for donations, including the benefits of civil society and wider support for taxes and public spending.

We end with a brief discussion of large gifts in Section 5. The past decades have seen an increasing concentration of giving in the United States, which means that discussion about tax subsidies for giving increasingly leads to a discussion about tax subsidies for large gifts. Consideration of large gifts brings with it slightly different issues to that of donations by regular donors.

 DOI: 10.4324/9781003139201-12

Three current challenges make discussion of these issues very topical. First, there is a documented stagnation of giving and a decline in the number of givers in countries such as the United States (Osili et al., 2019) and United Kingdom (Charities Aid Foundation, 2012). The share of Americans who do not give has been rising in recent years, with an accelerated trend following the 2008 financial crisis. Meer et al. (2016) report that in 1960, under 5 per cent of itemizing households reported no contributions. In 2016, the share had quadrupled to about 20 per cent. Second, there is an increasing concentration of giving in the hands of a few (relatively rich) donors, whose donations may be distributed differently than those of the general population (Duquette, 2020; Duquette and Mayo, this volume). Finally, the current COVID pandemic may reduce (and/or redirect) donations at the same time as sharply increasing social need. The wealth of many of the world's billionaires has also increased by an estimated 20 per cent during the pandemic, leading many to ask how the super-wealthy – whether through taxes or philanthropy or both – can be part of the solution to the many social and economic problems that COVID has created.

2 Giving and the tax treatment of donations out of income

2.1 Giving

Table 9.1 shows that donating to charity is a widespread activity in most OECD countries: more than half of the population gives in one-third of the 38 countries listed. These numbers suggest high levels of engagement in philanthropy across the population, but a recent study by Rooney et al. (2020) finds that a static lens (i.e., looking at a snapshot of who gives in a single year) may be misleading because many donors give infrequently and not in every year. In their analysis of giving data from the Panel Survey of Income Dynamics, Rooney et al. find that half the U.S. population (more than half of those who donate) are 'switchers' who move in and out of donating over time. This means that more people have ever given than the static lens suggests but that there is a smaller number of regular donors who give every year. Regular donors typically donate larger amounts conditional on their other characteristics and, indeed, whether someone is a regular or switcher donor has greater predictive power for how much they give than observable characteristics. Greater understanding of what characterizes these different groups of donors (regular donors versus switchers) would be helpful for charities and policy-makers.

Turning to amounts donated, the United States tops the rankings – by some margin – for the amount donated as a share of GDP (at 1.44 per cent). Outside the United States, the value of donations (for the countries for which the information is available) is below 1 per cent GDP. New Zealand, Canada, the United Kingdom, and the Netherlands make up the "top five." As discussed further in the following, the trend in the United States has been towards greater concentration of giving. The share of the population that gives is in decline, and the share of total giving accounted for by big givers has been increasing (Duquette, 2020). There is evidence of similar trends in the United Kingdom (Charities Aid Foundation, 2012).

In every country, giving as a share of GDP – and the level of public goods and services funded out of private donations – is dwarfed by government spending. However, donations play a crucial role in the provision of public goods and services in many ways. They are critical to some services – for example, the UK lifeboat service, which carries out sea rescues, is funded entirely in this way; private donations also represent around one-quarter of total funding for international aid in the United Kingdom/United States. The COVID pandemic has also revealed the crucial importance of, for example, privately funded food banks in meeting a dramatic and sudden increase in need.

Table 9.1 Summary of tax incentives

	% who give	*Giving as % GDP*	*Gini*	*GovExp as share of GDP*	*Tax relief*	*Cap on value of donations attracting relief*	*Floor to tax relief*
Argentina	18%		0.414	0.263	Deduction	5% annual earnings	
Australia	68%	0.23%	0.344	0.270	Deduction	A deduction cannot add to/create a tax loss	AUD 2
Austria	53%	0.14%	0.297	0.456	Deduction	10% total income	
Belgium	39%		0.274	0.414	Credit	Donation amount may not exceed 10% of global net income nor EUR 375,350 per spouse	EUR 40 per institution
Bulgaria	16%		0.404	0.324	Deduction	65% taxable income (after the deduction)	
Canada	63%	0.77%	0.333	0.173	Credit	Up to 75% of net income can be claimed	
Chile	44%		0.444	0.222	Credit	Credits received for donations to charity and education, culture, and sport are limited at 20% of the amount of the donation subject to beneficial tax treatment or UTM 320 (approx. USD 20,558)	
Colombia	22%		0.504	0.302	Credit	Credit received is limited to 25% of the income tax liability	
Czech Republic	22%	0.04%	0.249	0.329	Deduction	15% of taxable income	2% of the tax base or CZK 1,000
Estonia	20%		0.304	0.024	Deduction	EUR 1 200 and 50% of the taxable income	
Finland	42%	0.13%	0.274	0.399	Deduction	EUR 500,000	EUR 850
France	27%	0.11%	0.316	0.483	Credit	20% taxable income	
Germany	49%	0.17%	0.319	0.279	Deduction	20% total amount of income	
Greece	7%		0.344	0.488	Credit	Donation amount may not exceed 5% of taxable income	EUR 100
Hungary	20%		0.306	0.439	Allocation		
India	24%	0.37%	0.357	0.166	Deduction	10% of gross total income	

(Continued)

Table 9.1 (Continued)

	% who give	*Giving as % GDP*	*Gini*	*GovExp as share of GDP*	*Tax relief*	*Cap on value of donations attracting relief*	*Floor to tax relief*
Indonesia	69%		0.378	0.149	Deduction	5% from current net income	
Ireland	69%	0.22%	0.328	0.251	Matching		
Israel	51%		0.39	0.365	Credit	The credit cannot exceed 30% of taxable income or NIS 9,000,000	
Italy	38%	0.30%	0.359	0.423	Deduction credit allocation	10% of the taxable income	
Japan	23%	0.12%	0.329	0.169	Deduction credit	40% of total income	JPY 2 000
Latvia	25%		0.356	0.429	Deduction	EUR 600 and 50% of the annual taxable income	
Lithuania	12%		0.373	0.095	Allocation		
Luxem-bourg	51%		0.349	0.392	Deduction	EUR 1,000,000 or 20% of net income	EUR 120
Mexico	20%	0.03%	0.454	0.210	Deduction	For donations to private institution: 7% of last year's cumulative income. For donations to governmental institutions: 4% of last year's cumulative income	
Netherlands	71%	0.30%	0.285	0.390	Deduction	10% of the total income	1% of total income and over EUR 60.
New Zealand	65%	0.79%		0.308	Credit	Total amount of the donation may not exceed 100% of taxable income	NZD 5
Norway		0.11%	0.27	0.396	Deduction matching	NOK 50,000	NOK 500
Portugal	20%		0.338	0.414	Credit allocation	The credit cannot exceed 15% of tax liability (no limit for donations to public institutions)	
Romania	20%		0.36	0.313	Other		
Singapore	48%	0.39%		0.149	Deduction matching	No limits	
Slovak Republic	28%		0.252	0.402	Allocation		

	% who give	*Giving as % GDP*	*Gini*	*GovExp as share of GDP*	*Tax relief*	*Cap on value of donations attracting relief*	*Floor to tax relief*
Slovenia	36%		0.242	0.403	Deduction allocation	0.5% of taxable revenue	
South Africa	18%		0.63	0.345	Deduction	10% of taxable income	
Sweden	55%	0.16%	0.288	0.314	Credit	The credit cannot exceed SEK 1,500	SEK 2,000 total donations and at least SEK 200 per individual donation
Switzerland	56%	0.09%	0.327	0.174	Deduction	20% of taxable income	CHF 100
United Kingdom	71%	0.54%	0.348	0.373	Matching		
United States	61%	1.44%	0.411	0.227	Deduction	60% or 30% of adjusted gross income depending on the beneficiary	

Notes to table: *% who give* refers to the % population who report having given to charity in the last month, taken from the World Giving Index, averaged over 2010–18, collected by Gallup as part of its World Poll initiative published by Charities Aid Foundation. *Giving as % GDP* refers to money donated to not-for-profits by individuals as a share of GDP, compiled by Charities Aid Foundation. All other information provided by the OECD.

2.2 Tax treatment of donations out of income

Most OECD countries offer favorable tax treatment for private donations. Information collected by the OECD on the type of tax relief offered by different countries is summarized in Table 9.1.[1]

- **Tax deductions**, by far the most common form of relief, reduce the taxable amount of income before calculating the tax liability that is due. They are more generous to taxpayers who face a higher marginal tax rate.
- **Tax credits** are an amount subtracted directly from the tax liability once the liability has been computed. The value of the credits is equal for all taxpayers.
- In a **matching scheme**, the government effectively tops up donations so that the entity receiving the donation can claim the tax relief. The UK system of Gift Aid allows charities to claim the tax that was paid on donations that are made of net of taxable income (at the basic rate of tax). Higher-rate tax payers can claim back the difference between their marginal rate and the basic rate.
- **Allocation schemes** are not formally a type of tax relief for giving, but they are a device through which taxpayers are able to allocate a fixed amount or a share of their income tax to a beneficiary directly through their tax return (e.g., in Lithuania, taxpayers can allocate up to 2 per cent of their income tax to their chosen NGO). They are more commonly

found in countries which have a lower share of givers and a limited tradition of philanthropy. See Bilodeau (1994) for an analysis of this type of funding system.

As well as differences in the type of tax-favorable treatment offered, there is also variation in the scope of tax relief. Almost all countries set a maximum amount of donations which are eligible for tax relief – either in absolute terms or as a percentage of taxable income. In more limited cases, there is also a minimum threshold for tax relief to apply.

We use a simple ordinary least squares (OLS) regression to explore correlations between the share of the population who gives and alternative types of tax incentives, conditional on characteristics such as inequality, government spending, and per capita GDP. The results are reported in Table 9.2.

There is no difference in giving (the share of the population who gives) between countries offering a tax deduction compared to countries offering a tax credit. Countries offering a match have higher giving (p = 0.076) compared to a deduction, but this is a small sample. Countries with an allocation scheme have lower giving compared to a deduction (p = 0.092), indicating the role of allocation schemes in trying to foster a culture of giving. Of the other factors, per capita GDP has a positive effect on giving; doubling GDP is associated with a 10 percentage point increase in the share of the population that gives (p = 0.070). More inequality (a higher Gini coefficient) is associated with lower giving, though the estimated relationship is not statistically significant at conventional levels (p = 0.195). There is no systematic relationship between levels of government spending and giving. As indicated by the R^2, these factors collectively account for 40 per cent of the overall variation in giving. Although tax incentives are important, there is a limit to the role that they play, and other deep-seated factors such as culture and values also matter. As a striking reminder of this, Adena, this volume, reports a sizeable difference in levels of giving between East and West Germany, which share common institutions.

In the next section, we discuss the effectiveness of tax incentives in encouraging donations, discussing both 'tax-price elasticity', that is, how much donations respond to changes in the tax-price of giving, and the effects of different features of tax incentives, drawing on standard economic theory and behavioral insights.

Table 9.2 Accounting for variation in giving

OLS regression. Dependent variable = Giving (proportion of population)

	Coeff	*SE*	*p-value*
(Deduction)			
Match (0/1)	0.243	0.131	0.076
Credit (0/1)	–0.004	0.066	0.958
Allocation (0/1)	–0.144	0.082	0.092
Other (0/1)	–0.244	0.179	0.185
Gini	–0.555	0.418	0.195
Ln (GDP per capita)	0.107	0.057	0.070
Gov spending (share)	–0.216	0.277	0.442
Constant	–0.467	0.638	0.471

Note to table: N = 35. R^2 = 0.40. Deduction, Match, Credit, Allocation, Other are defined for any country that has this type of incentive (i.e., the categories are not mutually exclusive). Variables defined as in Table 9.1.

3 Tax efficiency

The effect of offering tax incentives is to lower the tax-price of giving. Suppose a donor wants to give money to a charity and cares about the dollar income amount (*$d*) that the charity receives. Tax incentives lower the price (in terms of other consumption foregone) of giving this amount to *$(1 – r)d*, and this lower price is expected to increase donations. The tax-price elasticity of donations (i.e., how much donations respond to changes in the tax-price) has been a key policy parameter of interest in the empirical economics literature. It is important because it is a key factor in determining the tax efficiency of tax incentives in boosting charity incomes, compared to the alternative of the government giving grants. As discussed by Steinberg (this volume), the comparison of grants versus tax incentives also needs to take account of the degree of crowd-out from government grants to private donations (see also Saez, 2004; Diamond, 2006). Broadly speaking, if donations are responsive to changes in the tax-price, then tax incentives are more likely to be tax efficient. Absent crowd-out, then, if the tax-price elasticity is greater than one in absolute value, tax incentives are to be preferred to grants if the only objective is to maximize charity incomes.

Lohse and Scharf (this volume) provide a summary of the findings from the economics literature. Most studies focus on the United States, but there has been a range of estimates. In early studies, price elasticities of giving were found to be negative and greater than one in absolute value. More recently, estimates have been shown to be sensitive to the empirical strategy and in particular to the time horizon (short-term versus long-term) – most studies estimate a long-term price elasticity that is less than one in absolute value (although for an exception, see Auten et al., 2002). Summarizing the empirical literature, Andreoni (2006a) concluded that 'the sensitivity of the estimates to the estimation technique and the identification strategy has left the literature unsettled as to the true values of price and income elasticities'. In addition to sensitivity to estimation methods, it has more recently been shown that there is heterogeneity in the tax-price elasticity across income classes. There is evidence, for example, that the tax-price elasticity is greater for richer taxpayers (see Adena, this volume). Hence, the estimated value will depend on the sample of donors being used for estimation.

In the next section, we discuss additional factors that might affect the tax-price elasticity, providing some reflections on what the tax-price elasticity is measuring. We draw on other chapters in this volume to discuss aspects of the tax treatment of donations (beyond the 'tax-price') that might affect how donors respond to tax incentives, including fixed costs, salience, match-versus-rebate, and minimum thresholds. The discussion offers some insights for policy-makers who are keen to maximize the effectiveness of tax incentives.

3.1 What does the tax-price elasticity measure?

The distinction between short- and long-term tax-price elasticities recognizes that tax-price changes may affect the timing of donations rather than the amount that is donated and that what is observed in response to a tax-price change may not be a change in underlying donations but a shift in the timing of donations to take advantage of preferential tax treatment.

Another obvious but often overlooked point is that the estimated tax-price elasticity (based on administrative data) captures the responsiveness of 'taxable donations', that is, donations declared for tax-favorable treatment, which may not be the same as total donations. At least part of an observed response to a tax-price reduction may be an increase in the share of donations that are declared, regardless of whether the total donations rise or fall. The decision to claim tax relief on donations is an important margin that is likely to be affected by the amount of tax relief available. Using administrative data and exploiting a UK tax reform in 2010, Almunia et al. (2020) estimate an intensive-margin price elasticity of giving of –0.2 – but they also estimate the fixed cost of declaring donations is £47. There are two implications from this. One is that extensive-margin responses are important. The second is that part of what is captured in the extensive-margin responses may be the decision to declare.

Other fixed costs, such as the cost of changing regular giving commitments ('hassle costs'), are likely to reduce the extent to which donors change out-of-pocket donations, particularly for small tax-price changes – for evidence, see Scharf and Smith (2015). Adena (this volume) reports that around two-thirds of private donations in Germany (including to big charities such as Greenpeace and the World Wildlife Fund) are paid in the form of membership fees. These are usually of a fixed, pre-specified value and are often automatically debited from members' bank accounts. They do not adjust when the tax-price changes.

Hassle costs may dampen the effect of *deduction-style* tax-price changes. One of the benefits of a match-style incentive is that more generous tax treatment of charities (i.e., higher match rates) are automatically passed on to charities as higher incomes even if donors do not change their out-of-pocket donations. In the case of a more generous tax deduction, on the other hand, donors must make changes to out-of-pocket donations for the income received by a charity to increase (Scharf and Smith, 2015).

Donation responses to changes in the tax-price necessarily reflect the behavior of those who are aware of the presence and level of tax incentives. The evidence suggests that awareness of charitable tax incentives is sometimes low. Insights from behavioral tax policy show that making sales taxes more salient increases consumer responsiveness (Chetty et al., 2009), and the same is likely to be true for donation tax incentives. The match element of Gift Aid is arguably very salient in the United Kingdom – charities need a declaration by the donor to reclaim the tax and will provide a prompt to 'tick the Gift Aid box' every time someone donates in a structured way. For evidence on the importance of awareness in the context of bequest giving, Sanders and Smith (2016) find large responses to a simple prompt to people who are writing their wills as to whether they have thought about making a charitable bequest. Using a regression discontinuity design, they estimate a sizeable tax-price elasticity effect around the bequests tax threshold. Discussions with will writers revealed that the presence of the tax threshold created an opportunity for conversations about making a charitable bequest and avoiding bequest tax. Some of these responses may capture some element of a social norm as well as salience, but clearly, awareness of tax incentives matters.

3.2 Design features of tax incentives

Table 9.1 shows that countries vary in the *form* in which tax relief is offered to donors – and this may matter for the tax-price elasticity in ways we discuss in the following. We review some insights from the economics literature on differences between the effects of match-style incentives and deduction-style incentives (see also Cutler, Adena, and Ugazio et al., this volume), and we discuss minimum thresholds for donations to benefit for tax relief and ask whether there are lessons from psychology and neuroscience that might be relevant for tax incentives.

3.2.1 Match versus rebate

Tax incentives can be offered as a match (for every *$1* donated out of pocket, the charity receives an additional *$m* from the government in the form of a match) or as a deduction [such that every *$1* donated out of pocket only costs the donor *$(1 – r)*]. If the donor cares about the income received by the charity, referred to by Hungerman and Ottoni-Wilhelm (forthcoming) as the impact of a donation, then both types of tax incentives lower the tax-price of impact in terms of other consumption foregone and should be equivalent in their effect on donations. However, estimated tax-price elasticities associated with changes in price driven by changes in the match rate are typically greater than the estimated tax-price elasticities associated with equivalent changes in price driven by changes in the rebate rate. This evidence comes from lab and field experiments with individual charities (Eckel and Grossman, 2003, 2017), from a hypothetical experiment varying the match/rebate elements of the UK Gift Aid scheme (Scharf and Smith, 2015), and from natural experiments studied by Hungerman and Ottoni-Wilhelm (forthcoming).

The literature discusses several explanations for the observed difference, including timing differences (matches are typically upfront, whereas deductions may benefit a donor with a delay) and pure framing effects (a deduction may be seen as selfish, whereas a match may be seen as co-operative). One explanation, already discussed, is that, if out-of-pocket donations do not adjust, for example, because of hassle costs, then the income received by the charity (impact) will vary mechanically with changes in the match rate and not at all with variations in the rebate rate (Scharf and Smith, 2015). More recently, Hungerman and Ottoni-Wilhelm (forthcoming) note that if the donor cares about the impact and also gets warm glow utility (Andreoni, 1989, 1990) from their own gift, a deduction affects the opportunity cost of both the impact and warm glow, while the match reduces the cost of impact but does not alter the cost of one's out-of-pocket donation. This adds to the explanations of why the two types of incentive might differ in their effect.

Matching done through the tax system, is different from matching used as a fundraising scheme. It is not uncommon for charities to use a large private gift as a fund to "match" the donations of other donors, until the fund is exhausted. In practice, large donors usually let the charities keep the full amount in the unlikely case that the fund is not exhausted. This means that a matched gift will not actually increase total donations and the matching fund is entirely infra-marginal. Consistent with this interpretation, Karlan and List (2007) find no effects of the rate of the match (1-for-1 versus 2-for-1). Rather, as shown by Huck and Rasul (2011), it is the fact that one donor has made a very large grant, not the match rate, that makes the difference to other donors, perhaps because it sends a signal of quality for that charity (Andreoni, 1990).

3.2.2 Thresholds

Several countries operate minimum thresholds for donations to qualify for tax relief. Recent field experiments provide insights into how these might increase donations compared to a system with no minimum threshold. Setting minimum thresholds can incentivize donors below the threshold to give at or above it. They can also set a social norm for acceptable donations – however, this can cause donations to go down as well as up, depending on the level of the threshold relative to individuals' donation amounts (Harbaugh, 1998, Andreoni and Petrie, 2004). Huck et al. (2015) show that non-convex matching with a lower price for higher gifts outperforms simple linear matching, but thresholds need to be high and ideally personalized such that they cause each donor to adjust their donations upwards (Adena and Huck, 2017). In a real-world setting, varying thresholds by income or by tax-rate in a progressive system would be one possible way forward.

3.2.3 Framing

The lessons from dictator and ultimatum games are that fairness, efficiency, equity, and reciprocity are important for people's decision to give (see Cutler, this volume). Sentiments such as 'giving back' and 'a sense of duty' feature prominently in the narratives of Giving Pledgers, billionnaires who have pledged to give away at least half of their wealth. Giving Pledgers also frequently mention that their giving is shaped by values from religion or from their upbringing. To date, most experimental findings focus on how values affect the *level* of giving, but they may also affect how people respond to tax incentives – hence, the framing of tax incentives may matter for the response.

Studies have found that 'social information', in particular, information about other people's giving, affects donations. Shang and Croson (2009) study messages about other people's donations in the context of a donation phone-in, while Smith et al. (2015) find that donors respond to seeing information on how much other donors have given on a social fundraising platform. Behavioral tax policy has demonstrated that social norm messages from the government can increase tax compliance (Hallsworth et al., 2017). In the context of bequest giving, Sanders et al. (2016) show that social norm messages ('leaving a bequest is something that many people do') increases take-up among those writing a will for the first time compared to a simple awareness message ('have you thought about leaving a bequest'). Reciting the 'golden rule' and other moral suasion also increases giving (Dal Bó and Dal Bó, 2014). Such messages about donations could both increase awareness and also reinforce social norms about giving that could increase the effectiveness of tax incentives.

Recently, List et al. (2019) ran a field experiment on fundraising campaign in Alaska, where identical mailings about the "Pick-Click-Give" program were sent to thousands of households. While each mailing had the same information, their headline banner differed. Half appealed to their love of Alaska, and half appealed to the good feeling donors will have about themselves. They found significantly more giving among those who were invited to think about themselves when giving rather than the good the donation will do for the community.

4 Social efficiency

Tax efficiency is a relatively narrow concept focusing on the effect of tax incentives on the revenues of charities. Consideration of the social efficiency of tax incentives moves from a focus on the size of the 'income pie' to the size (and composition) of the 'output pie' and the social benefits derived from charitable income.

4.1 Maximizing the 'output pie'

One argument for using tax revenue to support charities emanates from the claim that non-profit provision is more (cost-)effective. The argument is supported by the observation that because private charities often work directly with the populations served, unlike bureaucrats and legislators, and so can generate greater socially beneficial impact for a given revenue cost compared to government provision. Offering tax incentives puts allocation decision in the hands of donors, rather than government grants and will result in an allocation of resources within the charitable sector that is more (cost-)effective if donors care about charity cost-effectiveness and have more information than the government about which charities are most cost effective.

Evidence on whether donors care about cost-effectiveness is mixed (Lohse and Scharf, this volume). Donors respond to information about the magnitude of overhead costs (Gneezy et al., 2014) and to simple ratings by watchdog organizations like Charity Navigator that combine several metrics, including overhead (Gordon et al., 2009). However, such measures may not be good indicators of cost-effectiveness. In lab and field experiments, donors do not appear to respond to scientific measures of effectiveness, such as the ability of a charity to improve outcomes for recipients. Moreover, donors and are not willing to pay to acquire information on effectiveness (Karlan and Wood, 2017; Burum et al., 2020). We show in the following that many Giving Pledgers are strongly motivated by the potential impact of their gifts and prefer to transfer results-based methods from business to non-profits. However, many (large and small) donors are motivated by a range of factors besides charity effectiveness, including personal interests, values, social pressure (Andreoni et al., 2017; DellaVigna et al., 2012, Andreoni and Serra-Garcia, 2021a, 2021b), and socially motivated fundraising that takes place in the context of workplaces or peer networks (Scharf and Smith, 2015).

The effective altruism movement, started in the late 2000s, promotes the twin ideas of directing giving to where it can do most good and determining what is the most good by using evidence and reasoning. However, there is debate about some of the practical implications of the effective altruism principle. First, there may be a limit to what impact has been measured, so donors can only choose from a limited range of organizations. More fundamentally, there may be a limit to what can be measured (at least on a comparable basis). A de-worming organization can measure how many people were treated, n, at an estimated value v per treatment: effectiveness is nv. An organization providing mental health services can count the number of people helped, but may find it harder to monetize the benefit. A suicide hotline may find it hard to know how many lives they have saved.

Second, when measures of effectiveness are available, they capture marginal benefits that are unlikely to extrapolate to a case for directing all donations to the (currently) most effective charity. Providing an additional mosquito net has been demonstrated to be a cheap and highly effective way to save a life by preventing malaria, but there is a limit on how many mosquito nets are needed.

Finally, many have argued that focusing on the interventions that work/don't work ignores the potential of systemic changes in power and institutions that might bring about even greater benefits in the longer term. Adherents of effective altruism would argue that donors should support systemic change if it does the most good, but it is hard to fulfill the second principle of using evidence-based reasoning: typically marginal interventions, carried out within existing institutional structures, are the easiest to evaluate in order to produce the required evidence base.

The principle of effective altruism makes sense for a donor who is considering which charity to give to out of a set of charities doing similar work where measures of effectiveness are available. However, it may be a 'social distortion' in the case of decisions across different charities, favoring charities for which effectiveness can easily be measured, potentially at the expense of charities engaged in less tangible, more risky, more experimental, more novel, or more long-term investments, that could ultimately be of greater value but whose rewards are, as yet, unclear.

This brings us to what Reich (2017) calls the 'discovery case' for tax incentives. Tax incentives may help to support a plurality of organizations supplying public goods and services, and this plurality may be more likely to foster innovation, recognize real needs more quickly, and respond to changing circumstances. Precisely because individual donors do not all give to the (currently) most cost-effective charities but give to many different charities, donations can help to create and sustain a vibrant charity sector. There may be a short-term cost in not giving to the (currently) most cost-effective charity, but there may be longer-term benefits of sustaining a diverse charitable sector that are even greater.

Going further, there may be additional benefits to supporting a plurality of charitable organizations in terms of fostering a healthy civil society that exists between the public and the government. As well as the instrumental value from delivering public services, charitable organizations engage in advocacy on issues such as health, the environment, and human rights. They may be part of a vibrant civil society that is important for a healthy democracy – influencing policy and providing marginalized groups (including non-voters) with a voice. In some countries, they may also play a 'checks and balances' role and hold governments accountable. Tax-favoring donations, by introducing a degree of separation between the source of funding and the allocation decision, are likely to be a more effective way to promote civil society than government grants in a way that is free from direct political influence. This in itself may be a valuable output from a system of tax subsidies.

4.2 Composition of public services

Tax incentives for donations are likely to lead to a different allocation of funding across charitable causes (religious giving, social services, health, education, culture, etc.) compared to government grants/provision. According to standard political economy models, government provision will target the preferences of the 'median voter'. By contrast, donors may allocate funding across charities according to their personal preferences (which will be reflected in different levels of warm glow from giving to different causes). More specifically, however, and this is a common criticism of tax incentives for giving, the allocation associated with tax subsidies will be weighted towards the preferences of richer donors both because they give more and also because they enjoy a greater subsidy under deduction-style incentives.

Evidence shows that the distribution of donations by the rich differs from that of the rest of the population. Reich (2017) reports that, among donors with incomes less than £100k, 67 per cent of donations went to religious causes, 10 per cent to basic needs, 4 per cent to health, 3 per cent to education, and 3 per cent to arts, whereas, among donors with incomes greater than £1 million, 17 per cent went to religious causes, 5 per cent to basic needs, 25 per cent to health, 25 per cent to education, and 15 per cent to arts. The important questions are whether directing funding in line with donor preferences, not median voter preferences, is socially efficient and whether it is equitable.

Inherent in the mechanism for allocating government money via tax subsidies is a tension between personal motivations for giving to different causes (which drive donor decisions) and the associated social benefits of donations, which, we assume, the government wants to maximize. Of course, many donors care about maximizing social benefits in the short or long term; arguably, richer donors are more likely to act on this, not least because they can pay for the information and advice needed to make cost-effective donation decisions (Andreoni, 1998). But many donor choices are motivated by personal (reputational) benefits or personal preferences that have nothing to do with social welfare – there are many examples of the latter in the narratives of those billionaires taking the Giving Pledge. In this case, the allocation by donors will not be socially optimal. In itself, this does not invalidate the case for tax incentives, but it would point to a system that targets tax subsidies at charities which generate greater perceived social benefits, possibly varying tax incentives by cause. Whether a government could do this objectively, without being swayed by political considerations, is, however, a separate issue.

The second consideration is equity. Giving weight to the strength of people's preferences in directing funding in public service provision is arguably a potential advantage of tax subsidies over grants – it allows people to express their willingness to pay for different goods and services in markets where there is no price. However, tax deductions give greater weight to the preferences of richer votes, and this is seen by many as inequitable. Again, this does not invalidate the case for tax incentives, but if this is a concern, then the value of tax subsidies should be equalized across donors through a system of tax credits. Here, there is a possible tension between designing a system of tax incentives that is tax efficient (which would imply giving more generous tax incentives to richer donors, who are more tax-price sensitive) and designing a system of tax incentives that is seen as 'fair' (which would imply equal-value tax subsidies for all donors).

A final argument in relation to the provision of public goods and services is that tax subsidies for giving may help to increase voter support for government provision, particularly in diverse societies. Allowing donors to direct the allocation of (some) government funding provides a mechanism for publicly funded services to reflect a wider range of preferences beyond those of the median voter. In a diverse society, government-provided services (meeting the preferences of the median voter) may be a long way from the preferences of different groups in society, and this may reduce voters' willingness to pay taxes (Alesina et al., 1999). Levels of public spending, support for redistribution, and the legitimacy of the tax system are lower in more diverse societies (Li, 2010). More ethnic and religious diversity in a community also predicts lower donations (Andreoni et al., 2016). Giving people a voice in the composition of public services provides an opportunity to overcome this by better reflecting diverse preferences, and this may increase support for tax and public spending more generally (De Neve et al., 2014). Tax incentives in the form of allocation mechanisms provide a voice in the tax system explicitly. Other types of tax incentives (deductions, credits, matches) could be framed in this way.

4.3 Happiness

As well as potential benefits to charity recipients, it is well recognized that act of spending or the decision to spend money on others generates good feelings, often called a warm glow (Andreoni, 1989, 1990). To what extent should tax incentives take account of personal benefits to individual donors? This is perhaps a philosophical question as much it is an economic one (Andreoni, 2006a).

According to the Haig-Simons ideal, warm glow from giving is outside the definition of social welfare; that is, the government should not count warm glow as part of social welfare even if donors care about warm glow when choosing donations. The argument is that the money a donor gives away rather than consumes is no longer the donor's income and should be taxed at the rate of the ultimate recipients' income, which in the case of poverty relief is likely zero, as argued by Diamond (2006). At the other end, Kaplow (1995) fully supports counting all warm glow in welfare, so even gifts to friends should be tax deductible for the giver. Steinberg, this volume, explores the implications of this argument, suggesting that there is a case for tax incentives to facilitate mutually beneficial donations that would otherwise not occur.

There are several reasons warm glow considerations do not belong in social welfare calculations. First, unlike utility from consuming 'real' goods and services, warm glow from giving is a 'decision utility' and may be affected by the context and framing of giving decisions. Andreoni (1995), for instance, finds giving depends significantly on whether the positive action is to choose how much to give (the remainder is not given) or how much to not give (the remainder is given), with the former giving more, despite having identical payoff spaces. Should these be treated differently? Second, there is evidence that fundraising creates social pressure and that people will pay to avoid it (Andreoni et al., 2017; DellaVigna et al., 2012). Does the warm glow from alleviating the guilt that fundraising creates count towards social welfare? It is also clear that some sources of warm glow from giving, such as personal reputation or prestige, have no social benefit and may create social harm by making others feel worse off. Should the billionaire donor who enjoys personal satisfaction from endowing a fancy new university building receive a large tax benefit solely as a result? Andreoni (2006a) makes the case that if there is no compelling social interest argument for the donation itself, then the fact the donation has been made should have no effect on the calculation of the socially optimal level of the public good itself. The social welfare calculation should no more consider the additional utility from donating than the lost utility from other consumption foregone.

As discussed by Sellen (this volume), individual donors will consider the warm glow from donating in deciding whether and how to give – and in making trade-offs between donating and other spending. He explains that experiments show that spending on other people can generate more happiness than spending on oneself, as revealed by self-reported measures of happiness and he argues for promoting awareness of what he calls these "positive externalities", but are personal benefits. What do these self-reports tell us? Kahneman and Deaton (2010) used happiness data to ask the question directly: Does money buy happiness? In brief, their answer is that money can relieve unhappiness but only for incomes reaching about the median household income in the area the respondent resides. Beyond that, association of income to happiness flattens out.

5 Large gifts

In this section, we briefly discuss large gifts, exemplified by donors who have made good on their Giving Pledge (https://givingpledge.org/). Launched in June 2010 by Warren Buffet and Bill and Melinda Gates, the Giving Pledge is a public commitment by billionaires, initially from the United States but now from 25 countries worldwide, to donate at least half of their wealth during their lifetimes. The site itself has information on the pledges rather than donations and whether the pledges have been fulfilled, but many Pledgers have given away billions of dollars. In recent years, large gifts have become increasingly important. Analyzing U.S. tax data, Duquette (2020) shows that in 1960, 9.8 per cent of potential donors gave half of all donations; by 2012, half of total giving came from just 1.8 per cent of potential donors. The increasing concentration is due both to a decline in the share of the population who gives and also an increase in the value of the largest gifts. Hungerman (2020) reports that the increase in giving concentration is steeper than the estimated increases in income inequality reported in the literature. Any discussion of tax subsidies for giving is therefore increasingly a discussion about tax subsidies for large gifts made by the very wealthy.

Following the COVID pandemic, which has brutally exposed global inequalities, there has also been an increased focus on the fact that just a handful of the world's billionaires, who have seen their combined wealth increase by 20 per cent, have the capacity to tackle many of the major social problems that governments and the charitable sector are facing. For billionaire donors, there is no 'public goods problem' of coordinating contributions from many donors. Rather, billionaire donors have the resources to fund the whole of provision of some public goods/services individually. The head of the World Food Program USA recently called directly on billionaires to come forward to help tackle global food poverty, arguing that they have enough money (many times over) to solve the problem. The money spent by the Bill and Melinda Gates Foundation equals that of many individual countries – in fact, it is the around the same level as Office of Development Assistance spending by the Netherlands, the world's seventh-largest donor country. Large gifts can also be used to make big investments in risky medical research that could be transformative. The increasing concentration in giving, and the growing importance of billionaire donors with the capacity for very large gifts, raises fundamental questions about the implications for the charitable sector and also about what the appropriate policy toward large gifts is.

Tonin and Vlassopoulos (2018) present an interesting analysis of the Giving Pledgers. They show that, compared to the sample of all billionaires (defined by the Hurun Global Rich List), those who are self-made billionaires compared to those who inherited their wealth and those who are richer are more likely to pledge. Age and gender do not have an effect. Although Pledgers are more likely to be self-made billionaires, their giving narratives often refer to the 'luck' that they have experienced over their lives and a sense of wanting to give back and give others similar chances. Education – and the opportunities that education provides – is a common theme.

The giving narratives of Pledgers provide insights into their self-reported motivations for giving. In many respects, the motivations of Pledgers are similar to those of other givers (see also Andreoni et al., 2021). Many Pledgers refer to values that come from religion or from their personal upbringing. Joy-of-giving motivations are also important. Pledgers describe giving as providing happiness and satisfaction in a way that further material spending does not ('the more I do for others, the happier I am'). Perhaps different from regular donors, however, they see the (opportunity) cost of giving as low and perhaps effectively zero ('my family and I will give up nothing we need or want by fulfilling this 99% pledge'). Many explicitly say that they have no need for further material items and also see passing (a lot of) wealth on to their children as actively causing harm ('I do not believe that those who provide their offspring with luxuriously upholstered lives serve them well but rather saddle them with a terrible burden').

For major donors, however, a sense of agency and impact is more important than for regular donors (Kessler et al., 2019). Many Pledgers talk about translating methods and insights from their successful business careers to solving social problems ('I don't just write checks – we try to make the organizations we fund better. The results have been rather outstanding'). Not surprisingly, with the amount of money that they have to give away, many Pledgers talk about investing in solutions to problems rather than treating the symptoms ('I am not looking for band aids; I am looking for solutions').

As is the case for regular donors, preferences and personal passions are important in determining where large gifts are directed. One difference with large gifts is that each large gift has a bigger impact on the overall distribution. The evidence shows that richer donors – including the Pledgers – give to different charitable causes than do regular donors. Education, health, and the arts are the leading causes that are cited. This spread of causes contrasts with donors in the general population, who give a larger percentage of total donations to religious organizations than to any other subsector. The observed decline in the number of givers and an increasing concentration of giving is therefore likely to change the causes that benefit from donations, with a shift away from dominance by religious giving. Again, this is not an argument in itself to take away tax subsidies but to ensure that they are attached to charitable activities which are agreed to be genuinely in the social interest.

Should large gifts be treated differently by the tax system from regular donations? Currently many large gifts are likely to enjoy larger tax subsidies (per dollar), but only because they are likely to be made by higher-income donors who pay a higher marginal rate of tax, not because of the size of the gift per se. In many countries (see Table 9.1), larger donations may also be capped in terms of the relief they get if they exceed annual tax-free donation limits. There is a tax-efficiency argument for more generous tax treatment of large gifts are more sensitive to tax incentives. Studies that explore heterogeneity by income show that the tax-price elasticity is greater for high-income donors, which would justify a greater subsidy if the sole objective were to maximize the size of the (income) pie for charities, albeit for higher income donors, not larger gifts per se.

Hungerman (2020) makes an explicit argument for giving greater subsidies to large gifts if giving is more concentrated. The intuition behind his argument that increasing large gifts will have fewer negative crowd-out effects in a system where giving is more concentrated and large gifts account for a greater share of total giving. The argument may be stronger still with evidence that large gifts from well-known billionaire donors crowd *in* other gifts by acting as a signal of quality (Vesterlund, 2006; Andreoni, 2006b; Karlan and List, 2020), although this argument applies to donations to a single charity rather than aggregate donation. In particular, it may be more about influencing the allocation of the pie rather than growing the pie.

Looking at the income pie only tells part of the story, and it is important to also look at what the donations are funding – and the social welfare that is generated. Many large gifts appear to be motivated to maximize the prestige (and other personal benefits) to the donors. This applies to the praise that is given for major philanthropists' giving (in aggregate); billionaire donors are now rightly being challenged for flaunting their philanthropy while doing everything they can to avoid paying tax on their business activities. However, even if they do pay all the tax that is due, many of the world's billionaires could still afford to give away huge sums of money. Much criticism by the effective altruism movement is of large donations made to cultural and higher education institutions, which seem to have little to do with wider social benefits. There is also criticism of donor advised funds, which allow donors to claim tax benefits up front – including benefits of avoided capital gains taxation – and pay money into a fund which may not be disbursed and may do no social good for many years (Andreoni, 2018).

Many of the narratives provided by those making the Giving Pledge focus on the desire to achieve impact. According to the analysis by Tonin and Vlassopoulos (2018), this is by far the most prevalent theme in their narratives. Reich's discovery case for subsidizing philanthropy (that is, promoting a plurality of organizations in order to build capacity for social innovation) likely applies more to large gifts than to smaller donations, since the latter will typically go to established organizations with fundraising capacity. Large donations can be used for risky investments with the potential for large pay-offs, such as investment in medical research. This type of funding may be particularly important in a sector where borrowing to invest may be difficult. Many large gifts also go to political/advocacy organizations, such as investing in ways intended to sustain a vibrant civic society. This evidence suggests that large gifts can generate sizeable social benefits, which would justify some subsidy. However, transparency and accountability are important where such large sums, including of public funding, are involved.

6 Discussion

Tax incentives are a key policy tool that governments have to affect the level and composition of donations to charities. There has long been a focus in economics on estimating tax-price elasticities, but responses to tax incentives will be affected not only by the tax-price but also by the design and framing of tax incentives. Relevant factors are likely to include salience, fixed costs, minimum thresholds, social norms, and social information. These are important design features for policy makers to consider.

The design and scope of tax incentives should aim to maximize social benefit while also giving a voice to citizens. The definition of social benefit goes beyond channeling giving to the (currently measurable) most cost-effective charities and encompasses a 'discovery case' for supporting a plurality of organizations offering the possibility of a wide range of benefits and longer-term innovation. By allowing citizens to have a say in the allocation of some government funding via tax-subsidized donations, governments may also help to build support for tax/spending more generally. To date, there has been little discussion of these wider externalities, but understanding what it means to have a healthy charitable sector and a strong civil society – and the role of tax subsidies in that – is an important topic for discussion (see Lohse and Scharf, this volume).

Tax credits, rather than deductions, offer a way to give citizens equal voice. On social efficiency grounds, it is not clear that there is a case for offering greater tax subsidies (per dollar) for large gifts, not least since the opportunity cost of donating for the very wealthy is practically zero. The case for giving a subsidy is that large gifts have the potential to achieve big social benefits, particularly when used in ways that small donations cannot be to fund higher-risk/reward projects. If there is concern about the purpose of large gifts, the government can use tax subsidies to direct large gifts to causes where they will have maximal positive benefit, although there is a risk of excessive political interference. No matter the policy, however, ensuring transparency around large gifts and a degree of accountability is clearly important to include. The current trend towards increased use of donor advised funds works against this. A first step would be to focus as much attention on the donations that deliver on the Pledges as on the Pledges themselves.

Note

1 https://www.unige.ch/conference-philanthropy-taxation/files/4616/0646/4944/Full_report_oecd-taxation-and-philanthropy.pdf

References

Adena, M. and Huck, S. (2017) "Matching donations without crowding out? Some theoretical considerations, a field, and a lab experiment." *Journal of Public Economics*, 148(April), 32–42.

Alesina, A., Baqir, R. and Easterly, W. (1999) "Public goods and ethnic divisions." *Quarterly Journal of Economics*, 114.

Alumnia, M., Guceri, I., Lockwood, B. and Scharf K. (2020) "More giving or more givers? The effects of tax incentives on charitable donations in the UK." *Journal of Public Economics*, 183, 1–16

Andreoni, J. (1989) "Giving with impure altruism: Applications to charity and Ricardian equivalence." *Journal of Political Economy*, 97(6), 1447–1458.

Andreoni, J. (1990) "Impure altruism and donations to public goods: A theory of warm-glow giving." *The Economic Journal*, 100(401).

Andreoni, J. (1995). "Warm-glow versus cold-prickle: The effects of positive and negative framing on cooperation in experiments." *The Quarterly Journal of Economics*, 110(1), 1–21.

Andreoni, J. (1998) "Toward a theory of charitable fund-raising." *Journal of Political Economy*, 106(6), 1186–1213.

Andreoni, J. (2006a) "Philanthropy." In Kolm, S. C. and Mercier Ythier, J. (Eds.), *Handbook of Giving, Reciprocity and Altruism* (pp. 1201–1269). Amsterdam: North Holland.

Andreoni, J. (2006b) "Leadership giving in charitable fund-raising." *Journal of Public Economic Theory*, 8(1), 1–22.

Andreoni, J. (2018) "The benefits and costs of donor advised funds." In Moffitt, R. (Ed.), *Tax Policy and the Economy*. Washington, DC: NBER.

Andreoni, J., Nikiforakis, N. and Stoop, J. (2021) "Higher socioeconomic status does not predict decreased prosocial behavior in a field experiment." *Nature Communications*, 12(1), 1–8.

Andreoni, J. and Payne, A.A. (2013) "Charitable giving." In Auerbach, A., Chetty, R., Feldstein, M. and Saez, E. (Eds.), *Handbook of Public Economics* (Vol. 5, pp. 1–50). Amsterdam: North Holland.

Andreoni, J., Payne, A. A., Smith, J. and Karp, D. (2016). "Diversity and donations: The effect of religious and ethnic diversity on charitable giving." *Journal of Economic Behavior & Organization*, 128, 47–58.

Andreoni, J. and Petrie, R. (2004) "Public goods experiments without confidentiality: A glimpse into fund-raising." *Journal of Public Economics*, 88(7–8), 1605–1623.

Andreoni, J., Rao, J. M. and Trachtman, H. (2017) "Avoiding the ask: A field experiment on altruism, empathy, and charitable giving." *Journal of Political Economy*, 125(3), 625–653.

Andreoni, J. and Serra-Garcia, M. (2021a) "Time inconsistent charitable giving." *Journal of Public Economics*, 198, 104391.

Andreoni, J. and Serra-Garcia, M. (2021b) "The pledging puzzle: How can revocable promises increase charitable giving?." *Management Science*, forthcoming.

Auten, Gerald, Sieg, H. and Clotfelter, C. (2002) "Charitable giving, income, and taxes: An analysis of panel data." *American Economic Review*, 92(1), 371–382.

Bilodeau, M. (1994) "Tax-earmarking and separate school financing." *Journal of Public Economics* 54, 51–63.

Burum, B., Nowak, M. and Hoffman, M. (2020) "An evolutionary explanation for ineffective altruism." *Nature Human Behavior*, 4.

Charities Aid Foundation. (2012) *Mind the Gap*. https://www.cafonline.org/about-us/publications/2012-publications/mind-the-gap

Chetty, R., Kroft, K. and Looney, A. (2009) "Salience and taxation: Theory and evidence." *American Economic Review*, 99.

Dal Bó, E. and Dal Bó, P. (2014). "Do the right thing: The effects of moral suasion on cooperation." *Journal of Public Economics*, 117, 28–38.

DellaVigna, Stefano, List, J. A. and Malmendier, U. (2012) "Testing for altruism and social pressure in charitable giving." *Quarterly Journal of Economics*, 127(1), 1–56.

De Neve, J., Lamberton, C. and Norton, M. (2014) *Eliciting Taxpayer Preferences Increases Tax Compliance*. CEP Discussion Papers DP1270. London: CEP.

Diamond, P. (2006) "Optimal tax treatment of private contributions for public goods with and without warm glow preferences." *Journal of Public Economics*, 90(4–5), 897–919.

Duquette, N. J. (2020) "The evolving distribution of giving in the United States." *Nonprofit and Voluntary Sector Quarterly*, 36(December).

Dunn, E. W., Aknin, L. B. and Norton, M. I. (2008) "Spending money on others promotes happiness." *Science*, 319(5870), 1687–1688.

Eckel, C. C. and Grossman, P. J. (2003) "Rebates and matching: Does how we subsidize charitable contributions matter?" *Journal of Public Economics*, 87(3), 681–701.

Eckel, C. C. and Grossman, P. J. (2017) "Comparing rebate and matching subsidies controlling for donors' awareness: Evidence from the field." *Journal of Behavioral and Experimental Economics*, 66, 88–95.

Fack, G. and Landais, C. (2016) *Charitable Giving and Tax Policy: A Historical and Comparative Perspective*. Oxford: Oxford University Press.

Gneezy, A., Gneezy, U. and Keenan, E. (2014) "Avoiding overhead aversion in charity." *Science*, 346(6209), 632–635.

Gordon, T. P., Knock, C. L. and Neely, D. (2009) "The role of rating agencies in the market for charitable contributions: An empirical test." *Journal of Accounting and Public Policy*, 28(6), 469–484.

Hallsworth, M., List, J., Metcalfe, R. and Vlaev, I. (2017) "The behavioralist as tax collector: Using natural field experiments to enhance tax compliance." *Journal of Public Economics*, 148.

Harbaugh, W. T. (1998) "What do donations buy?: A model of philanthropy based on prestige and warm glow." *Journal of Public Economics*, 67(2), 269–284.

Huck, S. and Rasul, I. (2011). "Matched fundraising: Evidence from a natural field experiment." *Journal of Public Economics*, 95(5–6), 351–362.

Huck, S., Rasul, I. and Shephard, A. (2015) " Comparing charitable fundraising schemes: Evidence from a natural field experiment and a structural model." *American Economic Journal: Economic Policy*, 7, 326–369.

Hungerman, D. M. (2020) *On the Tax Treatment of Large Charitable Gifts*. Working Paper, Department of Economics. Notre Dame: University of Notre Dame.

Hungerman, D. M. and Ottoni-Wilhelm, M. (forthcoming) "Impure impact giving: Theory and evidence." *Journal of Political Economy*, preprint. https://doi., org/10.1086/713190.

Kahneman, D. and Deaton, A. (2010). "High income improves evaluation of life but not emotional well-being." *Proceedings of the national academy of sciences*, 107(38), 16489–16493.

Karlan, D. and List, J. A. (2007). "Does price matter in charitable giving? Evidence from a large-scale natural field experiment." *American Economic Review*, 97(5), 1774–1793.

Kaplow, L. (1995) "A note on subsidizing gifts." *Journal of Public Economics*, 58(3), 469–477.

Karlan, D. and List, J. A. (2020) "How can Bill and Melinda Gates increase other people's donations?" *Journal of Public Economics*, 191.

Karlan, D. and Wood, D. H. (2017) "The effect of effectiveness: Donor response to aid effectiveness in a direct mail fundraising experiment." *Journal of Behavioral and Experimental Economics*, 66, 1–8.

Kessler, J., Milkman, K. and Zhang, C. (2019) "Getting the rich and powerful to give." *Management Science*, 65(9), 4049–4062.

Li, S. (2010) "Social Identities, Ethnic Diversity, and Tax Morale." *Public Finance Review*, 38.

List, J. A., Murphy, J. J., Price, M. K. and James, A. G. (2019) *Do appeals to donor benefits raise more money than appeals to recipient benefits? Evidence from a natural field experiment with Pick. Click. Give* (No. w26559). National Bureau of Economic Research.

Meer, J., Wulfsberg, E. and Miller, D. (2016) *The great recession and charitable giving*, December. NBER Working Paper No. w22902. https://ssrn.com/abstract=2880340

Osili, U. O., Clark, C. J. and Han, X. (2019) "Heterogeneity and giving: Evidence from U.S. households before and after the Great Recession of 2008." *American Behavioral Scientist*, 63(14), 1841–1862.

Reich, R. (2017) *Just Giving: Why Philanthropy Is Failing Democracy and How It Can Do Better*. Princeton: Princeton University Press.

Rooney, P. M., Ottoni-Wilhelm, M., Wang, X. and Han, X. (2020) "Dynamics of American giving: Descriptive evidence." *Nonprofit and Voluntary Sector Quarterly* (December). doi:10.1177/0899764020977661

Saez, E. (2004) "The optimal treatment of tax expenditures." *Journal of Public Economics*, 88(12), 2657–2684.

Sanders, M. and Smith, S. (2016) "Can simple prompts increase bequest giving? Field evidence from a legal call centre." *Journal of Economic Behavior and Organisation*, 125.

Sanders, M., Smith, S., Groot, B. and Nolan, D. (2016) *Legacy Giving and Behavioral Insights, Behavioural Insights Team*. https://www.bi.team/wp-content/uploads/2016/10/Legacy-Giving-Report-final.pdf.

Scharf, K. and Smith, S. (2015) "The price elasticity of charitable giving: Does the form of tax relief matter?" *International Tax and Public Finance*, 22(2), 330–352.

Shang, J. and Croson, R. (2009) "A field experiment in charitable contribution: The impact of social information on the voluntary provision of public goods." *Economic Journal*, 119, 1422–1439.

Smith, S., Windmeijer, F. and Wright, E. (2015) "Peer effects in charitable giving: Evidence from the (running) field." *Economic Journal*, 125(585), 1053–1071.

Tonin, M. and Vlassopoulos, M. (2018) "Why give away your wealth? An analysis of the billionaires' view." In Costa-Font, J. and Macis, M. (Eds.), *Social Economics* (pp. 61–78). Cambridge, MA: MIT Press.

Vesterlund, L. (2006) *Why Do People Give. The Nonprofit Sector: A Research Handbook*. CT: Yale University Press.

10
THE DESIGN OF TAX INCENTIVES FOR GIVING

Richard Steinberg

Ever since Vickrey (1962) first proposed the treasury efficiency criterion for evaluating the charitable giving tax deduction in the United States, economists have argued over whether personal giving should receive special treatment through the personal income tax system and, if so, what form that treatment should take. It is time to bring these disparate analyses from economics and selected other fields together, and that is my goal in this chapter on tax design. This chapter focuses on the design of taxes levied against personal income and consumption[1] – the tax treatment of corporations and other profit-distributing organizations, nonprofit organizations (that is, organizations that cannot distribute their profits), and charitable bequests is beyond the scope of the chapter. I focus on considerations of efficiency, fairness, and legitimacy and omit important administrative considerations (processing and enforcement costs, enforceability of restrictions, and taxpayer compliance costs) in the interest of space.

In the first section, I discuss some results that are commonly believed to be correct but are in fact misleading, incomplete, or just plain wrong. In the next section, I catalog four elements of tax incentive design and gather the many variations of each element that have been used or proposed in the United States. I conclude with some approaches to choosing among the available options. While I am primarily concerned with economic aspects of tax design, tax systems affect the perceived fairness and legitimacy of government, and I discuss these impacts within the limits of my expertise.

What's wrong: accepted wisdom that misleads

In this section, I discuss four erroneous, incomplete, or misleading approaches that are commonly cited as correct. First, the literature shows that tax deductions for charitable giving provide a greater subsidy to the rich than to the poor. This conclusion is correct but incomplete and misleading. Second, the literature asserts that a tax incentive is treasury efficient (that is, results in an increase in donations that exceeds the loss of tax revenue) if and only if the price elasticity of giving is greater than one (in absolute value). This conclusion is incorrect. Third, the literature asserts that when giving passes the proper test for treasury efficiency, tax incentives for giving are socially efficient. They are not. Finally, it is commonly believed, at least among economists, that efficiency is the primary objective of public policy. As most non-economists know, this is an exaggeration, and I discuss other important objectives for tax policy.

DOI: 10.4324/9781003139201-13

Pro-rich aspects of charitable tax deductions

In a progressive income tax, the average tax rate[2] increases with the amount of income. Progressivity is implemented through some combination of a zero bracket (the first few dollars of income on which no tax is owed) and marginal tax rates[3] that increase with income. In the United States, the zero bracket has been replaced by the "standard deduction," which is \$24,400[4] in tax year 2019. Those with incomes of less than \$24,400 face a zero marginal and average tax rate and pay no income tax. The marginal tax rate is 10% for income between \$24,400 and \$43,450 and rises in a series of steps to 37% for income exceeding \$624,400. Taxpayers can reject the standard deduction and instead list their actual expenditures on certain tax-favored items including charitable donations (itemized deductions) whenever they calculate this would reduce their tax burden.

Those who itemize reduce their taxable income (and hence their taxes) in proportion to the amount given, but taxes do not depend on the amount of donations made by non-itemizers.[5] We measure the impact of these tax considerations using the "tax price of donations," which represents the net cost to the taxpayer of a dollar of charitable giving. This tax-price is \$1 for nonitemizers, but is reduced to $\$1 - m$, where m is the marginal tax rate, for itemizers.[6] For example, when an itemizing taxpayer in the 37% bracket gives \$1,000, her taxable income is reduced by \$1,000, so she avoids \$370 in taxes. The net cost to the high-income taxpayer of giving \$1,000 is \$630, so the tax-price (per dollar) is \$0.63.

The tax-price of giving declines as income rises for two reasons. First, those with more income are more likely to itemize and hence receive a price reduction. Second, the marginal tax rate increases as income rises, causing further reductions in the tax-price for itemizers as they move up through the income distribution.

This pattern of subsidizing the wealthy in a "bizarre upside-down fashion" (Surrey 1973: 229–230) results in a "plutocratic bias" (Vickrey 1947: 131). Precisely what is wrong with this pattern is not made clear in some publications, but it seems to offend notions of distributional justice based on norms of progressivity. Plutocratic bias may be objectionable on other grounds, but this is the misleading part of the claim, because tax deductions are not generally regressive.

Tax codes are too complex with too many discontinuities to fully characterize when the deduction is progressive or regressive, so I provide a few examples to illustrate my point in Figure 10.1. In all the examples, I assume that the tax code incorporates the simplest linear progressive structure[7] and calculate average tax rates with and without a charitable donations deduction. To further simplify, I set the standard deduction to \$0 so that every donor itemizes. Finally, I make the very reasonable assumption that the deduction is not refundable, which means that anytime the formula suggests a negative amount of tax (government paying the taxpayer), that number is replaced by \$0.

The usual definition of a progressive tax is that the average tax rate rises with income. I report average tax rates but also another measure, consumption as a share of gross income. Absent donations, the average tax rate plus consumption as a share of gross income add up to one, so that an equivalent definition of progressivity is that the consumption share decreases with added income. But are donations part of consumption, used to purchase "warm glow," or are donations a part of income that is not available to the donor for consumption? If donations are part of consumption, both measures of progressivity tell the same story, but otherwise, the tax system can be regressive by the first measure and progressive by the second. I therefore report both measures in Figure 10.1.

The first table in Figure 10.1 is the base case, with numbers that seemed plausible plucked out of thin air. The first two columns, containing income and donations, show the behavior

Base Case		*Without Deductibility*			*With Deductibility*		
Income	*Donations*	*Tax*	*Average tax rate*	*Consumption as a share of income*	*Tax*	*Average tax rate*	*Consumption as a share of income*
$50	$5	$0	0	0.9	$0	0	0.9
$100	$15	$0	0	0.85	$0	0	0.85
$200	$50	$30	0.15	0.6	$15	0.075	0.675
$400	150	$90	0.225	0.4	$45	0.1125	0.5125

Double Donations		*Without Deductibility*			*With Deductibility*		
Income	*Donations*	*Tax*	*Average tax rate*	*Consumption as a share of income*	*Tax*	*Average tax rate*	*Consumption as a share of income*
$50	$10	$0	0	0.8	$0	0	0.8
$100	$30	$0	0	0.7	$0	0	0.7
$200	$100	$30	0.15	0.35	$0	0	0.5
$400	$300	$90	0.225	0.025	$0	0	0.25

Income Elastic[1]		*Without Deductibility*			*With Deductibility*		
Income	*Donations*	*Tax*	*Average tax rate*	*Consumption as a share of income*	*Tax*	*Average tax rate*	*Consumption as a share of income*
$50	$5	$0	0	0.9	$0	0	0.9
$100	$20	$0	0	0.8	$0	0	0.8
$200	$80	$30	0.15	0.45	$6	0.03	0.57
$400	$360	$90	0.225	-0.125	$0	0	0.1

Income Inelastic[2]		*Without Deductibility*			*With Deductibility*		
Income	*Donations*	*Tax*	*Average tax rate*	*Consumption as a share of income*	*Tax*	*Average tax rate*	*Consumption as a share of income*
$50	$5	$0	0	0.9	$0	0	0.9
$100	$7.5	$0	0	0.925	$0	0	0.925
$200	$11.25	$30	0.15	0.794	$26.62	0.133	0.811
$400	$16.87	$90	0.225	0.733	$84.94	0.212	0.745

Notes:
1 Assuming the income elasticity of donations is 2
2 Assuming the income elasticity of donations is 0.5

Figure 10.1 The charitable donations tax deduction need not be regressive

of four different taxpayers (rows) arranged in order of income. The next three columns report taxes owed and the two measures of progressivity when charitable donations are not deductible from gross income. This tax is clearly progressive under either method when donations are not deductible. The last three columns replicate these calculations when donations are deductible. Despite the lower price of giving for itemizers, the tax system remains progressive, with increasing average tax rates and decreasing consumption shares.

The next three tables vary the amount of donations at each income level to show that the progressivity conclusion is somewhat robust. The second table doubles the amount of donations at each income level to see whether tax deductions are regressive for the most generous. They are not. Without deductibility, we confirm that the linear income tax is progressive. With deductibility, our four taxpayers pay zero in taxes, so the average tax rate is constant (neither progressive nor regressive). However, consumption as a share of income does decline dramatically with income, so the system remains progressive by this measure. The last two tables vary donations so that the income elasticity of donations is elastic and equal to 2, then inelastic with elasticity equal to ½. In the elastic case under deductibility, the average tax rate is stable at zero, then jumps to a small positive number, then returns to zero, indicating that it is possible that the deduction makes the tax regressive over some income ranges using the traditional measure of progressivity. However, even here, the system remains progressive in terms of consumption.[8] Finally, when giving is income inelastic, deductibility has a much smaller effect on progressivity by both measures, and the system is approximately equally progressive with and without deductibility of donations.

The treasury efficiency test is wrong

Early writers such as Vickrey (1962) worried whether the amount of giving stimulated by a tax deduction or credit was large enough to justify the foregone taxes. Subsequent work located these concerns in the "tax expenditure" framework, where government can collect taxes to directly subsidize charity or offer indirect subsidies in the form of tax breaks that encourage increased donations. In this framework, the indirect route is superior ("treasury efficient") if the added donations exceed the loss in tax collections, which happens whenever tax credits or deductions for charitable donations are employed and the (absolute value of the) price elasticity of giving exceeds unity (e.g., Clotfelter 1985).[9] As a result, hundreds of empirical studies focus on obtaining valid estimates of the price elasticity of giving, almost all of which report tests of whether the elasticity is greater than one. Recent surveys of this literature continue to report this as the proper test of treasury efficiency (e.g., Bakija 2013; Monnet and Panizza 2017). But this is not the proper way to test for treasury efficiency.

Feldstein (1980) was the first to recognize that the traditional test ignored interactions between direct government spending and charitable donations. Simply put, government spending changes the volume of charitable donations for similar goods and services – "crowding out" (when donations fall in response to government spending) or "crowding in" (when government spending increases donations) (e.g., Steinberg 1987; Andreoni 1989; Ribar and Wilhelm 2002). However, Feldstein made some technical errors, and so the proper test for treasury efficiency was devised by Roberts (1987). He found that the critical price elasticity for treasury efficiency is less than unity when there is crowding out and greater than unity when there is crowding in.

Why is this true? Taxes create economic distortions, so government policy should look for the cheapest route to financing a given expenditure on collective goods. Equivalently, government should maximize "bang for the buck." Collective-good expenditure comes from both government spending and charitable donations, and charitable donations are provided even when the government offers no tax subsidies. Suppose first that government spending crowds out charitable donations dollar-for-dollar (100% crowdout). Then direct government subsidies accomplish nothing – each time government grants increase donations fall by the same amount and total spending on the collective good does not change.[10] Indirect subsidies accomplish something provided the price elasticity of donations is not zero, and something is better than nothing. Hence, any elasticity greater than 0 suffices to show that tax breaks are more treasury efficient than direct government spending. The traditional rule, with a critical elasticity of unity is only correct when there is zero crowdout.

Empirical studies provide a complex picture of the extent of crowdout. De Wit and Bekkers's (2017) meta-analysis found that about 2/3 of the studies found crowding out and 1/3 found crowding in. The form of government direct support seemed to matter, as direct government production of collective goods has a larger effect than government grants to nonprofits. Crowdout estimates produced from experimental data were many times larger than those produced from natural data. This is consistent with the results of Ribar and Wilhelm (2002), whose theory showed that the size of the donor group matters, and with Ottoni-Wilhelm, Vesterlund, and Xie (2017), who found that crowdout decreases with output. Finally, the studies use different techniques to deal with econometric problems such as endogeneity bias, and De Wit and Bekkers found that this also affects estimates.

So, are deductions or credits treasury efficient by the proper test? The question is poorly posed, because there is not a single price elasticity of giving for all kinds of giving and for giving to all kinds of causes (e.g., Brooks 2007; Backus 2010; Hossain and Lamb 2012; Zampelli and Yen 2017), nor is there a single level of crowding out. Unless governments are willing and able to differentiate credits across these many factors accordingly, the concept of treasury efficiency is far more limited than previously thought.

Treasury efficiency is not social efficiency

Treasury efficiency was conceived as a simple and operational test to compare direct and indirect support for nonprofit organizations, but it measures social efficiency only under some very special circumstances. Other times, it can be massively misleading, because it supports a deduction or credit in cases where three threshold questions have not been answered: Should the nonprofit be subsidized? Should the subsidy apply to private donations? Should we subsidize organizations or activities? Finally, treasury efficiency does not suffice to determine the best subsidy rate. For all these reasons, we need a full-fledged measure of social efficiency for tax system design.

When used by an economist, efficiency has a precise mathematical definition that is more stringent than use of the word in common discourse would suggest. Efficiency is based on the outcomes throughout the entire *economy* which consists of all available resources, all the ways resources can be transformed into goods, all the individuals present, and all the ways of dividing each good among consumers. Economy A *Pareto-dominates* economy B if no individual in that economy prefers B and at least one individual prefers A. Economy A is *efficient* (synonyms: *Pareto-optimal, socially efficient*) if it is *feasible* (can be produced from available resources) and all economies that Pareto-dominate A are not feasible. Equivalently, an economy is socially efficient if the only way to make any consumer better off in her own estimation requires that at least one other consumer be made worse off.

In common discourse, efficiency means that resources are not wasted in production of goods or services. Social efficiency has additional requirements: that the right mixture of goods be produced and that each consumer's bundle of goods match that consumer's preferences. When the economy is inefficient, there is a feasible way to help people without hurting anyone else, and most agree that society should do so. But there are many socially efficient economies that cannot be mutually compared by the Pareto standard because one person prefers socially efficient economy A and another prefers socially efficient economy B. In effect, the various socially efficient economies differ in the distribution of income, so a theory of distributive justice is needed to determine the best efficient economy. Mathematically, efficiency and equity are combined in the form of a *social welfare function*, which provides a complete and transitive rank order over economies so that you can identify the *social optimum* (the best economy). Theories of distributive justice enter the function in the form of distributional weights for comparing monetary equivalent gains of one consumer with losses of another. There are substantial disagreements over how egalitarian social welfare functions should be, but any view can be accommodated by this tool.

The sources of social inefficiency in economic equilibrium are called *market failures*. In the next subsections, I first detail two market failures relating to gifts and donations and discuss how these inefficiencies can be fixed by proper tax design. Both these problems relate to the fact that transfers of income are collectively consumed as benefits to the giver, other givers, and ultimate recipients. A *pure collective good*[11] has two properties – *nonrivalry* (each unit of production can be enjoyed multiple consumers) and *nonexcludability* (once the good is made, it is not feasible to keep anyone from consuming it). Next, I turn to the treatment of charitable donations in the literature on socially optimal income taxes, which also incorporates other market failures affected by the tax treatment of donations. Finally, I return briefly to the threshold questions from a social welfare framework.

A remediable market failure due to donor motivations

Arrow (1972) noted a peculiarity about gift-giving and charitable donations – the act of giving is valuable to the donor independently of the consequences of that gift. This idea was developed further, most notably by Andreoni (1990) in his impure altruism model. *Altruistic motives* value the consequences of the gift, *warm glow* values the act of giving, and a donor with a mixture of both motivations is an *impure altruist*. Pure altruists want to others to be helped, but donations are inadequate because of the *free-rider problem* – one potential donor can enjoy the level of collective goods supported by other donors without personally contributing, and in any case the personal benefit of giving (enjoying a small increase in collective good provision) is far less that the benefits to the group (simultaneously enjoying that small increase).[12] Warm glow reduces free-riding because non-donors must forgo the special personal benefit associated with personally giving. Kaplow (1995) found that there is a new kind of market failure due to warm-glow preferences.[13] The failure is best illustrated with an example. Suppose Fred is considering a $10 gift for Wanda. If he makes the gift, he receives warm glow because he feels better about himself for being so generous or because his prospects with the ladies have improved as he gets a reputation for being generous. If Fred's warm glow is equivalent to $15 (that is, he would have to toss a coin to decide whether to accept $15 additional income for not making the gift in place of the $10 gift expenditure), then he makes the gift. The money-equivalent net benefit to Fred is $5, the value of his warm glow minus the monetary cost of the gift. For simplicity, assume that Wanda's value of receiving the gift is $10.[14] Both parties benefit from the exchange, no one else is harmed, and the outcome is socially efficient.

But suppose instead that Fred only receives $7.50 in warm glow from giving the gift. Then he does not give Wanda the gift, but mutual gains would be possible if he did, so this outcome is inefficient. Government could fix this inefficiency by giving Fred a $3.00 subsidy. Now, the sum of warm glow and subsidy exceeds the cost, Fred makes the gift and receives net benefits of $0.50, and Wanda gets $10. The sum of gains to Fred and Wanda exceeds the cost to the taxpayers who pay for the subsidy, so it is possible to redistribute gains so that Fred, Wanda, and the taxpayers are all better off. The subsidy is socially efficient if the sum of the net benefits exceeds the so-called *dead-weight loss*, the money-equivalent value of unintended harmful side-effects due to financing the subsidy.[15] This provides a rationale for subsidizing charitable donations through the tax system, but Fred's gift was to a single person and not to some charitable cause. Kaplow's (1995) argument would justify a tax deduction for any kind of gift motivated by warm glow.

A remediable market failure in voluntary donations for a pure collective good

Donative nonprofits, and even some commercial nonprofits, focus on providing pure collective goods.[16] Helping people in need of income and services is a collective good for the community that cares about these people, so when one donor gives, other donors benefit. Educational institutions, ideally, help voters make better decisions, and the quality of government is collectively consumed. Religious institutions produce social capital, also collective. We have already commented on the free-rider problem, leading to underprovision of collective goods, but now we will take a different look at it.

Collective goods are a specific form of a broader market failure due to externalities. An externality is a side effect of a market transaction on those who were not parties to the transaction, such as pollution inhaled by my neighbors when I buy fossil-fuel electric power. Specifically, donations produce reciprocal external benefits (meaning if any member of the group donates, every member of the group benefits). Externality theory was developed by Arthur Cecil Pigou in 1920, and his proposed solutions are known as Pigouvian taxes and subsidies in his honor. Because donations produce external benefits, they should receive Pigouvian subsidies, and if the marginal subsidy rate (amount of additional subsidy provided to the last dollar donated) is set equal to the marginal external benefits (the sum across external beneficiaries of benefits resulting from the last dollar donated), the optimal quantity of donations will be provided.

It is unknown but extremely unlikely that the charitable deduction in the United States provides optimal Pigouvian subsidies, as the marginal subsidy rate is zero for non-itemizers and equal to various marginal tax rates for itemizers. This could be approximately optimal if non-itemizers supported charities without marginal external benefits and the highest-income taxpayers supported causes with the largest marginal external benefits, a dubious supposition. But a Pigouvian subsidy set too low still helps, moving the economy towards social efficiency. Unfortunately, if the subsidy rate is set sufficiently above the optimum, efficiency will be lower than it would be when unsubsidized. My own opinion is that the current system, crude as it is, is helpful from a Pigouvian standpoint but could be more helpful if there were an above-the-line charitable contributions deduction or if the deductions were replaced by tax credits set at the appropriate rate.[17]

The optimal income tax treatment of donations

Optimal tax structures maximize the social welfare produced within a class of tax structures, such as the optimal linear or nonlinear income tax or the optimal set of commodity taxes. Results depend on parameterized social weights embodying a particular notion of distributive justice and, without consensus on that, cannot be made operational. Nonetheless, the literature provides some guidance for policy makers concerned with tax design.

Saez (2004) considers a government that wants to maximize social welfare by choosing an amount to spend on public provision of a single collective good, an amount of money that accomplishes redistribution in the form of a uniform cash transfer to all households, and a subsidy rate for private donations in a linear tax on labor income that balances the budget. His formulation incorporates a warm-glow term reflecting Kaplow's (1995) concern, a Pigouvian-subsidy term reflecting externalities, and a crowdout term reflecting Roberts's (1987) modeling of revenue interactions. He separately analyzes two *polar cases* (logical extremes spanning realistic cases), where the government-produced good is unrelated to the nonprofit good and where the two are identical.

In the first polar case, government produces a good that is unrelated to the good financed by donations. Then the crowdout term drops out (unrelated goods do not crowd each other in or out). The optimal subsidy rate increases with a) the magnitude of external benefits from the nonprofit good, b) the tax-price elasticity of giving, and c) the size of average weighted warm-glow benefits. All else equal, when donations are sufficiently price inelastic, the optimal subsidy rate is negative – donations are taxed, not subsidized. This is because price inelastic goods can be taxed without substantially reducing the quantity of warm glow, with the tax revenues used to reduce the dead-weight loss resulting from distortions in the labor market. Social weights also matter. If the weights are sufficiently egalitarian (supportive of redistribution from rich to poor) and average weighted warm-glow benefits are high, then the optimal subsidy depends on whether the rich give disproportionately more than others. The optimal subsidy is smaller if the rich give disproportionately more and larger otherwise.

In the second polar case, the government provides exactly the same good as the nonprofits. Now the Pigouvian term drops out because government adjusts its direct spending to ensure that the sum of donations and government spending provides the optimal quantity of the collective good. Saez (2004) assumes that the price elasticity of giving is not constant but gets smaller (in absolute value) as the price decreases.[18] To find the optimum subsidy rate, you increase the rate (decrease the price of giving) until the price elasticity reaches a critical value equal to $(1 - \textit{marginal crowdout}) * (1 - \textit{wtd.average marginal warm glow benefit})$

Both parenthetic quantities are less than 1 (unless there is crowding-in), so their product is less than 1.

If we reformulate the proper and common tests for treasury efficiency when the price elasticity is a variable, then subsidy rates should be increased until the elasticity declines to equal 1 (by the common test for treasury efficiency) or (1 – *marginal crowdout*) (by the correct test). Thus, the suggested subsidy is largest in optimal tax theory, smaller by treasury efficiency, and smallest by the traditional misapplication of treasury efficiency. The three measures are the same only when marginal crowdout and marginal warm glow are zero.

Subsequent work has generalized the model in various ways. Diamond (2006) makes some different assumptions and considers the optimal nonlinear income tax. He makes a serious argument that although warm glow affects behavior,[19] it should not be included in social welfare determination of the optimum. He then characterizes optimal taxes with and without warm glow in the social welfare function. Blumkin and Sadka (2007) consider a different form of warm glow stemming from status competition. At least in some settings, donors are motivated to give the largest donations because that comes with the highest level of status (Harbaugh 1998). Unlike the other reasons for warm glow, status is a zero-sum game. One individual's gain in status produces negative externalities in the form of lower status of others. Harbaugh focuses on how nonprofits can manipulate the status competition by creating elite categories of givers (e.g., "golden, silver, and bronze donors") that increase total giving, but Blumkin and Sadka take a different approach. Following the optimal tax literature tradition, government adjusts spending to maintain the optimal level of the collective good, so the positive externalities of giving vanish, the negative remain, and the proper Pigouvian solution is to tax donations. In contrast, preliminary work by Hungerman (2020) builds on Saez (2004) to analyze large gifts. He adds a measure of skewness in the distribution of gifts and finds that large subsidies are optimal even when giving is fairly price inelastic. Almunia et al. (2020) note that many donors do not claim their eligible donations on tax returns because the transaction costs exceed the tax benefits. They estimate an adjusted optimal subsidy rate using a structural model of tax reporting.

The threshold questions

Should nonprofits be subsidized by government in any fashion? From an efficiency standpoint, this depends on whether there are any market failures that could be addressed with subsidies. We have talked about two such market failures – the under-provision of collective goods and the under-provision of warm-glow-motivated gifts.[20] Still, the picture is more complicated than just that. Government provides many non-tax subsidies that can make up for free-rider-induced shortages[21] and also directly produces collective goods. If non-tax subsidies and/or government direct provision suffice to provide the optimal quantity of collective goods, then tax subsidies for giving would cause over-provision.[22] The free-rider problem is reduced by warm glow and could be further reduced if nonprofits employed the provision-point mechanism or the raffle mechanism.[23] No free-rider problems affect sales of goods and services that do not create externalities, so the problem does not clearly apply to commercial charities (those that derive the bulk of their revenues from sales of goods and services, such as private nonprofit hospitals and universities). There may be other externalities associated with commercial nonprofits (such as effects of education on crime rates and democratic function) that call for Pigouvian adjustments to tax rates, but in other cases (advocacy), the positive and negative externalities may cancel out. In sum, there is an efficiency case for subsidizing some nonprofits and not others, and it is unclear whether uniform subsidies are, on balance, more helpful than harmful.

When subsidies should be given to nonprofit organizations, should they be in the form of favorable tax treatment for donations; favorable treatment under sales, property, corporate income, and other entity taxes; and/or favorable contracts, grants, and other non-tax benefits? Surprisingly little is known about this question. The optimal tax literature has not included mixtures of optimal personal and entity tax structures, typically selecting the optimum within a restricted class of tax instruments. Clotfelter (1988) took an early look at the harmful side effects of property, income, and sales tax exemptions but provided no empirical estimates to compare with the dead-weight losses stemming from adjustments to tax rates that hold tax revenues constant in the face of income tax deductions and credits. Steinberg and Bilodeau (1999) provide a debater's guide to the advantages and disadvantages of sales and property tax exemption, and scattered papers have been published since then, but none provide a comprehensive view.

The scant literature on the second question helps to answer the final threshold question – should we subsidize organizations or activities? Income tax breaks encourage donations, which is the right choice for solving the problem of under-provision of warm-glow but is only a means to an end for solving the under-provision of collective goods and perhaps not the best means to that end. An alternative is a tax break based on organizational expenditures on collective goods such as the Historic Preservation Tax Credit, a 20% tax credit for the rehabilitation of certified historic structures.[24] Tax breaks like this more clearly ensure that revenues are spent on collective goods provision.[25] The same is true for entity taxation. Exemption from a sales tax on purchases and/or sales directly subsidizes nonprofit commercial activity, only incidentally benefiting nonprofit provision of collective goods. Exemption from a property tax directly subsidizes nonprofit land use, and exemption from a corporate income tax (depending on details of the tax) directly subsidizes nonprofit use of capital. Instead, corporate taxes can be used to subsidize organizations, for-profit or nonprofit, for their expenditures on remedying market failures. This analysis only scratches the surface, and I mention it to raise more questions deserving attention.

Social optimality is overrated

When a student is sent to the factory that turns him into an economist, he is exposed to social efficiency from day one and develops a natural bias that efficiency is the most important way to evaluate public policies. A few enlightened students move on to the distribution center, where they learn about distributional weights and social welfare functions and emerge thinking that social optimality is the most important thing. Rarely does the student move on to the human resources division of the firm, as Nobel Laureate Amartya Sen did, where he learns the fuzzier but truly important notion of human flourishing (Nussbaum 2011).

At the political scientist factory, distribution, just or otherwise, is where it's at. Every meaningful piece of legislation creates winners and losers, and legislation is passed when the winners are more numerous or more organized than the losers. Re-election sometimes depends on nothing more than that, but at other times, rewarding supporters and punishing oppositional members is seen as corrupt or unfair to the detriment of re-election. At the organizational theory factory, particularly in the sociology wing, graduates are trained to pay attention to the legitimacy and perceived legitimacy of institutions, organizations, and their decisions. The sociology and political science clubs may even focus on issues of power, fairness, and rights and may even conceive of a social contract granting and limiting personal rights in return for government's monopoly of legitimate coercive power.

What of the benevolent social planner, concerned with doing what's right for society? I am increasingly of the opinion that the other political science and organizational theory factories come closer to "doing what's right" than the economics factory does. I do not think that an efficient or socially optimal tax system makes as much difference to human flourishing as a fair tax system created by a political system widely regarded as legitimate. While the economic consequences of tax reform are quite significant in some cases, minor tweaks for optimality are hard to understand and are unlikely to be very salient in the minds of most citizens. The perceived unfairness and power maldistribution seen in the tax treatment of the very rich may be far more salient and important for human flourishing than efficiency. This is a reason to end the plutocratic bias resulting from the charitable tax deduction even if this form of subsidy is progressive and socially optimal.

What's useful: a catalog of tax designs

Literatures from different fields and disciplines focus on different dimensions of tax design. I think that an interdisciplinary catalog might prove useful to inform tax lawyers what economists are considering, to inform economists what tax lawyers are considering, and to help both understand the complexity of comprehensive tax reform. I consider four dimensions of tax policy: what kinds of entities are eligible to receive tax-favored donations with what restrictions on entity behavior, what kinds of donations are favored by the tax system, what kinds of restrictions are placed on taxpayers as a condition of eligibility to benefit from the tax-favored treatment, and what type of tax benefit is best.

Eligible entities

The common choice around the world restricts tax benefits to donations made to nonprofit entities. Gifts made to beggars on the street, to family members, and to unincorporated and informal community organizations are not eligible for support, but it is worth questioning whether they should be. Now is a good time to consider the question, because there are two relatively new kinds of entities that perhaps should become eligible: donor-advised funds (which may be administered in a nonprofit community foundation or a nonprofit subsidiary of a for-profit investment company) and new hybrid corporate forms that combine features of nonprofit organizations with features of for-profits. In the United States, donations to donor-advised funds are generally tax deductible, but as donors retain large elements of control over how the funds are distributed,[26] perhaps they should not be. Perhaps donors should not be allowed to deduct their contributions *to* a donor-advised fund but should be allowed to deduct their contributions *from* a donor-advised fund because that is when all control is relinquished.

A variety of hybrid forms have been created by recent legislation around the world. In the United States, we are experimenting with low-profit limited liability companies (L3Cs), B-corporations, and flexible purpose corporations. In the United Kingdom, there are community interest companies, and similar forms are popping up in other countries. These entities all distribute profits but with governance structures and restrictions designed to limit distribution and devote the rest of the profits to social purposes. There are also organizations that use a traditional corporate structure but call themselves social enterprises and try to devote some of their profits to providing collective goods (like reducing pollution). Currently, donations to hybrid organizations are not deductible and are not tax favored in any other way. Considering the threshold question regarding subsidizing donations or activities, this should be reconsidered.

U.S. nonprofits must restrict several kinds of activities to qualify for exemption from the Federal Corporate Income Tax. The federal nondistribution-of-profits tests differ in minor ways from those embodied in the various state corporation statutes,[27] as does the list of eligible nonprofit purposes.[28] Additional restrictions are placed on organizations seeking tax-favored donations. Political activities and advocacy are restricted,[29] and organizations that provide commercial-type insurance as a substantial part of activities,[30] as well as terrorist organizations,[31] are denied exemption and deductibility. Nonprofit hospitals must meet additional requirements.[32]

Some writers talk about tax deduction as a privilege, not a right, and emphasize that in return for receiving this privilege, nonprofits must give up some control over activities and expenditures. I do not agree with denying advocacy on this ground (as denial of deductibility amounts to taxing the exercise of free-speech rights), but the policy question is a reasonable one – how far can the state go in restricting political speech, fundraising practices, support of controversial causes, executive compensation, or other practices because the organization has accepted deductible donations?

Policy makers have discussed limiting favorable tax treatment to various nonprofit subsectors. Political parties are already excluded, but sometimes there are proposals to restrict favorable tax treatment to nonprofits concerned with the poor and needy and exclude organizations like those in the arts and education that do not primarily benefit these groups. At the state level, there are many tax credits and deductions for gifts to named charities and to nonprofits in a particular field. Indiana, for example, provides state personal income tax filers with a 50% credit for contributions to public and private colleges and universities in the state, capped at $400 (Indiana Department of Revenue 2020). All faculty are urged to donate and take this credit, and the university facilitates qualifying gifts that can be earmarked for the faculty donor's research and travel allowance, making a mockery of the restriction on donor control.

Although the matter is understudied, there is some evidence that special subsidies for charitable subsectors do not increase total giving. A laboratory experiment by Chatterjee et al. (2020) finds that targeted tax credits do not increase total giving; rather, they reallocate giving from ineligible to eligible organizations. An analysis of 46 tax credits in 23 states by Duquette et al. (2018) finds that estimated price elasticities do not statistically differ from zero, and the resulting confidence intervals rule out large effects.

Eligible gifts

In the United States and many other countries that favor donations, gifts of cash, appreciated assets, and in-kind goods and services made to eligible nonprofits receive favorable treatments. There are variations and controversies. For appreciated assets, should the appreciated value or original cost be favored? If the former, should any adjustments be made when the capital gains tax rate is different from the labor income tax rate? Should the appreciation portion of the asset gift be exempt from the capital gains tax when the asset is given directly but not when the asset is sold and the proceeds donated (the current practice in the United States)? How should in-kind gifts be valued, particularly when the good is no longer traded in markets (when outdated models are donated) or when trading markets are thin (for example, when donating a painting to a museum)?

But it is also worthwhile to consider extending favorable treatment to gifts of blood and body organs, although I will not open that can of worms here. How about gifts of time? Some writers support explicit subsidization of volunteer hours, not recognizing that there are already implicit subsidies. To a first approximation, the donor's hourly opportunity cost of volunteering is the after-tax hourly wage rate, so the tax-price of volunteering is already reduced by one minus the marginal tax rate for both itemizers and nonitemizers. The relative price of money to time gifts is unaffected by taxes for itemizers (one minus the marginal tax rate cancels out) but is distorted in favor of time gifts for nonitemizers. This distortion would end if an above-the-line charitable deduction were made permanent or the deduction were replaced by a tax credit.

Many donors donate by subscription, that is, through some system of regular automatic contributions (monthly, annually) for some period. Subscription giving is more valuable to recipient organizations, as it is more predictable and stable. Should subscription gifts be encouraged through more generous tax benefits? Others commit their future and posthumous giving through various kinds of trusts such as a split-interest trust, a charitable remainder trust, or a charitable lead trust. Should the tax treatment of charitable bequests be integrated with that for lifetime giving? Finally, some people make a current gift to create a private foundation. How should taxes regard these intertemporal donations?

Eligible donors

To benefit from a charitable deduction, one needs taxable income and a positive marginal tax rate. Low-income high-wealth taxpayers, if they make sufficiently large deductible gifts, would have negative taxable income. Under current law, the marginal tax-price of giving would be $1 for these taxpayers, but it is possible to design a non-standard *refundability provision* (a negative tax obligation implies the government pays you) that would incentivize giving. The situation is slightly different with a tax credit, which is subtracted from taxes owed instead of from the income that is taxed. A constant credit rate could be used (e.g., subtract 50% of donations from taxes owed), and the tax-price of giving would be ($1 – the credit rate) or 50 cents when the credit rate is 0.5. If the credit is *nonrefundable*, then the total credit is capped at taxable income, so the tax-price of giving rises to $1 for especially generous taxpayers. If the credit is refundable, the negative tax liability stemming from especially generous taxpayers turns into a payment from the government to the taxpayer, and then the tax-price of giving remains constant across all ranges of generosity.

Taxes can be designed with a variety of other donor-level restrictions, and some have been used. In the United States, a taxpayer can deduct a maximum of 60% of adjusted gross income in any year, limiting favorable tax treatment of giving for the most generous in a way that seems hard to justify. However, the excess over 60% can be carried over and deducted over the next five years, limiting the impact of the restriction to the time value of money.

The tax code includes an alternative minimum tax (AMT) payable instead of the regular income tax when the taxpayer has excessively reduced tax liability through aggressive use of all deductions and credits. The intent of the AMT is that very high-income taxpayers should not escape taxation entirely, but the devil is in the details, and the details change from time to time. Taxpayers subject to the AMT lose the right to take certain tax deductions, but under the current tax code, they retain the right to use the charitable tax deduction. Should that change, we would have an additional restriction on access to tax-price reductions. Finally, the United States has instituted partial phase-outs for specific itemized-deductions (including the charitable deduction) taken by high-income taxpayers.[33]

How should the favorable treatment of donations be structured?

The main question here is whether there should be a tax deduction or a tax credit for charitable donations, with several variations related to floors and ceilings and one related to the choice between seemingly equivalent tax rebates or tax matches (see also Adena 2021). But there are other forms of support, such as the checkoff system that is increasingly popular in state income taxes. Taxpayers who have over-withheld income for taxes can check a box on their state income-tax form authorizing the state to donate part of their refund to specified charities (Huffpost 2011). Some states allow the taxpayer to increase their tax liability to fund their donations through the checkoff (Tower and Angell 2007). The checkoff system does not affect the tax-price of giving; it merely saves the donor the transaction costs of donating, which may encourage modest increases in giving and/or shift giving from ineligible to eligible charities. There may still be transaction costs due to documentation requirements, which have been found to be a problem with credits and deductions (e.g., Almunia et al. 2020).

Whether government matches donations dollar for dollar or provides a 50% tax credit or a tax deduction with a 50% marginal tax rate, the results are the same – a dollar of forgone after-tax income provides the recipient with two dollars.[34] The deduction and credit return money to the donor and so are called "rebates" in the literature, as opposed to matching, which adds to donations at the recipient end. Since the Tax Reform Act of 1990 and the resulting Gift Aid program, the United Kingdom allows donors to claim a combination of matches and rebates, and Almunia et al. (2020) estimate a combined price elasticity for the two. However, Eckel and Grossman conducted a series of experiments[35] and concluded that when a tax break is described as government match for charitable donations, donations are higher than when the tax break is described as a tax rebate proportional to the size of the gift even though the purely economic incentives are identical in the two frames. Subsequent papers address a long list of methodological challenges, including those posed by two field experiments. Karlan and List (2007) experimented with matching and did not have a corresponding rebate frame, finding very low price-elasticities with respect to the match rate. Huck and Rasul (2011) also looked at only the matching frame and concluded that the seal of approval implicit in the choice to set up a matching fund may have been more important than the price established by the matching rate. Eckel and Grossman (2017) addressed both papers, finding that many subjects in these studies may not have paid attention to the matching scheme (described in a direct mail solicitation that subjects may have only glanced at). In the Eckel and Grossman (2017) experiment, subjects had to check a box indicating that they wanted their donation to be matched (some subjects donated without checking the box). They used both frames, with wordings that equalized the seal of implicit approval, and replicated their earlier findings. Overall, the evidence seems convincing, suggesting that current framing in the United States (which suggests a tax refund or rebate) is less effective than matching.

Does the difference between rebate and match elasticities reflect a framing effect (where the way something is described and not the substance of that thing affects behavior), or does it represent the structure of preferences with broader implications? Hungerman and Ottoni-Wilhelm (forthcoming) suggest the latter, detailing a theory of impure-impact giving in which donors enjoy warm glow from giving in a rebate condition but not a matching condition. Equivalent-price rebates and matches have the same impact on charitable revenues, and the warm glow and impact elements of utility interact to result in different price elasticities. They provide estimates from a natural experiment at a university in Indiana that the match-price elasticity is –1.2 and the rebate-price elasticity is –0.2 and, in the process, reject the simpler pure-impact, pure warm-glow, and impure altruism models nested in impure-impact preferences.

I have previously described the plutocratic bias inherent in progressive income taxes with a charitable tax deduction – the tax-price of giving declines as income rises. This is why advocates support replacement of the deduction with a tax credit, a reform that was adopted by Canada in 1988.[36] Refundable tax credits offer tax advantages to every donor. However, transitioning to tax credits is tricky, because it is not possible to simultaneously hold tax collection and resulting total donations constant (Lindsey 1988). Reforms can be budget neutral or donation neutral but not both.

Even if the replacement is donation neutral, the pattern of giving to different nonprofit subsectors will change, because, say, a uniform tax credit of 12% produces a tax-price of giving of $0.88 for everyone. This is an increase in price for most itemizers and a decrease in price for non-itemizers. The two groups support different kinds of charities, different kinds of charities may have different price elasticities, and the price elasticity of aggregate donations may differ between itemizers and nonitemizers. I am unaware of any studies that incorporate all these effects, but Cordes (2011) applied percentage changes to data on donations by subsector and income class from the Philanthropy Panel Study. He found that replacing deductions by a 12% nonrefundable tax credit would reduce aggregate donations by 8.7%.[37] Gifts to religion and basic needs would fall by less (7% and 8.1%), and gifts to arts and culture, education, health, and combined purposes fall by more than aggregate donations (14.2%, 13.8%, 9.9%, and 9.4%).

Tax credits have an additional advantage of policy independence. Any tax reform targeted at reducing marginal tax rates (the main goal of the U.S. Tax Reform Act of 1986) has the unintended side effect of reducing charitable donations under a deduction system but not under a credit system. This simplifies the task of addressing non-charity distortions caused by income taxes.

Deductions and credits may apply only to the portion of donations exceeding a specified dollar amount (such as $500) or share of taxable income (such as 2% of adjusted gross income). These are called floors. Alternatively, tax relief may apply up to some specified maximum amount (a ceiling). Floors can also have multiple parts (such as a tax credit of 10% for the excess of donations over $200 and a credit of 20% for the excess of donations over $10,000), and income-based phase outs can be thought of as multi-part ceilings. The key economic effect of floors and ceilings is that the marginal tax-price and the average tax-price are not constant.

Suppose we have a taxpayer who would donate $2,000 absent tax incentives to give and $3,000 if offered a 50% tax credit. The tax credit reduces tax payments by $1,500 but only encourages $1,000 in added donations and is not very efficient – taxes on other taxpayers must increase by $1.50 for each dollar donated by the first taxpayer to balance the budget. Now calculate the same numbers when there is a floor of $2,000. To a first approximation, that taxpayer would still donate $3,000, but the tax credit costs the government only $500, reducing the effect on other taxpayers to $0.50 per dollar donated.[38] Intuitively, the government gets more bang for its tax expenditure buck by restricting subsidies to the margin rather than subsidizing the part that needs no subsidy. In practice, government does not know what would have been given anyway, but provided that the floor is below what most people would otherwise give, floors increase efficiency in a static model.

Should the floor be a fixed dollar amount or a percentage of income amount? When floors are provided for tax deductions, the percentage floor would better address concerns over plutocratic bias. Another consideration is accommodating differences between taxpayers in generosity. To maximize efficiency, taxpayer-specific floors would be set, but as a practical and political matter, taxpayer-specific floors cannot be used. Because income is correlated with giving, I think that a percentage floor will come closer to this theoretical ideal and do a better job restricting the subsidy to its marginal effect on giving. Finally, the behavioral economics of floors have not been extensively studied, but to the extent that the floor sends a social signal on what each donor is expected to give, a reasonable dollar-amount floor (one that most taxpayers could afford to reach) might decrease the norm of giving by higher-income taxpayers and, in a worst case, major donors would shift to giving the dollar floor amount, and less generous donors, who do not reach the floor, would stop giving altogether.

Floors look like a good idea in a static model, but in practice, we must consider dynamics. Would less generous taxpayers stop giving annually and bunch their gifts in particular years to reach the threshold and obtain tax relief? There is already considerable evidence of bunching by high-income donors, whether because they participate in intermittent capital campaigns or they wish to achieve prestige and naming rights with their gifts (Auten and Rudney (1990), but the added bunching created by floors has not been estimated.

In contrast, ceilings (a maximum amount that can be deducted or credited) make little economic sense. True, ceilings limit the government's exposure to collecting less tax money than needed in a worst-case scenario, but a capped subsidy is a waste of subsidy dollars because it mostly rewards taxpayers for gifts that they would have made without the subsidy and provides no incentive to increase donations above the capped level.

Duquette (2020) proposes a two-tiered charitable contribution tax credit for U.S. taxpayers like that adopted by Canada in 1988. Under his proposal, the first dollars donated (up to 2% of adjusted gross income) receive a 10% tax credit, and giving in excess of that threshold receives a 37% credit. Like a floor, the increasing marginal credit-rate increases bang for the buck; like a single-tier tax credit, everyone receives the same subsidy regardless of income. Generosity, rather than higher income, is rewarded by larger subsidies to giving. He simulates the effect of his proposal and various alternatives using tax data, imputing giving by non-itemizers by matching taxpayers with those surveyed in the Panel Study of Income Dynamics and simulates the effect on total giving and foregone tax collections for his proposal compared with various alternatives. Results confirm that expected total donations increase (from $290 billion under the 2018 post-reform tax law to $349 billion if the itemized deduction is replaced by his two-tiered tax credit), while foregone tax revenues increase only slightly (from $74 to $77 billion). Results are even stronger when he compares the post-CARES Act law (with its non-itemizer deduction for gifts of up to $300). Then giving would increase from $304 to $349 billion, while tax expenditures would fall from $91 to $77 billion.

Concluding thoughts

There are many options for reforming the tax treatment of charitable donations, and tax design is a complicated business. One point made by Feldstein (1976) bears repeating – there is a difference between tax design (creating a tax system where there was none before) and tax reform (changing a tax system in place). There is considerable investment in charitable institutions based on the pattern of donations fostered by the current tax system, much of it irreversible. Fixing the plutocratic bias will likely result in major reductions in giving to education, the arts, and health, and wages and employment in these industries would likely decrease. To address this, reforms may need long phase-in periods, and government should consider compensating the losers through temporary income support and retraining. Current patterns of taxation are also capitalized in the value of physical assets held by nonprofits, and this is another cost of reform that government should consider helping with.

When we consider the threshold questions, the economic case for the favorable tax treatment of charitable donations is quite uneasy. Nonetheless, on noneconomic grounds, I support favorable treatment following some reforms. The argument concerns statements of civic values, fairness, and reciprocity. When a donor supports a collective good, she is helping all the free riders. Society should not cheapen the warm glow experience of donors by making giving costless, but it seems just and proper to raise taxes a bit on the free riders and use this to ease the burden on donors who sacrifice part of their personal consumption to help others. The tax authorities can make a valuable public statement that giving is valued and worthy of support.

Notes

1 Consumption taxes, like the value-added tax (VAT), tax consumer spending. The VAT is producer focused, assessed at each stage of production so that the final consumer pays the tax when purchasing goods or services. A taxpayer-focused consumption tax is administered like a personal income tax. Taxpayers report their income and savings and calculate consumption expenditures as income minus net additions to savings. In this form, charitable expenditures can receive favorable tax treatment through tax credits or deductions from the consumption base.

2 The average tax rate is taxes paid divided by income.

3 The marginal tax rate is the additional amount of tax due if income increases by one unit of currency.

4 This is the standard deduction for "married filing joint returns or qualifying widow(er)s." There are two other categories for the standard deduction and all tax brackets, but the numbers in the text will uniformly refer to married filing jointly. See IRS (2020a).

5 Twice in the history of the charitable giving tax deduction, nonitemizers could take the standard deduction and also subtract all or part of charitable donations from gross income. This is the "above-the-line" charitable donation deduction, in effect temporarily due to the COVID-19 crisis. Currently, non-itemizers can deduct up to $300 of donations to calculate taxable income.

6 Of course, U.S. taxes are far more complicated. Deductible donations are limited to 60% of adjusted gross income in any year. Gifts exceeding this amount receive no current tax-price reduction on the excess, but the excess can be carried over to a subsequent year and deducted then. Time donations (volunteering) are not deductible, but because volunteer time comes at the expense of after-tax labor income, the tax-price of giving an hour of time is the marginal after-tax hourly wage rate regardless of itemization status. Gifts of appreciated assets have a lower price of giving because, in addition to the charitable donation deduction, they are exempt from the capital gains tax applied to the appreciated portion of asset value. There are also complex interactions between federal, state, and local personal income taxes that cause geographic variation in the tax-price of giving, and other factors have affected the price of giving in some years.

7 The simplest linear progressive tax applies a constant marginal tax rate to income in excess of some threshold. The illustrated calculation sets the marginal tax rate to 0.3 and the threshold (top of the zero bracket) at $100. Letting T denote tax obligations, $T = 0.3 \times (Y - 100)$ when donations are not tax deductible, where Y is income. When donations are deductible, $T = 0.3 \times (Y - 100 - D)$ where D is donations.

8 As a result of our simplifications, the fourth taxpayer's donations plus taxes add up to more than gross income, indicating a negative consumption share that would need to be financed out of savings. This is an artifact of maintaining a constant income elasticity of 2 even for high levels of income.

9 The tax-price elasticity of giving is a proportional measure of how sensitive donations are to variations in the tax-price of giving. Specifically, it is the percentage change in the level of donations resulting from a 1% change in the tax-price of giving. That elasticity is always a negative number (people buy less when the price goes up), which leads to awkward textual constructions (if elasticity is –1.2, giving is more elastic than if it is –0.6), so I follow convention in reporting the absolute value of elasticity in the text.

10 He does consider the fact that if government spending exceeds charitable giving in the absence of government spending and tax subsidies, donations will fall to zero and can fall no further. Thus, the first dollars spent by government add nothing, the last dollars add dollar for dollar, and the average bang for the buck is less than one.

11 Many economists call nonrival and nonexcludable goods "public goods" because of an older tradition where government was thought to be the sole producer. But private nonprofits also produce "public goods," so "collective" is a more accurate description.

12 Technically, the free rider problem is that the competitive Nash equilibrium of the simultaneous donations game results in under-provision of collective goods. Similar problems arise with sequential donations and donations games repeated a known number of times.

13 My exposition of both this and the optimal taxes subsections follows the wonderful exposition in Bakija (2013).

14 Wanda could value the gift above its cost ("it's the thought that counts") or below the cost ("and I dearly wish you had thought before giving me this monstrosity").

15 Technically, the subsidy is *potentially Pareto-improving* rather than Pareto-improving. This means that the gains to the winners exceed the loss to the losers so that it is possible to transfer money from winners to losers so that everyone benefits. It is only Pareto-improving if those transfers are made.

16 Donations themselves are a pure collective good when donor utility includes an altruistic component. The altruistic term represents concern with the outcome resulting from total donations, so if one donor increases his gift, this causes a nonrival and nonexcludable benefit to all other donors through the summation term. The only time donations are not a pure collective good is when all donors are motivated exclusively by warm glow.

17 I am not aware of empirical studies that calculate the size of external effects of giving generally. Also, warm glow suggests that the optimal Pigouvian subsidies do not need to be as large as contemplated by Pigou himself.

18 This is a reasonable assumption and would hold, for example, if the demand curve for warm glow was a downward-sloping straight line.

19 There is no consensus that Diamond's position is correct, and the detailed debate on this matter is beyond the scope of this chapter.

20 There are other market failures such as contract failure (failure to deliver the promised quality or quantity of a good when there is a particularly difficult problem of asymmetric information) and over-exclusion (for excludable collective goods). The ability of nonprofits to address these market failures depends on the level of competition, and a subsidy or "cushion" for nonprofits is necessary when there is sufficient for-profit or for-profit-in-disguise competition (Steinberg, 2006).

21 Although many nonprofits need additional government and private support, they already receive it in the form of fees for service and goods from government (20.4% of 2005 revenues for reporting public charities) and government grants (9.0%). The largest share comes from fees for services and goods from private sources (50.0%), with only 12.3% of revenues coming from private donations (Blackwood et al. 2008). In addition, government directly provides many of the goods also provided by nonprofits.

22 When governments are modeled as responsive to voters, they do not always behave as social welfare maximizers. However, when the median-preference voter is decisive, as in the simplest such model of political equilibrium, government spending on the collective good is efficient when voter preferences are distributed symmetrically about the median, and any donations on top of political equilibrium would result in overprovision. See Steinberg (1987) for additional complications when voters are cognizant of voluntary donations.

23 In the provision-point mechanism, fundraising occurs in two stages. In the first stage, a goal is set (the provision point) and conditional pledges are solicited. In the second stage, donors are asked to honor their pledges if total pledges exceed the provision point and keep their money otherwise. Kickstarter

employs a variation on this method. Provision-point mechanisms reduce free riding by pure and impure altruists, because rather than providing a small increase in total spending, their pledged donations can make an all-or-nothing difference. In the raffle mechanism, donors buy tickets that give them a probability of winning a tangible prize, and the prospect of possibly winning a prize while donating increases the incentive to give. Bose and Rabotyagov (2018) summarize empirical confirmations that these mechanisms reduce free riding and propose a combination of the two for further gains.

24 This credit is available to individuals and business entities. At first glance, this seems useless, because a tax credit is of no use to an organization that is already tax exempt, but the IRS explains why it would be beneficial to a nonprofit involved in a limited partnership for rehabilitation with a taxable entity (IRS 2020b).

25 Contract failure (fn. 19, *infra*) cannot be handled this way. To subsidize an activity, the activity must be observable by the tax authorities. Contract failure concerns activities that are either unobservable by the buyer/donor/client or are not third-party verifiable. For such activities, for-profits have the incentive and opportunity to deliver less than the promised quality or quantity of a good. Nonprofits are less likely to shortchange donors and consumers, but because the IRS, as a third party, cannot verify the extent of for-profit contract failure, it cannot verify the portion of nonprofit expenditures devoted to fixing this market failure (see, e.g., Steinberg 2006 for a more complete exposition and some caveats).

26 Although donor-advised funds (DAFs) existed before formal recognition in the tax code, they were first defined and regulated under Title XII of the Pension Protection Act of 2006. As discussed in a report to Congress by the U.S. Department of the Treasury (2011: 2), "The Code now defines a DAF as a fund or account at a qualified public charity . . . over which a donor or a donor-appointed advisor retains advisory privileges regarding the investment and/or distribution of assets in the account; thus the name 'donor-advised fund.' The sponsoring organization generally heeds the recommendations from the donor but is not compelled to do so." In practice, donor advice is always heeded, so the term "advised" seems like a polite fiction.

27 There are multiple subsections to the Internal Revenue Code (IRC) section 501(c) about exempt organizations. The bulk of donations go to 501(c)(3) and 501(c)(4), and the operational test for non-distribution is different across subsections. In 501(c)(3) organizations, the test is "no part of the net earnings of which inure to the benefit of any private shareholder or individual."

28 For 501(c)(3) organizations, "organized and operated exclusively for religious, charitable, scientific, testing for public safety, literary, or educational purposes, . . ., or for the prevention of cruelty to children or animals."

29 "[N]o substantial part of the activities of which is carrying on propaganda, or otherwise attempting, to influence legislation (except as otherwise provided in subsection (h)), and which does not participate in, or intervene in (including the publishing or distributing of statements), any political campaign on behalf of (or in opposition to) any candidate for public office."

30 IRC Section 501(m).

31 IRC Section 501(p).

32 These involve community health needs assessment, financial assistance policies, and some restrictions on billing. IRC Section 501(r).

33 During the first year of the Obama administration, the American Taxpayer Relief Act reinstated a phase out of tax deductions for individuals (couples) with income exceeding $250,000 ($300,000) that had lapsed under legislation passed by the Bush administration (Weisman 2013).

34 More generally, letting t be the marginal tax rate and m the match rate and c the tax credit rate, if $t = c = m/(1 + m)$, the tax deduction, credit, and match all produce the same price of giving.

35 The first such article is Eckel and Grossman (2003). The latest is Eckel and Grossman (2017), which contains references (omitted here) to all their other studies and studies by others.

36 The Canadian charitable tax credit is complicated. Credit can be taken for up to 75% of net income, but for gifts of certified cultural property or ecologically sensitive land, up to 100% of net income can be credited, and carryovers are available. Credits are offered at the federal and provincial level, and the credit rates vary with the size of the gift and taxable income (for example, in 2016, the federal charitable donation tax credit was 15% of the first $200, and either 29% [for taxable income up to $200,000] or 33% [for taxable income over $200,000] of the excess up to gifts of $200,000, then 29% for the remainder of gifts over $200,000). Alberta added a provincial tax credit of 10% on the first $200 and 21% on the remainder of the gift. A special bonus credit was available to first-time credit claimants in some years. (Government of Canada 2017).

37 These estimates assume a uniform price elasticity of −1. He finds a different pattern when he assumes the price elasticity is −0.5.

38 Using standard microeconomics, floors complicate donor choice. Graphically, imagine a budget line between spending after-tax income on personal consumption or donations. When there is no floor, the 50% tax credit causes the budget line to rotate outward around the personal consumption intercept, reducing the slope to −0.5. With the floor, the budget line consists of two connected line segments. Below the floor, the slope of the budget line is −1, but above the floor, it is −0.5. These line segments create a nonconvex budget set, with the usual implications. There is a tangency at the kink point, but this is on a lower indifference curve than the taxpayer could reach by looking for a tangency on one or both line segments. Depending on the exact shape of the taxpayer's indifference curves, the new equilibrium could be the amount the taxpayer would give if there were no tax incentives for giving (which is lower than donations under a floorless tax credit) or an amount (depending on income effects) roughly comparable to the amount given under the floorless tax credit, or both tangencies might tie for the optimum. In terms of elasticities, nonlinearity means you have to use virtual price and virtual income changes to predict the policy impact of a tax credit. Most tax simulators used to evaluate the effect of tax reforms on charitable giving ignore these complications; the sole exception I know of is Feldstein and Lindsey (1983).

References

Adena, M., 2021. How can we improve tax incentives for charitable giving? Lessons from field experiments in fundraising. In Henry Peter and Giedre Lideikyte Huber, eds. *The Routledge Handbook of Taxation and Philanthropy*, forthcoming.

Almunia, M., Guceri, I., Lockwood, B. and Scharf, K., 2020. More giving or more givers? The effects of tax incentives on charitable donations in the UK. *Journal of Public Economics*, *183*, 104114. https://doi.org/10.1016/j.jpubeco.2019.104114.

Andreoni, James, 1989. Giving with impure altruism: Applications to charity and Ricardian equivalence. *Journal of Political Economy*, *97*(6), pp.1447–1458.

Andreoni, James, 1990. Impure altruism and donation to public goods; a theory of warm glow giving. *Economic Journal*, *100*, pp.464–477.

Arrow, Kenneth J., 1972. Gifts and exchanges. *Philosophy & Public Affairs*, pp.343–362.

Auten, Gerald and Rudney, Gabriel, 1990. The variability of individual charitable giving in the US. *Voluntas: International Journal of Voluntary and Nonprofit Organizations*, *1*(2), pp.80–97.

Backus, Peter, 2010. *Is Charity a Homogenous Good?* Warwick Economic Research Paper No. 951. Warwick: University of Warwick.

Bakija, Jon, 2013. Tax policy and philanthropy: A primer on the empirical evidence for the United States and its implications. *Social Research: An International Quarterly*, *80*(2), pp.557–584.

Blackwood, Amy, Wing, Kennard T. and Pollak, Thomas H., 2008. *The Nonprofit Sector in Brief. Facts and Figures from the Nonprofit Almanac 2008: Public Charities, Giving, and Volunteering*. Washington, DC: Urban Institute Press.

Blumkin, Tomer and Sadka, Efraim, 2007. A case for taxing charitable donations. *Journal of Public Economics*, *91*(7–8), pp.1555–1564.

Bose, Bijetri and Rabotyagov, Sergey, 2018. Provision of public goods using a combination of lottery and a provision point. *Journal of Behavioral and Experimental Economics*, *73*, pp.99–115.

Brooks, Arthur C., 2007. Income tax policy and charitable giving. *Journal of Policy Analysis and Management*, *26*(3), pp.599–612.

Chatterjee, Chandrayee, Cox, James C., Price, Michael K. and Rundhammer, Florian, 2020. *Robbing Peter to Pay Paul: Understanding How State Tax Credits Impact Charitable Giving*. NBER Working Paper 27163. Cambridge: NBER.

Clotfelter, Charles T., 1985. *Federal Tax Policy and Charitable Giving*. Chicago: University of Chicago Press.

Clotfelter, Charles T., 1988. Tax-induced distortions in the voluntary sector. *Case Western Reserve Law Review*, *39*, p.663.

Cordes, Joseph J., 2011. Re-thinking the deduction for charitable contributions: Evaluating the effects of deficit-reduction proposals. *National Tax Journal*, *64*(4), p.1001.

De Wit, Arjen and Bekkers, René, 2017. Government support and charitable donations: A meta-analysis of the crowding-out hypothesis. *Journal of Public Administration Research and Theory*, *27*(2), pp.301–319.

Diamond, Peter, 2006. Optimal tax treatment of private contributions for public goods with and without warm glow preferences. *Journal of Public Economics*, *90*(4–5), pp.897–919.
Duquette, Nicolas, 2020. A two-tiered charitable contribution credit for all American taxpayers. *Nonprofit Policy Forum*, *11*(4). https://doi.org/10.1515/npf-2019-0063.
Duquette, Nicolas, Graddy-Reed, Alexandra and Phillips, Mark, 2018. *The Effectiveness of Tax Credits for Charitable Giving*. https://ssrn.com/abstract=3201841 or http://dx.doi.org/10.2139/ssrn.3201841.
Eckel, Catherine C. and Grossman, Philip J., 2003. Rebates and matching: Does how we subsidize charitable contributions matter? *Journal of Public Economics*, *87*(3), pp.681–701.
Eckel, Catherine C. and Grossman, Philip J., 2017. Comparing rebate and matching subsidies controlling for donors' awareness: Evidence from the field. *Journal of Behavioral and Experimental Economics*, *66*, pp.88–95.
Feldstein, Martin S., 1976. On the theory of tax reform. *Journal of Public Economics*, *6*(1–2), 77–104.
Feldstein, Martin S., 1980. A contribution to the theory of tax expenditures: The case of charitable giving. In Henry J. Aaron and Michael J. Boskin, eds. *The Economics of Taxation*. Washington, DC: The Brookings Institution.
Feldstein, Martin S. and Lindsey, Lawrence B., 1983. Simulating nonlinear tax rules and nonstandard behavior: An application to the tax treatment of charitable contributions. In *Behavioral Simulation Methods in Tax Policy Analysis*. Chicago: University of Chicago Press, pp.139–172.
Government of Canada, 2017. *Charitable Donation Tax Credit Rates for 2017 and 2016*. https://www.canada.ca/en/revenue-agency/services/charities-giving/giving-charity-information-donors/claiming-charitable-tax-credits/charitable-donation-tax-credit-rates.html, accessed 17/11/2020.
Harbaugh, William T., 1998. What do donations buy?: A model of philanthropy based on prestige and warm glow. *Journal of Public Economics*, *67*(2), pp.269–284.
Hossain, Belayet and Lamb, Laura, 2012. Price elasticities of charitable giving across donation sectors in Canada: Is the tax incentive effective? *International Scholarly Research Notices*, *1*.
Huck, Steffen and Rasul, Imran, 2011. Matched fundraising: Evidence from a natural field experiment. *Journal of Public Economics*, *95*(5–6), pp.351–362.
Huffpost (no author given), 2011. *States Offer Charity 'Checkoffs' to Give Through Taxes*, 23/3/2011, updated 12/6/2017. https://www.huffpost.com/entry/taxes-checkoff-for-charity_n_839868, accessed 16/11/2020.
Hungerman, Daniel M., 2020. *On the Tax Treatment of Large Charitable Gifts*. Working Paper, Department of Economics. Notre Dame: University of Notre Dame.
Hungerman, Daniel M. and Ottoni-Wilhelm, Mark, forthcoming. Impure impact giving: Theory and evidence. *Journal of Political Economy*, preprint. https://doi.org/10.1086/713190.
Indiana Department of Revenue, 2020. *Tax Credits*. https://www.in.gov/dor/individual-income-taxes/filing-my-taxes/tax-credits/, accessed 16/11/2020.
IRS, 2020a. *Form 1040 U.S. Individual Income Tax Return 2019*. https://www.irs.gov/pub/irs-pdf/f1040.pdf, accessed 3/11/2020.
IRS, 2020b. *Tax Aspects of the Historic Preservation Tax Incentives – FAQs*. https://www.irs.gov/businesses/small-businesses-self-employed/tax-aspects-of-the-historic-preservation-tax-incentives-faqs, accessed 9/11/2020.
Kaplow, Louis, 1995. A note on subsidizing gifts. *Journal of Public Economics*, *58*(3), pp.469–477.
Karlan, Dean and List, John A., 2007. Does price matter in charitable giving? Evidence from a large-scale natural field experiment. *American Economic Review*, *97*(5), pp.1774–1793.
Lindsey, Lawrence B., 1988. Budget neutral options to encourage charitable giving. In *Looking Forward to the Year 2000: Public Policy and Philanthropy: Spring Research Forum Working Papers*. Washington, DC: Independent Sector, p.25.
Monnet, Nathalie and Panizza, Ugo, 2017. *A Note on the Economics of Philanthropy*. Graduate Institute of International and Development Studies Working Paper No. 19. Geneva: Graduate Institute of International and Development Studies.
Nussbaum, Martha, 2011. *Creating Capabilities: The Human Development Approach*. Cambridge, MA: The Belknap Press of Harvard University Press.
Ottoni-Wilhelm, Mark, Vesterlund, Lise and Xie, Huan, 2017. Why do people give? Testing pure and impure altruism. *American Economic Review*, *107*(11), pp.3617–3633.
Ribar, David C. and Wilhelm, Mark O., 2002. Altruistic and joy-of-giving motivations in charitable behavior. *Journal of political Economy*, *110*(2), pp.425–457.
Roberts, Russell D., 1987. Financing public goods. *Journal of Political Economy*, *95*(2), pp.420–437.

Saez, Emmanuel, 2004. The optimal treatment of tax expenditures. *Journal of Public Economics*, *88*(12), pp.2657–2684.

Steinberg, Richard, 1987. Voluntary donations and public expenditures in a federalist system. *The American Economic Review*, pp.24–36.

Steinberg, Richard, 2006. Economic theories of nonprofit organizations. In Walter W. Powell and Richard Steinberg, eds. *The Nonprofit Sector: A Research Handbook, Second Edition*. New Haven, CT: Yale University Press, pp.117–139.

Steinberg, Richard and Bilodeau, Marc, 1999. *Should Nonprofit Organizations Pay Sales and Property Taxes?* Washington, DC: National Council of Nonprofit Associations (out of print; contact the authors).

Surrey, Stanley, 1973. *Pathways to Tax Reform: The Concept of Tax Expenditures*. Cambridge, MA: Harvard University Press.

Tower, Ralph B. and Angell, Chase E., 2007. Charitable checkoffs: Taxpayer convenience or blueprint for controversy? *State Tax Notes*, *44*(1), pp.43–50.

U.S. Department of the Treasury, 2011. *Report to Congress on Supporting Organizations and Donor Advised Funds*. https://www.treasury.gov/resource-center/tax-policy/Documents/Report-Donor-Advised-Funds-2011.pdf, accessed 16/11/2020.

Weisman, Jonathan, 2013. Senate Passes legislation to allow taxes on affluent to rise. *The New York Times*, 1.1.2013.

Vickrey, William S., 1947. *Agenda for Progressive Taxation*. New York: Ronald Press Company.

Vickrey, William S., 1962. One economist's view of philanthropy. In Frank G. Dickinson, ed. *Philanthropy and Public Policy*. Cambridge, MA: NBER, pp.31–56.

Zampelli, Ernest M. and Yen, Steven T., 2017. The impact of tax price changes on charitable contributions to the needy. *Contemporary Economic Policy*, *35*(1), pp.113–124.

11

TREASURY EFFICIENCY OF THE CANADIAN TAX REGIME FOR PRIVATE FOUNDATIONS AND THEIR FOUNDERS

Brigitte Alepin

Introduction

In November 2020, the OECD released its most important report on taxation and philanthropy, and in it, the organisation strongly suggests that countries "conduct studies that evaluate the efficiency" of their incentives that subsidise philanthropy. This suggestion takes on even greater importance when one considers that the COVID-19 pandemic has caused the worst global economic crisis since the Great Depression and that in order to get through the crisis, all countries are currently in debt and the needs are glaring in several public sectors, particularly in health, social services and education. These are sectors to which several private charitable foundations have dedicated their purpose in the past.

Private foundations hold about $1 trillion worth of assets in North America, and that figure continues to grow every year. Even as urgent needs go unmet with the COVID-19 crisis, private foundations continue to spend only a tiny fraction of their wealth on charities, mostly due to the tax laws that permit and encourage this build-up of philanthropic wealth. In Canada, founders can take a full tax credit of a maximum of 57% of the value of their donation in the year of the creation of the foundation, while at the same time, that foundation can invest that money tax free forever and never spend its capital on charity.

Philanthropy is on the rise, and although many of its facets could be discussed further, the basic question in this chapter is to assess whether the tax incentives that private charitable foundations and their founders may benefit from in Canada are treasury efficient. In other words, are they a good or fair deal for Canadian taxpayers? The Canadian tax regime is studied because it is one of the most advantageous tax regimes for private foundations and their founders among the G7 countries. This chapter concludes that the tax regime in Canada is not efficient as it presently exists, with a disbursement quota of 3.5%, a full tax holiday for the foundation and a tax incentive that may reach as high as 57% of the donation for the founder. To become treasury efficient within 20 years, it is demonstrated that the disbursement quota should be increased to 5.5%.

The chapter is organised as follows. In the next section, the tax incentives that private charitable foundations and their founders may benefit from in Canada are explained. In the second section, the theoretical framework for analysing the treasury efficiency of these incentives is

 DOI: 10.4324/9781003139201-14

analysed. The last section establishes the necessary facts and reasonable assumptions for the evaluation and concludes with the calculation of the treasury efficiency of the tax regime regarding private foundations in Canada.

1 Tax incentives that private charitable foundations and their founders may benefit from in Canada

Tax incentives towards charitable giving have existed in Canada for over 100 years. The policy has been significantly modified over time, and the last major review of the tax regime regarding private foundations in Canada dates back almost 50 years.

The first tax deductions for charitable donations were introduced to finance the First World War through the creation of wartime relief funds. The Income War Tax Act (IWTA) of 1917 instituted unlimited tax deductions for all donations, primarily to the Canadian Patriotic Fund (CPF) as well as to the Canadian Red Cross (CRC) Fund.

With a 1930 amendment to the 1917 IWTA, the federal government defined the first official foundations on which charitable activities would operate on Canadian soil. Establishing the rules and obligations governing tax deductions for charitable donations, this amendment designated the Ministry of Finance as the regulator of the sector (Elson 2010).

Until the First World War, no major foundation had been created in Canada, and it was not until the end of the war that the Massey Foundation was created in 1918 (Granatstein and Kucharsky 2008). In 1976, as part of a broader tax reform flowing from the Royal Commission on Taxation (Carter Royal Commission), the obligation for the foundation to allocate at least 5% of its assets annually to charitable organisations and activities was introduced in the Income Tax Act. These rules were designed to ensure that tax-receipted charitable gifts were applied for the benefit of charities and not simply held in investment accounts (Bourgeois 2010: 184). Today, the law is essentially the same, but the charitable obligation has been lowered to 3.5%.

1.1 Tax incentives for the founder

The giving incentive for the founder is designed to support charities that serve the needs of the people. The tax treatment of the donation varies whether the donation is being done by an individual or a corporation.

Individuals: Until 1988, the incentive was a tax deduction, and the tax credit was introduced in Canada in 1988 for individual donors. An individual who has income taxed at the maximum marginal rate may benefit from a tax credit of 57% of the donation, taking into consideration both federal and provincial taxes. The federal government limits monetary donations to be included in the calculation of a tax credit to 75% of the taxpayer's net income, and any unused credit balance can be carried over for a period of five years.

When capital property is donated, there is a disposal at fair market value (FMV) for tax purposes, which may result in a capital gain, and this FMV represents the donation for tax purposes. Capital gains can be eliminated by donating certain types of capital property such as certain securities listed on a stock exchange in Canada (shares, debt, participation in a mutual fund trust or in a segregated fund trust, etc.).

Corporations: Donations to a registered charity made by a corporation are deductible from its taxable income, which will result in a reduction of the corporation's tax liability. In addition, there are additional tax incentives when publicly traded securities are donated. As in the case of individuals, the federal government limits monetary donations to be included in the calculation of the tax credit to 75% of the corporation's net income, and any unused credit balance can be carried over for a period of five years.

Without underestimating the importance of donations made by corporations, only donations made by individuals are analysed in this research because they represent by far the largest source of charitable donations made in Canada.

1.2 Tax incentives for private foundations

In Canada, organisations dedicated to charitable purposes and that are registered with the Canada Revenue Agency can issue donation receipts and are tax exempt.

A private foundation in Canada is established as a corporation or a trust. It has only charitable purposes and carries on its own charitable activities, and/or it funds other qualified donees. More than 50% of the foundation's directors deal with each other at arm's length and/or 50% or more of the foundation's funding comes from a person or group of persons that control the charity in some way [Income Tax Act, 149.1(1)].

Private foundations must file financial statements with the prescribed information form T3010 annually to the Canada Revenue Agency. The top sectors for private foundations in Canada are health, education and social services (Philanthropic Foundations Canada 2017).

Private foundations have to spend 3.5% of their capital annually on charitable activities or gifts to qualified organisations. There was a time in Canada when the "disbursement quota" imposed on charitable foundations was higher than 3.5%. According to Finance Canada's 2004 budget,

> analysis indicates that the current 4.5% disbursement quota is high relative to long-term investment returns. Accordingly, the budget proposes to reduce the 4.5% disbursement quota on capital assets to 3.5%. This rate will be reviewed periodically to ensure that it continues to be representative of long-term rates of return.

The reduction in the disbursement quota allows Canadian foundations to keep their start-up capital and ensure that their foundations last indefinitely.

The annual expenses of the foundation are considered in the calculation of the disbursement quota, and generally, the annual expenses of foundations range from 0.75% to 1.5% of their assets (Philanthropic Foundations Canada 2015).

Private foundations cannot engage in any commercial activities, and a private foundation that owns more than 20% of a class of shares of a corporation's stock faces a penalty of 5% of the FMV of those excess shares, and its registration can be revoked.

Tax incentives for private charitable foundations and their founders, in general: In short, in Canada, the regime grants a donation credit to the founder that can reach 57% of the donation in the year of the donation, regardless of when the money will be spent by the foundation. The foundation benefits from a total tax holiday, and its annual charitable obligation is limited to 3.5% of its capital. Compared to G7 countries (see Table 11.1), Canada offers one of the most generous tax regimes to private foundations and their founders.

2 How to measure the "treasury efficiency" of the tax incentives that private charitable foundations and their founders may benefit from?

There has been a lot of research into the efficiency of the tax incentives in philanthropy, but most of it has concentrated on the tax credits or deductions for giving. There has been less

Table 11.1 Tax regime for private foundations and their founders among the G7 countries

Country	*Maximum tax exemption/tax credit for founder*	*Foundation: tax holiday on income*	*Foundation: annual distribution obligation on the income*	*Foundation: annual distribution obligation on the capital*
Canada	Tax credit of 57% maximum, subject to limitation of 75% of income	Yes	No	Yes, 3.5% annually
France	Income tax reduction for 66% of the value of the gift (75% for specific donations), up to 20% of the donor's taxable income	Yes	No	No
Germany	Tax deduction up to 20% of the taxable income, or donations to a foundation can be deducted up to an amount of up to €1 million for an assessment period of up to 10 years	Yes	Yes, income has to be distributed within 2 years	No
Italy	Donations to ONLUS are deductible up to 10% of income with a maximum of €70,000. Alternatively, tax credit of 26% for donations to ONLUS and other kinds of charities, up to the value of € 30,000	No	Yes for foundations of banking origin: at least half of the profits of the year must be granted in the following years. Other: Yes, within a reasonable period of time	No
Japan	The donor claims a tax credit or a deduction up to 40% of its income	Yes	No	No
United Kingdom	The donor claims a deduction from taxable income or capital gains for the amount of the donation grossed up by the basic rate of tax (20%)	Yes	Yes, income has to be spent within a reasonable period of time, generally accepted as 3 years	No
United States	Tax deduction up to 60% or 30% of adjusted gross income depending on the beneficiary	No, tax on investment income	No	Yes, 5% annually

research into the efficiency of the global tax regime that may benefit private foundations, including the incentives for giving, the tax holiday for the foundation and the design of the disbursement quota.

This section analyses how to measure the treasury efficiency of private foundations. Before doing so, the treasury efficiency of the tax incentives of giving will be briefly reviewed to see if it is a good idea to fiscally encourage giving. If it would not be a good idea to begin with, then there would be no point in carrying the analysis further.

After, how to measure the treasury efficiency of private foundations' tax systems as a whole is analysed. This requires questioning the necessity of discounting the future value of the charity made by the foundation over the years and whether the cost of the tax holiday that benefits the foundation should be considered.

2.1 Treasury efficiency of the tax credit/deduction on the donation

The treasury efficiency suggests that the revenue losses to the treasury resulting from the tax incentives are equalled or exceeded by the value of the funds generated for public purposes through the incentives (Simon 1987: 72). In terms of tax incentives for giving, the treasury efficiency means that money raised by the tax exemption/credit exceeds the cost for the treasury in foregone revenue.

To reflect on this, it is therefore necessary to analyse the elasticity of giving. The demand for a product is considered inelastic with respect to the price if the percentage of change in quantity demanded is less than the percentage change in price (the elasticity is less than 1). And the demand for a product is said to be elastic with respect to the price if the percentage change in quantity demanded is greater than the percentage change in price (the elasticity is greater than 1).

In terms of tax policy, if the price elasticity of a tax incentive is greater than 1, it means that the taxpayers who claim tax deductions/credit for charitable contributions are likely to increase their giving by more than the estimated revenue cost of the subsidy. In such a case, the subsidy would be said to be "treasury efficient." If the elasticity is smaller than 1.0, the extra giving prompted by the charitable deduction is less than the revenue cost for the public finances and it is said to be "treasury inefficient."

Several experts have investigated the price elasticity of giving, and unfortunately their estimates vary greatly. In 1985, Charles Clotfelter found that the price elasticity for the population of taxpayers was probably greater than –1 (with a range of –0.9 to –1.4). In 1995, William C. Randolph used different methodologies and concluded differently, with a much lower price elasticity (Randolph 1995: 710). In 2005, John Peloza and Piers Steel concluded, after an analysis of 40 years of research, that tax deductions were treasury efficient (Peloza and Steel 2005: 269). Peter G. Backus and Nicky L. Grant concluded in 2019 that the top 10% of income earners had an elasticity of at least –1 and middle-income earners had a lower price elasticity (Backus and Grant 2019: 319).

Thus, after 100 years of using the tax system in different countries to encourage giving, it is still unclear if effectively, these tax policies have proved to be efficient or not. What about when these donations are given to private charitable foundations, which often withhold them, thereby paying no tax ever? Is the global tax regime for private foundations and their founders treasury efficient?

2.2 Treasury efficiency of the tax regime for private foundations and their founders

Let's return to the definition of treasury efficiency, which suggests that tax exemption is efficient if the revenue losses to the treasury resulting from the exemption are equalled or exceeded by the value of the funds generated for public purposes through the exemption (Simon 1987: 72).

Translated into the foundation context, the tax regime of the foundation is efficient and appropriate as long as it ensures that future grants distributed by the foundation exceed the deductions/credits given to the donor (Toepler 2004: 736).

Since these grants distributed by the foundation are made most of the time in the future, and the foundation does not pay tax in the meantime, two questions need to be answered in order to be able to calculate the treasury efficiency of a foundation:

> Should a present-day discount of future grants be considered?
>
> Should the cost of that tax holiday, in terms of public revenues lost, be considered?

Should present-day discounts of future grants be considered?

This question has been analysed mainly by American experts. In 1965, the United States Treasury Department and Congress were troubled by the fact that a donor to a foundation takes a tax deduction at the time of the donation, but the donated funds might not reach actual operating charities until many years later. Congress and the Treasury believed that because of this delay, donors were getting a tax benefit worth more than the charitable benefit they produced. In other words, they thought there was a mismatch between the value of the tax deduction and the value of charity given in the future. In the Treasury report on foundations submitted to Congress in February 1965, the United States Treasury Department stated that:

> The tax laws grant current deductions for charitable contributions upon the assumption that the funds will benefit the public welfare. This aim can be thwarted when the benefits are too long delayed.
>
> In such cases there is usually a significant lag between the time of the contribution, with its immediate effect upon tax revenues, and the time when the public benefits by having an *equivalent* amount of funds devoted to charitable activities.

Several elements in these two quotes show that the Treasury Department recognises that a dollar given today to charity does not have the same value as a dollar given in the future, including the fact that the Department chooses the word "equivalent" and not "equal" to compare the value of the tax savings resulting from the donation with the value of the charity created by the foundation in the future. This problem was addressed by introducing a 5% charitable obligation into tax law, requiring U.S. foundations to spend at least 5% of their capital on charity each year.

In 2002, McKinsey & Company experts Paul J. Jansen, David M. Katz and Bill Bradley also recognised the need to consider present-day discounts of future grants. They argued that we should view foundation grants as an investor would view an investment. In other words, just as investors would choose to receive a dollar today rather than a dollar a year from now, a dollar of charity given today is worth more than a dollar of charity given in the future.

The McKinsey team refer to what is being done in the business world when an investment is considered. To decide if the business should invest in a project or not, the present value of its future returns is calculated by discounting those returns at a certain rate to reflect the time value of money, and the project is considered only if those returns have a present value that exceeds its initial cost.

Thus, for the McKinsey team, the business concept of "discounting" should be applied by foundations to evaluate what is best between investing in a social project today or investing the money for future projects. However, as Jansen and Katz explain, "Applying this methodology to non-profits is admittedly complicated, since their return on investment accrues to society rather than to the donor and comes in the form of hard-to-quantify social benefits" (2002).

In 2003, Professor Michael Klausner brought an important clarification to the reflection to the effect that donations today are not necessarily worth more than donations tomorrow simply because of the time value of money. He said, "there are good reasons for foundations to favour high payout rates under certain circumstances, and there may be reasons for the law to mandate minimum payout rates, but the time value of money is not one of them" (Klausner 2003: 54).

Professor Klausner supports his theory by explaining that in reality, delayed spending by the foundation does not cost anything, since future charity benefits from compound growth, and therefore, "receiving 34 cents today and receiving $241 in 48 years are equivalent." Thus, assuming that the foundation's assets are invested as profitably as the government's money would have been, Klausner supports the conclusion that the delay does not reduce the present value of the government's subsidy via the deduction/credit allowed on the donation in the first place (Klausner 2003: 53).

From that perspective, when we compare a grant to charity today with one made in 48 years' time, we are in fact comparing the benefit of helping one group of people today with the benefit of helping another group in 48 years. By invoking the discounted cash flow approach, Professor Klausner explains that it is similar to adopting what economists refer to as a "pure time preference" in allocating resources over generations. If future grants are discounted to present value, Klausner explains that it is the same thing as saying that "future people's lives are less important simply because [they] live at different times." (Klausner 2003: 54).

Even if Professor Klausner brought this important nuance in relation to the value of money over time, he does not reject the idea that it is necessary to analyse "how cost-effective a grant to current charity would be, compared to future charity." Doing otherwise would cheat future generations as much as it would cheat present-day taxpayers (Klausner 2003: 57).

In 2009, David A. Weisbach and Cass R. Sunstein also recognised that we can value future and present lives equally and still want to consider the government's opportunity cost. By applying a market discount rate, in effect, we are asking, "Which project would produce more wealth for the future: funding this project or investing the money?" If the project would pay less than an investment would, how does it serve the future to fund the project? (Weisbach and Sunstein 2009: 449).

In 2016, Professor Brian Galle reiterated in his article "Pay It Forward? Law and the Problem of Restricted-Spending Philanthropy" that, "present value is and must be a key part of serious policy analysis." He explained that to justify *government support* for restricted spending, foundation savings should have to beat two benchmarks. First, the utility payoff to future spending – net of all the costs and benefits that delay might bring – should exceed the government's investment opportunity: when the government gives foundations a dollar, the utility of future spending should equal or exceed the utility we could get from a dollar of present spending. Second, the net payoff should exceed any returns that the foundation could achieve by spending now on projects whose useful life is expected to be just as "perpetual" as the foundation itself (Galle 2016: 1159).

In conclusion, the topic of how time and value interact in philanthropy is important and, somewhat surprisingly, "remains under-explored and under-analysed over time".[1] Despite Professor Klausner's inevitable finding that delayed spending by the foundation does not cost anything, since future charity benefits from compound growth, and therefore, "receiving 34 cents today and receiving $241 in 48 years are equivalent," a comparative analysis is nevertheless necessary in order to evaluate "how cost-effective a grant to current charity would be, compared to future charity" (Klausner 2003: 54). In other words, as Professor Galle explains,

> it is important to consider whether the future payoffs that a restricted-spending foundation can deliver are better than the alternatives of unrestricted spending, or of eliminating the government's subsidy and investing that money for some other kind of future spending instead.
>
> *(2016: 1159)*

Should the cost of that tax holiday for the foundation, in terms of public revenues lost, be considered?

Investment income is normally taxable income, and therefore, its exemption from tax should be considered a subsidy, even if earned by a charity (Hansmann 1981: 54).

The tax regime of private charitable foundations, which allows the donor to take their tax deduction/credit at the time of donation, while the foundation spends this money on charity several years later, allows foundations not to be taxed on investment income, whereas if the founder had owned the property himself, he would have been taxed on said investment income (Halperin 2011: 307).

As for the capital gain that accumulates while the investment is held by the foundation, its effect on public finances depends on the type of asset donated. For example, in the case of shares of public companies, the fact that the foundation is non-taxable does not in itself represent an additional cost, because it is a capital gain exempt from tax for the donor at the time of donation. The impact on public finances is therefore already considered with the calculation of the loss of tax revenue at the time of the donation. For other assets, those that do not benefit from special tax treatment allowing exemption from tax at the time of donation, the capital gain exemption from income tax also represents an additional subsidy offered to the foundation.

In addition to these revenue losses for the public finances, the tax exemption granted to private charitable foundations can "create an unfair competitive advantage for philanthropic entities over for-profit businesses" (OECD Taxation and Philanthropy 2020).

Conclusion

To evaluate the treasury efficiency of the Canadian tax regime related to private foundations, it is therefore necessary to compare the revenue losses to the treasury resulting from the different incentives given to the founder (via the donation tax credit) and the foundation (via the tax holiday), with the present value the charity the foundation will be doing over the years.[2] If the present value of the charity exceeds the revenue losses to the treasury, it generally means the regime represents a good deal for taxpayers.

However, if tax incentives related to private foundations and their founders are found to be treasury inefficient, it could still be a good initiative that benefits society. For example, the increased diversity that results from the fact that private foundations can provide services for which there is not enough demand to interest the state or the fact that private foundations, like other charities, allow taxpayers to use charitable donations and the tax benefits that flow from them as a means to vote on how public funds should be allocated (Levmore 1998: 411).

3 Are the tax incentives that private charitable foundations and their founders can benefit from in Canada treasury efficient?

There are no official statistics relating to private charitable foundations and their founders in Canada. To evaluate the treasury efficiency of the tax regime related to private foundations in Canada, it is therefore necessary to make assumptions about the charity that private foundations really provide, the tax credits received by their founders on their donation and the value of the tax holiday for the foundation. To do this, official statistics on all donations in Canada and studies on private foundations published by non-governmental organisations will be studied. The structure of the tax system also allows reasonable assumptions to be made.

3.1 Facts and assumptions

Charity made by private foundations: Canada had 5,738 private foundations with assets totalling $56.3 billion in 2018. Their total wealth has increased by almost 200% since 2010, from $19.4 billion in 2010 to $56.3 in 2018.

The Income Tax Act requires private foundations to disburse at least 3.5% of their total assets to charity annually. In June 2020, The Charity Report analysed the expenditures and charitable donations made by the 245 richest private foundations in Canada. According to this study, the combined assets of the top 245 private foundations in 2018 amounted to $42 billion and they spent 3.34% of their assets on average, on expenditures and donations (The Charity Report 2020).

The assets and the charity (including the expenses related to charity) of the top 10 private foundations in Canada, excluding the MasterCard Foundation, is presented in Table 11.2. This calculation reflects the results from 2019, excluding the MasterCard Foundation, because it is a private corporate foundation subject to a different tax system from private foundations founded by individuals, and this chapter focuses on the latter. Table 11.2 shows that on average, these 10 foundations together spent on charity, in proportion to their assets, an average of 3.84% in 2019, 3.69% in 2018 and 3.32% in 2017.

These findings are consistent with the study of Sansing and Yetman (2006), which concluded that private foundations respect the required disbursement quota to maintain their tax-exempt status, and when they exceed it, it is an immaterial amount above the minimum required (Sansing and Yetman 2006: 379).

Thus, to analyse the treasury efficiency, the disbursement quota of 3.5% required by the Canadian Income Tax Act will be used.

Donation tax credit: According to the Canadian tax system, donations that exceed $200 attract a tax credit of 29%, and if the individual has income in excess of $214,368 (in 2020) and is therefore subject to the maximum tax rate of 33%, he can benefit from a tax credit for donations calculated at the same rate of 33% on the excess of his donations over the threshold of $ 214,368. Since 5,738 private foundations held $56.3 billion in 2018, or an average of $9.8 million per foundation, founders of private foundations most probably benefit from the tax credit for donations that exceed $200 and receive savings that vary between 29% and 33% at the federal level. Table 11.3, which presents official 2017 statistics on the federal donation tax credits, demonstrates that on average, Canadians received a tax credit equal to 29.3% of their donation, and Canadians with income exceeding $250,000 received a tax credit of 32.5% of their donation.

Table 11.2 Top 10 private (non-corporate) foundations in Canada – ratio charity/total assets (charity listing; Canada Revenue Agency)

Foundation	*Year*	*Total assets*	*Total*	*Charity*	*Adm. expenses*	*Charity/assets*
Fondation Lucie and André Chagnon	2019	2,075,222,000	86,012,000	76,189,000	9,823,000	3.67%
	2018	1,955,782,000	55,891,000	46,863,000	9,028,000	2.40%
	2017	2,013,966,000	55,207,000	45,214,000	9,993,000	2.25%
Li Ka Shing (Canada) Foundation	2019	1,039,417,449	41,817,569	39,280,789	2,536,780	3.78%
	2018	867,319,784	35,861,713	34,282,695	1,579,018	3.95%
	2017	992,599,987	38,039,589	36,333,183	1,706,406	3.66%
The J W McConnell Family Foundation	2019	677,445,932	31,259,226	25,706,712	5,552,514	3.79%
	2018	628,873,297	30,686,639	26,021,051	4,665,588	4.14%
	2017	657,933,877	29,956,008	25,376,709	4,579,299	3.86%
La Fondation Marcelle-Jean Coutu	2019	623,428,000	24,484,753	21,590,193	2,894,560	3.46%
	2018	588,185,746	24,517,331	21,559,702	2,957,629	3.67%
	2017	583,182,186	26,234,976	23,488,495	2,746,481	4.03%
The Rossy Foundation	2019	728,975,044	24,200,293	23,729,335	470,958	3.26%
	2018	537,487,120	24,925,255	24,587,899	337,356	4.57%
	2017	834,902,674	24,100,260	23,792,295	307,965	2.85%
The Schulich Foundation	2019	369,588,285	16,362,594	15,041,288	1,321,306	4.07%
	2018	367,377,905	14,246,024	13,075,690	1,170,334	3.56%
	2017	403,086,459	13,901,815	12,541,020	1,360,795	3.11%
Audain Foundation	2019	331,863,419	5,119,178	4,585,414	533,764	1.38%
	2018	310,161,125	7,533,075	7,205,511	327,564	2.32%
	2017	229,294,091	8,571,226	8,313,797	257,429	3.63%
The W. Garfield Weston Foundation	2019	323,552,703	36,562,977	33,386,865	3,176,112	10.32%
	2018	296,149,220	32,375,883	29,356,340	3,019,543	9.91%
	2017	326,068,236	28,581,360	25,504,267	3,077,093	7.82%
Fondation Mirella & Lino Saputo	2019	370,237,537	10,770,080	9,894,202	875,878	2.67%
	2018	276,932,787	10,033,340	9,464,128	569,212	3.42%
	2017	262,413,537	7,930,029	7,347,132	582,897	2.80%
The Molson Foundation	2019	250,703,952	11,276,713	11,266,614	10,099	4.49%
	2018	266,728,803	12,749,308	12,738,662	10,646	4.78%
	2017	308,187,446	11,635,435	11,625,062	10,373	3.77%
			Ratio charity/total assets 2019			**3.84%**
			Ratio charity/total assets 2018			**3.69%**
			Ratio charity/total assets 2017			**3.32%**

The provinces also offer a tax credit on donations. The system is similar to that at the federal level, and the total tax credit on donations exceeding $200, including federal and the provinces, varies between 40% in Ontario and 57% in Quebec.

Value of the tax holiday for the foundation: The value of the tax holiday depends on the income earned by the foundation and the tax rate of the founder, because if these assets were not owned by the foundation, they would be owned and taxed at the founder's level.

Income earned by the foundation on its investment: The compounded annual gain in the S&P 500 between 1965 and 2019 was 10% (Berkshire Hathaway Inc. 2019). Even considering the COVID-19 crisis, the 2021 evaluation of the firm Vanguard is remarkably similar to last year's, and the outlook for global equities is 5%–7% over the next decade (Vanguard Economic and Market Outlook for 2021: Approaching the Dawn: 35). The rates on return earned by the

Table 11.3 Donation tax credit in Canada – Statistics 2017

CRA, Statistics on T1, *edition 2019 (taxation year 2017)*		
	Total	*Income >$250,000*
Donation		
– Number of taxpayers	5,529,010	199,000
– In thousands of CND$	$10,491,945	$3,487,992
Tax credits		
– In thousands of CND$	$3,076,860	$1,135,395 (37%)

Table 11.4 Tax rates for capital gains, dividends and interest incomes

For taxpayers in higher tax brackets established in Ontario and Quebec			
	Income of > $244,800		
	Interest	*Dividends*	*Capital gains*
Quebec	53,53%	40,11%	26,65%
Ontario	53,31%	39,34%	26,76%

top three richest private foundations in Canada during the years 2017–2018–2019 were 6% for the Fondation Lucie et André Chagnon, 3% for the Li Ka Shing (Canada) foundation and 7% for the Fondation Marcelle-Jean Coutu (Charity Listing, CRA). Thus, for the purposes of this analysis, a rate of return of 5% will be used, because it seems to be the most conservative rate, considering these different facts and expectations.

Tax rate of the founder: As explained previously, since private charitable foundations in Canada hold, on average, assets totalling $9.8 million, it makes sense to conclude that it is the wealthiest people who have the resources to set up such a structure, as well as to assume that these foundations are generally founded by individuals in the top 1% of earners in Canada. This represents a group of 283,015 individuals earning more than $244,800 per year in 2018 (Statistics Canada, High Income Filers in Canada 2020).

Furthermore, Table 11.3 indicates that in 2017, 37% of total tax credits benefited taxpayers with an income exceeding $250,000. While this is not a direct correlation with the founders of private charitable foundations, these statistics confirm that donations in Canada come largely from the top 1%.

In Canada, as in many jurisdictions, investment incomes are taxed differently depending on the nature of the income. Table 11.4 presents the tax rates on interest incomes, dividends and capital gains for the top 1% of earners in Ontario and Quebec, the most popular provinces for private foundations. It is not possible with the available data to calculate the exact tax rates, but for the purpose of this chapter, an average tax rate of 40% seems conservative and probable and will be used in the present analysis.

3.2 Treasury efficiency evaluation

As presented in Section 2, the analysis of treasury efficiency requires a comparison to be made of the present-day value of the charity that the foundation provides over time and the present value of the tax holiday from which it benefits, as well as the tax credit enjoyed by the founder at the time of the creation of the foundation.

To bring money back to today's value, the right discount rate needs to be determined. To think about the right rate, it is necessary to place yourself in the position of the Canadian government, since it is the one that has to take the final decision to grant the funds.

As in many countries, Canada must borrow presently to face the crisis, and the situation will stay the same in years to come. Total Canadian government borrowing was $1.421 trillion as of October 31, 2020, and an additional $323 billion in borrowing is expected through 2024. The needs are dire for health, education and social services, and if Canada gives tax incentives to the founders and their private foundations, who for the most part also have goals related to health, education and social services but who withhold these sums from a long-term perspective, the country faces a shortfall that it needs now and urgently. So, the current decision to invest in private charitable foundations results in more borrowing for Canada, and the cost of postponing health, education and social services into the future through private charitable foundations corresponds to the cost of its debt.

The average effective interest rate on the government's interest-bearing debt in 2019 was 2.3%, up from 2.2% in 2018, and the average effective interest rate in 2020 remained at 2.3% (Government of Canada-Public Accounts of Canada 2020). Although it is not certain what will happen to interest rates within the next few months and years, an interest rate of 2.3% seems to reflect the current tendency. Annexes 1–2–3 present an analysis of the treasury efficiency of the tax incentives that private charitable foundations and their founders may benefit from in Canada on a donation of $100 million, considering the different facts and assumptions presented previously and a discount rate of 2.3%.

Annexes 1 and 2 evaluate the treasury analysis of the tax regime over a period of 38 years and 53 years, respectively. Annex 1 demonstrates that it takes 38 years for the foundation to give back to society sufficient charity to balance the tax incentives the foundation and its founder receive at a rate of 44%. Annex 2 demonstrates that it takes 53 years for the foundation to give back to society sufficient charity to balance the tax incentives the foundation and its founder receive at a rate of 57%.

Annex 3 demonstrates that the disbursement quota would need to be increased to 5.5% if we want to reach treasury efficiency within a period of 20 years.

Conclusion

This chapter does not question the relevance and charitable nature of foundations or donors. Several qualified people have already spoken on this issue. For example, in 2006, Pope Benedict XVI clarified in his book *Deus caritas est*, or *God Is Love*, that charity is essential and that there is no substitute for charity, not even the state.

As private charitable foundations have become an important social pillar, it is important to ensure that tax regimes are an effective tool to put private foundations truly at the service of the state and its citizens. As demonstrated in this chapter, the current tax system in Canada is not treasury efficient, unless it is considered that 38 to 53 years is a reasonable time to balance the coffers of the state, which is obviously not the case, especially in times of crisis.

The last major tax reform of the Canadian tax system related to private foundations dates back almost 50 years, and the time may have come to rethink the subject in depth.

Notes

1 This concluding statement is presented in the report *On Time, Value, & Philanthropy* that followed the informal discussion that took place at the Atlantic Philanthropies on 10 May 2016. Available at: https://cspcs.sanford.duke.edu/sites/default/files/March%2010%20Time-Value%20Meeting%20Recap%205-13-16.pdf

2 Other considerations can be factored into the efficiency evaluation. The economies of scale that the state benefits from are a good example because, generally, private foundations cannot count on these reduced costs, and, to be exact, these costs should be accounted in the efficiency analysis (Parachin 2013: 39).

Bibliography

Afik, Z. and Katz, H., 2018. Reconsidering the philanthropic foundation minimum payout policy under a "new normal". *Journal of Policy Modeling*. Available at: https://doi.org/10.1016/j.jpolmod.2018.09.004.

Alberg-Seberich, M., 2018. Analyzing Canada's philanthropy support landscape to enhance giving. *The Philanthropist, European Philanthropy* [online]. Available at: http://file:///Users/gabriellasobodker/Downloads/analyzing-canadas-philanthropy-support-landscape-to-enhance-giving%20(1).pdf [Accessed 31 January 2021].

Backus, P. and Grant, N., 2019. How sensitive is the average taxpayer to changes in the tax-price of giving? *International Tax and Public Finance*, vol. 26/2, pp. 317–356.

Banque du Canada; Ministère des Finances du Canada, *Tableaux de référence financiers – 2018*, Tableau 13. Available at: https://www.canada.ca/fr/ministere-finances/services/publications/tableaux-reference-financiers/2019/partie-3.html#tbl13 [Accessed 31 January 2021].

Benshalom, Ilan, 2009. The dual subsidy theory of charitable deductions. *Indiana Law Journal*, vol. 84/4, Article 1.

Berkshire Hathaway Inc., 2020. *Berkshire's Performance vs. the S&P 500* [online]. Available at: https://www.berkshirehathaway.com/letters/2019ltr.pdf [Accessed 31 January 2021].

Bourgeois, Donald, 2010. Eliminating the disbursement quota: Gold or fool's gold? *The Philanthropist*, vol. 23/2, pp. 184–189.

Brody, Evelyn, 1997. Charitable endowments and the democratization of dynasty. *Arizona Law Review*, vol. 39, p. 873 [online]. Available at: https://scholarship.kentlaw.iit.edu/fac_schol/115 [Accessed 31 January 2021].

Brody, Evelyn. 1999. Charities in tax reform: Threats to subsidies overt and covert. *Tennessee Law Review*, vol. 66, p. 687 [online]. Available at: http://scholarship.kentlaw.iit.edu/fac_schol/116.

Canada Revenue Agency, *T1 Final Statistics 2019 Edition (for the 2017 Tax Year)* [online]. Available at: https://www.canada.ca/en/revenue-agency/programs/about-canada-revenue-agency-cra/income-statistics-gst-hst-statistics/t1-final-statistics/2017-tax-year.html.

Clotfelter, C., 1985. *Federal Tax Policy and Charitable Giving*. Chicago: University of Chicago Press.

Colinvaux, R., 2016. Using tax law to discourage donor-imposed restrictions on charitable gifts. *Ncpl.law.nyu.edu* [online]. Available at: https://ncpl.law.nyu.edu/wp-content/uploads/2017/03/Tab-E-Colinvaux-paper.pdf [Accessed 24 January 2021].

Department of Finance Canada, *Report on Federal Tax Expenditures 2019* [online]. Available at: https://www.canada.ca/en/department-finance/services/publications/federal-tax-expenditures/2020/part-1.html.

Department of Finance Canada, *Debt Management Report 2018–2019* [online]. Available at: https://www.canada.ca/en/department-finance/services/publications/debt-management-report/2018-2019.html

Donation States, 2016. An international comparison of the tax treatment of donations. *Charities Aid Foundation* [online]. Available at: https://www.cafonline.org/docs/default-source/about-us-publications/fwg4-donation-states [Accessed 31 January 2021].

Efc.issuelab.org., 2015. *Comparative Highlights of Foundation Laws: The Operating Environment for Foundations in Europe 2015* [online]. Available at: https://efc.issuelab.org/resource/comparative-highlights-of-foundation-laws-the-operating-environment-for-foundations-in-europe-2015.html [Accessed 31 January 2021].

Elson, P. R., 2007a. A short history of voluntary sector-government relations in Canada. *Thephilanthropist.ca* [online]. Available at: https://thephilanthropist.ca/original-pdfs/Philanthropist-21-1-358.pdf [Accessed 31 January 2021].

Elson, P. R., 2007b. *High Ideals and Noble Intentions: Voluntary Sector-Government Relations in Canada.* Toronto: University of Toronto Press.

Elson, P. R., 2010. The origin of the species: Why charity regulations in Canada and England continue to reflect their origins. *The International Journal of Non-for-Profit Law*, vol. 12/3, disponible en ligne.

Elson, P. R., Lefèvre, S. and Fontan, J., 2020. *Philanthropic Foundations in Canada, Landscapes, Indigenous Perspectives and Pathways to Change* [online]. Available at: https://philab.uqam.ca/en/publication/philanthropic-foundations-in-canada-landscapes-indigenous-perspectives-and-pathways-to-change/.

Fack, G. and Landais, C. 2010. Are tax incentives for charitable giving efficient? Evidence from France. *American Economic Journal: Economic Policy*, vol. 2/2, pp. 117–141.

Feld, Joel H., 1967. Unreasonable accumulation of income by foundations. *Cleveland State Law Review*, vol. 16, p. 362.

Feldstein, M., 1975. The income tax and charitable contributions: Part I – aggregate and distributional effect. *National Tax Journal*, vol. 28/1.

Fondationdefrance.org., 2015. *An Overview of Philanthropy in Europe* [online]. Available at: https://www.fondationdefrance.org/sites/default/files/atoms/files/philanthropy_in_europe_2015.pdf [Accessed 31 January 2021].

Fontan, J., Elson, P. and Lefèvre, S., 2017. *Les fondations philanthropiques: de nouveaux acteurs politiques?.* Quebec: Presses de l'Université du Québec.

Galle, Brian, 2016. Pay it forward? Law and the problem of restricted-spending philanthropy. *Washington University Law Review*, vol. 1143.

Government of Canada, 2020. *Public Accounts of Canada* [online]. Available at: https://www.tpsgc-pwgsc.gc.ca/recgen/cpc-pac/2019/vol1/s1/aef-fsda-eng.html [Accessed 31 January 2021].

Granatstein, J. and Kucharsky, D., 2008. Vincent Massey | The Canadian encyclopedia. *Thecanadianencyclopedia.ca* [online]. Available at: https://www.thecanadianencyclopedia.ca/en/article/massey-charles-vincent [Accessed 31 January 2021].

Halperin, Daniel I., 2002. A charitable contribution of appreciated property and the realization of built-in gains. *Tax Law Review*, vol. 56/1.

Halperin, Daniel I., 2011. Is income tax exemption for charities a subsidy?. *Tax Law Review*, vol. 64, p. 283, 15 July [online]. Available at: https://ssrn.com/abstract=1920430.

Hansmann, Henry, 1981 The rationale for exempting nonprofit organizations from the corporate income taxation. *Yale Law Journal*, vol. 98 [online]. Available at: https://digitalcommons.law.yale.edu/ylj/vol91/iss1/3 [Accessed 31 January 2021].

Income Tax Act, par. 149.1(1) 'qualified donees' ITA and s. 985.1b) *Taxation Act.*

Income Tax Act, RSC 1985, c. 1 (5th Supp.), as amended.

Jansen, P. J. and Katz, D. M., 2002. *For Nonprofits, Time Is Money*. Atlanta, GA: McKinsey & Co.

Klausner, Michael D., 2003. When Time Isn't Money: Foundation Payouts and the Time Value of Money. Available at SSRN: https://ssrn.com/abstract=445982 or http://dx.doi.org/10.2139/ssrn.445982

Levmore, S., 1998. Taxes as ballots. *University of Chicago Law Review*, vol. 65/2, pp. 387–432.

OECD, 2018. *Private Philanthropy for Development*, The Development Dimension. Paris: OECD Publishing.

OECD, 2020. *La fiscalité et la philanthropie.* Études de politique fiscale de l'OCDE, No. 27. Paris: OECD Publishing.

Parachin, A., 2013. The charitable contributions deduction, a tax debate or a question of charity versus government? *Urban.org.* [online]. Available at: https://www.urban.org/sites/default/files/publication/23616/412818-The-Charitable-Contributions-Deduction-A-Tax-Debate-or-a-Question-of-Charity-Versus-Government-.PDF [Accessed 24 January 2021].

Peloza, John and Steel, Piers, 2005. The price elasticities of charitable contributions: A meta-analysis. *Journal of Public Policy & Marketing*, vol. 24, pp. 260–272.

Pfc.ca., 2021. *A Portrait of Canadian Foundation Philanthropy: Canada National Report for the Global Philanthropy Project at Harvard Kennedy School.* Montreal: Philanthropic Foundations Canada [online]. Available at: http://pfc.ca/wp-content/uploads/2018/01/portrait-cdn-philanthropy-sept2017-en.pdf [Accessed 31 January 2021].

Philanthropic Foundations Canada, 2019. *Starting a Foundation, a Guide for Philanthropists.* Philanthropic Foundations Canada [online]. Available at: http://pfc.ca/wp-content/uploads/2019/06/starting_foundation_2019_en.pdf [Accessed 31 January 2021].

Philanthropic Foundations Canada, 2021. *Canadian Foundation Facts.*

Pope Benedict XVI. 2006, "God Is Love" [Deus Caritas Est].

Porter, Michael E. and Kramer, Mark R., 1999. Philanthropy's new agenda: Creating value. *Harvard Business Review*, vol. 77/6, pp. 121–122, November–December.

Randolph, W., 1995. Dynamic income, progressive taxes, and the timing of charitable contributions. *Journal of Political Economy*, vol. 91/1, pp. 703–738.

Roger, Colinvaux, 2013. Charitable contributions of property: A broken system reimagined. *Harvard Journal on Legislation*, vol. 50, p. 263.

Sansing, Richard and Yetman, Robert, 2006. Governing private foundations using the tax law. *Journal of Accounting and Economics*, vol. 41, pp. 363–384. doi:10.1016/j.jacceco.2005.03.003.

Sectorsource.ca., 2014. *Sector Impact: What Is the Charitable and Nonprofit Sector?* [online]. Available at: http://sectorsource.ca/research-and-impact/sector-impact [Accessed 31 January 2021].

Simon, J., 1987. The tax treatment of nonprofit organizations: A review of federal and state policies. In W. W. Powell (Ed.), *The Nonprofit Sector: A Research Handbook* (pp. 67–98). New Haven, CT: Yale University Press.

Simon, J., 1995. The regulation of American foundations: Looking backward at the tax reform act of 1969. *Voluntas: International Journal of Voluntary and Nonprofit Organizations,* vol. 6/3, pp. 243–254 [online]. Available at: http://www.jstor.org/stable/27927481 [Accessed 25 January 2021].

Statistics Canada, 2020. *Statistics Canada, High Income Tax Filers in Canada (Year 2018).* Available at: https://www150.statcan.gc.ca/t1/tbl1/en/tv.action?pid=1110005501 [Accessed 1 February 2021].

Statistics Canada, *Table 11-10-0130-01 Summary of Charitable Donors* [online]. Available at: https://www150.statcan.gc.ca/t1/tbl1/en/tv.action?pid=1110013001 [Accessed 31 January 2021].

Taxation Act, CQLR, c. I-3, s. 752.0.10.1 to 752.0.10.18.

The Charity Report, 2020. *Who Gives and Who Gets: The Beneficiaries of Private Foundation Philanthropy.*

Toepler, S., 2004. Ending payout as we know it: A conceptual and comparative perspective on the payout requirement for foundations. *Nonprofit and Voluntary Sector Quarterly*, vol. 33/4, pp. 729–738.

Treasury Department Report on Private Foundations, Comm. Print., Comm. On Finance, U. S. Senate 89th Cong., 1st Sess. 55, 2 February 1965.

Treasury Department Report on Private Foundations, 1966. *Real Property, Probate and Trust Journal*, vol. 1/3, pp. 292–306 [online]. Available at: http://www.jstor.org/stable/20780665 [Accessed 26 January 2021].

Weisbach, David A. and Sunstein, Cass R., 2009. Climate change and discounting the future: A guide for the perplexed. *Yale Law and Policy Review*, vol. 27, pp. 433–457.

Vanguard Research, 2020. Vanguard economic and market outlook for 2021: Approaching the dawn. *Vanguard* [online]. Available at: <https://pressroom.vanguard.com/nonindexed/Vanguard-economic-and-market-outlook-report-2021-120920.pdf> [Accessed 31 January 2021].

ANNEX 11.1 – TREASURY EFFICIENCY – ANALYSIS ON 38 YEARS

Year	*Cost of tax credit for the public finances (44%)*	*Cost of tax credit for the public finances (57%)*	*Cost of the tax holiday for the public finances*	*Distribution (charity)*	*Net benefit: distribution less the cost of the tax holiday*	*Net benefit: current value over 25 years*	*Balance of capital in the foundation, after distribution and expenses*
	44,000,000	57,000,000				44,412,781	
1			2,000,000	3,500,000	1,500,000	1,466,276	101,000,000
2			2,020,000	3,535,000	1,515,000	1,447,643	102,010,000
3			2,040,200	3,570,350	1,530,150	1,429,246	103,030,100
4			2,060,602	3,606,054	1,545,452	1,411,084	104,060,401
5			2,081,208	3,642,114	1,560,906	1,393,152	105,101,005
6			2,102,020	3,678,535	1,576,515	1,375,448	106,152,015
7			2,123,040	3,715,321	1,592,280	1,357,970	107,213,535
8			2,144,271	3,752,474	1,608,203	1,340,713	108,285,671
9			2,165,713	3,789,998	1,624,285	1,323,676	109,368,527
10			2,187,371	3,827,898	1,640,528	1,306,855	110,462,213
11			2,209,244	3,866,177	1,656,933	1,290,247	111,566,835
12			2,231,337	3,904,839	1,673,503	1,273,851	112,682,503
13			2,253,650	3,943,888	1,690,238	1,257,664	113,809,328
14			2,276,187	3,983,326	1,707,140	1,241,682	114,947,421
15			2,298,948	4,023,160	1,724,211	1,225,903	116,096,896
16			2,321,938	4,063,391	1,741,453	1,210,324	117,257,864
17			2,345,157	4,104,025	1,758,868	1,194,944	118,430,443
18			2,368,609	4,145,066	1,776,457	1,179,759	119,614,748
19			2,392,295	4,186,516	1,794,221	1,164,767	120,810,895
20			2,416,218	4,228,381	1,812,163	1,149,965	122,019,004
21			2,440,380	4,270,665	1,830,285	1,135,352	123,239,194
22			2,464,784	4,313,372	1,848,588	1,120,924	124,471,586
23			2,489,432	4,356,506	1,867,074	1,106,680	125,716,302
24			2,514,326	4,400,071	1,885,745	1,092,616	126,973,465

Year	*Cost of tax credit for the public finances (44%)*	*Cost of tax credit for the public finances (57%)*	*Cost of the tax holiday for the public finances*	*Distribution (charity)*	*Net benefit: distribution less the cost of the tax holiday*	*Net benefit: current value over 25 years*	*Balance of capital in the foundation, after distribution and expenses*
25			2,539,469	4,444,071	1,904,602	1,078,732	128,243,200
26			2,564,864	4,488,512	1,923,648	1,065,023	129,525,631
27			2,590,513	4,533,397	1,942,884	1,051,489	130,820,888
28			2,616,418	4,578,731	1,962,313	1,038,127	132,129,097
29			2,642,582	4,624,518	1,981,936	1,024,935	133,450,388
30			2,669,008	4,670,764	2,001,756	1,011,910	134,784,892
31			2,695,698	4,717,471	2,021,773	999,051	136,132,740
32			2,722,655	4,764,646	2,041,991	986,356	137,494,068
33			2,749,881	4,812,292	2,062,411	973,821	138,869,009
34			2,777,380	4,860,415	2,083,035	961,446	140,257,699
35			2,805,154	4,909,019	2,103,865	949,229	141,660,276
36			2,833,206	4,958,110	2,124,904	937,166	143,076,878
37			2,861,538	5,007,691	2,146,153	925,257	144,507,647
38			2,890,153	5,057,768	2,167,615	913,499	145,952,724

ANNEX 11.2 – TREASURY EFFICIENCY – ANALYSIS ON 53 YEARS

Year	*Cost of tax credit for the public finances (44%)*	*Cost of tax credit for the public finances (57%)*	*Cost of the tax holiday for the public finances*	*Distribution (charity)*	*Net benefit: distribution less the cost of the tax holiday*	*Net benefit: current value over 25 years*	*Balance of capital in the foundation, after distribution and expenses*
	44,000,000	57,000,000				56,801,545	
1			2,000,000	3,500,000	1,500,000	1,466,276	101,000,000
2			2,020,000	3,535,000	1,515,000	1,447,643	102,010,000
3			2,040,200	3,570,350	1,530,150	1,429,246	103,030,100
4			2,060,602	3,606,054	1,545,452	1,411,084	104,060,401
5			2,081,208	3,642,114	1,560,906	1,393,152	105,101,005
6			2,102,020	3,678,535	1,576,515	1,375,448	106,152,015
7			2,123,040	3,715,321	1,592,280	1,357,970	107,213,535
8			2,144,271	3,752,474	1,608,203	1,340,713	108,285,671
9			2,165,713	3,789,998	1,624,285	1,323,676	109,368,527
10			2,187,371	3,827,898	1,640,528	1,306,855	110,462,213
11			2,209,244	3,866,177	1,656,933	1,290,247	111,566,835
12			2,231,337	3,904,839	1,673,503	1,273,851	112,682,503
13			2,253,650	3,943,888	1,690,238	1,257,664	113,809,328
14			2,276,187	3,983,326	1,707,140	1,241,682	114,947,421
15			2,298,948	4,023,160	1,724,211	1,225,903	116,096,896
16			2,321,938	4,063,391	1,741,453	1,210,324	117,257,864
17			2,345,157	4,104,025	1,758,868	1,194,944	118,430,443
18			2,368,609	4,145,066	1,776,457	1,179,759	119,614,748
19			2,392,295	4,186,516	1,794,221	1,164,767	120,810,895
20			2,416,218	4,228,381	1,812,163	1,149,965	122,019,004
21			2,440,380	4,270,665	1,830,285	1,135,352	123,239,194
22			2,464,784	4,313,372	1,848,588	1,120,924	124,471,586
23			2,489,432	4,356,506	1,867,074	1,106,680	125,716,302
24			2,514,326	4,400,071	1,885,745	1,092,616	126,973,465

Year	*Cost of tax credit for the public finances (44%)*	*Cost of tax credit for the public finances (57%)*	*Cost of the tax holiday for the public finances*	*Distribution (charity)*	*Net benefit: distribution less the cost of the tax holiday*	*Net benefit: current value over 25 years*	*Balance of capital in the foundation, after distribution and expenses*
25			2,539,469	4,444,071	1,904,602	1,078,732	128,243,200
26			2,564,864	4,488,512	1,923,648	1,065,023	129,525,631
27			2,590,513	4,533,397	1,942,884	1,051,489	130,820,888
28			2,616,418	4,578,731	1,962,313	1,038,127	132,129,097
29			2,642,582	4,624,518	1,981,936	1,024,935	133,450,388
30			2,669,008	4,670,764	2,001,756	1,011,910	134,784,892
31			2,695,698	4,717,471	2,021,773	999,051	136,132,740
32			2,722,655	4,764,646	2,041,991	986,356	137,494,068
33			2,749,881	4,812,292	2,062,411	973,821	138,869,009
34			2,777,380	4,860,415	2,083,035	961,446	140,257,699
35			2,805,154	4,909,019	2,103,865	949,229	141,660,276
36			2,833,206	4,958,110	2,124,904	937,166	143,076,878
37			2,861,538	5,007,691	2,146,153	925,257	144,507,647
38			2,890,153	5,057,768	2,167,615	913,499	145,952,724
39			2,919,054	5,108,345	2,189,291	901,890	147,412,251
40			2,948,245	5,159,429	2,211,184	890,429	148,886,373
41			2,977,727	5,211,023	2,233,296	879,114	150,375,237
42			3,007,505	5,263,133	2,255,629	867,943	151,878,989
43			3,037,580	5,315,765	2,278,185	856,913	153,397,779
44			3,067,956	5,368,922	2,300,967	846,024	154,931,757
45			3,098,635	5,422,612	2,323,976	835,273	156,481,075
46			3,129,621	5,476,838	2,347,216	824,658	158,045,885
47			3,160,918	5,531,606	2,370,688	814,179	159,626,344
48			3,192,527	5,586,922	2,394,395	803,832	161,222,608
49			3,224,452	5,642,791	2,418,339	793,617	162,834,834
50			3,256,697	5,699,219	2,442,523	783,532	164,463,182
51			3,289,264	5,756,211	2,466,948	773,575	166,107,814
52			3,322,156	5,813,773	2,491,617	763,745	167,768,892
53			3,355,378	5,871,911	2,516,533	754,040	169,446,581

ANNEX 11.3 – TREASURY EFFICIENCY – ANALYSIS ON 20 YEARS, DISBURSEMENT QUOTA OF 5.5%

Year	*Cost of tax credit for the public finances (44%)*	*Cost of tax credit for the public finances (57%)*	*Cost of the tax holiday for the public finances*	*Distribution (charity)*	*Net benefit: distribution less the cost of the tax holiday*	*Net benefit: current value over 25 years*	*Balance of capital in the foundation, after distribution and expenses*
	44,000,000	57,000,000				51,012,127	
1			2,000,000	5,500,000	3,500,000	3,421,310	99,000,000
2			1,980,000	5,445,000	3,465,000	3,310,945	98,010,000
3			1,960,200	5,390,550	3,430,350	3,204,140	97,029,900
4			1,940,598	5,336,645	3,396,047	3,100,781	96,059,601
5			1,921,192	5,283,278	3,362,086	3,000,756	95,099,005
6			1,901,980	5,230,445	3,328,465	2,903,957	94,148,015
7			1,882,960	5,178,141	3,295,181	2,810,281	93,206,535
8			1,864,131	5,126,359	3,262,229	2,719,627	92,274,469
9			1,845,489	5,075,096	3,229,606	2,631,897	91,351,725
10			1,827,034	5,024,345	3,197,310	2,546,997	90,438,208
11			1,808,764	4,974,101	3,165,337	2,464,836	89,533,825
12			1,790,677	4,924,360	3,133,684	2,385,325	88,638,487
13			1,772,770	4,875,117	3,102,347	2,308,379	87,752,102
14			1,755,042	4,826,366	3,071,324	2,233,915	86,874,581
15			1,737,492	4,778,102	3,040,610	2,161,854	86,005,835
16			1,720,117	4,730,321	3,010,204	2,092,116	85,145,777
17			1,702,916	4,683,018	2,980,102	2,024,629	84,294,319
18			1,685,886	4,636,188	2,950,301	1,959,318	83,451,376
19			1,669,028	4,589,826	2,920,798	1,896,114	82,616,862
20			1,652,337	4,543,927	2,891,590	1,834,949	81,790,694

12

TAX-PRICE ELASTICITY OF CHARITABLE DONATIONS – EVIDENCE FROM THE GERMAN TAXPAYER PANEL

Maja Adena

1 Introduction

The tax system in many countries is designed to encourage private donations to charities. In some countries, including Germany, donations can be deducted from gross income and therefore reduce individual tax liability. However, this imposes a cost on governments in the form of foregone tax revenue. For example, in 2001 in Germany, taxpayers declared a total of €3.7 billion of donations, of which €2.9 billion was recognized as deductible, thus reducing the tax revenue by approximately €0.9 billion.[1] Thus, policy makers have a vital interest in assessing the effectiveness of allowing deductions to increase donations. The tax-price elasticity of donations is crucial for making this assessment and for evaluating potential policy changes. However, its value is unknown and has to be estimated. While there are numerous studies estimating tax-price elasticity of giving for the United States, the evidence for other countries is rather sparse.[2] However, one should not believe that the estimates for the United States are also valid for other countries. Specifically, Germany differs much from the United States when it comes to the role of the government and the tradition of charitable giving. Total public social expenditures in Germany in 2001 amounted to 27.4% of GDP. By contrast, they were 14.7% of GDP in the United States.[3] National giving levels are 1.67% of GDP in the United States, and they are 0.22% of GDP in Germany. Moreover, there are also strong regional differences in Germany. While in the former East Germany, the giving levels are 0.12% of GDP, they are 0.26% of GDP in West Germany.[4]

The United States and Germany also differ in the charitable goals that are primarily supported. While in 2010, 35% of U.S. donations went to support religious goals, 14% to educational goals, and 9% to support human services,[5] the numbers for Germany were: 33% for emergency relief, 24% for child welfare, and 24% for foreign aid.[6] Around two-thirds of private donations in Germany are paid in the form of membership fees for nonprofit associations and organizations.[7] Membership fees are usually of a fixed, prespecified value and are often automatically debited from members' bank accounts.[8] This could imply that German donors will be less responsive to small changes in price or that adjustments in contributions may occur after a time lag.

Given that donations have not been studied extensively in Germany,[9] this chapter contributes to closing this gap in a number of ways and fully exploits the advantages of the longitudinal

 DOI: 10.4324/9781003139201-15

character of the data set. First, it accounts for omitted variable bias coming from individual unobserved characteristics (like education, wealth or degree of altruism) that are potentially correlated with income and marginal tax and are known to be important determinants of donations. Second, it accounts for the endogeneity of the tax-price and after-tax income variables by appropriate instruments. Third, it helps to overcome the identification problems while using the tax reform implemented gradually in 2004 and 2005. Moreover, it allows to identify permanent and transitory tax-price and income elasticity and to understand whether donors adjust their charitable giving gradually in response to tax changes and whether they respond in advance to known future changes. Finally, this study allows tax-price and income elasticity to vary by income class.

The chapter is divided into the following parts. The next section presents a review of the relevant literature. Section 3 explains the treatment of donations in the German tax law. Section 4 explains empirical methodology. Section 5 presents estimation results. In Section 6, some robustness checks are presented, and Section 7 concludes.

2 Literature

There is a vast empirical literature investigating the tax-price and income elasticity of donations in the United States. Initial research was conducted with cross-sectional data, using ordinary least squares (OLS) or Tobit methods. Examples include Feldstein and Taylor (1976) and Feenberg (1988). The estimated price elasticity was large, on average −1.5 (United States). Later, the availability of panel data allowed researchers to exploit techniques accounting for individual heterogeneity of donors and found much lower price elasticities (for example, Broman 1989). Recently, a new line of research has tried to distinguish permanent from transitory effects using the availability of long panels (see, for example, Randolph 1995; Barrett et al. 1997; Bakija 2000). However, the discussion concerning the nature of the "true" tax-price elasticity is still ongoing.

Studies on tax-price elasticities from other countries are rather scarce, though tax deductions for donations are widely employed. Given different attitudes toward giving in different cultures as well as different roles governments play in the provision of public goods in different countries, the magnitude of the response to fiscal incentives in these countries might be very different from the United States. For example, Fack and Landais (2010), using a nonparametric method of quantile regression, found rather low elasticities for France, ranging from −0.6 to −0.2.

There are only a few empirical studies for Germany. Pioneering work was done by Paqué (1996). Using tax data aggregated on a state and income-group basis for 1961 to 1980 in three-year intervals and using the OLS method, he found an elasticity in the range of −1.8 to −1.4. Auer and Kalusche (2010) implemented a Tobit estimator on a 1998 cross section with individual data and found an elasticity of −1.11 to −1.05. Borgloh (2008) used a Tobit and a two-step Heckman model applied to pooled 2001–2003 individual tax data and provided estimates in the range of −2.08 to −0.84. Two more recent studies applied a censored quantile regression. Bönke et al. (2013) used (pooled) cross sections of the years 1998, 2001, and 2004 and obtained results ranging between −1.45 and −0.45. Bönke and Werdt (2015) used panel data for 2001–2006 and estimated heterogeneous elasticities depending on the level of donations. For donors at the lower and upper tails of the donation distribution, they estimated the price elasticity to be greater than 1 in absolute value and those in the middle of the donations distribution to be lower than 1.

This chapter makes use of the longitudinal characteristics of the available panel data for 2001–2006. Different from Bönke and Werdt (2015), I apply a different methodology which allows me to control for unobserved individual characteristics. Different from early studies for Germany, changes in tax rates were implemented in the years 2004 and 2005 (see Figures 12.1 and 12.2); thus, exogenous variation in price is available.

The methods used in this chapter are most similar to Bakija and Heim (2011). They worked with a very long panel of U.S. tax returns from 1979–2006. Bakija and Heim relied on both tax changes in the federal tax law and on the differences in tax evolution between different states. In Germany, there is only one uniform tax schedule. In this chapter, tax-price elasticity can be identified because individuals with different incomes were affected differently by tax schedule changes (see Figures 12.1 and 12.2). Instead of using the so called first-dollar (first-euro) price as proxy for the actual price, I apply an instrumental variable (IV) approach using the first-dollar price as an instrument for the actual price. I take the same approach for after-tax income.

3 Donations and the tax system in Germany

In Germany, both individual tax liability and the treatment of donations are regulated in the German Income Tax Act (ITA). The German fiscal year is equal to the calendar year. Roughly speaking, tax liability is determined in two steps. In the first step, all income from seven sources is added together, and then different deductions are subtracted. These include allowances for the elderly and farmers, loss deduction, special expenses deduction (including donations), deduction for extraordinary expenses, and personal allowances. The remaining amount is the taxable income (TI). If a couple opts for joint declaration, the taxable income for each spouse is determined as the average of the taxable incomes of both spouses. In the second step, the tax due is computed. The formula is $TAX = a_i TI^2 + b_i TI + c_i$, where $i = 0,1,2,3$ defines different income thresholds such that this function is continuous but not smooth. Marginal tax is then given by $MT = 2a_i TI + b_i$. Figure 12.2 presents the marginal tax as a function of taxable income for a single household in 2001–2006. A tax reform was implemented gradually in 2004 and 2005, lowering the marginal tax for all incomes but to a different extent. Figure 12.2 shows the changes in the tax-price for individuals with different values of taxable income. It indicates that individuals with €10,000, €30,000, and €60,000 taxable income experience a larger increase in the tax-price than, for example, individuals with €50,000 taxable income.

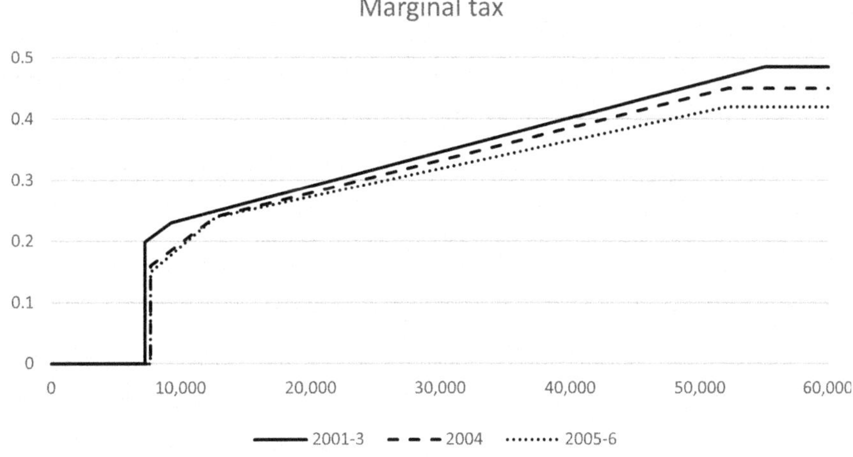

Figure 12.1 Marginal tax rates 2001–2006, single

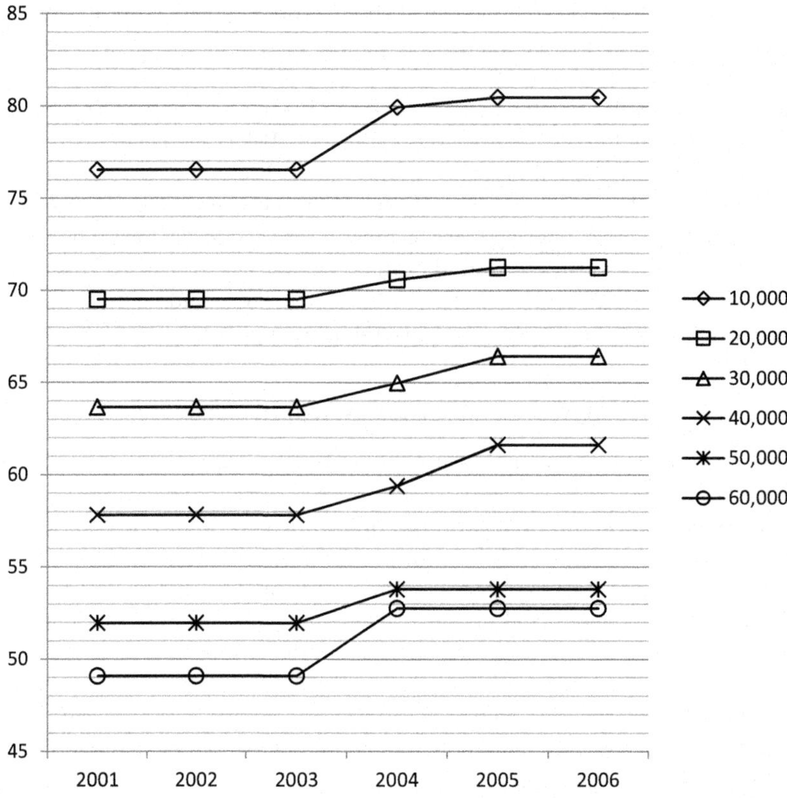

Figure 12.2 The evolution of the tax-price 2001–2006 for different values of taxable income per €100 (single)

The deductibility of donations is regulated in §10b and §34g ITA. §10b addresses donations and membership fees to organizations that pursue scientific, charitable and cultural goals that are recognized as eligible. These are deductible up to an amount 5% of gross income. Furthermore, §10b allows deductions of donations and membership fees to organizations pursuing church-related, religious, and charitable goals that are recognized as eligible. These are deductible up to an additional 5% of gross income. Additionally, one can deduct donations to foundations up to €20,450 and grants to newly established foundations up to €307,000. Donations to political parties are governed by §34g and §10b ITA. Fifty percent of the first €1,650 (singles) or €3,300 (married) given is directly deducted from due tax, having thus a fixed price of 0.5 for each €1 given. Each euro donated above this threshold up to €3,300 (singles) or €6,600 (married) reduces the taxable income in keeping with §10b. The price of those donations is given by 1 minus the marginal tax. In the following sections, I will focus specifically on those donations which can be deducted from gross income, the price of which is given by 1 minus the marginal tax.[10]

Among different separate deductions, German law allows for the deduction of extraordinary expenses (§10, §10a ITA). These include childcare, tax advice, alimony and other ongoing financial obligations, deductible church tax, education and training, expenses of a provident nature, school tuitions, donations, and other. Those who do not itemize any of those obtain a blanket allowance of €36 (€72 for couples choosing joint declaration).

Sommerfeld (2009) provided a statistical overview of charitable giving in Germany. Her survey revealed that 83.5% of taxpayers are aware of the deductibility of donations. According to Sommerfeld, 70% of the population donates and 43% declare donations in tax declarations.

4 Empirical methodology

4.1 Empirical specification

Usually, the literature assumes that the demand function for donations, $DON = f\left((1-\tau),Y\right)$, is linear in a natural logarithm and imposes the following empirical specification:[11]

$$lnDON_i = \mu + \delta ln(1-\tau_i) + \beta lnY_i + X_i\gamma + u_i \quad (1)$$

where for each individual i, DON_i is the amount of the donations, τ_i is the marginal tax, Y_i is a measure of disposable income, X_i is a vector of other characteristics,[12] μ is some constant, and u_i is an error term. Given the nonlinear dependence of the right-hand-side variables, that is, tax-price, income, marital status, and other characteristics leading to different deductions, there is the serious risk that if equation 1 is misspecified, the coefficients of interest might not be identified. The issues that accompany attempts to determine the tax-price effect and the income effect separately are discussed in Triest (1998). Identification is only possible if there is a variation in tax rates (price) independent of individual characteristics that may affect charitable giving. Feenberg's (1988) solution is to exploit the variations in state income taxes in the United States. For Germany, there is only one national income tax law. The needed variation in price is provided because changes in national income tax occurred in 2004 and 2005, and they affected individuals with different incomes differently (see Figure 12.2). Adopting the widespread approach from the previous literature on charitable giving, and in order to interpret the coefficients directly as elasticities, I estimate the previous log-log specification with some modifications explained in the following.

One of the most important issues is the omitted variable bias. The available data are missing characteristics such as education, wealth, and altruism which are known to be important determinants of charitable giving.[13] Likewise, these variables are known to be correlated with income.[14] Given that, a simple regression analysis will not identify the parameters of interest. Therefore, in the donation equation, I account for the individual-specific fixed effects α_i. I assume that these individual-specific fixed effects α_i do not vary (significantly)[15] over time. However, these fixed (time-invariant) individual-specific effect are potentially correlated with other explanatory variables, that is, $E\{X_{it}\alpha_i\} \neq 0$. To account for factors influencing donations from year to year, the time fixed effects δ_t are included in the specification. This might be especially important, as the Elbe flooding happened in 2002 and the tsunami at the end of 2004, thus increasing donations shortly afterwards. The time-varying, individual-specific error term denoted as u_{it}. I assume that $E\{X_{it}u_{it}\} = 0$ for each t. The donation equation becomes:

$$lnDON_{it} = \delta lnPRICE_{it} + \beta lnY_{it} + X_{it}\gamma + \alpha_i + \delta_t + u_{it} \quad (2)$$

The next important issue concerns endogeneity. Clearly, the tax-price is determined by income, marital status, the amount donated, and other deductions. For many levels of income, it holds true that the higher the amount of donations, the lower the marginal tax rate, and consequently the higher the tax-price. Similarly, after-tax income depends on taxes, which in turn depends on the amount donated. The simple OLS estimation of the equation of interest would yield biased estimates. Here, I address the endogeneity by using an instrumental variable estimator. For each individual, I calculate a hypothetical marginal tax at zero donations, which is clearly uncorrelated with the dependent variable. Similarly, for after-tax income, I calculate a hypothetical after-tax income at zero donations. Those instruments are correlated with the endogenous variables but uncorrelated with unobserved characteristics which determine donations. There is a convention in the literature on charitable giving of regressing donations directly onto these hypothetical variables, which are usually called first-dollar price and first-dollar income. This seems to be the second-best approach when the IV method is feasible. Not taking the IV approach leads to the estimation of what may be termed "first-dollar price elasticity." But this will be different from the actual tax-price elasticity, especially because first-dollar price elasticity is measured at a lower quantity and a lower price.

In the data, a significant portion of taxpayers do not itemize. Clotfelter (1980), Boskin and Feldstein (1977), and Reece and Zieschang (1985) suggest that excluding nonitemizers and border itemizers[16] might lead to a selection bias. Therefore, I follow Feldstein and Taylor (1976) by calculating a modified first-euro price as if the itemization were possible regardless of the actual value of donation.[17] This first-euro price is used in the IV approach as an instrument for the actual price, which is strictly lower than one for border itemizers and differs for each individual. I proceed accordingly for nonitemizers.

Many donors do not report donations in their tax declarations. It is difficult to account for censoring and fixed effects at the same time.[18] Panel studies from the United States widely employ demeaning or first differencing, for example, Bakija (2000) or Randolph (1995), and I follow this approach. Nonetheless, I will compare my results from the estimation of equation 2 with the results from an estimation that accounts for censoring in Section 6.3.

The availability of a six-year panel allows me to identify permanent and transitory effects. Therefore, specification 2 is extended to:

$$\begin{aligned} lnDON_{it} &= \delta_1 lnPRICE_{it-1} + \delta_2 lnPRICE_{it} + \delta_3 lnPRICE_{it+1} + \\ &+ \beta_1 lnY_{it-1} + \beta_2 lnY_{it} + \beta_3 lnY_{it+1} + \\ &+ X_{it}\gamma + \alpha_i + \delta_t + u_{it}. \end{aligned} \tag{3}$$

The permanent price effect is given by $\delta_1 + \delta_2 + \delta_3$, the transitory effect by δ_2, and the effect of an anticipated increase in price next year by δ_3.[19] Similarly, the permanent income effect is given by $\beta_1 + \beta_2 + \beta_3$ and the transitory income effect by β_2, respectively. When the actual values for the future tax-price and income are included into the equation 3, one assumes perfect foresight. However, future expectations are what matters for charitable giving and not realizations. To address this caveat, I implement a similar solution to the one chosen by Bakija and Heim (2011). In one specification (perfect foresight), I treat future realizations of price and income as erroneous measurements of future expectations. In an alternative specification (predictable tax change), I implement the IV approach in which I assume that the tax formula of the following year is known but one's own income in the following year is not known. This means that in the first step, I predict the following year's income using broad information available about the subjects, especially the income and price from the year in question and the year before as covariates. In the second step, I use this predicted income to calculate the (predicted) future after-tax-income and the (predicted) future price using the appropriate tax formula.

Finally, to allow for heterogeneous effects of price and nonprice variables, I multiply them by dummies for four different income classes (gross income in €: 1–29,999; 30,000–59,999;

60,000–89,999; and ≥ 90,000 for single households and twice the amount for married couples). Recall that the price is based on taxable income, which might be very different from the gross income. This means that the income groups are rather based on status than on disposable income and price. If there is indeed heterogeneity, the last step is also necessary due to the selectivity of the available sample in which high-income taxpayers are overrepresented (see the data description subsequently). Therefore, specification 3 is extended to:

$$\begin{aligned} lnDON_{it} = & \sum_{j=1}^{4} D_j * \\ & *[\delta_{j1} lnPRICE_{it-1} + \delta_{j2} lnPRICE_{it} + \delta_{j3} lnPRICE_{it+1} + \\ & + \beta_{j1} lnY_{it-1} + \beta_{j2} lnY_{it} + \beta_{j3} lnY_{it+1} + X_{it}\gamma_j + \delta_{jt}] + \\ & + \alpha_i + u_{it}, \end{aligned} \tag{4}$$

where D_j are dummies for the four income groups $j = \{1,2,3,4\}$. This approach allows, moreover, for a more flexible relationship between income and charitable giving, thus relaxing the assumption imposed by equation 1.

4.2 Data

The analysis in this chapter is based on 5% stratified sample from the German Taxpayer Panel 2001–2006 made available by the German Federal Statistical Office. It is a rich panel of individual income tax return data in which high-income taxpayers are strongly overrepresented. The strata are based on region, joint or separate declaration, main income source, and the average of the gross income over the six years. It contains around a million observations per year, detailed information on income and taxes, and some demographic characteristics such as age, state of residence, religion, and the number and age of children. The panel is available for distant computations with SAS. Tables 12.1 and 12.2 present some descriptive statistics.

4.3 Variables

The dependent variable, $ln(DON_{it} + 1)$, is the natural logarithm of donations declared according to §10bITA. Given that there are households that do not declare any donations and in order to assure that this variable takes values larger than zero, I add €1 to the amount of donations. The U.S. literature usually adds the amount of $10. However, the average donation in those studies is 5 to more than 250 times higher than in the data used for this study.[20] This suggests that €1 is a better choice. However, the choice is still arbitrary. Later, I present robustness checks adding, alternatively, €5 and €10 to the amount of donations.

The first independent variable, $lnPRICE_{it}$, is the natural logarithm of the price, which is 1 minus the marginal tax rate. The actual tax rate is endogenous, as it changes with the amount donated. Therefore, I calculate for each individual a hypothetical marginal tax at zero donations and use its natural logarithm, $lnPRICE_{it}$, as an instrument.

The second independent variable, lnY_{it}, is the natural logarithm of the after-tax income. Respectively, I calculate a hypothetical after-tax income at zero donations and use its natural logarithm, $ln\tilde{Y}_{it}$, as an instrument.

Additionally, I include other control variables: dummies for each of the six income sources other than income earned as an employee (income from agriculture and forestry, from business,

Table 12.1 Descriptive statistics 1

	2001	2002	2003	2004	2005	2006
Avg. donation (€)	474.73 (118.99)	537.54 (133.24)	511.34 (127.57)	580.72 (140.57)	647.77 (153.31)	665.48 (147.39)
Donor share (%)	45.55 (34.70)	47.64 (36.98)	46.75 (35.89)	48.77 (37.88)	50.34 (38.93)	47.71 (36.55)
Avg. price (per 100€)	71.03 (75.09)	71.32 (75.02)	71.36 (75.05)	72.20 (74.76)	72.03 (74.97)	72.85 (74.95)
Avg. gross income (€)	80,287 (33,344)	76,677 (33,272)	76,018 (33,297)	82,302 (34,531)	92,919 (33,346)	96,941 (36,753)
Avg. age	47.20 (44.10)	48.18 (45.09)	49.17 (46.08)	50.16 (47.07)	51.16 (48.07)	52.15 (49.06)
Joint declaration share (%)	60.30 (57.77)	60.53 (57.97)	60.71 (58.23)	60.86 (58.55)	61.12 (58.72)	61.06 (58.76)
West share (%)	84.77 (85.35)	84.79 (85.34)	84.80 (85.32)	84.83 (85.31)	84.85 (85.30)	84.87 (85.31)
Religion share (%)	23.36 (23.08)	23.18 (23.09)	22.92 (23.00)	22.40 (22.72)	21.97 (22.33)	23.61 (23.21)
Self-employment share (%)	18.13 (6.36)	18.26 (6.40)	18.50 (6.53)	18.77 (6.75)	18.86 (6.85)	18.77 (6.93)
Number of children	0.82 (0.75)	0.81 (0.75)	0.80 (0.74)	0.79 (0.73)	0.78 (0.72)	0.76 (0.71)
N in million	0.93	0.93	0.93	0.93	0.93	0.93

Note: This table presents raw sample averages. Population weighted averages are presented in brackets.

Table 12.2 Descriptive statistics 2

Single				
Gross income (€)	1–29,999	30,000–59,999	60,000–89,999	≥ 90,000
Avg. price	99.59	76.13	62.03	55.45
N in millions (total 6 years)	0.37	0.93	0.35	0.37
Joint declaration				
Gross income (€)	1–59,999	60,000–119,999	120,000–179,999	≥ 180,000
Avg. price	99.66	73.21	61.12	54.80
N in millions (total 6 years)	0.39	1.28	0.52	1.09

Note: This table presents raw sample averages.

from self-employment, from dependent employment, capital income, and from rent and leasing properties), a dummy for joint declaration, for living in West Germany, for religious affiliation, and one control variable for the number of children and for the age squared. Note that as those controls seldom change over time, they are mostly absorbed by individual fixed effects.

5 Estimation results

Table 12.3 presents the results from the estimation, which allows the coefficients for all nonprice variables to differ across income classes and uses the IV approach to price and income. The estimates for permanent price elasticity are –0.57 (Table 12.3, column I) assuming perfect foresight and –0.82 (Table 12.3, column II) when relying on predictable changes of future income and price.

Table 12.3 Permanent and transitory effects: the estimation allows coefficients on all nonprice variables to differ across income classes using the IV approach to price and income. The dependent variable is $lnDON_{i,t}$

	(I) Perfect foresight				*(II) Predictable tax change instruments*			
$lnPRICE_{i,t}$	−0.14***				−0.01			
	(0.01)				(0.01)			
$lnPRICE_{i,t-1}$	−0.33***				−0.41***			
	(0.01)				(0.02)			
$lnPRICE_{i,t+1}$	−0.10**				−0.39***			
	(0.01)				(0.04)			
Permanent price elasticity	−0.57				−0.82			
Income class	1–29,999	30,000–59,999	60,000–89,999	≥90,000	1–29,999	30,000–59,999	60,000–89,999	≥90,000
$lnY_{i,t}$	0.19***	0.16***	0.16***	0.15***	0.26***	0.23***	0.22***	0.21***
	(0.00)	(0.00)	(0.00)	(0.00)	(0.01)	(0.01)	(0.01)	(0.01)
$lnY_{i,t-1}$	0.00	0.01*	0.01*	0.01***	−0.01*	−0.01	−0.01	−0.00
	(0.00)	(0.00)	(0.00)	(0.00)	(0.01)	(0.01)	(0.01)	(0.01)
$lnY_{i,t+1}$	0.04***	0.03***	0.04***	0.04***	0.08**	0.08**	0.08**	0.08**
	(0.00)	(0.00)	(0.00)	(0.00)	(0.02)	(0.02)	(0.02)	(0.02)
Permanent income elasticity	0.23	0.20	0.20	0.31	0.34	0.31	0.30	0.28
Other controls × income class	Yes				Yes			
year effects × income class	Yes				Yes			
fixed individual effects	Yes				Yes			
N in millions	3.36				2.72			

Source: Taxpayerpanel 2001–2006, author's own calculations
Notes: Standard errors in parentheses
*** Significant at 0.01 level, ** significant at 0.05 level, * significant at 0.1 level

The estimates for permanent income elasticity are around 0.2–0.3, slightly varying among different income classes. The estimates of price elasticity are rather low when compared with previous cross-sectional studies from Germany.[21] However, if the price elasticity differs among income groups, those estimates are rather meaningless and depend strongly on the composition of the sample. Therefore, in the next table, we move on to relaxing the assumption of homogeneity of price elasticity.

Table 12.4 presents the results from the estimation, which allows the coefficients on all variables to differ across income classes (equation 4) and uses the IV approach to price and income. It allows for the heterogeneity of tax responsiveness among different income groups and corrects for the sample composition in which high income groups are overrepresented. The results show that permanent tax-price elasticity varies significantly between income classes. It is as low as −0.26 (perfect foresight) and −0.17 (predictable changes) for pretax incomes below €30,000 for singles and €60,000 for married couples, respectively. It is as high as −1.40 (perfect foresight) and −1.56 (predictable changes) for incomes €30,000–59,999 for singles and

Table 12.4 Permanent and transitory effects. Estimates allowing coefficients on all variables including price to differ across income classes. IV approach to price and income. Dependent variable: $lnDON_{i,t}$.

	(I) Perfect foresight				*(II) Predictable tax change instruments*			
income class	1–29,999	30,000–59,999	60,000–89,999	≥90,000	1–29,999	30,000–59,999	60,000–89,999	≥90,000
$lnPRICE_{i,t}$	−0.01	−0.54***	−0.38***	−0.37***	0.24***	−0.41***	−0.37***	−0.48***
	(0.01)	(0.03)	(0.04)	(0.04)	(0.02)	(0.04)	(0.07)	(0.05)
$lnPRICE_{i,t-1}$	−0.23***	−0.47***	−0.51***	−0.71***	−0.22***	−0.57***	−0.65***	−0.89***
	(0.01)	(0.03)	(0.04)	(0.03)	(0.02)	(0.03)	(0.05)	(0.04)
$lnPRICE_{i,t+1}$	−0.03**	−0.38***	−0.06	0.01	−0.19***	−0.58***	−0.32***	0.01
	(0.01)	(0.03)	(0.04)	(0.03)	(0.05)	(0.07)	(0.07)	(0.06)
Permanent price elasticity	−0.26	−1.40	−0.96	−1.07	−0.17	1.56	−1.33	−1.38
$lnY_{i,t}$	0.21***	0.16***	0.16***	0.15***	0.31***	0.25***	0.24***	0.23***
	(0.00)	(0.00)	(0.00)	(0.00)	(0.01)	(0.01)	(0.01)	(0.01)
$lnY_{i,t-1}$	0.01***	0.01*	0.01*	−0.00	0.01	−0.00	−0.01	−0.02**
	(0.00)	(0.00)	(0.00)	(0.00)	(0.01)	(0.01)	(0.01)	(0.01)
$lnY_{i,t+1}$	0.04***	0.03***	0.04***	0.05***	0.07**	0.05**	0.06**	0.08***
	(0.00)	(0.00)	(0.00)	(0.00)	(0.02)	(0.02)	(0.02)	(0.02)
Permanent income elasticity	0.27	0.19	0.21	0.20	0.39	0.30	0.30	0.29
Other controls × income class			Yes				Yes	
year effects × income class			Yes				Yes	
fixed individual effects			Yes				Yes	
N in millions			3.36				2.72	

Source: Taxpayerpanel 2001–2006, author's own calculations
Notes: Standard errors in parentheses
*** Significant at 0.01 level, ** significant at 0.05 level, * significant at 0.1 level

€60,000–119,999 for married couples. Higher incomes show elasticity of around −1 when assuming perfect foresight and around −1.35 when assuming predictable changes. Overall, there is evidence of heterogeneity among income classes. Consequently, this table presents results from the preferred specification (equation 4), and the results are referred to in conclusions from this chapter. Given that the distribution of the income classes in the whole population is approximately 50%, 30%, 10%, and 10%, and their shares of total giving are 23%, 26%, 14%, and 37%,[22] the average weighted permanent elasticity is slightly below −1. Overall, one can judge the fiscal incentives in Germany as being effective in stimulating charitable giving. However, the results also show that different treatment of donors depending on their characteristics could improve the efficiency even more. This could lead to a potential further decoupling of the price for charitable giving from the tax scheme.

The comparability with other empirical studies for Germany is limited because they all estimate "first-euro" elasticity. Regardless of the differences in the definition, my estimates predict rather lower responsiveness to tax incentives. This is especially true with respect to previous studies relying on OLS and Tobit methods.

The estimates for permanent income elasticity are around 0.2–0.3, slightly varying among different income classes.

I find evidence that donors adjust their charitable contributions gradually. They respond strongly to the former price. Moreover, I find evidence for all income classes, apart from the highest, that donors respond to predictable future changes in the price (see Table 12.4). The actual income and to some extent the future income drive the donations. The effects of past income are negligible.

6 Robustness checks

This section presents a number of important robustness checks.

6.1 Assuming that coefficients are uniform across income classes

Table 12.5 presents the results from a regression when assuming that all coefficients are uniform across income classes (equation 3) and using the IV approach to price and income. Column I presents the results from a regression that assumes perfect foresight, and column II presents the results when using predictable-tax-change instruments. The coefficient estimates of permanent price elasticity (–0.33 and –0.37) are low in magnitude when compared to the estimates from cross-sectional studies estimating a uniform price elasticity for Germany. Similarly, the coefficient estimates for permanent income elasticity (0.31 and 0.43) are rather low. However, given the selectivity of the available sample, those results cannot be carried over to the whole population. More importantly, the conclusions from Tables 12.1 and 12.2 are that the assumption of homogeneity among different income classes is clearly violated. This table, however, is the basis for the comparisons with the subsequent robustness checks.

Table 12.5 Permanent and transitory effects: assuming coefficients are uniform across income classes, using the IV approach to price and income. The dependent variable is $lnDON_{i,t}$

	(I) Perfect foresight	*(II) Predictable tax change instruments*
$lnPRICE_{i,t}$	–0.03** (0.01)	0.05** (0.02)
$lnPRICE_{i,t-1}$	–0.33*** (0.01)	–0.43*** (0.02)
$lnPRICE_{i,t+1}$	0.02** (0.01)	0.01 (0.03)
Permanent price elasticity	–0.33	–0.37
$lnY_{i,t}$	0.21*** (0.00)	0.26*** (0.01)
$lnY_{i,t-1}$	0.02*** (0.00)	0.02** (0.01)
$lnY_{i,t+1}$	0.07*** (0.00)	0.15*** (0.02)
Permanent income elasticity	0.31	0.43
Other controls	Yes	Yes
Year effects	Yes	Yes
Fixed individual effects	Yes	Yes
N in millions	3.36	2.72

Source: Taxpayerpanel 2001–2006, author's own calculations
Notes: Standard errors in parentheses
*** Significant at 0.01 level, ** significant at 0.05 level, * significant at 0.1 level

Table 12.6 Permanent and transitory effects. Assuming coefficients are uniform across income classes. First-dollar price. Dependent variable: $lnDON_{i,t}$

	(I) Perfect foresight	*(II) Predictable tax change instruments*
$lnPRICE_{i,t}$	−0.22*** (0.01)	−0.30*** (0.01)
$lnPRICE_{i,t-1}$	−0.38*** (0.01)	−0.55*** (0.01)
$lnPRICE_{i,t+1}$	0.00 (0.01)	−0.10*** (0.01)
Permanent price elasticity	−0.59	−0.95
$lnY_{i,t}$	0.17*** (0.00)	0.18*** (0.00)
$lnY_{i,t-1}$	0.02*** (0.00)	−0.01*** (0.00)
$lnY_{i,t+1}$	0.06*** (0.00)	0.03*** (0.00)
Permanent income elasticity	0.25	0.20
Other controls	Yes	Yes
Year effects	Yes	Yes
Fixed individual effects	Yes	Yes
N in millions	3.36	2.73

Source: Taxpayerpanel 2001–2006, author's own calculations
Notes: Standard errors in parentheses
*** Significant at 0.01 level, ** significant at 0.05 level, * significant at 0.1 level

6.2 First-euro price and income instead of IV approach

Table 12.6 presents the results when estimating the basic specification (assuming coefficients are uniform across income classes) without the IV approach and using the first-euro price and, similarly, hypothetical after-tax income at zero donations instead. The estimates of permanent tax-price elasticity are higher in absolute terms when compared to the basic specification with the IV approach (Table 12.5). It changes from −0.33 to −0.59 when assuming perfect foresight and from −0.37 to −0.95 when assuming predictable tax change instruments. This might suggest that the estimates of tax-price elasticity from previous studies for Germany are overestimated. The estimates for permanent income elasticity are somewhat lower, changing from 0.31 to 0.25 when assuming perfect foresight and from 0.43 to 0.20 when assuming predictable tax change instruments.

6.3 Censoring

Because I do not observe donations for around 50% of observations, there is a serious concern that due to censoring, my confidents are biased. Can the comparably low coefficient estimates of price elasticity be explained by neglecting the censoring? I estimate a Tobit model[23] on pooled data regressing donations directly on the first-euro price and other variables. I then compare the results with analogous OLS regression which does not account for censoring. The estimated coefficients as compared to simple OLS regression on pooled data are presented in Table 12.7. The marginal effects from the Tobit regressions are similar to those obtained from the OLS estimation. This does not support the hypothesis that the estimates of the elasticity obtained in previous sections are seriously biased due to censoring.

6.4 Adding different amounts to donations

Because of the numerous observations with zero donations and because the logarithmic function is not defined at zero, I have added an additional euro to the individual contribution.

Table 12.7 Accounting versus not accounting for censoring: Tobit versus OLS. First-euro price. Assuming perfect foresight. Dependent variable: $lnDON_{i,t}$

	Tobit marginal effects	*OLS*	*Tobit marginal effects*	*OLS*
$lnPRICE_{i,t}$	−1.16*** (0.24)	−1.11*** (0.03)	−0.60*** (0.11)	−0.68*** (0.08)
$lnPRICE_{i,t-1}$			−0.41*** (0.07)	−0.58*** (0.06)
$lnPRICE_{i,t+1}$			−0.14*** (0.02)	−0.18*** (0.07)
Permanent price elasticity			−1.14	−1.43
$lnY_{i,t}$	0.51*** (0.11)	0.51*** (0.01)	0.08*** (0.01)	0.13*** (0.02)
$lnY_{i,t-1}$			0.15*** (0.03)	0.13*** (0.01)
$lnY_{i,t+1}$			0.39*** (0.07)	0.36*** (0.02)
Permanent income elasticity			0.61	0.61
Other controls	Yes	Yes	Yes	Yes
Year dummies	Yes	Yes	Yes	Yes
N in thousands	366.5	366.5	306	252

Source: Taxpayerpanel 2001–2006, author's own calculations
Notes: Standard errors in parentheses
*** Significant at 0.01 level, ** significant at 0.05 level, * significant at 0.1 level

Given the steepness of the log function at low levels of donations, I conduct a robustness check by adding €5 or €10 alternatively. This results in somewhat lower absolute coefficient estimates of price elasticity due to the shift towards a less steep part of a logarithmic curve (see Table 12.8).

6.5 Excluding nonitemizers and border itemizers

Finally, I present the results from a regression in which I exclude nonitemizers and border itemizers (see Table 12.9). On average, 30% of the tax units take the standard deduction, and less than 1% are classified as border itemizers. As some individuals switch between itemizing and not itemizing in subsequent years, I lose around 42% of my sample. The estimates of tax-price elasticity are somewhat lower and those of income elasticity somewhat higher than those in Table 12.5.

7 Conclusions

This chapter analyzes the effectiveness of fiscal incentives for charitable giving in Germany. While there are numerous studies estimating tax-price elasticity of giving for the United States, we know little about European countries. Given this lack of knowledge as well as the different role of the government and different tradition of charitable giving, the widespread preferential treatment of donations in the income tax is striking.

This chapter provides new evidence from the German Taxpayer Panel 2001–2006. The availability of longitudinal data allows for the estimation of the permanent and transitory tax-price and income elasticity of donations while controlling for individual unobserved characteristics. The results suggest heterogeneous effects of the tax-price among different income groups.

Table 12.8 Permanent and transitory effects. Assuming coefficients are uniform across income classes. Adding different constants to donations. IV approach to price and income. Dependent variable: $lnDON_{i,t}$

	+1		+5		+10	
	Perfect foresight	*Predictable tax change instrument*	*Perfect foresight*	*Predictable tax change instrument*	*Perfect foresight*	*Predictable tax change instrument*
$lnPRICE_{i,t}$	–0.03**	0.05**	0.00	0.07**	0.01**	0.07***
	(0.01)	(0.02)	(0.01)	(0.01)	(0.01)	(0.01)
$lnPRICE_{i,t-1}$	–0.33***	–0.43***	–0.31***	–0.31***	–0.19***	–0.26***
	(0.01)	(0.01)	(0.01)	(0.01)	(0.01)	(0.01)
$lnPRICE_{i,t+1}$	0.02**	0.01	0.05**	0.05**	0.05**	0.06**
	(0.01)	(0.01)	(0.02)	(0.02)	(0.01)	(0.02)
Permanent price elasticity	–0.33	–0.37	–0.17	–0.19	–0.12	–0.12
$lnY_{i,t}$	0.21***	0.26***	0.17***	0.21***	0.15***	0.19***
	(0.00)	(0.01)	(0.00)	(0.00)	(0.00)	(0.00)
$lnY_{i,t-1}$	0.02***	0.02**	0.02***	0.02**	0.02***	0.01***
	(0.00)	(0.01)	(0.00)	(0.00)	(0.00)	(0.00)
$lnY_{i,t+1}$	0.07***	0.15***	0.05***	0.11***	0.05***	0.10***
	(0.00)	(0.02)	(0.00)	(0.01)	(0.00)	(0.01)
Permanent income elasticity	0.31	0.43	0.24	0.33	0.21	0.30
Other controls × income class	Yes	Yes	Yes	Yes	Yes	Yes
Year effects × income class	Yes	Yes	Yes	Yes	Yes	Yes
Fixed individual effects	Yes	Yes	Yes	Yes	Yes	Yes
N in millions	3.36	2.72	3.36	2.72	3.36	2.72

Source: Taxpayerpanel 2001–2006, author's own calculations
Notes: Standard errors in parentheses
*** Significant at 0.01 level, ** significant at 0.05 level, * significant at 0.1 level

The estimates of permanent tax-price elasticity range between –0.2 for lower incomes and –1.6 for higher incomes. The average permanent price elasticity weighted with the amount of giving by different income groups is slightly below –1, meaning that fiscal incentives for donations in Germany are effective. There is evidence that donors adjust their donations gradually after changes in the tax schedule and respond to future predictable changes in price. They respond mainly to changes in current and, to a smaller extent, in future income. The estimates for permanent income elasticity are around 0.2–0.3, slightly varying among different income classes. Actual income and to some extent future income drive donations. The effects of past income are negligible.

Table 12.9 Permanent and transitory effects. Assuming coefficients are uniform across income classes. IV approach to price and income. Excluding nonitemizers and border itemizers. Assuming perfect foresight. Dependent variable: $lnDON_{i,t}$

$lnPRICE_{i,t}$	0.06** (0.02)
$lnPRICE_{i,t-1}$	–0.29*** (0.02)
$lnPRICE_{i,t+1}$	–0.02 (0.02)
Permanent price elasticity	–0.25
$lnY_{i,t}$	0.27*** (0.01)
$lnY_{i,t-1}$	0.02*** (0.01)
$lnY_{i,t+1}$	0.10*** (0.00)
Permanent income elasticity	0.39
Other controls	Yes
Year effects	Yes
Fixed individual effects	Yes
N in millions	1.97

Source: Taxpayerpanel 2001–2006, author's own calculations
Notes: Standard errors in parentheses
*** Significant at 0.01 level, ** significant at 0.05 level, * significant at 0.1 level

Notes

1 The average marginal tax weighted by income in 2001 was around 32% (own calculations). For more income tax statistics, see Buschle (2006).
2 See the literature section of this chapter.
3 For more information, see Welfare Expenditure Report (2001), http://www.oecd.org/dataoecd/56/37/31613113.xls (viewed on 8.2.2021).
4 For more information, see International Comparisons of Charitable Giving (2006), https://www.cafonline.org/docs/default-source/about-us-publications/international-comparisons-of-charitable-giving.pdf (viewed on 8.2.2021). The numbers for Germany exclude the church tax, which is between 8 and 9% (depending on the state) of the tax due.
5 For more information, see Andreoni and Payne (2013, p. 10).
6 For more information, see Deutscher Spendenmonitor (2011), www.tns-infratest.com/presse/presseinformation.asp?prID=832 (viewed on 8.2.2021).
7 For more information, see Sommerfeld (2009).
8 Most of the organizations offer the possibility of membership; examples include the WWF and Greenpeace. The members usually receive a regular magazine informing about the program achievements and the like.
9 See the literature section of this chapter.
10 The church tax is not included, because it is automatically deducted from the income of all members of the Catholic and Protestant church as well as of some Jewish and some free church congregations and amounts to between 8 and 9% (depending on the state) of the tax due. For a study on the interrelation of church tax and charitable giving in Germany, see Bittschi et al. (2015).
11 See, for example, Feldstein and Taylor (1976) or Feenberg (1988).
12 See Section 4.3 for the enumeration of control variables used in the estimation.
13 For example, McClelland and Brooks (2004) find that more education is significantly correlated with donations, and Brooks (2002) finds similar effects for wealth.
14 Individuals can be more or less altruistic, which may affect the choice of occupation and consequently the income.
15 Most observations in my sample will have finished their education and, if not, education years will change linearly, which does not pose a problem. Wealth changes will be captured to some extent by time effects.

16 Those are the taxpayers who exceed their blanket allowance only due to their donation.
17 Indeed, in Germany, the blanket allowance for extraordinary expenses including donations is low (€36) as compared to the U.S. treatment.
18 The following programs offer partial solutions: Pantob implements Honoré (1992); LIMDEMP implements the fixed-effects Tobit model with up to 50,000 individual effects. However, Bradley et al. (2005) criticize applying such methods like Tobit or Heckman's two-stage method to address censoring in charitable donations. They observe that specification tests reject the assumptions about the form of the likelihood function in the selection equation, which is necessary for the consistency of these estimators. While they opt for semi- and nonparametric methods, they claim that their elasticities are similar to those obtained using panel data estimation methods.
19 Bakija and Heim (2011) include one more lag in their specification, but their panel is much longer. They estimate an equation equivalent to 3. Their price coefficients enter as $\gamma_1(lnPRICE_{it} - lnPRICE_{it-1}) + \gamma_2 lnPRICE_{it} + \gamma_3(lnPRICE_{it+1} - lnPRICE_{it})$. Rearranging, this gives $(-\gamma_1)lnPRICE_{it-1} + (\gamma_1 + \gamma_2 - \gamma_3)lnPRICE_{it} + \gamma_3 lnPRICE_{it+1}$ such that $\delta_1 = -\gamma_1$, $\delta_2 = \gamma_1 + \gamma_2 - \gamma_3$, and $\delta_3 = \gamma_3$. Then the persistent price effect is given by γ_2 $(= -\gamma_1 + \gamma_1 + \gamma_2 - \gamma_3 + \gamma_3)$, the transitory effect by $\gamma_1 + \gamma_2 - \gamma_3$, and the effect of an anticipated increase in price next year by γ_3. They treat their income coefficients analogously.
20 For example, in the sample used by Bakija and Heim (2011), the average donation is $125,000 (in 2007 dollars). However, the average after-tax income is greater than $1 million.
21 For example, Paqué (1996) found the price elasticity to be between −1.8 and −1.4 and Borgloh (2008) between −2.08 and 0.84.
22 See Priller and Schupp (2011).
23 Due to the computational constraint of the statistical office, this estimation was only possible with an 0.05% sample. Consequently, the number of observations is 10 times lower than in the other estimations.

References

Andreoni J. and Payne A. A. (2013) 'Charitable Giving', in Auerbach A. J. et al. (eds) *Handbook of Public Economics*. Amsterdam: Elsevier B.V., pp. 1–50. doi: 10.1016/B978-0-444-53759-1.00001-7.

Auer L. and Kalusche A. (2010) 'Steuerliche Spendenanreize: Ein Reformvorschlag, Jahrbuch für Wirtschaftswissenschaften', *Review of Economics*, 61(3), pp. 241–261.

Bakija Jon (2000) *Distinguishing Transitory and Permanent Price Elasticities of Charitable Giving with Preannounced Changes in Tax Law*. https://www.researchgate.net/publication/46468165_Distinguishing_Transitory_and_Permanent_Price_Elasticities_of_Charitable_Giving_with_Pre-Announced_Changes_in_Tax_Law.

Bakija J. and Heim B. T. (2011) 'How Does Charitable Giving Respond to Incentives and Income? New Estimates from Panel Data', *National Tax Journal*, 64(2), pp. 615–650. doi:10.3386/w14237.

Barrett K. S., McGuirk A. M. and Steinberg R. (1997) 'Further Evidence on the Dynamic Impact of Taxes on Charitable Giving', *National Tax Journal*, 50(2), pp. 321–334. doi:10.2307/41789261.

Bittschi Benjamin, Borgloh Sarah and Wigger Berthold U. (2015) 'Secularization, Tax Policy and Prosocial Behavior', *Beiträge zur Jahrestagung des Vereins für Socialpolitik 2015: Ökonomische Entwicklung -Theorie und Politik- Session: Public Good Contributions*. Kiel: ZBW – Deutsche Zentralbibliothek für Wirtschaftswissenschaften, Leibniz-Informationszentrum Wirtschaft.

Bönke T., Massarrat-Mashhadi N. and Sielaff C. (2013) 'Charitable Giving in the German Welfare State: Fiscal Incentives and Crowding Out', *Public Choice*, 154(1), pp. 39–58. doi:10.1007/s11127-011-9806-y.

Bönke T. and Werdt C. (2015) *Charitable Giving and Its Persistent and Transitory Reactions to Changes in Tax Incentives: Evidence from the German Taxpayer Panel*. https://ideas.repec.org/p/zbw/fubsbe/20152.html.

Borgloh Sarah (2008) *What Drives Giving in Extensive Welfare States? The Case of Germany*. ZEW Discussion Paper No. 8-123, Mannheim: ZEW.

Boskin M. J. and Feldstein M. (1977) 'Effects of the Charitable Deduction on Contributions by Low Income and Middle Income Households: Evidence From the National Survey of Philanthropy', *The Review of Economics and Statistics*, 59(3), pp. 351–354.

Bradley Ralph, Holden Steven and Robert McClelland (2005) 'A Robust Estimation of the Effects of Taxation on Charitable Contributions', *Contemporary Economic Policy*, 23(4), pp. 545–554.

Broman Amy J. (1989) 'Statutory Tax Rate Reform and Charitable Contributions: Evidence from a Recent Period of Reform', *Journal of the American Taxation Association*, 10, pp. 7–21.
Brooks Arthur C. (2002) 'Welfare Receipt and Private Charity', *Public Budgeting and Finance*, 22(3), pp. 101–114.
Buschle Nicole (2006) 'Spenden in Deutschland, Ergebnisse der Einkommensteuerstatistik 2001', *Wirtschaft und Statistik*, 2, pp. 151–159.
Clotfelter Charles T. (1980) 'Tax Incentives and Charitable Giving: Evidence from a Panel of Taxpayers', *Journal of Public Economics*, 13, pp. 319–340.
Fack Gabrielle and Landais Camille (2010) 'Are Tax Incentives for Charitable Giving Efficient? Evidence from France', *American Economic Journal: Economic Policy*, 2(2), pp. 117–141.
Feenberg Daniel (1988) 'Are Tax Price Models Really Identified: The Case of Charitable Giving', *National Tax Journal*, 40(4), pp. 629–633.
Feldstein Martin and Taylor Amy (1976) 'The Income Tax and Charitable Contributions', *Econometrica*, 44(6), pp. 1201–1222.
Honoré Bo (1992) 'Trimmed LAD and Least Squares Estimation of Truncated and Censored Regression Models with Fixed Effects', *Econometrica*, 60(3), pp. 533–565.
McClelland Robert and Brooks Arthur C. (2004) 'What Is the Real Relationship Between Income and Charitable Giving?', *Public Finance Review*, 32, pp. 483–497.
Paqué K. H. (1996) *Philanthropie und Steuerpolitik – Eine ökonomische Analyse der Förderung privater Wohltätigkeit*. Tübingen: Mohr Siebeck.
Priller Eckhard and Schupp Jürgen (2011) 'Soziale und ökonomische Merkmale von Geld- und Blutspendern in Deutschland', *DIW Wochenbericht*, 29, pp. 3–10.
Randolph W. C. (1995) 'Dynamic Income, Progressive Taxes, and the Timing of Charitable Contributions', *Journal of Political Economy*, 103(4), pp. 709–738. doi:10.1086/262000.
Reece W. and Zieschang K. (1985) 'Consistent Estimation of the Impact of Tax Deductibility on the Level of Charitable Contributions', *Econometrica*, 53(2), pp. 271–294.
Sommerfeld Jana (2009) 'Bericht zum Forschungsauftrag fe 17/07, Evaluierung von Auswirkungen des Gesetzes zur weiteren St ärkung des bu ̈rgerschaftlichen Engagements. Empirische Untersuchung der Entwicklungen im Regelungsbereich, insbesondere zum Spendenaufkommen', *DZI*.
Triest Robert K. (1998) 'Econometric Issues in Estimating the Behavioral Response to Taxation: A Nontechnical Introduction', *National Tax Journal*, 51(4), pp. 761–772.

13
ANALYSING THE ROLE OF TAX INCENTIVES FOR DONATIONS TO NON-PROFIT ORGANISATIONS IN INDIA

Malini Chakravarty and Priyadarshini Singh

Introduction

The recent amendments (October 2020) to India's Foreign Contributions Regulation Act (FCRA) are among the many challenges confronting the non-profit sector in the country. The act places significant hurdles to the receipt and utilisation of foreign donations by Indian NPOs. This development corresponds to similar global trends of increasing legal and regulatory hurdles on NPOs over the last decade, in both the world's most advanced economies and the developing countries facing the most complex civil strife and public health crises. Therefore, the current COVID-19 pandemic could not have been a more telling context for demonstrating the critical role of non-profits in supporting governments and citizens. Moreover, the pandemic has brought to light the discouraging regulatory environment in which NPOs operate worldwide.

Tax incentives are a key regulatory mechanism surrounding the non-profit sector, whose role is receiving increasing visibility during the pandemic. For instance, Russia, which did not initially provide any tax incentives for charitable donations, now allows a 1% tax break to businesses donating a portion of their profits to charity (CAF America, 2021). China has also significantly increased its tax incentives for philanthropic activities (Lexology, 2020). However, India has not increased tax incentives for donations to the non-profit sector, despite its pandemic-induced fund shortage in the last year. A study by Dasra (2020), a leading non-profit sector advisory and research organisation, highlights that there is likely to be significant reduction both in short and long term funding to the sector. Funding from corporate social responsibility (CSR) channels may see a long-term reduction as almost 2000–3000 crore INR will get redirected to the COVID-19–focused PMCARES fund[1]. Corporates are also likely to register a plunge in their profits and subsequently affect the funds they channel to their CSR contributions for the sector. Large donations from ultra-high net worth individuals (UHNWIs) may fall in the short term due to stock market volatility.

At a time when the Indian government has significantly relied on NPOs during the pandemic, it has not made any effort to ease their regulatory environment, particularly regarding funding and tax incentives. On the one hand, since March 2020, NITI Aayog, the apex national-level policy planning body of the government of India, has formally collaborated with 92,000 non-governmental organisations (NGOs) (Kulkarni, 2020) to manage socio-economic

DOI: 10.4324/9781003139201-16

challenges. On the other hand, new hurdles have been placed in accessing funding. Foreign funding will be hard to access because of the recent amendments in the FCRA. Recent changes in the tax regime for individuals and corporates allow donors to voluntarily opt out of tax incentives for philanthropic giving to benefit from lower rates of personal and corporate income tax.

Systematic studies on the role of tax incentive regimes as a whole and their contribution to strengthening the non-profit sector (and through that the national community), as well as their cost to the public exchequer, are limited, particularly in the Indian context.

A preliminary attempt to address this lacuna is being undertaken in a study by the Centre for Social Impact and Philanthropy (CSIP) at Ashoka University, Sonipat, in a research partnership with the Centre for Budget and Governance Accountability (CBGA) in Delhi. The study reviews the tax incentive structures of 12 select countries, including India,[2] evidence of their impact in encouraging philanthropic activities.

This chapter draws from the aforementioned project's findings. Centring around the Indian case, the study examines three critical aspects of tax incentives for charitable donations to NPOs. First, to what extent do tax incentives support the non-profit sector financially and legally? Second, what is the cost of such tax incentives for philanthropy to the Indian exchequer as a share of personal and corporate income tax collected? Third, how do the design and scope of the Indian tax incentives compare with other countries/the rest of the world? Overall, this chapter aims to provide policy recommendations to the Indian government for strengthening its tax incentive regime for philanthropic giving.

We address our research questions using a mix of qualitative and quantitative methods. To examine the financial and legal role of tax incentives, we examined the existing quantitative databases and research reports on the sources of financial inflows and their adequacy to the non-profit sector. Regarding the impact of tax incentives on public revenue, we analysed the data on the foregone revenues reported by the Indian government over 13 years from 2006–2019. Next, drawing on the previously mentioned tax incentives review project, we conducted the cross-country comparative review of the tax incentive regime in India. Additionally, we also reviewed secondary documents such as government and civil society reports as well as academic literature on the evidence of the impact of tax incentives on philanthropy. We validated our findings from the secondary document review by consulting tax and civil society experts and academics based in all the study countries except Norway and China. For these countries, our analysis relies entirely on secondary documents. All the material reviewed in this chapter is available in the public domain and mainly written in English. We commissioned French and Portuguese translations of some academic research set in France and Brazil. The language barrier in non-English-speaking countries was addressed by conversations with experts from these countries. Nonetheless, the limited access to the literature in the country's national languages is a limitation of this work.

The chapter is organised around our three research questions. In Section 1, we examine the financial and non-financial contribution of tax incentives in India. Here we argue that while the funds flowing into the sector due to tax incentives are minimal compared to those coming in from other sources, they are a prominent source of financial and legal legitimacy for this sector in India. Due to their small size and limited capacities, most NPOs lack access to alternative funding sources. In Section 2, we discuss India's tax incentive structure and present the trends in the revenue foregone by the Indian government. We illustrate that the revenue lost due to tax incentives for philanthropic giving is negligible. In Section 3, we present the global evidence on the state of tax incentives. We show that compared to other countries, India has a conservative tax incentive regime for philanthropic giving and is among the few countries without documented evidence on the effectiveness (or the lack) of tax incentives. Finally, in Section 4, we provide policy recommendations for strengthening the Indian tax incentive regime to increase philanthropic giving.

1 Tax incentives and India's non-profit sector: financial and regulatory environment

India lacks accurate and recent official data on its non-profit sector in terms of the number of NPOs, the nature of their work, their size, and the source of their financial inflows. The Darpan portal is an online, publicly accessible database established by the government of India where any Indian NPO applying for government grants-in-aid, and those receiving international funding, must register. However, it does not cover NPOs that do not use government or international grants. The portal provides a broad cross-section of data on the non-profit sector covering many thematic areas (such as health, education, skills, and livelihoods), service areas (advocacy, service delivery), and information on the quantum of grants-in-aid received. However, the quality of the data on the portal is poor. Other databases on the sector are in the context of legal and regulatory provisions such as the Income Tax Act, FCRA, and the Companies Act. These databases cover only a small subset of Indian NPOs and provide only the number of NPOs registered under these acts, leaving out other relevant information such as the area of work or the nature of their activities.

Our analysis of the financial and regulatory role of tax incentives draws on three major studies that provide an overview of the non-profit sector in India. The Indian Ministry of Statistics and Planning (MOSPI) in 2012 conducted a census-like exercise of the non-profit sector in line with the UN handbook on Non-profit Accounting. The study, however, focused only on those NPOs which are registered as 'societies', which is one of the three legal forms for the registration of NPOs in India. The other two are 'trusts' and 'Section 8' companies. This study reports that India has approximately 3.1 million registered 'societies' in India.[3] Of these, a little over half a million societies were physically 'traced' by the MOSPI study researchers. The detailed overview of the non-profit sector provided in the study includes data on the state-wise location of the traced societies, their operational areas (such as health, education, social service), and rural-urban distribution and funding sources. The second study was recently undertaken by the CSIP to understand the state of the support ecosystem available to the non-profit sector in India dealing with aspects such as fundraising, monitoring and evaluation, accounting, and communications. The study included 800 NPOs and 65 foundations (grant-making bodies) across India, using an online survey on 3,500-plus verified NPOs registered with GuideStar India.[4] The profile of the sampled NPOs gives a snapshot of the non-profit sector and includes indicators such as their state-wise location, thematic operation areas, and operating budgets. The third study was also undertaken by the CSIP, and it examined the total capital in the non-profit sector from various sources, including tax-incentivised donations, corporate social responsibility and foreign contributions (CSIP, 2020).

These reports highlight three distinct aspects of the non-profit sector in India. First, the sector is dominated by small NPOs. The CSIP study[5] of the non-profit ecosystem is the only one that provides a breakdown of the sample NPOs based on their operating budgets. The study estimates that over half of the sampled NPOs[6] have an annual operating budget of up to approximately 68,000 USD[7] approx. (less than INR 50 lakhs) a year. Additionally, 15% of the sampled NPOs have an annual operating budget of only up to 6,804 USD (up to INR 5 lakhs a year) (see Figure 13.1).

Second, the NPOs' focus areas as well as their geographical spread are disproportionately skewed. The CSIP study highlights that most NPOs are concentrated in the areas of education (with 75%) and health (with 65%)[8] (CSIP, 2019). However, within these thematic areas, there

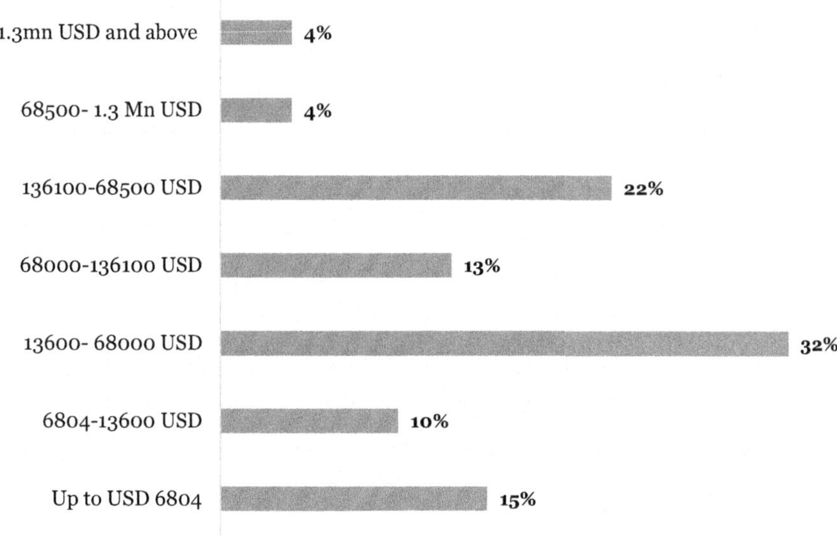

Figure 13.1 Distribution of NPOs in study sample according to the operating budget (in USD)

Source: (CSIP, 2019) Conversion rate 1 USD = 73 INR

Note: Lower and outer limit has been kept out of the estimates.

is no data available on the exact nature of the work undertaken by the NPOs, for example, whether it is service delivery, advocacy, or communications. Conversations with experts in the sectors highlight that the majority of the NPOs focus on service delivery activities, with relatively few working on research and advocacy. Maharashtra and Uttar Pradesh are the top states where the maximum number of sampled NPOs are located. Similarly, the MOSPI study highlights that more than 82% of the traced societies are registered in 24 states (this list excludes large states such as Rajasthan and Maharashtra). Of these, Uttar Pradesh, the most populous Indian state, has 37% of the traced societies. Andhra Pradesh (undivided; includes Telangana) has the second-highest population and only 11% of the traced societies. Bihar, another populous and poor Indian state, has only 0.6% of the traced societies (MOSPI, 2012, pp. 6–70). The concentration of NPOs in a limited number of thematic areas and states, and the availability of better funding opportunities through varied sources such as CSR, mutually reinforce each other. That is to say, as more NPOs work in certain sectors/issue areas, more funding flows into those specific areas than others and vice versa.

Third, tax-incentivised donations constitute the smallest share of funding sources into this sector as highlighted by the CSIP study (2018). Table 13.1 presents the share of individual and corporate donations incentivised through tax incentives (d1 and d3), which is much lower than other funding sources such as CSR funds (C), foreign contributions (A), and informal everyday giving (E).[9]

The data available on the non-profit sector indicates that an accurate assessment of the financial and legal role of tax incentives is highly difficult. However, the role of the tax incentives may be critical because of the specific nature of the Indian non-profit sector. For many NPOs, their operating budgets are low, and they operate from geographically remote areas. Consequently, they have limited resources to communicate the impact of their work or seek assistance of support organisations for communication, fundraising, and so on. In this context, a tax exemption

Table 13.1 Philanthropic capital flowing in the Indian NPO sector (in USD millions)

S. No.	*Philanthropic source*	*2017–18*	*Source*
A.	Foreign contribution	2289	www.fcraonline.nic.in
B.	Grants-in-aid to NGOs listed on DARPAN portal	1428	https://ngodarpan.gov.in/
C.	Grants through CSR Act	18582	https://csr.gov.in/CSR/
D. (d1+d2+d3)	Formal giving (income tax deductions* claimed on account of donations to charitable trusts and institutions)	315	https://www.indiabudget.gov.in/budget2018-2019/ub2018-19/rec/annex7.pdf
d1	Corporate taxpayer	215	
d2	Non-corporate taxpayers (firms/associations of persons [AOPs]/body of Individuals [BOI])**	16	
d3	Individuals/Hindu undivided family (HUF) taxpayers	82	
E.	Everyday/informal giving by individuals ***	4178	Report: 'Everyday Giving in India' by Sattva Consulting: https://www.sattva.co.in/publication/research-everyday-giving-in-india-report/

Source: Internal note prepared by CSIP, 2020 (reproduced here with permission)

* This is the sum total of amounts sanctioned by the central and state government to the NGOs registered on Darpan.

** This indicates the income tax deductions claimed by corporate, non-corporates, and individuals/HUF on account of donations to charitable trusts and institutions under section 80G. It is difficult to ascertain the total charitable contributions made, as the IT deduction claimed is a function of the tax bracket the taxpayers fall into, the deduction they are eligible for (50% versus 100% deduction), and the actual donation amount made by the taxpayer. Since individual charitable contribution data are not available at a disaggregate level, we cannot comment on the total charitable contributions made by these taxpayers.

*** A report by Sattva Consulting estimated that 90% of India's everyday giving is informal and largely in cash; it is mostly targeted to community members such as domestic helpers, homeless, and religious or spiritual institutions.

certificate provides legal legitimacy to NPOs and recognition of their work, including for those donors who do not seek to claim tax exemptions. Last, though tax incentives provide lower capital inflows to the sector compared to other sources, they remain the primary source of funding for a vast majority of NPOs that do not have access to foreign or CSR funds. Therefore, for these NPOs, even the limited funding support provided by tax incentives may be significant. However, a systematic study of these varied roles played by tax incentives in the non-profit sector is critical.

2 Does India's tax incentive structure encourage philanthropic giving towards NPOs?

India has a long history of tax incentives for philanthropic giving, which dates back to the British Raj (Sampradaan Indian Centre for Philanthropy, 2004). However, the basic structure of the tax incentive has remained unchanged since the mid-1970s and has seen a noticeable dilution in recent years. Moreover, the current tax incentive regime is designed to disproportionately incentivise philanthropic donations to government entities. The recent changes in the tax structure have either expanded the remit of philanthropic donations to the government or removed some incentive provisions for donating to NPOs.

There are two main provisions for tax incentives for philanthropic donations detailed in the Indian Income Tax Act, 1960. Under Section 80G, individuals and corporations are eligible to receive two categories of tax deductions, 100% and 50%, on donations given to government entities, government-run funds, trusts, societies, and other bodies that possess an 80G certificate (Puri, Nayak, and Dadrawala, 2018). Under Section 80GGA, donations can also be made for scientific research or rural development (Srinath, 2003). Section 80G is the broader and most widely used tax incentive provision, and under it, the donations made to government entities have the highest incentives. Donations made to NPOs attract only a 50% tax deduction, along with a ceiling. Other than this, since the financial year (FY) 2015, three main government programmes have been granted 100% donor exemption status under Section 80G. These are the 1) Swachh Bharat Abhiyan, 2) Clean Ganga Campaign, and 3) National Fund for Drug Abuse (VANI, 2016). Table 13.2 presents a summary of the 80G tax provisions for donations to NPOs and government entities.

Donations made under 80GGA (Srinath, 2003), while being fully deductible, apply only to institutions undertaking scientific, social science, or statistical research or rural development. Additionally, each institution eligible for a donation must be approved by the government under Section 35 (1) ii of the Income Tax Act. Moreover, here as well, the list of institutions eligible for donations under this section includes government entities and funds, such as public-sector companies, government-notified funds for rural development and afforestation, and a national fund for poverty eradication.

The 35AC tax incentive provision was introduced in the 1990s, which aimed to promote corporate donations. Under the provision, unlike the certificate granted under Section 80G (wherein donations made to qualifying NPOs entitles a donor to a 50% tax deduction), the 35AC certificate is given to NPOs running government-approved projects (Agarwal and

Table 13.2 Summary overview of India's tax incentive structure for philanthropy

Tax deduction	*Ceiling*	*Nature of entity*	*Examples*
100%	None	Central government funds and entities and some state government entities/funds	* National Defence Fund * Prime Minister's National Relief Fund
50%	None	Central and state government funds and entities and some government entities/funds	* Jawaharlal Nehru Fund * Prime Minister's Drought Relief Fund
100%	10% of the adjusted gross total income	Central government funds and entities and some state government entities/funds	* Government entities involved in family planning * Government entities involved in Olympic association
50%	10% of the adjusted gross total income	Non-profit organisations (known as civil society organisations)	All NPOs with an 80G certificate

Dadrawala, 2004) in areas such as drinking water projects, building homes for the poor, and building schools in economically vulnerable areas. While the provisions allowed the donors to deduct the full value of their donations against their taxable income, the exemptions were placed for a specific list of projects approved by the central government (VANI, 2016). This provision was, however, revoked in 2016–17.

In 2020, the tax incentives for philanthropic donations received further pushback by the Indian government with the introduction of a new 'optional' tax regime for individual and corporate taxpayers in the Union Budget 2020–21. Under this provision, individual taxpayers can avail themselves of lower tax rates if they forgo most of the tax incentives, including those for donations. Similarly, corporates who forgo tax incentives and exemptions are eligible for a reduction in the base tax rate to 22% from 30% (Rajakumar and Shetty, 2020).[10] While both these rules are optional at present, given that they entail an option of transitioning to a lower tax slab, it has far-reaching implications for tax incentives for philanthropic giving.

India's overall taxation policy, especially the changes in marginal tax rates since globalisation (i.e., the mid-1980s, when India began opening up to the world economy), further limits the attractiveness of the restricted tax incentives for donations to NPOs. As several experts note, tax reforms involving a reduction in marginal tax rates adversely affect donors' incentives for philanthropic giving (Clotfelter, 2012), unless these are compensated for with other incentives for inducing generous contributions. Therefore, analysing the marginal tax rate trends as part of a country's tax incentive regime is crucial for understanding the benefits derived by the donors and hence their incentive to give. Similar to many other countries across the world, India, too, since the mid-1980s[11] has seen a reduction in the marginal rates of personal income tax (PIT) and corporate income tax (CIT)[12] (see Figure 13.2 for peak PIT rates). In addition to these cuts, taxes affecting high-income groups such as the inheritance and wealth taxes, were also abolished in the 1980s and 2000s[13] (Rao and Rao, 2006).

The lower tax rates introduced for PITs in 1997–98 continue to date with three modifications: a) an increase in the number of tax brackets with the lowest marginal tax rate starting at 5% from the earlier 10% (as part of tax regime for individual taxpayers introduced in the Union Budget 2020–21); b) introduction of and thereafter increases in surcharge and cesses dedicated

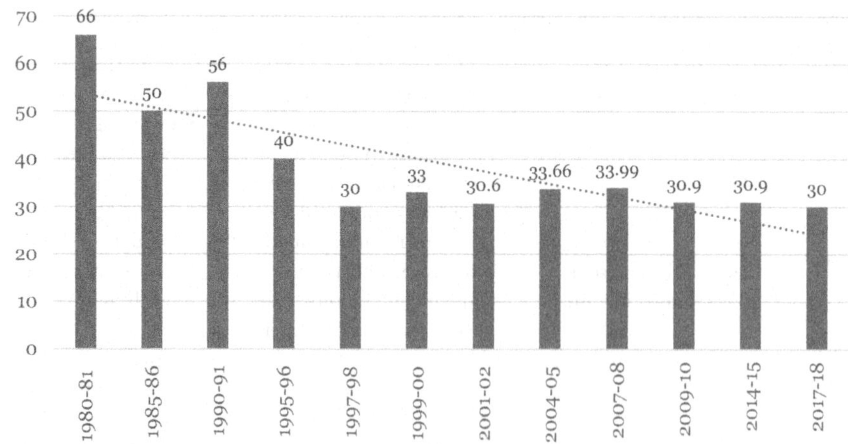

Figure 13.2 Trend in the peak rates of individual income tax (in %)

Source: Indian Public Finance Statistics, Ministry of Finance, various years

to primary education and health,[14] (Rao and Rao, 2006); and c) higher surcharges levied on the super-rich (since the Indian Union Budget 2019–20) (CBGA, 2019).[15]

Unlike the trends in PIT rates (which have stabilised and even increased to an extent) CIT rates in India have continued to register significant cuts, even in the recent years. Thus, in 1985–86, the peak corporate tax rate was reduced from around 60% to 50%, further reducing to 45% in 1994–95, 30% in 2005–06 (Pattnaik, 2009), and finally to 25% for existing companies as of 2019[16] and 15% for manufacturing companies established after October 2020 (Ministry of Finance, 2020).

However, the decline in tax rates in India did not accompany corresponding measures to increase tax incentives for charitable donations, thereby reducing their attractiveness over time (Viswanath and Dadrawala, 2004). Recent changes have in fact diluted the tax incentives for philanthropic donations.

Are tax incentives for philanthropic donations costly to the Indian government?

India is one of the lowest-taxed countries in the world, with the total (union plus state) tax to gross domestic product ratio being as low as 18% in 2020. Several experts suggest reducing the tax incentives[17] (including for philanthropic donations) to broaden the country's tax base and increase the potential tax revenue. However, regarding tax incentives for philanthropic donations to NPOs, it is important to assess whether the potential revenue generated by the withdrawal of tax incentives is large enough to warrant their removal. It is highly likely that the potential revenue generated from such a withdrawal may be negligible compared to the adverse impact on the functioning of the non-profit sector. As shown in Figure 13.3, the revenue foregone from individual and corporate donations as shares of PIT and CIT collections, respectively,

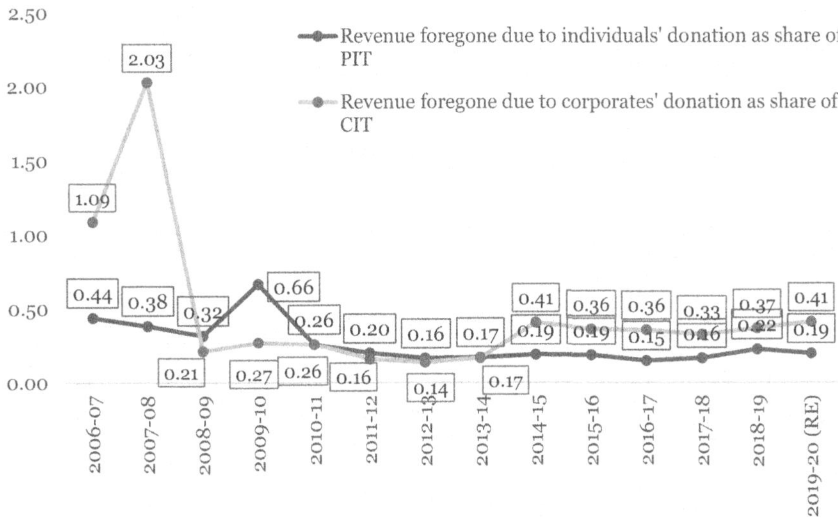

Figure 13.3 Revenue foregone on account of deductions claimed on donations by individuals and corporate taxpayers as a percentage of their respective tax revenues

Source: Author's calculation based on the Receipt Budget, Union Budget documents, various years

Note: RE: Revised estimate; the rest of the figures denote the actuals.

are quite small. Further, in the case of individual taxpayers, this share has consistently remained lower than the high reached in 2009–10. Revenue foregone on account of corporate donations as share of corporate income tax collection has returned to the high registered in 2014–15, but it still remains much below 1% of corporate income tax revenue collected.

Notably, the revenue foregone figures provided by the government are aggregate figures, which do not segregate between revenue foregone on account of donations to government entities and funds or donations to the NPOs. Given that the former attracts a more generous tax deduction, the revenue foregone on account of donations to NPOs is likely to be much lower than the aggregate figures cited in the budget documents.

The combined revenue lost due to tax incentives for philanthropic donations by both individual and corporate donors over the last decade (see Figure 13.4) constitutes less than 2% of total revenue foregone on income tax collection.

Given this context, the move towards a blanket removal of all types of incentives, without undertaking an in-depth cost-benefit analysis of their effectiveness against their basic objectives, does seem somewhat arbitrary. However, there is an acute lack of such literature in the case of philanthropic donations. The few studies available are dated and of little relevance for the present context when marginal tax rates for individuals and corporates have declined significantly (Aggarwal, 1989; GOI, 2001). Furthermore, there is a lack of publicly accessible data on the amount of donations, making a rigorous analysis of the implications for philanthropic activities in India difficult.

The previous analysis shows that with globalisation, while India's taxation strategy has seen a significant change, its tax incentive framework for charitable donations has either remained static (for the most popular tax incentive scheme under Section 80G) or has been completely dismantled (as in the case of the tax incentive under Section 35AC). Consequently, the benefit donors can derive from such tax incentives has shrunk over time. The analysis of the data on revenue foregone indicates that phasing out of tax incentives for charitable donations is unlikely to generate substantial additional potential revenue for the state exchequer. Such a move, however, is likely to have a disproportionately adverse impact on NPOs by blocking a major funding source.

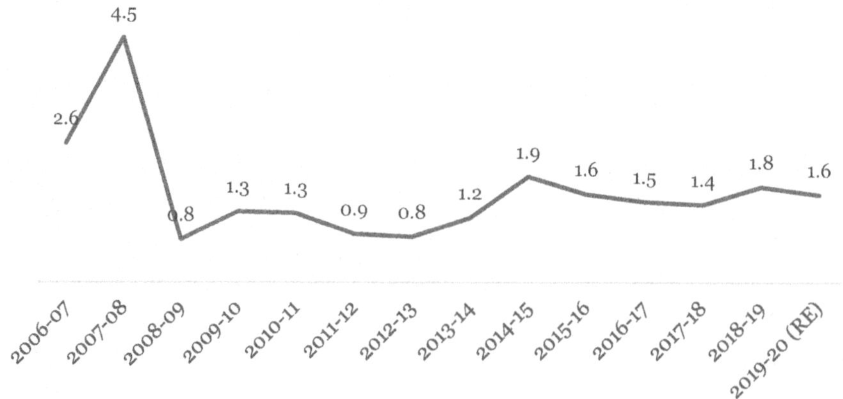

Figure 13.4 Revenue foregone on account of philanthropic donations as a percentage of revenue foregone on PIT and CIT

Source: Author's calculation based on the Receipt Budget, Union Budget documents, various years

Note: RE: Revised estimate; the rest of the figures denote the actuals.

3 India's tax incentives and their impact on philanthropy: a global overview

Compared to the 11 countries we studied in our project, India's tax incentive regime can be characterised as conservative in what we define as its 'provision' and 'scope'. Unlike countries such as Brazil, India's tax incentives for philanthropic donations do not disincentivise philanthropy; however, the existing structure does not prioritise tax incentives as an instrument to facilitate donations. The tax incentive structures of the 12 study countries (including India) are analysed under the 'provisions' of these incentives, which refers to the specific mechanisms for providing incentives on individual incomes and assets, and business income. We also examine it on the 'scope' of the incentives, which includes the rates of incentives, ceilings, and the sectors eligible for charitable giving.

Provisions of tax incentives

As presented in Table 13.3, our study countries have three forms of tax incentives on personal income tax (PIT), namely deductions, credit, and grossed-up donation. Deductions are the most common form and are available in all the study countries, except France and South Korea. In these two countries, tax incentives are given in the form of credit. The United Kingdom is a unique case, with two forms of incentives, deductions and grossed-up donations. India provides tax incentives on both personal and corporate income tax channelled only through standard deductions. The form of tax incentives influences charitable donations in important ways. Credits reduce the tax outflow of donors more than deductions.[18] Grossed-up donations are most beneficial to high-income donors, giving them the maximum reduction in tax outflows.[19] In a

Table 13.3 Summary of tax incentive provisions on personal income tax, individual assets, and cross-border donations

Countries	*Deductions*	*Credit*	*Grossed-up*	*Inheritance tax*	*Wealth tax*	*Capital gains tax*	*Donation/ gift Tax*	*Cross-border*
United States	Yes			Yes		Yes		Yes
UK	Yes		Yes	Yes		Yes		Yes
China	Yes							
South Africa[1]	Yes			Yes			Yes	Yes
Singapore	Yes							
Norway	Yes							Yes
Brazil	Yes			Yes			Yes	
Mexico	Yes							Yes
India	Yes							
Bangladesh	Yes						Yes	Yes
South Korea		Yes		Yes				Yes
France		Yes		Yes	Yes			Yes

Source: Based on Report on the State of Tax Incentives across the 12 countries under finalisation by CBGA and CSIP

1 Only businesses are allowed to make cross-border donations.

grossed-up donation-based approach, charities get greater monetary benefit as compared with deductions or credit-based provisions. Grossed-up donations seem to prioritise High Net Worth Individuals (HNWIs), as they are the most responsive to tax incentives.[20] For small donors, grossed-up donations provide greater worth to the monetary value of the donations they make. The government monetarily matches the amount donated to a charity, so for every amount donated, the charity receives an equal amount from the government, also increasing the value of the donation made. The use of either of these forms would significantly enhance the impact of tax incentives in India.

Furthermore, as Table 13.3 highlights, India does not have any of the other taxes (other than capital gains tax); hence, there are no incentives on those, examples being wealth tax, estate duty, or inheritance tax. The gift tax is applicable in India, Bangladesh, Brazil, and South Africa, which is included under the donation tax. However, only India does not provide an incentive for philanthropy on gift tax. It is also among the four sample countries (the others are China, Brazil, and Singapore) that do not provide incentives for cross-border donations.

Scope of tax incentives

Tax incentive provisions are primarily defined by their scope of implementation and are effective only when their scope targets a wide range of donors and philanthropic causes. The scope of tax incentives on individual incomes, assets, donations, and corporate taxes depends on factors such as the rate of incentives, the ceiling on income and the tax payable, and the eligibility of the sectors. Table 13.4 highlights the rate of incentives and the ceilings applicable on PIT in the study countries and shows that India is the only country that incentivises donations to government entities over and above NPOs. Most countries have implemented 100% incentives for NPOs with some ceilings, whereas India (along with two other countries) offers tax incentives at less than 100% with ceilings.

Table 13.4 Summary of tax incentives rates on personal income tax and applicable ceilings

Country	*Form*	*Rate of incentives*	*Ceiling (income and tax payable)*
Singapore	Deduction	250%	No limit
UK	Deduction and grossed up	100%	100% of tax payable
USA	Deduction	100%	60% of taxable income
China	Deduction	100%	30% of taxable income
S. Africa	Deduction	100%	10% of taxable income
Brazil	Deduction	100%	8% of tax payable with charity area-based exemptions
Mexico	Deduction	100%	7% of previous year's taxable income
Norway	Deduction	100%	NOK 50,000
India	Deduction	50%, 100%	10% of taxable income in most cases, 100% when donating to select government funds and entities
Bangladesh	Deduction	15%	Maximum donation allowed is 30% of taxable income or BDT 15 million, whichever is lower
France	Credit	66%, 75%	20% of taxable income
S. Korea	Credit	15%, 30%	100% of tax payable

Source: An interim report on the state of tax incentives across the 12 countries by CBGA and CSIP, 2021 (reproduced with permission)

Table 13.5 summarises the provisions and the scope for a tax incentive for businesses, revealing that here as well, India is the only country that incentivises donations to government entities.

Table 13.5 Summary of tax incentive rates for businesses

Country	*Form*	*Rate of incentives*	*Ceiling (income and tax payable)*
Singapore	Deduction	250%	No limit
UK	Deduction	100%	100% of tax payable
S. Korea	Deduction	100%	50% of taxable income
USA	Deduction	100%	30% of taxable income
China	Deduction	100%	12% of taxable income
S. Africa	Deduction	100%	10% of taxable income
Brazil	Deduction	100%	8% of taxable income
Mexico	Deduction	100%	7% of last year's income
Norway	Deduction	100%	NOK 50,000
India	Deduction	50%, 100%	10% of taxable income in most cases, 100% when donating to select government funds and entities
Bangladesh	Deduction	10%	Maximum donation allowed is 10% of taxable income or BDT 120 million whichever is lower
France	Credit	60%	0.5% of the annual revenue

Source: Report on the State of Tax Incentives across the 12 countries under finalisation by CBGA and CSIP, 2021 (reproduced with permission)

The list of causes eligible for tax incentives further determines the scope of the incentives[21]. India has a moderate range of causes eligible for tax incentives. While it does not include areas such as human rights, it has a generic area called 'objects of general public utility'. While this provision expands the scope of the eligible causes that are incentivised, it also significantly increases the discretionary powers of the government. Table 13.6 presents the most common philanthropic causes eligible for tax incentives among the study countries.

Table 13.6 Common causes eligible for tax incentives across the study countries[22]

	Health	*Education*	*HR**	*Religion*	*Arts/culture/ heritage*	*Science*	*Poverty reduction*	*Sports*	*Environment*
Bangladesh		Y							
Brazil	Y							Y	
China	Y	Y			Y	Y	Y	Y	Y
France	Y	Y			Y	Y		Y	Y
India	Y	Y			Y		Y		Y
Mexico									
Norway	Y		Y	Y	Y				Y
Singapore	Y	Y		Y	Y		Y	Y	Y
South Africa	Y	Y							Y
South Korea				Y				Y	
UK	Y	Y	Y	Y	Y	Y	Y	Y	
USA	Y	Y	Y	Y	Y		Y		

* Human Rights

4 Strengthening India's tax incentive regime: policy recommendations

India is among the six countries in our study cohort that have some documentation on the impact of tax incentives. But the Indian studies are dated and belong to an era when tax rates were high, which made tax incentives lucrative. Therefore, the recent changes in India's tax incentives regime were implemented without a systematic analysis of their economic, legal, and regulatory impact on civil society. Such a study would provide the foundational step in improving and strengthening the tax incentive regime in India, consequently improving the access to funding in Indian civil society. We strongly recommend that such a study be commissioned by an appropriate government authority.

The best studies on the effectiveness of tax incentives are available in the United States and the United Kingdom. They highlight the strengths and limitations of the evidence generated through such an analysis. The econometric analysis of price elasticities of tax incentives highlights their financial efficacy, although they do not shed enough light on the other roles tax incentives play for civil society. Most studies in this stream of research conclude that the increase in philanthropic giving generated through an increase in tax incentives, is either non-existent or marginal. A key variation is in the price elasticity of different income groups. In the context of France (Fack and Landais, 2010), the United Kingdom (Scharf and Smith, 2009), and the United States (Bijika, 2013; Backus and Grant, 2019), studies estimate higher elasticities for high-income groups, whereas in South Korea (Park and Jeon, 2017) and Singapore (Chua and Wong, 1999), the price elasticity of lower-income groups is higher than that of high-income groups. The characteristics of the dataset used can especially impact the estimates of the price elasticity of tax incentives. The study by Duquette (2016), which uses the data on donations received by charities in the United States, estimates that a 1% increase in the tax cost of philanthropy leads to a 4% fall in the donations received by charities. Focusing on the charity data, this study analysed the donations made to religious organisations and organisations with assets valued at less than 100 million USD that are not required to file tax returns. These organisations have been mostly excluded from the datasets used in other studies in the United States. We recommend that an income group-focused study that uses data from both the donors and charity organisations would be well suited to understand the financial impact of tax incentives in India. However, to undertake this study, data availability remains a critical challenge.

Among our study countries, India lacks sufficient data transparency on taxes (others include Bangladesh, China, Mexico, and South Africa) and the scale of donation activities (along with Bangladesh, China, Mexico, South Africa, Singapore, and South Korea), posing serious challenges in conducting a systematic analysis. Without these two data sets, the effectiveness of incentives cannot be understood. The United Kingdom and the United States are the only countries which provide high-quality data for the study of tax incentives. Table 13.7 summarises the types of data available in these two countries and the research analyses they enable from a policy perspective.

We also argue that a comprehensive study on the effectiveness of tax incentives should focus on the other benefits for donations such as legal recognition of the non-profit sector as a whole and individual charities, particularly in remote areas. Tax incentives also establish and anchor the state-civil society relationship through a formal and a historically well-established regulatory channel. While some sections of civil society are informal in nature and outside the regulatory ambit such as that of tax incentives, there is a prominent segment that works with the government in service delivery activities, which could benefit from legal recognition and tax incentives. At a normative level, such recognition of charitable activities enables civil society activism

Table 13.7 Summary of data required to study tax effectiveness and related research areas

Country	*Tax data*	*Scale of donations*	*Research areas*
United Kingdom	* Summary of individual income tax returns * Total number of donors and amount donated by both individuals and businesses * Deductions claimed by individuals as part of payroll giving, gift aid, self-assessment tax returns * Tax relief provided on inheritance, payroll and gift of shares and property, gift aid	* Scale of donation data available at the level of individual * Sector specific-data on level of donations, for example, on health, education, and so on	* Effectiveness of tax incentives for individuals and business in terms of level and number of donors at different income levels and charity sectors
United States	* Summary of income tax returns of individuals and businesses * Income group level details of itemised deductions claimed * IT returns of charitable organisations	* Overall quantum of charitable giving in billion USD further divided by donors, individuals, corporations * Individual giving as percentage of disposable income and business giving as a percent of profit	* Effectiveness of tax incentives for individuals and businesses in terms of level and number of donors at different income levels and charity sectors * Effectiveness of tax incentives based on donation data from charities

Sources: CAF/NCVO, 2010; NCVO, 2017; HMRC, 2019; NCVO Charity Tax Commission, 2019; *Giving USA*, 2020; IRS, 2020; U.S. Department of the Treasury, 2020

and provides a critical feedback loop on government policies, programmes, and actions. The formalisation of civil society strengthens the state-society relationships and creates an effective ground for democratic functioning. Thus, a comprehensive study of the multiple registers at which tax incentives link the state with the non-profit sector is a first step in strengthening India's tax incentive regime for civil society.

Conclusion

Despite its widespread destruction and challenges, the COVID-19 pandemic has highlighted the urgent need for a constructive relationship between the non-profit sector and the Indian state. The need to define the contours of the legal and regulatory environment of the non-profit sector to meet the demands of the current times has never been clearer, with the tax incentive regime being a critical component. Furthermore, evaluating the contributions of tax incentives to the non-profit sector is essential to strengthening the tax regime around the specific needs of the non-profit sector. As this sector has numerous small NPOs, small donors should be incentivised or enabled to avail themselves of tax incentives more easily. It is likely that high-income donors work with large NPOs, and therefore their incentive provisions could be modified to match the provisions for grossed-up donations like in the United Kingdom for better monetary benefits. Other types of incentives for high-income donors should be considered, for which new types of taxes such as wealth tax and inheritance tax may need to be introduced. Our analysis highlighted that although tax incentives are not the financial backbone of the non-profit sector, their removal may significantly and adversely alter the legal and regulatory relationship between the state and the non-profit sector, the consequences of which are not fully understood given the lack of research and data. Therefore, we strongly recommend that the government reconsider further removal of tax incentives and commission a rigorous study of the role of tax incentives in the non-profit sector in India.

Notes

1 Prime Minister's Citizen Assistance and Relief in Emergency Situations Fund (PM CARES Fund) has been set up as a public charitable trust. Its objective is to provide financial and other assistance and relief in the face of crisis and calamity such as COVID-19.

2 The countries are France, Norway, Brazil, Mexico, China, South Africa, India, Bangladesh, Singapore, South Korea, the United States, and the United Kingdom.

3 Each of these legal forms is governed by national and state-level acts and has different compliance requirements.

4 The study states that the distribution of NPOs registered in the GuideStar database reflects the distribution and thematic focus areas of other publicly available databases for Indian NGOs such as the Darpan database.

5 The study sampled 800 NPOs across India from a database of 3500+ verified NGOs available with GuideStar India. All 800 NPOs were the ones which responded to the survey. The GuideStar database reflects the distribution and focus area of other publicly available databases for Indian NGOs such as the Darpan database.

6 This cohort does not include foundations.

7 1 USD = 73.3 INR (see https://www.xe.com/currencyconverter/convert/?Amount=500%2C000&From=INR&To=USD).

8 Maharashtra, therefore, has a very well-developed NPO ecosystem whose NPOs receive wide recognition for their work. This is not the case with other states, although the causality is difficult to attribute.

9 An accurate assessment of the amount of tax incentivised for donations is not possible due to two prominent limitations of this data. First, the figure represents the revenue foregone by the government, which includes exemptions given to the donations made to government trusts and funds as well as other NPOs. Second, it may not include the contributions made by high-net-worth individuals because they 'typically make philanthropic contributions either independently or through a family-run foundation, and are neither required to report their philanthropic investments, nor to claim tax exemptions' (CSIP, 2020).

10 This move reduces the effective tax rate to 25.17%, (inclusive of surcharge and cess) as against the existing statutory tax rate of 34.32%.

11 See Chattopadhyay, 2011; Rao et al., 2016.

12 A part of this discussion is based on (Chakravarty, 2014); see (Chattopadhyay, 2011; Rao et al., 2016).

13 Long-term capital gains tax on securities has been re-introduced in the budget 2018–19.

14 These are applicable on all taxes.

15 Taxable income between INR 20 million and INR 50 million now attracts a 25% surcharge, while taxable income above INR 50 million attracts a 37% surcharge. The surcharge rate for both taxable income groups was 15% earlier.

16 Twenty-two percent in case companies do not avail of any tax incentives.

17 That is, tax concessions of all kinds.

18 To illustrate, on a monthly salary of 1000 INR, which receives a 20% tax cut for a 100-INR donation, in a deduction-based tax incentive. Here, the donated amount is deducted from the pre-tax salary (1000 INR), and the tax outflow reduces from 200 INR to 180 INR if there is no tax incentive on donations. However, in a credit-based incentive, the tax outflow will reduce to 100 INR because the

donated amount is deducted from the tax the donor will pay. In both cases, we assume that the entire amount donated is eligible for tax incentive.

19 The grossed-up donation-based approach to incentives has two components. First is the grossed-up section, in which both the amount donated and the tax applicable are given to the charity. Notably, this provision directs the revenue foregone by the government to the charity and not the donor. The donor benefits because this provision amplifies the monetary value of the amount donated. Second is the rebate component, which is applicable to high-income donors who face high (e.g., 40%) tax rates. In this, the government pays to the donor the tax amount over and above the standard rate, that is, the difference between the higher tax rate of 40% and the standard tax rate at 20%.

20 This does not include grossed-up donations in Ireland.

21 The eligible causes are only one among the many eligibility criteria for an organisation to fulfil to receive tax incentives.

22 In some countries, the causes for charitable donations differ for individuals and businesses. This table represents only the causes applicable to individual donations.

References

Agarwal, S. and Dadrawala, N. (2004) 'Philanthropy and Law in South Asia', in Sidel, M. and Zaman, I. (eds) *University of Iowa Legal Studies Research Paper*. Available at: https://papers.ssrn.com/sol3/papers.cfm?abstract_id=1126337.

Aggarwal, K. P. (1989) *Stimulative Effect of Tax Incentive for Charitable Contributions: A Study of Indian Corporate Sector.* New Delhi: National Institute of Public Finance & Policy.

Backus, P. and Grant, N. (2019) 'How Sensitive Is the Average Taxpayer to Changes in the Tax-Price of Giving', *International Tax Public Finance*, 26.

Bijika, J. (2013) 'A Primer on the Empirical Evidence for the USA and Its Implications', *Social Research*, 80.

CAF America (2021) *CAF Russia, CAF America Insider Blog*. Available at: https://www.cafamerica.org/caf-russia/ (Accessed: 21 January 2021).

CAF/NCVO (2010) *UK Giving 2010: An Overview of Charitable Giving in the UK, 2009/10*. Available at: https://cdoliv01sifi01.cafonline.org/docs/default-source/cafcdodocuments/UK-Giving-2010_101210.pdf.

CBGA (2019) *Promises and Priorities: An Analysis of Union Budget 2019–20*. New Delhi: CBGA.

Chakravarty, M. (2014) 'Public Finance Policy and Inequality: A Review of the Contrasting Experiences of India and Ecuador', in Flores, C. S. and Cortes, C. L. (eds) *Democratic Renewal Versus Neoliberalism: Towards Empowerment and Inclusion*. Buenos Aires: CLACSO (Latin American Council of Social Sciences).

Chattopadhyay, S. (2011) 'Assessing Tax Policy and Tax Compliance in the Reform Era', in *Progressive Fiscal Policy in India*. 1st edn. New Delhi: Sage Publishers, pp. 148–173.

Chua, V. C. and Wong, C. M. (1999) 'Tax Incentives, Individual Characteristics and Charitable Giving in Singapore', *International Journal of Social Economics*, 68.

Clotfelter, T. C. (2012) 'Ending Corporate Tax Avoidance and Tax Competition: A Plan to Collect the Tax Deficit of Multinationals', in Fack, G. and Landis, C. (eds) *Charitable Giving and Tax Policy: A Historical and Comparative Perspective*. Paris: School of Economics.

CSIP, A. U. (2019) *Enabling Philanthropy and Social Impact in India*. New Delhi. Available at: https://csip.ashoka.edu.in/research-and-knowledge/.

CSIP, A. U. (2020) *Estimating Philanthropic Capital in India: Approaches and Challenges*. New Delhi. Available at: https://csip.ashoka.edu.in/research-and-knowledge/.

DASRA (2020) *Institutional Resilience and Impact Optimisation Toolkit*. Mumbai: DASRA.

Duquette, N. (2016) 'Do Tax Incentives Affect Charitable Contributions? – Evidence from Public Charities' Reported Revenues', *Journal of Public Economics*, 137.

Fack, G. and Landais, C. (2010) 'Are Tax Incentives for Charitable Giving Efficient? Evidence from France', *American Economic Journal: Economic Policy*, 117–141.

GIving USA (2020). Available at: https://givingusa.org/ (Accessed: 13 October 2020).

GOI (2001) *Report of the Advisory Group on Tax Policy and Tax Administration for the Tenth Plan*. New Delhi: GOI.

HMRC (2019) *UK Charity Tax Relief Statistics, UK Charity Tax Relief Statistics Commentary*. New Delhi: HMRC.

IRS (2020) *Tax Statistics*. Available at: https://www.irs.gov/statistics (Accessed: 13 October 2020).
Kulkarni, S. (2020) 'NITI Aayog Reaches Out to 92,000 NGOs for Joint COVID-19 Fight', *Deccan Herald*, 5 April.
Lexology (2020) *China Tax Policies to Address the COVID-19 Pandemic*. Available at: https://www.lexology.com/library/detail.aspx?g=8c9bab9d-c184-4268-b0a6-ae59d00569fe (Accessed: 9 November 2020).
Ministry of Finance (2020) *Finance Act*. New Delhi. Available at: http://egazette.nic.in/WriteReadData/2020/218938.pdf.
MOSPI (2012) *Final Report on Non Profit Institutions in India: A Profile and Satellite Accounts in the Framework of System of National Accounts (including State-wise Comparison of Profiles)*. New Delhi: MOSPI.
NCVO (2017) *Getting Involved*. London. Available at: https://www.ncvo.org.uk/images/documents/policy_and_research/participation/NCVO_2017_Getting_Involved.pdf.
NCVO Charity Tax Commission (2019) *UK Charity Tax Statistics Overview*. Available at: https://www.ncvo.org.uk/images/documents/policy_and_research/funding/CharityCommissionResearchReport_3.pdf.
Park, M. and Jeon, B. (2017) *Impact of Tax Incentives on Charitable Contribution*. Korea: Institute of Public Finance.
Pattnaik, R. K. et al. (2009) *Empirical Fiscal Research in India: A Survey*. New Delhi: Reserve Bank of India.
Puri, A., Nayak, P. K. and Dadrawala, N. (2018) *Global Institutional Philanthropy: A Preliminary Status Report; Part Two, Country Profiles*, Johnson, P. D. (ed). Available at: https://www.civicus.org/images/Southern%20Philanthropy%20Social%20Justice%20and%20Human%20Rights_apr2016_FINAL.pdf.
Rajakumar, D. J. and Shetty, L. S. (2020) 'Corporate Tax Reductions: Weak Analytical Foundation', *Economic And Political Weekly*, 10, 62–66.
Rao, M. G. and Rao, R. (eds) (2006) 'Trends and Issues in Tax Policy and Reform in India', *India Policy Forum*, 2.
Rao, R. K. et al. (2016) *Corporate Tax: A Brief Assessment of Some Exemptions*, 165. Available at: https://ideas.repec.org/p/npf/wpaper/16-165.html.
Sampradaan Indian Centre for Philanthropy (2004) *A Review of Charities Administration in India*. Available at: https://niti.gov.in/planningcommission.gov.in/docs/reports/sereport/ser/stdy_cai.pdf.
Scharf, K. and Smith, S. (2009) *Gift Aid Donor Research: Exploring Options for Reforming Higher-Rate Relief: A Report for HMRC and MHT. Her Majesty's Revenue and Customs*. Available at: https://www.bristol.ac.uk/media-library/sites/cmpo/migrated/documents/giftaid.pdf.
Srinath, I. (2003) 'Donations and Deductions', *Outlook India*, March. Available at: https://www.outlookindia.com/website/story/donations-and-deductions/219358.
U.S. Department of the Treasury (2020) *Tax Expenditures*. Available at: https://home.treasury.gov/policy-issues/tax-policy/tax-expenditures (Accessed: 13 October 2020).
VANI (2016) *Income Tax Act for the Voluntary Sector – A Study Report*. New Delhi. Available at: https://www.vaniindia.org/publicationpdf/incometaxvani.pdf.
Viswanath, P. and Dadrawal, N. (2004) *Philanthropy and Equity: The Case of India*. Cambridge, MA: Global Equity Initiative, Harvard University.

14

TAX INCENTIVES FOR CHARITABLE GIVING

Evidence from the Swiss Canton of Geneva

*Giedre Lideikyte Huber, Marta Pittavino and Henry Peter**

1 Introduction

a Current Swiss legal framework

Switzerland is one of the countries whose legal framework includes a system of tax deductions to incentivize charitable giving (OECD 2020).[1]

Under the current Swiss law, taxpayers can deduct charitable donations from their taxable income (individuals) or taxable profits (corporations) subject to a specific threshold. In order to be deductible, the donation must be made to legal entities that benefit from a tax exemption as a result of the fact that they are pursuing public service or public-interest goals.[2] The law and case law specify the tax-exemption conditions for such entities, notably that economic goals cannot be considered public-interest purposes and that acquiring and managing significant corporate equity is considered a public-interest goal only when the interest in keeping such an entity is subordinate to the public-interest goals [Art. 56 (g) LIFD]. Such exoneration requirements apply to the entities subjected to limited and unlimited tax liability in Switzerland, that is, both to resident entities and to permanent establishments. Legal entities governed by public law and semi-public companies do not fall into this scope.[3]

A threshold applies to the amount of the deduction of charitable donations from taxable income and profits. At the federal level, this threshold is 20% of the net taxable income or profits with a minimum donation requirement of CHF 100. Nearly all cantonal legislations adopted the same limit of 20% (often without minimum donation requirement), even though federal law does not impose any requirement in this respect:[4] as a result of the principle of the cantonal autonomy in fixing tax rates, which is enshrined in the Art. 129 of the Swiss Federal Constitution, tax allowances applied by the cantons and the communes are in effect their sole prerogative. The threshold of a charitable deduction is calculated as follows: first, one must discount all deductions from the gross income that are mentioned in articles 26 to 33 of the DFTA (those include the deductions related to self-employed business activity, to wealth, social deductions, etc.). Second, the calculation of the 20% threshold is based on the remaining taxable income after these deductions. The charitable donation is deducted from the remaining income and capped – if necessary – at the aforesaid threshold.

* The authors greatly thank the Geneva Tax Administration for providing data for this study.

DOI: 10.4324/9781003139201-17

b The 2006 federal direct tax law reform

The 20% threshold of taxable income or profits was introduced on January 1, 2006, as part of a larger reform of the Swiss federal tax law.[5] Prior to this reform, the threshold was 10%. The goal of the 2006 reform was "the liberalization of the Swiss foundation law in order to boost the establishment of foundations".[6] Through this reform, the legislator in fact expressed its will to encourage more people "to give up part of their wealth" to charitable foundations, due to the fact that private foundations were the most popular vehicles (though not the only ones) in Switzerland for hosting charitable activities, as well as the fact that private wealth had risen sharply in the years preceding the reform.[7] The main part of this reform aimed at modifying civil law norms related to different aspects of foundations. However, tax law modifications were also carried out as the previous legal framework was considered an insufficient incentive for individuals to part with "important" portion of their wealth.[8] Thus, even though the objectives of these changes were only articulated in very general terms[9] (which in itself is problematic), it is safe to assume that at least one of its goals was to encourage *significant* donations.

The federal tax law amendments directly impacted charitable giving in three manners.[10] First, as already said, the existing threshold for deduction of charitable donations was increased from 10% to 20% of taxable income or profits. Second, the law introduced a possibility to deduct non-cash donations. Third, the law added a new clause stating that donations to the Swiss Confederation, the cantons, the communes and their institutions are deductible to the same extent as donations to charitable tax-exempt entities. Overall, those three tax law amendments significantly expanded the potential for tax deductions.

During the legislative process, the most important discussions concerned the first measure, that is, the increase in the threshold for deductible donations. The Economic Affairs and Taxation Committee of the Council of States,[11] reporting on this legislative proposal, was convinced that the activities of foundations pursuing public service or public utility goals would effectively be fostered through a more generous practice of deducting donations, as proposed by the reform.[12] In fact, the initial project suggested increasing the deductions for direct federal tax to 40% of net income or net profit. What is more, under certain specific conditions, such as a particularly important public interest, an enduring commitment to finance a foundation and at least an equivalent deduction granted by a canton and municipality (the latter norm had some logic of "matching" mechanisms), the tax deduction allowed by the direct federal tax would have been able to reach even 100%.[13] Thus, the initial suggested changes offered very generous tax deductions.

However, the large increases in deductible thresholds were dismissed in the context of the legislative procedure. During the consultation phase with the cantons, which is a part of the legislative process in Switzerland,[14] the vast majority of cantons resolutely rejected a quadrupling of the deduction (from 10% to 40%).[15] As a result, the 100% deduction, even in restrictive conditions, was also rejected, on the basis that it would affect the fiscal substance of the public authorities too profoundly.[16] The Federal Council used public law and finance arguments to reject the proposed increases. It highlighted that this type of deduction leads to unequal treatment, as taxpayers taxed at high marginal tax rates are favored over those with lower incomes. Also, extending too widely the possibility of making a deduction seriously undermines the distinctive fiscal character of taxes, whose goal is to finance the tasks of the State, whatever they may be.[17] In addition, the Federal Council pointed out that the norms instituting such deductions were questionable from a public finance perspective, because not only they do not respect the principle of "gross accounting", but they also ultimately restrict the financial sovereignty of the Federal Parliament. In particular, by allowing a taxpayer to decide on the allocation of certain funds to certain public tasks, the system would be delegating some budgetary authority to the taxpayer; such standards are not compatible with the requirements of the Federal Finance Act.[18] In the end, the threshold of 20% was adopted.[19]

Other tax law changes did not give rise to controversial discussions. The deductibility of non-cash donations was widely approved, with some cantons only pointing out the potential valuation problems that could arise.[20] The deductibility of voluntary contributions to the Confederation, the cantons, the communes and their related public institutions was also introduced without particular objections. In fact, the reason behind this provision was mainly to ensure that universities, which in Switzerland are mainly federal or cantonal institutions,[21] also benefit from the liberalization of the charitable deductions system: the proposal highlighted the need to fund considerable investments in teaching, research and science.[22] The Economic Affairs and Taxation Committee specifically highlighted in its Report that donations for research and education were very relevant for the State and could help to relieve its burden in this area.[23]

The federal law changes were followed by cantonal law modifications. In Geneva, the threshold of 5% of the taxable net income[24] was raised to 20% in 2010.[25] In 2009, deductions for legal entities were raised from 10% of the taxable corporate income to 20%.[26]

The introduction of different thresholds in the Swiss federal and Geneva cantonal law was introduced as shown in Table 14.1.

c Objectives

To our knowledge, the effectiveness of the 2006 income tax law reform has never been evaluated, neither at the federal nor at cantonal level.[27] In general, very little research and data exist in Switzerland regarding taxpayers' giving behavior in relation to tax incentives. Therefore, the aim of this chapter (which is a part of a larger project evaluating the efficiency of tax incentives for charitable giving in Switzerland) is to provide, using descriptive statistics, a first insight into the charitable giving behavior in the Canton of Geneva (GE) and to identify any possible changes in behavior – if any – correlated with the 2006 tax reform. The Canton of Geneva is one of the most important cantons in Switzerland, having the fifth-largest population and second-highest gross domestic product per capita.[28] Also, and importantly, it is a national as well as international philanthropy hub. As a result, observing the patterns of charitable giving behavior in relation to tax incentives among the Geneva population may provide significant information for policymakers.

Table 14.1 Deductible thresholds in federal and Geneva cantonal income tax laws during the studied timeframe

	Threshold	**2001**	**2001**	**2003**	**2004**	**2005**	**2006**	**2007**	**2008**	**2009**	**2010**	**2011**
Federal law	Individual	10%					20%					
	Corporate*											
Cantonal law (GE)	Individual	5%									20%	
	Corporate*	10%								20%		

* This table shows both individual and corporate income tax thresholds; however, the focus of the current chapter is only on individual income taxation.

The present chapter focuses on the tax filing data described in the following section. It analyses the giving behavior which can be observed on the basis of tax returns and not the overall charitable giving behavior (e.g. donations not claiming any tax deductions for their gifts) (see Adena, Chapter 12; Adena et al. 2014; Adena and Huck 2019).[29,30,31] This chapter will therefore not provide conclusions about the general giving behavior in the Canton of Geneva; it only focuses on specific tax-related patterns. In addition, based on this study, it will not be possible to draw definitive conclusions as to whether the changes of giving behavior – if any – were caused by a specific measure of the previously mentioned reform (increase in threshold, introduction of the possibility of non-cash deductions or the possibility to deduct donations to State entities), as segregated data for those categories were not available.

2 Material and methods

The outcomes presented in this chapter are related to taxpayer behavior for charitable giving over a time framework of 11 years (2001–2011) based on data from the Canton of Geneva.

Data were collected in the given years by the Tax Administration of the Canton of Geneva through its taxpayers' returns and were confidentially shared for the sake of our analysis. A different data set was provided for each year under study for a total of 11 data sets. Each data set consisted of the same eight variables, listed and described in the following with the original French name provided in the data set:

- "identifiant": a coded ID for each taxpayers. This variable allows, in principle, to follow the same taxpayer over time. In other words, the same coded ID is used for a given taxpayer for each fiscal year. As Switzerland has a joint filling system, married couples are considered and treated as one taxpayer in the same way as a single non-married individual and have only one coded ID (in this chapter, any deducting taxpayer, couple or individual is referred to as "deducter"). The code ID may change from one year to another in specific cases, mainly therefore: 1) replacement of one ID by another in the event of the death of a married taxpayer ("principal" taxpayer) by his surviving spouse; 2) disappearance of an ID in case of marriage between two taxpayers: the "main" taxpayer (often the husband) remains, and the spouse disappears; 3) appearance of a new ID in the case of divorce or separation of two taxpayers: the "main" taxpayer (often the husband) remains, and the spouse appears; 4) replacement of one ID by another in case of a change of surname or modification/correction of the date of birth. In all four situations, it is not possible to track a given taxpayer over time.
- "annee_de_naissance": the year of birth of a taxpayer. For married couples, it is the year of birth of the "principal" taxpayer.
- "revenu_net_imposable_GE": the net taxable income in the Canton of Geneva. In 2010 and 2011, the canton of Geneva has introduced several changes to its personal income tax law (e.g., extension of the deduction for family expenses). Those changes to a certain extent influenced the definition of taxable income for cantonal tax purposes. For this reason, the calculation of taxable income of 2001 through 2009 to a certain extent diverges from its calculation in 2010 and 2011.[30]
- "revenu_net_imposable_taux": the net taxable income applied to set the tax rate; it includes any foreign income.
- "fortune_brute": gross wealth.
- "fortune_imposable": taxable wealth.

- "bareme_revenu": the binary (0/1) indication of a possible "splitting" of income tax rate in the tax income computation, showing if a taxpayer is a couple (1) and not a single individual (0) (see the previous description of "identifiant").
- "versements_benevoles": the amount of deduction (if any) for charitable giving, representing the entire annual amount of the deducted donations (in case it is less than the deductible threshold) or capped amount of annual donations, if exceeding the deductible threshold.

Since the main relevant variables for the purpose of this study were "identifiant" and "versements_benevoles", a longitudinal data set representing the Canton of Geneva taxpayers from 2001 to 2011 was created and analyzed. In addition, we have used the variable net taxable income for tax rate overall ("revenu_net_imposable_taux") to identify patterns of giving behavior in 2001 and 2011. The outcomes are summarized in the "Results" section.

The characteristics of the available data do not allow checking whether the amounts deducted by taxpayers represent the full donation or only the part capped at the threshold level (10% prior to 2006 and 20% after 2006 for federal income tax purposes); as a result, in certain cases (which we cannot identify), only the deducted amount and not the whole amount of donation can be observed. In other words, the total amounts of all charitable donations are not known to us for the given 11 years (2001–2011) in the Canton of Geneva, as the present data encompass both the un-capped deductions (representing full amounts of donations) and the capped deductions (representing incomplete amounts of donations) without distinguishing between those two categories.[31]

3 Results

The total number of Geneva taxpayers was calculated. Its trend positively increased every year, from a minimum of 234,117 in 2001 to a maximum of 266,336 in 2011. The percentage change over the years is reported in the last column of Table 14.2, together with the percentage of Geneva deducting taxpayers (second-to-last column) computed for each of the 11 years in the given time framework period. From 2001 to 2011, the number of deducting taxpayers more than doubled, going from 8.3% of the total number of taxpayers in 2001 to 19.3% of the

Table 14.2 Descriptive statistics of taxpayers' population by year (2001–2011)

Year	*Number of taxpayers*	*Deducting*	*Non-deducting*	*% of deducting taxpayers*	*% yearly change in taxpayers*
2001	234,117	19,335	214,782	8.3%	
2002	236,341	25,272	211,069	10.7%	0.9%
2003	237,777	30,276	207,501	12.7%	0.6%
2004	240,254	35,192	205,062	14.7%	1.0%
2005	242,521	39,553	202,968	16.3%	0.9%
2006	245,224	39,511	205,713	16.1%	1.1%
2007	248,017	42,248	205,769	17.0%	1.1%
2008	250,886	44,707	206,179	18.0%	1.2%
2009	256,236	47,349	208,887	18.5%	2.1%
2010	261,703	49,389	212,314	18.9%	2.1%
2011	266,336	51,492	214,844	19.3%	1.8%

total number of taxpayers in 2011. The absolute numbers of these values are 19,335 (number of deducting taxpayers in 2001) and 51,492 (number of deducting taxpayers in 2011). Further, detailed information for the years under review can be found in Table 14.2, including the absolute number of non-deducting taxpayers and the percentage change of taxpayers from one year to the other.

Table 14.2 shows the absolute number of taxpayers, split between deducting and not deducting, from year 2001 to year 2011. The percentage of Geneva deducting taxpayers, and related changes, are also shown.

The total amount of deductions has been computed from year 2001 to year 2011. The amounts presented in the current chapter were not inflation-adjusted; however, the income classes were objectively computed by population percentages (25%, 25%, 25%, 20%, 4%, 1%). The absolute range for the amount of deductions is large, going from a minimum of CHF 29,133,697 in 2001 to a maximum of CHF 84,014,116 in 2010, with a substantial increase of 48% from 2008 to 2009. Overall, the total amount of deductions positively increased between 2001 and 2010, with a negligible (–0.7%) decrease from 2005 to 2006 and a slightly higher decrease (–13.4%) from 2010 to 2011, as shown in the third column of Table 14.3. While the mean deductions range varies from a minimum of CHF 1,098 to a maximum of CHF 1,701, with a CHF 603 difference and a mainly negative trend between the years, the median deduction range is smaller: from 270 to 393, with a difference of CHF 123 and a slow decrease over the years as seen in Figure 14.2. The latter result is validated by the outcome presented in the last column of Table 14.3, showing a prevalence of negative percentage of the change in median deductions among *deducters* from 2001 to 2011.

Table 14.3 represents the amount of deductions and related percentage change from 2001 to 2011. The mean and median deductions among *deducters*, together with the latter percentage change, are also reported.

In addition, we have carried out an analysis of giving by income using as a variable the taxable income for tax rate ("revenu_net_imposable_taux"). To that effect, we have divided the taxpayers by income classes into six categories, representing the following percentages of the taxpayer population (see Annexes 1 and 2): "low" (bottom 25% of taxpayers), "low-middle" (25% of taxpayers) and "middle" (25% of taxpayers). The remaining 25% of the taxpayers have

Table 14.3 Amount of deductions and related percentage change from 2001 to 2011

Year	*Amount of deductions (CHF)*	*% yearly change in the amount of deductions*	*Mean deductions among deducters (CHF)*	*Median deductions among deducters (CHF)*	*% change in median deductions among deducters*
2001	29,133,697		1,507	393	
2002	33,248,984	14.1%	1,315	360	–8.4%
2003	33,507,115	0.8%	1,098	305	–15.3%
2004	41,229,743	23.0%	1,171	300	–1.6%
2005	47,381,886	14.9%	1,197	300	0.0%
2006	47,056,580	–0.7%	1,190	298	–0.7%
2007	50,968,564	8.3%	1,206	280	–6.0%
2008	51,735,693	1.5%	1,147	270	–3.6%
2009	76,574,313	48.0%	1,617	280	3.7%
2010	84,014,116	9.7%	1,701	290	3.6%
2011	72,741,235	–13.4%	1,412	280	–3.4%

been divided into smaller income categories in order to make an in-depth analysis of the giving behavior of taxpayers belonging to the highest income classes. Thus, the following income class categories were established: "middle-high" (20% of taxpayers), "high" (4% of taxpayers) and "very high" (top 1% of taxpayers).

The analysis by income class shows that the amount of charitable deductions increases with the increase of the taxpayers' income. The largest amount of deductions is provided by the taxpayers belonging to the highest income class ("very high", i.e., 1%), accounting for 23.1% (2001) and 37.8% (2011) of deducting taxpayers as in Figure 14.1. The top 25% income classes (middle-high, high and very high together) account for 79.6% (2001) and 73.8% (2011) of the total deductions. The percentage of taxpayers deducting charitable donations in the respective income classes also increases along with income. Also, in every income class, we observe

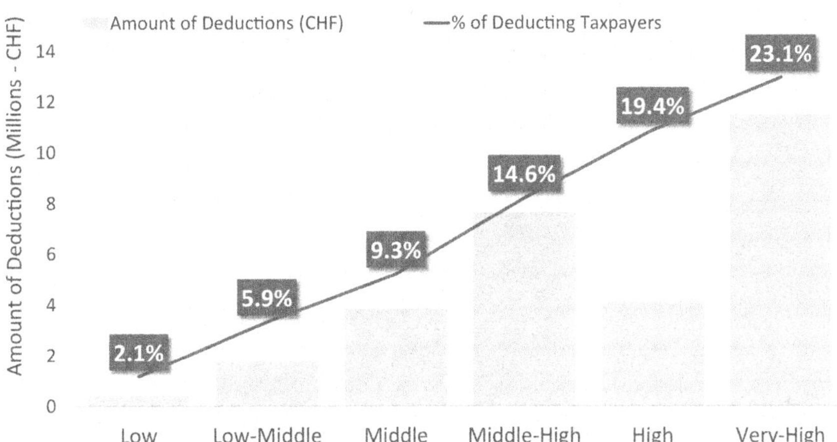

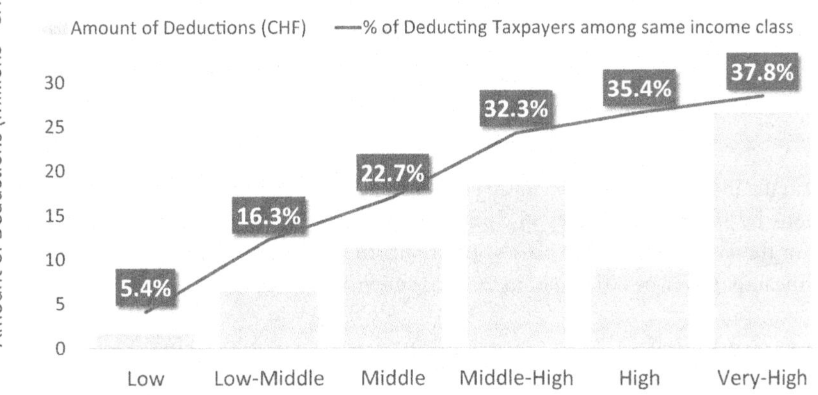

Figure 14.1 Amount of deductions and percentage of deducting taxpayers for each of the six income class categories in the year 2001 (above) and in the year 2011 (below). The six income class categories represent different percentages of the total income amount: Low, Low-Middle and Middle correspond to 25% each, while Middle-High indicates 20%, High 4% and Very-High the top 1%

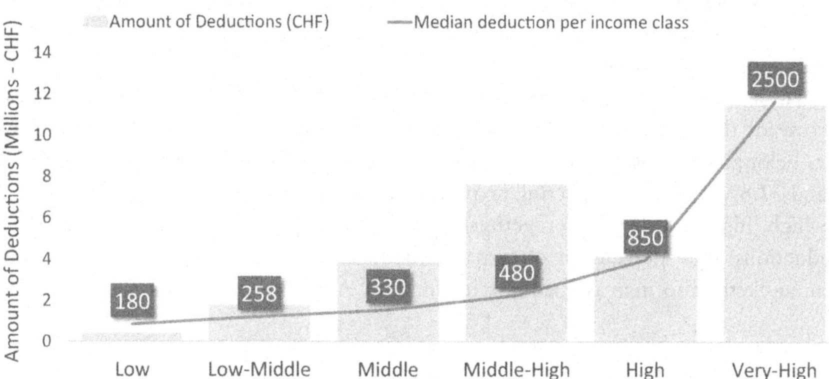

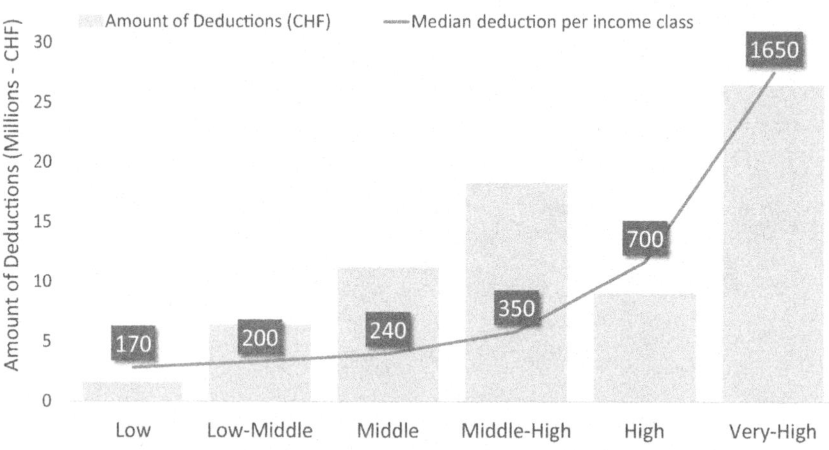

Figure 14.2 Amount of deductions and median deductions for each of the six income class categories in the year 2001 (above) 2011 (below). The six income class categories represent different percentages of the total income amount: Low, Low-Middle and Middle correspond to 25% each, while Middle-High indicates 20%, High 4% and Very-High the top 1%

an important increase in *deducters* in 2011 in comparison with 2001. Concerning the median deductions by income class, they also increase with the increase of income, rising especially sharply in the last three income classes. However, the median deductions in all income classes are significantly lower in 2011 than in 2001 as shown in Figure 14.2.

4 Discussion

The descriptive statistics presented in the "Results" section of this study provide several insights into taxpayer's giving behavior in the Canton of Geneva; these could be of interest for policy makers. In addition, it offers a first glimpse into the effects – if any – of the 2006 tax reform.

The first observation is that the percentage of *deducters* among Geneva's taxpayers more than doubled, from 8.3% to 19.3%, during the studied period from 2001 to 2011). In 2011, nearly one fifth of the Geneva population made charitable gifts for which they claimed charitable deductions, as opposed to less than one tenth of the taxpayers in 2001. Unambiguously, the use of these specific deductions has risen among taxpayers, and we observe this increase in every income class (Annex 1). Even though we can only speculate about the reasons for this increase (i.e., better awareness about the possibility to deduct gifts? An increase in the number of donors in the Canton of Geneva? An effect of the higher incentive? Other?), these data show that the relevant period claiming charitable deductions has become a common and not a marginal phenomenon during the process of filling tax returns.

This finding raises interesting questions when compared to other available data sources on giving behavior. For instance, the study of Freitag et al. reports that in 2014, 71% of the Swiss population made charitable donations. However, our data show that, at least in the Canton of Geneva, only 19% of taxpayers filed for charitable deductions in 2011. This number reflects tax fillings that occurred three years earlier than the study of Freitag et al., but judging from the level of increase in charitable deductions in Geneva during the 11-year period under review, it is quite unlikely that charitable deductions reached 71% in 2014. Therefore, further studies should look into the differences in various data sets describing individual charitable giving behavior in Switzerland. For instance, it would be interesting to assess whether and to what extent the estimated percentage (71%) of charitable giving by the Swiss population is accurate and, if it is, why an important portion of Swiss taxpayers still does not seem to deduct charitable donations.

In terms of the *amount* of deductions in relation to charitable donations, the total annual sum deducted by all taxpayers is steadily increasing during the observed period. It is in fact possible to observe a correlation with 1) the increase in the overall population of taxpayers and 2) the increase of charitable deductions among taxpayers. In terms of deductions *per taxpayer*, we observe a decrease both in the mean and in the median over time. While the median constantly decreases, the mean of donations fluctuates during the studied period but is overall lower in 2011 than in 2001. We observe the same trend when comparing median charitable deductions by income classes. In other words, the general trend seems to be lesser deductions, and this may be a clue showing that, considered individually, taxpayers tend to give less, that is, that the size of the individual donations is decreasing. However, a complementary set of data showing the exact amount of donations (and not only the deducted amounts) would be needed to verify such a hypothesis.

The data presented in the present chapter offers rare glimpse of the Swiss taxpayers' giving behavior per income class. In particular, having compared 2001 to 2011, we observe that the deductions made by the 1% of taxpayers having the highest income account for more than 35% of all deductions. The deductions for charitable donations carried out by the top 25% income classes (middle-high, high and very-high) account for more than 70% of all such deductions in the taxpayer population. This information is important for the policymaking, as it suggests that calibrating tax incentives for this particular class of taxpayers could potentially be a policy option to consider.

In those descriptive statistics, there is no obvious correlation with the timing of the reform. The increase of *deducters*, as well as the decrease in the median of individual amounts deducted, are mostly constant and linear, with no distinctive or drastic changes in 2006, when the new federal tax law norms took effect, nor in 2010, when cantonal adjustments were made. The increase in the overall amount of donations is not linear but subject to certain peaks, the largest of them (48%) being observed in 2009, several years after the reform. We can speculate about the reasons thereof, for instance, the fact that in 2009, taxpayers who were usually taxed at source were given the possibility, under certain conditions, to file a return and then be treated as resident taxpayers (so-called "quasi-residents"), thus claiming all personalized deductions, including for charitable giving.[32] It can be estimated that the number of such taxpayers was around 2,000 in 2009, 4,000 in 2010 and 5,600 in 2011.[33] This fact could influence both the amount of deductions and the number of *deducters*. However, the data transmitted by the Geneva Tax Administration for the purpose of this study are confidential, not allowing identification of the quasi-residents and thus verification of whether and to what extent their deductions explain this peak in giving.

Overall, three important observations should be highlighted: first, over the 11 years under review, it appears that an increased number of taxpayers deducted their donations; second, the amount of those deductions decreased in terms of both mean and median; third, an overwhelming part of deductions came from the upper 25% income class. With respect to the first two observations, the presented descriptive statistics do not show any conclusive evidence of the impact of the reform on those trends. As one of the goals of the 2006 reform was to encourage taxpayers to part with a substantial amount of their wealth, because the pre-reform level of giving was considered insufficient, the constantly decreasing median deduction could be a sign for legislators indicating that potentially the reform was unsuccessful on this point, at least for the lower 75% classes of income. Yet, this would call for further investigations about the 2006 reform effects, because while the total amount of deductions is known, the total amount of donations is not. In relation to another implicit goal of the reforms – to attract new deducters – it is not possible to detect any evidence of the reform's real impact, because the number of deducting taxpayers has steadily increased since 2001, with no visible increase during the year of the reform or the years immediately following the entry into force of the new law provisions. This finding in any event may indicate a constantly increasing awareness of the population of tax deductions for charitable giving, perhaps independently of any specific tax reform incentive. Overall, there is evidence which seems to show that that the reform might not have succeeded in attaining at least some of its goals. This impression is strengthened by the fact that the 2006 reform substantially increased the possibilities for tax deductions, because it not only allowed larger deductions but also offered a possibility to deduct non-cash donations (including real estate) as well as donations to various public entities. Therefore, one would expect to see at least some effects of those important changes in the descriptive data, which is not the case in the present study.

Overall, more research ought to be done to understand whether the 2006 reform had any effect on charitable giving behavior and, if so, to what extent. Ideally, every new tax measure that has been introduced – the increase of the deduction threshold and the introduction of the deductibility of non-cash donations, as well as the possibility to deduct gifts to public entities – should be evaluated separately, trying to disentangle their effects. Moreover, a more specific study stratified by income could reveal additional insights. For instance, alternative data sets should be used to enable researchers to understand the changes in the total amounts of donations (and not only of deductions) during this period. Furthermore, studying the patterns of charitable giving to higher education institutions could help establish whether the tax reform increased – as intended – their funding from charitable sources. Finally, studying charitable non-cash donations would contribute to determining to what extent such a policy measure was successful. In order to complete those studies, allowing an in-depth evaluation of the new tax measures, legislators and the administration should make tax measure-segregated data (for instance, indicating the total amount of charitable donations for different income categories indicated previously) available for scientific studies.

Conclusion

The present chapter provides unique descriptive statistics about taxpayer's giving behavior in the Canton of Geneva for the period from 2001 to 2011. Several important observations emerge. First, the number of taxpayers deducting charitable donations significantly increased. Second, in general, the median of individual amounts of charitable deductions decreased between 2001 and 2011 (even without inflation adjustment), and this effect is observed in all income classes comparing the years 2001 and 2011. This could suggest that even though the total number of *deducters* increased, they tended to make individually smaller donations; however, an alternative data set would need to be studied in order to confirm this hypothesis (in particular having access to the total amount of donations and not only to the deducted amounts). Third, the taxpayers with the highest income, especially the very high income class (top 1% of all the taxpayers) accounted for the largest percentage of deductions. Policy makers could consider whether tax incentives should target this specific group of taxpayers and whether to envisage other incentives which could be more attractive to a broader base of *deducters* (as proposed by other researchers).[34] Further interdisciplinary works studying the giving behavior of taxpayers belonging to the highest income classes could also usefully build on the present results in order to understand the rationale and what, in addition to tax incentives, moves taxpayers to make charitable donations.[35]

Notes

1 For examples of other jurisdictions, see OECD 2020, pp. 80–84.
2 Arts 33a and 56 let. g of the Direct Federal Taxation Act (DFTA).
3 For a more detailed description of the Swiss system, see Lideikyte Huber (2018).
4 Art. 9(1)(i) Direct Taxation Harmonization Act of 14 December 1990 (DTHA).
5 Code civil suisse (Droit des fondations), Modification du 8 octobre 2004, RS 4545.
6 Report 2003, p. 7426.
7 Schiesser initiative; Report 2003, pp. 7426–7427.
8 Report 2003, p. 7428.
9 Schiesser Initiative.
10 The reform also introduced changes in the Value Added Tax and Withholding Tax Acts, but they will not be considered in the framework of the present chapter.
11 FR: Commission de l'économie et des redevances.
12 Report 2003, p. 7431.
13 Draft Federal Act, p. 7458 et seq.
14 The consultation procedure is the phase of the preliminary legislative procedure during which federal projects of great political, financial, economic, ecological, social or cultural significance are examined as to whether they are materially correct, feasible and likely to be well accepted. https://www.fedlex.admin.ch/fr/consultation-procedures/explanations-cp access date 15.09.2021. Consultation procedures are defined by the Federal Act on the Consultation Procedure of 18 March 2005 (Consultation Procedure Act, CPA).
15 Federal Council, p. 7467.
16 Federal Council, p. 7467.
17 Federal Council, pp. 7466–7467.
18 Federal Council, p. 7467.
19 Federal Act Modifying CC, p. 4551.
20 In its message, this recognizes the need for rules to establish uniform practice and considers it advisable to provide for an ordinance to this effect. Federal Council, p. 7466.
21 Federal Parliament, deliberation 00.461 Pa. Iv. Schiesser Fritz. Revision of the Law on Foundations Report 2003, p. 7426.
22 Schiesser initiative; also see parliamentary deliberations on Schiesser initiative No. 00.461, p. 1216.

23 Report 2003, p. 7432.
24 Personal Income Tax Act – V (FR: Loi sur l'imposition des personnes physiques (LIPP-V) Détermination du revenu net – Calcul de l'impôt et rabais d'impôt – Compensation des effets de la progression à froid du 22 septembre 2000, D 3 16; in force: 01.01.2001).
25 Personal Income Tax Act of September 27, 2009 (FR: Loi sur l'imposition des personnes physiques du 27 septembre 2009; LIPP; D 3 08, in force: 01.01.2010).
26 Corporate Income Tax Act of September 23, 1994 (FR: Loi sur l'imposition des personnes morales du 23 septembre 1994, D 3 15; in force: 01.01.1995).
27 The authors of this chapter have contacted the Swiss Federal Office of Statistics, Swiss Federal Tax Administration, Swiss Federal Department of Finance and Swiss Federal Audit Office for these purposes. All the sources confirmed that no evaluations were carried out about the efficiency of this tax reform.
28 Federal Bureau of Statistics, regional comparison according to selected criteria, 2020, https://www.bfs.admin.ch/bfs/fr/home/statistiques/statistique-regions/portraits-regionaux-chiffres-cles/cantons.assetdetail.11587764.html access date 04.03.2021.
29 On this topic, also see Chapter 12 of this Handbook, Adena Maja, Tax-price elasticity of charitable donations – evidence from the German taxpayer panel.
30 See Adena et al., 2014.
31 See Adena et al., 2019.
32 Personal Income Tax Bill of the Canton of Geneva of 16.01.2008, PL 10199 https://www.google.com/url?sa=t&rct=j&q=&esrc=s&source=web&cd=&ved=2ahUKEwiB6MClrqHwAhXGsKQKHZ3CCIwQFjABegQIBhAD&url=https%3A%2F%2Fge.ch%2Fgrandconseil%2Fdata%2Ftexte%2FPL10199.pdf&usg=AOvVaw0HcXiLL1mRvpRmQH8HNvVz access date 28.04.2021; Art. 31 Art. 12 par. 1 of the Regulations for the implementation of the law on withholding tax on natural and legal persons of the Canton of Geneva [FR: Reglement d'application de la loi sur l'imposition a la source des personnes physiques et morales (RISP) du 30 September 2020; rsGE D 3 20.01].
33 Information provided by the Canton of Geneva together with the data for the present study.
34 See Chapter 15 of this Handbook, Nicolas J. Duquette/Jennifer Mayo, Who gives and who gets? Tax policy and the long-run distribution of philanthropy in the US.
35 For further developments on this topic, see the chapters of this handbook by Andreoni/Smith, Duquette/ Mayo, Bernardic et al. A study in progress by Lideikyte Huber and Pittavino, to be published in 2022, pursues the analysis of the Canton of Geneva further using a new set of tax data.

Bibliography

Adena, M. Huck, S. Giving once, giving twice: A two-period field experiment on intertemporal crowding in charitable giving, *Journal of Public Economics* 172, 127–134 2019. https://www.sciencedirect.com/science/article/pii/S0047272719300027

Adena, M. Alizade, J. Bohner, F. Harke, J. Mesters, F. Quality certification for nonprofits, charitable giving, and donor's trust: Experimental evidence, *Journal of Economic Behavior & Organization* 159, 75–100 2019

Adena, M. Huck, S. Rasul, I. Charitable giving and nonbinding contribution-level suggestions. Evidence from a field experiment, *Review of Behavioral Economics* 1 2014. https://papers.ssrn.com/sol3/papers.cfm?abstract_id=2407898

Draft Federal Act modifying the Civil Code, the Direct Federal Taxation Act, the Withholding Tax Act and the Federal Act on Value Added Tax (Draft Federal Act), FF 2003 7453 ("Draft Federal Act")

Federal Act of October 8, 2004 modifying the Civil Code, the Direct Federal Taxation Act, the Withholding Tax Act and the Federal Act on Value Added Tax, RO 2005 4545 ("Federal Act Modifying CC")

Freitag, M. Paul C. B. Was uns zusammenhält: Zwischenmenschliches Vertrauen als soziales Kapital in der Schweiz. In: Markus Freitag (dir.): *Das soziale Kapital der Schweiz*. Zurich: Verlag Neue Zürcher Zeitung, pp. 149–179 2016

Lideikyte Huber, G. Philanthropy and taxation: Swiss legal framework and reform perspectives. *Expert Focus* 3 20–24 2018

OECD. *Taxation and Philanthropy*, OECD Tax Policy Studies, No. 27, 2020. Paris: OECD Publishing. https://doi.org/10.1787/df434a77-en (access date 2 March 2021)

Opinion of the Federal Council of December 5, 2003 on the Parliamentary initiative "Revision of the Law on Foundations (Schiesser)" and on the Report of the Committee for Economic Affairs and Taxation of the Council of States of 23 October 2003 (FR: *Avis du Conseil federal – Initiative parlementaire Révision du droit des fondations (Schiesser), Rapport de la Commission de l'économie et des redevances du Conseil des Etats du 23 octobre 2003*)

Parliamentary Initiative No. 00.461 "Revision of the Law on Foundations of 14.12.2000" ("Schiesser initiative") (FR: *Initiative parlementaire No. "Révision de la législation régissant les fondations*"). https://www.parlament.ch/fr/ratsbetrieb/suche-curia-vista/geschaeft?AffairId=20000461 (access date 10 March 2021)

Report of the Economic Affairs and Taxation Committee on the Parliamentary initiative "Reform of the legislation governing foundations" of October 23, 2003), RS 00.461, ("Report 2003")(FR: *Rapport de la Commission de l'économie et des redevances du Conseil des Etats du 23 octobre 2003 Initiative parlementaire " Révision de la législation régissant les fondations*")

State Secretariat for Education, Research and Innovation, "Higher education and research in Switzerland" (FR: Secrétariat d'Etat à la formation, à la recherche et à l'innovation, "L'enseignement supérieur et la recherche en Suisse"). www.sbfi.admin.ch/campus-switzerland-f.html (access date 8 March 2021)

ANNEX 14.1

Summary statistics and related percentages for the number of taxpayers and of deducting taxpayers in the year 2001, by income class categories

Year	*Income class*	*Income (x) class categories (CHF)*	*Number of taxpayers*	*% of taxpayers per year*	*Number of deducting taxpayers*	*% of deducting taxpayers by income class*	*% of deducters among all taxpayers*	*Amount of deductions (CHF)*	*Median deduction by income class*
2001	Low	x <= 22,463	58,532	25.00%	1,220	2.08%	0.52%	395,442	180
	Low-middle	22,463 < x <= 47,743	58,531	25.00%	3,473	5.93%	1.48%	1,733,002	258
	Middle	47,743 < x <= 78,370	58,533	25.00%	5,430	9.28%	2.32%	3,804,624	330
	Middle-high	78,370 < x <= 172,000	46,825	20.00%	6,856	14.64%	2.93%	7,624,170	480
	High	172,000 < x <= 420,000	9,369	4.00%	1,818	19.40%	0.78%	4,100,334	850
	Very high	x > 420,000	2,327	0.99%	538	23.12%	0.23%	11,476,115	2,500
Total			**234,117**	**100.00%**	**19,335**		**8.26%**	**29,133,687**	

ANNEX 14.2

Table showing the summary statistics and related percentages for the number of taxpayers and of deducting taxpayers, in the year 2011, by income class categories

Year	*Income class*	*Income (x) class categories (CHF)*	*Number of taxpayers*	*% of taxpayers per year*	*Number of deducting taxpayers*	*% of deducting taxpayers by income class*	*% of deducters among all taxpayers*	*Amount of deductions (CHF)*	*Median deduction by income class*
2011	Low	x <= 14,419	66,585	25.00%	3,604	5.41%	1.35%	1,552,833	170
	Low-middle	14,419 < x <= 41,791	66,583	25.00%	10,828	16.26%	4.07%	6,337,844	200
	Middle	41,791 < x <= 79,104	66,584	25.00%	15,088	22.66%	5.67%	11,163,680	240
	Middle-high	79,104 < x <= 200,090	53,268	20.00%	17,195	32.28%	6.46%	18,232,544	350
	High	200,090 < x <= 532,200	10,655	4.00%	3,770	35.38%	1.42%	9,014,181	700
	Very high	x > 532,200	2,661	1.00%	1,007	37.84%	0.38%	26,440,153	1,650
Total			**266,336**	**100.00%**	**5,1492**		**19.33%**	**72,741,235**	

15

WHO GIVES AND WHO GETS? TAX POLICY AND THE LONG-RUN DISTRIBUTION OF PHILANTHROPY IN THE UNITED STATES

Nicolas J. Duquette and Jennifer Mayo

1 Introduction

It is commonly believed that giving in the United States is fairly stable. Historically, charitable contributions and philanthropic giving in the United States have remained close to 2% of GDP (Lilly School 2020). This quantitative stability has fed a qualitative sensibility that U.S. charitable giving is a stable, entrenched, and broadly shared civic activity little affected by public policy or social changes.

This chapter provides descriptive evidence that the reality is more complicated. We describe the predictors of charitable and philanthropic donations over time from the perspective of the donors who make the contributions and the charitable organizations that receive those contributions. Over time, that 2% of GDP has come from a very different set of donors, as economic inequality and changes in social structure and demography have remade the distribution of donative behavior.

These changes are reflected in charities' receipts, as giving has shifted away from churches to secular, or at least not solely religious, organizations. By other measures, however, the concentration of public support by size, geography, and mission has been largely stable. Comparing these two pieces of evidence, we infer that while secular charities have not seen a dramatic concentration or redistribution of resources over time, many are increasingly dependent on major donors.

These trends happen in parallel with important policy changes. Over the past 70 years, federal and state tax incentives for giving have favored specific charities and specific donors, which we argue may have contributed to the trends documented here. We conclude with suggested tax reforms to expand the distribution of charitable giving among more U.S. households and a greater diversity of charities.

2 The lopsided donation distribution

Average charitable contributions in the United States have been remarkably stable over time. Figure 15.1 reports the mean contribution of Americans at the personal, tax unit, and household

DOI: 10.4324/9781003139201-18

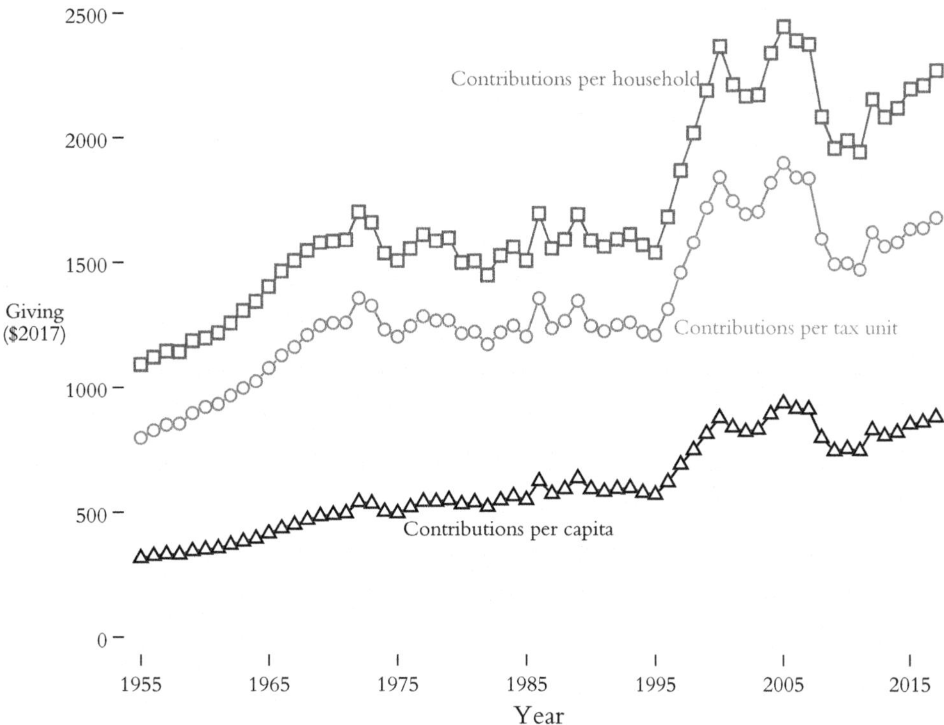

Figure 15.1 Aggregate giving in the United States

levels, calculated as *Giving USA* individual contributions divided by time series counts of those quantities and converted to real (2019) dollars using the Consumer Price Index. Contributions are quite stable over time, rising gradually in real terms over the very long run, with the exception of a more rapid rate of increase during the late 1990s economic boom. From these aggregates alone, it would be easy to conclude that U.S. giving is stable, predictable, and steadily increasing without cause for concern.

This apparent stability conceals important shifts in the distribution of giving activity. While scholars typically think of U.S. giving and philanthropy as a civic culture with wide participation, giving activity has become increasingly concentrated over the past 60 years. Figure 15.2 plots the share of giving by living Americans accounted for by the itemized contributions of the tax units who claim the most giving.[1] These shares are computed from publicly available Internal Revenue Service (IRS) cross-sectional data for available years 1960 to 2012.[2] These calculations show a rapid increase in the share of giving made by the top donors. In 1960, the top 1% of tax units made 18.9% of all charitable contributions from living individual donors. By 2012, this share had more than doubled to 43.5%.

This concentration is difficult to explain. Over this period, income has grown more concentrated, which likely accounts for a significant portion of the concentration of philanthropy. However, even the highest estimates of increased income inequality would imply a less steep increase than this rapid consolidation of giving into relatively few tax returns. It is likely that other social forces, such as the changing demography of the United States, also explain changes in who gives and how much they give.

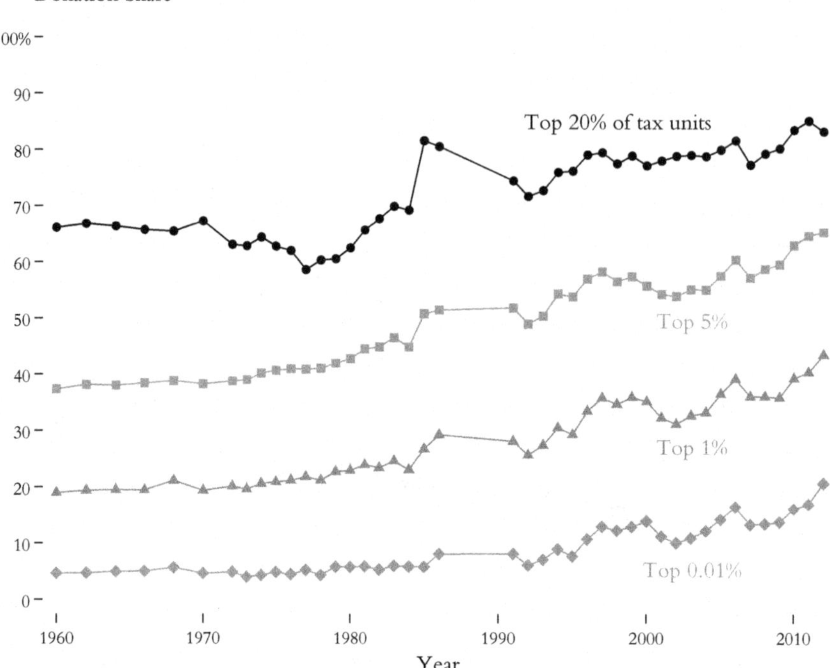

Figure 15.2 Top donors' share of annual giving

2.1 Income inequality

One plausible contributor to changes in the distribution of giving might be greater concentration of incomes in the United States over the same period. Rising concentration of income might mechanically increase concentration of giving to the extent that people give the same share of their incomes, but incomes are increasingly concentrated in a few top earners. A burgeoning literature quantifies economic inequality in the United States and finds, to varying degrees, an increase in inequality in recent years.[3]

The potential contributions of income shifts to giving are shown in Figure 15.3, which plots the average inflation-adjusted fiscal incomes of top donors over time.[4] The vertical axis is on a log scale, which both makes slopes interpretable as exponential growth rates and the large differences between series visible. The top 0.01% of tax units ranked by giving have very high incomes, consistently over $1 million in 2012 dollars over the period and then rising rapidly to over $8 million in 2012.

However, income concentration is unlikely to explain all of the observed concentration of giving among U.S. tax units. We can see this by comparing the 1% of returns with the highest charitable contributions to those with the highest reported incomes. Figure 15.4 compares the share of charitable contributions made by the top 1% and 0.01% of donors to the shares of giving made by the equivalent fractiles by reported income. Shaded areas show the difference in giving shares between each top-fractile group.

Over time, the top earners account for a greater share of overall charitable giving. However, there is a substantial amount of donor concentration above and beyond what is visible in the rising giving share of the top earners. In 1960, the giving share of top earners was very close to

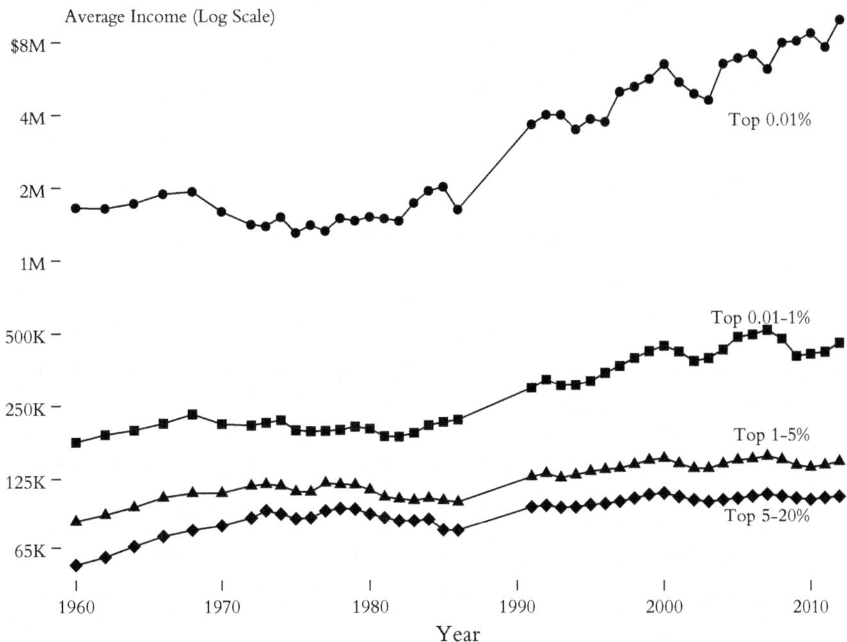

Figure 15.3 Incomes of top donors

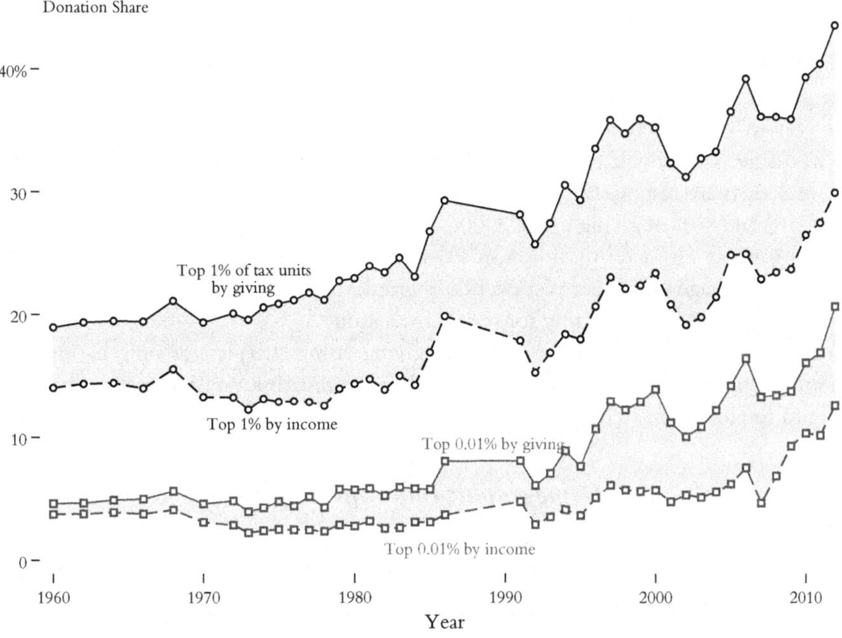

Figure 15.4 Top giving shares of top earners vs top donors

the share of the top givers, but over time, the two groups diverged substantially. The top 0.01% of *givers* provided 4.6% of giving in 1960, whereas the top 0.01% of *earners* were responsible for 3.7%, a gap of about one percentage point. By 2012, when the top 0.01% of givers were responsible for 20.6% of giving, the top 0.01% of earners gave 12.6%, a gap of 8.0 percentage points. The growth of the gap between the top 1% of earners and donors is less striking, but it is still substantial, going from about 5 percentage points in 1960 to about 14 percentage points in 2012.

This may be expected simply because the concentration of giving has risen more quickly than even the most extreme estimates of changes in income inequality. The Piketty and Saez (2003) estimates of changes in fiscal income report a steep rise in income concentration of the top 1% from 8.4% in 1960 to 18.9% in 2012, but this increase is not as large as the increase in giving. Moreover, Piketty and Saez's use of fiscal income from tax units likely overstates the degree of income concentration over this period; other inequality research that accounts for mechanical changes in inequality caused by the relationship between tax units and changing marital norms, as well as broader definitions of income not including those not reported on Form 1040, show much less dramatic increases.[5] While top income groups are giving a greater share of all individual contributions than before thanks to their higher income shares, this alone does not fully explain the rising concentration of giving.

As a final investigation into the relationship between income inequality and donor concentration, we examine the concentration within consistently defined high-income groups. If giving had become more concentrated solely because of changes in the distribution of income, then the concentration of giving within a set of similar tax units should not rise over time. We compute the concentration of giving within consistently defined high-income tax returns over the period 1960–2012. To do so, we restrict each year's data set to tax returns that are married filing jointly and within 20% of a target income level after adjusting for inflation to year-2012 dollars using the Consumer Price Index. We then compute the share of itemized contributions made by the top 1% of donors within each group each year. The income targets presented are real incomes of $1 million, $2 million, and $5 million. The top donor shares within these high-income groups are presented in Figure 15.5.

The year-to-year differences in the top donor shares within these groups are noisy, but the trend over time is unmistakably upward. Within each of the three high-income groups, the top 1% of donors are responsible for roughly 10% of giving through the 1960s, rising to shares between 20% and 40% of giving in the 2000s. A simple pooled regression of these top 1% shares on a trend variable estimates that the top 1% share within high-income groups has increased about 0.42 percentage points per year over this period; this estimate is statistically different from zero at the 5% level after correcting for serial correlation.

With the concentration of U.S. charitable giving rising sharply not only nationwide but within groups of similar incomes, other factors than the distribution of resources must be contributing to the long-run trend.

2.2 Demographic shifts affecting giving

Other trends have shaped the nature of giving beyond the distribution of resources. The demography of the United States has changed greatly since 1960, as families have grown smaller, the population has become older and more diverse, and gender and marital norms have shifted.

We consider the demographic information inferable from tax returns in Table 15.1. This reports the share of returns that report legal marriage status, that claim dependent children, and that report social security income (which proxies for being retirement age). We present shares for

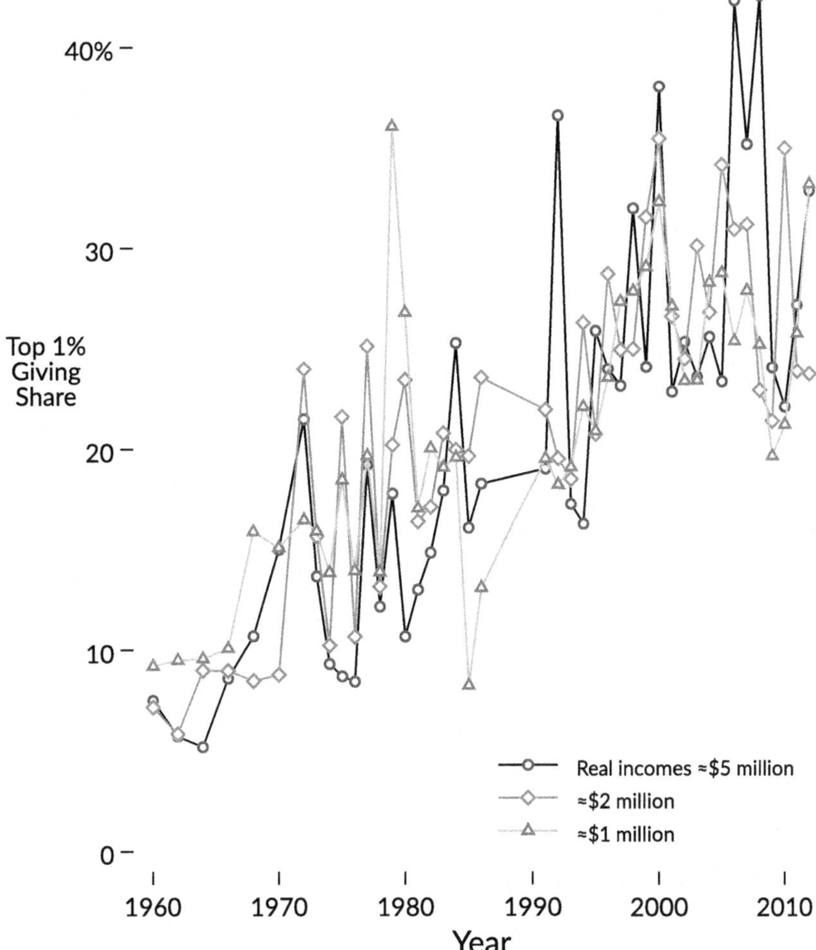

Figure 15.5 Top 1% donor share within high-income groups

1960 (the first year of tax return microdata), 1970 (the first year of data on children), 1984 (the first year of Social Security reporting), 1995, and 2012 (the last data year). For each variable and year, we report shares for "Top Givers," or those with itemized contributions in the top 1% of giving for all tax units, and "Other Filers," or tax filers not among the top givers (regardless of whether they itemized or took the standard deduction but excluding nonfilers). The final column presents the difference in percentage points between the first observed year and 2012, and the row below each variable group reports differences between top givers and other filers within each year.

It is clear that top givers and other filers are not alike and that these demographic differences between top givers and others change over time. All mean differences reported in Table 15.1 are statistically different from zero under a two-sided *t*-test with *p*-value less than 0.1%. The magnitudes of the differences are striking as well.

From 1960 to 2012, top donors' marriage rates are consistently high, declining by just over five percentage points, from about 89% to about 84%. Other filers' marriage rates are lower, and they drop much faster, from 64% in 1960 to just 39% in 2012. To the extent that it is necessary

Table 15.1 Demographics

	Share of filed 1040 returns					
	1960	*1970*	*1984*	*1995*	*2012*	*Change over span*
Is married						
Top givers	88.7%	87.9%	88.7%	84.3%	83.5%	−5.3 % pts
Other filers	64.3	59.8	48.2	43.3	38.5	−23.8
Difference	24.4	28.1	40.5	41.1	45.0	
Have children						
Top givers		59.3	52.7	47.1	39.6	−19.7
Other filers		42.5	37.8	35.3	32.8	−9.7
Difference		16.8	14.9	11.9	6.8	
Have Social Security income						
Top givers			17.9	22.9	30.2	+12.3
Other filers			7.2	8.6	18.1	+10.9
Difference			10.7	14.3	12.1	

Sources: Tax return micro data from Internal Revenue Service (2018); total tax units by year taken from the updated data files of Piketty and Saez (2003)

Notes: All variables are weighted by sampling weight. Reported mean differences within groups over time and within time across groups are all different from zero, with p-value < 0.001. "Top givers" are the 1% of tax units making the largest itemized charitable contributions. "Other filers" are all filed tax returns excluding the top givers. "Is married" is the percentage of each sample with a married filing status (joint or separate). "Have children" is the share of returns with children. "Have Social Security income" is the share of returns reporting social security income.

for most people willing to make large gifts to first feel economically and personally established, this differential in marriage rates may explain the greater share of the top givers, because the "long tail" of middle-income donors may have dwindled over time.[6]

Other differences between top givers and the general population are less dramatic than the differential marriage trends. The shares of both top givers and other filers with children decline over time, although top givers are consistently more likely to have children, with a larger decline over the period 1970–2012, narrowing the gap between these groups. Top givers are more likely to have a retirement-age person in the home than other filers in all years, with the share of both groups reporting social security income growing by about 10 percentage points over the observation period.

Although tax returns provide only limited data about donor demography, the evidence suggests that changes in marriage patterns are likely related to changes in the distribution of giving. In recent decades, American households have seen a bifurcation of household finances: lower-income people have married less and divorced more, whereas high-income households have become more likely to be two-income, dual-professional households who may give differently than a breadwinner-homemaker pair (Putnam 2000, 2016; Einolf et al. 2018). These speculations cannot be confirmed by tax return data alone, but the demographic information available suggests substantial changes in the distribution of marriage that are strongly correlated with giving behavior.

2.3 Giving according to charities' reported receipts

We can next examine whether the lopsidedness of individual giving is reflected in charities' reported receipts. Figure 15.6 plots the share of public support for 501(c)(3) charities according to the receipts of those that report the most. These shares are computed from publicly available

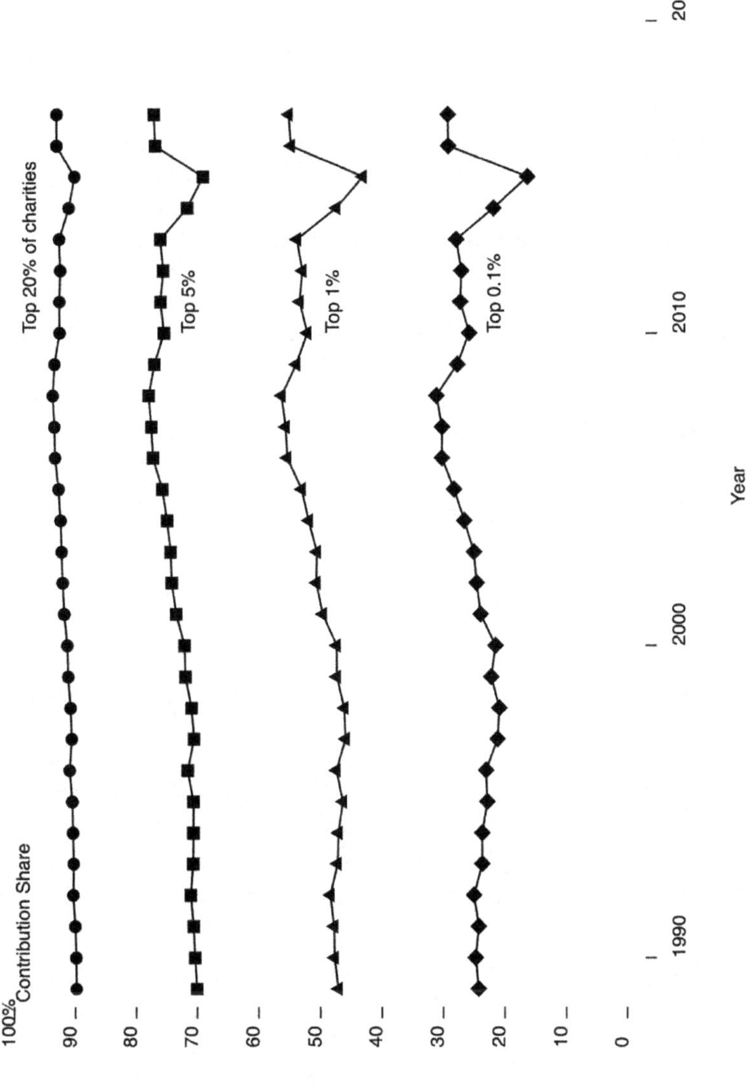

Figure 15.6 Top charities' share of public support

IRS Form 990 data for the years 1989 to 2017, where public support is defined as the sum of contributions, gifts, and grants. Specifically, public support from Form 990 data is rank-ordered and then summed to estimate total public support by top fractile. Unlike individual giving, the figure depicts the share of public support going to the top charities as being fairly flat across the period. The share going to the top 1% of charities remained below 50% throughout the 1990s before peaking at 56% around the Great Recession and then falling back down.

This pattern is in stark contrast to the distribution of individual giving, as although public support is fairly concentrated among the top fractiles, it has not become increasingly so. The divergence with the distribution of individual giving is somewhat of a puzzle.

One possible explanation is that the concentration in individual giving in fact reflects the decline in small-dollar donors. These types of donations are disproportionately religious tithes and can be linked to the growing secularization of giving. Figure 15.7 uses *Giving USA* data to plot real giving per household to religious and non-religious causes from 1967 to 2019. It depicts a steep rise in non-religious giving in the mid-1990s. In particular, real average giving to religious groups has remained fairly stable at around \$1000 per household, while giving to non-religious organizations has more than doubled, from \$1000 to \$2500 per household. While both religious and non-religious giving is recorded in 1040 data, only non-religious organizations are required to file an IRS Form 990 (religious organizations are exempt).[7] This difference in filing requirements means that any disappearance in small-dollar religious donors would be reflected in individual giving but not 990-filing charities' reported receipts. Of course, this hypothesis can only be tested with donor-level data, but it offers a possible explanation.

Another possible explanation is that the discrepancy is due to the distribution of big gifts across charities over time. Very large gifts from wealthy donors are rare events for the individual

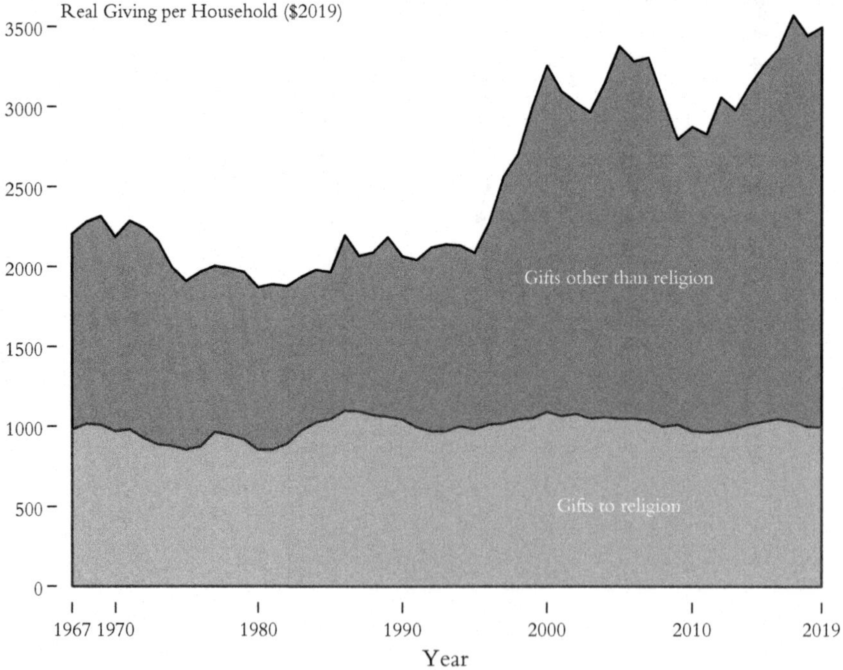

Figure 15.7 Giving USA gifts to religion and others

but not necessarily for the recipient. For example, one individual's $1 million donation to Harvard University would likely represent an outlier relative to that donor's other giving, as well as to other donors, but is not necessarily an outlier for Harvard. In other words, mega-donations are lumpy for the individual but not for the recipient, whose receipts relative to other charities have much lower variance. This means that the increasing number of big gifts would affect the concentration of individual giving but not necessarily the distribution of charities' receipts.

It is further possible that the composition of public support is changing. Form 990 public support, unlike 1040 giving, includes government grantmaking, foundation grants, and transfers from other public charities such as United Way. Figure 15.8 shows that public support and itemized contributions have evolved differently. Prior to 2005, 1040 giving exceeded Form 990 public support; however, that pattern has since reversed, with the latter continuing to rise, while itemized giving has remained fairly flat. This is likely due to the differing composition of 1040 and 990 totals. In particular, 1040 giving includes some components, such as religious giving, that are not included in Form 990 totals. However, given the secularization of giving, as well as the rise in foundation grants (which are not included in 1040 giving), it is unsurprising that Form 990 receipts have overtaken itemized contributions.

We conclude this discussion by looking at the distribution of 990 public support along other dimensions; compared to the dramatic changes in the distribution of Form 1040 contributions among U.S. tax units, Form 990 distributional statistics are remarkably stable.

Figure 15.9 uses Form 990 data to plot the share of public support by sector according to reported receipts for the period 1989 to 2017.[8] Throughout the period, education remained the sector with the largest share of public support, although this share has steadily declined. Human services remained the second-largest sector and was one of the few to see a rising share of public support during the Great Recession. According to a report by Reich and Wimer (2012), contributions to food banks increased from around $1.2 billion in 2007 and 2008 to just under $1.6 billion in 2009. Health-related charities form the third largest sector, with public support remaining fairly flat at around 10% throughout the period. Support for private grantmaking was flat throughout the 1990s and fell during the Great Recession but has climbed in recent years. Arts, culture, and humanities charities have experienced a gradual decline in support since the beginning of the period.

Finally, Figure 15.10 plots the share of public support for charities located in the five largest U.S. cities from 1989 to 2017. These shares are computed from 990 data, where charity location does not necessary reflect service area. For example, many charities are headquartered in New York City but in fact provide services across the country or world. Nevertheless, the share of public support for New York-based charities declined from around 11% in 1991 to 6% in 2014, although this trend has reversed in the most recent years. The remaining cities – Chicago, Los Angeles, Houston, and Phoenix – have maintained a fairly constant share of public support, with Chicago averaging 2.2% and Los Angeles 1.8%.

In summary, while U.S. philanthropic giving has become concentrated in a small share of U.S. tax units, 990-filing charities have not seen a similar concentration across charities. Some of this is likely explained by a shift of giving from non-990 charities favored by smaller donors to 990 charities favored by large donors (specifically, the proportional shift of giving from churches to other causes). But much of this also likely reflects a concentration of donors within the average charity, a trend that cannot be observed in the 990 data but which is consistent with the philanthropy trade press's coverage of major-gifts fundraising. For example, the May 2018 issue of the *Chronicle of Philanthropy* included new and republished articles with titles like "4 Ways to Ask Major Donors for Big Gifts" and "How to Make the Most of Your Meetings with Big Donors." Journal articles have also emphasized the need for special, highly personal strategies

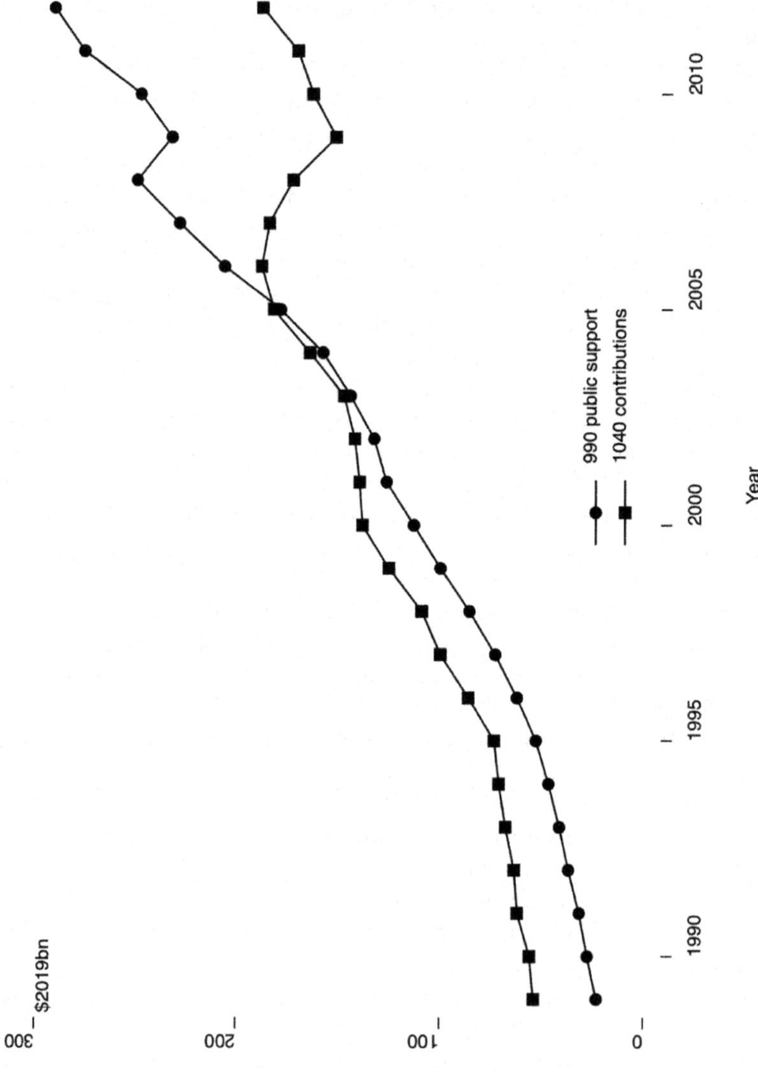

Figure 15.8 990 public support versus 1040 giving

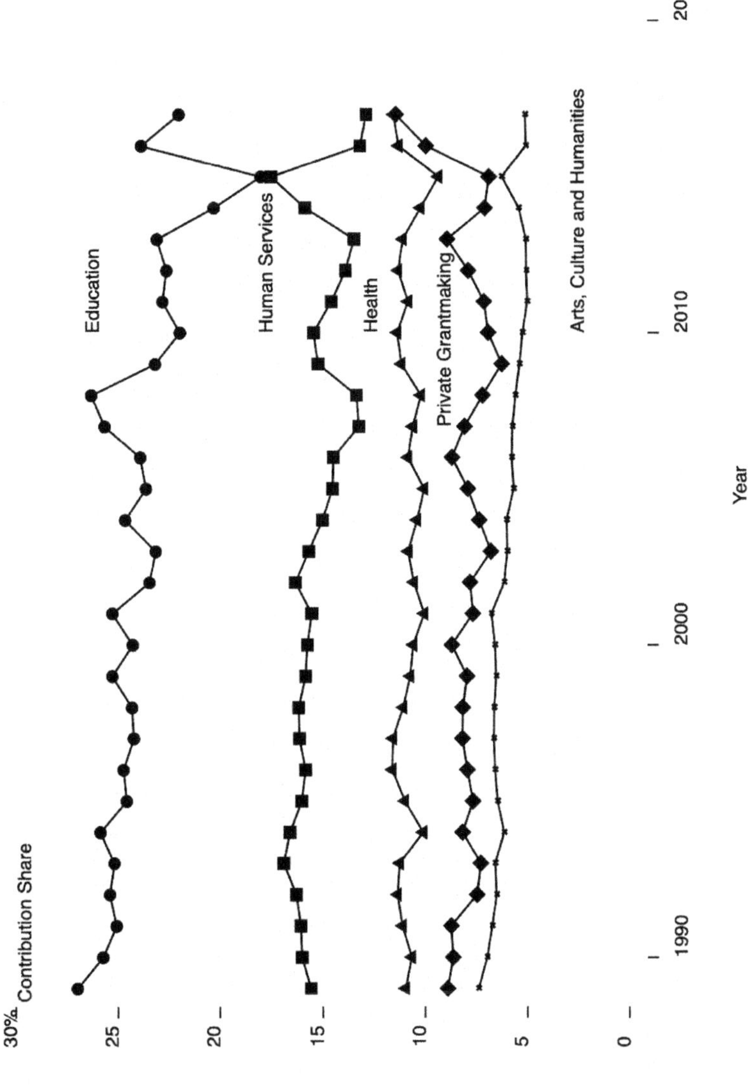

Figure 15.9 Share of public support by sector

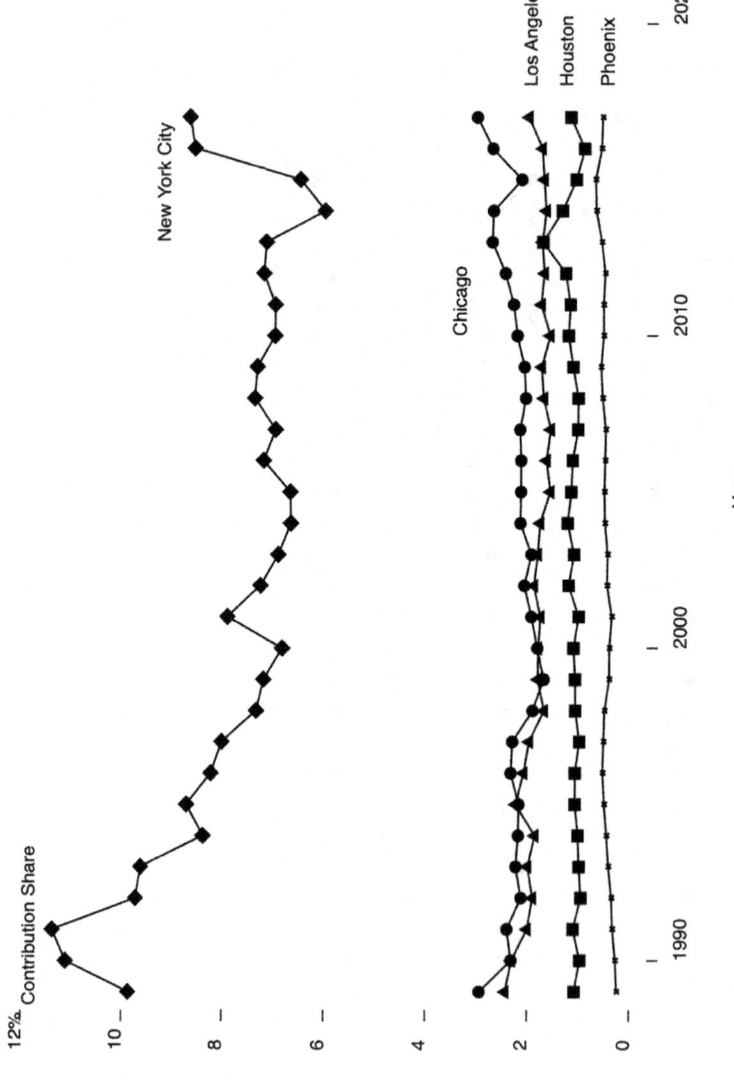

Figure 15.10 Share of public support by city

to cultivate large-dollar donors – which is necessarily more labor intensive per donor than mass fundraising (see, for example, Waters 2010; McLoughlin 2017; Drollinger 2018). The upshot: a large number of charities are likely more dependent on a shrinking number of donors to maintain stable public support revenues. In our final section, we consider the role of tax policy in this rising donor concentration.

3 Tax policy and the distribution of giving

Tax policy in the United States has a thoroughly studied incentive effect on philanthropy,[9] but those effects are not uniform across donors or across charities. In many instances, they have actively encouraged the trends described in this chapter or have ineffectively forgone tax revenue to little effect.

3.1 Tax policy affects the giving distribution

Tax incentives for philanthropy are especially valuable to high-income, high-wealth households, who deduct against high marginal rates and who are likely to get the most tax savings from the ability to avoid capital gains tax on donation of appreciated assets.[10] This is a deliberate policy choice; at times when reform of the federal contribution deduction has been considered, policy changes to reduce the deduction's value to wealthy donors (such as the appreciated asset double-benefit) have often not become law, while those that do benefit these donors (such as increases to the maximum adjusted gross income (AGI) that may be donated) often have (Duquette 2019b).[11]

In recent years, the AGI limitation on giving has increased twice; the 2017 tax reform raised the ceiling on the deductible share of AGI from 50 to 60% for cash gifts, while the 2020 CARES Act temporarily raised the limit to 100%. Though few donors give such large shares of their income away, there is a tiny minority of high-wealth households who make up a disproportionate share of contributions, and these tax changes are likely to have an observable effect on their giving decisions (Duquette 2019a) and on the spillovers to rival charities (Mayo, 2021).[12]

Changes in tax policy and the distribution also affect bequests to charity at death. While bequests are largely excluded from taxation at death, tax policy has not always been changed to encourage giving by bequest. The reduction in the top estate tax rate, coupled with the increase in the exemption from $600,000 in 1997 to $11.8 million in 2020, has reduced the appeal of tax-motivated charitable bequests by wealthy households. Notably, incentives for "giving while living" strictly dominate the bequest deduction from the estate tax itself, since money given away while alive is also no longer part of a future taxable estate (Joulfaian 2001).

At the state level, states offer both deductions modeled after the federal deduction, as well as targeted, often extremely generous credits supporting particular charity types. The state deductions appear to have donation elasticities comparable to the federal deduction (Bakija and Heim 2011). It is unclear whether state credits, which are narrowly targeted and often subject to low caps on deductible amounts, have a similar effect (Feldman and Hines 2003; Teles 2016; Duquette et al. 2018; Hungerman and Ottoni-Wilhelm 2018).

3.2 Policy changes to broaden giving

We recommend three policy changes to bolster policy effectiveness of tax subsidies for charitable contributions. These would expand the pool of potential donors, increase dollars given, and increase confidence in the nonprofit sector while controlling the cost of charitable contribution tax expenditures.

First, the federal itemized deduction could be replaced with a nonrefundable credit with a subsidy rate tied to the share of adjusted gross income donated, not marginal tax rate. Such a policy could expand tax subsidies for giving to all households with income tax liability (not just itemizers) and substantially increase total donations with little or no cost to tax expenditures (Duquette 2020). The 2020 CARES Act created a time-limited deduction for non-itemizers' cash donations up to \$300,[13] but this incentive is unlikely to have a large effect on giving relative to its tax cost; as this chapter has shown, giving is highly skewed, and donors who give more than \$300/year will have no marginal tax incentive to give more. An incentive with a floor or tiered rate to encourage last-dollar instead of first-dollar giving would be more efficient.

Second, we call for an overhaul of regulations governing the reporting of charitable contributions. The current compliance and reporting regime is open to manipulation and low-scale tax evasion. For example, the \$500 allowance for deduction of noncash gifts without documentation is widely abused (Tazhitdinova 2018). The United States should require non-public lists of donations linked to tax identifiers from charities, mandate information reporting of donor identities and in- and outflows from donor-advised funds, and expand the required filing of the Form 990 or similar to all organizations allowed to receive deductible contributions.

Third, we argue that charitable contributions for a given tax year should be allowed until the mid-April filing deadline for personal income tax returns in the following year, as is currently allowed for contributions to an individual retirement account. This would improve the effectiveness of the existing incentives in two ways: first, the time horizon for tax savings from charitable giving would be shortened from months to weeks or less and for many donors would be near immediate.[14] Second, such a policy would allow prospective donors to calculate their marginal tax rates before deciding how much to give. Relative to existing policy, these changes would give tax-motivated donors higher certainty and a timelier incentive without having to increase the generosity of tax expenditures per dollar given. This information would be especially valuable to middle-tier donors who in December would be unsure about whether they will be claiming the itemized deduction (and so have a tax incentive to donate) or the standard deduction (and so have no tax benefit for a modest contribution).

All of these reforms would have the potential to broaden access to tax incentives for giving, improve their effectiveness, and streamline their use. A two-tier tax credit instead of an itemized deduction would expand access to preferential tax treatment and link subsidy rates to the share of income given, not tax bracket. Better information reporting would increase confidence in charities and decrease scope for tax evasion. And a mid-April deadline would let middle-income donors have important information about their tax status before deciding whether and how much to give.

Notes

1 "Tax units" are a slightly cumbersome demographic unit corresponding to tax returns and return-equivalents who do not file. There are fewer tax units than people but more tax units than households (since cohabiting adults filing separately are one household but more than one tax unit).

2 Series taken from Duquette (2021), which explains the calculation of giving share ratios in detail. In brief, itemized contributions from tax return data are rank-ordered and then summed to estimate total giving by top-giving fractile (Internal Revenue Service 2018). The denominator is taken from *Giving USA* estimates of total individual charitable contributions (Lilly Family School of Philanthropy, Indiana University/IUPUI 2020). Some years within the 1960–2012 range are not calculated due to

data limitations or availability, and years after 2012 are not calculated because of the long lag in IRS distribution of new microdata.

3 Some of these estimates of income distribution statistics find very steep increases in U.S. income inequality since the middle 20th century (Piketty et al. 2018; Piketty and Saez 2003). Other methods find a substantially more modest increase, for example, Auten and Splinter (2019).

4 Since these calculations are made using Form 1040 data, income is measured and ranked using the Piketty and Saez (2003) measure of "fiscal income," which is observed in tax returns over time but which omits important income sources that are not reported (such as retained corporate profits) or observed inconsistently (such as Social Security income) or endogenously (such as realized capital gains).

5 See discussions in Auten and Splinter (2019) and Piketty et al. (2018).

6 Additionally, the large differential in trends in marriage rates means that the increasing share of contributions accounted for by the top donors is likely overestimated for mechanical reasons. Because top donor shares are computed as a share of tax units, and because a married couple represents one tax unit whereas an unmarried couple represents two, falling marriage rates among other filers will increase the number of tax units whose giving is summed to compute the top donor share relative to a world where marriage rates were constant across time and groups (see discussion in Auten and Splinter 2019). In the context of giving, average gifts within top donor tiers, which will be biased *downward* for the same mechanical reason, nevertheless show a dramatic rise over this period, suggesting that mechanical differences from changes in the composition of tax units are secondary to this broader trend (see Duquette 2021, Figure 3).

7 Organizations file the 990 if they are 501(c)3 public charities with at least $50,000 in revenue and are not churches or other houses of worship. Organizations eligible to receive tax-deductible contributions that do not file a Form 990 include private foundations (which file the Form 990-PF), low-revenue organizations, churches and other houses of worship, and governmental organizations such as public universities. Religiously affiliated charities that are not primarily religious, such as Catholic universities, do file the Form 990.

8 Sector is defined according to the National Taxonomy of Exempt Entities classification system. For a full list, see https://nccs.urban.org/publication/irs-activity-codes.

9 See OECD (2020) for a description of the tax treatment of giving across OECD countries.

10 For a broader discussion on the tax incentives for giving, see Steinberg (2021) and Lideikyte Huber et al. (2021).

11 When appreciated assets are given to qualifying organizations, donors can deduct the fair market value of the asset without first recognizing their capital gains for tax purposes, avoiding the income taxes on both the gains and on the market value's worth of income. Because of this double benefit for giving appreciated assets, there have been periods in American history when it was theoretically possible for very high-income households to wind up with more money by donating highly appreciated assets than liquidating the asset and consuming the after-tax proceeds (Duquette 2019a).

12 These increases may also change reported giving to the extent that giving in excess of the threshold may not be reported by donors on tax returns. Over the 1960–2012 period reported in most of the figures in this chapter, the AGI limitation was increased twice, in 1964 and 1969. Data for years 1987–1990 are not reported because the IRS public use data censors giving at the AGI limitation, creating a significant downward bias.

13 Internal Revenue Service, November 2020, "Special $300 tax deduction helps most people give to charity this year – even if they don't itemize." Press release. https://www.irs.gov/newsroom/special-300-tax-deduction-helps-most-people-give-to-charity-this-year-even-if-they-dont-itemize

14 Hickey et al. (2019) find that moving the timing of reporting of gifts closer to the timing of giving increases average donations by 9 percentage points.

References

Auten, G. E. and Splinter, D. (2019). *Income inequality in the United States: Using tax data to measure long-term trends*. Mimeo. http://davidsplinter.com/AutenSplinter-Tax_Data_and_Inequality.pdf.

Bakija, J. and Heim, B. (2011). How does charitable giving respond to incentives and income? New estimates from panel data. *National Tax Journal*, 64(2):615–650.

Drollinger, T. (2018). Using active empathetic listening to build relationships with major-gift donors. *Journal of Nonprofit & Public Sector Marketing*, 30(1):37–51.

Duquette, N. J. (2019a). Founders' fortunes and philanthropy: A history of the US charitable contribution deduction. *Business History Review*, 93(3):553–584.

Duquette, N. J. (2019b). Do share-of-income limits on tax-deductibility of charitable contributions matter for charitable giving? *Economics Letters*, 174:1–4.

Duquette, N. J. (2021). The evolving distribution of giving in the United States. *Nonprofit and Voluntary Sector Quarterly*, 50(5):1102–1116.

Duquette, N. J. (2020). A two-tiered charitable contribution credit for all American taxpayers. *Nonprofit Policy Forum*, 11(4), December.

Duquette, N. J., Graddy-Reed, A. and Phillips, M. D. (2018). *The extent and efficacy of state charitable contribution income tax credits*. Mimeo. http://www.nicolasduquette.com/research.html.

Einolf, C. J., Curran, H. D. and Brown, K. C. (2018). How married couples make charitable giving decisions. *Nonprofit and Voluntary Sector Quarterly*, 47(3):657–669.

Feldman, N. E. and Hines, Jr., J. R. (2003). *Tax credits and charitable contributions in Michigan*. University of Michigan, Office of Tax Policy Research Working Paper Series, no. 2007-3. Ann Arbor: University of Michigan.

Hickey, R., Minaker, B. and Payne, A. A. (2019). The sensitivity of charitable giving to the timing and salience of tax credits. *National Tax Journal*, 72(1):79–110.

Hungerman, D. M. and Ottoni-Wilhelm, M. (2018). *Impure impact giving: Theory and evidence*. Working Paper 24940. Washington, DC: National Bureau of Economic Research.

Internal Revenue Service (2018). *Individual public use tax file*. Statistics of Income Division, Data File. Years 1960–2012. Washington, DC: National Bureau of Economic Research.

Joulfaian, D. (2001). Charitable giving in life and at death. In Gale, W. G., James R. Hines, Jr., and Slemrod, J., editors, *Rethinking estate and gift taxation*, chapter 8, pages 350–369. Washington, DC: The Brookings Institution.

Lideikyte Huber, G., Peter, H. and Pittavino, M. (2021). Efficiency of tax incentives for charitable giving: Evidence from Switzerland. In Lideikyte Huber, G. and Peter, H., editors, *The Routledge handbook of taxation and philanthropy*, chapter C. London: Routledge.

Lilly Family School of Philanthropy, Indiana University/IUPUI (2020). *Giving USA 2020: The Annual report on philanthropy for the year 2019*. New York: Giving USA Foundation.

Mayo, J. (2021). How do big gifts affect rival charities and their donors. *Journal of Economic Behavior and Organization*, 191: 575–597.

McLoughlin, J. (2017). Advantage, meaning, and pleasure: Reframing the interaction between major-gift fundraisers and philanthropists. *International Journal of Nonprofit and Voluntary Sector Marketing*, 22(4):e1600.

OECD (2020). *Taxation and philanthropy*. OECD Tax Policy Studies, No. 27. Paris: OECD Publishing.

Piketty, T. and Saez, E. (2003). Income inequality in the United States, 1913–1998. *Quarterly Journal of Economics*, 118(1):1–41.

Piketty, T., Saez, E. and Zucman, G. (2018). Distributional national accounts: Methods and estimates for the United States. *Quarterly Journal of Economics*, 133(2):553–609.

Putnam, R. D. (2000). *Bowling alone: The collapse and revival of American community*. New York: Simon & Schuster.

Putnam, R. D. (2016). *Our kids: The American dream in crisis*. New York: Simon and Schuster.

Reich, R. and Wimer, C. (2012). Charitable giving and the great recession. *Nonprofit Management & Leadership*, 13(4):383–399.

Steinberg, R. (2021). The design of tax incentives for giving. In Lideikyte Huber, G. and Peter, H., editors, *The Routledge Handbook of Taxation and Philanthropy*, chapter C. London: Routledge.

Tazhitdinova, A. (2018). Reducing evasion through self-reporting: Evidence from charitable contributions. *Journal of Public Economics*, 165:31–47.

Teles, D. (2016). *Do tax credits increase charitable giving? Evidence from Arizona and Iowa*. Tulane Economics Working Paper 1606. http://repec.tulane.edu/RePEc/pdf/tul1606.pdf.

Waters, R. D. (2010). Increasing fundraising efficiency through evaluation: Applying communication theory to the nonprofit organization – donor relationship. *Nonprofit and Voluntary Sector Quarterly*, 40(3):458–475.

16

ALIGNING TAX INCENTIVES WITH MOTIVATIONS FOR PHILANTHROPY

Insights from psychology and neuroscience

Jo Cutler

Introduction

Tax incentives for philanthropy aim to increase the positive impacts of charitable activities, in some cases by promoting individual donations. There are many conceivable types of tax incentive to achieve this, and they differ in important ways. A vital component in determining the efficacy of each is the extent to which tax incentives increase the likelihood and size of philanthropic donations. Research addressing these questions has traditionally been concentrated within the fields of economics and public policy. However, alongside this progress, much work has been conducted in psychology and neuroscience to understand motivations for prosocial behaviour – actions to help other people – generally, and charitable giving specifically. There is also increasing recognition that psychological concepts, for example, wellbeing and happiness, may be critical in promoting philanthropy (Sellen 2021) and that the efficiency of government incentives cannot be quantified without taking into account citizens' responses to those incentives (Steinberg 2021). Research has also identified different responses to functionally equivalent subsidies (Eckel and Grossman 2003) and differences between individuals' responses to tax incentives (Lideikyte Huber 2020). These findings suggest that factors other than objective economic value are important for understanding philanthropy and the role of tax incentives. Here, I provide a review of the literature from psychology and neuroscience, tailored to be applicable to tax incentives and with a focus on gifts of money made by individuals. Only by understanding *why* people are philanthropic can the alignment of tax incentives with these motivations be assessed.

Studies on charitable giving in psychology and neuroscience constitute a subsection of research on prosocial decision-making, a specific application of research on decision-making generally. At this most general level, research identifies the costs and benefits associated with the different choice options and how these are integrated in value calculations in order to make a decision (Croxson *et al.* 2009). Value can be defined as the importance, worth, or usefulness of something and the process of estimating this. The idea of subjective value differentiates experienced desirability from objective worth (Peters and Büchel 2010). For example, the value of food changes depending on how much one has already eaten. In the context of philanthropy, choosing to donate suggests the total subjective value of this option is greater than the value of

 DOI: 10.4324/9781003139201-19

not donating. A comprehensive review of the literature on charitable giving identified psychological benefits as well as overall costs and benefits as some of the key mechanisms that drive giving (Bekkers and Wiepking 2010). As charitable giving is defined by giving away money, the subjective benefits must outweigh these costs.

From this perspective, tax incentives that aim to increase the frequency or levels of philanthropic giving must increase the subjective benefits or decrease the (subjective) costs of donating. These incentives will be efficient if they promote an increase in giving that is greater than the objective cost of the incentive to the government. The psychological or subjective benefits of philanthropic decisions can also be conceptualised as motivations for philanthropy and can be classified in different ways. In reality, it is likely that multiple motivations work together, even within a single decision. However, separating different motivations is necessary to understand and assess the possible motivations. Psychology and neuroscience can offer insight into different motivations for giving, how these can be increased or decreased, and how they may differ between individuals. Before outlining two distinctions between motivations for philanthropy that relate to tax incentives, I first give an overview of the methods used in the relevant psychology and neuroscience research.

Methods from psychology and neuroscience

Behavioural experiments

Perhaps the most obvious way to evaluate motivations for philanthropy is to ask people why they give. This can be done through questionnaires or scales quantifying different motivations (Konrath and Handy 2018) or qualitative interviews (Breeze 2013). While these approaches provide detailed information about donors' understanding of their own motivations, they cannot provide the experimental manipulations of motivations that are required to conclude a causal effect on giving. Behavioural experiments that provide these manipulations therefore offer a complementary approach to self-report and interview methods.

A large body of literature in experimental psychology and behavioural economics measures participants' decisions to give away or keep money in different contexts. Many of these studies use economic games such as the dictator game, ultimatum game, trust game, or public goods game. The dictator game is the most relevant to many forms of charitable giving. Participants in these studies are endowed with a certain amount of money and have the opportunity to give some or all of it away (Kahneman *et al.* 1986). The recipient can be another person or a charity. In the ultimatum game, the participant again receives an amount of money and has to decide whether to give some away, but now the recipient can decide whether to accept the offer or reject it, leaving both them and the participant who made the offer with nothing (Güth *et al.* 1982). Participants in the trust game endowed with money must decide what amount, if any, to 'invest' in another person. The recipient then receives the invested amount multiplied, for example, tripled, and has the opportunity to repay the participant by returning some of this amount (Berg *et al.* 1995). The ultimatum and trust games are used to study prosocial behaviours motivated by fairness, equity, and reciprocity, as well as responses to violations of these principles. Finally, the public goods game approximates contributions to a cause that the donor also benefits from. Groups of participants all receive an endowment and decide how much to contribute into a group fund or 'pot'. This amount is often multiplied, for example, by 1.25, to incentivise contributions, then equally divided between all group members, regardless of contribution (Rapoport and Chammah 1965). The greatest public good is therefore achieved by all participants contributing the full amount, but the greatest individual gain results from keeping one's own money and 'free riding' on others' contributions. These games all measure decisions to give money away, but by introducing different potential benefits, they create different motivations.

Within these economic games, additional manipulations can be introduced to measure whether they increase or decrease giving. For example, in a dictator game, participants gave more to a charity when they saw a photo of a child in need (Genevsky *et al.* 2013). Other studies have adapted the dictator game to ask how much money participants are willing to give to prevent another person experiencing pain (FeldmanHall *et al.* 2012) and show greater motivation to prevent the pain of someone else than oneself (Crockett *et al.* 2014). Evidence that these emotional factors promote donations, and link to participants' personality traits, suggests a role for psychological mechanisms such as empathy in some forms of giving (FeldmanHall *et al.* 2015).

Measuring decisions to give money away directly can be informative, given the reasonable assumption that choices generally reflect the option with the highest value (Rangel *et al.* 2008). However, an issue with just measuring donation decisions in experiments is that they can be biased if participants act in a socially desirable way, which does not reflect their true motivations (Fernandes and Randall 1992). Behavioural experiments are not limited to measuring decisions whether to donate. For example, an alternative to measuring willingness to pay (donations) is willingness to put in physical effort to earn money for other people (Lockwood *et al.* 2017). If a source of subjective value during philanthropy is creating positive outcomes for other people, prosocial behaviours that cause such positive outcomes will be experienced as 'rewarding', and donors are more likely to repeat them (Gęsiarz and Crockett 2015). Another alternative to measuring donation decisions is therefore a behavioural measure of whether people learn to repeat actions that benefit others (Lockwood *et al.* 2016; Cutler *et al.* 2021).

Neuroimaging

While there are many ways to measure behaviours relevant for prosociality and philanthropy, a focus on behaviour may miss the fact that similar behaviours can be motivated by a wide range of factors. The differences between motivations are crucial to understand, predict, and encourage prosocial behaviours (Hein *et al.* 2016). Neuroimaging tools can offer additional insights. The method from neuroimaging most used in studies relevant to philanthropy is magnetic resonance imaging (MRI). In these studies, participants lie inside a large tube containing powerful magnets and coils that transmit and receive pulses of radio waves. These can create images of the structure of the brain (or any part of the body for medical tests), as different tissues have different properties and generate distinct signals. For research on philanthropy, we are mostly interested in collecting functional MRI (fMRI) datasets that measure activity in different areas of the brain during an experimental task. Participants lying in the scanner can complete an experimental task by viewing a screen at the end of the tube via a mirror and pressing buttons to make responses or choices. During the task, the brain is scanned many times, approximately every two seconds. These data can provide information about brain activity due to the fact that blood full of oxygen has a different signal in the scanner to blood that is low in oxygen. When areas of the brain are active, they receive an increased supply of oxygenated blood. In analysis, we then match up these changes in signal that represent increased blood flow, and thus brain activity, to what was happening in the experimental task at the time.

The most common way of using fMRI in existing research on prosocial behaviour is to compare different conditions, often using one of the economic games described previously, and look for similarities and differences in regions of activity. For example, in several studies, participants decided whether to donate to charities and also received money for themselves during an fMRI scan. Results suggest that some areas may be involved in both giving away and receiving money (Moll *et al.* 2006; Harbaugh *et al.* 2007; Genevsky *et al.* 2013). Similarly, some regions of the brain were involved in both learning about actions that benefit ourselves and learning about actions that benefit other people. However, there were also differences between these types of learning (Lockwood *et al.* 2016). These findings offer insight into how the subjective benefits of giving may be calculated and represented in the brain, overlapping with networks involved in representing benefits for ourselves but also unique. In the following, I outline results on how these patterns of brain activity differ when financial incentives for giving introduce different motivations.

Motivations for philanthropy

To date, few studies have applied techniques from experimental psychology (Eckel and Grossman 2003, 2006; Davis *et al.* 2005; Peng and Liu 2020; Ugazio *et al.* 2021; see Adena 2021 for a review of field experiments), and to my knowledge no studies have applied neuroimaging methods, to the question of tax incentives in philanthropy. However, there is a large and rich literature in these disciplines on different motivations for giving. Here I outline two distinctions – between altruistic and strategic giving and between action-oriented and outcome-oriented giving – that are particularly relevant, as they align with different categories of tax incentive.

Altruistic or strategic giving?

Philanthropy could be considered a challenge for traditional theories in economics that suggest humans or *Homo economicus* are self interested (Adamus 2017). One possibility is that prosocial behaviours can lead to extrinsic – tangible, often financial – benefits for the donor as well as the recipient. A possible motivation for prosocial behaviour is therefore to *strategically* gain such rewards. However, people are also prosocial in contexts where this is not the case (Charities Aid Foundation 2019). I will describe these choices, to be generous when there is no opportunity to gain extrinsic rewards, as *altruistic*. This broad distinction between altruistic and strategic motivations aligns with several of the eight drivers for charitable giving identified in a review, particularly psychological benefits and 'altruism', as defined by the authors, compared to material costs and benefits (Bekkers and Wiepking 2010).

If altruistic choices to give are generous acts with no opportunity to gain extrinsic rewards, motivations for giving in these contexts rely on intrinsic rewards. Sources of intrinsic reward include 'warm glow' (Andreoni 1989, 1990), vicarious reward experience (Mobbs *et al.* 2009), relief of empathic concern (FeldmanHall *et al.* 2015), and self-enhancement from adherence to moral codes or social norms (Niemi *et al.* 2018). Intrinsic incentives to give are often studied through donations to charities, payments to prevent others from coming to harm (FeldmanHall *et al.* 2012), or dictator games (Kahneman *et al.* 1986). A meta-analysis of 616 dictator game treatments from 131 papers showed that on average, participants gave 28.35% of the total amount. Of the 328 treatments with full range information available, 16.74% of participants gave half of the total, and 5.44% gave away everything (Engel 2011). These results, combined with the extent of charitable giving in the real world, provide evidence of altruistic giving.

In contrast, strategic choices to give are generous acts that can also lead to extrinsic reward, which is thought to be the dominant factor in the decision process (Frey and Oberholzer-Gee 1997). Experimental tasks that measure strategic prosocial behaviour include the ultimatum game, trust game, and public goods game in which generosity can also benefit the donor through cooperation or reciprocity. For example, participants may contribute to the group pot or public good, as it leads to positive outcomes for the other group members and themselves. Interestingly, anonymous charitable donations are often considered a prototypical example of altruistic behaviour. However, there many examples of strategic benefits for philanthropy. Donations to some causes may be better characterised as providing a public good if the donor is among the beneficiaries. Membership schemes run by charitable organisations could be motivated by obtaining membership benefits, rather than donating for altruistic reasons. Such opportunities for strategic benefits may increase with the value of the gift and include indirect extrinsic benefits, for example, corporate philanthropy ultimately improving sales.

Crucially, some tax incentives create strategic benefits from charitable giving. Two of the most common tax incentives for philanthropy are matching grants and tax rebates (tax deductions or credits). A key distinction between these is whether the money contributed through the tax incentive goes to the charity or to the donor, respectively. This distinction in the way tax incentives are implemented aligns with the distinction between altruistic and strategic motivations for philanthropy. For matching grants to be effective, the donor must value benefits for the charity (altruistic motivation), whereas tax rebates create a strategic motivation for giving.

Situations and tax incentives that create opportunities for strategic motivations do not exclude the possibility that altruistic motivations also play a role (Capraro and Rand 2017). In other words, a donor could make donations through a scheme that offers tax rebates without taking into account the fact they will benefit financially from doing so. It is difficult to design experiments that exclude altruistic motivations. This is similar to the difficulty with separating whether someone does their job to earn money or because they enjoy it; we can test whether they would do the work for free, but it is difficult to manipulate levels of intrinsic motivation. If donors are giving for altruistic reasons and not considering tax rebates, the subsidy is at best irrelevant and wasteful and at worst conflicts with or 'crowds out' the altruistic motivations (Frey and Oberholzer-Gee 1997). However, there is evidence that strategic motivations do play a role in prosocial behaviour, as manipulations to increase the size or likelihood of the extrinsic rewards increase levels of prosocial behaviour (Camerer 2003; Camerer and Fehr 2003). A comparison of contexts where extrinsic rewards are possible with those where they are not can help identify how these motivations are different.

To understand the differences between altruistic and strategic prosocial decisions, we conducted a meta-analysis to summarise over a decade of fMRI studies on this topic, combining data from over 1000 participants (Cutler and Campbell-Meiklejohn 2019). We classified studies into an altruistic group and strategic group based on whether the experimental task meant that participants could gain extrinsic benefits, money for themselves, through being prosocial or whether the only reasons to give were altruistic.

Importantly, in this study, all charitable giving tasks were included in the altruistic decisions group, as no studies have used fMRI to look at financial incentives for the donor during charitable giving. However, looking at other types of decision which have both extrinsic and intrinsic benefits can help us understand how these motivations interact in the decision process.

Results showed that giving to others, compared to being selfish, in both altruistic and strategic contexts was associated with overlapping increases in activity across several areas of the brain. A common way of interpreting results from fMRI studies is to look at what other types of task or stimuli are associated with activity in these areas. The areas that were active during both types of generosity included the nucleus accumbens (NuAcc), ventromedial prefrontal cortex (vmPFC), orbitofrontal cortex (OFC), anterior cingulate cortex (ACC), and subgenual area of the ACC (sgACC). These are considered key elements of the reward and value-computation networks (Bartra *et al.* 2013). The sgACC has also been linked to charitable donations specifically (Moll *et al.*

2006), distinguishes altruism from decisions which benefit the individual (Pulcu *et al.* 2014), and signals learning which actions help others (Lockwood *et al.* 2016). Activity in the sgACC is also linked to a reduced propensity to harm others in utilitarian judgements (Wiech *et al.* 2013), as well as emotional processing in social contexts (Drevets *et al.* 2008). However, it is important to note we cannot conclude that sgACC activity during generosity necessarily means emotional processing, or any other previously identified process, was taking place during decisions to give money. The conclusions are broader: overlap in the brain between altruistic and strategic giving suggests commonalities in how intrinsic and extrinsic rewards are represented (Levy and Glimcher 2012).

We also compared activity between the two groups of studies and found key differences between altruistic and strategic choices to give. Altruistic choices to give correlated with greater activation than strategic choices in several regions. That any regions show greater activity during altruistic choices suggests there is something unique about decisions to give money away with no expectation of something in return. Of the areas of the brain involved in both types of giving, the one that showed even greater activity during strategic decisions was the right NuAcc. Activity in this region has been associated with multiple types of reward (Levy and Glimcher 2012), including money, intrinsic reward (Moll *et al.* 2006; Harbaugh *et al.* 2007; Genevsky *et al.* 2013), and social cooperation (Rilling *et al.* 2002). The issues of interpretation apply here too, but this finding could show the neural basis of how intrinsic and extrinsic benefits are combined during strategic decisions to give. The fact that activity in this area was highest during strategic decisions could fit with behavioural findings that people are more likely to be generous when they can get something in return (Zheng and Zhu 2013).

In summary, tax incentives following individual donations can be divided based on whether the benefit is to the philanthropic organisation or the donor. Incentives such as matching donations benefit organisations by increasing the overall value of gifts. For donors to value these incentives requires altruistic motivations. In contrast, making donations tax deductible provides financial incentives to individuals. Tax incentives for social enterprises may also provide benefits to the individual customer, as they obtain a desirable product while promoting social welfare. These situations with positive material benefits for both the benefactor and beneficiary mean generosity can be strategic rather than altruistic. Differences between patterns of brain activity during altruistic and strategic choices make a clear case that decisions in these two contexts rely on different processes and should not be considered interchangeable.

Our finding that some regions were most active during strategic decisions could suggest that contexts which benefit both the benefactor and beneficiary are the most desirable. However, there is evidence that altruistic behaviour can decrease following the introduction of extrinsic incentives (Frey and Oberholzer-Gee 1997). In the analogy of working to earn money or because of intrinsic motivation, this is like introducing payment for tasks someone is already doing just because they want to. Imagine someone who loves painting in their spare time being offered a small payment in return. It risks changing how the value of the activity is calculated and potentially undermining intrinsic motivations. Our results could show the neural basis of such 'crowding out' of altruistic motivations by selfish ones if these different motivations represented are within the same neural circuits. We also found other regions more involved during altruistic decisions, suggesting something unique about choices to help others with no opportunity for financial gain. In other words, introducing extrinsic incentives in an attempt to increase generosity could change the core motivations behind giving.

While the results of our meta-analysis and each of the individual studies on this topic provide insight into how the brain calculates the costs and benefits of giving, more work is needed to apply these ideas to tax incentives specifically. One key question for future research is whether tax incentives that offer money to the donor do alter, undermine, or increase their altruistic motivations. Perhaps there are contexts in which donors perceive them as reducing the cost of a donation and so increase the amount they donate. One interesting approach to this question could be to measure the impact of introducing tax incentives that benefit the donor in philanthropic contexts that differ in whether an extrinsic benefit is already available. For example, if tax deductions successfully increase donations through membership schemes but have a less positive impact on donations without an existing extrinsic benefit, considering the original motivations strategic or altruistic offers a possible interpretation.

As with much research in psychology and neuroscience, an important limitation is the artificial nature of experimental tasks, particularly those completed while lying in an MRI scanner. Examples of real-world tax incentives are often more complex than the distinction between altruistic and strategic motivations. UK gift aid applied to the basic rate of tax would align with altruistic motivations, as the charity claims 25% extra on donations. For donors to value this requires them to value the charity gaining more money from their gift. However, higher-rate taxpayers can personally claim back a tax deduction, creating an additional extrinsic benefit from their giving. Another more complex example is interacting tax rules, for example, appreciated property rules or donations of shares that have changed in value. In addition to complexities in the financial value of tax incentives for the donor, potential benefits of giving may not fall neatly into an intrinsic or extrinsic category. For example, donations to organisations that promote donor's political or cultural beliefs could be seen as strategically motivated to achieve the donor's aims, but these outcomes are less tangible than financial benefits. It may be possible to utilise the complex nature of real-world tax incentives, such as differences between individuals or countries, to design field experiments or observational studies on this topic. For example, donations that straddle tax rate or tax credit rate changes could offer interesting opportunities to study strategic motivations. While these situations offer natural examples of increased extrinsic rewards and opportunities for strategic motivation, it is important to reiterate that donors may still be giving for altruistic reasons.

Action or outcome-oriented altruism?

The findings outlined previously suggest that while giving can be strategic, there is also an intrinsic value to giving money away, which provides altruistic motivations for philanthropy. This raises the question: why are people altruistic? Previous work suggests a key distinction between motivations for altruism: pure and impure (Andreoni 1989, 1990), more recently also termed outcome-oriented and action-oriented altruism, respectively (Kuss *et al.* 2013). Pure or outcome-oriented altruism is motivated by the positive outcome for others or public good, independent of one's own contribution. In contrast, action-oriented altruism is motivated by positive emotions from the act of giving. This was originally described as warm-glow giving (Andreoni 1989, 1990), but recent uses of the term 'warm glow' do not necessarily exclude outcome-orientations (Västfjäll *et al.* 2015; Erlandsson *et al.* 2016; O'Brien and Kassirer 2019) so I use the terms action- and outcome-oriented altruism here.

As action-oriented altruism depends on the act of giving, it could be argued that a key component is feeling personally responsible for having a positive impact. In contrast, if someone is outcome oriented, they should see value in positive outcomes for others that they were not responsible for. This distinction in the role of personal responsibility links to the question of how effective it is to spend taxes on incentives to promote individuals' donations, compared to those that do not involve individuals. Examples of tax incentives that do not involve individuals are tax exemptions or special status granted to philanthropic organisations. More broadly, taxes can be spent directly on public policy goals that increase social welfare, rather than on any form of tax incentive. If people's motivations align with outcome-oriented altruism and so focus on the positive outcomes for philanthropic organisations and their causes, public support for these different ways of spending tax will be similar, to the extent they have equal social impacts. However, as these incentives remove individuals' agency, in order for them to align with motivations, people must value positive outcomes for others even when they do not feel personally responsible for the outcome. If personal responsibility plays a key role in motivating altruism, only tax incentives that involve individuals and make them feel their actions have a positive impact will be popular, but these will have the potential to increase donations.

Research in economics, psychology, and neuroscience provides evidence for both action- and outcome-oriented motivations for altruism. As outcome-oriented altruism is motivated by the benefit for the other person, separate from the act of helping, it can be difficult to measure based on behaviour alone. One prediction of outcome-oriented motivations is that donations by oneself and donations by others are perfect substitutes for each other if they create the same impact for the recipient(s). This means that if someone else contributes to a cause, an outcome-oriented donor should decrease their contribution by that amount. This is known as complete 'crowding out' (Ottoni-Wilhelm *et al.* 2017), but, importantly, this form of crowding out is distinct from the motivational crowding out described previously, when extrinsic incentives for prosocial behaviour undermine intrinsic ones. Experimental tests of crowding out have generally not shown support for outcome orientation (Andreoni 1990), and a review of crowding out in response to government support found mixed and context-dependent results (Wit and Bekkers 2017). However, an issue with experimental paradigms is that anything less than complete crowding out is considered evidence against outcome orientation, so the power to detect it is low. Another issue is that predictions of complete crowding out are specific to contexts where additional donations will not increase the size or strength of the positive outcome, and these are very unlikely in the real world.

Action-oriented altruism, motivated by the reward of personally having a positive impact on another person or cause, was introduced to explain the lack of complete crowding out found in behavioural economics experiments (Andreoni 1989, 1990). A similar pattern of behaviour is if donors fail to consider the marginal benefit of their gift, for example, donating to an appeal that has already raised enough to meet its aims rather than one that has not yet reached its target. Anecdotal and scientific evidence support the idea that many altruistic behaviours are not those that would bring about the greatest possible impact. In the charitable giving domain, for example, most donors do not choose causes or organisations based on the efficiency of their impact (Van Iwaarden *et al.* 2009). It is common to choose organisations based on the percentage they spend on projects (Caviola *et al.* 2014), and a lack of overhead costs promotes giving (Gneezy *et al.* 2014), even though this measure is often meaningless for comparing efficiency (Bowman 2006). Many other factors also lead to biases in altruistic behaviour, as they diverge from the common view that all lives have equal value (Slovic *et al.* 2011). These biases include preferring to help certain recipients over others (Everett *et al.* 2015) and the nonlinear relationships between the number of people in need and responses (Dickert *et al.* 2012). Warm-glow motivations within charities themselves have also been linked to inefficiency (Scharf 2014). If action-oriented motivations apply for responses to tax incentives for philanthropy, donors will respond to those that make them feel best about their own impact, even at the expense of objective impact for the beneficiaries or public good.

Using fMRI, work on observing others' gain, not because of altruism or prosocial behaviour, has identified the neural mechanisms of vicarious reward during positive outcomes for others one is not responsible for. Like donating to charity and receiving money for oneself, seeing others receive money was associated with activity in areas including NuAcc (Mobbs *et al.* 2009). This vicarious reward was powerful enough to drive learning, although learning rates were slower than for the self (Lockwood *et al.* 2016). A similar study measured activity in NuAcc during gains for the participant, a charity, and both the participant and a charity. The extent of activity in NuAcc when just the charity gained money correlated with how much the participant enjoyed winning for the charity (Spaans *et al.* 2018). While these results combined suggest that positive outcomes for others and charities have value, they do not consider costly prosocial behaviours to achieve these positive outcomes.

Several studies have developed measures of both outcome and action orientations using fMRI. In the first, participants made voluntary charitable donations and also observed tax-like involuntary transfers from their money to the charity. The NuAcc was active in both contexts, which the authors conclude shows participants did find the tax-like transfers rewarding. This region showed even more activity during voluntary donations, supporting the existence of both outcome-oriented and action-oriented giving (Harbaugh *et al.* 2007). In a different paradigm, participants also made costly charitable donation decisions in the scanner but on some trials, donations were discarded. As the action-oriented reward of being generous is unaffected by whether a donation is discarded, signals in the NuAcc on discarded donations were considered evidence for other-oriented motivations. This was present, but only for the most generous participants (Kuss *et al.* 2013), again supporting a relationship between outcome orientation and giving. In other words, most participants did not seem to care whether their donations actually reached the charity. Such differences between people suggest differences in motivations for altruism. These may also link to findings in the literature on tax and philanthropy of differences in how responsive people are to incentives. Understanding how incentives align with motivations may help explain these differences, and in future, if incentives were more aligned with individuals' motivations, it may boost their efficacy.

In summary, research using fMRI and building on theories from economics provides some evidence for pure or outcome-oriented altruistic motivation. Such motivation would align with support for directing taxes towards social welfare policies or tax exemption for charities to minimise outgoings. However, this was often only found in the most generous participants. For other people, being responsible for donations was crucial, in line with action-oriented altruistic motivation or warm-glow giving. This suggests people may prefer incentives that increase their feeling of responsibility for helping others. As with the section on altruistic and strategic giving, further research is needed to test these ideas and extend them to tax incentives specifically, especially including the complexities of real-world schemes. For example, matching grants could be perceived as the result of multiple donors' gifts. Moreover, the tax treatment of the entity holding the funds will also be relevant, so outcomes such as tax exemption may actually be linked to donation decisions rather than independent of them.

Previous work suggests there may be a partial crowding-out effect, with donors decreasing their donations if they will be matched (Lideikyte Huber 2020). However, warm-glow givers, as identified by a crowding-out task, increased their donations when matched and were more responsive to matching incentives than rebates (Gandullia 2019). One interesting possibility is whether conflicting previous findings are due to different motivations of participants. Another important question is whether matching is more effective if donors feel more responsible for the full, matched amount, perhaps if it is clear that matching only occurred because they personally gave.

Conclusion

In this chapter, I have provided an overview of the research from psychology and neuroscience on different motivations for prosocial behaviour and philanthropy that may be most relevant to tax incentives. Specifically, I first outlined the distinction between altruistic and strategic motivations for prosocial decisions. These motivations differ in whether there is an extrinsic benefit to being generous or not and so correspond to the distinction between tax incentives to the donor or to the charity. A key finding is that altruistic and strategic decisions were associated with overlapping activity in the areas of the brain that compute the value of different options, but there were also neural differences between these motivations. The second distinction I described was between pure and impure, or outcome and action-oriented, altruism. The key aspect here is whether participants value outcomes for others independently of being responsible for them, or whether they only get value from the act of personally giving. This aligns with tax incentives that are independent of or linked to individuals' donation decisions, such as tax exemptions or matching grants, respectively. Results from the studies described show evidence for both of these motivations but suggest feeling responsible for helping others, warm glow, is an important factor.

In addition to insight on how to maximise the effectiveness of tax incentives in promoting philanthropy, evidence that people experience warm glow from giving may reveal an overlooked component in calculating the utility of tax incentives. Perhaps encouraging philanthropy through tax incentives also has psychological benefits for donors (Sellen 2021). There is evidence that being altruistic enhances wellbeing (Dunn *et al.* 2008), with a recent meta-analysis suggesting a small to medium effect of being prosocial on happiness and no evidence of publication bias (Curry *et al.* 2018). Interestingly, recent evidence suggests that people adapt to the warm glow of giving more slowly than to the good feeling of receiving money (O'Brien and Kassirer 2019). Prosocial behaviours have also been linked to improved physical health outcomes (Crocker *et al.* 2017), decreased mortality (Konrath *et al.* 2012), and improved relationships (Crocker and Canevello 2008). While there are many potential mechanisms for these benefits, it is possible that promoting philanthropy through effective tax incentives can create positive social outcomes for both donors and beneficiaries.

References

Adamus, M., 2017. Reasons for doing good: Behavioural explanations of prosociality in economics. *Economics and Sociology*, 10 (1), 122–134.

Adena, M., 2021. How can we improve tax incentives for charitable giving? Lessons from field experiments in fundraising. *In*: *Handbook of Taxation and Philanthropy*. London and New York: Routledge.

Andreoni, J., 1989. Giving with impure altruism: Applications to charity and ricardian equivalence. *Journal of Political Economy*, 97 (6), 1447.

Andreoni, J., 1990. Impure altruism and donations to public goods: A theory of warm-glow giving. *The Economic Journal*, 100 (401), 464–477.

Bartra, O., McGuire, J.T., and Kable, J.W., 2013. The valuation system: A coordinate-based meta-analysis of BOLD fMRI experiments examining neural correlates of subjective value. *NeuroImage*, 76 (76), 412–427.

Bekkers, R., and Wiepking, P., 2010. A literature review of empirical studies of philanthropy: Eight mechanisms that drive charitable giving. *Nonprofit and Voluntary Sector Quarterly*.

Berg, J., Dickhaut, J., and McCabe, K., 1995. Trust, reciprocity, and social history. *Games and Economic Behavior*, 10 (1), 122–142.

Bowman, W., 2006. Should donors care about overhead costs? Do they care? *Nonprofit and Voluntary Sector Quarterly*, 35 (2), 288–310.

Breeze, B., 2013. How donors choose charities: The role of personal taste and experiences in giving decisions. *Voluntary Sector Review*, 4 (2), 165–183.

Camerer, C.F., 2003. Behavioural studies of strategic thinking in games. *Trends in Cognitive Sciences*, 7 (5), 225–231.

Camerer, C.F., and Fehr, E., 2003. Measuring social norms and preferences using experimental games. *Foundations of Human Sociality. Economic Experiments and Ethnographic Evidence from Fifteen Small-Scale Societies* (1214), 1–40.

Capraro, V., and Rand, D.G., 2017. Do the right thing: Experimental evidence that preferences for moral behavior, rather than equity or efficiency per se, drive human prosociality. *Ssrn*, 13 (1), 1–24.

Caviola, L., Faulmüllert, N., Everett, Jim, A.C.C., Savulescu, J., Kahane, G., Faulmüller, N., Everett, Jim, A.C.C., and Savulescu, J., 2014. The evaluability bias in charitable giving: Saving administration costs or saving lives? *Judgment and Decision Making*, 9 (4), 303–315.

Charities Aid Foundation, 2019. *UK Giving 2019*. London, UK: Charities Aid Foundation.

Crocker, J., and Canevello, A., 2008. Creating and undermining social support in communal relationships: The role of compassionate and self-image goals. *Journal of Personality and Social Psychology*, 95 (3), 555–575.

Crocker, J., Canevello, A., and Brown, A.A., 2017. Social motivation: Costs and benefits of selfishness and otherishness. *Annual Review of Psychology*, 68 (1), annurev-psych-010416-044145.

Crockett, M.J., Kurth-Nelson, Z., Siegel, J.Z., Dayan, P., and Dolan, R.J., 2014. Harm to others outweighs harm to self in moral decision making. *Proceedings of the National Academy of Sciences*, 111 (48), 17320–17325.

Croxson, P.L., Walton, M.E., O'Reilly, J.X., Behrens, T.E.J., and Rushworth, M.F.S., 2009. Effort-based cost-benefit valuation and the human brain. *Journal of Neuroscience*, 29 (14), 4531–4541.

Curry, O.S., Rowland, L.A., Van Lissa, C.J., Zlotowitz, S., McAlaney, J., and Whitehouse, H., 2018. Happy to help? A systematic review and meta-analysis of the effects of performing acts of kindness on the well-being of the actor. *Journal of Experimental Social Psychology*, 76 (May 2017), 320–329.

Cutler et al. 2021. https://doi.org/10.1038/s41467-021-24576-w

Cutler, J., and Campbell-Meiklejohn, D., 2019. A comparative fMRI meta-analysis of altruistic and strategic decisions to give. *NeuroImage*, 184 (January 2019), 227–241.

Davis, D.D., Millner, E.L., and Reilly, R.J., 2005. Subsidy schemes and charitable contributions: A closer look. *Experimental Economics*, 8 (2), 85–106.

Dickert, S., Västfjäll, D., Kleber, J., and Slovic, P., 2012. Valuations of human lives: Normative expectations and psychological mechanisms of (ir)rationality. *Synthese*, 1–11.

Drevets, W.C., Savitz, J., and Trimble, M., 2008. The subgenual anterior cingulate cortex in mood disorders. *CNS Spectrums*, 13 (8), 663–681.

Dunn, E.W., Aknin, L.B., and Norton, M.I., 2008. Spending money on others promotes happiness. *Science*, 319 (5870), 1687–1688.

Eckel, C.C., and Grossman, P.J., 2003. Rebate versus matching: Does how we subsidize charitable contributions matter? *Journal of Public Economics*, 87 (3–4), 681–701.

Eckel, C.C., and Grossman, P.J., 2006. Do donors care about subsidy type? An experimental study. *In*: R. Mark Isaac and D.D. Davis, eds. *Experiments Investigating Fundraising and Charitable Contributors*. Bingley, UK: Emerald Group Publishing Limited, 157–175.

Engel, C., 2011. Dictator games: A meta study. *Experimental Economics*, 14 (4), 583–610.

Erlandsson, A., Jungstrand, A., and Västfjäll, D., 2016. Anticipated guilt for not helping and anticipated warm glow for helping are differently impacted by personal responsibility to help. *Frontiers in Psychology*, 7 (September), 1–19.

Everett, J. A. C., Faber, N.S., and Crockett, M.J., 2015. Preferences and beliefs in ingroup favoritism. *Frontiers in Behavioral Neuroscience*, 9 (February), 1–21.

FeldmanHall, O., Dalgleish, T., Evans, D., and Mobbs, D., 2015. Empathic concern drives costly altruism. *NeuroImage*, 105, 347–356.

FeldmanHall, O., Mobbs, D., Evans, D., Hiscox, L., Navrady, L., and Dalgleish, T., 2012. What we say and what we do: The relationship between real and hypothetical moral choices. *Cognition*, 123 (3), 434–441.

Fernandes, M.F., and Randall, D.M., 1992. The nature of social desirability response effects in ethics research. *Business Ethics Quarterly*, 2 (2), 183–205.

Frey, B.S., and Oberholzer-Gee, F., 1997. The cost of price incentives: An empirical analysis of motivation crowding-out. *American Economic Review*, 87 (4), 746–755.

Gandullia, L., 2019. The price elasticity of warm-glow giving. *Economics Letters*, 182, 30–32.

Genevsky, A., Västfjäll, D., Slovic, P., and Knutson, B., 2013. Neural underpinnings of the identifiable victim effect: Affect shifts preferences for giving. *The Journal of Neuroscience*, 33 (43), 17188–17196.

Gęsiarz, F., and Crockett, M.J., 2015. Goal-directed, habitual and Pavlovian prosocial behavior. *Frontiers in Behavioral Neuroscience*, 9 (May), 1–18.

Gneezy, U., Keenan, E.A., and Gneezy, A., 2014. Avoiding overhead aversion in charity. *Science*, 346 (6209), 632–635.

Güth, W., Schmittberger, R., and Schwarze, B., 1982. An experimental analysis of ultimatum bargaining. *Journal of Economic Behavior & Organization*, 3 (4), 367–388.

Harbaugh, W.T., Mayr, U., and Burghart, D.R., 2007. Neural responses to taxation and voluntary giving reveal motives for charitable donations. *Science*, 316 (5831), 1622–1625.

Hein, G., Morishima, Y., Leiberg, S., Sul, S., and Fehr, E., 2016. The brains functional network architecture reveals human motives. *Science*, 351 (6277), 1074–1078.

Kahneman, D., Knetsch, J.L., and Thaler, R.H., 1986. Fairness and the assumptions of economics. *The Journal of Business*, 59 (S4), S285–S285.

Konrath, S., Fuhrel-Forbis, A., Lou, A., and Brown, S., 2012. Motives for volunteering are associated with mortality risk in older adults. *Health Psychology*, 31 (1), 87–96.

Konrath, S., and Handy, F., 2018. The development and validation of the motives to donate scale. *Nonprofit and Voluntary Sector Quarterly*, 47 (2), 347–375.

Kuss, K., Falk, A., Trautner, P., Elger, C.E., Weber, B., and Fliessbach, K., 2013. A reward prediction error for charitable donations reveals outcome orientation of donators. *Social Cognitive and Affective Neuroscience*, 8 (2), 216–223.

Levy, D.J., and Glimcher, P.W., 2012. The root of all value: A neural common currency for choice. *Current Opinion in Neurobiology*, 22 (6), 1027–1038.

Lideikyte Huber, G., 2020. Tax incentives for charitable giving as a policy instrument: Theoretical discussion and latest economic research. *World Tax Journal*, 12 (3).

Lockwood, P.L., Apps, M.A.J., Valton, V., Viding, E., and Roiser, J.P., 2016. Neurocomputational mechanisms of prosocial learning and links to empathy. *Proceedings of the National Academy of Sciences*, 113 (35), 201603198.

Lockwood, P.L., Hamonet, M., Zhang, S.H., Ratnavel, A., Salmony, F.U., Husain, M., and Apps, M.A.J., 2017. Prosocial apathy for helping others when effort is required. *Nature Human Behaviour*, 1 (7), 1–10.

Mobbs, D., Yu, R., Meyer, M., Passamonti, L., Seymour, B., Calder, A.J., Schweizer, S., Frith, C.D., and Dalgleish, T., 2009. A key role for similarity in vicarious reward. *Science*, 324 (5929), 900.

Moll, J., Krueger, F., Zahn, R., Pardini, M., de Oliveira-Souza, R., and Grafman, J., 2006. Human fronto-mesolimbic networks guide decisions about charitable donation. *Proceedings of the National Academy of Sciences of the United States of America*, 103 (42), 15623–15628.

Niemi, L., Wasserman, E., and Young, L., 2018. The behavioral and neural signatures of distinct conceptions of fairness. *Social Neuroscience*, 13 (4), 399–415.

O'Brien, E., and Kassirer, S., 2019. People are slow to adapt to the warm glow of giving. *Psychological Science*, 30 (2), 193–204.

Ottoni-Wilhelm, M., Vesterlund, L., and Xie, H., 2017. Why do people give? Testing pure and impure altruism. *American Economic Review*, 107 (11), 3617–3633.

Peng, H.-C., and Liu, W.-J., 2020. Crowding-out (-in) effects of subsidy schemes on individual donations: An experimental study. *Judgment and Decision Making*, 7.

Peters, J., and Büchel, C., 2010. Neural representations of subjective reward value. *Behavioural Brain Research*, 213 (2), 135–141.

Pulcu, E., Zahn, R., Moll, J., Trotter, P.D., Thomas, E.J., Juhasz, G., Deakin, J.F.W., Anderson, I.M., Sahakian, B.J., and Elliott, R., 2014. Enhanced subgenual cingulate response to altruistic decisions in remitted major depressive disorder. *NeuroImage: Clinical*, 4, 701–710.

Rangel, A., Camerer, C.F., and Montague, P.R., 2008. Neuroeconomics: The neurobiology of value-based decision-making. *Nature Reviews. Neuroscience*, 9 (7), 545–556.

Rapoport, A., and Chammah, A.M., 1965. *Prisoner's Dilemma: A Study in Conflict and Cooperation*. Ann Arbor, MI: University of Michigan Press.

Rilling, J.K., Gutman, D.A., Zeh, T.R., Pagnoni, G., Berns, G.S., and Kilts, C.D., 2002. A neural basis for social cooperation. *Neuron*, 35 (2), 395–405.

Scharf, K., 2014. Impure prosocial motivation in charity provision: Warm-glow charities and implications for public funding. *Journal of Public Economics*, 114, 50–57.

Sellen, C., 2021. Philanthropy as a self-taxation mechanism with happy outcomes: Crafting a new public discourse. *In*: *Handbook of Taxation and Philanthropy*. London and New York: Routledge.

Slovic, P., Zionts, D., Woods, A.K., Goodman, R., Jinks, D., Slovic, P., Zionts, D., Woods, A.K., Goodman, R., and Jinks, D., 2011. Psychic numbing and mass atrocity. *The Behavioral Foundations of Policy* (11), 11–56.

Spaans, J.P., Peters, S., and Crone, E.A., 2019. Neural reward-related reactions to monetary gains for self and charity. *Cognitive, Affective and Behavioral Neuroscience*, 19, 845–858.

Steinberg, R., 2021. The design of tax incentives for giving. *In*: *Handbook of Taxation and Philanthropy*. London and New York: Routledge.

Ugazio, G., Bernardic, U., Lebreton, M., Lideikyte Huber, G., and Peter, H., 2021. When and how do tax incentives promote prosocial behavior and charitable giving? *In: Handbook of Taxation and Philanthropy*. London and New York: Routledge.

Van Iwaarden, J., Van Der Wiele, T., Williams, R., and Moxham, C., 2009. Charities: How important is performance to donors? *International Journal of Quality & Reliability Management*, 26 (1), 5–22.

Västfjäll, D., Slovic, P., and Mayorga, M., 2015. Pseudoinefficacy: negative feelings from children who cannot be helped reduce warm glow for children who can be helped. *Frontiers in Psychology*, 6 (May), 616.

Wiech, K., Kahane, G., Shackel, N., Farias, M., Savulescu, J., and Tracey, I., 2013. Cold or calculating? Reduced activity in the subgenual cingulate cortex reflects decreased emotional aversion to harming in counterintuitive utilitarian judgment. *Cognition*, 126 (3), 364–372.

Wit, A. de, and Bekkers, R.H.F.P., 2017. Government support and charitable donations: A meta-analysis of the crowding-out hypothesis. *Journal of Public Administration Research and Theory*, 27 (2), 301–319.

Zheng, H., and Zhu, L., 2013. Neural mechanism of proposer's decision-making in the ultimatum and dictator games. *Neural Regeneration Research*, 8 (4), 357–362.

17

PHILANTHROPY AS A SELF-TAXATION MECHANISM WITH HAPPY OUTCOMES

Crafting a new public discourse

Charles Sellen

1 Introduction

As philanthropy can only be properly understood from a multidisciplinary perspective, I ground this chapter in observations and literature from various fields, including semantics, philosophy, economics, sociology, political science, psychology, anthropology, and neuroscience. Tax policy is generally considered a classical means for promoting philanthropy, and scholars have long debated the extent of its efficiency and suitability in policymaking toolboxes (OECD, 2020b). In economics only, Bekkers and Wiepking (2011, p. 933) identified over 50 studies published since the 1970s that empirically investigated such notions as "price and income elasticity," "crowding-out effects," and so on. These technical terms are generally taken for granted by economists, and other scientists cannot access this complex literature. There is an important need for clarification, synthesis, and accessibility to allow cross-fertilization. Building on these premises, I formulate the chapter around this nexus of questions:

- Beyond tax policy, what additional levers can be used for fostering a resilient culture of philanthropy and sustainably "grow the giving pie" via nonmonetary incentives?
- How can we then redefine the common understanding of the philanthropy-taxation conundrum to craft a new public discourse that spurs long-term generosity?

To answer these questions, I introduce new concepts and I elucidate preexisting ones in order to propose a novel analytical framework that is easy to grasp for the broadest community of philanthropy scholars. Second, I examine the usefulness and efficacy of tax policies using this novel prism. Third, I explore multidimensional rewards of altruistic behavior and propose adopting a new paradigm to understand philanthropy through happiness lenses. Fourth, I lay the foundation of a roadmap to promote philanthropy with a refreshed narrative.

2 Defining a new conceptual framework

The suggested novel approach requires the definition of several key concepts. Certain are known in the literature, while others are new.

DOI: 10.4324/9781003139201-20

a Philanthropy: broad vs. narrow understanding

"Philanthropy" is derived from the ancient Greek word *philanthrôpìa* (φιλανθρωπία), literally the "love of humankind" (Sulek, 2010b). To its broadest philosophical extent, the term may thus encompass notions such as being friendly to others or caring for the planet, behaving responsibly in all avenues of life, avoiding pollution, and so on.

The contemporary usage makes philanthropy equivalent to "voluntary action for the public good" (Payton & Moody, 2008) or "private means to public ends" (Sulek, 2010a). This essentially involves the gift of something not necessarily tangible (e.g., money, goods) but at least quantifiable (e.g., volunteered time, blood).

For simplicity – and although I do not plead for semantic restrictions – I adopt an even more restrictive definition of philanthropy in this chapter as tantamount to "monetary giving" (excluding in-kind donations). This is because taxation is most immediately related to economic values considered unquestionably measurable in financial terms. A restrictive definition is needed temporarily for demonstrating a case with greater clarity. The proposed approach can then be extended to other forms of generosity.

I will therefore use the terms "philanthropy," "generosity," and "giving" interchangeably, even though they are not absolute synonyms in the literature or in real life.

b Philanthropy: costly vs. costless

Economists have long surveyed what they call the "price of giving" (for instance, see Auten et al., 2002), defined as "the amount an individual must give for one dollar to accrue to the charitable activity itself" (Meer, 2014). Thus, it follows that the "tax-price of giving" is "the net cost to the taxpayer of a dollar of charitable giving" (Steinberg, 2021). From a semantic standpoint, "price" is ambiguous, as it can be synonym of "cost" and "valuable" at once. A "price" must be paid to purchase something; however, something desirable or precious can be said to have a "high price" to us (often in an emotional sense) or even to be "priceless." For that reason, I prefer employing the term "cost," which helps disambiguating and avoiding possible confusion in terminology.

If "philanthropy" is understood as "the gift of money," this gift must be costly to the donating entity – whether an individual or a corporation. Indeed, the dictionary defines "gift" as "Something, the possession of which is transferred to another without the expectation or receipt of an equivalent" (OED, 2020). Considering this definition, we may ask this philosophical question: If the sum of money from someone's pockets is repaid by other means (for instance, through a tax refund), does it still qualify literally as a "gift"? If the left hand takes back what the right hand has donated, where is the generosity? The notion of giving bears the implicit idea of incurring loss. In this vein, many wealthy philanthropists interviewed through a qualitative inquiry testified that a donation must cost you something to deserve being called "philanthropy" (Sellen, 2019). An extensive review of the literature also established that: "It is clear that giving money costs money" (Bekkers & Wiepking, 2011, p. 932).

In this chapter, I will not go as far as to establish a quality difference between the value of two equally costly gifts, depending on whether the donor is wealthy and taps into unnecessary surplus or if the donor has a modest background and shares a portion of vital resources[1]. Nevertheless, religious traditions certainly discriminate between those two instances and attribute higher moral value to greater efforts made by poor people who give from their livelihood, as illustrated in the Christian Lesson of the Widow's Mite (or the Widow's Offering)[2].

This moral distinction is somewhat corroborated by some rich people who see philanthropy as the "right use of surplus wealth" (Lloyd & Breeze, 2013). Certain major donors openly admit that their own surplus giving is less admirable than that of more deprived donors:

> There wasn't one single thing that I ever denied myself from the moneys I gave. Ever. But I think that there are people that I've seen that have denied themselves the moneys they give. Now the amounts might be different and the size. Those people are doing a lot more. So to them it's more meaningful.
>
> *(Schervish et al., 1994, p. 71)*

To avoid subjective judgment, let us assume here that all gifts have the same moral value. However, the aforementioned philosophical premises lead us to introduce a fundamental distinction between two objective subcomponents of a gift: the part that is "costless" and the rest that is "costly." Clearly, in the absence of tax incentives, the entirety of a gift is costly for the donor. However, in the presence of tax incentives, a more or less extensive portion of a gift may end up being "costless" to the donor, as this fraction will be paid back.

Equation 1 summarizes this subdivision of a monetary gift's cost components:

$$\text{Gift} = \text{Costly portion of gift} + \text{Costless portion of gift} \tag{1}$$

Figure 17.1a illustrates this equation. Note that the respective sizes of the costless and costly components are arbitrary at this point.

c Philanthropy: nominal vs. real

Economists normally discuss nominal wages versus real wages (i.e., adjusted for inflation) when examining a salaried person's income or to contrast nominal/real quantities such as gross

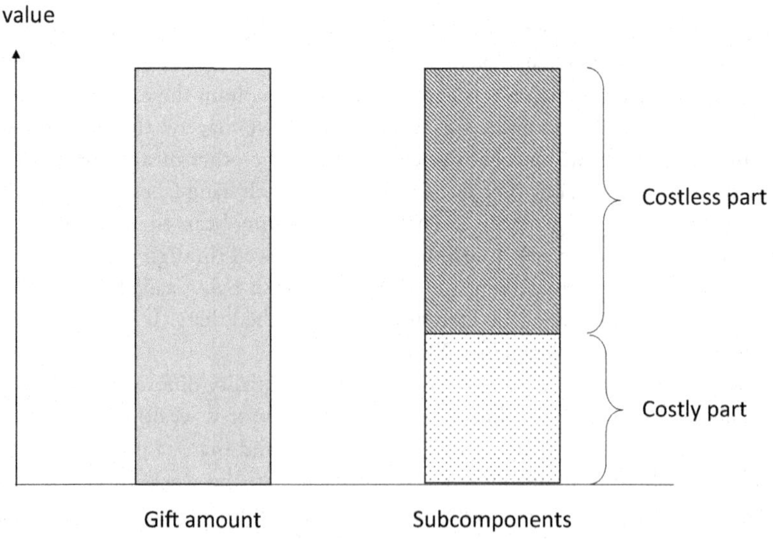

Figure 17.1a Cost components of a gift from the donor's perspective

domestic products, growth rates, or interest rates. I propose that philanthropy scholars distinguish between nominal and real generosity.

In this case, the inflation rate would not be the contrasting factor. "Nominal generosity" would reflect the face monetary value of the gift made. In contrast, "real generosity" would denote the costly value of the gift, that is, the portion permanently coming out of the donor's pocket. In the absence of tax incentives, nominal generosity equals real generosity. In the presence of a tax incentive scheme, the remaining portion of the nominal gift would be considered a "non-gift" insofar as the donor does not "give" this sum permanently (as it will be refunded through subsequent tax rebates).

This yields Equation 2:

$$\text{Nominal gift} = \text{Real gift} + \text{Non-gift} \tag{2}$$

Let us name the explanatory factors (or "causalities") behind each subcomponent of monetary generosity. The "non-gift" component is the direct result of a tax incentive scheme. The "real gift" component is unrelated to mandatory taxation. However, as it results from an individual's choice to voluntarily deprive oneself of a private resource oriented toward the public good, it has the same effect as a tax imposed from outside. Therefore, we can call it "self-taxation." Objections may arise that philanthropy is voluntary, whereas taxation is coercive; thus, "self-taxation" would only be appealing to "masochistic" individuals. Democracies were historically built on the principle of "no taxation without consent." In free countries, taxation ensues from a social contract made possible through elected representatives, whereby people agree that governments levy taxes for public purposes. Although "self-taxation" may sound like an oxymoron, I contend that it reflects the free will of citizens to voluntarily contribute to the public good. Without coercion, the donor's resources are depleted, just as if donated amounts had been taxed.

I therefore propose Equation 3:

$$\text{Nominal generosity} = \text{Voluntary self-taxation} + \text{Tax incentive scheme} \tag{3}$$

Equations 2 and 3 are summarized in Figure 17.1b, wherein the French tax scheme was used in reference. Individual donors can deduct 66% (up to 75% in some cases) of a charitable gift from

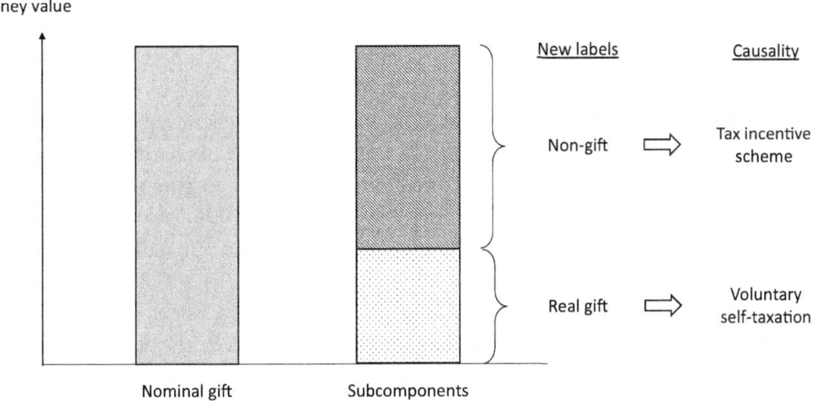

Figure 17.1b Splitting nominal gifts into real gifts and non-gifts

the amount owed in income tax.[3] Thus, a monetary gift costs only one-third (or one-fourth) of its nominal value. Because every country has a different tax scheme for incentivizing philanthropy – and sometimes none – the respective sizes of the "real gift" and "non-gift" components will sensibly vary across tax systems. The needle can also move up or down depending on the specific fiscal situation of a donor (person or corporation) within a given country. This can be used to describe the tax advantages at a certain moment and evolve over time. Therefore, the proposed model offers potential universal applications.

d Philanthropy: conjunctural vs. structural

This section draws inspiration from economists' analysis of the unemployment rate. This variable usually rises during recessions and decreases with economic growth. Public policies can influence the upward or downward trajectory of employment levels in the labor market. Empirical evidence shows that unemployment rates are bound by historical minima and maxima. These extremity levels vary across countries. The long-term trend is called "structural rate," which means that unemployment seldom drops below that level under this labor market's specific conditions. The variations in this rate above/below the bottom line are called "cyclical unemployment." By definition, the "structural" value is relatively stable over time, whereas the "cyclical" part depends on circumstances and business cycles.[4]

Governments can influence conjunctural levels of unemployment by designing emergency plans in times of crisis; however, they cannot easily alter the structural bottom line. Only by modifying the labor market fundamental mechanics (e.g., suppressing/introducing requirements for minimal wages) can they obtain lasting consequences and get closer to the desired level.

Mutatis mutandis, this reasoning may apply to charitable donations with slight variations in semantics.[5] I define "structural" philanthropy as the lowest average amount of charitable giving observed in an individual donor's (person or corporation) history or recorded on a nation-wide scale over a significant period.[6] I define "conjunctural" philanthropy as the amplitude of variation of this generosity level, from lowest to the highest thresholds.[7] These concepts are not expressed in absolute currency values but in shares of wealth or income (at personal or national scopes).

This yields Equation 4:

$$\text{Total generosity} = \text{Structural giving} + \text{Conjunctural giving} \tag{4}$$

Figure 17.2 applies this subdivision to the total amount of giving as a percentage of the American GDP over the past 40 years.[8]

Figure 17.2 shows that "structural giving" in the United States never dropped below 1.6% of the GDP in nearly half a century. Conversely, the total amount of charitable donations in the country has never surpassed 2.2% of the global output over this lengthy period. Furthermore, we distinguish two subperiods. During the first 15 years (1979–1994), structural generosity was pegged at 1.6%, and higher levels evolved slightly above this floor. In addition, the corridor of annual variation of "conjunctural giving" was extremely narrow (0.1%–0.2%). Then, something occurred in the late 1990s that significantly altered the equilibria. Over the past 23 years (1997–2019), both structural and conjunctural levels have risen. Indeed, the floor has increased to 1.9% since 1997, while the rooftop reached 2.2% in 2017. The amplitudes of annual variations nearly doubled (0.3%). Explaining *why* the corridor was uplifted in the late 1990s is beyond our scope; however, I have noted a "threshold effect" between two relatively "homogenous

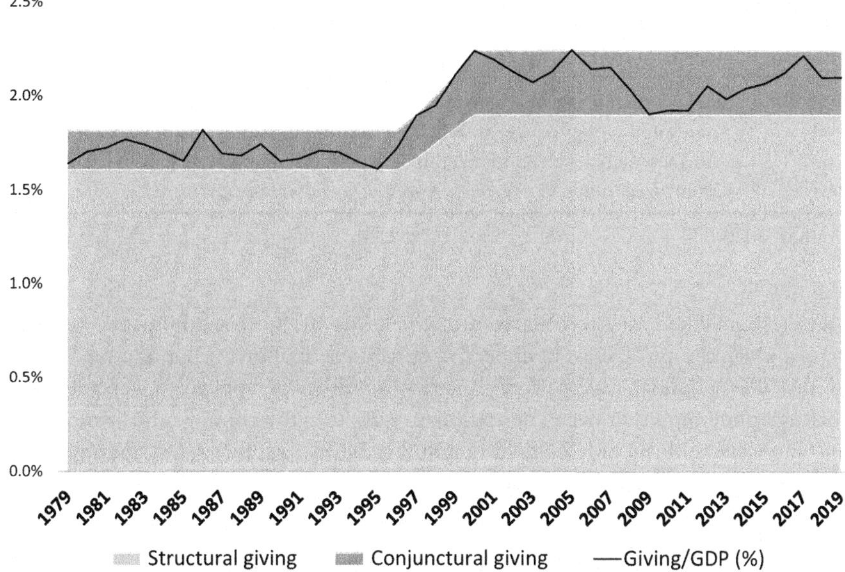

Figure 17.2 Structural and conjunctural giving in the United States, 1979–2019 (in current dollars)

Source: Data from GIVING USA 2020, Giving USA Foundation. Grey shades added by author, 2020

periods." Whether upsurges of generosity in response to disasters are part of conjunctural or structural giving remains an open question (see Box 17.1).

Box 17.1 Does "disaster philanthropy" belong to conjunctural or structural giving?

The term "disaster philanthropy" explains the waves of spontaneous giving that generally occur in the wake of major catastrophes, whether human-induced (terrorism, accidents, economic crises, etc.) or natural (earthquakes, tsunamis, hurricanes, pandemics, etc.). This source of giving typically illustrates the conjunctural fraction of giving defined in our framework, with higher peaks than usual observed at both the household and national scales. Although this phenomenon theoretically relates to one-time events, the more frequent occurrence of calamities over recent years (over 30 cases recorded in 2017–2018 in the United States alone) may lead to the incorporation of this type of giving as a recurrent part of the "structural giving" component (Indiana University, 2019).

e Micro, meso, and macro levels of analysis

To conclude this conceptual framework section, recall that the pairs of concepts of "nominal/real" and "structural/conjunctural" philanthropy are applicable to individuals, households, corporations, or nations as a whole. However, they also work for specific groups of actors, categorized by gender, age, wealth bracket, religion, ethnicity, political opinions, professions, and

Table 17.1 Application of new concepts at various scales

Scale of analysis	*Realities observed*
Micro level	Single economic agents (individuals, households, corporations, etc.)
Meso level	Aggregated groups of agents (sector-wise/professional occupation/age/gender/wealth or income bracket/religion/ethnicity/political opinion, etc.)
Macro level	Country, economy or society as a whole, worldwide mapping

Source: Author, 2020

so on. Researchers could seek to observe evolutive levels of "Catholic Hispanic women's real conjunctural philanthropy," "Swiss plumbers' nominal structural giving," and so on.

Note that the "nominal/real" pair of concepts can either be applied to a specific point in time (such as a photograph) or over a period (like a film). On the contrary, the "structural/conjunctural" binomial tool can only be used longitudinally (like a film, to describe an evolution). Both pairs fit a variety of scales of analysis, as summarized in Table 17.1.

3 How does tax policy fit in this new framework?

Let us reconsider the potential role and justification of tax incentives through the novel lenses offered by our proposed conceptual framework. When governments ask themselves, "How can philanthropy be encouraged?", they often ask, "How can *nominal* philanthropy be encouraged?" Commentators do the same. Indeed, debates surrounding philanthropy constantly revolve around a "nominal" level of charitable giving. So far, we have not witnessed in the literature or in political disputes (either by pros or cons of private giving) any such distinction between "nominal" and "real" philanthropy. Protagonists usually compare, appraise, or refute *nominal* figures of "how much is given" – or "how much is promised," as most public announcements are pledges rather than actual payouts. Even the harshest critics who question the legitimacy of incentivizing big philanthropy (Giridharadas, 2018, among others) tend to overlook the technical aspects of how "costly" a gift is to its donor. Few authors have detailed the inequities inherent to the tax treatment of charitable giving at a micro scale (Reich, 2018). They do this to demonstrate that the incentives tend to benefit the wealthy more than modest households, and they suggest pertinent avenues to reform the system in a fair way. However, they do not draw full conclusions about the soundness of the tax policy applied to each of the subcomponents of a gift described previously. This is what this section attempts to cover.

a Sequencing the tax policy debate

According to our framework, the legitimate question of "How do we encourage philanthropy?" actually translates into "How do we encourage [the four subcomponents of] philanthropy?" Policymakers should thus envision how to address each pillar, as tax policy may have different effects on them. Table 17.2 summarizes the main foreseeable mechanisms for public tax officials.

b Combining the subcomponents of tax policy

In a real-life situation, governments are unlikely acting on each subcomponent separately, as all four elements are intertwined. However, public decision-makers can attempt to target one

Table 17.2 Possible usages of tax policy in our novel framework

Subcomponents of philanthropy	*Conceivable effects of tax policy on each subcomponent of philanthropy*
Conjunctural part	**Principle**: Tax policy can predictably be effective in inducing greater conjunctural philanthropy by offering temporary high benefits to donors in response to exogenous shocks (e.g., economic recession, natural disaster, etc.). **Illustration**: In France, influential voices (including former Minister Aillagon, who passed the 2003 Act on *mécénat*) publicly asked to raise the rate of deductibility from 66% to 75% for gifts in response to the 2019 Notre Dame fire incident. Facing strong public criticism from the Yellow Vests movement, the government paid no heed to these calls. Again, in 2020, a multitude advocated the same shift to compensate for the losses faced by charitable organizations in the wake of the coronavirus crisis. This time, the law-makers relented.[1] **Analysis**: Such measures can only be temporary and moderate. They bear the risk of creating a form of "reliance on exceptionality" and removing the exceptions might become difficult once the non-profits begin to rely upon them. In that way, what was initially intended to be temporary becomes permanent. Conversely, deciding to remove the exceptions may create instability in the tax system and thwart donors' expectations, especially among major donors who engage in multi-year planned giving. This may also negatively affect the "learning curve" of all donors – small or big, current or prospective – who then face an ever-changing set of rules.
Structural part	**Principle**: Tax policy is intuitively suitable for structural philanthropy, provided that the tax scheme remains steady over long enough periods of time to generate a learning effect among donors, keen awareness among policy-makers, and longitudinal data for researchers to demonstrate the policy's impact. **Illustration**: In France, tax incentives introduced in 2007 to deduct some charitable giving from the wealth tax[2] failed to create a lasting behavioral change among wealthy taxpayers. When the tax base was reduced[3] in 2017, giving by these households eroded instantly and proportionally, from 52,000 to 20,000 households in F.Y. 2018 (Bazin et al., 2019, p. 16 ff.). This was a real catastrophe for major gifts fundraising campaigns in France: giving from that source collapsed from €270 million to €112 million (–60%). A decade of implementation of this scheme was obviously not sufficient to induce a lasting change in "structural" giving by the rich. Only 14% of wealthy French households deduct a gift from the wealth tax (Bazin et al., 2019), contrasting sharply with the 91% of the wealthy who give in the United States (Indiana University, 2016), where the culture of philanthropy is more pervasive. So far, France has not succeeded in replicating this culture through the sole use of tax incentives to encourage giving by the rich. **Analysis**: Given that structural philanthropy is defined as the floor below which the generosity levels never drop, raising that floor *sustainably* should be one of the objectives of tax incentives. Ideally, tax policies should be supplemented with an easing of philanthropic activities. Domestic tax policy constitutes only one of the five pillars of the enabling environment for philanthropy (Indiana University, 2018), along with cross-border tax policy, administrative regulations, governance and relations with government, and socio-cultural traditions related to giving. The fundamental parameters of the philanthropy sector must be altered by a diverse set of instruments (including but not limited to tax policy) so as to durably shift structural giving upward.
Non-gift part	**Principle**: Equations 2 (Nominal gift = Real gift + Non-gift) and 3 (Nominal generosity = Voluntary self-taxation + Tax incentive scheme) provide self-evident guiding principles to manage the "non-gift" part of a gift through incentives. Our conceptual framework indicates that tax policy has, *by definition,* a direct and

(*Continued*)

Table 17.2 (Continued)

Subcomponents of philanthropy	*Conceivable effects of tax policy on each subcomponent of philanthropy*
	powerful effect on "nominal philanthropy" insofar as one of its subcomponents originates exclusively from a tax scheme. However, in this respect, it is futile to expect an upsurge in giving through the *non-gift* part of a nominal gift, because it is caused by a pure transfer of public resources to refund private donors. **Illustration**: France introduced more generous percentages of deductibility of gifts from the income tax in 2003. In subsequent years, nominal giving rose in the same proportion as tax-incentive increase, which made experts infer that the apparent rise of generosity was only reflecting in more tax subsidies (Malet, 2005). In retrospect, the new incentives generated extremely moderate elasticity of the total value of gifts and tended to spur mostly the bigger ones (Fack & Landais, 2010). Our conceptual framework would have helped put this reality in plain light and perhaps adjust policies and reframe public debates in France accordingly. In the United States, econometrists have established that high-income taxpayers are particularly responsive to modifying their contributions swiftly after a tax-scheme change and even adjust their gifts in anticipation of projected reforms (Bakija & Heim, 2011). **Analysis**: Seeking to grow nominal philanthropy without growing real philanthropy means that only the "non-gift" part of a gift will be shifted. By focusing on this subcomponent only, tax policy may artificially boost philanthropy. This mechanism, by definition, will work instantly (because it is directly and fully correlated to the tax scheme), but it will bring only a delusional satisfaction to policy-makers and fuel an illusory bubble of apparent giving – indeed, entirely nurtured by public transfers.
Real part	**Principle**: As "real" philanthropy is defined as the residual portion of a gift that is 100% costly to the donor, it cannot be directly affected by tax policy. However, it may be affected indirectly, because tax schemes can draw new donors to philanthropic endeavors and provide them a taste of it, thereby costing them something (the "real" fraction), whereas some of these newcomers would never have practiced philanthropy in the absence of incentives. **Illustration**: France's introduction of generous tax breaks on the wealth tax in 2007 had a mixed impact (see previously) but spurred a new class of vocational philanthropists – at least for one decade. My interviews revealed that this wealth tax was so highly despised among rich people that several of them found the charitable scheme extremely attractive, because it allowed them "earmark/reallocate" to their preferred causes money that otherwise would have been "confiscated" by the State (Sellen, 2019). The "real," costly part incurred without refund was then assimilable to a "premium" disbursement they accepted to avoid paying the rest to the Treasury. It should, however, be noted that various types of French philanthropists co-exist and have different attitudes toward this wealth tax (Duvoux, 2021), which may influence real generosity levels from each of these profiles (see developments in the following about "perceived costs" of giving). **Analysis**: By using tax schemes judiciously, policy-makers can expect spillover effects on "real" giving. However, tax policy might not be the most direct or obvious option to straightforwardly enhance "real" generosity, which, by definition, remains unresponsive to tax reforms.

Source: Author, 2020

1 The Amending Finance Law (April 2020) temporarily raised to €1,000 (up from €552) the amount subject to a 75% tax refund when donations benefited "people in need" (including care and treatment).

2 The "TEPA" law n°2007–1223, enacted on August 21, 2007, allows one to deduct 75% of the gift value from the wealth tax, up to a ceiling of €50,000.

3 The former "*impôt de solidarité sur la fortune*" (ISF) became "*impôt sur la fortune immobilière*" (IFI). Stocks and private equity shares were removed from the tax base, which now essentially comprises real-estate assets.

of them in particular. Furthermore, understanding these various elements and their relative mechanics can only be beneficial in improving the soundness of tax policies.

To this end, our conceptual framework offers a new set of tools for policymaking. In Figure 17.3a, I design an entirely fictitious scenario and describe the underlying mechanics at work, drawing conclusions substantially different from the initial appearances.

Scenario: In fiscal year one (FY1), donors are presented with an incentive worth one-third (33%) of their gifts. Then, an economic crisis occurs, shrinking the overall level of giving in FY2 because the recession hits household income. The government decides to increase tax incentives to support the nonprofit sector and its unparalleled capacity to create social value in difficult times. Reform A doubles the deductibility of charitable donations to two-thirds of their value (66%). The new legislation is immediately implemented in FY3, while the economy bounces back to generate new growth. Due to economic recovery, FY4 sees more charitable giving within a stabilized framework. In this favorable context, the government then determines that greatly generous tax breaks are no longer justified and slightly reduces the advantage by allowing the deductibility of only half of donations (50%) through Reform B. The economic boom continues through FY5–FY6 in the presence of these new incentives.

Purpose: This scenario is hypothetical. It is intended to illustrate the mechanics at work according to our proposed framework, in contrast to the usual way of thinking about philanthropy and tax policy.

Analysis: Most analyses on the effect of fiscal incentives on charitable giving examine only nominal levels of gifts, either at the micro (e.g., a household or a company), meso (a group formed via certain criteria), or macro scale (e.g., a country). Applying our framework to a case study such as this one allows us to differentiate "conjunctural nominal" from "structural nominal" levels of gifts over time (see double-lined curves in Figure 17.3a). Based on the notion of "real giving" introduced previously, we can further distinguish "conjunctural real" from "structural real" levels (see single-lined curves in Figure 17.3a). The visual discrepancies between these four curves completely modify the assessment that decision-makers would make by observing the exact same situation from an outside perspective.

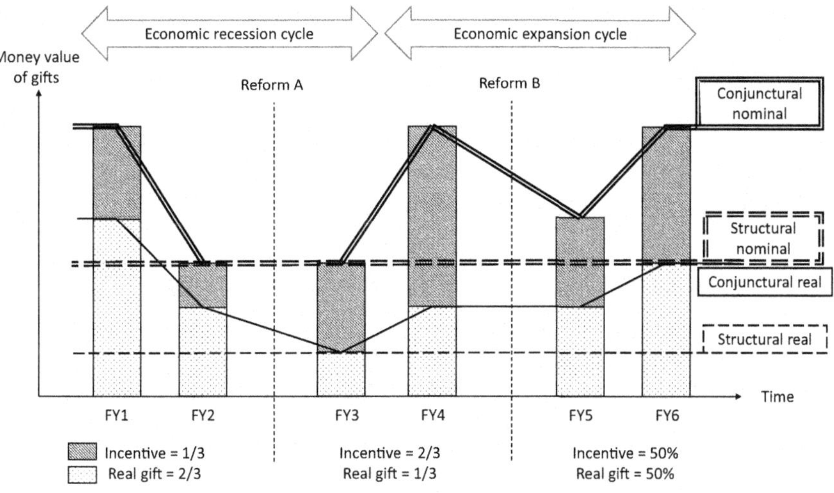

Figure 17.3a Mechanics of tax policy within our novel framework over time

Interpretations:

- The recession scenario imagined in FY1–FY2 translates into a temporary drop in giving (both nominal and real), a phenomenon that is often observed when the economy falters (Rooney & Bergdoll, 2020). Interestingly, Reform A doubles the government's efforts to support charitable giving. This leads to the stabilization of gifts, nominally speaking, in FY2–FY3, which means that donors gave the same face value and recipient organizations received the same annual budget. However, since the cost to donors was cut by 50%, "real generosity" was halved along the way. From a regulator's perspective, it can be correctly said that the reform succeeded in maintaining the same level of necessary funding for the nonprofit sector. However, this steadiness occurred only by transferring public funds to private beneficiaries – not by maintaining people's real generosity, which basically fell.
- Economic growth between FY3 and FY4 generated twice more, both nominal and real (in an unchanged fiscal environment, the growth in giving is homothetic). Note that while FY4's nominal giving has returned to the FY1 original peak level, FY4's real giving is only equivalent to FY2's lower level. Thus, public policy did meet its objective of restoring pre-crisis nominal giving; but, this is at a significant differential cost to state vaults (an additional 33% of gift value). However, the necessity to protect the national ecosystem of nonprofits may still be considered politically worthwhile at this price.
- Past the crisis, when the government evaluates that such a high incentive may no longer be legitimate, it resolves to pass Reform B, reducing the level of public support to 50% – which remains more than the initial 33% guaranteed during the first period. By examining only the nominal trend in giving (FY4–FY5), observers may primarily conclude that the reform had a negative impact on charitable behavior. However, even though donors have indeed adjusted their nominal giving downwards, their generosity actually remains steady in real terms during those two years; the visible drop is only the result of decreased public money transfers. Note also that this real generosity level in FY5 is exactly similar to that in FY2; however, nominal giving is higher due to tax incentives.
- Finally, continuous economic growth combined with a favorable tax treatment of gifts makes donors more comfortable to return to higher generosity levels in FY6. At that point, nominal giving is back at its all-time high. Real gifts have risen more effectively than those of FY4 (although the incentive is lower) but remain inferior to those of FY1 (despite a higher incentive).

As shown by these simulations, the proposed framework offers a completely new operational toolbox. If assumptions are refined and adapted to match local situations, these fundamental mechanics open a practical and straightforward way to assess public policy. At this point of reasoning, the key takeaway of this graph is yet to be considered.

c Centering policy efforts on "core philanthropy"

While tax policy is designed to primarily affect nominal levels – both structural and conjunctural – and to some extent "conjunctural real" giving, it is unhelpful to alter "structural real" generosity (see arguments developed in Table 17.2). In Figure 17.3a, this "structural real" is the lowest record of generosity, or the floor under which giving never drops. Figure 17.3b highlights this fundamental stripe, which I call "core philanthropy."

"Core philanthropy" is generosity that is entirely costly to the donor. It may be costless (like in France) or costly to the Treasury (like in the United Kingdom through the Gift Aid system,

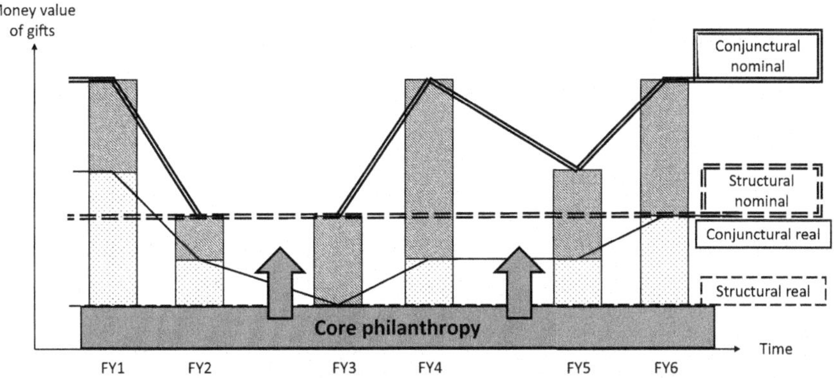

Figure 17.3b Focusing on the fundamental basis of generosity

Source: Author, 2020

whereby the government matches 25% of private giving). "Core philanthropy" existed before tax incentives were created and would certainly survive a total removal of those, as its essence is based on other types of motives completely unrelated to taxation.

Historical examples and contemporary empirical evidence demonstrate the undeniable existence of "core philanthropy." When Henry Dunant and a group of Genevan citizens created the International Committee of the Red-Cross (ICRC) in the 19th century, they established the basis for what has since become the world's largest humanitarian movement. Although the ICRC leveraged government collaborations early on, tax incentives did not exist at its foundational stages, and "core philanthropy" was arguably its primary source of funding. In the 20th century, when the Abbé Pierre called on French radio for an insurrection of generosity (*insurrection de la bonté*) during the terribly cold winter of 1954, millions of people responded instantly by sending an overwhelming flood of money and in-kind gifts. Sweden did not offer income tax incentives for charitable gifts until 2012; however, Swedish households traditionally supported charities long before this reform, which allows only modest tax incentives (OECD, 2020b, p. 86). Australia, for her part, does not incentivize giving to religious organizations, although they receive the lion's share of the country's total giving. These are only four examples taken from different epochs or contexts, showing that people did not wait for tax incentives to express their "core philanthropy."

Contemporary empirical evidence suggests that American high net-worth individuals[9] (HNWIs) would either maintain (48.3% in 2013) or moderately decrease (41.7% in 2013) their giving if income tax deductions were removed. I call "complete core philanthropy" the unchanged giving and "incomplete core philanthropy" the portion that would only be subject to slight changes (see Figure 17.4). Donors planning on increasing their giving are negligible (less than 2%). Those planning to significantly decrease their giving (8.7% in 2013) reveal the extent of the tax scheme's incidence on a minority, contrasting with relatively unalterable giving levels by the majority. Note that survey statements may differ from the respondents' actual deeds, partly due to a "social desirability" response bias.

To conclude this section, "core philanthropy" constitutes the fundamental brick upon which public authorities should seek to build policies designed to enduringly spur philanthropic growth at zero (or limited) cost to government. An upward shift in this ultimate building block of altruism (see plain grey arrows in Figure 17.3b) can raise the whole

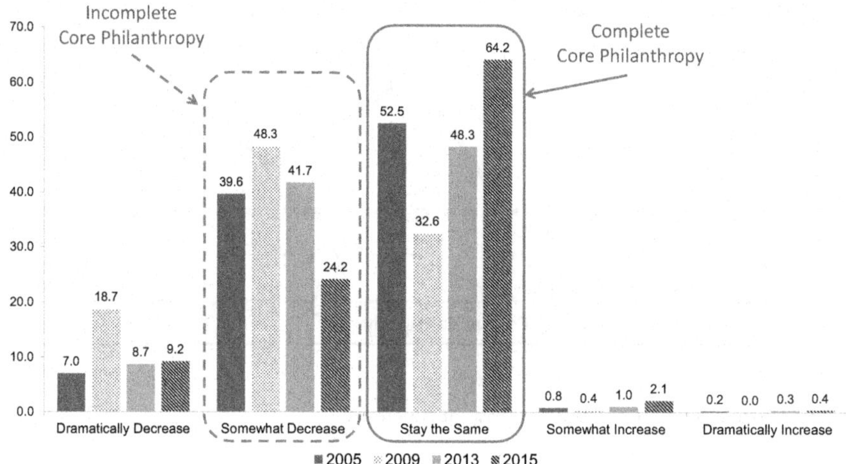

Figure 17.4 Change in giving by HNWIs if income-tax deductions for donations were eliminated: 2005, 2009, 2013, and 2015 (%)

Source: Data from Indiana University, 2006, 2010, 2014, 2016 Bank of America U.S. Trust Study of High Net Worth Philanthropy. Labels added by author, 2020

philanthropic tide in a country and allow tax policy to fully play its role in leveraging both conjunctural and nominal levels by riding on the crest of this wave.

4 Other ways to encourage real generosity

The previous section determined that tax policy is a necessary but insufficient tool for fostering philanthropy. It can prime the pump by providing a taste for generosity to donors who otherwise would not have donated. It can multiply pre-existing real giving by all donors into higher levels of nominal gifts. However, it cannot create a real-giving upsurge *ex nihilo*. Therefore, we ought to seek game-changing tools to boost this fundamental layer of generosity.

a Levers to stimulate "core philanthropy"

Figure 17.3b depicts "core philanthropy" as the lowest constant stripe of real giving in a nation or an individual's history. Thus, it is a synonym of "structural real giving," with a value inferior or equal to "conjunctural real giving." If taxation is decorrelated to core philanthropy, what are the other influencing factors?

The literature on donor motivations is extensive, and hundreds of publications have been condensed by several studies or meta-analyses (Bekkers & Wiepking, 2011; Lloyd & Breeze, 2013; Konrath & Handy, 2018). Table 17.3 summarizes the main factors identified to donate identified in these scholarly works. Note that the concepts of "mechanisms" and "motives" do not exactly match.

As shown in Table 17.3, avoiding taxation, or utilizing favorable tax breaks (depending on which side of the coin – negative or positive – the donor considers), count among many other factors in predicting or explaining charitable behavior. They are not necessarily the most prevalent ones triggering charity. Regarding major donors, Rooney and Osili (2016, p. 190) note

Table 17.3 Various underlying factors that explain giving

Main studies	*Identified mechanisms and motives to donate*
Bekkers and Wiepking (2011)	(a) Awareness of need, (b) solicitation, (c) costs and benefits, (d) altruism, (e) reputation, (f) psychological benefits, (g) values, (h) efficacy
Lloyd and Breeze (2013) *Note: this study is centered on major donors*	(a) Belief in a cause; (b) acting as a catalyst for change; (c) achieving self-actualization; (d) feeling a sense of duty and responsibility to share wealth; (e) enjoying the relationships that develop with the charity leadership, fellow donors, and beneficiaries; (f) belief that philanthropy is the rightful use of surplus money; (g) clarity on the complementary roles of government and philanthropy; (h) belief that philanthropy is a good parenting tool; (i) appreciating the public recognition that comes with being philanthropic; (j) having their own lives enriched by philanthropy
Konrath and Handy (2018, p. 359 ff)	(a) Trust, (b) altruism, (c) social ties, (d) tax, (e) egoism, (f) constraints

that "while the potential for tax benefits does influence the decision to give, the specific cause or organization is a more important factor." These authors report (p. 195) that "more wealthy people (34 percent) value tax benefits than respondents in the general population (11 percent) (HNW Inc., 2000)."

Even though richer families appear three times more sensitive to tax incentives than ordinary households, those figures clearly indicate that most citizens (from two-thirds to nine-tenths) declare their giving is not predominantly determined by tax schemes.

Consequently, if one wants to improve real philanthropy, the plethora of other non-monetary factors will be of the utmost importance in nurturing generosity. Some of them relate to social benefits (reputation, socializing, recognition, etc.), while others relate to psychological benefits (pleasure, joy of giving, opportunities to learn, guilt avoidance, etc.). These motives are either inner or outer oriented. Most of the time, they bring positive immaterial rewards to donors. However, there could be some adverse noneconomic consequences of displaying charitable behavior (see Box 17.2).

Box 17.2 Notable exceptions: When major giving may arouse public resentment

In France, public opinion rarely praises the good deeds of philanthropists and rather shows contempt or jealousy, according to the perception of wealthy interviewees (Sellen, 2019), who, therefore, generally give *quietly*[10]. Consequently, major donors often conceal their best actions (i.e., surrendering part of their "social benefits" of giving) in order to avoid the inconvenience of public resentment (i.e., reducing the negative side-effects of giving).

In their comprehensive review of literature, Bekkers and Wiepking (2011) focus on material costs and benefits, which are defined as "tangible consequences that are associated with a monetary value" (p. 932). I attempt to broaden this definition by encompassing immaterial rewards as well as a cost/benefit analysis of giving. This approach may seem akin to *rational choice theory* (Amadae, 2017), which has prompted skepticism. While it is not possible to provide further technical details here, we can still operate within a methodological individualism paradigm as long as we remain mindful of the probable framing effects on decisions (Tversky & Kahneman, 1986) and of the cognitive biases and *bounded rationality* of agents who seek to optimize utility under constraints (Gigerenzer & Selten, 2002).

b Embracing externalities to apprehend "perceived costs" of giving

Facing such a complex situation involving numerous factors of a diverse nature, economists would simplify and discriminate between a financial cost (or "price"; see previously) on the one hand and a set of psychological/social benefits on the other (known as "warm glow"). They would label the intangible gains "positive externalities" and the immaterial downsides "negative externalities." They would then seek to quantify and "internalize" externalities into a single utility function. Box 17.3 describes open avenues and persistent disagreements among economists to explain charitable behavior.

Box 17.3 Disagreements among economists about giving rationales

The economics literature offers several contradictory explanations for charitable giving. If *Homo economicus* is supposedly rational and selfish, why would s/he disburse resources without compensation? As predictions of neo-classical theory and empirical observations did not match, scholars proposed a variety of possible explanations. A few claim that the theory is inaccurate because individuals are neither completely rational (Kahneman & Tversky, 1979) nor completely selfish (Fontaine, 2007). They advocate, instead, for a renewed theory moving from *Homo economicus* to *Homo sapiens* (Thaler, 2000). Another stream of research justifies the mainstream theoretical framework by incorporating rewards into utility functions, which can then be logically maximized by rational economic agents. This yielded the notion of "impure altruism" (Andreoni, 1989, 1990). Various forms of recompense have been imagined: the satisfaction of contributing to a public good (Sugden, 1982, 1983), the reputation and pleasure derived from giving (Harbaugh, 1998a, 1998b), the thrill of "making a difference" in the world (Duncan, 2004), and so on. These explanations have different outcomes in terms of donor competition and cooperation. Whereas the "public good" model generates more happiness when everyone contributes (and, conversely, less contentment when some behave as "free riders"), the differential impact model follows an adverse correlation, with more joy derived from being the sole funder (someone who makes a relatively bigger difference to a cause when other contributors back off). The private consumption model and the prestige model rely on intrinsic or prestige motives, respectively, and, consequently, donors either derive contentment proportionate to their own giving – and irrespective of others' contributions – or they play a zero-sum game with co-contributors in their quest for "status."

The common denominator of several models is self-satisfaction, which is generally dubbed *warm glow*. As this notion remains arguably shallow and ambiguous (Tieffenbach, 2019), economists admit that "the warm-glow hypothesis provides a direction for research rather than an answer to the puzzle of why people give" and call for "more specific models of individual and social motivations" (Andreoni et al., 2017).

Another shared characteristic is that tax policy is unlikely to significantly affect donor behavior according to each model's predictions. All of them try to explain "real/costly giving" from a utilitarian or hedonic perspective, setting aside key moral dimensions (Ugazio, 2019).

By somewhat adapting the economics methodology, let us compare the "actual price" and the "perceived expense" of a "real gift" in a donor's mind. The latter price is equal to the former plus all immaterial rewards and minus all immaterial costs. I propose Equation 5:

$$PRC = ARC - (\mu + \psi + \sigma + \pi) + \varepsilon \tag{5}$$

where PRC stands for "perceived real cost" by the donor, ARC represents the "actual real cost" (monetary disbursement, net of tax rebates) to the donor, μ is the value of all material benefits or counterparts received in exchange for the gift, ψ is the sum of all positive psychological rewards, σ is the sum of all positive social rewards, and ε is the sum of all negative immaterial side effects incurred by the donor. Although underestimated and controversial, π characterizes the power relationships and dependencies gifting ineluctably creates (Mauss, 1954). The concept of *warm glow* (see Box 17.3) is often regarded in economics as a "black box"; here, it is proxied by the sum of immaterial rewards ($\psi + \sigma + \pi$).

A prior study introduced the notion of "perceived costs of giving" from a different standpoint. "Cost perception" on the supply side of giving is interpreted as the "ability to give" and pertain to donors' feelings of relative financial (in)security and more or less careful attitude toward money (Wiepking & Breeze, 2012). Integrating this approach could surely enrich our model in further developments; however, for simplicity, let us assume all donors feel equally capable of donating. This allows us to focus on rewarding mechanics.

According to our framework, to increase "core philanthropy" (a.k.a. "real structural giving"), policies must seek to persuade donors that the "actual real cost" (ARC) they seem to incur financially is dwarfed by the multifaceted rewards they will get in return. The more a donor becomes aware of these bonuses, the lower the "perceived real cost" (PRC). In extreme cases, PRC could become so low and so completely outbalanced by rewards in the donors' minds that the very notion of "cost" may wholly disappear. Moreover, donors will end up seeing mostly the "benefits." A number of qualitative enquiries attest to the validity of this statement, notably among major donors who have reflected long enough on their philanthropic endeavors to fully reap their immaterial benefits. One of these donors explains:

> I think, basically, when people give, they give for themselves. But I think that they get more out of it down the line than what they think they'll get out of it.
>
> *(Schervish et al., 1994, p. 70)*

Technically speaking, maximizing ψ can be achieved in many ways, for instance, by counseling and coaching donors individually or by allowing them to reflect upon their feelings and self-satisfaction through academic studies. Likewise, maximizing σ can be attained by celebrating philanthropists in society at large; through prizes, plaques, or medals of recognition; or by creating circles where they could share experiences among peers. Such marks of acknowledgment and select group membership are coveted by major donors, for whom philanthropy signifies accession to an elite status (Ostrower, 1995) or acquisition of "symbolic power" (Dean, 2020). Giving circles provide a similar type of mutual appreciation among donors in the general population (Eikenberry, 2009). Anonymous donors forgo σ but retain other rewards. Cynical donors may knowingly expect π, while others ignore it. Seeking to maximize μ might be foolish, as Bekkers and Wiepking (2011, p. 935) warn:

> There is a danger in offering material benefits for charitable contributions. When people receive material benefits for helpfulness, they tend to undermine self-attributions

of helpfulness, which reduces the effect of prosocial self-attributions on future helpfulness. Fringe benefits change the decision into an exchange (do I get value for money?).

Minimizing ε could be realized by teaching philanthropy in schools,[11] countering popular misunderstandings, or mainstreaming philanthropy in the media via more vivid reports or attractive educational shows.[12]

These actions could be partly funded by the state, meaning that they still bear the cost of public money. But this expenditure may be worthwhile, considering that the use of public funding through tax incentives is unlikely *per se* to lift "core philanthropy." The key point is that, unlike tax instruments, other tools available to reduce PRC are not state monopolies. Banks, wealth advisors, family offices, consultants, academia, nonprofits, media outlets, and many intermediaries can join the state's efforts in a sector-wide coalition to strengthen philanthropy.

Although the donor's financial cost is worth only the "real value" of a gift, the donor's intangible rewards derive from the full "nominal value" of donations. Suppose a donor gives $500, but this gift only costs him/her $200 in real terms due to tax breaks. Suppose charity dedicates recognition plaques for gifts above $300. The donor can earn this level of appreciation only thanks to the tax scheme. Recipient organizations would find it awkward to express gratitude only at the level of the "real cost" that donors incur. This means that public policies can indirectly award more social advantages to donors. Tax schemes are responsible for greater recognition. This is a key aspect, albeit often neglected, to remember when assessing usefulness.

To conclude this section, offsetting the (rare) intangible costs and magnifying the (frequent) psychological/social rewards associated with giving would be a relatively inexpensive method to use public funding while arousing collective action in support of national philanthropic policies.

c Cultivating the "joy of giving"

Hank Rosso, founder of the Fund Raising School at Indiana University in 1974, used to say that: "Fundraising is the gentle art of teaching people the joy of giving" (2016, p. 5). Over the past 50 years, research has established many connections between charitable giving or altruistic behavior and higher levels of wellbeing or life satisfaction. Bekkers and Wiepking (2011, pp. 938–939) provided a snapshot of key studies about the "joy of giving." The most comprehensive review of literature to date on this topic was conducted by Konrath (2016), comprising dozens of studies in psychology, sociology, neurosciences, economics, medicine, anthropology, and so on. By collecting this broad range of experiments, surveys, and empirical analyses, Konrath reveals a wide array of non-monetary benefits derived from acting altruistically. The key findings are as follows:

- Volunteering "*causes* people to have higher self-esteem and feel less depressed' (p. 13). Volunteering mitigates the psychological effects of aging (p. 16). Volunteering gives enjoyable feelings of "time affluence," even though the time volunteers spend on others is not used for themselves (p. 15).
- Spending money on others generates greater contentment than spending it on oneself. This holds true "regardless of the amount of money spent" (p. 13) and "even in relatively poor countries" (p. 22). Just remembering those good deeds creates "mood boosting effects," and such positive feelings subsequently stir more altruism, following a self-reinforcing loop (p. 13).
- Giving also helps cope with "post-traumatic stress disorder or social anxiety" (p. 15). Giving generally "enriches people's relationships, both in quantity and quality" (p. 16).

- In most cultures across the world, both volunteering time and donating money are associated with higher wellbeing (p. 18).
- Most importantly, donor awareness of the potentially beneficial effects of giving "does not diminish the psychological rewards." Such consciousness is also found to stimulate altruism (p. 14).
- Being generous is found to have direct positive consequences on health and longevity (pp. 16–17). In neuroscience experiments, the fact that reward centers of a donor's brain react similarly when giving and receiving money suggests that "physiological effects mirror psychological effects" (p. 16).
- Ultimately, "giving increases givers' sense of meaning and purpose in life" (p. 21).

The universality of these results appears to be consistent across cultures, countries, and generations. We must now envision how the "joy of giving" can be encompassed in a broader narrative, one that echoes and likely fulfills the donor's most intimate life aspirations.

d Happiness as a new paradigm

"Happiness" is commonly defined as "The state of pleasurable contentment of mind; deep pleasure in or contentment with one's circumstances" (OED, 2020). It has been pursued by the human race for centuries. It is both an individual quest and collective ambition. Political regimes of all sorts have attempted using "happiness" as a goal or a justification for pursuing their policies – with unequal wisdom and sometimes dreadful results. Countless philosophers have addressed this essential notion, which remains quite mysterious. Baruch Spinoza (1632–1677) is recognized as one of the most prominent thinkers of happiness in modern times. In his magnum opus, *Ethics*, he stated, "The desire to live a good or happy life, of acting well, etc., is itself the very essence of man" (Spinoza et al., 2020, Proposition No. 21).

From today's scientific perspective, "happiness" is not understood as fully equivalent to "joy." Although much overlap can be found between these notions, "happiness" tends to have a much broader meaning. A leading pioneer in this emerging field, Veenhoven (2006, p. 7) defines "overall happiness" as "satisfaction with one's life-as-whole". It includes two major components: a *hedonic level* reflecting the "balance of pleasant and unpleasant affect" and a *cognitive dimension* based on the "perceived realization of wants" (see Figure 17.5).

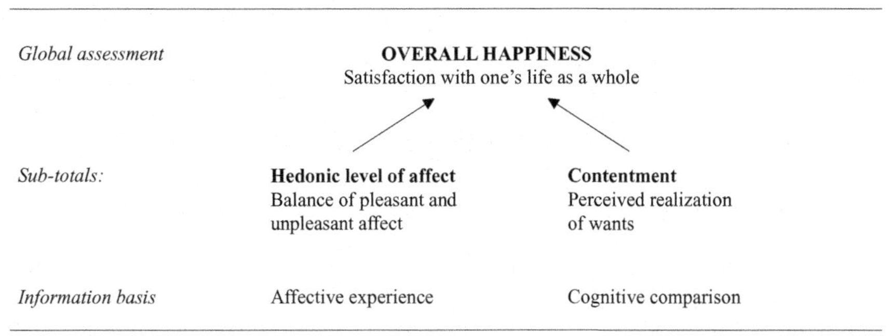

Figure 17.5 Defining happiness and its components

Source: Veenhoven, 2006, p. 7. Reproduced with permission

In his landmark contribution on the *Moral Biography of Wealth*, Schervish (2006) does explicitly refer to the notion of happiness in philanthropy. Drawing from Aristotle's ancient Greek concepts of *genesis* ("the set of metaphysical, social, and personal conditions within which agency transpires," i.e., "the conditions we receive") and *telesis* ("the destiny of outcomes toward which we aspire," i.e., "the consequences we strive to create"), he explains how philanthropy can serve an "agency moral biography" (pp. 482–483) defined as *capacity* combined with *moral compass*. Schervish concludes his demonstration by reckoning the necessity to "fulfill donors' desires simultaneously to increase their own happiness and the happiness of others" (p. 491). However, the notion of happiness appears to be a rather subordinate idea, used incidentally to support and illustrate his central paradigmatic description of "agency moral biography."

By connecting Veenhoven's clinical description of happiness with Schervish's holistic understanding of donors' ability to become change-makers, I propose to observe philanthropy through happiness lenses.

A preliminary exploration conducted in France from this angle yielded interesting results (Sellen, 2019). I initiated this study after reading Warren Buffett's letter of commitment to the Giving Pledge wherein he openly stated that he "*couldn't be happier* with that decision" [emphasis added] to "gradually give all of [his] Berkshire Hathaway stock to philanthropic foundations" (2010). Back then, French billionaires were invited to join the pledge; however, none had responded favorably.[13] I pondered the reasons for this monolithic rejection. A working hypothesis quickly emerged that issues of wellbeing (or lack thereof) regarding wealth and its public use could be at stake among the wealthy in France, where both conspicuous enrichment and ostentatious philanthropy are criticized in public opinion. Encountering high and ultra-high net-worth individuals (HNWIs and UHNWIs) through more than 30 in-depth one-on-one interviews revealed that "happiness" not only offered a key angle to explain attitudes towards philanthropy. They showed that "happiness" could also serve as a pivotal concept to explain many related issues, such as the respective roles of government and the nonprofit sector, the scope of individual freedom and responsibility, the legitimacy of taxation, the extent of national solidarity, and so on.

Although extremely abundant literature on "money and happiness," on the one hand, and on "money and giving," on the other hand (both streams comprising thousands of articles), exists, as do a growing number of publications on the "joy of giving," little research has been conducted at the intersection of the three ideas of wealth, happiness, and philanthropy. To summarize the qualitative findings around this nexus, I connected the tips of the triangular relationship depicted in Figure 17.6.

If, according to Spinoza, nearly all people search for happiness, and considering that everyone possesses some sharable wealth (usually defined by professional fundraisers as "time, treasure, or talent"), why doesn't everybody engage in philanthropic endeavors?

Answering this question goes beyond the scope of this study. However, I offer a clue derived from the testimonials heard through many interviews. Perhaps not everybody has had the chance to cross paths with philanthropy in their lifetime. One needs to be initiated in some ways to engage in philanthropy. It may be a childhood education, a one-time life event, an inspirational encounter, or something else, but something/someone has to give a prospective donor a taste for generosity before this person begins practicing it as a regular activity and, for some, going as far as to adopt altruism as a definite lifestyle.

This entry point is best illustrated by stories of successful business leaders who were converted into major donors after peers took them under their wings to start taking on adequate community engagement (Schervish et al., 1994, pp. 68–69, "Philanthropic initiation"). However, does not need to be a millionaire to begin looking for other goals in life aside

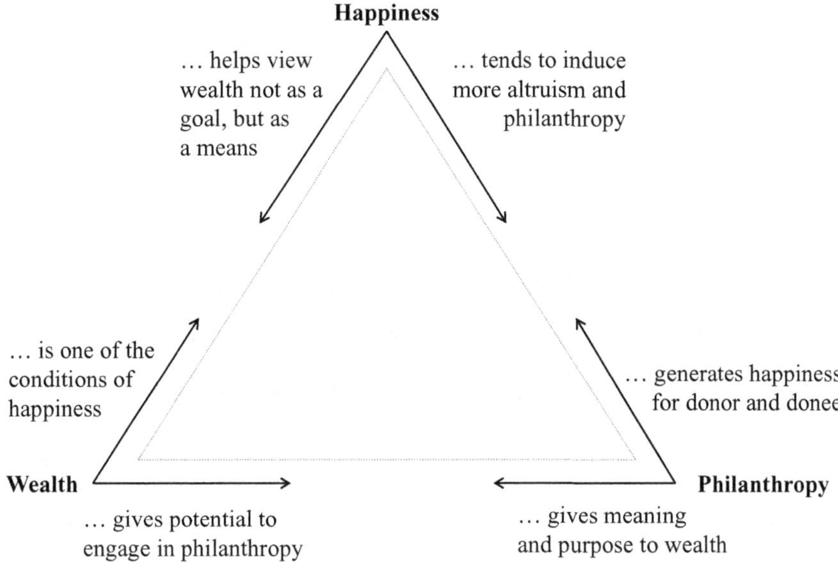

Figure 17.6 Triangular relationship between wealth, philanthropy, and happiness

Source: Sellen, 2019, p. 274

from amassing wealth. Indeed, it has been calculated that beyond an annual income of USD 75,000, ordinary people's happiness would not significantly increase with more wealth but rather be determined by factors such as relationships, leisure activities, and self-fulfillment (Kahneman & Deaton, 2010). Essentially, once basic needs are covered and financial security is assured, people find wellbeing in values other than money. These empirical results recall Maslow's "hierarchy of needs," a schematic pyramid dominated by a supreme desire for "self-actualization" (Maslow, 1954), although academically, this theory remains heavily contested. Sound policies may remedy the lack of awareness about the "feel-good" aspects of giving and palliating the lack of attractive opportunities that deter people from engaging in charitable behavior.

e *Why* happiness *transcends* warm glow

Since Andreoni (1990) established the *impure altruism* model, economists dissociate *altruistic* motives (outcome-oriented) from *warm glow* (action-oriented). However, philosophers have identified a core ambiguity whereby donors need to employ self-deception to persuade themselves that they are driven by pure altruism to enjoy the expected warm glow. This is called the "Valmont effect" (Elster, 2011). Conversely, behaving like a genuinely pure altruist does not preclude unanticipated pleasant rewards. It follows that the *pure altruism/warm glow* dichotomy may exist only in theory. In practice, all donors are *impure altruists* (having mixed motives) to various degrees. Neuroscience reveals evidence for both warm glow and more pure motivations, linking them with activity in the reward network of the brain, but finds that these motivations vary between people (Cutler & Campbell-Meiklejohn, 2019; Cutler, 2021). Psychology also recognizes this intertwined reality: wellbeing is derived both from prosocial behavior itself (warm glow) *and* from witnessing its positive impact (pure altruism) along a seemingly unified continuum. Thus, the "joy of giving" concept already goes far beyond the admittedly limitative scope of "warm glow." The paradigm of "happiness" currently developed by social scientists offers even more powerful avenues: it encompasses multidimensional factors (emotional, social, cognitive, ethical, aspirational, etc.), resulting in a holistic assessment of an individual's "life-as-whole" (Veenhoven, 2006, see Figure 17.5). Therefore, investigating happiness may help apprehend donor motivations and self-fulfillment more comprehensively in future research.

5 Roadmap for a new narrative on philanthropy

In light of the freshly acquired knowledge on happiness and wellbeing, what are the elements of a renewed approach to the philanthropy-taxation conundrum?

Changing the law or the administrative set of rules regulating nonprofits is not indispensable. Tax schemes may even remain identical. Essentially, novelty lies in framing things differently. Changing people's perceptions over the long run implies modifying the collective mindset, and the technique is a matter of narrative rather than tax pressure. Traveling along this novel route entails five steps.

a Transforming outlooks

The first step towards forging a novel approach is to change the way we look at the problem. The conceptual framework proposed previously offers a straightforward and workable method for policymakers to decide on the optimal level of tax incentives they deem legitimate in a given country. For citizens, understanding the scheme through these lenses will be easy. Citizens are all at once voters (i.e., constituents of decision-makers in a democracy), taxpayers (i.e., ultimate funders of tax incentives), and potential donors (i.e., beneficiaries of tax breaks), so their understanding and approval of the scheme is essential for its proper functioning. The adoption of new intellectual tools to address taxation in philanthropy ("nominal/real," "conjunctural/structural giving," "core philanthropy," "perceived cost of giving," etc.) will allow everyone to test their relevance and adjust their use.

b Taking happiness seriously

Second, policymakers must fully recognize and grasp the potential of "happiness" as a new paradigm sought after by citizens. A British poll determined that 85% of citizens agreed with this statement: "a government's prime aim should be to achieve the greatest happiness of the people, not the greatest wealth" (BBC, 2006, cited by Veenhoven, 2017, p. 1).

From 1975–2015, Bhutanese authorities officially computed an index of "Gross National Happiness." Recently, several countries have established indicators measuring citizens' wellbeing in real time. Some made audacious moves toward assessing the performance and soundness of public policy on these grounds. Even the United Nations takes happiness seriously: a major conference on this topic was held at its headquarters in 2012 (Royal Government of Bhutan, 2012), and the General Assembly subsequently decided[14] to celebrate the "International Day of Happiness" annually on March 20. The related *World Happiness Report* is updated annually (Helliwell et al., 2020). Since 2011, the OECD multi-country project *Better Life Index*[15] has offered a practical toolbox to measure citizens' wellbeing through 11 dimensions that can be blended and weighted at will (OECD, 2020a).

c Promoting philanthropy differently

Policymakers should remember three key ingredients of Konrath's literature review on the joy of giving: cultivating the memory of good deeds, repeating small actions frequently, and raising awareness about the feel-good consequences. However, philanthropists should not be too self oriented (Konrath, 2016, p. 18) to fully reap these benefits. The goal is to leverage altruism to build greater resilience.

> Repeated giving interactions are like deposits into a resilience bank account with compound interest. All of the potential explanations of why giving is associated with better health have something in common: they help people to deal with unanticipated negative life events and stressors.
>
> *(ibid., p. 21)*

In short, government should recommend as part of public health policies that citizens take a daily dose of "vitamin G" (*ibid.*, p. 22–23). Policymakers should also be mindful of the timing of roll-out policies, since this factor may affect giving (Bekkers & Wiepking, 2011, p. 934).

d Measuring achievements

Measuring social progress is a growing issue. It is beyond this chapter's scope to address the methodological and epistemological controversies surrounding this idea. I only recommend that the happiness of donors be assessed scientifically (Veenhoven, 2017), as well as the happiness of "beneficiaries" or "end-users" (sometimes called "partners in philanthropy" to reflect equal footing) who are all too often forgotten, even in the nascent impact-investing industry whose distinctive identity rests on end-user's satisfaction (Karim, 2020).

By using the "positive social science" approach advocated by Thin (2014), scholars may observe and seriously consider subjectively assessed wellbeing (i.e., self-reported by respondents in surveys). Indeed, people's perceptions of their own feelings matter at least as much as the investigator's opinion.

e Embarking the ecosystem on a new journey

Numerous potential implications exist for non-governmental decision-makers. Private bankers and wealth managers could incorporate the wellbeing dimension as a full component of their philanthropic advisory services. Nonprofit executives and fundraisers could appeal more explicitly to donors and beneficiaries' shared joy and wellbeing when developing cases for supporting and managing their fundraising campaigns. Academics could elaborate on compelling case studies and include the happiness dimension in their teachings to sensitize next-generation leaders. Every player in the philanthropic ecosystem could contribute to reenchant giving along these lines.

f From a negative to a positive approach: reenchanting giving

The perceived "price" of philanthropy is shown to be subject to a framing effect. Despite a lack of evidence on how people respond to framing, we already know that presenting incentives as matches rather than rebates generates more giving (Bekkers & Wiepking, 2011, p. 948).

Following the same logic, we must abandon the claim that tax incentives reduce the price of giving, as it taints philanthropy in the donor's mind. For some donors who see their inherited wealth as a "social stigma," philanthropy is a "story of *purgation*," a method of proving to themselves that they deserve their inherited wealth (Schervish et al., 1994, Chapter 5, "Expunging the Guilt of Unmerited Wealth", pp. 111–125). Insisting repeatedly on the lesser cost of giving can only be discouraging – if not insulting – to them. Thus, the concept of "voluntary self-taxation" brings forth a practical way for dignifying the wealth these heirs received at birth by encouraging them to employ these extra resources in virtuous and honorable endeavors.

Likewise, Carnegie's moral commandment to his fellow tycoons still resonates today as an imperious instruction to give away the bulk of one's wealth before passing away: "The man who dies thus rich dies disgraced" (Carnegie, 1889). In fact, very few other moguls heeded his unfriendly advice to the letter. Born in 1930, Chuck Feeney is currently one of the rare billionaires who lost this prosperous status because of excessive giving (over $8 billion). He displays serenity and splendid contentment, and in his own words: "I see little reason to delay giving when so much good can be achieved through supporting worthwhile causes. Besides, it's a lot more fun to give while you live than give while you're dead" (Bertoni, 2020). However, his astonishing example symbolizes an exception rather than a rule amidst the ultra-wealthy. Even signatories of the *Giving Pledge*, who freely committed to donating at least half of their wealth during their lifetime or at death have not successfully managed to keep the promise so far (Schmitz et al., 2021). Furthermore, this initiative struggled to gather almost 10% of the world's billionaires, despite the extraordinary momentum for global philanthropy. After the original wonder effect, shortcomings tended to spur more reproaches than admiration (Hill, 2020). Perhaps the proposed narrative centered on happiness – not self-centered pleasure but dynamics of shared joy among donors and beneficiaries – could provide a more durable impetus to this type of pledge and circumvent otherwise inescapable criticism by mitigating the breach of public trust caused by mogul philanthropists who blur the lines between business and charity (Dean & Brakman Reiser, 2021).

Beyond compassionate reactions to tragedies, fear of social backlash, guilt avoidance, narcissistic pleasure, or quest for prestige, humankind remains collectively lacking an overarching set of positive reasons to inspire enthusiastic giving. Embracing the happiness paradigm would offer such an opportunity.

6 Concluding remarks

a On the conceptual framework

To the best of our knowledge, the proposed distinctions between "nominal/real" philanthropy or between "conjunctural/structural" giving and the concepts of "core philanthropy" and "voluntary self-taxation" have not been put forward in the literature in those terms. I advocate that these concepts be tested, challenged, refined, enriched (e.g., by incorporating factors like inequality), and potentially adopted as commonplace by the academic community to describe more precisely the realities debated in philanthropy research from an interdisciplinary perspective.

In society at large, aggregated levels of individual and corporate donations make up a total level of generosity. However, again, statistical reports on charitable giving rarely (if ever) present the share of those donations that are really "costly" to donors and the portion considered "costless" to them. Therefore, from a philosophical standpoint, it is difficult to determine the exact levels of a person's overall generosity or a people's charity at the country level.

b On policy implications

This new toolbox will assist policymakers in describing the issues at stake when it comes to tax policy and to adjust fiscal levers to stimulate philanthropy in a given country. Not all policymakers have embedded philanthropy in their strategic goals. Those who do must clearly state their objectives and priorities (e.g., boosting donations vs multiplying donors). Policymakers should also be aware that "growing the giving pie" is no panacea: consider issues of absorptive capacity (can nonprofits use all additional resources?) and of effectiveness (do nonprofits need more money or other forms of support?).

Aside from these caveats, our framework suggests that public authorities wanting to develop philanthropy should not seek to artificially raise "nominal" or "conjunctural" philanthropy. These measures have limited long-term impact and fail to create lasting generous behaviors. Evidence shows that stable incentives applied to a reduced tax base lead to an immediate meltdown of gifts (e.g., the 2017 wealth tax reform in France). Instead, governments should aim to create vibrant ecosystems encouraging a deeper shift in "real" and "structural" philanthropy. This can be done by using levers such as education, sensitization, advocacy, case studies, applied research, professional training, and so on. Forging a culture of philanthropy depends on many factors other than a fiscal year's planning horizon.

c On happiness as a new paradigm

To elicit greater altruism among potential donors, who supposedly maximize their utility function even in the presence of bounded rationality and unselfishness, promoting awareness about the positive externalities derived from such behavior appears necessary. A large body of research on the "joy of giving," combined with recent qualitative research on subjective wellbeing, has explored how donors found themselves with greater happiness along their philanthropic journey. Focusing on this fruitful lever can improve the "real/structural" or "core" component of giving (which exogenous tax incentives barely affect) and eventually trigger persistently higher generosity levels derived from donors' perceived satisfaction.

Refreshed narratives and discursive engagements are vital to rally hearts and minds toward the greater good. Beyond the likelihood of materially increasing donations, the happiness paradigm offers powerful ways to achieve a conceptual "reenchantment" of the act of giving.

Notes

The author is grateful for valuable comments by Fiona Martin, Hans Schmitz, and one anonymous referee.

1 Bazin et al. (2019, p. 9) put forward the interesting notion of "giving effort" ("*effort de don*"), which represents the ratio between average gift and average income (per tax bracket). However, this idea differs from the conceptual framework hereby developed, as it does not consider tax effects on the "price" of gifts.

2 This story is narrated in the Synoptic Gospels (Luke 21:1–4; Mark 12:41–44).

3 Deductibility is allowed within a threshold of 20% of their taxable income (French tax code, art. 200).

4 A third type of unemployment, called "frictional," denotes people moving or voluntarily changing occupations.

5 I call conjunctural only the upper part of the differential curve, while "conjunctural unemployment" fluctuates above/below the long-term structural trend.

6 "Significant" here means long enough to observe *threshold effects* that sustainably modify average giving levels.

7 Auten et al. (2002, p. 371) mention that donors may opportunistically take advantage of "unusually high transitory tax rates." They distinguish between "transitory" and "persistent price of giving." However, these concepts are not synonymous with "cyclical" or "conjunctural" generosity, which designate the amounts effectively donated.

8 Giving USA 2020's data spans giving by individuals (including bequests), foundations, and corporations.
9 HNWIs are individuals or households whose net wealth is at least US$1 million in investable assets (excluding their main residency) or whose annual income is at least US$200,000 for two consecutive years.
10 The philosophy according to which "the good does not make any noise, the noise does not make any good" is a widespread common trait among France's major donors.
11 Examples could be the innovative programs "L'Ecole de la Philanthropie" and "Le Cercle des Petits Philanthropes" in France.
12 French examples include the program "Philanthropia" broadcast on Radio Notre-Dame [https://radionotredame.net/emissions/philantropia/] or the newspaper "Sens & Finances" initiated by the Fondation d'Auteuil [http://sens-et-finances.apprentis-auteuil.org/].
13 This is still the case as of September 2021, over a decade later.
14 U.N. resolution 66/281 of 12 July 2012. https://undocs.org/A/RES/66/281
15 See: https://www.oecd.org/statistics/better-life-initiative.htm and http://www.oecdbetterlifeindex.org/

References

Amadae, S.M. (2017). Rational choice theory. *Encyclopaedia Britannica*. 17 November 2017. Retrieved from: https://www.britannica.com/topic/rational-choice-theory [Accessed 30 September 2020].

Andreoni, J. (1989). Giving with impure altruism: Applications to charity and Ricardian equivalence. *Journal of Political Economy*, 97(6), 1447–1458.

Andreoni, J. (1990). Impure altruism and donations to public goods: A theory of warm-glow giving. *The Economic Journal,* 100(401), June, 464–477.

Andreoni, J., Rao, J.M., & Trachtman, H. (2017). Avoiding the task. A field experiment on altruism, empathy, and charitable giving. *Journal of Political Economy*. University of Chicago Press, 125(3), 625–653.

Auten, G.E., Sieg, H., & Clotfelter, C.T. (2002). Charitable giving, income, and taxes: An analysis of panel data. *American Economic Review*, 92(1), 371–382.

Bakija, J., & Heim, B.T. (2011). How does charitable giving respond to incentives and income? New estimates from panel data. *Economic Analysis of Tax Expenditures. National Tax Journal*. National Tax Association, Part 2, 64(2).

Bazin, C., Duros, M., & Malet, J. (2019, November). *La générosité des, Français*, 24th edition. Lyon: Recherches & Solidarités.

BBC. (2006). The happiness formula. GfK-NOP poll 421059. Retrieved from: http://news.bbc.co.uk/2/hi/programmes/happiness_formula/4771908.stm [Accessed 29 September 2020].

Bekkers, R., & Wiepking, P. (2011). A literature review of empirical studies of philanthropy: Eight mechanisms that drive charitable giving. *Nonprofit and Voluntary Sector Quarterly,* 40(5), 924–973.

Bertoni, S. (2020). Exclusive: The billionaire who wanted to die broke . . . Is now officially broke. *Forbes*. 15 September 2020. Retrieved from: https://www.forbes.com/sites/stevenbertoni/2020/09/15/exclusive-the-billionaire-who-wanted-to-die-brokeis-now-officially-broke/#20e4bf1e3a2a [Accessed 30 September 2020].

Breeze, B., & Lloyd, T. (2013). *Richer Lives: Why Rich People Give*. London: Directory of Social Change.

Buffett, W. (2010). My philanthropic pledge. *The Giving Pledge*. Retrieved from: https://givingpledge.org/Pledger.aspx?id=177 [Accessed 29 September 2020].

Carnegie, A. (1889). Wealth. *North American Review*, 148(CCCXCI), June, 653–664.

Cutler, J. (2021). Aligning tax incentives with motivations for philanthropy: Insights from brain and behaviour. In Peter, H. & Lideikyte Huber, G. (Eds.). *The Routledge Handbook of Taxation and Philanthropy*. London and New York: Routledge.

Cutler, J., & Campbell-Meiklejohn, D. (2019). A comparative fMRI meta-analysis of altruistic and strategic decisions to give. *Neuroimage*, 184, 227–241.

de Spinoza, B., Eliot, G., & Carlisle, C. (2020). *Spinoza's Ethics*. Princeton: Princeton University Press.

Dean, J. (2020). *The Good Glow: Charity and the Symbolic Power of Doing Good*. Bristol: Policy Press.

Dean, S., & Brakman Reiser, D. (2021). Trust and for-profit philanthropy: From Surrey's private foundation to Zuckerberg's limited liability company. In Peter, H. & Lideikyte Huber, G. (Eds.). *The Routledge Handbook of Taxation and Philanthropy*. London and New York: Routledge.

Duncan, B. (2004). A theory of impact philanthropy. *Journal of Public Economics*, 88(9–10), 2159–2180.

Duvoux, N. (2021). Philanthropy, class, and tax in France. In Peter, H. & Lideikyte Huber, G. (Eds.). *The Routledge Handbook of Taxation and Philanthropy*. London and New York: Routledge.

Eikenberry, A.M. (2009). *Giving Circles: Philanthropy, Voluntary Association, and Democracy*. Bloomington, IN: Indiana University Press.

Elster, J. (2011). Chapter 4. The Valmont effect. In Illingworth, P., Pogge, T. & Wenar, L. (Eds.). *Giving Well: The Ethics of Philanthropy*. Oxford: Oxford University Press.

Fack, G., & Landais, C. (2010). Are tax incentives for charitable giving efficient? Evidence from France. *American Economic Journal: Economic Policy*, 2(2), 117–141.

Fontaine, P. (2007). From philanthropy to altruism: Incorporating unselfish behavior into economics, 1961–1975. *History of Political Economy*, 39(1), 1–46.

Gigerenzer, G., & Selten, R. (Eds.). (2002). *Bounded Rationality: The Adaptive Toolbox*. Cambridge, MA: MIT Press.

Giridharadas, A. (2018). *Winners Take All. The Elite Charade of Changing the World*. New York: Penguin Random House.

Giving USA. (2020). *The Annual Report on Philanthropy for the Year 2019*. Chicago: Giving USA Foundation.

Harbaugh, W.T. (1998a). What do donations buy? *Journal of Public Economics*, 67(2), 269–284.

Harbaugh, W.T. (1998b). The prestige motive for making charitable transfers. *The American Economic Review*, 88(2), 277–282.

Helliwell, J.F., Layard, R., Sachs, J., & De Neve, J.-E. (Eds.). (2020). *World Happiness Report*, 8th edition. New York: Sustainable Development Solutions Network.

Hill, S. (2020). Warren Buffett and the Gateses: 200-plus billionaires and 10 years later, is the Giving Pledge a success? *Newsweek*. 28 April 2020. Retrieved from: https://www.newsweek.com/warren-buffett-gateses-200-plus-billionaires-10-years-later-giving-pledge-success-1500497 [Accessed 30 September 2020].

HNW, Inc. (2000). HNW wealth pulse: Wealth and giving. *HNW Inc.*

Indiana University Lilly Family School of Philanthropy. (2016). *The 2016 U.S. Trust® Study of High Net Worth Philanthropy*. Indiana University Lilly Family School of Philanthropy, October. http://hdl.handle.net/1805/11234.

Indiana University Lilly Family School of Philanthropy. (2018). 2018 *Global Philanthropy Environment Index*. http://hdl.handle.net/1805/15958.

Indiana University Lilly Family School of Philanthropy. (2019). U.S. Household disaster giving in 2017 and 2018. http://hdl.handle.net/1805/19403

Kahneman, D., & Deaton, A. (2010). High income improves evaluation of life but not emotional well-being. *Proceedings of the National Academy of Sciences of the United States of America*, 107(38), 16489–16493.

Kahneman, D., & Tversky, A. (1979). Prospect theory: An analysis of decision under risk. *Econometrica*, 47(2), March, 263–291.

Karim, F. (2020). Riding the impact wave: The brave new world. *Alliance Magazine*. London. Retrieved from: https://www.alliancemagazine.org/blog/riding-the-impact-wave-the-brave-new-world/ [Accessed 30 September 2020].

Konrath, S. (2016), Chapter 2. The joy of giving. In Tempel, E., Seiler, T. & Burlingame, D. (Eds.). *Achieving Excellence in Fundraising*, 4th edition. Hoboken, NJ: John Wiley & Sons, pp. 11–25.

Konrath, S., & Handy, F. (2018). The development and validation of the motives to donate scale. *Nonprofit and Voluntary Sector Quarterly*, 47(2), 347–375.

Lloyd, T. (2004). *Why Rich People Give*. London: Association of Charitable Foundations.

Lloyd, T., & Breeze, B. (2013). *Richer Lives: Why Rich People Give*. London: Directory of Social Change.

Malet, J. (2005). *La générosité des, Français*, 10th edition. Paris: CerPhi, November.

Maslow, A.H. (1954). *Motivation and Personality*. New York: Harper & Row.

Mauss, M. (1954). *The Gift: Forms and Functions of Exchange in Archaic Societies*. Glencoe, IL: Free Press.

Meer, J. (2014). Effects of the price of charitable giving: Evidence from an online crowdfunding platform. *Journal of Economic Behavior and Organization*, 103, 113–124.

OECD. (2020a). Executive summary. In *How's Life? 2020: Measuring Well-Being*. Paris: OECD Publishing. https://doi.org/10.1787/ea714361-en.

OECD. (2020b). Taxation and philanthropy. In *OECD Tax Policy Studies*. Paris: OECD Publishing, p. 27. https://doi.org/10.1787/df434a77-en.

Ostrower, F. (1995). *Why the Wealthy Give. The Culture of Elite Philanthropy*. Princeton, NJ: Princeton University Press.

Oxford English Dictionary. (OED). (2020). Retrieved from: https://www.oed.com/ [Accessed 29 January 2021].

Payton, R.L., & Moody, M.P. (2008). *Understanding Philanthropy: Its Meaning and Mission*. Bloomington: Indiana University Press.

Reich, R. (2018). *Just Giving. Why Philanthropy Is Failing Democracy and How It Can Do Better*. Princeton, NJ: Princeton University Press.

Rooney, P., & Bergdoll, J. (2020). What happens to charitable giving when the economy falters? *The Conversation United States*. 23 March 2020. Retrieved from: https://theconversation.com/what-happens-to-charitable-giving-when-the-economy-falters-133903 [Accessed 30 September 2020].

Rooney, P., & Osili, U. (2016). Chapter 15. Understanding high net worth donors. In Tempel, E., Seiler, T. & Burlingame, D. (Eds.). *Achieving Excellence in Fundraising*, 4th edition. Hoboken, NJ: John Wiley & Sons, pp. 185–199.

Rosso, H.A. (2016), Chapter 1. A philosophy of fundraising. In Tempel, E., Seiler, T. & Burlingame, D. (Eds.). *Achieving Excellence in Fundraising*, 4th edition. Hoboken, NJ: John Wiley & Sons, pp. 3–10.

Royal Government of Bhutan. (2012). *The Report of the High-Level Meeting on Wellbeing and Happiness: Defining a New Economic Paradigm*. New York: The Permanent Mission of the Kingdom of Bhutan to the United Nations. Thimphu: Office of the Prime Minister.

Schervish, P.G. (2006). The moral biography of wealth: Philosophical reflections on the foundation of philanthropy. *Nonprofit and Voluntary Sector Quarterly*, 35(3), 477–492.

Schervish, P.G., Coutsoukis, P., & Lewis, E.G. (1994). *Gospels of Wealth: How the Rich Portray Their Lives*. Westport, CT: Praeger.

Schmitz, H.P., Mitchell, G.E., & McCollim, E.M. (2021). How billionaires explain their philanthropy: A mixed-method analysis of the giving pledge letters. *VOLUNTAS: International Journal of Voluntary and Nonprofit Organizations*, 1–12.

Sellen, C. (2019). Is philanthropy a way for the wealthy to convert wealth into happiness? Preliminary exploration in France. In Brulé, G. & Suter, C. (Eds.). *Wealth(S) and Subjective Well-Being*. Social Indicators Research Series, 76, June. Cham: Springer, pp. 247–278.

Steinberg, R. (2021). The design of tax incentives for giving. In Peter, H. & Lideikyte Huber, G. (Eds.). *The Routledge Handbook of Taxation and Philanthropy*. London and New York: Routledge.

Sugden, R. (1982). On the economics of philanthropy. *The Economic Journal*, 92(366), 341–350.

Sugden, R. (1983). On the economics of philanthropy: Reply. *The Economic Journal*, 93(371), 639–639.

Sulek, M. (2010a). On the modern meaning of philanthropy. *Nonprofit and Voluntary Sector Quarterly*, 39(2), April, 193–212.

Sulek, M. (2010b). On the classical meaning of *philanthrôpìa*. *Nonprofit and Voluntary Sector Quarterly*, 39(3), April, 385–408.

Thaler, R.H. (2000). From *Homo economicus* to *Homo sapiens*. *Journal of Economic Perspectives*, 14(1), Winter, 133–141.

Thin, N. (2014). Positive sociology and appreciative empathy: History and prospects. *Sociological Research Online*, 19(2), 1–14 https://doi.org/10.5153/sro.3230 [First Published 2 June 2014].

Tieffenbach, E. (2019). La science du don. Le warm glow feeling, une théorie de l'altruisme impur. *Expert Focus, Centre en philanthropie de l'Université de Genève*, 2019(3), 116–120.

Tversky, A., & Kahneman, D. (1986). Rational choice and the framing of decisions. *Journal of Business*, 59(S4), 251–278.

Ugazio, G. (2019). Personalized philanthropy. Estimating moral and financial subjective values to explain preferences for philanthropy. *Expert Focus, Centre en philanthropie de l'Université de Genève*, 2019(3), 121–124.

Veenhoven, R. (2006). How do we assess how happy we are? Tenets, implications and tenability of three theories. Paper presented at conference on 'New Directions in the Study of Happiness: United States and International Perspectives', University of Notre Dame, USA, October.

Veenhoven, R. (2009), Chapter 3. How do we assess how happy we are? In Dutt, A.K. & Radcliff, B. (Eds.). *Happiness, Economics and Politics: Towards a Multi-Disciplinary Approach*. Cheltenham: Edward Elger Publishers, pp. 45–69.

Veenhoven, R. (2017). Measures of happiness: Which to choose? In Brulé, G. & Maggino, F. (Eds.). *Metrics of Well-Being. II 'Measurement Issues'*. Dordrecht: Springer, pp. 65–84. DOI:10.1007/978-3-319-61810-4_4.

Wiepking, P., & Breeze, B. (2012). Feeling poor, acting stingy: The effect of money perceptions on charitable giving. *International Journal of Nonprofit and Voluntary Sector Marketing*, 17(1), 13–24.

18

INTER-CHARITY COMPETITION AND EFFICIENCY

Considerations beyond fundraising and tax incentives for giving

Johannes Lohse and Kimberley Scharf

Setting the scene: the non-profit sector in an uncertain economic environment

Recent national and global economic challenges have revived interest in understanding the extent to which market economies can rely on the non-profit sector's essential and complementary role in enabling economic stability and growth. The austerity measures put in place across many EU countries in the aftermath of the financial crisis of 2008 and post-pandemic government spending sprees have widened the scope and the role of some parts of the charitable sector in supplying vital public goods while narrowing the scope and role of other parts of the sector. At the same time, the economic burden of COVID-19 on household finances (Bhutta et al., 2020) has brought new challenges to the entire charitable sector by limiting fundraising opportunities, which again depend upon donor, charity and public-sector responses to a changing and uncertain sectoral landscape. Especially charities holding low financial reserves were negatively impacted by a sudden loss of funding opportunities due to COVID-19 (Mirae and Mason, 2020).

These financial strains have put additional pressure on charities to be innovative in their fundraising strategies. They have also renewed academic interest in the more general questions of whether the charitable sector is an efficient producer of charitable outputs and whether these outputs have the right characteristics, such as quality and composition. Questions about efficiency and characteristics are important because the charitable sector not only provides a significant proportion of public goods and services but also because substantial amounts of support from the public purse are directed towards it. For instance, in 2017/18, the charitable sector in the United Kingdom was composed of 166,592 voluntary organizations that contributed £18.2 billion (about 1.5% of GDP) to the economy and employed 909,088 people (UK Civil Society Almanac, 2020).

While we have reached a better understanding of how charities and donors interact on the input, or fundraising, side of the marketplace (see Andreoni and Payne, 2013), there are

 DOI: 10.4324/9781003139201-21

fewer answers to questions relating to the output side of the market, specifically with respect to measuring overall efficiency and the optimal size and composition of the charitable sector. Issues of efficiency and composition in the charitable market tie in to the more general problem of measuring the efficiency of public goods production and its importance for social welfare (Atkinson, 2005; Simpson, 2009).

Coercive taxation has traditionally been interpreted as a means of overcoming the free-riding problem in public good provision and therefore underlies the central argument for government provision of such goods. Charities, on the other hand, lack the coercive power of the state. Instead, if they are to provide any output, they have to acquire resources from others (volunteer time or government handouts) or from devising fundraising strategies aimed at increase charitable income through altering donors' free-riding incentives. Whether fundraising strategies are successful depends on how donors respond to them. There is a large and growing evidence base about this "science of philanthropy", which mainly focuses on donor motives and on understanding how a charity can design the "perfect ask", that is, how individual charities can maximize the total amount of donations received (see, e.g., List, 2011; Andreoni and Payne, 2013; Vesterlund, 2016). However, while insights into optimal fundraising strategies provide useful answers to the question of whether fundraising is profitable to individual non-profits seeking to maximize their charitable income, they do not speak to questions related to production efficiency or the optimality of the size and shape of the sector. Those questions require an even broader perspective than that taken thus far (see Andreoni and Payne, 2013, for a discussion).

Here we explore this broader perspective. We do this through the lens of recent research that speaks to these questions in settings of inter-charity competition and donor responses when the following considerations are taken into account: (i) the distribution of donations across charitable causes, across time and in aggregate; (ii) the technological choices charities make when deciding on how to convert donations and other inputs in the production of charitable outputs; (iii) the structure of charitable markets. Using insights from (i)–(iii), we then briefly examine the role of government and tax incentives.

In devising their fundraising strategies, individual charities compete with other charities for soliciting funds from the same pool of potential donors. Yet it is donor responses to these fundraising drives that ultimately determines what happens to aggregate donations in the sector and the distribution of those donations across organizations within the sector. We are only beginning to understand how donor motivations interact with fundraising efforts when charities engage in fundraising competition. In particular, the successful fundraising drive of one charity could come at the expense of reducing donations received by other charities, as would be the case, if donors had a fixed budget for altruism. Whether donors' budget for altruism is indeed fixed (leading to 'fundraising cannibalism') is ultimately an empirical question that has not yet been fully settled (Ottoni-Wilhelm et al., 2021; Gee and Meer, 2019). Some stylized facts and findings support the fixed budget hypothesis, while others contradict it. For instance, from 2002–2017, improvements in fundraising technologies that are a direct result of the "science of philanthropy" have not significantly increased the total pot of donations in many countries. In the United States, giving to non-profits has been around 2% of GDP each year (Giving USA, 2018). Therefore, to assess how inter-charity competition affects the charitable sector's total income and the way it is distributed across its members, we need to understand exactly how fundraising competition drives specific patterns of donor responses not only in aggregate but also across charity space and time.

We have more to learn about how donors' motives for giving influence charitable donations and their distribution across causes, but we also need to develop a better understanding of how charities choose the production technologies that they use to convert funds and other inputs into outputs. Fundraising competition between charities can result in one of three outcomes in terms of the charitable income of the sector 'net of fundraising costs', that is, the 'income pie' of the sector: this pie can become smaller, stay the same or increase due to competition. If and only if all charities are operating with the best production technology for transforming donations into charitable goods and fundraising competition does not influence these technology choices, one could safely argue that fundraising competition that results in a bigger income pie is also unambiguously welfare enhancing. However, this unambiguous link between welfare and the size of the income pie can easily be broken if engaging in fundraising competition redirects funding towards charities that do not choose the best technology for transforming donations into charitable goods. In other words, fundraising competition may well alter the incentives for charities to be efficient producers of charitable goods. If true, the reverse effect can equally materialize: fundraising competition that directly reduces the net income of the sector but at the same time results in better technology choices could still enhance the overall performance of the sector if the efficiency gains from better production technology choices outweigh income losses. In sum, the 'size of the income pie' is only an insufficient proxy for the 'size of the output pie', the thing that matters most for evaluating performance if charities are to be considered efficient producers of public goods.

Which of these cases occurs depends on how donors respond to fundraising competition and how charities respond to those donor responses in terms of the technology choices that they make. It may also be that donors are directly influenced by the technological choices of charities, and if their donations are directed towards inefficient producers, charities may compete with other charities by adopting inferior technologies.

There is not much research that looks at these issues, but there is some emerging evidence that, unlike in the private sector, inter-charity competition can lead to an inefficient selection of providers and/or adoption by charities of inefficient modes of production. There are two main reasons that have been proposed for this. First, even if donors are fully aware of charities' performance, they could fail to coordinate their donations on the most efficient provider (Name-Correa and Yildirim, 2013; Perroni et al., 2019). Second, efficiency considerations may not be the foremost driver of their donation decisions (van Inwaarden, 2009; Ryazanov and Christenfeld, 2018). Such inefficiencies will be exacerbated if donors are not able to verify the quality of charities' output, which can lead to a higher quantity of low-quality charities entering the market or remaining in operation (Scharf, 2014; Krasteva and Yildirim, 2016). These explanations suggest that there should be a refocusing of the discussion about fundraising itself towards a more holistic assessment of the determinants of economic performance (efficiency) and ways in which informed giving can be promoted.

There are a limited number of papers addressing the implications of inter-charity competition for the structure of markets in the charitable sector. Fundraising, donor responses, government incentives and societal needs all determine the size and shape of the charitable sector. The first question is whether fundraising competition has led to an excessive size of the charitable sector. Excessive size can be the direct result of lacking competition in other aspects of charitable markets, such as prices or product quality. Apart from size, spatial factors play a crucial role in determining the structure of the charitable market. Not only is there empirical evidence that donors display a preference for giving to local charities (Tremblay-Boire and Prakash, 2017; Kessler and Milkman, 2018; Gallier et al. 2019a, 2019b), but there are also theoretical reasons to expect charities to specialize and localize (Bilodeau and Slivinski, 1997).

The previous discussion not only raises important considerations that need to be taken into account when assessing the performance of the non-profit sector; it also highlights the need to re-evaluate the relationship between the charitable sector and the public sector (e.g., whether privately provided charitable goods are substitutes or complements for public provision) and potential policy instruments for incentivizing efficiency in the sector as a whole (Atkinson, 1995). As we discuss more fully in the following, there is no sound efficiency-based rationale for government to be a provider of private goods. Yet such rationale exists for government to step in as a provider of public goods and services. What is less clear is whether government is better equipped to provide these in comparison to the charitable sector. Getting at the answer requires us to consider under what conditions government would provide the same varieties of charitable goods and services as the charitable sector and which form of provision, public or charitable, is best aligned with recipient preferences. It may be that fundraising competition in the charitable sector leads to more efficient outcomes than public provision. In this case, questions arise as to whether tax incentives or direct government grants are more effective at incentivizing charitable contributions, as well as questions about how social welfare calculations take into account measures of crowding-out effects and the cost of frictions of being a donor and/or claiming incentives. Besides tax incentives for giving and direct government grants, alternative forms of government intervention will also matter for welfare calculations. These could include subsidization of verifying output quality when there are information asymmetries between charities and donors.

As a starting point for considering the broader perspective we propose here, let us consider how the effects of competition differ between the non-profit sector and the for-profit sector of the economy. The standard mechanism through which positive selection is promoted in the provision of private goods is market competition. In the case of competition between for-profit firms producing private goods, the profit maximization objectives of firms are in structural opposition to those of consumers and to those of other firms. This opposition can nevertheless result in the selection of efficient firms when prices are allowed to play their role of coordinating demand and supply in different markets. Absent other market frictions (e.g., incomplete markets and incomplete information), perfect competition in the markets for private goods will result in exit by all firms that cannot profitably engage in marginal cost pricing. Competition limits entry and in the long run ensures that firms with an inefficient production technology (i.e., firms that are bad at converting capital and labour inputs into outputs) will incur losses until they are driven out of the market, customers get the products and quality they pay for, the number and size of firms is optimal and firms use a combination of labour and capital that allows them to produce goods in a cost-efficient manner (Arrow and Debreu, 1954).

Competition in the non-profit sector is rather different. By definition, charitable providers do not operate as for-profit entities with profit maximization objectives. Furthermore, the public goods and services they supply are characterized by non-rivalry and non-excludability in consumption, so the price mechanism does not work to clear markets. The lack of a price mechanism means that the selection of efficient charities through competition will be less powerful than the selection of efficient private firms through market competition: a charity that values its own activities comparatively more than those of similar charities may choose to operate even when it is comparatively inefficient, as long as the opportunity cost of continuing to operate, in terms of output lost relative to the potential output that could be achieved by other, more efficient charities, is not too large. In sum, competition in the non-profit sector does not put a brake on entry of charities that use inefficient production technologies. These can enter into a new market or continue operating as long as their funds are sufficient to cover their fixed costs. This lack of the disciplining effect of prices can easily result in a market structure where multiple charities of various sizes and geographical scope offer comparable goods and services yet differ in how efficient they are at converting the resources supplied by donors into these goods. Similarly, when quality is not readily observable, or the recipients of charitable goods cannot choose between multiple locally differentiated charities, charities offering low-quality services can co-exist with higher-quality providers. In both settings, the overall level or quality of public good provision could be improved if charities with efficient production technologies prevail. However, such quality differences are not readily observable for potential donors or targeted by public sector interventions if outputs are hard to measure because they are intangible, non-homogenous or uncountable (Scharf, 2014). Competition between charities supplying such outputs hence mostly takes the form of competition for inputs in which charities try to convince donors to give. Similarly, with current government subsidies and tax policies as a second source of charitable income, it is difficult for government policies to differentiate between lower- and higher-quality providers. A more targeted approach of subsidizing the charitable activities of the most efficient providers would be needed to replace the disciplining role that market competition plays in the private sector.

In the remaining sections, we will elaborate on (i)–(iii) in greater detail first separately and then jointly before concluding with (iv) and an outlook on a research agenda that may help to better understand how competition between charities can but may not improve the quantity and quality of goods provided.

An overview of inter-charity fundraising competition

Charities' fundraising strategies aim at generating income, which is then used to fund the provision of cause-specific public goods and services. Fundraising strategies often involve using matches or rebate incentives to lower a donor's perceived price of giving.[1] Advertising is the private-sector analogue to fundraising in the charitable sector. In the private sector, advertising expenditures in a perfectly competitive market are a waste of resources. Products are homogenous, so advertising does not lead to higher product quality, more efficient methods of production or more income for the market. Nor does it lead to better information for consumers, since a perfectly competitive marketplace is characterized by complete information. Advertising serves only to influence a consumer's choice of which firm to buy from (Schmalensee, 1972). Whether advertising is also a waste of resources when private markets are characterized by imperfect competition is less clear. On the one hand, if advertising has no social value (e.g., providing better information to the consumer), it is wasteful, resulting in higher prices for consumers and/or barriers to entry for new firms. On the other hand, if advertising is informative, it could enhance competition (through lower prices or weaker barriers to entry for innovation on the part of competitors) and result in a positive social value.

Non-profit organizations are not the same as private firms. In particular, non-profit organizations do not have profit maximization as their objective and so, unlike for-profit firms, face a binding non-distribution constraint. They lack a residual claimant for surpluses or losses incurred. The jury is still out on what motivates charitable organizations instead, but the literature suggests that a mix of prosocial and self-interested motivations are at work. Rose-Ackerman (1982) was the first to link charity motives to fundraising behaviour by showing that competition in charity markets (as measured by the number of charities offering homogenous outputs) leads to excessive fundraising and does not generate an increase in total donations going to the sector. For any market size, inter-charity competition in fundraising efforts merely convinces donors to choose one of many otherwise identical charitable providers.[2]

Rose-Ackerman (1982) also showed that an increase in competition for donations in the sector leads to more entry by charities, which each increase their fundraising activities to the point where the marginal cost of fundraising approaches its marginal benefit. Although we are not aware of any evidence that speaks to this, from an empirical perspective, if charities are, at least in part, driven by self-interested motives, we would expect increases in the number of charities in the market to be reflected in changes in fundraising efforts and vice-versa.

The baseline excessive fundraising result of Rose-Ackerman occurs in a world where charitable outputs are homogenous. In the real world, charitable markets do not offer up homogenous outputs. The sector is incredibly diverse in terms of the differentiation of its various outputs. This differentiation could be defined over the output itself or over the location of the output. If charitable outputs are not homogeneous, the conceptual relationship between the degree of competition as measured by an increase in the number of charities and the amount of fundraising that a charity engages in is not a priori clear: having to compete with more charities may prompt a charity to do more fundraising (as in Castaneda et al., 2008), but it may also reduce the effectiveness of any given fundraising drive, inducing a charity to reduce its fundraising efforts.

Distribution of donations across charitable causes, across time and in aggregate

In a differentiated charitable sector where charities' fundraising efforts drive competition for donations, how does fundraising influence donors' decisions about how much to give and which charities to give to? The theoretical concerns about the efficiency costs of excessive fundraising on the input side largely depend on what donors do in response to fundraising initiatives. Do donors respond to fundraising drives by simply shifting their donations to the charity with the more successful fundraising initiative, do they lift the amount they give to all charities, or do they shift and lift their donations? This is mainly an empirical question. However, its answer is crucial from a social welfare perspective. Only when fundraising activities lead to a net increase of giving to the sector as a whole (i.e., if there is a lift) can they be seen as a non-wasteful way of raising the level of public goods provided. If, instead, one charity loses what the other charity gains (i.e., a shift), fundraising is wasteful if charities are otherwise homogenous.

The empirical literature on fundraising and charitable inputs has recently turned to answering the question of how fundraising activities by one charity affect the income of other charities and thereby the overall sum of donations available to the charitable sector (Ottoni-Wilhelm et al., 2021; Gee and Meer, 2019). Understanding these effects is empirically challenging, as it is rarely possible for the researcher to observe the whole universe of giving (of time, money or in-kind donations) over the whole space of charities while being able to change the fundraising activities of one charity or cause randomly. Even if sufficiently detailed data were available, they would also need to be available over a long time period to understand how earlier giving to one charity affect giving to another charity later or vice versa (Ottoni-Wilhelm et al., 2021). Despite these challenges, there is now a growing number of experimental and empirical papers that try to understand these effects of competition on the total amount of donations flowing into the charitable sector (see Andreoni and Payne, 2013).

Due to the empirical challenges described previously, none of the existing studies can provide a full answer to this question. However, together, they indicate several regularities in the patterns of giving that may result when charities compete for a given pot of funds.

Several studies investigate how promoting giving to one charity reduces the amount given to another charity project at the same point in time (Meer, 2017) and whether the additional amount given to one charity is the same, larger or smaller than the amount lost by the other charity. Such spill-over effects are probably largest when charities offer a homogenous public good such that donors may not hold strong preferences over who provides the public good. Evidence on this question comes in three forms: lab experiments, field experiments and empirical studies.

While highly stylized in nature, laboratory experiments on the extent of spill-over effects offer a high level of control over the observed outcomes by holding constant any other shift parameters that may affect giving. The findings from the experimental laboratory are mixed, however. In line with the theoretical concerns raised in Rose-Ackerman (1982), showing a promotional video does not raise total donations while shifting donations to the charity conducting this fundraising activity (Harwell et al., 2015). Similarly, Deck and Murphy (2019) find that introducing a match for donations reduces the amounts received by other charities that do not offer a similar price incentive for giving. Finally, Schmitz (2019) exogenously varies the size of the charitable market for a homogenous charitable good in the presence or absence of a match. In line with the other studies, matching results in a negative spill-over: Giving to the matched charity increases, while donations to the unmatched charities decrease such that aggregate giving remains unchanged. Evidence for the observation that competition between charities simply leads to a redirection of funds is not univocal across all laboratory studies, however. Filiz-Ozbay and Uler (2019) introduce differentiated tax rebates in a multi-charity setting. Their findings suggest that the extent of negative spill-overs may depend on whether the outputs of competing charities are complements or substitutes. Negative spill-overs only occur for substitutes but not for complements. Moreover, in contrast to the other studies, they do not find that negative spill-overs are sufficiently strong to offset additional giving. In both cases, offering a tax rebate for one charity increases not only the share of donations going to subsidized charity but total donations.

Evidence on competition effects from the field is scarce. Several papers investigate the effect of multiple mail solicitations in which potential donors receive fundraising calls in temporal succession. This approach reveals how earlier fundraising efforts of one charity affect giving to the same charity or other charities at a later point in time. Donkers et al. (2017) find that additional mail solicitations by one charity reduce giving to other charities in the short term but not in the long term. There is also field evidence when charities compete for donations within a shorter time window. Gallier et al. (2019b) investigate spill-over effects in a setting where charities compete in a spatially differentiated market. They find little evidence that a matching grant offered by one charity significantly reduces giving to a second un-matched charity, in particular when the two charities operate in two different locations and donors can observe this local differentiation. This finding differs from Adena and Hager (2020), who provide evidence for substantial negative spill-overs in an online fundraising campaign on a social network platform. Thus, in parallel to lab experiments, the size and direction of spill-over effects in the field settings studied crucially depend on the context, type of fundraising and timeframe under investigation.

Finally, there a several empirical studies that investigate the extent to which fundraising competition affects aggregate giving. Van Diepen et al. (2009) show that fundraising drives immediately reduce giving to the same charity at a later point in time but increase giving to other charities. In the long run, these effects are negligible. Even in the short term, spill-overs may be small in some settings. For instance, offering a match for projects on a crowd-funding platform did not result in lower giving to other projects (Meer, 2017). Moving towards a causal interpretation, several studies exploit natural catastrophes or other sources of random variation to identify potential spill-over effects on other charities. Ottoni-Wilhelm et al. (2021) investigate the effect of a disaster appeal on donations to disaster relief and to other causes both immediately after the natural disaster and 20 weeks later. Immediately after the disaster, they find more giving not only to disaster relief but also to other causes. This short-term increase is, however, offset by a decrease in donations later. This observation is in line with Deryugina and Marx (2021), who find little evidence that giving to disaster relief immediately after a tornado reduces giving to other causes in the short run. All in all, most empirical evidence suggests that negative spill-over effects of fundraising activities are minor and dissipate quickly.

Technology choices and performance

As charities mainly compete for funding, it is donors' understanding and perceptions of the usefulness of overhead costs, actual performance and indirect performance metrics that will influence whether funding is directed to the most efficient charities. In the longer run, donor preferences will factor into whether competing charities choose efficient modes of production and produce high-quality outputs. When charities rely on donors' perceptions of their productivity, this raises complications in their production decisions that are absent for private firms. If donors' understanding of efficient production modes, performance and indirect performance metrics does not coincide with objective efficiency indicators, charities will optimize along the wrong dimensions. Moreover, charity managers may be inclined to influence how donors perceive their organization. Their attempt to provide success metrics that aid their fundraising efforts could refocus measurement and communication of performance indicators from harder-to-measure but more meaningful outcomes to more accessible but less meaningful output metrics. Across the sector as a whole, a focus on quantifiable performance metrics may also influence the composition of charitable goods offered. For instance, donors interested in impact giving may redirect their giving towards charitable outputs that can readily be measured and reduce giving towards less tangible outcomes like promoting civil rights (Ebrahim and Rangan, 2010).

Among the various performance metrics commonly used, the overhead ratio of a charity (or more generally its fixed costs) have received the most attention. A low overhead ratio means that a large proportion of charitable income covers a charity's core program expenses, that is, the public goods they fund. Donors often perceive high overhead costs as wasteful and thus a negative indicator of a charity's performance (e.g., Charles et al., 2020). Other actors in the charitable sector share this negative perception of fixed costs, and there is considerable variation in cost structures across charities and charitable sectors, which is likely to reflect variation in technologies.[3] However, this negative view ignores that sometimes, as in the private sector, using more efficient production technologies can require incurring higher fixed costs (Perroni et al., 2019). Moreover, charities may have more control over some parts of their overhead costs (e.g., salaries and administration) than others (e.g., the administrative costs of complying with government regulation or providing performance metrics) (Samahita and Lades, 2021).

In their paper, Perroni et al. (2019) discuss conditions for which government funding of fixed costs may be called for when charities compete. They show that if non-profit entrepreneurs are pro-socially motivated, but impurely so, they will have an incentive to misrepresent their technologies to donors and to enter the non-profit sector and compete with other charities even when the technology that they have access to is dominated by that of other charities. This gives rise to two kinds of inefficiencies relating to charity selection, with the result that output is not maximized for the given resources that donors and government allocate to the third sector.

The first type of inefficiency relates to entry by new providers. In the presence of a non-distribution constraint, any surplus or shortfall experienced by a charity is reflected in the level of its provision rather than in its residual profit claims. This makes it unattractive for individual donors to switch towards a start-up charity even if it is more efficient because such a switch would result in lower rather than higher provision unless the switch is coordinated across donors. As a result, when private contributions are directed towards charity providers that face fixed costs, non-cooperative contribution equilibria – as characterized by Bergstrom et al. (1986) – can support an inefficient status quo. Thus, in the absence of a residual claimant, fixed costs can not only be used strategically by an individual charity to coordinate their own set of donors, as fundraising fixed costs do in Name-Correa and Yildirim (2013), but they can also translate into entry barriers when charities choose them strategically in order to capture donations from other charities, as in Perroni et al. (2019).

These results contrast with the case of for-profit firms, since coordination between donors towards efficient charities is more complex than achieving coordination of consumers towards efficient firms. In the case of for-profit firms, consumers can be 'herded' towards more efficient firms through price competition: a for-profit challenger can undercut the incumbent and induce all consumers to switch, and it can do so credibly because consumers need not concern themselves about whether the challenger will succeed in meeting its objectives.

The second type of inefficiency results from sub-optimal technology adoption by incumbents. Fixed costs bring a risk of zero provision if they cannot be covered. Therefore, individuals will face incentives to abandon charities that adopt technologies with fixed costs in favour of other charities that adopt inferior, variable-cost-only technologies. This donor response will induce incumbent charities to forgo opportunities for exploiting scale economies and will make them adopt inferior technologies instead. Adopting an inefficient technology can thwart entry by more efficient challengers. For example, it may be that an incumbent charity has flexibility in its choice of technology; in this case, the presence of a less inefficient challenger can induce the incumbent to switch to an inferior technology with no fixed costs to protect its position. The final result is the same.

In either of the two cases discussed, the presence of fixed costs can bring about inefficient entry and/or (equivalently) the adoption of inferior technologies by incumbents. These conclusions are consistent with the prominence given by charities to core funding strategies. Charities often lament that donors are unwilling to fund core costs – making it difficult for start-up charities to get off the ground and for more established charities to cover management and general administration costs – and consistently lobby government to step in with grants to cover their fixed operating costs.[4]

Other research has also contributed to the debate on conduct and performance in the charitable sector vis-à-vis the for-profit sector,[5] but the implications of organizational form for inter-charity competition and industry structure have received less attention. An exception is Philipson and Posner (2009), who study competition between providers that pursue non-profit objectives. They consider markets that are not contestable, that is, where there are barriers to entry, concluding that, as in the case of for-profit firms, antitrust regulation may be called for. Their arguments hinge on the incentives that charities have to defend their incumbency position even when it is not socially efficient to do so. While antitrust measures are not well suited to tackle the specific kinds of coordination failures identified by Name-Correa and Yildirim (2013) and Perroni et al. (2019), public support of core funding needs may be able to alleviate them.

The previous discussion assumes that donors understand the role of fixed costs in capturing scale economies and that they have a good understanding of charities' production functions. Suppose instead that a significant fraction of giving is uninformed or has to rely on imperfect performance metrics. Then most donors would need to infer whether a charity is efficient by being able to verify the quality of output produced or by resorting to performance metrics that third parties provide.

If both donors and charities cared only about the quantity and quality of charitable output, their interests would be aligned, and there would be no need for such performance metrics.

Problems arise either when donors are primarily motivated by warm glow, that is, the act of giving itself (Andreoni, 1988, 1990), and therefore pay less attention to charity performance or if donors are motivated by altruism (i.e., by the level of public good provided) but cannot rely on charities pursuing the same motive (i.e., they act like impure altruists with some warm glow motives present).

The ramifications of impure altruism on the production side of charitable activities have been largely ignored. Two exceptions are Scharf (2014) and Krasteva and Yildirim (2016), who explore the incentives of impurely motivated charities to enter and/or continue operations. Scharf (2014) explores the welfare effects of warm-glow charities for entry and efficient selection of providers in the charitable sector. They show that altruistic motives can be sufficient for the most ineffective charities to exit (or not to enter in the first place). However, the lack of a price-based mechanism means that the selection of charities through competition will be less powerful than the selection of private firms through market competition: a charity that values its activities comparatively more than those of similar charities might choose to stay active even when it is comparatively inefficient, so long as the opportunity cost of doing so, in terms of loss of output relative to the potential output that could be achieved by other, more efficient charities, is not too large.

This setting can also provide the basis for comparing the selection effects of private donations and direct government grants. Private donors can freely choose to give to one charity over another similar charity, and they can stop their contributions to a charity that they perceive (rightly or wrongly) to be unsuccessful or increase or decrease their donations to charities depending on a purely subjective performance assessment. In sum, private donors are not accountable to anyone for their choices. Because of legal and political constraints, on the other hand, public funding arrangements do not give government the same level of discretion. Government is accountable to the public for its funding choices and cannot arbitrarily discriminate amongst charities or arbitrarily terminate its grants. Thus, even if government can perfectly observe performance, legitimately conditioning public funding of individual charities on their observed performance requires reliance on verifiable third-party signals – a constraint private donors do not face.

If verification constraints make government relatively less flexible at conditioning funding on performance than private donors, the latter will be in a better position to promote positive selection of charities through their giving choices. To the extent that this is the case, diverting funding away from direct grants towards subsidizing private donations, such as via tax rebates, can improve efficiency, even when it leaves the level of total funding unchanged; and vice-versa, diverting funding away from subsidizing private donations towards direct grants can adversely affect provision. Thus, measuring the crowding effects of government grants in terms of their effects on the volume of funding can understate their true impact on the effective (productivity-adjusted) provision level.

For donors to contribute in this productive way to charity selection, they have to be reactive to various performance metrics in their giving decisions; that is, their giving needs to be informed. Nevertheless, how informed is giving, and what metrics do donors take into account? This is an empirical question mainly studied via experiments. Donors react to simple ratings by watchdog organizations like Charity Navigator (Gordon et al., 2009). However, presenting scientific evidence on a charity's effectiveness (i.e., its ability to improve outcomes for recipients) does not increase the average gift size, although it affects donors differently contingent on their donations in prior donation drives (Karlan and Wood, 2017). Similarly, Metzger and Günther (2019) find in a lab experiment that only a minority of potential donors is interested in purchasing information on charities' effectiveness and administrative costs. Information about the former has no detectable effect on average gift size. It appears that a majority of donors takes an uniformed decision to give and hence cannot fulfil their essential role of directing funds to the highest-quality providers. As pointed out in Coffman (2017), this problem can even be exacerbated when donations are collected by intermediaries (like a workplace campaign, the girl scouts or a charity run) in lieu of charities, as donors are even less reactive to performance metrics in these circumstances.

Market structure

One aspect of charity performance is related to market size. We know that for private firms, larger and more competitive markets are more efficient. However, it is unclear if that conclusion carries over to not-for-profit markets. Two questions are of particular importance: First, what is the relationship between market size (e.g., population) and market entry of charitable organizations? Second, under which conditions does the market deliver efficient allocation (e.g., number of firms, size of firms)? The answers to these questions can have important implications on optimal policies regarding the charitable sector.

A recent paper by La Pointe et al. (2018) addresses both questions.[6] They develop a simple oligopoly model of fundraising competition between charities offering differentiated products. Their model delivers theoretical predictions which can be tested and related to analyses of the same questions asked of competition and performance in the private sector (Bresnahan and Reiss, 1991; Bloom et al., 2013). They find evidence that charities make decisions based partly on prosocial motives. As for the private sector, this finding implies that increased competition can lead to a better allocation of resources. The mechanism, however, is a different one: for the charitable market, a larger market already serves more varieties, which makes it harder for a pro-socially motivated charity to justify entering an already crowded marketplace when that entry eats into donations going to existing varieties and thus results in the reduced provision of existing varieties.

Apart from market size, a second question pertains to the extent of spatial differentiation in the sector. For some types of charities, competition in spatially differentiated markets is common. As for private firms (Lederer and Hurter, 1986; Anderson and De Palma, 1988), this market structure implies that charities offering homogenous goods may compete for donations by using the location at which their goods or services are provided as a distinguishing feature. An alternative to spatial differentiation would be offering services via a larger umbrella organization that offers the same product or service at various locations without stressing this as a determining feature of their operation. Foods banks, animal shelters, religious organizations, neighbourhood associations, safe houses, soup kitchens and other instances where the beneficiaries of the charitable good are concentrated in a well-defined geographical area are just a few charitable causes for which spatial differentiation of providers is a commonly encountered market form (Bilodeau and Slivinski, 1997). For instance, in the London metropolitan area alone, multiple food banks compete for funds or in-kind donations. The location of the different food banks is the distinguishing feature and is explicitly referenced in fundraising drives via their names, and gift aid forms of each provider specify their name even when they belong to a larger trust or organization.

Gallier et al. (2019a, 2019b) extend a standard model of impure altruism (Andreoni, 1990) to account for location-specific altruism. Their model suggest donor sorting, that is, a tendency to give locally in markets where donors and charities can share a location and donors receive additional (warm glow or altruistic) benefits from donations that flow to a charity that is located in their geographic proximity. The theoretical model is further supported by experiments that provide strong evidence for donor sorting. This experimental finding gives one strong rationale why spatially differentiated competition may be one commonly encountered market structure in the charitable sector. Further evidence for location-specific altruism and the importance of identity considerations for giving is found in Kessler and Milkman (2018).

Gallier et al. (2019b) also explore how differences in the price of giving between two spatially differentiated charities affect the charity with the relatively higher price of giving. Reducing the price of giving – through offering a match – has a comparable effect in spatially differentiated settings compared to in settings without spatial differentiation; that is, it increases the amount given to the charity offering the match. Even more importantly, there are no negative spill-over effects (and some instances of positive spill-overs) on charities not offering the match and hence having a relatively higher price of giving. For a spatially differentiated non-profit, however, positive spill-over effects between separate branches within their network imply that subsidizing the giving of local donors to local branches is the most profitable strategy for raising their total charitable income.

Public policy

There are good reasons for why economists are sceptical of governments engaging in the production of private goods. Without the disciplining effects of market competition, governments will not be efficient in providing such goods in the quality, composition and quantity demanded by their citizens, and provision costs will be excessive. Government's role is more obvious when it comes to providing public goods and services. As is well understood, at least since Samuelson (1954), private markets will underprovide such goods. Underprovision justifies a government stepping in and funding the provision of public goods and services through coercive taxation as a means of trying to improve on the private market outcome (Bergstrom et al., 1986). The charitable sector can also privately provide public goods and services and fund their provision with donations as a substitute for government provision. Or it may be that government and the charitable sector act in a complementary fashion, both providing public goods and services that are financed with donations and government revenue (e.g., tax incentives for giving).

While there is an efficiency-based rationale for government intervention in the provision of public goods and services, we do not have clear evidence about whether public provision of public goods through a government results in outcomes that are closer to the social optimum than private provision of the same type of goods through charitable organizations. The outcomes of interest are the amounts of public goods provided, the composition of public goods and services (varieties, location) and the financing of provision (e.g., donations and/or public funding). This raises the general and age-old question about whether governments and/or charities are better able to efficiently produce public goods that correspond to what the public desires in terms of size, quality and composition and whether the public sector and/or charities are more efficient in transforming inputs into outputs.

Governments can employ coercive contributions to public goods through their power to tax, so they do not have to rely on potentially wasteful fundraising. The charitable sector does not have the same ability to raise income through taxes but instead has to rely on voluntary donations. Because donations are voluntary, causes contributed to and the distribution of amounts given to each charity reflect a donor's preferences for public goods and services, which depends on their motives for giving. If aggregate contributions across causes are also reflective of the population's preferences, then the private sector may be better poised than government to provide the 'right' composition and amount of public goods and services. This argument is even stronger if donors can identify a direct link between charities' fundraising activities and efficient outcomes. However, extending political economy arguments to charitable giving (Horstmann et al., 2007; Horstmann and Scharf, 2008) suggests that rich or more numerous donor types can exert more influence on the variety of output that a charity provides and may even be able to, by the size of their donations, drag smaller donors away from their preferred varieties. The social welfare implications in these scenarios would be unclear: on the one hand, the charitable sector could be concentrated in few varieties that receive donations from rich and poor, even if the poor would prefer to provide something else, or the sector could be overly fragmented but with a composition more closely reflecting societal preferences (Sandford and Scharf, 2013).

If we see government's role primarily as supporting the third sector in their fundraising activities and regulating it, what policies are preferable from an efficiency perspective? Classically, governments have supported fundraising through tax incentives,[7] which are based on inputs and so do not directly address the inefficiencies that we have discussed here. This prominence of tax incentives for giving raises the important and unresolved question of why tax incentives are used as a significant channel for delivering public support to charities instead of relying solely on direct government grants. This question has provoked much debate and still does, especially in light of the pandemic, the financial crisis and the steadily increasing size and importance of the charitable sector and the corresponding increase in the level of government support directed to not-for-profit enterprises.

Since tax relief lowers the price of giving for donors,[8] there is a presumption that its rationale is to encourage private giving and boost charity funding – compared to direct government grants, tax incentives may result in a higher overall level of charity funding for the same amount of public funds.[9] This rationale, however, does not seem to square with available empirical evidence: recent estimates of the effects of tax incentives for giving on gross donations by private donors find price elasticities of giving to be less than one in absolute value – implying that the cost to the government of raising gross donations by one dollar exceeds one dollar.[10] In other words, there is empirical evidence for crowding-out effects of tax incentives.

In itself, this need not imply that subsidies are an ineffective way of delivering public funding to charities: as Roberts (1984) pointed out, even if tax incentives for giving leave net donations unchanged or reduce them, they may still dominate direct grants as a way of channelling government funds to charities if direct grants also crowd out private donations. It might also be argued that tax incentives result in giving that reflects donor preferences, whereas the use of grants breaks this link. This further muddies the waters as to draw conclusions about social welfare effects.

Empirical evidence suggests less-than-full crowding out of donations by direct government grants: Andreoni and Payne (2011) estimate crowding out of fundraising by direct grants to be around 25%.[11] When combining this with available estimates on price elasticities of giving, it would seem that there is not a strong prima facie case for tax incentives over direct grants.[12]

Recent research also shows the importance of taking into account extensive and intensive margin responses. A recent paper by Almunia et al. (2020) use administrative tax data around a 2010 tax reform and estimate an intensive-margin price elasticity of giving of −0.2. They model the extensive-margin response through a fixed cost of declaring donations, which is estimated to be around £47. Building on Roberts' model, they show that the welfare effects of tax incentives for donations are modified when extensive-margin responses are allowed for. Based on that theoretical framework and empirical results, a case can be made for increasing the subsidy on charitable giving in the United Kingdom.

The previous discussion suggests that in order to assess the relative effectiveness of direct grants and tax expenditures, evidence on price elasticities must be combined with evidence on crowding out of private giving by direct grants and evidence about associated frictions.

Considering a broader sectoral perspective can provide an alternative, supply-side-based rationale for the use of tax incentives for private giving: relying on tax incentives as alternatives to direct government grants may improve charity selection and performance. This effect would remain unmeasured in empirical estimates that focus on effects on the cost of provision by charities as measured by their overall budgets (their inputs) rather than the provision itself (their output). As well as being relevant for evaluations of third-sector performance, this selection effect can have important implications for public policy – not just in terms of rationalizing existing policies but also for designing new ones.

Finally, it is important to keep in mind that this positive selection effect of taxes over direct grants hinges on how informed donors are in their decision making (relative to a bureaucrat administering government grants). If information on charity performance is highly localized and widely distributed across the population, then it may well be that donors' decentralized information status is superior to the centralized knowledge of a government. If centralized knowledge is available, a government official may still be unsure how this knowledge translates into individual preferences. Yet here oversight and information sharing might be a policy that promotes the positive selection effect of tax incentives over direct grants.

Conclusion

We started out with the basic observation that competition for funding in the non-profit sectors differs from competition in the for-profit sector because prices cannot fulfil their usual coordination function. Absent this coordination function of prices, fundraising competition will not automatically lead to an efficient size of the charitable sector, an efficient selection of production technologies or an efficient market structure. Instead, we pointed out several inefficiencies that may prevail despite inter-charity competition or may even be exacerbated by it. Government policy needs to consider these potential sources of inefficiency when thinking about subsidies to the charitable sector in the form of tax rebates or direct grants. It also needs to consider limiting cases where direct government provision can be superior to the private provision of public goods and services through the charitable sector. Answering these questions requires the "science of philanthropy" to move beyond questions of designing the perfect ask and focus on questions about inter-charity competition and production efficiency. Answering this new set of questions requires theoretical models and experimental and empirical evidence that facilitate a better understanding of (i) whether the budget of altruism is fixed, (ii) what motivates charities (instead of donors), (iii) how much donors take charities' production functions into account when distributing funds and (iv) how the answers to these questions vary with government interventions and tax policies.

Notes

1 There is a large body of literature that compares the effectiveness of different kinds of fundraising strategies. These strategies include the use of match and rebate subsidies (Karlan and List, 2007; Eckel and Grossman, 2008), door-to-door fundraising (Landry et al., 2006; Landry, 2010; DellaVigna et al., 2012; Andreoni et al., 2017), lotteries (Morgan, 2000; Morgan and Sefton, 2000; Lange et al., 2007; Carpenter and Matthews, 2017), lead donations (Huck and Rasul, 2011), gifts (Falk, 2007; Alpizar et al., 2008), social information (Meier, 2007; Shang and Croson, 2009) and recognition (Harbaugh, 1998). For reviews, see Andreoni and Payne (2013), List (2011).

2 See also Weisbrod (1991), Andreoni and McQuire (1993), Andreoni (1998) and Name-Correa and Yildirim (2013).

3 We observe considerable variation in the composition of the funding sources of different charities: for some, the bulk of funding is represented by government grants, whereas for others, government grants are a relatively minor component of funding. There also appears to be some correlation between charities' funding from public sources and cost structures. La Pointe et al. (2018) find evidence for a positive correlation between fixed costs and the level of government funding received by charities relative to the total funding received for Canadian charities' revenues and costs across different sectors of activities.

4 The difficulties that charities face in persuading donors (especially small ones) to make donations that are not earmarked towards project costs and can be used to fund core costs leads charities to formulate specific core funding strategies. See, for example, Scott (2003). Government funding choices do appear to be sensitive to charities' core funding needs, but what is not clear is whether this is motivated by the need to promote entry by new charities – overcoming the implicit entry barriers that fixed costs induce in the presence of a non-distribution constraint – or by the need to support efficient technology adoption by incumbents.

5 This has focused mainly on the implications of organizational form for internal performance along various dimensions – information and agency costs (Alchian and Demsetz, 1972; Hansmann, 1980; Easley and O'Hara, 1983; Glaeser and Schleifer, 2001), differential regulatory and tax regimes (Lakdawalla and Philipson, 2006) and access to pro-socially motivated workforce (Ghatak and Mueller, 2011).

6 Papers that study not-for-profit competition have mostly focused on the health care sector (e.g., Propper et al., 2008; Gaynor and Vogt, 2003; Gaynor and Town, 2011; Capps et al., 2010).

7 See the 2020 OECD Report on Taxation and Philanthropy (OECD, 2020).

8 Tax relief can take various forms: deductions of donations from taxable income as in the United States; tax credits at the marginal rate of income taxation, a system similar to the one used in Canada; a proportional match claimed directly by charities on donations received as used in the United Kingdom. All of these methods result in a lower price of giving for donors.

9 The question of why governments would want to encourage private giving has been the source of much debate in the economics literature and in the policy debate. Research that has focused attention on this question includes that of Feldstein and Clotfelter (1976), Warr (1982) and Scharf (2000). In the United Kingdom, tax incentives for giving are the result of the normalization of a late 19C fundraising scheme offering donors the chance to avoid paying tax on donations made by Deed of Covenant.

10 In early studies, price elasticities of giving were found to be negative and greater than one in absolute value (these results are summarized by Clotfelter, 1985, and Triest, 1998), but more recent studies have shown that estimates are highly sensitive to the empirical strategy and to whether there are corrections for short-term price effects. For example, Randolph (1995) uses panel data to find a long-run price elasticity of giving of –.51. Using a longer but similar panel to that used by Randolph but a different estimation technique, Auten et al. (2002) arrive at the significantly higher estimate of –1.26. More recently, Bakija and Heim (2011) find a long-run value of –.7 – close to Randolph's estimate. See also Fack and Landais, (2010) and Scharf and Smith (2015). In sum, it is difficult to exactly estimate the price elasticity of giving and results may reflect the availabitlity of data and the econometric methods used.

11 When changes in fundraising costs are taken into account, this estimate has been shown to be even higher (up to 60% in Andreoni and Payne, 2011).

12 On the basis of the aforementioned elasticity estimates, incorporating second-best optimal tax considerations in the presence of endogenous labour supply decisions (Saez, 2004; Diamond, 2006) does not substantially affect the conclusions. Yet another rationale could be preference revelation (see Horstmann and Scharf, 2008, who look at the implications for segregation outcomes when donations are positively correlated to income inequality): by donating to certain charities, individuals reveal their preferences towards alternative forms of collective consumption; government support of private giving then results in government funds being directed where individuals ostensibly wish them to be directed.

References

Adena, Maja, and Anselm Hager. 2020. "Does Online Fundraising Increase Charitable Giving? A Nation-Wide Field Experiment on Facebook." WZB Discussion Paper No. SP II 2020–302.

Alchian, Armen A., and Harold Demsetz. 1972. "Production, Information Costs, and Economic Organization." *American Economic Review* **62**(5): 777–795.

Almunia, Miguel, Irem Guceri, Ben Lockwood, and Kimberley Scharf. 2020. "More Giving or More Givers? The Effects of Tax Incentives on Charitable Donations in the UK." *Journal of Public Economics* **183**: 104114.

Alpizar, Francisco, Fredrik Carlsson, and Olof Johansson-Stenman. 2008. "Anonymity, Reciprocity, and Conformity: Evidence from Voluntary Contributions to a National Park in Costa Rica." *Journal of Public Economics* **92**(5): 1047–1060.

Anderson, S.P. and A. De Palma. 1988. "Spatial Price Discrimination with Heterogeneous Products." *The Review of Economic Studies* **55**(4): 573–592.

Andreoni, J. 1988. "Privately Provided Public Goods in a Large Economy: The Limits of Altruism." *Journal of Public Economics* **35**(1): 57–73.

Andreoni, J. 1990. "Impure Altruism and Donations to Public Goods: A Theory of Warm-Glow Giving." *The Economic Journal* **100**(401): 464–477.

Andreoni, James. 1998. "Toward a Theory of Charitable Fundraising." *Journal of Political Economy* **106**(6): 1186–1213.

Andreoni, James, and A. Abigail Payne. 2013. "Charitable Giving." In *Handbook of Public Economics*, Vol. 5, ed. Alan Auerbach, Raj Chetty, Martin Feldstein, and Emmanuel Saez: 1–50. Amsterdam: North Holland.

Andreoni, J., and A.A. Payne. 2011. "Is Crowding Out Due Entirely to Fundraising? Evidence from a Panel of Charities." *Journal of Public Economics* **95**(5–6): 334–343.

Andreoni, James, Justin M. Rao, and Hannah Trachtman. 2017. "Avoiding the Ask: A Field Experiment on Altruism, Empathy, and Charitable Giving." *Journal of Political Economy* **125**(3): 625–653.

Andreoni, James, and Martin C. McQuire. 1993. "Identifying the Free-Riders. A Simple Algorithm for Determining Who Will Contribute to a Public Good." *Journal of Public Economics* **51**: 447–454.

Arrow, Kenneth, and Gerard Debreu. 1954. "Existence of an Equilibrium for a Competitive Economy." *Econometrica* **22**(3): 265–290.

Atkinson, A.B. 1995. "The Welfare State and Economic Performance." *National Tax Journal* **48**(2): 171–198.

Atkinson, Anthony. 2005. *The Atkinson Review Final Report: Measurement of Government Output and Productivity for the National Accounts*. London: Palgrave MacMillan.

Auten, Gerald, Holger Sieg, and Charles Clotfelter. 2002. "Charitable Giving, Income, and Taxes: An Analysis of Panel Data." *American Economic Review* **92**(1): 371–382.

Bakija, Jon, and Bradley Heim. 2011. "How Does Charitable Giving Respond to Incentives and Income? New Estimates from Panel Data." *National Tax Journal* **64**(2): 615–750.

Bergstrom, Theodore, Lawrence Blume, and Hal Varian. 1986. "On the Private Provision of Public Goods." *Journal of Public Economics* **29**: 25–49.

Bhutta, Neil, Jacqueline Blair, Lisa Dettling, and Kevin Moore. 2020. "COVID-19, the CARES Act, and Families Financial Security." *National Tax Journal* **73**(3): 645–672.

Bilodeau, Marc, and Al Slivinski. 1997. "Rival Charities." *Journal of Public Economics* **66**(3): 449–467.

Bloom, Nicholas, Mark Schankerman, and John Van Reenen. 2013. "Identifying Technology Spillovers and Product Market Rivalry." *Econometrica* **81**(4): 1347–1393.

Bresnahan, Timothy F., and Peter C. Reiss. 1991. "Entry and Competition in Concentrated Markets." *Journal of Political Economy* **99**(5): 977–1009.

Capps, C., D. Dranove, and R.C. Lindrooth. 2010. "Hospital Closure and Economic Efficiency." *Journal of Health Economics* **29**(1): 87–109.

Carpenter, Jeffrey, and Peter Hans Matthews. 2017. "Using Raffles to Fund Public Goods: Lessons from a Field Experiment." *Journal of Public Economics* **150**: 30–38.

Castaneda, Marco, John Garen, and Jeremy Thornton. 2008. "Competition, Contractibility, and the Market for Donors to Non-Profits." *Journal of Law, Economics & Organization* **24**: 215–246.

Charles, C., Sloan, M.F., and Schubert, P. 2020. "If Someone Else Pays for Overhead, Do Donors Still Care?" *The American Review of Public Administration* **50**(4–5): 415–427.

Clotfelter, Charles. 1985. *Federal Tax Policy and Charitable Giving. National Bureau of Economic Research Monologue*. Chicago: University of Chicago Press.

Coffman, Lucas. 2017. "Fundraising Intermediaries Inhibit Quality-Driven Charitable Donations." *Economic Inquiry* **55**(1): 409–424.

Deck, Cary, and James J. Murphy. 2019. "Donors Change Both their Level and Pattern of Giving in Response to Contests Among Charities." *European Economic Review* **112**: 91–106.

DellaVigna, Stefano, John A. List, and Ulrike Malmendier. 2012. "Testing for Altruism and Social Pressure in Charitable Giving." *Quarterly Journal of Economics* **127**(1): 1–56.

Deryugina, Tatyana, and Benjamin Marx. 2021. "Is the Supply of Charitable Donations Fixed? Evidence from Deadly Tornadoes." *American Economic Review: Insights*, **3**(3): 383–398. Diamond, Peter. 2006. "Optimal Tax Treatment of Private Contributions for Public Goods with and Without Warm Glow Preferences." *Journal of Public Economics* **90**(4–5): 897–919.

Donkers, Bas, Merel van Diepen, and Philip Hans Franses. 2017. "Do Charities Get More When They Ask More Often? Evidence from a Unique Field Experiment." *Journal of Behavioral and Experimental Economics* **66**: 58–65.

Easley, David, and Maureen O'Hara. 1983. "The Economic Role of the Non-Profit Firm." *The Bell Journal of Economics* **14**(2): 531–38.

Ebrahim, Alnoor, and V. Kasturi Rangan. 2010. "The Limits of Non-Profit Impact: A Contingency Framework for Measuring Social Performance." Harvard Business School Working Paper No. 10–099.

Eckel, Catherine, and Philip Grossman. 2008. "Subsidizing Charitable Contributions: A Natural Field Experiment Comparing Matching and Rebate Subsidies." *Experimental Economics* **11**(3): 234–252.

Fack, Gabrielle, and Camille Landais. 2010. "Are Tax Incentives for Charitable Giving Efficient? Evidence from France." *American Economic Journal: Economic Policy* **2**(2): 117–141.

Falk, Armin. 2007. "Gift Exchange in the Field." *Econometrica* **75**(5): 1501–1511.

Feldstein, Martin, and Charles Clotfelter. 1976. "Tax Incentives and Charitable Contributions in the United States: A Microeconometric Analysis." *Journal of Public Economics* **5**: 1–26.

Filiz-Ozbay, Emel, and Neslihan Uler. 2019. "Demand for Giving to Multiple Charities: An Experimental Study." *Journal of the European Economic Association* **17**(3): 725–753.

Gallier, Carlo, Timo Goeschl, Martin Kesternich, Johannes Lohse, Christiane Reif, and Daniel Röme. 2019a. "Leveling Up? An Inter-Neighborhood Experiment on Parochialism and the Efficiency of Multi-Level Public Goods Provision." *Journal of Economic Behavior & Organization* **164**: 500–517.

Gallier, Carlo, Timo Goeschl, Martin Kesternich, Johannes Lohse, Christiane Reif, and Daniel Röme. 2019b. "Inter-Charity Competition Under Spatial Differentiation: Sorting, Crowding, and Spill-Overs." ZEW-Centre for European Economic Research Discussion Paper 19–039.

Gaynor, M., and R.J. Town. 2011. "Competition in Health Care Markets." *Handbook of Health Economics*, **2**: 499–637.

Gaynor, Martin, and William B. Vogt. 2003. "Competition Among Hospitals." *The RAND Journal of Economics* **34**(4): 764–785.

Gee, Laura K., and Jonathan Meer. 2019. "The Altruism Budget: Measuring and Encouraging Charitable Giving." NBER Working Paper w25938.

Ghatak, Maitreesh, and Hannes Mueller. 2011. "Thanks for Nothing? Not-for-Profits and Motivated Agents." *Journal of Public Economics* **95**(1–2): 94–105.

Giving USA Foundation. 2018. "Giving USA 2018." https://givingusa.org.

Glaeser, Edward L., and Andrei Schleifer. 2001. "Not-for-Profit Entrepreneurs." *Journal of Public Economics* **81**(1): 99–115.

Gordon, Teresa P., Cathryn L. Knock, and Daniel G. Neely. 2009. "The Role of Rating Agencies in the Market for Charitable Contributions: An Empirical Test." *Journal of Accounting and Public Policy* **28**(6): 469–484.

Hansmann, Henry. 1980. "The Role of the Non-Profit Enterprise." *Yale Law Journal* **89**(5): 835–901.

Harbaugh, William. 1998. "The Prestige Motive for Making Charitable Transfers." *American Economic Review* **88**(2): 277–282.

Harwell, Haley, Daniel Meneses, Chris Moceri, Marc Rauckhorst, Adam Zindler, and Catherine Eckel. 2015. "Did the Ice Bucket Challenge Drain the Philanthropic Reservoir? Economic Research Laboratory, Texas A&M University, Working Paper.

Horstmann, Ignatius, and Kimberley Scharf. 2008. "A Theory of Distributional Conflict, Voluntarism and Segregation." *Economic Journal* **118**: 427–453.

Horstmann, Ignatius, Kimberley Scharf, and Al Slivinski. 2007. "Can Private Giving Promote Economic Segregation?" *Journal of Public Economics* **91**: 1095–1118.

Huck, Steffen, and Imran Rasul. 2011. "Matched Fundraising: Evidence from a Natural Field Experiment." *Journal of Public Economics* **95**: 351–362.

Karlan, Dean, and John A. List. 2007. "Does Price Matter in Charitable Giving? Evidence from a Large-Scale Natural Field Experiment." *American Economic Review* **97**(5): 1774–1793.

Karlan, Dean, and Daniel H. Wood. 2017. "The Effect of Effectiveness: Donor Response to Aid Effectiveness in a Direct Mail Fundraising Experiment." *Journal of Behavioral and Experimental Economics* **66**: 1–8.

Kessler, Judd B., and Katherine L. Milkman. 2018. "Identity in Charitable Giving." *Management Science* **64**(2): 845–859.

Kim, Mirae, and Dyana P. Mason. 2020. "Are You Ready: Financial Management, Operating Reserves, and the Immediate Impact of COVID-19 on Nonprofits." *Nonprofit and Voluntary Sector Quarterly* **49**(6): 1191–1209.

Krasteva, Silvana, and Huseyin Yildirim. 2016. "Information, Competition, and the Quality of Charities." *Journal of Public Economics* **144**: 64–77.

La Pointe, Simon, Janne Tukiainen, Carlo Perroni, and Kimberley Scharf. 2018. "Does Market Size Matter Also for Charities?" *Journal of Public Economics* **168**: 127–145.

Lakdawalla, Darius, and Tomas Philipson. 2006. "The Nonprofit Sector and Industry Performance." *Journal of Public Economics* **90**(8–9): 1681–1698.

Landry, Craig E., Andreas Lange, John A. List, Michael K. Price, and Nicholas G. Rupp. 2006. "Toward an Understanding of the Economics of Charity: Evidence from a Field Experiment." *Quarterly Journal of Economics* **121**(2): 747–782.

Landry, Craig E., Andreas Lange, John A. List, Michael K. Price, and Nicholas G. Rupp. 2010. "Is a Donor in Hand Better Than Two in the Bush? Evidence from a Natural Field Experiment." *American Economic Review* **100**(2): 958–983.

Lange, Andreas, John A. List, and Michael K. Price. 2007. "Using Lotteries to Finance Public Goods: Theory and Experimental Evidence." *International Economic Review* **48**(3): 901–927.

Lederer, P.J. and A.P. Hurter Jr. 1986. "Competition of Firms: Discriminatory Pricing and Location." *Econometrica: Journal of the Econometric Society* **54**(3): 623–640.

List, John. 2011. "The Market for Charitable Giving." *Journal of Economic Perspectives* **25**(2): 157–180.

Meer, Jonathan. 2017. "Does Fundraising Create New Giving?" *Journal of Public Economics* **145**: 82–93.

Meier, Stephan. 2007. "Do Subsidies Increase Charitable Giving in the Long Run? Matching Donations in a Field Experiment." *Journal of the European Economic Association* **5**(6): 1203–1222.

Metzger, Laura, and Isabel Günther. 2019. "Making An Impact? The Relevance of Information on Aid Effectiveness for Charitable Giving. A Laboratory Experiment." *Journal of Development Economics* **136**: 18–33.

Morgan, John, 2000. "Financing Public Goods by Means of Lotteries." *Review of Economic Studies* **67**(4): 761–784.

Morgan, John, and Martin Sefton. 2000. "Funding Public Goods with Lotteries: Experimental Evidence." *Review of Economic Studies* **67**(4): 785–810.

Name-Correa, Alvero J., and Huseyin Yildirim. 2013. "A Theory of Charitable Fundraising with Costly Solicitations." *American Economic Review* **103**(2): 1091–1107.

OECD. 2020. *Taxation and Philanthropy*, OECD Tax Policy Studies, No. 27. Paris: OECD Publishing.

Ottoni-Wilhelm, Mark, and Sarah Smith. Forthcoming. "Lift and Shift: The Effect of Fundraising Interventions in Charity Space and Time," forthcoming in the *American Economic Journal: Economic Policy*, 2021; CEPR Discussion Paper 12338, September 2017.

Perroni, Carlo, Ganna Pogrebna, Sarah Sanders, and Kimberley Scharf. 2019. "Are Donors Afraid of Core Costs? Economies of Scale and Contestability in Charity Markets." *Economic Journal* **129**: 2608–2636.

Philipson, T.J. and R.A. Posner. 2009. "Antitrust in the Not-for-Profit Sector." *The Journal of Law and Economics* **52**(1), 1–18.

Propper, Carol, Simon Burgess, and Denise Gossage. 2008. "Competition and Quality: Evidence from the NHS Internal Market 1991–9." *The Economic Journal* **118**(525): 138–170.

Randolph, W.C. 1995. "Dynamic Income, Progressive Taxes, and the Timing of Charitable Contributions." *Journal of Political Economy* **103**(4): 709–738.

Roberts, Russell. 1984. "A Positive Model of Private Charity and Public Transfers." *Journal of Political Economy* **92**(10): 136–148.

Rose-Ackerman, Susan. 1982. "Charitable Giving and 'Excessive' Fundraising." *Quarterly Journal of Economics* **97**(2): 193–212.

Ryazanov, Arseny, and Nicholas Christenfeld. 2018. "On the Limited Role of Efficiency in Charitable Giving." *Non-profit and Voluntary Sector Quarterly* **47**(5): 939–959.

Saez, Emmanuel. 2004. "The Optimal Treatment of Tax Expenditures." *Journal of Public Economics* **88**(12): 2657–2684.

Samahita, Margaret, and Leonhard K. Lades. 2021 "The Unintended Side Effects of Regulating Charities: Donors Penalise Administrative Burden Almost as Much as Overheads." University College Dublin Working Paper WP21/06.

Samuelson, Paul. 1954. "The Pure Theory of Public Expenditure." *The Review of Economics and Statistics* **36**(4): 387–389.

Sandford, Sarah, and Kimberley Scharf. 2013. "Mission Impossible? Inequality and Inefficient Fragmentation in the Charitable Sector." London School of Economics, Unpublished Manuscript.

Scharf, Kimberley. 2000. "Why Are Tax Expenditures for Giving Embodied in Fiscal Constitutions?" *Journal of Public Economics* **75**(3): 365–387.

Scharf, Kimberley. 2014. "Impure Prosocial Motivation in Charity Provision: Warm-Glow Charities and Implications for Public Funding." *Journal of Public Economics* **114**: 50–57.

Scharf, Kimberley, and Sarah Smith. 2015. "The Price Elasticity of Charitable Giving: Does the Form of Tax Relief Matter?" *International Tax and Public Finance* **22**(2): 330–352.

Schmalensee, Richard. 1972. *The Economics of Advertising, Contributions to Economic Analysis 80*. Amsterdam: North-Holland Publishing Company.

Schmitz, Jan. 2019. "Temporal Dynamics of Pro-Social Behavior: An Experimental Analysis." *Experimental Economics* **22**: 1–23.

Scott, Katherine. 2003. *Funding Matters: The Impact of Canada's New Funding Regime on Non-Profit and Voluntary Organizations*. Ottawa: Canadian Council on Social Development.

Shang, Jen, and Rachel Croson. 2009. "A Field Experiment in Charitable Contribution: The Impact of Social Information on the Voluntary Provision of Public Goods." *Economic Journal* **119**: 1422–1439.

Simpson, Helen. 2009. "Productivity in Public Services." *Journal of Economic Surveys* **23**(2): 250–276.

Tremblay-Boire, Joannie, and Aseem Prakash. 2017. "Will You Trust Me? How Individual American Donors Respond to Informational Signals Regarding Local and Global Humanitarian Charities." *Voluntas: International Journal of Voluntary and Non-Profit Organizations* **28**(2): 621–647.

Triest, R.K. 1998. "Econometric Issues in Estimating the Behavioral Response to Taxation: A Nontechnical Introduction." *National Tax Journal* **51**(4): 761–772.

UK Civil Society Almanac. 2020. *National Council on Voluntary Organisations*. London. https://data.ncvo.org.uk/.

Van Diepen, Merel, Bas Donkers, and Philip Hans Franses. 2009. "Dynamic and Competitive Effects of Direct Mailings: A Charitable Giving Application." *Journal of Marketing Research* **46**(1): 120–133.

van Iwaarden, Jos, Ton van der Wiele, Roger Williams, and Claire Moxham. 2009. "Charities: How Important Is Performance to Donors?" *International Journal of Quality & Reliability Management* **26**(1): 5–22.

Vesterlund, Lise. 2016. "Using Experimental Methods to Understand Why and How We Give to Charity." *The Handbook of Experimental Economics* **2**: 91–151. Elsevier, Holland.

Warr, Peter. 1982. "Pareto Optimal Redistribution and Private Charity." *Journal of Public Economics* **19**: 131–138.

Weisbrod, Burton. 1991. *The Nonprofit Economy*. Cambridge, MA: Harvard University Press.

19

HOW CAN WE IMPROVE TAX INCENTIVES FOR CHARITABLE GIVING? LESSONS FROM FIELD EXPERIMENTS IN FUNDRAISING

Maja Adena

1 Introduction

When thinking about what tax treatment is optimal for donations, researchers to date have had to rely mostly on cross-sectional or longitudinal data from tax returns in their empirical analysis. Their ability to draw causal conclusions from such data is limited, and they have to rely on relatively strict identification assumptions. Even if the period studied contains tax changes over time, the identification problems will still include the following: all individuals are affected by the tax changes in the same way, different individuals are affected differently, or changes to the tax rate affect both the price of giving and disposable income at the same time. A type of experiment in which a random half of the population would face a different tax rate from the rest of the population in a particular year could provide causal assessment of the policy in question but is rather infeasible.

This is exactly what field experiments with donors to charitable organizations can achieve, even if at a much smaller scale. Recent advances in such experiments can provide us with valuable insights that could also inform the design of the tax code with respect to donations. In this chapter, I connect the literature on the tax treatment of donations with recent field experimental studies in fundraising. Although most of the field experiments I review subsequently are designed with the aim of informing charitable organizations about what works best for their fundraising campaigns[1] and not with a view to aiding tax authorities, many elements of their designs are similar to the tax code. Such elements include reductions in the price of giving and thresholds for such reduction. The advantage of field experiments is that they allow researchers to arrive at clean causal conclusions without strict identification assumptions that are needed when using naturally occurring data (List, 2008).

Although some of the questions discussed in this chapter have been analyzed in other types of experiments – mostly laboratory but also online and natural experiments – I will not cover these

DOI: 10.4324/9781003139201-22

(with some exceptions). The reasons for this are as follows: First, covering all the experimental literature would exceed the scope of this chapter. Second, I concentrate on the field experiments because they generally offer a higher external validity than laboratory or online experiments while providing causal inference without relying on potentially restrictive assumptions (in contrast to many natural experiments). There are limitations of relying on field experiments as well. While some might offer innovative designs leading to higher charitable contributions, there might be, of course, other reasons that make the integration of such designs into the tax system not desirable or feasible. And even for uncontroversial and feasible designs, there is no guarantee that they will work when they are integrated into the tax code. The tests in field experiments are usually performed with one organization and one type of potential donor such that the results obtained might differ from general equilibrium results, that is, for all charities and individuals. Still, I believe that reflecting on those studies might be helpful with a view to advancing our thinking about the tax treatment of charitable giving.

I will structure the chapter in the following way. In Section 2, I review studies showing that individuals have a poor idea about their tax-price of giving and that they are inattentive to the tax incentives at the point when they make their donations. In Section 3, I review the literature that studies thresholds for price reduction, including novel approaches based on personalization. In Section 4, I will turn towards the field experiments that compare the effects of price reduction with direct grants to charities. In Section 5, I compare matching with rebate subsidies. In Section 6, I point to the more basic question of whether total donation revenue can be increased or whether taxpayers merely shift donations between recipients and over time as a result of a change in incentives. In the latter case, any change in the tax code with respect to donation treatment would only change the amount of declared donations and not the total amount. Section 7 concludes.

2 Timing, awareness, and transaction costs

In several countries, the income tax is designed in such a way that charitable donations reduce taxable income, hence reducing the effective price of giving. The price becomes one minus the marginal tax. This is the case, for example, in the United States and Germany. In practice, this does not necessarily mean that donors have to pay a lower tax on their income at the time when they make the donation but rather that they receive a refund for some part of the donation later. This is the case for many individuals in Germany. The statistical office reports that in 2016, 13.7 million of the approximately 25.5 million individuals subject to income taxation filled in a tax declaration, and of those, 12 million received a refund,[2] while only 1.5 million had to make a supplementary payment.[3] The time point at which the individual receives the refund must then necessarily be some time after the donation decision(s). If a person in Germany donates at the beginning of year one, she may not file her tax declaration before the end of February of year three (if she uses a tax advisor or a neighborhood organization that offers tax help). If we assume it takes the tax office another three months to verify the declaration, the difference between the time of donation and a refund might amount to 29 months (and, of course, it might be even longer). Even a person who makes a typical end-of-year donation and timely tax declaration can expect a 5–8-month lag.

Another issue is that taxpayers are unlikely to know their exact marginal tax and thus their individual tax-price for giving until they file their tax declaration and the tax authority approves it. Depending on the complexity of the tax system, this number is difficult to calculate, particularly for donations at the beginning of the tax year, as many income-related factors might change (like a pay raise, loss of a job, or changes in family composition). But even for later donations, additional tax-deductible activities might arise or, finally, the tax authority might not recognize some of them. Moreover, donors seldom are reminded of the tax incentives when they make a donation, so they might easily be inattentive or forget about tax benefits. This leads to the following question: To what extent do individuals account for their individual tax-price when making their donations?

Even if a number of empirical studies show that tax incentives are effective in encouraging donations, at least for those with high incomes (see Chapter 12 and references cited therein), it is still unclear what fraction of donations are included in the tax declaration. Clearly, people do not list some donations at all (like money put in a donation box or spare change given to the homeless people), and some individuals might decide ex post on whether to include their donations in the tax declaration. They will not include them if the hassle costs of the deduction (which likely vary over time) are higher than the expected refund value.

To my knowledge, there is only one experimental work devoted to studying those questions in detail. In two large-scale field experiments, Teirlinck (2020) found that donors in Germany are inattentive to tax incentives and hold misperceptions about their individual tax-price. She showed that both making tax incentives salient at the donation stage and providing personalized information increases donations. She also showed that the effect was larger for high-income individuals and that the reason for that was higher hassle costs of tax filing and claiming deductions for low-income individuals. In contrast, in a field experiment in Italy, Casarico and Tonin (2018) documented that mentioning the possibility of a tax deduction in a fundraising campaign reduced donations. This reduction was greatest for small donors, which could relate to transaction/hassle costs as in Teirlinck (2020). The seemingly contradictory results between Teirlinck (2020) and Casarico and Tonin (2018) might arise because of a different content of the information provided (it is much more detailed and personalized in Teirlinck, 2020) or differences between the two countries. This clearly shows that more research on this topic is needed.

3 Thresholds

Some tax schemes include minimum thresholds for charitable donations – only donations above the threshold reduce taxable income and thus have lower price. Such thresholds are usually of a fixed value or defined as a percentage of income. Minimum thresholds lead to non-convex budget sets, and such non-convexities have been studied in a number of field experiments. Huck, Rasul, and Shephard (2015) introduced a treatment in which donations above €50 were matched 1:1 – that is, they had a price of 0.5 – while those below €50 were not matched and had a price of 1. They compared this non-convex matching scheme to a linear 1:1 and 1:0.5 matching and other schemes. Using a structural estimation approach, they concluded that if a matching scheme is preferred, then non-convex matching with a lower price for higher gifts outperforms simple linear matching. They also suggested tailoring such matching schemes to the characteristics of potential donors. Such personalization was explored by Adena and Huck (2019a). In a theoretical framework, they showed how personalized thresholds can increase donation values. Such thresholds should be set slightly above the individual's optimal donation in the absence of matching. Of course, in practice, the latter is not observed. The authors proposed to proxy it with past donation values or to estimate it. They tested this idea in a field experiment with past donors and past non-donors. For both groups, they observed a number of individual characteristics. For past donors, they proxied the optimal donation with the past donation and set the threshold for a fixed match amount at different levels relative to this past donation. They found that the best results were obtained if the threshold was set at around 60–75% above the past donation. While such personalization is not feasible and potentially also not desirable for the tax code, they also showed that similar results can be achieved when a fairly small number of individual characteristics are used to set a threshold. They predicted the optimal donation of non-donors by extrapolating from the group of past donors and their individual characteristics. On the basis of this prediction, they set the threshold around the estimated values and obtained similar results to those obtained when the individual past donation was actually known. Again, the most effective threshold was around 75% above the predicted donation. Stunningly, the amount of information on individuals used for the prediction was fairly limited. How could this idea be applied to the tax treatment of donations? Different thresholds could be implemented depending on, for example, income and the number of children instead of 'one size fits all'. And what if personalized or characteristic-dependent thresholds are not feasible or desirable? Castillo and Petrie (2021) studied an optimal choice of uniform thresholds. In a large-scale field experiment and using a structural estimation, they concluded that such thresholds should be set relatively high. While the maximum threshold used in the experiment was $500, the estimated optimum threshold should be set at $2,000.

As pointed out in Chapter 10, (minimum) thresholds might also impact behavior by imposing a particular norm of giving. Adena and Huck (2019a) discovered that their results from a field experiment with non-personalized thresholds closely followed the patterns from the literature on suggested donation amounts and defaults as reviewed in Adena, Huck, and Rasul (2014). Thresholds and suggestions increase the likelihood that the donation will be the exact or near the suggested value. They lead large donors to reduce their gifts, while small donors increase their donations or abstain (if they see that they are not able to conform to the imposed norm). As a result, the values of donations increase with the level of the threshold, while the probability of donating decreases. The statistical relationship for the total effect is less obvious, but it is likely that the sum of all donations decreases as the threshold value increases. Adena and Huck (2019a) conclude that the latter pattern does not hold if thresholds are properly personalized. The reason is an inverted U-shape relative to the individually optimal donation – the thresholds that are set too low and the thresholds that are set too high are inferior.

4 The price of giving: matching versus direct grants to charities

The popular treatment of donations in the tax code results in a deduction that reduces a taxpayer's taxable income and consequently the tax due. This results in a lower price of giving, where the price equals one minus the marginal tax (see Chapter 12 and Chapter 18). On the other hand, charitable organizations often like to attract a major donor before the fundraising campaign and to use this major donor's contribution to leverage subsequent small donations. In many cases, a major donor of this kind commits to matching subsequent donations at a specified match rate (oftentimes 1:1, but sometimes other rates are used) up to a prespecified total amount. There are numerous field (and lab) experiments that study the effects of changes in the price of giving through matching (see Epperson and Reif, 2019, for a thorough review of those studies). In those field experiments, the performance of different matching rates has been tested against a pure control without a major donor or with information about the major donor providing seed money unconditionally.

Two early field experiments tested different matching rates – high matches implying a price of giving of 0.5, 0.33, and 0.25 in Karlan and List (2007) and small matches implying a price of giving of 0.5 and 0.75 in Karlan, List, and Shafir (2011) – against a pure control. While in the first experiment, matching increased the probability of giving and the gift amount relative to the pure control, there was no such effect in the second experiment. The authors explain the results as relating to the heterogeneous responses by different types of donors. In both of the field experiments, the changes of the match rate had no effect. The latter result has also been confirmed by Meier (2007), who tested the prices of 0.8 and 0.66.

In another field experiment with a lead donor control condition, Adena and Huck (2017) showed that matching attracted more donors but that those additional donors predominantly gave small amounts. More importantly, they found substantial crowding out for large donors – they reduced their donation amounts when matching was in place. The authors used a lead donor treatment for comparison. They argued that a lead donor treatment should be used because potential donors interpret it as a signal that the charity and its output is of high quality, as they do in the case of matching. In the spirit of Vesterlund (2003), they assumed that the major donor has better information about the quality of the charity and its output and only donates if it is high enough.[4] Most experiments that rely on pure control for comparisons find that matching performed better, while the studies that used a lead donor treatment for comparisons often found opposite results.

A number of field-experimental studies provide estimates of the price elasticity of giving. However, they use different methods such that the results are not comparable across the studies. Adena, Hakimov, and Huck (2019) calculated the price elasticity for field experiments that used a match rate of 1:1 and a lead donor as a control. Out of five studies, they found the price elasticity to be lower than one in absolute value for three of the experiments (Rondeau and List, 2008; Huck and Rasul, 2011; Gneezy, Keenan and Gneezy, 2014) and higher than one in absolute value for two (Adena and Huck, 2017; Adena, Hakimov, and Huck, 2019). While Huck, Rasul, and Shephard (2015) found that no matching scheme can outperform a lead donor, this conclusion seems to apply only to specific samples, like those made up of rich Western individuals (Adena, Hakimov, and Huck, 2019).

An interesting insight emerged from a field experiment by Meier (2007). He found that matching has a negative long-term effect on donations that can undo the initial positive effect. Donors who were offered matching in year one and did not receive matching in year two reduced their subsequent gifts. The reduction was larger than the initial increase in giving from matching relative to a no-matching control. Meier (2007) argues that matching incentives might crowd out the intrinsic motivation for giving. Other studies, however, did not confirm this negative long-term-effect of matching (Karlan, List, and Shafir, 2011; Kesternich, Löschel, and Römer, 2016).

Another important result is that an announcement of a lead donor always seems to lead to better fundraising results than no such announcement (List and Lucking-Reiley, 2002; Rondeau and List, 2008). This is because (i) the donors are not pure altruists (that is, they do not derive utility solely from all donors' contributions to the public goods) but are (to some extent) warm-glow givers (that is they derive utility from their own donation per se; see Andreoni, 1990). Therefore, there is no crowding out, or it is not complete. (ii) A lead donor provides a signal of quality about the charitable organization and its output, thus leading to higher contributions. A treatment with a lead donor (seed money) resembles direct government grants to nonprofit organizations, and one might be tempted to conclude from the previous line of the field-experimental literature that direct governmental grants should be superior to price reductions. Again, such comparisons are subject to certain limitations, namely that field experiments can only provide partial equilibrium results. Maybe this is why, somewhat in contrast to the experimental literature outlined previously, the empirical literature studying the effects of governmental grants on individual giving has found (incomplete) crowding out (Andreoni and Payne, 2003) rather than crowding in.

Finally, in order to reduce crowding out, Adena and Huck (2017) proposed an innovative design in which the matching amount is not going to the same project but to another, ideally complementary, one. What kind of similar design is plausible for the tax code? One option is for the tax subsidy to benefit other social projects directly instead of being paid back to the donors.

5 Matching versus rebates

Matching is sometimes offered by a major donor who matches gifts to a charity directly or by employers who encourage payroll giving. In contrast, the preferential treatment of donations in the U.S. and German tax code takes the form of a rebate. In the UK tax system, both subsidy types exist in parallel – donations of UK taxpayers are matched at a rate of 25% up to the tax due amount, and eventually the rebate subsidy applies. Matching and rebates are both mathematically equivalent, and both reduce the price of giving. But they differ in the implementation – that is, in the timing and which actions are required by the donor for the subsidy to apply. While matching usually happens instantaneously and the donor usually does not need to take any action, the rebates are paid out much later and require the donor to claim donations in their tax declaration. Do those two instruments have the same effect on donors?

Throughout the experimental literature, rebates consistently perform worse than matching. This was shown, among others, by Eckel and Grossman (2003, 2006, 2008, 2017) both in the laboratory and field experiments. The inferiority of rebates was even higher in field experiments, where the rebate takes more time to materialize (Eckel and Grossman, 2008). See Vesterlund (2016) for a thorough review of the experimental literature on this topic and Chapter 20, of this Handbook for a laboratory study.[5] This raises a question: Why are rebates inferior to matches?

In order to understand the reasons behind the differences in the effectiveness of matches and rebates, Eckel and Grossman (2017) introduced a small twist into the design of their field experiment: The donors had to tick a box if they wanted the subsidy – matching or rebate – to materialize. Only 56% of donors ticked the box, and donors in the match treatments were twice as likely to do so. The authors suggested different explanations for the observed responses: they pointed to a lack of awareness of the incentives, an unwillingness to accept a subsidy, misperceptions, or a reluctance to deal with the additional costs of cashing in a rebate check. Those reasons may potentially lead to differences between the responsiveness to match versus rebate incentives. The researchers found a much lower price elasticity in the case of rebates – they were less than one in absolute value, while price elasticities in the matching treatments were estimated to be above one in absolute terms. However, when they only accounted for the donors who accepted the subsidy, the price elasticity estimates were very similar and very high. Ottoni-Wilhelm and Hungerman (2021) offer a different explanation for the non-equivalence between the match-price elasticity and the rebate-price elasticity. According to their theoretical model, the donor cares about the impact of the amount received by the charity (which includes the matched amount in the case of matching) and gets warm-glow utility from their own gift. While the rebate affects the opportunity cost of both the impact and warm glow, the match reduces the cost of impact but does not alter the cost of one's out-of-pocket donation.

All together, the experimental results suggest that encouraging charitable giving in the tax code through deductions might be inferior to other simple alternatives. A potentially better solution would be instead to allow donors to communicate their tax number together with a donation and for the charities to cash in the match. If there is a reason to prefer rebates in the tax code, Thaler und Sunstein (2008, p. 230) propose the following simplification: an introduction of a charity debit card which would be only used for donation payments. Each donor would receive a summary at the end of the year which they could simply add to their tax declaration. This would reduce the additional transaction costs, which might explain the differences in the performance between rebates and matches. Richard Thaler[6] has made a further proposal regarding the simplification of how donations are treated in the tax code. Instead of differential incentives for those with high versus low incomes (see Chapter 10 for a discussion), he proposes a fixed subvention of 15% for each and every donation, including those made by individuals who do not pay any taxes.

6 Is the total donation pie constant?

The effect of incentives for charitable giving in the tax code depends crucially on whether the donation pie is constant. Even if a change in tax incentives leads to a change in the volume of claimed donations, it is possible that it merely leads to a shift between the claimed and unclaimed donations, eligible and ineligible beneficiaries, or over time. Truly increasing total donations would require reducing spending on other goods (assuming a constant budget), ideally on those which are not desirable from the society's point of view (Heger and Cornish, 2021; Schmitz, 2021). This leads to another important question that has become topical but is difficult to answer. Is the total donation pie constant, or can it be made bigger?

Field experiments that observe giving to only one charity in the short term do not allow us to answer this question. What happens to giving to other charities if one charity increases its fundraising activities or offers additional incentives for giving? In a field experiment with blood donations, Lacetera, Macis, and Slonim (2012) found that individuals went to blood drives that offered incentives like a t-shirt or lottery ticket and avoided those without incentives while keeping their total blood donation volume constant. Adena and Hager (2020) conducted a field experiment with fundraising activities for one organization in a random half of the zip codes in Germany. They also analyzed zip code-level data for a large fraction of donations to other organizations. They found a significant crowding out of donations to other organizations of a similar type, which points to crowding out and a limited scope to expand the donation pie.[7]

Another take on the total giving question is offered by studies that look at giving over time. Adena and Huck (2019b) studied whether inducing a donor to give more today leads them to reduce their giving later on. Initially, they documented that individuals who were informed about a future fundraising campaign reduced their giving in the first year as if they were planning their long-term giving. However, individuals in the second year gave similar amounts to their first-year amounts.[8] This means that, ultimately, they did not optimize over time. Similarly, Shang and Croson (2009) found that new donors who learned about a high donation that was given by a previous donor gave more, and they did so again a year later without receiving such information. This means that increasing giving today leads to more giving tomorrow and contradicts the fixed-budget hypothesis. In comparison, the findings from the empirical literature on tax-price incentives suggest that taxpayers do account for future and past changes in their individual tax-price to some extent (see again Chapter 12).

All together, the experimental results presented previously are inconclusive[9] and suggest that more research is needed.

7 Conclusions

Researchers have long called for tax reform with respect to the treatment of donations (Saez, 2004). The results from the field experiments presented previously call into question several design elements of the tax treatment of donations: the complexity and timing, the price reduction for giving through deductions, and the somewhat random setting of thresholds for deduction. Still, the previously reviewed studies cannot provide the ultimate answer for how to optimally incentivize giving through taxes, as they are not designed to do so. While there are a number of existing field experiments with taxpayers meant to enhance tax compliance (Iyer et al., 2010; Gangl et al., 2014; Dwenger et al., 2016; Bott et al., 2019), to my knowledge, no one has conducted a real-world field experiment that varies the tax incentives for giving.[10] There may be scope for this, and for this reason, more research of this type is needed.

Notes

1 Another reason is to understand better the motivation of donors, though laboratory experiments are sometimes a better option to that end.
2 There are, of course, other reasons than charitable giving that might lead to a refund.
3 https://www.destatis.de/DE/Themen/Staat/Steuern/Lohnsteuer-Einkommensteuer/im-fokus-steuererklaerung.html (accessed on 19.01.2021).
4 See also Adena et al. (2017) for quality certification.
5 There are two studies with different designs that achieve equivalence of rebate and matches. The first is in the context of unit donations (Diederich et al., 2020), and the second relies on framing contributions in terms of charity receipts and not refunds (Davis, 2006).
6 18.12.2017, Richard R. Thaler, "It's Time to Rethink the Charity Deduction" https://nyti.ms/2pmvncz (viewed on 20.10.2017).
7 In contrast, in the small world of a laboratory experiment, Schmitz (2021) found that matching incentives shifted donations towards charities that offer price reductions but that the overall donations remained constant. In an experiment with survey participants, an extra budget for charitable giving provided by the researchers, and two charities, Gallier et al. (2019) found that matching raised overall donations.
8 Such positive path dependence has been also found in an online experiment by Heger and Slonim (2020).
9 See also Gee and Meer (2020) for a more detailed review of further literature on this topic.
10 There are experiments outside the lab that try to mimic the real tax context, for example, (Becchetti, Pelligra, and Reggiani 2017).

References

Adena, M. *et al.* (2017) 'Quality certifications for nonprofits, charitable giving, and donor's trust: Experimental evidence', WZB Working Paper SP II 2017–302.

Adena, M. and Hager, A. (2020) 'Does online fundraising increase charitable giving? A nation-wide field experiment on Facebook video fundraising'. WZB Working Paper SP II 2020-302.

Adena, M., Hakimov, R. and Huck, S. (2019) 'Charitable giving by the poor. A large-scale field experiment in Kyrgyzstan'. WZB Discussion Paper No. SP II 2019-306r.

Adena, M. and Huck, S. (2017) 'Matching donations without crowding out? Some theoretical considerations, a field, and a lab experiment', *Journal of Public Economics*, 148(April), pp. 32–42. doi: 10.1016/j.jpubeco.2017.02.002.

Adena, M. and Huck, S. (2019a) 'Giving once, giving twice: A two-period field experiment on intertemporal crowding in charitable giving', *Journal of Public Economics*, 172, pp. 127–134. doi: 10.1016/j.jpubeco.2019.01.002.

Adena, M. and Huck, S. (2019b) 'Personalized fundraising: A field experiment on threshold matching of donations'. WZB Working Paper No SP II 2019–306.

Adena, M., Huck, S. and Rasul, I. (2014) 'Charitable giving and nonbinding contribution-level suggestions evidence from a field experiment', *Review of Behavioral Economics*, 1(3), pp. 275–293. doi: 10.1561/105.00000010.

Andreoni, J. (1990) 'Impure altruism and donations to public goods: A theory of warm-glow giving', *The Economic Journal*, 100(401), p. 464. doi: 10.2307/2234133.

Andreoni, J. and Payne, A. A. (2003) 'Do government grants to private charities crowd out giving or fund-raising?' *American Economic Review*, 93(3), pp. 792–812. doi: 10.1257/000282803322157098.

Becchetti, L., Pelligra, V. and Reggiani, T. (2017) 'Information, belief elicitation and threshold effects in the 5X1000 tax scheme: A framed field experiment', *International Tax and Public Finance*, 24(6), pp. 1026–1049. doi: 10.1007/s10797-017-9474-z.

Bott, K. M. *et al.* (2019) 'You've got mail: A randomized field experiment on tax evasion', *Management Science*, 66(7), pp. 2801–2819. doi: 10.1287/mnsc.2019.3390.

Casarico, A. and Tonin, M. (2018) *Pay-what-you-want to support independent information – a field experiment on motivation*, IZA Discussion Paper.

Castillo, M. and Petrie, R. (2021) 'Optimal incentives to give'. IZA Discussion Paper 13321. doi: 10.2139/ssrn.3616460

Davis, D. D. (2006) 'Rebate subsidies, matching subsidies and isolation effects', *Judgment and Decision Making*, 1, pp. 13–22.

Diederich, J. *et al.* (2020) 'Subsidizing unit donations: Matches, rebates, and discounts compared'. AWI Discussion Paper Series No. 697. doi: 10.11588/heidok.00029236.

Dwenger, N. *et al.* (2016) 'Extrinsic and intrinsic motivations for tax compliance: Evidence from a field experiment in Germany', *American Economic Journal: Economic Policy*, 8(3), pp. 203–232. doi: 10.1257/pol.20150083.

Eckel, C. and Grossman, P. J. (2003) 'Rebate versus matching: Does how we subsidize charitable contributions matter?' *Journal of Public Economics*, 87(3–4), pp. 681–701. doi: 10.1016/S0047-2727(01)00094-9.

Eckel, C. and Grossman, P. J. (2006) 'Subsidizing charitable giving with rebates or matching: Further laboratory evidence', *Southern Economic Journal*, 72(4), p. 794. doi: 10.2307/20111853.

Eckel, C. and Grossman, P. J. (2008) 'Subsidizing charitable contributions: A natural field experiment comparing matching and rebate subsidies', *Experimental Economics*, 11(3), pp. 234–252. doi: 10.1007/s10683-008-9198-0.

Eckel, C. and Grossman, P. J. (2017) 'Comparing rebate and matching subsidies controlling for donors' awareness: Evidence from the field', *Journal of Behavioral and Experimental Economics*, 66, pp. 88–95. doi: 10.1016/J.SOCEC.2016.04.016.

Epperson, R. and Reif, C. (2019) 'Matching subsidies and voluntary contributions: A review', *Journal of Economic Surveys*, pp. 1–24. doi: 10.1111/joes.12337.

Gallier, C. *et al.* (2019) 'Inter-charity competition under spatial differentiation: Sorting, crowding, and spillovers'. ZEW-Centre for European Economic Research Discussion Paper 19-039.

Gangl, K. *et al.* (2014) 'Effects of supervision on tax compliance: Evidence from a field experiment in Austria', *Economics Letters*, 123(3), pp. 378–382. doi: 10.1016/j.econlet.2014.03.027.

Gee, L. and Meer, J. (2020). '24. The Altruism budget: Measuring and encouraging charitable giving', in W. Powell and P. Bromley (eds.). *The Nonprofit Sector: A Research Handbook, Third Edition* (pp. 558–565). Redwood City: Stanford University Press. doi: 10.1515/9781503611085-033.

Gneezy, U., Keenan, E. A. and Gneezy, A. (2014) 'Avoiding overhead aversion in charity', *Science*, 346(6209), pp. 632–635. doi: 10.1126/science.1253932.

Heger, S. A. and Cornish, A. D. (2021) *Vice and virtue behaviours: Substitution and non-substitution effects*. New York: Mimeo.

Heger, S. A. and Slonim, R. (2020) *Altruism begets altruism*. New York: Mimeo.

Huck, S. and Rasul, I. (2011) 'Matched fundraising: Evidence from a natural field experiment', *Journal of Public Economics*, 95(5–6), pp. 351–362. doi: 10.1016/j.jpubeco.2010.10.005.

Huck, S., Rasul, I. and Shephard, A. (2015) 'Comparing charitable fundraising schemes: Evidence from a natural field experiment and a structural model', *American Economic Journal: Economic Policy*, 7(2), pp. 326–369. doi: 10.1257/pol.20120312.

Iyer, G. S. *et al.* (2010) 'Increasing tax compliance in Washington state: A field experiment', *National Tax Journal*, 63(1), pp. 7–32.

Karlan, D. and List, J. A. (2007) 'Does price matter in charitable giving? Evidence from a large-scale natural field experiment', *American Economic Review*, 97(5), pp. 1774–1793. doi: 10.1257/aer.97.5.1774.

Karlan, D., List, J. A. and Shafir, E. (2011) 'Small matches and charitable giving: Evidence from a natural field experiment', *Journal of Public Economics*. doi: 10.1016/j.jpubeco.2010.11.024.

Kesternich, M., Löschel, A. and Römer, D. (2016) 'The long-term impact of matching and rebate subsidies when public goods are impure: Field experimental evidence from the carbon offsetting market', *Journal of Public Economics*, 137, pp. 70–78. doi: 10.1016/j.jpubeco.2016.01.004.

Lacetera, N., Macis, M. and Slonim, R. (2012) 'Will there be blood? Incentives and substitution effects in pro-social behavior', *American Economic Journal: Economic Policy*, 4(1), pp. 186–223. doi: 10.1257/pol.4.1.186.

List, J. A. (2008) 'Introduction to field experiments in economics with applications to the economics of charity', *Experimental Economics*, 11(3), pp. 203–212. doi: 10.1007/s10683-008-9201-9.

List, J. A. and Lucking-Reiley, D. (2002) 'The effects of seed money and refunds on charitable giving: Experimental evidence from a university capital campaign', *Journal of Political Economy*, 110(1), pp. 215–233. doi: 10.1086/324392.

Meier, S. (2007) 'Do subsidies increase charitable giving in the long run? Matching donations in a field experiment', *Journal of the European Economic Association*, 5(6), pp. 1203–1222.

Ottoni-Wilhelm, M. and Hungerman, D. M. (2021) 'Impure impact giving: Theory and evidence', *Journal of Political Economy*, 129(5), pp. 1553–1614.

Rondeau, D. and List, J. A. (2008) 'Matching and challenge gifts to charity: Evidence from laboratory and natural field experiments', *Experimental Economics*. doi: 10.1007/s10683-007-9190-0.

Saez, E. (2004) 'The optimal treatment of tax expenditures', *Journal of Public Economics*, 88(12), pp. 2657–2684. doi: 10.1016/j.jpubeco.2003.09.004.

Schmitz, J. (2021) 'Is charitable giving a zero sum game? – The effect of competition between charities on giving behavior', *Management Science*. doi: 10.2139/ssrn.2862479.

Shang, J. and Croson, R. (2009) 'A field experiment in charitable contribution: The impact of social information on the voluntary provision of public goods', *The Economic Journal*, 119(October), pp. 1422–1439. doi: 10.1111/j.1468-0297.2009.02267.x.

Teirlinck, M. (2020) *Tax incentives for charitable giving : Information frictions and hassle costs*. New York: Mimeo.

Thaler, Richard H., and Sunstein, Cass R. (2008) *Nudge: Improving decisions about health, wealth, and happiness*. London: Penguin Books.

Vesterlund, L. (2003) 'The informational value of sequential fundraising', *Journal of Public Economics*, 87, pp. 627–657. doi: 10.1016/j.envexpbot.2012.01.010.

Vesterlund, L. (2016) 'Using experimental methods to understand why and how we give to charity', in John H. Kagel and A. E. Roth (eds.) *The Handbook of Experimental Economics, Volume 2* (pp. 91–152). Princeton: Princeton University Press.

20

BEHAVIOURAL PHILANTHROPY

Harnessing behavioural sciences to design more effective tax incentives for philanthropy

Ursa Bernardic, Maël Lebreton, Giedre Lideikyte Huber, Henry Peter and Giuseppe Ugazio

1 Introduction: individuals and charitable giving

Philanthropy can be defined as voluntary giving for the common good and as such codified by the Sustainable Development Goals (SDGs).[1] Non-profit organisations and charities are among the most prominent actors in the context of philanthropy. They are essential contributors of public goods and services that governments often fail to provide (Kingma, 1997). Such organisations are mostly supported by individual donations (Havens, O'Herlihy and Schervish, 2006). For example, according to Giving USA (2020), individual donations amounted to 68.9% (or $309.66 billion) of the total $449.64 billion donated in the United States in 2019. These numbers are even more remarkable considering that donations by corporations only amounted to 4.7% (or $21.09 billion) during the same period. These patterns in donations have been consistently observed over time. Further, over the past 10 years, both total donations and individual donations have been increasing, which is another encouraging trend (see Figure 20.1). However, a closer look at Figure 20.1 reveals a worrisome fact: the upward trend of donations by individuals is losing momentum. For instance, in 2009, individual donations amounted to 74% of the total, whereas in 2019, they only amounted to 69% of the total. Moreover, the number of people who give to charity annually has significantly decreased over the past years (Osili, Clark and Han, 2019). Taken together, these findings underscore the importance of identifying mechanisms that can reverse these worrying trends and increase not only the amount of donations but also the number of donors (Laffan and Dolan, 2020).

In recent years, there has been an increasing focus on the relevance of behavioural science regarding individuals' everyday decisions as well as societal policies. Behavioural economics' insights have been used to develop new policy tools that increase organ donations (Johnson and Goldstein, 2003) and pension contributions (Thaler and Benartzi, 2004), improve carbon emission offset (Weber and Johnson, 2012), and help reduce poverty (World Bank, 2014). Thus, it is very likely that insights from behavioural sciences can contribute to philanthropy as well. For instance, one intriguing application of behavioural sciences in philanthropy is to inform and design optimal public policies and fundraising mechanisms aimed at promoting giving by individuals. To investigate why people contribute to public goods and charities, one can

DOI: 10.4324/9781003139201-23

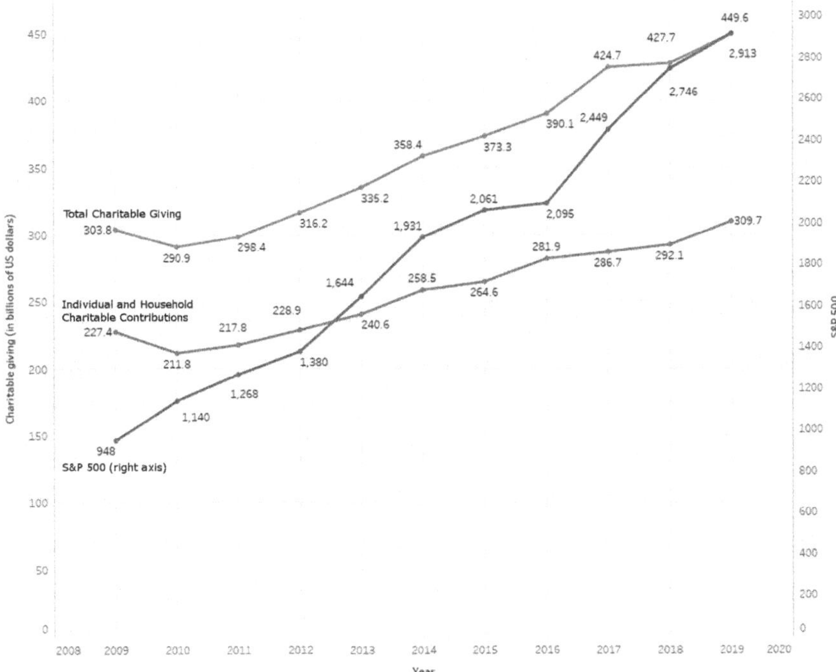

Figure 20.1 (Colour online):[2] Real charitable giving growth in the United States, along with the Standard & Poor's 500 Stock Index for comparison over time (2009–2019). The gap between total donations and individual donations is growing over the years

Source: Data on the trends of total charitable giving and individual charitable giving in the United States were retrieved from Giving USA Foundation. Yearly reports are based on the estimates of IRS Form 990 (a tax exemption form completed yearly by a non-profit organisation), which are econometrically adjusted based on information from other research institutions

empirically determine, in laboratory settings, individuals' motives that drive charitable giving. While such motives are difficult to determine from data on actual donations, such as surveys, tax returns, or charitable level data, laboratory experiments and experimental techniques offer a useful alternative.

In the following section, we introduce the new interdisciplinary field of behavioural philanthropy, an approach that combines insights and methods of disciplines that investigate philanthropy from a broader perspective, such as sociology that utilises surveys and case studies to investigate how policies may impact philanthropy at the societal level, with those of disciplines that analyse the determinants of philanthropy at the individual level, such as behavioural economics that relies on experiment-based research to provide a mechanistic understanding of philanthropic behaviour and its determinants.

Enter behavioural philanthropy

The academic literature on philanthropy has been growing over the past 20 years (see Figure 20.2). Although the literature is spread across the disciplines of economics, law, psychology, and sociology, among others, we simplified the categorisation of these approaches into two levels: macro-surveys and micro-experimental levels.

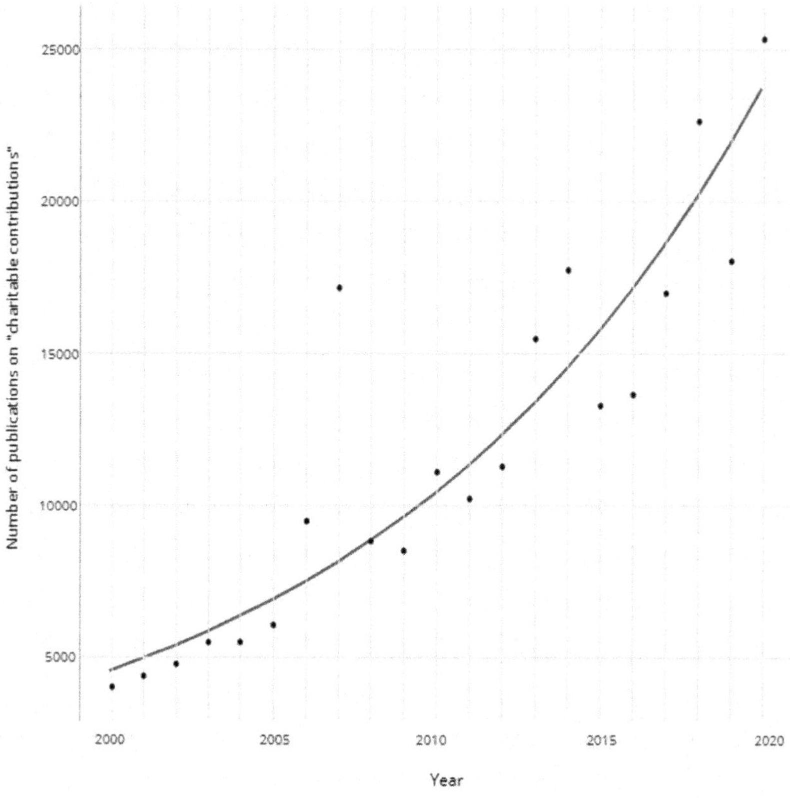

Figure 20.2 (Colour online):[3] Number of publications on 'charitable contributions' over time (2000–2020). The fitted line represents logistic regression

Source: Data on the number of publications were extracted using the Dimensions AI database (Hook, Porter and Herzog, 2018)

The prevailing approach in philanthropic research has been at the macro level, relying on archival tax data and cross-sectional surveys (Bekkers and Wiepking, 2011). Studies that use surveys have identified important correlates of charitable giving, such as religion, age, education, and socialisation practices (for review, see Wiepking and Bekkers, 2012). Such surveys usually involve a large number of respondents and are therefore relatively thorough and can detect small effects (see Figure 20.3). Most of these questionnaires often ask about real-life behaviour, as surveys are generalisable and ecologically valid such that they can be applied to other real-life situations. While survey and tax data provide an insightful line of research for philanthropy, the biggest flaw of this approach is the lack of evidence to support causal inferences; given that mostly correlational data are used, survey measures do not provide insights on the causality of the observed relationships between external factors, predictors, and behaviour. Therefore, due to the lack of a mechanistic explanation, findings in this domain often have several possible explanations for the relations identified, which are not mutually exclusive. For example, while there is a lot of descriptive knowledge about who gives, little is known about why some people give more than others or why some people may be more inclined to give to a specific cause instead of another. Cross-country surveys

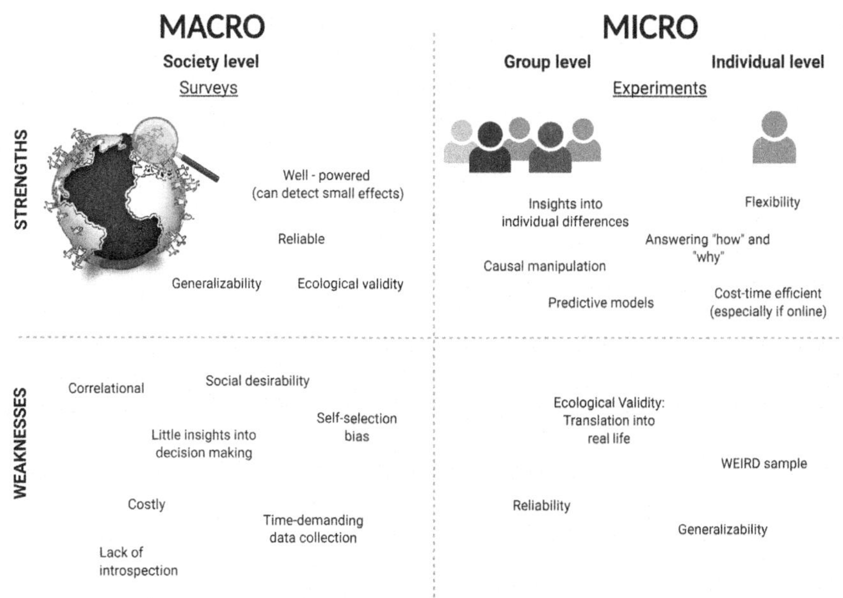

Figure 20.3 (Colour online):[4] Overview of the advantages (above) and disadvantages (below) of macro- and micro-level research

can also be a costly and time-consuming method of data collection, and while taxation studies frequently provide longitudinal data, they are usually collected only once a year. Another notable drawback of this type of data is that it relies on self-reports. Since philanthropy is a prosocial behaviour, it might be impacted by self-serving biases, such as social desirability and self-deception. As such, one could expect that people may report wrong information about desirable outcomes (i.e., more donations), thus impacting results. Even when participants want to be honest, the results might vary depending on the respondent's level of introspection (Wallendorf and Brucks, 1993).

In the past years, there has been a rise in micro-level research, especially in the fields of psychology and behavioural economics, which investigates philanthropic behaviour at the level of individuals or small groups by relying on controlled causal manipulations. Studies using such experiments provide an additional answer to how and why some people engage in philanthropy more than others and thus enhance the potential to inform policymakers looking for effective mechanisms to stimulate individual giving, for instance, through tax incentives. The experimental designs are flexible to different experimental manipulations and provide evidence of how philanthropic behaviour changes with environmental parameters. For example, how does philanthropic behaviour change when a country introduces a new tax subsidy scheme? Does an increase in taxation of individual wealth affect charitable donations? These manipulations can be studied in laboratory settings and are an important step in building predictive models that aim to capture the rationale behind people's decision-making. Such empirical knowledge provides insights into individual differences and establishes a basis for predictive models of philanthropic behaviour. However, experimental data are usually not reliable, generalisable, or ecologically valid because the evidence gathered in these controlled and simplified experiments often prevents drawing generalised inferences that could predict behaviour outside the laboratory setting. Another disadvantage of such experiments is that most of them are conducted on a 'Western, educated, industrialised, rich, and democratic' (WEIRD) (Henrich, Heine and Norenzayan, 2010) sample and therefore lack explanatory and predictive validity on the behaviour of the majority of the population. However, with recent advances in online platforms (such as Prolific and Mechanical Turk), online experiments are not only cost and time effective but also allow testing of the same designs on a country or global scale and across representative samples. Since tax cultures, and thus incentives, may differ depending on the region (see, for instance, the typology of the tax systems of the OECD countries proposed by Wagschal, 2015), such studies not only offer a very detailed overview at the country level but also extend and compare these findings to those of other cultures and countries.

Behavioural philanthropy proposes to generate novel theoretical models that are capable of providing mechanistic explanations of philanthropic behaviour by relying on evidence gathered in controlled experiments at the individual and group levels. Obtaining such evidence can be instrumental in forming policies and best practices for philanthropic actors. In the context of this book, it is important to stress the relevance of this approach by providing solid evidence regarding data-driven incentive schemes.

The challenge for behavioural philanthropy is to elaborate on existing economic models to deliver psychological realism that does not depend only on specific cases. We propose that combining the cognitive psychology studies on individual motivations for philanthropy and matching these insights with well-defined theories and methodologies of behavioural economics will allow a better understanding of the mechanisms that drive human (charitable) behaviour. To provide reliable evidence capable of informing policymaking and supporting other practical applications, we must carefully design research that ensures that behavioural philanthropy: 1) addresses socially and ecologically valid questions, 2) uses appropriate methods to answer these questions, and 3) develops theories that are well defined and supported by computational models that can predict philanthropic behaviour at both the micro and macro levels.

2 Literature review: identifying the motives of giving through psychology and economics

Understanding motives is crucial for solving one of the economic puzzles that philanthropy poses, namely why self-interested agents work hard to give away their earnings (apparently) unselfishly. In the following discussion, we analyse some of the most common motives that drive philanthropy as identified by researchers.

Personal material benefits – spillover effects

To address the donor's puzzle (see previously), the micro-donor-centric utility-based approach proposes that one of the crucial motives for philanthropy is that it provides benefits for both the recipients and the donors (Becker, 1974). In this spirit, early economic theories have proposed that philanthropy is not unselfish and that self-interested agents might give because they will benefit from these donations (for review, see Andreoni, 2006). For example, donating to medical research (for example, in COVID-19 times) may help donors benefit from the findings (i.e., vaccines) in the future. A second example is illustrated by so-called enlightened self-interest, which suggests that individuals may give to the poor to keep an institution in place that would take care of them in case they become impoverished (Andreoni, 2006).

Personal psychological benefits – self-image effects

While the personal spillover effects of charitable giving reconcile the apparent dissonance between self-interest and philanthropy, this motive fails to explain why individuals engage in philanthropic activities even when it is extremely unlikely that they might experience any benefits. For instance, why would individuals donate to relieve poverty on another continent, or why do people decide on charitable bequests (after their death)? In both of these scenarios, the individual has little to no chance of directly generating any personal benefit.

An alternative explanation is that donors do not derive a direct (or indirect) economic utility from giving but rather a psychological one: people feel good when they do good. This view has been referred to as 'warm-glow' giving, in which a donor gets an emotional reward by giving to others (Andreoni, 1990). This perspective has been supported by several empirical findings (Ottoni-Wilhelm, Vesterlund and Xie, 2014). Moreover, self-image theories use a dual self-approach to account for self-image as a motivation (Ariely, Bracha and Meier, 2009). As such, the dual self serves as an observer of one's own actions and provides signals about one's own identity (Bodner and Prelec, 2003; Bénabou and Tirole, 2006). Mazar, Amir, and Ariely (2008) suggested that people try to find a balance between two motivational forces (i.e., cheating and getting higher material payoffs and maintaining the self-image of being honest).

Long-term strategic benefits – social signalling

A large body of evidence demonstrates that one can use philanthropic giving as a strategy to promote or signal one's social image. For instance, previous studies found that public recognition increases not only volunteer work (Linardi and McConnell, 2011) and effort in charitable fundraising (Ariely, Bracha and Meier, 2009) but also the willingness to donate blood (Lacetera and Macis, 2010), as well as the likelihood that people will respond to fundraising appeals (Karlan and McConnell, 2014). Strategic motives for philanthropy have been captured by two main theoretical models that speculate that such motives are observed either because donors want to signal their altruism to others and receive social image benefits (i.e., 'I am generous') (Harbaugh, 1998a; Harbaugh, 1998b; Andreoni and Petrie, 2004; Rege and Telle, 2004) or because donors want to encourage others to give through social influence (i.e., 'follow my lead') (List and Lucking-Reiley, 2002; Shang and Croson, 2009; Bracha, Menietti and Vesterlund, 2011).

Intrinsic and extrinsic motives

Intrinsic moral motivation is another dominant driver of philanthropy. While it can be hard to directly assess the relevance of moral motives in promoting giving due to experimental demand effects, it is possible to quantify its relevance by measuring 'moral crowding-out', that is, the observed detrimental effects of adding extrinsic material incentives to stimulate a given behaviour (e.g., donating to charity, voting, etc.), which is motivated by intrinsic moral motives. Such effects have been documented in several studies that have demonstrated the economic inefficiency of extrinsic incentives on intrinsically motivated behaviour (for a review, see Promberger and Marteau, 2013). In 1970, Titmuss hypothesised that paying for blood donation would undermine the social utility of the intrinsic motivation of the act and have negative consequences on blood donations. Accordingly, a meta-analysis (Niza, Tung and Marteau, 2013) of Titmuss' hypotheses suggested that economic incentives are inefficient in the blood donation context. Similarly, Venkataramani et al. (2012) found that tax incentives do not boost organ donation. In the charitable giving context, Nelson et al. (2006) implemented egoistic (emphasising that donated money will benefit oneself as well as helping others) and altruistic (emphasising that donated money will benefit others in need) ads and found that altruistic ads were preferred by people whose charitable behaviour was motivated by intrinsic factors.

Despite these findings, it is still unclear how extrinsic incentives influence philanthropy. For instance, Falk and Zehnder (2013) found that the impact of gifts on possible donors influenced the frequency and amount donated in different directions. Compared to the no-gift condition, in which the relative frequency of donations was 12%, small gifts (one postcard with one envelope) increased the frequency of donations by 2% points (to 14%), and large gifts (four postcards with four envelopes) increased the frequency by 9% (to 21%). While these frequency differences were significant, the net donations were significantly lower between the no-gift and the large-gift conditions but not between the no-gift and small-gift conditions and between the small- and large-gift conditions. Interestingly, while only suggestive, those receiving no gift were more likely to donate large amounts (>200 CHF), whereas those receiving large gifts were more likely to donate smaller amounts. Furthermore, another study looked at how financial incentives in the form of tax-matching or tax-rebate schemes can impact individuals' donations to charitable giving. Here, it was shown that in a dictator game setting (see Section 3 and Forsythe et al., 1994), matching schemes had a stronger effect on incentivising donations as compared to the effect of rebate schemes (Peng and Liu, 2020). Finally, additional studies that have investigated the role of gifts in charitable donations found mixed results ranging from no effect in an online fundraising campaign offering products (Chen, Li and MacKie-Mason, 2006) to a negative effect on the amount contributed by donors to a natural park in Costa Rica (Alpizar, Carlsson and Johansson-Stenman, 2008). Such mixed evidence regarding the effect of incentives on charitable giving calls for future meta-analysis and replication studies.

Social norms, rules, and mimesis

Social norm theory in sociology (Schwartz, 1977) suggests that the likelihood that individuals will adopt charitable giving depends on whether such behaviour is approved, shared, and expected by the group or society and is considered a social norm. Social norms can be explicitly written in the teachings of many religions globally with a common consequence; that is, to give purely altruistically is the true essence of giving, as expressed in the Jewish Torah and the teachings of the Quran. The role of social norms in stimulating philanthropic behaviour has been established in existing studies that demonstrated that when participants are explicitly told that the social norm is to contribute to charity, the likelihood of their donating money increased (Agerström et al., 2016).

Modulators of individual motivations

The previous paragraphs provide an overview of some of the economic, psychological, and societal motives for charitable giving. Such motives are not important solely from the perspective of theoretical works (Bonar, 1926) but also because they provide a solid basis for designing experimental paradigms that can test predictions in a laboratory setting. For example, one could design an experiment to understand how the source (e.g., gifted vs. earned) of one's wealth may modulate the impact of self-image motivation and warm glow on one's decision to give. In this vein, a previous study (Erkal, Gangadharan and Nikiforakis, 2011) investigated whether participants' earnings were the result of effort or obtained through effort and luck. The results revealed that participants with the highest wealth were less likely to contribute to wealth redistribution among their social group's peers, irrespective of whether their wealth was obtained by exerting higher effort or due to effort and luck. Thus, these results demonstrate that the source of one's wealth does not seem to impact one's decision to give back to society. In the context of philanthropy, based on these findings, a theoretical model has been proposed (Mayo and Tinsley, 2009) which states that a similar behavioural pattern would be observed in the context of charitable giving; that is, perceptions of effort and luck as the cause of reward distribution would systematically reduce the warm glow giving of higher-earnings households and thus lead to lower contributions to charity by wealthier individuals.

Other possible modulators of individual motivations could be the perceived effectiveness of a philanthropic organisation or individual preferences for a given charity. In other words, are people more strongly motivated to give to charities that maximise impact and produce the greatest welfare gains? Or are more efficient philanthropic organisations the most popular ones? While normative economics models of charitable giving suggest that individuals should be motivated to give to charities that maximise welfare, descriptive accounts show that individuals often do not maximise the outcomes of their donations (Berman et al., 2018); however, they are more sensitive to efficacy when helping themselves or their families (Burum, Nowak and Hoffman, 2020). Therefore, lab studies could investigate and disclose whether and how individual preferences for charities and charity efficacy impact intrinsic moral motivation and therefore charitable giving.

To conclude, as the previous examples illustrate, there is a strong need for novel data that are capable of isolating the different factors that modulate individual motivations and informing computational models of individual philanthropic behaviour. To obtain this data, behavioural philanthropy proposes using methods from behavioural economics and game theory to investigate philanthropic decision-making with experimental games in controlled lab settings.

3 Testing models of individual charitable giving: behavioural/ experimental game theory and social preferences

Behavioural game theory has developed experimental games, wherein: 1) the decisions of the player can impact other individuals' payoffs, and/or 2) the player's payoff may not only depend on their own decisions but also on the decisions of others. By altering the payoff rules of different parties, such games can be used to reproduce the elementary tensions that govern decision-making in social contexts and therefore constitute the most convenient experimental tools to investigate individual motives in social contexts (Camerer, 2003).

The main goal of this section is to introduce behavioural game theory as a powerful and flexible framework for behavioural philanthropic research on charitable decision-making. First, we present two of the most pertinent games for the studies of philanthropy, namely the dictator game, which is the one most widely used games in the study of social preferences such as altruism and inequity aversion, among others (Vesterlund, 2016), and the public good game, which, although widely studied in the economics of cooperation (Fischbacher, Gächter and Fehr, 2001), is overlooked in charitable giving research. Following this, we highlight three major advantages of using these games for investigating charitable decision-making; that is, they measure actual behaviour and are properly incentivised, allow researchers to infer causality, and are highly generalisable and comparable.

Economic games to model charitable decision-making

Dictator game

The dictator game is one of the simplest games and a useful tool for investigating generosity and altruistic motives (Forsythe et al., 1994). It features two players: the dictator and the recipient. The dictator is endowed with an amount of money and asked to divide this endowment with the recipient. The recipients' role is entirely passive, since they can neither send some of the transferred money back (as in the trust game) nor reject the offer (as in the ultimatum game). For example, if the dictator is endowed with 10 dollars (E) and decides to allocate 2 dollars (x) to the recipient, the dictator receives 8 dollars ($E - x$), and the recipient receives 2 dollars (x). As such, the dictator game measures how much dictators give under experimentally manipulated conditions to mimic giving in charitable settings. The more money the dictators transfer, the more prosocial they are toward the recipient.

Rational choice theory predicts that the dictator will act solely out of self-interest, maximise his payoffs by keeping the largest amount possible, and thus give nothing (zero) to the recipient. However, empirical studies have reported that giving behaviour in a dictator game is consistently and significantly larger than zero. A recent meta-analysis reported that, on average, dictators gave 28.35%, while the distribution of means was left skewed; 36.11% of all participants gave nothing, 16.74% gave 50% (equal split), and as many as 5.44% of all participants gave 100% of their endowment to the recipient (Engel, 2011).

However, the classic setup features another (anonymous) participant as the recipient (e.g., Forsythe et al., 1994), and later studies looked at transfers to recipients outside the laboratory, such as Hurricane Katrina victims (e.g., Fong and Luttmer, 2009) or let an existing non-profit replace the role of the recipient (e.g., Eckel and Grossman, 2006b) and found contrasting results. Although changing the recipient does change the giving amounts, the theoretical predictions (everyone behaves self-interestedly and gives nothing) are never met, and most participants decide to give in laboratory as well as non-laboratory settings.

Public good game

While the dictator game focuses on binary interactions (one person deciding to give to another person, entity, or charity), the public good game was designed to investigate decision-making within group dynamics.

Participants in the public good game are first paired in groups and are each given an amount of money that they can individually allocate between a personal account and a public common pool. The money in an individual account benefits only the individual; the money in the public pool benefits the entire group and is typically also increased by the experimenters, as it is multiplied by a predefined rate. Importantly, group benefits are equally distributed across all individual members regardless of whether they contribute to the public good. The design of public and private earnings is set to mimic everyday situations/dilemmas of public goods (i.e., contributing to public transport, health insurance, and public education). In particular, on the one hand, the entire group earns the highest profit when all members contribute all of their resources to a public good (for a review, see Menietti et al., 2018). On the other hand, free riders can increase their payoff by contributing nothing and still benefit from the common pool (see Figure 20.4, a player in red). Such behaviour (as in real life) creates a socially inefficient situation and is called the free-rider problem.

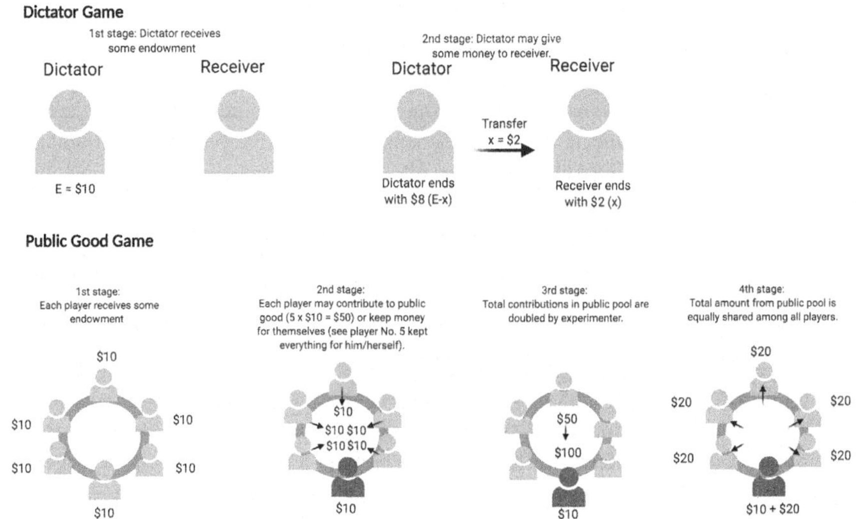

Figure 20.4 (Colour online):[5] Overview of the two economic games' settings for studying charitable decision making: Dictator game (upper part) and public good game (lower part)

Empirically, contributions in the public good game typically start off around 50% of endowments and then decrease with repetition but remain substantial even when participants have had time to gain experience in the game (see, e.g., Isaac and Walker, 1988; Ledyard, 1995; Croson, 2007, 2008; Holt and Laury, 2008 for reviews). Such contributions can be seen as evidence that individuals are concerned about others' welfare. Thus, by manipulating the incentives to give, we can determine how certain parameters and mechanisms influence contributions to others. For example, the introduction of an altruistic punishment option, in which individuals can punish free riders (who do not contribute to the common good), increases public cooperation. Interestingly, such punishments work even when they are costly for individuals who decide to punish, and there is some evidence that negative emotions toward defectors influence such altruistic punishment (Fehr and Gächter, 2002). This has been supported by a neuroscientific study by Strobel et al. (2011), who found that reward-related regions of the brain (nucleus accumbens) showed punishment-related activation.

In this context, studies in different disciplines (including law, management, economics, and public policy) have revealed that beliefs, feelings, and behaviours of people within groups influence individual decisions regarding cooperation and promotion of the group good over the selfish benefit. As such, the public good game captures how the incentive to behave selfishly affects the interaction between potential donors and groups.

Advantages of economic games

Accurately measuring behaviours

One of the main strengths of economic games is that they allow researchers to observe and assess actual behaviours. Such games connect the strategic decisions of multiple individuals to group-level outcomes through precisely defined mechanisms. In contrast, much of the research in law and social science has conducted surveys aimed at eliciting self-reports of behaviour and participant perceptions. Such self-reports and perceptions can be biased, especially when self-serving, social desirability, and self-deception biases come into play (Lee and Sargeant, 2011). The decision-making context in economic games is monetarily incentivised to increase value and create real stakes and dilemmas (between personal gains and cooperation) that will motivate individuals to reveal their true behaviour and mimic real-life situations. Although economic games are simplified and cannot include all factors from complex real-life settings, they nevertheless provide a setting that is more comparable to a real-life scenario as compared to hypothetical survey scenarios.

Inferring causality

An important element of any theory is the understanding and description of causal relationships (Muthukrishna and Henrich, 2019). Such insights are also important for practitioners and organisations that develop interventions based on theories and experimental findings. One of the biggest problems of field research is that it usually has an endogeneity problem, which refers to a scenario in which unmeasured or omitted variables could explain the resulting correlation. In contrast, participants in economic games are usually randomly assigned to different conditions and experimentally controlled to rule out alternative explanations. Such settings allow experimental manipulations to be imposed, thus providing mechanistic (i.e., causal) explanations of how people decide.

Adaptability, comparability, and replicability

Economic games provide great flexibility, and their baseline designs are usually simple and adaptable to the specific research questions that mirror situations in which people have to decide whether they would trust, cooperate, free ride, or be fair. While survey questionnaires are usually greatly varied, economic games have standard designs, and their richness and complexity can be modified as required. Economic games, therefore, provide an opportunity to achieve adaptability, comparability (to other studies), and replicability (of findings and their generalisability).

Economic games and behavioural philanthropy

A general framework

To further explore the different factors that influence charitable giving, we believe that both the dictator game and public good game can offer a clear and well-controlled setup for analysing charitable decision-making. By randomising experimental treatments, providing a baseline condition, and testing representative samples, such studies will provide implications more clearly and quickly and avoid the endogeneity issues in field experiments.

As in all economic games, there is no deception involved, and participants know that they receive real incentives and the money will go to the selected charity. This not only provides insights into personal preferences in which people's self-interest competes with self-image but also allows us to test the efficiency of different motivations that mirror decisions in real settings (such as tax incentives, warm-glow giving, social signalling, etc.). Furthermore, since public good games entail group interactions, this facilitates the study of the influence of social factors such as norms, social comparisons, and social signalling on individual and group behaviour.

Toward a more ecological framework

Although such games mirror everyday dilemmas, we believe that further improvements to provide an even more ecologically valid framework are possible. In the following paragraphs, we discuss some fundamental adaptations and manipulations that can increase the relevance of public good games as the tool of choice to investigate individual motives for philanthropy.

First, a common practice in dictator and public good games is to provide participants with endowments that serve as their capital and participants use such 'free' endowment when making decisions. There has been empirical evidence suggesting that such 'given' money, so-called house money, might be treated differently, and people take more risks when playing with it as compared to using their regular income (Thaler and Johnson, 1990). To avoid such distortion, a simple addition to economic games might be a working task in which participants earn money before playing economic games. Then, we will be able to provide insights into how varying sources of money (e.g., whether higher rewards are earned by luck or effort) impact decision making and how individual decisions are influenced by the nature of the money (i.e., free endowment vs. earned income) (Erkal, Gangadharan and Nikiforakis, 2011; Tonin and Vlassopoulos, 2017). Moreover, manipulating the level of effort can enable us to test how warm-glow motivation plays a role in giving, investigate the meritocratic aspects of giving (Mayo and Tinsley, 2009), and reveal how income inequality impacts giving behaviour (Gee, Migueis and Parsa, 2017). Importantly, these endowments should not be confused with the incentive schemes that are characteristic of public good games, which entail growing public wealth by multiplying the individual contributions of individuals to the public good by a pre-determined factor. These incentives are ecologically sound, as they mimic existing schemes, such as tax rebates or matching, that governments frequently decide to implement to stimulate private investments in a given area such as philanthropy.

Second, manipulating the participants' level of information in public good games can explain the role of subjective and objective social comparisons in giving. We believe that studies should also look into whether behaviour in games is generalisable with respect to real-life behaviour, for example, by combining experimental data with reports on real donations.

4 Behavioural philanthropy and tax incentives

In this section, we illustrate how the behavioural approach to philanthropic giving can help address important practical questions. Accordingly, we focus on individual reactions to tax subsidies. To incentivise more individuals to donate and greater amounts of donations, many countries have implemented subsidies as tax deductions, tax credits, allocation, or matching schemes. Identifying the best subsidy mechanism and understanding how it is perceived by individual taxpayers is fundamental to promoting charitable giving.

Incentives for charitable giving: rebate and match subsidy

Most empirical studies have investigated subsidies such as rebate or match subsidies. In a tax rebate subsidy, a fraction of the donor's contribution is refunded by a government and/or third party, while the charity still receives the entire amount donated. Alternatively, the match subsidy supplements the donated money; both the individual's contribution as well as a matching payment by the government and/or third-party subsidy are given to the charity. Theoretically, the rebate (r) and match subsidy (m) predict identical effects on individuals' net donations: $m = r/(1 - r)$, and the total amount a charity receives should be the same regardless of the subsidy type. For example, a 1 (donor contribution):1 (government contribution) matching scheme should be equivalent to a 50% rebate subsidy: when a 50% tax rebate (subsidy) is applied, an individual donor contributes 1 dollar, and the government refunds 50% of the donation (0.5 dollars) to the donor; thus, the charity receives 1 dollar, and the cost of donation for a donor is 0.5 dollars. When a 100% match subsidy is applied and an individual donor contributes 0.5 dollars, the government also donates 0.5 dollars; thus, the charity receives 1 dollar, and the cost of donation for a donor is 0.5 dollars, which is expressed by the following equation: $1 = 0.5 / (1 - 0.5)$. Similarly, a 2:1 matching scheme is equivalent to a 33% rebate, and a 4:1 matching scheme is equivalent to a 20% rebate.

Empirical studies: matching subsidy stimulates more giving to charities than rebate subsidy

Strikingly, despite the mathematical equivalence between the two subsidy mechanisms, both laboratory-and field-based empirical studies have repeatedly observed that match subsidies raise more money for charities as compared to rebates that are equally costly for the donor.

Eckel and Grossman (2003) conducted the first lab study to investigate whether charitable decisions are the same under equivalent match (100%, 33%, or 25% match) and rebate subsidies (50%, 25%, or 20% rebate). Employing a modified dictator game, participants (n = 181, students from the University of Texas) were asked to divide different amounts of endowments (40, 60, 75, or 100 tokens; each token value $0.10) between themselves and a charity of their choice. The findings showed that under the match subsidy condition, charity received 1.2 to 2 times more money than that of the rebate subsidy. Several experimental studies have replicated the finding that matching subsidies lead to higher charity receipts and larger price elasticity as compared to rebate subsidies (see Table 20.1). Moreover, findings from laboratory experiments were replicated in field studies; however, although the difference between the rebate and match subsidy in total charity receipts was significant, it was smaller than that of the findings reported in laboratory studies (see Eckel and Grossman, 2008, 2017; Bekkers, 2015).

Several previous studies have examined the impact of different rates under matching and rebate conditions (see a summary of the existing studies in Table 20.1). Karlan and List (2007) conducted a natural field experiment to investigate how different match ratios (donation: match of $3:$1, $2:$1, $1:$1) impacted revenue per solicitation and response rate. Contrary to intuition and standard economic theory predictions, higher match ratios ($3:$1, $2:$1) did not have a different impact on donations as compared to that of smaller match ratios ($1:$1). Moreover, this study also found that match subsidy increased both the likelihood of contributions (by 22%) and the amount given (by 19%) as compared to the no-subsidy condition. However, the effect of match subsidy relative to the control treatment could not be confirmed in a follow-up study (Karlan, List and Shafir, 2011). Therefore, future laboratory and field experiments are needed to establish how effective match and rebate subsidies are relative to the control treatment (i.e., the no-subsidy condition).

From both the non-profit and government perspectives, it is important not only to provide clear and replicable evidence on how effective specific subsidies are but also to examine the long-term consequences of implementing different subsidies. In other words, does more giving in match conditions result in less giving in the future? Meier (2007) conducted the first field experiment on student tuition among students at the University of Zurich. While the randomly assigned matching mechanism increased contributions at the start, once the matching subsidy stopped, the contribution rate declined. Furthermore, this decline was strong enough to outweigh the positive effect and ultimately had a negative net effect on the participation rate.

Table 20.1 Review of matching and rebate subsidies on charitable giving in laboratory experiments

Paper	*Methodology*	*Main manipulation*	*Design*	*Rebate vs. match rate*	*No. of subjects*	*Pool*	*Main findings*	*Differences on net donations*	*Comments*
(Eckel and Grossman, 2003)	Modified dictator game: subject makes a series of allocation decisions to divide an endowment between himself and a charity he chooses from a list of five charities	The decision problems differed by: 1) endowment (40, 60, 75, or 100 tokens), 2) the cost to the subject of contributing $1 to the charity ($1, $0.80, $0.75, and $0.50), and 3) match and rebate condition	Within-subject repeated dictator game.	Rebate rate: 20, 25, and 50% Match rate: 25, 33, and 100%	181 subjects	Undergraduate and graduate students at University of Texas at Arlington	Under match subsidy, charity received significantly more than under rebate subsidy	Authors did not report the net donations when no subsidy is applied ($1 costs $1) for three out of four conditions ($3, $7.50, $10); therefore, comparison is only possible for $6 endowment: there is a significant increase of net donations between no subsidy and match subsidy, as well as between no subsidy and rebate subsidy	The result of donations is reported for sample size = 135
(Davis, Millner and Reilly, 2005)	Modified dictator game: subject makes a series of allocation decisions to divide an endowment between himself and a charity (Feed the Children).	The decision problems differed by: 1) endowment: $8, $12, $2) the cost to the subject of contributing $1 to the charity ($1.00, $.67, and $.50), and whether the reduction in cost is a result of a rebate or a portion of matching	Within-subject repeated dictator game	Rebate rate: 33%, 50% Match rate: 50%, 100%	43 subjects	Mostly undergraduate students at Virginia Commonwealth University	Under match subsidy charity received significantly more than under rebate subsidy	There is no difference between net donation of match and no subsidy; however, rebate is significantly lower both from match and from no subsidy. This effect is the same for $8 and $12 endowments	Three experiments reported differ in: 1) control, 2) rewards in investment context, and 3) full information treatment (with table describing all possible outcomes)

(*Continued*)

Table 20.1 (Continued)

Paper	*Methodology*	*Main manipulation*	*Design*	*Rebate vs. match rate*	*No. of subjects*	*Pool*	*Main findings*	*Differences on net donations*	*Comments*
(Eckel and Grossman, 2006b): Subsidising	Modified dictator game: subject makes a series of allocation decisions to divide an endowment between himself and a charity (Feed the Children)	The decision problems differed by: 1) endowment ($4, $6, $7.5), 2) the cost to the subject of contributing $1 to the charity ($1, $0.80, $0.75, and $0.50), and 3) match and rebate condition	Between-subject (rebate vs. match) repeated dictator game	Rebate rate: 20, 25, and 50% Match rate: 25, 33, and 100%	96 subjects	Saint Cloud State University	Under match subsidy, charity received significantly more than under rebate subsidy	There is no control group which would not get any subsidy	
(Eckel and Grossman, 2006a): Do Donors	One-shot dictator game	Participants could decide whether they would like to implement match or rebate subsidy. Endowment was $20	Between-subject dictator game	Rebate rate: 50% Match rate: 100%	120 subjects (and 4 monitoring participants)	Saint Cloud State University	53 selected matching subsidy, and 67 selected rebate subsidy	While the net donations were not significantly different between match and rebate, the amount charities received was significantly higher in match than in rebate condition	
(Gandullia and Lezzi, 2018)	Modified dictator game: subject makes a series of allocation decisions to divide an endowment between himself and a charity from the list (The	The decision problems differed by: 1) endowment ($1.5 and $2), 2) the cost of contributing $1 ($1, $0.80, $0.75, and $0.50), and 3) match and rebate condition	Within-subject design	Rebate rate: 20, 25, and 50% Match rate: 25, 33, and 100%	333 participants	Amazon Mechanical Turk platform	Under match subsidy, charity received significantly more than under rebate subsidy	While the net donations were not significantly different between match and rebate, the amount charities received were significantly higher in match than in rebate condition	Correlational data: males are less altruistic than females, older participants donate more than participants younger than 35 in both subsidy

	Red Cross, WWF, Save the Children, and Doctors without Borders)								types, and Democratic participants are more altruistic than strongly Republican only under the rebate subsidy. Probability of giving increases monotonically along with subsidy rates, and participants who usually donate are more likely to give and less responsive to price changes
(Peng and Liu, 2020)	Modified dictator game: subject makes a series of allocation decisions to divide an endowment between himself and a charity (Feed the Children)	The decision problems differed by: 1) the cost of contributing $1 to the charity ($1, $0.75, and $0.50) and 2) match and rebate condition	Between-subject design	Rebate rate: 0, 20, and 50% Match rate: 0,25, and 100%	165 participants	National Taipei University	Under match subsidy, charity received significantly more than under rebate subsidy. Rebate subsidy was not significantly different between the three different costs of contributions	Individual net donations were higher under match than under rebate	

A large national study in the Netherlands (Bekkers, 2015) found that nine months after the matching campaign, there was no difference in contributions between individuals whose donations were matched and those whose donations were not matched. In contrast, other studies (Karlan, List and Shafir, 2011; Kesternich, Löschel and Römer, 2016) found a positive increase in contributions after the experiment but only in the specific condition of a 1:1 match subsidy. Overall, these findings report very mixed results of subsidies in the long term, and future longitudinal studies are needed to better address the factors that might explain these inconsistent results.

While previous studies established that match subsidies increase charity receipts, recently, Peng and Liu (2020) explored whether match subsidies increased individual net donations. Moreover, given the large amount (about 2% of GDP) donated annually in the United States, another important aspect is the amount donated by government or third-party donors under subsidies such as match or rebate. To provide evidence on these two important questions, further studies that compare match, rebate, and control (no subsidy) conditions and highlight not only the charity receipts but also net donations and cost for government and/or a third party who subsidises the donations are required. Therefore, the verdict for the most optimal donation design, which accounts for the costs and benefits of different subsidies, is still ongoing, and more research that implements representative samples and avoids using house money is needed.

Speculations on what drives the different behavioural outcomes

There have been some speculations and explanations from cognitive psychology regarding why theoretically similar match and rebate conditions would provide different behavioural outcomes. One of the first factors investigated was the role of confusion. In Davis, Millner, and Reilly's (2005) third experiment (referred to as full information treatment), a table on how much participants would earn and how much the charity would receive was included when participants made decisions. While this extra information moved the rates of match and rebate subsidies closer together, the charity receipts were still higher under the match subsidy than under the rebate subsidy. A recent study (Peng, 2020) followed up on this finding and reported a correlation between the money donated under the two different subsidies and the cognitive reflection task (CRT), which is a measure of cognitive abilities. While people with high and low CRT both gave significantly higher donations under the match subsidy condition, participants with higher cognitive ability are more likely to attain theoretical equivalence. Since rebate subsidies are even more complex to calculate and estimate in real life, future studies should address whether and how attention, complexity, and confusion play a role in the effectiveness of different tax incentives.

Davis and Millner (2005) argued that part of the effect might be attributed to rebate aversion, since participants might have more real-life experiences with rebate subsidies than with match subsidies. For example, in real life, rebates usually come with cost uncertainty. Such uncertainty depends on both the donor (i.e., time cost and additional effort or errors, or they might forget filling and mailing the form) and external, non-donor mistakes (i.e., the letter can be lost, errors can occur) regarding filling and mailing the forms. Comparing this to a typically immediate match subsidy, it might be that people are just rebate averse. To test this, Eckel and Grossman (2006a) asked participants to freely decide between the two subsidies before they were asked to contribute to the selected incentive. They predicted that if participants were rebate averse, more participants would decide to implement a match subsidy. Interestingly, more people decided on a rebate than a match subsidy, although this difference was not statistically significant. Furthermore, the donations from participants who selected the matching subsidy were twice the amount of donations from participants who selected the rebate subsidy. Another possible explanation could be that the different responses were due to an isolation effect (Davis, 2006), suggesting that participants focus on the variable they have under their control (i.e., money transfer), and net donations will be the same between rebate and match, which in turn implies that total contributions under the match exceed those under the rebate by precisely the magnitude of the match.

Lukas, Grossman and Eckel (2010) focused on the problem that the choice set under the rebate is smaller than under the match condition; that is, a participant in the rebate condition can never contribute everything. To minimise this effect, the authors allowed participants to borrow against future rebates to mirror possible contributions under the match. Additionally, they included the payoff table, yet the difference between the match and rebate conditions remained. Finally, although proposed in the first study by Eckel and Grossman (2003), to the best of our knowledge, no study has addressed whether different results are due to the differences in cooperative framing and reference groups. While the rebate subsidy is cast in a reward frame, the match subsidy might be perceived as a cooperation frame, and the experimenter can be seen as a reference group. Accordingly, it is plausible that rebate incentives may hurt an individual's intrinsic motivation to give.

To address these unanswered questions, we have developed a novel paradigm in an ongoing research project that asks participants to make donations in a public good game setting and allows us to manipulate whether donations are incentivised by matching or rebate schemes or in the absence of incentives. Our preliminary results revealed that in this social context, the matching scheme was the only one that effectively increased net donations to charities as compared to no incentives and rebate-type incentives. Importantly, we found no difference between the donations given by participants in the group incentivised through this scheme and those that had no incentive at all. This suggests that rebate schemes may be inefficient to promote philanthropy, as they cost the state a loss in tax revenues and do not achieve the objective of increasing the revenue of philanthropic organisations (see Figure 20.5).

5 Open questions and future research directions

We believe that behavioural philanthropy can make fundamental contributions to the understanding of why people engage in philanthropy and devise ways to increase the willingness of people to participate in the endeavour of promoting human wellbeing. Insights from this new field of research, combined with knowledge from other micro- and macro-level approaches to philanthropy, have the potential to deliver better-rounded evidence to support the design of effective tax policies and institutional practices aimed at promoting philanthropy. As can be seen in this chapter, recent years have seen a dramatic increase in the number of attempts to address the question of what motivates people to donate and how to boost this donation behaviour. However, much of this research regarding different factors that impact charitable giving has been largely correlational, leaving an open question of how different factors influence donation decision-making.

One of the most direct ways of stimulating giving among individual donors is to decrease the monetary cost of donating (for instance, through tax subsidies). While such a direct way of incentivisation decreases the cost of individual donors, it also increases the cost of government and/or third parties. To maximise public good, the 'most optimal' donation design (Haruvy et al., 2020) that produces the highest donor contributions at the lowest cost to the governments or third parties must be found (O.E.C.D., 2020). The first step in providing such applications for a behaviourally informed policy is to define which subsidies work, whether donors are price

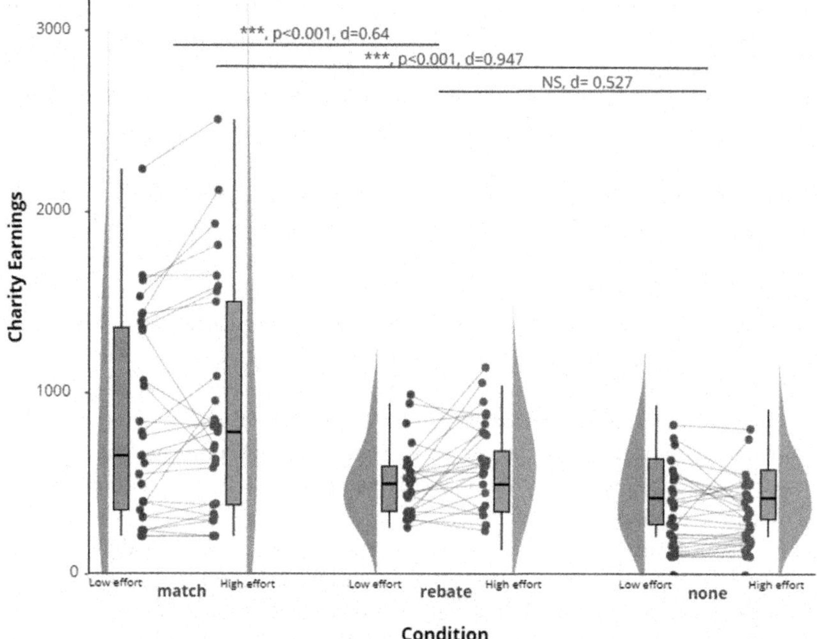

Figure 20.5 (Colour online):[6] Preliminary results on the effect of taxation subsidies on charity donations. Match subsidy significantly increases charity donations as compared to both rebate and no-subsidy schemes. Interestingly, the rebate scheme does not increase charity donations as compared to the no-subsidy condition. There is no main effect of effort tasks (low vs. high) within conditions

sensitive, and how donors respond to different frames of reduction in the cost of a donation. Since large amounts of money are involved in fundraising campaigns, such questions are not only important for the benefits of non-profit organisations but also have key implications for policymakers and overall public good maximisation.

While many studies have focused on monetary incentives that boost charitable giving, such as rebates and matches, recent neuroscientific studies have shown that altruism can also be mediated by mindfulness (Iwamoto et al., 2020). In particular, subjects who were in meditation treatment donated 2.61 times higher than the control. Such findings call for more research on how stress and emotional regulation impact social preferences and charitable giving.

Overall, field studies on the long-term effects of matching subsidies have reported mixed results, from no effect to positive and negative effects. We believe that laboratory studies, which are not only cheaper and faster to conduct but can also better control for heterogeneity of settings and samples, might be useful in the future to provide insights into what drives the differences. Once the behaviour in the laboratory is well understood, we believe field experiments could test whether such long-term findings are replicated in the representative samples and real-life behaviour.

While the experiments using match and rebate subsidies that were reviewed in this chapter treated taxes and donations as private ways of creating public value, economic literature (Slavov, 2014) seems to agree that taxes are public, while donations are a private way of creating public and social welfare. Therefore, laboratory studies that mirror the effects of tax reductions regarding different public or private ways of creating public value are needed.

As mentioned previously, we must stress that most studies (with the exception of Peng and Liu, 2020) have used WEIRD societies for their study samples, which has compounded the replication problem discussed in this chapter (Henrich, Heine and Norenzayan, 2010). To provide conclusions on a more general understanding of human behaviour, future studies should focus on cross-cultural samples and investigate how different donation behaviours are similar or vary across different countries and cultures.

Constructing theories of a more general understanding of human behaviour, linked between economics, psychology, and neuroscience, provides opportunities to address long-standing questions. By providing such theories, we will not only develop clear predictions through the use of formal modelling and set theoretical expectations but also determine whether novel findings are confirmatory or surprising and thus whether they require future replication and scrutiny. We hope to see behavioural philanthropy flourishing by addressing socially relevant and empirical studies with strong empirical methods that can answer these questions and provide models and evidence that predict charitable donations within and without the laboratory setting. We hope such practices will provide evidence on current mechanisms and build new ways 'to get the basket under the apple tree'.

Notes

1 The definition used by the Geneva Centre for Philanthropy: https://www.unige.ch/philanthropie/en/.
2 https://www.unige.ch/BehavioralPhilanthropyLab/files/2216/1916/8366/Ch15_Figure1.png
3 https://www.unige.ch/BehavioralPhilanthropyLab/files/3116/1916/8376/Ch15_Figure2.png
4 https://www.unige.ch/BehavioralPhilanthropyLab/files/2516/1916/8408/Ch15_Figure3.png
5 https://www.unige.ch/BehavioralPhilanthropyLab/files/9416/1916/8420/Ch15_Figure4.png
6 https://www.unige.ch/BehavioralPhilanthropyLab/files/4716/1916/8448/Ch15_Figure5.png

References

Agerström, J. *et al.* (2016) 'Using descriptive social norms to increase charitable giving: The power of local norms', *Journal of Economic Psychology*, 52, pp. 147–153. doi: 10.1016/j.joep.2015.12.007.

Alpizar, F., Carlsson, F. and Johansson-Stenman, O. (2008) 'Anonymity, reciprocity, and conformity: Evidence from voluntary contributions to a national park in Costa Rica', *Journal of Public Economics*, 92(5–6), pp. 1047–1060. doi: 10.1016/j.jpubeco.2007.11.004.

Andreoni, J. (1990) 'Impure altruism and donations to public goods: A theory of warm-glow giving', *The Economic Journal*, 100(401), pp. 464–477. URL: http://www.jstor.org/stable/2234133 Accessed: 02-03-2020.

Andreoni, J. (2006) 'Chapter 18 philanthropy', in S.-C. Kolm and J. M. Ythier (eds.) *Handbook of the economics of giving, altruism and reciprocity*. Elsevier, pp. 1201–1269. doi: doi.org/10.1016/S1574-0714(06)02018-5.

Andreoni, J. and Petrie, R. (2004) 'Public goods experiments without confidentiality: A glimpse into fundraising', *Journal of Public Economics*, 88(7–8), pp. 1605–1623. doi: 10.1016/S0047-2727(03)00040-9.

Ariely, B. D., Bracha, A. and Meier, S. (2009) 'Doing good or doing well? Image motivation and monetary incentives in behaving prosocially', *American Economic Review*, March, 99(1), pp. 544–555.

Becker, G. S. (1974) 'A theory of social interactions', *Journal of Political Economy*, 82(6), pp. 1063–1093.

Bekkers, R. (2015) 'When and why matches are more effective subsidies than rebates', *Research in Experimental Economics*, 18, pp. 183–211. doi: 10.1108/S0193-230620150000018007.

Bekkers, R. and Wiepking, P. (2011) 'Generosity and philanthropy: A literature review', *SSRN Electronic Journal*, pp. 1–67. doi: 10.2139/ssrn.1015507.

Bénabou, R. and Tirole, J. (2006) 'Incentives and prosocial behavior', *American Economic Review*, 96(5), pp. 1652–1678.

Berman, J. Z. *et al.* (2018) 'Impediments to effective altruism: The role of subjective preferences in charitable giving', *Psychological Science*, 29(5), pp. 834–844. doi: 10.1177/0956797617747648.

Bodner, R. and Prelec, D. (2003) 'The diagnostic value of actions in a self-signaling model', *The Psychology of Economic Decisions, Volume I: Rationality and Well-Being*, 1, pp. 105–126.

Bonar, J. (1926) '"The theory of moral sentiments," By Adam Smith, 1759', *Philosophy*, 1(3), 333–353. doi: 10.1017/S0031819100023536.

Bracha, A., Menietti, M. E. and Vesterlund, L. (2011) 'Seeds to succeed: Sequential giving to public projects', *Journal of Public Economics*. Elsevier B.V., 95(5–6), pp. 416–427. doi: 10.1016/j.jpubeco.2010.10.007.

Burum, B., Nowak, M. A. and Hoffman, M. (2020) 'An evolutionary explanation for ineffective altruism', *Nature Human Behaviour*. Springer: US, 4(12), pp. 1245–1257. doi: 10.1038/s41562-020-00950-4.

Camerer, C. F. (2003) *Behavioral game theory: Experiments in strategic interaction*. Princeton: Princeton University Press.

Chen, Y., Li, X. and MacKie-Mason, J. K. (2006) 'Online fund-raising mechanisms: A field experiment', *Contributions in Economic Analysis and Policy*, 5(2), pp. 75–113. doi: 10.2202/1538-0645.1477

Croson, R. T. (2007) 'Theories of commitment, altruism and reciprocity: Evidence from linear public goods games', *Economic Inquiry*, 45(2), pp. 199–216.

Croson, R. T. (2008) 'Differentiating altruism and reciprocity', *Handbook of Experimental Economics Results*, 1, pp. 784–791.

Davis, D. D. (2006) 'Rebate subsidies, matching subsidies and isolation effects', *Judgment and Decision Making*, 1(NA), pp. 13–22.

Davis, D. D. and Millner, E. L. (2005) 'Rebates, matches, and consumer behavior', *Southern Economic Journal*, 72(2), p. 410. doi: 10.2307/20062118.

Davis, D. D., Millner, E. L. and Reilly, R. J. (2005) 'Subsidy schemes and charitable contributions: A closer look', *Experimental Economics*, 8(2), pp. 85–106. doi: 10.1007/s10683-005-0867-y.

Eckel, C. C. and Grossman, P. J. (2003) 'Rebate versus matching: Does how we subsidize charitable contributions matter?' *Journal of Public Economics*, 87(3–4), pp. 681–701. doi: 10.1016/S0047-2727(01)00094-9.

Eckel, C. C. and Grossman, P. J. (2006a) 'Do donors care about subsidy type? An experimental study', *Research in Experimental Economics*, 11(0316), pp. 157–175. doi: 10.1016/S0193-2306(06)11007-8.

Eckel, C. C. and Grossman, P. J. (2006b) 'Subsidizing charitable giving with rebates or matching: Further laboratory evidence', *Southern Economic Journal*, 72(4), p. 794. doi: 10.2307/20111853.

Eckel, C. C. and Grossman, P. J. (2008) 'Subsidizing charitable contributions: A natural field experiment comparing matching and rebate subsidies', *Experimental Economics*, 11(3), pp. 234–252. doi: 10.1007/s10683-008-9198-0.

Eckel, C. C. and Grossman, P. J. (2017) 'Comparing rebate and matching subsidies controlling for donors' awareness: Evidence from the field', *Journal of Behavioral and Experimental Economics*. Elsevier Inc., 66, pp. 88–95. doi: 10.1016/j.socec.2016.04.016.

Engel, C. (2011) 'Dictator games: A meta study', *Experimental Economics*, 14(4), pp. 583–610. doi: 10.1007/s10683-011-9283-7.

Erkal, B. N., Gangadharan, L. and Nikiforakis, N. (2011) 'American economic association relative earnings and giving in a real-effort experiment', *Publish*, 101(7), pp. 3330–3348.

Falk, A. and Zehnder, C. (2013) 'A city-wide experiment on trust discrimination'. *Journal of Public Economics*, 100, pp. 15–27.

Fehr, E. and Gächter, S. (2002) 'Altruistic punishment in humans', *Nature*, 415(6868), pp. 137–140. doi: 10.1038/415137a.

Fischbacher, U., Gächter, S. and Fehr, E. (2001) 'Are people conditionally cooperative? Evidence from a public goods experiment', *Economics Letters*, 71(3), pp. 397–404. doi: 10.1016/S0165-1765(01)00394-9.

Fong, C. M. and Luttmer, E. F. (2009) 'What determines giving to Hurricane Katrina victims? Experimental evidence on racial group loyalty', *American Economic Journal: Applied Economics*, 1(2), pp. 64–87.

Forsythe, R. *et al.* (1994) 'Fairness in simple bargaining experiments', *Games and Economic Behavior*, 6(3), pp. 347–369. doi: 10.1006/game.1994.1021.

Gandullia, L. and Lezzi, E. (2018) 'The price elasticity of charitable giving: New experimental evidence', *Economics Letters*. Elsevier B.V., 173, pp. 88–91. doi: 10.1016/j.econlet.2018.09.012.

Gee, L. K., Migueis, M. and Parsa, S. (2017) 'Redistributive choices and increasing income inequality: Experimental evidence for income as a signal of deservingness', *Experimental Economics*. Springer: US, 20(4), pp. 894–923. doi: 10.1007/s10683-017-9516-5.

Giving USA. (2020) 'The annual report on philanthropy for the year 2019, giving USA foundation', researched and written by the Indiana University Lilly Family School of Philanthropy. Available at: www.givingusa.org. (Accessed: 7 January 2021).

Harbaugh, B. W. T. (1998a) 'The prestige motive for making charitable transfers author (s): William T. Harbaugh source: The American economic review, vol. 88, No. 2 papers and proceedings of the hundred and tenth annual meeting of the American', *American Economic Review*, 88(2), pp. 277–282.

Harbaugh, B. W. T. (1998b) 'What do donations buy?' *Journal of Public Economics*, 67(2), pp. 269–284. doi: 10.1016/S0047-2727(97)00062-5.

Haruvy, E. *et al.* (2020) 'Fundraising design: Key issues, unifying framework, and open puzzles', *Marketing Letters*, 31(4), pp. 371–380. doi: 10.1007/s11002-020-09534-8.

Havens, J. J., O'Herlihy, M. A. and Schervish, P. G. (2006) 'Charitable giving: How much, by whom, to what, and how?' *The Nonprofit Sector: A Research Handbook*, 2, pp. 542–567.

Henrich, J., Heine, S. J. and Norenzayan, A. (2010) 'The weirdest people in the world?' *Behavioral and Brain Sciences*, 33(2–3), pp. 61–83. doi: 10.1017/S0140525X0999152X.

Holt, C. A. and Laury, S. K. (2008) 'Theoretical explanations of treatment effects in voluntary contributions experiments',. *Handbook of Experimental Economics Results*, 1, pp. 846–855.

Hook, D. W., Porter, S. J. and Herzog, C. (2018) 'Dimensions: Building context for search and evaluation', *Frontiers in Research Metrics and Analytics*, 3(August), pp. 1–11. doi: 10.3389/frma.2018.00023.

Hui-Chun, P. and Wen-Jing, L. (2020) 'Crowding-out (-in) effects of subsidy schemes on individual donations: An experimental study', *Judgment and Decision Making*, 15(3), p. 346.

Isaac, R. M. and Walker, J. M. (1988) 'Group size effects in public goods provision: The voluntary contributions mechanism', *The Quarterly Journal of Economics*, 103(1), pp. 179–199.

Iwamoto, S. K. *et al.* (2020) 'Mindfulness meditation activates altruism', *Scientific Reports*, 10(1), 6511. doi: 10.1038/s41598-020-62652-1.

Johnson, E. J. and Goldstein, D. (2003) 'Do defaults save lives?' *Science*, 302(5649), pp. 1338–1339. doi: 10.1126/science.1091721.

Karlan, D. and List, J. A. (2007) 'American economic association does price matter in charitable giving? Evidence from a large-scale natural field experiment', *American Economic Review*, 97(5), pp. 1774–1793.

Karlan, D., List, J. A. and Shafir, E. (2011) 'Small matches and charitable giving: Evidence from a natural field experiment', *Journal of Public Economics*, 95(5–6), pp. 344–350. doi: 10.1016/j.jpubeco.2010.11.024.

Karlan, D. and McConnell, M. A. (2014) 'Hey look at me: The effect of giving circles on giving', *Journal of Economic Behavior and Organization*. Elsevier B.V., 106, pp. 402–412. doi: 10.1016/j.jebo.2014.06.013.

Kesternich, M., Löschel, A. and Römer, D. (2016) 'The long-term impact of matching and rebate subsidies when public goods are impure: Field experimental evidence from the carbon offsetting market', *Journal of Public Economics*. Elsevier B.V., 137, pp. 70–78. doi: 10.1016/j.jpubeco.2016.01.004.

Kingma, B. R. (1997) 'Public good theories of the non-profit sector: Weisbrod revisited', *VOLUNTAS*, 8(2), 135–148. doi: 10.1007/BF02354191.

Lacetera, N. and Macis, M. (2010) 'Social image concerns and prosocial behavior: Field evidence from a nonlinear incentive scheme', *Journal of Economic Behavior and Organization*. Elsevier B.V., 76(2), pp. 225–237. doi: 10.1016/j.jebo.2010.08.007.

Laffan, K. M. and Dolan, P. H. (2020) 'In defence of charity which benefits both giver and receiver', *Nature Human Behaviour*. Springer: US, 4(7), pp. 670–672. doi: 10.1038/s41562-020-0855-4.

Ledyard, J. O. (1995) 'Is there a problem with public goods provision', *The Handbook of Experimental Economics*, pp. 111–194.

Lee, Z. and Sargeant, A. (2011) 'Dealing with social desirability bias: An application to charitable giving', *European Journal of Marketing*, 45(5), pp. 703–719. doi: 10.1108/03090561111119994.

Linardi, S. and McConnell, M. A. (2011) 'No excuses for good behavior: Volunteering and the social environment', *Journal of Public Economics*. Elsevier B.V., 95(5–6), pp. 445–454. doi: 10.1016/j.jpubeco.2010.06.020.

List, J. A. and Lucking-Reiley, D. (2002) 'The effects of seed money and refunds on charitable giving: Experimental evidence from a university capital campaign', *Journal of Political Economy*, 110(1), pp. 215–233. doi: 10.1086/324392.

Lukas, I., Grossman, P. J. and Eckel, C. (2010) 'Preference or confusion: Understanding the differential impact of rebate and matching subsidies', Saint Cloud State University Working Paper.

Mayo, J. W. and Tinsley, C. H. (2009) 'Warm glow and charitable giving: Why the wealthy do not give more to charity?' *Journal of Economic Psychology*. Elsevier B.V., 30(3), pp. 490–499. doi: 10.1016/j.joep.2008.06.001.

Mazar, N., Amir, O. and Ariely, D. (2008) 'The dishonesty of honest people: A theory of self-concept maintenance', *Journal of Marketing Research*, 45(6), pp. 633–644. doi: 10.1509/jmkr.45.6.633.

Meier, S. (2007) 'Do subsidies increase charitable giving in the long run? Matching donations in a field experiment', *SSRN Electronic Journal*, (December), pp. 1203–1222. doi: 10.2139/ssrn.960959.

Menietti, M., Recalde, M. P. and Vesterlund, L. (2018) 'Charitable giving in the laboratory: advantages of the piecewise linear public goods game', in M. Tonin and K.A. Scharf (eds.) *The Economics of Philanthropy: Donations and Fundraising*. MIT Press.
Muthukrishna, M. and Henrich, J. (2019) 'A problem in theory', *Nature Human Behaviour*. Springer: US, 3(3), pp. 221–229. doi: 10.1038/s41562-018-0522-1.
Nelson, M. R. *et al.* (2006) 'Effects of culture, gender, and moral obligations on responses to charity advertising across masculine and feminine cultures', *Journal of Consumer Psychology*, 16(1), pp. 45–56. doi: 10.1207/s15327663jcp1601_7.
Niza, C., Tung, B. and Marteau, T. M. (2013) 'Incentivizing blood donation: Systematic review and meta-analysis to test Titmuss' hypotheses', *Health Psychology*, 32(9), pp. 941–949. doi: 10.1037/a0032740.
O.E.C.D. (2020) 'Taxation and philanthropy', *O.E.C.D. Tax Policy Studies*, 26.
Osili, U., Clark, C. and Han, X. (2019) *16 years of charitable giving research*. Indiana University Lilly Family School of Philanthropy, Indianapolis.
Ottoni-Wilhelm, M., Vesterlund, L. and Xie, H. (2014) 'Nber working paper series why do people give? Testing pure and impure altruism', Available at: www.nber.org/papers/w20497.
Peng, H. C. (2020) 'Effect of cognitive ability on matching and rebate subsidies', *Research in Economics*. Elsevier Ltd, 74(1), pp. 19–25. doi: 10.1016/j.rie.2019.11.003.
Promberger, M. and Marteau, T. M. (2013) 'When do financial incentives reduce intrinsic motivation? Comparing behaviors studied in psychological and economic literatures', *Health Psychology*, 32(9), pp. 950–957. doi: 10.1037/a0032727.
Rege, M. and Telle, K. (2004) 'The impact of social approval and framing on cooperation in public good situations', *Journal of Public Economics*, 88(7–8), pp. 1625–1644. doi: 10.1016/S0047-2727(03)00021-5.
Schwartz, S. H. (1977) 'Normative influences on altruism', *Advances in Experimental Social Psychology*, 10(C), pp. 221–279. doi: 10.1016/S0065-2601(08)60358-5.
Shang, J. and Croson, R. (2009) 'A field experiment in charitable contribution: The impact of social information on the voluntary provision of public goods', *Economic Journal*, 119(540), pp. 1422–1439. doi: 10.1111/j.1468-0297.2009.02267.x.
Slavov, S. N. (2014) 'Public versus private provision of public goods', *Journal of Public Economic Theory*, 16(2), pp. 222–258. doi: https://doi.org/10.1111/jpet.12058
Strobel, A., Zimmermann, J., Schmitz, A., Reuter, M., Lis, S., Windmann, S. and Kirsch, P. (2011) 'Beyond revenge: Neural and genetic bases of altruistic punishment', *Neuroimage*, 54(1), pp. 671–680.
Thaler, R. H. and Benartzi, S. (2004) 'Save more tomorrow™: Using behavioral economics to increase employee saving', *Journal of Political Economy*, 112(S1), S164–S187. doi: 10.1086/380085.
Thaler, R. H. and Johnson, E. J. (1990) 'Gambling with the house money and trying to break even: The effects of prior outcomes on risky choice', *Management Science*, 36(6), pp. 643–660. doi: 10.1287/mnsc.36.6.643.
Tonin, M. and Vlassopoulos, M. (2017) 'Sharing one's fortune? An experimental study on earned income and giving', *Journal of Behavioral and Experimental Economics*. Elsevier Inc., 66, pp. 112–118. doi: 10.1016/j.socec.2016.04.014.
Venkataramani, A. S. *et al.* (2012) 'The impact of tax policies on living organ donations in the United States', *American Journal of Transplantation*, 12(8), pp. 2133–2140. doi: 10.1111/j.1600-6143.2012.04044.x.
Vesterlund, L. (2016). *Edited by J. H. Kagel and A. E. Roth using experimental methods to understand why and how we give to charity*. Princeton: Princeton University Press.
Wagschal, U. (2015) 'Families of taxation: Convergence or divergence', Article Presented at the Conference the New Politics of Taxation from ECPR.
Wallendorf, M. and Brucks, M. (1993) 'Introspection in consumer research: Implementation and implications', *Journal of Consumer Research*, 20(3), p. 339. doi: 10.1086/209354.
Weber, E. U. and Johnson, E. J. (2012) 'Psychology and behavioral economics lessons for the design of a green growth strategy', *Policy Research Working Paper Series*, 6240(October), pp. 1–50.
Wiepking, P. and Bekkers, R. (2012) 'Who gives? A literature review of predictors of charitable giving. Part Two: Gender, family composition and income', *Voluntary Sector Review*, 3(2), pp. 217–245. doi: 10.1332/204080512X649379.
World Bank. (2014) '2015: Mind, society, and behavior, world development report 2015: Mind, society, and behavior', *World Development Report*. doi: 10.1596/978-1-4648-0342-0.

PART III

Tax incentives for cross-border philanthropy

21

DOUBLE TAXATION CONVENTIONS AS POTENTIAL TOOLS TO PROMOTE CROSS-BORDER PHILANTHROPIC PAYMENTS

Xavier Oberson

I The problem

Cross-border payments for philanthropic purposes raise various legal and notably tax concerns. Indeed, domestic laws of the states involved may characterize these payments in various ways and could apply different or even conflicting tax rules. In addition to the exception of the jurisprudence of the EU Court of Justice (EUCJ), which has introduced limits to the potential restrictions or discriminations caused by domestic taxation rules of EU Member States, taxation rules applicable to non-profit organizations are not coordinated. As a consequence, as we will demonstrate further, the risks of multiple or even contradictory taxation consequences of cross-border philanthropic payments could hinder their development and contradict their purposes, which, in essence, are not for profit.

In general, we can summarize the typical domestic tax problems as follows. First, often, states will treat resident and non-resident philanthropic entities differently. As a consequence, frequently, payments for philanthropic purposes in favor of a charitable entity sited abroad will not be allowed as a deduction in the payer's country. Conversely, the country of the recipient entity may also subject payments from foreign sources to profit (or income) tax. Second, resident philanthropic organizations often bear the burden of taxes levied in the source state, typically in a form of a withholding tax, on income received (dividends, interests, royalties and sometimes pensions). Third, the rules of inheritance and gift taxes are usually very different from one state to another. It follows that cross-border charitable inheritances or gifts may potentially be subject to heavy gift or inheritance taxes either in the residence country of the donor (or the deceased person), in the country of the beneficiary or even, in some cases, in the country of *situs* of specific assets (typically real estate or art collections).

This chapter will therefore try to analyze the extent to which the application of double taxation conventions (DTCs) could solve or at least alleviate the potential tax burden on cross-border philanthropic payments. To that aim, after a brief overview of the main domestic rules of some states in this area (hereafter II.), we will summarize the interesting jurisprudence of the EUCJ, which has developed a rather favorable tax perspective for cross-border charitable

 DOI: 10.4324/9781003139201-25

giving, including for non-EU third countries (hereafter III.). Finally, we will show how existing DTCs, or some new provisions of those legal instruments, may serve as tools to avoid excessive tax burden on cross-border philanthropic payments, alleviate potential double taxation or even create an incentive in favor of transnational charitable giving (hereafter IV.).

II Overview of the main domestic tax problems

A Direct taxes

1 Introduction

Without going into the details of the various domestic tax rules on cross-border payments, we will summarize the traditional tax issues that could arise in a typical cross-border transaction involving a donor (or a deceased person), a philanthropic entity, and beneficiaries, all sited in different states.[1] For the purpose of our analysis, we will focus on philanthropic entities, namely legal structures (typically an association or a foundation) with a non-for-profit purpose.[2] In this context, a first distinction should be drawn between the position of the beneficiary and the donor.

2 The philanthropic entity as beneficiary

In general, the entity *beneficiary* of the payments, will be a foundation, an association or a trust[3]. In most countries, foundations or associations, as legal persons, will be subject to domestic profit tax. To the extent they benefit from an exemption based on their philanthropic purpose, these entities would however usually not be subject to profit tax[4]. In general, this exemption should apply both for domestic and international payments, but the state of residence of the entity could apply different domestic rules based on the place of residence of the donor. In particular, it may be more difficult for the host state of the charitable entity to ascertain that a payment from abroad qualifies as a gift, that is, as a payment without any counterpart expected from the donee.

In addition, the conditions of a tax-exempt status are quite different between states and are governed by domestic law rules. For example, under Swiss law, foundations or associations which pursue charitable goals, characterized more generally as "public utility purpose" ("but d'utilité publique"), are exempted from profit and capital tax on payments exclusively and irrevocably affected to the charitable goals.[5] The concept of a public utility purpose corresponds to an altruistic activity, which serves the public good exclusively and directly.[6] Philanthropic entities should pursue a goal that benefits the collectivity as a whole and reach that objective based on disinterested sacrifices from their members.[7] In practice, tax exemption is granted by the competent tax authority under four cumulative conditions:[8] (i) the pursuit of a goal of general interest; (ii) the members, and notably board members, should follow a disinterested purpose; (iii) the philanthropic activity should be effectively pursued; (iv) the funds are irrevocably attributed to such activity. In practice, qualifying philanthropic activities are usually regarded as meeting the public utility test, namely a charitable, humanitarian, sanitary, ecological, educational, scientific or cultural purpose. The circle of beneficiaries should be opened and undetermined. However, the place of the activity is not relevant. Both domestic or foreign activities are eligible, to the extent that they meet the four conditions mentioned previously. In addition, once the conditions are met, a tax-exempt entity is not taxable on all payments received, notwithstanding their source. As a consequence, charitable payments stemming from Switzerland or abroad, including for gifts or inheritance purposes, will not be subject to profit tax. In other words, from the perspective of the beneficiary entity, Swiss domestic tax law does not make any difference between local- or foreign-source payments.

In the United States, in order to obtain a tax-exempt status, the qualifying organization must apply for recognition of the exemption and has to fulfill several requirements, notably to be organized and operated exclusively for the philanthropic purposes mentioned in the law.[9]

3 Tax position of the donor or payer

The situation is quite different from the perspective of the payer who makes a payment or a gift to a non-resident philanthropic entity. In most states, subject, however, to specific limits, the payer may deduct charitable payments to a tax-exempt entity resident in that state from income tax.[10] For example, under Swiss law, charitable gifts in favor of Swiss resident tax-exempt philanthropic entities are deductible, but the scope of the deduction is limited to 20% of the net taxable income for federal purposes. This percentage varies from canton to canton, but in most cases, cantonal law applies the same limitation as federal law.

However, payments in favor of *non-resident* philanthropic entitles are either not deductible or subject to complex limitations.[11] While some states, like Switzerland[12] and Australia, tend in principle not to grant any deduction for cross-border gifts, other states, like the United States, have a more favorable policy, subject to strict conditions, notably that the gift must be made to a qualifying organization.[13] Other states also allow for the deduction of cross-border charitable gifts but subject to specific requirements, such as, *inter alia*, the recognition of the foreign entity as a charitable entity following philanthropic purposes or some geographical limitations on the performance of the charitable activities.[14] In France, gifts to foreign non-profit organizations are in principle not deductible, but the tax administration may allow such deductions to the extent there is a reciprocal regime between France and the state of the beneficiary.[15]

Some international networks, however, exist, usually of private law nature, such as Transnational Giving Europe (TGE),[16] which allows, under specific conditions, a deduction of domestic charitable payments, which are then transferred to non-resident beneficiaries. The deduction is subject to strict conditions, and a fee is levied by the intermediate entity in order to cover, notably, the administrative costs of the "cash pool charity."[17] There are other exceptions based on domestic law.

This uncoordinated approach may result in a non-deduction from payments to a non-resident charitable entity and, in rare cases, in an additional taxation in the country of the recipient entity. Such consequences are generally the result of an absence of recognition of the philanthropic status of a non-resident charitable entity by the state of residence of the donor. Indeed, the conditions of the tax-exempt status are closely related to domestic rules. States may have quite divergent views on which activities may "deserve" a tax-exempt status. In other words, a charitable activity may be regarded as a "public utility activity" in one country and non-philanthropic in another. As we will see, however, within the EU, discriminations between resident and non-resident comparable public entities have been challenged by the case law of the EUCJ (see infra III.). In addition, the compatibility of such differences of treatment with the principle of non-discrimination anchored in DTCs similar to the OECD Model DTCs still needs to be addressed (see infra IV.).

B Inheritance or gift tax

In this area, domestic tax rules are in general completely uncoordinated and highly dependent upon local peculiarities.[18] In addition, even if an OECD Model of DTC for inheritance and gift tax purposes has been drafted,[19] there exist very few DTCs in this domain.[20] In order to demonstrate the potential disparities in the tax treatment of cross-border charitable inheritance or gifts, we may draw a distinction between the state of the payer and the state of the beneficiaries.

In most cases, countries will treat charitable payments to resident or non-resident beneficiary entities differently. In some countries, like Switzerland, we may even find different rules from one canton to the other. Indeed, under Swiss law, the ability to tax gifts or inheritances belong exclusively to the cantons.[21] It could even occur that charitable gifts or inheritance in favor of entities sited in other cantons could not benefit from a tax exemption available in the canton of residence of the payer. *A fortiori*, gifts or inheritances from a resident in one canton in favor of philanthropic entities abroad would, in most cases, be subject to a cantonal gift or inheritance tax at the highest cantonal rates applicable to unrelated parties. There are a few rare exceptions. For example, under Geneva law, a total or partial exemption for gifts of inheritance in favor of legal entities abroad may be granted, upon request, by a decision of the Geneva government.[22] In practice, this decision is difficult to obtain. The canton of Basel-City also seems to grant an exemption for inheritance or gifts of public utility entities, independently from their place of residence.[23] In addition, there are, under Swiss law, a limited number of intercantonal or international agreements based on the principle of reciprocity.[24]

Since the rules are completely uncoordinated, we could even be confronted with an additional gift or inheritance tax in the country of the recipient.

C Consequences

As a consequence, domestic law does not provide for appropriate solutions to the numerous tax obstacles of cross-border philanthropic payments. First, gifts paid in favor of nonresident philanthropic entities may not benefit from any deduction. Second, in the state of the beneficiary, there is even a potential risk that such payment could be subject to income or profit tax. Third, cross-border gifts and inheritance will often be subject to gifts or inheritance tax, potentially to the maximum applicable third-party rate, in the state of the payer and also, in some cases, even in the state of the beneficiary.

III The EU Law

A The EUCJ case law

The issue of potential excessive taxation of cross-border charitable payments has, however, been alleviated within the EU. In very interesting jurisprudence, illustrated notably by four landmark cases, the EUCJ has developed a framework which sets coordinated rules for cross-border charitable payments (including gifts or inheritance), notably on the basis of the freedom of movement of capital.[25]

In *Stauffer*, a musicology center operating as a tax-exempt foundation in Italy received rental income for a building it owned in Germany. This country refused to grant a tax exemption with respect to rental income on the grounds that the beneficiary did not reside in Germany. The EUCJ held that such discrimination was not justified, being contrary to the principle of free movement of capital.[26] That conclusion was based on the following motivation. First, the court ruled that the principle of freedom of establishment could not be invoked. In order to do so, the enterprise should have secured a permanent presence in the host Member State in which the real estate owned was actively managed. In the present case, the foundation did not have any premises in Germany for the purposes of pursuing its activities. Second, however, the freedom of movement of capital is applicable. In order to define the concept of capital movement, the nomenclature provided by Directive 88/361 has a relevant indicative value, even if the list is not exhaustive. Investment in real estate is included in this list, and, therefore, freedom of movement covers both ownership and management of such property. In this context, the fact that, under German domestic law, the tax exemption applies only to charitable entities which, as a matter of principle, have an unlimited tax liability in Germany puts non-resident comparable organizations at a disadvantageous position, which constitutes a *restriction* on the free movement of capital. In order to be justified, the difference in treatment between a foundation with unlimited tax liability and those with limited liability "must concern situations which are not objectively comparable, or be justified by overriding reasons in the general interest, such as the need to safeguard the coherence of the tax system or effective fiscal supervision."[27] In addition, the difference in treatment must not go beyond what is necessary in order to attain the objective of the applicable legislation.[28] The German government tried to justify the difference of treatment, notably, by arguing that a resident non-profit entity performs duties which usually would be a burden on the state budget, whereas the charitable activities performed by the foundation only concerned Italy and Switzerland. The ECJ did not follow that line of reasoning. In particular, the necessity of a link between the foundation and its activities was regarded as non-relevant. As a consequence, in the absence of a justification and overriding reasons of general interest, the ECJ found that the freedom of movement of capital had been infringed.

Having examined the scope of the rules on exemption from the perspective of the beneficiary, the ECJ then had to address the tax position from the point of view of a donor who was resident in an EU Member State and made a gift to a philanthropic entity sited in another EU state. In *Persche*, a German citizen had made a gift to a charitable organization in Portugal. The German tax authorities had disallowed the deduction, as the beneficiary did not meet German law requirements.[29] The ECJ was being asked to give a preliminary ruling on the admissibility of such a refusal. First, the court stated, in essence, that, when a taxpayer requests a tax deduction in one Member State with respect to gifts made to established organizations of acknowledged general interest in another Member State, such gifts "come within the compass" of the provisions relating to the free movement of capital, even if they are made in kind in the form of common consumer goods.[30] Second, the possibility of obtaining a deduction for tax purposes "can have a significant influence on the donor's attitude" so that the inability to deduct gifts to charitable bodies established in another Member State constitutes a restriction on the free movement of capital.[31] Third, this restriction is not justified. While the states have discretion to define the interests of the general public that they wish to promote by granting tax benefits, they cannot deny the right to equal treatment of a gift to a charitable body in another Member State, promoting the same interests of the general public recognized by the first Member State, "solely on the grounds that it is not established in that Member State"[32]. The ECJ considered, however, that, according to the principle of proportionality, nothing prevents the tax authorities of the Member State to require the taxpayer wishing to obtain the deduction to provide relevant evidence. In addition, the tax authorities concerned may contact the authorities of the other Member State in order to obtain information that may be necessary on the basis of Directive 77/799 on exchange of information.[33] As a consequence, since *Persche*, gifts from a taxpayer of one Member State to an institution with a public purpose in another Member State are governed by the principle of the free movement of capital and therefore cannot be the subject to tax discrimination in the case where the recipient is a charitable entity established in another Member State promoting similar interests of the general public.

In the third case, the ECJ had to examine tax discrimination in the area of gift and inheritance tax. The case *Missionswerk* involved a bequest from a Belgian resident on her death to an association with a religious purpose in Germany.[34] The Belgian tax authorities wanted to apply an 80% tax rate to the bequest, whereas the same bequest would have been taxed at a rate of 7% under domestic law. Once again, in keeping with its previous judgments, the ECJ held that the Belgian inheritance and gift rules were discriminatory. In order to reach that conclusion, the ECJ considered that a cross-border inheritance constitutes a movement of capital within the meaning of Art. 63 Treaty on the Functioning of the European Union (TFEU). Taxing an inheritance, whose beneficiary is a non-profit-making body, which has its center of operations in another Member State, in which the deceased neither actually resided nor worked, more heavily constitutes a restriction to the free movement of capital by reducing the value of that inheritance.[35] Indeed, this rule is liable to make those cross-border capital movements less attractive by dissuading Belgian residents from naming as beneficiaries persons established in Member States in which those Belgian residents have not actually resided or worked. In addition, this restriction is not justified. The Belgium government tried to argue that Member States are entitled to require, for the purposes of granting certain tax benefits, a sufficiently close link between non-profit-making bodies and the activities in which they are engaged. In the present case, Belgium collectivity takes an advantage from that regulation. However, according to the EUCJ, the fact that a Member State may be discharged from some of its responsibilities does not allow that state to establish a difference of treatment with the motive that the bequest made in favor of organizations with a public purpose in another state cannot result to a budgetary compensation in the state of source. Indeed, according to the court, the necessity to prevent a reduction of tax resources is neither a motive mentioned in Art. 65 TFEU nor an overriding reason in the general interest justifying a restriction to Art. 65 TFEU.[36] Therefore, the EUCJ, following its previous case law, considered the Belgium legislation discriminatory.

Finally, in *Commission vs Austria*, the EUCJ also confirmed that an Austrian tax rule, according to which deductions from tax are allowed solely for gifts to research and teaching institutions whose seats are in Austria, to the exclusion of gifts to comparable institutions established in other Member States of the EU or the EEA, is contrary to the free movement of capital, as guaranteed by Article 56 EC and Article 40 of the EEA Agreement.[37] The Court, in its reasoning, also referred to the previous case, *Laboratoires Fournier*, of 2005.[38] In the latter, while the ECJ held that the promotion of research and development may constitute a reason of overriding interest, the court nevertheless considered that national legislation reserving the benefit of a tax credit solely to research carried out in the Member State concerned was directly contrary to the objective of European Union policy in the field of research and technical development. In accordance with Article 163(2) EC, that policy aims in particular to remove the fiscal obstacles to cooperation in the field of research and cannot therefore be implemented by the promotion of research and development at the national level. The same is true of the tax rules concerning gifts at issue in the present case, insofar as the Republic of Austria relies on that objective to limit the deductibility of gifts to Austrian research establishments and universities.[39] It is interesting to note that, according to the Court, since the provisions of Article 40 of the EEA Agreement have the same legal scope as the substantially identical provisions of Article 56 EC, the considerations of the case law on that provision may, in similar circumstances such as those of the present case, be transposed *mutatis mutandis* to Article 40 EEA.

B Impact of EUCJ case law

It follows that Member States have an obligation to treat domestic and foreign charitable entities in another Member States equally. However, even if the principle of non-discrimination has to be observed within the EU, there are still many difficulties for charitable entities and donors to "effectively exercise their fundamental freedoms."[40] First, there is no global recognition of charitable entities. Indeed, as seen previously, the conditions of tax-exempt status are defined by the domestic law of the host state. Second, the charitable entity has to prove that it complies with the tax-exempt status conditions, as defined under the domestic law of the host state.[41] Third, the state of the donor has to be able to properly verify that such conditions are met, which requires an effective and adequate exchange of information clause in a Directive or a multilateral or bilateral treaty.

The case law of the EUCJ, in the context of the freedom of movement, could have an impact in non-EU third countries, such as Switzerland. Indeed, Art. 63 TFEU prohibits restrictions on the free movement of capital not only between Member States but also between Member States and third states. Consequently, gifts or payments derived from EU Member States to a third country, such as Switzerland, could benefit from this case law.[42] In the specific case of Switzerland, this is also justified by the fact that, even though Switzerland is not an EU Member State, it has adopted a European policy based on bilateral sectoral agreements. These agreements create broad, reciprocal access to markets and form the basis of close collaboration in several areas. As a consequence, in our view, attributions from an EU state towards non-EU countries should in principle be able to benefit from the case law developed by the EUCJ, following the *Persche* case. Following these cases, however, the EU state of residence of the donor should still be in a position to obtain relevant information from the state of the beneficiary. This condition should be met, to the extent that both states provide for an effective exchange of information, following the OECD standard of Art. 26 OECD Model DTC. This should notably be the case between Switzerland and an EU Member State, since the change of policy of Switzerland, as of 13 March 2009, in the area of exchange of information, to the extent of a DTC following the OECD standard, has been ratified between those countries.[43]

The question of whether a similar rule could also apply in the opposite direction, namely in the case of payments arising from a donor resident in a third country, such as Switzerland, in favor of a philanthropic institution sited in an EU state, is more delicate. In this context, an international agreement between the third country and the EU state providing for a freedom of movement of capital should exist. This should in particular be the case for EEA Member States. For third countries outside the EU or the EEA, it could be interesting to check whether a similar rule might be derived from the principle of non-discrimination under a tax treaty that incorporates a provision similar to Art. 24 of the OECD Model DTC with that EU Member State.[44]

C Proposal for a European Foundation

Despite the case law mentioned previously, the situation is still not satisfactory for cross-border donations within Europe. First, some Member States still have not implemented the rules of non-discrimination and either tend to discriminate against foreign-based EU nonprofit entities compared to local ones or provide very complex rules and processes in order for a foreign-based non-profit organization to be viewed as comparable to a resident entity.[45]

On 8 February 2012, as a multilateral solution to this problem, the EU Commission presented a Proposal for a Council Regulation on the Statute for a European Foundation (FE) (hereafter FE Prop. Regs).[46] This initiative intended to create a new European legal form which should facilitate the establishment and operation of foundations in the single market. It should allow "foundation to more efficiently channel private funds to public benefit purposes on a cross-border basis in the EU."[47] The proposed Regulation would also include a chapter on the tax treatment of the FE, donors and beneficiaries. First, with respect to income and capital gain taxes, gift and inheritance taxes, property and land taxes, transfer taxes, registration taxes, stamp duties and similar taxes, the Member States where the FE has its registered office would have to apply the same tax treatment as applicable to public benefit-purpose entities established in that Member State (art. 49 FE Prop. Regs). Second, the same tax treatment applicable to donations made to public benefit-purpose entities established in the Member State where the donor is resident should apply to any natural or legal person donating to the FE (Art. 50 FE Prop. Regs.). Third, beneficiaries of the FE should be treated as if they were given by a public benefit purpose entity established in the Member State or residence of the beneficiary (Art. 51 Prop. Regs). It was apparently difficult to reach the required unanimous approval of Member States.[48] A possibility to reach a consensus could have been to delete the tax chapter of this draft Directive. Finally, the proposal was withdrawn in March 2015.[49]

IV Impact of double taxation conventions

A In general

Non-profit organizations, as we have seen, may face complexities and even multiple taxation issues in cross-border payments. In addition, based on different domestic law rules, payments to foreign non-philanthropic entities could face adverse tax consequences, notably due to the absence of recognition by the host state of the tax-exempt status granted by a foreign state. DTCs could be used as tools to solve or alleviate or at least improve those issues.[50] In order to achieve these goals, a DTC should be applicable to philanthropic entities, despite their tax-exempt status (infra B.). In addition, specific treaty rules could either grant an exemption to income received by a non-profit entity resident in a contracting state (infra C.) or even offer a tax incentive, such as a deduction for cross-border gifts in favor of philanthropic entities sited in another contracting state (D.). Limitation on benefits (LOB) treaty rules, to the extent they are applicable, sometimes also grant qualifying status to non-profit entities (E.). DTCs could also ensure that cross-border gifts or inheritance will not be subject to multiple or burdensome tax (F.). Finally, an interesting possibility would be to rely on the non-discrimination provision of DTC to try to offer comparable tax treatment of payments to domestic and comparable non-profit entities sited in another contracting state (G.).

B Residence of charitable entity

The first issue is to ascertain that charitable entities may benefit from a DTC. It requires that these entities may be regarded as (i) persons, according to Art. 3 OECD Model DTC, which are (ii) resident in a contracting state, within the meaning of Art. 4 OECD Model DTC. According to the OECD Commentary, the term "person" should be interpreted broadly. A foundation or an association is notably considered a person. In order to be "resident," such an entity should meet the criteria to be fully taxable according to domestic law. It is, however, not important whether the state of residence makes use of the effective right to tax.[51]

The OECD Commentary confirms this position by stating that:

> In many States, a person is considered liable to comprehensive taxation even if the Contracting State does not in fact impose tax. For example, pension funds, charities and other organizations may be exempted from tax, but they are exempt only if they meet all of the requirements for exemption specified in the tax laws. They are, thus, subject to the tax laws of a Contracting State. Furthermore, if they do not meet the

> standards specified, they are also required to pay tax. Most States would view such entities as residents for purposes of the Convention.[52]

Following this approach, Art. 4 OECD Model DTC offers a protection against so-called virtual double taxation and provides for a limit towards the other contracting state, even if the state of residence does not levy a tax. The U.S. Model DTC (2016) is even more precise in that it provides, in Art. 4, that the term "resident of a Contracting State" includes:

> an organization that is established and maintained in that Contracting State exclusively for religious, charitable, scientific, artistic, cultural, or educational purposes; notwithstanding that all or part of its income or gains may be exempt from tax under the domestic law of that Contracting State.[53]

Many countries, such as Switzerland, follow this approach for charitable entities sited in their territory, despite tax-exempt status. As a consequence, notwithstanding the exemption of legal persons, which pursue public utility goals, these countries treat them as residents for tax purposes.[54]

According to the OECD Commentary, contracting states may solve the tax status of such entities in a specific provision of a DTC.[55] Following this approach, specific DTCs, following the approach of the U.S. Model, entail a provision providing that exempt charitable entities are regarded as resident. This is the case, for example, of many treaties concluded by the United States,[56] such as, inter alia, the U.S. treaties with the United Kingdom, Australia, Ireland and Switzerland.[57] The United Kingdom also includes specific clauses in many DTCs granting residence to non-profit organizations established in one contracting state.[58] Other states, however, consider tax exempt entities not resident for the purposes of DTCs.[59]

In order to continue to ensure the proper development of philanthropic activities, it should be recommended that states adopt the policy mentioned previously and simply confirm their positions that, as a matter of principle, charitable entities, despite their tax-exempt status, are in general regarded as resident for tax treaty purposes. Countries also have the possibility to confirm the application of tax treaties to non-profit entities in a mutual agreement procedure (MAP). Such agreements have already been concluded in practice.[60]

This would allow resident non-profit entities to claim the benefits of the allocation rules of the treaty, notably a reduced or nil withholding tax at source on any dividends, interests or royalties sourced in the other contracting state, as provided in provisions similar to Art. 10, 11, or 12 of the OECD Model of the applicable treaty.

C Exemption

As resident entities, non-profit organizations could claim the benefit of tax treaties, to the extent they comply with the potential limitation on benefits rules, if applicable[61]. In general, most DTCs entail distributions rules for specific foreign source income, notably for dividend, interest, royalties and sometimes services that may still suffer a residual withholding tax at source.

A few treaties go even further than confirming a residence status to philanthropic entities by providing a general tax exemption from income sourced in another contracting state.[62] These examples are, however, rare and exist mostly with some treaties concludes by the United

States.[63] As an interesting example, Art. 27 (Exempt Organizations) of the U.S.-Germany treaty provides that:

> 1. Notwithstanding the provisions of Article 28 (Limitations on benefits), a German company or organization operated exclusively for religious, charitable, scientific, educational, or public purposes shall be exempt from tax by the United States in respect of items of income, if and to the extent that:
>
>   a) such company or organization is exempt from tax in the Federal Republic of Germany, and
>   b) such company or organization would be exempt from tax in the United States in respect of such items of income if it were organized, and carried on all its activities, in the United States.
>
> 2. Notwithstanding the provisions of Article 28 (Limitations on benefits), a United States company or organization operated exclusively for religious, charitable, scientific, educational, or public purposes shall be exempt from tax by the Federal Republic of Germany in respect of items of income, if and to the extent that:
>
>   a) such company or organization is exempt from tax in the United States, and
>   b) such company or organization would be exempt from tax in the Federal Republic of Germany in respect of such items of income if it were organized, and carried on all its activities, in the Federal Republic of Germany.

In general, these provisions apply only to a non-profit organization resident in one contracting state that would also be exempt from tax in the other contracting state if it were organized and carried their activities in that state.

The advantage of such provisions is that they apply to all types of income and not only to dividends, interests or royalties. In addition, the exemption would go beyond the benefits of treaties with provisions similar to Art. 10, 11 or 12 of the OECD Model DTC in that it would grant a zero rate and not a reduced rate of tax at source, as the case may be.

In the case where a state uses the credit method for the avoidance of double taxation, the benefits of the tax exemption granted in another state, in the absence of a specific rule, would lead to a virtual double taxation.[64] Indeed, the exemption granted in one contracting state would lead to the absence of a credit in the other contracting state, unless that state includes a rule that would take this situation into account. States under a credit system could therefore be recommended to include a specific exception to the credit method for non-profit entities exempt in other states to the extent that they would qualify as exempt entity if they were resident in the state imposing the credit.

D Deductions of cross-border gifts

To the extent it is applicable, a DTC will then attribute, following the allocation rules, the right to tax income and, to the extent relevant, the assets of such entity between the contracting states. Under existing law, in principle, the allocation rules of a DTC focus on income (or profit) and, as the case may be, on capital (or wealth) but do not apply to the tax treatment of deductions. In particular, DTCs do not entail any specific rule applicable to cross-border deductions or allocations in favor of entities following philanthropic purposes. Tax treaties may, however, be used as promoting tools and could include an incentive for cross-border charitable giving in the form of a deduction, which is usually available to gifts to domestic non-profit entities in the host state.[65]

The Netherlands, admittedly in a fairly isolated case, and the United States, with some states that are tightly linked geographically, have included such clauses in their tax treaties.[66] It seems that the inclusion of a provision on charitable donation is also part of the tax treaty policy of the Barbados.[67] The possibility, under specific conditions, to deduct cross-border gifts does exist under the U.S.-Canada DTC (1980), the U.S.-Mexico DTC (1992) and the U.S.-Israel DTC (1995).[68] The provisions of these DTCs providing for a charitable deduction do, however, limit the deduction of donations to the other contracting state from income derived from that particular state.[69] Another interesting example is given by Art. 22 of the Netherlands-Barbados treaty,[70] which provides for the following rules for charitable contributions:

> Contributions by a resident of a Contracting State to an organization constituting a charitable organization under the income tax laws of the other Contracting State shall be deductible for the purposes of computing the tax liability of that resident under the tax laws of the first-mentioned Contracting State under the same terms and conditions as are applicable to contributions to charitable organizations of the first-mentioned State where the competent authority of the first-mentioned State agrees that the organization qualifies as a charitable organization for the purposes of granting a deduction under its income tax laws.

In order to encourage cross-border philanthropic giving, countries would be well advised to insert clauses in their tax treaties that would allow for recognition of a deduction for gifts to entities that have an acknowledged public purpose under the same conditions as those of the donor's state of residence. We will, however, analyze further the potential implications of the principle of non-discrimination.

E Limitation on benefits provisions

Under the influence of the United States treaty policy, so-called "limitation of benefits" provisions have been implemented in many treaties. Following the OECD Base Erosion Profit Shifting (BEPS) program, the 2017 version of the OECD Model DTC includes a new Art. 29, which opens the possibility to negotiate a LOB clause in a DTC. This approach is based on a list of alternative tests, which have to be fulfilled in order to be able to claim the benefits of a DTC. A LOB clause aims at discouraging treaty shopping by giving the advantages of the treaty only to qualifying persons.

Without any specific clauses, non-profit resident entities have to verify that they meet at least one of those tests in order to qualify for the benefit of the treaty. However, some treaties do consider philanthropic entities, as such, qualifying persons under LOB clauses.[71] For states that wish to include LOB clauses in their treaties, these types of specific qualifying provisions should provide for a simple and efficient mechanism to avoid a complex analysis of the LOB tests for philanthropic entities.

F Exemption of gift and inheritance tax to cross-border non-profit entities under gift and inheritance tax treaties

There are also a few DTCs in the area of inheritance tax and, rarely, in the field of gift tax. For instance, Switzerland has concluded only nine DTCs in the area of inheritance tax and no DTC for gift tax purposes. Again, and in the rare cases where such treaties do exist, they generally do not offer any specific tax treatment for cross-border inheritance or gifts in favor of philanthropic institutions. We have seen, however, that in the case of Switzerland, some cantons have concluded reciprocal agreements for gifts with religious, charitable or public utility purposes, but only with five states. However, the non-discrimination principle anchored in Art. 24 of the OECD Model for direct tax purposes, applies to "taxes of every kind and description."[72] The analysis of the impact of such a principle is thus relevant not only for direct but also inheritance and gift taxes.

There are, however, some rare treaty provisions that include rules which try to minimize the adverse tax consequences of cross-border payments for inheritance and gift tax purposes. Such treaties have been concluded mostly with the United States.[73] For example, Art. 9 of the DTC between the United States and Denmark provides the following rules for charitable gifts and estate (reductions):

> 1. The transfer or deemed transfer of property to or for the use of a Contracting State or a political subdivision or local authority thereof, or to a corporation or organization of a Contracting State operated exclusively for religious, charitable, scientific, literary, or educational purposes, if such transfer is exempt from tax or taxed at a reduced rate in that state shall be treated by the other Contracting State as if such transfer or deemed transfer were made to a similar corporation or organization of that other State.
> 2. In the case of property which passes from a decedent
>
>   a) domiciled (within the meaning of Article 4 (Fiscal Domicile)) in Denmark to the spouse of such decedent, the United States shall, in computing its tax, allow the same marital deduction that would be allowed with respect to a decedent domiciled in the United States, and in such case the tax rates that would be applicable if the decedent had been domiciled in the United States shall apply. If the United States tax determined without regard to the preceding sentence is lower than that computed under the preceding sentence, the lower tax shall apply.
>   b) domiciled (within the meaning of Article 4 (Fiscal Domicile)) in the United States to the spouse of such decedent, Denmark shall, if the spouse so requests, compute its tax as if the provisions of Danish law regulating matrimonial property rights were applicable to such property.

Art. 10 of the DTC between the United States and France, with respect to taxes on estates, inheritances and gifts, provides the following rule for charitable exemptions and deductions:

> (1) A transfer to a legal entity created or organized in a Contracting State shall be exempt from tax, or fully deductible from the gross value liable to tax, in the other Contracting State with respect to its taxes referred to in Article 2, provided the transfer would be eligible for such exemption or deduction if the legal entity had been created or organized in that other Contracting State.
> (2) The provisions of paragraph (1) shall apply only if the legal entity: (a) Has a tax-exempt status in the first Contracting State by reason of which transfers to such legal entity are exempt or fully deductible; (b) Is organized and operated exclusively for religious, charitable, scientific, literary, educational or cultural

purposes; and (c) Receives a substantial part of its support from contributions from the public or governmental funds.

(3) This Article shall not apply to transfers to a Contracting State or a political or administrative subdivision thereof unless specifically limited to a purpose described in paragraph (2)(b).

In general, these clauses tend to offer equivalent rules for domestic and foreign entities in the treaty partner, subject, however, to specific conditions. In other words, a contracting state should treat a transfer to a foreign charitable entity in the other contracting state at a reduced or zero rate, as if such transfer were made to a similar organization in the state of donor or deceased.[74]

G The non-discrimination principle

1 In general: Art. 24 par. 1 OECD model

DTCs in the area of direct taxes do generally provide for a non-discrimination clause corresponding to Art. 24 par. 1 OECD Model DTC, according to which:

> National of a Contracting State cannot be subject in the other Contracting state to any taxation or any requirement connected therewith, which is other or more burdensome than the taxation and connected requirements to which nationals of that other State in the same circumstances, in particular with respect to residence, are or may be subjected.

This rule applies to "taxes of every kind and description"[75] and therefore also to taxes falling outside the scope of the treaty in question, such as inheritance or gift taxes.[76] In actual terms, the non-discrimination principle means that a tax applied to nationals and foreigners in the same circumstances,

> must be in the same form, as regards both the basis of charge and the method of assessment, its rate must be the same and, finally, the formalities connected with the taxation (returns, payment, prescribed times, etc.) should not be more onerous for foreigners than for nationals.[77]

In the situation in question, partial or total exemption means a rate reduction that would be refused to foreign institutions due to their place of incorporation.

Consequently, the compatibility with such a non-discrimination clause of a reduced exemption or a more burdensome taxation of cross-border payments for philanthropic purposes in comparison to the potential more favorable tax regime applicable for comparable domestic charitable payments may be questioned.[78]

However, the non-discrimination clause of current DTCs, based on the OECD Model, still relies on the criteria of the nationality. In other words, and contrary to the case law of the EUCJ mentioned previously, Art. 24 par. 1 OECD Model only protects against *overt* and *direct* discrimination based on nationality.[79] In this respect, the principle of non-discrimination is different in scope from the EU principle, which also protects against so-called "hidden" and *indirect* discriminations, which, while not openly based on the concept of nationality, are in effect essentially targeting nationals.[80] As a consequence, until now, DTCs following Art. 24

par. 1 OECD Model have had limited impact, notably for individuals, because most states apply domestic tax rules, which are based on residence and not on nationality.[81]

The same is also true, in general, for philanthropic institutions, which are usually treated differently according to the criteria of residence, that is depending on their seat. In addition, the historical interpretation of Art. 24 par. 1 OECD Model tends to confirm that the initiators of this provision did not intend to offer the same tax advantages as comparable local entities to non-resident entities with public utility purposes.[82] The OECD Commentary follows the same line of reasoning. Indeed, it provides that Art. 24 par. 1 OCDE Model should not be interpreted as compelling contracting states, which offer certain tax privileges to private non-profit institutions, to extend those privileges to similar institutions which pursue non-profit activities.[83] At this stage, to the best of our knowledge, the jurisprudence does not seem to have interpreted Art. 24 OECD Model differently. In our view, only an evolutive interpretation of Art. 24 OECD Model, following the case law of the EUCJ, which would opt for a protection against hidden or indirect discrimination based on nationality, could justify such a broadening of the scope of the rule against non-discrimination.

As a consequence, even if in practice the differences of treatment between comparable resident and non-resident philanthropic entities may constitute "hidden" or indirect discrimination, because the exemption or the tax deduction would only apply to resident philanthropic entities, this discrimination is not overtly based on nationality. The leading and current interpretation of Art. 24 par. 1 of the OCDE Model tends therefore not to compel the state of residence to extend the same privileges offered to resident philanthropic entities to similar entities sited abroad.

2 Art. 24 par. 4 OECD model

Art. 24 par. 4 of the OECD Model DTC may, however, offer a broader scope of application. According to 24 par. 4 OECD Model DTC, interests, royalties and "other disbursements" paid by an enterprise of a contracting state to a resident of the other contracting state must, for the purpose of determining the taxable profits of such enterprise, be deductible under the same conditions as if they had been paid to a resident of the first-mentioned state. This time, such a rule does not allow for indirect discrimination based on residence, to the extent that this clause targets (non)residence of the person benefiting from the payment and not of the person who challenges the non-discrimination.[84] As a consequence, it should be analyzed whether this different perspective of the principle of non-discrimination may challenge the differences of treatment between domestic and cross-border philanthropic payments in favor of similar entities. In particular, we could wonder whether the refusal of a deduction for gifts towards philanthropic entities resident in a state other than the state of the donor would not be contrary to a provision of a DTC, including a rule similar to Art. 24 par. 4 OECD Model DTC.

The answer requires a careful analysis. First, it should be questioned whether "gifts" or other liberalities fall into the concept of "other disbursements" mentioned in this provision. According to commentators, contributions – such as gifts – which do not represent a counterpart are not governed by the OECD norm. Indeed, such a provision tends to apply to interest, royalties and other expenses which represent a remuneration for a transaction (services) or an investment (capital).[85] Such interpretation is, however, not the only conceivable one. Indeed, the OCDE Commentary admits that this provision could also include payments to a pension fund by the employer.[86] In any event, such a broad interpretation of the concept of "other disbursements" to gifts is undoubtedly disputable. In addition, this rule only applies to expenses paid by an enterprise. According to Art. 3 par. 1 lit. c OECD Model DTC, this term refers to the "carrying on of any business." The term "business" includes the performance of professional services and of other activities of independent nature.[87] According to commentators, this concept is difficult to assess and rather "ambiguous."[88] In addition, the question of whether an activity is performed in an enterprise or is deemed to constitute in itself an enterprise has always been interpreted according to the provisions of the domestic law of the contracting states.[89] It follows that at least the deduction from an individual, acting in a non-independent activity, in favor of a nonresident entity following philanthropic purposes, following a similar treatment in domestic law, could not benefit from this provision.

As a consequence, a potential violation of the non-discrimination principle could exist in the case of refusal of deductions in favor of non-resident public utility institutions, which are, however, allowed for similar domestic organizations but only under narrow limits. These deductions should at least be claimed by legal persons or individuals acting in an independent capacity that should be characterized as *enterprises* and only to the extent that we may characterize such gifts as "other disbursements" within the meaning of Art. 24 par. 4 OECD Model. In this framework, cross-border payments could be deductible under the same conditions as gifts in favor of residents in the state of the payer.[90] In this case, the amount of deduction, the timing and all other conditions should be the same.[91]

V Conclusion and recommendations

Our chapter has shown that DTCs may indeed offer interesting solutions in order to solve, or at least alleviate, the potential tax burdens of cross-border charitable giving. This possibility should, in our view, be developed further because, apart from the EU, "there is little tax support provided by counties for cross-border giving."[92] In some rare cases, DTCs may even be used as tax incentives to promote transnational giving by offering a deduction, under specific conditions, which would correspond to domestic gifts or payments to local non-profit entities. However, the practice is not well established, and there are in fact only a very few treaties that include specific clauses that favor cross-border charitable giving, mostly some United States and United Kingdom treaties, and, in the case of Barbados, part of a general policy. The author would recommend clarifying the position of states with regard to the application of DTCs in favor of non-profit entities and the application of similar rules between domestic gifts to philanthropic organizations and foreign comparable institutions in contracting states. This could be achieved by implementing the following recommendations.

First, states should be encouraged to clarify their position on the application of DTCs to charitable entities. Following the majority view described previously, states should admit that, despite their tax-exempt status, non-profit entities are recognized as resident for DTC purposes. Perhaps a clarification of the OECD Commentary on Art. 4 could solve this controversy. States that do not wish to accept this interpretation should then at least include specific rules in their treaties that confirm this point. This would allow philanthropic organizations to claim the benefits of the allocation rules of a DTC, including the reduced withholding treaty rates for dividends, interests or royalties sourced in the other contracting state.

Second, contracting states, in order to create an incentive for philanthropic payments, could be encouraged to include in their DTCs a specific clause which would allow for the recognition of the *deductibility* of gifts to entities with public utility purposes, under the same conditions as philanthropic entities, seated in the place of residence of the payer. In this respect, Art. 22 of the DTC between Holland and Barbados of 2006, which provides for a deduction of gifts to a charitable entity in the other contracting state under the same conditions as gifts to entities recognized as such in the state of residence of the donor, could serve as a reference.

Third, a new treaty rule could be introduced which would provide for a full *exemption* of foreign source income received by a philanthropic entity resident in a contracting states. Such provisions do already exist but only in rare cases. In general, they apply only to non-profit organizations resident in one contracting state that would also be exempted from tax in the other contracting state if they were organized and carried out their activities in that state. This rule applies to all types of income and not only to dividends, interests or royalties. In addition, the exemption would go beyond the benefits of treaties with provisions similar to Art. 10, 11 or 12 of the OECD Model DTC in that it would grant a zero rate and not a reduced rate of tax at the source, as the case may be.

Fourth, provisions could also be introduced in tax treaties in order to avoid multiple or adverse tax consequences of cross-border payments for inheritance and gift tax purposes. The recommendation, in order to have some impact, would require a broad change of policy among states and the conclusion of many more DTCs in the area of inheritance and gift taxes. In this respect, a provision similar to Art. 9 of the DTC between the United States and Denmark in the area of inheritance and gifts tax could serve a starting point of reference.

Fifth, under current law, DTCs based on the OECD Model do not offer a similar protection against non-discrimination for cross-border philanthropic payments as EU case law. Only an evolutive interpretation of Art. 24 par. 1 of the OCDE Model, which would go beyond the criteria of nationality, could broaden the scope of this principle. The current position, as confirmed by the OECD Commentary, does not seem to allow following the same line as the case law of the EUCJ. Furthermore, the non-discrimination principle applicable to "other disbursements," as governed by Art. 24 par. 2 OECD Model, does not seem under current law to undoubtedly apply to philanthropic gifts, even if sound arguments could be made, at least in the case of gifts or charitable payments from enterprises (including legal entities). As a consequence, the interpretation of the principle of non-discrimination in a DTC should be broadened to require a similar treatment of comparable non-profit entities in resident and non-resident states. While it appears difficult to adopt this rule from a political standpoint, a first step in this direction could be to clarify the interpretation of the concept of "other disbursements" in Art. 24 par. 4 OECD Model to include payments for philanthropic purposes.

Sixth, and in the long term, a more global solution, such as a multilateral approach, could be proposed. In this context, a mechanism similar to the multilateral treaty implemented in the context of the OECD BEPS program[93] in order to incorporate treaty modification rules recommended by the BEPS Action plan could serve as a model. Indeed, in this context, a multilateral instrument (a so-called MLI) entered into force on 1 July 2018 in order to modify DTCs which are covered by the MLI, under a complex mechanism of acceptance by the states party to the MLI. The purpose of this multilateral instrument is clearly different in that it intends to include in DTCs various rules against aggressive tax planning of multinational enterprises and against double non-taxation. In the future, in any event, this type of multilateral mechanism is, however, an interesting model also for philanthropy because it allows modification, upon ratification, of all covered tax treaties. We could therefore also imagine introducing rules favorable to cross-border philanthropic payments within a multilateral mechanism similar to or inspired by the MLI.[94]

However, even if the principle of non-discrimination towards non-resident public purpose entities would more generally apply, the problem would not be completely solved. Indeed, as the impact of the tax law of the EUCJ has demonstrated previously, complexities or discriminating approaches among states could still exist and qualify as restrictions on the free movement of cross-border charitable payments. In this respect, multilateral solutions, such as the implementation of the EU FE, represent an interesting approach, which appears, however, difficult to implement. An alternative would be at least to try to find a consensus, for example, at the OECD level, on a recommendation (soft law) which would offer basic elements on the acceptance of a similar treatment of payments to domestic and foreign comparable public purpose entities. In this respect, some basic elements on the conditions of comparability should be designed. Common factors should be defined on: (i) a definition of the public non-profit purposes qualifying for the similar tax treatment and (ii) the essential elements of an adequate supervision mechanism, which could be viewed as acceptable and equivalent to the supervision rules applicable in the host state.

Finally, it appears that, in order to ensure that the benefits of a treaty are fully granted to non-profit entities, the mains issue is to include a rule which recognizes, under clear conditions, the equivalence of non-resident entities and similar domestic entities.[95] In order to verify that this condition is met, various solutions have been introduced by some states. This issue is crucial and is the key to fostering the development of cross-border philanthropic payments without tax infringements. The case law of the EUCJ, mentioned previously, also confirms the necessity to compare non-profit domestic entities and foreign organizations with similar charitable purposes sited in another EU state. A specific treaty provision could also be introduced in this respect and provide for the key binding conditions of such recognition. It is also essential to ensure that the qualifying philanthropy entity does pursue a legitimate and effective activity for a non-profit purpose, which could be more precisely defined in a relevant treaty provision. Furthermore, the issue will be to safeguard the ultimate proper destination of the funds for charitable purposes, which requires extensive due-diligence rules and an adequate supervision mechanism.[96] To that end, the exponential development of the network of rules of international administrative assistance in tax matters, as of March 2009, has opened broad possibilities for states to verify all foreseeable relevant information, including financial data.[97] The development of anti-money-laundering rules, and the corresponding due diligence requirements, should also help to bring more certainty to the effective and adequate use of funds transferred for charitable purposes.

★★★

Notes

1 For a comprehensive report on the tax treatment of philanthropy across 40 OECD members and participating countries, see recently, OECD, Taxation and Philanthropy, OECD Tax Policy Studies, No 27, Paris 2020.

2 In this chapter, we will use the term philanthropic or non-profit entities or charitable organizations as synonyms.

3 The tax treatment of charitable trusts would require a further analysis, which goes beyond the scope of this chapter, since most states do not recognize trusts as such as legal entities.

4 See OECD, Philanthropy and Taxation, op. cit. 2020, pp. 41 ff.

5 See Art. 23 al. 1 lit. f of the Federal Harmonization Tax Law (FHTL); Art. 56 lit. g of the Federal Direct Tax Law (FDTL).

6 Under Swiss law, possibilities to exempt philanthropic entitles have been extended by a change of the law as of 1 January 2018 for legal persons pursuing "ideal goals" to the extent their profits are below CHF 20 000, under federal rules, and under a threshold applicable under cantonal law (see Art. 66a FDTL; 26a FHTL).

7 See, Federal Tax Administration (FTA), Circular N. 12, 8 July 1994, p. 3 (hereafter Circular FTA, par. 12).

8 See notably, "Swiss Tax Conference" (STC), "Exonération des personnes morales qui poursuivent des buts de service public, d'utilité publique ou des buts cultuels/Déductibilité des libéralités", 18 January 2008, pp. 38 ff (hereafter Circular STC 2008); see also Circular FTA no 12, 8 July 1994; X. Oberson, Droit fiscal Suisse, 5th ed., Basel, Helbing & Lichtenhahn 2021, pp. 254 ff.

9 See Sec. 501 (c) and (d) IRC; Sec 170 (e) to (o) IRC; S. Heidenbauer, B. Hemels, W. Muehlmann, M. Stewart, O. Thommes and T. Tukic, Cross-Border Charitable Giving and Its Tax Limitations, Bulletin for International Taxation, November 2013, p. 612.
10 See OECD, Philanthropy and Taxation, op. cit. 2020, p. 75 ff.
11 See Heidenbauer/Hemels/Muehlmann/Stewart/Thommes/Tukic, op. cit. 2013, p. 611; I. Koel, How Will International Philanthropy Be Freed from Landlocked Tax Barriers, European Taxation, September 2010, p. 409; recently, R. Buijze, Tackling the International Tax Barriers to Cross-Border Charitable Giving, IBFD, Amsterdam 2019, pp 72 ff.
12 X. Oberson, The Taxation of Philanthropy in Switzerland: Current Status and suggestions for improvement, IBFD Bulletin for International Taxation 2015, p. 237.
13 Heidenbauer/Hemels/Muehlmann/Stewart/Thommes/Tukic, op. cit. 2013, p. 612.
14 Heidenbauer/Hemels/Muehlmann/Stewart/Thommes/Tukic, op. cit. 2013, p. 616.
15 B. Gouthière, Les impôts dans les affaires internationales, 10th ed., Paris, 2014, n. 49020, p. 706.
16 See www.transnationalgiving.eu.
17 Heidenbauer/Hemels/Muehlmann/Stewart/Thommes/Tukic, op. cit. 2013, p. 624.
18 For a general overview on the disparities of the domestic tax rules on cross-border inheritance and gifts, see J.-E. Navez, La fiscalité des successions et des donations internationales, Bruylant, Bruxelles, 2011, pp. 75 ff.
19 See OECD, Report of the OECD Committee on Fiscal Affairs 1982: Model Double Taxation Convention on Estates and Inheritances and on Gifts.
20 Navez, op. cit. 2011, p. 13.
21 In a nutshell, all Swiss cantons, to the exception of Schwyz and, more recently, Obwald, do levy an inheritance and gift tax. Lucerne, however, does not levy any gift tax.
22 See Art. 6 par. 2 of the Geneva cantonal tax law on inheritance tax; Art. 28 par. 2 of the Geneva cantonal tax law on registration duties (including gift taxes).
23 STC, "Informations fiscales, Les impôts sur les successions et les donations", December 2016, p. 19.
24 Nowadays, 23 cantons have concluded international agreements on charitable gifts in the area of gift and inheritance tax, but only with France, Germany, Israel and Lichtenstein.
25 See European Foundation Centre, Taxation of Cross-Border philanthropy in Europe after *Persche* and *Stauffer*, 2014 (https://efc.issuelab.org/resources/18545/18545.pdf); B. Merkt and E. Zysset, Cross-Border donations, STEP Journal, May 2009, p. 33 ss. (https://www.step.org/step-journal/step-journal-may-2009/cross-border-donations).
26 Case *Centro di Musicologia Walter Stauffer v. Finanzamt München für* Körperschaften, ECJ C-386/04, of 14 September 2006 (hereafter *Stauffer* case).
27 *Stauffer* case, op. cit. par. 32.
28 Id.
29 Case *Persche v. Finanzamt* Lüdenscheid, ECJ C-318/2007, of 27 January 2009 (hereafter *Persche* case).
30 Art. 56 TFEU.
31 *Persche* case, par. 38 s.
32 *Persche* case, par. 49.
33 *Persche* case, par. 61.
34 Case *Missionswerk Werner Heukelbach v. Belgien*, ECJ C-25/2010, of 10 February 2011 (hereafter *Missionswerk* case).
35 Case *Missionswerk*, par. 24.
36 Point 31; see also *Persche* case, par. 46.
37 Case *Commission vs. Austria*, EUCJ C-10/2010, of 16 June 2011 (hereafter case *Commission vs. Austria*).
38 Case *Laboratoires Fournier*, ECJ C-39/2004, of 10 March 2005.
39 Case *Commission vs. Austria,* par. 37.
40 Heidenbauer/Hemels/Muehlmann/Stewart/Thommes/Tukic, op. cit. 2013, p. 618; Buijze, op. cit. 2019, p. 305.
41 See Heidenbauer/Hemels/Muehlmann/Stewart/Thommes/Tukic, op. cit. 2013, p. 618, who state that in the case of EU-wide projects, there are 28 comparability tests.
42 Oberson, op. cit. 2015, p. 237.
43 X. Oberson, L'imposition des prestations philanthropiques transfrontalières – L'apport potentiel des normes de droit fiscal international, notamment des conventions de double imposition, in: *Liber amicorum* pour Henry Peter, Geneva/Zurich/Basel 2019, p. 567.

44 See *infra* IV. G.
45 Philanthropy Advocacy, Comments on EC Roadmap: Action plan to fight tax evasion and make taxation simple and easy, 31 March 2020.
46 COM(2012) 35 final.
47 EU Commission, Proposed FE Regulation, n. 1.2.
48 Heidenbauer/Hemels/Muehlmann/Stewart/Thommes/Tukic, op. cit. 2013, p. 623.
49 Buijze, op. cit. 2019, p. 146.
50 Oberson, op. cit. 2019, pp. 557 ff; in the same vein, Buijze, op. cit. 2019, pp. 294 ff, 333, has also recently recognized the potential of DTCs for such goals but with many limitations.
51 M. Zweifel Martin and S. Hunziker, in: M. Zweifel, M. Beusch and R. Matteotti, Kommentar zum internationalen Steuerrecht, Basel, Helbing & Lichtenhahn, 2015, n. 15 ad Art 4 OECD-MA.
52 OECD Commentary to Model DTC, n. 8.11 ad art. 4.
53 See Art. 4 (2) (b) of the U.S. Model DTC (version 2016).
54 Oberson, op. cit. 2014, n. 360, p. 115.
55 See, for instance, Art. 4 (1) (c) [ii] DTT with the United States.
56 Koel, op. cit. 2010, p. 24.
57 See, inter alia, Art. 4 (3) (c) of the U.S.-UK treaty; Art. 4 (1) (a) U.S.-Australia treaty, Art. 4 (1) (c) U.S.-Irish treaty; Art. 4 (1) (c) (ii) of the U.S.-Swiss treaty.
58 See inter alia, Art. 4 (5) (b) of the UK-Belgium treaty; Art. 4 (1) (c) of the UK-Japan treaty; Art. 4 (2) (b) of the UK-Norway treaty; Art. 4 (2) (b) of the UK-Holland treaty; par. 1 (b) of the Protocol to the UK-Swiss treaty; Art. 4 (2) (c) of the UK-UAT treaty.
59 Zweifel/Hunziker, op. cit., 2015, n. 15 ad Art. 4 OECD-MA
60 See Th. Ecker, Taxation of Non-Profit Organizations with Multinational Activities – The Stauffer Aftermath and Tax Treaties, Intertax 2007, pp. 450 ff, 458, quoting the examples of MAP concluded by Austria with Luxembourg, Germany and the United Kingdom.
61 See *infra* E.
62 See, for example, Art. 27 of the U.S.-Germany treaty; Art. 36 of the U.S.-Holland treaty; Art. 15A of the U.S.-Israel treaty; Art. XXI of the U.S.-Canada treaty.
63 Koel, op. cit. 2010, p. 31; for an analysis of these provision, see M. Cerny and M. McKinnon, The Globalization of Philanthropy: International Charitable Giving in the Twenty-First Century, 45 *Real Property, Trust and Estate Law Journal* 2020, pp. 10 ss.
64 Koel, op. cit. 2010, p. 356.
65 See also, Heidenbauer/Hemels/Muehlmann/Stewart/Thommes/Tukic, op. cit. 2013, p. 620; OECD, Philanthropy and Taxation, op. cit. 2020, pp. 112 ff.
66 Koel, op. cit. 2010, p. 34; Heidenbauer/Hemels/Muehlmann/Stewart/Thommes/Tukic, op. cit. 2013, p. 620; Buijze, op. cit. 2019, p. 131.
67 Heidenbauer/Hemels/Muehlmann/Stewart/Thommes/Tukic, op. cit. 2013, p. 620.
68 See OECD, Philanthropy and Taxation, op. cit. 2020, pp. 112 ff.
69 Buijze, op. cit. 2019, p. 133.
70 See Convention between the Kingdom of the Netherlands and Barbados for the avoidance of double taxation ant the prevention of fiscal evasion with respect to taxes on income, 26 November 2006; see also Heidenbauer/Hemels/Muehlmann/Stewart/Thommes/Tukic, op. cit. 2013, p. 620.
71 See, for example, Art. 16 (g) of the U.S.-Austrian treaty; Art. 18 (g) of the U.S.-Canada treaty; Art. 16 (f) of the U.S.-Finland treaty; Art. 17 (e) of the U.S.-Mexico treaty.
72 Art. 24 par. 6 OECD Model DTC
73 See Koel, op. cit. 2010, pp. 36 ff (citing five U.S. treaties); see Milton/McKinnon, op. cit. 2020, pp. 10 ff (analyzing four U.S. treaties).
74 See, for example, Art. 9 (1) of U.S.-Denmark treaty, Koel, op. cit. 2010, p. 36.
75 See Art. 24 par. 6 OECD Model DTC.
76 Oberson, op. cit. 2014, p. 282.
77 OECD Commentary, n. 15 ad Art. 24.
78 Oberson, op. cit. 2015, p. 238.
79 A. Rust, in: E. Reimer and A Rust (ed.), Klaus Vogel on Double Taxation Convention, 4e ed., Kluwer, The Netherlands, 2015, n. 26 ad art. 24.
80 Oberson, op. cit. 2014, p. 283; Rust, op. cit. 2015, n. 14 ad art. 24.
81 Rust, op. cit. 2015, n. 26 ad art. 24.

82 K. van Raad and C. Landim, in: R. Danon, D. Gutmann, X. Oberson and P. Pistone (ed.), Commentaire du Modèle de Convention fiscale OCDE concernant le revenu et la fortune, Helbing & Lichtenhahn, Editions Françis Lefebvre, Basle 2014, n. 62 ad art. 24.
83 OECD Commentary, n. 11 ad Art. 24.
84 Van Raad/Landim, op. cit. 2014, n. 97 ad Art. 24.
85 Rust, op. cit. 2015, n. 95 ad Art. 24.
86 OECD Commentary, n. 37 ad Art. 18; Rust, op. cit. 2015, n. 95 ad Art. 24.
87 Art. 3 par. 1 lit. h OECD Model.
88 D. Gutmann and A. Lareau, in: Danon/Gutmann/Oberson/Pistone (ed.), op. cit. 2014, n. 29 ad Art. 24.
89 OECD Commentary, n. 4 ad art. 3.
90 Oberson, op. cit. 2019, pp. 557 ff.
91 Rust, op. cit. 2015, n. 99 ad Art. 24.
92 See OECD, Philanthropy and Taxation, op. cit. 2020, p. 131.
93 See, notably, OECD/G20, Base erosion and profit shifting (BEPS), Action 15, A multilateral instrument (MLI) to implement tax treaty related measures to prevent BEPS – Final Report 2015. The MLI has entered into force on 1 July 2018 and already covers more than 100 jurisdictions.
94 Oberson, op. cit. 2019, p. 572.
95 In the same vein, Koel, op. cit. 2010, p. 360.
96 Koel, op. cit. 2010, pp. 368 ff.
97 See X. Oberson, International Exchange of Information in Tax Matters – Towards Global Transparency, 2nd ed., United-Kingdom and United States, Elgar Tax Law and Practice, Cheltenham, UK, Northampton, USA, 2018, pp. 15 ff.

22

SOLUTIONS TO CROSS-BORDER CHARITABLE GIVING IN PRACTICE

The perspective of arts organisations

Renate Buijze

1 Introduction

An entity must typically meet a number of requirements in order to be considered a philanthropic organisation. In general, it must (i) be 'not-for-profit', (ii) have a 'philanthropic purpose', and (iii) exist for 'public benefit'. Besides, the entity must meet a range of administrative and oversight requirements. Common categories considered of 'philanthropic purpose' are welfare, education, scientific research, healthcare, culture, environmental support, and disaster relief (OECD, 2020). Despite the large consistency in domestic incentives for charitable giving (OECD, 2020; Quick et al., 2014), tax benefits on cross-border gifts are far less common. This is remarkable, especially considering the role cross-border philanthropy could play in tackling global challenges (OECD, 2020), as well as the willingness of donors to contribute to foreign philanthropic organisations. According to estimates in the *Global Philanthropy Tracker 2020,* the philanthropic outflow[1] in 2018 across the 47 countries included in the report totalled $68 billion (Indiana University Lilly Family School of Philanthropy, 2020).

Currently, there are few solutions that allow philanthropic organisations to work with foreign donors and ensure a tax benefit to them. Limited measures exist to overcome the tax barrier to international fundraising. Philanthropic organisations can, for example, set up a philanthropic entity for fundraising purposes in a foreign country – a foreign friends' organisation. This solution allows donors to give to a philanthropic organisation in their country of residence and obtain a tax benefit. The philanthropic organisation in the donor's country regrants the gift to the foreign philanthropic organisation that the donor intends to support. Other solutions rely on a giving intermediary or legislation that enables tax-efficient giving. Examples of the latter are the four fundamental freedoms in European Union (EU) Law,[2] tax treaties, or legislation in the donor's country that allows for tax benefits on donations to foreign philanthropic organisations. Legislation that allows for tax benefits on cross-border philanthropy is not widespread (OECD, 2020). The tax provision on qualifying philanthropic organisations typically limits the geographical scope of the tax incentive. Furthermore, some countries impose restrictions on the foreign spending of philanthropic gifts, which limits the use of a foreign friends' organisation or a giving intermediary as a solution for tax-efficient cross-border giving.

 DOI: 10.4324/9781003139201-26

The significant inapplicability of tax incentives on cross-border donations makes it less attractive for donors to give to a foreign philanthropic organisation. A cross-border gift becomes more expensive compared with a domestic charitable gift. For philanthropic organisations, attracting gifts from abroad can therefore be more challenging, as they are in a disadvantageous position in comparison with domestic philanthropic organisations. A level playing field, where both domestic and foreign philanthropic organisations are eligible to receive gifts with corresponding tax benefits, is preferred from a fundraising perspective. The European philanthropic sector even advocates for a 'single market for philanthropy', in which philanthropic organisations across EU Member States are treated equally, as is set out in the *Philanthropy Manifesto* (Donors and Foundations Networks in Europe and European Foundation Centre, 2019). To improve the environment for global philanthropy, the 2018 *Global Philanthropy Environment Index* also, amongst others, calls for the unification of a legal framework for cross-border philanthropy and tax incentives for gifts made directly to foreign philanthropic organisations (Indiana University Lilly Family School of Philanthropy, 2018).

This chapter evaluates optimal solutions from within the existing ones (which are briefly outlined in Section 2), more specifically in the context of arts organisations, to overcome the tax barriers of cross-border giving. The knowledge among fundraising professionals on tax incentives for cross-border gifts is discussed in Section 3B. The focus is on donations by individuals and the tax benefits that could facilitate these gifts.

Throughout this chapter, I refer to philanthropic organisations. These are organisations that make contributions towards public benefit and have a special tax status in their country of residence that makes them eligible to receive gifts in return for a tax benefit to the donor. These could be in the form of a tax deduction, tax credit, or any other type of incentive. In this chapter, arts organisations are used as a specific subtype of philanthropic organisations. The arts – more broadly, culture – are considered philanthropic causes in many countries, although not in all. In Argentina, Indonesia, and Malta, for example, culture is not considered a philanthropic purpose, and arts organisations do not qualify for a favourable tax status (OECD, 2020, p. 45). Whenever arts organisations are mentioned in this chapter, however, they are considered to have the same favourable tax status as other philanthropic organisations in their country of residence.

To assess the most optimal existing solution from a philanthropic perspective, arts organisations' experiences with different solutions are elaborated on in Sections 3C–3E. The methodology according to which this information is gathered is presented in Section 3A. The giving intermediary is perceived as the current best option in many cross-border situations (Section 4A). However, it has its disadvantages, which can be overcome with an optimal solution from the perspective of philanthropic organisations (Section 4B).

2 Solutions enabling tax-efficient cross-border giving

In most countries, the tax incentive for donations is limited to donations made to philanthropic organisations that are incorporated in the country that grants the tax incentives or they conduct (at least part of) their activities in the country that offers the tax incentive (Jochum and Savvaidou, 2015, pp. 69–70). If a donor wishes to give to a foreign philanthropic organisation, a tax incentive often does not apply. Depending on the tax law in the donor's country, it might be possible to obtain a tax benefit on a cross-border donation based on solutions at different legal levels.

At the national level, countries can partially or entirely remove geographical restrictions from tax incentives for gifts. By doing so, they allow donors to contribute to foreign philanthropic organisations with a tax benefit. I refer to this method of obtaining a tax incentive on a cross-border donation as the 'unilateral solution'.

In accordance with the four fundamental freedoms in EU law, EU Member States may not discriminate against equivalent philanthropic organisations located in other EU Member States.[3] Therefore, most EU Member States have modified their domestic legislation. Luxembourg, for example, allows Luxembourg taxpayers to contribute to qualifying organisations in Luxembourg as well as qualifying organisations in other Member States of the EU and those of the European Free Trade Association.[4] Dutch taxpayers can deduct their gifts to qualifying charities located in the Kingdom of the Netherlands, another EU Member State, or state designated by the Ministry of Finance from taxable income.[5]

For a foreign philanthropic organisation to qualify as a recipient of gifts with a corresponding tax benefit, the philanthropic organisation will have to meet the conditions of a qualifying organisation in the donor's country. This differs across countries. By imposing requirements on qualifying philanthropic organisations, governments target their tax benefits towards specific policy goals. Furthermore, the requirements help governments exercise control over the qualifying recipient philanthropic organisations and avoid abuse.

In the Netherlands, for example, foreign philanthropic organisations must be recognised as a Public Benefit Pursuing Entity (*Algemeen Nut Beogende Instelling)* by the Dutch tax authorities. To qualify as such, the organisation must meet a set of requirements. The foreign organisation must be located in the Kingdom of the Netherlands, another EU Member State, or a state designated by the Ministry of Finance. Most importantly, it must exclusively or almost exclusively (at least 90%) contribute to public benefit. It has to comply with a set of oversight rules and administrative requirements. These include, for example, a requirement to publish an annual report, policy plan, and other documents online.[6]

In the case of the Netherlands, the foreign philanthropic organisation must meet the Dutch requirements. This is what is referred to as host country control. Countries can also rely on supervision over the philanthropic organisation in the country of residence of the philanthropic organisation. This is referred to as home country control (Hemels, 2009). Luxembourg partially relies on home country control. In Luxembourg, the foreign philanthropic organisation must be a similar entity to a qualifying Luxembourg organisation. To establish that the organisation is similar to a qualifying Luxembourg organisation, the donor has to demonstrate that the foreign philanthropic organisation (i) 'pursues one or more non-lucrative aims' including art, education, philanthropy, worship/religion, science, social, sports, tourism, and/or development cooperation and (ii) is eligible to receive gifts with a tax benefit under the laws of its country of residence and that it is exempt from income tax and wealth tax.[7]

At the international level, countries can conclude tax treaties in which they bilaterally agree to apply their tax incentives to cross-border donations.[8] Since a tax treaty, in principle, decides which law is applicable and does not actually shape laws; the tax treaty solely regulates that the tax incentive available in the domestic situation applies in the specific cross-border situation and details the type of control exercised over the recipient charity – whether home country control, host country control, or a combination of the two. Most tax treaties are based on the model tax treaties of either the United Nations or the Organisation for Economic Co-operation and Development (OECD). These model tax treaties do not include a provision that enables tax-efficient charitable giving between the contracting states.[9] This is a possible reason for the existence of a limited amount of treaties that facilitate tax benefits on cross-border donations.

The United States has concluded tax treaties with Canada, Israel, and Mexico in which cross-border donations to philanthropic organisations qualify for a tax benefit. The deductibility of donations to philanthropic organisations in the other contracting state is, however, limited to the income derived from that country.[10]

At the supranational level, countries can overcome the inapplicability of tax incentives by (i) recognising equivalent philanthropic organisations in states with which they have concluded a supranational agreement or (ii) through the introduction of a common philanthropic status with the same tax preferences for organisations with a domestic philanthropic status. This requires countries to (partially) give up their sovereignty over their tax system. EU Member States, for example, must – in accordance with the four fundamental freedoms in EU law and specifically the free movement of capital[11] – apply the domestically available tax incentive to gifts to comparable philanthropic organisations located in other EU Member States. This was enforced by the European Court of Justice (ECJ) in the *Persche* case.[12] Thus, when a donor tax resident in EU Member State A donates to a philanthropic organisation in Member State B and the donation qualifies for a tax benefit in Member State A, the donor must also receive a tax benefit in the cross-border situation between Member States A and B. Discrimination on the basis of the country of residence of the philanthropic organisation is not allowed within the EU. Since 2005, the EC has instituted infringement procedures to ensure non-discrimination of philanthropic organisations and their benefactors in the EU. Nonetheless, Croatia, Portugal, Romania, and Spain do not apply the domestically available tax incentive in a comparable cross-border situation with other EU Member States.[13] The EC has ongoing infringement procedures against Spain.[14]

Countries could also supranationally agree to use a common philanthropic status. In 2012, the European Commission presented the Proposal for a Council Regulation on the Statute for a European Foundation. This proposal aimed to provide for a European uniform and supranational legal form for philanthropic organisations. This proposal, however, was withdrawn in 2015.[15]

These solutions at three different legal levels are initiated by governments and enable donors to overcome tax barriers across borders. Philanthropic organisations can also facilitate foreign donors with a tax benefit by circumventing the cross-border situation. This is done by facilitating the donor to donate to a domestic philanthropic organisation, which then spends the donation abroad. Philanthropic organisations can, for example, establish a separate entity with the specific purpose of raising funds in the donor's country, which I refer to as a 'foreign friends' organisation'. Donations are made to this legal entity with a philanthropic status in the donor's country of residence and they receive a tax benefit. The foreign friends' organisation then transfers the funds to the philanthropic organisation located abroad. The foreign friends' organisation offers tax authorities a certain degree of supervision over the philanthropic organisation while offering an option to facilitate tax-efficient cross-border charitable giving.

As an alternative to a foreign friends' organisation, which is typically dedicated to one philanthropic organisation, philanthropic organisations and their donors could also make use of a giving intermediary (also referred to as an intermediary organisation). This giving intermediary fulfils a similar role as the foreign friends' organisation. However, it serves multiple foreign causes in exchange for a limited fee. The giving intermediary has philanthropic status in the donor's country of residence. By donating to the giving intermediary, the donor obtains a tax benefit. The giving intermediary transfers the donation to the foreign philanthropic organisation. The fee, which can vary between 0.5% and 5% is usually deducted from the gift. To avoid infringement of domestic tax laws, the giving intermediary must ensure that the recipient charity spends the donations in line with the philanthropic status of the giving intermediary. Therefore, the giving intermediary must vet the foreign charitable organisation.

Usually, a giving intermediary attracts funds from donors in one country and enables them to contribute to philanthropic organisations in one or more foreign countries. There are also networks of giving intermediaries – entities with philanthropic status in multiple countries that allow donors from multiple countries to give to philanthropic organisations in other countries. The philanthropic organisation would, however, have to deal with entities in the different countries to ensure they act in line with the legislation in the donor's country.

Whether it is possible to obtain a tax benefit by donating to a giving intermediary depends on the legislation in the donor's country. Some countries, like the Netherlands, might perceive the giving intermediary as a fiscally transparent entity and, therefore, might consider the final beneficiary of the gift when deciding on the eligibility for a tax benefit. Other countries impose strict limitations on foreign spending of donations received, like Australia in the past (Silver and Buijze, 2020, pp. 123–128).

Solutions like the foreign friends' organisation, the giving intermediary, and other solutions cannot be used in every cross-border situation. This again is dependent on the legislation in the donor's country of residence.

3 Experiences with solutions to tax-efficient, cross-border philanthropy

A Methodology

To assess which of the existing solutions is optimal from the perspective of philanthropic organisations aiming to facilitate tax incentives for foreign donors, I used a qualitative case study design (Bryman, 2008, pp. 52–58; Yin, 2003, pp. 1–9).[16] In these qualitative case studies, I particularly focused on arts organisations as a specific group of philanthropic organisations. Amongst this group, some organisations are geographically bound to their physical location (like museums), whereas others can travel to foreign locations (like performing arts companies).

Semi-structured interviews were held with 47 employees of arts organisations responsible for international fundraising. These included managing directors, heads of development or heads of funding, coordinators of international friends circles, and the like. For clarity, I refer to these persons as 'fundraisers'. Furthermore, interviews were held with 25 tax and philanthropy experts, including tax and philanthropy advisors, employees of giving intermediaries, philanthropists, policy makers, and tax inspectors. Documents of arts organisations were analysed, including annual reports, websites, and media coverage on these organisations, and the gifts received and efforts made to attract funds from abroad were also examined. The cases were selected through a non-probability sampling strategy to ensure that a variety of organisations was included. All organisations have philanthropic status in their country of residence and are of some international relevance. They have either received donations from abroad or made a serious attempt to raise funds abroad. The results included 36 case studies on cross-border fundraising by arts organisations active across different disciplines and located in Austria, Belgium, Denmark, France, Germany, Italy, the Netherlands, the United Kingdom, and the United States.[17] More importantly, these arts organisations had international fundraising experience in various countries, as these were the resident countries of the donors. These countries stipulated whether a tax incentive was available in a cross-border situation and also which solutions should be used to obtain that incentive. The sample arts organisations received cross-border gifts from Belgium, Bermuda, Hong Kong, India, Italy, Mexico, Montenegro, the Netherlands, Peru, Poland, Russia, Sweden, Turkey, the United Arab Emirates, the United Kingdom, the United States, and Switzerland.

The interviewees were, amongst others, asked about their foreign fundraising and specifically their efforts to assist a foreign donor in obtaining a tax incentive on a donation, knowledge about tax incentives, experiences with the existing solutions, and preferences concerning these solutions.[18] The data gathered provide insight into the practice of cross-border philanthropy. They demonstrate what challenges an arts organisation faces when trying to facilitate a foreign donor with a tax benefit.

B The use of tax incentives for cross-border gifts

All arts organisations included in the research advertised tax incentives in the information for domestic donors. The interviewees seemed to be aware of the applicable domestic incentives and requirements involved. Those organisations that proactively raise funds abroad also address the possibility of obtaining a tax benefit on a cross-border donation in their brochures and on their websites. Fundraisers explain that they do so because the tax benefit persuades donors – although it is not the main motive behind giving. Arts organisations 13 and 35, for example, had foreign donors who contribute without receiving a tax benefit. It is not always known whether a donor utilises a tax incentive. Among the fundraisers interviewed, there was a general presumption that, when available, donors do use tax incentives. Arts organisations 1, 3, and 24 all had a donor for whom receiving a tax incentive was a prerequisite for giving. Arts organisation 3 used a giving intermediary to facilitate this gift, while arts organisation 24 even set up an American friends' organisation to provide the donor with a tax benefit. As fundraiser 24 says: 'Actually, it was he who said "I would like to support that exhibition. . . . I would like to support this exhibition with my American company, but I can only do so if you have a 501(c)3"'. Arts organisation 1 had to conclude that it was unable to facilitate the foreign donor with a tax benefit, after which the donor renounced his gift.

The fundraisers were, to some extent, familiar with the unilateral solution, foreign friends' organisation, or giving intermediaries. Some of them had experience with one or a few of these solutions. The best-known solutions were the foreign friends' organisation and the giving intermediary. Fundraisers had little to no experience with tax treaties and the fundamental freedoms in the EU. Not being aware of all the solutions does not seem to pose a problem for them. Fundraiser 9 mentioned the following when asked whether he wanted to know more about tax incentives for cross-border giving:

> Given that I know how [giving intermediary] works, I do know that it is feasible, and it will not take very long before it is arranged. So, if [arts organisation 9 receives a cross-border gift] we can still [provide a tax benefit via the giving intermediary].

C Experiences with foreign friends' organisations

For arts organisation 24, for example, the core reason for setting up a foreign friends' organisation was to facilitate their foreign benefactors with a tax incentive. Among the 36 arts organisations included in the research, 11 had, or used to have, a foreign friends' organisation. Setting up a foreign friends' organisation seemed to be of interest for arts organisations with a strong connection to one or a few foreign countries and a large support base in those countries that provides a steady stream of income. Fundraisers 26 and 35 stressed that having a foreign friends' organisation has positive ramifications, such as the ability to create a community abroad and a strong international network.

Experiences with foreign friends' organisations were not solely positive. Interviewees complained about the costs involved in setting up such an entity and the extensive and detailed administrative requirements that had to be met for the organisation to be recognised as a philanthropic organisation for tax purposes. Furthermore, the maintenance of a foreign friends' organisation – managing the entity and ensuring the entity continued to meet the general and administrative requirements of a philanthropic organisation (such as annual audits and board meetings) – imposed a large burden on the main organisation. For arts organisation 7, this was a reason to give up its American friends' organisation:

> The [board of the] American friends had the view that it was a big administrative burden, it was costly and took up too much of their time, which they would rather invest in meeting other people. Thus, they decided that nowadays this can be arranged in a much easier and different manner.

It was clear that voluntary efforts of dedicated individuals residing in the country where the foreign friends' organisation was established were key. As director 23 put it: 'Without the right people to pull the organisation, it is not a realistic option [to set up a foreign friends' organisation]'. For arts organisations, this means that they have to try to attract these persons and get them motivated to help the organisation, as well as keeping them aligned with the views of the arts organisation. Larger arts organisations even had staff at the main organisation to ensure smooth collaboration with the foreign friends' organisation. In fact, the experiences of several arts organisations demonstrated that active management of the foreign friends' organisations was necessary to ensure the foreign entity flourished and avoided any potential damage to the reputation of the main organisation.

D Experiences with giving intermediaries

Another well-known and widely used solution among arts fundraisers is the giving intermediary. All informants were familiar with this solution, and most of them had experience using it. The fact that the giving intermediary ensures the applicable legal and administrative requirements are met for the donor to obtain a tax benefit on a cross-border gift is a big relief for arts organisations. First, the arts organisation does not have to hire tax and legal experts in the donor's country to inform them. Second, the arts organisation does not have to meet specific provisions and detailed administrative requirements to be recognised as an eligible recipient according to a foreign legislation, in addition to the legislation in the arts organisation's country of residence.

Although a fee is charged by the giving intermediary, arts organisations do not perceive that as an obstacle. Compared with the costs involved for a foreign friends' organisation, the fee is perceived as reasonable. Fundraiser 10A explains:

> It is a very deliberate choice not to apply for charitable status, the 501(c)3 status, in the United States because then you need to have a board, take care of the administration, and you need an office. These costs are just too high in comparison to [the fee of a giving intermediary]. They cost us a minimum fee, as they are not for profit. So, in comparison, the [giving intermediary] is the cheapest option.

The fact that there are no other costs for legal advice or official translations of articles of association and other documents makes the giving intermediary relatively inexpensive. Most arts organisations pay the fee themselves. It is rather exceptional for a donor to pay this fee.

When making use of a giving intermediary, philanthropic organisations are usually vetted to ensure the giving intermediary does not put its own philanthropic status at risk by supporting the foreign organisation. For this procedure, the philanthropic organisation must submit several documents to the giving intermediary, such as annual reports, articles of association, and a policy plan. This was not considered an obstacle by the interviewees, as the vetting procedure was perceived as uncomplicated in comparison to the procedure of obtaining philanthropic status abroad for the arts organisation. Furthermore, once vetted, the arts organisation can actively inform foreign potential donors of the option to make a donation to the organisation with a tax benefit. If the organisation receives donations from multiple countries, however, the philanthropic organisation must deal with multiple giving intermediaries by whom it must be vetted. For organisations that only receive philanthropic gifts on an incidental basis, the giving intermediary proves to be an interesting solution.

E Experiences with the unilateral solution

A few arts organisations included in the research are familiar with the unilateral solution and have actual experience with it. The organisations that did rely on the unilateral solution have mixed experiences.

Arts organisation 20, an Italian cultural heritage organisation, hired tax advisors from the United Kingdom to help them obtain charitable status in the country. They tried twice but failed in both attempts.[19] According to the rejection letter, the articles of association of the arts organisation did not meet the exact requirements for recognition as a philanthropic organisation under United Kingdom law. First, the philanthropic aim of the organisation was defined too broadly. Where the articles of association referred to 'the defence of the environment and artistic and monumental heritage', according to the Charities Act 2006, they should have instead referred to 'the advancement of the arts, culture, and heritage' and 'the advancement of environmental protection or improvement'. Second, the dissolution clause stated that the organisation's remaining assets would be donated to other organisations 'with objectives of public utility'. 'Public utility' was considered too indefinite to ensure the funds would be distributed to 'charitable purposes'. Her Majesty's Revenue and Customs (HMRC) applied the Charities Act, 2006, in a strict and narrow manner. Despite the essence of the articles of association being in line with the Charities Act, 2006, the exact wording was lacking. Anecdotal evidence shared by the interviewed tax advisors suggests that not all supervising authorities are as stringent as the HMRC. France, for example, has a more lenient way of testing equivalence.

The example of arts organisation 20 illustrates that despite being similar, in the case of host country control, it can be impossible for philanthropic organisations to obtain philanthropic status in their country of residence, as well as in that of their foreign benefactors'. Conflicting requirements concerning the articles of association prohibit this.

Since arts organisation 20 wanted to maintain its philanthropic status in Italy, it could not change its articles of association, as it would then run the risk of not meeting the Italian requirements for philanthropic organisations. In this specific situation, applying for philanthropic status in the United Kingdom was a waste of resources, as the fundraisers had hired tax experts and official translators, as well as investing time themselves.

Other arts organisations were more successful. Belgian arts organisation 18 had an in-house tax lawyer, who applied for philanthropic status in four EU Member States. She reported that this process was relatively easy in two countries. In these countries, arts organisation 18 received philanthropic status. In the other two countries, the application procedure was complex and lengthy. Arts organisation 18 had to resubmit documents in one country and was still waiting for a response after one year from the other country. Tax lawyers also experienced these lengthy procedures when trying to register their clients as an equivalent philanthropic organisation in another EU Member State. In some EU Member States, the philanthropic status must be renewed after a certain period, which further increases the administrative burden (Hippel, 2014). For arts organisation 18, obtaining philanthropic status without having to establish or use the services of a separate legal entity proved advantageous.

4 Assessing the solutions to tax-efficient, cross-border giving

A Why is the giving intermediary currently the best option?

The optimal solution to facilitate a foreign donor with a tax benefit from the perspective of philanthropic organisations depends on the specific cross-border situation. Dutch donors, for example, can use a tax deduction when giving to philanthropic organisations located around the world as long as these organisations have Public Benefit Pursuing Entity (PBPE) status in the Netherlands. Arts organisations 33 and 34, both American arts organisations, are registered as a PBPEs in the Netherlands. Dutch donors, however, cannot use the giving intermediary to obtain a tax deduction on cross-border giving. American donors, on the other hand, can rely on the giving intermediary but not on domestic tax law to give to a foreign charity.

The optimal solution also depends on the specific context of the philanthropic organisation. Does it receive a steady stream of income from one specific country? Under these circumstances, it might be worthwhile to invest in a solution, like a foreign friends' organisation that facilitates a tax benefit for donors in the specific country. However, if international gifts are incidental and foreign donors are scattered across different countries, this might not be worthwhile.

Fundraisers included in this research who know and/or have experience using a giving intermediary are positive about this solution. The majority prefer the giving intermediary over other existing solutions, as they do not have to worry about legal and administrative requirements, and costs are limited. From their perspective, it is the optimal solution in many cross-border situations. Their knowledge on other solutions seemed to be limited. Therefore, the experiences of tax and philanthropy advisers are considered when assessing the solutions to cross-border, tax-efficient giving. When taking these views into account, the intermediary charity scores high as well.

An advantage of the intermediary charity over the foreign friends' organisation, unilateral solution, tax treaty, and supranational agreement is that it does not require much tax or legal knowledge. In the interviews, the fundraisers, for example, demonstrated that they were not familiar with tax treaties as a possible method to overcome the tax barrier to cross-border philanthropic giving. The following quote from fundraiser 28 of an American arts organisation that could potentially make use of a tax treaty to facilitate their Mexican, Canadian, and Israeli donors with a tax benefit illustrates that gathering the relevant knowledge is not their priority: 'it requires time, energy, and expertise to research this and so far we have not had enough staff, or we have not deemed it a big enough pay-off to invest in doing the research on this'. The frequent changes in tax laws further complicate the issue for arts organisations who have to keep up with legislation regarding charitable organisations in multiple countries. This itself is not surprising, as fundraisers are not tax experts. The arts organisations, however, must hire a tax adviser who is familiar with international tax law and the legislation in the donor's country.

Another advantage of the giving intermediary is that no separate legal entity needs to be established to facilitate foreign donors with a tax benefit. This is not the case in the option involving a foreign friends' organisation. Although setting up a legal entity abroad can have benefits when a philanthropic organisation wants to strengthen its relationship with a foreign country, setting it up solely for fundraising purposes is perceived as a rather costly and complex option that requires continuous attention and time. Besides the cost of setting up an entity and its maintenance, it is considered a rather time-consuming effort. As fundraiser 1 explains: '[The foreign friends' organisation] namely requires a lot of maintenance. I know how much investment is required to get a meeting with the board, to mobilise them, to bring them all together. That requires quite a lot of time'. Tax advisor 4 recognises the work involved in setting up a philanthropic organisation and says:

> I sometimes also tell my clients – who say 'I want my own foundation' – you have to know that you also take on a lot of hassle [when setting up a foundation]. You have to meet all Public Benefit Organisation requirements. You are not the sole board member. [The PBO] has to be officially independent. So, you have to gather some people [to join you on the board]. It also includes some administrative obligations. So, it is not just fun to have [a foundation]. It also has other sides to it.

For philanthropic organisations that do not want to set up a legal entity abroad, relying on one of the legal solutions – the unilateral solution, tax treaty, or the four fundamental freedoms in the EU – could be an option.

The four fundamental freedoms in the EU require the philanthropic organisation to be considered equivalent to domestic philanthropic organisations. Philanthropic organisations would, therefore, need to meet certain requirements like obtaining the necessary tax and legal knowhow or hiring an expert. The procedures to be recognised as an equivalent philanthropic organisation – the equivalence test – are often unclear and differ across EU Member States, which is the second hurdle. The proof that the donor must submit to demonstrate equivalence varies across countries, and sometimes there is lack of clarity regarding what proof is required. Then there are countries, such as Bulgaria, the Czech Republic, Estonia, Germany, Latvia, Lithuania, and the Slovak Republic, that decide whether a foreign charity is a charitable organisation on a case-by-case basis (for each donation filed for a tax benefit) (OECD, 2020, p. 111). This decision is made *ex post,* making it difficult for donors to anticipate on a potential tax benefit when donating to a foreign philanthropic organisation. Belgium also relies on a case-by-case approach. It is possible, though, to obtain a ruling on the equivalence of a foreign entity in Belgium (OECD, 2020, p. 111). Other countries make a general decision in which a foreign philanthropic organisation is granted equivalence to a domestic philanthropic organisation at once. In Finland, Ireland, Malta, the Netherlands, and Sweden, foreign philanthropic organisations must prove equivalence to a domestic charity and register themselves (OECD, 2020, p. 111). This *ex-ante* approach provides certainty on the applicability of a tax incentive to donors who want to contribute to a foreign charity and thus allows philanthropic organisations to use the available tax incentive as a tool to stimulate donations from foreign donors.

Philanthropic organisations that want philanthropic status in their country of residence as well as in the country where their foreign donors reside might have to meet the requirements in both countries. The interviewed tax advisors demonstrate that the key factor was whether a solution relied on home country control, host country control, or a combination of the two.

Koele (2007, pp. 389–390) and Oberson (2021) agree that in theory, a tax treaty can provide an effective solution to overcome the tax barrier to cross-border philanthropic giving. The tax advisors interviewed added that this provision is only useful from a practical point of view if it includes the concept that the philanthropic organisation under the legislation in one of the contracting states is essentially equivalent to a philanthropic organisation under the legislation of the other contracting state. If equivalence of philanthropic organisations is not included in the tax treaty, and the treaty thus relies on host country control, it might not provide an effective solution.

In the case of *Persche*, the ECJ ruled that an EU Member State does not automatically have to acknowledge a foreign philanthropic status when granting tax relief to donations. In the EU, the predominant type of control, therefore, is host country control, with a few exceptions, such as Luxembourg. Under host country control, the philanthropic organisation must meet the requirements of a philanthropic organisation for tax purposes in the EU Member State where the donor resides (Hemels, 2009). This imposes a large administrative burden on philanthropic organisations, as they have to demonstrate that they meet the requirements in the foreign country. Philanthropic organisations would potentially have to meet 28 different sets of requirements to meet the definition of a philanthropic organisation in all 28 Member States.

If requirements of the host country conflict with those of the home country of the philanthropic organisation or with those of another country where the philanthropic organisation has donors, it might not even be possible to facilitate donors in multiple countries with a tax benefit based on a legal solution. Tax advisor 1 pointed to the requirements regarding the legal form as conflicting between the home country and the host country. Tax advisor 10 had a foreign religious philanthropic organisation as its client who could not be recognised as such in the country of tax advisor 10 since religion was not considered a cause qualifying for special tax treatment. The definition of a public benefit purpose was conflicting in this case. Other conflicting requirements between countries that were mentioned included the reimbursement of board members, the articles of association – as experienced by arts organisation 20 – and the disclosure of documents. When relying on a giving intermediary, it is not necessary to meet every single administrative requirement in the donor's country of residence, as the giving intermediary ensures it meets all legal and administrative requirements. It is usually sufficient if the foreign philanthropic organisation is not for profit, benefits the general public, and pursues a philanthropic purpose. Not having to meet every detail of the requirements in countries where foreign donors reside to some extent neutralises the fact that taxation rules applicable to philanthropic organisations are not coordinated across countries. It allows philanthropic organisations to facilitate foreign donors in multiple countries with a tax benefit on their gift, despite varying requirements.

What further hinders the effectiveness of the legal solutions is their scope. The number of tax treaties that include a provision on cross-border charitable giving is limited. Only one of the tax advisers interviewed actually had experience in using a provision on cross-border charitable giving, specifically the provision in the Canada-U.S. tax treaty.[20] The effectiveness of the fundamental freedoms in the EU as a solution to ensure tax-efficient cross-border giving is in the first instance limited to cross-border giving from one EU Member State to another EU Member State or member of the European Economic Area (EEA).[21] To the best of my knowledge, the Netherlands is the sole country that has unilaterally extended the scope of its tax provision beyond the EEA. Canada and New Zealand allow foreign philanthropic organisations to become eligible recipients of gifts with a tax benefit (OECD, 2020 p. 113). The definition of qualifying philanthropic organisations, however, is limited.

B What the optimal solution would look like

Although the giving intermediary is currently the best available solution, it is not the optimal solution. The intermediary is a workaround, a service to avoid the actual cross-border situation for which a fee has to be paid. It does not allow the arts organisation to directly receive the international donation and requires them to collaborate with giving intermediaries in all the countries where they have donors.

For philanthropic organisations, it would be far more appealing if they could directly receive a foreign gift with a tax benefit. This could be done by allowing for cross-border gifts based on domestic legislation, tax treaties, or a supranational agreement. Ideally, the solution would be available in numerous cross-border situations. The experiences of arts organisations and tax and philanthropy experts demonstrate that the optimal solution would need to have clear procedures that apply an *ex-ante* approach to provide donors with certainty in advance on the tax benefit they obtain on their gift. Finally, and most importantly, the ideal solution relies on home country control. This would avoid philanthropic organisations having to meet multiple sets of (potentially conflicting) requirements. Furthermore, it would be a cost-efficient solution, as fundraisers themselves are usually well aware of the tax requirements that their organisation has to meet in its country of residence to be considered philanthropic.

The question is whether a solution that relies on home country control is feasible. Considering the high degree in overlap of requirements to qualify as a philanthropic organisation and the definition of philanthropic purpose (OECD, 2020), one would expect it to be feasible. It, however, would require countries to give up part of their sovereignty and trust each other's supervising authorities. The unsuccessful attempt to introduce a European-wide uniform and supranational legal form for philanthropic organisations[22] taught us that, thus far, this is an insurmountable barrier.

5 Conclusion

In the past three decades, extensive efforts have been made to overcome the tax barriers to cross-border giving. In line with the efforts within the EU to harmonise taxes, most EU Member States have opened their tax incentives to philanthropic organisations in other EU Member States. Networks of giving intermediaries like Transnational Giving Europe were established and grew from an annual turnover of €3 million in 2009 to almost €14 million in 2019 (Transnational Giving Europe, 2020). These efforts all contribute to create a level playing field for philanthropic organisations across countries. This stimulates international giving, which is important, as international philanthropy holds the potential to make a positive contribution to global challenges.

Still, a lot can be done to further ease cross-border philanthropy. The experiences of arts organisations show us that, despite legislation enabling tax-efficient cross-border giving in theory, in practice, obtaining a tax incentive on a cross-border donation is still challenging. Although the giving intermediary is effective and rather easy to use for arts organisations, this is no more than a workaround. Ideally, either at a national, bilateral, or supranational legal level, a provision should be introduced that allows for tax-efficient cross-border giving to equivalent foreign philanthropic organisations based on an *ex-ante* approach and home country control. The feasibility of such a solution is expected to be challenging, as states are not likely to give up a part of the sovereignty over their tax systems and trust each other's supervising authorities.

Notes

1 Philanthropic outflows are defined as 'a) the sum of charitable financial contributions sent by donors when the donor (individuals, corporations, foundations, or other grant-making organisations) and the beneficiary (individuals, philanthropic organisations, or intermediary organisations) are located in

different countries; or b) giving to domestic philanthropic organisations in a given country that focus on broad categories of international causes, such as foreign affairs, humanitarian assistance, international relations, promotion of international understanding, and international solidarity' (Indiana University Lilly Family School of Philanthropy, 2020, p. 10).

2 Treaty on the functioning of the European Union (TFEU) and EU Treaty (as amended through 2007).

3 TFEU and EU Treaty (as amended through 2007).

4 Article 112 Loi concernant l'Impôt sur le Revenue (Income Tax Act, Luxembourg).

5 Article 5b (1)b Algemene Wet Inzake Rijksbelastingen (Dutch General State Taxes Act).

6 Article 5b (1)b Algemene Wet Inzake Rijksbelastingen (Dutch General State Taxes Act).

7 Article 112 Loi concernant l'Impôt sur le Revenue (Income Tax Act) and Circulaire du directeur des contributions L.I.R. n° 112/2 du 7 avril 2010 (Circular of the director of Contributions, I.T.A. n° 112/2/ of 7 April 2010).

8 Oberson (2021) elaborates on the potential of tax treaties to promote cross-border philanthropic payments.

9 United Nations Model Double Taxation Convention between Developed and Developing Countries (1 January 2011) (22 July 2010), Treaties & Models IBFD, Treaties & Models IBFD, and OECD Model *Tax Convention on* Income *and on* Capital.

10 *Convention between Canada and the United states of America with respect to Taxes on Income and on Capital* (26 September 1980, as amended through 2007), Treaties & Models IBFD; *Convention between the United states of America and the Government of Israel with respect to Taxes on Income* (20 November 1975), Treaties & Models IBFD; and *Convention between the United Mexican states and the Government of the United states of America with respect to Taxes on Income* (18 September 1992, as amended through 2002), Treaties & Models IBFD.

11 TFEU and EU Treaty (as amended through 2007).

12 ECJ (27 January 2009) *Hein Persche v. Finanzamt Lüdenscheid, CASE*, p. C-318/07.

13 See *Country Profiles*. Available at: https://www.philanthropyadvocacy.eu/legal-environment-for-philanthropy-in-europe/last updated in 2020.

14 Case No 2013–4086, MEMO15/6006 19 November 2015, https://ec.europa.eu/commission/presscorner/detail/EN/MEMO_15_6006.

15 European Commission (7 March 2015) Withdrawal of Commission Proposals, OJ. *C80*(17), available at EUR-Lex-52015XC0307(02)-EN-EUR-Lex (europa.eu). For a detailed analysis of the potential of the European Foundation to overcome the tax barriers to cross-border giving, I refer to Hemels (2009) and Hemels and Stevens (2012).

16 This is part of a larger research on cross-border charitable giving to the arts and the tax barriers involved. It was carried out between 2012 and 2017; see *Tackling the International Tax Barriers to Cross-Border Charitable Giving* (Buijze, 2020).

17 For a full list of interviewees, see Appendix 1.

18 In this research, interviewees were questioned about actual experiences with cross-border giving (the *ex-post* perspective) as well as hypothetical situations based on a vignette (the *ex-ante* perspective). This resulted in rich data, from which criteria could be derived and parameters for the optimal solution could be set (to be met by the arts organisation) (Buijze, 2020). This chapter, however, focuses on the actual experiences of interviewees with fundraising abroad and the solutions to tax-efficient cross-border giving. Thus, this chapter takes the *ex-post* perspective.

19 When the interviews took place, the United Kingdom was still part of the European Union.

20 *Convention between Canada and the United states of America with respect to Taxes on Income and on Capital* (26 September 1980, as amended through 2007), Treaties & Models IBFD.

21 As the relevant EU case law refers to the free movement of capital, EU law could remove the tax barrier when donating from an EU Member State to a third country, based on article 63 TFEU. The scope of article 63 TFEU, however, is limited by article 64 TFEU, which stipulates that EU Member States may retain the restrictions that existed on 31 December 1993. As the tax provisions on charitable giving were in place before this date in many EU Member States, the tax benefits do not have to apply in cross-border situations between EU Member States and third countries.

22 On 8 February 8 2012, the EC presented a Proposal for a Council Regulation on the Statute for a European Foundation [COM (2012) 35 final, 2012/0022 (APP)]. These organisations and their benefactors would receive the same tax privileges as domestic charitable organisations in every EU Member State. By November 2013, the tax provision was excluded from the discussion of the Proposal. In March 2015, the Proposal was withdrawn.

References

Bryman, A. (2008) *Social Research Methods*. Oxford: Oxford University Press.

Buijze, R. (2020) *Tackling the International Tax Barriers to Cross-Border Charitable Giving*. Amsterdam: IBFD Publications.

Donors and Foundations Networks in Europe and European Foundation Centre. (2019) *Philanthropy Manifesto*. Brussels: Donors and Foundations Networks in Europe and European Foundation Centre.

Hemels, S.J.C. (2009) 'Are We in Need of a European Charity? How to Remove Fiscal Barriers to Cross-Border Charitable Giving in Europe', *Intertax*, 37(8), pp. 424–434.

Hemels, S.J.C., & Stevens, S. (2012) 'The European Foundation Proposal: A Shift in the EU Tax Treatment of Charities?' *EC Tax Review*, 21(6), pp. 293–308.

Indiana University Lilly Family School of Philanthropy. (2018) *The Global Philanthropy Environment Index 2018*. Indianapolis: Indiana University Lilly Family School of Philanthropy. Available at: http://hdl.handle.net/1805/15958 (Accessed on 12 September 2021).

Indiana University Lilly Family School of Philanthropy. (2020) *Global Philanthropy Tracker 2020*. Indianapolis: Indiana University Lilly Family School of Philanthropy. Available at: http://hdl.handle.net/1805/24144 (Accessed on 12 September 2021).

Jochum, H., & Savvaidou, A. (2015) 'Deduction of Gifts and Contributions and Other Tax Incentives in the PIT and CIT for Non-Profit Entities or Activities', in Vanistendael, F. (ed.) *Taxation of Charities*. 1st edition. Amsterdam: IBFD Publications, pp. 61–73.

Koele, I.A. (2007) *International Taxation of Philanthropy*. Amsterdam: IBFD Publications.

Oberson, X. (2021) 'Taxation of Cross-Border Philanthropy – The Potential of International Tax Law Standards and Double Taxation Treaties', in Peter, H. & Lideikyte Huber, G. (eds.) *Routledge Handbook of Taxation and Philanthropy*. 1st edition. London and New York: Routledge, pp. XX–XX.

OECD. (2020) *Taxation and Philanthropy, OECD Tax Policy Studies, No. 27*. Paris: OECD Publishing. Available at: https://doi.org/10.1787/df434a77-en.

Quick, E., Kruse, T.A., & Pickering, A. (2014) *Rules to Give By. A Global Philanthropy Legal Environment Index*. Washington: Nexus; McDermott Will & Emery LLP; Charities Aid Foundation.

Silver, N., & Buijze, R. (2020) 'Tax Incentives for Cross-Border Giving in an Era of Philanthropic Globalization: A Comparative Perspective', *Canadian Journal of Comparative and Contemporary Law*, 60(1), pp. 109–150.

Transnational Giving Europe. (2020). *Annual Report 2019*. Brussels: Transnational Giving Europe. Available at: https://www.transnationalgiving.eu/wp-content/uploads/2020/11/Annual-Report-2019.pdf.

Von Hippel, T. (2014) *Cross-Border Philanthropy in Europe after Persche and Stauffer: From Landlock to Non-Discrimination?* Brussels: European Foundation Centre and Transnational Giving Europe.

Yin, R.K. (2003) *Case Study Research: Design and Methods*. Thousand Oaks: Sage Publications.

APPENDIX 22.1

Experts and patrons

Location	*Interviewee*
NL	Tax expert 1
NL	Tax expert 2
NL	Tax expert 3
NL	Tax expert 4
NL	Accountant 1
NL	Tax expert 5
NL	Tax expert 6
NL	Tax expert 7
NL	Tax expert 8
NL	Tax expert 9
NL	Tax expert 10
NL	Philanthropy advisor 1
NL/UK	Philanthropy advisor 2
NL	Philanthropy advisor 3
BE	Philanthropy advisor 4
NL	Philanthropy advisor 5
NL	Philanthropy advisor 6
U.S.	Philanthropy advisor 7
NL	Expert 1
NL	Expert 2
NL	Expert 3
NL	Expert 4
BE	Expert 5
NL	Patron 1
NL	Patron 2

Arts organisations

#	Location	Interviewee	Discipline	Type	Size	FFO*	EA**
1	NL	Fundraiser 1	Cultural heritage	Fixed location	Medium		
2	NL	Fundraiser 2	Performing art	Company	Small		
3	NL	Fundraiser 3	Fine arts	Fixed location	Medium		
4	NL	Director 4	Fine arts	Fixed location	Small		
5	NL	Fundraiser 5	Performing art	Festival	Medium		
6	NL	Director 6	Cultural heritage	Fixed location	Medium	V	
6	NL	Fundraiser 6	Cultural heritage	Fixed location	Medium	V	
7	NL	Fundraiser 7	Performing art	Company	Major	V	
8	NL	Fundraiser 8	Fine arts	Fixed location	Medium	V	
9	NL	Fundraiser 9	Performing art	Company	Superstar		
10	NL	Fundraiser 10A	Fine arts	Fixed location	Superstar		
10	NL	Fundraiser 10B	Fine arts	Fixed location	Superstar		
11	NL	Fundraiser 11	Cultural heritage	Fixed location	Small		
12	NL	Fundraiser 12	Performing art	Company	Medium		
13	NL	Fundraiser 13	Fine arts	Fixed location	Superstar		
14	NL	Director 14	Fine arts	Fixed location	Small		
15	NL	Fundraiser 15	Performing art	Company	Medium	V	
16	NL	Director 16	Fine arts	Network organisation	Small		
17	NL	Director 17	Cultural heritage	Network organisation	Small		
18	BE	Fundraiser 18A	Fine arts	Fixed location	Major		
18	BE	Fundraiser 18B	Fine arts	Fixed location	Major		
18	BE	In-house lawyer 18	Fine arts	Fixed location	Major		
19	CH	Fundraiser 19	Fine arts	Fixed location	Small	V	
20	IT	Fundraiser 20A	Cultural heritage	Network organisation	Major	V	
20	IT	Fundraiser 20B	Cultural heritage	Network organisation	Major	V	
20	IT	Fundraiser 20C	Cultural heritage	Network organisation	Major	V	
21	DE	Fundraiser 21	Fine arts	Festival	Major		
22	FR	Fundraiser 22A	Fine arts	Fixed location	Superstar	V	
22	FR	Fundraiser 22B	Fine arts	Fixed location	Superstar	V	
23	BE	Director 23	Fine arts	Fixed location	Medium		
24	DK	Fundraiser 24	Fine arts	Fixed location	Medium	V	
25	UK	Fundraiser 25	Fine arts	Fixed location	Superstar	V	
26	BE	Director 26	Cultural heritage	Fixed location	Small		
27	AT	Fundraiser 27	Performing art	Festival	Superstar	V	
28	U.S.	Fundraiser 28	Performing art	Fixed location	Superstar		
29	BE	Director 29	Fine arts	Fixed location	Small		
30	FR	Fundraiser 30	Fine arts	Fixed location	Major	V	
31	U.S.	Fundraiser 31	Cultural heritage	Network organisation	Medium		V
32	U.S.	Fundraiser 32A	Fine arts	Fixed location	Superstar		
32	U.S.	Fundraiser 32B	Fine arts	Fixed location	Superstar		
32	U.S.	In-house lawyer 32	Fine arts	Fixed location	Superstar		
33	U.S.	Fundraiser 33	Fine arts	Fixed location	Medium		
33	U.S.	In-house accountant 33	Fine arts	Fixed location	Medium		
34	U.S.	Fundraiser 34A	Fine arts	Fixed location	Superstar		
34	U.S.	Fundraiser 34B	Fine arts	Fixed location	Superstar		
35	FR	Fundraiser 35	Performing art	Festival	Major		
36	U.S.	Fundraiser 36	Fine arts	Fixed location	Superstar		V

* Foreign friends' organisation
** Legal entity abroad with charitable activities

23
CROSS-BORDER PHILANTHROPY
A U.S. perspective

Eric M. Zolt

Americans are generous, at least with respect to charitable contributions. We contribute more money (and often highly appreciated property) to fund charitable activities (both domestic and foreign) than residents of any other country.[1] While this generosity exists among Americans of all income levels, over the past three decades or so, there has been a dramatic increase in charitable giving (and planned charitable giving) by those at the very top of the income distribution. We can see this in both the large growth of assets held in the non-profit, tax-exempt sector as well as the number of billionaires who have pledged to give a majority of their wealth for charitable purposes. The "Giving Pledge" highlights the generosity of the ultra-wealthy and their willingness to give back to a society that helped them achieve their success.[2]

Americans also lead in funding international charitable activities.[3] Many alternatives exist to help fund charitable activities outside the United States. For example, U.S. donors can contribute to U.S. charitable organizations that engage in direct operations in foreign countries or that make grants to foreign charitable entities, to U.S. "friends of" organizations that then transfer the funds to a designated foreign charitable organization, and to donor-advised funds with a recommendation that the funds be directed to a designated foreign charity. Tax subsidies to donors and to U.S. charitable entities support all these activities.

But Americans who contribute directly to foreign charities generally receive no income tax benefits (with exceptions for contributions made to charities in Canada, Mexico, and Israel, subject to limitations).[4] In examining whether this barrier to cross-border philanthropy makes sense, this chapter considers two key questions:

1 Should tax benefits support charitable activities outside the United States?
2 Should the U.S. tax system treat contributions to foreign charities differently from contributions to domestic charities?

Under current law, U.S. tax barriers to cross-border philanthropy are remarkably low.[5] Contributions to U.S. charitable organizations are deductible even if all charitable activity takes place outside the United States. Direct contributions to foreign charities are generally not deductible for income tax purposes. But, because many alternatives are available under U.S. law to channel contributions to foreign charities, this prohibition merely increases the complexity and transaction costs of giving to foreign charities. Nominally, the U.S. tax system treats contributions to

 DOI: 10.4324/9781003139201-27

foreign charities differently than contributions to domestic charities. Practically, donors generally can transmute non-deductible contributions to foreign charities into deductible contributions to domestic charities pretty easily.

The harder question is normative: what should the law be? It depends on how one frames the inquiry. One approach focuses on whether there are meaningful differences between U.S. and foreign charitable activities and between domestic and foreign charities that justify different tax treatment. This approach requires looking at the different rationales for charitable tax subsidies for guidance that might apply to warrant differential treatment. Unfortunately, the different theories that support using tax benefits to support charitable activities provide remarkably little guidance as to what types of activities merit favorable tax treatment and whether to extend such subsidies to foreign charitable activities or foreign charities. While strong arguments exist that the theories supporting charitable tax subsidies do not justify privileging domestic activity (or prohibiting or limiting subsides for foreign charitable activity), it is not clear a finding of "no sufficient difference" justifies tax subsidies for foreign charitable activities.

A second approach examines whether the current U.S. approach is the most effective way to achieve societal objectives for supporting charitable activities, including foreign activities. This second approach requires considerations of the efficacy of the current tax regime for both domestic and foreign charitable activities as well as other alternatives the U.S. government could adopt to provide financial support and other incentives to charitable activities. The question is easy to state: do the costs of the charitable tax subsidies exceed the benefits from the incremental charitable activities resulting from the tax subsidies? The answer is a lot more difficult. It requires looking at who benefits from charitable tax subsidies (both donors and recipients of charitable goods and services), who bears the costs of the tax subsidies, and who decides how to spend the funds attributable to these subsidies. It also requires consideration of factors that may justify greater tax incentives for domestic charitable activities than foreign charitable activities. Under this approach, it is not possible to answer the question of whether U.S. tax subsidies should support foreign charitable activities and foreign charities without going back to examine the U.S. charitable tax regime for both domestic and foreign activities.

Five observations help shape the discussion of using tax subsidies for domestic and foreign charitable activities.

First, we lack a comprehensive theory that marries tax subsidies to the current collection of qualified charitable activities and charitable organizations. The current tax regime reflects a set of trade-offs that result in a robust charitable sector and contributes to the diversity, pluralism, and even cacophony that are important in our society.[6] It is unclear whether these same trade-offs would apply to foreign charitable activities and foreign charities.

Second, the choice of whether to extend tax subsidies to foreign charitable activities or foreign charities need not be binary (that is, either deny tax subsidies for foreign activities or foreign charities or adopt tax subsidies that do not differentiate domestic and foreign charitable activities or charities). Another option provides tax subsidies for foreign activities and charities that are less expansive (either by adopting a different standard of charitable purpose or more restrictive contribution limitations) than those available to domestic activities.

Third, determining the efficacy of charitable tax subsidies requires consideration of all tax benefits for charitable activity, not just the charitable deduction under the personal income tax. These include income tax benefits for contributions of appreciated property, the reduced estate tax liability resulting from both lifetime and testamentary giving, and the loss of tax revenue from large transfers of assets from the taxable to the tax-exempt sector.

Fourth, the decision to provide tax subsidies for domestic and foreign charitable activities may require policy makers to compare the relative contribution of donors (the after-tax value of their donation) with the effective matching grant provided by government tax subsidies. They could then consider whether the current regime is at a "tipping point" where wealthy donors have too much control in deciding how government funds are spent.

Finally, accountability and oversight considerations play an important role in both understanding current aspects of the U.S. regime for cross-border philanthropy and providing a rationale for different treatment for foreign charitable activities and charities across different countries.

Part I reviews some of the important tax and other regulatory provisions that apply to charitable organizations and to donors. Part II examines some of the implications of using the tax system to subsidize charitable activities. Part III examines whether tax subsidies should support charitable activities outside the United States. Part IV considers whether the tax law should treat contributions to foreign charities differently than contributions to domestic charities as well as some proposed reforms that would encourage cross-border philanthropy. Part V provides some conclusions.

I Regulatory regime for charitable activities

This section reviews briefly the current tax regime that applies to charitable organizations and to those donors who contribute to these charities.

A Tax rules for charitable organizations

U.S. tax law provides two major types of tax benefits for charitable organizations.[7] First, the tax law provides an exemption from income tax for income related to the organization's charitable purpose and for investment income. Second, qualified charities are eligible to receive tax-deductible contributions for income, estate, and gift tax purposes. These two tax subsidies substantially reduce the after-tax costs of contributing to these charities for donors. In addition to these federal tax benefits, charitable organizations may have access to tax-exempt financing and qualify for state and local income, sales, and property tax benefits.

To qualify for tax exemption, U.S. tax law requires that the charitable organization be organized and operated for one of the enumerated charitable purposes. These activities include the usual suspects (religious, charitable, scientific, and educational purposes) as well as some activities that are less obvious (fostering amateur sports competition and for the prevention of cruelty to children or animals).

Additional statutory requirements for qualification ensure that the charitable organizations do not spill over to other non-charitable goals. They include a prohibition against "private inurement" to prevent the organization from providing benefits to insiders and related persons. Similarly, organizations cannot engage in political campaign activity or excessive lobbying. Most important for our purposes is a geographical limitation. Only donations made to charities organized or created in the United States or its possessions can qualify for the charitable income tax deduction. Foreign charities can qualify for tax exemption by complying with the same application procedures that apply to domestic charities. This status allows foreign charities to avoid federal income tax on their charitable activities and investment income but does not allow U.S. donors to claim income tax deductions for contributions to these foreign charities.

Different types of charitable organizations. Charitable organizations in the United States come in different flavors. The tax law divides charities into private foundations and public charities. "Traditional public charities" are what most people think of as charitable organizations, such as the YWCA or the Red Cross. Different types of charitable organizations may qualify for public charity status.[8] The first category provides public charity status either because of the nature of an organization's activities or because of the broad financial support received.[9] This category includes educational organizations, religious institutions, and hospitals and medical research organizations. A second category of public charities are organizations that receive more than one-third of their support from gifts, grants, fees, and receipts of sales of goods and services related to their exempt purposes.[10] Public charity status provides more generous income tax benefits for donors than contributions to private foundations and allows charitable entities to avoid a host of excise taxes, minimum distribution requirements, and restrictions that apply to private foundations.[11]

Charitable organizations that do not qualify as public charities are private foundations. While they differ greatly in size and nature of activities, they share a common feature – that a small group of donors (individuals, families, or corporations) controls them. Two types of private foundations exists: one, private operating foundations that engage directly in charitable activities, and two, private foundations that hold assets for grants to other charitable organizations.[12] Because of a history of abuses involving private foundations, U.S. tax law provides for several measures to reduce self-dealing and other abuses and requires a minimum annual distribution.[13] For tax years beginning after December 20, 2019, private foundations are subject to a 1.39% excise tax on their net investment income.[14]

For purposes of cross-border philanthropy, the key difference between public charities and private foundations is the additional requirements imposed on private foundations for grants made to foreign charities. Unless the foreign charity has received a determination letter from the IRS that it meets the standards to qualify as a U.S. public charity, private foundations need to comply with certain regulatory requirements. Private foundations are required to either exercise expenditure responsibility with respect to the grant or make a good faith determination that the foreign charity is the equivalent of a U.S. public charity. Failure to comply results in tax and other penalties.

To exercise expenditure responsibility, a private foundation must conduct a pre-grant inquiry of the foreign charity to ensure that the funds will be used for the intended charitable purposes. Expenditure responsibility also requires the foundation (i) to enter into a written agreement with the foreign charity that requires the foreign charity to return any funds not used for the charitable purpose, (ii) to exert all reasonable efforts to ensure the funds are spent solely for the purposes the grant was made, (iii) to obtain full and complete reports from the foreign charity on how funds were spent, and (iv) to make full and detailed reports to the IRS about the funds transferred to the foreign charity.

Private foundations can also avoid excise taxes and other penalties on grants to foreign charities by making a good-faith determination that the foreign charity is the equivalent of a U.S. public charity. An organization is equivalent to a U.S. public charity if it is organized, operated, and funded like a U.S. public charity. Before 2015, private foundations could rely on an affidavit from a foreign charity establishing that the organization was the equivalent of a Section 501(c)(3) organization. Treasury regulations provide that private foundations can satisfy the equivalency requirement by obtaining written advice from a qualified tax practitioner that the foreign charity satisfies the requirements for qualified public charity status.[15] In 2017, the IRS issued guidelines that sets forth the types of documents, affidavits, representations, and financial information that tax practitioners should compile and review in providing written advice to private foundations to support an equivalency determination.[16] Organizations, such as NGOsource, have substantially reduced the costs and challenges of establishing equivalency determination by providing private foundations (and donor-advised funds) with access to their repository of foreign charities satisfying the U.S. public charity equivalency requirement or by providing legal assistance in confirming equivalency for foreign charities not in their repository.[17]

In the post-September 11, 2001 world, the differences between the oversight requirements for public charities and private foundations have narrowed substantially. As set forth in Part I.C, while public charities are not subject to expenditure responsibility or equivalency determinations for grants to foreign charities, they must engage in sufficient due diligence and monitoring of funds to avoid penalties under counter-terrorism and anti-money laundering laws.

Donor-Advised Funds. One major change in the U.S. charitable landscape over the last decade is the growth of donor-advised funds.[18] These funds offer a hybrid approach to charitable giving that allows a donor to achieve a substantial measure of informal control over the investment and ultimate disposition of the donated property while qualifying for the less onerous rules and more generous tax benefits of a public charity.[19] A donor-advised fund is a fund or account at a qualified public charity (called a "sponsoring organization") over which the donor or donor-appointed advisor retains advisory privileges regarding the investment or distribution of assets in the fund or account.[20] Donors irrevocably transfer funds to the sponsoring organization and can claim an income tax deduction when funds are transferred, even though donors generally retain the ability to provide advice as to the ultimate charitable beneficiary and often to direct how the funds are invested. While the sponsoring organization has legal authority over how the funds will be invested and transferred, as a practical matter the "advisory" power of the donor will almost always be respected.[21]

A rapidly growing phenomenon is the affiliation of sponsoring organizations with financial institutions (such as Fidelity Charitable Gift Fund, Vanguard Charitable Endowment Program, Schwab Charitable Fund, and Goldman Sachs Philanthropy Fund).[22] The charitable organizations affiliated with financial institutions have seen a rapid increase in both the number of donor-advised funds and assets placed in donor-advised funds.[23] These sponsors have succeeded in creating a relatively simple device that allows donors to time their charitable contributions to get the maximum tax benefits while retaining control over where and when the contributions to traditional public charities will be made (as well as determining how the assets will be managed in the interim).

Donor-advised funds provide an easy mechanism for donors to designate contributions to foreign charities, thus avoiding the non-deductibility rules for direct contributions to foreign charities. Similar to the requirements imposed on private foundations, donor-advised funds making grants to foreign charities must either make a determination that the foreign charity is equivalent to a U.S. public charity or exercise expenditure responsibility over the grants to avoid tax penalties.[24] Sponsors of donor-advised funds have adopted different policies for contributions to foreign charities recommended by donors. One approach allows donors to recommend distributions to foreign charities but limits potential recipients to those foreign charitable organizations that have received a Section 501(c)(3) determination letter. A second option allows contributions to foreign charities but effectively channels the contribution through an American intermediary charity that will then make a grant to the foreign charity.[25] Finally, sponsors of donor-advised funds can partner with organizations that can conduct due diligence of foreign charities and provide evidence of equivalency determination to a U.S. public charity.[26]

"Friends of" Organizations. U.S. tax law allows donors to claim a charitable deduction for contributions made to a U.S. intermediate entity even if the intermediate entity transfers funds to a designated foreign charity.[27] As long as the organization does not act as a "mere conduit" to the foreign charity, U.S. donors can secure deductions for charitable contributions that are effectively made to foreign charities.[28]

These "friends of" organizations must satisfy several requirements.[29] First, the organization must not be required to transfer funds to the foreign charity by either charter or bylaw provision or by the terms of the gift. Second, the gift to the foreign organization must be within the intermediate entity's mission and purpose. Finally, the organization must exercise due diligence in determining that the foreign charity qualifies as an eligible organization. If the "friends of" organization qualifies as a public charity, then it can avoid the expenditure responsibility requirements that apply to private foundations. IRS guidelines require that the "friends of" organization not be controlled by the foreign charity.[30] A search of the Charity Navigator reveals at least 1,000 friends of organizations that have "American Friends of" in the name of the charity.[31]

In addition to formal "friends of" status, foreign charities can get de facto status by contracting with an intermediary U.S. charity. For example, CAF America has established a "friends fund" that allows foreign charities to avoid the application and reporting requirements under U.S. tax law but still allow U.S. donors to receive charitable deductions for funds directed to foreign charities.[32]

B Tax rules for donors

Since 1917, the United States has allowed individuals and corporations to deduct contributions made to qualified charitable organizations for income tax purposes. Various limitations on the amounts deductible apply depending on the type of donee (public charity or private foundation) and type of property contributed (cash or non-cash property contributions).

Under current temporary provisions, individuals can deduct cash contributions to public charities subject to a limitation of 60% (100% for contributions made in 2020) of their adjusted gross income.[33] For non-cash individual charitable contributions to public charities, the limitation is 50% of adjusted gross income unless the property is long-term capital gain property, in which case a 30% limitation applies.

Less favorable rules apply to contributions to private foundations. Generally, individuals can deduct 30% of their adjusted gross income for contributions of cash and short-term capital gains property and only 20% of their adjusted gross income for contributions of long-term capital gain property. For contributions to either public charities or private foundations, individuals can carry forward charitable contributions that exceed the limitations for up to 5 years.

Except for a temporary exception provided in the Coronavirus Aid, Relief, and Economic Security (CARES) Act[34] and extended by the Consolidated Appropriations Act, 2021,[35] individuals who take the standard deduction rather than itemizing receive no income tax benefits for charitable contributions. One major consequence of the Tax Cuts and Jobs Act of 2017 (TCJA) is the dramatic increase in the number of taxpayers in this category. Before the TCJA, about 69% of taxpayers took the standard deduction. Because of the increase in the amount of the standard deduction (and limitations put on other personal deductions – most notably the state and local tax deductions), more than 90% of taxpayers will elect to claim the standard deduction – and get nothing for their charitable contributions.[36] The itemizers are disproportionately from the upper end of the income distribution.

Donors contributing appreciated property generally receive a less widely recognized second tax benefit on top of the well-known charitable deduction. They can claim a deduction equal to the fair market value of the appreciated property without paying any capital gains tax on the pre-transfer appreciation.[37] While contributions of appreciated property to private foundations are generally limited to the tax basis in the property, a special exception applies to contributions of appreciated publicly traded stock.[38] As examined further in Part II.D, for many donors, the economic value of avoiding any tax on pre-transfer appreciation (and the resultant loss of potential tax revenue) dwarfs the tax benefit from claiming a charitable deduction for income tax purposes.

Individuals (and estates) can also receive tax benefits for charitable contributions under the estate and gift tax. For 2020, the estate and gift tax exemption is $11.58 million per individual (a married couple will have an exemption of $23.16 million). For taxable estates of $1 million or more, the estate tax rate is 40%. In 2019, charitable giving through estates amounted to about $43 billion, resulting in reduced estate tax revenue of roughly $17 billion (about one-third of the annual revenue loss from the charitable income tax deduction).[39]

Wealthy donors generally engage in more charitable giving at death than through lifetime charitable contributions. For net estates between $50 to $100 million, testamentary giving exceeds charitable giving in the last 5 years of life by a factor of 10.[40] For estates over $100 million, testamentary transfers are 20 times greater than giving in the last five years of life.[41] The amounts of charitable contributions are substantial. For estates over $50 million, charitable contributions as a share of the net estate exceed 40%.[42]

C Non-tax requirements for U.S. charitable organizations

While the IRS is responsible for recognizing tax-exempt status and monitoring charities' activities, charitable organizations are also subject to regulation at the state level. In the United States, charitable entities are organized or incorporated under state law and are subject to supervision by various state agencies. Each state has a non-profit statute that governs the allowable purposes for non-profit status as well as rules governing the operation and dissolution of charities. States vary greatly in the resources devoted to monitoring charitable activity as well as types of enforcement activities.[43] Many states require non-profits to register before engaging in fundraising activities and have local solicitation laws to protect donors from deceptive charities.

In addition to IRS and state supervision, charitable organizations are subject to several regulatory regimes that seek to prevent diversion of charitable assets for illicit purposes. These include counter-terrorism laws as well as laws targeting money laundering and corruption. Shortly after the September 11, 2001, terrorist attacks, President George W. Bush signed Executive Order 13224, which required the U.S. Department of Treasury to maintain a list of known and suspected terrorists and impose sanctions on those individuals or organizations who support or are associated with those on the list. The primary U.S. terrorist list is the Specially Designated Nationals List maintained by the U.S. Treasury's Office of Foreign Asset Control.[44] Charitable organizations that provide funds, goods, or services to listed terrorists or terrorist organizations can have their assets frozen or their tax-exempt status revoked, even if they did not knowingly support terrorist activity.

Additional potential penalties are included in the Uniting and Strengthening America by Providing Appropriate Tools Required to Intercept and Obstruct Terrorism (USA PATRIOT ACT) Act of 2001,[45] which was enacted about a month after Executive Order 13224 was signed. The Patriot Act imposes civil and criminal penalties on nonprofits and their directors if they are found to have provided material support to terrorists. In 2002, Treasury issued Voluntary Guidelines (later revised) that sought to provide "best practices" for charitable organizations to follow in making grants to foreign grantees.[46] The Voluntary Guidelines set forth the types of information that the nonprofit should obtain from grantees as well as the appropriate due diligence the nonprofit should conduct before making any grants.

U.S. charitable organizations can subject themselves to additional governance and operating requirements by joining organizations that require members to meet certain standards to maintain membership. InterAction is an alliance of 190 U.S.-based non-governmental organizations that work in developing countries. Members of InterAction agree to comply with a set of standards that provide a broad code of conduct covering governance, financial reporting, fundraising, public relations, management practice, human resources and program services.[47]

II Charitable tax subsidies

Before focusing on foreign charitable activities and foreign charities, this part examines four key questions related to tax subsidies: first, what theories justify favorable tax treatment; second, what the optimal level of charitable tax subsidies is; third, what the funding and allocation alternatives are for charitable contributions; and fourth, when one considers all charitable tax subsidies (not just the charitable deduction under the federal income tax), what we can say about the relative split between donors (amount of the after-tax contribution) and the government (reduced tax revenue) of funding for charitable activities.

A Theories justifying charitable tax subsidies

Tax scholars in the United States have taken different approaches in examining the justifications for tax subsidies for charitable activities.[48] The literature falls into two general categories. One group of scholars focuses primarily on the donor. They justify allowing tax deductions for charitable contributions based on considerations of designing the proper base for taxation and income measurement. A mostly different group of scholars justifies tax benefits for charitable deductions and for charitable organizations as a subsidy for collective goods and services. The difference is important. The donor-based theories are rooted in the design of a tax system. In contrast, the subsidy-based theories seek to use the tax system as a means to achieve non-tax objectives, in this case increasing incentives for private donors to support and monitor charitable activities and providing matching funds to supplement their efforts.

Donor-oriented approaches. Early examinations of the role of charitable deductions in an ideal tax system worked within the *Haig-Simons* framework, which defines income as the sum of personal consumption ("private preclusive use") plus wealth accumulation over a given time period.[49] Considering this definition of income, amounts transferred as charitable contributions are not income to the donor because they do not result in exclusive personal consumption. Instead, such contributions create common goods whose enjoyment is not limited to contributors nor apportioned among contributors according to amounts of contributions. Under the donor-oriented approach, no government subsidy for charitable contributions exists, as the contributed amounts are not income in the first place.

One could also allow a charitable deduction because it equitably accounts for loss of welfare by the donor.[50] Society should reward those who transfer private resources for the public good. In addition, as donations often derive from perceived moral obligations, the involuntary nature of the transfer should not require taxing the donor on such amounts.

Tax scholars have offered serious challenges to both donor-oriented approaches.[51] While these theories reflect a common intuition that money (or other property) transferred to charity should qualify for income tax deductions, the theoretical basis for charitable deductions as a way of accurately measuring income remains shaky.

These donor-oriented theories provide little or no guidance as to what types of charitable activities warrant support or whether giving for domestic activities should be preferred over giving for foreign charitable activities. As long as the donor gives up control of the property, it does not matter how or where the donated resources are actually used. These theories justify the tax deduction because donors are worse off because of their charitable donations. Interestingly, to the extent that geographic distance between the donor and the beneficiaries makes it harder for a donor to achieve reputational, social, or financial advantages from donations, one could argue that donor-centric theories justify preferences for foreign charitable activity over domestic activity.[52]

Subsidy-oriented approaches. A second approach justifies the charitable deduction (and other tax benefits) as a subsidy for certain types of under-provided collective goods and services. There are several strands of the subsidy literature, focusing on different types of market or government failure. The market failure arguments generally start with examination of public goods – those goods where one person's consumption does not reduce availability to others ("non-rival"), and there is no way to exclude others from enjoying the good ("non-excludable").[53] Such goods will be under-supplied because self-interested individuals will choose to free ride on the charitable activities of others rather than paying to support the goods and services themselves. As a practical matter, most goods provided by governments (and charities) are rival and excludable. These goods and services include schools, hospitals, roads, and various transfer payments. However, these goods and services can generate externalities that are not fully captured by market participants. There is thus a role for governments (and charities) to supply such goods where there are substantial secondary benefits. Allowing a tax deduction for charitable contributions thus both increases the amount of funds going to these types of activities (correcting a suboptimal level of funding) and imposes costs on those uncharitable individuals (making them involuntary contributors to these causes).

Support for tax subsidies for charitable contributions also rests on potential failures that may be inherent in the government decision-making process. If we leave all spending decisions to the political process, the level of collective goods and services would be decided by majority rule. The tax subsidy for charitable contributions allows, at least for certain types of goods and services, the preferences of a minority of voters who have a greater taste for certain collective activities to receive government support, as long as they are willing also to pay for them.[54] This decentralized approach allows for greater diversity and innovation, among other benefits.[55] Under this view, the greater the heterogeneity of preferences for collective goods, the stronger the case for tax subsidies for charitable contributions.

For our purposes, it is remarkable how little guidance these subsidy theories provide on such basic questions as which types of activities should qualify for favorable tax treatment and whether to extend tax deductions for foreign charitable activities of foreign charities. While the subsidy theories may provide general support for the government matching of private contributions, it does not tell us which types of activities to support, how much support to provide, or in which countries to provide support. Attempts to rank charities as to their relative worthiness based on their purpose and effectiveness of performance face substantial obstacles.[56] These challenges are perhaps unsurprising given both the difficulty of achieving political consensus on what activities are more or less worthy and of assessing the relative efficiency and effectiveness of performance.

Rather than relying on academic theories, we can view charitable tax subsides as a necessary part of the bargain to encourage charitable activities. The current tax regime reflects a series of trade-offs that occurred in the U.S. legislative and administrative process that result in a robust charitable sector.

The first trade-off focuses on the types of activities that merit tax subsidies. Policy makers can choose between a relatively narrow group of activities to support (for example, limiting to organizations that help the poor or prevent disease) or a more expansive approach (adopting a broad definition of what is "charitable"). The narrow approach reflects a policy decision that some types of charitable activities deserve government support more than others. In contrast, the expansive approach gives donors greater choice on how to spend their funds (and matching government funds) that likely results in more diverse and innovative charitable sector. In taking the broad approach, Congress was willing to use tax subsidies to support many different types of charitable activities, recognizing that some of the activities that receive support are of questionable "worthiness."[57]

A second trade-off concerns the level of review in granting tax-exempt status and monitoring charitable activity. Here, governments can choose between an aggressive approach that allocates resources to substantive reviews of applications for tax-exempt status and to monitoring entities to ensure they are fulfilling their charitable mission and a more narrow approach that relies on a limited review of applications for tax-exempt status and relies heavily on reporting to monitor activity. In taking the narrow approach, Congress is encouraging the growth of the charitable sector, recognizing that a potential for abuse exists.

A third trade-off focuses on the design of tax incentives. Generally, the more generous incentives are, the higher the amounts of charitable contributions will be.[58] For example, favorable tax treatment for contributions of appreciated property will result in greater contributions, albeit at a cost of substantial lost tax revenues. Again, Congress has adopted a menu of tax incentives (more than just the charitable deduction under the personal income tax) that has resulted in a large and diverse charitable sector. If Congress scales back on favorable tax treatment, then the growth of the charitable sector will slow.

The important insight is that these (and other) trade-offs were instrumental in adopting and shaping tax subsidies for charitable activities. It may be that Congress focused on both domestic and foreign charitable activities and charities in making decisions as to the scope of charitable activity, the level of government supervision, and the design of tax subsidies (and revenue costs). However, it is also possible Congress made these choices focusing primarily on domestic charitable activities and charities. It is likely that for each of these three trade-offs, different considerations may apply for domestic charitable activities and domestic charities as compared to foreign charitable activities and foreign charities. This may change the focus from the binary question of whether to extend the current charitable regime to foreign charitable activities and charities to how might the tax regime differ for foreign charitable activities and charities.

B Optimal level of charitable tax subsidies

The nonprofit sector in the United States consists of 1.5 million charitable entities, with assets of about $4 trillion ($2.5 trillion in net assets) and total revenues of $2.1 trillion (about 11% of GDP).[59] The sheer number and size of charitable organizations raises the question of whether the nonprofit sector in the United States is too big or too small. I have no idea – but I am confident that bigger is not necessarily better.

What would we need to know to answer this question? To start, we would require information about the charitable organizations and the different types of activities they are engaged in. We would then have to engage in the messy process of determining the societal benefits generated by the charitable sector, a process that requires making value judgments of the relative merits of different types of charitable activities (soup kitchens versus operas). While at one time, the IRS adopted a rather narrow view of what activities constitute charitable activities,[60] the current approach provides for tax subsidies for a "kaleidoscope" array of organization that often have little to do with common perceptions of charitable activity, such as poverty reduction, education, and health services.[61]

One's view of the optimal size of the charitable sector is likely colored by confidence in the approval process for tax-exempt and nonprofit status and the success of the IRS and state governments in monitoring charitable activities. Here, much is lacking. The IRS and state government approve almost all applications for tax-exempt and non-profit status, and their ability to monitor the activities of over 1.5 million entities is extremely limited.[62] With some high-profile exceptions,[63] because of either a lack of political will or resources, there is remarkably little oversight of the charitable sector, especially in light of its size and importance.

Also important in thinking about the optimal size of the charitable sector is the relative efficiency of charities in using their assets to provide goods and services. Unlike the for-profit sector, for many charitable organizations, there is relatively little "market discipline" by consumers. Underperforming charitable organizations seldom go out of business. While organizations such as the Charity Navigator[64] and Charity Watch[65] provide information about the financial health, accounting and transparency, and fund-raising practices of different charitable organizations, these reviews focus more on financial management of the charities rather than on the effective use of their assets to fulfill their charitable purposes.

Attempts to rank charities by the effectiveness in providing societal benefits (for example, lives saved or lives improved per dollar spent) require assessments of the relative marginal benefits from new charitable contributions as well as value judgments as to the types of projects that merit support. Organizations such as GiveWell (a U.S. public charity) provide guidance to potential donors by identifying high-impact giving opportunities.[66] GiveWell has developed a cost-effectiveness algorithm that allows the organization to compare charities engaged in similar activities as well as across different charitable activities.[67]

The non-profit sector also faces major corporate governance challenges. In the for-profit sector, shareholders play a role in monitoring the behavior of managers and directors, and directors (with varying degrees of success) monitor the behavior of managers. Many charitable organizations (especially those with a large number of donors contributing small amounts) lack mechanisms for controlling the actions of managers and the board of directors.[68] A survey of corporate governance practices in U.S. non-profits highlights their failure to adopt measures that would improve accounting and transparency.[69] These challenges have led to calls to reduce the size of the board of directors of large nonprofit organizations as well proposals to bifurcate boards (with one board focusing on fund-raising and the other board with governance responsibility).[70] The American Red Cross[71] and FIFA[72] offer two examples of high-profile corporate governance failures that resulted in less effective performance of charitable activities and misappropriation of charitable funds.

The question of the optimal level of charitable tax subsidies is intertwined with the question of the optimal relative split between the size of the public sector, private sector, and the charitable sector. Whether governments should provide charitable tax subsidies depends on the relative marginal costs and marginal benefits of those subsidies. Determining costs and benefits requires some prediction of what the counterfactual would be – what would the charitable sector look like in a world without tax subsidies?

Countries differ in the relative split between goods and services provided by the public sector, private sector, and charitable sector.[73] One, two, or three sectors can provide health care; primary, secondary, and university education; or poverty relief programs. Not surprisingly, countries with more comprehensive and successful government-provided health, education, or poverty relief programs will likely have a smaller nonprofit sector than countries with less successful or less comprehensive government programs.

One explanation of why Americans are more generous in making contributions to support charitable activities than residents of other countries is because of a relatively low level of government spending (or effectiveness) for these activities. In the cross-border context, large charitable contributions funding foreign charitable activities could compensate for relatively low levels of U.S.-government provided foreign assistance. The key insight is that individuals can "purchase" these types of goods and services by either paying taxes or making charitable contributions, but they direct the "purchase" only by charitable contributions, while majority rules for taxes.

Countries preferring a larger charitable sector will likely provide greater charitable tax subsidies than countries preferring a smaller charitable sector. But while the total level of government support for charitable activities (either through direct government expenditures or charitable tax subsidies) may be relatively similar among countries, the key difference is who dictates how the funds are spent.

Who benefits from charitable tax subsidies? One answer is the charitable organizations. These organizations now have greater resources because of the tax benefits. We first need to see which types of charities receive substantial contributions.

Figure 23.1 sets forth the choices made by U.S. donors in their charitable giving in 2019. Similar to other countries, religious organizations receive the largest share of donations. Contributions to international organizations and to arts, culture, and humanities organizations are a lower percentage of total giving, though still substantial in amounts of donations.

We then need to determine who benefits from the charitable activity. Beneficiaries depend on the type of charitable activity – with gifts to poverty-reduction organizations helping low-income individuals, gifts to religious organizations primarily benefitting members of the congregation, and gifts to arts organizations and prestigious private schools skewed towards the wealthy.

Table 23.1. highlights how charitable giving varies by income levels.

Because the beneficiaries of tax subsidies vary greatly by income level, tax subsidies are going disproportionately to charities supported by the wealthy rather than charities favored by those at the bottom and middle of the income distribution. For all charitable giving, no more than one-third of the contributions are made to organizations that assist the poor. In contrast, for donors with income greater than $1 million, the share going to organizations that assist the poor is no more than one-fifth of total contributions.[74]

Another potential beneficiary of charitable tax subsidies is the donor. Again, we need to know the counterfactual – what would the amount of contribution be if there were no tax

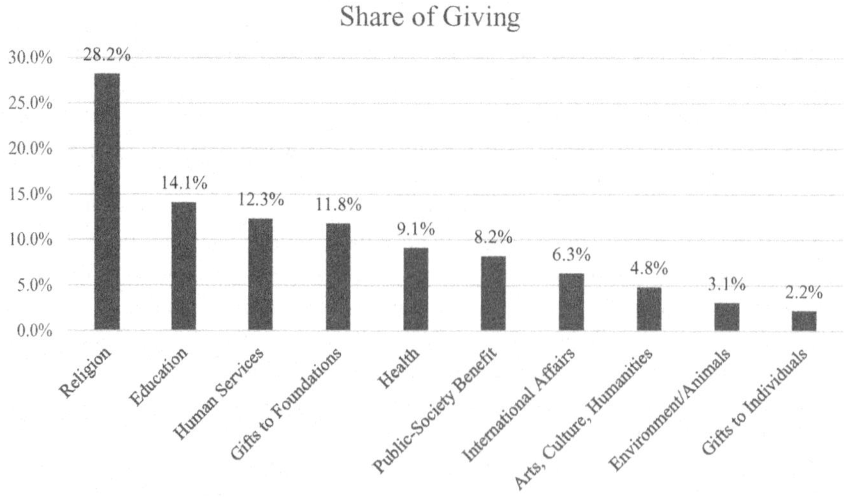

Figure 23.1 Share of charitable giving by type of recipient (2019)

Table 23.1 Household giving by income and charity type ($ in billions)

Household income	*Religion*	*Combined*	*Help meet basic needs*	*Health*	*Education*	*Arts*	*Other*	*Total*
<$100,000	59.96	7.70	9.34	3.06	2.69	1.01	6.16	89.92
$100,000 to $200,000	11.39	2.16	2.46	1.12	1.14	.44	1.17	19.88
$200,000 to $1 million	21.01	10.19	5.30	4.81	29.15	13.57	7.45	91.48
$1 million or more	8.64	2.06	1.93	12.97	12.94	7.88	4.85	51.27
Total	101.00	22.11	19.03	21.96	45.92	22.90	19.63	252.55

Source: The Center on Philanthropy at Indiana University, 2007. *Patterns of Household Charitable Giving by Income Group, 2005*. Bloomington, I.N.: The Center on Philanthropy at Indiana University at 12

subsidy? If a donor who makes a $1 million contribution would have contributed the same amount without a tax subsidy, then the donor is better off by the amount of the tax subsidy (and the financial position of the charity is not changed). The result is simply a tax reduction without any increase in charitable funding. If the amount of the contribution would be less if there were no tax subsidy (but not reduced by the full amount of the tax benefit), then the donor and the charity would share the tax subsidy.

As discussed earlier, only about 10% of U.S. taxpayers can take advantage of charitable deductions under the personal income tax (and only about 4,000 individuals who died in 2018 left estates large enough to require filing an estate tax return and to claim charitable deductions under the estate tax).[75] Figure 23.2 sets forth for different income levels the relative amount of the contribution supported by tax subsidies. Much greater tax subsidies are provided for contributions made by those at the top of the income distribution than contributions made by middle- or low-income donors.

Given how the current U.S. tax regime "matches" charitable contributions, it is not surprising that the top quintile captures almost all of the tax benefits, with over half going to the top 1%. Table 23.2 provides an estimate of the distribution of tax benefits for charitable deduction under the personal income tax system.

What about the costs of the tax subsidies? The economic consequences of providing subsidies through the tax system depend on who bears the burden of reduced tax revenues associated with charitable tax subsidies. Here are some alternatives. First, the government could compensate for the lost revenue from charitable tax subsidies by adopting revenue-raising income tax provisions (for example, through higher tax rates). Second, the government could recoup the lost revenue by increases in taxes other than the income tax. Finally, the lost revenue from charitable tax subsidies could simply result in reduced government spending (some of which might be offset by the charitable activities).

For each alternative, a different class of individuals bears the consequences of providing tax subsidies. For example, if governments recaptured lost revenue under the income tax system, the burden will fall primarily on wealthy individuals who are not charitable. In the United States, the income tax burden falls primarily on high-income taxpayers. For the 2017 tax year, the top 1% received 21% of total adjusted gross income and paid 38.5% of federal income taxes. The top 10% received about 48% of total income and paid about 70% of total federal income tax. In contrast, the bottom 50% received only about 11% of total income and paid about 3% of total federal income taxes. The poor are not subsidizing the charitable activities of the billionaires who signed the Giving Pledge; it is other millionaires and billionaires.

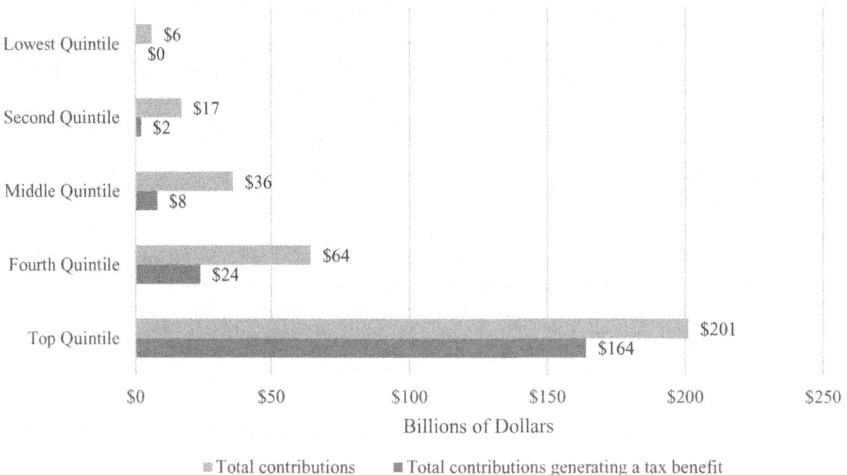

Figure 23.2 Tax benefits for contributions by income group (2020)

Table 23.2 Distribution of charitable deduction under the Federal Income Tax (2020)

Expanded cash income percentile	*Total contributions ($ billions)*	*Share of total tax benefit (%)*	*Marginal tax benefit per $100 of contributions ($)*	*Share of tax units with benefit (%)*
Lowest quintile	$6.3	*	$0.1	0.1%
Second quintile	$16.9	0.3%	$1.4	1.4%
Middle quintile	$36.1	1.7%	$3.2	5.6%
Fourth quintile	$63.9	6.5%	$6.6	14.1%
Top quintile	$200.9	95.1%	$21.8	36.3%
All	$324.4	100.0%	$15.3	8.9%
Breakdown of top quintile				
80th–90th percentile	$43.8	7.6%	$11.4	25.0%
90th–95th percentile	$30.4	8.2%	$15.5	37.4%
95th–99th percentile	$39.6	17.6%	$22.5	54.8%
Top 1 percent	$87.1	58.1%	$29.0	79.7%
Top 0.1 percent	$53.0	35.2%	$28.0	89.9%

Source: McClelland, R., Steuerle, E., Lu, C., and Boddupalli, A., 2019. *Tax Incentives for Charitable Contributions*. Washington, D.C.: Urban-Brookings Tax Policy Center

In contrast, if governments recoup revenue from other parts of the tax system, then the burden will fall on all taxpayers. Here, the distribution of the total tax burden falls more evenly across the population. When we focus on all federal taxes, the share of total taxes of the top 1% falls to about 25%, and for the top 10%, the share is about 54%.[76]

Finally, if governments choose to reduce government spending, then the burden falls on those individuals who would have received those goods and services. Here the economic cost of charitable tax subsidies is not limited to lost revenue; it also includes the opportunity costs associated with reduced government spending (which may or may not be more socially useful than privately directed charitable activity).

C Funding and allocation alternatives for charitable activities: why pay lobbyists to influence government spending?

We could, but do not, separate the decision to provide federal funds for charitable activities from the decision of who gets to decide how federal funds are spent. The following framework sets forth different combinations of funding and allocation decisions that reflect the public and private nature of using tax benefits to subsidize charitable activities.[77]

The upper-left box of Figure 23.3 reflects the use by individuals or corporations of their own funds to support activities that they choose. This is the after-tax cost of charitable contributions. For example, if an individual is subject to tax at the 37% marginal tax bracket and makes a $1,000 contribution, the value of the income tax deduction is $370, and the after-tax cost would be $630. Donors can further reduce the after-tax cost of making charitable contribution by taking advantage of tax subsidies afforded contributions of appreciated property as well as other income, gift, and estate tax savings. For those individuals who receive no tax benefits for their contributions, either because they do not itemize deductions or have no tax liability, the full amount of their contribution would be included in this box.

The upper-right box reflects the tax benefits associated with the contribution. Here private actors determine how public funds are allocated. Why pay lobbyists to persuade members of Congress on spending priorities when I can get my own private earmark to support medical services to combat cholera in Haiti simply by writing a check to the U.S. affiliate of Doctors Without Borders (Médécins Sans Frontières)? Here donors can direct government spending while bypassing majority approval. Minority preferences dictate government spending patterns.[78]

The bottom-left box reflects government regulation that influences the use of private funds for charitable purposes. This includes both incentives for funding certain types of activities and organizations and disincentives and prohibitions against certain types of activities, such as expenditures that may jeopardize an organization's tax-exempt status or that may result in excise taxes for private foundations.[79] In a post-September 11, 2001, world, it also includes requirements for charitable organizations to prevent diversion of charitable assets for illicit purposes (money laundering and counter-terrorist financing).

Finally, the bottom-right box reflects public actors spending public funds. Here taxpayers are subject to the whims of the majority (through their elected representative), who dictate how revenues are spent (including funds for many of the same types of activities supported by charitable tax subsidies). Congress can decide directly how to spend funds from general tax revenues, or Congress can delegate spending decisions to state and local governments, to government agencies, or to some band of experts, such as the governing boards of the National

		Funding alternatives	
		Private funds	*Public funds*
Allocation alternatives	*Private actors*	Unmatched portion of charitable contributions	Matching portion of charitable contributions
	Public actors	Government regulation (incentives and restrictions on the use of private funds)	Direct government programs (spending authorized by elected representatives)

Figure 23.3 Allocation and funding alternatives

Science Foundation or the National Endowment of the Arts. Important for our purposes, this bottom-right box includes amounts provided to U.S. Agency for International Development (US AID). In 2019, US AID provided about $2.7 billion in grants for U.S.-based charities for foreign humanitarian and development assistance.[80]

Viewing the charitable deduction (and other income and estate tax subsidies) as a matching grant program provides a lens to view charitable tax subsidies under different academic theories. As discussed earlier, we could allow charitable tax deductions because amounts contributed should not be included in an individual's tax base. Under these "base defining" theories, the existence of a federal matching program does not change the donor's tax base but does have tax revenue consequences.

Subsidizing charitable activity could also be justified because of market or government failure. Tax subsidies allow the minority to support activities that might be underprovided by the majority or under a "pluralistic" view that values greater participation, innovation, and supervision by donors to charitable activities. Under these theories, who gets to take advantage of tax subsidies and the relative split between donors and governments matters. The attractiveness of tax benefits for domestic or foreign charitable activities and charities may depend on the scope and degree of the subsidy, as well as the relative cost sharing between donors and government.

Here are a couple of alternatives for tax regimes that highlight the matching component of charitable tax subsidies. First, consider a tax regime with a relatively low top marginal income tax rate (say, a 20% tax rate), and a very large percentage of the population pays income taxes and is able to benefit (if they desire) from the charitable deduction. Here donors are bearing 80% of the cost (and reduced tax revenues cover the other 20%), and a large part of the population could participate in the matching grant program. For those in favor of using tax subsidies to support domestic or foreign charitable activities, the combination of donors providing the lion's share of the funding and the possible high levels of citizen participation provide substantial support for the tax subsidies.

In contrast, consider a tax regime with a top marginal tax rate of 80%, and only individuals subject to the top rate can claim charitable deductions. Here donors are contributing a relatively small amount of the costs of the charitable activities (20%), with the rest shifted to the government in the form of reduced tax revenues. Wealthy donors are able to dictate government spending even though their out-of-pocket costs are relatively low.

D Whose money is it (and should it matter)?

While the U.S. top marginal income tax rate currently is 37%[81] (much less than the 90% tax rate of many decades ago), total current and future tax benefits may increase the relative split between donors and government to much higher levels (with the cost to the government much closer to or exceeding 80% rather than the 20% of the example previously). Even where the income tax benefits from charitable tax deductions are relatively low, other income and estate tax savings (both federal and state) could substantially alter the relative contributions between donors and governments.

Let's start with what is one of the strongest cases for tax subsidies for charitable activities: the Bill and Melinda Gates Foundation.[82] The Gates Foundation allocates roughly 60% of its spending on foreign charitable activities and 40% on domestic charitable activities. An OECD survey of philanthropic giving by foundations to developing countries found that the Gates Foundation provided half of total giving.[83] By any formulation of "worthy" charitable activities, the types of foreign activities supported by the Gates Foundation easily qualify. The Gates Foundation funding generates substantial benefits in foreign countries but also generates positive externalities across borders. The foreign projects supported by the Gates Foundation likely address both political and market failures in foreign countries and are designed and monitored by talented and dedicated employees. The Gates Foundation provides a high level of transparency for grant and financial information to allow for a review of their activities.

What are the tax revenue consequences for Bill Gates and the Gates Foundation? First, Bill Gates gets an income tax deduction for his contribution of Microsoft stock to the Gates Foundation. Let's assume that Bill Gates contributes $40 billion of Microsoft stock to the Gates Foundation, that he is subject to income tax at a 37% rate, and that in the year of the contribution he has $50 million in adjusted gross income. What is the value of the charitable deduction under the personal income tax? As noted in the Gates Foundation 2019 Annual Report, the income tax benefits are relatively insignificant.[84] If Gates were able to fully use the charitable deduction to reduce his taxable income for the year to zero (with large carryforwards), the potential charitable tax benefit would be $18.5 million ($50 million multiplied by 37% = $18.5 million). The contribution reduces U.S. tax revenues by $18.5 million.

However, limitations apply. U.S. tax law provides for less generous rules for contributions to private foundations. Applying the 20% adjusted gross income limitation for contributions of property to private foundations reduces the amount of the charitable deduction to $10 million dollars ($50 million multiplied by 20%) and the amount of the tax savings to about $3.7 million ($10 million multiplied by 37%). The amount of lost revenue to the U.S. government from the charitable deduction (even if Gates staggered his stock contributions over several years and he took advantage of charitable carryforwards) is trivial compared to the size of the $40 billion contribution.[85]

But this is not the end of the story. By funding the Gates Foundation with appreciated property rather than cash, Bill Gates permanently avoids any tax on pre-transfer appreciation of Microsoft stock. What would the tax liability be if Bill Gates sold the stock (either to fund the Gates Foundation or other purposes)? If we assume a tax basis of 5% of the value of the stock ($2 billion), the gain recognized by Bill Gates is $38 billion. Assuming current capital gains rates of 23.8%, the tax liability of the sale would be roughly $9 billion, leaving Bill Gates with $31 billion in after-tax proceeds. While Bill Gates' state of residence (Washington) has no personal income tax, the effective capital gains tax rate in many states are much higher. If Bill Gates gave up rain in Seattle for sunshine in Los Angeles, he would face a potential capital gains tax rate of over 37%.

Of course, Bill Gates has techniques to monetize the $40 billion of Microsoft stock without incurring tax liability. For example, he could borrow against the stock and engage in hedging transactions to minimize (but not completely eliminate) the potential decline in Microsoft stock. He could then hold the stock until death and under current U.S. tax law avoid any tax on pre-death appreciation of the Microsoft stock. But he has a long time to wait. Using IRS guidance on life expectancy, Bill Gates at age 64 has life expectancy of 23.6 years (his friend and charitable partner, Warren Buffett, is 90 years old and has an IRS-predicted life expectancy of 5.7 years).

Bill Gates' generosity has additional tax revenue consequences to the U.S. government. Gates has irrevocably moved $40 billion of his assets (and additional billions from Warren Buffett and others) from the taxable to the tax-exempt sector. In the 2019 Annual Report, the Gates Foundation reported $6 billion of investment income. One approach in determining the value of the tax exemption is the amount of potential tax liability on the $6 billion in excess of any tax imposed on the investment income of private foundations. For current tax years, private foundations pay a tax on investment income of 1.39%. If the $6 billion of investment income were currently taxable and subject to tax at 21% (the corporate tax rate) or the 23.8% rate applicable to dividends and capital gains of individuals, the lost tax revenue to the U.S. government would be roughly $1.4 billion per year.[86] This tax subsidy will continue as long as the Gates Foundation has substantial investment assets.

Finally, at time of death, the size of Bill Gates' estate is likely smaller because of the $40 billion contribution to the Gates Foundation (and other contributions to the Gates Foundation and other charities). The amount of the reduction in the size of the taxable estate from the contribution of Microsoft stock to the Gates Foundation as well as the amount of the tax benefits depends on many factors, including assumptions as to how the assets and proceeds would have been used, how they would have appreciated, the life expectancies of Bill and Melinda Gates, and what other tax minimization strategies Bill and Melinda Gates might exploit. Here are some plausible estimates. One approach just focuses on the $40 billion contribution and assumes the taxable estate shrinks by that amount. Current estate tax rates are 40%, resulting in a tax benefit of $16 billion. Alternatively, we could assume that Gates retained the $40 billion in Microsoft stock until death, in which case the value (and resulting tax benefit) could be less (if Microsoft stock declined in value or Bill and Melinda Gates engaged in high levels of consumption that generated no residual value) or substantially more (if Microsoft continued to appreciate in value).

We are back to the original question of funding and allocation alternatives for charitable activities: Who should decide how to spend the funds resulting from charitable tax subsidies? Should the Gates Foundation have sole discretion in choosing which diseases to combat and which African countries deserve financial support?

This is no correct or easy answer. One view of Bill and Melinda Gates' funding of the Gates Foundation is resoundingly positive. One can make a strong case that the Gates Foundation is funding exactly the types of foreign charitable activities that merit government subsidies, especially given the cross-border challenges for disease prevention. Organizations like the Gates Foundation may be better positioned to design and monitor these types of programs than government agencies (such as US AID) or international organizations. Bill and Melinda Gates could simply have spent the funds contributed to the Gates Foundation on houses, artwork, and Stave puzzles[87] or made additional investments to increase their wealth. Compared to consumption and investment, their philanthropy should be celebrated.[88] And although the lost tax revenue from the counterfactual sale of appreciated Microsoft stock, the loss of investment income for assets transferred to the tax-exempt sector, and the smaller taxable estate on death is substantial, I have little doubt that Bill and Melinda Gates (with the assistance of well-qualified and well-compensated lawyers and accountants) would be able to arrange their finances to reduce greatly any tax liability.

But examining the political and economic consequences of charitable contributions provides a different perspective on philanthropy.[89] Here the desirability of large charitable gifts may depend on the relative size of the tax subsidies for Bill Gates and other mega-donors. If the split is 80% by the donor and 20% by the government, then a strong case can be made that the tax subsidies play an important role in encouraging charitable activities (whether domestic or foreign). However, a different answer may result if the size of the aggregate tax subsidies (charitable income tax deduction, no capital gains tax on the contribution of appreciated stock to charity, the tax exemption for investment income, and foregone estate state tax liability) approaches or exceeds 80%.

It is not possible to determine whether the split of the funding of the Gates Foundation between the Gates and the government is closer to 80%/20% or 20%/80% without making various assumptions about the Gates' charitable and investment activity and potential tax liability if they did not fund the Gates Foundation. It is also difficult to determine Gates' level of charitable giving in a world where tax subsidies were less generous. But with the current collection of charitable tax subsidies available to many mega-donors, we may well have reached a "tipping point" whereby these donors decide how to spend potential current and future tax revenues even though their after-tax contribution may be substantially less than the government's share of funding.

If policy makers consider the aggregate tax subsidies too generous, they have several options to scale them back.[90] For example, the tax regime for gifts of appreciated property could be changed to tax donors on any appreciation of the gifted property to charities or to limit the charitable deduction to the tax basis of the property (or just allow charitable contributions only for cash contributions). An Obama-era proposal would cap itemized deductions (including the charitable deductions) at 28% regardless of the taxpayer's tax rate.[91] Congress could change the unlimited estate tax deduction for charitable contributions by imposing limitations based on a dollar amount of contribution or a percentage of the total estate. Congress could also increase existing taxes on investment income of private foundations, increase mandatory distribution rules (and extend distribution requirements to donor-advised funds and public charities), and expand the taxation of investment income of public charity. All these proposed changes will generate additional tax revenue but also will reduce incentives to transfer property to charitable organizations.

Under current law, the charitable income tax deduction plays little or no role for many ultra-wealthy individuals. This partly explains why several ultra-wealthy donors use for-profit limited liability companies rather than tax-exempt private foundations for their philanthropic activities. But with the election of Joe Biden and a Democratic-controlled Congress, this could change. President Joe Biden has proposed increasing the top marginal tax rate and eliminating the rate preference for investment income and capital gains.[92] The Democratic members of the Senate Finance Committee have proposed taxing accrued but not realized gains on certain assets, most notably stock.[93] All these changes would increase the tax burden on the ultra-wealthy as well as increasing the tax subsidy for charitable contributions. If one was concerned in the current tax environment that the relative contributions by ultra-wealthy donors and the government was skewed too much towards the use of public funds, then changes to increase the income tax burden on the wealthy would exacerbate the problem of wealthy donors deciding how government funds are spent.

III Should tax subsidies be available to support charitable activities outside the United States?

The United States adopted much of the current tax regime covering the tax treatment of charitable entities and the deductibility of charitable contributions at a time when U.S. donors had relatively little interest in foreign charitable activities or entities. Whether Congress would have adopted a similar regime if contributions for foreign charitable activities or to foreign charitable entities played a much greater role in total charitable giving is unknowable. One way to address this question is to start with a baseline of tax subsidies for contributions to domestic charities or domestic charitable activities and then determine whether to extend these subsidies to contributions for foreign charitable activities and to contributions to foreign charitable entities.

A Home field advantage: should we privilege domestic charitable activity over foreign charitable activity?

Consider this thought experiment.[94] Assume the United States and another country (or two countries in the European Union) are identical in every respect, including a currently under-provided public good or quasi-public good (for example, disease prevention programs or university education). Assume also the benefits of the externalities from the public good are enjoyed entirely locally. Should the United States tax its individual and corporate taxpayers to provide the same level of public goods in both countries?

As a matter of domestic tax policy, the answer is probably no. Despite calls by moral philosophers advocating greater cosmopolitan responsibilities, tax and spending policies in the United States are driven by the gains to its citizens and residents rather than to foreign beneficiaries. There is a strong intuitive appeal to helping those closer to us (both geographically and culturally) than those outside our borders. We give greater weight to the utilities of our citizens and residents and discount the utilities of foreigners. If we focus only on the overall welfare of our society (defined by national borders), then the externalities generated by domestic charitable activities will remain in our country, while the externalities from foreign charitable activities accrue to others. Finally, if we view part of the bargain of providing tax benefits for charitable contributions as relieving government of the obligation of providing the goods and services directly, then favoring domestic activities over foreign activities may reduce the demand for domestic government spending.

All of these arguments are subject to strong counterclaims. It is hard to make comparisons between deserving individual recipients in the United States and abroad. Questions as to who are more deserving beneficiaries raise difficult value judgments that are hard to evaluate without some normative framework or political compromise. It is also not clear whether we should take such a narrow view of society in measuring general welfare, especially given the international consequences of many local challenges. Finally, providing tax subsidies for foreign charitable activities may well result in reducing the burden on the U.S. government, as it may allow for less direct U.S. government assistance to foreign countries.[95]

The important observation from the experiment is that if we cannot justify using general tax revenue to fund the foreign charitable activities, we should not use the charitable deduction as a means of providing public goods outside the United States. This provides a strong case for preferring tax benefits for domestic rather than foreign charitable activities.

Relaxing some of the assumptions of this experiment strengthens the case for U.S. tax subsidies for foreign charitable activities. First, let's assume that the U.S. government spending on charitable activities supported by tax subsidies in the other country generates positive externalities for the United States. For example, the foreign spending could result in political and strategic advantages to the United States. This help explains why we provide official development assistance to certain countries and not to others. Similarly, U.S. government spending and charitable activities on health and environmental programs in foreign countries could generate benefits that are global rather than local in nature. For these types of expenditures, a strong case could be made for taxing its individuals and corporations to fund these activities (or providing charitable tax subsidies).

Second, let's relax the assumption as to the two countries being identical. Now substantial differences may exist across countries as to relative income levels, poverty levels, disease prevention, or suffering from natural or man-made disasters. Countries could also differ in the relative success in providing basic services and the relative size and make-up of the charitable sector in both countries. This again presents a much stronger case for U.S. government spending – either directly or through charitable tax subsidies.[96]

How could we determine the optimal split for tax subsidies between domestic and foreign charitable activities? Here is another thought experiment. Assume a philosopher queen could decide how to allocate government charitable tax subsidies, say, $50 billion a year. She could determine which charitable projects merit funding by adopting the approach used by for-profit managers and non-profit grant makers in determining how to allocate resources among competing projects. With information about the costs of the investment, the amount, and timing of potential returns and an appropriate discount rate, grant makers would fund those projects with the greatest returns. So, theoretically, if the philosopher queen had $50 billion a year to spend on charitable projects, she could rank projects from the highest return to the lowest return and fund projects until the funds were exhausted.

If there were only domestic charitable activities, she would only need to rank domestic charitable projects. In a world with both domestic and foreign charitable activity and a policy of not granting preferences to domestic charitable activities over foreign charitable activities, then the process is again a straightforward ranking, with those projects with the highest returns funded without regard to geographical location.

But now assume some or great preference for domestic activity over foreign activity. She would then need to adjust the returns on foreign charitable activity by some factor, ranging from 0 to 1. In an America First world, the factor would be 0. In a world where the location of the charitable activity did not matter, the factor would be 1. Under this approach, a mix of domestic and foreign charitable projects would receive funding, with the relative mix determined by the relative discount applied to foreign projects.

B Overview of foreign charitable activities

Challenges exist in determining the size and scope of foreign charitable activities supported by U.S. donors and U.S. charities. Tables 23.3 and 23.4 seek to provide some sense of the types of foreign charitable activities receiving substantial support.

The National Center for Charitable Statistics has compiled data from the tax returns of U.S. charities to determine which organizations have substantial international activities.

These organizations provide a variety of services (health care, poverty relief, disaster relief, scholarships, environmental, and humanitarian aid). While it is difficult to make

Table 23.3 List of U.S. nonprofits that give the most to foreign charitable activities

	Non-profit	*NTEE classification*	*Grant expenditures*
1	Gavi Alliance	International Relief	$1,470,812,729
2	Food for The Poor, Inc.	International Relief	$866,573,810
3	Direct Relief	International Relief	$794,960,941
4	World Vision	International Relief	$706,466,654
5	Compassion International Incorporated	International Relief	$588,458,666
6	MAP International	International Relief	$576,398,289
7	Catholic Medical Mission Board, Inc.	International Relief	$554,862,050
8	Save The Children Federation, Inc.	International Relief	$498,746,784
9	Population Services International	Scientific Organization	$387,371,578
10	United States Fund for UNICEF	United Nations Association	$365,514,922

Source: National Center for Charitable Statistics (NCCS)

Note: The amounts of grant expenditures presented are derived from responses to question 3(A) in Part IX of the IRS Form 990 filed by each organization for fiscal year 2017 that asks for the total expenses related to "grants and other assistance to foreign organizations, foreign governments, and foreign individuals." The National Taxonomy of Exempt Entities (NTEE) is a classification system for tax-exempt organizations created by the IRS and the NCCS. All organizations on this list fall within the "International, Foreign Affairs, and National Security" NTEE major group area.

Table 23.4 "Friends of" organizations based on grants made to foreign affiliates (2017)

	Non-profit	*NTEE classification*	*Grant expenditures*
1	Cambridge in America	International, Foreign Affairs, and National Security	$78,750,336
2	Friends of The Israel Defense Forces	International, Foreign Affairs, and National Security	$69,042,549
3	American Technion Society	Education	$55,334,498
4	American Friends of The Israel Museum	Arts, Culture, and Humanities	$51,199,921
5	American Friends of The Hebrew University, Inc.	Education	$46,108,488
6	American Associates of Ben-Gurion University of the Negev, Inc.	Education	$37,738,195
7	Americans for Oxford, Inc.	Education	$36,343,411
8	American Friends of Tel Aviv University, Inc.	International, Foreign Affairs, and National Security	$30,194,134
9	American Friends of Magen David Adom	International, Foreign Affairs, and National Security	$19,668,102
10	American Friends of IDC	International, Foreign Affairs, and National Security	$19,055,7530

Source: National Center for Charitable Statistics (NCCS)

Note: This list contains only organizations that are classified by the IRS as organized for the purpose of providing monetary support for either a single entity (11) or multiple entities (12) under the National Taxonomy of Exempt Organized (NTEE). The amounts of grant expenditures presented are derived from responses to question 3(A) in Part IX of the IRS Form 990 filed by each organization for fiscal year 2017 that asks for the total expenses related to "grants and other assistance to foreign organizations, foreign governments, and foreign individuals."

direct comparisons between domestic and international charitable activities, a review of the largest foreign charitable organizations supports the position that international activities better fit traditional notions of charity than the current array of activities of domestic charitable entities.

A different story may emerge if we just focus on "friends of" organizations. Significant challenges exist in identifying which charities are "friends of" organizations if the words "friends of" are not included in the name of the organization. Table 23.4 sets forth a listing of some of the largest "friends of" organizations. Here, donors target contributions to foreign entities that donors may have a more direct affinity (such as educational institutions, cultural organizations, religious organizations, and foreign countries).

For some readers, providing U.S. tax subsidies for contributions to these foreign entities has less appeal. U.S. taxpayer dollars may yield greater returns (at least in the United States) for support of U.S. educational institutions than subsidies for Cambridge, Oxford, and Israeli universities.[97] Similarly, one can make strong arguments for using U.S. government resources for funding for U.S. military veterans rather than members and former members of the Israeli Defense Forces.

Whether these concerns merit differential treatment for contributions related to foreign charitable activities is unclear. For many observers, an advantage of the current charitable tax regime is that it provides donors the ability to direct their funds (and matching federal funds) to those charitable activities they wish to support. Just as it is difficult to compare the relative worthiness of different types of domestic charitable activities, it is hard to compare the relative value of domestic and foreign charitable activities.

Is there an optimal division of tax subsidies between domestic and foreign charitable activities? Assume a country decides to provide $50 billion per year in tax subsidies. How should it divide those subsidies between domestic and foreign charitable activities? Several alternatives exist: we could allocate all the subsidies to domestic charitable activities, allocate between domestic and foreign charitable activities based on some criteria, or allocate by letting donors decide where the subsidies should go. The first and third options are easy to implement. The second option raises a host of challenging issues, such as whether U.S. policymakers should give greater weight to domestic over foreign charitable activities and how to assess the relative "worthiness" of different types of domestic and foreign charitable activities.

Focusing only on foreign charitable activity, Congress could reach a different result in two main ways. First, it could adopt narrower standards for foreign charitable activity than the broad scope allowed for domestic charitable activity. For example, Congress could enact a "worthiness" approach limiting tax subsidies to certain types of activities (poverty reduction and disease prevention) but not to other activities (perhaps religious and cultural). If Congress decides to provide blanket preferences for domestic over foreign charitable activity, it could reduce the tax subsidies for foreign activity (or increase the tax subsidies for domestic activity).

IV Should contribution to foreign charities be treated differently from contributions to U.S. charities?

This section examines whether the United States should treat contributions to foreign charities differently than contributions to domestic charities. It first reviews the legislative history for restricting charitable deductions under the income tax to U.S. charities. It then reviews the different alternatives for structuring contributions to foreign charitable activities or foreign charities to qualify for charitable income tax deduction. Finally, it examines the benefits and costs for allowing direct contributions to foreign charities.

A Geographical limitations

With limited exceptions, U.S. tax law adopts a "water's-edge" policy by allowing donors to deduct for income tax purposes only contributions made to donees created or organized in the United States; or in any possession thereof; or under the laws of the United States, any State, the District of Columbia, or any possession of the United States.[98] The income tax regime initially allowed tax deductions for contributions made to foreign charities.[99] Congress adopted this "place of organization" restriction in 1938.[100] Here is the often-cited passage in the legislative history of the Revenue Act of 1938:

> The exemption from taxation of money or property devoted to charitable or other purposes is based upon the theory that the Government is compensated for the loss of revenue by its relief from financial burdens which would otherwise have to be met by appropriations from public funds and by benefits resulting from the promotion of general welfare. The United States derives no such benefit from gifts to foreign institutions, and the proposed limitation is consistent with the above theory.[101]

Professor Harvey Dale has persuasively described this passage as "bad history, bad philosophy, and bad logic."[102] It is bad history, because there was no Congressional quid pro quo requirement that charitable activities relieve government of an expense before allowing deductibility. Many types of domestic activities that qualify for tax benefits even though the government is not relieved of obligations to provide similar goods or services would not satisfy this requirement. Conversely, because of the current level of private assistance for foreign charitable activities, the U.S. government may be relieved of the burden of providing different types of foreign aid. It is also bad philosophy, as even in the 1930s, this was a narrow view of the world in general and global philanthropy in particular.[103] Finally, it is bad logic. It makes little sense to deny a charitable deduction based on where the entity is organized but to allow charitable deductions to domestic entities that use some or all of their funds outside the United States.[104]

The strongest rationale for requiring a domestic entity as a pass-through for funds sent overseas is to increase accountability and transparency. This allows the IRS and state governments to have some oversight over the activities, even though the funds are spent outside the United States. If deductibility under Section 170 requires the IRS to determine that the contributions are used exclusively for charitable purposes and that no part of the earnings inure to the benefit of any private individual, it is important to have a U.S. intermediary, especially where the IRS lacks the ability and authority to audit activities outside the United States.[105]

Oversight concerns take on added importance in the post-September 11, 2001, world. The use of charitable organizations to support terrorist activities makes the costs of abuses related to foreign charitable activities greater than wasted U.S. tax dollars. While requiring foreign charities to use a U.S.-based intermediary may not be entirely effective in limiting the flow of funds to terrorist organizations, it potentially provides some help in limiting such abuses.[106]

B Options for funding foreign charitable activities and foreign charities through a U.S.-charitable organization

The place of organization restriction merely increases the transaction costs of providing funds for foreign charitable activities and foreign charities. U.S. donors have multiple options to funnel their contributions towards foreign charitable activities and foreign charities:[107]

1 The easiest method is for donors to contribute to U.S. public charities engaged in foreign charitable activities either directly or through making grants to foreign charities;
2 U.S. individuals or corporations can use private foundations to make grants to foreign charities. As discussed earlier, to avoid excise taxes and other penalties, private foundations must either exercise expenditure responsibility or determine that the foreign charity is the equivalent of a Section 501(c)(3) organization;
3 Donor-advised funds present similar opportunities for foreign charitable activities as private foundations. Donors can effectively direct funds to foreign activities and even to foreign charities as long as they exercise expenditure responsibility. Sponsors of donor-advised funds impose different restrictions, but as a practical matter, donors can select a sponsor that will allow them to achieve their objectives;
4 "Friends of" organizations also provide an easy path to fund foreign charitable activities and foreign charities. As long as the organization does not act as a mere conduit, U.S. donors can use these organizations to engage in cross-border philanthropy;
5 Internet and other platforms allow for U.S. donors to choose foreign beneficiaries by effectively using the public charity status of a charitable intermediary. These platforms reduce transaction costs for individuals seeking to fund foreign projects. For example, CAF America, Give2Asia, and GlobalGiving provide individuals with funding opportunities for

education, health, and other types of projects in different countries and may offer foreign charities an opportunity to achieve de facto friends of status.[108]

Because of the availability of these alternatives for funding foreign charitable activity and foreign charities, the tax barriers for cross-country philanthropy are remarkably low. The general rule remains that direct contributions to foreign charities are not deductible for income tax purposes. But the availability of U.S. intermediaries to channel contributions to foreign charities and the ability of private foundations and donor-advised funds to obtain equivalency determinations of U.S. public charity status for foreign charities relatively quickly and inexpensively (through organizations such as NGOsource) means the U.S. regime is more a toll charge for contributions to foreign charity rather than a roadblock.[109]

C Benefits and costs of allowing deductibility for direct contributions to foreign charities

Assume for purposes of this discussion that there were no problems in monitoring the activities of domestic or foreign charities (or that the proportion of charities behaving badly were the same) and that we do not value domestic charitable activity over foreign charitable activity. Under these assumptions, we would want those organizations that were the most efficient providers of charitable services to receive tax subsidies. Many reasons exist why foreign charities would be more effective than U.S. charities in providing assistance in foreign countries. These could include better knowledge of local conditions, lack of language challenges, greater receptivity of beneficiaries to receive assistance from local providers, and lower operating costs. We should want the donations and the matching federal funds to go to the charities that provide the highest-quality assistance. Allowing direct contributions to foreign charities will have the additional benefits of encouraging the growth and development of charitable sectors outside the United States.

Another reason to provide deductibility for contributions to foreign charities is that some foreign countries may have regulatory regimes that are more effective in approving and monitoring charities than the IRS and state attorney generals. For example, the United Kingdom's Charity Commission likely provides more effective oversight of U.K. charitable organizations than U.S. oversight mechanisms.[110]

Allowing direct contributions to foreign charities avoids the complexity and transaction costs of the current regime. Given that it is relatively easy to get around the "place of organization" restriction, why make donors go through this extra step? U.S. charitable intermediaries would no longer collect a percentage of foreign contributions.

There are several potential costs of allowing direct contributions to foreign charities. The most important cost is giving up some or all of U.S. oversight over foreign charitable activity. While there may be incomplete vetting of applications for tax-exempt status and not robust monitoring of charitable activity by the IRS and state officials, there is at least some level of oversight by IRS and state officials. The tax returns (Form 990) provide helpful information in understanding the charities' operations and place oversight responsibility on officers and directors. Having an intermediate U.S. entity will also help in enforcing laws related to anti-terrorist financing and money-laundering. While other countries and organization may have similar measures to address these concerns, it may be in U.S. interests to directly involved in monitoring the activities of foreign charities receiving contributions from U.S. donors.

Several alternatives have been offered to extend tax benefits to foreign charities while minimizing opportunities for abuse.[111] First, foreign charities could apply for the right to receive tax-deductible contributions in the same way they can currently apply for tax-exempt status.[112] Second, the IRS could establish an "approved foreign charity list" of those foreign charities that satisfied certain criteria based on a review by the IRS, the State Department, or some other agency. This approach shares much in common with the current Canadian and Irish systems, where individual taxpayers can deduct contributions to foreign charities as long as the Canadian or Irish government has also contributed to those charities.[113] Third, the existing tax-treaty network could be used to provide for deductibility of contributions to foreign charities on a country-by-country basis. Currently, the United States provides treaty relief for U.S. residents with Canada, Israel, and Mexico.[114] These provisions generally allow U.S. residents to reduce their foreign source income by donations to foreign charities.[115] Finally, we could adopt a "substantial equivalent" approach, where charities in those countries whose charitable regulation meets some minimum guidelines would be eligible to receive deductible contributions.

This last alternative presents both opportunities and challenges. This substantial equivalent approach would reduce barriers to cross-border giving and provide donors greater choices in making charitable contributions. However, this approach may result in competition among countries to attract charitable organizations, not unlike tax competition for foreign investment. Even where countries adopt similar charitable regulation regimes, countries can vary greatly in their appetite for monitoring and enforcing charitable regulations.

V Conclusions

The U.S. regulatory regime provides relatively low tax barriers for U.S. donors to engage in cross-border philanthropy. From the beginning of the charitable deduction, U.S. tax law allowed tax benefits for contributions to domestic charities even if these charities spend some or all of the funds on charitable activities outside the United States (either directly or through grants to foreign entities). Since 1938, U.S. donors generally receive no income tax deductions for contributions made directly to foreign charities.

But the bark is worse than the bite. Donors have many alternatives (with different levels of complexity and administrative costs) to direct funds to foreign charities and still receive U.S. income tax benefits. These include contributions to (i) domestic public charities or private foundations that effectively forward the funds to foreign charities, (ii) "friends of" organizations with affiliated foreign charities, (iii) donor-advised funds with recommendations that the funds be transferred to designated foreign charities, and (iv) different platforms (such as CAF America, Give2Asia, and GlobalGiving) that facilitate transfers to foreign charities at a nominal charge). While the lack of deductibility for direct contributions may increase complexity and administrative costs, requiring a U.S. intermediary provides at least some degree of oversight and accountability for U.S. regulators.

Whether the U.S. charitable tax regime is desirable depends on how the inquiry is framed. One approach looks at the existing rationales for charitable tax subsidies and asks whether meaningful differences exist between domestic and foreign charitable activities and between foreign and domestic charitable entities that justify different tax treatment. Here, one can make a strong argument that the tax law should extend subsidies to foreign charitable activities and to foreign charitable entities (with some mechanism for confirming charitable status and monitoring). The relative strength of the argument depends on how foreign activities and foreign charities fit within the theoretical basis for charitable tax subsidies. Unfortunately, the U.S. lacks a coherent, comprehensive theory on why we should allow charitable tax subsidies for domestic charities engaged in domestic charitable activities. Just as current theories provide little guidance on how to compare the worthiness of different types of charitable domestic activities, they are of limited use in comparing the relative value between domestic charitable activities and entities and foreign charitable activities and entities. It is not surprising we struggle with the proper tax treatment for foreign activities and foreign charities. The current regime allows donors almost complete discretion in determining which countries should benefit from their share of the contributions (the after-tax amount of the contributions) as well as the government's share (the amount of the tax subsidy).

The question then becomes (for both domestic and foreign activities and charitable entities) whether the current charitable regime is the best way to achieve certain societal objectives. In the domestic context, the current regime has produced a robust charitable sector that increases the level of underprovided goods and services and allows donors to direct funds to activities that they believe merit support. Donors do many good things that local or federal government would not, or could not, provide. We can adopt a "take or leave it" approach that asks whether we are better off with the current tax regime than we would be without it. This recognizes a set of trade-offs that reflect decisions made as to which charitable activities deserve tax subsidies, the role of government in granting charitable status and monitoring activities, and the form of these subsidies under the income and estate and gift regimes.

In the foreign context, it is not clear whether the same types of trade-offs would apply and whether the benefits of tax subsidies for foreign activities justify the costs. These differences may support providing tax subsidies for foreign charitable activities and entities but not necessarily in the same form as the current domestic charitable regime.

In both the domestic and foreign context, a "bang for the buck" approach may support proposals for reforming the tax subsidies regimes to maximize returns for government revenues foregone. This requires examining the value of all tax benefits for charitable activity, not just the charitable deduction under the personal income tax. Part of this analysis would focus on who can take advantage of the tax subsidies and the relative contributions of donors and government in funding charitable activities. For both domestic and foreign charitable activities and entities, there may be a "tipping point" whereby the size of the tax subsidies relative to the donors' after-tax contribution no longer justifies allowing donors to determine where and how the matching portion of the government's contributions are spent.

Notes

1 Giving USA estimates that U.S. charitable giving was about $450 billion in 2019. Giving USA Foundation and Indiana University Lilly Family School of Philanthropy, 2020. *Giving USA 2020: The Annual Report on Philanthropy for the Year 2019*. Chicago, IL: Giving USA Foundation, 65. In addition, Americans engaged in about 8.8 billion hours of charitable activity (with a value estimated at $195 billion). Urban Institute, 2020. *The Nonprofit Sector in Brief 2019* [online]. National Center for Charitable Statistics, Urban Institute. Available from: https://nccs.urban.org/publication/nonprofit-sector-brief-2019 [Accessed 20 September 2020].

2 Over 200 wealthy individuals have pledged to donate the majority of their wealth to charities. *The Giving Pledge* [online]. Available from: https://givingpledge.org/ [Accessed 5 October 2020]. The Chronicle of Philanthropy each year publishes a list of the biggest donors. The Chronicle of Philanthropy, 2020. *The Philanthropy 50: Who Gives the Most to Charity* [online]. Washington, DC: The Chronicle of Philanthropy. Available from: https://www.philanthropy.com/specialreport/the-philanthropy-50-who-gives/228 [Accessed 5 October 2020].

3 Global Giving estimates that the amount of foreign donations for 2019 was $29 billion. Adelman, C., Schwartz, B., and Riskin, E., 2017. *Index of Global Philanthropy and Remittances 2016*. Washington, DC: Center for Global Prosperity, Hudson Institute. Available from: https://www.hudson.org/research/13314-index-of-global-philanthropy-and-remittances-2016 [Accessed 21 September 2020]. For cross-country comparisons, see OECD, 2020. *Taxation and Philanthropy*. OECD Tax Policy Series No. 27. Paris, France: Organization for Economic Co-operation and Development, 16–17. Available

from: https://www.oecd-ilibrary.org/taxation/taxation-and-philanthropy_df434a77-en [Accessed 10 January 2021].

4 Bilateral treaties between the United States and these countries allow U.S. citizens and residents to claim foreign charitable deductions against foreign source income. *United States–Canada Income Tax Convention, art. XXI,* 1984. Opened for signature 28 June 1984, entered into force 16 August 1984. Available from: http://www.irs.gov/pub/irs-trty/canada.pdf [Accessed 5 October 2020]; *Convention Between the Government of the United States of America and the Government of the State of Israel With Respect to Taxes of Income*, 1975. Opened for signature 20 November 1975, entered into force 1 January 1995. Available from: http://www.irs.gov/pub/irs-trty/israel.pdf [Accessed 5 October 2020]; *United States – Mexico Income Tax Convention, Art. 22,* 1993. Opened for signatures and entered into force 28 December 1993. Available from: http://www.irs.gov/pub/irs-trty/mexico.pdf [Accessed 5 October 2020].

5 As discussed in Part 1.C, U.S. charities are subject to a host of non-tax requirements, including laws covering counter-terrorism, anti-money laundering, foreign corrupt practices, boycotts, and sanctions. These regimes likely pose a greater barrier to cross-border philanthropy than tax requirements.

6 Dale, H.P., Commentary on Zolt, E.M., 2011. Tax Deductions for Charitable Contributions: Domestic Activities, Foreign Activities, or None of the Above [presentation]. NYU School of Law Colloquium on Tax Policy and Public Finance, 10 March 2011 (on file with the Author).

7 This discussion is adapted from Oh, J., and Zolt, E., 2021. Wealth Tax Design: Lessons from Estate Tax Avoidance. *Tax Law Review*, 74.

8 Dale, H.P., and Colinvaux, R., 2015. The Charitable Contributions Deduction: Federal Tax Rules. *Tax Lawyer*, 68(2), 331–366.

9 I.R.C. §§ 509(a)(1), 509(a)(2)(A) (2006); I.R.C. § 170(b)(1)(A)(i)-(iv) (2018).

10 I.R.C. § 509(a)(2)(B) (2006). A third category of public charity status is for supporting organizations qualifying under I.R.C. § 509(a)(3) (2006).

11 I.R.C. §§ 4940–4948 (2019).

12 The major distinction between the two types of private foundations is how they spend their funds. A private operating foundation must annually spend at least 85% of its investment income on direct charitable expenditures, while a private non-operating foundation must annually distribute at least 5% of its assets in charitable grants and related expenses. *Id.* at § 4942.

13 I.R.C. §§ 4940–4945 (2019).

14 I.R.C. § 4940 (2019).

15 Treas. Reg. § 53.4945–5.

16 Rev. Proc. 2017–53.

17 NGOsource is a project of TechSoup and the Council on Foundations that seeks to increase the level of cross-border philanthropy by facilitating the availability and reducing the cost to private foundations and donor-advised funds of satisfying the equivalency determination requirement. *NGOsource* [online]. Available from: https://www.ngosource.org/ [Accessed 11 November 2020].

18 In 2018, contributions to donor-advised funds exceeded $37 billion, or about 12.7% of individual charitable giving, and assets in donor-advised funds exceeded $120 billion. National Philanthropic Trust, 2019. *2019 Donor-Advised Fund Report.* Jenkintown, PA: National Philanthropic Trust, 7–13.

19 Donor-advised funds are not the only approach that weds the substantial control of private foundation with the benefits of a public charity. Donors can work with an existing charitable organization to set up so-called "supporting organizations," which the Internal Revenue Code establishes as a third category of public charities. These supporting organizations derive their public charity status through their relationship with their supported organization. IRS, 2020. *Supporting Organizations – Requirements and Types* [online]. Washington, DC: Internal Revenue Service. Available from: https://www.irs.gov/charities-non-profits/charitable-organizations/supporting-organizations-requirements-and-types [Accessed 5 October 2020]; see generally Bjorklund, V.B., 2003. *Choosing Among the Private Foundation, Supporting Organization, and Donor-Advised Fund. Charitable Giving Techniques*, Chicago, IL: ALI-ABA, 73.

20 I.R.C. § 4966(d)(2) (2006).

21 Department of the Treasury, 2011. *Report to Congress on Supporting Organizations and Donor Advised Funds.* Washington, DC: Department of the Treasury. Available from: https://www.treasury.gov/resource-center/tax-policy/Documents/Report-Donor-Advised-Funds-2011.pdf [Accessed 20 September 2020]. Traditionally, sponsoring organizations were either community foundations or single-issue charities. Community foundations are charitable organizations with a particular geographic or regional focus. Single-issue charities are organizations formed to promote a single issue, a religion, or an institution. For a good discussion of the different types of donor-advised funds and the growth

in number of funds, grants to charitable institutions, and total contributions to donor-advised funds, see National Philanthropic Trust, 2019. *2019 Donor-Advised Fund Report.* Jenkintown, PA: National Philanthropic Trust. Available from: https://www.nptrust.org/reports/daf-report/ [Accessed 20 September 2020].

22 Hester, M.C., 2008. Donor-Advised Funds: When Are They the Best Choice for Charitably Minded Clients? *Journal of Taxation*, 108(6), 330–346.

23 Feinschreiber, S., 2007. *Smart Giving*. Research Insights Report. Boston: Fidelity Investments. Available from: http://personal.fidelity.com/myfidelity/InsideFidelity/NewsCenter/mediadocs/Smart_Giving_Report.pdf [Accessed 5 October 2020].

24 Treas. Reg. § 53.4945–5(b).

25 For example, the Fidelity Charitable Gift Fund facilitates contributions to foreign charities through CAF America, Give2Asia, Global Giving, and King Baudouin Foundation United States. Fidelity Charitable, 2020. *Giving Internationally* [online]. Available from: https://www.fidelitycharitable.org/private-donor-group/giving-internationally.html [Accessed 6 October 2020].

26 See, for example, *Giving to International Charities* [online]. Schwab Charitable. Available from: https://www.schwabcharitable.org/public/charitable/features/where_to_give/giving_internationally [Accessed 5 October 2020].

27 See generally Dale and Colinvaux, *supra* note 8, Rev. Rul. 66–79, 1966–1 C.B. 48 and Rev. Rul. 74–229, 1974–1 C.B. 142. Bjorklund, V.B., and Reynoso, J.I., 2005. *How a Private Foundation Can Use "Friends of" Organizations* [online]. Council on Foundations. Available from: https://www.cof.org/content/how-private-foundation-can-use-friends-organizations [Accessed 20 September 2020].

28 Rev. Rul. 74–229, 1974–1, C.B. 142.

29 Dale and Colinvaux, *supra* note 8 at 334–335.

30 Bjorklund and Reynoso, *supra* note 27 at 1–2. Tax advisors generally recommend a governance structure whereby U.S. citizens not affiliated with the foreign charity can exercise control.

31 While it is common to have the "American Friends of" in the name of the intermediary organization, it is not required. Therefore, the total number of "friends of" organization is likely greater than those included in the Charity Navigator search. https://www.charitynavigator.org/index.cfm?FromRec=0&keyword_list=american+friends+of&bay=search.results. A high percentage of these organizations are affiliated with religious charities, mostly in Israel.

32 The cost to the foreign charity is an annual fee of $3,500 plus a transaction cost on funds received from U.S. donors and transferred to the foreign charity. For a description of the CAF America friend fund, see CAF America, 2019. *"Friends of" Organization vs. Friends Fund.* Available from: https://www.cafamerica.org/wp-content/uploads/FriendsFundv501c3_CAFAmerica.pdf [Accessed 11 November 2020].

33 Contributions to private operating foundations generally qualify for the same limitations as contributions to public charities. I.R.C. § 4942(j)(3).

34 Section 2204 of the CARES Act amends I.R.C. § 62(a)(22) to provide for a $300 deduction for cash charitable contributions made in 2020 by taxpayers who do not itemize personal deductions. Coronavirus Aid, Relief, and Economic Security Act, Pub. L. No. 116–136, 134 Stat. 281.

35 Section 212 of the Taxpayer Certainty and Disaster Tax Relief Act of 2020 contained within the Consolidated Appropriations Act, 2021 extends and modifies the $300 charitable deduction for non-itemizers for tax year 2021 and increases the maximum amount that may be deducted to $600 for married couples filing jointly. Consolidated Appropriations Act, 2021, Pub. L. No. 116–260, 134 Stat. 1182.

36 For an analysis of how the TCJA reduced the percentage of taxpayers who will claim itemized deductions (including the deduction for charitable contribution), see Tax Policy Center, 2020. Key Elements of the U.S. Tax System [online]. *In: Tax Policy Briefing Book.* Washington, DC: Urban-Brookings Tax Policy Center. Available from: https://www.taxpolicycenter.org/briefing-book/how-did-tcja-change-standard-deduction-and-itemized-deductions [Accessed on 8 October 2020].

37 Halperin, D., 2002. A Charitable Contribution of Appreciated Property and the Realization of Built-in Gains. *Tax Law Review*, 56(1), 1–38; Colinvaux, R., 2013. Charitable Contributions of Property: A Broken System Reimagined. *Harvard Journal of Legislation*, 50(263), 263–329.

38 Donors can deduct the fair market value of "qualified appreciated stock" without reduction for any long-term capital gain that the donor would have recognized on the sale of the stock. I.R.C. § 170(e)(5). For these purposes, qualified appreciated stock is stock traded on an established securities market and donated stock may not be more than 10% of the corporation's outstanding stock.

39 Giving USA, *supra* note 1.

40 Steurle, C.E., *et al.* 2018. *Patterns of Giving by the Wealthy*. Washington, DC: Urban Institute. Available from: https://www.urban.org/research/publication/patterns-giving-wealthy [Accessed 20 September 2020]. For support for the proposition that the estate tax increases both charitable bequests at death and charitable donations during life, see Greene, P., 2009. *Federal Estate and Gift Taxes*. Economic and Budget Issue Brief. Washington, DC: Congressional Budget Office. Available from: https://www.cbo.gov/sites/default/files/111th-congress-2009-2010/reports/12-18-estate_gifttax_brief.pdf [Accessed 5 October 2020] (citing Joulfaian, D., 2009. On Estate Tax Repeal and Charitable Bequests. *Tax Notes*, 123(10), 1221–1229; McClelland, R., and Greene, P., 2004. *The Estate Tax and Charitable Giving*. Washington, DC: Congressional Budget Office. Available from: https://www.cbo.gov/sites/default/files/108th-congress-2003-2004/reports/07-15-charitablegiving.pdf [Accessed 5 October 2020]).

41 Steuerle *et al.*, *supra* note 40, at tbl.4.

42 *Id.* at tbl.5. For estates of all sizes making charitable bequests, the charitable bequests were approximately 20% of total gross assets of the estate.

43 Adelstein, S., and Borise, E.T., 2018. *State Regulation of the Charitable Sector: Enforcement, Outreach, Structure and Staffing*. Washington, DC: Urban Institute. Available from: https://www.urban.org/research/publication/state-regulation-charitable-sector [Accessed 20 September 2020].

44 Office of Foreign Assets Control, 2020. *Specially Designated Nationals and Blocked Persons List*. Washington, DC: U.S. Department of the Treasury. Available from: https://www.treasury.gov/ofac/downloads/sdnlist.pdf [Accessed 9 October 2020]. The U.S. Department of Justice maintains a Terrorist Exclusion List. Bureau of Counterterrorism, 2020. *Terrorist Exclusion List*. Washington, DC: U.S. Department of State. Available from: https://www.state.gov/terrorist-designations-and-state-sponsors-of-terrorism/ [Accessed 20 September 2020]. Both the United Nations and European Union maintain list of suspected terrorists and terrorist organizations. United Nations Security Council, 2020. *United Nations Security Council Consolidated List*. New York: United Nations. Available from: https://scsanctions.un.org/fop/fop?xml=htdocs/resources/xml/en/consolidated.xml&xslt=htdocs/resources/xsl/en/consolidated.xsl [Accessed 20 September 2020]; The Council of the European Union, 2020. *EU Terrorist List*. Brussels: European Council and Council of the European Union. Available from: https://www.consilium.europa.eu/en/policies/fight-against-terrorism/terrorist-list/ [Accessed 20 September 2020].

45 Uniting and Strengthening America by Providing Appropriate Tools Required to Intercept and Obstruct Terrorism (USA PATRIOT ACT) Act of 2001, Pub. L. No. 107–56, 115 Stat. 272.

46 U.S. Department of the Treasury, 2002. *U.S. Department of Treasury Anti-Terrorist Financing Guidelines: Best Practices for U.S.-Based Charities*. Washington, DC: U.S. Department of the Treasury. Following comments from the charitable sector and others on a 2005 revised draft issued for public comments, the Treasury Department issued new, revised guidelines. U.S. Department of the Treasury, 2006. *U.S. Department of Treasury Anti-Terrorist Financing Guidelines: Best Practices for U.S.-Based Charities*. Washington, DC: U.S. Department of the Treasury. Available from: https://www.treasury.gov/resource-center/terrorist-illicit-finance/Pages/protecting-charities-intro.aspx [Accessed 21 September 2020].

47 Silver, N., 2017. *Regulating the Foreign Activities of Charities: A Comparative Perspective*. Edmonton, Alberta: The Pemsel Case Foundation at 14. Available from: https://www.pemselfoundation.org/wp-content/uploads/2017/07/Regulating-the-Foreign-Activities-of-Charities-July-25-2017.pdf [Accessed 11 November 2020]; InterAction, 2018. *InterAction NGO Standards*. Available from: https://www.interaction.org/documents/interaction-ngo-standards/ [Accessed 11 November 2020].

48 This section borrows heavily from Zolt, E.M., 2012. Tax Deductions for Charitable Giving: Domestic Activities, Foreign Activities, or None of the Above. *Hastings Law Journal*, 63(2), 361–410.

49 Andrews, W.D., 1972. Personal Deductions in an Ideal Income Tax. *Harvard Law Review*, 86(2), 309–385 at 313.

50 Bittker, B.I., 1972. Charitable Contributions: Tax Deductions or Matching Grants. *Tax Law Review*, 28(1), 37–64 at 46–49.

51 See generally Gergen, M.P., 1988. The Case for a Charitable Contributions Deduction. *Virginia Law Review,* 74(8), 1393–1450; Kelman, M.G., 1979. Personal Deductions Revisited: Why They Fit Poorly in an "Ideal" Income Tax and Why They Fit Worse in a Far from Ideal World. *Stanford Law Review*, 31(5), 831–884.

52 Pozen, D.E., 2006. Remapping the Charitable Deduction. *Connecticut Law Review*, 39(2), 531–602 at 573.

53 See Gergen, *supra* note 51, at 1396–1406; see also Boadway, R., and Wildasin, D., 1984. *Public Sector Economics*. 2nd ed. Boston: Little, Brown and Company. Market failures could also result from other causes, such as information asymmetries.

54 Weisbrod, B.A., 1972. *Toward a Theory of the Voluntary Non-Profit Sector in a Three-Sector Economy*. Madison, WI: University of Wisconsin; Levmore, S., 1998. Taxes as Ballots. *University of Chicago Law Review*, 65(2), 387–431.

55 *Id.*

56 Schmalbeck, R., 2010. Reforming Uneven Subsidies in the Charitable Sector. *Exempt Organization Tax Review*, 66(3), 237–251.

57 Fleischer, M., 2009. *Theorizing the Charitable Tax Subsidies: The Role of Distributive Justice*. Illinois Law and Economics Research Paper Series No. LE09–006. Champaign, IL: University of Illinois College of Law. Available from: https://papers.ssrn.com/sol3/papers.cfm?abstract_id=1348772 [Accessed 3 November 2020].

58 The level of charitable giving is influenced by price effects (changes in the after-tax cost of giving from changes in tax rates or the design of tax subsidies) and by income effects that affect the income available for charitable donations (economic growth, inflation, and tax rates). These effects may work in opposite directions. Clotfleter, C.T., and Salamon, L.M., 1982. The Impact of the 1981 Tax Act on Individual Charitable Giving. *National Tax Journal*, 32(2), 171–187.

59 Gravelle, J.G., Marples, D.J., and Sherlock, M.F., 2020. *Tax Issues Relating to Charitable Contributions and Organizations*. Washington, DC: Congressional Research Service, R45922 at 14. Available from: https://fas.org/sgp/crs/misc/R45922.pdf [Accessed 21 September 2020]; Urban Institute, *supra* note 1.

60 Colombo, J.D., 2009. The Role of Redistribution to the Poor in Federal Tax Exemption for Charities. *Shades of Virtue: Measuring the Comparative Worthiness of Charities,* 29–30 October 2009 New York. National Center on Law and Philanthropy at 3–4. Available from: https://ncpl.law.nyu.edu/wp-content/uploads/resources/Conf2009JColomboPaper.pdf [Accessed 2 November 2020]; Schmalbeck, R., 2009. Reforming the Charitable Sector to Account for Relative Worthiness? *Shades of Virtue: Measuring the Comparative Worthiness of Charities*, 29–30 October 2009 New York. National Center on Law and Philanthropy. Available from: https://ncpl.law.nyu.edu/wp-content/uploads/resources/Conf2009RSchmalbeckPaper.pdf [Accessed 8 October 2020].

61 Reich, R., 2018. *Just Giving: Why Philanthropy Is Failing Democracy and How It Can Do Better*. Princeton, NJ: Princeton University Press at 84.

62 *Id.* at 93.

63 See, for example, the N.Y. State Attorney General investigation of Trump Foundation. New York State Attorney General, 2019. *Donald J. Trump Pays Court-Ordered $2 Million for Illegally Using Trump Foundation Funds* [press release]. 10 December 2019. Available from: https://ag.ny.gov/press-release/2019/donald-j-trump-pays-court-ordered-2-million-illegally-using-trump-foundation [Accessed 6 October 2020].

64 Charity Navigator, 2020. *Charity Navigator's Methodology* [online]. Available from: https://www.charitynavigator.org/index.cfm?bay=content.view&cpid=5593#rating [Accessed 6 October 2020].

65 Charity Watch, 2021. *Our Charity Rating Process* [online]. Available from: https://www.charitywatch.org/our-charity-rating-process [Accessed 10 January 2021].

66 *GiveWell* [online]. Available from: https://www.givewell.org/ [Accessed 6 October 2020].

67 GiveWell's cost-effectiveness formula provides for GiveWell (and other donors) to make subjective determinations of the relative worthiness of different charitable activities. Their list of top charities reflects a heavy weighting towards disease prevention in low-income countries. GiveWell, 2020. *Top Charities* [online]. Available from: https://www.givewell.org/charities/top-charities?utm_expid=.uFVmrEFITdeqKbE25XDcxA.0&utm_referrer=https%3A%2F%2Fwww.givewell.org%2F [Accessed 6 October 2020].

68 Brody, E., 2007. The Board of Nonprofit Organizations: Puzzling Through the Gaps Between Law and Practice. *Fordham Law Review*, 76(2), 521–566.

69 Ostrower, F., 2007. *Nonprofit Governance in the United States: Findings on Performance and Accountability from the First National Representative Study*. Washington, DC: Urban Institute. Available from: https://www.urban.org/sites/default/files/publication/46516/411479-Nonprofit-Governance-in-the-United-States.PDF [Accessed 21 September 2020]. See also Donatiello, N., Larcker, D.F., and Tayan, B., 2015. *What Can For-Profit and Nonprofit Boards Learn from Each Other About Improving Governance?* Stanford Closer Look Series No. CGRP49. Stanford, C.A.: Rock Center for Corporate Governance

at Stanford University. Available from: https://www.gsb.stanford.edu/sites/default/files/publication-pdf/cgri-closer-look-49-profit-nonprofit-learn.pdf [Accessed 6 October 2020].

70 Klausner, M., and Small, J., 2005. Failure to Govern? The Disconnect Between Theory and Reality in Nonprofit Boards, and How to Fix It. *Stanford Social Innovation Review*, 3(1), 93–100.

71 American Red Cross Board of Governors, 2006. *American Red Cross Governance for the 21st Century*. Washington, DC: American Red Cross. Available from: https://www.redcross.org/content/dam/redcross/atg/PDF_s/Governance/BOGGovernanceReport.pdf [Accessed 21 September 2020].

72 Besinger, K., 2018. *Red Card: FIFA and the Fall of the Most Powerful Men in Sports*. New York: Simon & Schuster, Inc.

73 Challenges exist in comparing charitable sectors across countries because of differences in the size and composition of government social spending programs. One can divide countries into four categories of states (liberal states, social-democratic states, corporatist states, and statist states) depending on the relative size of the welfare state and charitable sector. OECD, *supra* note 3 at 12.

74 Reich, *supra* note 61 at 88–89.

75 Tax Policy Center, 2020. Key Elements of the U.S. Tax System: Who Pays the Estate Tax? [online]. *In: Tax Policy Briefing Book*. Washington, DC: Urban-Brookings Tax Policy Center. Available from: https://www.taxpolicycenter.org/briefing-book/who-pays-estate-tax [Accessed 11 November 2020]. COVID-19 relief legislation provides non-itemizing taxpayers a temporary $300 deduction for cash contribution made in 2020.

76 Congressional Budget Office, 2019. *Projected Changes in the Distribution of Household Income, 2016 to 2021*. Washington, DC: U.S. Congress. Available from: https://www.cbo.gov/publication/55941 [Accessed 21 September 2020].

77 This framework was suggested by Mitchell Kane in his Comment on Zolt, E.M., 2009. 'Tax Aspects of Private Development Assistance' [presentation]. NYU School of Law Rubin International Law Symposium, 4 December 2009 (on file with the Author).

78 Benshalom, I., 2009. The Dual Subsidy Theory of Charitable Deductions. *Indiana Law Journal*, 84(4), 1047–1098; Madoff, R.D., 2010. What Leona Helmsley Can Teach Us About the Charitable Deduction. *Chicago-Kent Law Review*, 85(3), 957–974.

79 See Sanders, M.I., and Roady, C. *Private Expenditures – Tax Expenditures (Sec. 4945)*. Bloomberg Tax Portfolio No. 474. Bloomberg Tax and Accounting. Available from: https://pro.bloombergtax.com/portfolio/private-foundations-taxable-expenditures-sec-4945-portfolio-474/ [Accessed 6 October 2020]; I.R.C. § 4945 (2010).

80 Calculated based on data published by USASpending.gov on awards made by US AID in 2019. This calculation only includes payments of new and continuing grant awards made to entities that were confirmed to be U.S.-based NGOs for charitable projects in foreign locations. USASpending.gov, 2020. *Custom Award Data*. Available from: https://www.usaspending.gov/download_center/custom_award_data [Accessed 10 January 2021]. For a review of U.S foreign assistance activities, see Lawson, M., and Morgenstern, E.M., 2020. *Foreign Aid: An Introduction to U.S. Programs and Policy*. Washington, DC: Congressional Research Service, R40213. Available from: https://crsreports.congress.gov/product/pdf/R/R40213 [Accessed 11 November 2020].

81 The top marginal tax rate exceeds 37% when social insurance taxes and state and local income taxes are included.

82 The Gates Foundation consists of two related entities: the Bill and Melinda Gates Foundation that has responsibility for the operations of the foundation and the Bill and Melinda Gates Foundation Trust that holds and manages the donated investment assets from Bill and Melinda Gates and Warren Buffett. For this discussion, the reference to the Bill and Melinda Gates Foundation refers to the combined entities.

83 OECD, 2018. *Private Philanthropy for Development, The Development Dimension*. Paris, France: Organization for Economic Co-operation and Development, Annex A. Available from: http://dx.doi.org/10.1787/978264085190-en [Accessed 18 October 2021].

84 The Bill and Melinda Gates Foundation's 2019 Annual Report has a section featuring Frequently Asked Questions. Here is a question and answer related to tax benefits for contributions to the foundation:

Q: Do Bill and Melinda get tax breaks for their donation to the foundation?

A: Many individuals enjoy tax benefits because of making charitable contributions. The amount of tax savings depends on both the size of the charitable contribution and the person's annual income.

Bill and Melinda have been exceptionally generous in making contributions to the foundation, donating sums much larger than their annual income. As a result, the tax savings they receive from these contributions represent a very small percentage of the contributions.

Bill & Melinda Gates Foundation, 2020. *Annual Report 2019* [online]. Seattle: Bill & Melinda Gates Foundation. Available from: https://www.gatesfoundation.org/Who-We-Are/Resources-and-Media/Annual-Reports/Annual-Report-2019 [Accessed 21 September 2020].

85 The relative unimportance of the charitable income tax deduction is not uncommon for many ultra-wealthy donors. For example, for 2015, Warren Buffett had an adjusted gross income of $11,565,931 and claimed charitable deductions of $3,469,179. Buffett's charitable contributions for 2015 were about $2.8 billion. Because of Section 170 limitations, the income tax benefits were about 0.12% of total contributions ($3,469,179 divided by $2.8 billion). Reuters Staff, 2016. Buffet Hits Back at Trump Over Tax Comments [online]. *Reuters*. Available from: https://www.reuters.com/article/us-usa-election-buffett/buffett-hits-back-at-trump-over-tax-comments-idUSKCN12A1Z0.

86 A recent report by the Congressional Research Service examines the tax revenue consequences of the tax exemption for investment income. Using data from the IRS, they find that for 2016 tax year, charities had $36.8 billion in investment income, $45.1 billion in net capital gains, $3.9 billion in net rental income and $3.5 billion in royalties. If this income were subject to then 35% corporate tax rate, the U.S. government would have received $31.3 billion of additional tax revenue. Gravelle *et al.*, supra note 59.

87 See Leonard, D., 2020. For Customers Addicted to Stave Puzzles, the Torture Is the Point [online]. *Bloomberg Businessweek,* 13 February. Available from: https://www.bloomberg.com/news/features/2020-02-13/for-some-puzzle-obsessives-getting-tormented-is-the-point [Accessed 11 November 2020].

88 Reich, *supra* note 61 at 14–15.

89 *Id.*

90 Joint Committee on Taxation, 2013. *Present Law and Background Relating to the Federal Tax Treatment of Charitable Contributions*. Washington, DC: Congress of United States; Colinvaux, R., and Madoff, R.D., 2019. Charitable Tax Reform for the 21st Century, *Tax Notes Federal*, 164(12), 1867–1875.

91 See Harris, B.H. et al., 2013. *Analysis of Specific Tax Provisions in President Obama's FY2014 Budget.* Washington, DC: Urban-Brookings Tax Policy Center. Available from: https://www.urban.org/sites/default/files/publication/23611/412817-Analysis-of-Specific-Tax-Provisions-in-President-Obama-s-FY-Budget.PDF [Accessed 11 January 2021].

92 For a summary of former Vice-President Biden's tax proposals, see Biden for President, 2020. *A Tale of Two Tax Policies: Trump Rewards Wealth, Biden Rewards Work* [online]. Available from: https://joebiden.com/two-tax-policies/# [Accessed 2 November 2020]; A comprehensive analysis of the economics effects of the Biden tax proposals is set forth in Mermin *et al.*, 2020. *An Analysis of Former Vice President Biden's Tax Proposals*. Washington, DC: Urban-Brookings Tax Policy Center. Available from: https://www.taxpolicycenter.org/sites/default/files/publication/158624/An_Analysis_of_Former_Vice_President_Bidens_Tax_Proposals_1_2.pdf [Accessed 2 November 2020]. For an overview of proposals to increase taxes on the wealthy, see Batchelder, L.L., and Kamin, D., 2019. *Taxing the Rich: Issues and Options* [online]. Available from: https://papers.ssrn.com/sol3/papers.cfm?abstract_id=3452274 [Accessed 2 November 2020].

93 Wyden, R., 2019. *Treat Wealth Like Wages*. Washington, DC: Senate Finance Committee. Available from: https://www.finance.senate.gov/imo/media/doc/Treat%20Wealth%20Like%20Wages%20RM%20Wyden.pdf [Accessed 2 November 2020].

94 Kane, *supra* note 77.

95 Giving preference to domestic, rather than foreign, altruism for revenue reasons is also not clear cut. If the revenue cost from charitable contributions is considered too large, it is not obvious without some normative framework that the place to start chopping is support for foreign charitable activities. The U.S. generally provides the same tax benefits to all types of charitable activities, even though one could imagine a regime where certain activities that generate higher levels of societal benefits (through greater externalities) receive greater tax benefits than activities where most of the benefits are captured by those making the contributions.

96 Even if we decide as a matter of tax policy not to extend the charitable deduction to foreign charitable activities, this does not mean that there is no role for government's use of tax benefits to support foreign charitable activities. Assume, for example, the U.S. government decides to provide $1 billion in funding in 2020 for humanitarian aid to victims of the Beirut explosion. We could choose to provide the $1 billion directly through direct foreign assistance funded out of general tax revenue, or allow charitable deductions at a revenue cost of $1 billion to subsidize private assistance efforts in Lebanon. The question then becomes which alternative (or combination of the two) yields the greatest benefit – both in terms of choice of projects and the quality of the outputs.

97 Similar arguments apply in the domestic context. The U.S. provides about $10 billion of charitable tax expenditures for contributions to U.S. educational institutions, with a large share going to Harvard,

Yale, Stanford, and UCLA rather than more financially challenged universities, colleges, and junior colleges.

98 The limitation applies even if the foreign charity qualifies for tax exemption under I.R.C. §501(c)(3).

99 Dale, H.P., 1995. Foreign Charities. *Tax Lawyer*, 48(3), 655–704 at 660.

100 *Id.*

101 HR Rep. No. 75–1860, at 19–20 (1938).

102 Dale, *supra* note 99, at 660–662; Pozen, *supra* note 52 at 542–546.

103 *Id.*

104 Rev. Rul. 71–460, 1971–2 C.B. 231 provides that "a [domestic corporation's] activities are charitable within the meaning of section 501(c)(3) of the Code when carried on within the United States, the conduct of such activities elsewhere does not preclude the organization form qualifying as an exempt organization under that section."

105 Wiedenbeck, P.J., 1985. Charitable Contributions: A Policy Perspective. *Missouri Law Review*, 50(1), 85–139.

106 See note 46, *supra.*

107 In addition to these five alternatives, other options exist, including having U.S. charities engaging in foreign charitable activity by setting up a foreign charity. Borrowing from the U.S. international tax-planning toolkit, the U.S. entity can elect to treat the foreign entity as a disregarded entity under the "check-the box" regulations. For U.S. tax purposes, the foreign entity is disregarded, even though under foreign law, the foreign entity is treated as a separate entity. For a discussion of the use of a "disregarded" foreign subsidiary charity in cross-border philanthropy, see Lewin, C. and Moran, C., 2019. *Charity Abroad: U.S. Donors' Options for International Philanthropy* [online]. Venable, LLP. Available from: https://www.venable.com/insights/publications/2019/07/charity-abroad-us-donors-options-for-international [Accessed 21 September 2020].

108 See, for example, GlobalGiving [online]. Available from: http://www.globalgiving.org/ [Accessed 6 October 2020].

109 For foreign charities that cannot qualify for equivalency to a U.S. public charity, contributions may qualify for deductibility for income tax purposes if the private foundation or donor-advised fund exercises expenditure responsibility.

110 Davis, K.E., and Gelpern, A., 2010. Peer-to-Peer Financing for Development: Regulating the Intermediaries. *NYU Journal of International Law and Politics*, 42(4), 1209–1268 at 1261–63.

111 Pozen, *supra* note 52, at 594–596.

112 Foreign charities currently can apply for tax-exempt status in the U.S. to qualify for certain Federal, state and local tax benefits.

113 See Canada Revenue Agency, 2010. *Gifts to Certain Charitable Organizations Outside Canada.* Income Tax Information Circular No. IC84–3R6. Ottawa: Canada Revenue Agency. Available from: https://www.canada.ca/content/dam/cra-arc/formspubs/pub/ic84-3r6/ic84-3r6-e.pdf [Accessed 6 October 2020].

114 See note 4, *supra.*

115 If this alternative is adopted, then the benefits could be expanded by relaxing limitations with respect to foreign source income.

24

REMOVING TAX BARRIERS TO CROSS-BORDER PHILANTHROPY

Lessons from Australia

Natalie Silver

I Introduction

Australia offers a tax deduction to encourage philanthropy, making charitable gifts less expensive for donors than they would be otherwise. Until quite recently, this tax incentive generally did not extend to cross-border philanthropy,[1] notwithstanding its significance for Australian charities[2] engaged in international charitable activities. The Australian government's justification for this strict approach derived from policy concerns relating to the fiscal consequences of extending tax concessions to cross-border donations and the potential for charities operating overseas to be misused for terrorist financing and other criminal purposes (Silver, McGregor-Lowndes and Tarr, 2016, pp. 85, 109–113). As a result of this policy position, Australian donors were subject to one of the most restrictive legal regimes among OECD donor countries for the tax treatment of cross-border philanthropy.

Ironically, instead of ensuring that the benefits of these charitable tax subsidies remained in Australia, the government's restrictive approach enabled largely unregulated tax deductible cross-border giving to take place through giving intermediaries. During this period, the government's insufficient oversight and monitoring of cross-border charity and philanthropy was highlighted by the Financial Action Task Force (FATF), an intergovernmental body that promotes the implementation of measures for combating terrorist financing and money laundering in compliance with its recommendations.[3] In an evaluation of Australia's domestic regulation of charities operating overseas, FATF found that Australia's supervisory framework for nonprofits was wanting, leaving them "vulnerable to misuse by terrorist organisations" (FATF and APG, 2015, p. 16).

Confronted with these regulatory shortcomings, combined with an increased number of Australian charities – almost 5,000 or 10 percent – operating and transferring funds overseas, (Australian Charities and Not-for-profits Commission, 2018, p. 8),[4] the government was forced to reconsider its regulation of cross-border charity. In doing so, changes were proposed to the regulatory regime governing international charitable activities. These changes included new tools to regulate charities operating and transferring funds overseas as part of a reform package introduced to "strengthen governance arrangements, reduce administrative complexity and ensure continued trust and confidence in the sector" (O'Dwyer, 2017).

 DOI: 10.4324/9781003139201-28

At the same time, as a result of two judicial decisions challenging the legislative efficacy of the geographic restrictions placed around Australia's charitable tax concessions, the government decided to change policy course, culminating in a new tax ruling reflecting a more permissive approach to the tax treatment of cross-border donations (Australian Taxation Office, 2019). While the government did not provide a rationale for this policy shift, its new approach represented a change in the longstanding justification for the provision of a tax deduction for charitable gifts. In Australia, the gift deduction is characterised as a government subsidy to promote charitable activities having a public benefit (Krever, 1991, pp. 1, 5). The subsidy was justified in that it supported the domestic charitable sector provide public goods that would otherwise need to be provided by the fiscal state (Krever, 1991, p. 5; Stewart, 2014, pp. 251–252). This traditional rationale corresponds to a narrow conception of public benefit in the tax law, confining it to the fiscal state.

With a less restrictive approach to the tax treatment of cross-border donations, a more geographically expansive conception of public benefit is possible that recognises the growth in Australian cross-border charitable activities. Indeed, an Australian inquiry into the definition of charities found that "public benefit is a universal concept and cannot be contained within the boundaries of any country" (Sheppard, Fitzgerald and Gonski, 2001, p. 257). Under this pluralist rationale, the gift deduction can be justified as supporting the decentralised provision of public goods through a diverse charitable sector wherever that may be (Reich, 2011, pp. 187–190; Stewart, 2014, pp. 251–252). As a result, the public benefitting from the gift deduction can be justified as extending beyond Australia's borders to the wider global community.

This chapter examines the removal – albeit incomplete – of some of Australia's tax barriers to cross-border philanthropy. Part II focuses on the evolution of the legislative architecture governing Australian cross-border philanthropy and identifies important changes to the regulatory regime that accompanied these developments. Part III employs the traditional tax policy criteria of efficiency, equity and simplicity to evaluate the Australian's government's shift to a less restrictive approach to the tax treatment of international giving. Part IV concludes by considering how the Australian experience can inform other governments seeking to reform their own tax and regulatory regimes affecting cross-border philanthropy.

II Legislative architecture governing cross-border philanthropy

Australia provides a deduction to its taxpayers as an incentive to encourage philanthropic giving. To be eligible to receive tax-deductible donations,[5] an Australian organisation must obtain deductible gift recipient (DGR) status and be registered with the Australian Charities and Not-for-profits Commission, Australia's national charity regulator [Australian Charities and Not-for-profits Commission Act 2012 (Cth) s 10–5]. Most DGRs are charities, although less than 40 percent of charities are DGRs (Australian Charities and Not-for-profits Commission, 2018, p. 27).[6] Charities are defined in s 5 of the Charities Act 2013 (Cth) as not-for-profit organisations established for charitable purposes that are for the public benefit. The concept of public benefit is central to the legal definition of charity, derived from the seminal English case, *Commissioners for Special Purposes of Income Tax v Pemsel* ([1891] AC 531 (Lord Macnaghten)). The charitable purposes enumerated in s 12 of the Charities Act 2013 (Cth) are reflected in the broad categories of deductible gifts contained in the income tax legislation, each of which contains "special conditions" (ITAA 1997, div 30).

One of the special conditions that must be met to achieve DGR status is that an organisation must be "in Australia" (ITAA 1997, s 30–15). However, the tax legislation does not provide a definition of "in Australia" for the purposes of this residency requirement. Instead, the

Australian Tax Office, which is responsible for administering and enforcing tax law for charities and other not-for-profits, has issued public tax rulings to explain the meaning of the "in Australia" residency requirement for DGRs.

A longstanding restrictive approach to the tax treatment of cross-border donations

For more than 50 years, the Australian Tax Office interpreted the "in Australia" residency requirement for DGRs strictly. The policy imperatives underlying this restrictive approach to the tax treatment of cross border donations were to protect the national tax base by ensuring that publicly-funded tax concessions are used for the broad benefit of the Australian community and to prevent non-profit organisations being used for tax abuse purposes of money laundering, offshore avoidance arrangements and terrorist financing [Explanatory Memorandum, Tax Laws Amendment (Special Conditions for Not-for-profit Concessions) Bill 2012 (Cth), pp. 5–12; Explanatory Materials, Exposure Draft: Tax Laws Amendment (2014 Measures No #) Bill 2014 (Cth), pp. 5–12].

The Australian Tax Office's strict interpretation of the "in Australia" residency requirement for DGRs was set out in a public tax ruling for a common sub-type of charity in Australia known as public benevolent institutions (Australian Taxation Office, 2003, para 129). Public benevolent institutions provide direct services to those in need of benevolent relief or raise funds for the purpose of providing benevolent relief [Australian Charities and Not-for-profits Commission Act 2012 (Cth) s 25–5(5) column 2, item 6]. They encompass organisations whose purpose it is to relieve poverty, sickness, suffering or disability. The Australian Tax Office's "in Australia" ruling for public benevolent institutions stated that for a public benevolent institution to be endorsed as a DGR it was required to be "in Australia", such that it "must be established, controlled, maintained and operated in Australia and its benevolent purposes must be in Australia" (Australian Taxation Office, 2003, para 128). The tax ruling further clarified that because the purpose of a public benevolent institution was to provide direct relief to persons in need, "this will mean that relief will be provided to people located in Australia" (Australian Taxation Office, 2003, para 129).

In practical terms, the result of this "in Australia" tax ruling was that donations by Australian taxpayers made directly to a charity outside Australia were never tax deductible. It also meant that donations made to an Australian DGR to use the gift for its own programs outside Australia were also not tax deductible, unless such activities were relatively minor or incidental to the organisation's Australian operations (Australian Taxation Office, 2003, para 130). Importantly, some limited exceptions to the "in Australia" residency requirement for DGRs are contained in the tax legislation. An organisation can obtain DGR status and use tax deductible donations for its activities outside Australia if it establishes an overseas aid fund undertaking development and humanitarian activities, a developed country disaster relief fund or a public fund on the Register of Environmental Organisations or if it is specifically listed by name in the tax legislation under the category of international affairs (ITAA 1997 ss 30–55, 30–80, 30–85). However, due to the high entry barriers resulting from initial heavy vetting, relatively few organisations have obtained DGR status through one of these purposefully limited exceptions (Silver, McGregor-Lowndes and Tarr, 2016, pp. 96–103).

Australia's restrictive approach to the provision of tax incentives for cross-border philanthropy was significant when compared to other OECD donor countries. A comparative analysis of the tax laws and policies governing cross-border philanthropy in the functionally comparable jurisdictions of Belgium, Canada, France, Germany, Japan, Luxembourg, the

Netherlands, Spain, the United Kingdom and the United States revealed that Australia's use of domestic tax policy to place geographic barriers around charitable tax relief for donors located it at the most restrictive end of the spectrum of approaches to the tax treatment of cross-border donations. At the other, most permissive, end of the spectrum was The Netherlands, which applies the same tax treatment to domestic and cross-border donations by allowing the registration of eligible foreign entities as Dutch charities. Other countries at the restrictive end of the spectrum are those which, like Australia, have tax laws with "in country" residency requirements, including Canada, Japan and the United States. However, because these jurisdictions generally permit a tax deduction for cross-border donations made indirectly through domestic charities, they were classified as less restrictive than Australia (Silver and Buijze, 2020, pp. 119–122).

In addition to limiting the ability of Australian donors seeking to obtain a tax deduction for donations directed overseas, the Australian Tax Office's longstanding interpretation of the "in Australia" residency requirement for DGRs had other unintended consequences. With few options for engaging in tax-effective overseas giving, many Australian nonprofit organisations and their donors resorted to using workarounds to channel tax-deductible funds abroad. This was achieved by using organisations that had obtained DGR status pursuant to one of the limited exceptions to the "in Australia" residency requirement as giving intermediaries (Australian Bureau of Statistics, 2015, table 10.1).[7] These channelling arrangements, involving a servicing fee being paid to the intermediary DGR,[8] created a workaround for organisations and their donors, enabling them to circumvent the strict "in Australia" residency requirement for DGRs in order to engage in tax-effective cross-border charitable activities (Silver, McGregor-Lowndes and Tarr, 2016, pp. 95, 103). In doing so, this fee-paying workaround compromised the government's ability to regulate cross-border charity through the tax laws. This in turn made monitoring cross-border charitable flows far more difficult and increased the risks that these funds could be used for tax abuse and terrorist financing purposes.

The Australian government's inadequate oversight and supervision of cross-border charity was exposed in a report by FATF, which assesses terrorist financing vulnerabilities and threats faced specifically by the nonprofit sector through its Recommendation 8. This Recommendation serves as an international policy standard influencing the domestic regulation of charities operating overseas. In its evaluation report of Australia in 2015, FATF rated Australia "non-compliant" with Recommendation 8, finding that Australia had "not implemented a targeted approach nor [had] it exercised oversight in dealing with nonprofit organisations that are at risk from the threat of terrorist abuse" (FATF, 2015, p. 6).

During this period where the efficacy of the "in Australia" residency requirement for DGRs was being scrutinised internationally, the government's restrictive position on this issue was also being challenged in the Australian courts. A landmark decision of the High Court of Australia in *Federal Commissioner of Taxation v Word Investments Ltd* (2008) 236 CLR 204 considered the "in Australia" residency requirement for income tax exemption, which differs slightly to that for DGRs. The Court found that this requirement did not mean that charitable funds transferred through a suitably qualified charitable intermediary needed to be expended in Australia; it only imposed a requirement that the charitable intermediary incur its expenditure and pursue its objectives principally in Australia (p. 239 [73]). This decision was affirmed in *Federal Commissioner of Taxation v The Hunger Project Australia* (2014) 221 FCR 302, where the issue was whether Hunger Project Australia qualified as a public benevolent institution in Australia. Hunger Project Australia was part of a global network of entities whose purpose was to relieve hunger in developing countries. While Hunger Project Australia was primarily a fundraising arm for other Hunger Project entities engaged in the direct provision of hunger relief outside

Australia, the organisation had some involvement in global and program decision-making. The Federal Court of Australia found that despite the fact that Hunger Project Australia did not itself directly give or provide relief but rather did so via its related entities, it nonetheless qualified as a public benevolent institution and was therefore eligible to apply for income tax exemption and DGR status (p. 314 [67]).

These two judicial decisions had significant implications for the Australian Tax Office's strict interpretation of the "in Australia" residency requirement for DGRs. By interpreting the "in Australia" residency requirement for income tax-exempt entities as not mandating that the ultimate purposes or beneficiaries be in Australia, these decisions suggested that, similarly, an organisation's purposes or beneficiaries may not need to be "in Australia" to qualify for DGR status.

A new less restrictive approach to the tax treatment of cross-border donations

Faced with both legal and practical challenges to its longstanding interpretation of the "in Australia" residency requirement for DGRs, in 2017, the Australian Tax Office withdrew its "in Australia" public tax ruling for public benevolent institutions (Australian Taxation Office, 2017). At the same time, the Australian Tax Office cited a statement issued by the Commissioner of the Australian Charities and Not-for-profits Commission that an organisation "is not precluded from being registered as a [public benevolent institution] subtype of charity if it has a main purpose of providing benevolent relief to people residing overseas" (2016, s 5.8). This was followed by an announcement that the Australian Tax Office would be issuing a new public tax ruling on the "in Australia" residency requirement for DGRs and income tax-exempt entities (Australian Taxation Office, 2018).

The new public tax ruling was issued in December 2019. This tax ruling is not limited to public benevolent institutions. Instead it is concerned with DGRs and income tax-exempt entities more broadly. The tax ruling states that a DGR satisfies the "in Australia" residency requirement for DGRs in the tax legislation so long as it is "established or legally recognised in Australia, and makes operational or strategic decisions mainly in Australia" (Australian Taxation Office, 2019, para 7). Importantly, there is no requirement that the organisation's purposes or beneficiaries be in Australia. The practical result of this new tax ruling is that while donations by Australian taxpayers made directly to a charity outside Australia are still not tax deductible, donations made to a qualified Australian DGR to use the gift for its own programs and those of its eligible related entities outside Australia are now tax deductible, provided that organisation's operational or strategic decisions occur "mainly in Australia" (Australian Taxation Office, 2019, paras 19, 35).[9] With this less restrictive approach to the provision of tax incentives for international philanthropy, Australia's location on the tax treatment of cross-border giving spectrum has shifted further towards the permissive end of the spectrum, albeit far from The Netherlands' equivalency ideal.

In the intervening years, while the charitable sector in Australia awaited the new public tax ruling, Australian organisations and their donors took advantage of the legal vacuum that existed by establishing public benevolent institutions with DGR status for the purpose of sending funds and engaging in charitable activities outside Australia.[10] By the end of 2017, approximately 10 percent of all charities in Australia reported operating overseas (Australian Charities and Not-for-profits Commission, 2018, p. 8),[11] a significant increase from approximately 6 percent of all charities in 2013 (Cortis et al., 2016, p. 11). More than three-quarters of these charities reported transferring funds overseas (Powell et al., 2017, p. 11). The rise in Australian charities operating and sending funds outside Australia signified the need for increased regulatory oversight and monitoring of these organisations.

New regulatory tools governing cross-border charitable activities

The Australian government responded to the criticism it had received from FATF in 2015 by conducting a national risk assessment into the charitable sector (AUSTRAC, 2017). The risk assessment found that while there were few proven instances of money laundering and terrorism financing – consistent with other assessments (AUSTRAC, 2014; AUSTRAC, 2016) – there remained a "medium" risk level of organisations being misused for such purposes (AUSTRAC and Australian Charities and Not-for-profits Commission, 2017, p. 39). Recommendations from the risk assessment focused on measures to strengthen the oversight and monitoring of international charitable activities. FATF conducted a follow-up report in 2018 analysing Australia's progress in implementing new requirements relating to recommendation 8 (FATF, 2018). In the period between its two reports on Australia, FATF amended Recommendation 8, emphasising the need for governments to adopt "effective and proportionate measures commensurate to the risks identified through a risk-based approach that respects countries' obligations under the Charter of the United Nations and international human rights law" (FATF, 2016, pp. 54–55).[12] FATF's follow-up report concluded that Australia was "largely compliant" with the revised Recommendation 8, citing the comprehensive risk assessment Australia had taken of its nonprofit sector. However, the report also noted "concerns that some smaller charities, which are identified as potentially higher-risk, are not subject to adequate monitoring" (FATF, 2018, p. 6), signalling that changes to Australia's regulatory framework governing these organisations were required.

To ensure compliance with its international obligations under FATF Recommendation 8 and to address the concomitant rise in Australian charities operating overseas, the Australian government undertook an assessment of the regulatory regime governing cross-border charity, resulting in a DGR reform package (The Treasury, 2018). The Australian Charities and Not-for-profits Commission has had a range of regulatory tools at its disposal, provided for in the Australian Charities and Not-for-profits Commission Act 2012 (Cth), including registration and reporting requirements, governance standards, penalties for non-compliance and revocation of charitable status. However, the DGR reform package introduced new tools specifically for regulating the sub-sector of charities with DGR status that operated outside Australia.

The most significant new reform measure introduced to strengthen the oversight and monitoring of cross-border charitable activities was the issuance of external conduct standards, which came into effect in 2019 [Australian Charities and Not-for-profits Commission Amendment (2018 Measures No. 2) Regulations 2018]. While Australia's charity legislation had made provision for external conduct standards since the inception of the Australian Charities and Not-for-profits Commission in 2012, these standards were only developed and implemented as part of the DGR reform package in 2018.

The regulations adopted to implement the external conduct standards stated that the objectives are

> to provide greater confidence that funds sent, and services provided, outside Australia are reaching legitimate beneficiaries and are being used for legitimate purposes . . . and to prevent a registered entity from being misused by a criminal organization.
>
> *(s 50.1)*

Pursuant to the regulations, the external conduct standards apply to a registered entity if it operates outside Australia or works with third parties that operate outside Australia, unless its overseas activities are "merely incidental" to its operations and pursuit of its purposes in Australia (s 50.4). There are four external conduct standards, which require charities engaging in cross-border charitable activities to appropriately manage their overseas activities and control of resources (s. 50.20), conduct an annual review of their overseas activities on a country-by-country basis (s 50.25), ensure they have appropriate anti-fraud and anti-corruption measures in place (s 50.30) and protect vulnerable individuals outside Australia from exploitation or abuse (s 50.35).

These external conduct standards combined with the new "in Australia" tax ruling represent an opportunity for the Australian government to provide the necessary regulatory oversight and monitoring of cross-border charity to facilitate legitimate cross-border charitable flows. The next section analyses Australia's new approach to cross-border charitable activities utilising normative tax policy considerations that inform policy-making across jurisdictions.

III Tax policy analysis

A review of the Australian tax system found it to be generally "accepted that a well-designed tax system will meet its revenue raising objective, while balancing the core principles of equity, efficiency and simplicity" (The Treasury, 2015, p. 14). Reform of domestic tax laws are frequently shaped by these traditional tax policy concerns of equity, economic efficiency and simplicity of administration and compliance (Graetz, 1995, p. 609; O'Connell, 2008, p. 19). With a new interpretation by the Australian Tax Office of the "in Australia" residency requirement for DGRs, it is worthwhile considering how the current legislative architecture for the tax treatment of cross-border giving in Australia holds up against these tax policy considerations.[13] The following tax policy analysis evaluates the benefits of the gift deduction as it applies to cross-border donations against the potential inequities, inefficiencies and complexities the deduction might produce.

Equity

There are two conceptions of equity to be considered when evaluating a national tax system: horizontal equity and vertical equity. The former involves the idea that "people with equal ability to pay taxes pay equal amounts of tax", while the latter is concerned that "those with greater ability to pay, pay more" (Graetz, 1995, p. 610). For domestic donations, the gift deduction is generally seen as satisfying horizontal equity because taxpayers with a similar capacity to pay are treated the same. For example, in Australia, taxpayers in the highest tax bracket of 49 percent each pay 51 cents after tax for each dollar donated, while taxpayers in the lowest 19 percent bracket each pay 81 cents. However, the gift deduction has been criticised on vertical equity grounds for decreasing the equity of the tax system. This is because progressive rates of personal income tax result in the deduction having greater value for those taxpayers on higher incomes (Australia's Future Tax System Review Panel, 2010, p. 726). The result is an "upside down effect" whereby the wealthier the donor, the less a charitable gift costs (Krever, 1991, pp. 219–220; Gergen, 1988, p. 1405). This inequity is compounded given that higher-income taxpayers are allocated more of the tax subsidy, as they have the resources to make larger donations compared to lower-income taxpayers. Vertical inequity can therefore be seen as a "critical flaw" of the gift deduction that renders it "at best, 'undemocratic' and at worst unacceptably elitist" (Krever, 1991, p. 21).

Applying these concepts of horizontal and vertical equity to cross-border donations requires a further level of analysis. Horizontal equity is arguably not achieved if the gift deduction is only available for donors in the same tax bracket who choose to give domestically but not for those whose donations are directed internationally. Instead, equal tax treatment for domestic and cross-border donations would be required. While Australia's more permissive approach to the tax treatment of cross-border donations does not meet this horizontal equity ideal in that gifts made directly to foreign charities are still not tax deductible, it does create greater horizontal equity than existed under the government's more restrictive approach. This is because the Australian Tax Office's new interpretation of the "in Australia" residency requirement for DGRs allows a deduction for Australian taxpayers in the same tax bracket for gifts made to qualified Australian charities that operate abroad.

An additional consideration for vertical equity is whether a higher level of income has a significant effect on the likelihood of giving internationally. This would make Australia's more permissive approach to the tax treatment for cross-border donations arguably more justifiable. In Australia, income has been shown to have a negative correlation with support for foreign aid and is not statistically significant for private donations to aid organisations. Instead, tertiary education is the strongest positive socio-economic determinant of both support for foreign aid and private donations to aid organisations (Wood, Humphrey Cifuentes and Pryke, 2014). This is consistent with studies in other jurisdictions (Casale and Baumann, 2015, p. 117; Micklewright and Schnepf, 2009, p. 335; Wiepking, 2010, p. 1081). As a result, even with a new interpretation by the Australian Tax Office of the "in Australia" residency requirement for DGRs, vertical equity issues remain.

Beyond the conceptions of horizontal equity and vertical equity which focus on a national tax system, equity can also be considered from a broader perspective that extends beyond national borders. Under this broader view, a generous tax deduction for cross-border donations may reduce global inequities given that most cross-border giving from wealthy countries is directed to developing countries (Roodman and Standley, 2006, pp. 5–6). This redistributive effect "might have especially powerful welfare effects for the world's most disadvantaged" (Pozen, 2006, p. 583). Australia's more permissive approach to the tax treatment of cross-border giving has the potential to assist in reducing global inequities as more charitable funds are redistributed from Australia to poorer countries.

Efficiency

The gift deduction is widely viewed as a government subsidy or tax expenditure, the fiscal equivalent of a direct government spending program, because it "triggers a reduction of taxable income and, as a result, a tax saving, that would not be available in a benchmark income tax system which treated charitable gifts similarly to all other gifts or uses of income" (Krever, 1991, p. 5). Because of the tax savings arising from gift deductibility, the donor does not bear the entire cost of the gift, and the government forgoes tax revenue. This raises the question of whether the gift deduction is a cost-effective way to subsidise charitable organisations. Economic (or treasury) efficiency is concerned with understanding whether the public benefit derived from the gift deduction exceeds the costs of the subsidy – specifically, whether a dollar of forgone taxes creates at least an extra dollar of charitable donations or (if not) whether the subsidy should be replaced with direct spending (Colinvaux, Galle and Steuerle, 2012, p. 8).

One measure of whether the gift deduction is efficient in encouraging donors to give to charity is to consider the price elasticity of giving. If giving is price elastic, then lowering the price of giving through tax incentives can potentially increase both the amount donated and the number of individuals donating (Simon, Dale and Chisolm, 2006, p. 272; Colinvaux, Galle and Steuerle, 2012, p. 9). On the other hand, if giving is price inelastic, then the tax deduction is an inefficient way to fund charitable organisations. On balance, empirical studies indicate that the price elasticity of giving has absolute value greater than one, at least among individuals with high incomes (Gergen, 1988; Peloza and Steel, 2005; Bakija and Heim, 2011; List, 2011). Indeed, high top marginal tax rates in Australia suggest that for wealthy taxpayers, the gift deduction would have a significant impact on giving (McGregor-Lowndes and Crittall, 2015, pp. 7, 61). While there have not been studies to determine the price elasticity of cross-border giving, one comparative study of charitable giving to developing countries found that individuals in countries with targeted income tax incentives give more to developing countries (Roodman and Standley, 2006, p. 35). This suggests that the gift deduction may be a cost-effective way to subsidise international charitable activities.

Whether a tax deduction for cross-border donations increases economic efficiency also depends on the wider social objectives of the deduction and the scope of the public who should benefit. The Australian government historically took a narrow view of treasury efficiency, largely confining the benefits of the deduction to the Australian public. According to this view, a generous deduction for cross-border donations would decrease treasury efficiency within Australia due to the consequences for the public purse. However, with the government's shift in policy and a new interpretation of the "in Australia" residency requirement for DGRs, a broader view of economic efficiency appears to have been adopted pursuant to which a deduction for cross-border donations is economically efficient in its cost-effective delivery of support to beneficiaries overseas. Under this broader view of treasury efficiency, it is also arguable that globally net social welfare will be increased with a more permissive approach to the tax deductibility of cross-border donations (Pozen, 2006, p. 580). Indeed, all Australians stand to benefit from cross-border gifts that fund organisations involved in the production of global public goods, such as medical breakthroughs associated with the development of vaccinations for COVID-19 or solutions for the climate change crisis. In such situations, the Australian government receives a return or benefit for the public funds expended.

Simplicity

Tax laws should be simple for taxpayers to comply with and for administrators to implement (Graetz, 1995, p. 609). Tax expenditures such as the gift deduction "can add complexity to the tax system [in that they] complicate the law and create additional choices for people" (Australia's Future Tax System Review Panel, 2010, p. 726). A recurring theme in the Australian nonprofit tax literature is criticism of the not-for-profit tax concessions for their complexity (O'Connell, 2008, pp. 19–20). For example, not only is the process for obtaining deductible gift recipient status in Australia complicated, "there are five initial categories of recipient and then a further 14 categories (different to the categories for income tax exemption) that each have a general category and a specific category for specifically listed entities" (O'Connell, 2021, p. 30). Such complexity is not surprising given that the charitable tax concessions in Australia developed by way of "ad hoc decision-making" rather than "considered policy analysis" (O'Connell, 2021, p. 36).

When applied to cross-border donations, the complexity surrounding the gift deductibility provisions generally increases. In Australia, the complex legislative architecture governing the tax treatment of cross-border donations had lacked clarity, particularly as the meaning of "in Australia" is not stated in the tax legislation and has required interpretation by the Australian Tax Office. Organisations engaging in international charitable activities and their donors are required to navigate the complex laws and cumbersome processes surrounding the "in Australia" residency requirement for DGRs and its exceptions to determine whether they are eligible for DGR status.

The new "in Australia" tax ruling provides some clarity for organisations operating overseas and their donors and in doing so reduces the need for complex workarounds to facilitate tax-effective cross-border giving. When regulatory reforms for cross-border charity are also taken into account, the overall result is a less complicated, more streamlined system for both taxpayers and administrators.

Summary

The Australian government's longstanding approach to the tax treatment of cross-border donations prioritised fiscal consequences over other tax policy considerations. This resulted in a reduced capacity of the traditional tax concerns to influence policymaking with respect to cross-border philanthropy. With a new, less restrictive approach, it is possible to evaluate the benefits of the gift deduction as it applies to cross-border donations against these tax considerations. A tax policy analysis reveals that while there are some costs to the public purse and vertical inequities persist, on balance, the government's more permissive approach to cross-border philanthropy better promotes economic efficiency in the broad sense as a cost-effective way to subsidise international charitable activities and ultimately contributes to a reduction in global inequities due to the redistributive effect on the global allocation of resources. This approach also has the potential to reduce the complexity associated with tax deductibility for cross-border donations by providing legislative clarity and regulatory specificity for charities operating overseas and their donors while simplifying administration for regulators.

IV Conclusion

A recent OECD report on taxation and philanthropy found that "[d]espite fairly widespread use of incentives for domestic philanthropy, the landscape for a more global approach to philanthropy remains fairly guarded" (2020, p. 109). For many years, the Australian government epitomised this guarded approach with its longstanding policy prohibiting tax concessions for cross-border philanthropy mitigated by special exemptions with high entry barriers. The result was that Australia, like many donor countries around the world, was faced with a legal and regulatory environment for cross-border giving where a tension existed between effective government regulation and a desire for donors to engage in tax-effective international philanthropy.

In theory, the government's strict approach limited the ability of Australian donors to get a tax deduction for cross-border donations by requiring these gifts to be made through organisations that had succeeded in obtaining DGR status under one of the very limited exceptions to the "in Australia" residency requirement. Yet in practice, instead of ensuring that the benefits of these charitable tax subsidies remained in Australia, this approach enabled largely unregulated tax deductible cross-border giving to take place through giving intermediaries. The channelling workaround used to circumvent the restrictive tax laws was costly for donors and stifled their ability to engage in tax effective cross-border giving. At the same time, it compromised the ability of the Australian authorities to appropriately monitor cross-border charitable flows, underscored by FATF's evaluation of Australia's regulation of charities operating overseas. As a result, the government was unable to provide effective regulatory supervision of cross-border philanthropy. This failed approach, recognised by the Australian courts, is a lesson for other jurisdictions in what not to do.

Following these judicial decisions challenging the geographic restrictions placed around the charitable tax concessions, the Australian government has acknowledged the shortcomings of its overly restrictive approach to the tax treatment of cross-border donations. In doing so, it has changed policy course by issuing a new "in Australia" tax ruling for DGRs that provides greater scope for some Australian charities and their donors to engage in tax effective cross-border charitable activities. While restrictions remain in place, such that Australian "cross-border donations are not incentivized as a general principle" (OECD, 2020, pp. 109–110, Table 5.1), for those organisations that qualify for DGR status, the government's new approach alleviates the need for charities and their donors to engage in workarounds of the tax laws. Indeed, a tax policy analysis demonstrates that although the government's new approach to the tax treatment of cross-border donations is not without domestic costs, the benefits to both the Australian community and the wider global community are difficult to ignore. With the establishment of a more appropriate supervisory framework for monitoring cross-border giving, there is potential for greater transparency of cross-border charitable activities which will advance Australia's tax abuse risk profile.

The government's reduction of some of the territorial barriers around charitable tax relief for donors, combined with new tools for regulating international giving, is a first step towards reforming Australia's legal and regulatory regime governing cross-border philanthropy. The extent to which this less guarded approach achieves a more appropriate balance between ensuring adequate oversight of cross-border charitable flows while enabling Australian citizens to effectively contribute to the wider global community remains to be seen.

Notes

1 Defined as a charitable gift from a donor in one jurisdiction to a recipient in another. This term will be used throughout this chapter interchangeably with "international philanthropy" and "international giving".

2 Charities are a subset of not-for-profit organisations that meet the statutory definition of charity under the Charities Act 2013 (Cth).

3 Australia is a founding member of FATF, which was established in 1989.

4 This includes transferring funds or goods, or delivering programs, outside Australia.

5 Under the Income Tax Assessment Act 1997 (Cth), s 30–15 (ITAA 1997), Australian residents can deduct from their taxable income the value of donations of AUD $2 or more made to a DGR.

6 Other not-for-profit organisations eligible to become DGRs include government institutions, income tax-exempt funds, and organisations with purposes that are primarily sporting or recreational in nature. The Treasury Laws Amendment (2021 Measures No. 2) Act 2021 amends the ITAA 1997 to require non-government DGRs (other than ancillary funds) to register as a charity from 14 December 2021.

7 'Grants and other payments' made by Australian non-profit organisations to 'non-resident organisations' (defined as any organisation domiciled overseas, including foreign branches and subsidiaries of Australian organisations) amounted to more than AUD $1 billion, highlighting the widespread use of domestic nonprofits for cross-border giving, a significant component of which is likely to be intermediary giving.

8 This servicing fee was typically 7–10 percent of the amount distributed. See Letter from Philanthropy Australia to Prime Minister Tony Abbott, 21 April 2015, 1 (on file with author).

9 The location of decision making is determined on the basis of where the organisation's decision-making powers are mainly exercised, such that if the decision makers are located in more than one place, operational or strategic decisions would be made "mainly in Australia" provided the balance of decision-making power usually lies in Australia.

10 Data from the Australian Charities and Not-for-profits Commission's registration database as at 24 May 2017 shows that the number of public benevolent institutions operating overseas has been steadily increasing since 2013–2016 by an average of approximately 300 per year (on file with author).

11 This includes transferring funds or goods, or delivering programs, outside Australia.

12 This change represented an acknowledgment be FATF that the non-profit sector's vulnerability to terrorist abuse may previously have been overstated given that "not all non-profit organisations are inherently high risk (and some may represent little or no risk at all)".

13 A tax policy analysis of Australia's long-standing restrictive approach to the tax treatment of cross-border donations was undertaken in Silver and Buijze (2020, pp. 136–148).

References

AUSTRAC (2014) *Terrorism Financing in Australia* 2014, Canberra: Commonwealth of Australia.

AUSTRAC (2016) *Regional Risk Assessment on Terrorism Financing 2016: South East Asia and* Australia, Canberra: Commonwealth of Australia.

AUSTRAC and Australian Charities and Not-for-profits Commission (2017) *Australia's Non-Profit Organisation Sector: National Risk Assessment on Money Laundering & Terrorism Financing*, Canberra: Commonwealth of Australia.

Australian Bureau of Statistics (2015) *Australian National Accounts: Non-Profit Institutions Satellite Accounts 2012–13*, Catalogue No 5256, Canberra: Commonwealth of Australia <www.abs.gov.au/AusStats/ABS@.nsf/MF/5256.0>.

Australian Charities and Not-for-profits Commission (2018) *Australian Charities Report 2017* <https://www.acnc.gov.au/tools/reports/australian-charities-report-2017>.

Australia's Future Tax System Review Panel (2010) *Australia's Future Tax System: Report to the Treasurer*, Canberra: Commonwealth of Australia.

Bakija, J. and Heim, B. (2011) 'How Does Charitable Giving Respond to Incentives and Income? New Estimates from Panel Data' *National Tax Journal* 64(2), p. 615.

Casale, D. and Baumann, A. (2015) 'Who Gives to International Causes? A Sociodemographic Analysis of US Donors' *Nonprofit and Voluntary Sector Quarterly* 44(1), p. 98.

Colinvaux, R., Galle, B. and Steuerle, E. (2012) *Evaluating the Charitable Deduction and Proposed Reforms*, Washington: The Urban Institute.

Cortis, N. et al. (2016) *Australian Charities Involved Overseas 2014*, Sydney: University of New South Wales.

FATF (2016) *International Standards on Combatting Money Laundering and the Financing of Terrorism & Proliferation: The FATF Recommendations,* Paris: OECD/FATF.

FATF (2018) *Anti-Money Laundering and Counter-Terrorist Financing Measures – Australia: 3rd Enhanced Follow-Up Report & Technical Compliance Re-Rating*, Paris: FATF <http:www.fatf-gafi.org/publications/mutualevaluations/documents/fur-australia-2018.html>.

FATF and APG (2015) *Anti-Money Laundering and Counter-Terrorist Financing Measures – Australia, Fourth Round Mutual Evaluation Report*, FATF, Paris and APG, Sydney <www.fatf-gafi.org/topics/mutualevaluations/documents/mer-australia-2015.html>.

Gergen, M. (1988) 'The Case for a Charitable Contributions Deduction' *Virginia Law Review* 74(8), p. 1391.

Graetz, M. (1995) 'Paint-by-Numbers Tax Lawmaking' *Columbia Law Review* 95(3), p. 609.

Krever, R. (1991) 'Tax Deductions for Charitable Donations: A Tax Expenditure Analysis' in Krever, R. and Kewley, G. (eds.), *Charities and Philanthropic Institutions: Reforming the Tax Subsidy and Regulatory Regimes*, Sydney: Australian Tax Research Foundation, pp. 1–28.

List, J. (2011) 'The Market for Charitable Giving' *Journal of Economic Perspectives* 25(2), p. 157.

McGregor-Lowndes, M. and Crittall, M. (2015) *An Examination of Tax Deductible Donations Made by Individual Australian Taxpayers in 2012–13*, Australian Centre for Philanthropy and Nonprofit Studies, Queensland University of Technology Working Paper No. 66.

Micklewright, J. and Schnepf, S. (2009) 'Who Gives Charitable Donations for Overseas Development?' *Journal of Social Policy* 38(2), p. 317.

O'Connell, A. (2008) 'The Tax Position of Charities in Australia – Why Does It Have to Be So Complicated?' *Australian Tax Review* 37(1), p. 17.

O'Connell, A. (2021) *Taxation of Charities and Not-for-Profits*, Australia: LexisNexis.

O'Dwyer, K. (2017) *Reforming Administration of Deductible Gift Recipients*, Media Release, <http://kmo.ministers.treasury.gov.au/media-release/114-2017/>.

OECD (2020) *Taxation and Philanthropy*, OECD Tax Policy Studies, No. 27, Paris: OECD Publishing. <https://doi.org/10.1787/df434a77-en>.

Peloza, J. and Steel, P. (2005) 'The Price Elasticities of Charitable Contributions: A Meta-Analysis' *Journal of Public Policy & Marketing* 24(2), p. 260.

Powell, A. et al. (2017) *Australian Charities Report 2016*, Sydney: Commonwealth of Australia.

Pozen, D. (2006) 'Remapping the Charitable Deduction' *Connecticut Law Review* 39(2), p. 531.

Reich, R. (2011) 'Toward a Political Theory of Philanthropy' in Illingworth, P., Pogge, T. and Wenar, L. (eds.), *Giving Well: The Ethics of Philanthropy*, Oxford: Oxford University Press, pp. 177–195.

Roodman, D. and Standley, S. (2006) *Tax Policies to Promote Private Charitable Giving in DAC Countries*, Center for Global Development Working Paper No. 82.

Sheppard, I., Fitzgerald, R. and Gonski, D. (2001) *Report of the Inquiry into the Definition of Charities and Related Organisations*, Canberra: Commonwealth of Australia.

Silver, N. and Buijze, R. (2020) 'Tax Incentives for Cross-Border Giving in an Era of Philanthropic Globalization: A Comparative Perspective' *Canadian Journal of Comparative and Contemporary Law* 6, p. 109.

Silver, N., McGregor-Lowndes, M. and Tarr, J. (2016) 'Should Tax Incentives for Charitable Giving Stop at Australia's Borders?' *Sydney Law Review* 38(1), p. 85.

Simon, J., Dale, H. and Chisolm, L. (2006) 'The Federal Tax Treatment of Charitable Organisations' in Powell, W. and Steinberg, R. (eds.), *The Non Profit Sector: A Research Handbook*, 2nd edn., New Haven: Yale University Press, p. 267.

Stewart, M. (2014) 'The Boundaries of Charities and Tax' in Harding, M., O'Connell, A. and Stewart, M. (eds.), *Not-for-Profit Law: Theoretical and Comparative Perspectives*, Cambridge: Cambridge University Press.

The Treasury (2015) *Better Tax System, Better Australia*, Tax Discussion Paper, Canberra: Commonwealth of Australia <http://bettertax.gov.au/publications/discussion-paper/>.

The Treasury (2018) *Deductible Gift Recipient (DGR) Reforms: Consultation Paper*, Canberra: Commonwealth of Australia <https://treasury.gov.au/consultation/c2018-t321162/>.

Wiepking, P. (2010) 'Democrats Support International Relief and the Upper Class Donates to Art? How Opportunity, Incentives and Confidence Affect Donations to Different Types of Charitable Organisations' *Social Science Research* 39(6), p. 1073.

Wood, T., Humphrey Cifuentes, A. and Pryke, J. (2014) *Putting Our Money Where Our Mouths Are? Donations to NGOs and Support for ODA in Australia*, Discussion Paper 37, Development Policy Centre, Australian National University.

Cases

Commissioners for Special Purposes of Income Tax v Pemsel [1891] AC 531

Federal Commissioner of Taxation v The Hunger Project Australia (2014) 221 FCR 302

Federal Commissioner of Taxation v Word Investments Ltd (2008) 236 CLR 204

Legislation

Australian Charities and Not-for-profits Commission Act 2012 (Cth)

Australian Charities and Not-for-profits Commission Amendment (2018 Measures No. 2) Regulations 2018 (Cth)

Charities Act 2013 (Cth)

Income Tax Assessment Act 1997 (Cth)

Other legal authorities

Australian Charities and Not-for-profits Commission (2016) Commissioner's Interpretation Statement: Public Benevolent Institutions, CIS 2016/03

Australian Taxation Office (2003) Taxation Ruling TR 2003/5, 'Income Tax and Fringe Benefits Tax: Public Benevolent Institutions'

Australian Taxation Office (2017) Taxation Ruling TR 2003/5W, 'Income Tax and Fringe Benefits Tax: Public Benevolent Institutions, Notice of Withdrawal'

Australian Taxation Office (2018) Draft Taxation Ruling TR 2018/D1, 'The 'in Australia' Requirement for Certain Deductible Gift Recipients and Income Tax Exempt Entities'

Australian Taxation Office (2019) Taxation Ruling TR 2019/6, 'Income Tax: The 'in Australia' Requirement for Certain Deductible Gift Recipients and Income Tax Exempt Entities'

Explanatory Materials, Exposure Draft: Tax Laws Amendment (2014 Measures No #) Bill 2014 (Cth)

Explanatory Memorandum, Tax Laws Amendment (Special Conditions for Not-for-profit Concessions) Bill 2012 (Cth)

PART IV

Tax incentives for hybrid entities and social entrepreneurship

25

TAX REACTIONS ON ENTREPRENEURIAL PHILANTHROPY

The case of the Netherlands

Sigrid Hemels

1 Introduction

Traditionally, philanthropy is thought to be an activity of rich individuals and charities funded by individuals. In this context, donations, transfers without a direct return, are the typical form of philanthropy. It is important to stress that these are transfers without a *direct* return, as in many cases, donors do expect an indirect return. In their literature survey on philanthropy, Bekkers and Wiepking (2011) identified eight key mechanisms that in combination drive individual philanthropy: (1) awareness of (perceived) need, (2) solicitation (being asked for a donation), (3) cost and benefits of a donation, (4) altruism, (5) psychological benefits (warm glow), (6) reputation, (7) values and (8) (perceived) effectiveness of a donation. Such a combination of motives was already present when the typical Dutch *hofjes* were founded in the 14th century. These *hofjes* are an early form of private social housing: small city houses gathered around a green which provided free or cheap housing for the elderly and the poor. For founders, the indirect return could be an increase or confirmation of prestige, social status and better chances to get to heaven after death: the poor as treasurer of heaven (Hooijer 2019, Chapter 2). A similar mix of charitable, social status and immortality motives can be found in the context of, for example, current-day art patrons. Donating to the arts can give access to certain social networks and is expected of those in certain circles. It can even make the donor immortal when a room or an entire gallery is given her name. It is, therefore, important to recognize that individual philanthropy is usually not purely altruistic. Bekkers and Wiepking (2011, p. 936) even found in their literature survey that private benefits dominate altruistic motives.

Nowadays, philanthropy is no longer an activity of individuals only. Companies have also become important players. Some well-known examples of corporate foundations are the Carlsberg Foundation (one of the oldest corporate foundations, founded in Denmark in 1876), the IKEA Foundation and the Wal-Mart Foundation. Philanthropy has, in this development, followed the general economy in which economic activities were no longer only enterprises of individuals but also bundled in legal forms, companies.

Companies and (former) entrepreneurs initiating philanthropic activities brought their entrepreneurial customs, values and expectations into the world of philanthropy. This influenced philanthropic activities. Entrepreneurs and companies have certain expectations and introduce

 DOI: 10.4324/9781003139201-30

their business attitude into the philanthropic world. This leads to new forms of philanthropy next to the conventional form of donations. Examples of such new forms of philanthropy are program-related investments and donations to for-profit companies.

These developments in the world of philanthropy lead to several questions related to tax incentives for charitable donations and charities. A tax incentive is a provision in tax legislation, regulation or practice that leads to a reduction or postponement of tax income for the government and deviates from the ordinary or benchmark structure of a tax system.[1] In short: tax legislation is used to give fiscal rewards for certain desired behaviour. Tax incentives for corporate philanthropy include, for example, deductibility of gifts and an exemption of gift tax.

Many questions that arise as a result of corporate philanthropy in relation to tax incentives are at the top of the charitable agenda in the Netherlands. As the Dutch tax rules for charitable activities are still based on traditional forms of philanthropy, the Dutch tax administration and the philanthropic world are currently struggling to fit the more entrepreneurial forms of philanthropy into this system. This chapter takes, therefore, after a short discussion of the general business rationales for corporate philanthropy, the Netherlands as an example. I give a brief overview of corporate philanthropy in the Netherlands and discuss problems which have been encountered in the Netherlands in relation to deductibility of corporate gifts, donations of shares, donations to for-profit entities and program-related investments, solutions that have already been found and solutions that are proposed. Furthermore, I discuss the threats a proposal for an EU Directive on a common corporate tax base entails for an EU level playing field of corporate giving and competition for corporate donations.

2 Business rationale for corporate philanthropy

Just as individuals do not only have altruistic motives for philanthropy, corporate philanthropic activities are usually not done without a business rationale. I, therefore, respectfully disagree with OECD (2020, pp. 102–103) that seems to make a sharp distinction between sponsoring (business costs) and donations (not business cost). According to OECD (2020), sponsoring is fully deductible as business costs as in return, "corporations purchase publicity and advertising from philanthropic entities for the fair market value of those services". Donations do not seem to be regarded as business costs by OECD (2020), as there is deemed not to be a return. This echoes the French system, where all payments to philanthropic entities are considered donations (OECD 2020, p. 103) and hence not business costs. However, this disregards the fact that businesses usually have a clear rationale for their actions and that although donations do not lead to a direct return from the philanthropic entity, they do lead to indirect returns, which provide a business rationale for the donation.

There is a large strand of management literature on the impact of so-called corporate social responsibility (CSR) activities on firm performance.[2] CSR firms are found to have a better long-run performance. CSR is regarded to contribute to an organization's reputation and thus to increase sales and profits. A well-designed CSR policy can reinforce the authenticity of a brand. However, CSR is not only a marketing strategy but also a recruiting strategy, especially for millennials who, both as consumers and as employees, are found to value CSR even more than previous generations (McGlone, Winters Spain and McGlone 2011). CSR has also been found to be increasingly important for competitiveness, because it can lead to innovation. Furthermore, CSR can not only lower the cost of equity but also of debt (El Ghoul et al. 2011; Goss and Roberts 2011).

Expectations for CSR performance have progressed from "net zero" practices aimed primarily at reducing or offsetting negative impact toward "net positive" contributions: minimizing negative impact while also contributing positively to society and the environment. Customers and employees expect CSR efforts from companies.

A 2017 KPMG survey found that CSR reporting is by now standard practice for large and mid-cap companies around the world, an upward trend also driven by investor pressure. Amongst the world's 250 largest companies, the reporting rate was 93%, and in the worldwide sample of the top 100 companies by revenue in each of the 49 countries studied by KPMG, the reporting rate was 75% (KPMG 2017).

In short: corporate philanthropy is regarded a strategic activity that may play an important role in the process of stakeholder management, including enhancing relations with employees, customers and regulators (Brammer and Milington 2006). Management literature, therefore, shows that there is a valuable indirect return for donations and gives a clear business rationale for philanthropic activities. Given this business rationale, it would follow that such donations are to be regarded as business costs.

3 Corporate philanthropy in the Netherlands

Several Dutch companies have incorporated charitable foundations that are registered charities in the Netherlands.[3] According to Lonneke Roza in Venema (2018), there were at least 75 corporate foundations in the Netherlands in 2018. This does not seem like much, given the fact that there are almost 44,000[4] registered charities in the Netherlands, but Roza noted that she made a conservative estimate, as corporate foundations are not registered separately. Furthermore, many companies do not incorporate their own foundation but donate directly to the causes they want to support. In addition, charities like the Prins Bernhard Cultuur Fonds offer companies the possibility to create an endowed fund.[5] This means that the company does not have to incorporate and maintain a charity itself.

In order to obtain charity registration, corporate foundations must meet the same requirements other charities must meet for registration, such as the expenses being for more than 90% in the public benefit; having an independent board (meaning that at least half of the board members must be independent from the company or its shareholders); restrictions regarding the remuneration of board members; the obligation to publish information, including recent accounts and a policy plan, on a website; and articles of association stating that any liquidation proceeds must go to a similar charity.[6]

Given the 90% public benefit requirement, corporate foundations are not allowed to spend more than 10% of their expenses for the benefit of the company or its shareholders. In cases where there is a very close bond between the activities of the company and the CSR activities, a corporate foundation might not be the best solution for corporate philanthropy. If, for example, the philanthropic activities focus on premises of the company and are all done with employees of the company, it might be more cost effective to perform the activities from a business unit within the company. The same applies when the philanthropic activities are relatively limited or are mainly in the form of donations to charities.

4 Deductibility of corporate donations and Dutch tax law in general

In the Netherlands, business costs, for example, costs made for business reasons, are, in principle, fully deductible.[7] There are exceptions to this principle. For example, gifts that are made for business reasons but meet the definition of bribes in criminal law are not deductible.[8] However, bribes are usually not part of a corporate philanthropy policy and can safely be regarded as being out of scope for purposes of this chapter.

From the discussion of management literature in Section 2, it can be derived that in most cases, corporate charitable gifts will be done for business reasons such as meeting expectations of consumers and employees. In my view, it is not necessary that there be a direct return provided by the recipient, such as in the case of sponsoring. An expected indirect return, for example, in terms of reputation, brand value or employee or customer expectations would also suffice for the gift to be business-like. In those cases, corporate gifts are fully deductible as business costs in the Netherlands, without a threshold or a maximum. For these business gifts, it is not relevant whether the recipient is a registered charity. This deduction can, in my view, not be regarded a tax incentive, as it stems from the ordinary Dutch tax system that allows deduction of business costs.

If, however, costs are not made for business reasons but for shareholder reasons, these are, in principle, not deductible. This means that if, for example, a company gives a large amount to the church the sole shareholder, an individual, is member of, one must establish what the reason was for this gift. If there is no business reason for the gift and it was only done because the shareholder wanted the company to do so, this would not be a deductible gift. For Dutch tax purposes, this would be deemed a hidden non-deductible distribution of profit (dividend) to the shareholder and subsequently a gift from the shareholder to the church. The dividend will be taxed with personal income tax (PIT) in the hands of the individual shareholder, but she can claim a deductible gift for the same amount if all PIT requirements for gift deduction are met. One exception to this rule is that corporate gifts that are substantiated with written documents and are made to charities registered in the Netherlands[9] are deductible up to a maximum of the highest of 50% of the profits or EUR 100,000 (the gift deduction).[10] For business gifts made for business reasons, this provision is irrelevant, as such gifts are fully deductible in the same way as any other business costs are. Especially for small and medium-sized enterprises (SMEs), it is of importance that it is stated in a decree that an entity making a gift because of personal charitable wishes of the shareholder can deduct this gift, making use of this gift deduction (and within the boundaries of the gift deduction).[11] This is a deviation from the ordinary application of the Dutch corporate income tax and, therefore, a tax incentive.

This tax incentive is attractive for a shareholder if her private funds do not suffice to donate directly. However, if the shareholder has enough private funds and sufficiently high taxed income, donating directly might be more attractive from a tax point of view. In 2021, the Dutch corporate income tax rate is 15% for the first EUR 245,000 and 25% for the remainder. The highest tax rate in personal income tax is 49.5% in 2021 (this rate applies, for example, to wages and income from independent activities; the lowest rate for these activities in 37.1% in 2021), and the lowest rate (for income from a substantial shareholding) is 26.9% in 2021. A gift to a charity registered in the Netherlands can, if certain requirements are met, be deducted in full.[12] Even though the tax rate against which a gift can be deducted is no longer the top rate of 49.5% but a rate that is gradually reduced to 37.1%, a shareholder who (or whose partner, as gifts can also be taken into account by one's partner for tax purposes) has sufficient taxed income can, therefore, benefit more from donating in private than from having the donation being made by her company.

The cap of EUR 100,000 makes the corporate gift deduction unattractive for larger companies that will usually be expected to spend much more on corporate giving. However, if the gifts can be regarded as business expenses, this restriction is not of relevance.

5 Gifts in the form of shares

In the Netherlands, gifts can be done in cash and in kind, including in the form of shares. In this respect, there is no difference between gifts that are deducted as business expenses or that are deducted under the gift deduction.

However, for charities that receive shares of a company, this is not without difficulties. The Dutch tax administration requires a yearly mark-to-market valuation of shares owned by a charity, demanding that an increase in value of the shares, including unrealized gains, lead to an increase of charitable spending, as otherwise, according to the tax administration, the requirement that a charity may not own more assets than necessary for the continuity of its activities (in short: anti-hoarding requirement) is not met.

It is questionable whether this view is correct. It is disputed in literature, but it was never tested in court. However, in 2019, the Ministry of Finance announced a policy change according to which a mark-to-market would not be necessary (anymore). In case of large shareholdings, the Ministry suggested requiring that the charity have enough control to ensure that enough funds will flow to the charity to fund its activities. The Ministry of Finance announced it would, together with the charitable sector, develop guidance on this requirement.[13] This guidance might be included in a decree. The latter would give the guidance a stronger status, also in relation to the principle of legal expectations and an obligation for the tax administration to apply the guidance. The Ministry of Finance promised that this guidance would be published in 2020,[14] but this promise was not met.

6 Donations to for-profit companies

Some entrepreneurial charities donate to for-profit companies. An example is the Bill and Melinda Gates Foundation that gives donations to pharma companies to develop vaccines. The reason for such donations us usually a market failure. For example, from a humanitarian point of view, vaccines that can protect against infectious diseases in developing countries should preferably be cheap and free from patents. However, developing such vaccines requires substantial resources. These can only be recovered through high prices for vaccines protected by patents. That makes the vaccines out of reach for the poor. The market mechanism encourages developing medicines that can be protected by patents and cure diseases found in rich countries that can pay high medicine prices.

The market failure is that not all positive external effects are included in the price. Rich countries benefit if infectious diseases are contained in poor countries. Through mutations, these diseases can also become dangerous for people living in rich countries. Furthermore, developing such medicines might lead to valuable knowledge which can be used again later. Such positive external effects can be a reason for governments to support research. Developing countries usually lack the resources to fund such research. Charities may step in and enable companies to develop vaccines and medicines that are of importance for developing countries.

The Dutch tax administration can be reluctant to regard such donations to for-profit entities as charitable. As the Dutch charitable status requires that at least 90% of the spending be for the public benefit, this point of view can be problematic. The philanthropic sector has asked the Dutch Ministry of Finance to regard donations to for-profit entities as charitable if the donation pursues one or more of the philanthropic objects of the charity. It is not yet clear whether the Ministry of Finance is willing to meet this wish of the sector.

7 Program-related investments

An alternative for a donation is a loan at a low interest rate or taking a minority share. The high risk of such investments is not compensated by financial means. A financial reward is also not the primary purpose of such investments. Well known are micro-financing initiatives in developing countries supporting people to support themselves instead of becoming dependent on donations, following the well-known quote, "Give a man a fish, and you feed him for a day. Teach a man to fish, and you feed him for a lifetime".[15]

This kind of philanthropy is not new. At his death in 1790, Benjamin Franklin bequeathed £1,000 to both Boston and Philadelphia. This bequest had to be used the following 200 years to give loans to young apprentices as he had once been. The interest-bearing loans had to be paid back and then be used to provide new loans. In 1990, the balance in the Boston trust was $4.5 million, while the Philadelphia account was valued at $2 million (Yenawine 2016).

This revolving fund made Franklin the founding father of what were called program-related investments (PRIs) by the Ford Foundation in 1968. According to the Ford Foundation (1974), PRIs could achieve certain philanthropic goals more effectively than donations. Already in 1969, the United States included this kind of philanthropic spending in tax legislation. PRIs generally come out of a foundation's grant budget and count toward the 5% of assets that U.S. foundations are required, under tax law, to pay out every year. The U.S. Internal Revenue Code defines PRIs as those investments in which (1) the primary purpose is to accomplish one or more of the foundation's exempt purposes, (2) production of income or appreciation of property is not a significant purpose and (3) influencing legislation or taking part in political campaigns on behalf of candidates is not a purpose (Internal Revenue Service 2020). Such PRIs must be distinguished from so-called mission-related investments (MRIs, also referred to as impact investments) that are designed to generate both a social and a financial return. MRIs are not deemed a charitable activity, nor do they qualify as charitable distributions in the United States (Levitt 2011).

The U.S. Internal Revenue Service (IRS) provides for extensive guidance on PRIs (Internal Revenue Service 2020). In determining whether a significant purpose of an investment is the production of income or the appreciation of property, it is relevant for U.S. tax purposes whether investors who engage in investments for profit only would be likely to make the investment on the same terms as the private foundation. If an investment incidentally produces significant income or capital appreciation, this is not, in the absence of other factors, regarded as conclusive evidence that a significant purpose is the production of income or the appreciation of property. To be program related, the investments must significantly further the foundation's exempt activities. They must be investments that would not have been made except for their relationship to the exempt purposes. The investments include those made in functionally related activities that are carried on within a larger combination of similar activities related to the exempt purposes. Recipients of PRIs do not have to be charitable themselves and may even be for profit. The IRS guidance mentions various examples of PRIs, including low-interest or interest-free loans to needy students, high-risk investments in non-profit low-income housing projects and investments in businesses in low-income areas.

Based on the Charities (Protection and Social Investment) Act 2016, the United Kingdom also recognizes PRIs for charitable purposes. PRIs that further the object of the charity are considered for the UK expenditure requirement (Charity Commission for England and Wales 2017).

The situation is completely different in the Netherlands. The Dutch tax administration regards PRI in the same way as other investments. This means that charities that invest in PRI on a large scale may be confronted with the anti-hoarding requirement that was discussed in Section 5. This problem has been brought to the attention of the Ministry of Finance. The Ministry announced that in collaboration with the philanthropic sector, guidance would be published in 2020 on PRI (confusingly called impact investments by the Ministry of Finance) that do not breach the anti-hoarding requirement.[16] However, this promise was not met.

8 Corporate giving, EU law and the Common Consolidated Corporate Tax Base

The decision whether to provide tax benefits for corporate giving is at the discretion of national governments, also in the European Union (EU). As is the case with all tax legislation, the fiscal sovereignty of EU Member States is, however, restricted by EU law, including the fundamental freedoms included in the Treaty on the Functioning of the EU (TFEU). In various judgments, the ECJ held that a different treatment of non-resident charities solely based on their place of residence is a restriction of the free movement of capital of article 63 TFEU and, therefore, not allowed.[17] Member States are not obliged, however, to mutually recognize each other's charities. They can still impose their own charity requirements on foreign charities, including a registration requirement. This means that also after this case law, tax benefits for corporate charitable giving vary widely in the EU.

On 16 March 2011, the European Commission published a Proposal for a Common Consolidated Corporate Tax Base (CCCTB).[18] This proposal aimed to provide large companies with a single set of corporate tax rules for doing business across the internal market and included a provision on charitable gifts. However, the Member States could not come to an agreement on this proposal. It was withdrawn and replaced on 25 October 2016 by a proposal for a two-step process: first a CCTB without consolidation and then a full CCCTB.[19] The 2016 CC(C)TB is still in discussion. The provision on charitable gifts differs significantly from the 2011 proposal. It would significantly change the landscape for corporate donations in the EU.

The 2011 CCCTB seemed to be derived from the French corporate gift deduction. Based on article 12 of the 2011 CCCTB, gifts to charities would be deductible up to a maximum of 0.5% of revenues in the tax year. Furthermore, only gifts to charitable bodies as defined in article 16 of the 2011 CCCTB could be deducted.[20] In a proposal for amendments,[21] it was suggested to add that the purpose had to be included in a list in Annex III to the Proposal.[22] The aim of including this list was to align the CCCTB definition of charitable bodies with that in Proposal for a Council Regulation on the Statute for a European Foundation (FE).[23] The latter would have enabled the incorporation of a separately constituted EU entity for a public benefit purpose. Member States had to regard an FE as equivalent to resident charities and give them, their donors and their beneficiaries the same tax treatment as resident charities. However, Member States could not unanimously agree to the FE Proposal, and in March 2015, it was withdrawn.[24]

It seems that also within the context of the CC(C)TB, Member States could not come to an agreement on what constitutes a public purpose. Article 9(4) of the 2016 CCTB simply provides that Member States may provide for the deduction of gifts and donations to charitable bodies. A definition of "charitable body" is missing. Formulating such definition seems to be left to the Member States. This means that if the 2016 CC(C)TB would be adopted, tax benefits for corporate charitable giving would be as divergent in the EU as they are today. The CC(C)TB will not lead to a level playing field for businesses providing donations to philanthropic activities. Depending on the Member State in which a donation is made, there will be more or fewer possibilities to deduct the gifts.

One could question whether corporate charitable gifts that are part of a CSR strategy could not simply be deducted as business costs under the CC(C)TB. Given the fact that the CC(C)TB would only apply to large corporations, it would not be very likely that charitable gifts would be based on shareholder motives, and one would expect a business rationale. Article 9(1) 2016 CCTB provides that expenses are deductible only to the extent that they are incurred in the direct business interest of the taxpayer. Article 9(2) elaborates that the expenses referred to in article 9(1) include all costs of sales and all expenses, net of deductible value added tax, that the taxpayer incurred with a view to obtaining or securing income, including costs for research and development, acquisition or construction costs of assets less than EUR 1,000 and costs incurred in raising equity or debt for the purposes of the business. If these provisions would apply to charitable gifts, there would not be any divergence between Member States with respect to corporate charitable giving. This would enhance the internal market.

However, given the fact that the deduction of charitable gifts is specifically included in article 9(4) and that the treatment of gifts in the CC(C)TB seems to be derived from the French system that does not regard donations as business costs, it might be argued that charitable gifts are not regarded as deductible expenses within the meaning of section 9(1). It might be that these costs are not regarded as being in the *direct* business interest of the taxpayer and cannot be regarded as being incurred with a view to obtaining or securing income. This would not be in accordance with the evidence from management literature that CSR, including charitable corporate giving, has a clear business rationale, just as other marketing and recruitment strategies do, and can increase profits and reduce the costs of attracting debt.

It is difficult to understand why regular marketing and recruitment costs would be deductible under article 9(1) and CSR costs in the form of charitable donations would be restricted by national provisions based on article 9(4). For companies that would be taxed in the Netherlands under the CC(C)TB, this would, for example, mean that they could no longer fully deduct these gifts as business costs but would be limited by the maximum of EUR 100,000. The latter amount might suffice for an SME but is not even close to the amount of corporate giving that the public expects from large companies.

When questioned by Parliament on the impact of the CC(C)TB on corporate charitable giving by Dutch companies, the Dutch State Secretary of Finance answered that given the various objections of several Member States, including the Netherlands, it is not to be expected that Member States will come to an agreement soon on the CCTB proposal.[25] However, this is beside the point that it would be important for a level playing field in the EU internal market that the Member States give more thought to the business rationale for corporate charitable giving by large businesses within the CC(C)TB scope and consider including such gifts in the already quite specific enumeration of article 9(2).

9 Conclusion

Corporate philanthropy is here to stay in the Netherlands. Corporate donations as such are not problematic from a Dutch tax perspective, as these will usually be deductible in the same way as regular business costs are. This might change, however, if the CC(C)TB Directive were adopted. In that case, such donations might only be deductible up to an amount of €100,000. The CC(C)TB would, therefore, negatively affect the level playing field in the EU for corporate philanthropic donations and receiving philanthropic organizations and thus have a negative effect on the internal market.

Currently, in the Netherlands, it gets complicated when charities become entrepreneurial in the way they want to achieve their objectives. In this respect, the tax legislation is lagging behind in the Netherlands. It is problematic for charities to comply with the requirements for charitable status when shares were donated to them, when they engage in PRI or when they donate to for-profit entities. This charitable status is necessary to be eligible for tax incentives. It is to be hoped that the Dutch Ministry of Finance will publish the promised guidelines soon and that these will be more adaptive to modern forms of philanthropy. As it is, Dutch tax law is a hindering factor for charities that want to apply more entrepreneurial forms of philanthropy to achieve their goals.

Notes

1 Various terms are used for this phenomenon, including tax expenditure, tax break, tax subsidy and tax concession. For an extensive discussion on what tax incentives are, I refer to Hemels 2017.
2 For an overview of sources, I refer to Orlitzky and Benjamin (2001), Bocquet et al. (2013), Bernal-Conesa, de Nieves Nieto and Briones-Peñalver (2017) and Carini et al. (2017).
3 For example, the Philips Foundation, ING Nederland Fonds and Facilicom Foundation.
4 Kamerstukken II, 2019–2020, 35 437, no. 7, p. 18.
5 For example, endowed corporate funds within the Prins Bernhard Cultuurfonds: Ahrend Fonds, Amsterdam Institute of Finance Fonds and AVRO Cultuurfonds (Prins Bernhard Cultuurfonds 2021).
6 Article 5b AWR in connection with article 1a Uitvoeringsregeling AWR 1994 (Implementing Decree AWR, UAWR).
7 Article 8(1) Wet op de vennootschapsbelasting 1969 (Corporation Tax Act 1969; CITA) in connection with article 3.8 Wet inkomstenbelasting 2001 (Personal Income Tax Act 2001, PITA.
8 Article 8(1) CITA in connection with article 3.14(1)(h) PITA.
9 These charities do not necessarily have to be resident in the Netherlands, as charities resident in other countries (both EU and third countries) can also apply for registration in the Netherlands (article 5b Algemene wet inzake rijksbelastingen (General State Tax Act, AWR). It is not relevant if non-resident charities are registered in their country of residence, but they have to meet all Dutch charity requirements. Various non-resident charities, including corporate charities, are registered in the Netherlands. Just to mention some examples: Alliance Foundation (Switzerland), the Fondazione Prada (Italy) and Shell Foundation (United Kingdom). This can be found on the public register https://www.belastingdienst.nl/rekenhulpen/anbi_zoeken/.
10 Article 16 CITA.
11 Decree of 31 October 2016, no. BLKB2016/152, Staatscourant 2016/58695.
12 So called periodic gifts are, in short, gifts to a charity registered in the Netherlands that are agreed on in a deed and that are made in yearly instalments for a minimum of five years (articles 6.34 and 6.38 IB). These gifts are fully deductible without a threshold or a maximum. Other gifts (gifts that do not meet the requirements of a periodic gift) are deductible insofar as these exceed 1% of the income up to a maximum of 10% of the income. In practice, all substantive gifts are given the form of a periodic gift.
13 Kamerstukken II, 2018–2019, 35 026, no. 63, p. 9.
14 Kamerstukken II, 2019–2020, 35 437, no. 7, p. 6.
15 For the unclear origins of this quote, I refer to Quote Research (2015).
16 Kamerstukken II, 2019–2020, 35 437, no. 7, p. 6.
17 Case C-386/04, Stauffer, 14 September 2006, ECLI:EU:C:2006:568; Case C-318/07, Persche, 27 January 2009, ECLI:EU:C:2009:33; Case C-386/04, Stauffer, 14 September 2006, ECLI:EU:C:2006:568; Case C 25/10, Heukelbach, 10 February 2011, ECLI:EU:C:2011:65; Case C 10/10, Commission v Austria, 16 June 2011, ECLI:EU:C:2011:399; Case C-485/14, Commission v. France, 16 July 2015, ECLI:EU:C:2015:506. In the latter case, the Court pointed out that Art. 40 of the European Economic Area (EEA) Agreement on the free movement of capital between nationals of States party to the EEA Agreement must be interpreted in the same way as Art. 63 TFEU.
18 COM(2011) 121 final. Hereinafter: 2011 CCCTB.
19 COM(2016) 685 final and COM(2016) 683 final. The latest Presidency compromise text on the CCTB proposal is dated 6 June 2019 https://data.consilium.europa.eu/doc/document/ST-9676-2019-INIT/en/pdf. It is this version that is used as reference in this chapter, and it will be referred to as 2016 CC(C)TB.

20 The requirements were that: (1) the body had legal personality and was a recognized charity in its state of establishment; (2) its sole or main purpose and activity were one of public benefit; an educational, social, medical, cultural, scientific, philanthropic, religious, environmental or sportive purpose was considered to be of public benefit, provided that it was of general interest; (3) its assets were irrevocably dedicated to the furtherance of its purpose; (4) it was subject to requirements for the disclosure of information regarding its accounts and its activities; (5) it was not a political party as defined by the Member State in which it was established.

21 Council of the EU, Presidency comments on the compromise proposal for a CCCTB, 16 April 2012, no. 8790/12, FISC 52, http://www.uva.nl/binaries/content/documents/personalpages/n/o/m.f.nouwen/nl/tabblad-een/tabblad-een/cpitem%5B14%5D/asset?1368633253789.

22 The purposes included were: (1) arts, culture or historical preservation; (2) environmental protection; (3) civil or human rights; (4) elimination of discrimination based on gender, race ethnicity, religion, disability, sexual orientation or any other legally prescribed form of discrimination; (5) social welfare, including prevention or relief of poverty; (6) humanitarian or disaster relief; (7) development aid and development cooperation; (8) assistance to refugees or immigrants; (9) protection of, and support for, children, youth or the elderly; (10) assistance to, or protection of, people with disabilities; (11) animal protection; (12) science and research; (13) education and training; (14) European and international understanding; (15) health, physical well-being and medical care; (16) assistance to, or protection of, vulnerable and disadvantaged persons; (17) the promotion of philanthropy.

23 COM(2012) 35 final, 2012/0022 (APP).

24 Withdrawal of commission proposals, 2015/C 80/08, *Official Journal of the EU*, C80/17.

25 Kamerstukken II, 2018–2019, 35 026, nr. 67, p. 6.

References

Bekkers, R.H.F.P. and Wiepking, P. (2011) 'A literature review of empirical studies of philanthropy: Eight mechanisms that drive charitable giving', *Nonprofit and Voluntary Sector Quarterly*, 40(5), pp. 924–973.

Bernal-Conesa, J.A., de Nieves Nieto, C. and Briones-Peñalver, A.J. (2017) 'CSR strategy in technology companies: Its influence on performance, competitiveness and sustainability', *Corporate Social Responsibility and Environmental Management*, 24(2), pp. 96–207.

Bocquet, R., Le Bas, C., Mothe, C. and Poussing, N. (2013) 'Are firms with different CSR profiles equally innovative?' *European Management Journal*, 31(6), pp. 642–654.

Brammer, S. and Milington, A. (2006) 'Firm size, organizational visibility and corporate philanthropy: An empirical analysis', *Business Ethics*, 15(1), pp. 6–18.

Carini, C., Comincioli, N., Poddi, L. and Vergalli, S. (2017) 'Measure the performance with the market value added: Evidence from CSR companies', *Sustainability*, 9(12), pp 1–19.

Charity Commission for England and Wales. (2017) *Charities and investment matters: A guide for trustees (CC14)* [Online]. Available at https://assets.publishing.service.gov.uk/government/uploads/system/uploads/attachment_data/file/857987/CC14_new.pdf (Accessed: 19 January 2021).

El Ghoul, S., Guedhami, O., Kwok, C.C.Y. and Mishra, D.R. (2011) 'Does corporate social responsibility affect the cost of capital?' *Journal of Banking & Finance*, 35(9), pp. 2388–2406.

Ford Foundation. (1974) *Program-related investments. A different approach to philanthropy*. New York: Ford Foundation.

Goss, A. and Roberts, G.S. (2011) 'The impact of corporate social responsibility on the cost of bank loans', *Journal of Banking & Finance*, 35(7), pp. 1794–1810.

Hemels S. (2017) 'Tax incentives as a creative industries policy instrument', in Hemels, S. and Goto, K. (eds.), *Tax incentives for the creative industries*. Singapore: Springer, pp. 33–64.

Hooijer, G.F. (2019) *. . . geen beter renten. Een studie naar de functie van het begrip hemelrente in opschriften in de Republiek der Zeven Verenigde Nederlanden tussen 1600 en 1800*. Amsterdam: Free University Amsterdam.

Internal Revenue Service. (2020) *Program-Related Investments* [Online]. Available at https://www.irs.gov/charities-non-profits/private-foundations/program-related-investments (Accessed: 19 January 2021).

KPMG. (2017) *The road ahead* [Online]. Available at https://assets.kpmg/content/dam/kpmg/be/pdf/2017/kpmg-survey-of-corporate-responsibility-reporting-2017.pdf (Accessed: 19 January 2021).

Levitt, D.A. (2011) 'Investing in the future: Mission-related and program-related investments for private foundations', *The Practical Tax Lawyer*, 25(3), pp. 33–43.

McGlone, T., Winters Spain, J. and McGlone, V. (2011) 'Corporate social responsibility and the millennials', *Journal of Education for Business*, 86(4), pp. 195–200.
OECD. (2020) *Taxation and philanthropy*. OECD Tax Policy Studies no. 27. Paris: OECD Publishing.
Orlitzky, M. and Benjamin J.D. (2001) 'Corporate social performance and firm risk: A meta-analytic review', *Business and society*, 40(4), pp. 369–396.
Prins Bernhard Cultuurfonds. (2021) *Cultuurfondsen op Naam* [Online]. Available at https://www.cultuurfonds.nl/fondsen (Accessed: 19 January 2021).
Quote Research. (2015) *Give a man a fish, and you feed him for a day. Teach a man to fish, and you feed him for a lifetime* [Online]. Available at https://quoteinvestigator.com/2015/08/28/fish/#:~:text=Foreign%20aid%E2%80%94%E2%80%9CYou%20give%20a,.%E2%80%9D%20(Chinese%20proverb (Accessed: 19 January 2021).
Venema, E. (2018) *Bedrijfsfilantropie & fundraising: ff wennen . . .* [Online]. Available at https://www.dedikkeblauwe.nl/news/corporate-philanthropy-fundraising (Accessed: 19 January 2021).
Yenawine, B.H. (2016) *Benjamin Franklin and the invention of microfinance*. London/New York: Routledge.

26

CULTURE CHANGE IS HARD

Evidence from a tax reform in the Netherlands[1]

Stephanie Koolen-Maas, Claire van Teunenbroek and René Bekkers

1 Context

All around the world, governments stimulate individuals and corporations to give to nonprofit organizations by providing tax incentives. How can such tax incentives be designed to encourage individuals and corporations to support nonprofit organizations? In this chapter, we provide evidence on a legal reform in the Netherlands introduced in 2012. The reform (Weekers, 2012) not only changed conditions for all registered charities in the Netherlands but also targeted one specific sector: the cultural sector. In this chapter, we answer the following two research questions: (1) How did giving to cultural nonprofit organizations change after the charity law reform between 2011 and 2018? and (2) How did fundraising by and entrepreneurship within cultural nonprofit organizations change after the charity law reform between 2012 and 2019?

Giving in the Netherlands. The Netherlands is a country with a long and rich philanthropic history (Wiepking & Bekkers, 2015, p. 211). Data on giving behavior in the Netherlands became available in the mid-1990s. We have evidence that amounts donated to charitable cases increased substantially since then (Bekkers, Gouwenberg & Schuyt, 2020). Philanthropic giving in the Netherlands to all causes amounted to €5.7 billion in 2018 (Bekkers, Gouwenberg & Schuyt, 2020). There is a widespread participation in charitable giving in the Netherlands, with about 80% of Dutch households giving to charity (Bekkers & Van Teunenbroek, 2020; Van Teunenbroek & Bekkers, 2020). This puts the country in the top 10 of the World Giving Index (CAF, 2019). Yet philanthropy entails only a small fraction of the economy; the total value of philanthropy in the Netherlands amounts to 0.85% of GDP (Bekkers, 2018; Bekkers, Gouwenberg & Schuyt, 2020). In the Netherlands, philanthropy is generally viewed as a complement rather than a substitute to government intervention (Wiepking & Bekkers, 2015). In 2018, on average, a household donates 265 EUR per year, with a median gift of 55 EUR (Van Teunenbroek & Bekkers, 2020).

Reform objectives. One goal of the reform of the law on giving ("Geefwet") was to reduce the dependency of the cultural sector on government grants. The reform intended to encourage philanthropic giving by both private donors and corporations, and to stimulate entrepreneurship by cultural nonprofit organizations (De Nooij, Bekkers & Felix, 2017; Franssen & Bekkers, 2016; Koolen-Maas, Van Teunenbroek & Bekkers, 2021). To achieve these objectives, the government enhanced the deductibility of donations to cultural nonprofit organizations and cultural organizations were given more freedom to earn commercial income.

DOI: 10.4324/9781003139201-31

How the reform could diversify income sources. In theory, the legal reform in the Netherlands facilitated a more diverse income portfolio for cultural nonprofit organizations, such that their dependence on government funding would reduce. Generally speaking, nonprofit organizations draw financial support from multiple sources, including private and corporate donations, commercial activities, government support and other sources of income – resulting in a mix of income sources. Generating a sufficiently robust and diversified mix of income is critical to sustaining the nonprofit organization (Chikoto-Schultz & Sakolvittayanon, 2020; Hung & Hager, 2019). Strong dependence on a single source of income could endanger the organization if income from that source is suddenly reduced. Thus, nonprofit organizations are advised to diversify their income sources. Earning more non-government income could substitute for reduced income from government grants. Private donations and commercial activities provide sources of income that may help organizations survive and thrive when income from government grants is reduced. To provide cultural nonprofit organizations with more freedom to earn commercial income, the legal reform permitted organizations to engage in commercial activities, as long as 90% of the activities benefit a public goal and total income does not exceed expenditure.

Tax incentives for donations. Governments can support nonprofit organizations with direct subsidies in the form of government grants or tax exemptions and rebates, as well as with indirect subsidies such as tax incentives for donors. Tax incentives can take many forms (European Fundraising Association, 2018; OECD, 2020). The Netherlands is one of many countries to offer charitable deductions for donations from taxable income of individuals or corporate profits. Both tax deductions and tax credits are indirect subsidies because they benefit nonprofit organizations indirectly through a price effect on donors. The lower tax-price allows donors to give more at the same cost to themselves. The tax incentives benefit nonprofit organizations only when donors are price sensitive and increase their donations as a result of a lower price of giving. Therefore it is crucial to know to what extent donors to the cultural sector are actually using the deduction and are aware of the enhanced deductibility through the multiplier.

Tax treatment of philanthropic organizations in the Netherlands. Before the reform, the Netherlands was already providing an excellent environment for charitable causes (Hudson Institute, 2013). The Netherlands has favorable tax treatment of philanthropic organizations, ranking number 1 on the Index for Philanthropic Freedom (Hudson Institute, 2015) and the Global Philanthropy Environment Index (2018). Philanthropic organizations in the Netherlands are exempt from income tax, estate tax and gift tax. There is no spending requirement for foundations and no mandatory disclosure of large gifts. On the donor's side, the Dutch tax deduction scheme offers tax incentives on individual and corporate donations. For instance, donors can deduct the value of their gift from the income tax up to 10% of total income when the recipient is registered as a public benefit organization ("ANBI"). Planned gifts are deductible from the income tax for private taxpayers when they are declared in an official deed by a notary. Occasional gifts are deductible when they exceed the threshold of 1% of pre-tax income. Corporate taxpayers can deduct the annual value of their donations up to 50% of their annual profit or revenues.

A separate status for cultural nonprofit organizations. The charity tax reform created a separate category of tax-exempt nonprofit organizations: cultural nonprofit organizations registered as a public benefit organization ("Culturele ANBI"). To register as a cultural ANBI, the nonprofit organization must be for at least 90% committed to and focus on activities in the cultural field (Belastingdienst, 2021). The tax code itself does not specify exactly which purposes and activities belong to the sphere of culture. In practice, a wide range of nonprofit organizations qualify. Registered cultural nonprofit organizations include museums, archives, theatres, libraries and heritage preservation societies, as well as (pop) music, dance and film festivals. The more than

4,000 organizations registered in 2020 include museums with collections of global significance attracting millions of visitors per year, as well as many small, locally bound associations run by volunteers that do not have their own building that is open to the public.

A multiplier for donations. The legal reform in the Netherlands enhanced the deductibility of donations by individuals and corporate taxpayers to registered cultural nonprofit organizations through a multiplier. The multiplier of 1.25 for individuals is capped at a deduction of 10% of tax income. The multiplier of 1.5 for corporate taxpayers is capped at 50% of profit with a maximum of €100,000. Through the multiplier, households and corporations could give higher amounts at the same price. An example: consider a €1,000 gift to a registered cultural nonprofit organization by a household with an income of €60,000 and a marginal tax rate of 52%. In the old situation, the charitable deduction would reduce the price of the gift to €480. For the calculation of the tax deduction after the reform, the gift may be multiplied by 1.25. The tax-deductible amount of €1,250 results in a tax benefit of €650 (1,250 × 0.52). Thus, the net cost of the €1,000 donation is only €350. If the household uses the tax benefit to increase the amount donated up to the previous price point of €480, it may give €1,371 at no additional cost (Bekkers & Franssen, 2015). By making donations to cultural nonprofit organizations more attractive, the Dutch government expected that donations would increase. The government budget for 2012–2015 included a projected decrease in the income tax as a result of an increase in the charitable deduction, amounting to €22 million per year (De Jager & Weekers, 2012, p. 45).

Concerns about substitution. Because the reform made giving to culture more attractive than giving to other charitable causes, donors may have redirected their giving to cultural nonprofit organizations. When introducing the tax reform, the minister stated that such substitution effects are unlikely to occur because amounts donated to culture tend to be low (Bekkers & Mariani, 2012) and sought approval from the European High Court (De Nooij, Bekkers & Felix, 2017). This process took a long time. While the reform took effect on January 1, 2012, the court approved the reform only on March 20, 2013. Pending approval, cultural nonprofit organizations were uncertain whether the law would in fact apply and were barely active promoting the enhanced deductibility to donors. The charity tax reform initially applied until December 31, 2017. On October 10, 2017, the Dutch government decided that the law on giving will remain in effect for an indefinite period of time (Nijboer, 2017).

Cutbacks. The legal reform coincided with sizeable cutbacks in direct government funding to cultural nonprofit organizations (Raad voor Cultuur, 2017). The national government announced that it would cut about 20% of the budget for arts and culture. In practice, between 2011 and 2015, the cuts amounted not only to €200 million in direct funding from the national government but also included cuts worth €47 million from provincial governments and €250 million from municipalities. During these periods of government cutbacks, the resources available to support cultural nonprofit organizations have been restricted. The uncertainty and decline in government funding – combined with the charity tax reform – necessitated income diversification among cultural nonprofit organizations. The reduction in government grants reduced the income for some cultural nonprofit organizations more strongly than others; those relying more on government funds were affected most. There were, however, instances in which some cultural nonprofit organizations received protection from the government cutbacks. These organizations included, for instance, the largest museums in the tourism industry in the biggest cities (e.g., Amsterdam, Rotterdam and The Hague). Initially, the charity tax reform was seen as a test case for other nonprofit sectors that the government wanted to cut back on (e.g., international relief and development).

When announcing the cutbacks in 2011, the newly appointed minister for Culture, Education and Science lamented dependence on government funding and called upon cultural nonprofit organizations to become more entrepreneurial and to diversify their income, for example, by increasing income from donations, corporate sponsorships and commercial activities (Broer & Niemantsverdriet, 2011). At the time, the cultural sector largely depended on direct funding from the national government and from local governments. The cutbacks threatened the existing basis of support for the future of the cultural sector. Protests were futile. One of the parties supporting the minority government at the time even justified cutbacks by qualifying culture as a "leftist hobby" not worthy of government support. In the caricature, cultural nonprofit organizations appeared to be passive welfare recipients waiting for handouts and lacking creativity and a business mindset. Indeed, because of their dependency on government funding, few cultural organizations will have developed skills and capacity for fundraising among private donors. Due to the legal restrictions, commercial activities were largely absent within cultural nonprofit organizations.

To support a culture change within the cultural sector to become more entrepreneurial and attractive for donors and sponsors, the Ministry of Culture, Science, and Education subsidized two training programs: a leadership program, "Leiderschap in Cultuur", and a workshop on fundraising, "Wijzer Werven" (De Nooij et al., 2017; Franssen & Bekkers, 2016). In addition, the Ministry of Culture, Education and Science executed a public awareness campaign to inform the public about the charity tax reform ("Cultuur, daar geef je om").

Previous research

At least five strands of literature are relevant for the analyses we present in this chapter. The first pair of strands concerns the donor side: 1. research on tax incentives for charitable giving; 2. research on the effects of changes in government funding. The other three strands concern nonprofit organizations: 3. research on entrepreneurship, 4. research on fundraising and 5. the Matthew effect.

1 Tax-price effects on charitable giving

A considerable body of literature in economics studied how changes in the tax-price of giving influence private giving. Though most donors report that the price of giving is not a relevant motivation to donate (Konrath & Handy, 2018), previous research indicates that tax incentives do in fact affect charitable giving (Peloza & Steel, 2005; Steinberg, 1990). In their 16-year-old meta-analysis, Peloza and Steel (2005) find a considerable price elasticity of giving. Subsequent research continued to demonstrate strong price effects (Adena, 2014; Almunia etal., 2020; Bönke, Massarrat-Mashhadi& Siela, 2013; Duquette, 2016 ; Eckel & Grossman, 2008; Fack& Landais, 2010; Hungerman & Ottoni-Wilhelm, 2021; Karlan & List, 2007; Meer, 2014; Scharf& Smith, 2015). In the United Kingdom, Almunia et al. (2020) concluded that gift aid may have increased the amounts donated but not the proportion of donors.

Several studies also analyze differences between individuals and causes in their sensitivity to tax incentives of charitable giving, finding that the wealthy are more responsive to changes in the price of giving (Bekkers & Wiepking, 2011). As a result, it is likely that giving to culture is more price sensitive than giving to other causes, because giving to culture is much more prevalent among the wealthy than among non-wealthy households (Bekkers, Gouwenberg & Schuyt, 2020).

Previous research in the Netherlands confirms that taxpayers in the Netherlands are also sensitive to price changes (Bekkers, 2012, 2015; Bekkers & Mariani, 2009; Brennenraedts etal., 2016; De Jong, 2012; Ministerie van Financiën, 2008), suggesting that giving in the Netherlands is price sensitive, though much less so than studies from other countries indicate (Peloza & Steel, 2005). We can rule out the possibility that taxpayers are not responsive to the price of giving because they don't know about it. Fewer than 10% of taxpayers are unaware of the charitable deduction (Franssen & Bekkers, 2016, p. 34). We can, however, question the extent to which taxpayers are aware of the enhanced deductibility as a result of the legal reform. A majority of taxpayers gave incorrect answers in a knowledge quiz consisting of two questions on the legal reform (De Nooij, Bekkers & Felix, 2017).

2 *Effects of changes in government funding*

Because the legal reform coincided with significant government cutbacks, it is important to take note of the vast body of literature that has examined the relationship between government funding and private giving. In theory, a crowding-out effect occurs when a decrease in government funding leads to an increase in philanthropic giving for a cause or when an increase in charitable giving reduces government funding (Abrams & Schitz, 1978; De Wit & Bekkers, 2017; Lu, 2016). Reduction of government funding could lead nonprofit organizations to invest more in fundraising (Andreoni & Payne, 2003). A crowding-in effect occurs when an increase in government funding leads to an increase in charitable giving or vice versa (Khanna & Sandler, 2000). Institutional signaling theory predicts a crowding-in effect, as government support can signal that nonprofit organizations are trustworthy, leading to a positive relation between government funding and charitable giving (Handy, 2000; Heutel, 2014). Conversely, a reduction of direct government funding may signal to citizens that a charitable cause and the organizations supporting it are not worthy of support. In our case, it was an explicit objective of the government to create a crowding-out effect by replacing direct funding in the form of government grants by indirect support in the form of charitable deductions. If the signaling explanation holds, however, the pejorative remarks about the cultural sector by policy makers may have undermined the desired crowding-out effect.

The empirical evidence on the effects of changes in government funding is mixed. Though early studies (Kingma, 1989) suggested that an increase in government funding may decrease charitable giving, subsequent estimates have been less clear and may as well go in the opposite direction. Two recent meta-analyses (De Wit & Bekkers, 2017; Lu, 2016) showed that estimates vary widely from study to study, depending on the data, methods and context. De Wit and Bekkers (2017) show that laboratory studies are more likely to find crowding-out effects than studies relying on surveys or administrative data. There is little support for crowding-out (or crowding-in) outside the laboratory. The assessment by Payne (1998, p. 338) still holds: "a severe cut in government funding to nonprofit organizations is not likely, on average, to be made up by donations from private donors". One interpretation of the finding that estimates from experiments are stronger is that most citizens are not aware of changes in government funding, while participants in experiments receive explicit information (De Wit & Bekkers, 2020; Horne, Johnson & Van Slyke, 2005). The meta-analysis by Lu (2016) found a *positive* correlation between government funding and charitable giving to arts organizations in the United States, United Kingdom and Canada. This finding suggests a crowding-in, though it is not clear whether it holds in the Netherlands.

Four years before the legal reform, when the Netherlands government announced cutbacks after the 2008–2009 financial crisis in which it bailed out national banks, we asked participants in the Giving in the Netherlands Panel Study whether they would be willing to increase donations in various areas. At that time, it was not yet clear how much the government would cut in which areas. Among donors to cultural organizations, a mere 12% said they would be willing to increase donations. At the same time, among donors to culture, there was also a group of 9% that said they would be reducing their gifts in response to government cutbacks (Bekkers & Mariani, 2012). Because those who reported a willingness to increase their gifts gave low amounts anyway, and larger donors were reluctant to increase their gifts, the net effect in the entire population is likely to be minimal. After the cuts were announced, we asked similar questions and found even less positive results. Among those who gave to culture and were aware of the enhanced deductibility, only 8% expressed willingness to increase gifts to culture (Bekkers, Mariani & Franssen, 2015). Ten percent of these participants said they would give *less* in the coming year.

In sum, the effects of the legal reform on donor behavior by households are likely to be rather small: the tax-price effect on giving in the Netherlands is weak, and the willingness of citizens to increase donations after government cutbacks is small. Now we consider the changes that the legal reform may have had on the behavior of cultural nonprofit organizations.

3 Revenue diversification and entrepreneurship in nonprofit organizations

All organizations need to acquire and maintain financial resources for their operations (Pfeffer & Salancik, 1978). Nonprofit organizations are generally advised to adopt a revenue diversification strategy, as nonprofit organizations operate in a resource-scarce, competitive and therefore uncertain environment (Chang & Tuckman, 1994; Gronbjerg, 1993). Strong dependence on a single source of income could endanger the nonprofit organization if income from that source is suddenly reduced. Thus, nonprofit organizations are advised to avoid "putting all their eggs in one basket". Revenue diversification is a financial strategy in which the organization relies on diverse and multiple sources of income. It improves the financial health and stability of nonprofit organizations because it lowers the risk of financial crisis, provides the organization with a financial cushion and improves the likelihood for financial organizational survival (Chikoto-Schultz & Sakolvittayanon, 2020). A particularly relevant finding by Hager (2001) is that arts nonprofit organizations with a higher degree of revenue diversification were less likely to close down. Kingma (1993) advises nonprofit organizations to consider the expected return, risk and correlation between different income sources when they are making decisions about the level of revenue diversification they seek to achieve.

Despite the theoretical relevance of revenue diversification, empirical estimates of its association with the financial health of nonprofit organizations, operationalized by either financial capacity, vulnerability or sustainability, do not reveal a clear pattern. Hung and Hager (2019) and Lu, Lin and Wang (2019) conducted meta-analyses of revenue diversification. Both found a large degree of heterogeneity in the association between revenue diversification and nonprofit financial health. Some studies reveal positive results, others reveal negative results. Lu, Lin and Wang (2019) find that a majority of studies that examined the association between revenue diversification and financial capacity report a negative correlation, though the average is very close to zero. The bottom line is that there is no simple pattern in the association between revenue diversification and financial health, not even in the differences between the results.

In addition to government funding, nonprofit organizations can also raise income from private or corporate donations, engage in corporate sponsorships, apply for grants from foundations, sell goods and services, raise membership fees or obtain income from investments or other resources (Chikoto-Schultz & Sakolvittayanon, 2020; Garcia-Rodriquez & Romero-Merino,

2020). These other sources have gradually been considered more relevant in recent years (Garcia-Rodriquez & Romero-Merino, 2020). In particular, nonprofit organizations gradually adopted business practices and are said to become "business-like" (Maier, Meyer & Steinbereithner, 2016; Vaceková et al., 2020). One example of such business practices is implementing commercial activities to generate commercial income to support the nonprofit organization's mission. This involves, for instance, selling goods or products related to the nonprofit's mission but also asking admissions fees for nonprofit services (e.g., admission tickets to a museum, orchestra or theatre). Commercial activities may generate a substantial source of income for cultural nonprofit organizations.

Entrepreneurship. The charity tax reform in the Netherlands not only sought to encourage the financial independence of cultural nonprofit organizations by allowing them to generate more commercial income. The reform aimed to enhance their entrepreneurship. Entrepreneurial orientation involves three components: 1. innovation, 2. risk-taking and 3. pro-activeness (Lumpkin & Dess, 1996). Organizations with low scores on these dimensions are characterized as conservative (e.g., Morris, Webb & Franklin, 2011). Innovation is the degree of creativity and the extent to which new services, products or processes are introduced. Risk-taking refers to the degree to which an organization is willing to bear the risks and invests in services, products or projects that still have to prove successful. Pro-activeness refers to the extent to which an organization actively seeks opportunities and anticipates on future market needs.

The trend among nonprofit organizations to adopt business-like practices, however, also raises serious concerns (e.g., De Goede, Schrijvers& De Visser, 2018; Eikenberry& Kluver, 2004; Maier et al., 2016; Trommel, 2018; Vaceková etal., 2020; Weisbrod, 2004). One concern is mission drift. Weisbrod (2004, p. 40) recommends that "nonprofit organizations should get out of commercial ventures", as becoming business-like produces mission drift: a diversion of resources away from a nonprofit organization's mission. Maier, Meyer and Steinbereithner (2016) echo this warning. Vaceková and colleagues (2020) also highlight that income from commercial activities can be a risky approach. As nonprofit organizations adopt business-like practices, their commitment to public welfare may be in danger, at least in the public's perception. Commercial activities could cause a loss of income from private donations and government grants. On the other hand, they may also help to secure survival of the organization (Vaceková et al., 2020). The arguments supporting the legal reform ran along these lines.

Nonprofit organizations may demonstrate an entrepreneurial orientation in the programs and services they offer, as well as in the activities they engage in to generate income. Investments in fundraising activities are an important example of entrepreneurship (Mourdaunt & Paton, 2013).

4 Fundraising: If you don't ask, you don't get

Historically, private donations are the most distinctive source of income for nonprofit organizations (Garcia-Rodriguez & Romero-Merino, 2020; Weisbrod, 1998). While the literature is replete with studies examining the individual determinants and motivations of donating behavior (e.g. Bekkers & Wiepking, 2011; Konrath & Handy, 2018), very few studies investigated how fundraising activities by nonprofit organizations affect giving behavior. Without fundraising, however, nonprofit organizations would receive very few donations. In the Netherlands, more than 95% of all donations by individuals occur in response to some form of solicitation (Bekkers, 2005). As a result, differences between households in giving behavior are strongly affected by the likelihood of exposure to fundraising solicitations (Bekkers, 2005, 2019).

Approaches to fundraising "are nearly as diverse as the types of nonprofit organizations that populate the nonprofit sector" (Hager, Rooney & Pollak, 2002, p. 312). Effective fundraising activities attract contributions by private individuals or corporations at a scale that exceeds their costs. Effective fundraising requires practical knowledge that can be taught and learned (Breeze, 2017). On the other hand, fundraising also benefits from social skills that some people have more of than others.

The prevalence and effectiveness of fundraising activities vary considerably across countries and organizations. Though the Netherlands has a long philanthropic tradition, the current degree of professionalization of fundraising in the Netherlands is not as high as in Anglo-Saxon countries (Wiepking & Handy, 2015; Wiepking et al., 2021). Fundraising activities in the Netherlands rely heavily on volunteers who have not been trained as fundraisers. The most common fundraising method in the Netherlands is door-to-door collection. This method is highly effective in terms of compliance but inefficient in terms of return on investment (Bekkers, 2005), because strong social norms direct low gift amounts, irrespective of income (Wiepking & Heijnen, 2011). Moreover, the reduced availability of volunteers has made it more difficult for charities to organize fundraising campaigns. As a result, households receive a lower number of solicitations to contribute to charities.

Fundraising efforts also depend on a range of organizational factors, including the field of activity, organizational age, organizational size in terms of paid staff and total revenues, geographical scope and location and tax status (Lyon & Zappala, 2006). For instance, younger nonprofit organizations experience greater difficulty in raising funds, as they have not yet earned a solid reputation and donor trust. This is a problem for new organizations in the market for charity.

Fundraising investments and effectiveness are a function of capacity (size, paid staff) and experience. This implies that cultural nonprofit organizations with more fundraising experience and more capacity in terms of size and the presence of paid staff are more likely to attract donations (Hager, et al., 2002). Chang and Tuckman (1994) find that higher spending on fundraising is positively associated with revenue diversification. Larger organizations arguably have more capacity to invest in fundraising. When facing cuts in government funding, they will be more able to replace that amount by income from fundraising. Thus, fundraising experience and capacity determine the ability to deal with reductions in government grants.

The Matthew Effect. The previous can result in the so-called "Matthew effect", labeled by Merton (1968) after a phrase in Matthew (13:12): "to him who has will more be given, and he will have abundance; but from him who has not, even what he has will be taken away". Matthew effects occur when previous advantage leads to further advantage and previous disadvantage leads to further disadvantage (Merton, 1968). Matthew effects exacerbate existing resource disparities and are essential in understanding the dynamics of inequality. Matthew effects are observed across a broad spectrum of social, economic and political institutions and systems (Rigney, 2010).

In our study context, larger cultural nonprofit organizations are most likely to invest in fundraising, gaining experience and capacity, and thus obtain more income from fundraising. Smaller cultural nonprofit organizations, on the other hand, are most likely unable to make investments in fundraising and will thus lack fundraising experience and capacity and receive less income from fundraising. Thus, larger cultural nonprofit organizations will obtain more fundraising income, while smaller cultural nonprofit organizations will obtain less fundraising income. The larger cultural nonprofit organizations are advantaged by being able to make necessary investments and being more experienced, while smaller organizations are disadvantaged. A dynamic analysis of income changes among the 465 largest charities in the Netherlands in the period 2005–2010 indicated that, indeed, government funding and fundraising capacity are positively related (Bekkers, 2013). In flat contrast to the crowding-out hypothesis, charities that saw their income from government funding increase in a given year were more likely to increase investments in fundraising in subsequent years. Charities that lost government funding, in contrast, were less likely to increase investments in fundraising. Such patterns suggest that in the Netherlands, government funding and private donations are complements rather than substitutes. To better understand this complementarity, it is crucial to examine the dynamics of different revenue sources (De Wit, Bekkers & Wiepking, 2020, p. 83). Hung (2020) performed a meta-analysis on the relationship between commercialization and private donations, finding that commercialization and private donations were not related in cultural nonprofit organizations – again in studies that were largely from the United States, United Kingdom and Canada. Examining earned revenue activities, Levine Daniel (2021) showed that earned revenue activities complement donations when the activity entails offering new products or services to existing donors.

The Dutch government cutbacks and the charity tax reform will most likely widen the income gaps between larger and smaller cultural nonprofit organizations. Resources accumulate among the larger cultural nonprofit organizations, carrying them in a upward spiral towards further advantage as they gain more experience and gain more financial means to make further investments in fundraising. Smaller cultural nonprofit organizations will experience a downward spiral.

One reason larger organizations may be advantaged compared to smaller organizations with regard to the government cutbacks is that it takes resources to be resilient (Barasa, Mbau & Gilson, 2018). Organizations with fewer resources at their disposal are less likely to fully recover from adverse events such as cutbacks. In an analysis of register data, the national audit chamber found that 16% of cultural nonprofit organizations that had received government grants prior to the cutbacks went out of business after the cutbacks (Algemene Rekenkamer, 2015). This is an important caveat for the following analyses of changes in the behavior of cultural nonprofit organizations: we are essentially looking at a population of relatively resourceful and resilient survivors.

Data and methods

In the following analyses, we examine changes at both the donor and recipient side of the market for giving to cultural nonprofit organizations in the Netherlands. On the donor side, we document changes in giving behavior of households, corporations and high-net-worth households. Have donations to culture increased after the charity tax reform? On the recipient side, we document changes in the income sources as well as entrepreneurial behavior among cultural nonprofit organizations. An analysis of this data allows us to estimate to what extent the reduction of direct government support has been compensated by other sources of income.

Data. We collected longitudinal data covering the period between 2011 and 2019. For the donor side, we rely on data from the Giving in the Netherlands (GIN) studies, an initiative of the Center for Philanthropic Studies at the Vrije Universiteit Amsterdam. Since 1995, the research provides biennial macro-economic estimates of philanthropy by households, corporations, foundations, bequests and lotteries. For the recipient side, we rely on data gathered among cultural nonprofit organizations in the Netherlands. The appendix provides details on both data sets.

As income diversification and entrepreneurial behavior by cultural non-profit organizations vary with the level of income, we divide the responses from cultural nonprofit organizations into five groups: very small (max €2,000), small (€2k–€50k), medium-sized (€50k– €1.5 million), large (€1.5– €10 million), and very large (more than €10 million). In some analyses, we combined the two highest income levels into one group of (very) large cultural nonprofit organizations. Table 26.1 provides an overview of the composition of the sample for 2012, 2015 and 2019.

Table 26.1 Sample composition in number of cultural nonprofit organizations per income class (n), the share of the response per year (%) and the average income (€) for 2012, 2015 and 2019

	2012			*2015*			*2019*		
	n	%	€	n	%	€	n	%	€[1]
Very small Max 2K	229	23	267	51	12	436	33	6	745
Small (2–50K)	407	41	17.942	203	46	17.816	219	38	18.743
Medium-sized (50K–1.5 mln)	243	25	353.265	126	29	366.789	182	32	401.979
Large and very large (>1.5 mln)	103	10	8.366.911	58	13	9.493.479	140	24	8.974.125
Total sample	982	100	904.337	438	100	1.370.950	574	100	2.323.462
Excluding the very large organizations (>10 mln)	964	98	455.132	428	98	601.447	539	76	909.422

The composition of the response varies from year to year as a result of changing priorities in the data collection strategy. In the first edition, we sought to obtain the broadest possible representation of the cultural sector. We included as many organizations as possible and invested a lot of effort to recruit them. As a result, the response consisted mainly of small organizations with no paid staff. In the second edition, we had fewer resources available but sought to retain as many organizations as possible that participated in the first edition. This proved difficult for the smallest organizations. In the third edition, we focused on the largest organizations to capture the majority of all economic activity in the cultural sector. As a result, almost one-fourth of the response consisted of large institutions. To control for changes in the income distribution of the response by organizations, we stratified the analyses per year by income class.

This chapter provides a descriptive analysis of changes in giving behavior by households and corporations and in income sources and entrepreneurial behavior among cultural nonprofit organizations over the course of the period 2011–2019. Unfortunately, the nature and chronology of the policy decisions do not allow for a clean causal identification of the effects of the legal reform. Most importantly, the legal reform coincided with severe government cutbacks in the cultural sector. As a result, we cannot identify the effect of either one of the two. At best, we obtain an aggregate estimate of the combined effects of the charity tax reform and the government cutbacks. In the more likely scenario, however, numerous other unmeasured factors such as ongoing trends in giving behavior, technological advancements and fluctuations in the economy created changes in giving behavior and the behavior of cultural nonprofit organizations. On the donor side, we can to some extent control influences on giving to culture that also occur in other sectors. Because the multiplier favored cultural nonprofit organizations, the proportion of total giving that goes to cultural nonprofit organizations should have increased. Even when the exact size of the price effect due to the introduction of the multiplier cannot be identified, we can observe its sign. Theoretically, the reduction in the price of giving should lead to an increase in the amount donated, particularly among those who use the charitable deduction. If we do not observe such a change, we can either assume that the price effect is absent or that it has been neutralized by a negative effect of the reduction in direct government funding. In both cases, we can infer that the price effect is weaker than the effect of the reduction in direct government funding.

Results: a small increase in total amounts donated to culture after the reform

A first result is that giving behavior to culture and arts increased from €293 million in 2011 to €439 million in 2018 (see the light grey line in Figure 26.1). This seems like a large increase. In the same period, however, contributions to other causes (religion, health, international assistance, environment, nature and animal protection, sports and recreation and education and research) increased as well, roughly at a similar pace.

Total giving (the dark grey line) increased from €4.3 billion in 2011 to €5.7 billion in 2018. As a result, the share of culture (the striped black line) remained small and did not increase much. In 2011, culture received 6.8% of all contributions; in 2018, the share was 7.8%.

Figure 26.2 breaks down the sources of contributions. Households provide a small share of all contributions to culture. In 2018, households donated €78 million to culture, amounting to 18% of all contributions to culture. In 2011, the amount donated was €26 million, amounting to 9% of all contributions. We cannot attribute the full increase to changes in giving behavior by households, because the method improved. We will revisit this issue in the following when we discuss amounts deducted, particularly by wealthy households.

In the Netherlands, charity lotteries also provide a significant share of funding to cultural nonprofit organizations. The amount was €80 million in 2018, 18% of all contributions to culture. In 2011, lotteries gifted a total of €68 million (23%). Gifts from lotteries are mostly coming from one lottery: the BankGiro Loterij.

An increasing share of total income for cultural nonprofit organizations comes from bequests. In 2018, the total amount to culture and arts received through bequests amounted to €33 million, 8% of total contributions. The amount in 2018 is much higher than in previous years, mostly as a result of a single very large bequest of €22 million to the Prins Bernhard Cultuurfonds. Excluding this bequest, we still observe an increase in bequests, from €5.7 million in 2011 to €10.8 million in 2018.

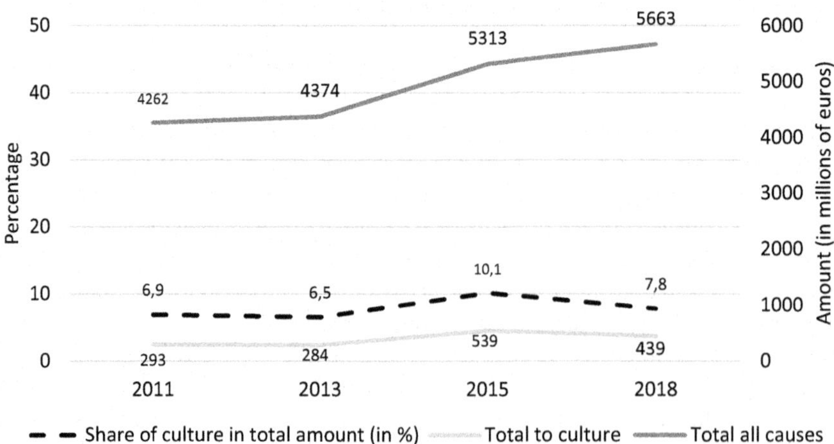

Figure 26.1 Total amounts donated to charitable causes, to culture and the share of culture in the total amount, 2011–2018

Note: Data for 2018 are based on a new estimation method in which the donations of high-net-worth households are also included.

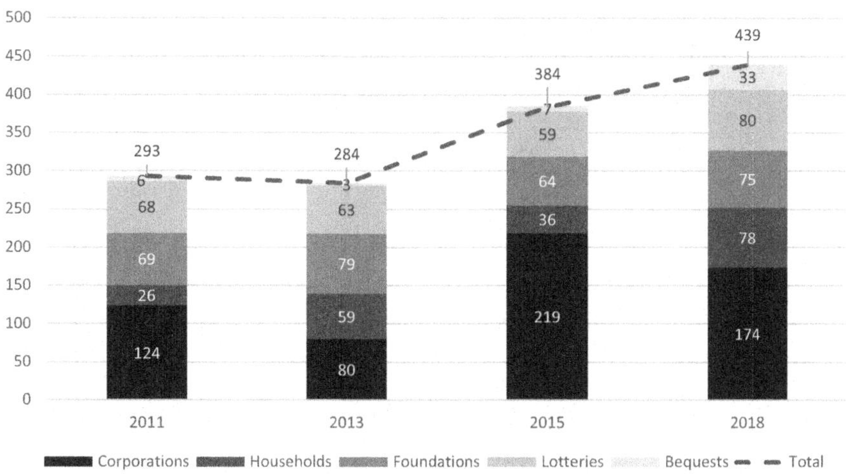

Figure 26.2 Total contributions to culture and arts in millions of euros, 2011–2018

Note: Data for 2018 are based on a new estimation method in which donations by high-net-worth households are better represented.

The largest share of contributions to culture typically comes from corporations. In 2018, corporations gave a total of €174 million to culture and arts. This was 40% of all contributions to culture. Compared to 2011, when corporations gifted a total of €124 million (42% of all contributions), this is an increase. The share of corporate donations to culture, however, remained small throughout the period (see Figure 26.3). In 2011, it was 9%. In 2013, it declined to 6%, then jumped to 11% and plateaued at that level in 2015 and 2018.

The total amount contributed by corporations consists of sponsorship and gifts. Corporations prefer sponsorships over gifts; almost three quarters (73%) of the total amount consists of sponsorships. About one third (36%) of corporate contributions to culture and arts were gifted in the form of manpower or in-kind donations (e.g., offering office space to host an exposition). Culture and arts is probably a sector where corporations can easily connect their name to a one-time event. The percentage of corporations supporting the culture and arts sector with gifts is small. Since 2011, the percentage of corporations using sponsorships is 10%. For gifts, this was 7% in 2011 and 5% in 2018.

Giving by households increased slightly

In 2018, about one in nine households donated to culture and arts (see Table 26.2). This proportion has not increased much since 2011. The average amount donated to culture and arts among those who give to culture has increased, from €37 in 2011 to €48 in 2018. We also see an increase in the median amount donated. The average amount among all donors (where we assigned those households that did not donate to culture a value of 0) also increased, from €3,50 in 2011 to €4,70 in 2018. While the amount donated to culture increased, the share of culture in total giving did not increase by much; it was 1.5% in 2011 and 2.0% in 2018.

High-net-worth households give less to culture

In 2018, about one in five high-net-worth households to culture (see Table 26.3). Unexpectedly, the proportion of high-net-worth households that give to culture has decreased since

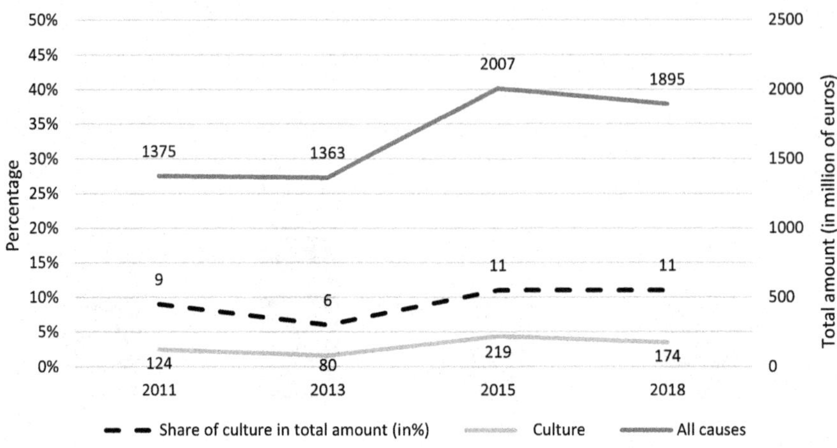

Figure 26.3 Share of culture in the total amount given by corporations, 2011–2018

Table 26.2 Percentage and average amount given to culture and arts by households, 2011–2018

	2011	*2013*	*2014*	*2015*	*2018*
% giving to culture	10	10	10	11	11
€ Average amount donated to culture (among donors)	37	34	28	36	48
€ Median amount donated to culture (among donors)	15	13	10	10	20
€ Average amount donated to culture (among all households)	3,50	3,50	2,80	4,90	4,70
€ Average amount to all causes (among all households)	225	240	216	247	236
Share of culture	1.5%	1.5%	1.3%	2.0%	2.0%

Table 26.3 Percentage and average amount given to culture and arts by high-net-worth (HNW) households, 2011–2018

	2011	*2013*	*2014*	*2015*	*2018*
% giving to culture	29	29	30	22	21
€ Average amount donated to culture (among HNW donors)	607	318	343	589	295
€ Median amount donated to culture (among HNW donors)	100	50	76	100	79
€ Average amount donated to culture (among all HNW households)	176	92	102	139	63
€ Average amount to all causes (among all HNW households)	2.254	1.009	1.267	1.657	1.071
Share of culture in total giving by HNW households	7.4%	9.1%	8.1%	8.4%	5.9%

2011, when it was 29%. The average amount donated to culture among those who give to culture has decreased as well, from €607 in 2011 to €295 in 2018. We also see a decrease in the median amount donated among high-net-worth households. The average amount among all donors (where we assigned those households that did not donate to culture a value of 0) also decreased, from €176 in 2011 to €63 in 2018. Thus, the share of culture decreased from 7.4% in 2011 and 5.9% in 2018.

Use of the charitable deduction by Dutch households decreased

Since 2012, donations to cultural ANBIs are eligible for an additional gift deduction. The percentage of households that use the deduction, however, has not increased since 2011. On the contrary, the proportion of households deducting gifts has declined from 8.9% in 2011 to 7.2% in 2018 (see Figure 26.4). Among high-net-worth households with a net worth exceeding €1 million, the proportion using the deduction has also decreased, from 17.0% in 2011 to 15.6% in 2018.

At the same time, we see that the average amount deducted increased, from €1.113 in 2011 to €1.423 in 2018. As a result, the total volume of donations for which Dutch households use the charitable deduction increased slowly from €723 million in 2011 to €792 million in 2018. The increase of €69 million over a period of 7 years is less than half the budgeted amount of €22 million per year.

Among households with a net worth exceeding €1 million, the percentage of households using the deduction decreased, but the amounts deducted increased slightly (see Table 26.4). We see the reverse pattern among the most wealthy households in the country with net worth exceeding €10 million. The net result is that the most wealthy households in the Netherlands have a higher share of all amounts deducted in 2018 (9.1%) than in 2011 (8.4%). For comparison, it is important to note that this group forms only 0.06% of all households in the Netherlands. This means that the inequality in the use of charitable deduction is large and increasing. The even more disconcerting conclusion is that the increase in the use of the charitable deduction was not accompanied by an increase in the amounts donated to culture among wealthy households.

Changes among cultural nonprofit organizations

Now we turn to the behavior of cultural nonprofit organizations. Were they able to diversify their income? Did their dependency on government funding decrease? Have cultural nonprofit organizations become more entrepreneurial?

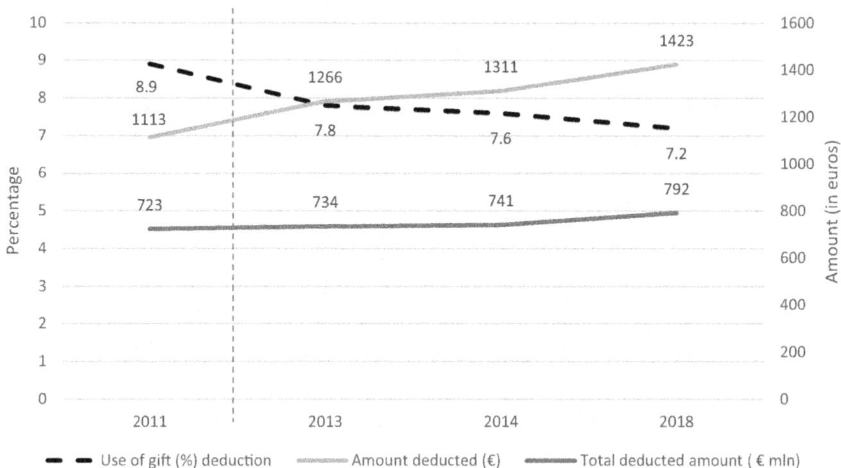

Figure 26.4 Percentage of Dutch households using the gift deduction, 2011–2018

Source: Statistics Netherlands (CBS)

Note: The vertical dotted line represents the legal reform (2012).

Table 26.4 Charitable deductions by wealthy households, 2011–2018

		2011	*2013*	*2014*	*2018*
Net worth >€1 million	%	17.0	16.2	16.0	15.6
	€	5.803	6.550	6.461	6.047
Net worth >€10 million	%	19.4	19.4	20.5	22.2
	€	16.800	18.200	15.600	16.000

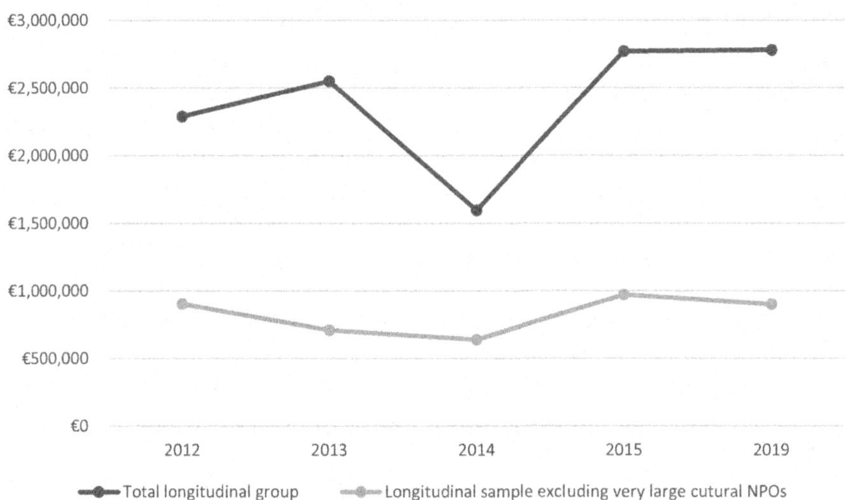

Figure 26.5 Total average income, longitudinal group 2012–2019

Were Dutch cultural nonprofit organizations able to diversify their income?

Table 26.1 shows the changes in total income of cultural nonprofit organizations for every income class in the period 2012–2019. Although the average income is subject to sample fluctuations, we see an increase in average total income within the very small and medium-sized cultural nonprofit organizations. There is no increase in revenues visible within the small and large cultural nonprofit organizations as the average amount in 2019 is roughly the same as in 2012. To obtain a more reliable view on revenue development over the years, we examine the longitudinal group.

Figure 26.5 shows the total income for the entire longitudinal group increased slightly over the period 2012–2019 with a decrease in 2014. This decrease can be a result of the small *n* and the lack of larger cultural nonprofit organizations in the response for that year. If we exclude the largest organizations, we see a smaller fluctuation in total income in the period 2012–2019 with no clear trend.

Income diversification

We divide the income of cultural nonprofit organizations into income sources: government funding, commercial revenues, private income, sponsorships, indirect revenues and other income. Government funding was furthermore divided into national or state government funding and other government funding (i.e., funding provided by the European Union, provincial government, municipalities). Commercial revenues refer to commercial activities related to the core activities of the nonprofit organization, such as entrance fees and tickets. Private income refers to donations, gifts, bequests from individuals and corporations. Sponsorships consist of income received from corporations in exchange for something in return that benefits the corporation. Private income and sponsorships together form fundraising income. Indirect revenues refer to generated income that is not directly related to the core activities of the organization. This includes for example, revenues generated by renting out facilities and other indirect commercial activities.

We examine the income mix over the years for every income class separately to control to some extent for the sample fluctuation. Important to note is that we calculate the share of each income source in total income using the sum of all seven income sources as the total income. This sum, however, differs from the total reported income as reported in Table 26.1. After discussing the income mix, we examine each source of income separately.

Income mix

Figure 26.6 shows the income mix for all income classes in 2012, 2015 and 2019. Our data indicate that the income mix differs substantially between cultural nonprofit organizations when we divide them into the four income classes. Figure 26.6 shows that based on their income class, cultural nonprofit organizations differ not only in the sources from which the organizations derive income but also where the center of gravity lies in the income mix.

Very small cultural nonprofit organizations are less dependent on government funding in 2019 than in previous years. Moreover, sponsorships and other income sources are an important income source. Very small cultural nonprofit organizations rely on private revenues,

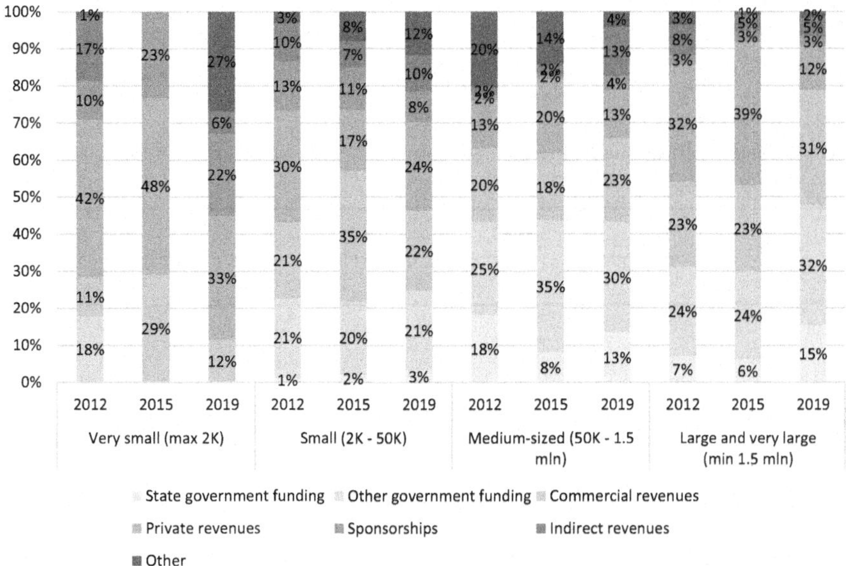

Figure 26.6 Income mix in share (in %) of total income for each income class in 2012, 2015 and 2019

sponsorships and other income, as these sources generate most of their income. Other cultural nonprofit organizations still rely for a large part of their income on grants and public activities. State government funding, other government funding and commercial revenues make up a large part of the total income of medium-sized, large and very large organizations. As the nonprofit organization grows, grants and public activities form a more important source of income. A smaller portion of the income comes from sponsorship, private, indirect and other sources. Private revenues, sponsorship and other income form a more important part of the total income for the (very) small nonprofit organizations. Private income and sponsorships increase importance when the cultural non profit organization is smaller.

The income mix of small cultural nonprofit organizations did not change much between 2012 and 2019. Other government funding, commercial and private revenues remain the most important sources of income. The income mix of medium-sized organizations remained largely unchanged. The main sources of income are still other government funding and commercial revenues. The income mix of large and very large cultural nonprofit organizations appears more unbalanced in 2019 than in 2012 and 2015. Income from state government funding, other government funding and commercial revenues is more important in 2019. Private revenues, on the other hand, seem less important; sponsorships within the large and very large institutions still only generate a very small part of their total income.

Government funding

Table 26.5 strikingly shows that the share of state government grants in total revenues of the large and very large cultural nonprofit organizations is *higher* in 2019 compared to previous years. Very small cultural nonprofit organizations did not receive any government funding by the state during the entire period. The share of state government funding in medium-sized organizations fluctuates over the years. The share of state government funding in the class of small cultural nonprofit organizations seems to be stable over the years.

Table 26.6 shows the average income from other government funding for each income class over the years. We see that the share of other government funding in the total income in 2019 is higher for large and very large cultural nonprofit organizations. Very small cultural nonprofit organizations did not receive other government funding. Among small and

Table 26.5 State government funding in average amount (in €) and share (in %) in the total revenues per income class 2012–2019

	2012		*2013*		*2014*		*2015*		*2019*	
	%	€	%	€	%	€	%	€	%	€
Very small (Max 2K)	0	2	0	3	0	0	0	0	0	0
Small (2K–50K)	1	178	3	399	1	212	2	339	3	1.018
Medium-sized (50K–1.5 mln)	18	53.865	14	39.672	17	50.177	8	22.735	13	80.925
Large and very large (>1.5 mln)	7	648.060	5	487.822	5	489.483	6	540.656	15	1.659.939

Note: Share in % calculated based on the sum of the seven income sources as total income.

Table 26.6 Other government funding in average amount (in €) and share (in %) in the total revenues per income class 2012–2019

	2012		*2013*		*2014*		*2015*		*2019*	
	%	€	%	€	%	€	%	€	%	€
Very small (Max 2K)	17	101	1	8	0	0	0	0	0	0
Small (2K–50K)	21	2.770	19	2.787	19	2.834	20	3.048	21	6.508
Medium-sized (50K–1.5 mln)	25	75.400	33	96.636	26	78.447	35	98.454	30	179.545
Large and very large (>1.5 mln)	24	2.221.084	20	1.942.755	20	1.886.522	24	2.058.428	32	3.473.801

Note: Share in % calculated based on the sum of the seven income sources as total income.

medium-sized cultural nonprofit organizations, the share of other government funding in total income in 2019 did not change compared to 2012, although slight fluctuation is visible between the years.

When we add both government funding sources together, we see that government funding remains an important source of income for the majority of Dutch cultural nonprofit organizations. Government funding accounts for 24%, 43% and 47% of the total revenues for small, medium-sized and (very) large cultural nonprofit organizations. Contrary to the objective of the legal reform and the cutbacks, dependence on government funding among (very) large cultural nonprofit organizations is much higher in 2019 than in previous years. The dependence on government funding among small and medium-sized cultural nonprofit organizations is similar in 2019 and 2012. Only the dependence on government funding among very small nonprofit organizations fell sharply when we compare 2019 with 2012.

Commercial revenues

Table 26.7 shows that the share of commercial revenues is subject to fluctuation for all income classes. In 2019, it appears that commercial revenues have become a more important source of income for larger cultural nonprofit organizations. The share of commercial revenues in total income for (very) small organizations does not differ too much in 2012 and 2013; in 2014 and 2015, there appears to be an upward trend. Nonetheless, the trend did not continue in 2019. Among medium-sized cultural nonprofit organizations, the share of commercial income is slightly higher in 2019 after a small decrease in 2014 and 2015. When we look at (very) large cultural organizations, commercial revenues constitute a bigger share of the total income.

Private revenues

The share of private revenues in the total income fluctuates over the years for all income classes; it appears that private revenues such as donations, gifts and bequests from individuals and corporations is a less important source of income when the cultural nonprofit organization is larger. In Table 26.8, we see that the share of private revenues in the total income among (very) small cultural nonprofit organizations is lower in 2019 compared to 2012. The share of private

Table 26.7 Commercial revenues in average amount (in €) and share (in %) in the total revenues per income class 2012–2019

	2012		*2013*		*2014*		*2015*		*2019*	
	%	€	%	€	%	€	%	€	%	€
Very small (Max 2K)	10	60	10	62	27	90	29	259	12	154
Small (2K–50K)	21	2.682	27	3.844	24	3.539	35	5.416	22	6.568
Medium-sized (50K–1.5 mln)	20	59.281	20	57.565	18	53.619	18	50.117	23	136.787
Large and very large (>1.5 mln)	23	2.097.792	24	2.362.998	20	1.905.460	23	2.025.139	31	3.333.086

Note: Share in % calculated based on the sum of the seven income sources as total income.

Table 26.8 Private revenues in average amount (in €) and share (in %) in the total revenues per income class 2012–2019

	2012		*2013*		*2014*		*2015*		*2019*	
	%	€	%	€	%	€	%	€	%	€
Very small (Max 2K)	42	240	25	152	57	191	48	423	33	444
Small (2K–50K)	30	3.902	21	3.066	30	4.494	17	2.564	24	7.292
Medium-sized (50K–1.5 mln)	13	38.016	18	53.655	14	43.938	20	55.667	13	77.773
Large and very large (>1.5 mln)	32	2.900.695	27	2.652.564	27	2.552.921	39	3.365.523	12	1.259.389

Note: Share in % calculated based on the sum of the seven income sources as total income.

revenues in the class of medium-sized organizations remains relatively stable. Interestingly, the share of private revenues of the (very) large organizations fluctuates over the years. When we compare the share of 2019 with 2012, the share of this income source fell sharply in the class of (very) large organizations. Commercial revenues seem to be an important source of income over the years for smaller cultural nonprofit organizations.

Sponsorships

Similar to private revenues, sponsorships also appear to be a more important source of income for smaller cultural nonprofit organizations. See Table 26.9. The share of sponsorship income in the total income is higher in 2019 compared to 2012 among the very small organizations. Again, we see strong fluctuation over the years without a clear trend. Within the group of small cultural organizations, sponsorships constitute a smaller share in 2019 than in previous years; sponsorships thus became a less important income source for these organizations. The share of sponsorships remains the same for medium-sized and large organizations over the years; sponsorships generate only a small portion of their income.

Table 26.9 Sponsorship revenues in average amount (in €) and share (in %) in the total revenues per income class 2012–2019

	2012		*2013*		*2014*		*2015*		*2019*	
	%	€	%	€	%	€	%	€	%	€
Very small (Max 2K)	10	59	5	29	2	6	23	206	22	294
Small (2K–50K)	13	1.718	14	1.974	10	1.433	11	1.748	8	2.514
Medium-sized (50K–1.5 mln)	2	4.757	2	5.621	2	5.342	2	4.276	4	22.900
Large and very large (>1.5 mln)	3	243.145	3	330.556	3	283.373	3	252.981	3	289.597

Note: share in % calculated based on the sum of the seven income sources as total income.

Table 26.10 Indirect revenues in average amount (in €) and share (in %) in the total revenues per income class 2012–2019

	2012		*2013*		*2014*		*2015*		*2019*	
	%	€	%	€	%	€	%	€	%	€
Very small (Max 2K)	17	97	50	306	13	45	0	0	6	81
Small (2K–50K)	10	1.349	13	1.878	13	1.882	7	1.087	10	2.963
Medium-sized (50K–1.5 mln)	2	6.535	3	8.127	10	30.895	2	6.585	13	80.573
Large and very large (>1.5 mln)	8	763.930	7	638.919	11	1.021.566	5	398.608	5	537.567

Note: Share in % calculated based on the sum of the seven income sources as total income.

Indirect revenues

Our data show that the importance of indirect revenues on the total income fluctuates for all income classes and is a relatively small source of income in 2019. For instance, we see that the share of indirect revenues in the total source of income in the group of very small, large and very large institutions in 2019 is lower compared to 2012 but higher or equal to the years in between. In the class of medium-sized organizations, the share of indirect revenues is also subject to strong fluctuations from year to year without a clear trend.

Changes in fundraising

Private revenues such as contributions, donations, gifts, sponsorships and bequests from individuals and corporations can be considered fundraising income. The data show that larger cultural nonprofit organizations engage more often in fundraising and invest more in fundraising. In 2019, 55%, 50%, 73%, 89% and 100% of very small, small, medium-sized, large and very large cultural nonprofit organizations engaged in fundraising. On average, in 2019, very small nonprofit organizations invest on average €113 in fundraising; small, medium-sized and (very) large organizations invest on average €507, €7.127 and €97.970, respectively. In addition, we find that smaller organizations more often rely on volunteers for fundraising activities, whereas larger cultural nonprofit organizations hire more paid staff to raise funds.

We also asked respondents one question inquiring their knowledge on the legal reform. Our inquiry, asked the height of the multiplier for individual donations to cultural nonprofit organizations (1.25). Large(r) organizations were more likely to answer this question correctly and have more knowledge about the reform.

The data also show a relation between the size of the organization and whether a cultural nonprofit organization communicates about the multiplier to potential donors. The larger the cultural nonprofit organization, the more likely it is that the organization communicates about the multiplier. Cultural nonprofit organizations that do not communicate about the multiplier generate substantially fewer revenues than those that do communicate about the reform.

Did cultural nonprofit organizations become more entrepreneurial?

Besides stimulating individual and corporate donations to cultural nonprofit organizations, the legal reform also aimed to stimulate cultural nonprofit organizations to become more entrepreneurial. This would subsequently reduce their dependency on government funding and would diversify their income. Within our study, we provided respondents with various statements related to entrepreneurship to measure their attitudes towards and levels of entrepreneurship within their organization. Our statements stem from the theoretical concept of entrepreneurial orientation (EO). Were cultural nonprofit organizations able to become more entrepreneurial, and which cultural nonprofit organizations have been most successful in achieving this? We can conclude that the cultural nonprofit organizations that participated in our study had a more positive attitude towards entrepreneurship in 2020 than in previous years.

We included one statement related to entrepreneurship in general. We asked to what extent respondents agreed or disagreed with the statement "Working in an entrepreneurial way is important for our organization" on a 6-point Likert-scale ranging from "totally disagree" (1) to "totally agree" (6). Figure 26.7 shows that, over the years, an increasing proportion of respondents (fully) agreed with this statement.

We presented three statements to respondents about innovation – with the same 6-point Likert scale. Figure 26.8 shows that the majority of respondents indicated that their organization behaves rather innovatively by exploring new opportunities, improving and innovating programs and projects and by constantly seeking new projects and activities. The percentage of cultural nonprofit organizations that have a positive attitude towards innovation was higher in 2019 than in 2015 and 2016.

To measure pro-activeness, we provided respondents in 2020 with two statements in which they had to choose between two alternatives on a 7-point Likert scale. At the one end is a "reactive" alternative (1), while the other end gives a "pro-active" alternative (7). Reactive organizations wait, while pro-active organizations take the lead. Respondents could also choose a middle position (4). We organized the responses in such a way that respondents choosing 1–3 were classified as "reactive", while respondents choosing 5–7 were classified as "pro-active". Figure 26.9 shows that cultural nonprofit organizations are very divided when it comes to their attitude towards being proactive.

Third, we investigated the extent to which respondents indicated their organizations are willing to take risks. Similar to pro-activeness, we provided respondents with two statements in

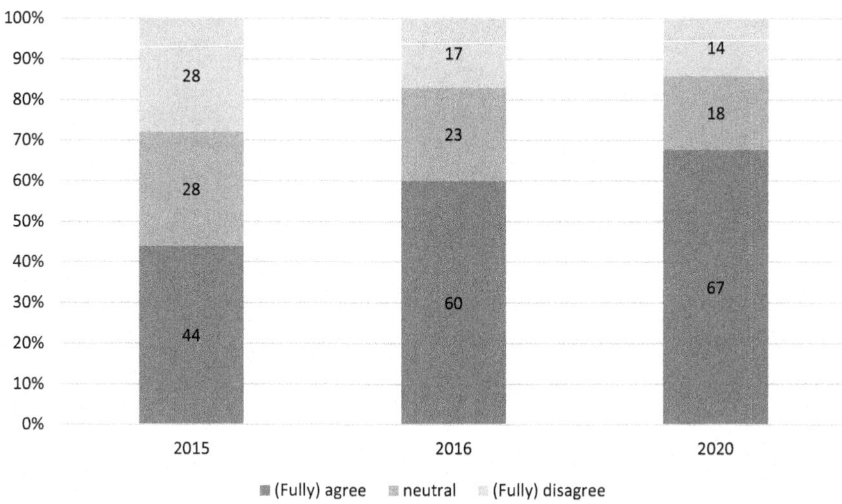

Figure 26.7 Agreement to the statement "Working in an entrepreneurial way is important for our organization" in 2015, 2016 and 2020 (in %)

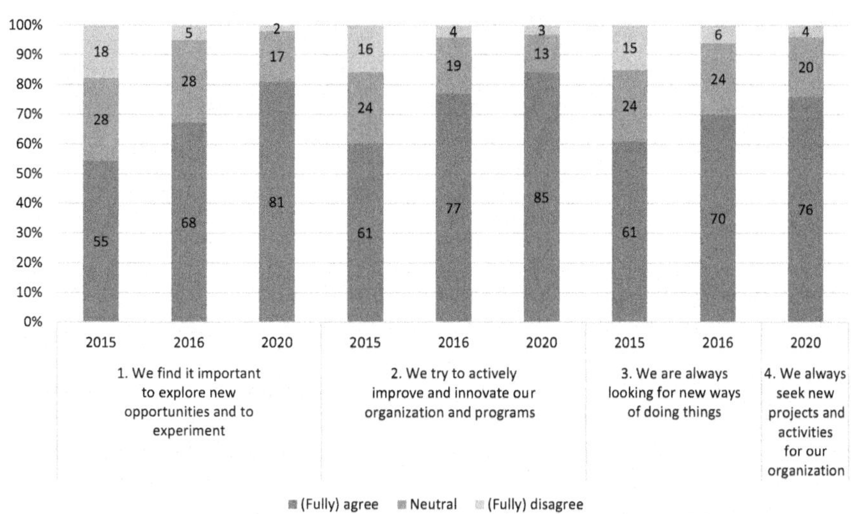

Figure 26.8 Agreement to statements on innovation in 2015, 2016 and 2020 (in %)

which respondents needed to choose between two alternatives on a 7-point Likert scale. Both statements provide a risk-averse alternative (1) versus a risk-taking alternative (7). Figure 26.10 shows that respondents in 2020 more often say that their organization takes risks when it comes to projects and activities. This increase stems from a decrease in organizations that did not make a clear choice (4; neutral). The percentage that indicates their organization avoids taking risks remained the same over the years. We do not see a clear change in the more general statement about uncertain situations.

We also asked respondents about their attitudes towards being independent as an organization. These statements relate to the respondent's attitude towards government funding and

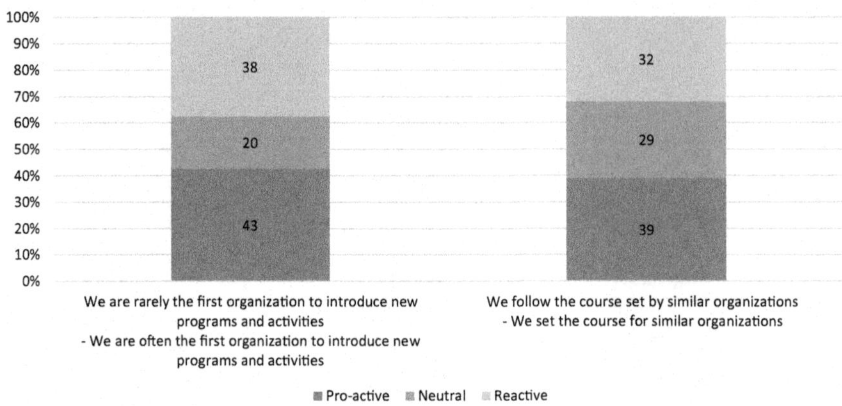

Figure 26.9 Responses to statements on pro-activeness in 2020 (in %)

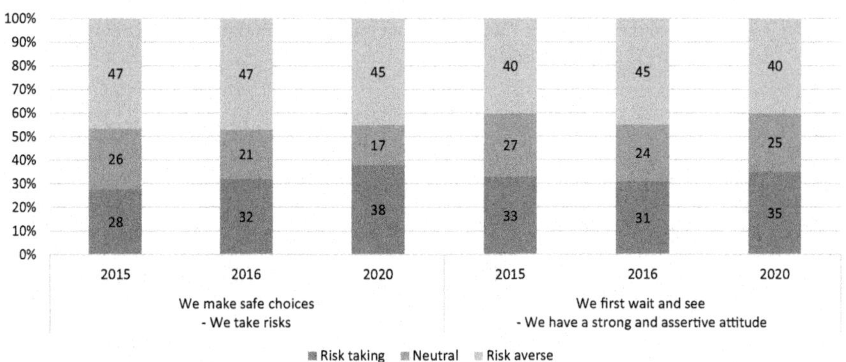

Figure 26.10 Responses to statements on risk-taking in 2015, 2016 and 2020 (in %)

income diversity: "It is good to be less dependent on the government" and "We rather engage in fundraising than receive government funding". Both statements had a 6-point Likert scale ranging from "fully disagree" (1) to "fully agree" (6). Figure 26.11 shows that the attitudes towards these two statements did not change substantially since 2015. Cultural nonprofit organizations attach greater importance to increasing their fundraising income to a lesser extent, they value independence from the government.

Finally, we provided two statements to respondents regarding the organization's collaboration with corporations and partnerships more broadly. Figure 26.12 shows that the attitudes towards cross-sector collaboration did not change substantially over the years. Most cultural nonprofit organizations in our sample indicate they are not reluctant when it comes to collaborating with corporations; attitudes towards collaboration with other parties outside the cultural sector are even more positive.

In Table 26.11, we look at four different aspects related to entrepreneurship per income class in 2020. It is evident that larger cultural nonprofit organizations score higher on entrepreneurship. The four aspects are innovation, risk-taking, cross-sector partnerships and independence. For innovation, we only look at the first three statements on innovation. When we look at

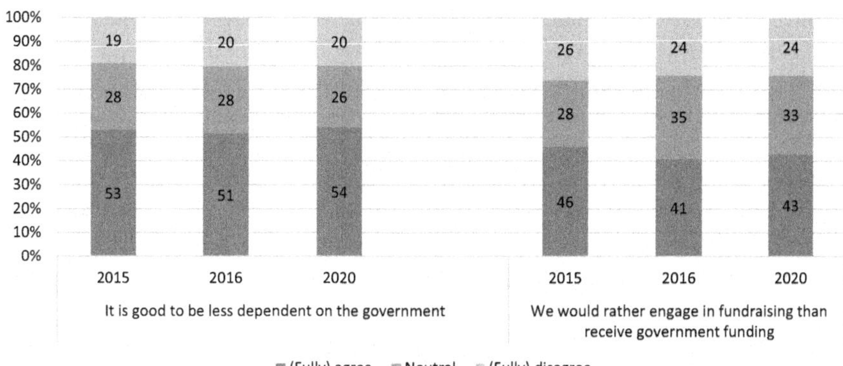

Figure 26.11 Responses to statements on independence in 2015, 2016 and 2020 (in %)

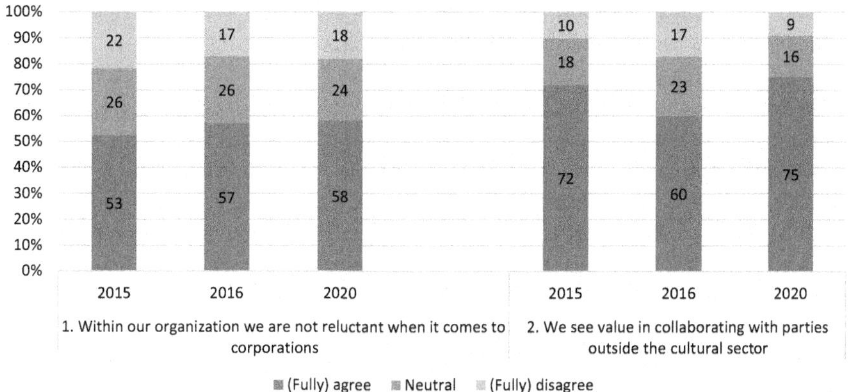

Figure 26.12 Responses to statements on cross-sector collaboration in 2015, 2016 and 2020 in (%)

Table 26.11 Highest score on four aspects of entrepreneurship per income class in 2020 (in %)

	Innovation	*Risk-taking*	*Cross-sector partnerships*	*Independence*	*Entrepreneurship*
Very small (Max 2K)	57	35	42	47	44
Small (2K–50K)	60	43	45	32	44
Medium-sized (50K–1.5 mln)	72	61	61	39	58
Large and very large (>1.5 mln)	92	71	66	48	68
Total sample	69	53	53	38	52

innovation, 57% of very small cultural nonprofit organizations (fully) agree with all three statements. In contrast, 92% of the largest organizations (fully) agree with these three statements. The same applies to risk-taking and the attitude towards cross-sector partnerships. Large(r) cultural nonprofit organizations have more positive attitudes. We see a different pattern when we look at independence. Very small organizations and (very) large cultural nonprofit organizations all score similarly. Their scores are more positive compared to medium-sized organizations. The total score in the last column is calculated based on the number of times that respondents have a positive attitude towards the four aspects of entrepreneurship. We see that the percentage of organizations that say they engage in entrepreneurial behavior increases markedly with the size of the organization.

Conclusions

We studied developments in donations to cultural nonprofit organizations and changes in their income sources and entrepreneurial orientations. On the donor side, we find that donations to culture increased somewhat after the charity law reform. The increase comes solely from an increase in the amount donated. The increase roughly kept pace with the increase in giving to other causes. This means that we do not see much of a substitution effect away from other causes to the cultural sector. Because the reform coincided with large cutbacks in direct government funding, we cannot isolate the tax-price effect on giving to culture. It is, however, unlikely that the effect comes from a crowding-out effect of reduced government funding. Before the reform, we found that households were not willing to compensate government cuts. The joint effect of the reduced tax-price of giving and the cutbacks is much less than projected by the Ministry of Finance. The increase in the amount deducted from the income tax was roughly half of the projected increase. Finally, we see that the increase does not come from the group of wealthy households that gives the highest amounts to culture and benefits most from the tax deduction. As a matter of fact, donations to the cultural sector made by wealthy households even decreased after the introduction of the charity law reform, though at the same time, the amounts deducted by the most wealthy households increased. This makes it unlikely that the increase in giving to culture is the result of the multiplier for donations to culture that the legal reform introduced.

The results on the side of cultural nonprofit organizations are very different. Our findings indicate that cultural nonprofit organizations succeeded in earning more income from private sources and became more entrepreneurial. The increase in entrepreneurship is evident both from the attitudes of cultural nonprofit organizations as well as from their behavior. These results are in line with the objectives of the reform.

At the same time, cultural nonprofit organizations are still relying on government funding quite heavily. Contrary to the objective of the charity tax reform, cultural nonprofit organizations relied more strongly on government funding in 2019 than in previous years. Their sources of income did not become more balanced or diversified. We also see that a Matthew effect occurred: differences between smaller and larger organizations increased. In part, this development is due to more investments in fundraising by larger organizations and more effective communication about the reform to prospective donors.

We conclude with a few insights for policymakers in other countries. What can they learn from the Dutch charity tax reform for the effective design of tax incentives for charitable giving? A first lesson is that one should not expect miracles: enhanced deductions do not easily expand the pie of total giving. A second lesson is that it is important to help organizations to become entrepreneurial and learn how to successfully engage in fundraising. Cultural nonprofit organizations that invested in fundraising were more likely to increase their fundraising income.

These were larger organizations. Prior experience and current income allow these organizations to build capacity and invest in fundraising, enabling them to obtain the necessary skills and capacity for fundraising. Subsequently, these investments generate income out of fundraising and commercial activities. Finally, we warn policy makers to be aware of adverse consequences such as the Matthew effect or substitution effects. Though we did not see much of a substitution effect in giving behavior, we do see a Matthew effect among cultural nonprofit organizations.

Note

1 This text and supporting materials are available at https://osf.io/qrdfc/.

References

Abrams, B.A., & Schitz, M.D. (1978). The 'crowding-out' effect of governmental transfers on private charitable contributions. *Public Choice*, 33(1), 29–39.

Adena, M. (2014). Tax-price elasticity of charitable donations: Evidence from the German taxpayer panel. Discussion Paper No. SP II 2014-302. Berlin: Wissenschaftszentrum Berlin für Sozialforschung (WZB).

Algemene Rekenkamer (2015). *Bezuiniging op cultuur: Realisatie en effect.* Den Haag: Algemene Rekenkamer. https://www.rekenkamer.nl/binaries/rekenkamer/documenten/rapporten/2015/02/12/bezuiniging-op-cultuur/Bezuiniging_op_cultuur.pdf

Almunia, M., Guceri, I., Lockwood, B., & Scharf, K. (2020). More giving or more givers? The effects of tax incentives on charitable donations in the UK. *Journal of Public Economics*, 183, 104114.

Andreoni, J., & Payne, A.A. (2003). Do government grants to private charities crowd out giving or fundraising? *American Economic Review*, 93(3), 792–812.

Barasa, E., Mbau, R., & Gilson, L. (2018). What is resilience and how can it be nurtured? A systematic review of empirical literature on organizational resilience. *International Journal of Health Policy and Management*, 7(6), 491.

Bekkers, R. (2005). It's not all in the ask: Effects and effectiveness of recruitment strategies used by nonprofits in the Netherlands. Paper presentation at the 34th ARNOVA Annual Conference, Washington, DC, November 17–20, 2005.

Bekkers, R. (2010). Giftenaftrek in Nederland: Evaluatiemethoden en hun interpretatie. *Weekblad Fiscaal Recht*, 139(6873), 1140–1148. http://renebekkers.files.wordpress.com/2011/08/bekkers_wfr_2010.pdf

Bekkers, R. (2012). The Limits of Social Influence on Giving. Paper presented at the workshop "Social influences and charitable giving", Centre for Market and Public Organisation, University of Bristol, February 24, 2012. https://renebekkers.files.wordpress.com/2015/11/limits-of-social-influence-on-giving-paper5.pdf.

Bekkers, R. (2013). De maatschappelijke betekenis van Filantropie [The societal significance of philanthropy]. Inaugural lecture, Vrije Universiteit Amsterdam. https://renebekkers.files.wordpress.com/2013/04/bekkers_filantropie.pdf.

Bekkers, R. (2018). *Values of philanthropy. Keynote address, ISTR conference.* Amsterdam: Vrije Universiteit Amsterdam. https://renebekkers.files.wordpress.com/2018/07/values-of-philanthropy.pdf.

Bekkers, R. (2019). De waarde van filantropie [The value of philanthropy]. Inaugural lecture, Vrije Universiteit Amsterdam, 6 June 2019. https://renebekkers.files.wordpress.com/2019/06/waarde-van-filantropie.pdf.

Bekkers, R., & Franssen, S.E. (2015). *De Geefwet en donaties aan cultuur in Nederland.* Pp. 16–19 in: Boekman 103. Amsterdam: Boekman. https://renebekkers.files.wordpress.com/2015/06/bekkers_franssen_boekman.pdf.

Bekkers, R., Gouwenberg, B.M., & Schuyt, T.N.M. (Eds.). (2020). *Geven in Nederland 2020.* Amsterdam: Lenthe. https://www.geveninnederland.nl/publicatie-geven-in-nederland-2020/ Summary in English: https://renebekkers.files.wordpress.com/2020/04/giving-in-the-netherlands-2020-summary.pdf.

Bekkers, R., & Mariani, E. (2009). Is the charitable deduction in the Netherlands treasury efficient? Paper presented at the Economics of Charitable Giving conference, Mannheim, October 8–9, 2009. http://test.giving.nl/wp-content/uploads/2013/09/Bekkers_Mariani_09-2.pdf.

Bekkers, R., & Mariani, E. (2012). Gedragseffecten van de Geefwet. *Weekblad voor privaatrecht, notariaat en registratie*, 143(6917), 133–139. https://renebekkers.files.wordpress.com/2011/08/bekkers_mariani_12_gedragseffecten-van-de-geefwet_pub.pdf

Bekkers, R., Mariani, E.E., & Franssen, S.E. (2015). Special: De multiplier in de Geefwet en het geefgedrag aan cultuur. Pp. 217-236 in: Bekkers, R., Shuyt, T.N.M., & Gouwenberg, B.M. (Eds.). *Geven in Nederland 2015: Giften, sponsoring, legaten en vrijwilligerswerk*. Amsterdam: Reed Business.

Bekkers, R., & Van Teunenbroek, C. (2020). Generatieverschillen in geefgedrag en vrijwilligerswerk. Pp. 22–48 in: Bekkers, R., Gouwenberg, B.M., & Schuyt, T.N.M. (Eds.). *Geven in Nederland 2020*. Amsterdam: Lenthe. https://renebekkers.files.wordpress.com/2020/04/bekkers_vanteunenbroek_20_special.pdf.

Bekkers, R., & Wiepking, P. (2011). A literature review of empirical studies of philanthropy: Eight mechanisms that drive charitable giving. *Nonprofit and Voluntary Sector Quarterly*, 40(5), 924–973.

Belastingdienst. (2021). Culturele ANBI. https://www.belastingdienst.nl/wps/wcm/connect/bldcontentnl/belastingdienst/zakelijk/bijzondere_regelingen/goede_doelen/algemeen_nut_beogende_instellingen/culturele_anbi/.

Bönke, T., Massarrat-Mashhadi, N., & Sielaff, C. (2013). Charitable giving in the German welfare state: Fiscal incentives and crowding out. *Public Choice*, 154(1–2), 39–58.

Breeze, B. (2017). *The new fundraisers: Who organises charitable giving in contemporary society?* Bristol: Policy Press.

Brennenraedts, R., Vankan, A., Veldman, J., Rienstra, Y., Bongers, F., Gielen, M., & Gercama, L. (2016). *Evaluatie giftenaftrek*. Utrecht: APE/Dialogic. https://www.dialogic.nl/wp-content/uploads/2016/12/Dialogic-2016.083-Evaluatie-Giftenaftrek.pdf.

Broer, T., & Niemantsverdriet, T. (2011). Halbe Zijlstra: Niet Raad voor Cultuur maar publiek moet bepalen wat goede kunst is. Vrij Nederland, January 12, 2011. https://www.vn.nl/halbe-zijlstra-niet-raad-voor-cultuur-maar-publiek-moet-bepalen-wat-goede-kunst-is/.

Chang, C.F., & Tuckman, H.P. (1994). Revenue diversification among non-profits. *Voluntas*, 5(3), 273–290.

Charities Aid Foundation. (2019). CAF World Giving Index: 10th edition, Ten years of giving trends. West Malling: CAF. https://www.cafonline.org/docs/default-source/about-us-publications/caf_wgi_10th_edition_report_2712a_web_101019.pdf.

Chikoto-Schultz, G., & Sakolvittayanon, N. (2020). Revenue diversification, growth, and stability. pp. 99–113 in: Garcia-Rodriguez, I., & Romero-Merino, M.E. (Eds.), *Financing nonprofit organizations*. London: Routledge.

De Goede, P., Schrijvers, E., & De Visser, M. (2018). Filantropie op de grens van overheid en markt. Naar een beleidsvisie. Pp. 11–65 in: De Goede, P., Schrijvers, E., & De Visser, M. (Eds.), *Filantropie op de grens van overheid en markt*. Den Haag: Wetenschappelijke Raad voor het Regeringsbeleid.

De Jager, J.C., & Weekers, F.H.H. (2011). Wijziging van enkele belastingwetten en enige andere wetten (Belastingplan 2012). Memorie van toelichting 33003. https://zoek.officielebekendmakingen.nl/kst-33003-3.pdf.

De Jong, A. (2012). Price elasticity of giving in the Netherlands. Master thesis, Erasmus University Rotterdam. https://thesis.eur.nl/pub/12390/12390-deJong.pdf.

De Nooij, F., Bekkers, R., & Felix, S. (2017). *Ontwikkelingen in giften, sponsoring en andere inkomsten van culturele instellingen in Nederland*. Amsterdam: Werkgroep Filantropische Studies, Vrije Universiteit Amsterdam. https://fci14.files.wordpress.com/2017/07/ontwikkelingen-in-giften-sponsoring-en-andere-inkomsten.pdf.

De Wit, A., & Bekkers, R. (2017). Government support and charitable donations: A meta-analysis of the crowding-out hypothesis. *Journal of Public Administration Research and Theory*, 27(2), 301–319.

De Wit, A., & Bekkers, R. (2020). Can charitable donations compensate for a reduction in government funding? The role of information. *Public Administration Review*, 80(2), 294–304.

De Wit, A., Bekkers, R., & Wiepking, P. (2020). Crowding-out or crowding-in: The dynamics of different revenue streams in: Garcia-Rodriguez, I., & Romero-Merino, M.E. (Eds.), *Financing nonprofit organizations*. Abingdon: Taylor & Francis.

Duquette, N.J. (2016). Do tax incentives affect charitable contributions? Evidence from public charities' reported revenues. *Journal of Public Economics*, 137, 51–69.

Eckel, C., & Grossman, P. (2008). Subsidizing charitable contributions: A natural field experiment comparing matching and rebate subsidies. *Experimental Economics*, 11, 234–252.

Eikenberry, A.M., & Kluver, J.D. (2004). The marketization of the nonprofit sector: Civil society at risk? *Public Administration Review*, 64(2), 132–140.

European Fundraising Association. (2018). Tax incentives for charitable giving in Europe. European Fundraising Association. https://efa-net.eu/wp-content/uploads/2018/12/EFA-Tax-Survey-Report-Dec-2018.pdf.

Fack, G., & Landais, C. (2010). Are tax incentives for charitable giving efficient? Evidence from France. *American Economic Journal: Economic Policy*, 2(2), 117–41.

Franssen, S.E., & Bekkers, R. (2016). *Culturele instellingen in Nederland: Veranderingen in geefgedrag, giften, fondsenwerving en inkomsten tussen 2011 en 2014*. Amsterdam: Werkgroep Filantropische Studies. https://fci14.files.wordpress.com/2021/04/franssen_bekkers_16_culturele-instellingen-in-nederland-2012-2014.pdf.

Garcia-Rodriguez, I., & Romero-Merino, M.E. (Eds.). (2020). *Financing nonprofit organizations*. New York: Routledge.

The Global Philanthropy Environment Index. (2018). The Lilly family school of philanthropy. http://hdl.handle.net/1805/15958.

Gronbjerg, K.A. (1993). *Understanding nonprofit funding: Managing revenues in social services and community development organizations*. San Francisco: Jossey-Bass.

Hager, M.A. (2001). Financial vulnerability among arts organizations: A test of the Tuckman-Chang measures. *Nonprofit and Voluntary Sector Quarterly*, 30(2), 376–392.

Hager, M.A., Rooney, P., & Pollak, T. (2002). How fundraising is carried out in US nonprofit organisations. *International Journal of Nonprofit and Voluntary Sector Marketing*, 7(4), 311–324.

Handy, F. (2000). How we beg: The analysis of direct mail appeals. *Nonprofit and Voluntary Sector Quarterly*, 29(3), 439–454.

Heutel, G. (2014). Crowding out and crowding in of private donations and government grants. *Public Finance Review*, 42(2), 143–175.

Horne, C.S., Johnson, J.L., & Van Slyke, D.M. (2005). Do charitable donors know enough – and care enough – about government subsidies to affect private giving to nonprofit organizations? *Nonprofit and Voluntary Sector Quarterly*, 34(1), 136–149.

Hudson Institute. (2013). *Philanthropic freedom: A pilot study*. Washington: Hudson Institute. https://s3.amazonaws.com/media.hudson.org/files/publications/FinalOnlineVersionPhilanthropicFreedomAPilotStudy.pdf.

Hudson Institute. (2015). *The index for philanthropic freedom*. Washington, DC: Hudson Institute. https://www.hudson.org/research/11363-index-of-philanthropic-freedom-2015.

Hung, C. (2020). Commercialization and nonprofit donations: A meta-analytic assessment and extension. *Nonprofit Management and Leadership*, 31(2), 287–309.

Hung, C., & Hager, M.A. (2019). The impact of revenue diversification on nonprofit financial health: A meta-analysis. *Nonprofit and Voluntary Sector Quarterly*, 48(1), 5–27.

Hungerman, D.M., & Ottoni-Wilhelm, M. (2021). Impure impact giving: Theory and evidence. *Journal of Political Economy*, 129(5), 1553–1614.

Karlan, D., & List, J. (2007). Does price matter in charitable giving? Evidence from a large-scale natural field experiment. *American Economic Review*, 97, 1774–1793.

Khanna, J., & Sandler, T. (2000). Partners in giving: The crowding-in effects of UK government grants. *European Economic Review*, 44(8), 1543–1556.

Kingma, B.R. (1989). An accurate measurement of the crowd-out effect, income effect, and price effect for charitable contributions. *Journal of Political Economy*, 97(5), 1197–1207.

Kingma, B.R. (1993). Portfolio theory and nonprofit financial stability. *Nonprofit and Voluntary Sector Quarterly*, 22(2), 105–119.

Konrath, S., & Handy, F. (2018). The development and validation of the motives to donate scale. *Nonprofit and Voluntary Sector Quarterly*, 47(2), 347–375.

Koolen-Maas, S.A., Van Teunenbroek, P.S.C., & Bekkers, R. (2021). *Geven en werven in de culturele sector in Nederland, 2011–2020*. Amsterdam: Werkgroep Filantropische Studies.

Levine Daniel, J. (2021). All Earned Revenue is Not Created Equal: Revenue Embeddedness as a Framework for Exploring Crowding-In/Crowding-Out Effects. Voluntas. https://doi.org/10.1007/s11266-021-00373-3

Lu, J. (2016). The philanthropic consequence of government grants to nonprofit organizations: A meta-analysis. *Nonprofit Management and Leadership*, 26(4), 381–400.

Lu, J., Lin, W., & Wang, Q. (2019). Does a more diversified revenue structure lead to greater financial capacity and less vulnerability in nonprofit organizations? A bibliometric and meta-analysis. *Voluntas*, 30(3), 593–609.

Lumpkin, G.T., & Dess, G.G. (1996). Clarifying the entrepreneurial orientation construct and linking it to performance. *Academy of Management Review*, 21(1), 135–172.

Lyons, M., & Zappala, G. (2006). Factors associated with fundraising dependency among nonprofit organisations in Australia. *The Australian Journal of Social Issues*, 41(4), 399–417.

Maier, F., Meyer, M., & Steinbereithner, M. (2016). Nonprofit organizations becoming business-like: A systematic review. *Nonprofit and Voluntary Sector Quarterly*, 45(1), 64–86.

Meer, J. (2014). Effects of the price of charitable giving: Evidence from an online crowdfunding platform. *Journal of Economic Behavior & Organization*, 103, 113–124.

Merton, R.K. (1968). The Matthew effect in science: The reward and communication systems of science are considered. *Science*, 159(3810), 56–63.

Ministerie van Financiën. (2008). Evaluatie Giftenaftrek 1996–2006. Ministerie van Financien, Den Haag. https://zoek.officielebekendmakingen.nl/blg-37049.pdf.

Morris, M.H., Webb, J.W., & Franklin, R.J. (2011). Understanding the manifestation of entrepreneurial orientation in the nonprofit context. *Entrepreneurship Theory and Practice*, 35(5), 947–971.

Mourdaunt, J., & Paton, R. (Eds.). (2013). *Thoughtful fundraising: Concepts, issues and perspectives*. London: Routledge.

Nijboer. (2017). Wijziging van enkele belastingwetten en enige andere wetten (Overige fiscale maatregelen 2018). Kamerstuk nr. 34786, 31 oktober 2017. https://zoek.officielebekendmakingen.nl/kst-34786-8.html.

OECD. (2020). *Taxation and philanthropy*. OECD Tax Policy Studies, No. 27. Paris: OECD Publishing. https://doi.org/10.1787/df434a77-en.

Payne, A.A. (1998). Does the government crowd-out private donations? New evidence from a sample of non-profit firms. *Journal of Public Economics*, 69(3), 323–345.

Pfeffer, J., & Salancik, G. (1978). *The external control of organizations*. New York: HarperCollins.

Peloza, J., & Steel, P. (2005). The price elasticities of charitable contributions: A meta-analysis. *Journal of Public Policy & Marketing*, 24(2), 260–272.

Raad voor Cultuur. (2017). Verkenning cultuur voor stand, land en regio. https://www.raadvoorcultuur.nl/documenten/adviezen/2017/11/29/verkenning-cultuur-voor-stad-land-en-regio

Rigney, D. (2010). *The Matthew effect: How advantage begets further advantage*. Columbia: Columbia University Press.

Scharf, K., & Smith, S. (2015). The price elasticity of charitable giving: Does the form of tax relief matter? *International Tax and Public Finance*, 22(2), 330–352.

Steinberg, R. (1990). Taxes and giving: New findings. *Voluntas*, 1(2), 61–79.

Trommel, W. (2018). Staat, filantropie en veerkracht. Over gulle gaven en gulzig bestuur. Pp. 241–263 in: De Goede, P., Schrijvers, E., & De Visser, M. (Eds.), *Filantropie op de grens van overheid en markt*. Den Haag: Wetenschappelijke Raad voor het Regeringsbeleid.

Vaceková, G., Svidroňová, M.M., Plaček, M., & Nemec, J. (2020). Business practices in nonprofit funding. Pp. 161–172 in: Garcia-Rodriguez, I., & Romero-Merino, M.E. (Eds.), *Financing nonprofit organizations*. London: Routledge.

Van Teunenbroek, C., & Bekkers, R. (2020). Geven door huishoudens. Pp. 53–86 in: Bekkers, R., Gouwenberg, B.M., & Schuyt, T.N.M. (Eds.). *Geven in Nederland 2020*. Amsterdam: Lenthe.

Weekers, F. (2012). Wijziging van de Uitvoeringsregeling inkomstenbelasting 2001, de Uitvoeringsregeling schenk- en erfbelasting, de Uitvoeringsregeling Algemene wet inzake rijksbelastingen 1994 en de Uitvoeringsregeling Belastingdienst 2003. Staatscourant Nr. 12737, 22 juni 2012. https://zoek.officielebekendmakingen.nl/stcrt-2012-12737.pdf.

Weisbrod, B.A. (1998). The nonprofit mission and its financing: Growing links between nonprofits and the rest of the economy in: *To profit or not to profit: The commercial transformation of the nonprofit sector*. Cambridge: Cambridge University Press.

Weisbrod, B.A. (2004). The pitfalls of profits. *Stanford Social Innovation Review*, 2(3), 40–47.

Wiepking, P., & Bekkers, R. (2015). Giving in the Netherlands: A strong welfare state with a vibrant nonprofit sector. Pp. 211–299 in: Wiepking, P., & Handy, F. (Eds.), *The Palgrave handbook of global philanthropy*. London: Palgrave Macmillan.

Wiepking, P., & Handy, F. (Eds.). (2015). *The Palgrave handbook of global philanthropy*. London: Palgrave Macmillan.

Wiepking, P., Handy, F., Park, S., Neumayr, M., Bekkers, R. Breeze, B., De Wit, A., Einolf, C.J., Gricevic, Z., Scaife, W., Bethmann, S., Breen, O.B., Kang, C., Katz, H., Krasnopolskaya, I., Layton, M.D., Mersianova, I., Lo, K.-T., Osili, U., Pessi, A.B., Sivesind, K.H., Yamauchi, N., & Yang, Y. (2021). Global philanthropy: Does institutional context matter for charitable giving? *Nonprofit & Voluntary Sector Quarterly*. https://doi.org/10.1177/0899764021989444.

Wiepking, P., & Heijnen, M. (2011). The giving standard: Conditional cooperation in the case of charitable giving. *International Journal of Nonprofit and Voluntary Sector Marketing*, 16(1), 13–22.

APPENDIX

Data on giving behavior

The results on giving behavior to culture and arts in the Netherlands are based on data from the Giving in the Netherlands (GIN) studies. GIN is an initiative of the Center for Philanthropic Studies at the Vrije Universiteit Amsterdam. Since 1995, GIN biennially publishes macro-economic estimates of philanthropy by households, corporations, foundations, bequests and lotteries. The data among households and corporations include weighted responses to survey questionnaires on giving in the past calendar year. The data among foundations, bequests and lotteries are based on annual reports (and in the case of foundations, an additional survey).

The data on households include two samples: 1. a general sample among Dutch households and 2. a targeted sample among Dutch high-net-worth households. The high-net-worth sample is included to improve the coverage of the high end of the income and wealth distribution in the Netherlands. The sample includes respondents with a capital (freely disposable) of at least €50,000. Most of the households in the high-net-worth sample (37%) have a capital above €500,000. Besides being a Dutch resident and the age restriction of being 18 years or older, there were no restrictions for the general household sample. The general household sample has a longitudinal design: the same respondents are approached every two years. Both samples are weighted based on age, gender, region, household size and education level. See Table 26.A.

The data on corporations are collected via a survey among a representative sample of corporations located in the Netherlands. The questionnaires were completed by an employee responsible for the corporation's sponsorships and donations. In the questionnaire, sponsorships are described as donations with a "business interest" and where the corporation receives someting in return, while gifts are donations without a business interest without a return. We extrapolated the data from the sample to the total population of corporations in the Netherlands. The sample was weighted based on the total number of corporations in the Netherlands per sector, including data on the number of employees per company.

The data on lotteries are based on annual reports of all nine lotteries in the Netherlands. The data on foundations are based on contributions by foundations from surveys and annual reports. For foundations, we report a minimum estimate, since not all foundations are represented (i.e., incomplete data). For 2018, the data include 122 endowed foundations (with a budget of more than €500,000) and 676 fundraising foundations.

Table 26.A Sample sizes on giving behavior

	2011	*2013*	*2014*	*2015*	*2018*
Households	2.193	980	1.001	1.192	1.201
Corporations	1.164	1.201	1.115	1.007	1.022
High-net-worth households	1.307	1.356	836	891	1.087

Table 26.B Sample sizes of cultural nonprofit organizations

	2012	*2013*	*2014*	*2015*	*2018*	*2019*
Cultural nonprofit organizations	928	928	512	438	21	574
Response rates (in %)	39	39	–		–	10

Data on cultural non-profit organizations

We collected data on cultural nonprofit organizations via a survey administered three times: in 2014, 2016 and 2020. We collected the data on 2012 and 2013 in the autumn of 2014. We collected the data on 2014 and 2015 in the summer of 2016. In the winter of 2020, we collected the data on 2019. As some cultural nonprofit organizations did not have their annual report ready for 2019, we allowed them to provide their revenues and expenses for the year 2018. In this chapter, we refer to the year 2019 for both 2018 and 2019, as the responses for 2018 were negligible (see Table 26.B). We rely on survey data, as we cannot rely on income tax returns. Tax returns only contain information about the donations that households declared as deductible gifts. Not all households that could make use of the gift deductibility do so in practice. As a result, the insight into the giving behavior via tax returns is incomplete (Bekkers, 2010). Moreover, tax returns do not distinguish between in-kind and monetary gifts.

To obtain a wide and varied data set, we invited all Dutch cultural nonprofit organizations registered with the tax authority as a cultural nonprofit organization with a public benefit (Culturele ANBI). We invited these cultural nonprofit organizations several times using multiple methods. When email and/or correspondence addresses were available, we sent an invitation per postal service and via email. In 2020, the email invitation was sent three times. In 2020, we also called the cultural nonprofit organizations that participated in our study in all previous years (i.e. longitudinal sample group) and the largest cultural nonprofit organizations by telephone to solicit participation. As we were particularly interested in the largest cultural nonprofit organizations, we supplemented our survey data on 2019 with publicly available annual reports from 82 largest Dutch cultural nonprofit organizations.

The survey included questions on the organization's revenues and expenses, as well as attitudes towards entrepreneurship (i.e. innovation, risk-taking, and pro-activeness). As we expected that the effect of the charity tax reform became only noticeable after several years, we mainly focussed on the data gathered in 2020. Our sample is unlikely to be representative of the entire Dutch cultural nonprofit sector. The sample of cultural nonprofit organizations for which we gathered data in 2014 and 2015 consisted to a greater extent of medium-sized and large cultural nonprofit organizations. The 574 cultural nonprofit organizations that provided data in 2020 are also unlikely to be representative of the entire cultural sector, especially since we were particularly interested in the largest Dutch cultural nonprofit organizations. As we supplemented the data with annual reports of the largest Dutch cultural nonprofit organizations, the largest cultural organizations are probably overrepresented, while smaller organizations are underrepresented in the data collected in 2020. To account for this, we carried out certain analyses over the years for different income classes (i.e., very small, small, medium-sized and (very) large cultural nonprofit organizations).

27

TRUST AND FOR-PROFIT PHILANTHROPY

From Surrey's private foundation to Zuckerberg's limited liability company

Steven Dean and Dana Brakman Reiser

Philanthropy has left an indelible mark on the United States over the last half century. To offer just one example, a foundation proved instrumental in the creation of the nation's emergency 911 response system in the 1970s (Kohler, 2007, p. 1). Unfortunately, the foundation rests on an increasingly fragile foundation. Wealthy donors have begun to avoid the very structures created to support philanthropy, forgoing the generous tax benefits they provide. In 2015, Mark Zuckerberg and Priscilla Chan proudly announced the creation of the Chan Zuckerberg Initiative – a limited liability company – to give away 99% of their net worth.

This chapter offers an unconventional explanation for the diminished allure of foundations and the rise of for-profit philanthropy embodied in alternative philanthropic vehicles such as the limited liability company. In our previous work, we have shown how trust plays a critical role in hindering the rise of social enterprise (Brakman Reiser and Dean, 2017, pp. 11–13). Designed to pursue profits and social goals simultaneously, an absence of trust between investors and social entrepreneurs chokes off access to capital these ventures need to grow.

Rousseau famously observed that hunters unable to trust one another will never share the big prize – the stag – and will instead be condemned to hunt hares on their own. Both untrusting and untrusted, social enterprises have been unable to raise capital from investors. Trust remains out of reach because each lacks the means to make a reliable commitment to the other.

In 1969, a legislative compromise we call the Grand Bargain solved a similar trust gap between philanthropists and the public. Gilded Age industrialists like Rockefeller and Carnegie pioneered the concept of a philanthropic foundation, designed to manage and distribute funds for charitable purposes. Newly minted moguls followed suit in the ensuing decades. By mid-century, concern was running high about abuses within these organizations. A series of inquiries by administrative agencies and congressional committees led to major reform legislation in 1969.

The Tax Reform Act of 1969 can be viewed as "a necessary part of the bargain to encourage charitable activities . . . reflect[ing] a series of trade-offs that occurred in the U.S. legislative and administrative process that result in a robust charitable sector" (Zolt, 2021, p. 26). Now officially dubbed "private foundations" by statute, they retained the capacity for perpetual life and significant tax benefits in exchange for government regulation and transparency.

 DOI: 10.4324/9781003139201-32

The Grand Bargain channeled foundation resources toward public-regarding activities and at least some significant current spending and away from entanglements with business interests and politics. It demanded heightened accountability through new prophylactic rules against non-charitable distributions and transactions between foundations and their donors and managers. The enhanced disclosure scheme it imposed allowed for tracking and enforcement of this strengthened regulatory framework. By imposing these affirmative obligations on foundations, the Grand Bargain directly targeted two of the main criticisms of modern-day philanthropy and its "tax incentives for giving . . . that they may be regressive and undemocratic" (OECD, 2020, p. 2).

Today, alternatives to the private foundation, notably philanthropy LLCs, commercially affiliated donor-advised funds and strategic corporate philanthropy defy the Grand Bargain. These for-profit philanthropy tools allow elites to evade the regulatory architecture the Grand Bargain erected. Just as social enterprise blurs the boundaries between doing business and doing social good, for-profit philanthropy phenomena upend the Grand Bargain's balance between elite power and public control. The possible dissolution of that bargain and the cautionary tale of social enterprise suggest how easily trust can slip through our fingers.

We trace the Grand Bargain's decline to developments in tax policy designed to enhance transparency that, in no small irony, can in turn be traced to the Grand Bargain itself. The tax expenditure budget that grew out of the Tax Reform Act of 1969 may have doomed the Grand Bargain simply by clearly and publicly tallying its costs. That lost innocence transformed philanthropy from a shared act of faith into a transaction, with the Chan Zuckerberg Initiative as its logical conclusion.

1 Trust to transaction

The link between taxation and philanthropy has been indisputable since Carnegie wrote his famous essay "Wealth." Not one to mince words, Carnegie concluded that by "taxing estates heavily at death the state marks its condemnation of the selfish millionaire's unworthy life" (1889, p. 659). In practice, carrying out the threat implicit in such progressive taxes has proven difficult. Even when rates are high, loopholes and lax enforcement shield wealthy taxpayers from the harsh judgment Carnegie envisioned.

Philanthropic reforms Congress embraced in 1969 targeted perceived abuses by curbing tax benefits and enacting exacting penalties on political activity and a range of transactions deemed suspect. As Carnegie predicted, philanthropists seized on that sternly worded invitation to transform "the surplus wealth of the few" into "in the best sense, the property of the many, because administered for the common good" (Carnegie, 1889, p. 660). Since 1969, the Gates Foundation and countless others have had an enormous impact in areas ranging from health to education.

The Tax Reform Act of 1969 would – by fueling the subsequent work of one of its chief architects, Stanley Surrey – plant the seeds of the Grand Bargain's undoing. As Surrey put it, he "came to recognize that most of the matters considered in 1969 – whether they were adopted or rejected in the final legislation – related to items in the Tax Expenditure Budget" (Surrey, 1973, p. viii). The Grand Bargain succeeded for any number of reasons, but perhaps the most important was that both wealthy elites and the public could believe they got the better of it. The tax expenditure budget, by design, made that impossible. Stripping all mystery from the exchange of tax breaks for philanthropic largesse may have doomed the Grand Bargain.

A The picaresque story of the income tax

The world has changed in the half-century since the Grand Bargain created a fruitful and unlikely partnership between the public and wealthy philanthropists. The most striking changes, the rise of new technologies and old inequalities, may not pose the greatest threat to the Grand Bargain and its philanthropic stag hunt. This chapter highlights deeper challenges fueled by legal changes so gradual they often go unnoticed. From election law to the income and estate taxes, a slowly remade landscape has left the Grand Bargain intact while stripping it of the power to generate trust.

In this chapter, we tell the picaresque story of the income tax to show how legal change has made trust between philanthropists and the public harder to come by. Enshrined in the U.S. Constitution a century ago to "put the burdens of government justly upon the backs of the people," the income tax began modestly, paid by an elite few (Jennings Bryan, 1896). In the decades that followed the ratification of the 16th Amendment, the income tax evolved into a shared ritual at the heart of our civic life. Today, more Americans file federal tax returns than vote.

By 1969 – when the Grand Bargain was struck – top marginal income tax rates above 70% had become an enduring presence for high-income taxpayers. Those rates tell a compelling story of the power of taxation to constrain elite influence. Recent calls to raise top marginal rates to match those prevailing at the time of the Grand Bargain underscore the continuing appeal of that narrative. The Grand Bargain reveals a more complex reality, highlighting both unexpected limits and surprising power.

The specter of high tax rates played the role Carnegie once envisioned, but not because the rich felt bound to pay them. The Grand Bargain allowed the wealthy to avoid high marginal rates. Although they had already mastered that feat, the 1969 Tax Reform Act allowed them to do so respectably. In the 1950s and 60s, support for high wartime tax burdens might have waned, but the rates themselves had not. That confluence of high rates and skepticism made tax avoidance widespread (Bank, 2017, p. 128).

Nominal rates were high, but well-advised taxpayers could blunt their impact. Aggressive tax planning fueled a very different reality in which charitable contributions could, as described in the following, quite literally pay. Today, by any measure, the burden of the income tax falls lightly on elite shoulders. Reduced marginal income tax rates tell only part of the story. Technical changes – applying capital gains treatment to most dividends, for example – mean that corporate earnings distributed to shareholders once taxed at rates above 90% now face a maximum rate of 20%.

Other changes matter as much or more to the fate of the Grand Bargain but can be seen neither in the rise and fall of rates nor the fate of loopholes. A half century ago, tax planning could tame the threat of high rates, but not without risk. Today, wealthy individuals have little to fear. A report by the Treasury's Inspector General for Tax Administration issued in 2020 revealed that "high-income nonfilers owing billions of dollars" were simply being ignored by an underfunded Internal Revenue Service. Together, lower rates, larger loopholes and weakened enforcement reveal an altered landscape that makes the Grand Bargain's benefits far less appealing than 50 years ago.

B Regulating philanthropy

Simply doubling top marginal tax rates would be both too much and not enough to reinvigorate the Grand Bargain. As early as 1957, Surrey highlighted how "high rates of the individual income tax, and of the estate and gift taxes" powered tax preferences like the foundation (Surrey, 1957, p. 1149). Yet as Surrey understood all too well, translating high rates into revenues can be surprisingly difficult.

Carnegie and Surrey both understood how tax law could play a central role in the rise and fall of the Grand Bargain, but tax does not tell the whole story. While the value of tax benefits shrank, the opportunity costs of embracing the Grand Bargain's constraints on political activity, in-kind contributions and privacy ballooned. The Grand Bargain brought federal oversight to almost every component of foundation operations in service of restraining the real and potential excesses of these powerful institutions and the people behind them. It tells foundations how to spend the money they distribute; how to invest the money they retain; and how to manage their relationships with fiduciaries, employees and donors.

Federal tax law regulates foundation spending on virtually all possible dimensions. A payout requirement addresses both the timing and the amount of foundation spending by penalizing foundations that fail to distribute at least 5% of their assets each year for charitable purposes. Through excise taxes imposed on certain types of expenditures, it also limits the potential recipients of foundations' resources and the purposes for which they may be distributed. Faced with these constraints, philanthropists such as Zuckerberg and Chan have rejected the private foundation in favor of a limited liability company. Although it may seem otherwise, that offers reason for optimism.

Nowhere can the magnitude of the growing sacrifice choosing a private foundation represents be seen more starkly than in the changing role of money in politics. In an election law environment that imposes ever fewer limitations on political spending by elites, pledging political abstinence by forming a private foundation has become costly. So philanthropists find ways to avoid them.

Allowing foundations to engage in political activity – replacing outright prohibitions with limits and minimum standards of accountability – could replicate the Grand Bargain's success, nudging elites towards benign forms of political engagement. It could help to turn the clock back to 1969, preserving the philanthropic partnership between the public and elites against the entropic pull of profit. The Grand Bargain harnessed tax avoidance. The same might be accomplished with political spending.

This chapter explores three distinct ways to breathe new life into the Grand Bargain. A return to steeply progressive post-war rates – and all that goes with them – represents only one path back towards a reinvigorated Grand Bargain. As detailed in the following, that route may be the least promising. Reducing the opportunity costs of embracing regulated philanthropic forms by remaking the relationship between politics and philanthropy could have an even greater impact. Finally, a wealth tax could deliver accountability in timing, transparency and targeting for the age of for-profit philanthropy.

C The evolving income tax

In 2019, Congresswoman Ocasio-Cortez alluded to a 70% marginal tax rate on income, and many found the idea astonishing. A century of history shows that we might be equally surprised by the rates in effect today.[1] A careful study of the income tax reveals many more twists and turns than the steadily falling tax rates of the last three decades suggest. In countless ways, today's income tax bears little resemblance to the one embraced after the ratification of the 16th Amendment.

At first, the vast majority of Americans paid no income tax at all. In terms of its reach, the first modern U.S. income tax can be roughly compared to today's estate tax, targeting only the most affluent. And the tax was only imposed on amounts far in excess of anything a typical worker could hope to earn (or, in the case of the estate tax, to accumulate). After the Second World War, that would change as the role of the income tax in American life grew.

Initially a tool designed blunt the excesses of inequality by compelling the wealthiest to contribute more, a vast expansion would make the income tax part of most American lives. Once a tax on elites, the income tax became a tax on the masses. In the years since, a further expansion – notably in the form of negative taxes designed to subsidize the wages of the working poor – ensured that the income tax plays an important part in the lives Americans from every background.

Many struggling workers today have reason to exclaim "thank God for tax day!" In terms of those it touches, the story of the income tax has been one of relentless expansion. How much any given taxpayer pays has been much more complicated. At the most basic level – the rate of tax set by Congress – the burden of the income tax grows along with how much a taxpayer earns. How they earn income also matters. The results – famously illustrated by Warren Buffet's observation that he pays a lower rate of tax than his secretary – can be counterintuitive.

Despite such quirks, an overarching pattern on rates appears clear. First one World War then another triggered a sharp rise in rates only to be followed by a steady fall. Recent critiques focused on top marginal rates seize on that pattern to highlight the failure of the income tax to curb inequality.

D Rates, loopholes and enforcement

The Grand Bargain hints at why a focus on rates misses the mark. When the Grand Bargain was struck, growing evasion and avoidance had already made the U.S. income tax surprisingly porous, with "high rates tempered by many avoidance possibilities" (Surrey, 1957, p. 1150). Legislative loopholes had made many affluent taxpayers learn to stop worrying and love the income tax.

Falling rates alone do not explain the Grand Bargain's diminished appeal. The tax breaks that would compel Stanley Surrey to create the tax expenditure budget highlight a very different balance of power between tax authorities and elites at the time the Grand Bargain was struck than those high nominal rates might suggest. Thanks to such tax breaks, in Surrey's day, planning could often deflect the blow of rates above 70%.

But they could not do so without risk. Even half a century ago, tax authorities could neither detect nor defeat every avoidance scheme. Yet enforcement remained a real threat. Top rates have fallen significantly since the Grand Bargain was struck, but an accelerating decline in the ability of tax authorities to challenge aggressive taxpayer behavior matters more. As tax rates fell, the value of the tax benefits the Grand Bargain promised did the same. Even those sharp declines fail to paint an accurate picture of the falling burden the income tax poses for wealthy taxpayers. Tax rates have fallen in half. The drop-off in enforcement has been steeper.

A decade ago, a typical U.S. taxpayer faced an audit risk four times smaller than they would have in the 1960s (Slemrod and Bakija, 2008, p. 181). And since then, that trend has only gained momentum. A systematic effort to reduce funding to the Internal Revenue Service has further hobbled tax enforcement, as highlighted by the 2020 Treasury report titled "High-Income Nonfilers Owing Billions of Dollars Are Not Being Worked by the Internal Revenue Service." If shrugging off the burden of the income tax has become as simple as not filing a return, the tax advantages of the private foundation mean nothing at all.

The Grand Bargain's power can be explained in part by an implicit threat such high tax rates might be enforced. Today, the likelihood of enforcement has fallen even more sharply than rates. Lower rates were precisely what Surrey hoped to achieve with his tax expenditure budget, with "all economic income . . . taxed, and the top rate lowered to 35 percent" (Surrey, 1973, p. 226). But he intended "tax-rate reductions for the wealthy" to be paired with "the closing of a number of loopholes which the public cannot understand" (Surrey, 1957, p. 1151).

2 Entitlement and entitlements

The Grand Bargain was struck at a moment when high post-World War II rates had yet to fall but had already worn out their welcome. The Grand Bargain did not invent, but did reinvent, the foundation. Surrey once considered foundations symbols of a tax system that stealthily favored insiders. He drily noted, for example, that "[o]n July 30, 1955, Congressman Curtis of Missouri introduced a private bill for the relief of the Cannon Foundation, which had been established by Congressman Cannon of Missouri" (Surrey, 1957, p. 1178).

The Grand Bargain rehabilitated foundations by imposing clear limits on their activities and on the tax benefits of giving. As his tax expenditure budget expanded the tax base by thrusting loopholes into the spotlight, the Grand Bargain steered elites towards philanthropy by forcing them to make an easy choice between the possibility of lurid headlines for tax avoidance and the certainty of flattering coverage for charitable giving. The resulting truce between wealthy taxpayers and the public would help philanthropy flourish in the United States.

Central to the Grand Bargain's success was the myth that it made both sides winners. While taxpayers and the public each yielded on key points, they had little information about the value of the tax breaks at stake. Both the public and elites could believe that the costs of philanthropy were borne by someone else thanks to a virtuous counterpart to Murphy and Nagel's everyday libertarianism. Murphy and Nagel note that by the 1990s, many taxpayers had come to believe themselves entitled to the entirety of their pre-tax holdings and to see any imposition of tax as an affront (Murphy and Nagel, 2002, p. 9). In the 1950s and 1960s, those battle lines had not yet hardened.

Trust comes much more easily when you can believe you have an opportunity to gamble with house money, with nothing to lose and everything to gain. Against a backdrop of high nominal rates and rampant planning, elites and the public could each place very different values on the tax breaks delivered by the Grand Bargain. The Grand Bargain, as Surrey tells it, drove him to put a price tag on the tax law's hidden subsidies, fueling the creation of the tax expenditure budget.

When the Grand Bargain was struck, taxpayers and policymakers lacked even that rudimentary framework to shape their expectations. The tax expenditure budget Surrey popularized fundamentally changed the way policymakers approach tax breaks, highlighting that tax breaks for charitable giving reduce tax revenues by more than $50 billion each year. No longer would "tax expenditures tumble into the law without supporting studies, being propelled instead by clichés, debating points, and scraps of data and tables that are passed off as serious evidence" (Surrey, 1973, p. 6).

A Control

The architecture of the Grand Bargain also allowed each to feel they controlled the disposition of foundation assets. Public control took the form of clear expectations on the timing, transparency and targeting of foundation spending. For their part, philanthropists could rightly claim authorship of foundation achievements as they both exercised day-to-day control and continued to manage the capital that fueled their efforts. The Grand Bargain again let both be sides be winners.

Rob Reich describes a long-ago antecedent to the Grand Bargain that helps explain its power. He examines an Athenian "system whereby wealthy citizens could make voluntary contributions to various state projects that were of benefit to the entire citizenry, or *demos*." Even when vital to its survival, Athens did not quite compel these philanthropic – here liturgical – efforts. In Reich's words, "[l]iturgies in democratic Athens became a system of public finance via private contribution, something akin to a system of taxation" (2018, p. 31). Rather than compulsory, the Athenian system made contributions voluntary.

The liminal nature of that system – almost, but not quite, a tax – achieved much the same result as the Grand Bargain. Wealthy Athenians could qualify for a safe harbor – a "temporary exemption" – from that near-tax by, say, voluntarily funding the construction of a trireme warship. Reluctant elites knew they might be enlisted to build and captain such a vessel by selection from the registers of wealthy people kept by the state. But even then, the liturgical system allowed the chosen individual an alternative. By identifying a wealthier citizen – not already exempt – they could shift the burden by invoking the antidosis procedure, which would require whichever citizen a trial determined was wealthier to fund the effort.

That liturgical system relied only indirectly on state power. The wealthiest citizens might recognize the logical inevitability of being called on to make a contribution. Anticipating their selection by the state or a challenge by a less wealthy neighbor, they enjoyed the luxury of transforming an obligation into an act of generosity. Ensuring that civic burdens fell fairly on the backs of the Athenian people while "preserving certain privileges for the wealthy, such as honor, gratitude, and status as a civic benefactor" that liturgical process accomplishes just what Carnegie envisioned (Reich, 2018, p. 34).

The Grand Bargain did much the same. With triremes replaced by private foundations and antidosis by audits, the Grand Bargain allowed wealthy Americans to trade the complexities and risks of tax planning for the simplicity of honor and gratitude. But today, we live in Surrey's world. Any bargains struck will not be paid for with house money.

Just like their liturgical counterparts, for the past half century, philanthropists have been able to trade state compulsion for public gratitude. Both the Grand Bargain and the Athenian liturgical system represented a partnership between the public – the demos – and wealthy elites. Against the backdrop of (nominally) high tax rates, the Grand Bargain achieved what Reich describes as a "balance between plutocratic voice and democratic voice" that did not depend on the government's power over elites (2018, p. 140). The mere possibility that their tax planning might unravel in the harsh glare of public scrutiny would have made "honor, gratitude and status as a civic benefactor" every bit as appealing as it once was to wealthy Athenians.

B Optimal rates

Encouraging future Chans and Zuckerbergs to embrace private foundations could be as straightforward – and every inch as difficult – as recreating the conditions that prevailed in 1969. The income tax presents a particularly tempting opportunity to turn the clock back. Doubling the top marginal income tax rate from 37% to 74%, for example, should, after all, make tax breaks twice as appealing.

That simple math obscures a more complex reality. Recent interest in sharply higher tax rates can be traced to the work of economists focused on a narrow question. Diamond and Saez worked to identify the "optimal" tax rates for high-income earners. Relying on key assumptions, they concluded that tax rates twice as high as those in effect currently could be imposed without distorting behavior over the short run. Diamond and Saez do note that over the long term, high rates could affect choices about education and careers in ways that would be decidedly suboptimal.

Diamond and Saez show that even surprisingly high rates would have little immediate impact on top earners. But they offer an important caveat. If avoidance and evasion remain possible, those high rates would mean little in terms of increased revenues. In order to have an impact, they would need to be paired with "base broadening and tax enforcement" (Diamond and Saez, 2011, p. 173). Simply put, taxpayers must have none of the escape hatches Surrey worried about.

In practice, returning rates to levels not seen for decades may be the easy part. Base broadening might mean, for example, reversing changes that now result in dividends paid to stockholders once taxed at 90% benefitting from capital gain rates of 20%. Without countless such adjustments, doubling the top marginal rates might not impact the treatment of elites at all.

C Philanthropic windfalls

High tax rates on their own will not produce the trust once supplied by the Grand Bargain and will not generate big tax payments by wealthy individuals. Surrey's tax expenditure budget illustrates why. Since the concepts embodied in the tax expenditure budget were in their infancy – and despairing of the prospect of explaining the excessive generosity of the tax treatment of charitable gifts the tax expenditure budget targeted – Surrey offered a stylized example. He underscored how entirely legal tax planning could produce surprising results:

> If a person in the 70 percent top bracket informs the Government he is selling fully appreciated stock to pay his tax bill or to obtain cash for other reasons and would like $100 paid to a philanthropy, the Government pays the $100 to that philanthropy and also pays the person $5 – or perhaps $6.50 or even $15.50.
>
> *(Surrey, 1973, p. 227)*

His point was simple. Combining the tax benefits granted to contributions of appreciated property – deduction of its full value plus exclusion of all gain from income – can transform a gift into a windfall. Before the Grand Bargain was struck, philanthropy might cost philanthropists less than nothing.

A charitable contribution of appreciated property could be more than fully paid for with the tax breaks it would generate, resulting in a net after-tax payment to – not from – a donor. For the Grand Bargain, that would prove a help rather than a hindrance. When a charitable gift can more than pay for itself while loopholes cause marginal rates above 70% to loosen their grip, notions of entitlement like those Murphy and Nagel found problematic become meaningless. From the taxpayer's perspective, the pain of curtailed tax preferences and increased accountability trumped even a modest risk of being dragged into court and compelled to pay tax at a 70% rate. From the public's perspective, curbing abuses to boost tax revenues while asserting firmer control over the operations of foundations would have been equally appealing.

With high rates and robust enforcement, philanthropic tax preferences would, of course, once again become appealing for the wealthy. But not for the demos. Why not just keep the revenues and allow philanthropic entrepreneurs to compete for funding?

The same would be true if current rates were imposed broadly and enforced vigorously. A top tax rate approaching 40%, if wealthy taxpayers actually expected to pay it, could nudge them towards private foundations. High rates, unenforced and under threat by loopholes, would not.

3 Interests, not price

The Grand Bargain's success lay in its ability to elude the question of how heavy a tax burden should fall on elites. Rather than focusing on price (here, tax), elites and the demos had the luxury of focusing on interests.[2] The Grand Bargain offered both respectability and the modern-day equivalents of triremes. Impossible in the zero-sum world Surrey fought for, the Grand Bargain made winners of both the public and elites.

In the pre-tax expenditure budget era, the Grand Bargain's price remained obscure. While precisely what Surrey lamented, the resulting lack of salience of cost made agreement possible. The private foundation gave the wealthy license to gamble their fortunes on idiosyncratic visions of public benefit. And it allowed the public to believe that elite philanthropy cost them nothing.

An exchange of respectability elites could secure nowhere else for a rescue the public could hope to receive from no one else forged the trust at the heart of this modern-day liturgy. Rekindling that trust through the income tax would be difficult precisely because of the tax expenditure budget. Because of Surrey's great success, price has taken center stage (Sellen, 2021, p. 1).

A Converging political interests

Fortunately, the Grand Bargain itself suggests another approach. Although its tax aspects loom large, the Grand Bargain did much more than remake the tax treatment of elite philanthropy. Today, political spending presents a tableau of unconstrained power hardly more reassuring than the one Surrey described half a century ago. Surrey's cartographic feat – mapping the terrain of tax breaks – has not been, and perhaps could not be, replicated for political spending. Certainly, no one has yet created political influence budget.

In principle, that absence creates an opening. Rather than attempting to craft an optimal suite of tax incentives – bargaining over price – to cement a new philanthropic partnership between elites and the public, it offers an opportunity to bargain over interests. What minimum standards elites and the public might jointly impose on political spending matters less than the ability to find common ground.

Private foundations could, for example, be allowed to make contributions on the same terms as individuals, effectively "tak[ing] a more general approach that is consistent across both the political entities and charitable organisations performing them" rather than merely attempting "to regulate the definition of charitable purposes and the types of activities that may advance them" (Carmichael, 2021, pp. 1–2). Many philanthropy LLCs make such political contributions. In 2020, the Emerson Collective contributed over a quarter of a million dollars to the Democratic party. Limiting – and clawing back the value of any tax benefits from – any political contributions by foundations, rather than punishing them as current law does, could make foundations more appealing without making them more costly in terms of either direct or tax expenditures.

Just as the Grand Bargain nurtured expectations regarding philanthropic activity, a new compromise could draw clear lines between forms of philanthropic political engagement. By ensuring accountability for those types of political expenditure deemed philanthropically compatible, such an arrangement would reduce the opportunity costs of embracing private foundations without creating new sources of unobserved political influence. Crafted carefully, such minimum standards could benefit both elites and the demos by preserving a balance between plutocratic and democratic voice.

B Bargaining in the shadow of a wealth tax

One could also draw a different lesson from the Grand Bargain's success. That both elites and the public could claim victory in the Grand Bargain does not, of course, mean that either was correct. The public may have been hoodwinked into believing that a combination of high nominal and low effective tax rates could constrain elite influence by promoting philanthropy. Wealthy taxpayers arguably agreed to minimum standards and modest tax burdens to ward off what they did not yet recognize as a waning threat of enforcement. Whatever they believed, neither truly gambled with house money.

Today's wealth tax proposals – and the fundamental disagreements that surround them – could allow elites and the public to replicate the Grand Bargain's feat. The wealth tax remains nearly as unmapped today as the income tax was before Surrey conquered it. Its advocates, perhaps naively, see an opportunity to realize the unfulfilled promise Jennings Bryan once saw in the income tax, finally "put[ting] the burdens of government justly upon the backs of the people." Its critics see little more than a return of the evasion and avoidance that Surrey decried. Both cannot be true, but since no U.S. wealth tax has ever been enacted, this particular Schrödinger's cat remains both alive and dead.

Today, estimates of the revenues a wealth tax would raise vary by an order of magnitude. The success of the Grand Bargain suggests that there will be no better time to forge an agreement between elites and the demos on the wealth tax's treatment of philanthropy than before we know its measure. Absent a compromise, both sides risk being left with a losing hand.

High effective wealth tax rates would profoundly impact elites. A wealth tax riddled with loopholes and saddled with inadequate enforcement would leave the public with little to show for their efforts. Neither can discount the possibility that the strong version its advocates envision or the weak version its critics fear will materialize. Better, perhaps, to gamble on the impact philanthropy can have on public problems and elite reputations than to risk a toothless or crushing wealth tax.

The public would, of course, prefer a wealth tax able to bring elite influence to heel with high rates, a broad base and robust enforcement. Elites, on the other hand, undoubtedly prefer the freedom the opposite would bring. Given the wide range of possible outcomes, a substantial opportunity to find common ground would exist.

A wealth tax that falls more lightly on assets placed in a private foundation than it does on assets placed in a philanthropy LLC might nudge elites rather burdening them. The results could revive the Grand Bargain, capitalizing on the uncertainty surrounding the wealth tax today to burnish the appeal of private foundations at a time when some of the wealthiest philanthropists have turned to other vehicles. The public might just accept the possibility of substantial lost tax revenues as the price of reimposing minimum standards on elite philanthropy. For their part, elites would eliminate a non-trivial risk that a strong wealth tax would leave them footing the bill for today's triremes, without the benefit of gratitude or honor.

Conclusion

In some ways, philanthropists and social entrepreneurs could not be more different. But both depend on trust to have access to capital. Social entrepreneurs have been unable to persuade investors to trust them, just as they find themselves unable to trust investors. The results for the growth of social enterprise have been as predictable as they have been disappointing.

Philanthropists hope to retain, rather than gain, access to capital. The Grand Bargain allowed them to do that in exchange for embracing a suite of rules that limited their freedom and heightened transparency. Chafing under the burdens of the Grand Bargain, philanthropists have turned to alternatives to the private foundation. Renewed interest in steeply progressive taxes highlights the fragile benefits the Grand Bargain offers to the wealthy and the potential consequences of lost trust. A potent wealth tax would not leave the wealthiest philanthropists entirely without access to capital, but it could represent the end of the fruitful partnership forged by the Grand Bargain a half century ago.

Notes

1 In 1913, 7 cents would have been collected in tax on the last dollar earned by a prosperous taxpayer. In 2020, after more than a century, that burden would rise more than fivefold to 37 cents. While striking, that contrast actually understates the changes that have marked the income tax's tenure (Roberts, 2014, pp. 932–939).

2 In *Getting to Yes*, the classic vision of bargaining (over positions such as price) is contrasted against bargaining over interests. Bargaining over interests allows two sides to reach agreement by focusing on aspects of an arrangement that are not zero sum. The authors offer an example of farmers and oil producers realizing that since it would take at least that long to begin drilling, waiting three months to evict farmers after oil was discovered rather than doing so immediately would benefit both the farmers (harvesting crops crucial to their livelihoods) and the oil companies (drilling as soon as possible) (Fisher et al., 2011, pp. 5–6).

References

Bank, S. (2017) 'When Did Tax Avoidance Become Respectable', *Tax Law Review*, 71(1), pp. 123–178.

Brakman Reiser, D. and Dean, S. (2017) *Social Enterprise Law: Trust, Public Benefit and Capital Markets*. New York: Oxford University Press.

Carmichael C. M. (2022) *Charitable ends (perhaps) by political means: what are the governments regulating?*, Routledge, pp. 95–114

Carnegie, A. (1889) 'Wealth', *The North American Review*, 148(391), pp. 653–664.

Diamond, P. and Saez, E. (2011) 'The Case for a Progressive Tax: From Basic Research to Policy Recommendations', *Journal of Economic Perspectives*, 25(4), pp. 165–190.

Fisher, R., Ury, W. and Patton, B. (2011) *Getting to Yes: Negotiating Agreement Without Giving in*. New York: Penguin.

Jennings Bryan, W. (1896) 'The Cross of Gold', Speech Delivered before the National Democratic Convention at Chicago, 9 July 1896.

Kohler, S. (2007) 'The Emergency Medical Services Program of the Robert Wood Johnson Foundation', available at https://cspcs.sanford.duke.edu/sites/default/files/descriptive/emergency_medical_services_program.pdf (accessed: 27 January 2021).

Murphy, L. and Nagel, T. (2002) *The Myth of Ownership: Taxes and Justice*. New York: Oxford. [OECD Policy Brief].

OECD. (2020) 'Taxation and Philanthropy', available at https://doi.org/10.1787/df434a77-en (accessed: 13 September 2021).

Reich, R. (2018) *Just Giving: Why Philanthropy Is Failing Democracy and How It Can Do Better*. Princeton: Princeton University Press.

Roberts, T. (2014) 'Brackets: A Historical Perspective', *Northwestern University Law Review*, 108(3), 925–958.

Sellen C. (2022) *Philanthropy as a self-taxation mechanism with happy outcomes: crafting a new public disourse*, Routledge, pp. 298–324

Slemrod, J. and Bakija, J. (2008) *Taxing Ourselves: A Citizen's Guide to the Debate Over Taxes*. Cambridge: MIT Press.

Surrey, S. (1957) 'The Congress and the Tax Lobbyist: How Special Tax Provisions Get Enacted', *Harvard Law Review*, 70(7), 1145–1182.

Surrey, S. (1973) *Pathways to Tax Reform: The Concept of Tax Expenditures*. Cambridge: Harvard University Press.

Treasury Inspector General for Tax Administration. (2020) 'High-Income Nonfilers Owing Billions of Dollars Are Not Being Worked by the Internal Revenue Service', available at https://www.treasury.gov/tigta/auditreports/2020reports/202030015fr.pdf (accessed: 13 September 2021).

[Zolt (2021) from collected volume].

28

THE GROWING CONCEPT OF SOCIAL ENTERPRISE IN AUSTRALIA

Can a social enterprise take advantage of tax concessions by operating through a charity?

Fiona Martin

I Introduction

Social enterprise is a broad term beneath which sit entities ranging from for-profit businesses that, for example, use only ethically sourced suppliers, to, in some cases, not-for-profits (NFPs) and charities that carry on businesses that support their underlying charitable purposes (Nehme and Martin, 2019). The importance of the latter entities is seen by many researchers as rapidly increasing in western democracies. The report 'Global Civil Society: An Overview' (Salamon, Sokolowski, and List, 2003) found that the number and variety of NFPs or charitable institutions had grown enormously in the 1990s, and there is nothing to suggest that this growth is not still occurring. Expansion of this sector is more marked in developed nations, but it is also occurring in the developing world. These organisations occupy a unique space within the community in that they are private in nature; however, they exist for a public or community purpose (Salamon, Sokolowski and List, 2003). Furthermore, most developed nations offer a variety of tax concessions for charities and NFPs, the most common being the exemption from income tax. For example, the income of charities in England,[1] the United States,[2] Hong Kong,[3] New Zealand,[4] and Australia[5] is generally exempt from income tax. Although not all social enterprises are NFPs, many are (Social Traders, 2016), and all charities must be.[6]

There is no legal definition of NFP in Australia; however, the Australian Taxation Office (ATO) advises that a non-profit (or NFP)[7] organisation does not operate for the profit or gain (direct or indirect) of individual members both while operating and winding up. Any profit made must be used to carry out the organisation's purposes (Dal Pont, 2000, pp. 22–25). The ATO accepts an organisation as an NFP where its constituent or governing documents prevent it from distributing profits or assets for the benefit of particular people (Australian Taxation Office, 2007, p. 6).

In 'Global Civil Society: An Overview', the researchers found that in the late 1990s, the NFP sector had aggregate expenditures of US$1.3 trillion. This represented 5.1 per cent of the combined gross domestic product (GDP) of the 35 countries examined. If this figure is looked at in terms of national economies, it would make it the seventh-largest world economy at that

DOI: 10.4324/9781003139201-33

time behind the United States, Japan, China, Germany, the United Kingdom, and France and ahead of Italy, Brazil, Russia, Spain, Canada, and Australia (Salamon, Sokolowski and List, 2003). There are currently over 57,000 charities in Australia (Australian Charities and NFO Commission, 2017), and they employ 1.26 million staff (Australian Charities and NFO Commission, 2017). In June 2018, there were 12.6 million people employed in Australia, which means that employees of charities make up almost 10 per cent of all employees in Australia. Charities in Australia, the United States, and other developed nations are major providers of welfare, education, and health services (Powell et al., 2017; Boris, 2012).

As well as seeing the number of charitable entities increase, the number of NFPs in Australia increased from 520,000 in 1996 to 700,000 in 2008 (ATO, 2008–09, p. 61). In Australia, this sector is therefore of growing significance both economically and socially. But not only is there a growth in NFPs and charities, the number and type of what are termed social enterprises are also growing. A 2016 Australian report estimates that there are 20,000 social enterprises in Australia (Social Traders, 2016, p. 9), and 68 per cent of these are in the services sector, of which 24 per cent are in retail and 23 per cent in healthcare (Social Traders, 2016, p. 9).

There are many reasons for the growth of NFPs and social enterprises, including the withdrawal of government from areas which it traditionally dominated, such as disability services, education, and health; the increasing complexity of today's society; and awareness of international issues such as the environment (Koele, 2007, p. 1). The business sector has been criticised for ignoring human needs and producing untenable social inequities (Salamon, Sokolowski and List, 2003, pp. 1–2). The issues with both government and business are considered to foster the growth of the third sector and social enterprises.

This chapter seeks to analyse the overlap, advantages, and disadvantages between social enterprises and charities. It has commenced with an introduction that describes the parameters and impact of the third sector. Part II considers the term 'social enterprise' and reviews the literature around this concept. Part III establishes the legal definition of charity, whether charities can carry on businesses, and the advantages and disadvantages of carrying on a business through a charity. Part IV uses three case studies to illustrate this last point, and Part V is the conclusion.

II What is a social enterprise?

Most social enterprises see themselves primarily as businesses in that they emphasise the importance of trading to build long-term sustainability. In that sense, they are part of the market economy in that they earn revenue from the production and sale of goods and services. However, while traditional businesses trade for the purpose of creating profit, social enterprises operate for a social purpose – profit (or surplus) is only a means to that end. These entities also see themselves as distinct from charities, which have traditionally relied on donations and grants for their operations. However, as charities become more commercial and entrepreneurial, and government grants decrease, many now consider themselves part of the social enterprise sector. This point is discussed in more detail later in this chapter.

Social enterprise is also seen from different perspectives by the stakeholder groups involved in their development and operation. For example, users and consumers of their goods and services value the fact that meeting investor needs is not the main priority of the business model and that they aim to re-invest profits in the social mission of the enterprise. Social enterprises are also gaining recognition because of the developing focus on ethical business practices in the broad community (Reiser and Dean, 2017, pp. 9–10). Many social entrepreneurs and philanthropists see social enterprises as a new way of doing good outside the constraints of charitable status. Governments see social enterprise as a new way of tackling wicked problems, building social capital, creating community wealth, and outsourcing public services. Community groups and staff of the enterprises see social enterprise as a new way of becoming involved in the governance of business enterprises. Indeed, ownership and control are essential questions in social enterprise, and ideally the social enterprise should be owned and controlled in the interest of its social or environmental mission. This also means that it may not be an NFP, as some of its profits or capital on a winding up may go back to the original investors.

Review of literature surrounding social enterprise

As there is no legal definition of social enterprise in Australia, it is not surprising that many practitioners and researchers in this area rely on the 2010 'Finding Australia's Social Enterprise Sector' Report (FASES Report), which is also used in the subsequent 2016 FASES report (Barraket, Mason and Blain, 2016, p. 3). The Report states that social enterprises are organisations that are led by an economic, social, cultural, or environmental mission consistent with a public or community benefit; trade to fulfil their mission; derive a substantial portion of their income from trade; and reinvest the majority of their profit/surplus in the fulfilment of their mission (Barraket et al., 2010, p. 16).

This definition is cited by the Australian Law Reform Commission in their 2019 report 'The Future of Law Reform' (Australian Law Reform Commission, 2019, p. 48). It is also cited by the Australian Institute of Company Directors (Australian Institute of Company Directors, 2015, p. 1). It is 'the definition utilised in the most substantial public policy investments to date' (Barraket et al., 2017, p. 345, 347).

A slightly different view was taken by a group of researchers and academics who came together through the University of New South Wales, Centre for Social Impact. This group, known as the Legal Models Working Group (Rodgers et al., 2015, p. 8), stated in its 2015 report that the defining features of social enterprise are contained in three essential elements. These are first, trading for social purposes; second, achieving financial sustainability; and third, re-investing profit into the social mission of the enterprise (Rodgers et al., 2015, p. 2).

The authors include 'financial sustainability' as a feature of social enterprises (a feature which is not explicitly stated in the FASES definition), because they consider successful trading and profitability a 'necessary factor for success' of these enterprises. The Report states that '[s]uccessful trading is a necessary factor for success as a SE and an enterprise's social mission can be achieved only if the enterprise continues to be a viable, profit-making, business venture' (Rodgers et al., 2015, p. 13).

The Legal Models Working Group relied for its definition of a social enterprise on the characteristics provided by Social Enterprise, United Kingdom. According to this organisation, social enterprises should (Social Enterprise, 2012, p. 1)

- Have a clear social and/or environmental mission set out in their governing documents;
- Generate the majority of their income through trade;
- Reinvest the majority of their profits;
- Be autonomous of the state;
- Be majority controlled in the interests of the social mission; and
- Be accountable and transparent.

These characteristics make social enterprises clearly different from ordinary businesses, but they also differ from charities and many not-for-profits. The fundamental difference is that not all charities and NFPs generate most of their income through trade.

The Social Innovation Entrepreneurship and Enterprise Alliance (SIEEA) has been disbanded but described itself as a strategic partnership of intermediary organisations working to support the growth and improve the impact of the 'social economy' in Australia (Pro Bono Australia, 2014). The SIEE Alliance's 2014 report outlined six characteristics of social enterprises. These were:

- Driven by an economic, social, cultural, or environmental mission for public benefit;
- Place people at the centre of their business;
- Trade profitably to fulfil their mission;
- Reinvest profits/surplus in the fulfilment of their mission;
- Engage a wide group of stakeholders in governance and decision-making; and
- Operate with transparency (Social Innovation, Entrepreneurship and Enterprise Alliance, 2014).

Although the core principles are the same, the last two points are interesting additions to the criteria of social enterprises which are not included in the FASES definition.

Social Traders is an organisation which 'connects social enterprises with social procurement opportunities' by certifying social enterprises and facilitating procurement contracts (mostly for government projects/policy) for social enterprises in Australia (Social Traders, 2019a). They are partially funded by the Victorian state government. They have three criteria for social enterprises. First, that they have a defined primary social purpose, environmental, or other public benefit; second, they derive a substantial portion of income from trade; and third, they reinvest 50 per cent or more of their annual profits towards achieving the social purpose (Social Traders, 2019b).

Victoria has a 'strong concentration of social enterprises' which 'may reflect the effects of more consistent public policy support for social enterprise in this state' (Barraket, Mason and Blain, 2016, p. 13). The Victorian government defines social enterprises as organisations that are driven by a public or community cause, be it social, environmental, cultural, or economic; derive most of their income from trade, not donations or grants; and use at least 50 per cent of their profits to work towards their social mission (State Government of Victoria, 2019).

The Australian Institute of Company Directors views social enterprises through the lens of the type of activities that they perform and the audience that they benefit (Australian Institute of Company Directors, 2015, pp. 1–2). They consider that social enterprises can be one of eight types of entities. First are intermediate labour market companies. These are for-profit commercial businesses developed as a method of training and providing work for the unemployed. Second are social firms; these are commercial businesses developed to provide employment for people with a disability. Again, they are for-profit entities. Third are Australian disability enterprises, an Australian government term for businesses developed to employ people with a disability who are unable to work in mainstream organisations; these are also for-profit entities. The final group of five are entities that are more community led and focused. They tend to be NFPs. These comprise cooperatives, associations, and mutual, as in member-run, member-benefiting businesses which are designed to meet a specific need of members (for example, childcare); community enterprises which are businesses designed purely to benefit the local community (for example, a credit union or petrol station); community development finance institutions, which are businesses created to provide access to financial products for people who find it difficult to access mainstream financial services; fair trade organisations, businesses created to improve the conditions and pay for producers of goods, usually in developing countries, through selling accredited goods to developed world consumers; and charitable business ventures, an income-generation arm of a charity.

Researchers are now publishing in this area, and a body of academic literature is emerging. Young and Lecy consider that social enterprises are organisations or ventures which pursue financial success in the private marketplace in combination with a social purpose. They also argue that social enterprises are more diverse than NFPs and that they are not willing to be confined to one particular sector (Young and Lecy, 2012, p. 3).

III The legal definition of 'charity'

At common law, a 'charity' must be an NFP.[8] No payment can be made to a charity's members other than for wages or allowances to employees, reimbursement of expenses, or payment for services. This requirement also means that on a winding up, any excess funds must be transferred to an entity with similar purposes.

Prior to the introduction of a statutory definition of 'charity' and 'charitable purpose' in Australia, the Australian courts recognised a legal definition as developed through the common law.[9] This common law dates back to the Preamble to the 1601 *Statute of Charitable Uses*,[10] which listed a range of charitable purposes that included relief of poverty, assistance to scholars and orphans, help to returned soldiers, and repairs to highways and churches.

Subsequently, the House of Lords accepted the guidelines suggested by Lord Macnaghten in *Commissioners for Special Purposes of Income Tax v Pemsel*[11] in applying the spirit and intendment of the Preamble in a tax scenario. Lord Macnaghten suggested that charitable purposes fall within four divisions. These are the relief of poverty, advancement of education, advancement of religion, and other purposes beneficial to the community not falling under any of the preceding heads.[12] The classification of charitable purpose into these four areas has been consistently used as a guideline in Australian judicial considerations.[13] Furthermore, as well as requiring a charitable purpose, entities that aim to qualify as charities must also be of public benefit.[14]

In 2013, Australia followed several other countries and enacted a statutory definition of charity.[15] The Charities Act 2013 (Cth) (Charities Act) was enacted in 2013 and came into force on 1 January 2014. This legislation includes a definition of charity and charitable purpose. Under the Charities Act, an entity is 'charitable' for federal law purposes if it is a 'charity' within this term as defined in the legislation.[16] The Act requires that the organisation satisfy four requirements. First, it must be NFP; second, all the entity's purposes must be *charitable* and for the *public benefit* (or ancillary or incidental to *and* in furtherance or in aid of such purposes); third, none of the entity's purposes can be disqualifying purposes; and finally, the entity cannot be an individual, political party, or government entity.[17]

Charitable purposes are defined in s 12(1)(a)–(l) and expanded upon in ss 14, 15, 16, and 17 of the Charities Act. These purposes include the traditional categories of relief of poverty, advancement of education, and religion,[18] together with others such as promoting reconciliation and protection of the natural environment. Section 12(1)(l) of the Charities Act states that a charitable purpose includes the purpose of promoting or opposing a change to any matter established by law, policy, or practice in the Commonwealth, a State, a Territory, or another country, but the promotion or opposition to change must be in furtherance or in aid of one or more of the purposes set out in s 12(1)(a)–(k).

The public benefit requirement has two overlapping aspects. The purpose or object of the NFP must be 'beneficial' in itself, and it must be of benefit to the community or a sufficient section of the community (with the exception of entities for the relief of poverty, where a more relaxed test is followed). The case law establishes that for the first three heads of charitable purposes, 'the court will assume it to be for the benefit of the community and, therefore charitable, unless the contrary is shown'.[19] It is usually where the charitable purpose falls within the general heading under the common law 'other purposes beneficial to the community' that argument surrounding charitable benefit in this sense arises.

As stated previously, the first aspect of public benefit is that the charity's objectives must provide some actual public benefit. This benefit can, however, extend beyond material benefit to other forms including social, mental, and spiritual. An example of where the courts in Australia have found that a purpose was beneficial was the 1971 decision of *The Incorporated Council of Law Reporting of the State of Queensland v The Commissioner of Taxation*.[20] In this case, the High Court of Australia, Australia's highest judicial authority, held that the production of law reports was a matter that was beneficial to the community in a charitable sense.

The public benefit test also requires that the public or a section of the public be benefitted by the charity's objectives. In other words, it cannot be a charity that merely assists a family group or a group of employees. The public benefit test, however, does not mean that the entire public must be benefitted. The case law has accepted that a benefit to a 'sufficient section of the public' is sufficient.[21] The rationale is that not all charities are for the benefit of the entire community; after all, charities are often motivated by the need to assist a section of the community with special needs or disadvantages. The Chief Justice of the High Court of Australia in 1959, Dixon CJ, expressed it clearly in *Thompson v Federal Commissioner of Taxation* when his Honour said that the public benefit test can be determined 'by reference to locality, to conditions of people, to their disabilities, defects or misfortunes and by reference to many other attributes of men and things, yet the trusts may retain their "public" character'.[22]

The requirement that a charity must be of public benefit commonly arises in the context of tax concessions. The concern is that private individuals might take advantage of the favourable tax position available to charities for what is essentially a private purpose.[23] The tax advantages of charities was a strong consideration for Lord Greene in *Re Compton* when deciding whether a trust for the education of descendants of a named person was a family trust and not charitable because it was not for the benefit of the community. His Lordship came to this conclusion even though the advancement of education is a recognised charitable purpose.[24]

The public benefit test is not applied with the same degree of strictness by courts where the charitable purpose is the relief of poverty. In *Re Scarisbricks Will Trust*,[25] the Court approved a charity for the relief of poor relatives ('the relations of my son and daughter'). Further, in *Dingle v Turner*,[26] the House of Lords granted charitable status to a trust for the relief of poor employees, even though this group was defined through their employment relationship. This approach has been accepted in many cases in England[27] and Australia.[28] The rationale seems to be that relief of poverty is overwhelmingly charitable and beneficial to the community.

Can charities carry on businesses?

In 2008, the common law of Australia confirmed that a charity that engaged in carrying on a business could still maintain its charitable status. This confirmation is found in the High Court decision of *Federal Commission of Taxation v Word Investments Limited*.[29] Word Investments Limited was established as a company limited by guarantee in 1975 by members of the Wycliffe Bible Translators Australia. Wycliffe engaged in Christian evangelical purposes and was recognised by the Australian Taxation Office as a charity for the advancement of religion. The memorandum of association of Word Investments allowed it to carry on business activities in connection with its other purposes (which were all clearly charitable as being for the advancement of religion). Any funds from these activities were to go directly to Wycliffe and other entities to support the evangelical work and therefore the religious charitable purpose. Word engaged in the business activity of running a funeral business along commercial lines and distributed all surpluses towards its charitable purposes.

The crucial issue was whether an entity could still be considered charitable when it had the capacity to carry on a business, the funds from which would go towards its purposes, which were all charitable. The funeral business was conducted along commercial lines and was open to the general public. The majority in the High Court emphasised that Word's powers to carry on business activities were a means to Word achieving its religious charitable purposes and therefore did not preclude its charitable status. The rationale of the court was:

> Word endeavoured to make a profit, but only in aid of its charitable purposes. To point to the goal of profit and isolate it as the relevant purpose is to create a false dichotomy between characterisation of an institution as commercial and characterisation of it as charitable.[30]

Therefore, as long as the entity is an NFP and satisfies all the other requirements, in that it has solely charitable purposes and operates for the benefit of the community or a section of the community, it can retain its charitable status and operate a commercial business. The income from this business will be exempt from income tax in the same manner as all other income of the charity.

The Australian situation is very different to many other jurisdictions (OECD, 2020).[31] For example, the business income of charities in the United States is taxable under what is referred to as the Unrelated Business Income Tax (UBIT). The UBIT, found in ss 511–514 of the Internal Revenue Code, generally imposes income tax at the corporate tax rate on the unrelated business income of certain tax-exempt entities. The business income must arise from a trade or business that is regularly carried on by the charity and is unrelated to its purposes. 'Unrelated trade or business' is defined in s 513 as

> any trade or business the conduct of which is not substantially related (aside from the need of such organization for income or funds or the use it makes of the profits derived) to the exercise or performance by such organization of its charitable, educational, or other purpose or function constituting the basis for its exemption.

Certain exempted types of U.S. unrelated passive income, including dividends, interest, loan proceeds, annuities, royalties, rent from real property, capital gains, and certain other types of income such as research income, are not subject to the UBIT.[32] However, any kind of investment income is subject to UBIT to the extent that it is debt financed.[33]

Examples of how Australian charities commonly carry on business can be seen through such organisations as the St Vincent de Paul Society and Oxfam. The St Vincent de Paul Society operates stores around Australia that sell second-hand clothing, books, toys, and so on that have been donated by the public. This is not only an efficient means of recycling goods and providing them at low cost to low income earners, but all the profits from the shops go right back into the community, funding local programs like soup vans, food hampers, tutoring programs for disadvantaged children, emergency relief, and accommodation. If we consider the criteria that the Legal Models Working Group set out for a social enterprise, the St Vincent de Paul Society has much in common. It is trading for a social purpose, in that it is assisting low income earners in purchasing clothes and other essentials and is recycling existing goods; second, it is achieving financial sustainability: the goods are donated and then on sold at a small profit, and they are re-investing profit into the social mission of the enterprise. The only ostensible difference between this organisation and an NFP social enterprise is that the St Vincent de Paul Society must have charitable purposes to retain its charitable status. In this case, it is for the relief of poverty and advancement of religion.

Until recently, Oxfam[34] sold 'fair trade' goods manufactured in developing countries both through its stores and online. A decrease in demand and high overheads has meant that this part of the organisation has closed; however, it still supplies fair trade coffee and drinking chocolate to supermarkets, other outlets, and online. This coffee is sourced from communities in developing countries. Oxfam ensures that the producers are paid a fair price, and all the proceeds are reinvested into Oxfam's projects of alleviating world poverty.[35] Again, there is little difference in this organisation's aims and how it operates as compared to a social enterprise.

The advantages of being a charity

For a variety of reasons, both historical and political, most developed nations offer a variety of tax concessions for charities and not-for-profits. In England,[36] the United States,[37] Hong Kong,[38] New Zealand,[39] and Australia,[40] the income of charities is generally exempt from income tax. Tax concessions to NFPs represent a significant amount of public sector revenue in Australia, the United States, and other nations. In Australia, the Treasury estimates that the tax deductibility of donations to specific eligible NFPs (including some charities) costs the Commonwealth revenue around $1.3 billion per year.[41] In the United States, this amount is estimated to be $69.1 billion dollars for the 2016 fiscal year.[42]

However, just because an organisation is an NFP does not mean that it is eligible for exemption from income tax. An NFP organisation will only be exempt from income tax if it falls into a category of exempt entity. Section 50–5 ITAA97 lists the categories of entities that are exempt from income tax. These entities fall into specific 'main' categories (each category has sub-categories), and this includes charities (ITAA97 s 50–5).

An organisation that is NFP and a charity will therefore be exempt from income tax. Such an organisation is also able to access other Commonwealth tax concessions under the Fringe Benefits Tax[43] and Goods and Services Tax (GST).[44] In Australia, charities are also able to obtain a range of tax concessions under state and local government legislation.[45]

Tax deductibility of donations to eligible charities

Section 30–15 ITAA97 provides that a donation of $2 or more to what is referred to as a Deductible Gift Recipient (DGR) is deductible from a taxpayer's assessable income whether the donor is a company or an individual. If the donation is property, then the property must be valued at greater than $5,000.[46] If the donation is jointly owned property, the owners work out the share based on each owner's interest in the property.[47]

Australia is unlike the United States and other countries in that it does not place a percentage cap on the deduction for donations. The Australian federal government has instead protected the revenue by limiting the types of organisations that are eligible for donation status. In other words, just because an entity is a charity does not mean that it is a DGR.

The ITAA97 sets out how to determine whether an entity is eligible to be endorsed as a DGR.[48] The number of DGR categories is more than 40, which provides insight into the complexity of the system. To be eligible for endorsement under one of what are referred to in the legislation as the general categories, the organisation must fall within a category specified in the ITAA97 and itemised in subdivision 30-B. These general categories are Health, Education, Research, Welfare and Rights, Defence, Environment, The Family, International Affairs, Sports and Recreation, Cultural Organisations, Fire and Emergency Services, and Ancillary funds. Examples of the types of entities that are included under the general headings include Public Benevolent Institutions (PBIs), public hospitals, health promotion charities, school building funds (both government and NFP), and necessitous circumstance funds.

The largest group of charities that are eligible for DGR status are PBIs (Cortis et al., 2015, pp. 49–50). The PBI was developed by the legislature to ensure that the tax concession of deductibility of donations was not available to all charities. There are several explanations for this, although currently the paramount one seems to be the protection of the revenue as the donation tax concession is estimated by Treasury to cost the Federal revenue approximately $1.3b per year.[49] Further reasons that flow from some of the Parliamentary debates and judicial statements at the time the term was inserted in the legislation suggest that the phrase PBI was developed to capture those entities more closely aligned to the traditional view that charities are for the relief of poverty (Martin, 2017) and therefore are the NFPs that should have most significant tax concession privileges (Martin, 2017; Chesterman, 1999, pp. 340–341).

It is the responsibility of the Commissioner of Taxation, the head of the Australian Taxation Office to ensure that the administration of the general categories of DGRs is applied impartially. Furthermore, since 2013, regulation and registration of charities has been vested in the Australian Charities and Not-for-profit Commission (ACNC).[50] NFPs must register with the ACNC before they can be endorsed by the ATO as charities,[51] and for charities that wish to become DGRs, this registration is an essential pre-requisite.[52] Charities therefore face the administrative burden of making separate and different applications to two different government agencies.

Section 30–120 of the ITAA97 provides that the Commissioner may use his endorsement powers according to Division 426 in Schedule 1 to the Taxation Administration Act 1953 to endorse DGRs. The endorsement may be for an organisation or for the operation of a fund, authority, or institution. This means the Commissioner can endorse the organisation or fund itself or endorse the legal person that operates the organisation or fund. Section 30–125 ITAA97 lists the requirements for application for endorsement. The ATO also publishes guides for the NFP sector. These include a Gift Pack to help NFPs to apply for DGR status.

If the organisation or fund does not meet the requirements for the general categories, it may apply for a ministerial decision to change the ITAA97 to specifically list it in the legislation as a DGR. To commence this process, the organisation must write to the Treasurer (ATO, 2013). DGRs listed by name include organisations such as the National Trust and the Australian Sports Foundation. The federal government announced that from 1 July 2019, DGRs that are not government entities will be automatically registered with the ACNC (O'Dwyer, 2017). There is no detail in the media announcement about how this process will occur.

Other benefits of being a charity

A charitable or a not-for-profit social enterprise may access a range of grants specifically available to promote the mission of those enterprises. However, once the social enterprise becomes a for-profit business, these grants will no longer be accessible to them even though the social enterprise's social mission remains in place (Justice Connect, 2014, p. 15).

The limitations of being a charity

As discussed earlier, charities must have a charitable purpose as established under the Charities Act. A social enterprise with a mission that does not fall within one of these purposes would therefore not qualify. However, a potentially more significant limitation is that charities cannot access investment funds or provide a return to investors from their profits. This is because they must be NFP structures. If a social enterprise is run through a proprietary limited for-profit company, it can issue shares to investors, who can then anticipate a return on their investment and have some say in the management of the company. Chuffed, which is one of the case studies discussed later in this chapter, is a good example of where a charity transitioned to a for-profit model for just these reasons.

IV Blending social enterprises and charities: three case studies

Some organisations have managed to work around the previous issues and limitations by either carrying on business through a charity or forming hybrid structures or joint ventures with reputable charities. In this part, I discuss three case studies. Each case study demonstrates a different way of carrying on a social enterprise. The first is a charity, the second a for-profit entity, and the third a hybrid of charity and for-profit structures. I have chosen each situation as a case study for the following reasons. First, each has been written about, and therefore there is publicly available documentation regarding their effectiveness, longevity, or otherwise. Second, each either uses a charity or has used a charity in the past to carry on its social enterprise. Third, each represents a very different way of approaching the carrying on of a social enterprise.

The first case study is Vanguard Laundry Services, a hospital laundry service that provides employment for people suffering from mental illness. The following is a description of this entity:

> Vanguard Laundry Services is a social enterprise commercial laundry service based in Toowoomba, Queensland, which provides jobs and employment pathways for people with a lived experience of mental illness who have a history of unemployment. In 2019, the third year of business, Vanguard grew rapidly and increased laundry revenues. While it did not make an operating profit in FY2019, this was achieved early in 2020.
>
> *(Vanguard Laundry Services, 2019, p. 2)*

Vanguard operates as a PBI, so it is a charity and DGR, and it partners with several organisations, both charities, businesses, and government, to access operating funds (Vanguard Laundry Services). It operates a commercially successful business, which it can, due to the *Word Investments* decision. As a charity, it has the advantages of tax concessions, including income tax exemption. As a PBI, donations to it are tax deductible. As discussed in Section III, being a PBI allows it to gain DGR status, and therefore any donations from the public are tax deductible. This is a major incentive to members of the public to make donations. Being a charity does mean that its social mission is limited to charitable purposes. In this case, the social mission of Vanguard Laundry Services fits squarely within charitable purposes to assist the disadvantaged. The other major limitation of operating through a charity is that Vanguard has limited access to investment funds; however, by partnering with business and government, it has managed to obtain funds without losing its charitable status. This is through both donations and grants. In addition, it is making a profit from the business undertaking.

My second case study found the charity structure too confining and moved to a wholly for-profit social enterprise. This organisation is Chuffed. Chuffed.org was established in 2013, and its stated mission was to transform and improve the nature of non-profit fundraising. The organisation was first registered as a company limited by guarantee, and it was a charity. However, the desire to grow the business and attract venture capital while at the same time maintaining its social mission resulted in this organisation transforming from an NFP entity to a hybrid for-profit business which is incorporated as a proprietary company (Paramanathan, 2016). In this way, it could raise capital through issuing shares and retain its social mission by embedding this in its constitution.

Chuffed assists in fundraising for projects that have a social, community, or political cause, and promoters can include charities and NFPs (Chuffed, 2018). Chuffed charges fees and also operates courses that are fee paying. Chuffed is clearly carrying on a business, and all proceeds of the business will be assessable income. Some of the ventures that Chuffed engages with would clearly fit within charitable purposes, for example, its many projects raising funds to assist refugees and asylum seekers; however, others, such as 'Ophelia's broken tail' (Ophelia's Broken Tail, 2020), are targeted to assist individuals (in this case a rescued greyhound) and therefore unlikely to fit within a charitable purpose or the public benefit (being targeted at a particular animal and its owners). Chuffed is therefore free from restrictions regarding its social mission and can more easily gain investment funding than a charity; however, it is not income tax exempt, and amounts paid to it are not eligible for a tax deduction. Another advantage is that operating through a proprietary limited company means it has fewer restrictions and reporting requirements than a charity (Nehme and Martin, 2019).

The third case study is a social enterprise that forms a corporate group grouping a DGR with a proprietary company. An example of this corporate group structure may be found in the STREAT organisations.

STREAT Ltd is a Melbourne-based NFP social enterprise that originally operated café businesses that employed young homeless Australians. In 2012, STREAT Ltd bought two cafes and a coffee roasting business from another social enterprise. To protect itself from liability, it created a corporate group that resulted in a hybrid model being created and in which a proprietary limited company would operate the businesses (e.g., Diagram) (Justice Connect, 2014, pp. 14–15).

Diagram of Hybrid structure of STREAT

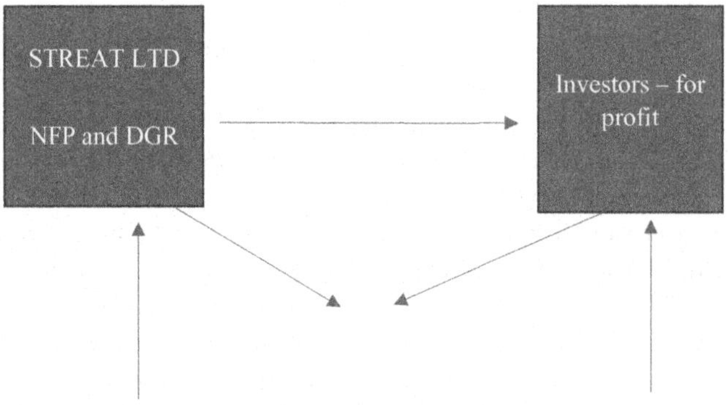

STREAT and Investors own shares in STREAT Enterprises Pty Ltd

STREAT Enterprises pays profits to STREAT and Investors in the form of dividends

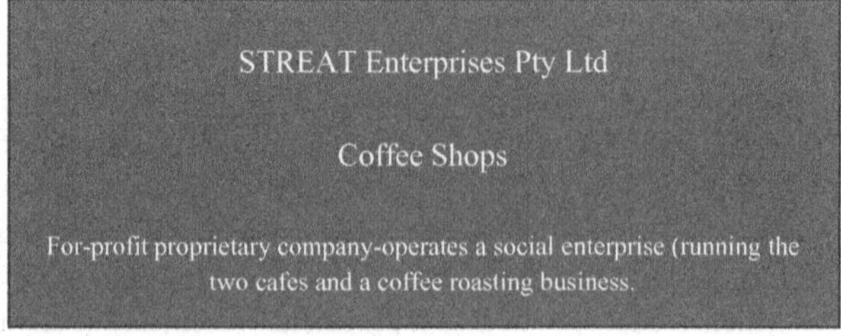

STREAT is exempt on all the income that it receives from STREAT Enterprises Pty Ltd. This will be in the form of dividends and, if franked (tax credit on the dividend), STREAT is entitled to a refund of the franking credits. The investors will receive taxable dividends. But, if franked, can access a franking credit. As it is a charity and a DGR, STREAT can access grants and tax-deductible donations. By having a separate entity own the coffee shops, STREAT and the investors are protected from liability if the enterprise is unsuccessful. STREAT Enterprises can also raise funds through issuing shares.

However, it is important to note that running such a structure can be expensive, as there will be a range of legal obligations that need to be complied with, for example, to gain DGR status, the organisation must comply with legal rules that are set out in div 30 ITAA97 and be endorsed by the Australian Taxation Office. Charities are subject to regulation by the ACNC. This cost may stop newly incorporated social enterprises from adopting this model. However, it may be a realistic option once the social enterprise becomes successful.

Clearly, all these entities have the characteristics of social enterprises as established in the FASES Report (Barraket, Mason and Blain, 2016, p. 3). They are led by an economic, social, cultural, or environmental mission consistent with a public or community benefit. In the case of Vanguard, this is to provide employment opportunities for people with mental health issues, which will in turn keep them out of poverty. Chuffed is a crowdfunding platform that raises funds for projects that have a social, community, or political cause. In the case of STREAT, it is homeless youths who are being assisted to gain employment, which will ultimately result in their being able to find affordable housing and lift them out of poverty. All these organisations trade to fulfil their mission, derive a substantial portion of their income from trade, and reinvest most of their profit/surplus in the fulfilment of their mission (Barraket et al., 2010, p. 16).

It appears that there is a spectrum in Australia along which social enterprises may move and develop but that with some developments in their structure, certain opportunities are either lost or gained. At the furthest end of the spectrum is the traditional charity which operates a business that is linked to its charitable purpose, such as a charity shop operated by the St Vincent's de Paul Society. Such an entity must be an NFP, have charitable purposes, and be registered with the ACNC to gain charitable status and therefore income tax exemption. Moving further along the spectrum are also charities, but they operate businesses that are more akin to social enterprises, such as the examples of Vanguard and STREAT. If they are NFPs and have solely charitable purposes, they can maintain charitable status and income tax exemption. If they are also DGRs, donations to them are tax deductible, which is a motivating factor for donations. At the furthest end of the spectrum are social enterprises operating as for-profit businesses. They are liable to income tax; however, they can also access investment funds and pay profits to investors. Somewhere in the middle are hybrid structures such as the STREAT example. However, this requires legal advice and may be costly to establish and maintain.

V Conclusion

This chapter has established that whilst social enterprises and charities can be very different and have very different aims and outcomes, there is also considerable overlap. Many social enterprises have social outcomes that are like charitable purposes. For example, Vanguard Laundry Services describes itself as a social enterprise, but it is also a charity with the charitable purposes of assisting the disadvantaged and alleviating poverty. A social enterprise that puts the environment at the forefront of all decisions and workplace practices would look very similar to a charity for the promotion of the environment. STREAT is a charity and a social enterprise with the aim of educating and assisting the unemployed and thereby ultimately relieving poverty.

Whilst there is considerable overlap between social enterprises and charities, there are also differences and limitations. Charities have the advantage of being income tax exempt and being able to access grants from both government and charitable organisations. In some cases, they can attract donations that are tax deductible. For-profit social enterprises cannot access these advantages; however, they can access investment from shareholders and, if successful, can provide a return to investors. If a social enterprise operates through a proprietary limited company, it has fewer restrictions and reporting requirements than a charity (Nehme and Martin, 2019).

It is possible in Australia to carry on a business through a charity, and this chapter has provided examples of some charities that have successfully done this. It is also possible that a hybrid structure can be established, as was done by STREAT. However, no one structure will suit all outcomes, and it is important that entrepreneurs take the considerations discussed in this chapter into account before launching a social enterprise.

Notes

1 Income Tax Act 2007 (UK) ch 3, s 518, ss 524–537. Also, Corporation Tax Act 2010 (UK) c 4 and Taxation of Chargeable Gains Act 1992 (UK) c 12.
2 Inland Revenue Code § 501(c)(3) (IRC).
3 Inland Revenue Ordinance (Hong Kong) cap 112, s 88.
4 Income Tax Act 2007 (NZ) CW 41.
5 Income Tax Assessment Act 1997 (Cth) s 50–5 (ITAA97).
6 Charities Act 2013 (Cth) s 5–6.
7 The term not-for-profit is used throughout this chapter as it is generally accepted as the more appropriate term refer I Sheppard, R Fitzgerald and D Gonski, *Report into the Inquiry into the Definition of Charities and Related Organisations* (2001) 13.
8 *Re Smith's Wills Trusts; Barclays' Bank Ltd v Mercantile Bank Ltd* [1962] 2 All ER 563; Ann O'Connell, 'The Tax Position of Charities in Australia – Why Does It Have To Be So Complicated?' (2008) 37 *Australian Tax Review* 17, 24.
9 *Salvation Army (Victoria) Property Trust v Shire of Fern Tree Gully* (1952) 85 CLR 159.
10 43 Eliz. 1, c.4, commonly referred to as the Statute of Elizabeth.
11 [1891] AC 531.
12 [1891] AC 531, 583.
13 See the High Court of Australia in *Commissioner of Taxation v Word Investments Limited* [2008] HCA 55; *Salvation Army (Victoria) Property Trust v Shire of Fern Tree Gully* (1952) 85 CLR 159, 173; *Ashfield Municipal Council v Joyce* (1976) 10 ALR 193; *Commissioner of Taxation v The Triton Foundation* (2005) 226 ALR 293, 299 (Kenny J).
14 *Commissioners for Special Purposes of Income Tax v Pemsel* [1891] AC 531; *Salvation Army (Victoria) Property Trust v Shire of Fern Tree Gully* (1952) 85 CLR 159.
15 For example, in England and Wales, there is now a statutory definition of 'charity' under the Charities Act 2006 (UK).
16 Charities Act, s 5.
17 Charities Act, ss 5–6, 11 and 12.
18 As established by the common law – see *Commissioners for Special Purposes of Income Tax v Pemsel* [1891] AC 531.
19 *National Anti-Vivisection Society v Inland Revenue Commissioners* [1948] AC 31, 65.
20 *The Incorporated Council of Law Reporting of the State of Queensland v The Commissioner of Taxation* (1971) 125 CLR 659.
21 *Dingle v Turner* [1972] AC 601, 623 (Lord Cross); *Oppenheim v Tobacco Securities Trust Co Ltd* [1951] AC 297.
22 *Thompson v Federal Commissioner of Taxation* (1959) 102 CLR 315, 321 (Dixon CJ).
23 *Re Compton* [1945] Ch 123, 136; *Perpetual Trustee Co (Ltd) v Ferguson* (1951) 51 SR (NSW) 256, 263 (Sugerman J).
24 *Re Compton* [1945] Ch 123, 136.
25 *Re Scarisbricks Will Trust* [1951] 1 Ch 622.
26 *Dingle v Turner* [1972] AC 601.

27 See *Re Hobourn Aero Components Limited's Air Raid Distress Fund* [1946] Ch 194, 203–07 (Lord Greene MR); *Re Scarisbricks Will Trust* [1951] 1 Ch 622, 649–52 (Jenkins LJ); *Gibson v South American Stores* [1950] Ch 177.
28 *Alice Springs Town Council v Mpweteyerre Aboriginal Corporation* [1997] 139 FLR 236, 252.
29 [2008] HCA 55.
30 [2008] HCA 55, [24].
31 See generally 'Taxation and Philanthropy', OECD Tax Policy Series, November 2020.
32 Internal Revenue Code s 512(b).
33 Internal Revenue Code s 514.
34 Oxfam https://faircoffee.com.au/ (Accessed: 30 September 2020).
35 Oxfam https://faircoffee.com.au/pages/about-us (Accessed: 30 September 2020).
36 Income Tax Act 2007 (UK) ch 3, s 518, ss 524–537. Also, Corporation Tax Act 2010 (UK) c 4 and Taxation of Chargeable Gains Act 1992 (UK) c 12.
37 Inland Revenue Code § 501(c)(3) (IRC).
38 Inland Revenue Ordinance (Hong Kong) cap 112, s 88.
39 Income Tax Act 2007 (NZ) CW 41 and CW42.
40 Income Tax Assessment Act 1997 (Cth) s 50–5 (ITAA97).
41 Standing Committee on Tax and Revenue, House of Representatives, *Tax Expenditures Statement 2015* (2016), 26–27. No amount is estimated for revenue foregone with respect to the income tax exemption. Tax expenditure is a term used to refer to tax exemptions, deductions; or offsets; concessional tax rates; and deferrals of tax liability.
42 The U.S. Joint Committee on Taxation breaks down the tax expenditures (cost) of charitable deductions into three categories: (1) charitable contribution deductions to educational institutions, $54.2 billion; (2) charitable contribution deductions to health organisations $28.7 billion; and (3) a catchall category of charitable contribution deductions other than for education and health, $230.5 billion: Joint Committee on Taxation, 115th Congress, *Estimates of Federal Tax Expenditures for Fiscal Years 2016–2020* (JCX0–3–17), 30 January 2017, 36–38.
43 For example, s 57A Fringe Benefits Tax Act 1986 (Cth) for benefits to employees of health promotion charities and public benevolent institutions (PBIs). PBIs are not-for-profit institutions that are organised for the direct relief of poverty, sickness, and so on and are considered a subset of charities. Refer Taxation Ruling TR 2003/5 'Income Tax and Fringe Benefits Tax: Public Benevolent Institutions' [7], [24]; Gino Dal Pont, *Charity Law in Australia and New Zealand* (Oxford University Press 2000) 37.
44 For example, charities have a higher GST turnover threshold ($150,000 as compared to $75,000) before being required to register for GST, s 23–15 A New Tax System (Goods and Services Tax) Act 1999 (Cth) and certain supplies by charities are GST free under Subdivision 38-G.
45 At the state and local government level, a range of exemptions or concessions in relation to payroll tax, land tax, stamp duty, and local government rates are available to certain charities. For a summary, refer to I. Sheppard, R. Fitzgerald and D. Gonski, *Report into the Inquiry into the Definition of Charities and Related Organisations* (2001); Commonwealth of Australia Productivity Commission Research Report, *Contribution of the Not-for-Profit Sector*, (2010), [7.1]; also refer to Fiona Martin, 'Local Government Rates Exemptions for Indigenous Organisations: The Complexities of a State by State System' (2010) 14 *Australian Indigenous Law Review* 35.
46 ITAA97 s 30–15. Unless it is specific types of shares; see ITAA97 s30–15 items 7, 8.
47 ITAA97 s 30–225.
48 ITAA97 s 30–15.
49 Standing Committee on Tax and Revenue, House of Representatives, *Tax Expenditures Statement 2015* (2016), 26–27. No amount is estimated for revenue foregone with respect to the income tax exemption.
50 Australian Charities and Not-for-profits Commission Act 2012 (Cth) ss 10–5 to 15–10.
51 ITAA97 ss 50–4750–110.
52 ITAA97 ss 30–20, 30–25, 30–45, 30–50.

References

Australian Charities and Not-for-profits Commission, Australian Charities Report 2017, www.acnc.gov.au/tools/reports/australian-charities-report-2017 (Accessed: 30 September 2020).

Australian Institute of Company Directors, Social Enterprise: Role of the Board (NFP Director Tools, 2015).

Australian Law Reform Commission, The Future of Law Reform: Suggested Program of Work 2020–25 (December 2019).

Australian Taxation Office Income Tax Guide for Non-Profit Organisations NAT 7967-03. 2007.

Australian Taxation Office 2008–09 Compliance Program www.ato.gov.au/content/downloads/COR_0015516_CP0809.pdf 61 (Accessed: 30 September 2020).

Australian Taxation Office, DGRs Listed by Name (5 December 2013) www.ato.gov.au/law/view/document?docid=SAV/GIFTPACK/00001#H6 (Accessed: 30 September 2020).

Barraket, Jo, Nick Collyer, Matt O'Connor, and Heather Anderson, *Finding Australia's Social Enterprise Sector 2010: Final Report* (Australian Centre for Philanthropy and Nonprofit Studies, June 2010).

Barraket, Jo, Heather Douglas, Robyn Eversole, Chris Mason, Joanne McNeill, and Bronwen Morgan, 'Classifying social enterprise models in Australia' 13(4) (2017) *Social Enterprise Journal* 345.

Barraket, Jo, Chris Mason and Blake Blain Finding Australia's Social Enterprise Sector 2016: Final Report (Centre for Social Impact, Swinburne University of Technology, and Social Trader, 2016).

Boris, Elizabeth T. 'The Nonprofit Sector in the United States: Size and Scope' *Urban Institute* (2012) https://pdfs.semanticscholar.org/presentation/47af/24c3b53ba5554a7bf4086b4d9f06b4ac01de.pdf.

Brakman Reiser, Dana, and Steven A. Dean, *Social Enterprise Law* (Oxford: Oxford University Press, 2017), 9–10.

Chesterman, Michael, 'Foundations of Charity Law in the New Welfare State' (1999) 62 *Modern Law Review* 333, 340–341.

Chuffed, Before You Start, Are You Eligible? (2018) https://chuffed.org/how-it-works-crowdfunding/before-you-start (Accessed: 30 September 2020).

Chuffed, How to Build a Team to Crowdfund $91,400 for Asylum Seekers https://chuffed.org/academy/articles/detail/against-the-odds-how-libby-and-caroline-crowdfunded-91400-for-people-seeking-asylum 2020 (Accessed: 30 September 2020).

Chuffed, Our Fees Are the Lowest (2018) https://chuffed.org/fees (Accessed: 30 September 2020).

Chuffed, We Help You Take Action on Issues You Care About (2018) https://chuffed.org/ (Accessed: 30 September 2020).

Cortis, Natasha et al., 'Australian Charities Report 2015' Centre for Social Impact and Social Policy Research Centre, UNSW Australia, 2015.

Justice Connect Not-for-Profit Law, Social Enterprise Guide, 2014.

Koele, Ineke, Alien, International Taxation of Philanthropy (IBFD 2007) 1.

Martin, Fiona, 'The Sociopolitical and Legal History of the Tax Deduction for Donations to Charities in Australia and How the 'Public Benevolent Institution' Developed' (2017) 38 *Adelaide Law Review* 195.

Nehme, Marina, and Fiona Martin, 'Social Entrepreneurs: An Evaluation of the Pty Ltd Company from a Corporations Law and Taxation Law Perspective' (2019) *Australian Law Journal* 125.

O'Dwyer, Kelly, 'Reforming Administration of Tax Deductible Gift Recipients' *Media Release*, 5 December 2017.

OECD, 'Taxation and Philanthropy', OECD Tax Policy Series, November 2020.

Ophelia's Broken Tail https://chuffed.org/project/ophelias-broken-tail 2020 (Accessed: 30 September 2020).

Oxfam https://faircoffee.com.au/ (Accessed: 30 September 2020).

Oxfam https://faircoffee.com.au/pages/about-us (Accessed: 30 September 2020).

Oxfam https://faircoffee.com.au/pages/our-promise (Accessed: 30 September 2020).

Paramanathan, Prashan, 'Introducing the Social Benefit Company – A New Legal Structure for Australian Social Enterprises' *Chuffed Blog* (January 2016) https://chuffed.org/blog/the-social-benefit-company (Accessed: 30 September 2020).

Powell, Abigail et al., 'Australian Charities Report 2016' (2017) Centre for Social Impact and Social Policy Research Centre, UNSW Australia.

Pro Bono Australia, 'Creating a Thriving Social Enterprise Sector in Australia' (26 February 2014) https://probonoaustralia.com.au/news/2014/02/creating-a-thriving-social-enterprise-sector-in-australia/ Accessed: 30 September 2020).

Rodgers, Malcolm, Bronwen Morgan, Fiona Martin, Alan Greig, Robyn Donnelly, Joanne McNeil, Andrew Perry, and Stephen Bennet, Legal Models Working Group, Legal Models Working Group Final Report (2015).

Salamon, Lester M., S. Wojciech Sokolowski, and Regina List, *Global Civil Society: An Overview* (Baltimore: Centre for Civil Society Studies The Johns Hopkins University, 2003).
Social Enterprise, United Kingdom, 'What Makes a Social Enterprise a Social Enterprise?' (2012) www.socialenterprise.org.uk/wp-content/uploads/2019/05/What_makes_a_social_enterprise_a_social_enterprise_April_2012.pdf (Accessed: 30 September 2020).
Social Innovation, Entrepreneurship and Enterprise Alliance (SIEE) Social Enterprise: Doing Business Differently for a More Inclusive Society (2014) 5 https://pollinators.org.au/wp-content/uploads/2013/09/social_manifesto_13.pdf (Accessed: 30 September 2020).
Social Traders, 'About Us' *Social Traders* (2019a) www.socialtraders.com.au/about-us/about-social-traders/ (Accessed: 30 September 2020).
Social Traders, 'About Social Enterprises' *Social Traders* (2019b) www.socialtraders.com.au/about-social-enterprise/what-is-a-social-enterprise/social-enterprise-definition/ (Accessed: 30 September 2020).
Social Traders and the Centre for Social Impact Swinburne, 'Finding Australia's Social Enterprise Sector' (FASES) 2016.
The St Vincent de Paul Society www.vinnies.org.au/page/Shops/NSW/ (Accessed: 30 September 2020).
Standing Committee on Tax and Revenue, House of Representatives, Tax Expenditures Statement 2015 (2016), 26–27. No Amount Is Estimated for Revenue Foregone in Respect of the Income Tax Exemption.
State Government of Victoria, 'Social Enterprise' *Business Victoria* (17 October 2019) www.business.vic.gov.au/setting-up-a-business/business-structure/social-enterprise (Accessed: 30 September 2020).
The US Joint Committee on Taxation Breaks Down the Tax Expenditures (Cost) of Charitable Deductions into Three Categories: (1) Charitable Contribution Deductions to Educational Institutions, $54.2 Billion; (2) Charitable Contribution Deductions to Health Organisations $28.7 Billion; and (3) a Catchall Category of Charitable Contribution Deductions Other Than for Education and Health, $230.5 Billion: Joint Committee on Taxation, 115th Congress, Estimates of Federal Tax Expenditures for Fiscal Years 2016–2020 (JCX¬¬0–3–17), 30 January 2017, 36–38.
Vanguard Laundry Services, '2019 Three Years of Business' 2.
Vanguard Laundry Services, Our Partners www.vanguardlaundryservices.com.au/ (Accessed: 30 September 2020).
Vanguard Laundry Services www.vanguardlaundryservices.com.au/ (Accessed: 30 September 2020).
Young, Dennis, and Jesse Lecy, 'Defining the Universe of Social Enterprise: Competing Metaphors' (2012) *Voluntas: International Journal of Voluntary and Nonprofit Organizations*, 1.

29

SOCIAL ENTREPRENEURSHIP

Is it social or entrepreneurship? Tax treatment of social entrepreneurship in Switzerland

Raphaël Gani

1 Introduction

In Switzerland, legal tax-exempt entities are exhaustively listed in the law (Oberson/Hull, 2011, p. 41). Such an exemption includes institutions of public or private law to the extent that they are dedicated to purposes in the public or cultural interests. It classically applies to charity-type entities that are completely "not-for-profit." On the contrary, "for-profit" entities are subject to full corporate tax on profit and capital. In recent decades, in Switzerland, as in other developed countries, a hybrid form of entities that blurs the boundaries of the classical binary model (for- or not-for-profit) has emerged. For these social entrepreneurs, generating revenue (clearly outside profit maximization) from their enterprises is a key driver, ensuring financial sustainability, generating returns for investors, and avoiding the need to rely on charitable donations or grants. Even if they consider generating revenue, their purpose remains in the public interest, as they pursue a mission solely focused on the promotion of public benefit purposes.

This hybrid characteristic may, as we shall see under the current Swiss tax environment, prevent them from benefiting from a tax exemption (the hybrid nature of the social entrepreneur may also carry some problems in other fields of the tax law, like VAT: see, Vogelsang, 2021, p. 501). We therefore explore which conditions to fulfill under Swiss tax law and, in particular, which could be an obstacle for those social entrepreneurs.

2 Notion of social entrepreneurship and selected model

The notion of social entrepreneurship is difficult to precisely define. Recent research indicates that the conceptualization and definition are differentiated under the applicable subject and methodology (Shapovalov *et al.*, 2019). Broadly defined, social entrepreneurship is the field in which entrepreneurs tailor their activities to be directly tied to the ultimate goal of creating social value. In doing so, they often act with little or no intention to gain personal profit (Abu-Saifan, 2012; Zahra *et al.*, 2008). In this sense, "the social entrepreneur is a mission-driven individual who uses a set of entrepreneurial behaviors to deliver a social value to the less privileged, all through an entrepreneurially oriented entity that is financially independent, self-sufficient, or sustainable" (Abu-Saifan, *op. cit*, 2012).

DOI: 10.4324/9781003139201-34

As this definition is too broad to examine whether a tax exemption is possible under the current Swiss tax environment in each particular case, we arbitrarily select a special model of social entrepreneurship among this definition. Indeed, among these social enterprises, there are companies in the technology sector that are considering developing devices specifically for the world's poorest countries or that are seeking a medicine for diseases that are only found in such countries. These markets are commercially unattractive to ordinary market oriented enterprises because customers are not able to pay a high price. Therefore, there is a lack of research and development in this sector, which requires a social enterprise to take an interest in it.

These companies generally operate with start-up capital that comes from a donation or public or private subsidy. With this seed money, development is conducted, and, in the best case, a product is developed and then sold at a price that is just enough to cover research and production costs and to enable the company to start researching a new product or drug. It is a production and selling model with a minimum margin, clearly having its place in development policies.

3 Current tax environment under Swiss tax law

Under current Swiss tax law, the granting of an exemption for public utility or public service purposes is subject to the fulfillment of several conditions. Under the terms of Article 56, let. g of the Direct Federal Tax Act (DFT), legal persons pursuing public service or pure public utility purposes are exempt from tax on profits exclusively and irrevocably allocated to these purposes (first sentence). The law adds the following: "economic purposes cannot, in principle, be considered to be of public interest" (second sentence). We first examine the general and specific conditions (3.1 to 3.2) and then will specifically analyse the prohibition of economic purpose (see Section 3.3). The practice of the Swiss tax authorities is reflected in circulars that are available online (in particular, "2008 Circular"; and the "Circular AFC, 1994").

3.1 General conditions

The tax exemption of a legal person on the basis of Art. 56 (g) DFT presupposes the fulfillment of three cumulative *general* conditions: being a legal person, the exclusive and irrevocable use of the funds, and the effective continuation of the activity in accordance with its articles of association.

3.1.1 Being a legal person

This condition is not as innocuous as it may seem at first glance. Of course, this means that an entity applying for exemption must be incorporated in a legal form. The type of entity does not matter (foundation, association, or even corporations, like Swiss société anonmye, société coopérative, or another type of legal person), provided that it is a legal person. Nevertheless, this raises the question of trusts. Thus, if a trust, by definition now governed by foreign law, carries out activities that may be exempt in Switzerland, it is not certain that it can be tax exempted; it is not a person under Swiss law. However, this condition demonstrates another essential point of the Swiss legal framework: the exemption applies to entities and not to activities.

3.1.2 Exclusive and irrevocable use of funds

The funds must be used purely for public purposes. This allocation must be exclusive and irrevocable. The means must exclusively serve the exempted purpose and not be used for any other statutory purpose. The allocation of funds is irrevocable when the available means cannot be returned to the founders or donors. This destination of the funds must be made in an irrevocable provision contained in the founding act of the legal entity. This condition may be relatively easy to fulfill for entities that are not owned by anyone. For example, a foundation or an association has only assets for the former or members for the latter. In such cases, it is sufficient to state in an irrevocable statutory clause that the funds will revert upon dissolution of the entity to another legal person, which will also be exempt for a similar purpose. This condition appears to be more complicated for corporations. Indeed, the funds initially entrusted (share capital) are remunerated in the form of dividends. According to the Circular AFC 1994, corporations that pursue purely public utility purposes must renounce, in their articles of association, distributing dividends and directors' fees (on this last point, see Section 3.2.2). However, it seems that this element mixes the irrevocable allocation of capital and its remuneration. A stock company should not be prohibited from remunerating its shareholders, but the articles of association should irrevocably provide that the funds initially made available may not be distributed. Furthermore, on liquidation, as in the case of a foundation or an association, the initial capital must be allocated to another entity benefiting from a similar exemption.

Regardless of the existence or lack of a limitation to the distribution of a dividend for companies, this element should not constitute a significant obstacle for the social enterprise. Indeed, in the model chosen previously, the initial financing can be carried out either as "non-refundable" in the form of a subsidy or a donation or in the form of an equity investment. In the first hypothesis, there is, by nature, neither the return of funds to the investor nor remuneration for the donation.

In the second hypothesis, it may occur in practice that the investor who wants to invest in a hybrid social enterprise is attracted by its social function but nevertheless demands some form of remuneration for its funding. In practice, it is often the case that this investor agrees to a lower return than they could obtain from an ordinary commercial enterprise but nevertheless demands a return. In such cases, it should be noted that the previously mentioned practice of the tax administrations presents an obstacle, since it appears to prohibit any payment of dividends. In our view, this prohibition is not related to the principle from which it is supposed to derive, which is the irrevocability of the funds allocated to fulfill the statutory purpose. Thus, it should not be strictly prohibited to distribute a dividend but rather limit the distribution in relation to the outlay so that the "social" investor can still obtain a limited form of remuneration, without which they will not make the investment.

3.1.3 Effective continuation of the activity

The purpose according to the articles of association must be the same as that actually fulfilled in reality. In this sense, there is no point in indicating as a statutory aim of pure public utility while pursuing a different aim, whether it is profit-oriented or not. There is also no actual purpose if no activities are carried out at all, and the funds are only hoarded. The prohibition of the accumulation of assets has been emphasized in case law (in particular ATF 120 Ib 374 consid. 3a p. 377) on the grounds that hoarding removes the altruistic character of the institution in question. The question of whether an entity devotes sufficient resources to the pursuit of its statutory aims or, on the contrary, has hoarded its assets, is in principle a question of accounting. An operating loss should hence exclude any claim of hoarding (cf. RDAF 2016 II 144 recital 5.5.3). In the aforementioned judgment, it was thus held that an entity that allocated 1/3 of its profits to its corporate purpose was not deemed to be accumulating assets. Distributing 62,000 fr. in a financial year in which a profit of 156,428 fr. was made "cannot represent a fraction out of proportion to its means." If, as indicated by case law, the examination of whether the statutory purpose is actually being pursued is made with regard to the use of profits (and not with regard to available assets), the criterion must be deemed to have already been satisfied in the case of a loss over a financial year.

This condition is not a specific problematic of social enterprises. Any entity benefiting from a tax exemption may prove problematic if the entity cannot immediately start its activity of pure public utility.

3.2 *Specific conditions*

In addition to these three *general* conditions, in accordance with the text of Article 56. g DFT, it is necessary that the legal entity pursue either *a public service* or *pure public utility*. Hence, Swiss tax law distinguishes between these two types of activities that are eligible for tax exemption, on the one hand, activities of pure public utility and, on the other hand, public service activities. Each of these types of activities must meet specific conditions; for example, an exemption for an activity of pure public utility will not be exempted under the same conditions as a public service activity (Federal Supreme Court, case 2C_147/2019 of August 20, 2019, and case 2C_740/2018 of June 18, 2019). According to case law, an exemption based on a public service purpose must be interpreted restrictively. A legal person pursues public service goals if it performs tasks closely related to state tasks (cf. ATF 131 II 1, recital 3.3. p. 6; case 2C_740/2018 of 18 June 2019, recital 5.3).

Exemption based on the pursuit of purely public utility objectives, which is our selected case (see previously 2.), presupposes the fulfillment of two more specific conditions, namely the exercise of an activity in the general interest in favor of an open circle of recipients and disinterestedness (Federal Supreme Court, cases 2C_484/2015 of December 10, 2015, recital 5.3 and 2C_251/2012 of August 17, 2012, recital 2.1).

3.2.1 General interest

According to the Circular AFC 1994 (p. 2), activities of charitable, humanitarian, health, ecological, educational, scientific, and cultural nature may be considered to be of general interest. For example, public assistance, the arts, science, education, the promotion of human rights, the safeguarding of heritage, the protection of nature and animals, and development aid are likely to promote the general interest. Public utility presupposes that the entity carries out an activity in the general interest (as opposed to selfish individual interests), that is, an activity that serves to promote the interests of the community and meets the needs of a significant part of the population (Urech, 2017, art. 56 LIFD N 60). It must be an activity that is particularly worthy of encouragement and support according to the conception of a significant part of the population, one which is carried out for the good of the community. The general interest should not necessarily be confused with the (presumed) interest of a majority of the population, nor with the activities normally carried out by the state.

In the leading case, ATF 113 Ib 7 (= RDAF 1990, p. 197) concerning the "Welttheatergesellschaft Einsiedeln," the Federal Court confirmed that the elements constituting the exemption on grounds of public utility must be interpreted strictly and that it does not cover every activity enriching the community in cultural terms. In particular, the condition of "public utility" cannot be considered as satisfied in the presence of events which constitute a pure entertainment. In addition, an association of public utility cannot simply be tax exempted because it receives subsidy from a public authority. This was also emphasized by the Federal Supreme Court in an old judgment (ATF 63 I 316 consid. 1), according to which musical culture is to be considered as being in the public interest if the entity makes sacrifices in this respect.

In a recent decision by the Federal Supreme Court (August 20,2019, 2C_147/2019), the tax exemption was requested by a foundation whose aim was, among other things, to promote respect for animals, mainly horses, as a symbol of nature. This foundation acquired horses destined for death from their former owners so that the animals could continue their retirement. After analyzing the general conditions of the exemption, the Court considered whether this aim was truly in the general interest; it held that it was not. It thus stated (recital 5.1) that the concept of general interest should not be understood in a broad sense, which would include any activity in the service of the community and would also include all efforts to promote the economic or social interests of certain categories of the population. Public-interest goals are those that, from the perspective of the community as a whole, are particularly worth pursuing. In this case, the Court considers that even if the majority of the population does not share the view that the animal is a mere object, the acquisition of a horse is a personal choice, the consequences of which remain the primary responsibility of the owners concerned. Therefore, there is no public-interest goal in the sense of tax exemption. As said previously, the Court stated that public interest is not the sum of every community interest but interests that, from a community (as a whole) perspective, are particularly worth pursuing. This could not be construed as the addition of all personal interests. In any case, this condition should not present a specific problem for social enterprises.

3.2.2 Disinterest

In addition to the objective element of general interest, the notion of public utility includes a subjective element, disinterestedness. An activity is disinterested in the sense of tax law only if it serves the public interest and is based on altruism, in the sense of dedication to the community. Therefore, the notion of pure public utility presupposes not only that the activity of the legal person is carried out in the general interest but also that it is disinterested. That is, it requires a sacrifice on the part of the members of the corporation or third parties in favor of the general interest overriding their own interests. In this sense, it is required that the legal person requiring the benefit of Article 56 let. g LIFD acts in a non-profit-making capacity.

First, disinterestedness presupposes a sacrifice for the benefit of third parties in the interest of the community. This sacrifice may materialize (i) in the form of financial or work contributions made by the institution, the founder, the members of the institution's board or third parties, or (ii) through what may be termed a "collective sacrifice." That is, the activity is only carried out thanks to public or para-public subsidy or even naturally through a mixture of these different means. The sacrifice must be significant and allow the institution to have sufficient funds to achieve its statutory goals (Urech, op. cit., art. 56, LIFD N 67). In this respect, members of the institution's bodies must perform their duties on a voluntary basis, subject to reimbursement of their actual expenses, and/or in the event of activities exceeding the activity of a member of the Foundation Board/Association Committee. Hence, because they perform their duties on a voluntary basis, the managing members of the legal person are in principle subject to reimbursement of their actual expenses (Urech, op. cit. N 67 ad art. 56). This sacrifice must be of some importance in relation to the means available to the legal person. The condition of disinterestedness presupposes that an institution's activity is based on altruism.

In a judgment by a lower Court (Fribourg – RDAF 2012 II 569), the Court recognized this disinterest by stating

> it should be noted on the one hand that the members of the committee and more than a hundred volunteers work free of charge. Indeed, sacrifices can be made not only in the form of cash, but also through benefits in kind. On the other hand, it is important

> to note that income is also earmarked to a large extent for the provision of free events and the realization of special cultural promotion projects (at least indirect support for young talent and youth choirs, original creations, additional offers of introduction to musical culture, provision of documentation, etc.). In addition, the applicant apparently aims for the lowest possible price policy, which makes admission to paid concerts more accessible to a wide audience.

In the same vein, activity in one's own interest is deemed to exist when the aim of a foundation is to build high-quality, moderately priced housing and the personal interests of an economic group in the construction industry, which is close to it, depend on this activity, even though the latter could be a public interest (ATF 114 Ib 277).

The question of disinterestedness does not, in our view, pose a specific problem for social enterprises. Admittedly, the remuneration of the board of directors can be an obstacle as soon as tax practices require such disinterestedness. However, the 2008 Circular (p. 38) specifies that when a member of a foundation board or a committee of an association assumes tasks that exceed the ordinary activity of such group from a quantitative or qualitative viewpoint, an appropriate compensation may be paid to him. This is particularly the case if a member of a board or association committee is primarily engaged in this professional activity and is remunerated in accordance with market rates. In such a case, compensation does not preclude the notion of disinterest, since the institution would have to use the services of third parties or perform said tasks through a commercial entity. In any case, these would have to be compensated in accordance with the professional tariff applicable in the matter according to the nature of the assets to be managed or the deployed activity. Thus, the same applies to paid members of a social enterprise.

3.2.3 Unlimited circle of potential recipients

The exempt entity must not pursue its own interests, which excludes the exemption for mutual assistance institutions. Furthermore, the case law has made it clear that it is not so much the statutory purpose that is decisive but the actual use of the funds. Thus, in a recent judgment (case 2C_835/2016 of March 21, 2017, in RDAF 2018 II 437), the Supreme Court held that the exemption had rightly been withdrawn from an entity which, although having an open circle of beneficiaries in its statutes, carried out its activity – a public utility activity – exclusively in favor of members of a specific religious community. The funds paid out only went to a very limited circle of recipients, that is, institutions with the same religious affiliation. It is decisive that the restricted circle of recipients belonging to the same religion is contrary to the necessary openness.

The activity cannot generally be aimed at the entire population. However, it must be carried out for the benefit of an unspecified part of the population and is therefore aimed at an open circle of potential recipients (Urech, op. cit., art. 56 LIFD N 64). This is not the case if the circle of recipients is too narrowly limited (e.g., limited to a family circle, members of an association, or persons exercising a specific profession) (Circular AFC 1994, p. 3).

3.3 What about the prohibition of economic activities?

Once all conditions described previously are met, one should nevertheless control that the entity is not pursuing an economic goal (see especially Lideikyte Huber, 2019). This condition, which is probably the most important for our subject, that is, in relation to social enterprises as defined previously, is the prohibition for an exempted enterprise to pursue an economic purpose. To the best of the author's knowledge, there is no direct case law in relation to social entrepreneurship under Swiss tax law that has been confronted with this condition. Nevertheless, the prohibition of a predominant economic activity has increased in some cases, notably linked to cultural activities.

Generally speaking, a profit-making purpose exists when a legal person, in a situation of real competition or economic monopoly, commits capital and labor to obtain a profit and demands a remuneration for its services similar to that normally paid in economic life. The exemption of such an entity would be contrary to the principle of economic neutrality, even if the institution were to devote itself exclusively to an exempt purpose or to allocate the entire profit to this purpose (Circular AFC 1994, p. 3; Urech, op. cit., art. 56, LIFD N 74).

Thus, the criterion of market participation relates more to the services provided (outbound) (and, if applicable, invoiced) by the entity than to those it acquires (inbound). This condition is the corollary of the selflessness and sacrifice that the latter implies. However, this condition does not require that persons carrying out activities in favor of the institution should not be remunerated. An exception to this principle is the case of secondary gainful employment or when the aims of pure public utility are paramount. An economic activity (even with a certain lucrative purpose) is permissible if it remains subsidiary and of secondary importance in relation to the activity of general interest or serves to achieve the goal of public utility (Circular AFC 1994, p. 4). In this case, economic activity must be a means and not an end in itself. Hence, not every gainful activity leads to the refusal of tax exemption, provided that this activity does not constitute the final goal of the institution. Gainful activity, which remains subsidiary to altruistic activity, does not preclude an exemption based on public utility. For example, a meditation center dedicated to Buddhist practice and meditation can accommodate participants and provide courses by charging for its services, including a share of administrative costs, at cost price even if the entity is tax exempted (Supreme Court of August 17, 2012, case 2C_251/2012). The activity may either be subordinate or allow the legal entity to have the means to be allocated to the exempt purpose.

In this context, a recent case law of the Swiss Supreme Court, Supreme Court July 22, 2020, published in ATF 146 II 359, is very interesting. International School A in Geneva sought a full tax exemption, arguing that it served as a public service objective. The Supreme Court rejected its claim, stating that an exemption due to the pursuit of a public service purpose is, in principle, excluded when a legal person pursues mainly profit-making purposes, even if these simultaneously serve public-interest purposes. In any case, the exemption can only be admitted if the profit-making purposes are secondary to the main public service purpose of the legal person. Thus, an exemption, even partial, is excluded when the legal person pursues profit-making purposes that exceed a certain measure (see a previous case in ATF 131 II 1). The principle of competitive neutrality must be respected in the case of a lucrative activity of the legal person. However, this principle only applies between legal persons in comparable situations of competition.

The court responded to the appellant's argument that making a profit was a matter of medium-term survival for any public school and that it should therefore be distinguished from the goal of doing so. While it is certain that a private school must aim for minimum profitability to survive, the presence of deferred profits is an element to be taken into account in the weighting of the criteria established to determine the granting of a tax exemption. Indeed, a school run as a commercial enterprise with the aim of making a profit cannot benefit from it. Hereafter, we examine what can be derived from this case law.

4 (Deemed) obstacles for our selected social enterprise model

4.1 Obstacles

As previously mentioned, a profit-making activity occurs when a legal person, in a situation of real competition or economic monopoly, commits capital and labor to obtain a profit and demands a remuneration for its services similar to what is normally paid in economic life. The exemption of a commercial enterprise is thus contrary to the principle of economic neutrality. Even if it devotes itself exclusively to an exempt purpose or uses the entire profit for that purpose, for tax purposes, such enterprises must be treated as those that do not pursue a disinterested purpose (Urech, op. cit., N 77 ad Art. 56). There is nevertheless a commercial purpose if the natural persons behind the legal person seek gain through the latter.

In the social enterprise model described previously, several phases need to be distinguished. First, an initial research phase, which is made possible by an initial foundation. In this phase, the device to be developed or medicine is developed and researched. In this phase, there is no production or sale. Let us take the example of an X-ray machine that is designed to withstand power cuts, high temperatures, and high dust levels and must be transportable. It is already questionable whether the imperative of Swiss tax law ("Economic goals cannot in principle be considered to be in the public interest") is respected at this early stage. The aim of the entity is to produce and sell its products, which is clearly an economic goal that, according to the law, cannot be construed as a public interest.

In fact, the law makes it clear that the *purpose of an entity* cannot be an economic one. Thus, the different phases of research and production should not change the purpose of the company. In our hypothesis, the purpose of the social enterprise is to find, develop, produce, and eventually deliver technological solutions specific to developing countries or impoverished communities. Therefore, regardless of the phase of research or development, the prohibition of economic purposes could prevent our company from benefiting from the exemption. This consequence is even truer in the following phases, especially when selling to third parties. Admittedly, this sale is made with a very small margin, allowing only basic financing for future researches. It is thus relatively clear that the activity described previously cannot benefit from a tax exemption for the purpose of pure public utility, the conditions of which are strictly described in the law.

However, why is it important that such social enterprises benefit from a tax exemption? There are several reasons. First, the entity itself is tax exempt, allowing it to lower its production costs. Indeed, this exemption covers both profit and capital taxes. Second, the exemption also allows a deduction for donations made by an entity in favor of legal persons that are exempt from tax due to their public service or public utility purposes up to a maximum of 20% of the income. In other words, as soon as the social enterprise would be exempt, all entities that finance it without any counterpart are likely to deduct this donation up to 20% of the taxable profit from their own tax. To obtain a private subsidy, in particular to finance the start of research, the exemption presents an element facilitating the search for funds for the social enterprise, since it ensures the funder a reduction in its own taxes. There is at least one final very important element in Switzerland linked to the status of tax-exempt entities. It is a type of label that indicates recognition of its utilitarian status by the state. It is a form of "State stamp" that guarantees that the entity receiving it brings some kind of special utility through its activity. If one considers these three consequences of the tax exoneration status, the last one is probably the most important.

By definition, the social enterprise does not aim to maximize its profits, and it is practically certain that it will only cover its expenses in the medium term, at least, without making large profits. Therefore, it is not very interested in the direct effects of tax exemptions. As far as its financers are concerned, it may certainly be interesting to be able to deduct a donation from a tax burden, but the entities that are willing to finance social enterprises are themselves generally exempt entities and therefore do not pay tax. It is therefore really this quasi-"State guarantee" effect that is most interesting for social enterprises such as in the model examined herein. This will serve to make it easier for them to find funding, and it is not uncommon for funders to require such an exemption to grant a subsidy.

In summary, given the state of the Swiss tax context, the prohibition to pursue an economic purpose expressly mentioned in the law constitutes a major obstacle to any granting of a tax exemption for the social enterprise model. As currently understood in the practice of tax administrations in Switzerland, the selected model of social enterprise would probably not be granted a tax exemption. However, this situation is regrettable, since it prevents the development of this type of social enterprise, which is of great social importance.

4.2 Are these obstacles only deemed?

However, it could be argued that the prohibition of the economic purpose should not be directly applied to some types of social enterprises. If we examine the scholarly writings and the latest case law of the Federal Court as indicated in its latest ruling on a privately owned school, it is striking that the prohibition of an economic purpose must above all avoid disrupting competition between enterprises that are in comparable situations. This can also be viewed as in line with the issue raised in the OECD report (2020), Taxation and Philanthropy, OECD Tax Policy Studies (ch. 2.3.3 p. 31), according to which commercial operations run by non-profit entities have an unfair advantage when competing with for-profit organizations offering the same or similar goods and services. It is clear that the prohibition of an economic purpose must prevent a company subject to tax from having to compete on the market with a competitor that is exempt from tax. If the prohibition did not exist, the exempted company would have lower production costs (by the amount of the net tax burden) than its competitors. This is also why the prohibition of economic activity in the context of tax exemption is always linked to competition. A profit-making activity can only occur when legal persons are in a situation of "real competition." This is also the main concern of courts that have to decide cases of tax exemption in the field of culture. Exemptions for cultural purposes should not disrupt competition with non-exemptible entities operating in the entertainment field.

However, in our social enterprise hypothesis, there is, strictly speaking, no market. What is at stake in the production of a medical device for developing countries is that the market by definition is not interested in it due to lack of economically interesting outlets. Since potential customers cannot pay a market price, development and production must be carried out by a social enterprise. If there is no market, there can be no disruption of competition. More specifically, a company that produces "ordinary" medical devices is not in competition with our social enterprise because not only does it not sell the same type of products, but above all, it is also not present in the same market. Thus, assuming that there is a market, only social enterprises can, by definition, be in that market. There is therefore ultimately no disruption to free competition or to the market. An enterprise that produces ordinary medical devices is not in a comparable situation with a social enterprise that develops a medical device specific to developing countries.

It follows that the reason for which the legislator established the profit motive as a categorical prohibition of tax exemption does not allow this prohibition to be applied to our social enterprise model. In other words, it seems that the sentence in Art. 56 DFT stating that "economic purposes cannot in principle be regarded as being in the public interest" should not prevent social enterprises considered herein from obtaining a tax exemption. As long as such enterprises do not disrupt competition between market players in similar situations, there is no need to prohibit economic purposes. The current prohibition of economic activity should therefore be substituted with a "level playing field test" in which the tax administration should control that the exemption requesting entity is interfering with legal persons in comparable competitive situations. This point seems to be compatible with the current legal text, since the law makes it clear that the prohibition is only applicable "in principle." In this respect, the legislator did not want to prohibit all economic activity, and the substitution of the prohibition of an economic activity by a "level playing field test" allows this exception to be in line with the current law.

The current practice of tax administration can hence appear to be too restrictive compared to the *ratio legis*. This is also derived from the most recent Supreme Court's case law, which tends to avoid disrupting competition between entities in comparable situations. However, we have sought to demonstrate that certain activities carried out by certain social enterprises do not disrupt this competition and thus should be tax privileged.

5 Conclusion

In conclusion, it must be noted that in the current Swiss tax environment, a social enterprise in the sense defined herein will face several obstacles before obtaining a tax exemption. In particular, these are the prohibition of economic purposes, as currently applied in Switzerland, which, in our view, does not take sufficient account of the hybrid nature of social enterprises. As has been proposed, if one accepts that the legal prohibition of economic purposes for tax-exempted entities ultimately serves to protect competition between similar actors, this obstacle could be removed without the need to change the law. Under this hypothesis, the social enterprise, like the model herein, which does not disrupt competition, that is not in competition with other enterprises not exempted from taxes should not be prohibited from having a "hybrid" economic purpose.

References

Abu-Saifan, Samer, Social Entrepreneurship: Definition and Boundaries, *Technology Innovation and Management Review*, February 2012.

Circular on Tax exemption for legal persons pursuing the aims of public service, public utility, or religious purposes, January 2008, www.steuerkonferenz.ch/downloads/merkblaetter/praxishinweise_steuerbefreiung_2008_f.pdf

Circular on Tax exemption for legal persons pursuing public service or pure public utility purposes, 1994, www.estv.admin.ch/dam/estv/fr/dokumente/bundessteuer/kreisschreiben/2000/W95-012.pdf.download.pdf/w95-012f.pdf

Greter, Alexander and Greter, Marco, in Martin Zweifel and Michael Beusch (eds.), *Kommentar zum Schweizerischen Steuerrecht*, ad art. 56 DBG, 3rd ed., 2017.

Lideikyte Huber, Giedre, Activité à but lucratif d'une entité d'utilité publique exonérée d'impôt, *Expert Focus*, 2019, p. 215.

Locher, Peter, *Kommentar zum DBG – Bundesgesetz über die direkte Bundessteuer, II.* Teil – Art. 49–101 DBG, 2004.

Oberson, Xavier and Hull, Howard, *Switzerland in international tax law*, 4th ed., Amsterdam: IBFD Publications BV, 2011.

Opel, Andrea, Ehrenamtlichkeit als Voraussetzung der Steuerbefreiung – ein alter Zopf? *Revue fiscale*, 2019, p. 84.
Peter, Henry and Merkt, Benoît, Utilité publique et activité économique, *Expert Focus*, 2019, p. 209.
Shapovalov, Valery *et al.*, Practices of Defining the Notion of Social Entrepreneurship, *International Journal of Innovative Technology and Exploring Engineering (IJITEE)*, Vol. 9, No. 1, November 2019.
Urech, Nicolas and Noël, Aubry Girardin (eds.), *Commentaire Romand de la loi fédérale sur l'impôt direct*, 2nd ed., ad art. 56 LIFD Bâle: Helbing Lichtenhahn, 2017.
Vogelsang, Marc, GEMEINNUETZIGE ORGANISATIONEN IM MEHRWERTSTEUERRECHT, ExpertFocus 10/21 p. 501.
Zahra, Shaker A. *et al.*, Globalization of Social Entrepreneurship Opportunities, *Strategic Entrepreneurship Review*, June 2008.

30

IMPACT OF THE OVERLAP OF PUBLIC AND PRIVATE INITIATIVES ON THE PHILANTHROPY TAX REGIME IN FRANCE

Philippe Durand, Dominique Lemaistre and Laurence de Nervaux

Introduction

In most European countries, philanthropy has seen rapid and conspicuous development over the past 20 years. This is notably visible in France, where donations from individuals subject to tax deductions increased by 70% between 2006 and 2016. Moreover, two-thirds of the foundations in France have been created since 2000.[1] This phenomenon, whereby private actors voluntarily collaborate with public authorities to serve the 'common good,'[2] enables a synergy between vastly different cultures and different parts of society.

However, at the same time, some actors serving the public interest can be driven to include a degree of profit-making activities to complement their resources or to achieve their goals, depending on the challenges they face and according to the mechanisms described in this study.

The hybridisation of economic models among an ever-increasing number of actors is not unique to France and is well documented in international academic research.[3] In practical terms, such hybridisation led to a profound upheaval in the major categories of reference in social and economic spheres. Consequently, the redistribution of roles between the public and private sectors blurred the traditional boundaries between commercial activities and activities that fall within the scope of public interest. This unavoidable evolution of economic models corresponds to regulations aiming to define clear boundaries between public and commercial interests.

The difficulties in distinguishing commercial and public-interest activities discussed in this chapter pertain to European competition regulations, which limited state subsidies in accordance with the *de minimis* rule.[4] However, this problem is highly apparent in the French context because, after decades of restricting public-interest financing to the state and public authorities nearly 20 years ago, France decided to encourage private generosity by providing significant tax benefits.[5] The rapid growth of philanthropy, or the transfer of proceeds from economic success to serve the common good, is a notable indicator of the redistribution of roles between the public and private sectors, increasing the number of interactions between actors with diverse interests and the complexity of the resulting models.

 DOI: 10.4324/9781003139201-35

Using the French context, this chapter aims to describe this gradual increase in porosity between economic activities and public interest by reviewing the background of such developments and the problems they pose. It also outlines proposals for adapting the definition of public interest to specific economic activities to restore consistency between the law and the official guidelines by administrative authorities and avoid depriving organisations and actors of scarce funding while addressing some of the most acute problems facing today's society.

I Transformation of relationships between non-profit actors, the commercial world and the public sector

The deep transformation of the relationships between various actors supporting public interest and their economic models is rooted in the socio-historical context of the last quarter of the 20th century. The Glorious Thirties, the 1970s and the 1980s failed to remove poverty and exclusion mainly because of two factors of economic relegation. The first is the growing urbanisation and the desertion of some rural areas which created geographical pockets of poverty. The second is the consequence of unemployment induced by successive economic downturns after the oil crises became both a cause of economic hardship and social relegation.[6] Consequently, job creation for long-term unemployed became a matter of public interest, with a special focus on the causes of poverty and relegation; that is, the vulnerabilities of territories and individuals.[7] While this two-fold effect is prevalent even after 40 years, the challenge today is to establish clearly defined criteria to identify these vulnerabilities.

This socio-historical context, which is shifting the dividing line between the economic and social spheres, is simultaneously experiencing a radical reorganisation of public-interest financing. An increasing complexity is visible in two areas: a change in the ecosystem, with the multiplication and diversification of donors, and a change in their relationships with public funders, with the nature of the funding transforming from a subsidy into a form of service rendered for value.

A Developments in the public sector

1 Growing scarcity of public resources and the recourse to private funding

In the past 20 years, there has been an inexorable rise in the cost of some of the state's sovereign missions (e.g., education and healthcare, with the increased duration of compulsory schooling,[8] the ageing of the population[9] and the growing technology of healthcare). In this context, philanthropy has become a popular method of financing or supplementing the financing of certain initiatives.

Thus, in search of additional revenues, the French legislature frequently extended the list of bodies or the scope of actions that may benefit from philanthropic contributions to sectors which have been almost entirely financed by public money until now.[10] This is notably the case for higher education, research, culture and heritage protection. Apart from direct legislative intervention, public bodies also created 'friends' associations'[11] to raise funds while providing donors with tax benefits for voluntary contributions. The scarcity of resources thus encourages public bodies to compete with associations and foundations in the philanthropic fundraising 'market'.

2 *Transformation of subsidies into a service subject to public procurement rules*

Over the past 30 years, public actors have had to review the scope and methods of their actions under the combined effect of shrinking public resources and a decrease in public subsidies.

Initially, associations receiving regular subsidies were generally considered *de facto* representatives of the state or some other public entities responsible for public missions. However, this situation met increasing criticism because it was viewed as a kind of 'debudgeting'. This connection between subsidised associations and the state is challenged for two main reasons.

- First, the purpose or scope of subsidies and the methods of assessing the achievements of such subsidies lack sufficient regulation.
- Second, the European Union (EU) rules regarding fair competition oblige public entities to select their suppliers and providers through a tender process. But if one of the bidders receives subsidies, this would be considered an infringement to fair competition rules. Therefore, entities receiving public subsidies should frequently be excluded from public tenders.

Thus, supervisory bodies also contributed to the rise in the suspicion of public subsidies granted to public-interest actors.

To comply with the EU's principles of fair competition, public authorities gradually dressed subsidies as a price paid in exchange for services within the framework of public tenders. However, private companies can also bid on these tenders. This approach is likely to attract both associations and new service providers from the commercial world. National surveys on associations indicate a major change in their resource structure between 2005 and 2011: a decrease in public funding from 34% to 25%, combined with an increase in public procurement from 17% to 24%.[12]

Therefore, public authorities treat associations as service providers, which has serious consequences for their economic and fiscal models. What was previously a matter of public interest is shifting towards a traditional commercial relationship, which now falls within the ambit of the legal and fiscal rules specific to such a relationship.

B Developments in the commercial sector

Parallel to the changes concerning public actors, the relationship between the commercial sector and public interest is also evolving.

1 *Progressive institutionalisation of corporate philanthropy*

In France, the first foundation, Fondation de France, was created in 1990[13] based on the American model. Twenty years after its emergence, a corporate foundation, the new 'American uncle' of the French non-corporate service sector, led to private donors supplementing and taking over state action. Private actors in the field welcomed this development, as they constitute an additional source of revenue. However, these actors are in an awkward position between profit and not profit. This is a characteristic of what we refer to as the hybridisation of their model.

Regarding the dividing line between commercial activities and activities for the 'common good', despite undertaking a public-interest mission lying beyond the scope of the company's corporate purpose, in the early 1990s, corporate giving was deductible from the company's revenue, similar to its expenses. This provision, which is still applicable in most developed countries,[14] helps to blend philanthropy into the company's business model. In France, this regime changed in 2003,[15] following which philanthropic activities were incentivised through tax deductions rather than being deducted from the companies' taxable income. This development emphasises the benefits of public subsidies. It had consequences when the 'doctrine of causes', a historical framework defining the scope of tax shelters according to the charity's objectives and formed the cornerstone of philanthropy in France, was shaken up by European competition law, as discussed in the next section.

2 Corporate social responsibility and the introduction of an endogenous corporate mission of public interest

Article 116 of the Law of 15 May 2001 on 'the new economic regulations'[16] proposed that companies listed on the stock exchange must include information regarding their corporate social responsibility (CSR) activities in their annual reports.

Thus, the associations gained new funding, accompanied by new constraints. Already providing services to the state, they now became service providers for CSR activities with similar consequences for the complexity of their economic and fiscal models (e.g., the obligation to implement specific analytical accounting, known as 'sectorisation', or even to create subsidiaries, among others).

The case of Simplon, examined further in the following, provides a telling example of the impact of the rise in CSR on the relationship between companies and public-interest operators. This social business offers free training in digital professions to low-income and marginalised people. Thus, companies trying to improve the diversity of their human resources, an important component of CSR reporting, no longer remain donors but have also become the clients of Simplon by sponsoring the remuneration of the trainers for those lacking solvency.

With the increasing demand for private intervention in social issues, CSR and sustainable development have become key arguments for companies to resist the scrutiny and short-term views of some of their shareholders; therefore, to improve their position in this challenge, some American companies found a solution that includes such social issues in their corporate purpose, with the B-corp (benefit corporation) status. Hiller's study describes the context of the development of this new model in the United States,[17] while Reiser analysed its advantages and limitations.[18] In France, this movement culminated in the *Plan d'action pour la croissance et la transformation des entreprises* [Action Plan for Corporate Growth and Transformation] Law enacted on 21 May 2019, which created mission-based companies. However, unlike in the United States,[19] this new model does not have a legal status in France.

II 'Public interest market': A grey area

A Historical subjectivity in the concept of public interest

The concept of public interest, which is sometimes portrayed as universal and unchallengeable, is, conversely, truly subjective. This observation was not new. For instance, sociologist Chloé Gaboriaux analyses the recognition of the public utility of associations and foundations by the *Conseil d'Etat* (French Supreme Administrative Court) during the Third Republic (1870–1914). When the *Conseil d'Etat* was just renewed by the republicans and thus sought to establish its legitimacy and the impartiality of its opinions, Gaboriaux nevertheless demonstrates the impact of the subjectivity of the members of the highest administrative court, their value systems and their personal relations.[20]

Beyond personal positions and ideological convictions, the borders of public interest saw historical and geographical fluctuations, depending on the context. Notwithstanding some points of stability, such as solidarity and access to education and healthcare, some causes appear, while others disappear. However, in the long term, the scope of public interest increased significantly. For example, in France, access to culture, once accepted as a privilege of the powerful, was included as a public interest cause since the end of the 19th century,[21] whereas the environment was included within its scope only in the past few decades.[22]

Another example of this volatility of public utility in France can be found in the early 20th century idea of 'municipal socialism'. This historical concept was analysed by the legal expert Katy Sibiril in an article on the notion of interest in French administrative law.[23] In this case, some local elected officials utilised public utility to justify their intervention to address the inadequacy of the private sector in meeting the requirements of trade, management of water or electricity and distribution services or public transport in rural areas. This interventionist stance was justified only because the local authorities deemed it necessary to satisfy universal needs. From this perspective, market competition, which has considerable significance today in the assessment of public interest, was not considered a relevant criterion.

While the present economic logic is returning to the concerns of public interest, unlike municipal socialism, it operates less as an aim but rather as a means of integrating citizens through work. Thus, the desire to promote integration by enabling people to find employment is clearly in the public interest and therefore within the scope of philanthropy.

B New distinction in economic markets between the public and private sectors

New private markets are now developing in sectors that were financed mainly by public authorities 50 years ago. An ageing and dependent population is a key example of this development. The 'silver economy' is now a regular economic market which is estimated at over 130 billion euros[24] and is regulated in France by a supply chain contract since 2013.

These changes led to a fundamental evolution in the concept of public interest. Today, the distinction is no longer determined by the sector of intervention and the purpose of activity by applying the 'doctrine of causes' but by other criteria such as the fragility or vulnerability of populations and territories. This new mechanism is probably more relevant, as it allows for a more specific consideration of the needs of the target population rather than predetermining eligible areas. However, defining its boundaries remains challenging.

C The social and welfare sectors as alternatives to the liberal capitalist model

In 2014, the French legislature recognised a specific field of the economy known as the *économie sociale et solidaire* [social and welfare economy (ESS)], composed of four types of organisations: mutual companies, cooperatives, associations and foundations[25].

The 2014 law also introduced *Entreprise Solidaire d'Utilité Sociale* [Welfare Company of Social Utility (ESUS)] accreditation for ESS companies serving the public interest or public utility that have democratic governance and reinvest most of their profits in the company. This accreditation entitles the holder to specific resources, including welfare-based employee savings schemes and tax reductions.

The ESUS accreditation aimed to urge private investors to encourage greater participation in corporate projects with social utility through tax incentives. Their investments have a purpose other than profit, enabling the creation of an environment for developing welfare-based enterprises. However, this accreditation led to a new form of hybridisation by bringing together associations, mutual companies, cooperatives and even traditional companies seeking to distinguish themselves from other commercial enterprises. Despite the intent to create a credible alternative to the global capitalist enterprise, this new mechanism further increased the complexity in defining a scope that is already fragmented and composite, as organisations eligible for accreditation (associations, mutual companies, cooperatives and foundations) have very different missions and operations.

The diagram (e.g., Stages 1, 2 and 3) shows three successive stages of the growing complexity of the relations and flows (donations or investments) between the actors in the French context: those traditionally working under general interest vs. private interests. In the middle, the grey area represents the 'public interest market', where private actors integrate some of their economic activities to serve the public interest.

Stage 1: Traditional actors on the spectrum from public to private interests

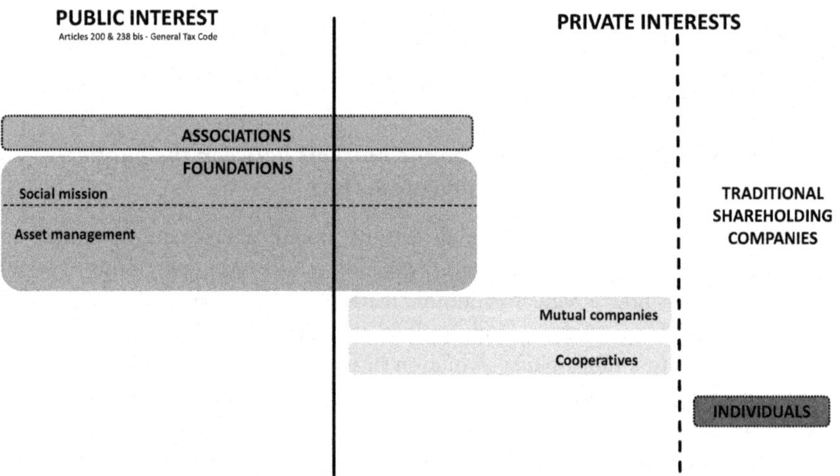

Figure 30.1 Stage 1: Traditional actors on the spectrum from public to private interests

Stage 2: Three-stage legislative evolution of the interactions between economic actors and the public-interest sphere

- *1990 law: creation of the corporate foundation marking the emergence and recognition of the private donor to supplement and take over state action*
- *2001 law: introduction of CSR, an endogenous corporate mission for public interest*
- *2014 Law on Social Economy: The legislature-recognised economic field, ESS, composed of four types of organisations: mutual companies, cooperatives, associations and foundations.*

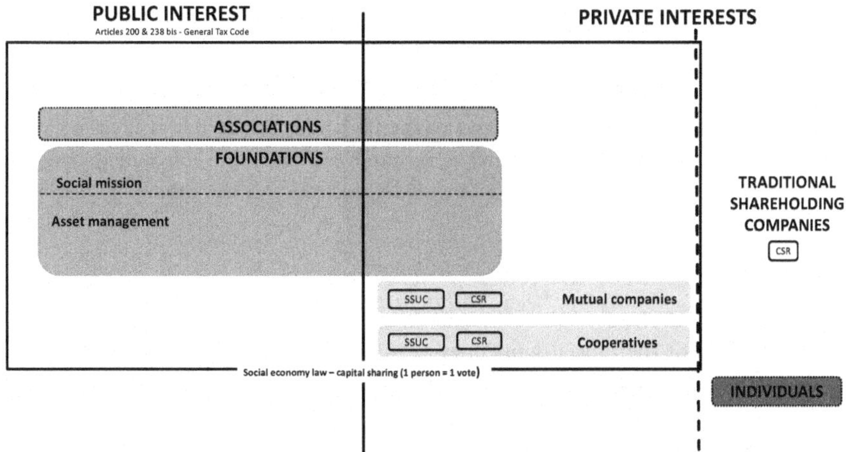

Figure 30.2 Stage 2: Three-stage legislative evolution of the interactions between economic actors and the public-interest sphere

Stage 3: New models and complex flows defining the grey area of the 'public interest market'

- *Private resources funding public interest*
- *New economic models (hybrid social enterprises, benefit corporations)*
- *Impact investment targeting hybrid models.*

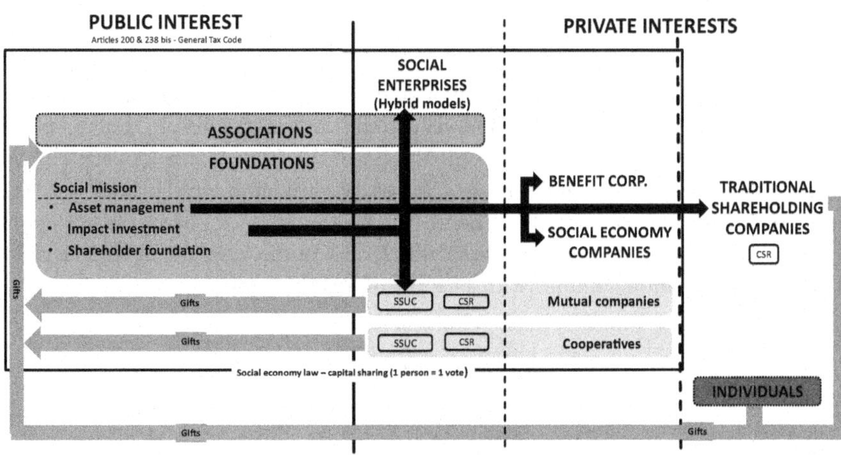

Figure 30.3 Stage 3: New models and complex flows defining the grey area of the 'public interest market'

The proposals formulated in this chapter focus on shifting the limit of public interest to the dotted line in the middle to include hybrid social enterprises, according to the conditions described in the subsequent sections.

III History of the tax regulatory framework in France

A Set of rules and three definitions

This section interprets the eligibility criteria of the philanthropic shelter tax regime according to its regulatory context. For this, we delineate three relevant concepts and their associated rights arising from the *Conseil d'Etat* case law, tax legislation and the official guidelines of the tax authorities.

1 Public utility

This concept is part of the official guidelines of the administrative authorities, recognised by the case law of the *Conseil d'Etat*, upon the proposal of the Ministry of the Interior.[26] Public utility depends theoretically and explicitly upon the concept of public interest, as mentioned in Articles 200 and 238 of the French General Tax Code. Nevertheless, in practice, the *reconnue d'utilité publique* [recognition as being of public utility (RUP)], a body regulating public utilities, rarely casts doubt on whether an activity constitutes public interest.

2 Public interest

This second concept also follows the official guidelines of the administrative authorities,[27] in this case, tax authorities, which are under the Ministry of Finance.

- Donations to public interest, which form the basis of the philanthropy tax regime, are regulated by Article 200 of the General Tax Code. It entitles donors to a 66% reduction in income tax equal to the gift amount, subject to a ceiling of 20% of the taxable income. The reduction is applicable to donations and payments, including the express abandonment of income or proceeds made by taxpayers domiciled in France to organisations listed under Article 4 B.
- Article 238 *bis* of the General Tax Code adapts Article 200 to corporate giving by defining an almost identical scope. The reduction of up to 60% of the donation amount is applicable to income or corporation tax (and 40% reductions for donations over 2 million euros).
- In terms of the wealth tax, Article 885–0 V *bis* A of the General Tax Code relating to the *Impôt de Solidarité sur la Fortune* [Solidarity Tax on Wealth] reproduced in Article 978 for the *Impôt sur la Fortune Immobilière* (Real Estate Wealth Tax) defines a narrower scope which is different from Article 200 of the General Tax Code. In this case, the applicable reduction is 75% of the donation amount, with a ceiling of 50,000 euros.

3 Social utility

Law No. 2014–856, regarding the social and welfare economy, provides a precise definition of social utility. Under this law, enterprises (i.e., associations, foundations, cooperatives and mutual companies) whose objectives satisfy at least one of the following three conditions are recognised as being of 'social utility'.

- Their aim is to support economically and socially vulnerable people or those with adverse personal circumstances or who need social or socio-medical support due to their health condition. Such persons may be employees, users, clients, members or beneficiaries of this enterprise.

- Their aim is to help prevent exclusion and inequality in healthcare, socio-economic and cultural matters to provide education to citizens, particularly through community centres, to protect and support social and territorial cohesion.
- They contribute towards sustainable development in its economic, social, environmental and participatory dimensions to support energy transition or international solidarity, provided that their activities are related to one of the aims mentioned in 1) and 2).

After public interest, social utility has its own doctrine of causes with no reference to public interest, the tax treatment or the fiscal framework of philanthropy.

The two fiscal frameworks do not fall within the ambit of the same set of rules. Nevertheless, while they overlap, they do not duplicate each other and have a fundamentally distinct set of provisions. The concept of social utility is split between the *Conseil d'Etat's* conception, which *de facto* presumes public interest, and the definition of the ESUS accreditation regulated by the ESS law, which differentiates itself from the official guidelines of the tax authorities. In practice, this split is particularly confusing for public-interest funders who must determine whether the organisation seeking involvement is eligible for philanthropic tax benefits. Nevertheless, in France, the distinction between for-profit and non-profit remains fundamentally determined by its tax law.

B Official guidelines of the administrative authorities and their limits

1 Introduction of the '4Ps' rule

In the mid-1990s, the administrative authorities' guidelines[28] originally intended to settle a tax investigation problem regarding the criteria for determining cases when associations and assimilated organisations should be subject to commercial taxes, namely corporation tax, value-added taxes (VAT) and territorial economic contributions. However, the concept of public interest was subsequently extended to regulate the scope of the philanthropy tax regime.

The boundary between taxed and non-taxable activities was previously based on the 'doctrine of causes' and depended upon the aim of the organisation's activities: pursuing a philanthropic goal and conducting a for-profit economic activity. From a tax perspective, this teleological approach was a source of great insecurity as inspectors were obligated to question the tax status of non-profit organisations upon finding that their management used similar methods or activities that placed the organisation in competition with private enterprises. Thus, the doctrine of causes was unsuitable for determining the scope of commercial taxes, despite its coherence with the statutory definition of the scope of donations eligible for the philanthropic tax benefits provided by Articles 200 and 238 *bis* of the General Tax Code. The objective or cause of the organisation prevails while establishing the scope of non-profitability, determining fiscal liability and delineating the right to benefit from the philanthropy tax regime. The presumption of eligibility for the philanthropy tax regime is, therefore, almost systematic when the funds received by the organisations fall within the ambit of this doctrine.

However, Articles 200 and 238 of the General Tax Code do not define the concept of public interest. They refer to the official guidelines of the tax authorities, which have three conditions to be satisfied beyond the cause doctrine:

- disinterested management,
- widespread beneficiaries that are not limited to a small circle of people, and
- non-profitability.

From the outset, the semantic conflation of profitability with economic activity blurs the reasoning of eligibility for philanthropic tax benefits.

When the guidelines were introduced, the public-interest sector had a limited scope of activities requiring donations. Therefore, non-profitability was analysed solely in terms of the volume of economic activity. As far as their economic activities were not preponderant, organisations would not be liable for commercial taxes and would remain eligible for philanthropic benefits.

However, by the late 1990s, the EU imposed new rules in line with the policies of competition law.[29] The non-profit sector was affected by the state subsidies received, especially those received indirectly through philanthropic tax incentives. France was particularly affected because, since 1995, such incentives took the form of a tax reduction rather than a simple deduction from the taxable base. A law enacted in 2003[30] significantly increased tax reductions. However, this measure also led to the suspicion of French non-profit organisations benefiting from the philanthropic regime.

Therefore, the analysis of non-profitability is not limited to the preponderance of economic activity. The French tax administration devised a '4Ps' grid, which is better suited to verify whether an association with commercial activities competes unfairly with other businesses.[31] This inquiry focuses on the following aspects:

- **Product**: Does the 'product' offered cater to a need that is either not catered to or inadequately catered to by the market? In other words, the product offered should not be available in any market where it can be procured under similar terms, which is tantamount to ensuring that there is no risk of competition with businesses in the commercial sector.
- **Public**: Do the target beneficiaries ('public') suffer from any difficulties (unemployment, disability, age etc.) that make them worthy of philanthropic interest and justify the grant of special benefits?

The beneficiaries in this case refer to direct 'clients' or recipients of the activity and not those for whom the activity could be a source of employment.

- **Prices**: If the product is not gratuitous, are the prices significantly below the market prices (beyond the effect of tax exemptions), such that they facilitate access to similar services for people in difficulty?
- **Publicity**: Advertising ('publicity') or, more broadly, marketing and sales methods that lead to the presumption of competition, may only be used to appeal to the public's generosity while considering the type of target beneficiaries the organisation serves. The purchase of advertising inserts, sale of a catalogue on newsstands or participation in trade shows may call into question the non-commercial nature of the organisation's approach. However, in the age of digital communication and social media, this criterion is losing relevance.

The non-profit nature of the organisation should be assessed by all four criteria and not just based on one criterion. Furthermore, the presence of competition must be assessed '*in concreto*', implying that a product or service would not be considered competitive if it has no competitors within a radius of several dozen kilometres. However, this concern has been undermined by the fact that, in the case of VAT, the EU Court of Justice subsequently retained the importance of competitive potential rather than the presence of actual competition.[32]

As European law applies to circumstances of hybridisation of for-profit and non-profit markets, reasoning based on unfair competition prevails over the doctrine of causes.

This new dominant paradigm to assess the scope of public interest has several limitations, as seen in the case of Montessori schools. Although the law states that private education is a matter of public interest, in 2013 and 2014, the local authorities of the tax administration considered one Montessori school in the form of an association ineligible for philanthropy. This was because this school had three other Montessori schools operating as limited liability companies (and therefore subject to commercial taxes) within a radius of less than 30 km. Thus, these schools fell within the same 'geographical area of attractiveness'[33] defined under the tax code.

The liberal approach characterising Europe favours private companies' interventions in public-interest issues. Despite public service constraints, European tax laws prefer to apply the normal rules of competition, even if it means allowing private companies to assume any public service obligations while scrupulously preventing it from becoming a means of distorting market competition. This approach exemplifies the regulation on the 'Services of General Economic Interest (SGEI)'.

2 Public interest and the exclusion of profit-making activities: A nonlinear movement

The official guidelines issued by the tax authorities favoured the 4Ps rule in certain cases. For instance, these guidelines resolutely protect the disability sector against scrutiny over unfair competition. The administrative authorities accept that *Etablissements et services d'aide par le travail* [establishments and assistance services through employment] would not fall within the scope of competition[34] distortion because the additional costs incurred by disabled workers significantly exceed the advantages of the tax benefits. Moreover, disabled workers are considered beneficiaries or the 'public' of the 4Ps and not clients to whom the products or services are sold.

In other cases, the doctrine of causes prevailed. France was an early campaigner in Europe to exclude the cultural sector from a competitive analysis. Recently, this exception includes the audio-visual and press sectors.

Conversely, some early examples of the rejection of the doctrine of causes due to evidence of competition include a decision by the tax authorities based on an old case of the *Conseil d'Etat* relating to the Association de médecine du travail du département de la Mayenne.[35] In this case, it was held that any activity aimed at providing services to businesses is necessarily 'profit-making'. Accordingly, administrative instructions state that for an activity to remain of public interest, its main purpose must not consist of applying resources to enable enterprises to conduct or delegate tasks to third parties that are either compulsory or useful to their main activity. In other words, to determine its tax regime, an organisation conducting non-profit operations may assume a non-profit role solely to satisfy tax eligibility based on the identity of the beneficiaries and the services it provides.

3 Weaknesses of the hybrid model

- Supremacy of guidelines over tax law.
- After the introduction of the '4Ps' analysis grid, rather than revising the law or putting the doctrine of causes into perspective, France chose to allow two different types of reasoning to coexist. This led to the paradoxical application of the current tax law guidelines in France.
- Distorted link between commercial taxes and ineligibility for philanthropic tax benefits.
- Ideally, the shift from a purpose-based definition of non-profitability to that based on an absence of competition with businesses should have ended the connection between the

payment of commercial taxes by non-profit organisations and their ineligibility for philanthropic tax benefits. However, the tax authorities did not foresee the consequences of this evolution and continued to restrict the eligibility of non-profit organisations engaged in profit-making activities to enjoy philanthropic tax benefits. In some respects, this amounts to considering that the mere fact of conducting an activity for payment implies that it is no longer of public interest.

- Stopgap proposal of the sectorisation of profit-making activities with 'preponderance' of the non-profit-making activity.

The sectorisation of profit-making activities could enable organisations to retain philanthropic tax benefits without creating a separate legal person, provided that the donation amount is not utilised for profit-making activity and does not act as a subsidy that could distort competition. However, sectorisation is only suitable for organisations that can clearly distinguish and isolate an economic activity that is not preponderant from other activities.

Several conditions must be satisfied to be allowed to sectorise an economic activity:

- **Separation of commercial activities from non-profit-making activitie**s: An organisation's activities must correspond to services of a different nature, which does not exclude an element of complementarity as far as the two activities are effectively separated.
- **Principle behind sectorisation**: According to the 16 February 1999[36] instruction, sectorisation must be based on a 'principle of a physical separation or individualisation of the relevant activities in relation to the association's main activity, notably with respect to the place of production, human and material resources and investments'. However, the tax instruction of 18 December 2006[37] specifically curtailed this requirement and allowed associations to apply the same resource simultaneously if they could justify it based on the association's purpose (e.g., achieving social diversity). In such cases, the separation of activities may be limited to the accounting aspect by separating the expenses and incomes from various activities or for various kinds of beneficiaries.
- **Preponderance of non-profit-making activities**: An association must not be guided by commercial activities, while its non-profit-making activities must remain materially preponderant. This distinction must be assessed to reflect the true weight of the association's non-profit activity, such as by measuring the ratio of commercial income to an association's overall financial resources (operating income, subsidies, subscriptions, donations, etc.), without a set percentage of margin of appreciation set by tax authorities. However, the example published in the 1998 tax instruction indicated a ratio of 75% of resources from the non-profit sector to 25% of commercial income. However, additional criteria may be considered, such as the magnitude of voluntary work and the number of staff and resources devoted to profit and non-profit-making activities, respectively. This preponderance was assessed based on a multi-annual average.
- **Isolating income and expenditure of exempt activities vs. taxable profit-making activities**: Cost accounting should enable the isolation of income and expenditure relating to the sectors of exempt activities and taxable profit-making activities, where each sector must bear its incumbent costs. This requires the allocation of operating resources to either the profit or non-profit sector. In the case of assets for common use, a distribution mechanism must be devised.

The application of sectorisation is particularly complicated for small organisations that are often underequipped to deal with legal issues. Therefore, it does not resolve the requirements of organisations whose purpose depends on a predominant economic activity or whose economic activity would be considered extremely similar to the other activities.

The Simplon case: an emblematic hybrid

The Simplon project, a socially conscious welfare enterprise, was co-founded by Frédéric Bardeau in 2013. It leverages digital technology to promote the inclusion of disadvantaged or vulnerable groups (migrants, older adults, people with disabilities) while supporting the digital transformation of organisations. Simplon.co is a network of socially aware and inclusive factories that offer its clients free training in digital technical professions, both in France and abroad.

Through its 109 factories worldwide, Simplon has already trained more than 11,476 people, 78% of whom are job seekers, with a positive outcome rate of 67%[38] after training.

The project is widely recognised for providing free training to insolvent persons on a large scale. The majority of the project's budget now comes from public funds. However, to remain economically feasible, the Simplon project was forced to create three organisations in the course of its development:

- An ESUS-approved **simplified limited liability** company, a commercial body positioned in a market consisting of companies seeking to improve their recruitment diversity in the age of CSR and that of the state, local authorities (regions) and the Employment Agency. This entity brings together ESS investors and receives public subsidies and issues invoices in its capacity as a training organisation for third-party funders (trainees are not liable for payment).
- **An endowment fund**, with the capacity to collect donations and issue receipts for receiving tax deductions. The endowment fund supports activities that are complementary to training such as social support, French lessons for refugees, mobility assistance, housing assistance and drop-out prevention scholarships.
- **An association** that receives grants from donors that cannot be channelled through the ESUS-approved SAS or the endowment fund and that which assist a part of the support activities, excluding training and occupational integration.

According to Frédéric Bardeau, 'this forced hybridisation of our model is the source of many complications in the management of the project, particularly in terms of governance and human resources'. In a 2019 report by the Court of Auditors that addressed this emblematic case,[39] the state expressed its regret regarding the Simplon Foundation directly subsidising free and inclusive activities conducted by the ESUS-approved SAS as an umbrella foundation but without proposing a solution nor questioning the impact of Simplon's actions.

IV Proposed changes and methods

The proposals in this chapter have a three-fold objective: (i) to modernise the concept of public interest to adapt it to new circumstances (as in other periods of its history), (ii) to make administrative authorities' official guidelines comply with the law and (iii) to urgently simplify the work of public-interest operators and protect their access to essential resources to fulfil their missions.

A Constraints

The regulation and application of public interest face two types of constraints.

The first constraint is the predominance of the objective of public interest in conducting an activity. This primarily involves ensuring that the pursuit of gain ('profit') does not determine the activities of the relevant organisation. Tax authorities already mostly consider this constraint by requiring disinterested management, executive remuneration and the democratic functioning of the organisation. While some adaptations might seem appropriate, the present rules for non-corporate bodies do not require any significant modifications.

The second constraint is the rules pertaining to competition and state subsidies. Measures to prevent unfair competition due to philanthropic tax benefits are not unique to Europe. From a global perspective, it is also one of the recommendations of the 2020 OECD report on taxation on philanthropy (recommendation 6.6.2).[40] As discussed earlier, the guidelines of the French Tax administration give paramount importance to the numerous and stringent constraints of European law.

However, the general opinion supports upgrading the doctrine of causes upheld by Articles 200 and 238 *bis* of the General Tax Code, accounting for the constantly evolving list of subjects eligible for philanthropy, which corresponds not only to the structural changes in society but also to economic cycles. Consequently, the assistance provided to a small business after a natural disaster or in a severely underdeveloped region would not be analysed in the same way as under 'normal' circumstances in a developed country.

- Analysis of competition: A complex undertaking

The analysis of competition is a complex process. Competition may arise directly because of the actions of the organisation seeking benefits from the philanthropy tax regime if its services overlap with those provided by commercial enterprises. However, indirect competition occurs when the benefits enjoyed by the organisation are transferred, notably in the form of lower prices, to businesses to conduct activities to meet their aims.

Tax authorities' comments redefining the condition of non-profit organisations regarding 'commercial taxes' already attempted to define competition. They emphasised that competition can be effective in certain geographical areas and not in others and is limited to certain categories of products or services while being assessed based on their target clients.

However, these efforts were partly undermined by the European courts' adoption of a stricter approach, particularly regarding VAT. In 2017, the Court of Justice focused on the potential rather than the effective nature of competition regarding this tax.[41] This allowed non-profit organisations to compete with each other or with companies, despite operating in different geographical areas. Similarly, it obliged the tax authorities to adopt a more restrictive approach to VAT exemption on services provided by an entity, especially created by non-profit organisations, for their own needs (Article 261 B of the General Tax Code). This is a real concern for these associations.

The lesson to be drawn from these regulations is that rather than using the theoretical analysis of competition to define the tax treatment of transactions, it would be better to try to use the exceptions or derogations provided in the sixth VAT Directive, particularly Article 13. By relying too much on the commentaries of the FTA, taxpayers, including non-profit organisations, cannot be sure that such commentaries could not be challenged by the EU Commission or by the ECJ.

- *De minimis* subsidies[42]

The European regulation regarding subsidies compatible with the internal market provides some criteria for restricting and relaxing subsidies. The latter is applicable for *de minimis* subsidies that may be granted to small enterprises or for amounts that are considered too insignificant to distort competition.

These regulations enabled the introduction of an amendment on support offered to small businesses (cf. Article 238 *bis* (4) of the General Tax Code regarding the grant of financial subsidies to or equity investments in SMEs). This provision was adapted to the European regulation on state subsidies compatible with the internal market, which required prior approval from the European Commission.

Article 17 of Commission Regulation (EU) No. 65/2014 of 17 June 2014, mentioned in Article 238 *bis* (4) of the General Tax Code, concerns organisations accredited for paying certain financial subsidies or providing non-financial support services, such as advice to SMEs. This reference provides a framework for utilising financial subsidies by targeting new investments or acquiring assets from organisations. Financial subsidies must not be remunerated, whereas the assessment of their value should treat support services as donations in kind.

The conditions for accreditation notably require the relevant organisations to be managed in a disinterested manner, the subsidies to satisfy the criteria for *de minimis* aid and the amount paid each year to an enterprise to not exceed 20% of the organisation's resources. This example illustrates the complexity of the system and the hierarchy of EU rules over national regulations.

Moreover, it seems clear that the benefits of the provisions favouring philanthropy and the nature of organisations' non-profit activities are obsolete. Therefore, it warrants a revision of this connection along with the overly global and systematic approach of the tax authorities towards organisations that complement the activities of profit-making enterprises, particularly *associations intermédiaires* [intermediary associations], *entreprises d'insertion* [job seekers' support organisations or the ESUS].

- Organisations' use of legal forms other than associations

  The provisions of Articles 200 and 238 *bis* of the General Tax Code could be applied to companies, even in the cultural or research sectors. Organisations operating in various sectors, including those supporting integration through employment, housing and dependent support, constitute different forms, such as cooperative companies or even traditional corporations. However, legal statutes should not justify, by themselves, exclusion from the scope of the philanthropy tax regime.

Accordingly, a parallel could be drawn with Article 107 of the Treaty of Lisbon, which determines the areas of subsidies considered compatible with the internal market, as listed in the following.

- Promoting economic development of regions with an abnormally low standard of living or serious under-employment.
- Facilitating the development of certain economic activities or regions without altering trade conditions to be contrary to public interest.

However, the preference for a corporate form rather than an association should not be used to circumvent non-profit constraints, such as in terms of remuneration. If allowed to conduct an activity in public interest, companies must pay special attention to their governance and resource use, particularly regarding the devolution of assets in the event of cessation of activity.

The problem of executive remuneration or the risk of a diversion of philanthropic funding due to a privileged relationship between organisations and the beneficiaries of their actions must be scrutinised. However, this should apply to all organisations, regardless of their legal form.

B Proposals

The following proposals aim to arrive at a better definition of the scope of public interest in the context of Articles 200 and 238 *bis* of the French General Tax Code and the official guidelines of the administrative authorities. However, these proposals do not seek to extend the scope of the benefits provided by other legislation, nor do they deviate from the principles laid down by European law.

From this standpoint, we outline the following proposals for redefining the scope of public interest:

1 Three cumulative conditions to be presumed by public interest actions

We propose a three-stage approach to overcome the difficulties of assessing public interest. Moreover, in addition to the organisations mentioned previously, organisations that satisfy the following cumulative conditions should be eligible for the philanthropic regime:

- Disinterested governance

The first eligibility condition is to ensure that the organisation's governance is disinterested.

As discussed, Articles 200 and 238 of the General Tax Code already apply to certain companies. However, an increasing number of actors in public interest tend to opt for a commercial status to benefit from institutional investments, which, in the current context, deprives them of the potential for philanthropy that could aid their missions.

Following the progress made by associations and foundations, other social and welfare organisations (SSEs) should also diversify their resources as far as possible to guarantee disinterested governance.

- Purpose of the project

Once the first condition is satisfied, the next step is to analyse the purpose of the project. If the conditions relating to the purpose of the project are not satisfied, then the project will not be eligible.

We propose that the terms 'family', 'social' and 'humanitarian' in Articles 200 and 238 *bis* of the General Tax Code be interpreted based on the relevant tax instruction. To clarify the scope of these terms, such instruction could draw inspiration from the terms used to define the scope of ESUS accreditation (vulnerable people, prevention of exclusion, maintaining and strengthening territorial cohesion, the preservation and development of social cohesion, etc.). Alternatively, they could also refer to the definitions proposed by organisations representing the philanthropy sector as part of the working group set up in 2013 on the territoriality of donations led by Gilles Bachelier.[43] These proposals are inspired by the definitions of social and medico-social action provided in Articles L116–1 and L312–1 of the Code of Social Welfare and Families.[44]

Additionally, the conditions listed in III B 1 should apply not only to project operators but also to those who support them by providing advice and/or funding, provided they operate under public interest and from the non-profit sphere.

Furthermore, advocacy, when distinguished from the promotion of particular interests, should be considered a means of conducting actions related to a public interest cause and should therefore benefit from the rights attached thereto, provided that the cause served is eligible for philanthropic benefits. Some prominent and effective examples of public interest actions include Greenpeace's work to protect the environment or the fight against AIDS.

- Non-competitive nature of the project

The third issue is determining whether the nature of the project is non-competitive. This requires considering the three criteria (product, public and price) currently used by the tax authorities. The activity must offer a product or service that meets specific social needs.

- For products or services that are currently unavailable in the territory under consideration, a time-based criterion should be introduced to support activities in their starting phase. For instance, some activities that are useful in terms of public interest may be unprofitable before finding a suitable economic model.
- If the first condition is not satisfied, then the product or service must be offered at a price that is accessible to people in vulnerable circumstances.
- If the first two conditions are not satisfied, then the product or service should be provided to a group that does not currently have access to it (e.g., job seekers' support organisations helping people obtain employment).

2 Invert and clarify the conditions for implementing sectorisation

Rather than limiting economic activities, philanthropic resources should be sectorised to indicate the charges that they may legitimately cover. This mechanism would help to justify the additional costs incurred by a public-interest organisation when acting for people in difficulty or in deprived areas, thereby promoting transparency while avoiding any suggestion of unfair competition.

Nevertheless, the limitations of sectorisation listed earlier remain relevant and require further review. The conditions under which philanthropic funds can be traced should be specified. For example, regarding job integration initiatives, there is continuity between activities that are part of a competitive sector and those that are not. The same beneficiary may require both professional and social support, one of which may not fall under philanthropy. Thus, the funds intended for each of these activities may, in part, be common, yet administrative authorities are reluctant to address such situations. Therefore, a regulatory framework for the sectionalisation of activities should also consider such situations.

3 Amending the statutory provisions of the general tax code relating to philanthropy

As provisions on philanthropy are not limited to the official guidelines of the administrative authorities, the statutory provisions of the General Tax Code relating to philanthropy may require an amendment.

Given the risk of interference with EU law, some aspects of the contemplated amendments must be subject to prior notification to the European Commission. This precaution should be taken to forcing organisations that may have already received donations to reimburse the funds received in the event of a dispute. Dealing with such risk is all the more important to avoid donors' tax benefits from being challenged.

Frequently updating these regulations would be cumbersome because of the nature of the notification procedure. Therefore, the content and scope of the regulatory mechanism should be clarified before they are notified to the European Commission. This would require a detailed consultation and documentation outside legislative text, which could also serve as a basis for the administrative authority's comments on the proposed mechanisms. Such a process would also provide an opportunity to address two concerns: the challenge of anticipating answers to potential questions asked by the European Commission and the challenge of clarifying the rights and obligations of the organisations concerned.

Conclusion

The analysis of public and commercial interests overlaps with the economic and social spheres. Additionally, the increasing complexity of the relationships between public, private commercial and private non-profit actors highlights two main ideas:

- Public interest is and will necessarily remain a partially subjective concept, whose scope cannot be set in stone and whose interpretation would vary with time and space. Therefore, it is important to adapt its scope to societal evolution and train administrative authorities to interpret the same while understanding the true constraints and motivation of the actors in the field.
- The idea that the preponderance of profitable economic activities within an organisation should inevitably imply its for-profit motives, and therefore its incompatibility with public interest is largely erroneous.

Although this chapter focused on the French context, it is clear that methods to improve the untenable situation faced by several public-interest operators must be explored at both the national and European levels. To start, subsequent efforts should focus on identifying and analysing these issues in various national contexts to identify similar issues and converging action policies.

Notes

1 Fondation de France (2019). Panorama national des générosités [National panorama of donations]. And Fondation de France (2018). Enquête nationale fondations et fonds de dotation [National survey of foundations and endowment funds].

2 The term 'common good', which indicates a general, philosophical concept, will be used in quotation marks to clearly distinguish it from the concepts of public interest, public utility and social utility, each of which refers to specific legal and/or fiscal concepts.

3 Livia Ventura (University of Geneva) provided an excellent overview of the development of hybrid models internationally (L. Ventura [2019]. The social enterprise development and the birth of hybrid entities. A comparative law perspective. *Expert Focus*, 3, 170–174). Heather Sertial also analyzed the development of hybrid models in the United States and their limits and challenges (H. Sertial [2012]. Hybrid entities: Distributing profits with a purpose. *Fordham Journal of Corporate & Financial Law*, 17, 261).

4 In EU Law, this principle of regulating state subsidies of economic operators takes its name from the Latin legal maxim *De minimis non curat praetor* (the chief does not bother with the details).

5 Law n ° 2003–709 of August 1, 2003, on philanthropy, associations and foundations, introduced reductions on corporate tax (60% of the amount of the gift) and income tax (66%).
6 E. Malinvaud (1986). Les causes de la montée du chômage en France [The causes of the rise of unemployment in France]. *Revue française d'économie*, 1(1), 50–83.
7 P. Rosanvallon (1981). *La crise de l'Etat-providence* [*The crisis of the welfare state*]. Seuil, Paris.
8 Law n° 2019–791 of July 26, 2019 regarding 'a school of trust' increased the duration of compulsory schooling for 16–18-year-old children. Moreover, the age of entry for primary school was reduced from six years to three years.
9 People aged 65 and above constitute 20.5% of the population in 2020. Their share has increased by 4.7% in the past 20 years. (M. Martin & E. Rignols (2020). Tableaux de l'économie française. *Collection Insee Références Édition*, 24–25.)
10 F. Charhon (2016). *Vive la philanthropie!* Cherche Midi, Paris.
11 Created in 1871, Les amies et amis de la commune de Paris was the first friends' association in France.
12 V. Tchernonog & L. Prouteau (2019). *Le paysage associatif français: mesures et évolutions* [*An overview of French associations – measures and developments*]. Dalloz Juris Associations, Paris.
13 Law No. 90–559 of July 4, 1990, on the formation of corporate foundations and amendment to the provisions of Law No. 87–571 of July 23, 1987, on the development of philanthropy.
14 See OECD (2020). *Taxation and philanthropy, OECD tax policy studies*, n° 27. OCDE Editions, Paris, p. 96 and following.
15 Law n° 2003–709 of August 1, 2003 (article 40).
16 Law n° 2001–420 of May 15, 2001 on new economic regulations.
17 J. S. Hiller (2013). The benefit corporation and corporate social responsibility. *Journal of Business Ethics*, 118(2), 287–301.
18 D. B. Reiser (2011). Benefit corporations – a sustainable form of organization. *Wake Forest Law Review*, 46, 591.
19 In the United States, the B-corp legal status is not recognised at the federal level; however, 37 states have adopted this status in their legislation.
20 C. Gaboriaux (2017). Une construction sociale de l'utilité publique [A social construction of public utility. Associations and foundations before the Conseil d'Etat (1870–1914)]. *Genèses*, 4, 57–79.
21 M.-C. Gonet-Delacroix (1992). *Art et Etat sous la IIIème République* [*Art and state under the Third republic*]. Editions de la Sorbonne, Paris.
22 Law n° 76–629 of July 10, 1976 on the protection of nature.
23 K. Sibiril (2012). *La notion d'intérêt en droit administratif français* [*The notion of interest in French administrative law*]. University of Brest, France.
24 Ministère de l'économie des finances et de la relance. (2017). Qu'est-ce que la silver économie ou économie des seniors? [What is the silver economy?]. Retrieved from: https://www.economie.gouv.fr/entreprises/silver-economie-definition.
25 Law No. 201–856 of July 31, 2014 on the social and welfare economy.
26 Law of July 1, 1901 on the association contract (article 10).
27 Article 11 of the law August 11, 1954, which introduced a tax benefit for gifts to 'oeuvres ou organismes d'intérêt general' in France.
28 Instruction 4 (1998), 170 of September 15, H-5–98.
29 ECJ judgment of 1970 France c/Commission (61969CJ0047). Subsequently, on December 10, 1998, the European Commission published a notice on the application of the state aid rules relating to direct business taxation (98/C 384/03).
30 Law n ° 2003–709 of August 1, 2003.
31 The 4P rule is defined in *Bulletin Officiel des Finances Publiques* [Official Bulletin of Public Finances] BOl BOI-IS-CHAMP-10–50–20–20120912.
32 ECJ (19/01/2017) aff C 344/15. National Roads Authority.
33 Tax rescript refusal by letters of October 1, 2013, and March 24, 2014, received by the Association Ecole Maria Montessori from the local authorities of the tax administration of Essonne.
34 BOI No. 61 of 9 June 2008.
35 Conseil d'État (November 6, 1995). Association de médecine du travail du département de la Mayenne
36 Instruction 4 (1999), 33 of February 16, H-1–99 'Concerning the Tax Regime Applicable to Non-profit Organisations'.
37 Tax Instruction 4 (2006), 208 of December 18, H-5–06 'Concerning the Tax Regime Applicable to Non-profit Organisations'.

38 Simplon (2021). Rapport impact social [Social impact report]. Retrieved from: https://simplon.co/uploads/Site%20national/chiffres%20d%27impact/Rapport%20d%27impact%20T4%202020.pdf?_t=1613388190.
39 Cour des comptes (2019). *Fondation Agir Contre l'Exclusion: Exercices 2013 à 2017.* Rapport, pp. 58–59. Paris.
40 OECD (2020). *Taxation and philanthropy, OECD tax policy studies*, n° 27. OCDE Editions, Paris.
41 CJEU (19 January 2017). National Roads Authority.
42 *De minimis* subsidies are small state subsidies granted to businesses. For amounts below EUR 200,000 per company over a three-year period, the relevant EU countries are not obliged to notify the European Commission.
43 G. Bachelier (2013). *Les règles de territorialité du régime fiscal du mécénat* [*The rules of territoriality in the French philanthropy fiscal regime*]. Rapport au ministre de l'économie et des finances, Paris.
44 Code de l'action sociale et des familles [Code of Social Welfare and Families] (1956, last updated on April 5, 2021).

References

Bachelier, G. (2013). *Les règles de territorialité du régime fiscal du mécénat* [*The rules of territoriality in the French philanthropy fiscal regime*]. Official report to the Finance minister, Paris.

Charhon, F. (2016). *Vive la philanthropie!* Cherche-Midi, Paris.

European Commission (2015). *A map of social enterprises and their eco-systems in Europe*. Publications office of the EC, Luxembourg.

Fondation de France (2018). *Enquête nationale fondations et fonds de dotation* [*National survey of foundations and endowment funds*]. Paris.

Fondation de France (2019). *Panorama national des générosités* [*National panorama of donations*]. Paris.

Gaboriaux, C. (2017). Une construction sociale de l'utilité publique [A social construction of public utility]. *Genèses*, 4, 57–79. Paris.

Hiller, J. S. (2013). The benefit corporation and corporate social responsibility. *Journal of Business Ethics*, 118(2), 287–301.

Malinvaud, E. (1986). Les causes de la montée du chômage en France. *Revue française d'économie*, 1(1), 50–83. Paris

OECD (2020). *Taxation and philanthropy, OECD tax policy studies*, n° 27. OCDE Editions, Paris.

Reiser, D. B. (2011). Benefit corporations – a sustainable form of organization. *Wake Forest Law Review*, 46, 591.

Rosanvallon, P. (1981). *La crise de l'Etat-providence* [*The crisis of the welfare state*]. Seuil, Paris.

Sertial, H. (2012). Hybrid entities: Distributing profits with a purpose. *Fordham Journal of Corporate & Financial Law*, 17, 261.

Sibiril, K. (2012). *La notion d'intérêt en droit administratif français* [*The notion of interest in French administrative law*]. University of Brest, France.

Tchernonog, V., & Prouteau, L. (2019). *Le paysage associatif français: mesures et évolutions* [*An overview of French associations – measures and developments*]. Dalloz Juris Associations, Paris.

Ventura, L. (2019). The social enterprise development and the birth of hybrid entities. A comparative law perspective. *Expert Focus*, 3, 170–174.

APPENDIX

OECD Tax Policy Studies

Taxation and Philanthropy

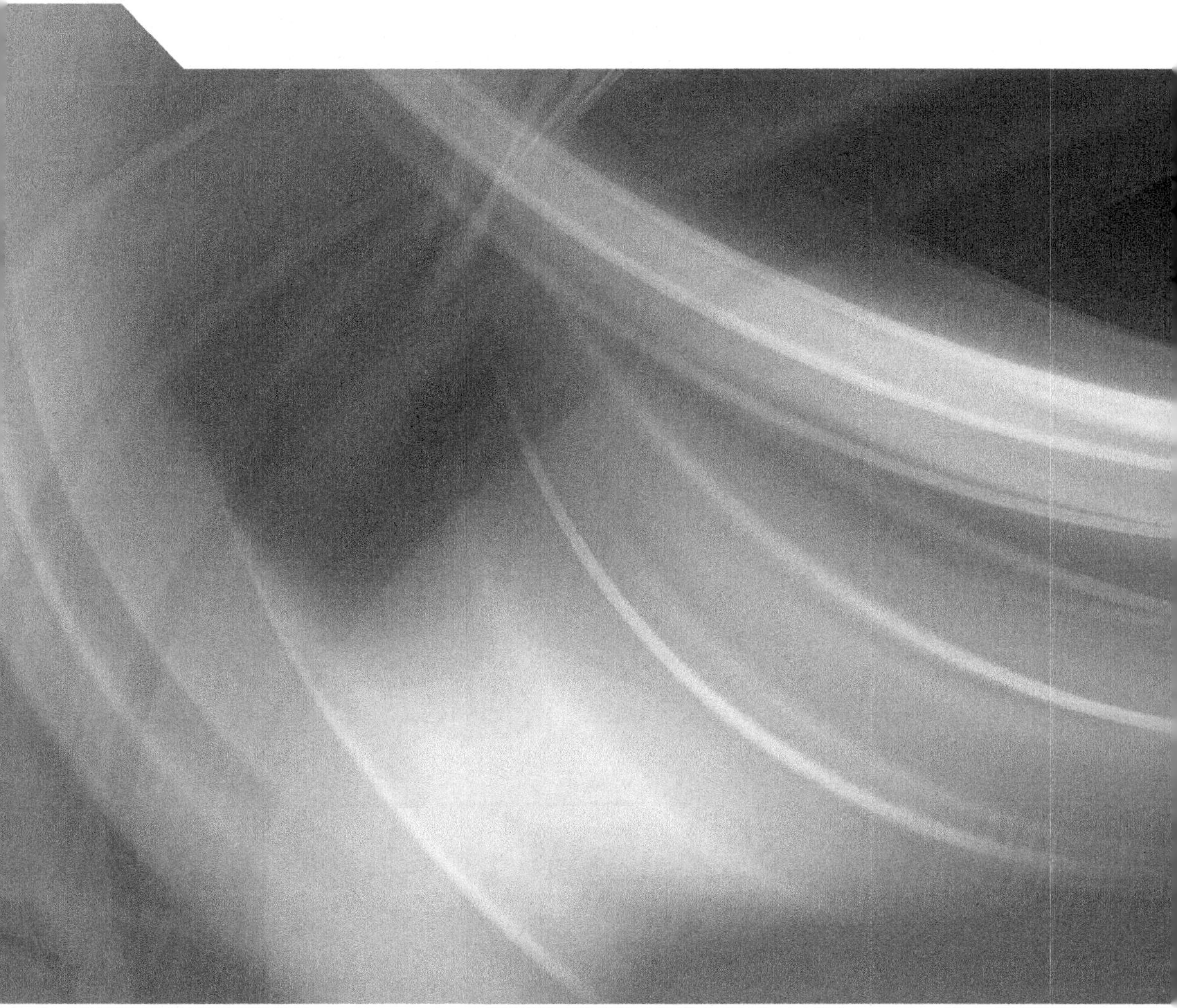

No. 27

OECD Tax Policy Studies

Taxation and Philanthropy

No. 27

This document, as well as any data and map included herein, are without prejudice to the status of or sovereignty over any territory, to the delimitation of international frontiers and boundaries and to the name of any territory, city or area.

The statistical data for Israel are supplied by and under the responsibility of the relevant Israeli authorities. The use of such data by the OECD is without prejudice to the status of the Golan Heights, East Jerusalem and Israeli settlements in the West Bank under the terms of international law.

Please cite this publication as:
OECD (2020), *Taxation and Philanthropy*, OECD Tax Policy Studies, No. 27, OECD Publishing, Paris, *https://doi.org/10.1787/df434a77-en*.

ISBN 978-92-64-63114-4 (print)
ISBN 978-92-64-40619-3 (pdf)

OECD Tax Policy Studies
ISSN 1990-0546 (print)
ISSN 1990-0538 (online)

Photo credits: Cover © selensergen/Thinkstock.

Corrigenda to publications may be found on line at: *www.oecd.org/about/publishing/corrigenda.htm*.

Foreword

Philanthropy plays an important role in most countries, providing private support to a range of activities for the public good. This differentiates the sector from government initiatives (i.e., public action for the public good) and profit-based initiatives (i.e., private action for the private good). Almost all OECD countries provide some form of preferential tax treatment for philanthropy. Entities with a philanthropic status typically receive tax relief directly in relation to their activities, while both individual and corporate donors to these entities are often able to receive tax incentives that lower the cost of giving. This report represents one of the most comprehensive attempts to catalogue the tax treatment of philanthropic entities and philanthropic giving across 40 OECD member and participating countries.

In many countries these tax preferences have been in place, unaltered, for many years despite changing social conditions. For example, when income tax exemptions for philanthropic entities were introduced in many countries around the beginning of the 20th century, there were relatively few eligible entities and most of their income was in the form of donations. Over time, the philanthropic sector has grown and many philanthropic entities now rely significantly on self-generated income, including business and investment income. Large philanthropic foundations have also become more prevalent, placing greater focus on the degree of influence of large donors on the use of taxpayer funds. Meanwhile, the increasingly global nature of many policy challenges – such as environmental and public health concerns (including the COVID-19 pandemic) – raises questions regarding the appropriate tax treatment of cross-border giving. These developments suggest that a review of the tax rules in place in many countries may be warranted.

This report provides a detailed review of the tax treatment of philanthropic entities and philanthropic giving in 40 OECD member and participating countries. The report first examines the various arguments for and against the provision of preferential tax treatment for philanthropy. It then reviews the tax treatment of philanthropic entities and giving in the 40 participating countries, in both a domestic and cross-border context. Drawing on this analysis, the report then highlights a range of potential tax policy options for countries to consider.

The report, which has been carried out as part of a collaboration between the OECD and the Geneva Centre for Philanthropy, draws heavily on country responses to a questionnaire on *Taxation and Philanthropy* by country delegates to Working Party No. 2 on Tax Policy Analysis and Tax Statistics of the OECD's Committee on Fiscal Affairs.

Acknowledgements

This study was produced by the Tax Policy and Statistics Division of the OECD Centre for Tax Policy and Administration (CTPA) in collaboration with the Geneva Centre for Philanthropy (GCP).

The study was led by Alastair Thomas, under the supervision of David Bradbury and Bert Brys. The main authors of the report were Daniel Fichmann and Alastair Thomas of the CTPA. Chapters 1, 2 and 5 were co-authored by Professor Ann O'Connell of the University of Melbourne. Chapter 5 was co-authored by Alexandre Jutand of the CTPA. The study draws heavily on information gathered from a questionnaire issued to OECD and participating countries in December 2019. This questionnaire was developed, and country responses collated, by Daniel Fichmann and Alexandre Jutand.

The study draws on the questionnaire responses and additional comments received from delegates to Working Party No. 2 on Tax Policy Analysis and Tax Statistics of the OECD Committee on Fiscal Affairs. The study has also benefitted from significant input and guidance provided by Pascal Saint-Amans, Director of the CTPA, as well as Dr Giedre Lideikyte Huber and Professor Henry Peter, Head of the GCP. Karena Garnier and Carrie Tyler assisted with the publication process. Violet Sochay provided administrative assistance.

Table of contents

Tables

Figures

Boxes

Follow OECD Publications on:

 http://twitter.com/OECD_Pubs

 http://www.facebook.com/OECDPublications

 http://www.linkedin.com/groups/OECD-Publications-4645871

 http://www.youtube.com/oecdilibrary

 http://www.oecd.org/oecddirect/

Executive Summary

Most countries provide some form of preferential tax treatment for philanthropy. Entities with a philanthropic status typically receive tax relief directly in relation to their activities, while both individual and corporate donors to these entities are typically able to receive tax incentives that lower the cost of giving. This report provides a detailed review of the taxation of philanthropic entities and philanthropic giving in 40 OECD member and participating countries, and draws on this analysis to highlight a range of potential policy options for countries to consider.

The report first examines the various arguments for and against tax concessions, highlighting that there is no single generally accepted rationale for the preferential tax treatment of philanthropy. Economic theory, for example, provides a limited rationale for preferential tax treatment of philanthropy where there is under-provision of a public good or where there are positive externalities associated with the philanthropic activity. Additional arguments include that the surplus of a philanthropic entity is different in nature to income (and therefore beyond the scope of the income tax base), and that philanthropic giving strengthens civil society and so should be encouraged. Arguments against tax concessions for philanthropy highlight, for example, their fiscal cost, as well as potential distributional and democratic concerns. In particular, richer taxpayers often receive larger tax incentives than poorer taxpayers. Meanwhile, as a tax incentive effectively reallocates tax revenue towards the favoured philanthropic entity, richer taxpayers who make larger donations may gain a disproportionate influence over how public resources are allocated.

The report then considers, in turn, the tax treatment of philanthropic entities and of giving to philanthropic entities, before considering cross-border issues. For an entity to receive philanthropic status and the associated tax benefits, it typically must meet "not-for-profit", "worthy purpose", and "public benefit" requirements, as well as being subject to other administrative and oversight requirements. Not-for-profit requirements prevent any form of profit distribution. Worthy purpose requirements specify the types of activities eligible for support – most commonly welfare, education, scientific research, and healthcare. Public benefit requirements typically stipulate that the benefit must be open to a sufficiently broad section of the public.

Most countries surveyed provide concessionary income tax treatment for approved philanthropic entities. The report identifies two approaches commonly taken: the first is to exempt all (or specific) income, and the second is to consider all forms of income taxable, but to allow the entity to reduce its taxable income through current or future reinvestments towards the fulfilment of its worthy purpose. Countries following the first approach generally exclude non-commercial income (received gifts or grants) from the tax base. Approaches to dealing with commercial activities and the income generated from those activities, diverge. A common approach is to exempt commercial income that is related to the worthy purpose and tax unrelated commercial income. A number of countries also provide preferential VAT treatment to philanthropic entities, and concessions regarding various other taxes (e.g. property taxes).

All the countries surveyed also provide some form of tax incentive to encourage philanthropic giving to eligible entities, although the generosity and design of the incentives vary. In the large majority of countries surveyed, donations are deductible from an individual's taxable income. Other countries offer tax credits instead and, in some cases, the donations of individuals are matched by government. Furthermore, as long as there is a sufficient nexus with earning income, most countries consider corporate sponsoring of philanthropic entities a deductible business expense. Additionally, most countries that levy inheritance or estate taxes generally provide preferential tax relief for philanthropic bequests. Restrictions on the size of tax incentives for giving are common and vary across countries. Some countries limit the size of the tax incentive by adopting a cap of a fixed amount, while others adopt caps based on a percentage of the donor's income or tax liability, and some adopt a combination of both. To limit the cost of matching schemes, countries set the rate at which the relief may be claimed by the receiving philanthropic entity. Lastly, the majority of countries that incentivise cash donations of individuals also incentivise non-monetary donations.

Regarding cross-border philanthropy, the report finds that, beyond the European Union, there is little tax support provided by countries for cross-border giving. With regard to philanthropic entities that operate across borders, beyond the European Union, most countries do not provide tax relief for foreign philanthropic entities operating domestically. However, many countries do allow domestic entities to operate abroad without losing their tax-favoured status, though they are potentially subject to additional restrictions or reporting requirements.

Drawing on the preceding analysis, the report highlights a number of key issues that countries face in the design of their tax rules for philanthropy. First, the report highlights that countries need to ensure that the design of their tax incentives for philanthropic giving is consistent with their underlying policy goals. For example, countries that are particularly concerned about restricting support to areas prioritised by government may wish to consider limiting the breadth of their eligibility criteria. Countries particularly concerned about the distributional impact of the tax incentive, may wish to provide a tax credit, which will ensure that the same proportionate tax benefit is provided to taxpayers irrespective of their income level. Conversely, countries with a progressive personal income tax system wishing to provide a greater incentive to richer donors in order to maximise total giving, may wish to provide a tax deduction.

Second, countries should reassess the merits of providing tax exemptions for the commercial income of philanthropic entities, at least insofar as this income is unrelated to the entity's worthy purpose. In undertaking such a reassessment, countries will need to consider the added complexities associated with distinguishing between taxable (i.e. unrelated commercial income) and exempt income and weigh the additional compliance and administrative costs against the pursuit of competitive neutrality. Furthermore, countries that currently provide an exemption should consider fully subjecting philanthropic entities to the VAT.

Third, the report identifies a number of ways countries can look to both reduce the complexity and improve the oversight of the concessionary tax regimes for philanthropy. These include: applying the same eligibility tests for both philanthropic entities and philanthropic giving; imposing a minimum value threshold for a non-monetary donation to receive a tax incentive; establishing a publicly available register of approved philanthropic entities; introducing an annual reporting requirement; implementing a combined oversight approach (e.g. tax administration and independent commission); clearly differentiating between corporate donations and sponsorship; improving data collection and tax expenditure reports; implementing limits to fundraising expenditures; implementing rules that limit certain types of operating expenses of philanthropic entities; and limiting the remuneration of staff, managers, and board members of philanthropic entities.

Finally, the increasingly global nature of many policy challenges – such as environmental and public health concerns (including the COVID-19 pandemic) – may require countries and institutions to cooperate across borders. In this context, there is merit in countries reassessing whether there may be some instances where equivalent tax treatment should be provided to domestic and cross-border philanthropy. To address concerns regarding oversight, countries could impose equivalent requirements as apply in the domestic philanthropy context, or require additional checks before providing tax-favoured status.

1 Introduction

This introductory chapter provides background information on the characteristics of the philanthropic sector, to set the scene for the detailed analysis of the taxation of philanthropy that follows in the report. It also provides an outline of the overall structure of the report.

Philanthropy plays an important role in most countries, providing support for a wide range of private activities and initiatives in support of the public good. This differentiates the sector from government initiatives (i.e., public action for the public good) and profit-based initiatives (i.e., private action for the private good). The use of the tax system as a means of supporting philanthropy is widespread. In addition to government grants and the contracting of services to philanthropic entities ("direct support"), governments typically support philanthropy ("indirectly") in two ways, by providing: tax incentives for giving to philanthropic entities; and (full or partial) exemptions of philanthropic entities from various taxes.

In many cases these tax preferences have been in place, unaltered, for many years despite changing social conditions. For example, when income tax exemptions for philanthropic entities were introduced in many countries around the beginning of the 20th century, there were relatively few eligible entities and most of their income was in the form of donations. Over time, the sector has grown, often in response to out-sourcing by governments of welfare and other services, and many philanthropic entities now rely significantly on self-generated income, including business and investment income. There have also been significant developments in research on the optimal design of tax incentives for giving that highlight, for example, a range of efficiency and distributional concerns. Furthermore, the increasing prevalence of large philanthropic foundations has placed greater focus on the degree of influence of large donors on the use of taxpayer funds. Finally, the global nature of many of the challenges facing the world such as environmental, medical research, and public health concerns (such as the COVID-19 pandemic), raises questions regarding the appropriate tax treatment of cross-border giving.

In light of these developments, a reassessment of the tax rules in place in many countries may be warranted. To aid such reassessment, this report provides a detailed review of the taxation of philanthropic entities and philanthropic giving in 40 OECD member and participating countries, and highlights potential reform options for countries to consider. The report draws heavily on country responses to a questionnaire on *Taxation and Philanthropy* ("the questionnaire") by country delegates to Working Party No. 2 on Tax Policy Analysis and Tax Statistics of the OECD's Committee on Fiscal Affairs.

This introductory chapter provides a range of background information on the philanthropic sector to aid the analysis to follow. It first discusses the exact meaning of philanthropy adopted in this report. It then highlights a number of key aspects of the philanthropic sector, before discussing the size of the philanthropic sector both in terms of the number of philanthropic entities and the total amount of giving to the philanthropic sector. Finally, the chapter provides an outline of the structure of the report to follow.

1.1. Defining philanthropy

The term "philanthropy" does not have a universally accepted meaning. The term derives from the Greek "philanthropia" meaning "love of humanity" or "love of gods for humanity". Various attempts have been made to define the term. Dictionary definitions include "the gratuitous transfer of funds or other property for altruistic purposes".[1]

Scholars from different disciplines have also sought to define the term, referencing various concepts such as the "voluntary" aspect of philanthropy, the notion of "generosity" or concern for others, or the application of private resources for public purposes. For example, philanthropy has been described as:

- voluntary giving, and voluntary association, primarily for the benefit of others; (Payton, 1988[1]) or
- the voluntary giving and receiving of time and money, aimed (however imperfectly) towards the needs of charity and the interests of all in a better quality of life; (Van Til, 1990[2]) or
- the use of personal wealth and skills to benefit specific public causes. (Anheier, 2005[3])

All of these 'definitions' are concerned with the act of giving, but the term philanthropy is also used in other contexts. For example, philanthropy has been defined as being 'one form of income of non-profit entities' (Salamon and Anheier, 1992[4]), equating philanthropy with donations and moving the focus from the act of giving to the recipient entities. The term is also sometimes used to refer to the entities themselves, with one researcher noting that the term 'typically applies to philanthropic foundations and similar institutions' (Anheier, 2005[3]).

Another definition is: 'The planned and structured giving of money, time, information, goods and services, influence and voice to improve the wellbeing of humanity and the community' (Philanthropy Australia[5]). This definition is narrower in that it emphasises planned and structured giving, but also notes different types of gifts and includes the notion of community. It has also been said that 'being a philanthropist is synonymous with the largesse of rich individual donors' (Anheier and Leat, 2006[6]). But generally the term is considered broad enough to cover all giving.

Despite the divergent uses of the term, there are some common threads: philanthropy is concerned with 'giving', and with 'worthy' and 'public', rather than private, causes. Several definitions refer to giving time as well as money. There is also a reference to 'altruism' or concern for others in some of the definitions, but this is not generally part of any definition that specifies which entities or activities qualify for tax relief. Indeed, some entities exist for the benefit of their members rather than for the broader public benefit e.g. a disability support group. The focus then, is on 'gifting' – the making of voluntary contributions without expectation of return; and on identification of appropriate worthy causes or purposes. This identification of 'worthy purposes' is likely to differ between jurisdictions and is an important part of the tax framework in this area.

In some common law countries, the term 'charity' is often used to refer to the act of giving or to the entities that either enable or carry out activities. Although the terms charity and philanthropy are sometimes used interchangeably, they do not necessarily have the same meaning. While charity and philanthropy both seek to accomplish the same outcome – to address needs and make the world a better place – the method that philanthropic entities and charitable entities each use to reach that outcome is different. Whereas charity refers to the direct relief of suffering and social problems, philanthropy systematically seeks out root causes of these issues and endeavours to find a solution (Anheier and Toepler, 2010[7]). This distinction has been significant in the emergence of modern philanthropic foundations, particularly in the United States.

This report will use the terms philanthropic giving and philanthropic entities, respectively, to refer to:

- the act of giving by individuals and corporations, to philanthropic entities with worthy purposes, and
- entities that are engaged in activities in pursuit of those purposes, including by providing funds to other entities.

1.2. The philanthropic sector

Although philanthropy has a long history, the idea of a philanthropic sector or 'third sector' beyond the realms of the state and the market is of fairly recent origin, certainly post-World War 2. This relatively recent recognition of the sector as having an economic and political presence may explain why there is limited research into the sector as such, with the notable exception being in the United States.[2] More recently other countries have undertaken research, and there have been a number of comparative world-wide studies[3] that have identified common characteristics and helped to inform decision-makers. The notion of a distinct sector remains a perplexing concept in modern political and social discourse, as it covers a tremendous diversity of institutions and behaviours.

It is difficult to compare philanthropic sectors across countries for a number of reasons. First, each country will have its own historical, economic and political background that will influence the size and scope of the sector. This has been described as the 'social origins' theory that considers inter alia, how and why welfare states took on different forms (Anheier and Salamon, 1996[8]). The theory suggests an inverse relationship between the extent of government social welfare spending and the size of the non-profit sector. This research identifies countries as having one of four characterisations:

- **'liberal states'** – where democratic government developed before the welfare state. The welfare state may be limited but available to the 'deserving poor'. These countries are likely to have a larger philanthropic sector;
- **'social-democratic states'** – where the working class gained power and pushed for a universal welfare state. As a result of the high level of welfare, these countries tend to have smaller philanthropic sectors;
- **'corporatist states'** – where the welfare state developed under the control of non-democratic states that later became democratic. These countries tend to have low welfare and large philanthropic sectors;
- **'statist states'** – where a country's elites are in control of the public good provision, and this leads to both low government spending on social welfare and a small philanthropic sector.[4]

The theory also suggests that there will be differences across countries in the predominant types of non-profits, shaped by historical development and class relations. Other country specific issues may include the role of religion in the development of the country, including in the development of philanthropic traditions. Economic development may also be significant both in terms of needy recipients and in the accumulation of the financial ability to provide welfare and for citizens to be able to contribute by way of philanthropy.

Other factors that may make comparisons difficult include notions of 'legal families', that is whether the country has a common law or civil law tradition. Common law countries tend to adopt the notion of 'charity' that dates from the Preamble to a Statute of Elizabeth of 1601,[5] as the basis for identifying worthy purposes and activities. Civil law countries will not be constrained by these notions but may have strong traditions of freedom of association and organising for workers' rights. The German non-profit sector has, for example, been influenced by the principle of 'subsidiarity' that gives priority to private over public action in many areas such as health and social services. The principle of 'self-administration' also gives independence to many public institutions and both of these features make it difficult to identify the non-profit or philanthropic sector as such. (Salamon and Anheier, 1992[4])

Given this diversity, identifying the philanthropic sector in a country for the purposes of comparison means identifying characteristics that are essential. The Johns Hopkins University Comparative Non-profit Sector Project (JHU Project) (Salamon, Sokolowski and List, 2003[9])[6] developed a set of factors to identify non-profit entities that they suggested could be applied across jurisdictions for the purpose of carrying out comparisons of the 'non-profit sector':

- **voluntary** – the voluntariness of those participating and of the entity acting is one of the factors that sets these activities apart from government;
- **self-governing** – not directed by government or others as to how to act;
- **private** – that is, not part of government. The Project notes that in some countries there may a blurring of the line between private and public activity;
- **non-profit distributing** – although these entities may make profits or generate a surplus, they are not formed for the purpose of profit making. The non-distribution requirement distinguishes these entities from for-profit entities;
- **formal**, that is institutionalised to some extent. This would preclude individual acts of philanthropy or assistance to another individual.[7]

1.2.1. Philanthropic activity

This report separates **philanthropic activity** into three dimensions: Giving; funds; and Public Benefit Organisations (PBOs). Each of these activities has different tax implications.

Giving

An important source of funds for philanthropic entities is donations. Philanthropic giving occurs at an individual or corporate level, typically in the form of gifts to funds or PBOs directly, and in the case of individual giving, it may also be in the form of bequests. Individuals may also contribute time or services i.e. volunteering. Businesses may also provide services on a pro bono basis.

Funds

Funds are entities such as grant-making foundations (or 'fundaçions') and trusts that hold assets with which they provide support in the form of grants to PBOs to advance a worthy purpose. This report uses the term 'funds' to refer to intermediaries that provide support to PBOs.

Public Benefit Organisations (PBOs)

Public Benefit Organisation or 'PBO' is the term used in this report to refer to entities that carry out the worthy purposes. However, the distinction between funds and PBOs is not always clear cut, for example, in some countries PBOs do not exclusively work directly with beneficiaries. Many jurisdictions use the term 'charity' to refer to these types of entities. PBOs can be distinguished from funds as they work directly with beneficiaries. There are two matters that are specific to PBOs – the fact that they obtain monies to carry out their worthy purpose from philanthropy – both directly and in the form of grants from funds, but also from government and from self-funded sources, including commercial activities. Secondly, PBOs can take a variety of legal forms. This may have significance for tax purposes e.g. if it is a condition of relief that an entity take a particular form.

In general, philanthropic entities may adopt, or be regarded as having, various legal forms. Some jurisdictions may exclude some legal forms from eligibility such as partnerships, political parties or government entities. Forms that may be adopted include:

- unincorporated associations – a number of people coming together to pursue a common purpose. Generally, these associations are not treated as having legal personality, although some form of registration process may confer legal status in certain jurisdictions. In civil law countries, the right to form associations is often enshrined in the Constitution;
- incorporated entities – the adoption of separate legal form e.g. corporations. Some jurisdictions also offer a special form of incorporation for charitable or philanthropic entities. Some jurisdictions may offer a modified form of incorporation to allow for the non-distribution requirement;
- foundations – may be either grant-making or operating foundations. This report uses the term 'funds' to refer to grant-making foundations. Foundations may take a variety of legal forms;
- trusts – a legal device used in common law countries to denote the separation of the legal rights to the (trust) property from the enjoyment of that property. The holding of trust property in this way ensures that the holder (the trustee) must comply with high standards in dealing with the property. The trust is commonly used for establishing foundations or other funds and denotes a setting aside of monies for the philanthropic purpose;
- co-operatives or mutual entities – are also associations of persons that come together for a common purpose, although they may also have a special form of incorporation. A non-profit co-operative e.g. a child-care co-operative, where the parents run a child care centre but do not distribute any surplus (a 'non-distributing co-operative'), may qualify as part of the philanthropic sector in some countries. Other countries may consider such co-operatives or mutual entities as providing more than an insubstantial benefit to private interests (e.g. the parents of the children being cared for) and therefore would not consider them a philanthropic entity. Co-operatives that distribute profits to members ('distributing co-operatives') will typically be taxed under special provisions. Generally, non-distributing co-operatives will not be taxed under specialist co-operative tax provisions;
- other – there may be other types of entities e.g. religious orders that do not fit into the other categories.

Whatever legal form is adopted; most jurisdictions will treat the entity as a corporation for tax purposes. The legal form may however be relevant for matters such as regulation and for other legal obligations.

1.2.2. The size of the philanthropic sector

The results of the *Taxation and Philanthropy* questionnaire highlight significant variety in terms of the size and scope of the philanthropic sector. Table 1.1 presents the approximate number of philanthropic entities that were eligible for some form of preferential tax treatment in 2018 (for the 27 countries that provided data).[8] The Table also contains the respective populations, expressed in millions.

What these numbers show is that there are a significant number of entities that are eligible for tax concessions, although the number of entities varies widely between countries.

The number of philanthropic entities in a country is, of course, only one measure of the size and significance of the sector in a country. Other measures include the economic contribution, the size of the workforce and, uniquely to the sector, the number of people volunteering. Reliable data on these measures across countries is notoriously difficult to estimate. Despite the limitations of measuring the contribution of the philanthropic sector, the JHU Project surveyed 35 countries in the period 1995 to 2002 and found that using expenditures as a proxy for economic contribution, the sector accounted for USD 1.3 trillion, or 5.1%

of combined Gross Domestic Product (GDP) (Salamon, Sokolowski and List, 2003[9]). The JHU Project also looked at the size of the workforce and found that there were 39.5 million full-time equivalent (FTE) workers, including 21.8 million paid workers and 12.6 FTE volunteers representing 4.4% of the economically active population. Further, they found that 190 million people were volunteers across the 35 countries surveyed. More recently, in 2013 the JHU project estimated for a smaller sample of 15 countries (drawing on data from 2002-2009) that the sector's economic contribution was 4.5% of GDP (Salamon et al., 2013[10]).

Table 1.1. Number of philanthropic entities across countries

Country	Approximate number of entities	Population in 2018 (million)
Argentina	17 756	44.5
Australia	188 000[1]	25.0
Austria	1 230	8.8
Belgium	2241[2]	11.4
Canada	86 000	37.1
Chile	311 319[3]	18.8
Colombia	44 000	49.8
Czech Republic	130 000[4]	10.6
Estonia	2 474	1.3
France	4 188[12]	66.9
Germany	600 000	82.9
Ireland	9 781[5]	4.9
Israel	40 000[6]	8.9
Italy	98 231[13]	60.4
Latvia	2 000	1.9
Lithuania	11 400	2.8
Mexico	8 763[7]	125.3
Netherlands	43 000[8]	17.2
New Zealand	27 000	4.9
Portugal	8 148	10.3
Romania	144	19.5
Singapore	2 277[9]	4.0
Slovak Republic	8 687	5.4
Slovenia	28 524	2.1
Sweden	99 300[10]	10.2
Switzerland	10 000	8.5
United States	1 682 091[11]	327.2

Notes:

1. Includes income tax exempt and gift deductible recipients.
2. Registered since 2018.
3. This is the total number of taxpayers registered as non-profit organizations, however it may include inactive entities. Additionally, it may include organizations that do not fit within the PBO definition.
4. Total number of not-for-profit entities
5. Tax exempt entities.
6. Not-for-profit, but not necessarily eligible for tax concessions.
7. Authorised donees.
8. PBOs; number of funds not available.
9. In Singapore, registered charities are eligible for income tax relief. Of these registered charities, 666 are Institutions of Public Character (IPCs) which receive 250% tax deductions on qualifying donations.
10. Registered as not-for-profit but not necessarily eligible for all concessions.
11. Recognised entities under s 501(c) Internal Revenue Code (this does not include churches).
12. 2 537 foundations and 1 651 active endowment funds (no data on total PBOs).
13. Data refer to ONLUS (Non-profit organisation of social utility) from data from tax returns and other fiscal-related administrative information.

Source: OECD Taxation and Philanthropy Questionnaire and OECD Labour Force Statistics 2020

1.2.3. Total amount of giving to funds and PBOs

The significance of philanthropy can also be seen in the level of donations to philanthropic entities, which is presented in Table 1.2. Data availability, and comparability, is however imperfect. In particular, not all countries were able to provide the total annual amount of donations to PBOs and funds in 2018, and, in some countries, only the amount of donations eligible for preferential tax treatment is available. Nevertheless, the questionnaire responses highlight that the amount of philanthropic giving varies widely across countries and that there is a significant amount of giving to philanthropic entities that gets the benefit of preferential tax treatment.

Table 1.2. Total amount of giving to funds and PBOs

Country	Total amount of giving to funds and PBOs	USD million
Argentina	ARS 5 019 million (2018)	72.0
Austria	EUR 630 million (2017)	704.0
Belgium	EUR 263.2 million (PIT donations) (2017)	294.0
Canada	CAD 9.6 billion (individuals) (2017) CAD 3.8 billion approx. (corporations) (2017)	7 100.0 2 790.0
Chile	CLP 276 479 million donations (2018) CLP 10 052 million inheritances (2018)	358.1 13.0
Czech Republic	CZK 5.9 billion (2017)	249.0
Estonia	EUR 9.4 million (2018).	10.5
France	EUR 2 545 million (PIT donations) (2018) EUR 112 million in donations reported by the real estate and wealth tax (2018) Between EUR 2.3 billion and EUR 2.5 billion in corporate donations (2015)	2 968.9 130.6 2 683.0 – 2 916.1
Germany	EUR 5.3 billion (2018)	5 920.0
Ireland	EUR 83.7 million 2018	93.5
Italy	EUR 705.5 million (2017)	788.4
Latvia	EUR 28 million (2017)	32.1
Lithuania	EUR 12.2 million (individuals) (2018) EUR 68 million (companies) (2018)	13.6 76.0
Mexico	MXN 47 659 million (2018)	2 477.0
Netherlands	EUR 845 million (including EUR 20 million from businesses) (yearly average from 2008-2014)	944.5
New Zealand	NZD 900 million approx. (2018)	577.0
Portugal	EUR 372 million, including EUR 59 million in goods in kind	415.0
Romania	RON 115.5 million in 2014-2017	26.0
Singapore	SGD 1 billion (2018)	715.0
Slovak Republic	EUR 14 million (2018)	15.6
Slovenia	EUR 29.6 million (2018)	33.0
United States	USD 180.5 billion in cash donations, USD 88.1 billion in non-cash donations, and USD 35.4 billion carried over from prior periods (individuals) (2017) C corporations USD 18.6 billion (2017), charitable bequests of USD 22.8 billion (2018)	345 400.0

Source: OECD Taxation and Philanthropy Questionnaire

The data provided does not, of course, reveal the total amount of giving in a country. It does not reflect, for example, giving to entities that are not eligible recipients. In Australia, giving to religious entities is not deductible, but nevertheless approximately 30% of annual giving is to a religious entity (Charities Aid Foundation, 2019[11]). The data will also not include giving where the donor has not claimed the tax relief. This may be inadvertent, or where giving falls below relevant thresholds, but there are also cases where donors choose not to access tax relief as a means of retaining greater control of the spending.[9]

Research by the Charities Aid Foundation in 2016, compared giving as a percentage of GDP for 24 countries using surveys and publicly available data. Table 1.3 shows the results for countries that are included in the questionnaire. It should be noted however that the results are not necessarily confined to giving that received subsidies and preferential tax treatment.

Table 1.3. Giving as a percentage of GDP

Country	Giving as a percentage of GDP
Australia	0.23
Austria	0.14
Canada	0.77
Czech Republic	0.04
Finland	0.13
France	0.11
Germany	0.17
India	0.37
Ireland	0.22
Italy	0.30
Japan	0.12
Korea	0.50
Netherlands	0.30
New Zealand	0.79
Norway	0.11
Singapore	0.39
Sweden	0.16
Switzerland	0.09
United Kingdom	0.54
United States	1.40

Source: Derived from Charities Aid Foundation, Gross Domestic Philanthropy: An international analysis of GDP, tax and giving, January 2016, https://www.cafonline.org/docs/default-source/about-us-policy-and-campaigns/gross-domestic-philanthropy-feb-2016.pdf

1.2.4. Sources of revenue for philanthropic entities

Another finding of the JHU Project is that philanthropic giving is significant but not the main source of revenue for philanthropic entities. The composition of the sources of revenue, namely which proportion of revenue is from philanthropy, from fee income and from government, also varies widely. According to the JHU Project, the classification they adopted refers to *philanthropic giving*, which includes individual giving, corporate giving and foundation giving (grants); *fees*, which includes private payments for goods and services, membership dues, and investment income; and *government* or public sector support, which includes grants, contracts, and payments from all levels of government. The results for countries in our survey are in Table 1.4.

The data shows that philanthropic giving is not the most significant source of funding for any country. Beyond that, it is not possible to say whether self-funding or government support is the most significant as the results vary substantially by type of philanthropic entity and country. Furthermore, averages can be misleading. In the United States, for example, non-profit schools, colleges and hospitals receive substantial revenues from tuition, fees and some government grants, reducing the average percentage from donations. Other types of philanthropic entities, however, such as food banks and other social welfare organisations depend much more on donations. It is also not possible to say whether there is any causal relationship – that is, whether entities turn to self-funding because the other sources of revenue are in decline, or whether the receipt of government funding means the entity has less need to generate its own income or to engage in fundraising. One issue that has generated significant literature is whether the receipt of government grants by non-profits has a crowding-out effect i.e. whether the receipt of such funding means that philanthropy is discouraged. This is considered in Chapter 2.

Table 1.4. Not-for-profit revenue sources across countries

Country	% Philanthropic giving	% Fees	% Government
Argentina	7	73	19
Australia	6	63	31
Austria	6	44	50
Belgium	5	19	77
Colombia	15	70	15
Czech Republic	14	47	39
Germany	3	32	64
Finland	7	58	58
Hungary	18	55	27
Japan	3	52	45
Korea	4	71	24
Ireland	7	16	77
Israel	10	26	64
Italy	3	61	37
Mexico	6	85	9
Netherlands	2	39	59
Norway	7	58	35
Romania	27	29	45
Slovak Republic	23	55	22
Sweden	9	62	29
United Kingdom	9	45	47
United States	13	57	31
South Africa	24	31	44

Source: Derived from Salamon, Sokolowski and List (2003[9]) Figure 11, p 32 and Salamon, Sokolowski and Anheiner (2000[12]) Figure 3, p 6, The Johns Hopkins Comparative Non-profit Sector Project.

1.3. Outline of the report

The rest of this report is structured as follows. Chapter 2 investigates the various arguments both for and against the provision of tax concessions for philanthropic entities, and the provision of tax incentives for philanthropic giving.

Chapter 3 examines the tax treatment of philanthropic entities across OECD member and selected participating countries, starting with the qualification process for entities to become recognised PBOs or funds, including worthy purpose, public benefit, and not-for-profit requirements, followed by an overview of the administrative application and regulatory process. The chapter then analyses the different forms of tax relief that philanthropic entities benefit from. Finally, the chapter highlights the potential risk of tax avoidance and evasion schemes involving philanthropic entities and the anti-abuse policies countries have put in place as a result.

Chapter 4 examines the tax treatment of donors and philanthropic giving across OECD member and selected participating countries. It first considers the tax design of incentives for giving by individuals, and then countries' tax incentives for corporate giving. It also highlights the potential risk of tax avoidance and evasion and the anti-abuse policies countries have put in place as a result.

Chapter 5 considers the taxation of cross-border philanthropy. It first considers tax incentives for giving: both donations and bequests; and also considers how gift and inheritance taxes apply and how capital gains tax might apply where the gift is non-cash. It then considers the tax treatment of philanthropic entities that operate across borders, examining whether tax relief is extended to foreign philanthropic entities operating domestically, and the tax treatment of domestic PBOs operating across borders. Finally, it considers the tax treatment of international grant-making by funds.

Chapter 6 brings together the key insights from the preceding chapters and discusses their tax policy implications. It highlights the importance of countries ensuring that the design of their tax incentives for philanthropic giving are consistent with their underlying policy goals. It also suggests that countries reassess the merits of providing tax exemptions for the commercial income of philanthropic entities, at least insofar as this income is unrelated to the entity's worthy purpose. More broadly, the chapter finds scope for countries to both reduce the complexity and improve the oversight of their concessionary regimes for philanthropic entities and philanthropic giving. Finally, in light of the increasingly global nature of many policy challenges – such as environmental and public health concerns (including the COVID-19 pandemic) – it suggests countries reassess the restrictions commonly imposed on access to tax concessions for cross-border philanthropy.

References

Anheier et al. (2020), *The Non-profit Sector: A Research Handbook*, Yale University Press, London. [13]

Anheier, H. (2005), *A Dictionary of Civil Society, Philanthropy and the Non-profit Sector*, Routledge, London. [3]

Anheier, H. and D. Leat (2006), *Creative Philanthropy: Toward a New Philanthropy for the Twenty-First Century*, Routledge, London. [6]

Anheier, H. and L. Salamon (1996), "The Social Origin of Civil Society: Explaining the Non-profit Sector Cross-Nationally", *International Journal of Voluntary and Nonprofit Organizations*, Vol. 9, pp. 213–248. [8]

Anheier, H. and S. Toepler (2010), *International Encyclopedia of Civil Society*, Springer Publishing, New York. [7]

Charities Aid Foundation (2019), *Australia Giving 2019*, https://www.cafonline.org/docs/default-source/about-us-publications/caf-australia-giving-report-2019-16master.pdf?sfvrsn=65e49940_2. [11]

Philanthropy Australia (n.d.), "Glossary", https://www.philanthropy.org.au/tools-resources/glossary/#P. [5]

Payton, R. (1988), *Philanthropy: Voluntary action for the public good*, Macmillan Publishing, London. [1]

Salamon, L. and H. Anheier (1992), "In search of the non-profit sector I: The question of definitions", *International Journal of Voluntary and Non-profit Organisations*, Vol. 3, pp. 125–151. [4]

Salamon, L., S. Sokolowski and H. Anheiner (2000), *Social Origins of Civil Society: An Overview*, Johns Hopkins Comparative Nonprofit Sector Project, Johns Hopkins University, Baltimore. [12]

Salamon, L., S. Sokolowski and R. List (2003), *Global Civil Society: An Overview*, Johns Hopkins Comparative Nonprofit Sector Project, Johns Hopkins University, Baltimore. [9]

Salamon, L. S. Sokolowski, M. Haddock and H.Tice (2013), "The State of Global Civil Society and Volunteering: Latest findings from the implementation of the UN Nonprofit Handbook", *Comparative Nonprofit Sector Working Papers*, No. 49, Johns Hopkins University. [10]

Van Til, J. (1990), *Defining Philanthropy*, Jossey Bass, San Francisco. [2]

Notes

[1] Merriam-Webster Dictionary (online).

[2] See, for example, the work of the Johns Hopkins University Comparative Non-profit Sector Project and the University of Indiana's Lilly Family School of Philanthropy.

[3] See for example, the Comparative Non-profit Sector Project at The Johns Hopkins University: http://ccss.jhu.edu/research-projects/comparative-nonprofit-sector-project/

[4] More recently one of the original authors has questioned the utility of the theory (Anheier et al., 2020[13]).

[5] The Preamble set out a range of (mostly) secular purposes that could be supported. The classification of 'charity' into four heads arises from the case of Commissioners for Special Purposes of Income Tax v Pemsel (1891) AC 531.

[6] JHU launched this project in the 1990s to gather systematically a body of internationally comparative data on community service organisations (CSOs), philanthropy, and volunteerism. The Project operates in more than 45 countries, spanning all of the world's continents and most of its major religious and cultural traditions. The Project has produced a rich body of comparative data, the Johns Hopkins Global Civil Society Index, several books, and more than 60 published working papers written or edited by Project staff, mostly with indigenous authors. More information about the JHU Project is available at: http://ccss.jhu.edu/research-projects/comparative-nonprofit-sector-project/

[7] Ibid.

[8] In the last years, the Italian philanthropic sector has been involved in a wide reform that aims to simplify philanthropic businesses and encourage public giving. The reform, approved by the Italian Parliament in 2017 (legislative decree 117/2017), is not yet entirely in force, because some technical ministerial decrees are still missing. In particular, as regards the fiscal aspects of the reform, an authorisation of the European Commission is necessary to allow the implementation of a preferential regime, according to the European Union State-aid rules.

[9] See, for example, the Chan Zuckerberg Initiative which is structured as an LLC rather than a traditional foundation: https://chanzuckerberg.com

2 The case for providing tax concessions for philanthropy

The chapter provides an overview of the different rationales for tax incentives for philanthropy domestically and internationally and some of the arguments against providing incentives. It starts by providing a brief overview of the different rationales for tax incentives for philanthropic entities and the case for tax incentives for giving to philanthropic entities. It then summarises the arguments against these tax incentives. Finally, the chapter also discusses the rationales for incentivising cross-border giving.

2.1. Introduction

While philanthropy plays an important role in most countries, this does not automatically mean that it justifies support through the tax system.[1] This chapter examines the different rationales for and against providing tax incentives for philanthropy[2] domestically and internationally. It considers both: (1) tax concessions for philanthropic entities; and (2) tax incentives for giving to philanthropic entities. The chapter highlights that there is no single generally accepted rationale for preferential tax treatment of philanthropic entities. Economic theory provides a limited rationale for providing tax concessions for philanthropy (potentially both for entities and giving) where there is under-provision of a public good or where there are positive externalities associated with philanthropic activity. In this regard, tax concessions will be justified if they result in a larger increase in social welfare than that which government could have otherwise achieved through direct spending. Legal scholars frequently refer to this as the subsidy rationale.

Another often articulated argument for exempting philanthropic entities from income tax is the "base defining" rationale which argues that the surplus of a philanthropic entity is different in nature to income and therefore beyond the scope of the income tax base. Additional arguments include that philanthropic giving, as well as the institutions it develops, strengthen civil society, and decentralise decision-making, and are thus an important feature of a democratic society and worth supporting.

A number of arguments have been raised against the provision of tax preferences for philanthropic entities and/or giving. The cost of providing concessions is often highlighted as a concern. By reducing government revenue, tax concessions for philanthropy require other taxpayers to bear an increased tax burden (or alternatively result in less government expenditure on other policy priorities). A concern regarding exemption of commercial income of philanthropic entities is that this may create an unfair competitive advantage for philanthropic entities over for-profit businesses.

Two related concerns that are raised regarding tax incentives for giving are that they may be regressive and undemocratic. Tax incentives may be regressive in that higher income taxpayers benefit from a larger tax incentive than lower income taxpayers. This can be the case in both aggregate terms, but also in proportionate terns as a tax deduction will provide a greater benefit to higher income taxpayers where they are subject to higher marginal tax rates than lower income taxpayers. The democratic argument highlights the concern that, as a tax incentive effectively reallocates tax revenue towards the favoured philanthropic entity, higher income taxpayers that make larger donations benefit from a disproportionate influence in the determination of how tax revenue is spent. This may be of particular concern where the priorities of donors are not consistent with those of society in general.

Irrespective of the arguments for and against tax concessions, most countries do provide tax incentives for giving, and in general provide exemptions from some taxes for philanthropic entities. The design of these tax concessions are examined in detail in the subsequent chapters of this report.

This chapter is organised as follows: Section 2.2 and 2.3 provide, respectively, an overview of the rationales for and against the provision of tax concessions for philanthropy in a domestic context. Section 2.4 then considers arguments for and against tax concessions for cross-border philanthropy.

2.2. Arguments for tax concessions for domestic philanthropy

A range of arguments can be made in favour of the provision of tax concessions for philanthropic entities and for tax incentives for giving to such entities. This section first considers arguments from economic theory that point to a potential market failure rationale for the subsidisation of both philanthropic entities and philanthropic giving. It then summarises a number of broader arguments drawing on legal, accounting and philosophical perspectives.

2.2.1. Economic theory

The section first outlines two economic theory-based rationales for government intervention to subsidise philanthropy: the under-provision of a public good; and the presence of positive externalities. It then considers whether such a subsidy, if warranted, should be provided via direct grants or via tax concessions (to philanthropic entities and/or philanthropic giving). Finally, it discusses the various trade-offs that must be made in determining the optimal level of a tax incentive for philanthropic giving.

Under-provision of public goods

The under-provision of public goods rationale requires three "failures" to occur to justify government subsidisation of philanthropy: "market failure", "government failure", and "voluntary failure" (Hansmann (1987[1]), Weisbrod (1975[2]) and Salamon (1987[3]) (2016[4]). A "market failure" case will exist for government to intervene and provide public goods that would be welfare improving, but that, due to their non-rival non-excludable nature, are not provided by the market. However, in some cases "government failure" may also occur where the government does not, or is unable to, provide (or unable to provide at a welfare maximising level) the public good. In such cases, philanthropic entities can play an important role in providing these public goods. However, "voluntary failure" may also occur in the sense that philanthropic entities provide an inefficiently low level of the public good, for example, due to insufficient resourcing.

In the presence of these three failures, there is a case for the government to subsidise the philanthropic activity in order to increase supply of the public good to the social optimal level. This subsidisation could occur via a tax incentive for giving, tax concessions to the philanthropic entities themselves, or direct grants to these entities.

Positive externalities

While not providing a public good in the technical sense of a non-rival non-excludable good, a philanthropic entity may provide goods and services that produce positive externalities that are not fully captured by the entity itself or by those contributing to the entity. The presence of externalities may justify government intervention to correct the market failure. In the case of negative externalities, the intervention generally consists of a tax. In the case of positive externalities, on the other hand, the intervention may consist of a subsidy which could take the form of a tax incentive for giving, a tax concession for the entity itself, or a government grant.

It is often argued that philanthropic activity may be viewed as having consumption externalities. To the extent that the private marginal benefit of a gift to a philanthropic entity (i.e. the donor's "warm glow" – see Box 2.1) is below the social marginal benefit of that gift, philanthropic giving has positive consumption externalities and may be 'under-consumed.' Although views in the literature differ to which extent this argument could justify tax subsidies for giving to philanthropic entities (in particular because the argument would provide a justification to subsidise giving to, for instance, other family members, but tax systems typically do not provide a tax subsidy for this type of giving).'

Therefore, to internalise the externality and correct the market failure, there may be a case for government to intervene. This intervention could occur via tax concessions or direct grants to the philanthropic entity. In the case of tax concessions to philanthropic entities, reducing the taxes borne will (directly or indirectly) lower the private marginal cost of producing the goods and services, which can increase the provision of these goods towards the social optimal level. In the case of philanthropic giving, a tax incentive lowers the price of giving so that the private marginal benefit of the donor increases towards the social marginal benefit, thereby increasing the level of giving towards the social optimal level.

Box 2.1. The drivers of philanthropic giving

Overview

Noting the importance of philanthropic giving has led researchers in various fields and the sector itself to consider what drives philanthropy. Such analysis is important in the context of tax policy because it may indicate whether tax policy is efficient in increasing philanthropy i.e. whether tax is a driver of philanthropy. Bekkers and Wiepking (2011[5]) have identified eight mechanisms that they say are key mechanisms determinants of philanthropy. They are (i) awareness of need; (ii) solicitation; (iii) costs and benefits; (iv) altruism; (v) reputation; (vi) psychological benefits; (vii) values; (viii) efficacy. The Charities Aid Foundation (2014[6]) carried out a survey of donors in 2012 and the top 5 factors identified for the decision to giver were: (i) personal values; (ii) sense of morality/ethics; (iii) particular belief in cause; (iv) faith and (v) personal experience. Other factors, including societal factor may also be relevant. Classifications of this kind are complex and rarely clear-cut. Research into the drivers of philanthropy can be seen as identifying three types of factors: personal; societal and 'other factors'.

Personal factors

Various researchers have identified that personal values; personal experience; belief in specific causes; faith and religion are likely to influence the decision to give. The notion of 'altruism' – the desire to help others, is likely to be part of an individuals' personal values. Individuals and social entities are said to have an altruistic view if they value positively what is good for others. Such an altruistic view leads to giving when the donor views the value of such a gift as greater than the cost to them. This is why a number of tax incentives are aimed at either lowering the price of giving (in the case of tax deductions and credits) or increasing its value (in the case of matching schemes such as Gift Aid). Altruism is, of course, not the only driver of giving, self-esteem as well as social norms and status are examples of other causes of philanthropy that have been identified.

Economic models of philanthropic giving have also identified 'warm glow' (or the 'joy of giving') as a key driver of private giving to philanthropy. Warm glow models suggest that donors receive some positive utility from giving to philanthropy. Andreoni (1990[7]) for example, models philanthropic giving with what he calls 'impure altruistic' motives. In the model, individuals have wealth which they can allocate between consuming a private good and a donation towards a public good. In a purely altruistic model, the donor does not get any utility from their gift and only receives utility from the level of the public good as well as their consumption of the private good. In a purely warm glow model, the donor only receives utility from their gift and their consumption of the private good. In the impurely altruistic model, individuals receive utility from both the level of the public good as well as the gift itself.

Personal experience, such as knowing someone assisted by the philanthropic entity or having some other connection to the entity or cause may also increase the likelihood of giving. Religious faith may also reinforce the sense of moral obligation. Other personal factors may include feeling good about oneself by giving or demonstrating virtue to others. Signalling virtue may be demonstrated by requesting acknowledgement, particularly for large donations, but this of itself may lead others to give. While these personal factors are generally related to individual giving, they may also translate into corporate philanthropy. Of course, it may not be possible to know whether a business gives money because they care or because they believe it will be good for business. Personal wealth will also be important in determining ability to donate to various causes, and much work has been done on the types of entities or causes that are likely to attract high wealth individuals. Several studies show that high end philanthropy is likely to be attracted to arts and cultural entities, with lower end donors favouring religion and welfare.

Societal factors

Some countries appear to have a stronger giving culture than others. This might be influenced by historical factors as well as cultural factors. The Johns Hopkins University Comparative Non-profit Project ('JHU Project') has carried out significant research on the 'social origins' of philanthropy. This theory posits that the political and economic history of a country will be a strong indicator of the size and scope of the non-profit sector. This theory has been considered in Chapter 1. Broader cultural and political factors may also be important e.g. whether the sector is regulated may impact on perceptions of the transparency and reliability of the sector and whether entities are viewed as trustworthy. The way in which the government supports the sector e.g. by making grants may also be significant, although researchers are divided as to whether government support will 'crowd-out' private giving or in fact have the effect of 'crowding-in', that is signalling to private donors that the worthy purpose and/or the entity engaged in carrying out the worthy purpose should be supported.

Government grants vs. tax concessions

The public good and positive externality arguments provide a case for government subsidisation of philanthropic entities and giving. However, as alluded to in the preceding discussion, an alternative to providing tax concessions to subsidise philanthropic activities, is for government to provide direct grants to a philanthropic entity. A grant may be preferable to a tax concession where the government wants greater control regarding the destination of the government support, where the level of "crowding out" of private contributions is low, or where a tax concession is not "treasury efficient" – that is, where it would result in a smaller increase in funding of the philanthropic entity than the tax revenue forgone. Equally, when government grants largely crowd out philanthropic giving, tax concessions may be preferable to government grants, even when tax incentives for philanthropic giving are not treasury efficient. More generally, a tax incentive may still be welfare increasing even if it is not treasury efficient if the benefit to society of the activity funded by the giving is sufficiently large.

The economic literature has focused on two key factors that may influence whether government grants or tax concessions are preferable: crowding out of private contributions and the treasury efficiency of a tax incentive. For the crowding out effect, the hypothesis is that since government grants are financed through taxes, taxpayers will be less inclined to donate to a philanthropic entity that has already received their tax dollars (Andreoni and Payne, 2003[8]). Research suggests that although government support for a non-profit entity might influence private donations, it is unlikely to fully 'crowd-out' private giving (references). There is, in fact, some support for the opposite conclusion, namely that government support for a philanthropic entity may be a signal of the entity's quality, resulting in a crowding-in effect. A variation on the notion of crowding-out is that government grants may discourage an entity from fundraising and that this might then lead to a decline in private support (Andreoni and Payne, 2003[8]).

Whether a tax incentive for philanthropic giving is "treasury efficient" is typically examined by empirical estimation of the price elasticity of philanthropic giving – with an elasticity greater than one indicating the tax incentive is treasury efficient.[3] More generally, the issue of whether philanthropic giving is responsive to tax incentives lowering the price of giving, has prompted significant debate in the econometric literature, mostly based on data from the United States, but more recently also on European data.

A major review by Clotfelter in 1985 found a notable consistency in the findings, with the consensus being that the price elasticity for the population of taxpayers was probably greater than -1, with a range of -0.9 to -1.4. As well, it was observed that the price elasticity appeared to rise with income; there are substantial lags in giving behaviour; and there is little effect of 'crowding out' individual contributions through government contributions (Clotfelter, 1985[9]). While there were tax effects on corporate giving, this appeared to be less than for individual contributions, and there was also evidence that corporations time-shift their donations (Clotfelter, 1985[9]).

The literature has examined both the 'price effects' (including tax rates), which influence the cost of giving, and the 'income effects', such as inflation or economic growth, that affect the income available for philanthropic giving (Clotfelter and Salamon, 1982[10]). Different methodologies used in other studies reported much lower price elasticities (e.g. Steinberg (1990[11]) and Randolph (1995[12])). Nevertheless, an analysis in 2005 of 40 years of research in this field concluded that tax deductions were treasury efficient, and (surprisingly) that the price elasticity was not significantly higher for high-income earners (Peloza and Steel, 2005[13]).

A more recent paper by Backus and Grant (Backus and Grant, 2019[14]) noted that results varied depending on whether studies were based on tax return data of individuals who itemise their deductions (a group substantially wealthier than the average taxpayer), or were based on general population survey data. Backus and Grant concluded that the top 10% of income earners had an elasticity of at least -1, but middle-income taxpayers were less sensitive (see also Fack and Landais (2010[15]), Bönke et. al. (2013[16]), and Bönke and Werdt (2015[17])).[4]

Determining the size of the tax concession

When there is a rationale for government intervention in the form of a tax concession for philanthropic entities or a tax incentive for philanthropic giving to these entities, determining the optimal subsidy level for philanthropic giving is complicated and involves various trade-offs. On the one hand, there are the welfare gains from increasing the provision of the public good or the externality generating activity. On the other, there is the opportunity cost in terms of what the tax revenue that would have otherwise been collected could have been used for (acknowledging the distortionary impact of taxation). Consideration must also be given to the distributional impact of the tax concession. In particular, if the benefit (e.g. the additional warm glow, or the reduced cost of generating the same warm glow) of the tax concession is primarily enjoyed by individuals at the top of the income distribution, this may conflict with the underlying redistributive preferences of government. That said, if the resulting increase in the philanthropic activity primarily benefits lower-income households this will aid redistribution goals. Moreover, tax concessions can only be enjoyed if individuals give away part of their income or wealth to a philanthropic activity, and the mere fact of giving by the rich will reduce income and wealth inequality, irrespective of the design of the tax concession.

The optimal tax literature has attempted to incorporate these trade-offs into a single welfare-maximising framework (see Box 2.2 for more detail on optimal taxation of philanthropic giving). In this regard, Saez (2004[18]) models the optimal tax rate for private contributions to a public good in the presence of warm-glow effects, externalities, crowding out, and the redistributive preferences of government. Subject to a number of strong assumptions, the model suggests that the optimal tax subsidy for philanthropic giving:

- increases with the size of the external effect of a marginal increase in the level of contributions;
- increases with the responsiveness of the donor to the subsidy;
- increases with the level at which public contributions crowd out private contributions;
- and decreases with the proportion of giving made by high-income individuals (assuming government values redistribution).

The optimal tax subsidy itself will depend on the interaction of all these factors. In the model, the optimal subsidy rate is found to decrease with the proportion of giving made by high-income individuals because government is placing a lower weight on the utility that higher income individuals derive from contributing as compared to lower income individuals. The model also suggests that the optimal tax subsidy for philanthropic activity does not necessarily have to be linked to the personal income tax rate schedule, which is the case in countries where contributions are deductible from the personal income tax base.

Box 2.2. Optimal taxation in the presence of externalities

The optimal taxation literature essentially formalises the equity-efficiency trade-off inherent in tax design. Saez (2004[18]) incorporates tax expenditures into the standard optimal tax model of Diamond and Mirrlees (1971[19]). Previous work in the area has considered the presence of externalities (Sandmo, 1975[20]) or public goods (Atkinson and Stern, (1974[21]); Boadway and Keen, (1993[22])).

In Saez's (2004[18]) model there are three goods: private consumption *c*, earnings *z* and a contribution good *g*. A lump sum payment, *R*, is made to all individuals to achieve the government's redistributional goals. The public good nature of charitable contributions or tax expenditures is reflected in the level of contributions per capita G. The model assumes that individuals derive utility from giving through what is often referred to as warm glow (discussed in more detail in Box 2.1). Therefore, the utility function of each individual, $u(c, z, g, G)$, is non-decreasing in c, g, and G and decreasing in z. The government's problem is to set

- the flat tax rate on earnings (τ),

- the tax rate on contributions (t),
- the level of the lump sum payment to all individuals (R),
- and possibly the amount G^0 of the contribution good that it finances directly (i.e. government grants),

in a way that maximises social welfare subject to the requirement that it collects enough tax revenues to finance R, G^0, and government consumption E. Welfare is measured by the weighted sum of individual utilities, where the weights β^h reflect the level at which government values redistribution. For example, if government values redistribution, $\beta^h$is higher for low-income individuals than for high-income individuals.

With a few simplifying assumptions[5], the model produces two sets of expressions for the optimal tax rate t on contributions in a setting where government cannot contribute to the public good, and in a setting where it can. In the first setting, the optimal tax rate t on contributions is given by:

$$t = -e + \frac{1}{\rho}[1 - \beta(G)], \qquad [1]$$

where e denotes the external effect of a marginal increase in the level of the contribution good, ρ is a measure of the price response of private contributions, and $\beta(G)$ denotes the average social welfare weight, weighted by contribution levels. Equation [1] shows that the optimal subsidy rate for contributions is larger when the external effect of a marginal increase in the level of the contribution good is larger. The optimal subsidy rate is lower if the price response of the contribution is small. If on the other hand contributions are perfectly elastic, the optimal subsidy rate would equal the external effect. Finally, if high-income individuals contribute disproportionately to the rest of the population, $\beta(G)$ is assumed to be low (meaning the utility derived from, for example, warm glow is weighted less because it is disproportionately experienced by high-income individuals) and thus the optimal subsidy rate for contributions is lower.

In a setting where the government can contribute directly to the public good (i.e. where crowding out is possible), the optimal tax rate on contributions is given by:

$$t = -1 + \frac{1}{\rho}(1 + \bar{G}_{G^0})[1 - \beta(G)], \qquad [2]$$

where public contributions crowd out private contributions when $\bar{G}_{G^0} < 0$. Equation [2] shows that the optimal subsidy rate increases in $\beta(G)$, the size of the price response, and in the absolute value of crowding out.

A weakness of the model may be that it assumes that private contributions are equally as efficient as direct government contributions. This is likely not the case, due to the fundraising activities that philanthropic entities frequently have to engage in to receive private contributions. On the other hand, the collection of taxes is not without inefficiencies either.

2.2.2. Base-defining rationale

Base-defining theories aim to identify what is properly taxable e.g. as income or profit. This approach recognises that some revenue of philanthropic entities may not be appropriately included in the tax base. These theories assert that income tax can only logically be levied on activities undertaken for profit (see for example, Bittker and Rahdert (1976[23])). For example, for many philanthropic entities, a not insignificant portion of revenue will comprise contributions or membership payments which may not fall within notions of 'income'. Similarly, many expenses incurred in operating the philanthropic entity e.g. the Red Cross providing relief after a disaster, may not fit within notions of deductible expenditure as ordinary and necessary business expenses. There will, of course be some philanthropic entities that derive most of their income from 'business' activities, e.g. hospitals or universities, and it would be relatively easy to calculate taxable income.

Brody (1999[24]) proposes what she describes as a 'sovereignty view' as a variation on the base defining approach. She argues that charities go untaxed because 'Caesar should not tax god' (or its modern secular equivalent). Brody acknowledges that although this might have something to do with the role of religion in early charity, its continued existence can be justified based on the independence of the sector. She argues that a sovereignty view also explains why a subsidy would take the form of tax exemption rather than more logical form of direct grants: for all its imperfections, tax exemption keeps governments out of charities day to day business and keeps charities out of the business of petitioning government for subvention.

Another variation on the tax base theory is that taxation of corporations is sometimes viewed as a proxy for taxation of shareholders, and the philanthropic entity will generally not have shareholders (Rushton, 2007[25]) (Buckles, 2005[26]). Rather those who are beneficiaries of the activities of the philanthropic entity, would not be viewed as appropriate subjects of taxation.

2.2.3. Distributive justice theory

Fleischer (2018[27]) has put forward an alternative to the traditional theories. She argues that support for philanthropy can be justified based on what she terms 'two bedrock principles of Western liberal democracies' namely: limited government and equal opportunity. She argues that the charitable tax subsidies reflect these principles, as expressed in the two theories of distributive justice respectively associated with them, libertarianism and resource egalitarianism. However, she acknowledges problems that may need to be tempered. In her view, the tax subsidies may undermine the principle of limited government by coercing taxpayers to subsidise activities that are not the legitimate purview of government. The subsidies' relation to resource egalitarianism is more complex: she argues that tax subsidies may undermine basic equality of opportunity notions both by subsidising activities that increase the head-start of the wealthy and by giving wealthy taxpayers more say over government resources than poorer taxpayers.

2.3. Arguments against tax concessions for domestic philanthropy

Although there were earlier critics of the tax concessions,[6] the case against the tax concessions was put most powerfully in the 1960s and 1970s by US scholars, most notably Kahn (1960[28]), and Rabin (1966[29]), in the context of the charitable contribution deduction. The arguments of the critics are considered below. Some, but not all of these arguments can be used to critique all tax concessions for philanthropic entities.

2.3.1. Cost of providing the concessions and tax expenditure analysis

The starting point is that tax concessions have a 'cost', that is, they reduce government revenue, and therefore shift the tax burden to other taxpayers. This is relatively uncontroversial. More controversial, however, is a second related argument that the loss in revenue amounts to a 'tax expenditure'. Tax expenditure analysis distinguishes between tax measures which seek to achieve the primary goal of income taxation and those ('tax expenditures') which reduce tax liability to support social or economic objectives. Tax expenditure analysis treats tax exemptions and concessions as government subsidies and evaluates them in the same way as direct expenditures. Tax expenditure analysis has its modern genesis in a seminal US Treasury analysis in 1968 (1968[30]) and subsequent explanations of its implications by Assistant Secretary of the United States Treasury, Stanley Surrey (1970[31])

It is necessary to consider whether tax concessions for philanthropy are, in fact, tax expenditures. This is likely to be the case for property tax exemptions. It is also relatively, although not universally, accepted in the case of the charitable contribution deduction or credit, since the outgoing does not fall into either the recognised category of expenses in the production of income, or expenses that are in a legal or moral sense necessary or involuntary. There has been significantly more contest over whether the income tax exemption (or other relief) is a tax expenditure or could be justified by principles of income taxation ('base-defining theories') (Brody, 1999[24]) as discussed above.

There are a number of issues relating to the notion of tax expenditure analysis in relation to the philanthropic sector:

- Tax expenditure analysis compares the current or prospective tax treatment of taxpayers who receive the concession to a 'benchmark' treatment. (Andrews, 1972[32]) For example, in relation to the gift concession it assumes that the same amount would be donated even without the concession. That is, it assumes that taxpayer behaviour is unchanged and for that reason may not accurately reflect revenue foregone.
- There is some debate about whether the tax exemptions for non-profits are, in fact, tax expenditures. For example, much of the revenue received by philanthropic entities would not be income in most countries, such as donations and government grants. In that sense the exemption may not be a concession in relation to that revenue (Krever, 1991[33]) . There is also an argument, discussed above, that philanthropic entities may be 'outside' the system for taxing corporations.
- There are also concerns about the reliability and accuracy of the tax expenditure statements. For example, tax expenditure estimates are only concerned with statutory provisions and do not take into account situations where income is not taxed for some other reason e.g. because of the common law principle of 'mutuality' or because of the exercise of an administrative discretion (Burton and Sadiq, 2013[34]).
- Perhaps most significantly, there is simply insufficient data available to quantify the tax expenditures in relation to the philanthropic sector across jurisdictions. There are a number of reasons for this: many countries do not calculate tax expenditures – of the countries responding to the survey, less than half were able to provide estimates of revenue foregone in relation to either gift concessions or exemptions from other taxes. In addition, information to estimate the amount of tax that might be payable is often not available e.g. if the philanthropic entity is not required to lodge a tax return, it will not be possible to quantify the amount of revenue foregone. Several countries that did provide responses to the questions relating to the cost of concessions, were only able to provide estimates, suggesting either that it is too soon to provide the data or that the data cannot be accurately identified.

What does appear from the responses provided to our survey is that there is an amount of tax revenue foregone, and hence the tax treatment of philanthropy is an important topic that needs to be considered in detail to ensure that the concessions are justified and well designed.

2.3.2. Inequality and the regressive nature of tax incentives for giving

The pluralism argument considered as part of the subsidy rationale carries with it the importance of a heterogeneous and large number of donors. However, the design of tax-subsidies may lead to incentivising large donations from a small number of wealthy donors rather than smaller donations from a large number of donors.

In this regard, it has been argued that one of the main objections to the philanthropic gift concessions is the inequity that results from its regressive nature (Rabin, 1966[29]). This arises because the deduction is tied to progressive tax brackets. A progressive income tax system results in all deductions 'benefiting' higher income taxpayers more, and the philanthropic contribution deduction has a similar effect of reducing the 'price of giving' more for higher income earners. This is said to conflict with the basic premise of a progressive income tax. It is also said to be inequitable because the evidence is that higher income taxpayers favour different types of charities, typically higher education and arts and culture, than lower income taxpayers which tend to favour religion and welfare (Rabin, 1966[29]) (Atkinson, 1997[35]). This may have implications for the potentially undemocratic nature of tax concessions for giving (discussed below). Incentivising the wealthy more may increase the treasury efficiency of the tax subsidies, that is, if those with higher income levels are more responsive to tax incentives for donations, a tax-subsidy would be more efficient if it focused on big donors[7]

Some authors have observed that this is the effect of all tax deductions and not peculiar to the charitable contribution (Bittker, 1972[36]) Most of the proposals that seek to redesign the philanthropic gift concession attempt to minimise this regressive effect by proposing tax credits or matching schemes (Duff, 2014[37]).

2.3.3. Competitive neutrality

It is often claimed that commercial operations run by non-profit entities have an unfair advantage when competing with for-profit organisations offering the same or similar goods and services (Brody and Cordes (2001[38]); Sharpe (1996[39])). A competitive advantage may result from tax concessions that apply to the income, inputs, or outputs of philanthropic entities, including when they operate businesses. In this context it is argued that philanthropic entities can undercut the competition. The notion of unfair competition underpinned the introduction of the unrelated business income tax ('UBIT') in the United States in the 1950s. Before that time, the tax system followed a 'destination of income' approach under which income, whatever the source, could be earned tax-free if profits were dedicated to a charitable or philanthropic purpose. The introduction of the UBIT was also said to be about preserving the corporate income tax base, and to have been the result of the infamous ownership of Mueller Macaroni by New York University Law School (Brody and Cordes, 2001[38]). The UBIT operates so that to the extent that an activity is 'substantially related' to the entity's tax-exempt purpose, the income is tax-free (and the associated expenses are, essentially, not deductible). By contrast, net income from 'unrelated business activities', is subject to the UBIT, which generally taxes such income at ordinary corporate (or trust) tax rates. Congress, however, has exempted dividends, interest, rents, and royalties from the UBIT.

It has also been argued that an income tax exemption (on all income or on income from related activities) does not provide an unfair advantage to philanthropic entities (Henry et al. (2009[40]); Steuerle (1998[41])). An income-tax exemption is not a subsidy on the cost of inputs; it does not reduce the charities cost of purchasing goods. One commentator has argued that:

> *the zero rate for charity is no more 'unfair' to a [fully] taxed competitor than are the progressive income-tax rates on individuals who conduct business activities in a sole proprietorship or through a partnership, [or a corporation]..... Nor is a non-profit organisation likely to under-price its for-profit competitor (the 'unfair' part of the competition), just as it would not accept a lower return on an (untaxed) passive investment (Weisbrod, 1988[42]).*

The UBIT in the United States, and similar arrangements in other countries to impose tax on 'unrelated' commercial profits, suffer from the difficulty of trying to identify what is related and what is unrelated. It has been noted that very little revenue is in fact collected in the United States from the UBIT. However, the income tax concessions available to philanthropic entities may provide them with some advantages over for-profit firms, such as in relation to cash flow.

In response to these concerns, many countries do tax income or profits derived from commercial operations. A variety of terms are used to signify the types of income being taxed e.g., commercial, business or trading income; and a distinction is often made between commercial activities that are part of the philanthropic activities of the PBO, such as operating a school or hospital (commonly referred to as 'related commercial income') and activities that are not part of the philanthropic activities, other than as providing revenue to undertake those philanthropic activities (commonly referred to as 'unrelated commercial income'). These distinctions are often difficult to make and complex to administer. Some countries either prohibit, or at least tax, commercial activities that are undertaken by for-profit competitors (see Chapter 3).

It has also been argued that concessions related to the cost of inputs, e.g., employee-related tax concessions, do provide a competitive advantage for the commercial activities of philanthropic entities compared with for-profits and that they could be distortionary because they provided an incentive for non-profits to favour the use of the inputs that attracted the concessional taxation treatment.

Distortions from VAT concessions for philanthropic entities typically arise from the exemption from VAT of the output of these entities. The distortion can result in either a competitive advantage or a competitive disadvantage to the philanthropic entity, depending on who is the recipient of the supply and what the recipient uses it for.

A VAT exemption can provide a competitive advantage to a philanthropic supplier if the recipient is a consumer or an entity that uses it as an input to the production of its own exempt supplies. This is because the total price paid by the recipient is lower than the VAT-inclusive price they would pay to a for-profit supplier.

A VAT exemption can create a competitive disadvantage for a philanthropic supplier if the recipient is an entity, such as a for-profit business, that uses the good or service as an input to a taxable supply. This is because input tax credits would allow the purchaser to fully recover any VAT paid on inputs purchased on a non-exempt basis (e.g., from another for-profit business), and the suppliers of those inputs are entitled to input tax credits on their own inputs. In contrast, the philanthropic supplier of exempt goods and services cannot recover the VAT it pays on its inputs. This VAT gets embedded into the cost of the good or service itself and is not recoverable by the purchaser.

When the exemption of the entity's outputs causes a competitive disadvantage, input concessions may reduce the distortion. Either way, philanthropic entities that make VAT exempt supplies will tend to favour the use of inputs with VAT concessions. The VAT treatment of philanthropic entities in countries is discussed in more detail in Chapter 3.

2.3.4. Inflexibility (once introduced difficult to change)

A somewhat related argument is that tax subsidies are not subject to the same periodic review that spending programs receive. As a result, once enacted, there is no need for the recipients to justify the concession. Further, the operation of a tax concession can result in unexpected budgetary outcomes. Tax incentives are usually 'open-ended' – that is, they do not limit the tax benefits a taxpayer can receive. In the case of direct expenditures, if the legislator considers that certain programmed costs in a given year are too high, it can cap them in advance. However, it is often impossible to apply such restrictions to existing tax incentives: they do not require annual approval from the legislator and remain valid as long as the tax law remains unchanged (Lideikyte Huber, 2020[43]).

Perhaps surprisingly it has been suggested that tax expenditure analysis, which aimed to highlight the 'cost' of providing various concessions has resulted in more 'tax expenditures' being included in tax legislation in many jurisdictions. One commentator has noted that the effect of producing tax expenditure statements, 'unintended by the advocates of tax expenditure analysis, has been to legitimate and expand tax expenditures (Zelinsky, 2012[44]).

2.3.5. Undemocratic (the power of large philanthropists)

Reich (2019[45]) argues that much philanthropy is undemocratic and unaccountable. His arguments are really concerned with 'big philanthropy' or large private foundations, and is focussed on the United States.

Reich notes that a fundamental commitment of a democratic society is that individuals have an equal opportunity to influence politics or public policy. This is enshrined in the constitutional protections for 'one person, one vote'. However, by operating through a private foundation, wealthy people are able to uniquely influence public policy. In other words, the power to spend money gives the philanthropist significant political power. This is not restricted to tax-preferred philanthropy e.g., Mark Zuckerberg and Priscilla Chan have established a limited liability company rather than a private foundation to undertake philanthropic activities. This means they will not be subject to IRS rules about disbursements or any reporting requirements. Furthermore, there is no guarantee that big philanthropy will relieve poverty or direct monies to reducing inequality.

Reich (2019[45]) also notes that large foundations are largely unaccountable – they do not have to account to customers or competitors and, unlike politicians, cannot be voted out of office. Reich notes that this was a matter of real concern in the 1880s when the first private foundations were mooted, and refers to the fact that Rockefeller had considerable trouble in setting up his private foundation – and that there were no tax concessions for doing so at the time. Moreover, he argues that instead of moderating the behaviour of big philanthropy, governments encourage it with tax concessions, and the charitable deduction in the US provides benefits that reinforce inequality. However, Reich does not argue that there should be no tax support, but rather that the contribution concession should be a credit rather than a deduction, so that the value of the concession does not give greater support to wealthy donors.

While not accountable to 'customers', foundations are accountable to the tax authorities in staying compliant with the tax rules including using funds for personal benefit and disposing of donated stock within a specified period. In the United States, for example, IRS audits periodically result in imposition of penalties, court cases or even the closing down of a foundation.

2.4. The rationale for incentivising cross-border philanthropy is distinct from that of domestic philanthropy

The discussion above has assumed that the donor and the recipient entity are located in the domestic or home jurisdiction and that the entity pursues its objectives domestically. The notion of cross-border philanthropy raises distinct issues for various stakeholders. Cross-border philanthropy has been defined as 'voluntary contributions from private donors in one country to a recipient in another country' (Moore and Rutzen, 2011[46]).

There is little comprehensive or comparable data on the extent of cross-border philanthropy, although the data that is available suggests that such giving is growing. In many cases, the discussion around cross-border philanthropy revolves around assistance for developing countries or in conflict situations. But potentially, cross-border philanthropy could relate to any of the worthy purposes identified previously. A philanthropic intermediary in Europe has reported that for the period 2010 to 2016 donations channelled related to education accounted for 42%, social matters 18%, heritage and culture 14%, health 11%, international development 11%, environment 3% and religion 1%. (European Foundation Centre, 2017[47]) There is some data on private philanthropy related to development. An OECD survey on private foundation giving for development found that the 147 foundations surveyed provided approximately USD7.96 billion per year to developing countries from 2013 to 2015, representing an average annual increase of 19% (OECD, 2018[48]). The OECD survey also noted that the sources of philanthropic giving for development are highly concentrated. Of the 143 foundations included in the data survey sample, the Bill & Melinda Gates Foundation was by far the most significant philanthropic donor, and 81% of the total philanthropic giving during 2013-15 was provided by only 20 foundations.

The increase in cross-border philanthropy has given rise to concerns in both donor and recipient countries. Donor countries are concerned that the money donated may be diverted for the purposes of terrorism and money-laundering. This was the view taken by the Financial Action Task Force ('FATF') – an intergovernmental body that promotes implementation of anti-money laundering and anti-terrorist financing measures through its recommendations and country evaluations – in its initial assessment of the terrorist financing vulnerabilities and threats faced by the non-profit sector (FATF, 2012[49]). Since 2012, FATF's Recommendation 8 has served as an international policy standard influencing the domestic regulation of cross-border philanthropy. FATF subsequently acknowledged that the non-profit sector's vulnerability to terrorist abuse in Recommendation 8 may have been overstated given that 'not all non-profit organisations are inherently high risk (and some may represent little or no risk at all)' (FATF, 2016[50]).

The initial view about the vulnerability of the non-profit sector has resulted in additional administrative and due diligence requirements being imposed on donors and philanthropic entities seeking to work abroad in many countries. It has also been put forward as one reason for imposing restrictions on tax deductibility of donations as revenue authorities refer to the lack of control over the recipient entity (Charities Aid Foundation, 2016[51]).

Some recipient countries have also viewed foreign funding or foreign activities as a threat to national sovereignty and have imposed restrictions that might include prohibiting foreign funding or requiring all funding to be channelled through the government or approved by government (Indiana University Lilly Family School of Philanthropy, 2018[52]). Concerns about cross-border philanthropy raise some of the same issues as official aid programs, although as noted, not all cross-border aid is concerned with humanitarian or development activities.

There are various ways that cross-border philanthropy can occur where:

- a donor in one country makes a donation directly to a philanthropic entity in another country ('direct cross-border philanthropy'); or
- the donation is made to a domestic philanthropic entity that pursues its programs abroad; or the donation is made to a domestic philanthropic entity that channels the funds to the foreign philanthropic entity ('indirect cross-border philanthropy').

2.4.1. Direct philanthropy

Most countries do not permit tax relief for donations to foreign philanthropic entities (direct cross-border philanthropy), subject to some exceptions that allow tax relief for donations within a geographic region.

The position in the European Union ('EU') is based on the fundamental freedoms of the *Treaty on the Functioning of the EU* ('TFEU') mandating the non-discrimination of philanthropic entities and their donors. This has been confirmed by the case law of the European Court of Justice ('ECJ'), which ensures that the tax autonomy of the Member States is exercised in accordance with the fundamental freedoms as enshrined in the TFEU. In the landmark judgement in *Stauffer* (Case C-386/04), the ECJ held that non-resident philanthropic entities should not be treated differently for tax purposes simply because they are resident in another Member State. Thus, if a Member State grants an income tax exemption to domestic philanthropic entities, it should extend such advantageous tax treatment to entities in other Member States which meet the same conditions as domestic philanthropic entities. In a subsequent judgement in *Persche* (Case C-318/07), which complements the Stauffer case with regard to the tax treatment of donors in respect of cross-border giving, the ECJ ruled that limiting the preferential tax treatment for donations to domestic philanthropic entities while excluding donations to comparable foreign entities is not compatible with the free movement of capital as guaranteed by the TFEU. This means that tax relief should be provided where the foreign charities in a Member State can be shown to be 'comparable' to domestic organisations holding charitable tax status. Practical difficulties remain in demonstrating comparability and the process for seeking tax incentives is complex and burdensome (European Foundation Centre, 2017[47]). The end result is that donors are more likely to use indirect channels (discussed below).

Another regional grouping that permits some cross-border donations to qualify for tax relief concerns the United States. The US permits deductions for philanthropic contributions in its treaties with Canada (USA-Canada DTA, Article XXI), Mexico (USA-Mexico DTA Article 22) and Israel (USA-Israel DTA Article 15A). Like the EU, the basis for the concession is 'comparability' with eligible domestic entities. The rationale for the philanthropic contribution provisions in the tax treaties with Canada and Mexico are close geographic and economic ties. In the case of Israel, the reasons for the preferential tax treatment appear to be the close political ties and the extensive funding of philanthropic activities in Israel by US citizens. There is however no equivalent provision in the Canada-Mexico DTA.

2.4.2. *Indirect philanthropy*

Some countries do permit domestic philanthropic entities to transfer funds or to operate overseas. There are various models that are used to facilitate this. Many international non-government organisations (NGOs) such as the Red Cross, Amnesty International, Greenpeace and World Vision, establish domestic entities in a large number of countries but essentially undertake all their activities offshore. There may also be a process for other domestic philanthropic entities to be approved so that they can undertake activities overseas. The approval processes for such entities tend to be quite onerous and may be restricted to entities that undertake humanitarian and/or development type of activities. In addition to an approval process, there may be a code of conduct imposed to ensure that entities operating overseas, that are eligible for tax preferred donations, meet certain standards. Some countries permit a wider group of domestic entities to be approved. One example is the proliferation of entities designated by the prefix 'friends of' which allows tax relief for donations that are to be used offshore. The need to go through an onerous approval process tends to penalise smaller philanthropic entities. However, a number of countries permit a 'work around' that is, entities can request an approved entity to act as a conduit and pass on donations to intended recipients overseas. The entity acting as a conduit will typically charge a fee of between 5% and 10% and will be responsible for the due diligence associated with the funds being passed on.

An alternative model has developed in Europe where, despite the rulings by the ECJ, cross-border giving is still not easy. A private initiative, the Transnational Giving Europe ('TGE') network, is a partnership of leading European foundations and associations that facilitates tax-efficient cross-border giving within Europe (Transnational Giving Europe[53]).The TGE network covers 19 countries and enables donors, both corporations and individuals, resident in one of the participating countries, to financially support non-profit organisations in other Member States, while benefiting directly from the tax advantages provided for in the legislation of their country of residence. (Transnational Giving Europe[53])

2.4.3. *Arguments in favour of tax incentives for cross-border philanthropy*

As the world becomes more interconnected, the argument that countries should treat cross-border philanthropy in much the same way as domestic philanthropy becomes harder to ignore. If governments accept that they should subsidise domestic philanthropy, arguments can also be made as to why they should subsidise cross-border philanthropy. The arguments in favour of tax incentives fall into two categories: arguments that rely on what might be described as the 'moral imperative' to assist others, especially those less well off, and arguments that are based on the 'self-interest' of the country providing the tax relief.

Moral imperative

The global nature of many of the challenges facing the world require global responses. If the relief of poverty, advancement of health and education and preservation of heritage are worthy purposes domestically, they should be seen as 'deserving' globally and so private contributions should be encouraged (Buijze, 2016[54]). Many issues also transcend borders e.g., environmental concerns, or medical research or public health issues such as fighting pandemics, can only be dealt with by countries cooperating. There is already considerable cooperation in the area of development and humanitarian aid, as well as in responding to international disasters. The global public benefit these causes relate to could be a possible reason for some governments to stimulate private contributions to these causes through tax incentives.

Self-interest

The provision of tax incentives for philanthropy directed abroad can also be justified using the subsidy rationale by refocussing on the notion of what constitutes the public benefit. There may be a number of benefits to a country from engaging with global causes by supporting cross-border giving. Just as aid programs enable a country to develop 'soft power' through cultural and economic influence, so does the provision of support for philanthropy (Jenkins, 2007[55]). Certainly, there appears to have been a level of acceptance of this argument by many countries, given the number of domestic philanthropic entities that already have this support. A more focussed notion of self-interest might be present in allowing tax relief in a regional context, where wellbeing of a region, increased sense of solidarity and strengthening of community ties, may generate benefits for the country in which the donors are present.

2.4.4. Arguments against tax incentives for cross-border philanthropy

There are, of course, a number of arguments that can be raised against providing support for cross-border giving. Those arguments tend to focus on the lack of benefit for the 'donor' country and the lack of oversight of the funds once they leave the country. There may also be concerns for the donors or intermediaries about navigating the legal and cultural terrain of the recipient country.

Public benefit

One possible argument is that the granting of tax relief is a cost to the donor country, and there is no matching benefit in terms of spending within the country (Buijze, 2016[54]). This is in effect confining the public in the public benefit requirement to the domestic sphere, although it could be argued that a country derives a benefit from the provision of assistance to less fortunate countries. In some cases, this is recognised as where there is already tax relief for donations to recognised disasters.

Lack of oversight

Lack of oversight of the actual spending of the private contributions is often raised as a concern (Buijze, 2016[54]). This has been exacerbated by the FATF Report in 2012 describing the vulnerability of the non-profit sector. Although the FATF has since moderated its view, the uneasiness remains. There are also issues concerning compliance of domestic entities operating abroad, often in partnership with local entities, to ensure they comply with any codes of conduct as well as the laws of the country in which they are operating e.g., Oxfam in Haiti. Philanthropic activities abroad are also more difficult to administer, which in some cases may raise accountability and transparency issues.

Costs to donors and/or entities operating overseas

Entities that operate across borders may also encounter additional costs of complying with a different legal regime, having to navigate supply arrangements in countries that may have an element of endemic corruption as well as translation and other costs associated with engaging with local populations (Charities Aid Foundation, 2016[51]). All of these costs may mean that less money is actually being spent on the worthy purpose and may discourage countries from supporting philanthropy across borders.

References

Andreoni, J. (1990), “Impure Altruism and Donations to Public Goods: A Theory of Warm-Glow Giving”, *The Economic Journal*, Vol. 100/401, pp. 464-477. [7]

Andreoni, J. and A. Payne (2003), “Do Government Grants to Private Charities Crowd Out Giving or Fund-raising?”, *American Economic Review*, Vol. 93/3, pp. 792-812. [8]

Andrews, W. (1972), “Personal Deductions in an Ideal Income Tax”, *Harvard Law Review*, Vol. 89, pp. 309-385. [33]

Atkinson, A. and N. Stern (1974), “Pigou, Taxation and Public Goods”, *The Review of Economic Studies*, Vol. 41/1, pp. 119-128. [21]

Atkinson, R. (1997), “Theories of the Federal Income Tax Exemption for Charities: Thesis, Antithesis and Synthesis”, *Stetson Law Review*, Vol. 27, pp. 395-431. [23]

Auten, G., C. Clotfelter and R. Schmalbeck (2000), "Taxes and philanthropy among the wealthy", in J. Slemrod (Ed.), *Does atlas shrug: The economics consequences of taxing the rich*, New York: Russell Sage. [56]

Backus, P. and N. Grant (2019), “How sensitive is the average taxpayer to changes in the tax-price of giving?”, *International Tax and Public Finance*, Vol. 26/2, pp. 317-356. [14]

Bekkers, R. and W. Pamala (2011), “A Literature Review of Empirical Studies of Philanthropy: Eight Mechanisms That Drive Charitable Giving”, *Nonprofit and Voluntary Sector Quarterly*, Vol. 40/5, pp. 924–973. [5]

Bittker, B. (1972), “Charitable Contributions: Tax Deductions or Matching Grants?”, *Tax Law Review*, Vol. 28, pp. 37-63. [36]

Bittker, B. and G. Rahdert (1976), “The Exemption of Non-profit Organisations from Federal Income Tax”, *Yale Law Journal*, Vol. 85/3, pp. 299-358. [24]

Boadway, R. and K. Michael (1993), “Public Goods, Self-Selection and Optimal Income Taxation”, *International Economic Review*, Vol. 34/3, pp. 463-478. [22]

Bönke et. al. (2013), “Charitable giving in the German welfare state: fiscal incentives and crowding out”, *Public Choice*, Vol. 154, pp. 39-58. [16]

Bönke, T. and C. Werdt (2015), “Charitable giving and its persistent and transitory reactions to changes in tax incentives: Evidence from the German taxpayer panel”, *School of Business and Economics Discussion Papers, No. 2015/2*, Free University Berlin. [17]

Brody, E. (1999), “Charities in Tax Reform: Threats to Subsidies Overt and Covert”, *Tennessee Law Review*, Vol. 66/3, pp. 687-763. [25]

Brody, E. and J. Cordes (2001), *The Unrelated Business Income Tax: All Bark and No Bite?*, Urban Institue, Washington, D.C. [38]

Buckles, J. (2005), “Community Income Theory of the Charitable Contributions Deduction”, *Indiana Law Journal*, Vol. 80, pp. 947-988. [27]

Buijze, R. (2016), "Approaches towards the Application of Tax Incentives for Cross-Border Philanthropy", *Intertax*, Vol. 44/1, pp. 14-28. [54]

Burton, M. and K. Sadiq (2013), *The Tax Expenditure Concept in Tax Expenditure Management: a Critical Assessment*, Cambridge University Press, Cambridge. [35]

Charities Aid Foundation (2016), *Donation States: An international comparison of the tax treatment of donations,* https://www.cafonline.org/docs/default-source/about-us-publications/fwg4-donation-states. [51]

Charities Aid Foundation (2014), *Why we give*, https://www.cafonline.org/docs/default-source/about-us-publications/caf-why-we-give-jan14.pdf. [6]

Clotfelter, C. (1985), *Federal Tax Policy and Charitable Giving*, University of Chicago Press, Chicago. [9]

Clotfelter, C. and L. Salamon (1982), "The Impact of the 1981 Tax Act", *National Tax Journal*, Vol. 35/2, pp. 171-187. [10]

Diamond, P. and J. Mirrlees (1971), "Optimal Taxation and Public Production I: Production Efficiency, II Tax Rules", *American Economic Review*, Vol. 61/1, pp. 8-27 and 261-78. [19]

Duff, D. (2014), "The Tax Treatment of Charitable Contributions in a Personal Income Tax: Lessons from Theory and the Canadian Experience" in M. Harding, A. O'Connell and M. Stewart (eds.) *Not-for-Profit Law: Theoretical and Comparative Perspectives*, Cambridge University Press, Cambridge. [37]

European Foundation Centre (2017), *Boosting Cross-Border Philanthropy in Europe: Towards a Tax-Effective Environment*, https://www.efc.be/uploads/2019/03/Boosting-Cross-Border-Philanthropy-in-Europe-Towards-a-Tax-Effective-Environment.pdf [47]

Fack, G. and C. Landais (2010), "Are Tax Incentives for Charitable Giving Efficient? Evidence from France", *American Economic Journal: Economic Policy*, Vol. 2/2, pp. 117-141. [15]

FATF (2016), *Outcomes of the Plenary meeting of the FATF*, Paris. [50]

FATF (2012), *International Standards on Combating Money Laundering and the Financing of Terrorism & Proliferation - the FATF Recommendations*, Paris. [49]

Fleischer, M. (2018), *Research Handbook on Not-For-Profit Law: Subsidizing Charity Liberally*, Edward Elgar, Cheltenham. [28]

Hansmann, H. (1987), *Economic theories of non-profit organizations*, Yale University Press, London. [1]

Henry, K. et al. (2009), *Australia's Future Tax System*, https://treasury.gov.au/review/the-australias-future-tax-system-review. [40]

Indiana University Lilly Family School of Philanthropy (2018), *The Global Philanthropy Environment Index*, https://scholarworks.iupui.edu/handle/1805/15958. [52]

Jenkins, G. (2007), "Soft Power, Strategic Security and International Philanthropy", *North Carolina Law Review*, Vol. 85/3, pp. 773-846. [55]

Kahn, H. (1960), *Personal Deductions and the Federal Income Tax*, Princeton University Press, Princeton. [29]

Krever, R. (1991), *Tax Deductions for Charitable Donations: A Tax Expenditure Analysis*, Australian Tax Research Foundation, Sydney. [34]

Lideikyte Huber, G. (2020), "Tax Incentives for Charitable Giving as a Policy Instrument: Theoretical Discussion and Latest Economic Research", *World Tax Journal*, Vol. 12/3. [43]

Moore, D. and D. Rutzen (2011), "Legal framework for global philanthropy: Barriers and opportunities", *International Journal of Not-for-Profit Law*, Vol. 13/1-2, pp. 5-42. [46]

OECD (2018), *Private Philanthropy for Development*, OECD Publishing, Paris. [48]

Ott, J. and L. Dicke (2016), *The nature of the non-profit sector*, Westview Press, Boulder. [4]

Peloza, J. and P. Steel (2005), "The Price Elasticities of Charitable Contributions: A Meta-Analysis", *Journal of Public Policy and Marketing*, Vol. 24/2, pp. 260-272. [13]

Rabin, E. (1966), "Charitable Trusts and Charitable Deductions", *New York University Law Review*, Vol. 41, pp. 912-925. [30]

Randolph, W. (1995), "Dynamic Income, Progressive Taxes, and the Timing of Charitable Contributions", *Journal of Political Economy*, Vol. 91/1, pp. 371-382. [12]

Reich, R. (2019), *Just Giving: Why Philanthropy is Failing Democracy and How it Can do Better*, Princeton University Press, Princeton. [45]

Rushton, M. (2007), "Why are Non-profits Exempt from the corporate Income tax?", *Non-profit and Voluntary Sector Quarterly*, Vol. 36/4, pp. 662-675. [26]

Saez, E. (2004), "The optimal treatment of tax expenditures", *Journal of Public Economics*, Vol. 88/12, pp. 2657–2684. [18]

Salamon, L. (1987), "Of Market Failure, Voluntary Failure and Third Party Government: Towards the a Theory of Government-Non-profit Relations in the Modern Welfare State", *Non-profit and Voluntary Sector Quarterly*, Vol. 16, pp. 29-49. [3]

Sandmo, A. (1975), "Optimal Taxation in the Presence of Externalities", *The Swedish Journal of Economics*, Vol. 77/1, pp. 86-98. [20]

Sharpe, D. (1996), "Unfair Business Competition and the Tax on Income Destined for Charity: Forty-Six Years Later", *Forida Tax Review,* Vol. 3, p. 367. [39]

Steinberg, R. (1990), "Taxes and Giving: New Findings", *International Journal of Voluntary and Non-profit Organizations*, Vol. 1/2, pp. 61-79. [11]

Steuerle, E. (1998), *The Issue of Unfair Competition*, Center for the Study of Philanthopy and Voluntarism, Institute of Policy Sciences and Public Affairs, Duje University, Durham NC. [41]

Surrey, S. (1970), "Tax Incentives as a Device for implementing Government Policy: A Comparison of Direct Government Expenditures", *Harvard Law Review*, Vol. 83/4, pp. 705-738. [32]

Transnational Giving Europe (n.d.), *How Does it Work?* https://www.transnationalgiving.eu/how-does-it-work. [53]

Treasury Department United States (1968), *Annual Report of the Secretary of the Treasury on the State of Finances for the Fiscal Year Ended June 30,* Washington, D.C. [31]

Weisbrod, B. (1988), *To Profit or Not to Profit: The Commercial Transformation of the Non-Profit Sector*, Oxford University Press. [42]

Weisbrod, B. (1975), *Toward a Theory of the Voluntary Non-Profit Sector in a Three-Sector Economy*, Oxford University Press, Oxford. [2]

Zelinsky, E. (2012), "The Counterproductive Nature of Tax Expenditure Budgets", *Tax Notes*, Vol. 137/12, pp. 1-9. [44]

Notes

[1] The focus of this chapter is on the case for (and against) providing tax concessions for philanthropy. A broader discussion of the benefits to society of philanthropy and the philanthropic sector is beyond the scope of this chapter.

[2] The meaning of the term 'philanthropy' has been discussed in Chapter 1. The term 'philanthropic giving' is used in this report to refer to the act of giving to entities, rather than to individuals, as this is the type of giving that may qualify for tax relief. This report uses the term philanthropic entities to refer to not-for-profit entities with a 'worthy' purpose that typically provide public benefits, and the philanthropic sector to refer to the sector covering such entities.

[3] The price elasticity of philanthropic giving is generally estimated by analysing the effect a change in the price of giving (which, in a country where private contributions are tax deductible, is equal to $(1-t)$, where t is an individual's marginal tax rate) has on the level of philanthropic giving.

[4] There is also evidence that high income taxpayers are more likely to donate large amounts periodically rather than regular amounts every year (Auten, Clotfelter and Schmalbeck, 2000[56]).

[5] The three assumptions are that there are no income effects on earnings at the individual level, that aggregate earnings are not affected by the level of the contribution good and by the tax rate on contributions, and that the compensated supply of contributions does not depend on the tax rate on earnings.

[6] See for example, Chancellor of the Exchequer in UK, William Gladstone put forward a bill in 1863 to abolish the exempt status of charities on the grounds that it was an undiscriminating public subsidy for a large group of organisations not subject to adequate public scrutiny, including elite schools, but was defeated.

[7] See the discussion relating to 'efficiency'.

3 The tax treatment of philanthropic entities

This chapter provides an overview of the tax treatment of philanthropic entities, starting with the qualification process for entities to become recognised Public Benefit Organisations (PBOs) or funds. This includes a description of countries', worthy purpose, public benefit, and not-for-profit requirements, followed by an overview the administrative application and oversight process. The chapter then analyses the different forms of tax relief that philanthropic entities benefit from, starting with the tax treatment of income of philanthropic entities, followed by Value-Added Tax (VAT) benefits, and an overview of other forms of tax relief that PBOs or funds may be eligible for. Finally, the chapter highlights the potential risk of tax avoidance and evasion schemes involving philanthropic entities and the anti-abuse policies countries have put in place as a result.

3.1. Introduction

Philanthropic entities can be categorised as either funds or Public Benefit Organisations (PBOs). For the purposes of this report, funds are entities such as foundations, associations and trusts that hold assets with which they support PBOs to advance a social objective. The term PBO refers to entities that provide goods and services in pursuit of the public benefit. From a tax perspective, philanthropic entities can benefit from tax incentives in a number of ways. Generally, entities with a philanthropic status may be able to receive tax incentivised gifts from individuals and corporations, or receive tax relief directly in relation to their activities (e.g., exemption from income tax, property tax, VAT[1], etc.). For an entity to receive such a status (fund or PBO status), it must meet a number of requirements that can be separated into three broad categories:

- Not-for-profit requirements.
- Worthy purpose requirements.
- Public benefit requirements.

Additionally a number of administrative requirements must be met to determine that the requirements listed above are met. Countries' approaches to ensuring that the requirements are fulfilled, as well as the stringency of the requirements themselves, vary. Only once the requirements are fulfilled are philanthropic entities eligible to benefit from the tax incentives for philanthropy (such as receiving tax incentivised donations, income tax exemption, capital gains tax exemption, and VAT tax exemption or relief).

By subjecting philanthropic entities to the before mentioned requirements, governments may be able to better keep track of, and have some oversight over, their tax expenditures used to incentivise philanthropy. The not-for-profit requirement ensures that the recipients of tax incentives for philanthropy are entities whose primary objective is the public benefit (and not making profit). The not-for profit requirement does not prohibit a philanthropic entity from making a surplus, instead, it generally includes non-distribution requirements so that the surplus is not distributed as dividends or other benefits beyond the scope of the entity's worthy purpose. The worthy purpose requirement allows the government to direct philanthropic funds, as well as its tax expenditures, towards particular social objectives (and possibly away from others). The public benefit requirement ensures that tax expenditures are used to incentivise activities that benefit a large and inclusive enough section of the public. How large and open the circle of beneficiaries needs to be, depends on the country and is discussed in more detail below. Finally, the administrative requirements may help ensure that the state has (and will continue to have) all the information necessary to evaluate whether an entity meets all the other requirements, particularly if there is an administrative body to monitor approvals and compliance.

3.1.1. Key Findings

The main findings of this chapter are that:

- Countries tend to impose not-for-profit, worthy purpose and public benefit requirements to determine eligibility for tax concessions. Welfare, education, scientific research, and healthcare are deemed worthy purposes most frequently across countries. For the public benefit requirement, countries generally stipulate that the benefit must be open to all, that the benefit can be restricted to groups with specific characteristics, or that the characteristics used to specify who can benefit must relate to the fulfilment of the entities' worthy purpose.
- Almost all countries surveyed in this report require philanthropic entities to undergo a specific application process to become eligible for preferential tax treatment. Countries typically follow three broad approaches: the tax administration is responsible for the accreditation process; the responsibility is shared between the tax administration and a competent authority such as an independent commission; or the responsibility lies with another department and not the tax administration.
- Countries' tax relief for the income of philanthropic entities can be separated into two approaches: (1) to exempt all or specific income, or (2) to consider all forms of income taxable, but allow the entity to reduce its taxable income through current or future reinvestments towards the fulfilment of their worthy purpose. Countries following the first approach generally exclude non-commercial income (received gifts or grants) from the tax base. Approaches to dealing with commercial activities and the income generated from those activities, diverge. A common approach is to exempt commercial income that is related to the worthy purpose and tax unrelated commercial income.

- Finally, countries that offer preferential VAT treatment to philanthropic entities tend to exempt them from having to collect VAT on certain (or all) supplies. Because such an exemption can create an input tax burden, some countries have implemented rules that help philanthropic entities reclaim some of their input tax.

This chapter proceeds as follows. Section 3.2 below summarises the not-for-profit, worthy purpose, public benefit and requirements across countries. Section 3.3 gives an overview of the administrative requirements and application processes that countries have put in place to ensure that the other conditions are being met. Section 3.4 discusses the tax treatment of philanthropic entities' income. Section 3.5 gives an overview of countries' VAT treatment of PBOs. Section 3.6 discusses other taxes and tax benefits that apply to philanthropic entities in some countries. Lastly, section 3.7 analyses the potential risk of tax avoidance and evasion schemes that involve philanthropic entities.

3.2. Qualifying for fund or PBO status and preferential tax treatment

3.2.1. Not-for-profit entities and commercial activity

The first requirement is that entities must be 'not-for-profit'. The term originally used was non-profit but in the last 10 years it has been more commonly referred to as 'not-for-profit' to reflect that the entity may make a surplus, but that its purpose is not to make profits. Thus, the requirement does not in itself limit not-for-profit entities from engaging in commercial activity or even acquiring a surplus (as long as that surplus is not distributed as dividends or as unreasonably high salaries or payments). Nevertheless, countries may choose to limit the degree to which philanthropic entities benefitting from tax incentives are able to engage in commercial activity. Furthermore, in a number of countries philanthropic entities must reinvest their surplus towards activities aimed at fulfilling their worthy purpose. If philanthropic entities engage in too much commercial activity or do not reinvest the surplus into a worthy purpose, countries may choose to tax the commercial activity, as well as the remaining surplus, or strip the entities of their preferential tax status altogether.

When philanthropic entities with a preferential tax treatment engage in commercial activity, it may raise unfair competition concerns if the goods or services supplied by the entity are also supplied by non-philanthropic businesses. To overcome this challenge countries may limit the degree to which a philanthropic entity can engage in commercial activity, tax the commercial activity, limit the commercial activity they can engage in, or only limit the preferential tax treatment of commercial activities that lead to unfair competition with for-profit businesses. More detail on this requirement is provided in the section on the tax treatment of income of philanthropic entities below (Section 3.4).

3.2.2. Worthy purpose requirements

In general, a worthy purpose signifies a cause that is deemed by government to be deserving of the philanthropic gifts of a donor and the resources of a fund or PBO. This characteristic is subjective and can be determined by the donors or philanthropic entities that are choosing what cause to focus their philanthropy on. In this report, however, worthy purposes denote a set of causes that philanthropic entities, which are eligible for tax relief, are able to engage in. That is to say that for a philanthropic entity to receive preferential tax treatment, it must have a purpose that the state (e.g. the legislature or tax administration) accepts as worthy. In a number of countries (e.g. Germany and the United States), PBOs need to focus their resources on the worthy purposes they specified in their application for a PBO status. That is to say that they cannot simply change their objective to any of the accepted purposes without going through an administrative process. In Germany, for example, if a PBO wants to change its worthy purpose, or add a new one, it must report this to the fiscal authorities.

Table 3.1 presents a non-exhaustive list of worthy purpose categories that countries may choose to support by giving tax relief to philanthropic entities with such a purpose. In order to compare worthy purpose requirements across countries, the categories listed are umbrella terms that include any related philanthropic causes. Welfare, for example, includes organisations offering shelter to fight homelessness or foodbanks that distribute food to those in need. Other worthy purposes, such as culture, may include museums or particular movie theatres, but may also apply more generally to heritage organisations or entities supporting the arts through grants. The categories that are deemed worthy most frequently across countries are welfare (37), education (35), scientific research (34), and health care (34).

Welfare qualifies as a worthy purpose in all countries listed except for Bulgaria, which is an anomaly as it only extends preferential tax treatment to the Bulgarian Red Cross. However, Bulgaria does offer tax relief to corporate and individual donors that give to entities other than the Bulgarian Red Cross (for more information see Chapter 4). Of the countries listed, Argentina, Bulgaria and Malta are the only countries that do not include education in their list of eligible causes. All countries listed in Table 3.1, except for Chile, Indonesia, Malta, and Bulgaria, include healthcare in their worthy purposes. South Africa, Malta, and Bulgaria are the only countries listed for which scientific research does not qualify as a worthy purpose. On the other hand, consumer protection (22), civil protection (28), animal protection (28), amateur sports (29), and religion (29) are the least frequently recognised worthy purpose categories across the countries listed.

Table 3.1 also shows that some countries have broad definitions for what constitutes a worthy purpose, while other countries have a more narrow definition. For instance, all of the listed categories could be considered worthy purposes in the Czech Republic, Estonia, Germany, Greece, Ireland, Israel, Lithuania, New Zealand, Norway, Portugal, Romania, the Slovak Republic, Slovenia, and the United States. Argentina, Bulgaria, Chile, Indonesia, Malta, and South Africa, on the other hand, all have a more narrow definition of what constitutes a worthy purpose.

In the majority of countries, funds and PBOs that meet the worthy purpose and public benefit requirements to receive tax incentivised donations also meet the conditions to receive preferential tax treatment and vice versa. However, this is not the case in Australia, Bulgaria, Canada, Germany, New Zealand, Norway, Sweden, South Africa, and the United States.

In countries like Bulgaria, the worthy purpose conditions for incentivising giving are less narrow than those determining whether a fund or PBO can receive direct tax support. In Bulgaria, funds and PBOs with a qualifying worthy purpose can receive tax incentivised donations but only the Bulgarian Red Cross is eligible to receive preferential tax treatment directly.

In Canada, worthy purpose conditions for incentivising giving are not identical to those determining whether a fund or PBO can receive direct tax support. In Canada tax-favoured donations can be made to funds and PBOs that engage in the worthy purpose activities listed in Table 3.1 as well as to: journalism organisations; municipal or public bodies performing a function of government in Canada; universities outside of Canada with Canadians in the student body; registered funds and PBOs outside Canada to which Her Majesty has made a gift; and the United Nations and its agencies. In general, however, it is more onerous for an organisation in Canada to become a registered charity organisation benefiting from tax-favoured donations than it is to be considered a non-profit.

Conversely, in Norway, Sweden and South Africa, the conditions for receiving tax incentivised donations are more restrictive than those for receiving tax support directly. In Norway, for example, only a specific subset of the philanthropic entities eligible for tax exemption qualify to receive donations from which the donating party can claim a tax deduction. In order to qualify, the receiving entity's worthy purpose must fall within the following categories: healthcare; activities directed at children and young people engaged in culture or amateur sports; religion; human rights; development aid; disaster relief; and environmental and cultural preservation. In South Africa, funds and PBOs are only eligible to receive tax incentivised donations if their worthy purpose falls within healthcare, welfare and education.

Table 3.1. Worthy purposes by country

	Welfare	Education	Science	Health-care	Cultural	Environmental	Disaster relief	Civil society	Community service	Human rights	Development finance	Child-care	Humanitarian aid (abroad)	Religious	Amateur sport	Animal protection	Civil-protection	Consumer protection	Other
Argentina	X		X	X					X			X		X					X[1]
Australia	X	X	X	X	X	X	X	X	X	X	X		X	X	X	X	X		X[2]
Austria	X	X	X	X	X	X	X	X		X	X	X	X	X	X	X	X		
Belgium	X	X	X	X	X	X	X	X	X	X	X	X	X			X	X		
Bulgaria	X	X		X	X	X	X	X	X			X	X	X					X[3]
Canada	X	X	X	X	X	X	X	X	X	X	X	X	X	X	X	X	X		
Chile	X	X	X		X		X		X		X	X			x		X		
Colombia	X	X	X	X	X	X	X	X	X	X	X	X		X	X		X		
Czech Republic	X	X	X	X	X	X	X	X	X	X	X	X	X	X	X	X	X	X	
Estonia	X	X	X	X	X	X	X	X	X	X	X	X	X	X	X	X	X	X	
Finland	X	X	X	X	X	X		X	X			X			X			X	X[4]
France	X	X	X	X	X	X	X	X	X	X	X	X	X	X		X	X	X	
Germany	X	X	X	X	X	X	X	X	X	X	X	X	X	X	X	X	X	X	
Greece	X	X	X	X	X	X	X	X	X	X	X	X	X	X	X	X	X	X	
India	X	X	X	X	X	X	X	X	X	X	X	X	X	X	X	X	X	X	X[5]
Indonesia	X	X	X				X							X	X				X[6]
Ireland	X	X	X	X	X	X	X	X	X	X	X	X	X	X	X	X	X	X	
Israel	X	X	X	X	X	X	X	X	X	X	X	X	X	X	X	X	X	X	
Italy	X	X	X	X	X	X	X	X	X	X	X	X	X		X	X		X	
Japan	X	X	X	X	X	X	X	X	X	X	X	X	X	X	X	X	X	X	
Latvia	X	X	X	X	X	X	X	X		X		X	X		X	X	X		
Lithuania	X	X	X	X	X	X	X	X	X	X	X	X	X	X	X	X	X	X	
Luxembourg	X	X	X	X	X	X	X	X	X	X		X	X	X	X	X	X		
Malta	X									X			X						
Mexico	X	X	X	X	X	X	X	X	X	X	X	X				X	X	X	X[7]
Netherlands	X	X	X	X	X	X	X	X	X	X	X	X	X	X		X	X		
New Zealand	X	X	X	X	X	X	X	X	X	X	X	X	X	X	X	X	X	X	
Norway	X	X	X	X	X	X	X	X	X	X	X	X	X	X	X	X	X	X	X[8]
Portugal	X	X	X	X	X	X	X	X	X	X	X	X	X	X	X	X	X	X	
Romania	X	X	X	X	X	X	X	X	X	X	X	X	X	X	X	X	X	X	
Singapore																			X[9]
Slovak Republic	X	X	X	X	X	X	X	X	X	X	X	X	X	X	X	X	X	X	
Slovenia	X	X	X	X	X	X	X	X	X	X	X	X	X	X	X	X	X	X	X[10]
South Africa	X	X		X		X					X			X	X				
Sweden	X	X	X	X	X	X	X	X		X	X		X	X	X				
Switzerland	X	X	X	X	X	X	X	X	X	X	X		X			X		X	
United Kingdom	X	X	X	X	X	X	X	X	X	X	X	X	X	X	X	X	X	X	
United States	X	X	X	X	X	X	X	X	X	X	X	X	X	X	X	X	X	X	X[11]
Frequency	**37**	**35**	**34**	**34**	**33**	**33**	**33**	**32**	**31**	**31**	**30**	**30**	**30**	**29**	**29**	**28**	**28**	**22**	

Notes:

1. Charity, Art and Literature, Unions
2. Sporting clubs in general, employer and employee associations, trade unions, associations promoting primary and secondary resources and tourism.
3. The activities of the Bulgarian Red Cross.
4. Finland does not have an exhaustive list of worthy purposes and categories identified in this table are from a list of non-exhaustive examples in the income tax act.
5. Yoga and the advancement of any other object of general public utility.
6. Scholarship awarding; environmental preservation.

7. The worthy purposes for Mexico in this table, are limited to those that receive deductible donations. Other worthy purposes, such as amateur sports, religious or some mutual societies can only benefit from preferential income tax treatment.
8. The tax act does not contain a specification of what constitutes an entity with worthy purposes or activity of public benefit.
9. Recognises charitable purposes as defined in common: (i) relief of poverty; (ii) advancement of education; (iii) advancement of religion; and (iv) other purposes beneficial to the community, such as health-promotion, advancement of arts and heritage, and environmental protection.
10. Must be considered "generally useful" (*splošnokoristen*).
11. Amateur athletics (added for 1976 Olympics).
Source: OECD Taxation and Philanthropy Questionnaire

3.2.3. Public benefit requirements

For an entity to be philanthropic, its worthy purpose must be for the public benefit. Generally speaking this means that the worthy purpose of a fund or PBO has to benefit the public as a whole or a sufficient section of the public (sometimes referred to as a charitable or public class). If the circle of beneficiaries does not constitute a sufficient section of the public, the entity's purpose would only be for the private benefit of a few individuals and therefore not meet the necessary requirements to qualify as a philanthropic entity worthy of receiving preferential tax treatment.

Typically, some worthy purposes are considered to benefit the public as a whole, meaning that the benefit is not limited to people who satisfy a particular criteria. Such worthy purposes may include, for example, protecting the environment, scientific discovery, or animal protection. Other worthy purposes, however, tend to benefit a circle of beneficiaries and countries typically regulate the size and/or the criteria used to specify who can benefit. An example of a worthy purpose that specifies who can benefit, is a disability support group. Generally, countries consider a circle of beneficiaries that is defined by need to be a sufficient section of the public.

Some entities, however, define their circle of beneficiaries using characteristics such as age, disability, gender, sexual orientation, race, nationality, pregnancy, or religion. Public benefit rules addressing this issue can be categorised into three approaches: countries may restrict philanthropic entities from using individual characteristics to define who can benefit altogether; countries may approve a list of characteristics (sometimes referred to as protected characteristics) that philanthropic entities are permitted to use in order to specify who can benefit; or countries may only allow limiting benefits to people with these characteristics if the criteria can be justified in relation to the worthy purpose (e.g., under this approach, a PBO committed to the health and well-being of pregnant women can use pregnancy as a characteristic to limit the circle of beneficiaries but cannot specify that only individuals of a particular religion may benefit from its services).

The benefit must be open to all and cannot be restricted

Some countries (e.g. Austria, France, and Slovenia) stipulate that the circle of beneficiaries needs to be open to the public and cannot be restricted by specific characteristics of individuals such as gender, sex, religion, or origin. In Austria, the circle of beneficiaries has to be the general public in the sense that the activity is in line with public interest in regard to intellectual, cultural or material subjects. Furthermore, the circle of beneficiaries of public benefit activities cannot be restricted by specific characteristics, including sex and gender. In Slovenia, there is no minimum number of people that need to be in the circle of beneficiaries and the benefit cannot be limited by individual characteristics including skill, gender, religion, nationality, or origin.

In France, PBOs are referred to as general interest organisations (*association d'intérêt general*) and can issue tax receipts to their donors so that they can benefit from the tax incentive for giving. To be eligible for such a status, an entity must meet the public benefit requirement of not working for the benefit of a small circle of people. Furthermore, the interests and activities of a general interest organisation must be able to benefit everyone, without being limited to any criteria (e.g., race, sex, profession, or religion). Additionally, a general interest organisation can become an association of public utility (*association d'utilité publique*). An association of public utility can receive, in addition to gifts which any PBO can benefit from, donations and bequests. To become an association of public utility, a PBO must fulfil additional public benefit requirements, such as having an influence and outreach beyond the local context and a minimum of 200 members.

The benefit can be restricted by specified characteristics

A number of countries allow philanthropic entities to restrict who can benefit using certain characteristics (e.g., Chile, Colombia, Greece, Israel, Lithuania, Malta, Mexico, Norway, Romania, Singapore, the Slovak Republic, South Africa, and Switzerland). In Colombia and Switzerland, for example, entities are allowed to benefit only one gender but may not use any other characteristics to further restrict who can benefit. In Mexico, no restrictions are allowed regarding origin, religion, or nationality. However, restrictions based on gender and potentially other characteristics are possible. For instance, philanthropic entities can concentrate their support on single mothers. The rule is that they must fulfil their specific purpose.

In Israel philanthropic entities can target only one gender and can specify origin, or nationality. In Latvia a worthy purpose can benefit target groups such as children, young people, people in poverty, and disabled people but the philanthropic activity must reach people regardless of their skill, origin, religion or nationality.

In Lithuania there are no rules that prohibit entities selecting their beneficiaries based on gender or skill as long as the activity is in line with the Law on Equal Opportunities for Women and Men. The philanthropic activities of the entities must also reach people regardless of their origin, religion, or nationality. In Romania, on the other hand, entities cannot benefit only one gender but may specify their circle of beneficiaries using other individual characteristics such as skill, religion, or nationality. Singapore permits entities to target only one gender if their activities also benefit the public as a whole. For example, PBOs such as the Boys Brigade and Girls Brigade engage in activities that benefit the wider community. Chile, Greece, Malta and the Slovak Republic have no rules regarding whether or not entities can limit their philanthropic activity to individuals with particular characteristics.

The characteristics used to specify who can benefit must relate to the worthy purpose

Lastly, a number of countries (Australia, Belgium, Canada, Estonia, Germany, India, Japan, the Netherlands, New Zealand, Portugal, South Africa, Sweden, and the United States) only permit philanthropic entities to limit the circle of beneficiaries to people with particular characteristics if it can be justified with their worthy purpose.

In Australia, philanthropic entities must have a purpose that provides a benefit to the general public or a sufficient section of the general public. Whether a purpose benefits a sufficient section of the general public is to be assessed on registration. Certain PBOs are presumed to be for the public benefit, such as those involved in the relief of poverty. PBOs can limit their beneficiaries to a gender if such a restriction relates to the worthy purpose. For example, a charity providing support to victims of domestic violence may be permitted to provide services only to women, and a charity with a purpose of advancing health may provide services only to men with mental health concerns. Similarly, a tax-exempt PBO may promote a specific religion or provide services to people who have migrated to Australia from a specific country.

Belgian law prohibits discrimination on grounds of age, sexual orientation, marital status, birth, property, religious or philosophical belief, political conviction, language, present or future state of health, disability, physical or genetic characteristic or social origin. However, if the PBO receives its accreditation for the purpose of benefiting a defined category of people (e.g. disabled persons), it may limit its action to this specific section of the public. Such PBOs include associations that specifically defend women's rights with a view to achieving greater gender equality. Regarding the geographic reach of an entity's activities, specific criteria are defined by both the Ministry of Finance and the competent authority:

- Scientific research: Entities must be active throughout the national or regional territory and not only at the local level.
- Culture: Entities must be active throughout the national territory and not only at the local level, and may not be related to teaching activities which fall within the responsibility of the Ministry of Education.
- Protection of nature and the environment: Entities must demonstrate that their activities are of a continuous and sustainable nature, have an area of influence that extends to more than one municipality.
- Assistance to war victims, to the disabled, the elderly, minors of protected age and people living in poverty: Entities must be active throughout the national territory and not only at the local level.
- Aid to victims of natural disasters recognised in Belgium, aid to developing countries, assistance to victims of major industrial accidents and sustainable development: Entities must be active throughout the national or regional territory and not only at the local level.
- Donations to associations that assist the disabled may only benefit the disabled and not their families.
- For cultural associations, activities must be organised in three different provinces. Local associations are excluded. A calendar of activities and an activity report for the past year must be provided.

In Canada an entity that benefits only one gender may be eligible to be a registered PBO and receive preferential tax treatment if it can show that there is a need to do so. All types of limitations to access have the potential to prevent an entity from being registered as a PBO, although to differing degrees. Entities that want an outright restriction of benefit or exclusion of services have a far greater burden of establishing public benefit than those entities that want only to focus attention on a specific group, but extend service delivery to the general public. Most importantly, when a PBO proposes to restrict the beneficiaries of an activity in any way, the nature of the restriction must be clearly linked to the proposed benefit. For example, a religious charity may well be limited to those who are adherents of that particular religious faith, whereas that same limitation would not suffice for an organisation established to assist persons with a disability. Overall, an entity with an unreasonably limiting service or programme, will not meet the public benefit requirements, unless the restrictions are shown to be relevant to achieving the charitable purpose.

Within the public benefit requirements, there are several sub-requirements. For instance, the benefit should generally be tangible; the beneficiaries must be the public-at-large or come from a sufficient segment of the public as determined by the charitable purpose being considered; the entity may not otherwise benefit private individuals except under certain limited conditions; subject to some exceptions, the entity cannot exist for the benefit of its members; the entity cannot charge fees for its services where the effect of the charge would unduly exclude members of the public.

In Estonia, the benefits of the philanthropic activity must be identifiable and justifiable, but not quantifiable. Philanthropic activities cannot only be aimed at individuals with specific characteristics and need to benefit a sufficient section of the public. If targeting only one gender can be justified with the entity's worthy purpose, that would be considered a sufficient section of the public. The worthy purpose must not benefit a fixed number of people. If the not-for-profit entity has members, it must have two or more.

In Germany, the worthy purpose must be dedicated to the altruistic advancement of the general public. In 2017 the federal fiscal court in Germany decided that a PBO cannot be for the common-benefit if it excludes women from its membership without a relevant justification. The ruling has led to public debate. Member based entities are eligible for preferential tax treatment. There is a minimum number of seven members in order to establish a registered association. Non-registered associations may also be eligible for the preferential tax treatment.

In India a philanthropic entity cannot be for a private religious purpose or be a trust "for the benefit of any particular religious community or caste". Activities may cater to women, children and vulnerable sections of society. Similarly in Japan, the beneficiaries can be specified by characteristics such as gender, religion, or ability as long as the there is a relevant connection with the worthy purpose. For example, a women's rights organisation can target people based on gender, a religious organisation can target people based on religion, or an educational facility can target people based on skill or ability.

In Italy, most philanthropic entities are open to all, without restrictions to beneficiaries. However, some kinds of entities can restrict the benefits from their activities to some groups with characteristics related to the PBO's worthy purpose (for example, philanthropic organisations that help disadvantaged people to find employment).

In the Netherlands, there is no specific definition of 'public benefit'. In the legislation as well as in case law, this term is neutrally described, so that there may be different opinions as to whether the organisation benefits the public. The circle of beneficiaries can be restricted by the entity if, for example, its worthy purpose is promoting equal treatment of men and women and therefore focusses only on women. Importantly, however, the purpose and activities of a philanthropic entity may not violate the constitution or international treaties, which forbid discrimination based on (amongst other characteristics) gender, race and religion.

In New Zealand, philanthropic activity needs to benefit a sufficient section of the public. Imposing fees for access to a benefit can be acceptable if done reasonably. For example, by providing a benefit that can only be accessed by members of a certain group (e.g. a scholarship for Māori students). Limits on public access must be reasonable and appropriate. When members of an organisation can also benefit, any limitations on membership must also be reasonable in the context of the benefit to the public. For example, a society of doctors set up to improve medical practice may reasonably limit its membership to qualified doctors, because the real benefit is to the wider public from the improvement of public health.

In Sweden, member based entities are eligible if they are open to the public. Nevertheless, they are allowed to make certain restrictions (e.g., age limit for a shooting club, the ability to play an instrument for an orchestra etc.). Similarly, their activities can target only one gender only if this target is naturally associated with the objective of the member based entity.

In the United States, entities need to support a charitable "class", and not provide a more than insubstantial private benefit. There is not a specific number that constitutes a charitable class, however it must either be large enough that potential beneficiaries cannot be individually identified, or sufficiently indefinite that the community as a whole, rather than a pre-selected group of people receive benefits. Clubs and associations that are not charities are eligible for limited preferential tax treatment and there is not a specific minimum number of members needed.

3.3. Tax Administration and application processes

3.3.1. Application process

To ensure that the entities receiving preferential tax treatment meet the public benefit, worthy purpose, and not-for-profit conditions, almost all countries surveyed in this report require philanthropic entities to undergo a specific application process to become eligible for preferential tax treatment. The assessing body must therefore approve entities before they are able to receive the preferential tax treatment. In a number of countries (e.g., Canada, France, Ireland, New Zealand, Colombia, and Germany), entities are able to apply before starting to operate. An advantage of this approach may be that entities can address issues from the start and thereby reduce the chance that they do not receive preferential tax status after they have already started operating. On the other hand, the shortcoming of such an approach may be that countries grant entities preferential tax status without being able to evaluate their performance or operations. Following up with the entity after it receives its initial tax privileges is a potential way in which countries could address this issue. For example, within three years after the approval of the status, the German tax administration monitors whether the requirements of the preferential tax treatment are still met. In France, the tax administration has six months to respond from the date of receipt of the application. After six months without notification of an administration agreement, a general interest association can receive preferential tax treatment. When it is negative, the tax administration must justify its decision. If the general interest organisation does not agree with the tax administration, it can send a second application within two months.

On the other hand, some countries (e.g., Belgium, Romania, and Argentina), require entities to have already been operating for a minimum period of time before they can apply. In Belgium, for example, PBOs must provide an activity report for the past year as well as a detailed statement of the current year's projects. In Argentina, entities that apply to receive PBO status with preferential tax treatment must demonstrate an initial (and largely symbolic, given recent inflation rates) social capital of ARS 1 000 in the general case, and ARS 200 for entities with a worthy purpose to promote economic, social and cultural rights of vulnerable groups and/or ethnic communities with a poverty or vulnerability status. In the case of foundations, the minimum initial social capital required is ARS 80 000. In Romania, entities must have been operating for at least three years and have achieved part of their philanthropic objectives before they can apply for tax relief.

In some countries (e.g., Norway and Lithuania), there is no application process for philanthropic entities to receive some of the preferential tax treatments. The benefits of not having an application process for preferential tax treatment may be to reduce the administrative burden on the entities as well as on the assessing body but this may raise issues of accountability. In Norway, for instance, there is no application process for qualifying philanthropic entities to benefit from direct preferential tax treatment. For funds and PBOs to be able to receive tax-incentivised donations, however, the entity must apply to the tax administration and fulfil the accounting and auditing requirements. Similarly, in Lithuania, there is also no registration process for philanthropic entities to receive most forms of preferential tax treatment, but if a PBO would like to receive sponsorship, it must apply to become an eligible sponsorship recipient.

3.3.2. Assessing body

To ensure that philanthropic entities meet the necessary conditions to benefit from preferential tax treatment, countries task their tax administration, other ministries or independent commissions with accreditation and oversight responsibilities. Table 3.2 shows that the majority of countries (16) have specific departments or units within their tax administration and/or Ministry of Finance that are dedicated to the philanthropic sector. Such countries may or may not have another department or independent body that oversees the funds and PBOs. To ensure that tax relief is targeted efficiently, the oversight body has to be able to determine whether the entity is productively fulfilling its worthy purpose. For PBOs with a cultural purpose, for example, such a determination may require a very different set of expertise as for PBOs with a welfare or environmental objective.

Table 3.2. Departments devoted to the tax treatment of philanthropic entities

Countries <u>with</u> a specific department/unit in the Ministry of Finance and/or tax administration that is dedicated to philanthropy:	*Argentina; Australia; Belgium; Canada; Estonia; Germany; India; Ireland; Israel; Italy; Malta; Mexico; the Netherlands; New Zealand; Singapore; South Africa; Sweden; Switzerland; and the United Kingdom and the United States[1];*
Countries <u>without</u> a specific department/unit in the Ministry of Finance and/or tax administration that is dedicated to philanthropy:	*Austria; Bulgaria; Chile; Colombia; Czech Republic; France; Indonesia; Lithuania; Latvia; Norway; Portugal; Romania; the Slovak Republic; and Slovenia*

Note:

1. In the United States, the IRS has an office devoted to Exempt Organizations (including philanthropic entities).

Source: OECD Taxation and Philanthropy Questionnaire

Table 3.3 indicates where within the government the administrative process of accrediting and overseeing philanthropic entities takes place. Countries typically follow one of three broad approaches: the tax administration is responsible for the accreditation process; the responsibility is shared between the tax administration and a competent authority; or the responsibility lies with another department and not the tax administration.

Table 3.3. Administering body by country

	Tax administration	Ministry of Finance	Another ministry	Independent commissions	A combination	Other
Argentina	X					
Australia	X			X[1]	X[2]	
Austria	X					
Belgium	X	X			X[3]	
Bulgaria			X[4]			
Canada	X	X				
Chile	X				X[5]	
Colombia	X					
Estonia	X					
Finland	X					
France	X		X[6]			
Germany	X	X				
Greece	X				X[5]	
India	X					
Indonesia	X		X[7]			
Ireland	X			X[8]		
Israel	X					
Italy	X		X[9]			
Japan	X		X[3]			
Latvia	X					X[10]
Lithuania						X[11]
Luxembourg	X				X[12]	
Malta	X	X				
Mexico	X					
Netherlands	X					
New Zealand	X		X[13]			
Norway		X[14]				
Portugal	X				X[5]	
Romania			X[15]			
Singapore			X			
Slovak Republic	X					
Slovenia	X		X[3]			X[16]
South Africa	X					
Sweden	X					
Switzerland	X					
United Kingdom	X					
United States	X					X[17]

Notes:

1. The Charities Registration Board is responsible for all decisions regarding the registration and removal of organisations from the charities register; Australian Charities and Not-for-profits Commission.
2. Eligibility for some concessions requires endorsement by both the ATO and the ACNC.
3. PBOs must be accredited by the Ministry of Finance/ tax administration as well as the competent authority (e.g. Ministry for Development Cooperation for humanitarian NGO's).

4. Registry Agency to the Ministry of Justice.
5. Tax administration and other competent entities, depending on the activity (e.g., social security, ministry of education, etc.).
6. Ministry of Interior ("Ministère de l'Intérieur").
7. Ministry of Law and Human Rights (for the record of establishment and financial report.
8. The Charities Regulatory Authority.
9. With the implementation of the reform, the Ministry of Labour and Social Policies will be in charge of administering the new National Register of PBOs together with the Tax Administration.
10. The Commission is a collegial consultative body which includes, in equal number, authorized officials as well as representatives of associations and foundations.
11. Centre of Registers under the supervision of Ministry of the Economy and Innovation of the Republic of Lithuania.
12. The Ministry of Justice as well as the Direct Tax Administration play a role in the administration of PBOs and funds.
13. Charities Services (Department of Internal Affairs).
14. There is no accreditation process. However, organisations can request either a binding or advisory advance ruling from the tax administration with respect to whether it would qualify for tax exempt status.
15. General Secretariat of the Government.
16. Administrative office (as part of state).
17. Organizations are generally registered as non-profits by the states before they apply to the IRS to receive preferential tax treatment.
Source: OECD Taxation and Philanthropy Questionnaire

Tax administration

In the majority of countries, the responsibility over the accreditation process lies within the tax administration (see Table 3.3). This is the case in, for example, Argentina, Austria, Colombia, Estonia, Finland, India, Israel, Mexico, the Netherlands, Norway, the Slovak Republic, South Africa, Sweden, and Switzerland. In all of these countries, entities applying for preferential tax treatment need to apply directly to the tax administration, which is then tasked with reviewing the provided materials and determine eligibility. The majority of the countries following this approach (Argentina, Australia, Estonia, India, Israel, Mexico, the Netherlands, the Slovak Republic, South Africa, and Sweden) have a department or unit in their tax administration that is dedicated to philanthropy (see Table 3.2). For those countries in particular, a benefit of this approach may be to centralise the oversight process. On the other hand, this approach may require the tax administration to devote a significant amount of resources to entities that pay little to no taxes. Depending on the political environment, there could be competing pressures to prioritise revenue-raising activities over administering tax incentives for funds and PBOs. In such cases, there may be advantages in involving other parts of the government.

The Colombian approach is unique because it allows the public to be involved in the accreditation process. As Figure 3.1 below shows, once the submission of the request and the fulfilment of the online registry are correctly completed, the information of the entity will be published online, allowing the public to comment on it for five business days. After this, the Colombian tax administration will have four months to decide if it approves or denies the request of the entity to be classified as a philanthropic entity benefiting from the special tax regime (see the Figure 3.1 for more details on the timeline).

Figure 3.1. Colombian special tax regime application process

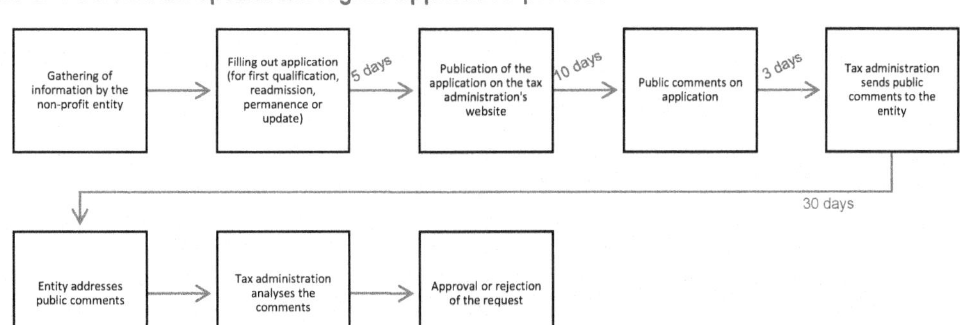

Note: The days in the infographic correspond to business days
Source: OECD Taxation and Philanthropy Questionnaire

Tax administration as well as other competent authority

In a number of countries (e.g., Australia, Belgium, Canada, Chile, France, Germany, Greece, Indonesia, Ireland, Japan, Latvia, Malta, Portugal, Slovenia, the Unites States) the administrative responsibilities are shared between the tax administration and other competent authorities. The range of activities that philanthropic entities may engage in is typically very broad and thus it could be challenging to properly assess and oversee entities that engage in fields that are not within the expertise of the tax administration or ministry of finance. Especially for countries that do not have a specific department or unit devoted to administering philanthropic entities (see Table 3.2), the additional resources and expertise of another competent authority may be an advantage. Some countries (e.g., Belgium, France, Slovenia, Portugal, and Chile) have addressed this challenge by assigning a competent authority in addition to the tax administration to oversee philanthropic entities. For example, the tax administration as well as the ministry of culture may process a cultural heritage organisation's application for PBO status. In France, general interest organisations must register with the tax administration, while those seeking to be additionally recognised as being of public utility, must send their application to the Ministry of the Interior.

Another approach is to make an independent commission of experts responsible for the accreditation and oversight process (e.g., Australia, Ireland, Latvia and New Zealand). Having a dedicated commission of experts as an oversight body may have the advantage of overcoming institutional constraints of tax administrations. The primary purpose of a tax administration is the collection of tax revenue on behalf of citizens to fund the work of the government (OECD, 2019[1]). Managing a largely untaxed philanthropic sector, may therefore compete with limited resources needed for revenue raising activities. Dedicated commissions are typically able to collect and analyse data, develop expertise in the field of philanthropic entities, publish reports, and offer a clear point of contact for funds and PBOs.

Nevertheless, tax administrations have a crucial proficiency of the applicable tax rules and the way in which they interact with the country's overall tax system. As a result, countries with commissions typically follow two approaches to incorporate the tax administration in the oversight process. The first approach, followed by Latvia, is to include tax administration officials in their commissions. The second approach, followed by Australia, Ireland and New Zealand, is to make use of a two-step process where entities must apply for approval to both a commission dedicated to philanthropic entities and the tax administration.

For example, in Latvia, entities are evaluated by a commission that is a collegial consultative body which includes (in equal number) authorized officials from the Ministry of Finance, the Ministry of Education and Science, the Ministry of Culture, the Ministry of Welfare, the Ministry of Justice and the Ministry of the

Environment and Regional Development, as well as representatives of funds and PBOs who are competent and have experience in one of the worthy purpose fields.

In Ireland, philanthropic entities must firstly apply to an independent charity commission in order to be granted philanthropic status. Following that, philanthropic entities can apply to the tax administration for tax exemption. To be eligible for tax concessions in New Zealand, charities must first register with the Charities Services (a group within the Department of Internal Affairs with an independent charities registration board of three people). As part of the registration process, entities must disclose to Charities Services if they operate, or intend to operate, overseas. This information is passed on to the tax administration to further consider the charity's eligibility for income tax concessions and for receiving tax-incentivised donations. Other PBO's that may be fully income tax exempt, but are not considered charities in New Zealand (e.g., amateur sports bodies, or 'friendly societies') must apply to the tax administration directly and provide a copy of their company rules to ensure their funds can only be applied to their worthy purposes before the tax exemption is approved. Other clubs and associations, which are not eligible for full income tax exemptions, are also required to supply the tax administration with copies of their rules as they may be entitled to a limited NZD 1 000 tax deduction but unlike registered charities, are expected to file a tax return.

In Australia, the assessing body responsible for all decisions, regarding the registration and removal of organisations from the charities register is the Australian Charities and Not-for-profits Commission (ACNC). A charity must be registered with the ACNC to be exempt from income tax and obtain other tax concessions. Furthermore, a charity must be endorsed by the tax administration to be exempt from income tax. An entity wishing to be a deductible gift recipient must be endorsed by the tax administration or specifically named in tax legislation. The tax administration's endorsement process typically takes less than 28 days.

Other department

Not all countries follow the above approaches of involving the tax administration in oversight responsibilities. In Lithuania, for example, the assessing body in charge of the application process to becoming a sponsorship recipient is the Centre of Registers under the supervision of the Ministry of the Economy and Innovation of the Republic of Lithuania. In Luxembourg, a PBO (like any other corporation) has to file annual accounts with the Company and Trade Register, which have to be supervised and approved by an independent auditor. PBOs may only own property or buildings necessary to carry out its mission. In Romania, the assessing body is the General Secretariat of the Government. In Bulgaria, the Registry Agency to the Minister of Justice is the body responsible for accrediting philanthropic entities, which enables them to receive tax-incentivised donations.

3.3.3. Additional reporting requirements

Regardless of what authority is tasked with approving philanthropic entities for tax privileges, the assessing body typically requires funds and PBOs to provide them with the information they need to evaluate whether or not the entities are, and continue to be, eligible to receive the philanthropic status as well as the associated preferential tax treatment. The requirements differ across countries and there is a trade-off between requiring entities to provide a lot of detailed information at the cost of a high administrative burden and minimal information at the cost of less oversight and perhaps more misconduct. The information requirements that countries implement can be categorised into record keeping requirements (so that entities can be audited effectively); annual reporting requirements (to help the administrative body oversee whether the entities continue to meet the worthy purpose, public benefit and not-for-profit conditions); constitutional requirements (to align the company rules with the tax rules); and an activities plan requirement (to help the assessing body evaluate the entity's future plans).

Application and record keeping requirements

Record keeping requirements are necessary for effective auditing. For example, the Canadian tax administration conducts selective audits of registered philanthropic entities each year to evaluate whether they continue to qualify for registration and ensure they follow the rules (the tax administration maintains an audit coverage of approximately 1%). Funds and PBOs are required to provide books and records to demonstrate that their resources were used for worthy purposes and to ensure that official donation receipts were issued. So that entities have all the necessary information available during an audit, registered funds and PBOs in Canada are obliged to:

- maintain direction and control of the use of all their resources;
- meet their annual spending requirement (disbursement quota);
- keep reliable and complete books and records;
- issue complete and accurate official donation receipts (see Chapter 4 for more details on requirements relating to donation receipts).

In Belgium, PBOs must provide a budget for the current fiscal year; and the accounts of the last two accounting years. Furthermore, they must formally commit to limit management fees to less than 20%, limit advertising costs to less than 30%, and make no profits. The minimum duration of the process of accreditation is three months. Similarly, in Ireland the application for tax-exempt status must include a full set of recent financial accounts; a constitution; a plan for activities for the year ahead; and proof of registration of PBO or fund status with an independent charity commission.

Philanthropic entities in the Netherlands must keep accounting records from which the following can be inferred:

- the nature and scope of the expense allowances and/or attendance fees granted to the separate members of the board;
- the nature and scope of the management activities, and the other costs incurred by the entity; and
- the nature and scope of the income and the assets held by the entity.

In Lithuania, philanthropic entities entitled to receive sponsorship must keep separate accounts for sponsorship received as well as for donations and/or services provided. Additionally, they must submit their monthly or annual reports to the tax administration. If the amount of the sponsorship received since the beginning of a calendar year from a single provider of sponsorship exceeds EUR 15 000, the entity must submit a monthly report.

In Colombia, the application process requires the following information:

- a description of the entity's worthy purpose;
- the amount and destination of the reinvestment of the net benefits or surpluses, when applicable;
- the amount and destination of permanent assignments that have been made in the taxable year;;
- names of the persons that manage, direct or control the entity;
- the salary of the members of the governing body of the entity;
- names of the founders;
- the amount of equity as of December 31st of the previous year;
- the identification of the donors and the amount of the donations, as well as the destination of such donation and the projected term for expenditure or investment (if applicable);
- an annual report of the results that establishes the information about ongoing projects and concluded ones, income, agreements entered into, subsidies and contributions received, as well as goals achieved for the public benefit;

- financial statements of the entity;
- a certificate of the legal representative or controller, as well as the income tax return that establishes that the entity has complied with all requirements for the taxable year;

In France, PBOs benefiting from a preferential tax treatment are subject to audit by the Court of Auditors. Organizations receiving more than EUR 153 000 in grants or more than EUR 153 000 in philanthropic gifts, must have their account records certified by an external auditor each year.

In Luxembourg, PBOs must determine who their beneficial owners are and have to declare them in the register of beneficial owners. A form must be completed with the information required by law in order to complete this declaration (in most cases, it will be the members of the board of directors).

Annual reporting requirements

A number of countries have annual reporting requirements (e.g., Australia, Colombia, Estonia, Lithuania, and Singapore). Typically, annual reporting helps the assessing body monitor an entity's activities and assess whether they are still meeting all the necessary requirements. In Australia, for example, a registered entity must provide annual reports – an Annual Information Statement and for medium and large entities, a financial statement - to the ACNC. If a philanthropic entity is income tax exempt, it does not need to submit an income tax return, although there is a requirement to do so if requested by the tax administration. However, if applicable, such an entity may need to submit statements in relation to the VAT. Similarly, in order for philanthropic entities to maintain their status in Colombia, funds and PBOs of the special tax regime must annually submit their financial and legal information to the Colombian tax administration. Furthermore, all entities belonging to the special tax regime must file an annual income tax return.

Some countries require funds and PBOs to make their information publicly available. This is the case in the Netherlands, where philanthropic entities must publish information about the organisation on their own website or on a communal website of a trade organisation for example. An advantage of this approach may be in fostering the public's trust in the philanthropic sector.

A number of countries require philanthropic entities to submit tax returns regardless of whether or not they are liable to pay taxes. In Germany, for example, funds and PBOs that receive preferential tax treatment can self-assess but are required to submit tax returns even if no tax is payable. Similarly, funds and PBOs in Slovenia can self-assess but are required to submit tax returns. On the other hand, for an entity to receive preferential tax treatment in the Slovak Republic, the only condition is to establish a business with a worthy purpose. The philanthropic entity is then required to submit tax returns but only if their income includes non-exempt income.

In the United States, philanthropic entities (other than churches) must apply for tax exemption from the tax administration and receive a tax-exempt status. After the tax-exempt status is granted, the entities (other than churches) must file annual information tax returns, which are available to the public. Additionally, if they engage in any unrelated trade or business activity, the philanthropic entities (including churches) must file a separate tax return, which is also available to the public.

Company rules and related requirements

Some countries (e.g., Ireland, New Zealand, Estonia, Mexico, and the Netherlands) require entities to report their company rules, constitution or bylaws with the administration, so that they can ensure that they are in line with the requirements necessary to receive preferential tax treatment. For example, to be qualified as a fund or PBO in the Netherlands, the articles of association of the philanthropic entity must stipulate that, in the event of liquidation, the assets remaining are to be passed on to a philanthropic entity with a similar purpose or on a foreign philanthropic entity that is (entirely or almost) exclusively committed to the public good and has a similar worthy purpose. In New Zealand, clubs and associations which are not eligible for full income tax exemptions are required to supply the tax administration with copies of their rules as they may be entitled to a limited NZD 1 000 tax deduction, but are also expected to file a tax return. Funds and PBOs in Mexico must include the current company bylaws in their application along with a proof of the nature of their activities.

Activities plan requirement

In a few countries (e.g., Belgium, Ireland, Colombia, Estonia, and Romania), entities have to provide the administration body with an activities plan. A benefit of this approach may be that countries can evaluate whether the entities have successfully made progress on their objectives but also allows them to flag any issues of eligibility ahead of time. For example, Belgium requires entities to provide a calendar of activities and an activity report for the past year as well as a detailed statement of the current year's projects.

In order to receive preferential tax treatment in Estonia, a philanthropic entity must submit an application complying with the requirements of the tax administration. The application should describe the activities of the association in the current year (including planned activities), explain the philanthropic activities carried out for the public benefit, describe the future visions of the entity and provide the necessary information on its founders. In addition to the application, the objectives set out in the articles of the entity and in the annual report are reviewed by the tax administration.

Philanthropic entities in Romania must present an activity report accompanied by annual financial statements as well as revenue statements and expenditure budgets for the three years prior to the application. The entity must also show proof of collaboration and partnership contracts with public institutions, associations or foundations in the country or abroad. Lastly, the entity should be able to show significant results in the fulfilment of its worthy purpose or present recommendation letters from competent authorities.

In Singapore, entities that wish to be a registered charity have to apply to the Commissioner of Charities, who assesses the application. Once registered, the philanthropic entity is required to make an annual submission to the Commissioner of Charities, which includes an annual report (including financial statements and a governance evaluation checklist).

3.4. Tax treatment of income of philanthropic entities

3.4.1. Sources of income

Philanthropic entities may have commercial and/or non-commercial income, but the distinction is not always clear or the same across countries. Generally, non-commercial income refers to income from philanthropic gifts (discussed in Chapter 4) and government grants, or (in the case of PBOs) grants from supporting funds. Income from philanthropic gifts includes donations from individuals and corporations and testamentary transfers from individuals. In relation to these transfers, in countries that levy an inheritance tax instead of an estate tax, the tax liability is with the beneficiary and therefore an inheritance tax incentive for giving would benefit the philanthropic entity receiving the inheritance.

Broadly, commercial income is income derived from the supply of goods or services in return for some form of payment. When a corporation makes a payment as sponsorship (i.e. in return for publicity) to a philanthropic entity, it may, in some countries, be considered commercial income. That is to say that to the extent that the publicity resulting from sponsoring a philanthropic entity is a service, such income could be considered commercial.

Countries' tax relief for the income of philanthropic entities can be separated into two approaches: (1) to exempt all or specific income (e.g. income from philanthropic gifts), or (2) to consider all forms of income taxable, but allow the entity to reduce its taxable income through current or future reinvestments towards the fulfilment of their worthy purpose. Table 3.4 shows that most countries tend to follow the first approach.

Colombia, Indonesia, Lithuania, and Ireland follow the second approach, where all income (including philanthropic gifts) is considered taxable unless it is reinvested towards the fulfilment or the worthy purpose (see Table 3.5 for a detailed explanation of how the income tax liability of philanthropic entities is determined in Colombia).

Table 3.4. Approaches to providing tax relief for the income of philanthropic entities

Countries following the exempt all or specific sources of income approach:	*Australia; Austria; Belgium; Bulgaria; Canada; Chile; Finland; Germany; Greece; Ireland; Israel; Italy; Latvia; Malta; Mexico; the Netherlands; New Zealand; Norway; Portugal; Romania; Singapore; the Slovak Republic; Slovenia; South Africa; Sweden; Switzerland; the United Kingdom, and the United States.*
Countries following the exempt income if reinvested towards worthy purpose approach:	*Colombia, Indonesia; Lithuania; and Ireland*

Source: OECD Taxation and Philanthropy Questionnaire

3.4.2. Exempting all or specific sources of income approach

Countries generally exclude non-commercial income (such as income from philanthropic gifts or government grants) from the tax base and do not consider it as taxable income. Countries with inheritance taxes tend to exempt philanthropic entities from paying such taxes on the testamentary transfers they receive (Belgium and France apply a reduced inheritance tax rate on income from bequests).

Approaches to the tax treatment of income from commercial activities diverge. The first subsection below, discusses a small number of countries that exempt all commercial income of philanthropic entities. The second subsection provides an overview of countries whose philanthropic entities are fully income tax exempt and restrict these entities from engaging in certain kinds of activities. The third subsection discusses the countries that want philanthropic entities to pay taxes on some of their income, and thus generally differentiate between income that is related to their worthy purpose and income that is unrelated (also referred to as related and unrelated business income). The fourth subsection covers countries that tax commercial income above a threshold. Finally, there are also countries that simply tax commercial income and are thus not included in the following subsections (this is the case in Greece, Luxembourg, and Slovenia, where income derived from commercial activities is taxed).

Exempting all income from commercial activity

In Australia, philanthropic entities are fully exempt from paying income tax on both commercial and non-commercial income. Notably, a 2008-2010 review of the Australian tax system considered the issue of taxing the unrelated business income of philanthropic entities. The review found that the tax exempt entities are not incentivised to undercut the prices of their for-profit counterparts and thus the income tax concessions do not violate the principle of competitive neutrality and should be retained (Henry et al., 2009[2]). Entities may also receive a refund for franking credits (see Box 3.1 for more information).

New Zealand follows a similar approach: philanthropic entities are exempt from paying corporate income tax on non-commercial income and are also exempt from income tax on commercial income if the philanthropic entity meets the not-for-profit requirement and has no activities overseas. The issue of competitive neutrality concerns arising from exempting the commercial income of philanthropic entities was considered in the recent New Zealand Tax Working Group report. The report concluded that the underlying issue was the extent to which the philanthropic entity directs its surplus to their worthy purpose activities for the public benefit. As a result, the Working Group recommended that the Government regularly review the philanthropic sector's use of tax expenditures to ensure that the intended social outcomes are being achieved (Tax Working Group, 2019[3]). In Malta too, philanthropic entities benefit from a tax exemption on all their income.

Restricting the commercial activities an entity can engage in

In Canada, qualifying philanthropic entities are exempt from paying income tax. PBOs are not permitted to undertake commercial activities unless they are related to the charitable purpose the entity is undertaking or the entity is run almost entirely with volunteer labour. Philanthropic entities are prohibited from carrying out unrelated commercial activities themselves and may have their registration revoked or be subject to financial penalties if they do so. A philanthropic entity may, however, carry out commercial activities through separate business corporations or trusts, provided the proper separations between the philanthropic entity and the business are in place. There are also expenditure requirements: if the average value of an entity's property not used directly in philanthropic activities (during the 24 months before the beginning of the fiscal year) exceeds CAD 100 000, the philanthropic entity's disbursement quota is 3.5% of the average value of that property.

In Belgium, philanthropic entities are subject to the legal entities income tax (LEIT). The LEIT is not specific to philanthropic entities and is applied to all legal entities that are not subject to the corporate income tax. A philanthropic entity can engage in economic activity if it does not constitute a principal activity, and is a secondary activity whose profits are reinvested in the entity's worthy purpose. Philanthropic entities liable to the LEIT are not taxed on their total annual net income, but only on:

- their real estate income,
- their income from capital and movable property, inclusive the first EUR 1 880 euro bracket of income from savings deposits and the first EUR 190 bracket of dividends from recognised cooperative companies and to companies with a social purpose.
- certain miscellaneous forms of income.

Thus, income from donations is exempt from the LEIT, but regional inheritance taxes may still apply to bequests.[2]

The LEIT is collected as a withholding tax. Where philanthropic entities receive income from movable property or miscellaneous income of movable origin without the withholding tax being deducted at source, the withholding tax is due by the recipient of the income. In the following cases specific assets are put on the Belgian tax roll:

- Certain types of real estate income, notably net income from land and buildings situated in Belgium and leased, are subject to a 20% tax.
- Capital gains made through the transfer of developed or undeveloped real estate are taxable at 16.5% or 33%.
- The transfer of important participations is taxable, at the 16.5% rate, according to the same arrangements as for personal income tax.
- Unjustified expenses, in-kind benefits or financial advantages, are taxable according to the same arrangements as for the corporate income tax (contribution of 100% on secret commissions and 50% if it can be established that the beneficiary for those expenses, in-kind benefits, and financial advantages is a legal person).
- Pension contributions and pensions considered as disallowed expenses under the corporate income tax, financial advantages or in-kind benefits, as well as the amount equal to 17% of the benefit in kind resulting from the private use of a company car, are liable to a 33% tax.
- Inter-municipal associations operating a hospital or an institution assisting war victims, disabled persons, etc., are taxable on dividends attributed to other legal entities except public administrations. The rate of this tax is 25% and the increase for lack or insufficiency of advance payments is applicable according to the same arrangements as for corporate income tax.

In Latvia, philanthropic entities are not subject to corporate income tax if the purpose of the establishment is not to make profit or achieve an increase in capital for their members, religious organisations, trade unions, and political parties. Furthermore, monetary assistance received from a public benefit organisation for covering expenditure for medical treatment (including in order to ensure transport of a patient and accompanying person to a medical treatment institution) is not included in the annual taxable income and is thus exempt from personal income tax.

Box 3.1. Imputation credits

Overview

The rationale behind imputation credits (also termed refundable franking credits') is to reduce the double taxation of dividends by imputing the corporate tax to the shareholder. Dividends paid from taxed profits are 'franked' (i.e. receive an imputation credit) if the company that distributes its dividends has paid tax on its profits. Therefore, individuals or corporations receiving the franked dividends may receive an imputation credit under certain conditions.

Imputation Credits in Australia and New Zealand

In Australia, some tax-exempt entities (i.e. charities and deductible gift recipients) that receive franked dividends are eligible to benefit from a refund of franking credit. Since these tax-exempt entities do not pay tax on the income received from dividends, the refundable credit is essentially additional income for the entity to use for its worthy purpose. In New Zealand, on the other hand, tax-exempt entities that receive franked dividends will not be taxed on those dividends but will not be able to use the imputation credits attached to the dividends. The effect is that they are effectively subject to tax at the company rate, 28%, on the income that is taxed within any companies they invest in.

Source: Australian Taxation Office website.

In Japan, the income of PBOs (that fulfil the not-for-profit requirement) is tax exempt. The commercial activities that exempt PBOs are permitted to engage in without losing their tax exempt status, are stipulated by the most applicable ministry (i.e. the ministry that has the most expertise regarding the particular worthy purpose). Furthermore, if half or more of the employees of a commercial activity are persons with disabilities and the PBO contributes to the protection of the lives of these persons, than the activity is not considered a profitable business, which would otherwise be taxable.

In Singapore, the income of all philanthropic entities registered under the Charities Act, is exempt from income tax. PBOs may engage in commercial activities to generate additional income, or to provide goods or services for their members or clients to further their worthy purposes. However, these commercial activities, may not undermine the philanthropic entity's focus and distract the charity from its exclusively worthy purpose. Charity boards should also be prudent and must not expose their charitable assets to significant risk. Where business activities may expose charitable assets to significant risk, they must be carried out by a business subsidiary. Business subsidiaries that are set up by charities are treated in the same manner as any other company. The income of these business subsidiaries is subject to income tax.

In Argentina, philanthropic entities are exempt from corporate income taxes. In Switzerland, PBO's are exempt from income and wealth taxes. In Israel, donations, inheritances, government grants and passive income are tax exempt. In Chile, some PBOs may be exempt from the corporate income tax when the exemption is granted by the President of the Republic. This benefit can only be requested by PBOs where their main and effective purpose is to provide aid directly to people with limited economic resources who are unable to meet their basic needs.

Exempting commercial income if related to worthy purpose activities

Austria distinguishes between three types of commercial activities: necessary, related, and unrelated. A commercial activity is considered necessary if the worthy purpose of the philanthropic entity cannot be achieved without it and the exempt entity does not significantly compete with other taxed entities that engage in a similar commercial activity. The income generated through necessary commercial activities (e.g., selling entry tickets as a museum) is fully tax exempt. A commercial activity is considered related if it is a means to achieving the worthy purpose, although not a necessary one. Income generated from related commercial activities is liable for the corporate income tax but a EUR 10 000 exemption remains. Philanthropic entities that engage in unrelated commercial activities risk losing their tax-exempt status all together. If, however, the commercial activities that a philanthropic entity engages in, generates under a threshold of EUR 40 000 in the tax year, the entity may keep its tax-exempt status. Furthermore, some capital gains of PBOs are tax-exempt. For example, the capital gain from shares (and interest from capital assets) that is verifiably used for worthy purposes is tax-free if the business is related to the PBO.

In Finland, philanthropic entities are liable to a tax on income derived from business activity, as well as a 6.26% tax on income derived from real property that is used for a purpose other than the eligible worthy purposes. For philanthropic entities in Finland, the income from the following activities is not considered to be income derived from business activity and is therefore tax exempt:

- income derived from organising lotteries, fairs, athletic competitions, dances, bingo and other entertainment events, as well as the income derived from buffets, sales and other similar activities;
- income derived from member magazines and other publications directly serving the purpose of the entity;
- income derived from collecting funds through selling remembrance cards, badges, cards, vanes or other such products;
- income derived from selling goods or services, which are manufactured or produced for the purposes of therapy, or teaching in hospitals, mental hospitals, penal institutions, workhouses, old people's or disabled people's homes or other similar care-taking institutions.

Income subject to tax can be deemed to be wholly or partly income tax exempt by the tax administration. A tax exemption can be granted only when the exemption can be regarded as justified with respect to the benefit that the entity produces for society. When an exemption is considered, attention is paid to what degree the entity's assets and income are used worthy purpose activity that is important for society. Attention must also be paid to whether the exemption for an entity's business leads to unfair competition.

In Germany, the income generated from activities related to the worthy purpose is exempt from corporate income and trade tax. Income attributable to economic activities which are not related to the designated worthy purpose are not subject to corporate income tax or trade tax if the total annual income including VAT from these commercial activities does not exceed EUR 35 000. Furthermore, the income of capital assets of philanthropic entities is exempt from the withholding tax on capital investments.

Philanthropic entities in Bulgaria are not taxed on their non-commercial income (such as income from grants or donations), i.e. the income that supports their main purpose, but income from commercial activities is subject to the corporate income tax for all philanthropic entities except for the Bulgarian Red Cross.

Similarly in Greece, any income acquired by philanthropic entities through the pursuit of the fulfilment of their worthy purpose (such as membership fees, public or private grants, donations, etc.) is not subject to income tax. On the other hand, any income generated from commercial/business activities is taxable, regardless of whether it is used to fulfil the worthy purpose of the not-for-profit entity (e.g., interest on deposits, public events etc.).

In Portugal, the income of philanthropic entities that is derived from donations is untaxed. Income derived from worthy purpose activities is generally also untaxed. Other sources of income, such as unrelated commercial activity or financial assets and investments are considered taxable income.

In Sweden, as in most other countries, PBOs are exempt from paying income taxes on income received or derived from donations, grants, investments, and worthy purpose activities. Furthermore, income earned by carrying out philanthropic activities, including under contracts with government, is also tax-exempt. This suggests that income from unrelated activities will be taxable income.

In the United States, PBO's are generally exempt from corporate income taxes. However, income from unrelated business activities (i.e. activities that are not substantially related to the exempt purpose), is taxable at the corporate tax rate. More specifically, such income is taxed at the top corporate tax rate with an exclusion of USD 1 000. Income related to the exempt purpose of the non-profit organisation is generally income tax exempt. The rules on income from outsourcing work depend on the way in which it is outsourced. If, for example, an entity pays a management company to run a business and transfer all of the income over to the entity itself, then the income would be taxable as unrelated business income. Similarly, if the philanthropic entity is a partner in a partnership and the partnership is running the business, then the income would be taxable also. If, on the other hand, the income is from a business that just pays the PBO rent, then the income would usually not be taxable. If the income is passive income, for example royalty or dividend income, it would also not be taxable.

Using a threshold to exempt commercial income

As noted in the section above, Austria, Germany and the United States apply thresholds as well as distinguish between related and unrelated commercial income. In Austria, philanthropic entities that generate related or unrelated commercial income above the respective thresholds, risk losing their tax-exempt status. In Germany and the United States, on the other hand, unrelated commercial income above the threshold is taxed. In addition, several other countries (France, Hungary, Mexico, the Netherlands, Norway, the Slovak Republic, and South Africa) use thresholds to determine how to tax the income of philanthropic entities.

In France, PBOs which carry out commercial activity on a regular or occasional basis, may be exempt from corporate taxes (value added tax, corporate income tax, corporate property tax) if the activity does not compete with the business sector and if the revenues collected during the calendar year for this activity do not exceed EUR 72 000. PBOs that benefit from the corporate tax exemption remain liable for corporate income tax at reduced rates for income from asset management such as:

- income from the rental of built and undeveloped buildings owned by the association (CIT rate at 24%);
- profits from the exploitation of agricultural or forestry properties (CIT rate at 24%);
- dividends (CIT rate at 15%);
- other securities (CIT rate at 10 % or 24%).

In Hungary, PBOs are exempt from corporate tax if their income derived from commercial activities (including managing real estate) does not exceed 15% of the total income. In India, philanthropic entities that are not engaged in certain specified charitable activities and are classified as being engaged in the advancement of any other object of general public utility can derive up to 20% of their income from trade, commerce or business, provided it is earned in the course of advancing the charitable purpose of the entity.

In Mexico, philanthropic entities are exempt from income tax on income from donations; government grants; the sale of fixed or intangible asset; membership fees; recovery fees; interest; economic rights derived from intellectual property; temporary use or enjoyment of real estate, or from yields obtained from shares or other credit instruments, provided they are used for the purposes for which they were authorised.

Additionally, they may obtain income from activities other than the purposes for which they were authorised, provided it does not exceed 10% of their total income.

In the Netherlands, philanthropic entities are only liable to the corporate income tax if (1) they participate in the market economy with labour and capital and thereby make a profit, or (2) if their activities compete with commercial businesses, or (3) if no exemption applies. The exemption applies if the entity's surplus is below EUR 15 000 a year or less than EUR 75 000 combined for the prior four years.

In Norway, a philanthropic entity is exempt from paying income taxes on received donations, inheritances and grants. The entity is exempt from income taxes on income generated from any commercial activity it undertakes that does not contribute towards the realisation of the institution's worthy purpose, provided that the annual revenue from the commercial activity does not exceed a threshold of NOK 140 000. This includes any capital gain as a result of economic activity. On the other hand, capital gains resulting from the tax-exempt worthy purpose activities are tax-exempt.

In the Slovak Republic, the income received by philanthropic entities is generally tax-exempt, except for commercial income, including income derived from property (rent), the sale of assets, membership fees and advertising income above EUR 20 000 per year.

In South Africa, only welfare, education, healthcare and conservation activities qualify for an income tax deduction. The other worthy purposes (shown in Table 3.1 are only exempt from gift tax. Furthermore, 15% of all commercial income of philanthropic entities is tax exempt, amounts above that are taxable at the corporate income tax rate.

3.4.3. Exempting income if reinvested towards the worthy purpose

For countries following the second approach (exempting income if reinvested towards the worthy purpose), the source of the income is generally secondary to its destination. That is to say that as long as the surplus of a philanthropic entity is reinvested towards the worthy purpose within a given time period, the income of the entity is exempt. If, on the other hand, the entity decides to defer reinvestment, stockpile its surplus or invest it towards something other than its worthy purpose, the surplus may become taxable.

In Colombia the income tax treatment of philanthropic entities is determined based on whether, and how, the net benefit or surplus is reinvested. Other countries discussed in this report tend to exempt non-commercial income automatically (i.e. not consider it taxable income). In Colombia, however, all forms of income are considered taxable and the tax relief instead allows the entity to reinvest the net benefit or surplus (resulting from the income) towards the fulfilment of its social objective.

In Indonesia, donations and grants to philanthropic entities are tax exempt income. If an entity engaged in education or research and development has a surplus, it is only tax exempt if the surplus is reinvested in its worthy purpose (education or research and development) within a four year period after the income was received. Similarly, in the Czech Republic, the corporate income tax exemption only applies to the income of a PBO if such income is or will be used for specified worthy purposes.

In Ireland, philanthropic entities do not enjoy automatic income tax exemption simply by virtue of registering with charities commission. As discussed at the beginning of the chapter, entities must apply to the revenue for the tax exemption separately. Once the tax-exempt status is approved, entities are also exempt from capital gains tax and tax on commercial income, provided that the income is applied towards the fulfilment of the entities' worthy purposes. Philanthropic entities also benefit from a matching scheme for donations which is described in more detail in Chapter 4.

Table 3.5. Tax liability formula for philanthropic entities in Colombia

+	Ordinary or extraordinary income of the taxable year
-	Expenses of the taxable year, including those not related to the worthy purpose
-	Investments made to strengthen the equity (for more than one year), which are not susceptible to amortisation or depreciation and generate returns for the worthy purpose.
=	Net Benefit or Surplus
-	The assets of the Net Benefit or Surplus reinvested during the following taxable year towards the worthy purpose of the philanthropic entity.
-	The assets of the Net Benefit or Surplus reinvested into long-term projects (between 2 to 5 years) towards the "worthy purpose" of the entity. These long-term reinvestment projects will be recognized as "Permanent Assignments". In case the long-term reinvestment project surpasses five (5) years, the entity must submit a request to the Colombian Tax Administration to extend the reinvestment term.
=	Taxable Net Benefit or Surplus
×	Income tax rate of 20%
=	**Total income tax liability**

Source: OECD Taxation and Philanthropy Questionnaire

In Lithuania, philanthropic entities are subject to the corporate income tax. The rules for calculating taxable profits of such organisations do not differ from the rules applicable for commercial entities. Nevertheless, the preferential tax treatment allows philanthropic entities to reduce the taxable surplus calculated in accordance with the general corporate income tax rules by deducting the funds directly allocated to a worthy purpose in the current or subsequent two tax periods. Where the amount of funds directly allocated to the financing of activities with a worthy purpose in the current tax period exceed the amount of taxable surplus calculated for that tax period, the funds exceeding this amount may be carried forward to reduce the amounts of taxable surplus calculated for the two subsequent tax periods. Donations in cash from a single donor which exceed EUR 9 750 during a tax period, and other donations not used for public benefit purposes are taxed at a general 15% corporate income tax rate.

3.5. Value-added taxes

Preferential VAT treatment may apply to a philanthropic entity's inputs (purchases) as well as its outputs (supplies - sales or disposals). Regarding its inputs, philanthropic entities pay VAT on their purchases (as long as those purchases are not exempt goods or services). If they are not registered for VAT purposes, the entity is likely treated as a final consumer and cannot recover the VAT paid on its inputs without specific tax relief. Similarly, if the entity is registered for VAT purposes but does not make any taxable sales, it will also not be able to recover the VAT paid on its inputs. A philanthropic entity may not make any taxable sales because its supplies (outputs) are exempt, or because they are out of the scope of the VAT. On the other hand, philanthropic entities that do charge VAT on their sales (including zero rated goods and services) are able to recover the VAT paid on their inputs.

Consequentially, countries may choose to allow philanthropic entities to not charge VAT on their supplies (or the entities may be under the revenue threshold), which could in return create an input tax burden for those entities. As a result, some countries offer tax relief to philanthropic entities that are not able to recover VAT paid on their inputs (or are only able to recover a share of it).

VAT exemptions, reduced rates, and zero rates can create unfair competition, especially if the VAT exempt goods or services supplied by a philanthropic entity are also provided by businesses that charge VAT on their sales. Thus some countries do not exempt from VAT certain goods and services provided by philanthropic entities in order to avoid unfair competition (e.g. Canada and Ireland). Belgium, Chile, Colombia, Estonia, Indonesia, Italy, and the Slovak Republic, do not have preferential VAT treatment for philanthropic entities and apply the standard VAT rules. Although Italy does not allow a preferential VAT regime for philanthropic entities, PBOs are exempt from the requirement to provide evidence of their sales through invoices and sales receipts.

3.5.1. VAT exempt

Entities (or the activities of entities) can be exempt from VAT due to their philanthropic nature (e.g., France), because their activities do not fall within the coverage of the VAT, or because they operate below a VAT registration threshold.

In Argentina, the services of philanthropic entities that are directly related to the PBO's main purpose are exempt from VAT. That means that donations by third parties, membership dues, and fees charged to members for specific statutory activities, are all VAT exempt services for PBOs. Other transactions of PBOs are subject to the standard VAT rules.

In Australia, philanthropic entities have a higher revenue threshold for registering for VAT. Eligible entities do not need to register for VAT until their turnover is AUD 150 000 or more (normally registration is required at AUD 75 000). In some cases, PBO may choose how activities are treated. If, for instance, a PBO (e.g., a parents association) operates a school canteen on the grounds of a primary or secondary school, the PBO can choose to be VAT exempt, meaning it does not need to remit VAT on its sales of food. However, the school canteen cannot claim VAT credits for its purchases. Once the PBO chooses to be VAT exempt (i.e. pay input tax) it cannot revoke that choice for 12 months. Similarly, all philanthropic entities can choose to exempt their fundraising events from VAT, which in turn means they will have to pay input tax on their purchases since they will not be able to claim the VAT credits. This is aimed at reducing the administrative burden.

In Austria, not all philanthropic entities are exempt from the VAT. Instead, only PBOs with a "cultural" or "sports promoting" worthy purpose, as well as those running care facilities or health institutions, or providing accommodation and food to trainees below the age of 27, are VAT-exempt. Other philanthropic entities are subject to the standard VAT rules.

In Greece, philanthropic entities are exempt from charging VAT on several goods and services, subject to certain conditions. Examples of exempted activities are: The provision of services closely related to sport to persons engaged in sports or physical education by philanthropic entities. The provision of services to their members by philanthropic entities and organizations pursuing religious, philosophical, charitable purposes. The provision of cultural or educational services by philanthropic entities operating for cultural or educational purposes (in particular those services provided to visitors of museums, monuments, archaeological or other similar sites, as well as the organisation of art events, exhibitions and lectures). And finally, services provided by the above-mentioned entities in the context of events organised by them for their financial support.

In Israel, PBOs pay VAT on the goods and services they purchase and use as part of the philanthropic activity. The VAT paid by the PBOs cannot be deducted as an input tax, as there is no VAT on goods or services supplied by the PBO as part of its philanthropic activity. Commercial activity by the PBO is subject to VAT and therefore the VAT paid on inputs for the commercial activity can be deducted against VAT collected from the commercial activity.

In Latvia, the non-commercial activities of PBOs are generally considered to be outside the scope of the VAT. On the other hand, the commercial activities of PBOs are subject to the standard VAT rules. However, the VAT treatment is evaluated on a case-by-case basis. For example, VAT paid on inputs that are used as part of the philanthropic activity are not deductible. VAT paid on inputs for the commercial activity on the other hand, are deductible. However, if a PBO 'sells' the goods and services as part of its philanthropic activity, this activity would be regarded as a taxable transaction. The taxable amount of this transaction shall be the purchase price of the goods or full cost to the PBO of providing these services.

In Mexico, philanthropic entities are exempt from VAT for the sale of goods, the provision of services and the temporary use or enjoyment of goods as part of their activities. However, the entities have the obligation to pay and withhold the VAT when they receive independent personal services or goods provided or granted by individuals.

In Portugal, philanthropic entities are exempt from charging VAT on goods and services related to:

- health, social security and social assistance (provided that they do not receive any compensation);
- education – including day-care centres, kindergartens, leisure centres, establishments for children and young people with no normal family environment, establishments for disabled children and young people, rehabilitation centres for the disabled;
- sport, art, and culture – including artistic, sporting, recreational, physical education and cultural activities (e.g., visiting museums, art galleries, and castles);
- civic activities (e.g., political, union);
- religious activities;
- and humanitarian activities.

Fundraising activities (such as access tickets, registration fees, buffet, bar, stand rental, advertising revenue, etc.) are also exempt from VAT, as long as the fundraising is on an occasional basis and for the exclusive benefit of these entities (and provided they do not distort competition) and is limited to a maximum of eight fundraising events.

In Romania, some activities for the public benefit are exempt from VAT. These activities include the supplies of services closely related to sports or physical training, performed by PBOs for persons who practice sports, as well as the supplies of cultural services by cultural PBOs, recognised by the Ministry of Culture.

In South Africa, PBOs need to apply separately to be exempt from VAT. However, in general a PBO will not have to register for VAT as a vendor since it cannot be a predominantly commercial enterprise. In Switzerland, the VAT threshold for PBOs is supplies of CHF 150,000. In Finland, philanthropic entities are only liable for VAT on their commercial activities.

In the Netherlands, VAT is not applicable to non-commercial activities and therefore the VAT paid on inputs is not deductible. Within commercial activities there is a distinction between activities that are exempt and not exempt from VAT. Where activities are exempt from VAT, the VAT paid on the inputs is not deductible either. If a PBO is located in the Netherlands and has sales of no more than EUR 20 000 a year, the PBO can choose to be exempt from charging VAT, like any other small business, but will not be able to deduct or claim VAT on inputs.

In Singapore, PBOs are subject to standard VAT rules. PBOs may be regarded as carrying on both business and non-business activities for VAT purposes. Non-business activities include the provision of free services that are funded by grants, donations or sponsorships. PBOs are liable for VAT registration in Singapore if the annual value of taxable supplies arising from business activities exceeds the registration threshold of SGD 1 000 000. Once VAT-registered, PBOs are required to charge and account for VAT on their taxable supplies made. These include supplies made in the course of commercial activities (e.g. school or course fees, and day-care facility fees), as well as subsidised services as part of their philanthropic or religious purposes (e.g. dialysis fees, medical consultation fees). Like other businesses under standard VAT rules, PBOs are allowed input VAT claims on business purchases if these inputs are incurred for the making of taxable supplies in the course or furtherance of their business. Input VAT incurred for carrying out wholly non-business activities or exempt supplies is not claimable, while input VAT incurred for carrying out subsidised activities (partly business and partly non-business) is to be apportioned such that only the portion relating to the business of making taxable supplies is claimable.

3.5.2. VAT exempt with possibility of reclaiming input tax

Exempting entities or activities from VAT can lead to entities having to pay VAT on their inputs and some countries have put in place policies that enable philanthropic entities to reclaim some of the VAT they paid on inputs.

In Canada, most supplies of services and some supplies of goods made by registered charities and other PBOs are exempt from VAT (e.g. supplies of food and lodging made for the relief of poverty or distress; meals on wheels; recreational programs established for children, individuals with a disability and disadvantaged individuals; memberships in organizations providing no significant benefit to individual members; and trade union and mandatory professional dues). However, the VAT generally applies to certain supplies of goods and services made by charities that are similar to goods and services supplied by non-charitable businesses. For example, VAT typically applies to admissions to a place of amusement (e.g., a theatre), even when supplied by a philanthropic entity. If all or substantially all (90%) of a philanthropic entity's supplies (outputs) are taxable, the entity would typically be entitled to full input tax credits for VAT paid on its purchases of inputs to those taxable supplies. For VAT paid on purchases that do not qualify for input tax credits, philanthropic entities are eligible for partial rebates. The typical rebate rate for PBOs is 50%, however, higher rebate rates are available if the PBO is also a public hospital or a non-profit school, college or university. Registered charities that produce or offer a mix of taxable and exempt supplies (outputs) use a special streamlined method for calculating their VAT obligations: registered charities generally retain 40% of the VAT they collect on their taxable supplies (outputs) and receive a rebate on the VAT paid on most of their inputs, but are not entitled to input tax credits on these inputs.

In Ireland, a PBO may have activities which are taxable from a VAT perspective, outside-the-scope of VAT or even exempt from VAT. If their activity is an outside-the-scope or exempt activity, they are neither obliged nor entitled to register and account for VAT on the income generated from those income activities. In certain circumstances, the activities of a PBO may be considered to be in competition with commercial traders and the charity may then be required to register and account for VAT on these activities. Additionally, where a PBO acquires, or is likely to acquire more than EUR 41 000 worth of goods from other EU Member States in any period of twelve months, there is an obligation to register and account for VAT in respect of those intra-Community acquisitions. Overall, the VAT status of the PBO's activities is important in determining the VAT treatment of any income generated and the resultant entitlement to deduct VAT on costs associated with that income. In other words, the activities of a PBO must be considered on a case by case basis to decide their VAT status.

Under Irish legislation, a PBO can only recover VAT on its costs if it makes taxable sales, that is, if it is registered for VAT and charges VAT (including sales subject to the zero rate) on its sales. If the PBO has taxable supplies, it can reclaim its VAT on inputs. If the supplies are exempt or out-of-the-scope of VAT, no VAT recovery is possible. If the PBO has a mix of both exempt income and income which is subject to VAT, and income which is outside the scope of VAT, it can reclaim VAT incurred on the direct costs of making its taxable sales as well as a proportion of the VAT incurred on its general costs using an apportionment method. Furthermore, Ireland has a unique VAT compensation scheme for PBOs, which is described in more detail in Box 3.2. Other reliefs from VAT are available for the following PBOs, goods and services:

- PBOs involved in the transport of severely and permanently physically disabled persons: a refund of the amount of VAT paid may be claimed in relation to the purchase and adaptation of vehicles for use by qualifying bodies for the transport of severely and permanently disabled persons.
- Radios for the blind: a refund of the amount of VAT paid may be claimed in respect of radios where the PBO has a primary objective of improving the circumstances of blind persons and where the radios are intended for the use of blind persons.

- Appliances for use by disabled persons: a refund of the amount of VAT paid may be claimed on certain aids and appliances purchased by or on behalf of a disabled person to assist that disabled person in the performance of essential daily functions or in the exercise of a vocation.
- Rescue craft and equipment: a refund of the amount of VAT paid may be claimed on certain small rescue craft, ancillary equipment and special boat buildings and also on the hire, repair and maintenance of these craft to PBO's who provide a sufficient standard of rescue and assistance services at sea and on inland waterways.
- Humanitarian Goods for Export: a refund for VAT can be granted for goods purchased for exportation by philanthropic organisations for humanitarian, charitable or teaching activities abroad e.g. Apostolic Societies, Chernobyl Children Projects etc.
- Donated medical equipment: a refund of the amount of VAT paid may be claimed by a hospital or a donor on the purchase of certain new medical instruments and appliances which are funded by voluntary donations. The VAT refund may be claimed by whoever suffers the tax i.e. the hospital or the donor, as appropriate, but not, of course, both.
- Donated Research Equipment: a refund of the amount of VAT incurred in the purchase or importation of any new instrument or appliance (excluding means of transport) through voluntary donations, to a research institution or a university, school or similar educational body engaged in medical research in a laboratory.

In New Zealand, PBOs that make taxable supplies of more than NZD 60 000 per annum are required to register for the VAT. PBOs that do not reach this registration threshold may voluntarily register so long as they do make taxable supplies of goods or services. The rules do not distinguish between different types of activities. PBOs can, as long as they make some taxable supplies, claim back the VAT on any inputs they have other than inputs used for making exempt supplies (i.e. rental accommodation or financial services). As such, they can claim back the VAT on inputs that are not actually used for making a supply of goods or services. This is more generous than the input tax deduction rules for other registered-persons who can normally only claim an input tax deduction if the input is applied towards making a taxable supply of goods or services. All goods and services sold by PBOs, other than exempt supplies, are subject to VAT. Whether the goods and services are sold as part of a commercial activity or a philanthropic activity is irrelevant for VAT purposes.

The United States does not have a VAT although the States and local authorities imposes retail sales taxes. In the United States, the specific rules about exemption from State and local retail sales taxes are made by the States and can vary. Philanthropic entities are generally exempt from paying sales tax on their purchases and from collecting sales taxes from related business activities provided they meet state requirements, which may include a certificate or application for eligibility.

Germany is an outlier, because it offers a reduced VAT rate for some supplies by philanthropic entities, while others are VAT-free (e.g. some medical services). Entities can reclaim the VAT paid on their inputs for supplies subject to a reduced VAT rate. If the activities of PBOs are not part of a commercial activity and meet the worthy purpose and public benefit requirements, philanthropic entities in Germany are subject to the reduced VAT rate of 7%.

Box 3.2. Irish VAT compensation scheme for charities

To mitigate the VAT cost for registered charities that cannot recover VAT on their costs, a VAT Compensation Scheme for PBOs was introduced in Ireland in 2019. This scheme aims to reduce the VAT burden on qualifying charities to partially compensate them for irrecoverable VAT which they have suffered in the previous calendar year. They are entitled to claim a refund of a proportion of their VAT costs based on the level of non-public funding they receive.

The scheme is capped at EUR 5 000 000 per year and, where the total amount of all eligible claims in each year exceeds the capped amount, claims are paid on a proportional basis. VAT may only be reclaimed on goods and services which were applied only to the PBOs charitable purpose. The charity must also provide proof that the charity was not entitled to a deduction or refund of the tax being claimed under any other legislation administered by the tax authority.

3.6. Other taxes

3.6.1. Recurrent taxes on immovable property

Philanthropic entities may own real-estate that they use to fulfil their social objectives, or they may own it as a source of income. If entities use their real-estate for their worthy purpose such as the location of offices or philanthropic activities such as treatment centres, athletic infrastructures, events, or distribution centres, some countries may exempt them from property taxes. Philanthropic entities that own immovable property as a source of income are generally liable for property taxes on those properties if such a tax is levied in their jurisdiction.

In certain cases philanthropic entities in Canada may be exempt from property taxes. However, property tax is predominantly levied at the municipal level and exemptions, rebates and credits vary provincially and by municipality. In Germany, real estate used by PBOs for charitable purposes is exempt from local property tax. In Ireland, residential properties that are owned by a PBO and used for the sole purpose of providing residential accommodation in connection with the facilitation of recreational activities are exempt from property taxes. This exemption is intended to benefit philanthropic entities who own residential properties that are used by its members when taking part in recreational activities. In Italy, local authorities (municipalities and regions) can exempt philanthropic entities from local taxes (such as real estate taxes). In Romania, there is an exemption from the tax on buildings for structures owned by the entities established either by will or set up according to the law, in order to maintain, develop and help national cultural institutions, as well as to support humanitarian, social and cultural actions. Local councils may decide to grant exemption or reduction of tax on buildings used for the supply of social services by philanthropic entities. In Singapore, PBOs benefit from a property tax exemption for real-estate that is used exclusively for public religious worship, as a public school, for charitable purposes, or for purposes conducive to social development in Singapore.

In the United States, property tax rules are determined by the States. Land and buildings of churches are generally exempt, although some States limit the amount of eligible land (such as one acre). Land and buildings of other non-profits are also generally exempt, although this exemption may not apply to all types of non-profits. In Sweden, a PBO is exempt from real estate tax if the real estate is mainly used in activities promoting the worthy purpose.

3.6.2. Miscellaneous tax benefits for philanthropic entities

Lastly, there are a number of unique tax benefits that some countries offer philanthropic entities in their tax jurisdiction. In Norway, philanthropic entities are exempt from employers' SSCs on wage costs related to their worthy purpose activity. This exemption is limited to total wage costs below a total of NOK 800 000, and NOK 80 000 per employee. Australia and New Zealand both impose a fringe benefits tax (FBT) but provide preferential tax treatment to philanthropic entities (see Box 3.3)

In Portugal, PBOs are exempt from taxes on vehicles if they are used to pursue their philanthropic activities. In the Netherlands, PBOs (including churches) are, under certain conditions, eligible to repayment of half of the energy tax they pay. In France a PBO which owns a television set on January 1 of the tax year is liable for the contribution to public broadcasting. However, organisations hosting people are generally exempt. It Italy, philanthropic entities are exempt from the stamp duty and license duty, normally charged for the certification of documents and for the authorisation of administrative procedures. The United States has recently introduced some additional taxes on income tax-exempt entities (see Box 3.4).

Box 3.3. Fringe Benefit Tax and philanthropic entities

Australia

In Australia, some PBOs are exempt and other tax-exempt entities pay a reduced rate of fringe benefit tax (FBT). The Australian States also impose payroll tax based on the total size of the payroll. Exemptions are available to charities where the employees are engaged solely in the philanthropic activities of the charity.

New Zealand

In New Zealand, charities generally do not have to pay FBT on benefits provided to employees while they are carrying out the entity's charitable activities. For example, if an employee uses the entity's car while doing charitable work, there will not be any FBT due on any private benefit they receive. The one exception is where the employee is provided with a credit card or similar facility for private use and the value exceeds NZD 300. This will be liable for FBT. If the charity operates a business that is unrelated to the philanthropic purpose, FBT will be payable on any benefits provided to employees. New Zealand does not impose payroll tax.

Box 3.4. Implications of the Tax Cuts and Jobs Act (TCJA) for philanthropic entities

Overview

Signed into law 22 December 2017, the TCJA is considered the biggest overhaul of the US tax system in more than thirty years. It includes corporate and individual tax changes, which have implications for giving and philanthropic entities.

Excise tax on net investment income of foundations

The law imposes a 1.39% excise tax on the net investment income of most domestic tax-exempt private funds, including private operating foundations. The tax itself has applied since 1969, but the rate was previously 2% (or 1% in some years if certain requirements were met) until the TCJA made it a flat 1.39%.

An exemption (unaltered by the TCJA) from the excise tax may apply to an operating foundation if:

- it has been publicly supported for the last ten years;
- Its governing body consists of individuals fewer than 25% of whom are "disqualified individuals";
- It has no officer who is a "disqualified individual".

A disqualified individual refers to

- a substantial contributor; or
- an owner of more than 20% of the total combined voting power of a corporation, the profits of a partnership, or the beneficial interest of a trust which contributes to the PBO; or
- a member of the family of any individual described in (1) or (2).

Excise tax on excessive executive remuneration of exempt organisations

The law imposes a 21% excise tax (based on the top corporate tax rate) on remuneration in excess of USD 1 000 000 per year paid by tax-exempt organisations. The tax applies to the highest paid employees of a tax-exempt organisation. The tax also applies to termination payments.

Source: Internal Revenue Service (IRS) website and OECD Taxation and Philanthropy Questionnaire.

3.7. Abuse of tax incentives for philanthropic entities

3.7.1. Examples of tax abuse

Abuse of tax incentives for philanthropy occurs when the preferred tax status of a fund or PBO is abused either by the entity itself, or by taxpayers and donors, or third parties, such as fraudsters who pose as philanthropic entities or tax return preparers who falsify tax returns to defraud the government (OECD, 2009[4]). The abuse of tax incentives, and the diversion of monies intended for public purposes, discussed in this chapter focuses on the entities themselves. Common types of abuse include:

- Excessive salaries and compensation for board members and employees of PBOs and funds;
- Diverting funds intended for public purposes to private benefit, e.g. misusing the entity's funds for personal expenses such as cars, office spaces, or the employment of unqualified family members;
- A for-profit business poses as a PBO to benefit from the tax relief;
- Investment by a philanthropic entity in corporations owned or controlled by employees of the entity
- Liquidation of a PBO and distribution to individuals, eluding tax liability
- Salaried employees concealed as volunteer workers (and non-declaration of salary or wages);
- An entity not registered for VAT that is undertaking taxable activities.

In Canada, arrangements involving transactions between philanthropic entities and non-arm's length individuals and entities are an ongoing concern. This can include transactions involving investments by a charity in corporations owned by individuals controlling the charity or low or zero interest loans to such individuals or corporations. Often such amounts are at significant risk of not being repaid. Another form of non-arm's length transaction is the above-fair-market value contracts for services between charities and individuals or corporations that control the charity. This includes above fair-market value salaries paid to those involved, payment of personal expenses and other fringe benefits. In Colombia abusive schemes have included the setting-up of fictional philanthropic entities to take advantage of tax benefits, such as those provided for in the Special Tax Regime for Non-Profit Entities. For example, company-M may donate money to PBO-X, which is an entity that enjoys preferential tax treatment. Company-M therefore obtains a benefit consisting of a 25% tax credit of the value donated while PBO-X allocates the received donations towards programs in which company-M is a contractor, thereby receiving the initially donated value as income. To avoid such schemes some countries have, among other policies, strict donor-benefit rules discussed in Chapter 4.

In a 2009 OECD report on the abuse of charities for money-laundering and tax evasion, a number of countries identified tax evasion schemes related to philanthropic entities. Canada, the Czech Republic, and the United States reported that they have tracked schemes in which a philanthropic entity is set up so it receives approval for issuing donation receipts, but does not engage in the worthy purpose activities and instead the individuals who set up the entity use the fund for their personal benefit (OECD, 2009[4]). According to the report, the Canadian tax authority has noticed that charities and tax return preparers who previously have been identified as being involved in false receipting continue to issue the false receipts. At the time, the 2009 report found that suspected fraudulent alteration and creation of receipts has become more prevalent due to advancements in printing technology. Most suspicious activities seemed to involve tax return preparers and the use of electronic services.

3.7.2. Risk of terrorist financing

Another important finding of the 2009 OECD report is that although terrorist abuse of the philanthropic sector is rare, it does occur and there are vulnerabilities and risks that countries should keep track of. In the United States, the designation, prosecution and investigation of philanthropic entities has shown that terrorist abuse of philanthropic entities exists.

The Australian Charities and Not-for-profits commission (ACNC, 2020[5]) has published some of the ways in which terrorist organisations can misuse philanthropic entities to raise and distribute funds for their activities:

- A resident PBO may have an overseas partner organisation that uses its funds to finance terrorism.
- Terrorist organisations may use a philanthropic entity's assets (e.g., vehicles, storage, etc.).
- Terrorist organisations may attempt to use a philanthropic entity's name and status to raise funds without the entity's knowledge.
- Terrorist organisations may attempt to infiltrate a philanthropic entity to redirect money to fund terrorist purposes.
- A terrorist organisation may set up and register a philanthropic entity and hide its true purpose.

3.7.3. Detection of tax abuse related to philanthropic entities

To prevent abuse of tax concessions for philanthropic entities (including tax evasion and terrorist financing schemes), countries need to ensure that the administrative requirements (such as the application process, or annual reporting in some cases) enable the oversight body to identify and track suspicious entities and activities. However, the philanthropic entities have a role to play in limiting abuse too. As discussed in this section, some schemes occur without the entity's knowledge. Therefore it is important that the entities themselves regularly conduct internal audits and investigations, and engage in due diligence before financing certain projects or partnering with another organisation.

For the government oversight body, in-depth audits during an application or renewal of status can help detect cases of abuse. In Belgium, the tax administration also verifies if the entity has followed the directives with respect to tax receipt preparation and issuance, even if an entity has already been certified in the past (OECD, 2009[4]).

In a number of countries, tax authorities investigate cases of tax abuse in the philanthropic sector in partnership with other law enforcement agencies. Exchanging good practices as well as information with tax administrations and law enforcement agencies helps countries better detect and track tax abuse schemes involving philanthropic entities.

Keeping the public and especially donors aware of schemes involving philanthropic entities is also important. According to the 2009 OECD report on the abuse of charities, countries such as Canada and the United States have introduced awareness campaigns to alert the public about the risks associated with the abuse of charities (OECD, 2009[4]). Canada and the United States have put out tax alerts on their websites about donation schemes (such as a tax shelters) and the abuse by intermediaries (such as tax return preparers) with respect to charitable donations. In Canada, taxpayers can search the online charities listing and have access to the list of the registered charities, newly registered charities, charities whose status have been revoked and suspended, and which charities have been permanently annulled or have been fined. The public can also review the annual information returns filed by registered charities.

3.7.4. Rules on remuneration and total spending on employment

Philanthropic entities, generally meet a non-distribution requirement while the entity is in existence. An issue that can arise is whether the payment of salaries to employees breaches this notion of 'non-distribution'. Generally, the requirement does not prevent the payment of 'reasonable' remuneration for services (or the provision of goods). Some countries may impose restrictions in this regard, while others may be less prescriptive. Disclosure requirements may lessen the opportunities for excessive inurement.

To ensure that the untaxed income and received donations from philanthropic entities are not used for the personal gain of people associated with the entity, some countries have strict rules on remuneration and the total spending on employment. In Canada, for example, board members of PBOs are entitled to reasonable remuneration for the services they provide. This includes attendance fees and reimbursement of expenses, but does not generally include a salary simply for being a board member. The members of the board of trustees (or the board of directors) in Switzerland work on a voluntary basis and are generally only entitled to compensation of their effective expenses and cash expenses. For special services of individual members of the board of trustees (board members) it is allowed that an adequate compensation is paid.

In Colombia, the budget destined to compensate, remunerate or finance any disbursement, in money or in kind, for purposes of payroll, fees or commissions to the persons who hold managerial and directive positions of a philanthropic entity, may not exceed 30% of the total annual expenditure of the entity. If such payments exceed this limitation, the entity will be excluded from the Special Tax Regime.

Board members and trustees of PBOs in Ireland cannot accept a salary specifically for acting as a charity trustee, or receive other benefits for acting as such. However, they may be reimbursed for reasonable expenses, which they incur in carrying out their duties. Similarly, in Australia board members are generally unpaid but can be reimbursed for expenses.

In Sweden, board members of the PBO are entitled to remuneration. The only condition is that the PBO must use the main part of the income for a worthy purpose. In the Netherlands, PBOs can have volunteers, who may receive a limited compensation for their work. If the compensation is in line with the market, the volunteer will be seen as an employee and the normal rules for employees are applicable. In South Africa, employees and board members of philanthropic entities are entitled to remuneration, which is taxed as their personal income. Further, 75% of all donations received by a philanthropic entity in South Africa must be distributed for worthy purpose annually. Therefore, 25% is available to remunerate employees and others involved in the entity and for other expenses. The United States levies a 21% tax on excessive (over USD 1 000 000) remuneration for the five highest paid employees of exempt organisations (see Box 3.4 for more details).

References

ACNC (2020), *Governance Toolkit: Financial Abuse*, https://www.acnc.gov.au/for-charities/manage-your-charity/governance-hub/governance-toolkit/governance-toolkit-financial. [5]

Henry, K. et al. (2009), *Australia's Future Tax System*, https://treasury.gov.au/review/the-australias-future-tax-system-review. [2]

OECD (2019), *Tax Administration 2019: Comparative Information on OECD and other Advanced and Emerging Economies*, OECD Publishing, Paris, https://dx.doi.org/10.1787/74d162b6-en. [1]

OECD (2009), *Report on abuse of charities for money-laundering and tax evasion*, http://oecd.org/dataoecd/30/20/42232037.pdf. [4]

Tax Working Group (2019), *Future of Tax: Final Report*, Tax Working Group, https://taxworkinggroup.govt.nz/resources/future-tax-final-report-vol-i. [3]

Notes

[1] Value Added Tax (VAT) and the equivalent Goods and Services Tax (GST) in some jurisdictions area are referred to as "VAT" in this report.

[2] In the Brussels-Capital Region, for example, a reduced rate of 7% is applied for bequests (movable and immovable assets).

4 The tax treatment of giving

This chapter provides an overview of the tax treatment of donors and philanthropic giving across OECD member and selected participating countries. The first two sections of the chapter discuss the tax design of incentives for giving by individuals and countries' tax incentives for corporate giving. The last section highlights the potential risk of tax avoidance and evasion and the anti-abuse policies countries have put in place as a result.

4.1. Introduction

4.1.1. Characteristics of philanthropic giving

Philanthropic giving is the act of voluntarily transferring private resources to qualified philanthropic entities without receiving, or expecting to receive, anything of equal value in return. Both natural and legal persons can engage in philanthropic giving. Any benefit to the donor that arises from the gift must be within the statutory limits that apply. A number of countries (e.g. Australia, Austria, Canada, the United Kingdom, and the United States) have rules in place to accommodate the above fair market value purchase of goods and services from a philanthropic entity. Examples of such forms of philanthropic giving may include the purchase of tickets to a fundraising event (in the case of individuals) or the sponsoring of funds and PBOs in return for advertisement (in the case of corporations).

Philanthropic giving is a significant source of funding for funds and PBOs. All of the countries surveyed provide some form of tax incentives to encourage philanthropic giving. The generosity and design of the incentives varies. Countries may choose to encourage only some forms of giving or offer more support to some donors based on their income or wealth, or whether they are individuals or corporations.

The design of tax incentives for philanthropic giving depends on four characteristics of the transfer: (1) who is giving; (2) how is it given; (3) what is the gift; and (4) who is the recipient? As shown in Figure 4.1, giving can occur at an individual or corporate level, which has implications on motives as well as the tax used to incentivise this behaviour. At the individual level, we differentiate between donations during one's lifetime and testamentary giving on death. At the corporate level, we differentiate between donations and sponsorship payments to philanthropic entities, which may be considered part of the donor's business expenses. The gifts (or donations) themselves can be in the form of cash, or non-monetary assets (e.g. real estate, stocks, cultural assets, and in some cases even blood or organ donations). Finally, the type of recipient is important as it determines the philanthropic nature of the gift. This chapter will compare and contrast how countries use their tax systems to incentivise giving and how those incentives are designed to apply to the different forms of philanthropic giving.

Figure 4.1. Different tax implications depending on the characteristics of philanthropic giving

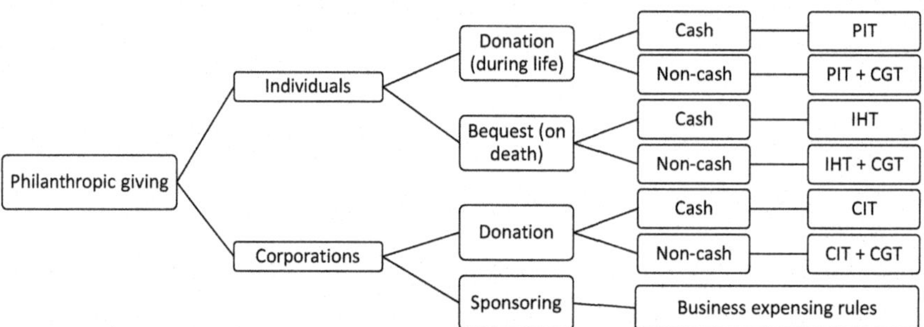

Note: This shows the most likely tax implications of philanthropic giving to funds and PBOs. Giving to individuals directly, in most cases, does not qualify as philanthropic and could instead lead to inheritance, estate or gift tax liabilities. Abbreviations: personal income tax (PIT); capital gains tax (CGT); Inheritance tax (IHT); corporate income tax (CIT).

4.1.2. Eligibility for tax incentives

For philanthropic giving, of any kind, to be eligible for tax incentives, the recipient must be an eligible (i.e. recognised) fund or PBO. None of the countries surveyed (see Box 4.1 for unique exceptions) offer tax subsidies to gifts made directly to individuals in need without passing through a fund or PBO. Moreover, such transfers may trigger estate, inheritance or gift tax liabilities. Gifts made to funds or PBOs that are earmarked for specific individuals usually do not benefit from tax incentives either. There are a number of reasons countries may want funds and PBOs to act as intermediaries between the donors and the final beneficiaries of philanthropy. Ensuring that each individual gift is distributed in a way that meets the not-for-profit, worthy purpose, and public benefit criteria would create a large administrative burden for governments and donors. As a result, it is more efficient to make funds and PBOs responsible for meeting the conditions necessary for philanthropic giving to be tax incentivised.

Box 4.1. Exceptions to the rules on giving to individuals directly

Chilean law concerning national emergencies

In Chile, philanthropic gifts to individuals directly (i.e. without passing through a fund or PBO) are exempt from any tax affecting them, and are deductible from the corporate income tax base, if they are given during a national emergency.

The Virginia Beach Strong Act in the United States

The Virginia Beach Strong Act states that a cash contribution made for the relief of the families of the dead or wounded victims of the mass shooting in Virginia Beach, Virginia, on May 31, 2019, shall be treated as a philanthropic donation despite being for the exclusive benefit of such families.

4.1.3. Key findings

The key findings of this chapter are that:

- The majority of countries surveyed, offer tax deductions to incentivise individual and corporate philanthropic giving. Other countries offer tax credits instead, and in some cases, donations are matched or facilitated through an allocation scheme. Furthermore, deductions are more common for corporate tax incentives than personal income tax incentives.
- Countries generally limit the value of their tax deduction or credit to a share of taxable or total income; a share of the income tax liability; a fixed value; a combination of ceilings; or limit the size of the donation itself.
- In countries with no tradition of philanthropic giving, an allocation scheme can create awareness among taxpayers, financially support funds and PBOs, and develop stronger ties between the general public and philanthropic entities.
- Countries that levy inheritance or estate taxes generally provide preferential tax relief for philanthropic bequests. In countries with an inheritance tax, the funds or PBOs receiving the bequest is liable for the tax and thus are the ones that receive the tax relief. In countries with an estate tax, on the other hand, the tax liability as well as the corresponding tax relief is with the estate of the deceased.
- The majority of countries that incentivise cash donations of individuals, also incentivise non-monetary donations. Countries may require appraisals if the value of a non-monetary donation exceeds a threshold, have different valuation rules for different types of assets, not require valuations or review valuations through audits.
- Corporate payments to philanthropic entities in return for advertising are considered business expenses in most countries, if they have a sufficient nexus with producing business income. However, these payments may have tax implications for the PBOs receiving them.
- Common types of tax avoidance and evasion issues with tax relief for philanthropic giving include: eligible philanthropic entities that wilfully participate in a tax evasion scheme to benefit their donors; falsified donation receipts prepared by the philanthropic entity, tax preparers or donors; payments for goods and services disguised as donations; overvalued gifts; and donations of assets in which the donor retains an interest in.

This chapter proceeds as follows. Section 4.2 summarises countries' tax policies that are intended to incentivise philanthropic giving by individuals. Within this section, the individual incentive schemes of countries are discussed in detail, followed by an analysis of tax rules for non-monetary donations by individuals. Section 4.3 provides an overview of tax policies incentivising philanthropic giving by corporations. This section covers the design of countries' tax incentives, as well as the tax rules concerning the sponsoring of the philanthropic entity in return for advertising. Finally, section 4.4 discusses the risks of tax avoidance and abuse that are related to the tax policies discussed in this chapter.

4.2. Philanthropic giving by individuals

In most of the countries surveyed, individual taxpayers that give to a qualifying fund or PBO during their lifetime receive some form of tax incentive. Philanthropic giving of individuals can occur during life, in the form of donations, or on death, in the form of philanthropic bequests. Donations by individuals are encouraged, directly or indirectly, through personal income and/or capital gains tax incentives. Almost all countries surveyed have tax incentives for individuals that donate during their lifetime to qualified funds or PBOs. In the absence of such an incentive, individual taxpayers that give would do so entirely from their post-tax income and with no change to their personal income tax liability or size of their gift (this is the case in Malta).

The design of tax incentives for individual donors differs across countries and depends on the nature of the gift. A philanthropic donation can be in the form of cash or non-cash, frequently referred to as non-monetary or in-kind donations. Non-monetary donations may include:

- real and intellectual property;
- stock or shares;
- trading stock;
- cultural assets;
- other personal property;
- services (volunteering); or
- blood and organ donations.

None of these forms of donating are always eligible for tax-subsidies. Countries may choose to limit their tax incentives to cash donations only (e.g., Austria, Finland, Israel, New Zealand, Norway and Sweden), or severely restrict the size and nature of non-monetary donations. Non-monetary donations also raise valuation concerns, which may have capital gains tax implications.

This section provides an overview of countries' tax treatment of donations made by individuals and is organised as follows: an overview of the design of the tax policies meant to support and incentivise philanthropy (deductions, credits, matching schemes, and allocation schemes), followed by a discussion of tax incentives for philanthropic bequests. Lastly, this section covers the tax policies for in-kind donations with a particular focus on the applicable valuation rules, as well as the potential capital gains tax implications.

4.2.1. Tax incentives for cash donations by individuals

In the large majority of countries surveyed, donations are deductible. Other countries offer tax credits and in some cases, donations are matched or facilitated through an allocation scheme. Although allocation schemes are not tax incentives, they are included in this discussion as they are part of the toolbox of tax policies intended to support philanthropy and are administered through the tax system. Table 4.1 shows that donations are deductible in 22 of the countries surveyed. Tax deductions effectively subtract the donation, or a portion of the donation, from the personal income tax (PIT) base before the tax liability is computed, thereby reducing the taxable amount before calculating the tax. Deductions that are tied to progressive tax brackets can become regressive since the value of tax deductions increases with marginal tax rates. In the context of deductible donations this means that in countries with a progressive personal income tax, the cost of giving is lower for the wealthy.

Another aspect to consider is whether countries have a comprehensive or schedular income tax system. In the case of the latter, the gross income, deductions, and credits are determined separately for each type of income (e.g., labour and capital income). Since rates may vary from type to type, the impact of the incentive may also. For example, countries with a dual income tax system may have a progressive tax rate for labour income, but a flat rate for capital income. As a result, a deduction would only be regressive if it is allowed against labour income.

Twelve countries incentivise donations through tax credits. A tax credit is an amount subtracted directly from the tax liability, after the liability has been computed. Unlike tax deductions, the value of tax credits is equal for all taxpayers (as long as their tax liability is equal to or larger than the value of the credit). If the value of the credit is larger than the tax liability of an individual, the credit would have to be refundable for the taxpayer to benefit fully from the incentive (this is the case in New Zealand for example). One country (Japan) offers donors a choice between a tax deduction and credit.

Table 4.1. Tax incentives for donations by individuals

Country	Deduction	Credit	Matching	Allocation	Other
Argentina	X				
Australia	X				
Austria	X				
Bulgaria	X				
Czech Republic	X				
Estonia	X				
Finland	X				
Germany	X				
India	X				
Indonesia	X				
Italy	X	X		X	
Japan	X	X			
Latvia	X				
Luxembourg	X				
Mexico	X				
Netherlands	X				
Norway	X		X		
Singapore	X		X		
Slovenia	X			X	
South Africa	X				
Switzerland	X				
United States	X				X[2]
Belgium		X			
Canada		X			
Chile		X			
Colombia		X			
France		X			
Greece		X			
Israel		X			
New Zealand		X[1]			
Portugal		X		X	
Sweden		X			
Ireland			X		
United Kingdom			X		
Hungary				X	
Lithuania				X	
Romania				X	
Slovak Republic				X	
Malta					X[3]

Note:
1. The tax credit is wholly refundable.
2. Some states have tax credits for certain donations.
3. In cases of shares and immovable property donations to a qualifying PBO, such transfers would not be subject to tax.
Source: OECD Taxation and Philanthropy Questionnaire and Ministry of Finance websites

The United Kingdom, Ireland, Norway, and Singapore have a matching scheme, where government tops up donations at a given rate so that the entity receiving the donation is able to claim the tax relief. In the United Kingdom and Ireland the matched amount is linked to the personal income tax rate of the donor.

Romania, Slovenia, Portugal, Hungary, Lithuania, and the Slovak Republic use a tax allocation scheme to support philanthropic entities. In countries with an allocation scheme, the tax administration allows taxpayers to designate a fixed percentage or amount of their income tax to a fund or PBO directly through their tax return. In itself, such a scheme is neither a tax incentive nor an act of giving. As discussed at the beginning of this chapter, philanthropic giving involves the voluntary transfer of private resources, and the money directed at funds and PBOs through a pure allocation scheme is public. Nevertheless, some have argued that allocation schemes can be used to help develop a culture of philanthropic giving in countries where there is no tradition of philanthropy (Bullain, 2004[1]). On the other hand, such a scheme may curb philanthropic giving as individuals will be less inclined to use their private resources to support funds and PBOs if they can do so with public resources (Bullain, 2004[1]).

4.2.2. Tax deductions

In countries with tax deductions, a donation (or a portion of it) is deductible from the personal income tax (PIT) base up to a limit that may be a fixed value and/ or expressed as a share of taxable or total income. To limit the size of the deduction, countries can: limit the share of the donation that is deductible (e.g. 50% of the donation is deducted from the PIT base); limit the size of the deduction to a share of taxable or total income (e.g. up to 20% of the PIT base); or limit the size of the deduction to a fixed value (e.g. up to EUR 1000). Table 4.2 shows that countries use any combination of tax deduction ceilings with different levels of generosity.

Decisions over what ceilings to use have policy implications on what income groups the tax subsidies target and what size of donations they most incentivise. For example, if the ceiling is a rather low share of total income but allows for a high fixed limit, high-income taxpayers will still receive a marginal benefit for large donations. If on the other hand, the ceiling is set to a high share of total income but the fixed limit on the deduction is low, the marginal benefit for any donation exceeding the fixed value limit will be zero. In Germany, for instance, deductions are simply capped at 20% of 'total income'[1], while in Estonia deductions are capped at 50% of 'taxable income' but may not exceed EUR 1 200.

Limiting the deduction to a share of taxable or total income

Table 4.2 shows that a number of countries (Argentina, Austria, Bulgaria, Switzerland, Germany, Indonesia, Italy, Mexico, the Netherlands, Slovenia, the United States, and South Africa) have ceilings that are only tied to income (as opposed to those limited to a fixed value). In these countries, the marginal cost of giving for large donations is lower for wealthy individuals regardless of the personal income tax rate, as higher income raises the deduction ceiling. Of course the fact that most countries have progressive personal income taxes leads to the cost of giving being even lower for those in higher tax brackets but this effect is independent of whether or not the ceiling is a function of total income or a fixed value.

Of the above mentioned countries, Argentina, Indonesia, Italy and Slovenia have the lowest ceilings. In Argentina, individuals can deduct donations up to 5% of 'annual earnings' of Argentinian source. In Indonesia, donations of up to 5% of current net income are deductible from the personal income tax base and for a taxpayer to be eligible for the deductible deduction, they must have net fiscal income (not a loss) based on the income tax return of the previous year, and the donation may not cause a loss in the current year. In Italy, individual taxpayers can choose between a deduction and a tax credit. Higher marginal tax rate taxpayers have a greater incentive to opt for deductions. Additionally, the gift may not be made through cash payments (i.e. it must be made through bank transfers, digital payments, etc.) in order to reduce the risk of abuse and tax evasion. For the tax deduction, individuals can deduct donations up to 10% of their taxable income. In Slovenia, a taxpayer with business and professional income can deduct donations but wage earners are incentivised through an allocation scheme. A taxpayer with business and professional income may claim a deduction for donations for humanitarian purposes, disabled persons assistance, social assistance, charitable, scientific, educational, health, sporting, cultural, ecological, religious and generally useful purposes. The deduction can be up to 0.3% of the taxpayer's 'taxable revenue' in the tax period. Additionally, a taxpayer may claim a deduction of up to an added 0.2% of the taxpayer's taxable revenue in the tax period concerned, for donations to cultural purposes and voluntary societies established for the protection against natural disasters. Donations for these purposes (culture and disaster relief) can be spread over three tax periods. As a general rule the sum of all tax incentives (not just those for philanthropic giving) cannot exceed 63% of the tax base.

Table 4.2. Limitations to personal income tax deductions

Country	Share of the donation that is deductible	Ceiling	Floor
Argentina	100%	5% of annual earnings	
Australia	100%	A deduction for a gift or contribution cannot add to or create a tax loss.	AUD 2
Austria	100%	10% of total income	
Bulgaria	100%	65% of taxable income (after the deduction)	
Czech Republic	100%	15% of taxable income	2% of the tax base or CZK 1 000
Estonia	100%	EUR 1 200 and 50% of the taxable income	
Finland	100%	EUR 500 000	EUR 850
Germany	100%	20% of total amount of income	
India	50% - 100%	10% of Gross Total Income	
Indonesia	100%	5% from current net income	
Italy	100%	10% of the taxable income.	
Japan	100%	40% of total income	JPY 2 000
Latvia	100%	EUR 600 and 50% of the annual taxable income	
Luxembourg	100%	EUR 1 000 000 or 20% of net income	EUR 120
Mexico	100%	For donations to private institution: 7% of last year's cumulative income. For donations to governmental institutions: 4% of last year's cumulative income.	
Netherlands	100%	10% of the total income.	1% of total income and over EUR 60.
Norway	100%	NOK 50 000	NOK 500
Singapore	250%	No limits	
Slovenia	100%	0.5% of taxable revenue	
South Africa	100%	10% of taxable income	
Switzerland	100%	20% of taxable income	CHF 100
United States	100%	60% or 30% of adjusted gross income depending on the beneficiary	

Source: OECD Taxation and Philanthropy Questionnaire and Ministry of Finance websites

In Bulgaria, Mexico, the Netherlands, and Slovenia the deduction rules vary across worthy purposes. In Bulgaria the limitations of deduction varies depending on the worthy purposes that the recipient fund or PBO is engaged in. Donations are deductible from the annual personal income tax base up to a total ceiling of 65% of the tax base after the deduction. For individual donations, the ceilings further differ depending on the beneficiary:

- Up to 5% of the annual tax base, where donations are in favour of:
  - healthcare and medical-treatment establishments;

    - social services for residential care, as well as of the Social Assistance Agency and of the Social Protection Fund under the Minister of Labour and Social Policy;
    - public nurseries, kindergartens, schools, higher schools or academies;
    - budgetary organisations, within the meaning given by the Accountancy Act;
    - any religious denominations registered in the country;
    - any specialised enterprises or cooperatives of persons with disabilities;
    - the Bulgarian Red Cross;
    - cultural institutes and community centres;
    - PBOs with the exception of any organisations supporting culture;
    - the Bulgaria Energy Efficiency and Renewable Sources Fund;
    - therapeutic communities for the treatment of drug-addicted persons;
    - the United Nations Children's Fund (UNICEF);
- Up to 15% of the annual tax base, where donations are in favour of culture;
- Up to 50% of the annual tax base, where donations are in favour of:
    - the National Health Insurance Fund: for activities related to the medical treatment of children.

In Mexico, the deduction limits vary depending on the nature of the receiving entity. Donations to private philanthropic entities are only deductible for an amount that does not exceed 7% of the 'cumulative income' earned by the taxpayer in the year immediately preceding the deduction. Mexico also incentivises donations to local government entities. Donations in favour of the Federation, the Federal Entities, the Municipalities, or their decentralized organisations, are only deductible in an amount that does not exceed 4% of the taxpayer's cumulative income in the previous year (donations to local government entities or institutions are outside the scope of this report and therefore not covered in more detail elsewhere). The sum of donations to private philanthropic entities and governments entities must not exceed 7% of the 'cumulative income' earned by the taxpayer in the year immediately preceding the deduction.

In the Netherlands donations are deductible if the amount of the donation is at least 1% (minimum EUR 60) and up to 10% of the donor's total income. A donation that is pledged for at least 5 years in a written statement (by a notary) can be deductible without the threshold and ceiling. For donations to a cultural PBO, there is a multiplier of 1.25 times the gift (up to a maximum of EUR 1 250). There are no rollover provisions and gifts are only deductible in the year they were given. Sole traders and unincorporated entities can deduct donations as business expenses as long as they do so for the purpose of producing income. Otherwise, the payment to philanthropic entities is deductible as a donation.

In the Czech Republic, donations to municipalities or qualifying philanthropic entities are deductible from the personal income tax base up to a ceiling of 15% of taxable income adjusted for deductible expenses. For the donation to qualify, it must be greater than the lesser of 2% of taxable income or CZK 1 000.

Austria, Australia, Germany, and the United States provide a deduction for donations to a broad range of philanthropic entities but also have rules to regulate donations for which the donor receives a benefit (donor-benefit rules). In Austria, cash donations of individuals are deductible from the personal income tax base in the year the money was donated. The only restriction is that the deduction may not exceed 10% of the total income. Donations cannot be carried over to a subsequent year. Austria also has very specific donor-benefit rules, for example, in relation to a fundraising event. Donors that give to funds and PBOs by purchasing an overpriced good or service, may deduct the amount paid that exceeds the fair market value of the good or service purchased. In a fundraising auction, where one individual donates a good and the other purchases it, the donor of the good may deduct its fair market value. The buyer of the good may in return deduct the amount paid in excess of the fair market value of the good.

In Australia, donations of more than AUD 2, are deductible from the personal income tax base. There is no specific upper limit on the value of a donation that may be deducted. The only limit is that deductions for donations cannot create or add to a tax loss. However, taxpayers can spread a donation over up to five income years. Furthermore, Australia differentiates between a gift for which the donor receives no benefit at all and a contribution for which the donor does receive a benefit. When the donor does receive a benefit (e.g. purchasing a ticket for a philanthropic fundraising event), the transaction is only tax deductible if the benefit to the donor is no more than AUD 150 and 20% of the value of the donation.

In the United States, deductions by individuals to philanthropic entities are generally limited to 60%[2] of 'adjusted gross income', although donations to private foundations are limited to 30% of adjusted gross income. Donations in excess of these limits can be carried over to up to 5 years. For taxpayers to benefit from the deductible deduction, they must itemise their deductions and cannot take the standard deduction (see Box 4.2). In the case of an above fair market value purchase of goods and services from a qualified fund or PBO (e.g. philanthropic fundraiser tickets), the excess payment (difference between the payment and the fair market value of the good or service) can be considered a philanthropic contribution and is tax deductible. However, for the excess amount to qualify, the individual must pay it with the intent of making a charitable contribution (i.e. the individual must be aware that they are paying more than the fair market value of the good or service).

In Germany, donations are considered special expenses and are deductible from the personal income tax base. The deduction is limited to 20% of 'total income' (or 4% of the sum of the total turnover and wages and salaries paid during the calendar year). Membership fees to entities that promote sports, certain cultural or heritage activities as well as customs and traditions are not deductible. Similarly, Germany has strict donor-benefit rules so that, unlike in the United States or Australia, the above fair market value purchase of goods and services from a fund or PBO (e.g. fundraiser tickets) is not tax deductible.

In Japan, the amount of a qualifying donation exceeding JPN 2 000 is deductible from donors' income up to 40% of total income. A donation qualifies for the tax incentive if it is made to public interest incorporated associations, public interest incorporated foundations and other corporations or groups that carry out business for the public benefit, which meet the requirements discussed in Chapter 3. Japan is a unique case because it allows donors to choose between a tax deduction and a tax credit (for some donations). The design of the tax credit is discussed in the next section.

In Switzerland, donations over CHF 100 are deductible up to 20% of 'taxable income' for federal income tax purposes. For cantonal (i.e. regional) income tax purposes, the thresholds are sometimes different. The majority of Swiss cantons have adopted the federal threshold and minimum donation amount. Some cantons, however, have eliminated the minimum donation amount or given its regional council the authority to wave the 20% threshold on a case by case basis if there is found to be 'a considerable public interest' in the relevant purpose. In South Africa, donations for the purposes of healthcare, conservation, education, and welfare activities, are deductible from the personal income tax base up to a limit of 10% of 'taxable income' (rollover provisions apply).

Limiting the deduction to a fixed value and/or a share of income

Countries with a fixed value limit (Estonia, Finland, and Norway) keep the size of the deduction under a certain maximum regardless of how high a donor's income is. This means that in these countries individuals with lower incomes can deduct a higher proportion of their income for philanthropic giving than those with high incomes. In Finland, donations between EUR 850 and EUR 500 000 are deductible from taxable income. Only donations for the purpose of promoting science, or art given to a publicly financed university, can qualify for the tax deduction. The ceiling is significantly lower in Norway, where the donation must be between NOK 500 and NOK 50 000 (~ EUR 4 500) to qualify for the tax deduction.

Furthermore, the design of the tax deduction in Estonia, Latvia, and Finland shows that there are regional similarities. In Estonia, donations of up to EUR 1 200 and 50% of the taxable income may be deducted. In

Latvia, donations can be deducted as part of the total eligible expenses including the acquisition of education and the use of health and medical treatment services. Total deductions are limited to 50% of the annual taxable income, and no more than EUR 600. So the deduction limit is set to the same share of total income in both Latvia and Estonia, but the fixed value limit is double the size in Estonia.

India is a unique case where the donations are limited if they are made in cash. All donations above INR 2 000 made in cash are not deductible and must be made by cheque or wire transfer. In India, 100% of the donation is deductible if it is given to certain funds (e.g. Prime Minister National Relief Fund) only 50% of the donation is deductible if it is given to most other philanthropic entities. In most cases, the deduction is capped at 10% of the gross total income (after all other eligible tax exemptions and deductions).

In Luxembourg, tax deductible donations must be at least EUR 120 and may not exceed 20% of the donor's total net income, or EUR 1 000 000. Donations that exceed these limits may be reported over the next 2 tax years. Additionally, the initial donation made by the founder of an eligible foundation or fund is also considered deductible donation.

Box 4.2. Implications of the Tax Cuts and Jobs Act (TCJA) for philanthropic giving

Signed into law on 22 December 2017, the TCJA is considered the biggest overhaul of the United States tax system in more than thirty years. It includes corporate and individual tax changes, which have implications for giving and philanthropic entities.

In the United States, taxpayers can choose between itemising their deductions on their income tax returns and claiming the standard deduction. Only taxpayers that itemise can deduct charitable contributions from their taxable income. Since the tax-subsidy for donations does not apply to those that claim the standard deduction, only itemisers have a tax incentive to give to philanthropic causes.

The TCJA just about doubled the standard deduction and capped the deduction for state and local taxes at USD 10 000. Since taxpayers only choose to itemise if the sum of their potential itemised deductions is larger than the standard deduction, this is likely to reduce the number of households claiming an itemized deduction especially among middle-income households.

Coupled with a slight decrease in PIT rates, the TCJA reduced the average tax subsidy for charitable giving considerably. In other words, the price of giving has increased and the overall design of the tax incentive has become even more focused on big donors.

Source: (Urban-Brookings Tax Policy Center, 2018[21]).

4.2.3. Tax credits

Belgium, Canada, Chile, Colombia, Greece, Israel, New Zealand, Portugal and Sweden all incentivise donations by individuals through tax credits. As discussed above, a tax credit is an amount subtracted directly from the tax liability, after the liability has been computed. Unlike a deduction, the value of a tax credit does not depend on the income tax rate paid by the donor and is, in itself, not regressive in countries with a progressive personal income tax.

To limit the size of tax credits countries may adjust the share of the donation that is creditable (e.g. 50% of the donation is creditable); limit the value of the credit to a share of taxable or total income (e.g. up to 20% of the PIT base); limit the value of the credit to a share of the total PIT liability (e.g. the credit cannot exceed 20% of the tax liability); limit the value of the credit to a fixed value (e.g. the credit cannot exceed EUR 1 000); or limit the size of the donation to a fixed value (e.g. up to EUR 1 000). Table 4.3 shows that countries use a combination of limitations to design their tax credits for philanthropic giving. The minimum amount necessary for a donation to qualify for the tax credit may be used to increase the efficiency of administrative costs and incentivise larger donations.

Table 4.3. Limitations to personal income tax credits

Country	Tax credit	Ceiling	Floor
Belgium	45%	Total amount of the donation may not exceed 10% of global net income nor EUR 375 350 per spouse	EUR 40 per institution
Canada	15% - 33%	Up to 75% of net income can be claimed (for cash donations)	
Chile	35-50%	Credits received for donations to charity, and education, culture and sport are limited at 20% of the amount of the donation subject to beneficial tax treatment or UTM 320 (approx. USD 20 558).	
Colombia	25%	Credit received is limited to 25% of the income tax liability (the excess may be carried over to the following year)	
France	66%	20% of taxable income	
Greece	20%	Total amount of the donation may not exceed 5% of taxable income	EUR 100
Israel	35%	The credit cannot exceed 30% of taxable income or NIS 9 000 000	
Italy	30% (35% for specific PBOs)	Up to EUR 30 000 of total giving	
Japan	40%	The donated amount cannot exceed 40% of total income and the value of the tax credit may not exceed 25% of the income tax liability.	JPY 2 000
New Zealand	33.33%	Total amount of the donation may not exceed 100% of taxable income.	NZD 5
Portugal	25%	The credit cannot exceed 15% of tax liability (no limit for donations to public institutions).	
Sweden	25%	The credit cannot exceed SEK 1 500	SEK 2 000 total donations and at least SEK 200 per individual donation

Source: OECD Taxation and Philanthropy Questionnaire and Ministry of Finance websites

Limiting the value of the credit to a share of taxable or total income

Canada offers tax credits for donations at the federal and provincial level. The federal tax credit is 15% on the first CAD 200 and 29% on donations above that amount, with the exception of individuals with taxable income exceeding the highest income tax bracket (which is indexed to annual inflation and approximately CAD 200 000), where the tax credit is 33% on all donations above the first CAD 200. Thus the value of the tax credit is larger for wealthier donors for all donations above CAD 200. Take, for example two donations of CAD 1 000 by donor A and donor B. Donor A has a taxable income above the highest income tax bracket (approximately CAD 200 000) and donor B does not. The monetary value of the tax credit for donor A and B is CAD 330 and CAD 290 respectively. Provinces tend to extend similar credits for provincial income tax at lower rates (e.g., Ontario provides a credit of 5.05% on the first $200 and 11.16% on donations above that). Generally, individuals are only able to claim up to 75% of their net income for the year but donations can be carried forwarded for 5 years. If the donor receives a benefit (e.g., the purchase of a ticket to a fundraising event), the fair market value of the benefit must be determined by the philanthropic entity (this is referred to as the 'split receipt' method) and deducted from the amount of the payment before the tax credit is applied. Furthermore, a donation is only eligible for tax relief if the value of the benefit received is less than 80% of the value of the donation. This is referred to as the 'intention to make a gift' threshold as gifts with a benefit to the donor above that amount are considered to have been made with no true intention of donating.

France provides a 66% tax credit for donations to philanthropic entities. The reduction applies within the limit of 20 % of taxable income. For donations to PBOs providing free meals, care or accommodation for people in need, the tax credit is 75% of a donation less than or equal to EUR 546. For the part of the donation that exceeds EUR 546, the tax credit is 66%. The 20 % of the taxable income limit remains constant. Additionally, France provides a reduction on the real estate wealth tax ("Impôt sur la fortune immobilière"). The reduction is 75 % of the amount of the donation with a cap at EUR 50 000.

In New Zealand, donors receive a fully refundable tax credit of 33.33% of the donation. Furthermore, the amount an individual can donate and claim a donation tax credit for is capped at 100% of their taxable income for the year the donation was made. The value of the tax credit is limited to 33.33% of the donor's taxable income. For a donation to qualify, it must be a gift of NZD 5 or more. The credits can be claimed by sole traders as well as individuals who are wage-earners.

In Japan, donors can select a 40% tax credit in place of the tax deduction for certain types of donations. However, the tax credit is only applied to the part of the donation that exceeds JPN 2 000. Furthermore, the donated amount cannot exceed 40% of total income and value of the credit cannot exceed 25% of the personal income tax liability.

Limiting the value of the credit to a share of the income tax liability

In Colombia and Portugal, the credit ceiling is tied to the tax liability instead of total taxable income. In Colombia, the tax credit is 25% of the value donated in the year or taxable period, limited to 25% of taxpayers' income tax liability of the year in which the donation was made. The excess may be offset against the income tax liability in the following tax year. For example, if an income taxpayer makes a donation of COP 150, such donation creates a credit of COP 37.5 (25% of COP 150). If the tax liability of the income tax payer is COP 80, the total amount of the credit that may be offset in the taxable year of the donation is COP 20 (25% of USD 80); the remaining COP 17.5 credit may be offset in the following tax year if it does not exceed 25% of the total income tax liability. In Portugal, the tax credit is set at 25% of the donation but limited to 15% of the tax liability which is ten percentage points lower than in Colombia.

Limiting the value of the credit to a fixed value

In Sweden, donors receive a 25% tax credit of up to SEK 1 500, corresponding to a maximum of SEK 6 000 a year in eligible donations. For the donation to be eligible for the credit it must be at least SEK 2 000 a year and SEK 200 at each giving occasion.

Limiting the value of the credit to a combination of ceilings

In Belgium, a 45% tax credit is granted for donations made to eligible philanthropic entities, provided the gifts amount to at least EUR 40 per beneficiary fund or PBO. The total amount of donations for which the tax credit is granted cannot exceed 10% of 'global net income' nor EUR 376 350 per spouse for a married couple.

In Chile, the size and limits of the tax credit depend on the worthy purpose of the entity receiving the donation. For donations to culture and sports, the tax credit can be 35% or 50%. Donations to social and public purposes and education, may receive a tax credit of 50%. The donation, however, is limited to 20% of the amount of the donation subject to beneficial tax treatment or 320 UTM (which is equal to about CLP 16 000 000 and EUR 18 000). For so called 'reconstruction donations', the tax credit is 40% and there are no limits to the size of the donation.

In Israel, the donor receives a tax credits equal to 35% of the eligible donations in the tax year. The value of the credit is limited 30% of the donor's yearly income or NIS 9 000 000.

Limiting the size of the donation

In Greece, donations are incentivised through a 20% tax credit provided that the sum of all donations exceeds EUR 100 during the tax year. The total amount of donations eligible for the tax credit cannot exceed 5% of taxable income and there are no carry over provisions. For individuals that have a business activity, donations can be considered business expenses without a limit or ceiling (as long as they comply with the business expensing rules).

Box 4.3. Tax measures to incentivise philanthropy in response to the Covid-19 pandemic

China

- In-kind donations to help combat COVID-19 are exempt from VAT and other consumption taxes. In addition, donations made by enterprises or individuals through qualified Public Benefit Organisations or government authorities can be fully deducted for corporate income tax and personal income tax purposes. Before the measure, Chinese taxpayers could only deduct part of their donation from their PIT base.

Chile

- Due to the Covid-19 crisis, a decree was issued by the Chilean government triggering the application of the tax benefits of Chilean law concerning national emergencies (see Box 4.1) to donations related with this catastrophe.

United States

- For 2020, up to USD 300 of monetary donations are deductible from the personal income tax base, whether or not the taxpayer itemises or takes the standard deduction (see Box 4.2).
- The United States also increased the limitations on deductions for charitable contributions by individuals who itemise, as well as corporations. For individuals, the 50% of adjusted gross income limitation is suspended for 2020. For corporations, the 10% limitation is increased to 25% of taxable income. This provision also increases the limitation on deductions for contributions of food inventory from 15% to 25%.

Italy

- Offered tax deductions of 30% for philanthropic donations linked to the COVID-19 emergency.

Belgium

- Companies donating medical material and equipment to hospitals do not have to pay VAT on these donations.

Iceland

- Persons and entities building, renovating or maintaining residential housing or vacation homes can seek reimbursement for 100% of the VAT incurred due to certain craftsman labour. The reimbursement rate has been increased from 60% to a 100% and now includes more types of labour, for example architects. This measure is further extended to PBOs such as charities and sports associations. These measures will remain in effect until end 2020.

Source: OECD Tax Policy Responses to COVID-19 database (http://www.oecd.org/tax/covid-19-tax-policy-and-other-measures.xlsm).

4.2.4. Matching schemes

In a matching scheme, the government tops up donations with a specific amount, which means that the fund or PBO receiving the donation is able to claim the tax incentive. The United Kingdom and Ireland both have matching schemes. The matching scheme in the United Kingdom is referred to as Gift Aid. The donation is treated as if the donor has had the basic tax rate (20%) deducted (i.e. a donation of GBP 1 000 is treated as GBP 1 250). The PBO or fund receiving the donation is then able to claim Gift Aid from the tax administration (HMRC in the United Kingdom) at the basic tax rate (see Table 4.4 for an illustration of Gift Aid). Higher rate taxpayers can claim the difference between the basic rate and the higher rate as personal tax relief.

The fiscal devolution of Wales and Scotland allows for differential tax rates across the United Kingdom. Nevertheless, Gift Aid claimed by charities regardless of their location within the United Kingdom is determined using the United Kingdom basic rate. On the other hand, the tax relief claimed by the Welsh or Scottish donor is determined using the difference between the United Kingdom basic rate and the Welsh or Scottish higher rate respectively.

Table 4.4. Example of Gift Aid in the United Kingdom

Income tax rate of the donor	Donation	Gift Aid claimed	PBO and fund receive	Personal tax relief
Basic (20%)	GBP 1 000	GBP 250	GBP 1 250	GBP 0
Higher rate (40%)	GBP 1 000	GBP 250	GBP 1 250	GBP 250

Note: (GBP 1000 / 80) * 100 = GBP 1 250.
Source: Government website (https://www.gov.uk).

In the United Kingdom, payments to funds and PBOs in return for goods or services (including the purchase of a ticket to a fundraising event or raffle) are not considered donations and cannot qualify for Gift Aid. However, specific rules apply to a charity auction where individuals are willing to pay substantially more than market value in order to support the philanthropic entity. For auctioned goods that have a retail price and are freely available, the benefit to the individual for Gift Aid purposes is considered to be the retail price. Any excess payment can be treated as a donation if the donor is aware of that the item's retail price and that it is freely available elsewhere (e.g., if an individual knowingly purchases a TV with a retail price of GBP 500 for GBP 700 at a charity auction, the excess GBP 200 pounds can qualify as a donation for Git Aid purposes). The value of goods that are not freely available and have no retail price (e.g., items belonging to celebrities) or services that are not usually available (e.g., babysitting for an evening) are considered to be worth the price that they are purchased for and therefore do not qualify for Gift Aid.

Ireland also has a matching scheme for incentivising charitable donations (called Charitable Donation Scheme). Philanthropic donations from an individual which are greater than EUR 250 per year, but do not exceed EUR 1 000 000 per year, attract tax relief. The relief may be claimed by the approved body to which the money is donated at a rate of 31%, or 10% if there is a connection between the donor and the organisation. The matching payment to an approved body cannot exceed the amount of tax that the donor has paid for that year. The donor cannot claim a refund of any tax that has been paid to the approved body.

In 2014, Norway introduced a matching scheme (also known as the gift reinforcement programme) in addition to the available deduction. The purpose of the program is to stimulate increased private sector funding for art and culture in the form of monetary donations. Recipients of donations receive an additional gift reinforcement sum, usually 25% of the donated amount. Applications for the receiving the reinforcement sum must be submitted to the Ministry of Culture.

4.2.5. Allocation schemes

In countries with no tradition of philanthropic giving, an allocation scheme (also referred to as 'percentage philanthropy' or 'tax percentage designation' scheme) can create awareness of philanthropy among taxpayers, financially support funds and PBOs, and develop stronger ties between the general public and philanthropic entities. Allocation schemes were introduced mainly in post-communist Europe during the transition period and reports have estimated that by 2016 these schemes have provided philanthropic entities in the region with around five billion in funding (Strečanský and Török, 2016[3]). Of the countries surveyed, Romania, Slovenia, Portugal, Hungary, Italy, Lithuania, and the Slovak Republic have a tax allocation scheme to support their philanthropic entities. Hungary was the first country to introduce an allocation scheme in 1997, followed by Portugal in 2001, the Slovak Republic in 2002, Lithuania in 2003, Poland, and Romania in 2004, and Slovenia in 2007 (Bullain, 2004[1]).

Allocation schemes decentralise the decision-making process of allocating a certain percentage of income tax revenues to the taxpayers themselves. As discussed above, allocation schemes are not a form of philanthropic giving because they does not involve the transfer of private funds. Instead, taxpayers are able to indicate to the tax authorities what philanthropic entities or causes a set percentage of their income tax liability should be allocated to. The details of the scheme vary across countries, but typically taxpayers need to choose the philanthropic entity or worthy purpose from a list provided by the tax authority.

Some countries that have allocation schemes do not have incentives for individual philanthropic giving (e.g., Hungary, Lithuania, and the Slovak Republic), while others (e.g. Slovenia and Portugal) also offer tax incentives such as deductions or credits. This is worth noting because while allocation schemes can complement deductions, credits, or matching schemes, they should not be viewed as a replacement of this kind of tax relief for philanthropic giving because the scheme comes at zero cost to the taxpayer making the allocation. In Hungary, taxpayers can designate 1% of their personal income tax to an eligible PBO since 1997 and since 1998 they can designate an additional 1% to churches. In Lithuania, a taxpayer can designate up to a total of 1.2% of their personal income tax to eligible PBOs. In the Slovak Republic, individuals can allocate 2% of their income tax to a philanthropic entity and they can do so when submitting their tax return. If the taxpayer has volunteered for a 'worthy' purpose entity, for at least 40 hours during the tax year, the amount that can be allocated increases to 3% of the personal income tax liability. In Romania, individuals can allocate 2% or 3.5% of their personal income tax liability to philanthropic entities by submitting a form with the list of preferred recipients to the tax authority. The 2% share can be directed to philanthropic entities that are established and operate according to legal provisions, but also to religious units (including parishes). The share of 3.5% can be directed to PBOs and religious units that are also providers of social services. From 2021, the share will become 3.5% and can be directed to all PBOs and religious units that operate according to legal provisions.

What distinguishes Italy, Slovenia and Portugal is that they have tax deductions and credits to incentivise philanthropic giving, but have also implemented a tax allocation scheme. In Slovenia, taxpayers can allocate either 0.1%, 0.2%, 0.3%, 0.4% or 0.5% of their personal income tax to eligible funds and PBOs by submitting a form online, in person, or by mail at any point before end of the year for which the personal income tax is assessed. In 2018, a total of about EUR 5 million was allocated to over 5 000 entities, in 2017 the total sum allocated this way was around EUR 4.6 million and in 2011 it was around EUR 3.8 million.[3]

In Portugal a taxpayer can allocate 0.5% of their personal income tax for religious or charitable purposes, to a church, religious community, or PBO. They can do so as part of their annual personal income tax declaration or through an online portal by April. In addition to the personal income tax allocation scheme, Portugal also introduced a VAT allocation scheme in 2019 (see Box 4.4 for a more detailed overview of how it works).

In Italy a large amount of the financing for the philanthropic sector comes from the "5 per mille" option, an allocation scheme which enables taxpayers to allocate the 0.5% of their PIT to public and private entities operating in cultural, educational, scientific and charitable fields. PBOs represent a relevant part of the entities entitled to receive these funds. In 2018 this kind of financing amounted to EUR 439.8 million for PBOs.

Box 4.4. The Portuguese VAT allocation scheme

In addition to being able to allocate a share of their personal income tax, individuals in Portugal can also direct a share of some of their VAT payments to the same entity that they specified for the allocation of their income tax.

Contrary to the allocation of personal income taxes, the VAT allocation scheme comes at a cost to the taxpayer and is therefore a form of philanthropic giving. In Portugal 15% of the VAT paid to car workshops, restaurants, accommodation services (e.g. hotels), hairdressers, beauty salons and veterinaries, and 100% of the VAT paid for social passes (i.e. public transportation) is tax deductible. The allocation scheme allows taxpayers to direct their VAT deductible VAT payments to a philanthropic entity and forgo the tax benefit themselves.

4.2.6. Philanthropic bequests

Countries that levy inheritance or estate taxes generally provide preferential tax relief for philanthropic bequests. In countries with an inheritance tax, the PBO or fund receiving the bequest is liable for the tax and thus entitled to receive any tax relief. In countries with an estate tax, on the other hand, the tax liability as well as the corresponding tax relief is with the estate of the deceased.

The Brussels-Capital region in Belgium, for example, has a reduced regional inheritance tax rate of 7% for bequests of moveable and immovable assets to accredited philanthropic entities (as opposed to the standard rate of 25%).

In France, bequests made to PBOs recognized as being of public utility (see Chapter 3) are subject to the inheritance tax rate provided for inheritances between siblings:

- 35 % up to EUR 24 430;
- 45 % above EUR 24 430.

For other PBOs which do not benefit from the public utility status, the tax rate is set at 60%. Nevertheless, some type of donations and bequests are exempted from the inheritance tax:

- endowment funds of a philanthropic, educational, scientific, social, humanitarian, sporting, family, cultural nature, or contributing to the enhancement of artistic heritage, the defence of the natural environment or the dissemination of culture , French language and scientific knowledge;
- endowment funds whose management is selfless and which transfer the income from donations to other non-profit organizations,

In Bulgaria, bequests to the Bulgarian Red Cross, registered religious denominations and community centres are exempt from inheritance tax. Funds and PBOs are also exempt from inheritance tax in the Netherlands, Slovenia and Finland.

In countries with an estate tax, the estate receives the exemption or other tax relief. In South Africa, for example, bequests to PBO's are exempt from estate tax. In the United States, philanthropic bequests are fully deductible from the estate tax base.

Norway, Canada and Australia do not have an inheritance or estate tax, but donations on death or in the year before can still qualify for tax deductions. In Canada, the tax credit for a donations made by an individual in the year of death (but prior to the date of death) can be claimed either on the deceased individual's final tax return or the return for the preceding year. Additionally, the limit of the tax credit for donations made in the year of death is raised to 100% of the deceased person's net income or the eligible amount of gifts made in the year of death (in addition to any eligible unclaimed portion of the amount of any gifts made in previous years). In Norway, testamentary donations (i.e. bequests) are deductible under the same conditions as donations made before death. If the conditions are fulfilled, philanthropic bequests are deducted from the estate when the tax for the estate of the relevant deceased person is calculated. In Australia, a gift on death is not subject to capital gains tax, if the gift would have been deductible if made during the donor's lifetime. In Japan, assets donated by the heir to a PBO, are not included in the taxable value of inheritance tax.

4.2.7. Non-monetary donations of individuals

In countries that extend tax incentives to non-monetary donations by individuals, the limitation rules or form of tax relief may differ from cash donations. Not all countries that incentivise philanthropic giving of individuals include non-monetary donations. Of the countries that do (Argentina, Australia, Belgium, Bulgaria, Canada, Chile, Colombia, Estonia, France, Germany, Greece, India, Indonesia, Ireland, Italy, Latvia, Mexico, the Netherlands, Portugal, Singapore, Slovenia, South Africa, Switzerland, and the United States), some have specific rules that are different from those for cash donations discussed above. Non-monetary, or in-kind donations, refer gifts such as property, services, and in some cases even blood and organ donations (see Box 4.5). Donations of property can include real and intellectual property; stocks or shares; trading stock; cultural assets; or other personal property. Donations of goods and services typically refer to the provision of the kind of goods and services that PBOs themselves provide to those in need (e.g. clothing, food, medicine, volunteering at a homeless shelter, etc.). Not all of these different forms of in-kind donations are eligible in all countries, but most allow for the donation of property. A disposal of property may also give rise to a capital gain in some countries.

In Australia, the same rules that apply to cash donations apply to donations of shares and items of trading stock. For donations of property other than shares, the gift must be valued at more than AUD 5,000 unless it is donated within 12 months of purchase. Shares listed on a stock exchange must be valued at less than AUD 5 000 and acquired within the last 12 months. A disposal of property to a philanthropic entity as a gift could give rise to a capital gain (or loss), but this may be offset, in whole or part, by the gift deduction. In Belgium, donations in the form of works of art are eligible to receive a tax credit, provided that the donations are made to state museums, public welfare centres or communities such as regions, provinces, and municipalities.

In Canada, the valuation rules and by extension limitations to tax incentives also depend on the nature of the donated assets. In Canada, generally speaking, non-monetary property can be donated and the donor is entitled to claim the charitable donation tax credit on the full fair-market value (FMV) of the donation. Dispositions of such property may be subject to capital gains tax. Generally, individuals are only able to claim a credit up to 75% of their net income for the year and may be carry forwarded for 5 years. However, gifts of ecologically sensitive land to certain qualified PBOs (not private foundations) are not limited to a percentage of net income and may be carried forward for up to 10 years. Gifts of certified cultural property are not limited to a percentage of net income.

In Italy, the monetary value of the donation is evaluated according to the open market value of the asset. If the giving is higher than EUR 30 000, the donor has to provide with a technical report certifying the estimated value of the given asset. Donations of primary goods, such as food, drugs and hygienic products, are not taxable for income tax purposes and are exempt from VAT.

Box 4.5. Tax incentives for volunteering and blood and organ donations exist in only a few countries

Tax incentives for donations of services

Tax incentives for donations of services are difficult to design since PBOs often have both employees and volunteers and distinguishing between the two can be challenging.

Germany, for instance, extends preferential tax treatment to income from civic engagements and volunteering. Income from a 'side-line' activity paid to individuals by a PBO is tax-exempt up to EUR 720 per year. For certain side-line activities (trainer, instructor, childcare work, support work, artistic activity, part-time care of an old, sick or disabled person), the tax exemption is EUR 2 400 per year.

In the United States, volunteers cannot deduct the value of their services for income tax purposes. Expenses incurred as a result of the volunteering may however be deductible. For expenses to qualify for tax relief they must be unreimbursed, directly connected with the volunteering, expenses that only occurred because of the services given, and not personal, living or family expenses.

In the Netherlands, volunteers can deduct expenses of up to EUR 1 500 per year (and not more than EUR 150 per month) without having to itemise. Expenses above EUR 1 500 have to be itemised and justified. If unjustified, any reimbursements that individuals receive for these expenses are treated as income and taxed accordingly.

The Slovak Republic's allocation scheme indirectly incentivises volunteering because it enables taxpayers that have volunteered to designate one percentage point more of their income tax to a philanthropic entity of their choice (see section 4.2.3 for more information).

Incentives for blood and organ donations are less frequent

In Ireland, compensation received by living donors of kidneys for transplantation are exempt from income tax and not included in computing the PIT rate.

In some states of the United States, organ donations are eligible for certain tax deductions. In New York state, for example, a taxpayer that, while living, donates one or more of their human organs for human organ transplantation can deduct up to USD 10 000 from their PIT base for any expenses incurred. The deductible expenses are limited to travel expenses, lodging expenses, and lost wages.

In the Czech Republic, blood donations are valued at CZK 3 000 per donation and can be deducted from the donor's PIT base. The donation of bone marrow is also deductible from the personal income tax base and valued at CZK 20 000.

In the United States, contributions of certain 'long-term capital gain property' is deductible but generally limited to 30% of adjusted gross income (AGI). Qualified farmers and ranchers (over 50% of gross income from farming) can deduct up to 100% of AGI, less any other contribution deductions, for donations of qualified real property provided that the property remains generally available for agriculture or livestock production. In addition, deductions for certain contributions are limited to the donor's basis in the property.

Valuation rules of non-monetary donations

For non-monetary donations to receive any form of tax relief the value of the gift has to be determined. Regardless of whether it is a deduction, credit or matching scheme, the valuation of a non-monetary gift determines the amount that can be deducted, credited, or matched. The undervaluation of a gift will decrease the incentive power of the tax relief. If a gift is overvalued, on the other hand, the donation will increase the benefit to the donor and, in extreme cases, could exceed the actual value of the gift. The valuation of non-monetary donations is therefore essential for tax incentives for philanthropic giving to function efficiently. Generally, the fair market value (FMV) is used to calculate the respective tax subsides but the regulations concerning who is responsible for the valuation, and how the fair market value is determined, typically depends on the size of the gift and varies across countries. The different approaches are discussed below.

Regardless of whether the donor, beneficiary, or tax administration is responsible for determining the monetary value of a gift, the valuation process comes at a cost. In some cases it may be as simple as looking up the retail price of an item or the market value (e.g., of shares), but for real estate, used goods, or artwork, the process tends to be more time and resource intensive. Therefore countries tend to make the probable value of a good a determining factor of whether or not it needs to go through a more extensive valuation process. Small non-monetary donations (such as gifts of used clothing) are not worth getting appraised by an expert and may therefore not qualify for tax relief.

Require appraisals if the value is likely to exceed a threshold

In Australia, property valued at over AUD 5 000 (other than shares in a listed company) must be valued by the revenue authority i.e. the Australian Taxation Office and the cost of the valuation must be paid by the donor. Additionally, the cost of the valuation may be claimed as a deduction if the sole purpose of the valuation was to determine the value of a gift.

In Canada, it is the responsibility of the PBO to ensure that donations are properly valued at their fair market value (FMV). If the FMV of the property is less than CAD 1 000, a member of the registered PBO, or another individual, with sufficient knowledge of the property may determine its value. If, on the other hand, the FMV is greater than CAD 1 000, the valuation or appraisal will generally be carried out by a professional third-party appraiser. If it is appraised, the name and address of the appraiser must be included on the official donation receipt. In the case of donations of ecologically sensitive land and donations of certified cultural property, special rules apply with respect to valuation. Generally, there are rules that provide, respectively, the Minister of Environment and the Canadian Cultural Property Export Review Board, with the responsibility of determining the FMV of the donation.

Valuation rules depend on the nature of the asset

In Colombia, the valuation rules depend on the nature of the asset. The value of gold and other precious metals is the commercial value of such goods. The value of motor vehicles is the commercial appraisal established annually by the Ministry of Transportation; the value of shares, contributions and other rights in companies is determined in the donors' tax basis of these assets. The value of real or immovable property is the one registered in the donor´s last tax return, according to special tax rules.

In Mexico, the value of donations of land or shares is equal to the Original Investment Amount (MOI), updated for the effects of inflation, generated from the date at which the land or shares were acquired until the month immediately prior to the donation. In the case of fixed assets, the value of the donation should be the updated Original Investment Amount. For other real estate the amount of the donation is valued by updating the amount paid to acquire the good for the period of the month in which it was acquired up to the month of the donation for inflation. In the event that merchandise/trading stock is donated it would not be deductible since it was already considered within the cost of sales for tax deduction purposes.

The valuation of real estate for tax purposes in Germany, depends on whether the property is developed. The value of undeveloped real estate is determined and published by the committee of land valuation experts responsible for the local area. In the case of developed property, the value is calculated using the comparative value method, the rental value method or the material value method depending on the situation.

- The comparative value method is generally used to value detached and semi-detached houses as well as residential apartments and non-residential rooms forming part of larger properties. The value of the property is determined by comparison with the prices of similar properties.
- The rental value method is used to value property rented for residential purposes, as well as mixed-use and business property, for which it is possible to determine the customary amount of rent paid on the local market. The value of the property is calculated by determining the value of the land in the same way as for undeveloped property and adding a value representing the yield from the building.
- The material value method is used for real estate, for which neither the comparative value nor the rental value method is practical. Under this method, the value of the property is determined on the basis of the standard construction costs for the building and for other facilities together with the value of the land. If the taxpayer provides evidence substantiating a lower market value, this is to be recognised instead.

In the United States, donations of property (except publicly traded stock) above USD 5 000 must have a qualified appraisal. The appraisal must be signed by a qualified appraiser using generally accepted appraisal standards and, in most cases, the receipt of the donation must be acknowledged by the receiving entity. For donations of artwork over USD 20 000 and any donations valued over USD 500 000, signed copies of the appraisal must be filed with the tax return in which the deduction is claimed. Donations of artwork to a philanthropic entity are subject to review by art advisory committee. In general, a deduction is not allowed if the donor retains any interest in the property, or if the donation is of a partial interest in property. The primary exception is that a contribution of a conservation easement is deductible even though it is a contribution of a partial interest. The valuation of the easement is based on the loss of value due to the easement restrictions determined by a qualified appraiser.

In France, securities (e.g., stocks, bonds) are valued according to the last price known on the stock market (closing price the day before the donation) and the value of real estate (e.g., individual houses, apartments, forests, etc.) is estimated according to its market value.

In the Netherlands, the value of listed shares and bonds is based on the stock market price. For other assets the value is based on the FMV, which has to be determined before the donation is made.

No appraisals are required and valuation may be reviewed through audits

In some countries the appraisal of donated assets is not required, but the donor's valuation may be audited, in which case the indicated price of the asset has to be confirmed. This is the case in Chile, Estonia, and Ireland. In Chile, as a general rule, appraisal of non-monetary donations should be made according to special provisions of the inheritance and gift tax law. Special appraisal rules may apply in some cases. In Indonesia, the value of a non-monetary donation is determined according to historical value, book value, or the retail cost of other goods sold. In the case of in-kind donations such as the construction of infrastructure, the value is determined using the actual construction cost necessary to build the donated infrastructure.

Capital gains tax relief

Donations of assets that have increased in value may have capital gains tax implications in countries that levy a capital gains tax (CGT). If, for example, an individual donates property to a PBO that they purchased for EUR 50 000 but is now valued at EUR 100 000, a capital gain will be realised. In a country where donations are exempt from capital gains tax, the individual may benefit from the tax incentive schemes, but may also not have to pay the capital gains tax they would have otherwise had to pay once they had either sold or disposed of the asset.

Canada provides a full capital gains exemption for donations of certain types of property (in addition to such donations receiving the charitable donation tax credit). Specifically:

- Gifts of publicly-traded shares and stock options may be eligible for an inclusion rate of zero on any capital gain realised, subject to certain conditions. The capital gains tax on donations of shares in private companies, on the other hand, does apply and is not subject to CGT relief.
- Gifts of ecologically sensitive land to certain qualified funds (not private foundations) are eligible for an inclusion rate of zero on any capital gain realised, subject to certain conditions.
- Gifts of certified cultural property are also not subject to capital gains tax, subject to certain conditions.

Ireland exempts from capital gains tax the disposal of a work of art that has previously been loaned to an approved gallery or museum or to the Irish Heritage Trust, for a period of 10 years or more (6 years or more for loans made before 2 February 2006) and has been on display to the public. To qualify for this relief, a work of art must have a value of at least EUR 31 740 at the time it is loaned to the gallery. For information on the capital gains tax relief for the donation of shares, see Box 4.6.

Box 4.6. Irish capital gains tax (CGT) relief

Donation of property

Capital gains tax (CGT) relief is available for donors (both individual and corporate) of tangible assets, such as real property. A donation of property will be deemed to have been made at the value it had on the date the property was acquired by the donor. This is an exception to the normal rule requiring the disposal consideration to be treated for tax purposes as the market value at disposal. The donor will therefore be treated as having made neither a gain nor a loss on the disposal and will not be subject to capital gains tax.

Donation of shares

If an individual donor in Ireland, makes a donation of shares which have increased in value since the date on which they were acquired by the donor, the disposal would give rise to a CGT liability. The donor can claim CGT relief on this disposal, but the PBO would then not be able to claim the income tax relief (described in Box 3.2). If the donor chooses not to claim the CGT relief, then the PBO will receive the FMV of the shares plus the relief of 31% (or 10% if there is a connection between the donor and the organisation).

The charity will have no CGT liability on any subsequent sale of the shares provided the proceeds on the sale are applied for its charitable purposes. The donor, however, may (subject to their personal exemption on capital gains of EUR 1 270 per year) be liable for capital gains tax at 33% on the difference between the value of the shares transferred and the original cost of the shares.

A company making a donation of shares to PBO may choose between claiming corporation tax relief at 12.5% and deducting the donation as a trading expense, or claiming CGT relief, whichever is higher. If corporation tax relief is claimed then the company will be liable for CGT on the disposal and the charity will not be able to claim a repayment.

In the United States, no capital gains tax is imposed on donations of appreciated property, provided that the one-year holding period requirement is met.

In Australia, a gift of property, including shares, may trigger a capital gain or loss event. This is treated separately, i.e. the taxpayer may claim a deduction for the gift and must also record a capital gain or loss as applicable. Such a gain or loss is treated normally, increasing or decreasing the tax liability as applicable. However, a donor is exempt from paying CGT on donations of property to PBOs under the Cultural Gifts Program and donations of exempt personal use assets to PBOs (and will also be able to claim a deduction for the value of the gift). Testamentary gifts are not subject to CGT provided the gift would have been deductible if made during the individual's lifetime.

In Norway, a non-monetary donation to a philanthropic entity is not considered an event of realisation/divestment for tax purposes. Therefore, potential capital gains arising from donations, do not trigger capital gains tax in the hands of the donor. This is also the case in Argentina and Israel. In Indonesia, non-monetary donations are exempt from capital gains tax if they are given to a religious body, educational or other social entity including a foundation, or cooperative. In Colombia, Estonia, Latvia, Portugal South Africa, and Switzerland, donations in the form of assets are not exempt from capital gains tax.

4.3. Philanthropic giving by corporations

Of the countries analysed in this report, all except for Sweden incentivise corporate philanthropic giving to qualifying funds or PBOs. Corporate giving can occur in the form of donations or sponsorship payments. However, for corporate giving to be considered philanthropic it must comply with the country's donor-benefit rules. Since sponsoring payments to funds and PBOs are in return for publicity that generates a benefit to the donor, it will only be considered philanthropic giving if the benefit is within the statutory limits that apply. Corporate donations are encouraged through corporate income and/ or capital gains tax incentives. In the absence of such an incentive, corporate taxpayers that donate to philanthropic entities would do so from their post-tax profits and receive no tax benefit. In some countries, the donation would be considered an expense unrelated to economic activity and therefore remain part of the corporation's taxable income.

4.3.1. Tax incentives for donations by corporations

Tax incentives for donations by corporations include tax deductions, credits, and matching schemes. Additionally, this section also discusses allocation schemes, on the same basis as for individuals. Unlike the incentives for individuals, businesses can also use business expensing rules, which are linked to deductions, to incentivise corporate sponsoring of philanthropic entities. Table 4.5 shows that corporate donations are deductible in 29 countries.

Compared to the information in Table 4.1, Table 4.5 shows that deductions are more common for corporate tax incentives than personal income tax incentives. For instance, three countries that have personal income tax credits to incentivise individual giving (Belgium, Canada, and New Zealand), encourage corporate giving through deductions instead. A possible explanation for this difference is that countries view corporate donations as business expenses and thus simply allow them to deduct the gift through the same mechanism that other business expenses are deducted. Another contributing factor for the difference between corporate and individual tax incentives is that countries use personal income tax credits to avoid the regressive effect of tax deductions when rates are progressive. Since corporate income tax rates are typically flat, tax credits are no longer necessary to avoid the regressive effect (this is not the case in the Netherland and discussed in more detail below).

Six countries incentivise donations using tax credits, three of which (Chile, Latvia, and Portugal) also offer deductions. Corporate tax credits allow corporations to subtract a share of the value of their donation from their income tax liability, after the liability has been computed. In a number of countries, corporations can choose whether they want to make use of the deduction or the credit depending on which incentive would benefit them more.

Table 4.5. Tax incentives for donations by corporations

X denotes the tax incentive for corporations; O denotes the tax incentive for individuals (if different from that of corporations).

Country	Deduction	Credit	Matching	Allocation	Other
Argentina	X				
Australia	X				
Austria	X				
Belgium	X	O			
Bulgaria	X				
Canada	X	O			
Chile	X	X			
Czech Republic	X				
Estonia	X				
Finland	X				
Germany	X				
Greece	X				
Hungary	X			O	
India	X				
Indonesia	X				
Ireland	X		O		
Italy	X	O		O	
Japan	X				
Latvia	X	X			
Lithuania	X			O	
Luxembourg	X				
Malta	X				O
Mexico	X				
Netherlands	X				
New Zealand	X	O			
Norway	X		X		
Portugal	X	X		O	
Romania	X			O	
Singapore	X				
Slovenia	X			O	
South Africa	X				
Switzerland	X				
United Kingdom	X		O		
United States	X				
Colombia		X			
France		X			
Israel		X			
Slovak Republic				X	
Sweden		O			X[1]

Note:

1. No tax incentive for donations by corporations

Source: OECD Taxation and Philanthropy Questionnaire

Norway is the only country with a matching scheme for corporate giving and the Slovak Republic is the only country with an allocation scheme. The advantages of allocation schemes – such as their ability to foster a culture of giving by increasing the awareness of the general public – relate mainly to donations of individuals. Thus a potential explanation of the difference in the frequency of allocation schemes between incentives for individuals compared to corporations, is that aside from directing public funds to philanthropic entities (which can be done through grants) their effect on the visibility of the philanthropic sector is not as powerful when the scheme is applied to corporations.

The design of tax incentives for corporate donors differs across countries and depends on the nature of the gift. A philanthropic donation can be in the form of cash or non-cash, frequently referred to as non-monetary or in-kind donations. In the case of corporations such gifts may include

- real and intellectual property, stocks, and cultural assets;
- the provision of goods (e.g., a medical equipment producer donating its wheelchairs);
- or the provision of services (e.g., a construction company building infrastructure).

As with non-monetary donations of individuals, countries have rules regulating the valuation of gifts. Section 4.2.7. (above) provides an overview of these valuation rules and unless countries have specific regulations for corporate donations the valuation rules are not repeated in this section of the report.

4.3.2. Limitations for tax incentives to corporate donors

Tax deductions and credits for corporate donations are tied to the corporate income tax and may be limited to: a share of total revenue; a share of total taxable income; a share of the sum of total turnover and wages and salaries paid; a share of the corporate income tax liability, a share of the gift itself, a monetary value; or a combination of these tax relief ceilings. Furthermore, unlike individuals, corporations can deduct business expenses, and thus the sponsoring of philanthropic entities, as well as donating, may partly be encouraged through normal business expensing rules.

Countries can use a combination of limits to their deductions and credits with different levels of generosity. In some cases those limits depend on the worthy purpose of the receiving fund or PBO (e.g., Bulgaria, Chile, Hungary, and Slovenia). Other countries may offer the taxpayer a choice of limits or even type of tax-subsidy (e.g., Germany and Latvia). A number of countries limit their tax relief to a fixed monetary value in addition to a ceiling defined as a share of, for example, total revenue or taxable income (e.g. India, Belgium, and Lithuania).

Offering similar incentives for individual and corporate donors

In Argentina, Australia, Austria, Bulgaria, Colombia, the Czech Republic, India, Indonesia, Luxembourg, Norway, Singapore, Slovenia, and Switzerland, the same or similar treatment applies to donations by individuals and corporations (thus see section 4.2.3. and 4.2.5. for more details). The difference between tax reliefs for corporate donations is that the tax credits or deductions apply to the corporate instead of the personal income tax. The floors, ceilings, and type of tax subsidy remain the same. In Argentina, corporations can deduct donations up to a limit of 5% of annual earnings. In Australia, donations are deductible from the corporate income tax base with no upper limit as long as the deduction does not create a negative tax liability (and the donation can be spread over 5 years). In Austria, donations by corporations are deductible but cannot exceed 10% of total profit. Contrary to donations made by individuals, however, corporate donations receive preferential tax treatment for both cash and in-kind donations. In Colombia, corporations that make donations to philanthropic entities receive a tax credit of 25%, limited to 25% of the corporation's income tax. In the Czech Republic, corporations can deduct cash and in-kind donations up to a ceiling of 10% of the corporate income tax base if the value of the donation is above CZK 2 000. In India 100% of the donation is deductible if it is given to certain funds (e.g. Prime Minister National Relief Fund) but only 50% of the donation is deductible if it is given to most other philanthropic entities. In most cases, the deduction is capped at 10% of the gross total income (after all other eligible tax exemptions and deductions). In Indonesia donations are deductible from the corporate income tax base up to a limit of 5% taxable income. In Luxembourg, the tax deduction cannot exceed EUR 1 000 000 or 20% of total net income, where total net income consists of the revenue remaining after deducting expenses incurred for the purpose of acquiring, ensuring and maintaining revenue. In Norway, corporate donations up to NOK

50 000 are deductible. Singapore provides a 250% tax deduction on certain types of donations, such as cash donations, gift of shares and works of art given to qualifying philanthropic entities. In South Africa donations can qualify for a tax deduction of up to 10% of taxable income. In Slovenia, a corporation can deduct donations up to 0.5% of their taxable revenue. Deductions for donations to worthy purposes such as social assistance science, and religion are limited to 0.3% and deductions for donations for culture and disaster relief are capped at 0.5% of their taxable revenue. In Switzerland, donations are deductible up to 20% of the corporation's taxable income.

In Bulgaria the ceiling of the tax deduction varies depending on the worthy purpose and the percentages are similar to those for individual donors. Donations are deductible from the corporate income tax base (annual accounting profit) up to a total ceiling of 65% of the tax base. The ceilings differ depending on the beneficiary as follows:

- Up to 10% of annual accounting profit where the expenses on donations are incurred in favour of::
  - healthcare and medical-treatment establishments;
  - social services for residential care, as well as of the Social Assistance Agency and of the Social Protection Fund under the Minister of Labour and Social Policy;
  - homes for medical and social care for children;
  - public nurseries, kindergartens, schools, higher schools or academies;
  - public-financed enterprises within the meaning given by the Accountancy Act;
  - religious denominations registered in the country;
  - specialised enterprises or cooperatives of persons with disabilities or the persons with disabilities as well as their technical aids;
  - victims of disasters, or of the families thereof;
  - the Bulgarian Red Cross;
  - socially disadvantaged persons including children with disabilities or parentless children;
  - cultural institutes and community centres;
  - PBOs with the exception of any organisations supporting culture;
  - the Bulgaria Energy Efficiency and Renewable Sources Fund;
  - therapeutic communities for the treatment of drug-addicted persons;
  - the United Nations Children's Fund (UNICEF)
  - social companies listed in the Register of Social Companies, for the conduct of their social activities and/or for attainment of their social goals
- Up to 15% of the accounting profit for the assistance provided gratuitously under the terms and according to the procedure established by the Financial Support for Culture Act;
- Up to 50% of the accounting profit where the expenses on donations are incurred in favour of:
  - the National Health Insurance Fund: for activities related to the medical treatment of children which are financed by transfers from the budget of the Ministry of Health, and of the Assisted Reproduction Centre.
- Any expenses for donations of computers and computer peripheral equipment, which are manufactured within one year prior to the date of the donation, and donated to Bulgarian schools, including higher schools, shall be recognized for tax purposes.

Any expenses for donations of computers and computer peripheral equipment, which are manufactured within one year prior to the date of the donation, and donated to Bulgarian schools, including higher schools, shall be recognized for tax purposes.

Finland, Ireland, Mexico, the Netherlands, Germany, France and Israel, have the same tax incentive for corporate donors as they do for individual donors, but their limits differ significantly from the personal income tax incentives. In Finland, corporations can deduct cash donations to publicly funded universities between EUR 850 and EUR 250 000 euros for the purpose of promoting science, art or the Finnish cultural heritage. Additionally, cash donations between EUR 850 and EUR 50 000 are also deductible if they are made for the purpose of promoting science, art or Finnish cultural heritage and given to associations, foundations or other institutions on the condition that they have been nominated by the tax administration and that their purpose is promoting art, science, or the maintenance of Finnish cultural heritage.

In Ireland, a corporation which donates over EUR 250 to an approved philanthropic entity may claim a deduction for the donation as if it were a trading expense or an expense of management for the accounting period in which it is paid. For the donation to be tax deductible it must not confer any benefit, either directly or indirectly, on the donor or any person connected with the donor, and it must not be conditional on, or associated with, any arrangement involving the acquisition of property by the approved philanthropic entity. Capital gains tax relief is available for donors of tangible assets, such as real property (for more information on the donation of shares see Box 4.6). The capital gains tax relief for donations of works of art is the same for individuals and corporations and is discussed in Section 4.2.7.

Corporations in Mexico can deduct donations to private institutions up to 7% of taxable profit obtained in the previous tax year. For donations in favour of the Federation, Federal Entities, Municipalities, or their decentralized agencies, the deductible amount cannot exceed 4% of fiscal profits. The sum of both must not exceed 7% of taxable profits.

In the Netherlands, corporate donations are deductible up to a limit of 50% of fiscal profit to a maximum of EUR 100 000. Additionally the deductibility of donations cannot lead to a loss and excess donations cannot be spread over multiple years. Donations to PBOs with a cultural worthy purpose are marked-up and can be deducted at 1.5 times the value of the gift with maximum EUR 2 500. Because the Netherlands has a progressive corporate income tax rate (16.5% for profits up to EUR 200 000 and 25% for profits above € 200 000) the value of the deduction is higher for corporations with profits over EUR 200 000.

In Germany, donations are deductible up to 20% of taxable income (before the deduction) or 4% of the sum of the total turnover and wages and salaries paid (this is similar to the design of the corporate tax incentive for giving in Latvia, summarised in Box 4.7. Carry-over provisions apply and donations can be considered business expenses. If goods are donated, the corporation can choose between the common value approach and the book value approach (see section on valuation rules for more details on the approaches).

France provides corporate donors a 60% tax credit for the share of the donation up to EUR 2 million and a 40% tax credit for amount over EUR 2 million. For organizations providing free meals, care or accommodation for people in need the tax credit is 60 % of the total amount of donation. The annual cap of the tax reduction is EUR 20 000 or 5 % (5 per thousand) of annual turnover excluding tax (ceiling applied to all payments made). If the ceiling is exceeded, it is possible to carry the excess over the next 5 years.

In Israel, corporations that donate to an eligible philanthropic entity can benefit from a 30% tax credit. For the donation to qualify for the credit it must be between USD 50 and USD 2.5 Million. The deduction cannot exceed 30% of gross income and excess donations cannot be spread over more than one year. Furthermore, donations cannot be considered a business expense and capital gains tax applies when a non-monetary donation is made.

In Italy, corporations can deduct philanthropic gifts from their taxable income in the same way as individuals. However, they cannot opt for tax credits.

Offering tax credits to individual donors and tax deductions to corporate donors

Belgium, Canada, and New Zealand offer tax credits to individual donors and tax deductions to corporate donors. In Belgium, corporate donations to accredited philanthropic entities are deductible up to 5% of the taxable profit or 500,000 euros. In Canada, donations are deductible up to a limit of 75% of the corporation's taxable income. The limit is increased by 25% of the amount of taxable capital gains arising from donations of appreciated capital property and 25% of any capital cost allowance recapture arising from donations of depreciable capital property. The net income percentage limit does not apply to certain gifts of cultural property or ecologically sensitive land. As with individuals, gifts of publicly traded shares and stock options, ecologically sensitive land, and certified cultural property may be eligible for an inclusion rate of zero on any capital gain realised. Donations in excess of the limit may be carried forward up to 5 years with the exception of gifts of ecologically sensitive land, which may be carried forward up to 10 years. In New Zealand, corporations can claim tax deductions for all donations made to an approved funds and PBOs providing the deduction does not exceed their total annual net income. For a donation to qualify for the deduction it must be a gift of NZD 5 or more of cash. Gifts of property are not eligible for the tax deduction and excess donations cannot be spread over multiple years.

Japan provided individual donors with a choice between a deduction and a credit. Corporate donors, on the other hand, may only benefit from a tax deduction. To determine the deduction limit of general donations, Japan uses the following formula: *[(Amount of capital at the end of the fiscal year × Number of months in the current fiscal year / 12 × 2.5 / 1 000) + (income in the current fiscal year × 2.5 / 100)] × 1/4.* The limit of donations to PBOs with a special status is determined through this formula: *[(Amount of capital at the end of the fiscal year x number of months in the current fiscal year / 12 x 3.75 / 1 000) + (income in the current fiscal year x 6.25 / 100)] x 1/2.* The deductible limit is calculated in each fiscal year when the donation is made. It is not possible to carry over the deductible limit amount which is not used.

Offering both tax credits and deductions

Chile, Latvia and Portugal, offer both tax credits and tax deductions to corporate donors. Corporate donors in Latvia are able to choose from three tax relief options to receive a tax benefit from their donation (see Box 4.7 for more information). The options are a deduction with a limit tied to profits, a deduction with a limit tied to total gross work remuneration, and finally a tax credit tied to the tax on income from dividends. In Portugal, corporate donations can be deducted from the tax base by up to 8/1000 of total turnover. Depending on the worthy purpose, the donations receive a mark-up of 120% to 150% of their total value for deduction purposes. For example, if a corporation makes a donation of EUR 1 000 to a PBO with an educational purpose, the corporation will be able to deduct EUR 1 200 from their taxable income.

In Chile, certain corporate donations can benefit from a 50% tax credit and a tax deduction equal to the remaining amount. Others can benefit from a full deduction as a tax incentive. National emergencies' donations and donations made under municipal law are deductible from the tax base. Donations for reconstruction are eligible for a 50% tax credit and the remaining is deductible. Cultural donations are eligible for a 50% tax credit caped at the lower value of 2% of the tax base or a fixed amount and the remaining is deductible. Donations to charities are eligible for a 50% tax credit which is caped to a fixed amount and the remaining is deductible. Cultural donations are eligible for a 50% tax credit caped at the lower of 2% of the tax base or a fixed amount and the remaining is deductible. Donations for sporting associations are eligible for a 50% or 35% tax credit which is capped at 2% of the tax base or a fixed amount and the remaining amount is deductible. Donations to philanthropic educational entities qualify for a 50% tax credit and the remaining amount is deductible with different limits according to the type of educational entity. Additionally, in the majority of cases a general limit on the amount of the donation applies corresponding to 5% of the taxable base (special limits apply to entities in a tax loss position and other cases).

Box 4.7. Tax incentives for corporate giving in Latvia

The three relief options

Corporations that have made an eligible donation to an eligible philanthropic entity are entitled to choose one of the following three tax relief options:

- Tax deduction: Deduct the donated amount from the corporate income tax base, where the value of the deduction is limited to 5% of the profits from the previous reporting year (after the calculated taxes);
- Tax deduction: Deduct the donated amount from the corporate income tax base, where the value of the deduction is limited to 2% of the total gross work remuneration (e.g. wages paid) calculated for employees in the previous reporting year;
- Tax credit: Reduce the corporate income tax liability but only on income from dividends by 85% of the donations, where the value of the credit does not exceed 30% of the income tax on income from dividends.

The conditions for a donation to be eligible for the tax relief

A corporate donation is only eligible for the three tax relief options if the following conditions are met:

- The donation is not directed at a specific recipient who is related to the donor, an employee of the donor or a family member of an employee of the donor;
- The recipient of the donation does not perform activities of a compensatory nature that are related to having received the gift (e.g. advertising, invitations to high-value entertainments).
- The total amount of tax debt of the donor on the first day of the taxation period does not exceed EUR 150.
- The beneficiary of the donation has not publicised the donor's brand. This could be the case if the name of the beneficiary of the donation has an obvious link to the donor's brand (e.g., *Company A* donates money to the *Company A Foundation*). If the recipient publicises a list of all the donors, the name of each individual donor must not exceed 1/20th of the text area.

Offering allocation schemes to individuals but not to corporations

Of the six countries that have an allocation scheme for individual taxpayers (Hungary, Lithuania, Portugal, Romania, the Slovak Republic, and Slovenia) the Slovak Republic is the only country that has an allocation scheme for corporations. In the Slovak Republic, corporations can attribute 1% or 2% of their income tax to an approved non-profit entity. The minimum amount that can be allocated is EUR 8. In Lithuania, corporations are allowed to deduct twice the total amount of donations (except for donations in cash exceeding EUR 9 750 each to a qualifying philanthropic entity in a tax year). The total deduction amount cannot exceed 40% of the corporation's taxable income during the tax year. In Hungary, a set share of corporate donations are deducted from pre-tax profits as a business expense. If a corporation donates to a PBO, it can deduct 20% of the total value of the donation. If the donation is made under a long-term agreement, the corporation can deduct 40%. Additionally, 50% of donations to the Hungarian Fund for Clean-up and Salvage, the National Culture Fund or the Agricultural Compensation Fund are deductible.

4.3.3. Sponsoring philanthropy in return for advertisement

This report distinguishes between two kinds of sponsorship payments to philanthropic entities: (1) corporations purchase publicity and advertising from philanthropic entities for the fair market value of those services; and (2) corporations donate to philanthropic entities and the fair market value of the publicity and advertisement they receive as a result is below the value of the donation and in line with the country's donor-benefit rules. In most countries (e.g., Belgium, Latvia, Mexico, the Netherlands, New Zealand, Norway, the Slovak Republic, Sweden, and the United States), the first form of sponsoring is fully deductible. In some cases, advertising contracts tend to be required to ensure that the PBO does in fact provide publicity for the corporation. In Belgium, donations are capped at 5% of taxable profits or EUR 500 000 but sponsoring is fully deductible. In France, on the other hand, all payments towards philanthropic entities are considered donations. However, there must an advertisement contract in which the PBO is obliged to ensure the visibility of the brand or its products. In New Zealand and Australia, a payment to a PBO could be considered a business expense and is deductible under the general rules if the payment is incurred in deriving assessable income. Thus a sponsorship payment to a PBO may be deductible under the general rules for business expenses if the sponsorship is likely to increase the business's taxable income. In the United States, contributions that are directly related to the taxpayer's trade or business that are made with a reasonable expectation of a financial return commensurate with the amount paid may be deductible as a business expense. The deduction for a business expense is not limited to the 10% of adjusted gross income that the charitable deduction is limited to.

Although payments can be considered business expenses in many countries (as long as they have a sufficient nexus with earning income), these payments may have implications for the PBOs receiving them. The income from activities different to those related to the worthy purposes for which they were granted PBO status for, may be regarded as commercial activity and limited accordingly. In Mexico, for example, income from advertising activity is regarded as commercial and cannot exceed 10% of the PBOs income if it wants to be able to receive tax-incentivised donations. PBOs receiving sponsorship payments rather than donations may impose a set of obligations on the PBOs, which they may not be able to fulfil or that may trigger an increase in their tax liability. The income tax rules for PBOs are discussed in more detail in a separate chapter of this report.

When sponsoring is part of philanthropic giving, corporations may give more than they receive in publicity. For example, if a business in Canada receives special recognition for its donation, or if it receives more than minimal recognition (for example, banners or advertising of products), this is considered philanthropic sponsorship, and donor-benefit rules may apply. In some countries, the payment may not be eligible for tax relief (e.g., see Latvia's strict donor-benefit rules discussed in Box 4.7). In Canada, the fair market value of the publicity given to the corporate donor, is subtracted from the amount of the donation for tax deductibility purposes. When the value cannot be calculated, the charity cannot issue the business an official donation receipt and the business may be entitled to claim the payment as a deduction against income as an advertising expense (i.e. not necessarily a form of philanthropic giving).

4.4. Tax avoidance and evasion risks

4.4.1. Abuse of tax incentives for philanthropic giving

The abuse of tax incentives for philanthropy occurs when the sanctioned government status of a fund or PBO is abused either by the entity itself, by taxpayers and donors, or third parties, such as fraudsters who pose as philanthropic entities or tax return preparers who falsify tax returns to defraud the government (OECD, 2009[4]). The abuse of the tax incentives discussed in this chapter do not just lead to losses in tax revenue but erode the public's trust in the philanthropic sector as a whole. Common types of tax avoidance and evasion issues with tax relief for philanthropic giving include: philanthropic entities that wilfully participate in a tax evasion scheme to benefit its donors (see Box 4.8 for an example); falsified donation receipts prepared by the philanthropic entity, tax preparers or donors; payments for goods and services disguised as donations; overvalued gifts; and donations of assets in which the donor retains an interest.

Box 4.8. The Cup Trust Case in the United Kingdom

Background

In 2009 the Charity Commission for England and Wales registered the Cup Trust as a charity, with a company based in the British Virgin Islands as its only trustee. Of the GBP 176 000 000 that the Cup Trust received in so-called donations, it claimed GBP 46 000 000 in Gift Aid and only gave GBP 55 000 to philanthropic causes.

Overview of the scheme

The Cup Trust charity was found to be involved in a circular transaction scheme with the objective of receiving Gift Aid from the government and obtaining personal tax relief for individuals. The infographic below shows a simplified version of how the scheme was designed to work in a 24-hour transaction. In summary, the Cup Trust charity took up a loan with which it bought a government bond worth GBP 50 000. Cup Trust then proceeded to sell the bond to a third-party intermediary for GBP 5, under the condition that it would either receive a donation of GBP 50 005 within 24 hours or the legal title to the bond would be returned to the charity. A tax-paying individual would then purchase the bond from the third-party intermediary for GBP 5, sell the bond for its full market value of GBP 50 000 and donate the sum of GBP 50 005 back to Cup Trust, with the intention of receiving personal tax relief for the full GBP 50 005. The Cup Trust then used the donation to pay back the loan, which was interest free as long as it was paid within 24 hours. The intention was then to claim Gift Aid on the donation it received.

One 24-hour transaction

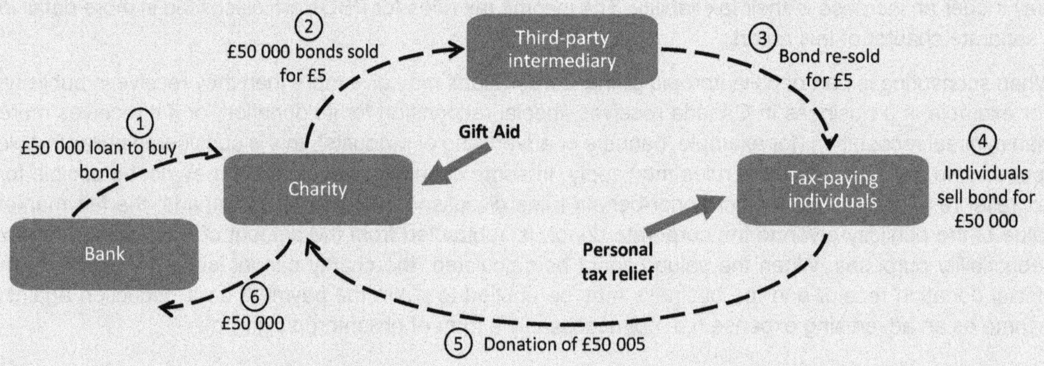

Lessons on how to prevent such schemes

- Regular exchange of information about philanthropic entities of common concern between a registering authority and the tax administration to help focus limited resources on suspicious entities and track tax avoidance and evasion schemes in the philanthropic sector.
- Due diligence by registering authorities to check whether there is a clear public benefit to an entities purpose before granting them the preferential tax status.
- The importance of regulation of philanthropic entities is important to safeguarding access to tax concessions. Need to improve accountability and transparency through reporting requirements and make better use of data from different agencies.

Note: The infographic is a simplification of the scheme using the transaction of one government bond.
Source: https://www.gov.uk/government/publications/the-cup-trust-charity-commission-inquiry-results/the-cup-trust-inquiry-results-formerly-a-registered-charity

Overvaluation of non-monetary gifts

Lax valuation rules and lack of oversight can lead to overvaluation schemes. Overvaluation schemes refer to cases in which taxpayers, for example, buy property at a low price and donate it at a much higher value (often with supportive valuations) thereby generating excess benefits when claiming the charitable donation tax relief. These schemes often utilize foreign entities (foreign PBOs and offshore trusts in tax havens) to obscure, but also legitimise, the transaction. In Canada, this was a significant problem in the 2000s. As a result, the country passed legislation and increased audit resources to address valuations of donations, which appears to have curbed the problem. Colombia and Germany too, have experienced schemes in which the value of the donations were artificially inflated to increase the tax benefit.

In the United States, the valuation of donated property has long been an issue. Over time, requirements for appraisals and other requirements have been made stricter by legislation or regulation when abuses were found. One example is the valuations of donations of used vehicles, which was frequently abused. To curb the overvaluation of used vehicles, legislation required appraisals for vehicles valued over USD 500 and forms required to be submitted to the revenue required information about the year, model and vehicle identification number for auditing purposes.

The falsification or sale of donation receipts

A lack of oversight and targeted tax audits has, in some countries, led to the sale or falsification of donation receipts. The sale of receipts involving PBOs, and tax preparers selling donation receipts for a fraction of the value indicated on the receipt, has resulted in an excess tax benefit when claiming the tax incentive. In Canada, this was a particular issue in the late 1990s and early 2000s.

In-kind donations deducted as business expenses

In some countries, in-kind donations have falsely been deducted as business expenses. This occurs in Indonesia, where in-kind donations are not deductible. In some cases, businesses will deduct an in-kind donation as a business expense and financial assistance is often misused as a personal expense.

Payments for goods and services disguised as gifts

Individual donors may, together with the entity involved, want to disguise a payment for goods or services as a donation. Common examples of these schemes involve charities that receive donations and then use the funds to provide a scholarship to a donor's child or pay tuition at a private school attended by a donor's child. This was identified as an issue by Canada as well as New Zealand (see Box 4.9).

4.4.2. Anti-abuse policies

To ensure that the tax expenditures used to encourage philanthropic giving is efficient, it is important for countries to tackle tax avoidance and evasion schemes related to philanthropic giving, and implement regulations and policies in response to these schemes. On the other hand, excessive rules and requirements can significantly increase the administrative burden to the tax administration/regulatory authority, as well as philanthropic entities and their respective donors. Thus countries report that the use of targeted audits, increased fines and legal consequences, better use of data, as well as clear tax rules have been effective anti-abuse policies.

The majority of anti-abuse policies, however, are in the form of regulations and transparency and reporting requirements for funds and PBOs discussed in chapter five. This is because, a key anti-abuse policy is that the recipients of philanthropic giving must be accredited philanthropic entities. This allows the tax administration to focus its resources on these entities and shifts the worthy purpose and public benefit requirement on to the funds and PBOs that receive the donation. The registration process for entities to qualify as funds and PBOs that are eligible to receive tax subsidies donations is intended also to legitimise philanthropic entities, which in return can foster public trust and financial support for the sector as a whole. This suggests that a key part of a regime that provides tax concessions for philanthropy is a robust system of approval and regulation of philanthropic entities.

Box 4.9. Common avoidance and evasion schemes related to philanthropic giving in New Zealand

Avoidance schemes

- Beneficiary and donors treat payments for goods and/or services as gifts (e.g. private school fees). Such a scheme would allow the 'donor' to receive the goods or services and claim 33% of the price paid as a tax credit on their personal income tax.
- In New Zealand, tax relief for individual donors is limited to gifts of cash. Thus some donors make cash 'gifts' to philanthropic organisations on the understanding that the organisation uses those funds to buy an asset owned by the donor (turning the effective gift of an asset into a gift of cash for tax purposes).
- Donors pay cash 'gifts' to a related charity on the understanding that it is immediately loaned back to the donor, or an associate, for use in its ongoing business activities (the donor claims a tax concession whilst the charity may effectively never have use of the funds).

Evasion schemes

- Fraudulent alteration or manufacturing of donation receipts.
- Using other people's ID to make a fraudulent donation claims.

References

Bullain, N. (2004), "Explaining Percentage Philanthropy: Legal Nature, Rationales, Impacts", *International Journal of Not-for-Profit Law*, Vol. 6/4, https://www.icnl.org/resources/research/ijnl/explaining-percentage-philanthropy-legal-nature-rationales-impacts. [1]

OECD (2009), *Report on abuse of charities for money-laundering and tax evasion*, http://oecd.org/dataoecd/30/20/42232037.pdf. [4]

Strečanský, B. and M. Török (2016), *Assessment of the Impact of the Percentage Tax Designations: Past, Present, Future*, ERSTE Foundation, http://www.erstestiftung.org/en/publication/percentage-tax-designations/. [3]

Urban-Brookings Tax Policy Center (2018), *How did the Tax Cuts and Jobs Act affect incentives for charitable*, https://www.taxpolicycenter.org/briefing-book. [2]

Notes

[1] In the German income tax code, the "total amount of income" (Gesamtbetrag der Einkünfte) is a precisely defined intermediate amount during the assessment process. It roughly refers to taxable income minus related business expenses or entrepreneurial costs, reduced by some special allowances for single parents and retirees.

[2] The TCJA created a 60% contribution limit for gifts of cash until 2026.

[3] Data published by the Slovenian Ministry of Finance. http://edavki.durs.si.

5 The tax treatment of cross-border philanthropy

This chapter examines the tax treatment of cross-border philanthropy. It first considers tax incentives for cross-border giving: both donations and bequests; and also considers how gift and inheritance taxes apply and how capital gains tax might apply where the gift is non-cash. It then considers the tax treatment of philanthropic entities that operate across borders, examining whether tax relief is extended to foreign philanthropic entities operating domestically, and the tax treatment of domestic PBOs operating across borders. Finally, it considers the tax treatment of international grant-making by funds.

5.1. Introduction

This Chapter considers the approach countries adopt in relation to cross-border philanthropy and tax. Cross-border philanthropy can occur where a person (and individual or corporation) makes a gift to an entity in another jurisdiction ('direct philanthropy'). Cross-border philanthropy can also occur where a domestic entity operates in another in another jurisdiction or where a foreign entity operates domestically ('indirect philanthropy'). This Chapter considers the tax treatment of both cross-border giving and cross-border operations by philanthropic entities.

The Chapter considers the extent to which countries provide tax incentives (deductions, rebates or matching) for giving to foreign philanthropic entities, either inter vivos gifts or gifts made on death (bequests). It also considers whether other taxes apply to the making of the gift i.e. gift taxes, inheritance taxes or, if it involves a transfer of property, capital gains taxes. Apart from the position in the European Union (EU) (that extends to countries in the European Economic Area (EEA)), that is governed by rulings of the European Court of Justice (ECJ), there is little tax support in other countries for cross-border giving. The position in the EU requires Member States to adopt a 'comparability' approach to ascertain whether a gift to a philanthropic entity in another Member State is entitled to tax relief. This may require a case-by-case approach to determine eligibility, and due to differences between Member States relating to tax relief, means that relief is not straightforward. There also appears to be less than complete adoption of the position in the ECJ rulings by all Members of the EU. Outside of the EU there are a few cases where there are limited tax incentives for cross-border giving. These limitations have led some philanthropic entities to establish 'work arounds' with entities in various jurisdictions, so that gifts can be made to domestic entities (that are eligible for tax relief) but are then passed on to entities in other countries.

This Chapter also considers whether tax relief is provided to entities that operate across borders – foreign philanthropic entities operating domestically, as well as domestic philanthropic entities operating, wholly or in part, outside the jurisdiction. Apart from the position in the EU, most countries do not provide tax relief for foreign philanthropic entities. The position in the EU is governed by ECJ rulings requiring Member States to adopt a 'comparability' test to determine the eligibility of an entity in another Member State for tax relief, and once again the position is complex. Beyond the EU, there are a few examples of other countries providing tax relief for foreign philanthropic entities on a case-by-case basis. The inability of foreign entities to qualify for tax relief has meant that many entities that operate internationally establish local entities that are eligible for tax relief. Many, but not all, countries provide tax relief to domestic entities that operate abroad, particularly where the activities are related to humanitarian relief or development assistance.

This Chapter proceeds as follows: Part 5.2 considers tax incentives for giving: donations and bequests; and also considers how gift and inheritance taxes apply and also how capital gains tax might apply where the gift is non-cash. Part 5.3 considers the tax treatment of philanthropic entities that operate across borders. This Part considers whether tax relief is extended to foreign philanthropic entities operating within the country, including any conditions that must be met for that tax relief. It then considers domestic PBOs, including domestic PBOs that are branches of international philanthropic entities, operating across borders. It also considers the tax treatment of the making of international grants by funds (grant-making).

5.2. Cross-border giving

Despite fairly widespread use of incentives for domestic philanthropy, the landscape for a more global approach to philanthropy remains fairly guarded. The issues that arise relate to:

- incentives for individuals and corporations for the making of a cross-border donation;
- incentives relating to cross-border bequests; and
- other tax treatment of cross-border donations or bequests e.g. exemptions from gift taxes; inheritance taxes and, where property is disposed of, capital gains tax.

5.2.1. Incentives for cross-border donations

This section gives an overview of the tax incentives for cross-border donations. The focus of the section are the tax incentives that countries may or may not extend to corporate or individual donors that give to a foreign PBO operating abroad. For the majority of countries, cross-border donations are not incentivised as a general principal (see Table 5.1). However, certain specific situations allow for a subsidy, if the foreign entity meets a set of domestic and/or international requirements. This section will cover three different scenarios: donations within the EU/EEA; donations between countries with bilateral tax agreements; and countries with other specific regimes.

Table 5.1. Tax incentives for cross-border donations

Country	Country incentivises cross-border donations
Argentina	No
Australia	No
Austria	Yes, if EU/EEA[1] and countries where administrative cooperation exists
Belgium	Yes, if EU/EEA
Bulgaria	Yes, if EU/EEA
Canada	No, except under DTA
Chile	No
Colombia	No
Czech Republic	Yes, if EU/EEA
Estonia	Yes, if EU/EEA
Finland	Yes, if EU/EEA and entity registered
France	Yes, if EU/EEA
Germany	Yes, if EU/EEA and some connection to Germany
Greece	Yes, if EU/EEA
Hungary	Yes, if EU/EEA (only corporate donors)
India	No
Indonesia	No
Ireland	Yes, if EU/EEA and entity registered
Israel	No, except under DTA
Italy	Yes, if EU/EEA
Japan	No
Latvia	Yes, if EU/EEA and DTA
Lithuania	Yes, if EU/EEA
Luxembourg	Yes, if EU/EEA
Malta	Yes, if EU/EEA and entity registered
Mexico	No, except under DTA
Netherlands	Yes, if entity registered
New Zealand	No, except for specific cases
Norway	Yes, if EU/EEA
Portugal	No (does not comply with ECJ rulings)
Romania	No (does not comply with ECJ rulings)
Singapore	No
Slovak Republic	No (no relief for domestic donations)
Slovenia	Yes, if EU/EEA
South Africa	No
Sweden	Yes, if EU/EEA and entity registered
Switzerland	No[2]
United Kingdom	Yes, if EU/EEA[3]
United States	No, except under DTA

Note:
1. EU' refers to countries that are Members of the European Union. They are Austria, Belgium, Bulgaria, Croatia, Republic of Cyprus, Czech Republic, Denmark, Estonia, Finland, France, Germany, Greece, Hungary, Ireland, Italy, Latvia, Lithuania, Luxembourg, Malta, Netherlands, Poland, Portugal, Romania, the Slovak Republic, Slovenia, Spain and Sweden. 'EEA' refers to the European Economic Area and includes EU countries and also Iceland, Liechtenstein and Norway. It allows them to be part of the EU's single market.
2. In general, as Switzerland is not in the EU, it is not subject to decisions by the ECJ. It may be that Switzerland can benefit from the ECJ ruling for incoming donations based on the principle of free movement of capital that prohibits restrictions on the free movement of capital not only between Member States but also between Member States and third states. Oberson notes that the question whether the same treatment can apply in the other direction, i.e. gift from Switzerland to an institution established in an EU Member State, is less clear: (Oberson, 2015[1]).
3. This may change post-BREXIT.
Source: OECD Taxation and Philanthropy Questionnaire

Apart from the position in the European Union, which applies to all members of the European Economic Agreement (EEA), the general position is that the relief available for donations to domestic philanthropic entities is not available for donations to foreign entities. Most countries limit the tax relief to donations to entities that are 'in', 'formed in', or 'established in' the jurisdiction or have some other connection to the jurisdiction. The nature of the connection required is important in determining whether tax relief is available and is discussed further below. Generally, the rules are the same whether the donor is an individual or a corporation, although Hungary only provides tax relief to corporations and Sweden only provides tax relief to individuals.

There are three situations where tax relief is available for donations to foreign entities: the first involves the Member States of the EU (and EEA) that are subject to rulings of the ECJ. The ECJ has developed a general non-discrimination principle relating to philanthropic giving (see Box 5.1). Second, some countries have bilateral agreements that permit cross-border tax relief. Third, some countries have a process for recognising foreign PBOs in limited circumstances and allowing tax relief for donations to those entities.

EU law

The EU Treaties provide for the free movement of capital between Member States and freedom of establishment. European Community law therefore requires Member States not to discriminate against a gift to a PBO in another Member State. This does not mean a gift to a foreign PBO will automatically benefit from the same treatment as a domestic PBO, it means that the nationality of a PBO is not sufficient to justify a difference of treatment. The ECJ in *Hein Persche v Finanzamt Ludenscheid* [2008] Case 318/07 (14 October 2008) (*Persche's* case), stated that European Community law does not require Member States to automatically acknowledge a foreign charity status when granting tax relief to donations. However, where a taxpayer in one State (in that case Germany) makes a donation to an entity that has philanthropic status in its own State (in that case Portugal), the State of the taxpayer cannot deny the right of equal tax treatment solely because the recipient entity is not resident in its territory. In that case, Mr Persche, a German resident, claimed a deduction from personal income tax for an in-kind donation of bed and bath linen, walking frames, and other equipment. The donation was made in favour of a Portuguese PBO working on a number of social issues including providing care homes for the elderly. The ECJ did not go so far as to require Member States to provide mutual recognition of philanthropic entities, but rather required Member States to accord tax benefits when there was 'comparability', and in this case Germany had not considered whether the Portuguese PBO satisfied such a test. Following this, and other ECJ cases, the burden is on the taxpayer to prove that the entity would be entitled to tax relief in the Member State in question but for its establishment elsewhere; and if the taxpayer can prove this the authority must consider the evidence presented.

Almost all Member States have amended their legislation and/or procedures to recognise donations to comparable or similar entities in other Member States. A number of Member States assess comparability on a case-by-case basis which is often a time-consuming and costly exercise for taxpayers, including the requirement to provide translations of relevant documents. This approach typically requires individual donors to obtain approval, often from a regional authority, in each case; no record is retained, and no precedent is established. This is the case in Belgium, Bulgaria, Czech Republic, Estonia, Germany, Hungary, Latvia, Lithuania and the Slovak Republic, although in Belgium it is possible to obtain a Ruling that the foreign entity is comparable from the central authority. Other Member States require the philanthropic entity to demonstrate comparability and/or be registered in that State as well as in their home jurisdiction. This is the case in Austria, Finland, Ireland, Malta, Netherlands, Norway and Sweden. This approach has the advantage that once registered, other donors can rely on the registered status to support the tax relief. However, due to the difficulties of establishing comparability, very few entities are registered under this approach.

Determining whether a gift to a foreign entity is comparable is problematic because of the diversity of approaches to the question of tax relief for donations in the Member States. Differences between the jurisdictions that might be relevant include whether the gift is money or in-kind (Finland and Portugal only provide tax relief for cash donations) and whether the donor is an individual or corporation (as noted above, Hungary only provides relief for corporations and Sweden only provides relief for individuals). There may also be differences related to the eligibility of the entity: whether it is a PBO or a fund and the nature of its purposes (Austria, Germany, Finland, Malta and Romania have more limited purposes), how monies are disbursed including on overheads (Austria, Belgium, Estonia, Latvia and Lithuania all restrict the expenditure on 'overheads' in different ways). There are also differences relating to directors' remuneration (most countries prohibit payments to board members, but Sweden does not), whether the entity engages in activities abroad (Germany imposes restrictions) and on timely disbursement of funds (Portugal and Sweden impose specific time limits while others require the monies to be expended in a 'reasonable period').

Some Member States impose additional requirements on foreign entities. For example, Latvia only provides relief in relation to Member States with which it has a Double Tax Agreement. The German tax legislation also requires that the activities of all philanthropic entities 'either have to support individuals which have their permanent residence in Germany, or the activities could benefit Germany's reputation'.

The Netherlands is the most open of the countries responding. The Netherlands makes no distinction between domestic and foreign entities, whether from the EU/EEA or elsewhere. Providing the entity can satisfy the requirements of the tax law, they are entitled to be registered and donors can claim deductions. These entities must be comparable and satisfy other requirements such as integrity requirements, to demonstrate that those involved with the entity are 'fit and proper persons'.

Finally, it should be noted that some Member States (Portugal, Romania and the Slovak Republic) do not comply with the ECJ rulings.

Bilateral agreements

The second situation in which a donation may obtain tax relief when made to a foreign PBO is where there has been a bilateral agreement between countries to provide such relief. This is the case for the United States that has such agreements with Canada, Mexico and Israel. A similar provision applies in the treaties between the Netherlands and Barbados and between Mexico and Barbados.

The US-Canada tax treaty (1980) provides for limited cross-border deductions in certain circumstances. Article XXI allows US donors to deduct gifts to Canadian 'registered charities', subject to US percentage limitations, *but the deduction can only be offset against Canadian-source income*. The treaty also allows US donors a deduction against their US-source income for donations to Canadian colleges and universities attended by the donor or a member of the donor's family (again, subject to US percentage limitations). The treaty also provides for reciprocal charitable credit for gifts by Canadian residents to US tax exempt organisations that could qualify in Canada as 'registered charities' if they were Canadian organisations *but the deduction can only be claimed against US-source income*, (subject to Canadian percentage limitations). Gifts to US colleges or universities attended by the donor or a member of the donor's family are creditable against Canadian-source income (again, subject to Canadian percentage limitations).

A further issue is whether the Canadian charity will be treated as a private foundation or a public charity under US law – as these types of entities have different percentage limits i.e. the deductible donation is limited to a maximum of 50% of the donor's adjusted gross income for public charities or 30% for private foundations. A Protocol to the US-Canada treaty recognises that Canadian law governing tax exempt status is materially equivalent to US law governing charities. Under the Protocol, the public charity status of a Canadian entity is now recognised by the United States, without a separate determination by the IRS or a requirement to lodge financial information by the Canadian entity, and vice versa.

The US-Mexico tax treaty (1992), also contains provisions allowing deductions for cross-border charitable gifts. Article XXII of the treaty allows income tax deductions to US donors for contributions to Mexican charities. The deductions are allowed *only with respect to Mexican-source* income and are subject to US percentage limitations. Mexican donors are allowed reciprocal deductions *only against US-source income* (subject to Mexican percentage limitations) for contributions to US charities. The responsibility for determining public charity status resides with the taxing authority of the nation in which the charity is organised. Although the deduction is limited to particular sources of income, the status of the foreign charity is recognised.

The US-Israel tax treaty (1995), Article 15-A, permits US donors to deduct contributions to Israeli charities *against their Israeli-source income*, but only if the Israeli charity would have qualified for tax exemption under US law had it been established there (a comparability test). The deduction is capped at 25% of Israeli-source 'adjusted gross' income for individual donors and 25% of *Israeli-source taxable income* for corporate donors. Israeli donors are permitted a reciprocal deduction against *US-source income* for contributions to US charities that would qualify for tax exemption under Israeli law if organised there. The deduction is limited to 25% of US-source taxable income.

Another example of bilateral relief can be found in The Netherlands- Barbados Tax Treaty (2006), and in the Mexico-Barbados Income Tax Treaty (2008). Article 22 of The Netherlands-Barbados Treaty provides that a contribution by a resident of State A to a charity in State B is deductible in State A where the competent authority of State A agrees that the entity qualifies as a charity in State A (i.e. it satisfies a comparability test). The Mexico-Barbados Treaty provides that a resident of State A can claim a deduction for a contribution to an entity that is a qualifying charity in State B. The competent authority in State A can consult with the competent authority in State B to ensure that the entity is qualified in State B (that is, there is mutual recognition).

The inclusion of a provision on charitable donations seems to be part of the tax treaty policy of Barbados. A similar provision on donations to charitable institutions is included in article 21 of the Barbados-Seychelles Income and Capital Tax Treaty (2007), Article 22 of the Barbados-Mauritius Income Tax Treaty (2004), and Article 23 of the Barbados-Ghana Income Tax Treaty (2008).

Specific recognition

There are also a few examples of countries that have a process for providing tax relief for gifts to approved foreign PBOs in limited circumstances, namely Canada and New Zealand. In Canada, a tax credit is available (to an individual) for a gift to a 'qualified donee'. This generally means a registered charity, that is, a charity that is created in and resident in Canada. However, a foreign entity can become a qualified donee if it is:

- a university outside Canada, the student body of which ordinarily includes students from Canada, that has applied for registration by the Minister, or
- a foreign charity that has applied to the Minister for registration. The Minister may register, in consultation with the Minister of Finance, a foreign charity for a 24-month period that includes the time at which Her Majesty in right of Canada has made a gift to the foreign charity, if the Minister is satisfied that the foreign charity is:

  (i) carrying on relief activities in response to a disaster;

  (ii) providing urgent humanitarian aid; or

  (iii) carrying on activities in the national interest of Canada.

  There are currently only 4 approved foreign charities.

New Zealand also has a process for foreign PBOs to become approved donees. In such a case, an application is made to the Minister through the Inland Revenue Department (IRD) for approval and inclusion on a list in Schedule 32 of the *Income Tax Act 2007* (NZ). The criterion for approval is that the money received must go towards at least one of these things:

- relieving poverty, hunger, sickness, damages from war or natural disaster;
- the economy of developing countries recognised by the United Nations; or
- raising the educational standards of a developing country recognised by the United Nations.

Charities are specifically excluded from being listed if they form to foster or administer any religion, cult or political creed. There are currently approximately 120 listed charities.

The non-recognition of a foreign philanthropic entity does not preclude a foreign entity establishing an entity or branch in the other jurisdiction. Where an entity is set up in one country but will perform some or all of its activities in another country, the issue will be whether a domestic entity is allowed to undertake activities abroad. This is considered in Part 5.3.2.

Finally, it should be noted that in those countries such as the Slovak Republic, that do not provide tax relief for donations to domestic PBOs, such relief does not apply to cross-border donations.

Box 5.1. Cross-border philanthropy in the European Union regulatory framework

Emergence of a non-discrimination principle

Historically, EU Member States did not grant tax privileges to foreign PBOs. Indeed, the general rule was that tax incentives were restricted to domestic PBOs and donors giving to domestic PBOs. However, this regulatory framework was overhauled by a series of judgements by the European Court of Justice (ECJ).

Between 2005 and 2011, these judgements developed a general non-discrimination principle as regards to tax law in the area of public-benefit activities. It has set the below-mentioned rules for Member States.

Design of the non-discrimination principle

It is at the discretion of Member States whether or not they wish to provide tax privileges for PBOs and their donors (1). Similarly, Member States are in principle free in determining the relevant conditions and requirements. Among admissible conditions, Member States may theoretically limit the beneficiary circle of PBOs' activities to domestic citizens or persons living within the domestic territory (2). There is also no obligation of automatically granting a PBO status to an entity recognised as a PBO in another country (3)

However, limits to the Member States regulatory powers are established by the fundamental freedoms of the Treaty on the Functioning of the EU. Indeed, Member States may not exclude a foreign EU-based PBOs and their donors from eligibility for tax privileges if they fulfil all requirements for domestic PBOs (4). Moreover, it is not permitted that a Member State requires a PBO to undertake its philanthropic activities solely in its jurisdiction in order to benefit from a preferential tax treatment (unless there are compelling objective reasons for this). For example, Member States may not restrict tax benefits for donations strictly to domestic universities or laboratories (5)

Member States should carry out a comparability test to determine whether a foreign EU-based PBO meets the requirements of national tax law. Such tests are to be carried out by the national authorities and courts of the Member State concerned. (6). While conducting the comparability test, Member States may ask that a foreign EU-based PBO provides any document useful for the carrying out of the test (7).

Note: (1) ECJ, 27. 1. 2009 - C-318/07 (Hein Persche/Finanzamt Lüdenscheid). (2) ECJ, Stauffer, paras. 37f., 57, Missionswerk, para. 30 (3) ECJ Stauffer, para. 39; Persche, para. 48. (4) ECJ, Persche, para. 46, Missionswerk, paras. 30-31. (5) ECJ, Laboratoires Fournier, para. 23; or Commission/Austria, paras. 35-38 (6) ECJ, Persche, para. 49, Missionswerk, paras. 33-34. (7) ECJ, Persche, paras. 53-58.

5.2.2. Incentives for cross-border bequests

This section summarises the tax treatment of bequests to foreign PBOs (also referred to as cross-border bequests). Although a number of countries did not provide information on this issue, Table 5.2 suggests that countries that grant tax incentives to domestic philanthropic bequests also incentivise cross-border bequests to PBOs, although exceptions exist. These are predominantly members of the EU, and the responses indicate that the same comparability requirements that apply for donations would apply to bequests.

Table 5.2. Tax incentives for cross-border bequests

Country	Countries incentivise domestic and cross-border philanthropic bequests
Australia	No (but CGT relief available)
Austria	Yes
Belgium	Yes
Bulgaria	Yes if EC/EEA
Canada	Yes (limited)
France	Yes, if EU/EEA
Japan	Yes
Netherlands	Yes
Norway	Yes
Slovenia	Yes
United Kingdom	Yes (limited)
United States	Yes

Source: OECD Taxation and Philanthropy

Canada states that in limited circumstances a cross-border bequest is possible. This would apply where the bequest is to a foreign universities or foreign charities approved under the *Income Tax Act 2007* (Can) (discussed above) or where the US-Canada tax treaty provides comparable tax relief.

The survey asked whether different rules applied for bequests to funds rather than PBOs. There were no differences indicated.

5.2.3. Gift tax, inheritance tax and capital gains tax

This section provides an overview of other taxes that countries may levy upon cross-border giving. The taxes covered are gift taxes, inheritance/estate taxes and capital gains taxes. Although the approaches differ across countries, the majority of countries do not levy taxes on cross-border giving (see Table 5.3). Finally, this section provides examples of countries that do levy the before listed taxes on cross-border giving.

Many countries (22) do not levy gift taxes or inheritance taxes. In some countries that do not levy such taxes, a disposal of property could give rise to capital gains tax (5) or stamp duty (1).

The US provides an exemption from gift duty (s 2522(a) of the *Internal Revenue Code*) and from inheritance tax (s 2055(a) of the *Internal Revenue Code*) for donations and bequests that could apply to gifts to foreign PBOs.

European countries that do impose such taxes generally noted that an exemption may be available to other Member States, presumably on the basis of comparability. This is supported by the case of *Missionswerk Werner Heukelbach eV v Belgium* [2011] Case 25/2010,10 February 2011 (*Missionwerk* case). Missionswerk was a religious association and PBO registered in Germany. Mrs R, a Belgian citizen, who had lived her whole life in Belgium, died in 2004 in Belgium, having left her estate to Missionswerk. The

Belgian regional tax authority applied inheritance tax at a rate of 80% on the amount Missionswerk was to receive. Missionswerk sought to have the reduced tax rate of 7% applied instead, which was the rate applied for legacies to resident PBOs. The Belgian tax authority rejected the request for the application of the reduced tax rate on the grounds that it was only to be applied to foreign EU-based PBOs in cases where the testator had lived or worked in the country in which the foreign entity was based. The ECJ ruled that legacies are protected under the free movement of capital and that a restriction on tax incentives would be permissible only in the case that the German PBO was not comparable to a Belgian PBO. The *Missionwerk* case means that revenue authorities in Member States are at least obliged to apply the comparability test – the practical difficulties of applying the comparability test, including that some States assess comparability on a case-by-case basis, have been discussed above.

Table 5.3. Cross-border giving and gift taxes, inheritance tax, and capital gains tax (CGT)

Country	Gift Tax	Inheritance tax	Exemption	Other taxes
Argentina	No	No		
Australia	No	No		disposals of assets may be subject to CGT
Austria	No	No		
Belgium	No	Yes	may be exempt including within EU/EEA	
Bulgaria	Yes	Yes	may be exempt including within EU/EEA	
Canada	No	No		disposals of assets may be subject to CGT
Chile	Yes	Yes		
Colombia	No	No		disposals of assets may be subject to CGT
Czech Republic	No	No		
Estonia	No	No		
Finland	Yes	Yes	may be exempt including within EU/EEA	
France	Yes	Yes	may be exempt including within EU/EEA	
Germany	Yes	Yes	may be exempt including within EU/EEA	
Greece	Yes	Yes	lower rate for PBOs, including within EU/EEA	
Hungary	Yes	Yes		
Indonesia	No	No		
Ireland	No	Yes	may be exempt including within EU/EEA	
Israel	No	No		disposal of assets may be subject to CGT
Italy	Yes	Yes	May be exempt including within EU/EEA	
Japan	No	No		
Latvia	No	No		
Lithuania	No	No		
Malta	No	No		may be stamp duty
Mexico	No	No		
Netherlands	Yes	Yes	may be exempt if entity registered	
New Zealand	No	No		
Norway	No	No		
Portugal	No	No		
Romania	No	No		
Singapore	No	No		
Slovak Republic	No	No		disposals of assets may be subject to CGT
Slovenia	Yes	Yes	may be exempt including within EU/EEA	
South Africa	Yes	Yes		
Sweden	No	No		
Switzerland	Yes	Yes		
United Kingdom	No	Yes	may be exempt within EU/EEA	
United States	Yes	Yes	exemptions available	

Source: OECD Taxation and Philanthropy Questionnaire

Three countries appear have a gift tax or inheritance tax that might be imposed on the making of a donation or bequest to a foreign PBO: Switzerland, Greece, and South Africa. In Switzerland, in most cantons, gifts and bequests by Swiss residents in favour of foreign resident PBOs are subject to gift and inheritance taxes, unless a 'reciprocity declaration is concluded with the country where the foreign charity is registered. Almost all Swiss cantons have so-called reciprocity declarations with France, and some of them with the US, Germany and Israel. Greece taxes bequests and donations to philanthropic entities at a lower rate, including where the entity is within the EU/EEA. In South Africa, the bequest is taxed in the hands of the recipient, so a foreign recipient may be beyond the reach of the domestic taxing authorities.

In countries that do not impose gift tax or inheritance tax, a donation or bequest that takes the form of a disposal of property may be subject to CGT. This is the case in Australia, Canada, Colombia, Israel and the Slovak Republic. Malta indicated that stamp duty may be payable on the disposal.

5.3. Cross-border treatment of PBOs and funds

This section considers the tax treatment of philanthropic entities that operate across borders. This includes the tax treatment of foreign philanthropic entities engaging in activities in another country. It also includes domestic PBOs carrying out activities in other countries and funds transferring assets or, more commonly, making grants to PBOs or other entities in other countries. Although most countries do not provide tax preferences for foreign philanthropic entities, many countries do permit domestic tax-preferred entities to operate abroad in various situations.

5.3.1. Tax treatment of foreign PBOs

This section analyses the tax treatment of foreign PBOs that engage in activities domestically. An entity that was granted a PBO status in one country may engage in activities in another jurisdiction, which raises numerous tax questions related to the treatment of income arising from domestic sources. The section focuses on the following issues: the extension of the PBO status granted abroad, the test applied by domestic jurisdictions allowing for a preferential treatment of domestic income received by the foreign entity and the taxation of these incomes in cases where the foreign entity fails to meet domestic requirements

Table 5.4 shows whether countries provide preferential tax treatment to foreign PBOs operating domestically. Most European countries treat comparable philanthropic entities within EU/EEA in the same way as domestic entities. The requirement to accord comparable treatment arises from the ruling of the ECJ in *Centro di Musicologia Walter Stauffer v Finanzamt München für Körperschaften* [2006] Case-386/04, 14 September 2006 (*Stauffer's* case). In that case, an Italian philanthropic entity awarded scholarships to young people from Switzerland, particularly those from Bern, to pursue studies in music. The entity owned a building in Germany from which it obtained rental income. Under German tax law this type of income was exempt from corporate tax for domestic philanthropic entities. However, the exemption was said to not be available to foreign philanthropic entities. The ECJ stated that European Community law does not require Member States to automatically acknowledge a foreign charity status. However, where an entity that has philanthropic status in its own State (in that case Italy), also satisfies the requirements in another State (in that case Germany), the Member State cannot deny that entity the right of equal tax treatment solely because it is not resident in its territory. The operation of the comparability test to cross-border donations and cross-border bequests has already been noted. Philanthropic entities deriving income in another Member State will need to satisfy the revenue authorities in the source jurisdiction as to comparability and this can be complex and costly. Three Member States, Ireland, Malta and The Netherlands, require registration of the relevant foreign PBO. The Netherlands is the most generous of all countries as it permits entities from any country to register provided it meets the eligibility requirements in the legislation. Belgium allows the foreign PBO to assess whether it is exempt from corporate tax on one of two criteria. The first criterion is that the PBO does not carry out operations of a for-profit nature. The exemption based on this criterion can be claimed by both domestic and foreign PBOs. The second criterion (which may enable a wider exemption) is that the PBO belongs to one of the privileged sectors enumerated by Article 181 of the *Income Tax Code* (for instance, education). However, this basis for exemption is only applicable to domestic PBOs.

A large number of countries (16) indicated that they did not provide tax concessions to foreign PBOs, including some Member States of the EU.

Table 5.4. Preferential tax treatment of foreign PBOs

Country	Country provides preferential tax treatment to foreign PBO
Argentina	No
Australia	Generally no, but may obtain approval
Austria	Yes, if within EU/EEA and countries where administrative cooperation exists
Belgium	Yes, if within EU/EEA but only for one of two alternative grounds
Bulgaria	Yes
Canada	Foreign charities are not exempt; foreign NPOs may be
Chile	No
Colombia	No
Czech Republic	Yes, if within EU/EEA
Estonia	No
Finland	Yes, if within EU/EEA
France	Yes, if within EU/EEA
Germany	Yes, if within EU/EEA
Greece	Yes, if within EU/EEA
Hungary	Yes, if within EU/EEA
India	No
Indonesia	Some foreign PBOs may be recognised
Ireland	Yes, if within EU/EEA but must be registered
Israel	No
Italy	Yes, within EU/EEA
Japan	No
Latvia	No
Lithuania	Yes, if within EU/EEA
Luxembourg	Yes, if within EU/EEA
Malta	Yes, if within EU/EEA but must be registered
Mexico	No
Netherlands	Yes, must be registered
New Zealand	Generally no, but may obtain approval
Norway	Yes, if within EU/EEA
Portugal	No
Romania	No
Singapore	No
Slovak Republic	No
Slovenia	Yes, if within EU/EEA
South Africa	No
Sweden	Yes, if within EU/EEA
Switzerland	No
United Kingdom	Yes, if within EU/EEA
United States	No

Source: OECD Questionnaire on Taxation and Philanthropy

The remaining countries had some limited arrangements for recognition of foreign PBOs. For example, Indonesia has an arrangement that involves some foreign PBOs being granted a permit by the Central Government (see Box 5.2). Canada allows a foreign PBO to qualify as a 'non-profit organisation' if it meets the conditions under the legislation, specifically that it is not a charity and that it is organised and operated for social welfare, civic improvement, pleasure, sport, recreation, or any other purpose except profit. If it qualifies as a non-profit organisation its income will generally not be subject to tax but unlike a registered charity, it is not eligible to receive tax preferred donations. In Australia, a small number of foreign PBOs are approved by regulation as income tax exempt (but not as deductible gift recipients). The New Zealand revenue has the ability to approve foreign entities as tax charities, which means that they can become approved donees (see Part 5.2.1) and also eligible for tax exempt status. It is however necessary to have a strong connection with New Zealand, meet the requirements for registered charities, apart from residency and demonstrate that they are eligible for charity tax concessions in their home jurisdiction. This approval and inclusion on a list in Schedule 32 of the Income Tax Act 2007 means the foreign entity will be able to derive non-business income (i.e. passive investment income) and not be subject to income tax. They will, however, be subject to income tax on any business income in New Zealand if all of their charitable purposes are carried out overseas. As noted above there are currently approximately 120 listed foreign charities.

South Africa notes that foreign PBOs may establish 'branches' and the United States, allows the establishment of entities that are closely aligned with foreign PBOs e.g. as 'friends of' a foreign PBO (these types of entities are discussed in Part 5.3.2).

To the extent that a foreign PBO does not qualify as a tax-exempt entity, it would likely be taxed as a corporation. As a result of these limitations, many philanthropic entities establish separate entities in each jurisdiction to take advantage of the tax concessions available to domestic entities (see Part 5.3.2).

Box 5.2. Foreign PBOs operating in Indonesia

In Indonesia, a PBO status issued by another country will be verified by relevant ministries before the PBO gets an approval to operate in Indonesia. Foreign PBOs must obtain a **principal permit** and an **operational permit** from the Central Government

Obtaining of principal permit

- The country issuing the PBO status has diplomatic relations with Indonesia
- The PBO has a non-profit principle and worthy purpose

Obtaining an operational permit

- The PBO needs a principle permit from the central government
- It also need a written agreement with relevant ministries/ government agencies according to its operational field.
- An annual work-plan with the relevant regional government is required

Source: Government Regulation No. 93 Year 2010

5.3.2. Tax treatment of PBOs that operate abroad

This section provides an overview of the tax rules concerning domestic PBOs engaging in activities abroad. Preferential tax treatment is usually granted to a PBO's domestic activity and thus PBOs with activities abroad may risk losing its preferential tax status. In most cases however, responding countries allow a domestic PBO to conduct activities abroad. Typically, this authorisation is reliant upon the respect of worthy purpose requirements imposed by the national legislation, usually similar to requirements imposed to domestic PBOs. This forces the imposition of strong documentation requirements for PBOs in order to respect the national criteria. Some countries allow these requirements to be lifted in certain specific cases, such as the occurrence of a natural disaster or humanitarian crises.

The question is, of course, concerned with what the tax provisions have to say about operating overseas. There may in addition be other requirements or restrictions on cross-border financial flows or activities. For example, most countries have regulations aimed at illicit financial flows and anti-money laundering, including following FATF recommendations about not permitting monies to be transferred to high-risk countries.[1] Many countries also have regulations aimed at foreign interference, including restrictions on contributions to political parties (Canada, United States) and in some cases restrictions on contributions to philanthropic entities (Hungary, India, and Israel). There may also be restrictions on fundraising, both domestically and internationally, that restrict the ability of philanthropic entities to operate abroad. For example, in Singapore, if funds are raised from the public, a permit is required, and the applicant has to apply at least 80% of the net proceeds of the funds raised within Singapore (and the donations will not be tax-deductible). The rule may be waived for private donations or for appeals in aid of providing immediate disaster relief. These non-tax restrictions may affect the ability of philanthropic donor or entities to transfer funds or engage in activities in other countries.

Most countries provide tax support to domestic PBOs to carry out activities in another country (see Table 5.5). Most countries indicated that the requirements for approval were the same for entities that carried out their activities abroad as those that operated domestically. Some countries indicated that there may be restrictions relating to purpose and some countries impose additional reporting requirements when PBOs operate abroad. It is also important to consider how philanthropic entities can permit donors to support overseas activities ('indirect philanthropy').

Purpose requirements

Countries that do allow domestic PBOs to engage in such activity typically require the PBO to meet the domestic worthy purpose requirement. For example, 17 countries indicated that the same purposes were relevant whether the entity would be operating domestically or overseas. In some other countries, the relevant purpose must be related to assistance for developing countries or to assistance following disasters. For example, the Slovak Republic notes that a donation for material humanitarian aid provided abroad is a deductible tax expense for the donor, if donated through the Ministry of Interior of the Slovak Republic (s 19(2)(u) of the *Income Tax Act* No 595/2003 as amended). Presumably such donations are tax exempt in the Slovak Republic. In Australia, a registered charity can establish a 'developing country relief fund' if the Foreign Affairs Minister has declared the country to be a 'developing country' and has approved the entity. There is also a provision for the Minister to recognise a 'disaster', including in countries other than developing countries, if the disaster develops rapidly and results in death, serious injury or other physical suffering of a large number of people, or in widespread damage to property or the natural environment. In India, if a charitable trust derives income from property held for a charitable purpose which 'tends to promote international welfare in which India is interested' and is applied to such purposes outside India, the income is exempt, subject to special approval processes.

In the case of natural disasters and humanitarian crises, some countries note special arrangements. For example, in Canada, the Canada Revenue Agency (CRA) has indicated that following a natural disaster, such as an earthquake or flood, many organisations want to provide immediate assistance and relief to those affected, and as a result, the CRA often receives applications from such organisations seeking to be registered. The CRA has indicated that it will typically assign priority to these applications. In Germany, in cases of natural disasters or humanitarian crisis the tax administration may publish a catastrophe decree ('Katastrophenerlass'). These decrees allow entities with preferential tax treatment to collect donations for worthy purposes not set out in their constitutions. In Indonesia, the government permits tax relief for natural disasters, although it is not clear whether the disaster must be within Indonesia or whether it could be in some other country (Government Regulation No. 93 Year 2010). In New Zealand, a domestic registered charity must apply 75% of its funds within New Zealand, allowing up to 25% to be devoted to charitable purposes outside New Zealand. The Inland Revenue Department (IRD) indicates that if the figure is below 75% in any year, the cumulative total of its funds applied over the current and preceding two years can be used for the purposes of determining whether a tax credit or deduction is available. This allows some year-on-year variation for exceptional years, for example in response to natural disasters: IRD Interpretation Statement 18/05. Importantly the 75% requirement does not apply to foreign charities listed under Sched 32 of the Income Tax Act 2007 (see Part 5.3.1).

Table 5.5. Domestic PBOs allowed to carry out activities abroad

Country	Country permits PBOs to carry out activities abroad
Argentina	Yes
Australia	Yes+
Austria	Yes
Belgium	Yes
Bulgaria	Yes
Canada	Yes+
Chile	Yes
Colombia	Yes
Estonia	Yes
Finland	Yes
France	Yes
Germany	Yes+
Greece	Yes
Hungary	Yes
India	Yes+
Indonesia	Yes+
Ireland	Yes
Israel	Yes
Italy	Yes+
Latvia	No
Lithuania	Yes
Luxembourg	Yes+
Malta	Yes
Mexico	No
Netherlands	Yes
New Zealand	Yes+
Norway	Yes
Portugal	Yes
Romania	No
Singapore	Yes+
Slovak Republic	Yes+
Slovenia	Yes
South Africa	Yes
Sweden	Yes
Switzerland	Yes+
United Kingdom	Yes
United States	Yes

Source: OECD Taxation and Philanthropy Questionnaire
Note: Yes+ indicates that there are additional requirements that must be satisfied or restrictions. These are discussed below.

Additional requirements

Another group of countries, namely Australia, Canada, New Zealand and Switzerland, require the domestic entity to meet the specified worthy purpose but also to satisfy additional reporting requirements (documentation, justification of activity, proof of control of the activity abroad etc.). For example, in Australia domestic entities will only be approved to engage in activities abroad, whether on their own or in partnership with in-country entities, if they can demonstrate that the entity's focus is on supporting development and/or humanitarian assistance activities in developing countries (under the Overseas Aid Gift Deduction scheme); that they have the capacity to manage and deliver overseas aid activities and that they have appropriate safeguards in place to manage risks associated with child protection and terrorism. Some other philanthropic entities that pursue activities abroad may be eligible for income tax exemption provided that the entity has a physical presence in Australia and 'pursues its objectives and incurs its expenditure principally in Australia'. This does not mean that the beneficiaries must be in Australia. The requirement in Canada that to be tax exempt, the PBO must carry on its activities itself, does not prevent the PBO from entering into contracts with local providers or appointing a local agent, but it is important that the domestic entity retains direction and control over any intermediaries. Switzerland notes that there must be suitable documentation for activities abroad.

In Luxembourg, a PBO can carry out activities abroad as long as it does not do so exclusively and its main activities are domestic. If the PBO has a non-government organisation status (which is authorised by the Ministry of Foreign and European Affairs), it is able to carry out activities abroad more extensively.

In Italy, domestic PBOs can carry out activities abroad only if related to humanitarian aid. If a PBO gives funds abroad, the allocation is allowed only for a humanitarian purpose. In such a case, the domestic entity has to comply with additional accounting requirements, with reference to the accountability of the foreign beneficiary entity/institution and with reference to how the funds will be spent.

A few countries, such as Singapore and Romania, indicated that they do not provide tax relief to domestic PBOs that engage in activities beyond the borders of the country, although it appears that they may permit certain international philanthropic entities such as the Red Cross, World Vision or Oxfam to operate with tax relief available.

Indirect philanthropy

The restrictions on tax relief for foreign philanthropic entities, but widespread acceptance of domestic entities operating overseas, means that donors wishing to support overseas causes need to find a suitable domestic entity to make donations to. From the perspective of the philanthropic entity, there are essentially two models available for entities to raise funds in one jurisdiction and spend money or carry out activities in another jurisdiction:

- the separate entity model; or
- use of an intermediary.

Separate entity model

An entity that seeks tax-preferred status in a particular jurisdiction, perhaps with a view to fundraising in that jurisdiction, but carrying out activities in another jurisdiction, may set up a domestic PBO. The entity will, of course need to comply with the tax and other requirements of that jurisdiction. There are two types of this model – the international PBO and the specific purpose PBO.

Many international organisations, sometimes referred to as International Non-Government Organisations (INGOs), establish separate entities in different countries e.g. Red Cross, CARE, Amnesty International, Greenpeace, World Vision, Oxfam and Médecins Sans Frontiere, because of the inability to make tax-preferred gifts to foreign PBOs or for a foreign PBO to obtain tax relief. For example, there are 192 national

Red Cross societies carrying out the work of the international Red Cross movement. The critical point is that the funds are to be used in a foreign country by a domestic entity as opposed to being donated to and used by a foreign entity.

Another type of cross-border PBO will typically relate to a particular purpose, perhaps an educational or arts-related purpose in another jurisdiction, but because of the inability of donors to obtain tax relief for cross border donations, the PBO will establish a separate entity in jurisdictions where potential donors may be located. For example, there are a number of entities in the US that support various museums and art galleries e.g. the Tate, Museo del Prado and the Rijksmuseum. There are also entities that support educational institutions, such as The University of Oxford – including in the US, Canada, Switzerland, Germany and Australia. In some countries the entity might be referred to as a 'branch' or 'affiliate' of the foreign entity, but will be treated as a separate domestic entity for tax purposes. Some entities will simply adopt a name that reflects the purpose e.g. the Oxford Australia Scholarship Fund. The US has a tradition of allowing US taxpayers to support overseas PBOs through a 'Friends of' PBO e.g. American Friends of Oxford University, and this nomenclature has now been adopted in Switzerland (Swiss Friends of Oxford) and Germany (German Friends of Oxford). South Africa permits a foreign organisation that is incorporated, formed or established in a country outside South Africa, which is exempt from income tax in that other country to obtain tax relief as a PBO. The critical point in each of these cases is that it is a domestic entity (and so subject to regulatory oversight) that will generate monies that will be passed onto the foreign entity in accordance with the stated purposes.

Use of intermediaries

An increasingly common phenomena is the use of intermediaries to transfer funds to a foreign PBO. A donor may be able to make a donation to a domestic PBO or fund that is authorised to make grants to foreign PBOs. It is likely that such entities will have to satisfy various requirements to be able to make grants overseas (see Part 5.3.3) and will need to have some oversight of the spending of the monies. Examples of intermediaries that operate in this way include the Charities Aid Foundation (CAF), Global Giving, Transnational Giving Europe and the King Baudouin Foundation.

Where a local intermediary is used to direct monies from donors to a nominated foreign PBO, the donation will get the benefit of domestic tax relief and the monies will be applied abroad in accordance with the donors' wishes. In some cases, the intermediary may allow the donor to have an account (sometimes called a 'Donor Advised Account') and have some say about how the monies are to be applied. The domestic PBO or fund agrees to act as a 'conduit' and pass on donations to nominated foreign PBOs. This will typically generate a fee for the entity acting as a conduit (which is likely to be treated as business income of the recipient intermediary). For example, Transnational Giving Europe charges a fee equivalent to 5% of the donation up to EUR 100 000 and 1% above this, capped at a maximum fee of EUR 15 000.

Some countries have restrictions on philanthropic entities acting as conduits. For example, in Canada a PBO is required to carry on its charitable activities itself. If the purpose of a PBO was to raise funds for another entity, the PBO would not be entitled to registration as a charity. A Canadian foundation can make grants to other entities, but the entity would need to be a qualified donee. However, a Canadian PBO may enter in contracts with foreign entities, provided that the domestic entity ensures that the funds are applied for philanthropic or charitable purposes by the foreign PBO. This imposes an obligation on the PBO to take 'reasonable steps' to ensure that the funds are applied appropriately.

In some countries, the earmarking of a contribution by a donor for a particular entity or project may impact on the tax relief. For example, In the United Kingdom, tax reliefs are not available if the charity makes payments overseas unless the charity takes reasonable steps to ensure that the funds remitted overseas are not only intended for use for a purpose that would qualify as a charitable purpose according to UK law, but that the funds are in fact so used. Simply passing on monies to another entity is unlikely to satisfy this requirement. In the US, a donor cannot deduct a contribution made to a qualifying philanthropic entity if the contribution is directed to go to a foreign PBO (or some other entity). However, it may be possible to express a preference, rather than a direction, as to how the monies are to be used. In the US, the qualified entity must approve the program as furthering its own exempt purposes and must keep control over the use of the contributed funds. Simply passing on monies would not suffice. However, where the foreign entity is an administrative arm of the qualified US entity, a deduction will be available.

5.3.3. International grant-making

This section provides an overview of rules concerning international grant-making. Indeed, donations of assets or grants to foreign PBOs by a fund can have tax implications. While some countries support this form of cross-border giving, others may withdraw the tax-preferred status if grants are made to foreign PBOs.

Some countries indicated that funds were able to make grants to PBOs in other countries without losing their tax preferred status. The relevant countries are Austria, Belgium, Bulgaria[2], Germany, Ireland, Malta, the Netherlands, Sweden and the US.

Although many countries have funds that make international grants, the US is home to some of the largest funds making such grants and accounts for a significant proportion of grants worldwide. According to a report by COF and Foundation Centre in 2018, 'The State of Global Giving by US Foundations', covering the period 2011-2015, private US foundations give around USD10 billion a year to organisations that work on social and environmental problems outside of the country, particularly in Africa, South Asia, and other low-income parts of the world. Since the early 2000s, international grant-making has increased from about 14 to about 30 percent of all foundation giving in the US, which itself has grown dramatically. Half of international giving comes from the Bill & Melinda Gates Foundation; the remainder is from other large foundations, which might be either independent, community, corporate or operating foundations. According to the report, the top 10 international grant-makers are:

1. Bill & Melinda Gates Foundation
2. The Susan Thompson Buffett Foundation
3. Ford Foundation
4. Foundation to Promote Open Society
5. The William and Flora Hewlett Foundation
6. Walton Family Foundation
7. The Rockefeller Foundation
8. The David and Lucile Packard Foundation
9. Open Society Institute
10. Silicon Valley Community Foundation

There are different types of recipients of these types of grants. Foundations may seek to build relationships with governments; or to support international NGOs or develop relationships with in-country NGOs (often referred to as 'local partners'). The Council on Foundations and the Foundation Centre found that about 88% of all international grants went to or through INGOs.

The US Internal Revenue Service (IRS) imposes some restrictions on international grant-making by private foundations (i.e. foundations that are tax exempt under the Code), to ensure that grant proceeds will be used by the foreign grantee for appropriate charitable purposes. Private foundations may demonstrate compliance with such requirements through one of two methods: 'expenditure responsibility' which requires a level of oversight by the grantor, or 'an equivalency determination' that requires the grant-maker to form opinion that the foreign organisation it wishes to support is essentially the equivalent of a US s 501(c)(3) public charity.

US public charities may also make international grants and are generally not subject to the same restrictions on international grant-making as private foundations. A public charity must ensure that the foreign recipient of its funds engages in activities that are consistent with the public charity's exempt purpose. This invariably means having a grant agreement in place requiring progress reporting and return of the funds if they are used for an improper purpose.

Other countries indicated that a fund may lose its tax-preferred status if grants are made to PBOs in other countries. For example, in Australia an approved fund (which may be a Private Ancillary Fund or a Public Ancillary Fund) can only make grants to PBOs in Australia (although those PBOs may undertake activities in other countries, see 5.3.2).

Similarly, in Canada, tax-preferred charitable foundations are only allowed to gift funds to 'qualified donees' which are generally only situated in Canada. Foundations that donate assets or make grants to PBOs in other countries may have their registration temporarily suspended or revoked or be subject to a monetary penalty. However, foundations are able to carry out activities through intermediaries. This means that foundations can transfer funds to PBOs in other countries, provided that they maintain sufficient direction and control over their resources such that the activity can be considered their own.

In New Zealand, as is the case for PBOs (see 5.3.2), funds will lose their donee status (so donors will not be eligible for tax concessions) if monies are not applied 'wholly or mainly to charitable, benevolent, philanthropic or cultural purposes within New Zealand'. This means that a maximum of 25% of funds could be applied to purposes outside NZ. These restrictions do not apply to foreign charities listed in Sched 32 of the Income Tax Act 2007 (see 5.3.1)

Colombia, Israel and Mexico indicated that funds that make grants abroad may lose their preferential tax treatment.

Notes

[1] The FATF recommendations in relation to non-profit entities are discussed in Chapter 2.

[2] The Bulgarian income tax legislation does not place any restrictions on making grants to PBOs in other countries.

6 Conclusions and policy options

This concluding chapter brings together the key insights from the report and discusses their tax policy implications. It highlights the importance of countries ensuring that the design of their tax incentives for philanthropic giving are consistent with their underlying policy goals. It also suggests that countries reassess the merits of providing tax exemptions for the commercial income of philanthropic entities, at least insofar as this income is unrelated to the entity's worthy purpose. More broadly, it finds scope for countries to both reduce the complexity and improve the oversight of their concessionary regimes for philanthropic entities and philanthropic giving. Finally, in light of the increasingly global nature of many policy challenges – such as environmental and public health concerns (including the COVID-19 pandemic) – it suggests countries reassess the restrictions commonly imposed on access to tax concessions for cross-border philanthropy.

6.1. Introduction

Philanthropy plays an important role in most countries, providing private support to a range of activities for the public good. This differentiates the sector from government initiatives (i.e., public action for the public good) and profit-based initiatives (i.e., private action for the private good). Almost all OECD countries provide some form of preferential tax treatment for philanthropy. Entities with a philanthropic status typically receive tax relief directly in relation to their activities, while both individual and corporate donors to these entities are typically able to receive tax incentives that lower the cost of giving.

This report has undertaken a detailed review of the tax treatment of philanthropic entities and philanthropic giving in 40 OECD member and participating countries. It has first examined the various arguments for and against the provision of preferential tax treatment for philanthropic entities and giving. It has then reviewed the tax treatment of philanthropic entities and giving in a domestic context, before then examining the cross-border taxation of philanthropy. This final chapter brings together the insights from this analysis and discusses their tax policy implications.

This chapter is structured as follows. Sections 6.2-6.5 summarise the key messages from the preceding chapters in the report. Section 6.6 then presents the resulting conclusions and discusses a range of policy options.

6.2. The case for preferential tax treatment for philanthropy

Chapter 2 summarised the various arguments for and against the use of tax concessions for philanthropic entities and philanthropic giving. This highlighted that there is no single generally accepted rationale for preferential tax treatment of philanthropic entities. Economic theory provides a limited rationale for providing tax concessions for philanthropy (potentially both for entities and giving) where there is under-provision of a public good or where there are positive externalities associated with the activity of the philanthropic entity. The under-provision of a public good rationale requires there to have been a combination of “market failure”, “government failure” and “voluntary failure”, in the sense that the private market, government, and voluntary sector are all unable to provide the welfare-maximising level of public good provision.

A related public good-based rationale put forward by legal scholars posits that tax favoured status (again potentially for both entities and giving) is justified on the basis that it provides a subsidy for the provision of public goods that would otherwise be required to be provided by the state (the “subsidy” rationale). Another often articulated argument is the “base defining” rationale which argues that the surplus of a philanthropic entity is different in nature to income and therefore beyond the scope of the income tax base. Additional arguments include that philanthropic giving, as well as the institutions it develops, strengthen civil society and decentralise decision-making, and are thus an important feature of a democratic society and worth supporting.

A number of arguments have been raised against the provision of tax preferences for philanthropic entities and/or giving. The cost of providing concessions is often highlighted as a concern. By reducing government revenue, tax concessions for philanthropy require other taxpayers to bear an increased tax burden (or alternatively result in less government expenditure on other policy priorities). Another argument, is that taxpayers are often relatively unresponsive to tax incentives for philanthropic giving, suggesting they may not be “treasury efficient” in the sense that they increase giving by less than the tax revenue lost. Empirical evidence on the elasticity of giving provides some support for this argument. However, it is important to note that a tax incentive could be treasury inefficient but still welfare improving if the benefit to society of the activity funded by the giving is sufficiently large. While grants could in this case be more effective, concerns of government grants crowding out private donations may in some instances still justify the use of tax incentives. A concern regarding exemption of commercial income of philanthropic entities is that this may create an unfair competitive advantage for philanthropic entities over for-profit businesses.

Two related concerns that are raised regarding tax incentives for giving are that they may be regressive and undemocratic. Tax incentives may be regressive in that higher income taxpayers benefit from a larger tax incentive than lower income taxpayers. This can be the case in both aggregate terms, but also in proportionate terms as a tax deduction will provide a greater benefit to higher income taxpayers if they are subject to higher marginal tax rates than lower income taxpayers. The democratic argument highlights the concern that, as a tax incentive effectively reallocates tax revenue towards the favoured philanthropic entity, higher income taxpayers that make greater donations benefit from a disproportionate influence in the determination of how tax revenue is spent. This may be of particular concern where the priorities of donors are not consistent with those of society in general. Greater control by the government over the range of entities for which donations are eligible for tax incentives may limit this concern to some extent.

Irrespective of these arguments, most countries do provide tax incentives for giving, and in general provide exemptions from some taxes for philanthropic entities. The next sections summarise the approaches countries have taken.

6.3. Taxation and philanthropic entities

In almost all of the countries analysed in this report, entities with a philanthropic status (funds and PBOs) can receive tax incentivised gifts from individuals and corporations, as well as receive tax relief directly in relation to their activities. The report finds that for an entity to receive a philanthropic status with the associated tax benefits, it must meet not-for-profit, worthy purpose, and public benefit requirements.

The not-for profit requirement does not prohibit a philanthropic entity from making a surplus, instead, it generally includes non-distribution requirements so that the surplus is not distributed as dividends or other benefits beyond the scope of the entity's worthy purpose. An issue that can arise is whether the payment of some salaries to employees breaches this notion of 'non-distribution'. This report finds that generally the requirement does not prevent the payment of 'reasonable' remuneration for services (or the provision of goods). Some countries may impose restrictions in this regard, while others may be less prescriptive.

With regard to the worthy purpose requirement, welfare, education, scientific research, and health care are deemed worthy purposes most frequently across countries. Countries generally stipulate that the benefit must be open to all, that the benefit can be restricted to groups with specific characteristics, or that the characteristics used to specify who can benefit must relate to the fulfilment of the entity's worthy purpose.

Additionally, to help assess whether entities meet these requirements, countries tend to impose a number of administrative requirements. Almost all countries surveyed in this report require philanthropic entities to undergo a specific application process to become eligible for preferential tax treatment. Countries typically follow one of three broad approaches in determining the administrative and oversight body. Under the first approach, the tax administration is responsible for oversight of the sector (including the accreditation process). The second approach is to assign the responsibility to both the tax administration and a competent authority such as an independent commission. Lastly, in some countries the accreditation and oversight responsibility lies entirely with another department and not the tax administration.

The report identifies two approaches for providing tax relief for the income of philanthropic entities: the first is to exempt all or specific income, and the second is to consider all forms of income taxable, but allow the entity to reduce its taxable income through current or future reinvestments towards the fulfilment of its worthy purpose. Countries following the first approach generally exclude non-commercial income (received gifts or grants) from the tax base. Approaches to dealing with commercial activities and the income generated from those activities, diverge. Countries, whose philanthropic entities are fully income tax exempt, restrict these entities from engaging in certain kinds of activities. On the other hand, countries that want philanthropic entities to pay taxes on some of their income generally differentiate between commercial income that is related and unrelated to the worthy purpose.

The report also finds that countries that offer preferential VAT treatment to philanthropic entities tend to exempt them from having to collect VAT on certain (or all) supplies. As such an exemption can create an input tax burden, some countries have implemented rules that enable philanthropic entities to reclaim a portion of their input tax.

Philanthropic entities may own real estate that they use to fulfil their social objectives, or they may own it as a source of income. The report finds that, in some countries, entities that use their real estate for their worthy purpose, such as the location of offices or philanthropic activities, may be exempt from property taxes.

A number of common types of abuse of the preferential tax treatment provided to philanthropic entities are identified in this report. For example, they include diverting funds intended for public purposes to private benefits, for-profit businesses posing as PBOs to benefit from the tax relief; philanthropic entities investing in corporations owned or controlled by employees or managers of the entity; salaried employees concealed as volunteer workers; or entities not registered for VAT that are undertaking taxable activities.

6.4. Taxation and philanthropic giving

In most of the countries surveyed, individual taxpayers that give to a qualifying fund or PBO receive some form of tax incentive. In the large majority of countries surveyed, donations are deductible. Other countries offer tax credits instead and, in some cases, the donations of individuals are matched or facilitated through an allocation scheme. In countries with a matching scheme, government tops up donations at a given rate so that the entity receiving the donation is able to claim the tax relief. In countries with an allocation scheme, the tax administration allows taxpayers to designate a fixed percentage or amount of their income tax to a fund or PBO directly through their tax return. Although allocation schemes are not tax incentives, they are included in this discussion as they are administered through the tax system and their objective is to support philanthropy. Unlike individual donors, companies can also claim deductions (under standard business expensing rules) for corporate sponsoring of philanthropic entities. As a result, the report finds that deductions are more common for incentives for corporate donors than for individual ones.

In countries with no tradition of philanthropic giving, an allocation scheme can create awareness among taxpayers, financially support funds and PBOs, and develop stronger ties between the general public and philanthropic entities. The report finds that allocation schemes were introduced mainly in eastern European countries and may thus be a part of a regional trend.

Countries' approaches to limiting the fiscal cost of their incentives vary. Countries that provide tax deductions, may cap the share of the donation that is deductible, cap the size of the deduction to a share of taxable or total income, cap the size of the deduction to a fixed value, or use a combination of these ceilings. Countries that provide a tax credit, may cap the value of their tax credit to a share of taxable or total income; a share of the income tax liability, a fixed value, a combination of ceilings, or cap the size of the donation that is creditable. To limit the cost of matching schemes, countries set the rate at which the relief may be claimed by the receiving philanthropic entity.

The report also finds that countries that levy inheritance or estate taxes generally provide preferential tax relief for philanthropic bequests. In countries with an inheritance tax, the PBO or fund receiving the bequest are liable for the tax and thus are the ones that receive the tax relief. In countries with an estate tax, on the other hand, the tax liability as well as the corresponding tax relief is with the estate of the deceased.

The majority of countries that incentivise cash donations of individuals also incentivise non-monetary donations. Nevertheless, some countries choose to limit their tax incentives to cash donations only, and some severely restrict the size and nature of non-monetary donations. With respect to countries that incentivise non-monetary donations, the report identifies a number of different approaches to designing valuation rules: some countries require appraisals if the value of a non-monetary donation exceeds a threshold, others have different valuation rules for different types of assets and a number of countries do not require appraisals and review valuations through audits.

Corporate sponsoring of philanthropic entities (i.e. payments in return for publicity or advertisement) is considered a business expense in most countries, as long as there is a sufficient nexus with earning income. However, the report finds that, in a number of countries, these payments may be considered commercial income of the philanthropic entities receiving them and thus have tax implications.

Common types of tax avoidance and evasion issues with tax relief for philanthropic giving include: falsified donation receipts prepared by the philanthropic entity, tax preparers or donors; payments for goods and services disguised as donations; overvalued gifts; and donations of assets in which the donor retains an interest. Given that a key anti-abuse policy is that the recipients of philanthropic giving must be accredited philanthropic entities, the majority of anti-abuse policies identified in the report are in the form of transparency and reporting requirements for funds and PBOs. This allows the tax administration to focus its resources on these entities and generally shifts the onus of demonstrating that the worthy purpose and public benefit requirements have been satisfied on to the philanthropic entities that receive the donations.

6.5. Taxation and cross-border philanthropy

The report has also examined the tax treatment of cross-border philanthropy. Cross-border philanthropy can occur where a person (an individual or a corporation) makes a gift to an entity in another jurisdiction ('direct philanthropy'). Cross-border philanthropy can also occur where a domestic philanthropic entity operates in another jurisdiction or where a foreign entity operates domestically ('indirect philanthropy').

The report finds that, beyond the European Union (EU), there is little tax support provided by countries for cross-border giving. Within the EU, Member States are governed by European Court of Justice (ECJ) rulings requiring Member States to adopt a 'comparability' approach to ascertain whether a gift to a philanthropic entity in another Member State is entitled to tax relief. This typically requires a case-by-case analysis to determine eligibility, and due to differences between Member States relating to tax relief, can result in considerable complexity and uncertainty. The report finds that the ECJ rulings have not been fully adopted by all Members of the EU. Beyond the EU, there are a small number of bilateral treaties (such as the US-Canada and US-Mexico treaties) where tax relief may be obtained for a donation in the partner country. There are also a small number of countries (e.g. Canada) that provide tax concessions for donations to certain approved foreign PBOs. The limitations imposed on tax support for cross-border giving have led some philanthropic entities to establish 'work arounds' with entities in various jurisdictions, so that gifts can be made to domestic entities (that are eligible for tax relief) but are then passed on to entities in other countries.

With regard to PBOs that operate across borders, most countries do not provide tax relief for foreign philanthropic entities. The position in the EU is again governed by ECJ rulings requiring Member States to adopt a 'comparability' test to determine the eligibility of an entity in another Member State for tax relief. Beyond the EU, there are a small number of countries that provide tax relief for foreign philanthropic entities on a case-by-case basis (e.g. Australia, Canada, Indonesia). The inability of foreign entities to qualify for tax relief has meant that many entities that operate internationally establish local entities that are eligible for tax relief.

Many, but not all, countries provide tax relief to domestic entities that operate abroad, particularly where the activities are related to humanitarian relief or development assistance. Typically, this authorisation is reliant upon the philanthropic entity respecting the worthy purpose requirements imposed by the national legislation, usually similar to the requirements imposed on domestic PBOs.

6.6. Policy options

While, as noted above, there are arguments both in favour of and against the use of tax incentives for philanthropy, in practice most governments judge them as worthwhile. This section draws on the preceding analysis to highlight a number of key issues that countries face in the design of their tax rules for philanthropic entities and philanthropic giving.

First, it is important that countries ensure that the design of their tax incentives for philanthropic giving are consistent with their underlying policy goals. Second, there is scope in many countries to reassess the design of tax concessions for philanthropic entities. More broadly, countries should also look to both reduce the complexity and improve the oversight of their concessionary regimes for philanthropic entities and philanthropic giving. Finally, there may be merit in countries reassessing the restrictions that are typically imposed on cross-border philanthropic activity. These issues are discussed in more detail below.

6.6.1. Ensuring the design of tax incentives for philanthropic giving meets policy goals

Designing tax incentives for philanthropic giving is complicated due to the need to balance a range of potential policy goals. While the overall aim of a tax incentive can be seen as maximising social welfare, determining how to achieve this is challenging and requires various value judgements to be made. Broadly speaking, trade-offs must be made between incentivising giving, limiting fiscal cost, and managing both the distributional and democratic (in terms of influence over how tax revenue is spent) impacts of the tax incentive. A range of design choices impact on these goals.

Choice of eligibility criteria

Most countries allow tax incentives for a broad range of worthy purposes. The choice of eligibility criteria offers policy makers a means of targeting the benefit of tax concessions. Narrower eligibility conditions will ensure tax concessions more tightly target activities that align with the priorities of policy makers, but may result in a lower level of total giving. In contrast, wider eligibility conditions will ensure that the philanthropic priorities of a wider range of taxpayers are eligible for concessionary treatment and may therefore lead to increased giving.

Countries that are particularly concerned about restricting support to those areas prioritised by government may wish to consider limiting the breadth of eligibility. For example, by restricting eligibility to activities that directly support those suffering from poverty, illness and disability. Ensuring that tax incentives are limited to a narrow scope of activities is likely to be a more effective means of targeting support than by imposing fiscal caps (see below).

Tax deductions vs tax credits

As noted above, the most popular tax incentive for philanthropic giving across the countries examined in this study is a tax deduction. However, for countries with a progressive personal income tax (PIT) system, a deduction will disproportionately benefit higher income taxpayers because the benefit of the deduction increases with the marginal tax rate of the giver. This may create distributional concerns in light of the broader goals of progressivity and redistribution associated with the progressive PIT systems adopted in most countries. Furthermore, it may also create concern regarding the increased degree of influence that high-income taxpayers are given in the determination of how tax revenue is spent (with richer households potentially favouring different types of philanthropic activities than poorer households), and the consistency of this with democratic principles. This, in turn, may exacerbate distributional concerns if higher income taxpayers not only benefit more in terms of the tax concession they receive, but also in terms of the benefit they derive from the type of activities the tax-incentivised giving funds. At the same time, providing a greater tax incentive to richer taxpayers is likely to result in greater increases in aggregate philanthropic giving both because the bulk of giving comes from higher income as compared to lower income taxpayers and they are also more responsive to tax incentives.

In contrast, countries particularly concerned about distributional impacts, may wish to consider moving to a tax credit. A tax credit will ensure that the same proportionate tax benefit is provided to taxpayers irrespective of their income level. Providing a credit that is lower than the deduction currently available to top-PIT rate taxpayers may reduce the incentive to give among high-income earners. Alternatively, matching the top-rate may come at some additional fiscal cost. This creates a trade-off that governments will need to balance. At a minimum, countries with deductions should reassess the merits of maintaining the deduction to ensure that the decision to maintain the deduction is based on a clear policy decision to provide a greater incentive to higher income taxpayers.

Fixed vs percentage-based fiscal caps

Restrictions on the size of tax incentives are common in light of countries' desire to restrict the fiscal cost of their tax incentives for giving. Some countries adopt caps on the size of the tax incentive set equal to a specific fixed currency amount, while others adopt caps based on a percentage of the donor's income or tax liability, and some adopt a combination of both.

The adoption of such caps do, however, have an impact on both the degree of incentive provided by the concession and their distributional impact. A fixed cap will result in no taxpayers above the cap receiving any additional incentive to give on their marginal earnings, thereby reducing the amount of giving. The extent of the restriction will depend on the level of the cap set. Such a cap may improve distributional outcomes as it will ensure that the maximum potential aggregate benefit available to both poor and rich households will be the same. It will also cap the influence of high-income taxpayers in the determination of how tax revenue is spent. However, the imposition of a relatively high cap may be binding on high-income taxpayers but not on low-income taxpayers and will still result in a greater concession being provided to high-income taxpayers in practice.

A percentage-based cap will instead equalise the maximum potential proportional benefit available to both poor and rich households. Richer households will still benefit more in aggregate terms, but not in proportional terms (with a proportionate cap more likely to be binding on lower income households than a high fixed cap). For a given fiscal cost, this may result in a greater increase in giving than a fixed cap due to the greater responsiveness of higher income taxpayers. As such, if a country aims to maximise total giving for a given fiscal cost then it should consider applying a percentage based cap, rather than a fixed cap. If instead distributional concerns are of high importance then consideration may be given to applying a fixed cap. An alternative option in balancing these goals may be to combine a percentage-based cap together with a generous fixed cap. Such an approach may be of particular merit for countries concerned about the disproportionate influence of high-income taxpayers in the determination of how tax revenue is spent.

Allocation schemes

A small number of countries apply allocation schemes, where taxpayers can designate a fixed percentage or amount of their income tax to a fund or PBO directly through their tax return. Allocation schemes can increase the visibility of the philanthropic sector and create a culture of giving in a country where there is no such a culture. However, allocation schemes do not provide a tax incentive to give and so are unlikely to have a significant impact on the level of giving. As such, the use of tax incentives should generally be preferred where the aim is to increase the level of giving.

6.6.2. Preferential tax treatment of philanthropic entities

As stated above, a common approach of countries that provide tax concessions to philanthropic entities, is to exempt all or specific income of these entities. Furthermore, a number of countries exempt philanthropic entities from having to collect VAT on certain (or all) supplies. This section discusses the challenges that may arise as a result of these concessions and provides policy options that may reduce complexities and distortions as well as increase compliance.

Commercial income of philanthropic entities

Philanthropic entities may have commercial and/or non-commercial income, but the distinction is not always clear or the same across countries. Generally, non-commercial income refers to income from philanthropic gifts (discussed in Chapter 4) and government grants, or (in the case of PBOs) grants from supporting funds. Broadly, commercial income is income derived from the supply of goods or services in return for some form of payment.

If there are no restrictions on the commercial activities a philanthropic entity can engage in and the income from those activities is fully tax exempt, it may give rise to competitive neutrality and revenue loss concerns. To avoid such concerns, the report identifies a number of policy options. A common approach is to only exempt income generated from commercial activities that are related to the philanthropic entity's worthy purpose. However, the definitions of related and unrelated commercial income vary widely across countries and such tax rules often result in significant complexity.

Other approaches are less complex, but may not fully exclude unrelated income from the preferential tax treatment. One approach is to only exempt income generated from commercial activities where it is reinvested towards the entity's worthy purpose in a timely fashion. To facilitate some flexibility on behalf of the entities, such a policy could potentially be subject to an exception or allowance for the creation of small reserves that may be necessary to support the ongoing pursuit or expansion of the philanthropic entity's activities that are directly connected to its worthy purpose. Another approach may be to limit the size of the expansion through a threshold beyond which income from commercial activities is taxed.

The competitive neutrality concerns associated with exempting the commercial income of philanthropic entities gives rise to an important issue that requires the attention of policy makers. For this reason, countries should reassess the merits of providing tax exemptions for the commercial income of PBOs, at least in so far as this income is unrelated to the entity's worthy purpose. However, in undertaking such a reassessment, countries will need to consider the added complexities associated with distinguishing between taxable (i.e. unrelated commercial income) and exempt income and weigh the additional compliance and administrative costs against the pursuit of competitive neutrality.

VAT

Exempting philanthropic entities, or their activities from VAT may also lead to competitive neutrality concerns between for-profit and philanthropic entities. Furthermore, policies intended to refund parts of the tax paid on inputs tend to be very complex. Therefore, countries that currently provide an exemption should consider fully subjecting philanthropic entities to the VAT. As is typically the case with for-profit businesses, a registration threshold could be applied to exclude small philanthropic entities for whom compliance costs are likely to be disproportionate relative to the VAT revenue collected.

6.6.3. Reduce complexity

Another challenge for designing tax incentives for philanthropy is to find a balance between tailoring policies to the wide range of philanthropic activities and limiting the complexity of the tax system. This report identifies three key areas that could benefit from reducing the complexity of the tax rules in a number of countries: eligibility requirements for different kinds of tax incentives, tax rules for non-monetary donations and the valuation processes, and payroll giving.

Overly complex tax rules risk increasing compliance costs and uncertainty. This, in turn, can lead to both accidental and deliberate tax compliance issues. Complex tax rules and the related compliance costs that ensue may also put low-income donors and smaller philanthropic entities at a disadvantage compared to high-income donors and larger philanthropic entities. This is because the compliance costs may be lower in relative terms for high-income donors and large entities, which may also be more likely to afford tax advice from experts. Therefore, limiting complexity where possible has the potential of making tax incentives for philanthropy more efficient, less regressive, and increase overall compliance.

Eligibility requirements for different kinds of tax incentives

The report finds that in most countries, entities with a recognised philanthropic status are able to receive tax-incentivised gifts from individuals and corporations, or receive tax relief directly in relation to their activities. For an entity to be eligible for these incentives, it must meet not-for-profit, worthy purpose, and public benefit requirements. To reduce complexity, countries should consider applying the same eligibility tests for both kinds of incentives.

Non-monetary donations

A philanthropic donation can be in cash or non-cash form, with the latter frequently referred to as non-monetary or in-kind donations. Non-monetary donations may include: real and intellectual property; corporate stock or shares; trading stock; cultural assets; other personal property; services (volunteering); or blood and organ donations. To apply a tax incentive to non-monetary donations, the gift must be assigned a value. The valuation rules and process increase compliance and administration costs for donors, government, and in some cases the receiving entities. The valuation of a non-monetary donation determines the value of the tax incentive for the donor, and thus creates an incentive for donors to inflate the value of their donation. As such, valuation rules for non-monetary donations are intended to limit the possibility of abuse. Furthermore, the value of assets can fluctuate significantly. To the extent that the value of assets is subjective, valuation rules need to establish a process through which the value is determined as objectively as possible. This, in turn, may require a professional assessment (e.g., the valuation of artwork), which increases the compliance cost to whoever is responsible for the valuation.

In light of the complexities around valuation and the associated compliance costs, imposing a minimum value threshold for a non-monetary donation to receive concessionary tax treatment, may be warranted. Furthermore, countries may consider reassessing the kinds of non-monetary donations eligible for the tax incentives. When considering what kind of non-monetary donations to incentivise, the benefit resulting from the donation being non-monetary (as opposed to cash), should be weighed against the additional cost associated with the required valuation process and risk of abuse.

On the other hand, determining the kinds of non-monetary donations that could more effectively be made through cash donations, may be challenging as future needs are uncertain. For example, the COVID-19 health crisis has shown how an unexpected shortage in personal protective equipment (PPE) created a demand for non-monetary donations of masks and other PPE products. Similar needs can arise where natural disasters occur and often the provision of goods and materials that are urgently needed, may be more helpful than the provision of cash donations.

Payroll giving

A number of countries have introduced payroll giving schemes. These schemes enable employees to elect to have donations to approved philanthropic entities deducted from their income by their employer, and for them to receive the relevant tax incentive (deduction or tax credit), within an extended pay-as-you-earn withholding tax system. Effectively, they shift the compliance costs associated with giving from employees to employers – who may be able to more efficiently bear this compliance burden. Such schemes may therefore be an administratively efficient way to increase the effectiveness of a tax incentive for giving.

6.6.4. Improve oversight

Improving oversight of the philanthropic sector is important for protecting public trust in the sector as well as ensuring that the tax concessions used to subsidise philanthropy are not abused through tax avoidance and evasion schemes. This section provides an overview of policy options that may help protect public trust, increase compliance, limit loopholes and ultimately improve oversight of the philanthropic sector and its activities.

Publicly available register of approved philanthropic entities

Public trust and confidence in the philanthropic sector is a key priority for government as well as the sector itself. In part due to philanthropy's reliance on private philanthropic giving, public trust is an essential component of financing the sector. Additionally, because philanthropy benefits from considerable tax support, public trust is also important in justifying and upholding the tax concessions used to subsidise philanthropic activities. A key way in which many countries improve transparency, certainty and accountability regarding what entities are eligible for receiving tax concessions as well as tax incentivised gifts, is to make publicly available a register of approved philanthropic entities. Countries that do not currently do so, should consider adopting such a publicly available register of approved philanthropic entities.

Such a policy may also help combat schemes in which fraudulent entities pretend to be eligible funds or PBOs in order to receive donations. Having a publicly available register would enable donors to cross-reference the information. Furthermore, a publicly available register invites public scrutiny, which may help to increase compliance and improve the detection of abuse.

Annual reporting requirements

A key challenge for oversight bodies (whether that is the tax administration, an independent commission or other department within the government) is to be able to collect the information needed to evaluate whether the philanthropic entities are complying with existing regulations and meeting the necessary requirements of organisations benefitting from preferential tax status. This report finds that in the majority of countries, entities have to go through an application process in order to qualify for the preferential tax status. Such a process, however, can only ensure that entities are compliant and meet the requirements at the time of their application (which frequently is at the start of their operations).

Imposing annual reporting requirements on funds and PBOs could improve oversight. This is because the oversight bodies are able to use the annual reports to keep track of philanthropic entities even after they have been granted preferential tax status. Such a policy may also help countries better identify errors or compliance issues early on, which may be beneficial for the entities as well. Furthermore, annual reports also have the potential to increase public trust, especially if some of the information in the report is made public. As annual reporting requirements may increase compliance costs, countries may wish to consider the adoption of a *de minimis* amount of revenue above which the reporting requirements would apply.

Combined oversight approach

The range of activities that philanthropic entities may engage in is typically very broad and thus it may be challenging for a tax administration to properly assess and oversee entities that are involved in fields that are not within the expertise of the tax administration. Additionally, it may be difficult for a revenue administration to justify the allocation of significant resources to the oversight of a largely untaxed philanthropic sector, resulting in a degree of under-supervision. To both improve the level of oversight in areas that require specific expertise, and alleviate the workload on the tax administration, countries should consider the adoption of a combined oversight approach. In a combined oversight approach, the tax administration and a competent ministry or commission with experts in a field related to the worthy purpose, would oversee the philanthropic entity and its activities.

Tax avoidance and evasion schemes

Abuse of incentives for philanthropic giving could deprive governments of much-needed revenues and risks undermining public trust in the government and the philanthropic sector. To reduce the risk of tax abuse, countries should consider a number of policy options:

- Maintaining a database of suspicious activities to help identify trends and develop expertise on tax abuse related to tax concessions for philanthropy. Collecting data on suspicious activities may also assist the oversight bodies to conduct more targeted audits and thus become more efficient.
- Exchanging good practices as well as information with tax administrations and law enforcement agencies may improve the efficiency of the oversight process as non-compliant actors in the philanthropic sector may already be on the radar of other law enforcement agencies. More specifically, exchanging information across law enforcement agencies may also strengthen the effort to ensure that organisations involved in illegal and inappropriate activities do not abuse the concessions afforded to the philanthropic sector to finance their activities.
- Implementing limits to fundraising expenditures may be an effective approach to restrict tax-exempt entities from overspending on fundraising events.
- Similarly, implementing rules that limit certain types of operating expenses of PBOs that are at an increased risk of being misused for the private benefit of people associated with the entity (e.g., vehicles, residential real estate, etc.) may limit schemes in which managers, employees, board members, or large donors use the assets of tax-exempt entities for their private benefit.
- Limiting the remuneration of staff, managers, and board members of PBOs may help ensure that the untaxed income and donations received by philanthropic entities are not used for the personal gain of people associated with the entity. Unreasonably high remuneration may also be an indication of a scheme to circumvent the non-distribution requirement of the not-for-profit status. Therefore, limiting the remuneration that people associated with the entity can receive could be an effective policy at ensuring the not-for-profit requirement is met.
- Screening non-resident PBOs and funds eligible for receiving tax-incentivised donations helps ensure that the requirements countries impose on resident entities that may receive tax-incentivised donations are also met abroad. Furthermore, screening non-resident PBOs is a key strategy of a number of countries to combat terrorist financing schemes involving philanthropic entities.
- Implementing clear and transparent procedures for authorities to deal with non-compliance quickly.

Rules for corporate and individual giving

As discussed in Chapter 4, corporate philanthropic giving can occur in the form of donations or sponsorship payments. Sponsoring funds and PBOs are payments in return for publicity and thus generate a benefit to the donor. This report has highlighted that in many countries, sponsorship or advertising payments (which have a sufficient nexus with earning income) are deductible under business expensing rules and not subject to the limitations placed on deductions for corporate donations. This in turn may create an incentive for managers or owners of businesses to support causes through business sponsorship payments instead of personal donations in order to circumvent the limits placed on the tax incentives for philanthropic giving in a number of countries. Therefore, countries should better align rules for corporate and individual giving to limit distortions and ambiguities. This may be achieved by, for example, implementing similar limits for tax incentives for corporate and individual donations.

To do so, tax rules should clearly differentiate between donating and sponsoring. This may be done by, for example, requiring a sponsorship contract that clearly specifies the publicity the corporation will receive. This, in turn, allows policy makers to only provide deductions for sponsorship equal to the market value of the publicity/advertisement received in return for the payment. The amount of the payment in excess of the fair market value should be treated as a donation and subject to the respective limits.

Clearly differentiating between donations and sponsorship may also have important tax consequences for the philanthropic entity receiving the donation or the sponsorship payment. Countries that tax the commercial income of philanthropic entities may consider advertising to be a commercial activity and tax the sponsorship payments accordingly (while the income from donations is generally exempt).

Data collection and tax expenditure reports

Part of improving oversight of the tax incentives provided for philanthropy is to be able to estimate the cost of these incentives. To do so, countries should collect data and estimate as well as publish tax expenditures used to subsidise philanthropy. Furthermore, tax expenditure data may also enable countries to conduct studies that evaluate the efficiency of their individual incentives.

6.6.5. Reassess the current restrictions for international giving

Concerns regarding the degree of benefit (or lack thereof) to the country providing the tax concession, as well as regarding a potential lack of oversight, have resulted in only a very limited degree of tax support for cross-border philanthropy. However, the global nature of many of the challenges facing the world emphasises the importance of countries taking a global rather than an insular perspective. In particular, responding to issues such as poverty, war and conflict, environmental concerns, medical research, and public health issues such as pandemics, may require countries and institutions to cooperate across borders. A number of countries now also see a role for cross-border philanthropy in limited circumstances such as the provision of development assistance, and in relation to conflict situations.

In this context, there is merit in countries reassessing whether there may be some instances where equivalent tax treatment should be provided to domestic and cross-border philanthropy. For example, countries may wish to consider ensuring that domestic PBOs operating overseas for certain health, environmental and development assistance purposes, or those providing direct humanitarian support in conflict situations, should receive equivalent tax treatment to those operating domestically.

To address concerns regarding oversight and risks of abuse of tax concessions, countries could impose equivalent requirements as apply in the domestic philanthropy context, or require additional checks before providing tax-favoured status. Given the difficulties associated with monitoring and ensuring the compliance of philanthropic entities operating overseas, it would seem appropriate that additional checks and mechanisms would be required to ensure that the tax support provided is being directed towards the entities' worthy purposes and that these entities are complying with all requirements that would be expected of entities operating domestically.

In the European Union, countries may wish to examine the possibility of explicitly incorporating the non-discrimination requirements of European Court of Justice (ECJ) rulings as they pertain to philanthropic entities into their domestic legislation. This may reduce uncertainty for both philanthropic entities and donors, and minimise compliance and administrative costs associated with the current case-by-case comparability analysis required under the ECJ rulings.

OECD Tax Policy Studies

Taxation and Philanthropy

This report provides a detailed review of the tax treatment of philanthropic entities and philanthropic giving in 40 OECD member and participating countries. The report first examines the various arguments for and against the provision of preferential tax treatment for philanthropy. It then reviews the tax treatment of philanthropic entities and giving in the 40 participating countries, in both a domestic and cross-border context. Drawing on this analysis, the report then highlights a range of potential tax policy options for countries to consider.

PRINT ISBN 978-92-64-63114-4
PDF ISBN 978-92-64-40619-3

INDEX

Note: Page numbers in *italic* indicate a figure and page numbers in **bold** indicate a table on the corresponding page.

Printed in the United States
by Baker & Taylor Publisher Services